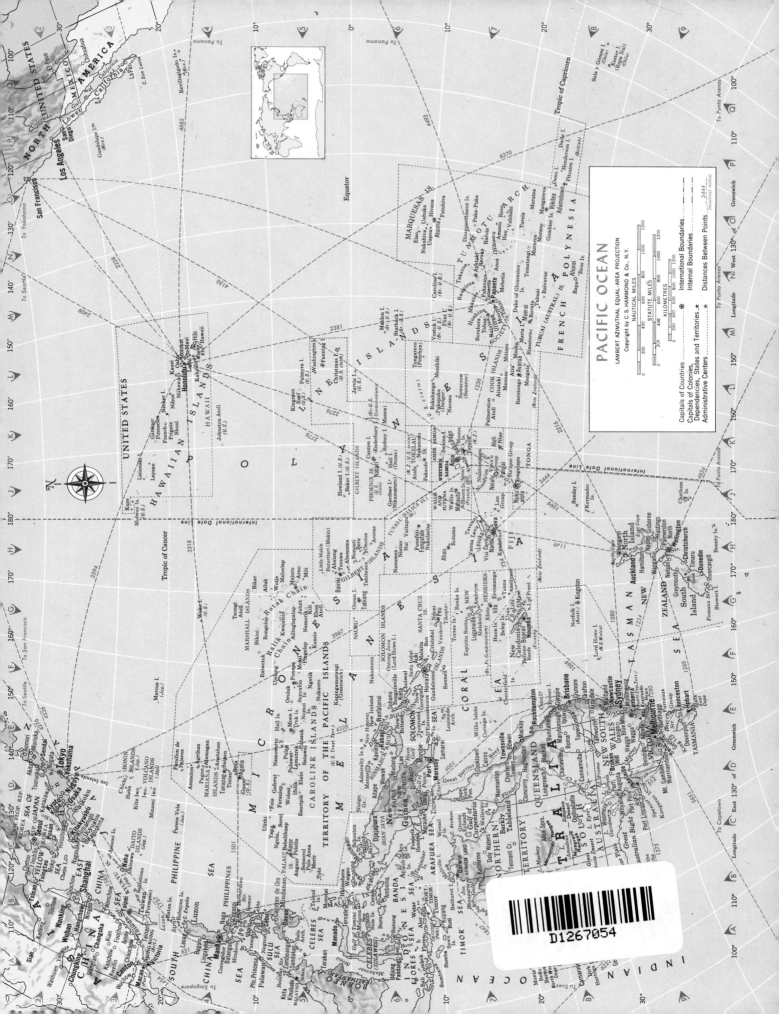

PACIFIC OCEAN

LAMBERT AZIMUTHAL EQUAL-AREA PROJECTION

Copyright by C. S. HAMMOND & Co., N.Y.

NAUTICAL MILES

STATUTE MILES

KILOMETRES

Capitals of Countries	⊛
Capitals of Colonies, Dependencies, States and Territories	★
Administrative Centers	⊛

International Boundaries

Internal Boundaries

Distances Between Points 5444 (nautical miles)

Volume 4

A practical guide to the geographic, historical,

political, social, & economic status of all nations, their international

relationships, and the United Nations system.

WORLDMARK
ENCYCLOPEDIA
OF THE NATIONS

ASIA & AUSTRALASIA

WORLDMARK PRESS, LTD.

JOHN WILEY & SONS, INC. NEW YORK AND TORONTO

Goode projection of the world Copyright by the University of Chicago.

Typography by Graphicomposition, Inc., and
U.S. Lithograph Inc., New York, N. Y.

Production by Vail-Ballou Press, Inc., Binghamton, N. Y.

Printed in the United States of America

Map endsheets prepared by Hammond, Inc., Maplewood. N.J.

Issued in the United Kingdom and Ireland as
ENCYCLOPEDIA OF THE NATIONS.

DISTRIBUTED IN THE UNITED STATES OF AMERICA AND CANADA BY
JOHN WILEY & SONS, INC. NEW YORK AND TORONTO.

LIBRARY OF CONGRESS CATALOGING IN PUBLICATION DATA

Worldmark Encyclopedia of the Nations.
Includes bibliographies and index.
Contents: v.1. United Nations.—v.2. Africa.—v.3. Americas.
—v.4. Asia & Australasia.—v.5. Europe.

1. Geography—Dictionaries. 2. History—Dictionaries.
3. Economics—Dictionaries. 4. Political Science—Dictionaries.
5. United Nations.

G63.W67   1976   910′.3   76-26857
ISBN 0 471 74833 1 (Wiley)

Staff

Editor and Publisher	MOSHE Y. SACHS
Executive Editor	FREDRIC M. KAPLAN
Senior Editor	LOUIS BARRON
Associate Editor	GEOFFREY HORN
Managing Editor	ADELE SACHS
Chief Copy Editor and Consulting Editor	MARY JANE ALEXANDER
Assistant Editors	LESLIE A. GLEW MARILYN BURLESON
Research Editors	MAUREEN RILEY SUSAN O. GILBERT
Cartographers	FRANCIS BARKOCZY MIKLOS PINTHER
Proofreaders	MARION R. BAKER BARRY BENJAMIN ROBERT S. MILNE MARTIN MITCHELL EUGENE F. SHEWMAKER MELVIN WOLFSON
Artists	HIDEO IETAKA LYDIA OKUMURA GAUNHA Q. SINGHO
General Staff	ISABEL STEIN DANIEL H. NEUDELL CHRISTINA NELSON

Contributors

TOUFIC ABOUCHAER, Second Secretary, Embassy of Syria, Washington, D.C.: SYRIA (in part).

NARINDER K. AGGARWALA: INDIA, JORDAN, KUWAYT, SA'UDI ARABIA, SYRIA (in part).

JOHN ANTHONY, Assistant Professor of Middle East Studies, School of Advanced International Studies, Johns Hopkins University: BAHRAYN* (in part), QATAR* (in part), UNITED ARAB EMIRATES* (in part).

EDMUND ASFOUR, formerly Bureau of Economic Affairs, United Nations: LEBANON (in part).

MOSHE AUMANN, Counselor, Embassy of Israel, Washington, D.C.: ISRAEL (in part).

JAMES H. D. BELGRAVE: BAHRAYN,* QATAR,* UNITED ARAB EMIRATES.*

PETER BLECHINGER: BHUTAN, INDONESIA (in part), JAPAN, REPUBLIC OF KOREA, THAILAND, VIET-NAM.

M. YUSUF BUCH: AFGHANISTAN, IRAN, IRAQ, JORDAN, KUWAYT, LEBANON, NEPAL, OMAN, PAKISTAN, SA'UDI ARABIA, SYRIA, YEMEN ARAB REPUBLIC.

ANGÈLE BUCK: BAHRAYN* (in part), LEBANON (in part), OMAN, QATAR* (in part), UNITED ARAB EMIRATES* (in part), PEOPLE'S DEMOCRATIC REPUBLIC OF YEMEN.

RICHARD BUTWELL, Dean for Arts and Science, State University of New York at Fredonia: AUSTRALIA, BURMA, ISRAEL, KAMPUCHEA, LAOS, NEW ZEALAND, SINGAPORE, THAILAND, TURKEY, VIET-NAM.

A. S. CHANG, Hong Kong Correspondent, Institute of Foreign Studies, Tokyo; formerly Professor of Economics, National Chi-nan University, Shanghai: CHINA.

WILLIAM W. COVER, Colonel, US Army (retired): JORDAN.

BRUCE G. CUMINGS, Professor of Political Science, Swarthmore College: DEMOCRATIC PEOPLE'S REPUBLIC OF KOREA, REPUBLIC OF KOREA.

LAURENCE EVANS, Professor of History, Harpur College: JORDAN, SYRIA.

BERNARD B. FALL, late Professor of Government, Howard University: KAMPUCHEA, LAOS, VIET-NAM.

WILLARD ALLEN FLETCHER, Professor and Chairman, Department of History, University of Delaware: CYPRUS.

MOHAMMAD H. GANJI, Professor Emeritus, Tehran University; Chancellor, Amir Showkatul-Mulk University, Birjand, Iran: IRAN.

JUDITH GLICKMAN: AFGHANISTAN.

THOMAS E. GOUTTIERRE, Dean, International Studies and Programs; Director, Center for Afghanistan, University of Nebraska at Omaha: AFGHANISTAN.

RALPH GREENHOUSE, US Information Agency: MALAYSIA.

PATRICIA EILEEN HIGGENS: JAPAN (in part).

BUSHROD HOWARD, JR.: OMAN.

WARREN S. HUNSBERGER, Professor of Economics, American University (with the assistance of Alan D. Smith, Information Officer, Consulate-General of Japan, New York): JAPAN.

INDOCHINA RESOURCE CENTER, Washington, D.C., D. Gareth Porter, Director: KAMPUCHEA (in part), LAOS (in part), VIET-NAM (in part).

NORMAN ITZKOWITZ, Associate Professor of Oriental Studies, Princeton University: SA῾UDI ARABIA (in part), YEMEN ARAB REPUBLIC.

MIRIAM KARR: FRENCH PACIFIC DEPENDENCIES, PORTUGUESE ASIAN DEPENDENCIES, TONGA, UK ASIAN AND PACIFIC DEPENDENCIES (in part), US PACIFIC DEPENDENCIES.

SALLY KENNEWICK: PHILIPPINES.

ROBERT C. KINGSBURY, Assistant Professor of Geography, Indiana University: INDIA, THAILAND.

HUEY LOUIS KOSTANICK, Professor of Geography, University of Southern California: CYPRUS.

ROBERT H. G. LEE, Assistant Professor of History, State University of New York at Stony Brook: TAIWAN.

H. A. G. LEWIS, O.B.E., Fellow, Royal Geographical Society (United Kingdom): UNITED KINGDON ASIAN AND PACIFIC DEPENDENCIES.

JAMES L. LEWIS: FIJI, UNITED KINGDOM ASIAN AND PACIFIC DEPENDENCIES, UNITED STATES PACIFIC DEPENDENCIES, WESTERN SAMOA.

ILSE LICHTENSTADTER, Center for Middle Eastern Studies, Harvard University: IRAQ.

SANDRA LITT: IRAN, ISRAEL (in part), LEBANON, MALDIVES, OMAN, SA῾UDI ARABIA (in part), SYRIA (in part), UK ASIAN AND PACIFIC DEPENDENCIES (in part), WESTERN SAMOA.

WILLIAM A. McGEVERAN: AUSTRALIA (in part), BANGLADESH* (in part), ISRAEL (in part), JORDAN (in part), LEBANON (in part), SYRIA (in part).

ERIC MACRO, Wing Commander, Royal Air Force: YEMEN ARAB REPUBLIC.

L. JOHN MARTIN, US Information Agency: NEPAL.

MARJORIE E. MAZEL: KUWAYT (in part), NEW ZEALAND (in part).

JOHN A. MILES: INDONESIA.

R. S. MILNE, Professor of Political Science, University of British Columbia: NEW ZEALAND.

ANN MOFFAT: PHILIPPINES.

JOHN K. C. OH, Professor of Political Science, Marquette University: DEMOCRATIC PEOPLE'S REPUBLIC OF KOREA, REPUBLIC OF KOREA.

ROBERT T. OLIVER, Head, Department of Speech, Pennsylvania State University: REPUBLIC OF KOREA.

ROBERT E. O'MELIA: FRENCH PACIFIC DEPENDENCIES.

RAPHAEL PATAI, Editor, The Herzl Press: JORDAN.

VICTOR P. PETROV, Professor of Geography, California State College: MONGOLIA, TAIWAN.

WILLIAM R. POLK, Director, Adlai E. Stevenson Institute, University of Chicago: LEBANON (in part).

M. RASHIDUZZAMAN, Professor of Political Science, Glassboro State College: BANGLADESH.*

BERNARD REINES: SINGAPORE.

MARILYN ROBERTS: TURKEY (in part).

RICHARD D. ROBINSON, Lecturer on Middle Eastern Studies, Center for Middle Eastern Studies, Harvard University: TURKEY.

DONOVAN ROWSE: CYPRUS, NEPAL.

ROBERT A. RUPEN, Associate Professor of Political Science, University of North Carolina: MONGOLIA.

WILLIAM SANDS, Editor, The Middle East Journal: LEBANON, SA'UDI ARABIA.

THEODORE SHABAD, Correspondent, The New York Times: CHINA, DEMOCRATIC PEOPLE'S REPUBLIC OF KOREA (in part), MONGOLIA, VIETNAM (in part).

RICHARD SORICH, East Asian Institute, Columbia University: CHINA.

AMRY VANDENBOSCH, Director Emeritus, Patterson School of Diplomacy and International Commerce, University of Kentucky: INDONESIA, MALAYSIA, SRI LANKA.

NANCY VIVIANI: Department of Economics, Australian National University: AUSTRALIA, FIJI, MALDIVES, NAURU, PAPUA NEW GUINEA,* TONGA.

EDWARD W. WAGNER, Associate Professor of Korean Studies, Department of Far Eastern Languages, Harvard University: DEMOCRATIC PEOPLE'S REPUBLIC OF KOREA, REPUBLIC OF KOREA.

MARY FRANCES WEIDLICH: MONGOLIA.

LAURENCE WEINSTEIN: BURMA, KAMPUCHEA, PAKISTAN, SRI LANKA.

MANFRED W. WENNER, Associate Professor of Political Science, University of Northern Illinois: PEOPLE'S DEMOCRATIC REPUBLIC OF YEMEN, YEMEN ARAB REPUBLIC.

FREDERICK L. WERNSTEDT, Associate Professor of Geography, Pennsylvania State University: PHILIPPINES.

DONALD N. WILBER, author of *Iran Past and Present*, etc.: AGFHANISTAN (in part), IRAN, PAKISTAN.

R. BAYLY WINDER, Chairman, Department of Near Eastern Languages and Literatures, New York University: SAʿUDI ARABIA (in part).

FLETCHER WORRELL: YEMEN ARAB REPUBLIC.

GRETCHEN ZOLLENDECK: ISRAEL (in part).

*Countries so marked indicate entirely new articles written for the present edition.
NOTE: Many articles have been written and/or revised by several contributors since the First Edition.

Acknowledgment is given to the governments of most countries whose articles are included in this volume. In particular, the editors wish to express their gratitude for the exceptional help extended by the governments of Afghanistan, Australia, Bahrayn, Bangladesh, Bhutan, Burma, Cyprus, Fiji, Indonesia, Iraq, Israel, Japan, Jordan, Republic of Korea, Kuwayt, Malaysia, Maldives, Mongolia, Nauru, Nepal, New Zealand, Oman, Pakistan, Papua New Guinea, Philippines, Saʿudi Arabia, Singapore, Sri Lanka, Syria, Taiwan, Thailand, Tonga, United Arab Emirates, and Yemen Arab Republic. Special thanks are given to Anne Adamcewicz and to Antonio Romualdez, Cultural Attaché, Philippines Embassy, Washington, D.C.

Contents

For Index to Countries and Territories, Conversion Tables, Abbreviations and Acronyms, Glossary of Intergovernmental Organizations, List of Nongovernmental Organizations, and Notes to the Fifth Edition, see Volume I.

Key to Subject Headings

All information contained within a country article is uniformly keyed by means of small superior numerals to the left of the subject headings. A heading such as "Population," for example, carries the same key numeral (5) in every article. Thus, to find information about the population of Argentina, consult the table of contents for the page number where the Argentina article begins and look for section 5 thereunder.

Introductory matter for each nation includes: Coat of arms
Capital
Flag
Anthem
Monetary unit
Weights and measures
Holidays
Time

FLAG COLOR SYMBOLS

 yellow   red   green   blue   orange   brown white   black

Flag descriptions are given from hoist to fly or from top to bottom.

1 Location, size, and extent	26 Mining	Agriculture 22
2 Topography	27 Energy and power	Animal husbandry 23
3 Climate	28 Industry	Armed forces 16
4 Flora and fauna	29 Domestic trade	Balance of payments 31
5 Population	30 Foreign trade	Banking 32
6 Ethnic groups	31 Balance of payments	Bibliography 50
7 Language	32 Banking	Climate 3
8 Religion	33 Insurance	Communications 10
9 Transportation	34 Securities	Customs and duties 37
10 Communications	35 Public finance	Dependencies 49
11 History	36 Taxation	Domestic trade 29
12 Government	37 Customs and duties	Economic policy 39
13 Political parties	38 Foreign investments	Economy 19
14 Local government	39 Economic policy	Education 43
15 Judicial system	40 Health	Energy and power 27
16 Armed forces	41 Social welfare	Ethnic groups 6
17 Migration	42 Housing	Famous persons 48
18 International cooperation	43 Education	Fishing 24
19 Economy	44 Libraries and museums	Flora and fauna 4
20 Income	45 Organizations	Foreign investments 38
21 Labor	46 Press	Foreign trade 30
22 Agriculture	47 Tourism	Forestry 25
23 Animal husbandry	48 Famous persons	Government 12
24 Fishing	49 Dependencies	Health 40
25 Forestry	50 Bibliography	History 11

Housing 42
Income 20
Industry 28
Insurance 33
International cooperation 18
Judicial system 15
Labor 21
Language 7
Libraries and museums 44
Local government 14
Location, size, and extent 1
Migration 17
Mining 26
Organizations 45
Political parties 13
Population 5
Press 46
Public finance 35
Religion 8
Securities 34
Social welfare 41
Taxation 36
Topography 2
Tourism 47
Transportation 9

EXPLANATION OF SYMBOLS

Data not available...
Nil (or negligible) —
Figures on tables not included in totals and subtotals are usually given in parentheses ( ).
A fiscal or split year is indicated by a stroke (e.g., 1974/75).
The use of a hyphen (e.g., 1973–74) normally signifies the full period of calendar years covered (including the end year indicated).

AFGHANISTAN

Republic of Afghanistan
Dawlati Jamhuri Afghanistan

CAPITAL: Kabul. **FLAG**: The national flag is a tricolor of black, red, and green horizontal stripes. In the upper left corner, in gold, is a device composed of an eagle encircled by a wreath of wheat ears bearing a scroll lettered "Republic of Afghanistan" in Pashto (Arabic script); below the eagle is the date 26 Changaash 1352 (17 July 1973), the founding of the Republic. **ANTHEM**: *Suroodi Millee (National Anthem)* beginning "So long as there is the earth and the heavens." **MONETARY UNIT**: The afghani (A) of 100 puls is a nonconvertible paper currency. There are coins of 50 puls and 1, 2, and 5 afghanis, and notes of 10, 20, 50, 100, 500, and 1,000 afghanis. As of 29 February 1976, A1 = $0.0222 (or $1 = A45). **WEIGHTS AND MEASURES**: The metric system is the legal standard, although some local units are still in use. **HOLIDAYS**: Now Rooz (New Year's Day), 1st day of spring; Roozi Istiqlaal (Independence Day), 27 May; Jashni Jumhooriyat (Republic Day Holidays), 17–19 July; Pashtoonistan Day, early September; Establishment of the National Assembly, 2d Wednesday in September; and Jashn Nijaat (Deliverance Day), middle of October. Movable religious holidays include First Day of Ramadan, 'Id al-Fitr, 'Id al-'Adha', 'Ashura, and Milad al-Nabi. **TIME**: 4:26 P.M. = noon GMT.

¹LOCATION, SIZE, AND EXTENT

Afghanistan is a landlocked country in Central Asia with a long, narrow strip in the northeast (the Wakhan). Its total area has never been definitely established, but it is estimated to be 647,500 sq km (250,000 sq mi), extending *1,239* km (*770* mi) NE–SW and *563* km (*350* mi) SE–NW. Afghanistan is bounded on the N by the USSR (Turkmen, Uzbek, and Tadzhik Soviet Socialist Republics), on the extreme NE by China, on the E and S by Pakistan, and on the W by Iran, with a total boundary length of *5,770* km (*3,585* mi).

²TOPOGRAPHY

Although the average altitude of Afghanistan is about 4,000 feet, the Hindu Kush mountain range rises to more than 20,000 feet in the northern corner of the Wakhan panhandle in the northeast and continues in a southwesterly direction for about 600 miles, dividing the northern provinces from the rest of the country. Central Afghanistan, a plateau with an average elevation of about 6,000 feet, contains many small fertile valleys and provides excellent grazing for sheep, goats, and camels. To the north of the Hindu Kush and the central mountain range, the altitude drops to about 1,500 feet, permitting the growth of cotton, fruits, grains, and other crops. Southwestern Afghanistan is a desert, hot in summer and cold in winter. The four major river systems are the Amu Darya (Oxus) on the north (which flows into the Aral Sea), the Hari Rud and Murghab in the west, the Helmand in the southwest, and the Kabul in the east (which flows into the Indus). There are few lakes.

³CLIMATE

The ranges in altitude produce a climate with both temperate and semitropical characteristics, and the seasons are clearly marked throughout the country. Wide temperature variations are usual from season to season and from day to night. The temperature in Kabul may vary as much as 39 centigrade degrees (70 Fahrenheit degrees) in a single day. The maximum summer temperature in Jalalabad is about 46°C (115°F). There is much sunshine and the air is usually clear and dry. Rainfall averages about 10 to 12 inches, precipitation occurring in winter and spring, most of it coming in the form of snow. Wind velocity is high, especially in the west. There are 32 stations in operation for meteorological observation.

⁴FLORA AND FAUNA

There are hundreds of varieties of trees, shrubs, vines, flowers, and fungi. The country is particularly rich in such medicinal plants as rue, wormwood, and asafetida. Fruit and nut trees are found in many areas. Animals include the fox, lynx, wild dog, bear, mongoose, shrew, hedgehog, hyena, jerboa, hare, and wild varieties of cats, asses, mountain goats, and mountain sheep. Trout are the most common fish. There are more than 100 species of wild fowl and birds.

As of 1975, endangered species in Afghanistan included the wolf, Indian tiger, Caspian tiger, leopard (*panthera pardus*), snow leopard, Asiatic cheetah, Bactrian deer, three species of markhor (common, Kabul, and straight-horned), Cheer pheasant, and Central Asian grey monitor.

⁵POPULATION

A demographic survey was completed in 1975, but the results have yet to be released. Population estimates vary from approximately 12 million to more than 19 million; 18.7 million is the official government estimate. The UN projected a population of 22,038,000 for 1980, based on a 1975 population of 19,280,000 and an annual growth rate of 2.7% (assuming a crude birthrate of 48.1 per 1,000 population, a crude death rate of 21.4, and a net natural increase of 26.7). Between 2 and 3 million persons are nomadic or seminomadic. Based on the government estimate, the population density was 29.3 per sq km (76 per sq mi) in 1975. Approximately 15% of the people live in cities or towns of 3,000 or more. Kabul, the capital, has a population estimated by the government at 553,000; Qandahar, 143,200; Herat, 112,300.

⁶ETHNIC GROUPS

About the mid-2d millennium B.C., Indo-Aryans began to move into and through the present area of Afghanistan. Much later came other tribal groups from Central Asia—Pactyes (from whom the present-day name Pashtoons derives), Sakas, Kushans, Hephthalites, and others—and a procession of Iranians and Greeks. In the 7th century A.D., Arabs arrived from the south, spreading the new faith of Islam. In the same century, Turks moved in from the north, followed in the 13th century by Mongols, and, finally, in the 15th century by Turko-Mongols. This multiplicity of movements made the country a loose conglomeration of racial and linguistic groups.

All citizens are called Afghans, but the Pashtoons (the name may also be written as "Pushtun" or "Pukhtun," and in Pakistan as "Pathan") are often referred to as the "true Afghans." Numbering about 55% of the population, they are known to have centered in the Sulaiman range in the east; it is only in recent centuries that they moved into areas inhabited by Dari-speaking Tajiks and Hazaras. They have long been divided into two major divisions, the Durranis and the Ghilzais, each with its own tribes and subtribes. Pashtoons hold a predominant place in the government.

The Tajiks, of Iranian stock, comprise about 30% of the population. In the south-central ranges are found some half million Hazaras, who are said to have descended from Mongols who moved into the region from the 13th to the 15th century. To the north of the Hindu Kush, Turkic and Turko-Mongol groups were in the majority until 1940. Each of these groups is related to groups north of the Amu Darya and within the USSR. Other groups include the Chahar Aimak and the Baluchi. In the northeast are the Kafirs, or infidels. After their conversion to Islam at the end of the 19th century, they were given the name of Nuristanis, or people of the light.

⁷LANGUAGE

Both Pashto and Dari (Afghan Persian) are the official languages of the country. Although Pashto has a literature of its own, Dari is the principal language of cultural expression, of the government, and of business. Baluchi belongs to the same linguistic group, as do several obscure tongues spoken in the high Pamirs. The Hazaras speak their own dialect of Dari. The Turkic languages include Uzbek, Turkoman, and Kirghiz, and the Nuristanis speak some seven different dialects belonging to the Dardic linguistic group.

⁸RELIGION

At least 99% of the Afghans are Muslims. Of these, 80% are Sunnis; the rest are Shi'is, including some Isma'ilis. The Pashtoons, most of the Tajiks, the Uzbeks, and the Turkomans are Sunnis, while the Hazaras are Shi'is. There are also small colonies of Hindus, Jews, and Parsis (Zoroastrians). Islam is the official religion of Afghanistan.

⁹TRANSPORTATION

There are no railways, and only the Amu Darya is navigable. Many roads have been built in recent years to connect the principal cities and to open up formerly isolated areas. In 1976 there were approximately 12,000 miles of roads, of which about 1,500 miles were paved. Roads connect Kabul with the provincial capitals and with Peshawar in Pakistan through the Khyber Pass. The road from Herat to Mashhad in Iran was completed in 1971. The Salang Tunnel through the Hindu Kush, completed in 1964, considerably shortened the distance between Kabul and northern Afghanistan. The Qandahar-Torghundi highway was completed in 1965. In 1975 there were 20,275 passenger cars and 7,483 commercial vehicles registered in Kabul.

The Khyber Pass is the best known of the passes providing land access to Afghanistan. Transit arrangements with Iran provide an alternate route for its commercial traffic. However, the great bulk of the country's trade moves through the USSR.

Ariana Afghan Airlines (in which Pan Am has a 49% interest) offers service to neighboring countries, the Middle East, and Europe. There are scheduled flights to Kabul on the national airlines of the USSR, Pakistan, Iran, India, and Czechoslovakia. Kabul and Qandahar have international airports, and there are civil airports of varying quality in about 30 other cities. The Bakhtar Afghan Airline, established in 1971, operates domestic service, connecting the larger cities with remote areas of the country.

¹⁰COMMUNICATIONS

Principal cities and some smaller towns and villages are served by the government-operated telegraph and telephone system.

Radio and telegraph connect the country with the rest of the world. In 1975 there were 20,842 telephones and about 400,000 radios. The only radio broadcasting station is at Kabul.

¹¹HISTORY

Afghanistan did not exist as an extensive, cohesive country until about two centuries ago. Areas of present-day Afghanistan were conquered by the Persian emperor Darius I in the 6th century B.C., and three centuries later by Alexander the Great on his way to India. As the power of his successors, the Seleucids, waned, an independent Greek kingdom of Bactria was established with its capital at Balkh, but after about a century it fell to invading tribes (notably the Sakas, who gave their name to Sakastan or Seistan). Toward the middle of the 3d century B.C., Buddhist religion and philosophy spread to Afghanistan, and from the beginning of the Christian era until the opening of the 9th century A.D., Buddhism was the religion of at least half the population of eastern Afghanistan.

For a millennium or more, Afghanistan remained divided. Tribal rulers strove against one another and resisted invaders from east and west. The Muslim conquest, however, which began as early as the 7th century, provided the area with the religion it has today. For almost two centuries, Ghazni was the capital of a powerful kingdom, the greatest of whose rulers, Mahmood (r. 997–1030), conquered most of the area from the Caspian Sea to the Ganges River in India. The Ghaznavids were displaced by the Seljuks, who mastered Persia and Anatolia (eastern Turkey); Sultan Sinjar (r. 1095–1157) was a powerful ruler; his capital was at Khurasaan. The Ghaznavids and the Seljuks were of Turkish origin. They were followed by the Iranian Ghorids, who, rising from Ghor, southeast of Herat, destroyed Ghazni, invaded India in 1175, and established an empire stretching from Herat to Ajmir in India. Next came the Khwarezm shahs, the rulers of the Khiva oasis in Transoxiana, who, by 1217, had created a Turco-Persian state that included the whole of Afghanistan. This empire disintegrated when Genghis Khan attacked it in 1219. The Barlas Turk, Timur (Tamerlane), occupied the whole of Afghanistan from 1365 to 1384. The Timurids established a court of intellectual and artistic brilliance at Herat but came under challenge from the Uzbeks. The Uzbeks drove the Timurids out of Herat in 1507. One of their princes, Babur, occupied Kabul in 1504, Qandahar in 1522, and conquered Delhi in 1526, establishing the great Mughal empire. Eastern Afghanistan was ruled from Delhi, Agra, or Lahore (now in Pakistan), while Herat and Seistan were provinces of Persia.

In the 18th century, Persians under Nadir Shah conquered the area. After Nadir's death in 1747, one of his military commanders, Ahmad Shah, was elected emir of Afghanistan. Ahmad's formation of a unified Afghanistan marked its real beginning as a political unit. His family remained in control until Dost Muhammad established himself in 1826 and gained the emirate in 1835. Although the British defeated Dost in the first Afghan War (1838–42), they restored him to power; but his attempts and those of his successors to play Russian interests against the British for control of Central Asia led to other conflicts. In the second Afghan War (1878), the forces of Sher Ali, Dost's son, were defeated, and his entire party was ousted in 1880. Abdur Rahman Khan, recognized as emir by the British in 1880, organized a standing army, established a central administration, and supported British interests against the Russians. Fighting with the border tribes continued even after the establishment in 1893 of the boundary (the Durand line) between Afghanistan and British India, now Pakistan. The Anglo-Russian agreement of 1907 guaranteed the independence of Afghanistan under British influence.

Afghanistan remained neutral in World War I, but Afghan forces briefly invaded India in 1919 under Amanullah, who had become emir after Habibullah (Abdur Rahman Khan's son and his successor in 1901) was assassinated. In the Treaty of Rawalpindi (1919), Afghanistan obtained freedom to conduct its own foreign affairs. Emir Amanullah's Westernization program was strongly opposed, and he was forced to abdicate in 1929. After a brief civil war, Muhammad Nadir Shah was elected king by a tribal assembly in October. He restored peace and continued Amanullah's modernization efforts. Assassinated in 1933, he was succeeded by his son Zahir Shah. For 20 years, however, real power resided with Zahir's uncles, who served as the prime ministers. In 1964 a new constitution was introduced, converting Afghanistan into a constitutional monarchy. The country's first general election was held in 1965.

12 GOVERNMENT

Between 1964 and 1973, Afghanistan was a constitutional monarchy. The head of government was the prime minister, appointed by the king and responsible to the legislature. The legislature (Shura) was bicameral. The 215-member House of the People (Wolesi Jirgeh) was elected by direct universal suffrage; the 84-seat House of the Elders (Meshrano Jirgeh) consisted of members appointed by the king, elected by each of the provincial councils, or directly elected by the residents of each province. The Great Council (Loya Jirgeh) included members of both houses and the chairmen of the provincial councils.

Since 17 July 1973, Afghanistan has been a republic, headed

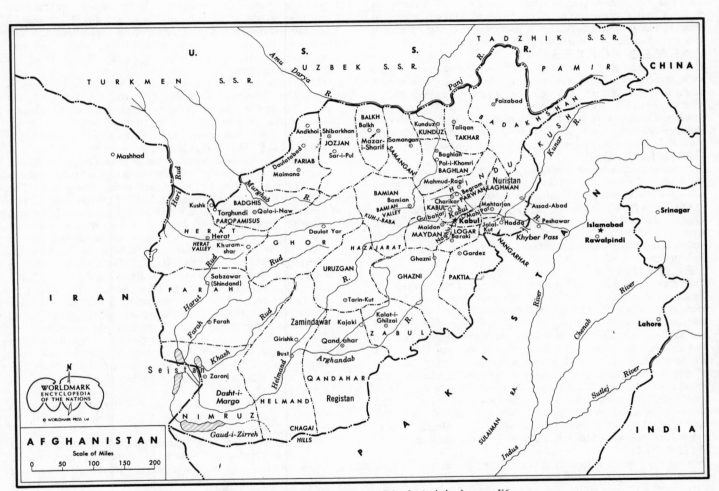

See continental political: front cover K6; physical: back cover K6

LOCATION: 29°28′ to 38°30′N; 60°30′ to 74°53′E. **BOUNDARY LENGTHS**: USSR, 2,383 km (1,481 mi); China, 71 km (44 mi); Pakistan, 2,466 km (1,532 mi); Iran 850 km (528 mi).

On 17 July 1973, Muhammad Daoud Khan, Zahir Shah's first cousin and brother-in-law, who had served as prime minister from 1953 until early 1963, was returned to power in a near-bloodless coup as founder, president, and prime minister of the Republic of Afghanistan. The monarchy was abolished, and Zahir Shah and his immediate family went into exile. The legislature was formally dissolved on 28 July, and the powers of the Supreme Court were transferred to the Ministry of Justice. Under Daoud Khan, Afghanistan has sought better relations with India and Iran and pursued the border dispute with Pakistan, which dates from the founding of that state in 1947.

by Muhammad Daoud Khan, who serves as president and prime minister. Power rests with the military and gendarmerie, both of which are firmly within Daoud Khan's camp. Government operations are carried out under 15 ministers who also serve as members of Daoud Khan's cabinet.

13 POLITIAL PARTIES

The 1964 constitution provided for the formation of political parties. However, since the framers of the constitution decided that political parties should be permitted only after the first elections, all candidates for the parliamentary elections of August and September 1965 stood as independents. Subsequently, no formal political parties were permitted, although many rival groups put forth divergent political philosophies. Nor has the new military government permitted the establishment of competing political organizations.

14 LOCAL GOVERNMENT

Afghanistan is divided into 26 provinces, which are subdivided into 175 districts and 118 subdistricts. There is a governor for each province, a district governor for each district, and a sub-governor for each subdistrict.

15 JUDICIAL SYSTEM

The Supreme Court was abolished after the July 1973 coup. The judiciary is now administered by the Ministry of Justice. The highest judicial body is called the Judicial High Council, with one of its members serving as administrative chief. The members of the Council are appointed by President Daoud, who also chooses the administrative chief. There are 7 courts of appeal and 26 provincial, commercial, and district courts.

16 ARMED FORCES

There is compulsory conscription and two-year military service for a percentage of men from 22 to 45 years of age. Officers are recruited for long-term service. The armed forces had 88,000 men in 1975. The army had 80,000 personnel, plus reserves of 150,000. The air force had 8,000 men and 160 combat aircraft, plus reserves of 12,000. The gendarmerie totaled 25,000 personnel. The military budget was A2,022 million in 1973/74.

17 MIGRATION

External migration is negligible and, owing to government policy and control, very difficult; but special border arrangements allow for the seasonal emigration of nomads.

18 INTERNATIONAL COOPERATION

Afghanistan has been a member of the UN since 1946 and is a member of most of the specialized agencies. It participates in various intergovernmental conferences and joined the Colombo Plan group in 1963.

19 ECONOMY

Until recently, Afghanistan lacked an integrated economy. With the building of roads in the 1950s linking the financial and commercial centers with the wool- and fruit-producing areas, a unified national economy began to emerge. Still largely agricultural and pastoral, Afghanistan's mainstays are the cultivation of fruits and cotton, the production of wool and karakul skins, and traditional handicrafts like carpet weaving. Modern industry consists of cotton and wool textiles, sugar refining, cement, and food processing. The country has valuable mineral resources but only coal, salt, lapis lazuli, barite, and chrome are being exploited. The discovery of large quantities of natural gas in the north, for which a pipeline to the USSR was completed in 1967, has meant increased fuel resources and export earnings.

20 INCOME

In 1974/75, the estimated GNP at current prices was A66.88 billion. Assuming an estimated population of 18.7 million in 1975, the GDP per capita was A3,576 (about $80), one of the lowest in the world.

21 LABOR

Of the active labor force, about 3.29 million persons were employed in agriculture and 750,000 in trade, industry, administration, and other services in 1975. There are some 2 million to 3 million nomads. The textile industry is the largest employer of industrial labor. The weaving of cloth and carpets is the most important home industry. There are no trade unions or other labor organizations.

22 AGRICULTURE

Afghanistan grows about 95% of its needs in wheat and rye, and more than meets its needs in rice, potatoes, pulses, nuts, and seeds; it depends on imports only for some wheat, sugar, and edible fats and oils. Agricultural production, however, is a fraction of its potential. Of the country's total land area of about 160 million acres, some 35 million acres, or 22%, is agricultural land. But only 19.5 million acres are considered cropland. Of the 14.5 million irrigable acres, only 60% are actually cropped, because of lack of water. The extension of irrigation, increased use of fertilizers and modern farming methods, and the provision of agricultural credit are the country's prime economic objectives. The Helmand Valley reclamation project made about 200,000 acres of new land available for farm settlers. Similar projects are under way in Nangarhar, Ghazni, Parwan, and Kunduz.

The variety of the country's crops corresponds to its topography. The areas around Qandahar, Herat, and the broad Kabul plain yield fruits of many kinds. The northern regions from Takhar to Badghis and in Herat and Helmand provinces produce cotton. Corn is grown extensively in Paktya and Nangarhar provinces and rice mainly in Kunduz, Baghlan, and Laghman provinces. Wheat is common to several regions. The wheat crop in 1974/75 was 2.75 million tons. Other crops were corn, 770,000 tons; rice, 420,000 tons; barley, 380,000 tons; and cotton, 145,000 tons.

The installation of facilities for cleaning and packing raisins has enabled the country's dried fruits to enter the European market. Pistachios and almonds are widely grown, and substantial quantities are exported. Fresh and dried fruits together accounted for more than 40% of Afghanistan's exports in 1974/75.

23 ANIMAL HUSBANDRY

The availability of land suitable for grazing has made animal husbandry an important part of the economy. Natural pastures cover some 8 million acres but are being overgrazed. The northern regions around Kataghan, Mazar-i-Sharif, and Maimana are the home range for about 6 million karakul sheep. In 1974/75 there were 21.5 million sheep, 3.1 million goats, 3.6 million head of cattle, 1.3 million asses, and 403,000 horses.

Export of karakul sheepskins is a declining source of foreign exchange revenue; annual production totals between 1.5 and 2.4 million skins, practically all of which are shipped to the US, the Federal Republic of Germany (FRG), and the UK. In 1974/75, karakul skins brought $11.5 million, or 5.5% of all export earnings, less than one-third their share of export earnings in 1968/69. Annual wool production, mainly from fat-tailed sheep, is about 25,000 tons, of which more than two-thirds is locally used in carpet weaving and cloth manufacture. Export of raw wool amounted to 4,000 tons in 1974/75 but earned less than $6.2 million, down from $7.5 million in 1968/69.

24 FISHING

Some fishing takes place in the lakes and rivers, but fish do not constitute a significant part of the Afghan diet.

25 FORESTRY

The formerly abundant forests have been greatly depleted, and only about 4% of the land area is now forested, mainly in the east. Exploitation has been hampered by lack of power and access roads. Although most of Afghanistan suffers from a chronic timber shortage, much timber is exported because it can be moved from Nangarhar and Paktya provinces by river to Pakistan more easily than to other parts of Afghanistan. In 1973, about 6.8 million cu meters of round wood and 415,000 cu meters of sawn wood were produced.

26 MINING

Afghanistan has valuable deposits of barite, beryl, chrome, coal, copper, iron, lapis lazuli, lead, mica, petroleum, salt, silver, sulfur, and zinc. Reserves of high-grade iron ore are estimated to total 2 billion tons.

Some 186,800 tons of coal were mined in 1974/75. Of the 10 million or more tons of high-grade talc found in the Shinwari tribal territory in the northern part of Nangarhar, fewer than 1,000 tons are produced annually. In 1974/75, Afghanistan produced 48,700 tons of salt. Deposits of lapis lazuli in Badakhshan are mined in small quantities.

Natural gas reserves are estimated to total 150 billion cu meters. Production started in 1967 with 342 million cu meters but rose to 2.9 billion cu meters in 1974/75. A pipeline carries gas to the USSR. Gas exports brought in $23.3 million in 1974/75, as compared with $9 million in 1968/69. With technical assistance from the USSR, oil was discovered near the Soviet border. A small refinery with a capacity of 200,000 tons was to be built under the seven-year development plan beginning 21 March 1976.

27 ENERGY AND POWER

In 1974/75, production of electricity totaled 527.2 million kwh, of which about 300 million kwh were generated by public power plants. Total installed capacity in 1973 was 268,000 kw; 192,000 kw were hydroelectric. Industrial consumption amounted to about 60 million kwh. Three hydroelectric plants were opened between 1965 and 1970 at Jalalabad, Naghlu, and Mahipar near Kabul; another at Kajakee in the upper Helmand River Valley was opened in the mid-1970s. Development of natural gas resources has had increasing impact on domestic power consumption.

28 INDUSTRY

Industry is in a primary stage of development, limited to processing of local materials. The principal industry is cotton textile production. Several plants, including a modern one at Gulbahar, produced 68.1 million meters of cotton fabrics and 240,000 bundles of cotton yarn in 1974/75.

There are also small woolen and rayon textile industries. The latter produced 20.9 million meters of fabrics in 1974/75. Other industries are cement (144,200 tons in 1974/75), raisin cleaning (about 6,000 tons a year), fruit preservation, leather tanning, preparation of casings, sugar refining (8,900 tons in 1974/75), and vegetable oil extraction (6,300 tons of margarine in 1974/75). A large urea plant, financed on credit from the USSR, started production in 1975 with an annual capacity of 105,000 tons.

Carpet making is the most important handicraft industry. The most famous carpets come from Daulatabad. Production varies from year to year; 537,000 sq meters (valued at $19.4 million) were exported in 1974/75. Other handicrafts include feltmaking and the weaving of cotton, woolen, and silk cloth. Most of Afghanistan's household consumer requirements are met by its own cottage industries.

29 DOMESTIC TRADE

Kabul, Qandahar, Mazar-i-Sharif, and Herat are the principal commercial cities of eastern, southern, northern, and western Afghanistan, respectively. The first two are the main distribution centers for imports arriving from the direction of Pakistan, the latter two for materials arriving from Iran and the USSR.

Hours of business vary from city to city, from season to season, and from one line of business to another.

There is one advertising agency, controlled by the government. Advertisements appear in newspapers, billboards, and on radio.

30 FOREIGN TRADE

Trade balances are generally favorable, if imports coming to Afghanistan as commodity loans and grants are excluded. Principal exports in 1974/75 (in millions of dollars) were:

Dried fruits and nuts	57.6
Cotton	32.2
Fresh fruits	30.3
Natural gas	23.3
Carpets	19.4
Karakul skins	11.5
Wool and other animal hair	6.2
Other exports	30.2
TOTAL	210.7

Principal imports in 1974/75 (excluding commodity loans and grants, in millions of dollars) were:

Textiles	23.5
Rubber tires and tubes	15.3
Petroleum products	14.1
Chemicals	13.6
Tea	12.5
Base metals	8.4
Machinery	8.3
Motor vehicles	6.6
Other imports	68.2
TOTAL	170.5

Principal trade partners in 1974/75 (excluding commodity loans and grants, in millions of dollars) were:

	EXPORTS	IMPORTS	BALANCE
USSR	80.0	14.7	65.3
India	34.4	24.5	9.9
Japan	—	53.6	−53.6
Pakistan	24.0	10.6	13.4
UK	20.6	8.4	12.2
FRG	5.7	7.7	− 2.0
US	3.4	5.8	− 2.4
Other countries	42.6	45.2	− 2.6
TOTALS	210.7	170.5	40.2

Donors of commodity loans and grants totaling $49.4 million in 1974/75 were the USSR, $17.6 million; the US, $4.4 million; others, $27.4 million.

31 BALANCE OF PAYMENTS

As a recipient of large-scale commodity aid from the USSR and the US, Afghanistan is not confronted with the balance-of-payments problem that its previous export-import gaps might otherwise have created. Between 1951 and 1973, Afghanistan's year-end international reserves were never lower than $38 million or higher than $65 million. Development of the natural gas industry and favorable prices for some of the country's agricultural exports led to increases in international reserves, to $67.5 million in 1974 and to $115.4 million as of 31 December 1975. Exploitation of natural gas also freed Afghanistan from extreme dependence on petroleum imports and from the rapid increase in import costs that most countries experienced in 1973 and 1974.

32 BANKING

The government central bank, the Bank of Afghanistan, founded in 1939, with a paid-up capital of A500 million and 28 branches in the chief cities, issues bank notes, administers government loans, grants loans to municipalities and to other banks, and provides short-term loans at interest rates ranging from 4% to 7%. In December 1975, its assets included A6,533 million in foreign assets, A15,189 million in claims on the government, A1,627 million in claims on the private sector, and A805 million in claims on commercial banks. Currency in circulation totaled A11,515 million in December 1975.

All banks in Afghanistan were nationalized in 1975. In December 1975, reserves of commercial banks totaled A315 million; time, savings, and foreign currency deposits were A1,476 million; and demand deposits totaled A663 million.

The Agricultural and Cottage Industries Bank was reorganized in 1969 as the Agricultural Development Bank to provide credit to farmers for modern agricultural implements and inputs. The Construction and Mortgage Bank provides building loans and short-term commercial credits. Foreign banks are not permitted in Afghanistan.

33 INSURANCE

In 1974 there were three foreign insurance companies and one domestic company doing business in Afghanistan. The Afghan Insurance Co. covers fire, transport, and accident insurance; net premiums in 1974 amounted to A14,077,205 and net claims were A6,208,818.

34 SECURITIES

Afghans may not own foreign securities. There is no organized domestic securities market.

35 PUBLIC FINANCE

The budget is divided into separate components for ordinary and development revenues and expenditures. The fiscal year ends 21 September. Consolidated government revenues and expenditures for 1972/73 and 1973/74 (in millions of afghanis) were:

	1972/73	1973/74
REVENUES		
Taxes on income	573.4	819.4
Import duties	1,702.8	1,998.9
Export duties	223.4	208.4
Other indirect taxes	1,012.3	1,385.2
Sales and charges	1,049.3	1,158.1
Other receipts	2,807.9	2,322.3
TOTALS	7,369.1	7,892.3
EXPENDITURES		
Current expenditures	3,830.0	3,960.7
Development expenditures	2,386.7	1,985.9
Subsidies	799.7	984.6
Interest on public debt	1,026.7	1,586.0
TOTALS	8,043.1	8,517.2
Balance	−674.0	−624.9

The domestic public debt totaled A12,147.8 million as of 21 September 1974.

36 TAXATION

Indirect taxes account for more than 40% of government revenues, direct taxes for about 8–10%. Income taxes are limited to business income of individuals. Agriculture is exempt. Most taxable income earners pay 10% (plus a surtax ranging from 3% to 43%) on all income over A4,000 a year). The maximum personal income tax for Afghans and foreigners is 40% of taxable income, allowing for deductions. The maximum corporate tax for both Afghan and foreign businesses is 20% of net profits.

37 CUSTOMS AND DUTIES

Customs duties, levied as a source of revenue rather than as a protective measure, comprise more than one-fourth of total government revenue. Ad valorem in character, the duties range from 1% to 50%. There are no preferential duties. In addition to customs duties, a surtax of 3% to 30% is levied on all imports of luxuries. The importation of products whose use is contrary to Islamic tenets is prohibited to all except foreigners. No goods or merchandise may be imported, exported, or transported from one city to another without a declaration or customs permit. There are no free-trade zones. Afghanistan is a signatory to GATT.

38 FOREIGN INVESTMENTS

A 1967 law encouraging investment of private foreign capital in Afghanistan provides that such capital invested in approved enterprises shall enjoy (1) the leasing for long periods on liberal terms of government-owned land, (2) exemption from tariff duties or moderate tariff protection on products exported, and (3) three-year exemptions from (a) corporate income taxes on profits not exceeding 15% per annum of the registered capital, (b) duties on imports, and (c) income taxes on the investments of shareholders or owners of capital. Annual profits or dividends arising out of such investments may be repatriated provided they do not exceed 15% of the registered capital. Owners of enterprises that may be nationalized or taken over by the government are to be equitably compensated.

Afghanistan is heavily dependent on foreign loans and grants. Between 1950 and 1974, Afghanistan received about $1.5 billion in foreign assistance, of which the US contributed $450 million and the USSR more than $600 million. As of 30 June 1975, Afghanistan had $40,834,000 in development credits outstanding with IDA, of which $10,516,000 had been disbursed.

39 ECONOMIC POLICY

Between 1956 and 1972, Afghanistan completed three five-year plans (1956–61, 1962–67, and 1967–72). The first two plans aimed primarily at establishing the basic socioeconomic infrastructure that was lacking until then, and developing the mineral resources. The third plan marked the country's entry into a new phase of development, when it undertook such quick-payoff projects as irrigation and chemical fertilizer and food-processing plants. Development outlays for the first plan were $350 million, for the second $696 million, and for the third an estimated $856 million. The implementation of the first plan was impeded by a severe shortage of technical and administrative skills. The second plan was also only partially realized; as against the target of $807 million, only five-sixths of that amount was actually utilized. On the other hand, although the increase in agricultural output merely kept pace with population growth, the country did acquire transportation, communication, and power facilities that should spur further progress. The third plan aimed to increase agricultural production so as to yield an exportable surplus in raw materials; to increase and diversify industrial output; to encourage private investment, which had been markedly sluggish; and to train technical and administrative personnel. The fourth plan (to have begun in 1973) was interrupted by the 1973 coup. Afghanistan's economic policy was thereafter switched to a seven-year cycle. The new plan, to extend from March 1976 to March 1983, was expected to entail a proposed expenditure of $3.5 billion.

40 HEALTH

In 1975, 901 qualified physicians, almost 800 nurses, 183 dentists, and 153 midwives were attached to 170 hospitals and clinics with a total of 3,587 beds. Most doctors live in the capital city. There are modern pharmacies in Kabul and in provincial centers. A national medical school was established in 1931; many Afghan medical students are sent abroad to study. In 1932, the first tuberculosis hospital was built with funds donated by Muhammad Nadir Shah. Muhammad Zahir Shah donated funds toward the construction of three women's hospitals.

Public health advanced considerably under the first two five-year plans. In addition to the construction of several hospitals, mobile medical units were established to bring medical services, particularly vaccination and inoculation, to remote villages. According to UN estimates, average life expectancy for both males and females was only 30 years in 1930. By 1975, estimated life expectancy had risen to 42 years for males and 43.4 years for females. In 1971, the infant mortality rate was estimated at a very high 182 per 1,000 live births.

41 SOCIAL WELFARE

Social welfare in Afghanistan has traditionally relied on family and tribal organization. In the villages and small towns, a tax is levied on each man to benefit the poor. Disabled people are cared for in social welfare centers in the provincial capitals. Most other welfare activities are still unorganized and in private hands.

42 HOUSING

Houses in farming communities are largely of mud brick and frequently grouped within a fortified enclosure, to provide protection from marauders. The roofs are flat, with a coating of mixed straw and mud rolled hard above a ceiling of horizontal poles, although in areas where timber is scarce, separate mud brick domes crown each room. Every town has at least one wide thoroughfare, but other streets are narrow lanes between houses of mud brick, loftier than those in the villages, and featuring decorative wooden balconies.

The government moved into the field of housing with the construction of the first modern factories. At Pol-i-Khomri, adjacent to the textile mills, workers' houses were built in an extensive green area, and at other sites similar housing projects have been constructed. Government banks and agencies aid in the financing of homes for government employees at Kabul and its suburbs, and provide loans to stimulate the construction of medium- and low-cost housing units by the private sector. The Helmand Valley Authority has built houses for the farmers who settle on newly irrigated lands along the Halmand and Arghandab rivers.

43 EDUCATION

It has been estimated that fewer than 30% of the people are literate. Education is free at all levels, and primary education is theoretically compulsory, but only about one in eight boys completes the six years of primary education. Primary schools are now coeducational, but most secondary schools remain separate. In 1974/75, only 2,897 of the 10,680 teachers in primary schools were women. Children are taught in their mother tongue (Dari or Pashto) during the first three grades; the second official language is introduced in the fourth grade. Children are also taught Arabic so that they may be able to read the Qurʾan. The school year extends from early March to early December. In 1974/75 there were 653,514 pupils at the village school and primary level, of whom 95,094 were girls. In remote or mountainous communities, where primary schools are not yet available, one-teacher village schools provide four years of rudimentary education.

Students who successfully pass their primary-school examination are qualified for admission to middle schools (grades 7 to 9) or to lycées (grades 7 to 12) patterned on French and German secondary schools. Vocational schools in Kabul train youths in agriculture, commerce, theology, teaching, secretarial studies, arts and crafts, mechanics, and technology. In 1974/75 there were 8,521 teachers (1,286 female) teaching 171,843 students at the secondary level, including those in vocational schools.

The University of Kabul, which is now coeducational, was founded in 1933 with the inauguration of the faculty of medicine, to which faculties of law and diplomacy, science, literature, theology, engineering, agriculture, economics, and pharmacy were subsequently added. There were 10,962 students at university level in 1974/75. In 1963, a faculty of medicine was established at Jalalabad in Nangarhar Province. This faculty is responsible to the central administration in Kabul. Current development plans provide for this faculty to be the nucleus in the establishment of a second university for Afghanistan.

44 LIBRARIES AND MUSEUMS

For centuries, manuscript collections were in the hands of the rulers, local feudal lords, and renowned religious families. Printing came fairly late to Afghanistan, but with the shift from the handwritten manuscript to the printed book, various collections were formed. One of the largest (at least 800 manuscripts and 28,000 volumes), housed in a special building of the Department of Press and Information, includes many works in Dari, Pashto, and Arabic. New libraries are being developed through exchange programs with foreign institutions. Kabul has a public library with more than 60,000 volumes and about 500 manuscripts. The library of the University of Kabul has 85,000 volumes.

On the outskirts of the capital, the Kabul Museum possesses an unrivaled collection of stone heads, bas-reliefs, ivory plaques and statuettes, bronzes, mural paintings, and Buddhistic material from excavations at Hadda, Bamian, Begram, and other sites. It also contains an extensive collection of coins and a unique collection of Islamic bronzes, marble reliefs, and ceramics from Ghazni. There are provincial museums at Ghazni, Herat, Mazar-i-Sharif, Parwan, and Qandahar. Major religious shrines have collections of valuable objects.

45 ORGANIZATION

Organizations to advance public aims and goals are of recent origin, and most are sponsored and directed by the government. Unions, political parties, and student associations do not exist. The most active organizations are those concerned with cultural and charitable activities. The Pashto Tolanah promotes knowledge of Pashto literature, and the Historical Society (Anjumani Tarikh) amasses information on Afghan history. Both organizations issue periodicals. Literary societies meet in the larger towns.

The Women's Welfare Society carries on educational enterprises, provides training in handicrafts, and dispenses charitable aid, while the Maristun, a social service center, looks after children, men, and women and teaches them crafts and trades. The Red Crescent, the equivalent of the Red Cross, is active in every province.

The Utaqi Tejarat is the national chamber of commerce. Institutional and industrial employees have their own clubs.

46 PRESS

The only Afghan newspapers and magazines permitted are operated by the government. In 1975 there were 15 daily newspapers. The three leading daily newspapers in Kabul (with estimated 1974 circulations) are *Anis* (25,000), published in Dari and Pashto; *Hiwad* (5,000), in Pashto; and *Jumhooriyat* in Dari and Pashto. All are published under the supervision of the Ministry of Information and Culture. Foreigners may not publish newspapers.

47 TOURISM

A passport and visa are required for entrance into Afghanistan. The visa is valid for varying periods depending on the nature of the visit. The government has established the Afghan Tourist Organization to help tourists. These numbered 44,500 in 1968 and more than 96,195 in 1974/75. A modern hotel was opened in Kabul in 1969, and modern hotel facilities at some of the country's most scenic spots have been built with help from IBRD.

48 FAMOUS AFGHANS

The most renowned ruler of medieval Afghanistan, Mahmood Ghazni (971–1030) was the Turkish creator of an empire stretching from Ray and Isfahan in Iran to Lahore in India (now in Pakistan) and from the Amu Darya (Oxus) River to the Arabian Sea. The Iranian Muʿizz ud-Din Muhammad of Ghor (d.1206) founded Muslim rule in India. Zahir ud-Din Babur (1483–1530), a Timurid prince of Ferghana (now in USSR), established his base at Kabul and from there waged campaigns leading to the expulsion of an Afghan ruling dynasty, the Lodis, from Delhi and the foundation of the Mughal empire in India.

Many eminent figures of Arab and Persian intellectual history were born or spent their careers in what is now Afghanistan. Al-Biruni (973–1048), the great Arab encyclopedist, was born in Khiva but settled in Ghazni, where he died. Abdul Majid Majdud Sanaʿi (1070–1140), the first major Persian poet to employ verse for mystical and philosophical expression, was a native of Ghazni. Jalal ud-Din Rumi (1207–1273), who stands at the summit of Persian poetry, was born in Balkh but migrated to Konya (Iconium) in Turkey. The last of the celebrated Persian classical poets, Abdur Rahman Jami (1414–92), was born in Khurasaan but spent most of his life in Herat. So did Behzad (c.1450–1520), the greatest master of Persian painting.

The founder of the state of Afghanistan was Ahmad Shah Abdali (1724–73), who changed his dynastic name to Durrani. He conquered Kashmir and Delhi and, with his capital at Qandahar, ruled over an empire that also stretched from the Amu Darya to the Arabian Sea. Dost Muhammad (1789-1863) was the founder of the Muhammadzai (Barakzai) dynasty. In a turbulent career, he both fought and made peace with the British in India, and unified the country. His grandson, Abdur Rahman Khan (1844-1901), established order after protracted civil strife. Amanullah Khan (1892-1960), who reigned from 1919 to 1929, tried social reforms aimed at Westernizing the country but was forced to abdicate. Nadir Shah (d.1933), who was elected king by a tribal assembly in 1929, continued Amanullah's Westernization program. His son, Zahir Shah (b.1914), was king until he was deposed by a coup in July 1973. Muhammad Daoud Khan (b.1909), cousin and brother-in-law of King Zahir, was the leader of the coup and is the founder and first president of the Republic of Afghanistan.

[49] DEPENDENCIES
Afghanistan has no territories or colonies.

[50] BIBLIOGRAPHY

Adamec, Ludwig. *Afghanistan, 1900-1923.* Berkeley: University of California Press, 1967.

Ahmad, Jamal-ud-din, and Muhammad Abdul Aziz. *Afghanistan: A Brief Survey.* London: Longmans, Green, 1936.

Ali, Muhammad. *The Afghans.* Lahore: 1965.

Ali, Muhammad. *A New Guide to Afghanistan.* Lahore: Northern Pakistan Printing and Publishing Company, 1959.

Bell, Marjorie Jewett. *An American Engineer in Afghanistan.* Minneapolis: University of Minnesota Press, 1948.

Caroe, Olaf. *The Pathans.* New York: St. Martin's Press, 1958.

Dupree, Louis. *Afghanistan.* Princeton, N.J.: Princeton University Press, 1973.

Dupree, Louis, and L. Albert. *Afghanistan in the 1970s.* New York: Praeger, 1974.

Fletcher, Arnold. *Afghanistan: Highway of Conquest.* Ithaca, N.Y.: Cornell University Press, 1966.

Fox, Ernest Franklin. *Travels in Afghanistan, 1937-1938.* New York: Macmillan, 1943.

Franck, Peter Goswyn. *Afghanistan Between East and West.* Washington, D.C.: National Planning Association, 1960.

Fraser-Tytler, Sir William Kerr. *Afghanistan.* 3d ed. Revised by M. Gillett. London: Oxford University Press, 1967.

Grassmuck, G., L. Adamec, and F. Irwin (eds.). *Afghanistan: Some New Approaches.* Ann Arbor: University of Michigan Press, 1969.

Gregorian, Vartan. *The Emergence of Modern Afghanistan.* Stanford, Calif.: Stanford University Press, 1969.

Griffiths, John C. *Afghanistan.* New York: Praeger, 1967.

Hackin, Ria, and Ahmad Ali Kohzad. *Légendes et coutumes Afghans.* Paris: Presses universitaires de France, 1953.

Humlun, Johannes. *La Géographie d'Afghanistan.* Copenhagen: Gyldenal, 1959.

Ikbal Ali Shah. *Modern Afghanistan.* London: Sampson Low, Martson, 1939.

King, Peter. *Cockpit in High Asia.* New York: Taplinger, 1967.

MacMunn, Sir George Fletcher. *Afghanistan, from Darius to Amanullah.* London: Bell, 1929.

Michel, Aloys Arthur. *The Kabul, Kunduz and Helmand Valleys and the National Economy of Afghanistan: A Study of Regional Resources and the Comparative Advantages of Development.* Washington, D.C.: National Academy of Sciences, 1959.

Poullada, Leon. *Reform and Rebellion in Afghanistan, 1919-1929: King Amanullah's Failure to Transform a Tribal Society.* Ithaca, N.Y.: Cornell University Press, 1973.

Sale, Lady Florentia. *A Journal of the Disasters in Afghanistan, 1841-42.* New York: Harper and Bros., 1843.

Sassani, Abul H. K. *Education in Afghanistan.* Washington, D.C.: Office of Education, U.S. Department of Health, Education, and Welfare, 1961.

Sykes, Sir Percy. *A History of Afghanistan.* 2 vols. New York: Macmillan, 1941.

Tarn, William Woodthorpe. *The Greeks in Bactria and India.* London: Oxford University Press, 1938.

Wilber, Donald Newton (ed.). *Afghanistan: Its People, Its Society, Its Culture.* New Haven, Conn.: Human Relations Area Files, 1962.

Wilber, Donald Newton. *Annotated Bibliography of Afghanistan.* New Haven, Conn.: Human Relations Area Files, 1962.

AUSTRALIA

Commonwealth of Australia

CAPITAL: Canberra. **FLAG**: The flag has three main features: the red, white, and blue Union Jack in the upper left quarter, indicating Australia's membership in the Commonwealth of Nations; the white five-star Southern Cross in the right half; and the white seven-pointed federal star below the Union Jack. The flag has a blue ground. Of the five stars of the Southern Cross, four have seven points and one has five points. **ANTHEM**: There is no official national anthem. *God Save the Queen* is reserved for regal and state occasions; *Waltzing Matilda* was used at the 1976 Olympics. **MONETARY UNIT**: The Austalian dollar (A$) of 100 cents is a nonconvertible paper currency. There are coins of 1, 2, 5, 10, 20, and 50 cents, and notes of 1, 2, 10, 20, and 50 Australian dollars. A$1=US$1.25 (or US$1=A$0.80). **WEIGHTS AND MEASURES**: Metric weights and measures are used. The Australian proof gallon equals 1.37 US proof gallons. **HOLIDAYS**: New Year's Day, 1 January; Australia Day, 26 January; Christmas, 25 December; Boxing Day, 26 December. The Queen's Birthday is celebrated in June, except in Western Australia, where it is observed in November. Movable religious holidays include Good Friday, Holy Saturday, and Easter Monday. **TIME**: Western Australia, 8 P.M.=noon GMT; South Australia and Northern Territory, 9:30 P.M.; Victoria, New South Wales, Queensland, and Tasmania, 10 P.M. Summer time is 1 hour later in all states except Western Australia and Queensland.

¹LOCATION, SIZE, AND EXTENT

Lying southeast of Asia, between the Pacific and Indian oceans, Australia, the world's smallest continent, is almost completely surrounded by ocean expanses. Australia has a total area of 7,686,879 sq km (2,967,909 sq mi). The five mainland states are New South Wales, 801,431 sq km (309,433 sq mi); Queensland, 1,727,529 sq km (667,000 sq mi); South Australia, 984,381 sq km (380,070 sq mi); Victoria, 227,619 sq km (87,884 sq mi); and Western Australia, 2,527,631 sq km (975,920 sq mi). The island state of Tasmania has an area of 68,332 sq km (26,383 sq mi); the Northern Territory, 1,347,524 sq km (520,280 sq mi), and the Australian Capital Territory, 2,432 sq km (939 sq mi). The country, including Tasmania, extends *4,000* km (*2,485* mi) E–W and *3,837* km (*2,384* mi) N–S. Australia is bounded on the N by the Timor and Arafura seas, on the NE by the Coral Sea, on the E by the Pacific Ocean, on the SE by the Tasman Sea, and on the S and W by the Indian Ocean, with a total coastline of *27,930* km (*17,355* mi). Neighboring areas include Irian Jaya (part of Indonesia) and Papua New Guinea to the north, New Zealand to the southeast, and Indonesia to the northwest.

²TOPOGRAPHY

The continent of Australia is divided into four general topographic regions: (1) a low, sandy eastern coastal plain; (2) the eastern highlands ranging from 1,000 to more than 7,000 feet in altitude and extending from Cape York Peninsula in northern Queensland southward to Tasmania; (3) the central plains, consisting largely of a north-south series of drainage basins, including the Great Artesian Basin, which underlies about 1,751,480 sq km (676,250 sq mi) of territory and is the most extensive area of internal drainage in the world; and (4) the western plateau, covered with great deserts and "bigger plains" (regularly spaced sand ridges and rocky wastes), 1,000 to 2,000 feet high and comprising most of the western half of the continent. Australian mountains have eroded over recent geological periods, and less than 7% of the continent is above 2,000 feet. The highest point is Mt. Kosciusko (7,310 feet) in the Australian Alps of the southeastern corner of New South Wales; the lowest point is Lake Eyre in South Australia, 39 feet below sea level.

The most important river system, and the only one with a permanent, year-round flow, is formed by the Murray, Darling, and Murrumbidgee rivers in the southeast. The Murray River itself, Australia's largest, rises in the Australian Alps of New South Wales and flows 1,600 miles west and southwest to empty into the sea below Adelaide, South Australia. Several other rivers are important, but for the most part they carry great amounts of water in the wet season and are dry for the rest of the year. The largest lakes have no outlet and are usually dry. The coastline is smooth, with few bays or capes. The two largest sea inlets are the Gulf of Carpentaria in the north, between Arnhem Land and the Cape York Peninsula, and the Great Australian Bight in the south. The Great Barrier Reef, the longest and most spectacular coral reef in the world, extends for about 1,200 miles off the east coast of Queensland.

³CLIMATE

Although it has a wide diversity of climatic conditions, Australia is generally warm and dry, with no extreme cold and little frost, its temperatures ranging from comfortably mild in the south to hot in the central interior and north. July mean temperatures average 9.4°C (49°F) in Melbourne in the southeast and 11.6°C (53°F) in Darwin in the north. January mean temperatures average 20°C (68°F) in Melbourne and 29°C (84°F) in Darwin. Summer readings often reach 38°C (100°F) or more in almost any area of the continent, and may exceed 46°C (115°F) in interior regions. Long hours of sunshine are characteristic. Winds are light to moderate, except along the coasts, where cyclones have occurred.

The continent is subject to great variations in rainfall, but except for a few areas rainfall is insufficient, and the rate of evaporation is high. About 40% of the continent is desert, and 40% is subhumid. About 20% has more than 30 inches of rain annually, but some parts suffer from a long dry season while others have too much rain. Only Tasmania, Victoria, and parts of New South Wales have enough rainfall all year round. Droughts and floods occur irregularly but frequently over large areas. On 25 December 1974, a cyclone and flood devastated most of Darwin; at least 49 people were killed; some 20,000 were left homeless.

⁴FLORA AND FAUNA

Many distinctive forms of plant and animal life are found, especially in the coastal and tropical areas. There are some 500 species of eucalyptus and 767 species of acacia (wattle). Other outstanding trees are the baobab, blackwood, red cedar, coachwood, jarrah, Queensland maple, silky oak, and walnut. Native trees shed bark instead of leaves. Numerous types of wild flowers grow in the bush country, including boronia, Christmas bush, desert pea, flanner flower, Geraldton wax plant, kangaroo paw, pomaderris, and waratah. There are 470 varieties of orchids.

About 400 kinds of animals, 200 kinds of lizards, and 700 kinds of birds are indigenous. Apart from marsupials (bandicoots, kangaroos, koalas, opossums, tree-kangaroos, and wallabies), the most unusual animals are the dingo, echidna, flying fox (fruit bat), platypus, Tasmanian devil, and wombat. Birds include the anhinga, bellbird, bowerbird, cassowary, emu, galah, kookaburra (laughing jackass), lyrebird, fairy penguin, rosella, and many native types of cockatoos, parrots, hawks, and eagles.

Many species of trees, plants, and domestic animals have been imported, often thriving at the expense of indigenous types. Herds of wild buffalos, camels, donkeys, horses, and pigs, descendants of stock that strayed from herds imported by pioneers, roam the sparsely settled areas. The proliferation of rabbits resulted in a menace to sheep, and in 1907, a thousand-mile-long fence was built to keep rabbits out of Western Australia. Subsequently, a similar fence was put in the east to prevent the incursion of dingos.

As of 1975, endangered species in Australia included 6 species of wallaby, (parma, bridle nail-tailed, crescent nail-tailed, western hare, banded hare, and yellow-footed rock), 3 species of rat-kangaroo (desert, northern, and Lesueur's), scaly-tailed possum, Leadbeater's possum, Queensland hairy-nosed wombat, pig-footed bandicoot, rabbit bandicoot, red-tailed phascogale, dibbler, narrow-nosed planigale, Kimberley planigale, long-tailed sminthopsis, eastern jerboa marsupial, thylacine, dugong, Cape Barren goose, Australian night parrot, 3 species of ground parrot (ground parrot, western, and Tasmania), 6 species of parakeet, (orange-bellied, turquoise, splendid, golden-shouldered Paradise, hooded Paradise, and beautiful), noisy scrub-bird, rufous scrub-bird, 3 species of western whipbird (sw, se and s), Eyrean grass-wren, western bristlebird, western rufous bristlebird, helmeted honey-eater, short-necked turtle, 2 species of crocodile (Australian freshwater and estuarine), reticulated velvet gecko, dragon lizard, and miniature blue-tongued skink.

⁵POPULATION

A government estimate put Australia's population for June 1975 at 13,502,300. Populations of the six states and two mainland territories in 1974 were New South Wales, 4,743,400; Victoria, 3,631,900; Queensland, 1,967,900; South Australia, 1,218,200; Western Australia, 1,094,700; Tasmania, 400,400; Australian Capital Territory, 180,500; and Northern Territory, 101,200. Population growth of more than 27% from 1945 to 1957 was due to a large excess of births over deaths (more than 1 million) and a net migration of 1.5 million. Between 1961 and 1973, the population grew 24%.

In the year ending 30 June 1975, there were 239,764 live births and 114,501 recorded deaths, for a net natural increase of 125,263. The net overseas migration gain was 38,709 in 1974/75. The UN population projection for Australia in 1980 was 15,140,000, assuming a crude birthrate of 21.4 per 1,000 population, a crude death rate of 8, and a net natural increase of 13.4.

Density in 1975 was 1.8 persons per sq km (4.5 per sq mi). The population is unevenly distributed. One-third of Australia is virtually uninhabited; another third is sparsely populated. Most of the people live in the southeast section and in other coastal areas. Less than one-fourth of the population is rural. Estimates of 30 June 1973 placed more than 60% of the population in the six state capitals: Sydney, New South Wales, 2,874,380; Melbourne, Victoria, 2,583,900; Brisbane, Queensland, 911,000; Adelaide, South Australia, 868,000; Perth, Western Australia, 739,200; and Hobart, Tasmania, 157,870. The national capital is Canberra (185,000) in the Australian Capital Territory, a specially designated area within New South Wales. Three other large cities are Newcastle, New South Wales, 357,770; Greater Wollongong, New South Wales, 205,180; and Geelong, Victoria, 126,500.

⁶ETHNIC GROUPS

Most Australians are of British ancestry. More than four-fifths are Australian born; of the foreign born, one-half were British subjects.

The aborigines probably numbered between 150,000 and 300,000 before the coming of the Europeans. In 1971 there were 106,290 aborigines of pure or mixed blood. Many of them live in primitive, tribal conditions on government reservations in the north and northwest; some 18,000 are in the Northern Territory. Their social organization is among the most complex known to anthropologists. They do not cultivate the soil but are nomadic hunters and food gatherers, without settled communities. A few are stockmen on cattle stations. Some serve as trackers for the police. The Aranda are the best-known group. Many aborigines are now settling in urban areas and changing their style of life.

Specialists believe the Australian aborigines are relatively homogeneous, although they display a wide range of physical types. Their serological, or blood-group, pattern is unique, except for a faint affinity with the Paniyan of southern India and the Veddas of Sri Lanka. The aborigines probably originated from a small isolated group subject to chance mutation but not to hybridization. There seems to be a sprinkling of Australoid groups in India, Sri Lanka, Sumatra, Timor, and New Guinea. In 1963, aborigines were given full citizenship rights, although as a group they continued to suffer from discrimination and a lower living standard than European Australians generally.

⁷LANGUAGE

More than 99% of the population speaks English. There are no class variations of speech and few if any local dialects.

Many languages or dialects are spoken by the aboriginal tribes, but phonetically they are markedly uniform. There is no written aboriginal language, but the markings on "letter sticks," sometimes carried by messengers from one tribe to another, are readily understood by tribal headmen.

⁸RELIGION

Constitutionally, there cannot be a state religion or state aid to any religion, the exercise of any religion cannot be prohibited, and a religious test as qualification for public office is forbidden. About two-thirds of Australians are Protestants, 30% being Anglicans. Methodist (8%), Presbyterian (8%), Baptist (1%), and Lutheran (1%) are the other major Protestant denominations. About 27% are Roman Catholic. Nearly 3% are Orthodox Christian. Less than 1% are Jewish.

⁹TRANSPORTATION

With a railway network totaling 65,137 km as of 30 June 1973, Australia ranks low among developed nations in total railway length, but high on a per capita basis. As of 31 March 1975, there were 40,349 km of open railway track. Owned and operated by Commonwealth and state governments, the railway systems do not interconnect well, and rail travel between principal cities involves changing of trains. Modern equipment is gradually replacing older stock. In 1973/74, railroads in Australia carried 97 million tons of revenue freight.

Highways provide access to many districts not served by railroads. As of 1973 there were 1,390,478 km of roads, about half of which were improved. As of 30 June 1975 there were about 6,300,000 motor vehicles, including 4,900,000 passenger cars, 1,100,000 commercial vehicles, 28,000 buses, and 281,700 motorcycles.

Inland water transport is negligible, but ocean shipping is important for domestic and overseas transport. Most overseas trade is carried in non-Australian ships, while most coastwise vessels are of Australian registry. Although the fine natural harbors of Sydney and Hobart can readily accommodate ships of 11-meter draft, many other harbors have been artificially developed. All main ports have ample wharfage, modern cargo-handling equipment, and storage facilities. In Australian ports in 1972/73, 132,362,000 tons of cargo were loaded for distribution overseas, and 20,167,000 tons were unloaded from overseas.

Domestic air services are operated primarily by the

10 COMMUNICATIONS

The Department of the Postmaster General is responsible for the public postal, telephone, and telegraph services. Local and long-distance telephone services are rated highly. In 1975 there were 5,266,845 telephones, about 1 for every 2.6 Australians. More than 95% of the total service is automatic. More telegrams are sent per capita than in any other country. The government administers and supervises broadcasting through a control board. The federal government stations are financed from budget revenues, and the private commercial stations derive their income from business advertising. In 1974 there were 118 private commercial radio stations, 99 federal government radio stations, 48 private commercial television stations, and 55 government

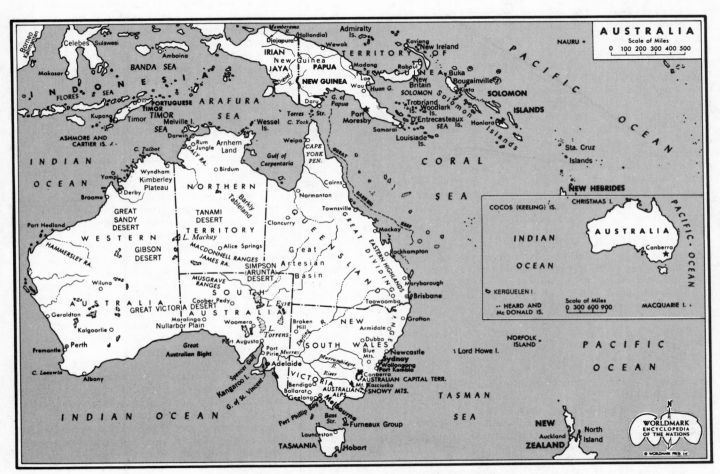

See Pacific Ocean map: front cover D8; physical: see back cover
LOCATION (including Tasmania): 112°55' to 153°39'E; 9°9' to 43°44's. **TERRITORIAL SEA LIMIT**: 3 mi.

government-owned Trans-Australian Airlines and the privately owned Ansett Airlines. The Australian overseas airline, Qantas, is owned and operated by the Commonwealth government. Foreign airlines operating in Australia include JAL, Alitalia, BA, Canadian Pacific Airlines, KLM, Pan Am, PAL, MAS, and Air New Zealand. There are international airports at Brisbane, Darwin, Melbourne, Perth, and Sydney, and more than 400 airfields throughout Australia. Australian-owned airlines, in 1974/75, carried 100.9 million ton-km of freight within Australia and 213.7 million ton-km of freight on overseas services. There were 10.8 million paying passengers on domestic and overseas flights by Australian-owned airlines in 1974/75.

television stations. On 30 June 1974 there were 2,851,000 listeners' licenses and 3,022,000 viewers' licenses, indicating increased ownership and popularity of television. Licenses have since been abolished.

11 HISTORY

The first recorded sightings of the Australian continent took place early in the 17th century when the Dutch, Portuguese, and Spanish explorers, sailing along the coast, discovered what is now Tasmania. None took formal possession of the land, and not until 1770, when Capt. James Cook charted the east coast and claimed possession in the name of Great Britain, was any major exploration undertaken. Up to the early 19th century, the area was known as New Holland, New South Wales, or Botany Bay.

The first settlement—a British penal colony at Port Jackson (now Sydney) in 1788—was soon enlarged by additional shipments of prisoners, and (until the system was abolished 1840–68) about 161,000 of the settlers were transported convicts. With the increase of free settlers, the country developed, the interior was penetrated, and six colonies were created: New South Wales in 1786, Van Diemen's Land in 1825 (renamed Tasmania, 1853), Western Australia in 1829, South Australia in 1834, Victoria in 1851, and Queensland in 1859. Sheep raising and wheat growing were introduced and soon became the backbone of the economy. The wool industry made rapid progress during the period of squatting migration, which began on a large scale about 1820. The graziers followed in the wake of explorers, reaching new pastures or "runs," where they squatted and built their homes. Exports of wool increased from 245 lb in 1807 to 2.5 million lb in 1831. The increased flow of immigrants following the Ripon Land Regulations of 1831, as well as natural increase, raised the population from about 34,000 in 1820 to some 405,000 in 1850. The discovery of gold in Victoria (1851) attracted thousands, and in a few years the population had quadrupled. Under the stimulus of gold production, the first railway line—Melbourne to Port Melbourne—was completed in 1854. Representative government spread throughout the continent, and the colonies acquired their own parliaments. Until the end of the 19th century, Australia's six self-governing colonies remained separate. However, the obvious advantages of common defense and irrigation, and many other joint functions, led eventually (1901) to the federation of the states into the Commonwealth of Australia. (A constitution was approved by the British Parliament at the end of the 19th century.) In 1911, territory was acquired from New South Wales for a new capital at Canberra, and in 1927, the Australian Parliament began meeting there. Liberal legislation was introduced, providing for free and compulsory education, industrial conciliation and arbitration, the secret ballot, female suffrage, old age pensions, invalid pensions, and maternity allowances (all before World War I). Child subsidies and unemployment and disability benefits were introduced during World War II.

Australian forces fought along with the British in Europe during World War I. In World War II, the Australian forces supported the UK in the Middle East between 1940 and 1942 and, after the Japanese attack on Pearl Harbor, played a major role in the Pacific theater. After the war, a period of intense immigration began. The Labour government was voted out of office in 1949, beginning 23 years of continuous rule by a Liberal-Country Party (now National Country Party) coalition. During that period, Australian foreign policy stressed collective security and support for the US presence in Asia. Australian troops served in Viet-Nam between 1965 and 1971. When Labour returned to power in December 1972, it began the process of dissociating Australia from US and UK policies and strengthening ties with non-Communist Asian nations; in addition, diplomatic relations with the People's Republic of China were established. After a constitutional crisis late in 1975, when the Opposition in the Senate successfully blocked the Labour Party's budgetary measures and thereby threatened the government with bankruptcy, the governor-general dismissed the Labour prime minister, Gough Whitlam, and new elections were called for December. The Liberal-National Country Party coalition won majorities in both the House and Senate and swept back into power.

12 GOVERNMENT

The Commonwealth of Australia, an independent, self-governing nation within the Commonwealth of Nations, has a federal parliamentary government. The federation was formed on 1 January 1901 of six former British colonies, which

thereupon became states. The constitution combines the traditions of British parliamentary practice with important elements of the US federal system. Powers of the federal government are enumerated and limited.

The government consists of the British sovereign, represented by a governor-general, and the Australian Parliament. Nominally, executive power is vested in the governor-general and an executive council, which gives legal form to cabinet decisions, but in effect it is normally exercised by a cabinet chosen and presided over by a prime minister, representing the political party or coalition with a majority in the House of Representatives. The number of cabinet ministers is variable.

Legislative power is vested in the Parliament, which is composed of a 64-member Senate, representing the states and territories, and a 127-member House of Representatives, representing electoral districts. Members must be Australian citizens of full age, possess electoral qualification, and have resided for three years in Australia. Ten senators are elected by proportional representation from each state voting as a single electorate and two senators each from the Northern Territory and Capital Territory; they are elected for six years, with half the members retiring at the end of every third year. House membership is approximately double that of the Senate, with a minimum of five representatives for each state. House members are elected according to population by preferential voting in specific electoral districts; they serve for three years, unless the House is dissolved sooner. There are two members from the Australian Capital Territory and one from the Northern Territory; they have been able to vote on all questions since 1968. Parliament must meet at least once a year. Taxation and appropriation measures must be introduced in the lower house; the Senate has the power to propose amendments, except to money bills, and to defeat any measure it may choose to.

The parties in the House elect their leaders in caucus. The party or coalition with a majority of seats forms the government. The leader of the majority party becomes prime minister, and selects his cabinet from members of his party who are members of Parliament, while the leader of the principal minority party becomes leader of the official Opposition. The party in power holds office as long as it retains its majority or at the pleasure of the governor-general, who exercised his inherent constitutional powers during the 1975 crisis.

Suffrage is universal for all persons 18 years of age and older, subject to citizenship and certain residence requirements, and voting is compulsory. In general elections since 1931, ballots have been cast by 94% to 96.3% of the registered voters.

13 POLITICAL PARTIES

Since most Australians have been shaped by the same language and by a similar cultural and religious heritage, their internal differences are largely based on economic issues. Attachments to the UK are compounded of sentiment, tradition, and economic advantage. Australian nationalism has been associated more closely with the domestic Labour Party than with its rivals, who tend to regard Australian interests as almost identical with those of the UK. Because of Australia's geographical position as a "European people on an Asian limb," the economic element in its nationalism has been mixed with the fear of external conquest or domination.

Except in 1929–31, when a Labour government was in office, interwar governments were dominated by non-Labour groupings. When war seemed certain in 1939, the government was resolutely imperial, considering that Australia was at war automatically when the UK went to war. This view, however, was challenged by the Labourites, who, though not opposing a declaration of war on Germany, wanted the step to be taken in such a way as to show Australia's independence.

Labour was in office from 1941 to 1949. The Liberal and Country parties were in office as a coalition for a long period afterward, from 1949 to 1972, and again beginning in December 1975 (after the Country Party had become the National Country Party). A direct descendant of the governments of the 1920s and 1930s, the coalition is principally linked with business and farming, and is officially antisocialist. In economic and foreign affairs, its outlook is still involved with the Commonwealth, but it supports the UN as well as the alliance with the US in the ANZUS pact. It is sympathetic toward the new Asian countries and values the link with these countries afforded by the Colombo Plan.

The Labour Party is a trade-union party, officially socialist in policy and outlook. It initially maintained an isolationist posture, but since the early 1940s, its policy has been a mixture of nationalism and internationalism. For security, it looks to the UN, to the US, and to regional security arrangements.

Smaller parties include the Democratic Labour Party, the Communist Party, the Australia Party, and the Working Party.

In the general elections of 13 December 1975, a caretaker government, formed the preceding month by the Liberal-National Country Party coalition after the dismissal of the Labour government of Prime Minister Gough Whitlam, obtained large majorities in both houses of the legislature. The coalition won 91 seats in the House (a gain of 29) while the Labour Party won only 36 seats (compared to its previous 65). The coalition, which in the previous Senate had held 30 of the 60 seats (as against 27 held by Labour and 3 held by independents), gained 5 seats, to hold 35 of 64 seats in a newly expanded body. Of the remaining 29 seats, Labour retained the 27 it had won in 1974, with independents holding the other 2 seats.

¹⁴LOCAL GOVERNMENT

Powers not specifically granted to the federal government in the constitution are reserved to the states, although some powers (such as health, labor, and social services) are held concurrently. Except for Queensland, which has a unicameral legislature, the parliament in each state is composed of two houses. The lower houses—the dominant legislative bodies—are popularly elected; the upper houses are elected by franchise limited to property holders and to those with certain academic or professional qualifications. The state prime minister achieves office and selects his cabinet in the same fashion as does the Commonwealth prime minister.

Local communities (variously designated as boroughs, cities, district councils, municipalities, road districts, shires, and towns)—even the great cities—have limited powers of government; but they are responsible for some health, sanitation, light, gas, and highway undertakings. They do not provide police protection nor do they conduct or support education; these are state functions. Local aldermen or councillors ordinarily are elected on a property franchise, and mayors are elected annually or biennially by the aldermen from among their own number or by taxpayers. State departments of local government regulate and oversee the organization of local government. Some large interior areas are directly controlled by the state governments. In some areas ad hoc authorities carry out important activities.

¹⁵JUDICIAL SYSTEM

Cases in the first instance are tried in local or circuit courts of general and petty sessions, magistrate's courts, county courts, children's courts, or higher state courts. Capital crimes are tried before state supreme courts. The High Court of Australia, consisting of a chief justice and six other justices, may hear and determine appeals from judgments of other federal courts or of state supreme courts. It is the supreme authority on constitutional interpretation, except that in certain instances appeals may be taken from it to the Privy Council in the UK, the final court of the Commonwealth of Nations. For special cases, there are such courts as the Commonwealth Court of Concilia-

tion and Arbitration, the Federal Court of Bankruptcy, and territorial supreme courts.

¹⁶ARMED FORCES

Since 1973 there has been no conscription in Australia. The regular army in 1974 had an official strength of 30,235 men; the navy, 16,141; the air force, 21,119; and a part-time citizens' force, 36,000. All three services are supplemented by trainees and reservists. Military hardware in 1975 included 143 medium tanks, 4 submarines, 1 aircraft carrier, 6 destroyers, 6 frigates, and more than 150 combat aircraft. Two air force squadrons were deployed in Malaysia and Singapore.

Australia's annual defense expenditure rose from A$1,137.6 million in 1970/71 to an estimated A$1,628 million in 1974/75.

¹⁷MIGRATION

The government promotes immigration of the maximum number of persons Australia can absorb without economic disequilibrium. There is no discrimination on the grounds of race or nationality, although for many years whites (especially English-speaking whites) were more readily admitted than nonwhites. Priority is given to reunion of families sponsored by Australian residents. The net overseas migration gain was 73,237 in the year ending 30 June 1974 and 38,709 in the year ending 30 June 1975.

Most of the 3 million immigrants to Australia since World War II have been of working age, but, although the government encouraged rural settlement, many immigrants had skills in short supply and preferred to work in the cities. The main countries of origin of such workers were the UK, Italy, and Greece. Two and a half million migrants (including 250,000 refugees) received government passage assistance. The number of permanent settlers arriving in 1973 was 105,003 and in 1974, 121,324. In 1974, 44% of the settlers arriving came from the UK and Ireland; 4% from Yugoslavia; 3% each from New Zealand, the US, Greece, and Uruguay; and smaller numbers from many other countries.

¹⁸INTERNATIONAL COOPERATION

Australia is a member of the Commonwealth of Nations, of the UN and its specialized agencies, and of ANZUS. It was also a member of SEATO up to the time of its dissolution. It is also a member of ASPAC, IPFC, ICEM, ICAC, IRC, IRSG, the International Sugar Council, the International Tin Council, the International Tin Study Group, the International Whaling Commission, IWC, IWSG, SPC, and other Commonwealth and intergovernmental organizations. In February 1966, Australia joined the Development Assistance Committee of the OECD.

In 1974/75, Australia contributed about A$350 million in foreign aid for economic and technical assistance, provided training for thousands of Asian students, and sent experts and advisers on numerous aid assignments abroad. Under the UN Expanded Program for Technical Assistance, foreign nationals receive training in Australia and Australian experts are assigned to other countries.

¹⁹ECONOMY

Wool, food, and minerals provide raw materials for home processing industries and are the main source of foreign earnings. Australia grows all needed basic foodstuffs and has large surpluses for export. Australia is the world's largest wool-producing country. About 30% of the world's wool and 45% of all wool traded are produced in Australia. One of the world's great wheat exporters, Australia also exports large quantities of meat and dairy products. The late 1960s saw a major minerals boom, led by iron ore and bauxite. Australia also has considerable deposits of lead, zinc, and copper. Coal and nickel have become major industries. Chief lacks are petroleum, rubber, and certain chemicals, but oil needs are being increasingly met domestically. By 1975, Australia was 70% self-sufficient in oil.

Although Australia is a great primary producer, the growth of manufacturing was the major development in the 1960s. By 1974, less than 7% of the work force was engaged in agriculture. In the past, Australian manufactures almost wholly served domestic needs, but since the 1960s they have provided an ever-increasing share of the country's exports. Heavy industry expansion has taken place at a rapid pace, with steel output more than quadrupling from 1960 to 1970.

[20] INCOME
Australia's national income in 1973/74 totaled A$49.8 billion (representing a 36% increase in current prices since 1971/72). The 13.3 million citizens had a per capita income of A$3,744, among the world's highest. For 1974/75, gross fixed capital formation was A$14.4 billion, the GDP at market prices was A$58.5 billion, and national income at market prices was A$54.3 billion.

The origins of the GDP (in percentages of total for 1972/73) were: industry, 21%; wholesale and retail trade, 14%; agriculture, 7%; construction, 7%; transport and communication, 7%; and other sectors, 44%.

Income tax returns for 1972/73 (assessed in 1973/74) showed that 1,965,752 Australians, or 38.7% of those filing returns, had net incomes ranging from A$4,000 to A$6,999 per annum. Only 33,677 persons had net incomes of A$20,000 or more. A total of 581,166 persons, or 11.4%, reported incomes under A$2,000 per annum.

[21] LABOR
In November 1975, the Australian work force was estimated at 6,061,500, or about 45% of the population. From 1970 to 1974, the work force grew by 434,000, with the married female work force rising by a significant 26%. Married women represented 22% of the total labor force in mid-1975, and females in general accounted for 35%. In a seasonally adjusted total, 277,200 workers were classified as unemployed in November 1975.

The occupational distribution for civilian employees in September 1975, as estimated by the government, partly on the basis of comprehensive data from the 1966 census, was as follows: manufacturing, 27.1%; community and business services, 17.6%; commerce, 17.4%; building and construction, 7.9%; amusements, hotels, and personal services, 6.9%; transportation and storage, 5.4%; public authority activities, 5.3%; finance and property, 5%; and other, 7.4%.

Australia's record for time lost through industrial disputes compares favorably with that of most industrialized nations. In 1974, an average of 3.1 days per employee was lost. Australia is highly unionized; more than 50% of all wage and salary earners are trade unionists. At the end of 1974, 286 trade unions had a membership of 2,773,600.

Awards by federal and state industrial tribunals contain minimum or award rates of pay. The minimum wage of adult males under federal awards averaged A$94.17 weekly in 1974. Management and labor can negotiate pay rates above the award rates, and overaward pay varies with the employment situation. Overaward payments, together with overtime and bonus payments, are reflected in the Office of the Commonwealth Statistician's figures on average weekly earnings, which in the last quarter of 1975 averaged A$163.80 for adult males. The standard workweek is 40 hours, generally from Monday through Friday. Under legislation passed by the Labour government of Prime Minister Gough Whitlam, Australian workers receive 4 weeks of annual vacation, at rates of pay 17.5% above regular pay. In 1973–75, total wages in industry rose about 70%, while industrial productivity increased less than 1%.

[22] AGRICULTURE
Australia is an important producer and exporter of agricultural products and a major world supplier of cereals, sugar, and fruit. Its 244,000 rural holdings comprise about 500 million hectares, representing about 65% of total land area. However, more than 90% of the utilized land area is in its natural state or capable of

only limited improvement, and is used largely for rough grazing. The area cultivated for agriculture and intensive grazing is little more than 8% of all utilized land. Lack of water is the principal limiting factor, but unsuitable soil and topography are also important determinants.

In the five years ending in 1973, farm income averaged about 7% of national income, while rural production contributed approximately 9% to GNP at factor cost. Total crop value in 1974/75 was estimated at A$3,142 million.

Grain crops have been cultivated since the first year of settlement. In November 1790, plantings around Sydney of wheat, barley, and corn totaled 85 acres. Today, winter cereals are cultivated in all states. Three cereals are often grown on one farm for grain, green fodder, and hay for livestock. Most wheat and barley and about half the oats are grown for grain.

The wheat area sown for grain increased from 6,478,000 hectares in 1970/71 to 8,948,000 hectares in 1973/74; there was a slight decline in 1974/75, to an estimated 8,308,000 hectares. Production of wheat for grain in 1974/75 was an estimated 11,357,000 tons, up 44% from 1970/71, and the yield per hectare was about 1.4 tons. Western Australia and New South Wales are the chief wheat-producing states. In 1973/74, it was estimated that Australia produced more than 2,398,000 tons of barley, 1,107,000 tons of oats, 106,000 tons of corn, 636,000 tons of potatoes, and 1,034,000 tons of hay.

Sugarcane is grown along a 2,000-km stretch of coastal land in New South Wales and Queensland. About 95% of sugar production comes from Queensland. A normal crushing season is from June to December. The 1973/74 harvest, totaling 19.2 million tons of cane, yielded about 2.5 million tons of raw sugar. Although tobacco growing is a relatively small industry, it is important in some areas. During 1972/73, 10,000 hectares were planted in tobacco, and about 17,100 tons were produced.

Cotton has been grown in the coastal river valleys of Queensland for more than a century, but on a limited scale, and it has provided only a small percentage of Australia's lint requirements. In recent years, however, successful development of cotton-growing areas in New South Wales and Western Australia has resulted in spectacular production increases. In 1972/73, 97,000 tons of cotton were produced.

Australia's wide climate differences permit the cultivation of a range of fruit, from pineapples in the tropical zone to berry fruits in the cooler areas of the temperate zone. About 116,000 hectares are under fruit cultivation, and some 69,000 hectares are vineyards. Although these comprise less than 1% of the total area cultivated for crops, the products—notably apples, pears, bananas, and grapes—represented close to 10% of the gross value of principal crops produced. In 1972/73, 598,368 tons of grapes were produced.

[23] ANIMAL HUSBANDRY
More than 50% of Australia's land is used in stock raising. Animal husbandry is concentrated in the eastern highlands, but it spreads across the wide interior spaces and even to low rainfall areas where up to 12 hectares are required to support 1 sheep, or where cattle must be brought overland hundreds of miles to coastal meat-packing plants. In 1973/74, the total estimated gross value of livestock slaughters and other livestock sales was A$1,026 million; the value of livestock products was A$1,663 million.

Sheep raising has been a mainstay of the economy since the 1820s, when mechanization of the British textile industry created a huge demand for wool. In 1850 there were 17.5 million sheep in Australia; by 1894, some 100 million; and in 1970, a record high of some 180 million. Australia's flocks now comprise less than one-sixth of the world's sheep, but produce about 30% of the world's wool and about 45% of all wool entering world trade. Wool production in 1973/74 was an estimated 701,000 tons.

About 80–90% is exported; wool represented 50% of Australia's merchandise exports (by value) in 1957/58, though only 17% in 1973/74.

During periods of great drought, the number of sheep has diminished by 30 million or more. In the better lands, however, animal husbandy ranks high on a world scale. Large, scientifically managed stations have produced some of the earth's finest stock. A majority of the 151.6 million sheep (March 1975) were of the Merino breed, noted for its heavy wool yield. In 1975 there were 2.2 million hogs and 32.8 million head of cattle. Animal products—wool, meats, dairy products, hides and skins, and live animals—now make up about 40% of all Australian exports. In 1974/75, meat production totaled an estimated 2.2 million tons. Of these, beef and veal constituted 1,533,752 tons; mutton and lamb together, 519,819 tons; and ham, pork, and bacon, 175,072 tons. Total poultry production in 1974/75 was estimated at 189,425 tons (dressed weight) and included 165,977 tons of chicken. Butter production in 1974/75 (in factories) amounted to an estimated 161,000 tons, whole milk was an estimated 6,543 million liters, cheese (factory production) was about 99,000 tons, and an estimated 60,000 tons of condensed, concentrated, and evaporated milk was produced.

24 FISHING
Fishing is relatively unimportant. Even with a low per capita fish consumption, Australia must import about half its normal requirements. Pearl and other shell fishing are relatively significant. The 1972/73 catch included 59,400 tons of fish; 30,300 tons of crayfish (lobster tails), prawns, and crabs; and 33,000 tons of oysters and other mollusks. Exports of fisheries products were valued at A$66.8 million in 1973/74. The total value of shell (pearl and trochus) taken in Australian waters was estimated at A$203,000 in 1972/73.

Whaling has declined in recent years; it employed only 51 persons in 1973, compared to 688 in 1965 and 1,481 in 1961.

25 FORESTRY
Forest land is 42.5 million hectares, or about 5.5% of the total area, and only slightly more than half of that is exploited or potentially exploitable. Native forests consist principally of hardwood and other fine cabinet and veneer timbers. Softwood resources—never large—are now seriously depleted. Hardwood constitutes about 80% of all timber used. Two-thirds of Australia's timber requirements are domestically provided, the rest being imported mostly from New Zealand, North America, and Scandinavia. Annual lumber production, with 1,258 mills employing about 16,000 persons (1972/73), totals about 11.5 million cu feet; timber valued at about A$8 million was exported in 1973/74, while imports were worth A$116 million. Some 1.8 million hectares has been set aside permanently for reserves; extensive reforestation has been undertaken to combat soil erosion. Since hardwoods grow slowly, Australia will probably have to import much lumber in future years to meet its timber needs.

26 MINING
More than 60 varieties of minerals and metals have been commercially produced in Australia, and successful exploration in the late 1960s led to a long-term mineral boom and a sharp increase in exports. The country now exports coal, iron ore, zinc, silver, gold, rutile (a titanium ore), tungsten, nickel, and bauxite. Uranium deposits were discovered at the end of World War II, and treatment plants have been opened. Newly prospected bauxite reserves produced more than 18 million tons in 1973/74, and provided the foundation for an aluminum industry. Bauxite deposits in northern Queensland are among the world's largest. In addition, bauxite deposits in the Northern Territory are in production. Extensive drilling for oil is also being carried out, and output in 1973/74 totaled 23 million cu meters, nearly 70% of the total Australian consumption. Natural gas production in 1972/73 was 6.7 billion cu meters.

The structure of mineral production and equity changed dramatically in Australia in the early 1970s. Production of iron ore doubled between 1969/70 and 1973/74, to 91.7 million tons. Manganese ore production in 1973/74 was 1.7 million tons; bauxite, 18.6 million tons; coal, 86 million tons; copper, 249,000 tons; and nickel concentrates, 298,000 tons. In 1974/75, an estimated 92,853,000 tons of coal were mined. Total mineral production was valued at A$1,998.6 million in 1972/73, as compared with less than A$900 million in 1968. Mineral exports represent more than 10% of the value of total Australian exports.

The policies of successive Australian governments concerning exploitation of Australia's mineral wealth have differed, although both private companies and government agencies have been involved. There is, however, an emphasis on significant Australian equity in new projects.

27 ENERGY AND POWER
Because of its relatively small hydroelectric resources and only recently discovered oil, Australia has had to rely on more than 350 coal-burning steam plants for about 72% of its power requirements. The remainder was supplied by hydroelectricity (about 26%) and diesel-oil plants (about 2%). Total power capacity in 1973 was 29.5 million kw (as contrasted with 11.77 million kw in 1968). Power generation in 1972/73 totaled 64,802 million kwh. Major electric power undertakings, originally privately owned and operated, were by 1952 under the control of state organizations. Manufacturing has been developed most extensively in or near coal areas, and distribution of electricity to principal users is therefore relatively simple. Voltage ranges from 200 to 250 and is mostly 50-cycle, three-phase alternating current. All major cities except Perth use 240-volt, 50-cycle alternating current, and Perth has 250-volt, 40-cycle, single-phase alternating current.

The Snowy Mountains hydroelectric scheme in southeast New South Wales, Australia's most ambitious public works project, comprises power stations generating 5 million kw of electric power annually. The Snowy Mountains scheme and other large power projects in New South Wales, Victoria, and Tasmania, have greatly increased the nation's aggregate installed capacity. The only state with water resources sufficient for continuous operation of large hydroelectric power stations is Tasmania, which possesses 50% of Australia's hydroelectric energy potential. Production and use of such power are on the increase throughout the country, however: Output was up 156% in 1968 over 1958.

Since 1969, natural gas has been used as a local energy source. Major pipelines for New South Wales were under construction in 1976.

28 INDUSTRY
In proportion to its total population, Australia is one of the world's most highly industrialized countries. In 1973/74, its 37,137 factories employed 1,338,910 persons, or less than 25% of the work force. Nevertheless, although manufacturing has tripled since 1939, and Australian steel is the cheapest in the world, domestic and overseas markets are small, costs of production, transportation, and some imported materials are generally high, and productivity is insufficiently developed. Industrial products are consumed mainly at home, only about 7% being exported. Australia still imports about 20% of the manufactures it needs.

Servicing and repair plants employing fewer than 10 persons make up about 60% of the factories, but about 50% of the employees are in factories having more than 100 workers. Total capital expenditures by industries amounted to A$1,360 million in the third quarter of 1975. Emphasis is shifting from consumer goods industries to those making heavy machinery, electrical and transport equipment, chemicals, fuels, lubricants, and power. More than half the automobiles in Australia are made domestically, and the motor industry, which produced an estimated 453,800 vehicles in 1974/75, is now the largest employer of labor.

Australia is self-sufficient in beverages, most foods, building materials, many common chemicals, some domestic electrical appliances, radios, plastics, textiles, and clothing; and most of its needed communications equipment, farm machinery (except tractors), furniture, leather goods, and metal manufactures are domestically produced. A large proportion of Australian needs in aluminum, locomotives, rolling stock, drugs and chemicals, electric motors, power-generating equipment, paper goods, and rubber products is domestically provided. It was estimated that, in 1974/75, Australian factories produced 5,086,000 tons of pig iron and ingot steel, 5,086,000 tons of cement, 4,516,000 electric motors, 182,825 million megajoules of gas, 9,708,000 pairs of hosiery, 1,957 million liters of beer, 86,959 tons of margarine, 196,000 tons of newsprint, 91,009,000 liters of ready-mixed paints and enamels, 266,092,000 grams of refined silver, and 32,000 tons of cigars and cigarettes.

Industry tends to concentrate in the population centers, and there is much duplication of light industry. But some dispersal is taking place, and many plants are moving to country towns. Many manufacturing companies are closely connected—financially and technically—with manufacturers in the UK, the US, or Japan.

²⁹DOMESTIC TRADE

There are many small specialty shops, but in the larger cities department stores sell all kinds of items. Supermarkets like those in the US have been widely established, and telephone shopping and delivery services are becoming popular. Retail sales for February 1976 (seasonally adjusted, excluding motor vehicles, automobile parts, gasoline, and some other products) were A$1,559 million. Installment selling, called hire purchase, is widespread, and used in the sale of many products. In July 1974, installment credit debt totaled A$7,838 million, more than four times the debt outstanding in 1969. Reliable commercial credit agencies cover all the main cities and many smaller towns. Collection agencies and firms furnishing credit information are located in the state capital cities.

Usual business hours are from 9 A.M. to 5:30 P.M., Monday through Friday.

Most advertising is done through the press, radio, and television. Principal advertising agencies are in Sydney and Melbourne.

³⁰FOREIGN TRADE

Measured by foreign trade volume per capita, Australia is one of the great trading nations, and it continues to show a steady rise in trade volume. Between 1970 and 1974, total trade rose 87% (by value). In most recent years, exports have exceeded imports. In 1974/75, the value of Australian exports amounted to A$8,672,762,000 and the value of imports amounted to A$8,079,471,000 leaving a trade surplus of A$593,291,000. Australia is mainly an exporter of primary products and an importer of manufactured and semifinished goods. Transport or reexport trade is negligible.

Primary industries now account for about half of all exports. Wool provides about 20% of export earnings, and provided export revenues of A$1,164 million in 1973/74. Meat, wheat (including flour), minerals (principally iron ore), sugar, and fruits are other principal exports. No one commodity dominates the imports. Heavy import restrictions formerly applied to many consumer goods, but many have now been eliminated.

Principal exports in 1973/74 (in millions of Australian dollars) were:

Crude materials (except fuel)	2,223
Food and live animals	2,185
Manufactured goods	853
Machinery and transport equipment	447
Fuels	436
Chemicals and pharmaceuticals	350
Miscellaneous manufactured articles	102
Animal and vegetable oils and fats	45
Beverages and tobacco	17
Other exports	247
TOTAL	6,905

Principal imports in 1973/74 (in millions of Australian dollars) were:

Machinery and transport equipment	2,091
Manufactured goods	1,405
Miscellaneous manufactures	722
Chemicals	580
Inedible crude materials	415
Mineral fuels and lubricants	377
Food and live animals	237
Beverages and tobacco	65
Animal and vegetable oils and fats	28
Other imports	165
TOTAL	6,085

Japan is Australia's chief trading partner, accounting for 31% of its exports and 18% of its imports. The US and the UK rank second and third. The US accounts for 11% of Australia's export market and 22% of its imports. Principal trade partners in 1973/74 (in millions of Australian dollars) were:

	EXPORTS	IMPORTS	BALANCE
Japan	2,143	1,085	1,058
US	750	1,348	−598
UK	457	847	−390
FRG	181	451	−270
New Zealand	449	168	281
Canada	175	192	− 17
France	200	80	120
Hong Kong	114	160	− 46
Italy	133	141	− 8
China	163	72	91
Malaysia	118	70	48
India	99	53	46
Other countries	1,923	1,418	505
TOTALS	6,905	6,085	820

³¹BALANCE OF PAYMENTS

Australia's balance of payments on current accounts fluctuated during the 1950s and 1960s, mainly because of changes in imports and exports. In 1956/57, because of a large trade surplus, international reserves rose by A$482 million. Over the period 1957/58-1958/59, reserves dropped by A$100 million, as a result of lower export receipts and higher import payments. In 1959/60, despite increased exports, imports, and net receipts from capital transactions, reserves fell by A$8 million. Nevertheless, import restrictions, which had been progressively relaxed, were virtually abolished early in 1960. In the first half of 1960/61, therefore, imports increased in value and, since export receipts declined (partly because of lower wool prices), reserves fell by A$272 million to A$752 million in December 1960, the lowest level in 4 years. In April 1961, the government drew A$156 million from the IMF and arranged for a standby credit of A$90 million. An increase in net capital inflow and a more favorable trade balance brought reserves back up to A$1,102 million by 30 June 1961. In 1961/62, the trade balance improved as exports increased and imports decreased; short-term debts were repaid, the standby credit was canceled, and the IMF drawing was repaid in March

1962. In 1963/64, the net capital inflow (apparent) reached A$1,036 million, with a positive trade balance of A$978 million, but in 1964/65 a A$338-million trade deficit led to a A$388-million loss in net monetary movement and a A$44-million increase in Australia's IMF position. In June 1968, Australia's trade deficit was A$218 million; its deficit in invisibles was A$1,127 million. But there was a net capital inflow in the same year of A$1,205 million, as well as a favorable net official monetary movement of A$78 million.

Australia's payments position was favorable in the early 1970s but fell into deficit in 1973 and 1974, despite trade surpluses in both years. The overall deficits were attributable to mounting deficits in invisibles, leading in 1974 to a substantially negative balance on current accounts. The following table summarizes the balance of payments situation in 1973 and 1974 (in millions of US dollars):

	1973	1974
CURRENT ACCOUNTS		
Trade, net	2,782	92
Services, net	−1,937	−2,292
Transfers, net	− 368	− 507
TOTAL	477	−2,707
CAPITAL ACCOUNTS		
Long-term capital	− 702	893
Short-term capital	129	− 220
TOTAL	− 573	673
Errors and omissions	− 259	391
Net change	− 355	−1,643

Australia's international reserves, US$1,693 million in 1970, rose to US$6,141 million in 1972 before declining to US$5,697 million in 1973, US$4,269 million in 1974, and US$3,256 million in 1975.

32 BANKING

The Reserve Bank of Australia, the central bank, reconstituted in 1960, functions as a banker's bank and financial agent of the federal and some state governments, issuing notes, controlling interest and discount rates, mobilizing Australia's international reserves, and administering exchange controls and government loans. It is connected through a common governor and board with the Commonwealth Trading Bank—a general bank—the Commonwealth Savings Bank, and the Commonwealth Development Bank. Its departments provide special services, such as rural credits, mortgage banking, and industrial financing. As of 31 December 1975, the Reserve Bank had A$2,907 million in foreign assets (net), A$2,736 million in claims on the government, and A$147 million in claims on the private sector.

The 9 major commercial banks, 4 minor commercial banks, 3 foreign banks, and 3 specialized state banks have some 4,733 branches and 1,417 agencies. Trading banks are primarily concerned with financing commerce and industry. There are 13 savings banks, 1 of which is federally owned, 5 state-owned, and 7 privately owned. There are also agricultural or rural banks, finance companies, trust companies, building societies, and life insurance companies.

Bank balances and savings deposits are high; in June 1974, the figure for check-paying was A$13,880.8 million. Combined deposits in savings banks amounted to A$14,150 million in February 1976, or about A$1,048 per capita. As of June 1975, commercial loan rates ranged from 6% to a maximum of 12% per annum. As of June 1974, the treasury bill discount rate was 1%; and rates for fixed deposits with trading banks varied from 6.75% for 3 months to 8% for 6 years. On 30 June 1974, the total value of notes in circulation was A$25,010 million (of which A$1,949

million was held by the public). Decimal currency was introduced in 1966.

33 INSURANCE

In 1972/73, income from premiums of fire, marine, and general insurance in Australia was A$1,321 million, and net return on investment was A$95 million, a total of A$1,416 million. Expenditure on claims was A$901 million; contributions to fire brigades, A$35 million; commissions and agents' charges, A$105 million; expenses of management, A$217 million; and taxation, A$38 million, for a total of A$1,296 million.

Life insurance firms, through premiums on policies and interest earned on accumulated funds, account for substantial annual savings. The companies invest in government securities, in company securities (including shares and fixed-interest obligations), and in mortgage loans and loans against policies in force. Most loans (to individuals and building societies) are for housing. At 30 June 1975, major assets of life insurance firms included A$4,017 million in claims on the private sector, A$2,069 million in claims on government, A$1,957 million in fixed assets, and A$810 million in claims on official entities.

34 SECURITIES

Stock and bond markets are active in new issues, especially equities, and are important sources of funds for businesses and mineral exploration. Most underwriting is performed by member firms of the stock exchanges—in Sydney, founded in 1859, and in Melbourne, founded in 1861.

Foreign affiliates listed on one or both exchanges include those partly owned by Rio Tinto, Imperial Chemicals, Schweppes, and Consolidated Goldfields of the UK, and Borg Warner, AMF, American Smelting, Caltex, Union Carbide, Continental Oil, W.R. Grace, and Philip Morris of the US. Large capital investments, such as for the Mt. Newman iron ore complex and the ICI-Conzinc Rio Tinto Eastern nitrogen fertilizer plant, are commonly assumed by insurance companies or other institutional investors.

35 PUBLIC FINANCE

The fiscal year begins 1 July and ends 30 June. In postwar years, the Commonwealth government assumed greater responsibility for maintaining full employment and a balanced economy, as well as for providing a wide range of social services. Social security and welfare payments are the largest category of government expenditure, accounting for 20.8% of the total budget in 1974/75. The central government has financed almost all its defense and capital works programs from revenue and has made available to the states money raised by public loans for public works programs. Deficits are common. The budget deficit was A$293 million in 1973/74 and A$2,567 million in 1974/75.

Budget figures for 1973/74 and 1974/75 (in millions of Australian dollars) are listed in the accompanying table.

	1973/74	1974/75
REVENUES		
General taxes	10,734	13,977
Interest, rent, and dividends	1,031	1,174
Receipts from enterprises (net)	11	−12
Other revenues	162	125
TOTALS	11,938	15,264
EXPENDITURES		
Social security and welfare	2,486	3,703
Economic services	1,489	2,346
Education	859	1,672
Defense	1,326	1,628
General public services	1,009	1,294
Health	947	1,284
Other expenditures	4,114	5,904
TOTALS	12,230	17,831

The public debt as of 30 June 1974 was A$15,306 million, of which A$1,032 million was foreign. The domestic debt included A$12,956 million in long-term obligations and A$1,318 million in short-term obligations; A$11,219 million of the domestic debt represented debts to the states.

In 1973/74, state and local public authorities collected A$2,766.5 million in taxes and recorded a gross fixed capital expenditure on new assets of A$2,959 million.

36TAXATION

The main taxes (personal and corporate income, payroll, and sales taxes) are levied by the Commonwealth, but the states and municipalities impose other levies. Federal rates are determined in legislation that is foreshadowed in the budget, presented each August; rates apply to the fiscal year beginning in July, except for company tax rates, which apply to the previous year's income.

Corporate taxation is slightly higher for public companies than for private companies. The 1973 rate was 47.5% for public firms and 45% for private firms. Undistributed profits of private firms are taxed at 50%, but some profit can be retained without tax liability.

A domestic corporation paying dividends to a nonresident foreign parent with no permanent establishment in Australia must withhold income tax at the rate of 30%. Tax is reduced to 15% if dividends go to the UK, US, Canada, New Zealand, Singapore, or Japan. Foreign branches are not subject to withholding; there is no withholding on dividends distributed to Australians. Taxes on royalties and fees paid abroad are the same as on corporate income.

Wholesalers pay a federal sales tax, levied on almost all products, generally on the last transaction, in which goods are sold to a retailer. The rates vary widely, e.g., 2.5% on sewing machines and 25–30% on private motor cars, but the usual rate is 15%. Agricultural machinery is exempt.

Other Commonwealth taxes include a levy of 2.5% on payroll wages and salaries in excess of A$20,800 a year. Both the Commonwealth and states can levy land taxes, and states levy stamp duties on various documents.

Personal taxation is levied by the Commonwealth on a sharply progressive basis. The PAYE (pay as you earn) system is used. Taxes (on income, after deductions) range from zero on income up to A$416, to A$6,037 on income of A$20,000, with a marginal rate of 60.3% on amounts above this figure. Social security taxes are included as part of income taxes. Deductions are allowed for dependents, donations, medical expenses, and children's educational expenses; up to 5% of the base salary may be deducted for payment of life insurance or pension premiums.

37CUSTOMS AND DUTIES

Federal policy is to use the tariff to protect local industries (especially the automobile industry), and tariff debates are non-party affairs. Intermediate and most-favored-nation rates, established for many products, apply to most foreign countries. Preferential or lowest rates are for imports from the UK and other Commonwealth countries. A free-trade agreement concluded with New Zealand on 31 August 1965 eliminated duties up to 10% and reduced higher duties by 20% at two-year intervals. As a contracting party to GATT, Australia has consented to a number of other tariff reductions since 1947. There is also a preference scheme for developing nations. Tariffs on industrial machinery and plant equipment ordinarily are low where they do not compete with Australian enterprise, and machinery and equipment required by new industries may be imported duty-free or at concessional rates. There are no free ports.

Besides the duties levied under the customs tariff, revenue duties are imposed on a wide range of goods. Tax on imports subject to sales tax is collected at port of entry and is based on duty-paid value increased by 20%.

38FOREIGN INVESTMENTS

Approximately A$15 billion had been invested in Australia from abroad as of June 1973. Total annual overseas investment ranged from A$1 billion in 1968/69 (the UK led, followed by the US) to A$1.5 billion in 1971/72 (the US was the largest investor, followed by the UK, other EEC members, and Japan). Inflow of capital fell sharply in 1973/74 to A$441 million because of global recession conditions and Australian policies on ownership and control. In 1973/74, of a total of A$968 million in overseas payments made by companies in Australia, A$377 million went to UK companies and A$445 million to US companies.

More than 400 US companies have subsidiaries or joint ventures in Australia, while another 1,100 US firms have some kind of licensing arrangement. Originally strong in manufacturing, the US has become greatly interested in mineral exploration and development. US investments in petroleum refining and marketing total more than US$700 million; in auto manufacturing, about US$600 million; and in mineral exploration and production, about US$500 million.

Australia prefers the inflow of long-term development capital to that of short-term speculative capital. It also welcomes the technical competence usually accompanying foreign investment. UK investment has been important in Australian development, and further British investment is favored. Since the UK has been unable to supply all the necessary capital, Australia looks to the US and to Japan for much of its overseas capital requirements.

39ECONOMIC POLICY

Commonwealth and state governments have devoted special attention to the production and marketing of main primary products, and since 1920, legislation has provided subsidies or other marketing aids to certain commodities. Direct subsidies, however, are not common, and butter, cheese, and cotton are among the few export commodities subsidized. Federal and state aid is given to industries established in approved fields of manufacture. The Exports Payment Insurance Corporation (set up in 1957 by the Commonwealth) insures Australian exporters against losses or delays in payment by importers of Australian goods, thus enabling insured exporters to find new markets and expand existing ones. During fiscal 1972/73, the Corporation issued policies covering A$822 million worth of Australian exports.

The government endeavors to prevent undue fluctuation in the economy. Price controls were in effect during World War II and part of the postwar period and are now imposed on a few essential household items. Inflationary pressures, however, began growing as the 1960s ended; in the period 1973–75, inflation reached an annual rate of about 17%. Consumer prices in the fourth quarter of 1975 were an average of 72% higher than 1970 prices. As an alternative to price controls, the Commonwealth government, in mid-1975, introduced a policy of wage indexation, allowing wages to rise as fast as, but no faster than, consumer prices; major labor unions, however, opposed this restraint. The consumer price index in March 1976 was up 13.4% from March 1975.

The need for foreign capital is recognized by the major political parties, and conventions for the avoidance of double taxation have been entered into with the UK, the US, and other countries.

All the states try to spread landownership among owner-operators of economic, family-sized farms.

40HEALTH

Australia is one of the most healthful countries in the world. Tropical and malignant diseases are negligible. The common cold and other respiratory infections are the most prevalent forms of illness. Arteriosclerosis is the most common cause of death. Water in most cities is good and safe for household purposes. In all capital cities garbage and trash are collected.

All levels of government are concerned with public health, the municipalities functioning largely as agents for the administration of state policies. State health departments are responsible for infant welfare, school medical and dental services (provided free of charge), treatment and eradication of infectious and contagious diseases and tuberculosis, industrial hygiene programs, maintenance of food and drug standards, public and mental hospitals, and the regulation of private hospitals. The Commonwealth government makes grants for medical research, coordinates state health programs, and maintains specialist medical research institutions and laboratories.

Health services are efficient. Hospitals are generally modern and well equipped, but space often is at a premium. On 30 June 1972 there were 778 public hospitals, with 77,557 beds, and 1,428 private hospitals, with 52,630 beds. There were also 78 mental hospitals, with 26,861 beds. In 1971 there were 16,107 physicians, 3,477 dentists, 8,046 pharmacists, and 89,520 nurses and midwives. Competent general physicians and specialists are available in most larger cities, and the Royal Flying Doctor Service provides medical care and treatment in remote areas. Medibank, a comprehensive universal health insurance program funded by the Commonwealth, was introduced in 1975. Since 1950, certain drugs have been provided free of charge when prescribed by a medical practitioner. All patients other than pensioners must pay A$2 for every prescription supplied under the scheme; the remainder is met by the government.

In 1974, the death rate was 8.7 per 1,000 population, and infant mortality was 16.1 per 1,000 live births. The estimated life expectancy in 1975 was 76 years for females and 69.7 years for males.

41 SOCIAL WELFARE

The Commonwealth Social Services Act of 1947, as amended, provides for invalid and old age pensions and a variety of other benefits. Invalid pensions are payable to persons 16 years of age and older who have lived at least 5 years in Australia and have become totally incapacitated or permanently blind. Old age pensions are payable to men 65 years of age and over, and to women 60 years of age and over, who have lived in Australia for at least 20 years.

The Commonwealth Maternity Allowance Act of 1912, as amended, provides for allowances for every child born, and the Commonwealth Child Endowment Act of 1941 provides for weekly payments to children under 16 years of age.

The Commonwealth Widows' Pension Act of 1942 provides for monthly payments to widows maintaining at least one child under 16 years of age and to widows 50 years of age and older not maintaining children. Special allowances, paid for not more than 26 (in some cases, 39) weeks following death of the husband, are also provided for widows under 50 years of age in straitened circumstances. A weekly allowance is made to women over 50 years of age or maintaining one or more children under 16 whose husbands have been imprisoned for more than six months.

The Commonwealth Unemployment and Sickness Benefits Act of 1945 provides weekly payments to persons between the ages of 16 and 65 (60 for females) who are not qualified to receive old age, invalid, widows', or service pensions.

Health insurance is universal and government-funded. In 1974/75, the Australian government expended A$2,826.7 million from national welfare funds on social services and A$3,691 million from these funds on health services. As of 30 June 1975, 1,097,225 persons were receiving old age pensions averaging A$33.14 per week.

42 HOUSING

As of 30 June 1971 there were an estimated 3,670,553 occupied dwellings. A total of 128,100 houses and apartments were commenced in 1975, as compared with an annual average of about 85,000 before 1961. A striking feature of postwar housing has been the remarkably high proportion (80%) of new owner-built houses. Central heating, formerly available only in the most modern and expensive homes and apartments, is now generally available in the coldest areas of the country. Most apartments and houses are equipped with hot-water service, refrigeration, and indoor bath and toilet facilities.

Under the Commonwealth-State Housing Agreement of 1941, the federal government subsidized the building by state governments of good houses for families in the lower income groups and subsidized rents in inverse proportion to occupants' income. During World War II, the Commonwealth controlled rents and evictions, but in 1948 these controls reverted to the states.

In 1974/75, about A$161,000,000 in housing subsidies was provided by the government.

43 EDUCATION

Illiteracy is virtually nonexistent except among the aborigines. Education is compulsory for children from 6 until 14, 15, or 16, varying according to the state. Free education is provided in municipal kindergartens and in state primary, secondary, and technical schools. There are also state-regulated private schools. Correspondence courses and educational broadcasts are given for children unable to attend school because of distance or physical handicap. Although each state controls its own system, education is fairly uniform throughout Australia. The federal government directly controls schools in the Northern Territory and in the Australian Capital Territory. In 1974, there were 2,257,845 pupils in government schools and 618,841 pupils in private schools. There were 7,295 government schools and 2,157 private schools in 1974, with a combined total of 135,473 full-time teachers.

There is a state university in each capital city and each provincial area; there is also a national postgraduate research university at Canberra, and a university of technology at Sydney with a branch at Newcastle. In 1975 there were 18 universities in the country, including Murdoch University in Perth, inaugurated in 1975. A total of 148,338 students attended these institutions, and full-time faculty members totaled 9,929 as of 1975.

44 LIBRARIES AND MUSEUMS

The National Library of Australia traces its origins back to 1902, but it was not until 1960 that it was legislatively separated from the Commonwealth Parliamentary Library and made a distinct entity. The Library is now housed in modern facilities in the national capital and has over 1 million volumes. Three other libraries in Australia of comparable size are the library of the University of Sydney (1.9 million volumes), founded in 1852; the State Library of Victoria (1 million), founded in 1853; and the Public Library of New South Wales (1.3 million), founded in 1826. The state capital cities have large noncirculating reference libraries as well as municipal public circulating libraries. The university libraries in Brisbane, Adelaide, Canberra, and Melbourne all have sizable collections.

There are eight large museums, two each in Sydney and Melbourne and one in each of the other state capital cities. Some of the smaller towns also have museums. The National Gallery of Victoria in Melbourne has a fine collection of paintings and other art works, and the South Australian Museum in Adelaide has excellent collections relating to Australian entomology, zoology, and ethnology. Botanical gardens are found in every capital city.

45 ORGANIZATIONS

Chambers of commerce and chambers of manufacture are active throughout Australia, especially in the state capital cities. The Associated Chambers of Commerce coordinates their activities. The Australia Council (founded in 1943) encourages amateur activities in the arts and sponsors traveling exhibitions of ballet, music, and drama. The Australian Academy of Science (founded

1954) promotes research in many branches of science; it took over the functions of the Australian National Research Council in 1955. There are associations or scholarly societies in the fields of architecture, art, international affairs, economics, political and social science, engineering, geography, history, law, literature, medicine, philosophy, and the natural sciences. Many publish scholarly journals. Theatrical, musical, and choreographic groups perform in the larger cities and towns.

Australians are probably more sports-conscious than any other people in the world. Cricket and football competitions are highly organized. Most towns have racecourses. Equestrian contests are featured at agricultural shows. Skiing and tobogganing clubs function in the mountainous areas. Sydney, Melbourne, Hobart, and several other cities have large yacht clubs, and every state capital city has swimming and surfing clubs.

46 PRESS

Many small-town newspapers are scattered throughout Australia. In 1974 there were an estimated 58 dailies and 502 nondailies; the dailies had a total circulation of 4,028,000 per day. All are popular in varying degrees. No metropolitan daily paper presents the point of view of the Labour Party, but even the dailies listed as conservative in orientation are not so closely tied to the political party as to be regarded as party papers. In general, news is straightforwardly presented and political criticism is fair and responsible. The *Australian*, the only national newspaper, was established in 1964 and is published in all state capitals. It is independent and had an estimated daily circulation in 1974 of 141,837.

Other leading dailies and their estimated 1974 circulation figures are listed in the following table:

	ORIENTATION	CIRCULATION
Sun-News-Pictorial (Melbourne, m.)	Conservative	649,585
Herald (Melbourne, e.)	Conservative	484,307
Daily Mirror (Sydney, e.)	Independent	361,549
Sun (Sydney, e.)	Conservative	352,700
Daily Telegraph (Sydney, m.)	Conservative	309,857
Morning Herald (Sydney, m.)	Conservative	270,904
Courier-Mail (Brisbane, m.)	Conservative	265,008
West Australian (Perth, m.)	Conservative	223,305
Advertiser (Adelaide, m.)	Conservative	222,657
Age (Melbourne, e.)	Independent	210,000
Telegraph (Brisbane, m.)	Conservative	169,000
News (Adelaide, e.)	Independent	143,000

Major Sunday newspapers in Sydney include the *Sun-Herald*, 658,440; *Telegraph*, 654,419; *Mirror*, 502,542; and *Times*, 213,260. Other major Sunday newspapers are the *Mail* (Brisbane), 358,803; *Sun* (Brisbane), 288,000; *Mail* (Adelaide), 251,905; and the *Observer* (Melbourne), 123,000.

Among the nondailies in 1974 there were 40 foreign-language newspapers, including 13 in Greek, 5 in Italian, 3 in Maltese, 3 in Polish, and 3 in Hungarian.

The major news agency is the Australian Associated Press, founded in 1935; it has been associated with Reuters since 1946. The Australian United Press was founded in 1932 through the merger of several smaller agencies. Many international news services have bureaus in Sydney.

47 TOURISM

Visitors must have valid passports duly visaed by an Australian or British consul or passport officer, be in possession of sufficient funds to maintain themselves while in Australia, and hold return tickets for travel to a destination beyond Australia. Health examinations are made at all Australian ports of entry. Persons traveling by sea need not have a vaccination or inoculation certificate unless they come from or by way of Eastern countries. Every person entering Australia by air must present an official certificate of vaccination against smallpox dated more than 14 days but not more than 3 years before arrival in Australia. In 1973, some 472,000 tourists visited Australia, as compared with 327,000 in 1967/68.

48 FAMOUS AUSTRALIANS

The most highly regarded contemporary Australian writer is Patrick White (b.1912), author of *The Vivisector, The Eye of the Storm*, and other works of fiction, and winner of the 1973 Nobel Prize for literature. Other well-known novelists include Henry Handel Richardson (Henrietta Richardson Robertson, 1870–1946), author of *The Fortunes of Richard Mahoney*, and Thomas Keneally (b.1935). Henry Lawson (1867–1922) was a leading short-story writer and creator of popular ballads.

Three renowned scholars of Australian origin are Sir Gilbert Murray, O.M. (1866–1957), classicist and translator of ancient Greek plays; Samuel Alexander, O.M. (1859–1938), influential scientific philosopher; and Eric Partridge (b.1894), authority on English slang. An outstanding bacteriologist is Sir Frank Macfarlane Burnet, O.M. (b.1899), director of the Melbourne Hospital, and cowinner of the 1960 Nobel Prize for medicine. Elizabeth Kenny (1886–1952) made important contributions to the care and treatment of infantile paralysis victims. Sir John Carew Eccles (b.1906) shared the 1963 Nobel Prize for medicine for his work on ionic mechanisms of the nerve cell membrane. John Warcup Cornforth (b.1917) shared the 1975 Nobel Prize for chemistry for his work on organic molecules.

Leading Australian-born figures of the theater include the actors Dame Judith Anderson (b.1898) and Cyril Ritchard (b.1898), and the ballet dancer, choreographer, and stage director Sir Robert Helpmann (b.1909). Musicians of Australian birth include the operatic singers Dame Nellie Melba (1861–1931), John Brownlee (b.1901), Marjorie Lawrence (b.1909), and Joan Sutherland (b.1928) and the composers Percy Grainger (1882–1961), Arthur Benjamin (1893–1960), Peggy Glanville-Hicks (b.1912), and Peter Sculthorpe (b.1929). Alfred Hill (1870–1960) is regarded as the founder of the art of musical composition in Australia. Albert Namatjira (1902–59), a full-blooded Aranda, achieved renown as a painter, as has Sidney Nolan (b.1917). The aviator Sir Charles Edward Kingsford-Smith (1897–1935) pioneered flights across the Pacific Ocean.

In recent years, the tennis world has been dominated by such Australian players as Frank Sedgman (b.1927), Lewis Hoad (b.1934), Kenneth Rosewall (b.1934), Rod (George) Laver (b.1938), John Newcombe (b.1944), and Evonne Goolagong (b.1951). Sir Donald Bradman (b.1908) was the outstanding cricket player of modern times. Record-breaking long-distance runners include John Landy (b.1930) and Herb Elliott (b.1938). Jon Konrads (b.1942) and his sister Ilsa (b.1944) have held many world swimming records, as did Dawn Fraser (b.1937), the first woman to swim 100 meters in less than a minute, and Murray Rose (b.1939).

The principal modern Australian statesman is Sir Robert Gordon Menzies (b.1894), who served as prime minister from 1939 to 1941 and again from 1949 to 1966. Other postwar prime ministers have included (Edward) Gough Whitlam (b.1916), who held office from 1972 to 1975; and Malcolm Fraser (b.1930), who succeeded Whitlam late in 1975.

49 DEPENDENCIES

Since 1936, Australia has claimed all territory in Antarctica (other than Adélie Land) situated south of 60°s and between 45° and 160°E, an area of 6,402,475 sq km (2,472,000 sq mi). Three scientific and exploratory bases are now in operation: Mawson (established February 1954), Davis (established January 1957), and Casey (established February 1969).

Territory of Ashmore and Cartier Islands

The uninhabited, reef-surrounded Ashmore Islands, three in number, and Cartier Island, situated in the Indian Ocean about 480 km (300 mi) north of Broome, Western Australia, have been under Australian authority since May 1934. In July 1938, they were annexed to the Northern Territory.

Christmas Island
Situated at 10°30's and 105°40'E in the Indian Ocean, directly south of the western tip of Java, Christmas Island is about 2,330 km (1,450 mi) northwest of Perth. About 18 km (11 mi) long and from 6 to 18 km (4 to 11 mi) wide, it has an area of about 155 sq km (60 sq mi). Total population in June 1973 was 2,884, of whom roughly two-thirds were Chinese, and one-sixth Malay. The only activity, phosphate extraction, is carried out by the governments of Australia and New Zealand. In 1972/73, 1,255,170 tons were exported to Australia and New Zealand; in addition, 134,698 tons of phosphate dust were exported to Southeast Asia and 8,269 tons to Australia. A British crown colony since 1888, Christmas Island was transferred to Australia on 1 October 1958.

Cocos (Keeling) Islands
The Territory of Cocos (Keeling) Islands is a group of coral atolls consisting of 27 islands with a total land area of 13 sq km (5 sq mi) in the Indian Ocean, at 12°5's and 96°53'E, about 2,770 km (1,720 mi) northwest of Perth. The population of 654 on 30 June 1973 consisted mainly of Cocos Islanders. A British possession since 1857, the islands were transferred to Australia in 1955 and are administered by the minister for territories. The climate is pleasant, with moderate rainfall. Principal crops are copra, coconut oil, and coconuts. The airport is a link in a fortnightly service between Australia and South Africa.

The Clunies-Ross Estate, which employs most of the islanders, provides two to three years of elementary education in the vernacular to the children of its employees.

Coral Sea Islands
The Coral Sea Islands were declared a territory of Australia in legislation enacted during 1969 and amended slightly in 1973. The islands, spread over a wide ocean area between 10° and 23°30's and 154° and 158°E, contain only a few sq km of land area. They are administered by the minister for the Capital Territory and have no permanent inhabitants.

Territory of Heard and McDonald Islands
Heard Island at 53°6's and 72°31'E, about 480 km (300 mi) southeast of the Kerguelen Islands and about 4,000 km (2,500 mi) southwest of Perth, is bleak and mountainous, about 910 sq km (350 sq mi) in size, and dominated by a dormant volcano, Big Ben, 9,000 feet high. There was a station at Atlas Cove from 1947 to 1955, but the island is now uninhabited and visited occasionally by scientists. Just north is Shag Island and 42 km (26 mi) to the west are the small, rocky McDonald Islands. The largest island of the group was visited for the first time, it is believed, on 27 January 1971, by members of the Australian National Antarctic Expedition. The Territory was transferred from the UK to Australia at the end of 1947.

Macquarie Island
Macquarie Island, at 54°30's and 158°40'E, is about 1,600 km (1,000 mi) southeast of Hobart. The rocky, glacial island, 34 km (21 mi) long and about 3 to 5 km (2 to 3 mi) wide, is uninhabited except for a base maintained at the northern end since February 1948. Macquarie Island has been a dependency of Tasmania since the early 19th century. At the most southerly point, the island has what is believed to be the biggest penguin rookery in the world. Two small island groupings are off Macquarie Island: Bishop and Clerk and Judge and Clerk.

Norfolk Island
Norfolk Island, with an area of 36 sq km (14 sq mi) and a population (1971) of 1,683 is situated at 29°3's and 167°57'E, some 1,500 km (930 mi) northeast of Sydney. Discovered in 1774 by Capt. James Cook, it was the site of a British penal colony in 1788–1813 and 1826–55, and in 1856 was settled by descendants of the *Bounty* mutineers. Since 1914, it has been administered by the minister for territories. There are about 240 km (150 mi) of usable roads, and transport is almost exclusively by motor vehicle. The soil is fertile and the climate conducive to the growing of fruits and bean seed. There is a small whaling industry, and tourism is important. As of 1975, endangered species on Norfolk Island included the Norfolk Island starling, gray-headed blackbird, Norfolk Island parakeet, and scarlet-breasted robin.

[50]BIBLIOGRAPHY

Aitken, Jonathan. *Land of Fortune.* New York: Atheneum, 1971.

Albinski, Henry S. *Politics and Foreign Policy in Australia: The Impact of Vietnam and Conscription.* Durham, N.C.: Duke University Press, 1970.

Andrews, John. *Australia's Resources and Their Utilization.* Sydney: Department of Tutorial Classes, University of Sydney, 1957.

Atlas of Australian Resources. Canberra: Department of National Development, 1953–date.

Australia Handbook. Melbourne: Australian National Travel Association, 1941–date.

Australian Encyclopaedia. Sydney: Angus and Robertson, 1957.

The Australian Environment. Melbourne: Melbourne University Press, 1960.

Australian Parliamentary Handbook. Sydney: Angus and Robertson, 1952–date.

Baker, Sidney John. *The Australian Language.* Sydney: Angus and Robertson, 1945.

Baker, Sidney John. *Australia Speaks: A Supplement.* Sydney: Shakespeare Head Press, 1953.

Barnard, Marjorie. *History of Australia.* New York: Praeger, 1963.

Barnes, Victor S. *Modern Encyclopaedia of Australia and New Zealand.* Cleveland: World, 1965.

Battarbee, Reginald Ernest. *Modern Australian Aboriginal Art.* Sydney: Angus and Robertson, 1951.

Berney, Maurice. *Australia.* Chicago: Rand McNally, 1965.

Bleakley, J. W. *The Aborigines of Australia.* Brisbane: Jacaranda, 1959.

Blunden, Geoffrey. *Australia and Her People.* London: Lutterworth, 1959.

Boxer, A. H. (ed.). *Aspects of the Australian Economy.* Melbourne: Melbourne University Press, 1966.

Butler, David. *The Canberra Model.* New York: St. Martin's Press, 1974.

Caiger, George. *The Australian Way of Life.* New York: Columbia University Press, 1954.

Cameron, Roderick. *Australia.* New York: Columbia University Press, 1971.

Coleman, Peter. *Australian Civilisation.* Sydney: Angus and Robertson, 1962.

Condliffe, John B. *Development of Australia.* New York: Free Press, 1964.

Crisp, Leslie Finlay. *The Parliamentary Government of the Commonwealth of Australia.* Melbourne: Longmans, Green, 1955.

Crowley, F. K. (ed.). *A New History of Australia.* New York: Holmes & Meier, 1974.

David, Sir Tannatt William Edgewater. *Geology of the Commonwealth of Australia.* 3 vols. London: Arnold, 1950.

The Federal Guide: A Handbook of the Organization and Functions of the Commonwealth Government Departments. Canberra: Commonwealth Government Printer, 1924–date.

Feeken, Erwin H. J. and Gerda E. E. *The Discovery and Exploration of Australia.* Melbourne: Nelson, 1970.

Fitzpatrick, Brian Charles. *The Australian Commonwealth: A Picture of the Community, 1901–1955.* Melbourne: Cheshire, 1956.

Fitzpatrick, Brian Charles. *The Australian People, 1788–1945.* Melbourne: Melbourne University Press, 1946.

Gillett, Keith, and Frank McNeill. *The Great Barrier Reef and Adjacent Isles.* Sydney: Coral Press, 1960.

Grattan, Clinton Hartley (ed.). *Australia*. Berkeley: University of California Press, 1947.

Greenwood, Gordon (ed.). *Australia: A Social and Political History*. Sydney: Angus and Robertson, 1966.

Gunther, John. *John Gunther's Inside Australia*. New York: Harper & Row, 1972.

Harper, Norman Denholm (ed.). *Pacific Orbit*. New York: Humanities Press, 1968.

Harper, Norman Denholm, and David Sissons. *Australia and the United Nations*. New York: Manhattan, 1959.

Horne, D. *The Lucky Country; Australia in the Sixties*. London: Penguin, 1964.

Howitt, Alfred William. *The Native Tribes of South-East Australia*. London: Macmillan, 1904.

Inglis, K. S. *The Australian Colonists: An Exploration of Social History, 1788-1870*. Carlton, Victoria: Melbourne University Press, 1974.

LaNauze, J. A. *The Making of the Australian Constitution*. Melbourne: Melbourne University Press, 1972.

Levi, Werner. *Australia's Outlook on Asia*. Sydney: Angus and Robertson, 1959.

London, H. I. *Non-White Immigration and the "White Australia" Policy*. New York: New York University Press, 1970.

McCubbin, Charles. *Australian Butterflies*. Melbourne: Nelson, 1971.

McKnight, Thomas L. *Australia's Corner of the World*. Englewood Cliffs, N. J.: Prentice-Hall, 1970.

McLead, A. L. (ed.). *The Pattern of Australian Culture*. Ithaca, N.Y.: Cornell University Press, 1963.

McNally, W. *Australia: The Challenging Land*. London: Hale, 1965.

Massola, Aldo. *The Aborigines of Southeastern Australia*. New York: Scribner, 1974.

Miller, John Donald Bruce. *Australian Government and Politics: An Introductory Survey*. London: Duckworth, 1959.

Miller, John Donald Bruce (ed.). *Australia Trade Unionism*. Newport, New South Wales: 1952.

Miller, T. B. *Australia's Foreign Policy*. Sydney: Angus and Robertson, 1968.

Nicholas, Harold Sprent. *The Australian Constitution: An Analysis*. Sydney: Angus and Robertson, 1952.

Official Year Book of the Commonwealth of Australia. Canberra: Commonwealth Government Printer, 1908–date.

Osborne, Charles (ed.). *Australia, New Zealand and the South Pacific*. New York: Praeger, 1970.

Overacker, Louise. *The Australian Party System*. New Haven, Conn.: Yale University Press, 1952.

Parliamentary Handbook and Record of Elections. Canberra: Commonwealth Government Printer, 1915–date.

Phillips, Arthur Angell. *Australian Tradition: Studies in a Colonial Culture*. Melbourne: Cheshire, 1958.

Pike, Douglas. *Australia: The Quiet Continent*. Cambridge: Cambridge University Press, 1961.

Preston, Richard (ed.). *Contemporary Australia*. Durham, N.C.: Duke University Press, 1969.

Reese, Trevor R. *Australia in the Twentieth Century*. New York: Praeger, 1964.

Robinson, K. W. *Australia, New Zealand and the Southwest Pacific*. London: University of London Press, 1960.

Sawer, Geoffrey. *Australian Federal Politics and Law*. Vol. 1 (1901–1929). Melbourne: Melbourne University Press, 1956.

Sawer, Geoffrey. *Australian Government To-day*. Melbourne: Melbourne University Press, 1954.

Scott, Sir Ernest. *A Short History of Australia*. Melbourne: Oxford University Press, 1951.

Spate, O. H. K. *Australia*. New York: Praeger, 1968.

Spencer, Sir Baldwin. *Wanderings in Wild Australia*. London: Macmillan, 1928.

Spencer, Sir Baldwin, and Francis James Gillen. *The Arunta: A Study of a Stone Age People*. London: Macmillan, 1927.

Taylor, Thomas Griffith. *Australia: A Study of Warm Environments and Their Effect on British Settlement*. London: Methuen, 1955.

Wannan, Bill. *The Australian: Yarns, Ballads, Legends and Traditions of the Australian People*. Melbourne: Australasian Book Society, 1954.

Ward, Russel. *Australia*. Englewood Cliffs, N. J.: Prentice-Hall, 1965.

Who's Who in Australia. Melbourne: Colorgravure Publications, 1906–date.

Wynes, William Anstey. *Legislative, Executive and Judicial Powers in Australia*. Sydney: Law Book Co. of Australasia, 1956.

BAHRAYN

State of Bahrayn
Dawlat al-Bahrayn

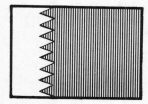

CAPITAL: Al-Manamah. **FLAG:** Red with a white vertical stripe on the hoist, serrated with seven points. **MONETARY UNIT:** The Bahrayn dinar (BD) is divided into 1,000 fils. There are coins of 1, 5, 10, 25, 50, and 100 fils, and notes of 100, 250, and 500 fils and 1, 5, and 10 dinars. BD1 = $2.531 (or $1 = BD0.395). **WEIGHTS AND MEASURES:** The metric system is used. **HOLIDAYS:** New Year's Day, 1 January; National Day, 16 December. Movable Muslim religious holidays include Hijra (Muslim New Year), Ashura, Birthday of Muhammad, 'Id al-Fitr, and 'Id al-'Adha'. **TIME:** 3 P.M. = noon GMT.

¹LOCATION, SIZE, AND EXTENT
Situated in the western Persian Gulf, 29 km (18 mi) NW of Qatar, the State of Bahrayn, the fourth-smallest Asian country, consists of a group of islands with a total area of 622 sq km (240 sq mi), extending *48* km (*30* mi) N–S and *19* km (*12* mi) E–W. Al-Manamah is situated on Bahrayn, the main island, which is linked by causeways and bridges to Muharraq and Sitrah islands. Other islands include the Huwar group, Nabi Salih, Umm al-Na'san, Muhammadiyah, and Jiddah. The total coastline is *126* km (*78* mi).

²TOPOGRAPHY
A narrow strip of land along the northern coast of Bahrayn is irrigated by natural springs and artesian wells. South of the cultivable area, the land is barren. The landscape consists of low rolling hills with numerous rocky cliffs and wadis. From the shoreline the surface rises gradually toward the center, where it drops into a basin surrounded by steep cliffs. Toward the center of the basin is Jabal al-Dukhan, a rocky, steep-sided hill that rises 250 feet above the surrounding plain and 450 feet above sea level. Most of the lesser islands are flat and sandy, with the Nabi Salih group covered in date groves.

³CLIMATE
Summers in Bahrayn are hot, although, surrounded as it is by the sea, temperatures are somewhat lower than in neighboring Gulf countries. Maximum temperatures recorded in recent years were 44.4°C (112°F) in June and 43.4°C (110°F) in July. Winters are relatively cool, with temperatures ranging from 10°C to 20°C (50°F to 68°F). Rainfall averages 3 to 4 inches annually. Prevailing southeast winds occasionally raise dust storms.

⁴FLORA AND FAUNA
Outside the cultivated areas there is a considerable variety of wild desert flowers that flourish most noticeably after rain. Desert shrub, grass, and self-planted date palms are also found.

Animal life is limited to the jerboa (desert rat), gazelle, and hare; some 14 species of lizard and 4 types of land snake are also found. Bird life is especially varied. Larks, song thrushes, and terns are frequent visitors, and residents include the bulbul, hoopoe, parakeet, and warbler.

⁵POPULATION
Of the total population of 216,815 (1971 census), 89,728 lived in al-Manamah, 37,577 in al-Muharraq, and 10,780 in Rifa' al-Gharbi. The 1975 population was estimated at 265,000, with a density of 426 persons per sq km (1,104 per sq mi). The annual growth rate in the 1970s was about 3.5%.

⁶ETHNIC GROUPS
In 1975, about 75% of the population (some 200,000 persons) were indigenous Bahraynis, the vast majority of whom are of northern Arab (Adnani) stock, infused with black racial traits. Other Arabs, principally Omanis, form the largest nonindigenous group (about 14% of the total), followed by Indians, Pakistanis, Iranians, and some 7,500 persons from the UK and US.

⁷LANGUAGE
Arabic is the universal language; the Gulf dialect is spoken. English is widely understood, Farsi less so.

⁸RELIGION
The Muslims of Bahrayn are equally divided between the Sunni, adherents of the orthodox sect, and the Shi'i, who are mostly in Bahrayn's rural areas. About 200 Bahraynis follow Christianity and other faiths.

⁹TRANSPORTATION
The outline of the present network of roads was traced in the early 1930s, soon after the discovery of oil. The three main islands of Bahrayn and all the towns and villages are linked by an excellent road network. A four-lane, 2.8-km causeway and a bridge connect al-Manamah with Muharraq Island, and a bridge joins Sitrah to the main island.

The port of Bahrayn, Mina Sulman, accommodates six oceangoing vessels drawing up to 30 feet. Six additional berths are being planned, along with additional transit and storage sheds.

Bahrayn's international airport, opened near al-Muharraq in 1971, was undergoing a major expansion in 1976. Some 15 international airlines serve Bahrayn. Gulfair, headquartered in Bahrayn, is owned equally by the governments of Bahrayn, Qatar, the United Arab Emirates, and Oman, and had some 17 aircraft in service in mid-1976.

¹⁰COMMUNICATIONS
The external and internal telephone services in Bahrayn are operated by Cable & Wireless Ltd. In 1975, the government acquired a 60% interest in the company. A satellite station, opened in 1969, provides communications with every part of the world. Internally, some 14,000 telephone lines (26,000 telephones) serve the country. New exchanges at Isa Town, al-Rifa' al-Gharbi, and al-Muharraq were completed in mid-1976. The government operates a radio and a color television station.

¹¹HISTORY
The history of Bahrayn has been traced back 5,000 years to Sumerian times when, known as Dilmun, Bahrayn was a thriving trade center. It was visited by the ships of Alexander. Bahrayn accepted Islam in the 7th century A.D., after which it was ruled alternately by its own princes and by the caliphs' governors. The

Portuguese occupied Bahrayn from 1522 to 1602. The present ruling family, al-Khalifah, who are related to al-Sabah of Kuwayt and the Sa'udi royal family, captured Bahrayn in 1782.

Following an initial contact in 1805, the ruler of Bahrayn signed the first treaty with Britain in 1820. A binding treaty of protection was concluded in 1861 and revised in 1892 and, again, in 1951.

In the 20th century, Iran put forward a number of claims to Bahrayn. After a UN mission had ascertained that the Bahraynis wished to remain independent, Iran abandoned its claims. Between 1968 and 1971, Bahrayn participated in discussions aimed at forming a federation of the nine shaykhdoms of the southern Gulf. On 14 August 1971, Shaykh Isa bin Sulman al-Khalifah declared that, in view of the failure of the larger federation to materialize, Bahrayn was declaring its independence as a sovereign state. Bahrayn's treaties with the UK were replaced, on 15 August, by a treaty of friendship and cooperation. On that date, the country effectively became the independent State of Bahrayn. Bahrayn promulgated its first constitution in 1973, which occasioned the convening of an elective National Assembly. The Assembly was dissolved in August 1975 amid charges of Communist influences. A new 16-member cabinet was announced on 25 August and the prime minister, Shaykh Muhammad bin Mubarak al-Khalifah, promised elections as soon as a new electoral law had been drafted and certain legislative articles in the constitution revised.

12 GOVERNMENT

Under the constitution ratified in June 1973, Bahrayn is a constitutional monarchy headed by the amir who, since 1961, has been Shaykh Isa bin Sulman al-Khalifah. The government is administered by a cabinet appointed by the amir and presided over by the prime minister. Since 1973, a majority of ministers have been selected from outside the ruling family. The constitution provides for a National Assembly composed of 30 elected members and 14 cabinet ministers. Suffrage is restricted to men over age 21.

13 POLITICAL PARTIES

Prior to the 1970s, political activity in Bahrayn was limited to a reform-seeking committee in 1954–56. In the 1970s there have been numerous manifestations of radical ferment. Working-class militants are mainly involved with the Arab Nationalists' Movement (ANM) and the Iraq-centered Ba'th Party. As political parties were not allowed, some ANM sympathizers campaigned successfully as independents for the 1973 National Assembly. The dissolution of the Assembly in August 1975 was aimed directly at the leftist movement.

14 LOCAL GOVERNMENT

In March 1956, the amir of Bahrayn decreed that the country's major towns—al-Manamah, al-Muharraq, al-Rifa' al-Gharbi, Sitrah, and Judd Hafs—would be administered by municipal councils. Half of the councilmen are elected; the remainder, including the council presidents (who are members of the ruling al-Khalifah house), are appointed by the amir. In rural communities, administration continues to be conducted along traditional lines by mukhtars (village headmen), also appointed by the amir.

15 JUDICIAL SYSTEM

The law of Bahrayn represents a mixture of Shari'ah (Islamic religious law) and government decrees dealing with criminal and commercial matters. Professional judges serve at all levels of the judiciary, which provides a progression of levels for appeals.

16 ARMED FORCES

The Bahrayn Defense Force was set up in 1968 in anticipation of the UK's withdrawal from the region. In 1975, the armed forces numbered some 1,200 officers and men and were equipped with light artillery and armored cars. An equivalent number of personnel serve in the state police, established in 1926.

17 MIGRATION

The 20% proportion of non-Bahraynis is by far the lowest immigration figure in any Gulf state. However, the construction boom of 1974–75 brought in a higher-than-normal number of immigrants, including 1,600 construction workers from the Republic of Korea. Nearly 10,000 workers entered the country in 1974, with 1975 estimates running to double that number.

18 INTERNATIONAL COOPERATION

Prior to independence, Bahrayn became an associate member of UNESCO, FAO, and WHO, and since 1971 has become a full member of these and other international organizations, including the UN, Arab League, IMF, and IBRD. It is also a member of OAPEC. Close ties with the UK have been maintained.

19 ECONOMY

For centuries, Bahrayn depended almost exclusively on trade, pearl diving, and agriculture. The discovery of oil in 1932 came at a providential time, when the pearl trade was being drastically undercut by the development of cultured pearls.

Although its economy has been oil-based for the last four decades, Bahrayn's development has been tempered by relatively limited reserves. Oil provided more than 85% of the national income in the mid-1970s, but with present oil supplies not expected to last much beyond 1995, the government has pressed for the evolution of auxiliary sectors, such as petroleum refining and aluminum production. Significant progress has also been made in enhancing Bahrayn as an entrepôt and a service and commercial center for the Gulf region. Bahrayn now provides ample warehousing for goods in transit and dry-dock facilities for marine engine and ship repairs.

20 INCOME

Bahrayn derives more than 85% of its national income from petroleum revenues. Income from oil increased from BD96 million in 1974 to BD126 million in 1975. Roughly half of the remainder is derived from customs and port duties.

21 LABOR

The total labor force in 1975 was estimated at 70,000–80,000, of whom about half were Bahraynis. Bahrayn boasts a high proportion of skilled workers, both among its foreign residents and the indigenous population, many of whom have benefited from local technical and vocational training programs.

Bahrayn enacted a comprehensive labor law in 1958, which provided for an 8-hour day, 48-hour week, overtime and severance pay, paid vacations, sick and maternity leave, collective bargaining, and conciliation and arbitration. A minimum wage for laborers stood at BD1.50 per day in 1975. In that year, civil servants were covered by social security and pension law provisions.

22 AGRICULTURE

There were some 15,000 acres under cultivation in 1975. The date palm industry, which once employed 4,000 people, is now at a relative standstill; dates have become a luxury item. About 6,000 acres of former date plantations are now neglected. Alfalfa and vegetables account for most of the rest of Bahrayn's agriculture.

The FAO is working on pilot projects in Bahrayn. Essential services, such as plowing and spraying with insecticides, are offered free by the government and an Agricultural Credit Fund provides interest-free loans to help farmers purchase equipment.

23 ANIMAL HUSBANDRY

Most domestic meat consumption is supplied through the import of live cattle, goats, and sheep. A few herds of cattle are kept for milk production, and the Ministry of Agriculture is importing cows from Australia to form the nucleus of a new dairy herd. There is a thriving poultry industry. A Federal Republic of Germany (FRG) concern has contracted to produce 15 million eggs a year at a new poultry farm.

24 FISHING

Although more than 300 varieties of fish found in Bahrayni waters constitute an important food source for much of the population, local fishing and pearl diving have declined to the point where there are now as few as 20 Bahrayni fishing dhows still in use. Shrimp production, however, has been growing rapidly, and shrimp exports of the Bahrayn Fishing Co., 40% UK-owned, averaged $3 million annually in the 1970s, with the US and Japan the chief markets.

25 FORESTRY

There are no forests in Bahrayn.

26 MINING

The Middle East's first oil well was drilled in Bahrayn in 1931, and production began in 1933. In 1928, Standard Oil of California had formed the island's sole concession, the Bahrayn Petroleum Co. (BAPCO), which subsequently came under the ownership of Caltex (a Standard Oil-Texaco conglomerate registered in Canada). In 1974, the Bahrayn government acquired a 25% holding in BAPCO, and in 1975 increased its share to 60%.

Total daily onshore production has never exceeded the 1972 peak of 76,000 barrels and has begun a steady decline, reaching 55,000 barrels in 1975. Officials have forecast a continuing decline, averaging 3% annually. A major impetus to the state's petroleum income for the immediate future is expected from Bahrayn's 50% share in the Abu Safa field. This small offshore field lies entirely within Saʿudi Arabia's offshore boundaries, but its daily production of around 60,000 barrels is split between Bahrayn and Saʿudi Arabia under an arrangement reached with Saʿudi Arabia's King Faysal in 1972.

Bahrayn's natural gas resources are a second income factor, although the Khriff gas field has failed to meet earlier expectations. In 1976, 250 million cu feet were being produced daily. Reserves are now put at 8,000–11,000 billion cu feet.

27 ENERGY AND POWER

In mid-1975, Bahrayn had a total installed power capacity of 150 Mw, derived from a municipal power station at Jufayr and the new Sitrah power and water station. By mid-1976, capacity was to be 220 Mw, with the addition of a second unit at Sitrah and two new gas turbines at al-Muharraq. Unlike most Gulf states, Bahrayn has always enjoyed a constant fresh water supply, borne through natural aquifers from Saʿudi Arabia. But population expansion during the 1960s and 1970s caused a serious drop in the ground water level, prompting the construction of the Sitrah seawater desalination and electric power facility, designed for fresh water production of 20 million gallons per day.

28 INDUSTRY

Petroleum refining, modestly begun in 1942, was Bahrayn's first modern industrial enterprise. By early 1976, the BAPCO refinery at Awali had a daily output of 250,000 barrels, with a 10% increase expected by the year's end. The refinery's capacity has far outstripped the local supply of crude oil, and about three-fourths of the oil is now pumped from Ra's Tanurah in Saʿudi Arabia through 34 miles of sea and land lines. World demand for low-sulfur fuels has prompted the introduction of hydro-desulfurization processes. By the early 1970s, much of the refinery's basic equipment had become antiquated and a low sulfur fuel oil project, completed in 1973 at a cost of $60 million, has had outstanding results. The refinery can now produce 50,000 barrels of fuel oil daily with a sulfur content of 0.5%.

An aluminum industry was launched by Aluminium Bahrayn in 1971 and in 1975 it had a smelter capacity of 120,000 tons annually. The Bahrayn government has increased its share from 17% to 77.9%, with 22.1% held by US and FRG firms.

The Arab Shipbuilding and Repair Yard, a pan-Arab industrial venture, undertaken by OAPEC, was due to become operative by mid-1977.

29 DOMESTIC TRADE

The shops of Bahrayn are becoming increasingly modernized and there is a growing tendency toward specialization. Local regulations encourage the granting of agencies to Bahrayni citizens. Working hours for shops and most offices are from 8 A.M. to 12:30 P.M. and from 4 to 6 P.M., Saturday through Thursday. Fridays are holidays. Government offices, banks, and some large companies work in the mornings only. Of all the Gulf states, Bahrayn offers the most scope for consumer advertising through its publications, theaters, direct mail, and radio.

30 FOREIGN TRADE

Refined oil products are the principal exports, comprising about 75% of the annual export volume in the mid-1970s. In 1975, total exports were valued at about BD395 million, of which BD315

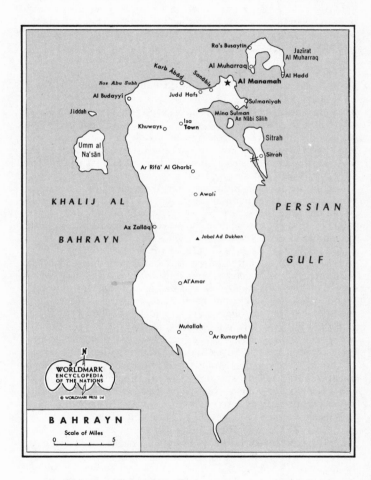

See continental political: front cover J7; physical: back cover J7
LOCATION: 25°47′10″ to 26°17′3″N; 50°22′45″ to 50°40′20″E.
TERRITORIAL SEA LIMIT: 3 mi.

million derived from oil. Aluminum, frozen shrimp, paper goods, air-conditioning units, and flour are other main export earners. During 1970–73, imported equipment for Bahrayn's industrialization projects produced trade deficits, but these purchases dropped off after 1973 and the sharp rise in oil prices produced surpluses during 1974–75. Imports in 1975 totaled BD240 million, with foodstuffs the major category, followed by machinery, textiles and clothing, construction materials, and transport equipment. The principal markets for Bahrayn's non-oil exports (oil recipients are not published) are Japan, Saʿudi Arabia, Dubayy, China, Kuwayt, and the UK.

³¹BALANCE OF PAYMENTS
Bahrayn has traditionally relied on a substantial influx of funds from Saʿudi Arabia, Kuwayt, Abu Dhabi, and Iran to offset capital outlays. Following a payments deficit in 1973 brought on by an unusual volume of capital expenditures, Bahrayn registered payments surpluses of BD43 million in 1974 and BD44 million in 1975. Official gross reserves meanwhile jumped from $72 million at the end of 1973 to $271 million as of 30 June 1975.

³²BANKING
The Bahrayn Monetary Agency (BMA), the central banking authority in Bahrayn, issues and redeems bank notes, regulates the value of the Bahrayn dinar, and supervises interest rates. To establish Bahrayn as a major regional center for commerce and finance operations in the Gulf, the BMA introduced a licensing scheme in September 1975 to set up Bahrayn as an offshore banking center. By April 1976, 32 banks had set up offshore operations in the country, including international banks from the Middle East, Far East, Western Europe, and the Americas.

³³INSURANCE
Twenty-one insurance companies have offices in Bahrayn.

³⁴SECURITIES
There is no stock exchange. Share trading is through banks.

³⁵PUBLIC FINANCE
Total revenues in the 1975 budget stood at BD142 million, of which BD126 million (88.7%) derived from oil receipts. Expenditures for 1975 were projected at BD130 million, double the level for 1974, with notable increases for labor and social welfare, health, education, housing, utilities, and transportation.

³⁶TAXATION
There are no taxes in Bahrayn, apart from an income tax on oil production and a municipal tax of 10% on rented property in al-Manamah and a lesser sum on owner-occupied property. To establish Bahrayn as an offshore tax haven, foreign firms may remit accumulated profits and capital without taxation.

³⁷CUSTOMS AND DUTIES
Import licenses are not required for most commodities. Principal prohibited items are arms, ammunition, liquor (except by authorized importers), and cultured pearls. Custom duties are 5% on foodstuffs and essential goods, and 10% on all other commodities except for tobacco (15%) and liquor (50%).

³⁸FOREIGN INVESTMENTS
While continuing to encourage foreign investment, the government acted in the mid-1970s to acquire majority holdings in most of the country's major foreign-held enterprises. Complete acquisition of BAPCO was under negotiation in 1976. Certain other companies remain wholly overseas-owned. Bahrayn offers considerable incentives to companies wishing to establish plants in Bahrayn if these will provide employment and/or exports.

³⁹ECONOMIC POLICY
Since the late 1960s, the government has concentrated on policies and projects that would provide sufficient diversification in industrial, commercial, and financial activities to sustain growth in income, employment, and exports into the post-oil era.

⁴⁰HEALTH
In 1960, Bahrayn inaugurated a free national health service, available to both foreign and indigenous segments of the population. Bahrayni patients who require sophisticated surgery or treatment are sent abroad at government expense. In 1971 there were 5 state and private hospitals, with more than 1,000 beds; 135 physicians, surgeons, and dentists; 863 nurses and midwives; and 161 professional medical workers and technicians. Ten new health centers were planned for the late 1970s, bringing the total number to 22, including a 450-bed hospital in al-Muharraq.

⁴¹SOCIAL WELFARE
Education and medical care have been provided free in Bahrayn for more than 50 years. Impoverished families receive subsistence allowances from the Ministry of Labor and Social Affairs. Free child guidance clinics—the first in the Gulf—were introduced in 1975.

Expanded benefit and pension provisions for government employees came into force in 1975, and a nationwide social security scheme was before the cabinet in 1976. Faced with an unprecedented rise in the cost of living, the government has introduced subsidies for essential commodities.

⁴²HOUSING
The newly established Ministry of Housing plans the construction of 1,000 units a year for lower-income groups; a crash program for the first 700 was launched in 1975. Isa Town was the first low-cost government housing scheme, initiated in 1963 in barren desert between al-Manamah and al-Rifa' al-Gharbi.

⁴³EDUCATION
Education is free and was the largest single item in Bahrayn's 1975 budget, accounting for 18% of recurrent expenditures. Schooling is not compulsory; about one-fourth of the islands' school-age population was enrolled in the mid-1970s. The literacy rate is about 45%. In 1974/75 there were about 42,000 pupils attending primary schools, of whom about 16,000 (38%) were girls. In 1972/73 there were 13,575 students (6,567 girls) at general intermediate and secondary schools, 614 boys at technical schools, and 139 at religious schools. There were 1,465 male and 1,125 female teachers in 1973; enrollment at the teacher-training colleges totaled 204 women and 151 men.

The Gulf Technical College, founded in 1968 in Isa Town, had about 1,100 students in 1974/75, pursuing courses in engineering and business. A teacher-training school in Isa Town accommodating 500 students was established in 1975.

⁴⁴LIBRARIES AND MUSEUMS
The Ministry of Education maintains public libraries in al-Manamah and al-Muharraq as well as a mobile library. There is a public library run by the British Council, and a museum on Muharraq Island.

⁴⁵ORGANIZATIONS
In addition to the Chamber of Commerce and Industry, there are a considerable number of Bahrayni and multinational clubs, including the Bahrayn Red Crescent Society, Children's and Mothers' Welfare Society, and Rotary Clubs.

⁴⁶PRESS
Bahrayn's first daily newspaper in Arabic, *Akhbar al-Khali*, began publication in February 1976. There are 4 Arabic weeklies, a weekly English newspaper, and 3 monthlies.

⁴⁷TOURISM
The government encourages tourism and in April 1974 joined with private interests in setting up the Bahrayn Tourism Co. to develop Bahrayn's tourism potential.

⁴⁸FAMOUS BAHRAYNIS
There are no internationally famous Bahraynis.

⁴⁹DEPENDENCIES
Bahrayn has no territories or colonies.

⁵⁰BIBLIOGRAPHY
Abu Hakima, Ahmad. *History of Eastern Arabia*. Beirut: Khayyats, 1965.
Bibby, Geoffrey. *Looking for Dilmun*. New York: Knopf, 1969.
Busch, B. C. *Britain and the Persian Gulf, 1894–1914*. Berkeley: University of California Press, 1967.
Hay, Sir Rupert. *The Persian Gulf States*. Washington, D.C.: Middle East Institute, 1959.
Kelly, John B. *Britain and the Persian Gulf, 1795–1880*. Oxford: Oxford University Press, 1968.
Marlowe, John. *The Persian Gulf in the Twentieth Century*. London: Cresset, 1962.
Miles, Samuel Barrett. *The Countries and Tribes of the Persian Gulf*. London: Cass, 1966 (orig. 1919).
Wilson, Sir Arnold. *The Persian Gulf*. London: Allen & Unwin, 1954.

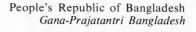

BANGLADESH

People's Republic of Bangladesh
Gana-Prajatantri Bangladesh

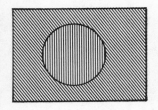

CAPITAL: Dacca. **FLAG**: The national flag is a red circle against a dark green background. **ANTHEM**: *Amar Sonar Bangla (My Golden Bengal)*. **MONETARY UNIT**: The taka (T) of 100 paisa is a nonconvertible paper currency set on a par with the Indian rupee. There are coins of 1, 2, 5, 10, 25, and 50 paisa, and notes of 1, 5, and 10 taka. T1 = $0.0639 (or $1 = T15.6535). **WEIGHTS AND MEASURES**: The imperial system is in use, but a conversion to the metric system is under consideration. Numerical units include the crore (equal to 10 million). **HOLIDAYS**: New Year's Day, 1 January; National Mourning Day (Shaheel Day), 21 February; Independence Day, 26 March; May Day, 1 May; Victory Day, 16 December; Christmas, 25 December; Boxing Day, 26 December. Movable religious holidays include Good Friday, Jamat Wida, Shab-i-Bharat, 'Id al-Fitr, 'Id al-'Azha', and Durga Puja. **TIME**: 6 P.M. = noon GMT.

¹LOCATION, SIZE, AND EXTENT

Situated in the northeastern corner of the Indian subcontinent in southern Asia, Bangladesh, before it became an independent state, was the eastern province of Pakistan, known as East Bengal and, later, as East Pakistan. It comprises an area of 142,776 sq km (55,126 sq mi), extending 767 km (477 mi) SSE–NNW and 429 km (267 mi) ENE–WSW. Bangladesh is bordered on the N and E by India, on the SE by Burma, on the S by the Bay of Bengal, and on the W by India, with a total boundary length of 3,390 km (2,107 mi).

²TOPOGRAPHY

Bangladesh is a tropical country, mainly situated on the deltas of large rivers flowing from the Himalayas. The Brahmaputra River, known locally as the Jamuna, unites with part of the Ganges to form the Padma, which, after its juncture with a third large river, the Meghna, flows into the Bay of Bengal. Offshoots of the Ganges-Padma, including the Burishwar, Garai, Kobadak, and Madhumati, also flow south to the Bay of Bengal. No part of the delta area is more than 500 feet above sea level. Its soil consists mostly of fertile alluvium, which is intensively farmed; mineral deposits are negligible. During the rainy season floodwater covers most of the land surface, damaging crops and injuring the economy. The northwestern section of the country, drained by the Teesta River, is somewhat higher and less flat, but the only really hilly regions are in the east, notably in the Chittagong Hill Tracts to the southeast and the Sylhet District to the northeast. Near the Burmese border, in the extreme southeast, is the Keokradang, which at 4,034 feet is the highest peak in Bangladesh.

³CLIMATE

Bangladesh has a tropical monsoon climate. Annual rainfall is high, averaging 85 inches throughout the country and up to 250 inches in the northeast. There are three distinct seasons. The winter, which lasts from November through February, is cool and dry. The average January temperature for most of the country is about 7°C (45°F); total winter rainfall averages about 7 inches in the east and less than 3 inches in the northwest. Temperatures rise rapidly in early March, and during the summer season (March through May) average about 32°C (90°F). Rainfall also increases during this period, and severe thunderstorms are common. However, nearly 80% of the annual rainfall falls from June to October, when moisture-laden winds blow from the south and southeast. Temperatures drop somewhat, seldom exceeding 31°C (88°F), but humidity remains

high. In April and May and from September through November, devastating tropical cyclones, accompanied by high seas and heavy flooding, are common. There were severe cyclones in May 1963, May 1965, December 1965, October 1966, and most notably during the night of 12/13 November 1970, when a storm and resultant flooding killed more than 200,000 persons.

⁴FLORA AND FAUNA

Bangladesh has the plant and animal life typical of a tropical and riverine swamp. The landscape, which for most of the year is lush green, is dotted with palms and flowering trees. The large forest area of the Sunderbans is the home of the endangered Bengal tiger; there are also leopards, crocodiles, elephants, spotted deer, boars, pheasants, and many varieties of birds and waterfowl.

As of 1975, endangered species in Bangladesh included the wolf, Asiatic wild dog, clouded leopard, leopard (*Panthera pardus*), Sumatran rhinoceros, river terrapin, marsh crocodile, gavial, and Indian python.

⁵POPULATION

Bangladesh is one of the world's most densely populated nations. The census population in 1974 was given as 71,316,517. Unofficial estimates are higher; the UN estimate for 1975 was 73,746,000, with a population of 84,803,000 projected for 1980 (based on an annual population growth rate of 2.8%). In 1975, the crude birthrate was estimated at 49.7 per 1,000 population, the crude death rate at 21.8, and the net natural increase at 27.9. Using the government census figure, the population density in 1974 was still about 500 persons per sq km (1,300 per sq mi). However, the distribution is uneven, with extremely heavy concentrations (up to 1,550 per sq km) in the districts of Noakhali, Dacca, and Comilla. Nearly 45% of the total population is under 15 years of age.

The cities of Dacca, Chittagong, and Khulna have had large influxes of population from rural areas in recent years, although the population of Bangladesh remains about 90% rural. In mid-1975 there were about 2 million people in Dacca and neighboring towns, about 1 million in Chittagong, and about 530,000 in Khulna. Other cities with more than 50,000 people were Mymensingh, Narayanganj, Barisal, Saidpur, Dinajpur, Rajshahi, Bogra, Pabna, Sylhet, Comilla, Chandpur, Brahmanbaria, and Faridpur.

⁶ETHNIC GROUPS

Most of the people are Bengalis, predominantly a mixture of Aryan and Dravidian strains. About 12 tribes inhabiting the

Chittagong Hill Tracts are ethnically distinct from the Bengalis; their facial features and language are closer to the Burmese. In addition, there are a few million non-Bengali Muslims who migrated from India to what was then East Pakistan, after the partition of the subcontinent in 1947. There is evidence that many non-Bengalis who were part of the Mughal legion also settled in Bengal. In the coastal areas of Bangladesh, Arab, Portuguese, and Dutch settlers have gradually come to adopt the Bengali life-style.

7 LANGUAGE

Bengali, an Indo-Aryan tongue, is the official language of Bangladesh and is spoken by about 98% of the population. The successful move to make Bengali coequal to Urdu as an official language was a hallmark of Bengali nationalism in the early 1950s. Non-Bengali migrants from India still speak Urdu today, and this language is widely understood in urban areas. A few tribal groups, notably the tribal peoples of the Chittagong Hill Tracts, also speak a distinct language akin to Burmese and Assamese. Among those speaking Bengali, there are differences of dialect according to region. The people of Chittagong, Noakhali, and Sylhet are known for their distinctive dialects. Although Bengali has replaced English as the medium of instruction, English remains the most important foreign language and is widely understood among the educated.

8 RELIGION

Nearly 90% of the people are believers in Islam, making Bangladesh the world's second-largest Muslim country (after Indonesia). Most of these are of the Sunni sect. About 10% of the population is Hindu. There are small numbers of Christians, mainly Roman Catholic, and some Buddhists, mainly among the tribal people of the Chittagong Hill Tracts.

9 TRANSPORTATION

The large number of rivers and the annual flooding hazard make it difficult to build and maintain adequate transportation facilities in Bangladesh. Railways and waterways are the chief means of transportation. The railways are managed by the government. Most districts of the country can be reached by the railway networks, which have an overall length of more than 3,000 km and include about 4,000 bridges. Passenger traffic has increased substantially during the 1970s, but the quality of service has declined since it is expensive to import the necessary new equipment. The railway system was also damaged by guerrilla warfare during the 1971 liberation struggle. Enlarging and improving the railway network is expensive, partly because of the number of bridges required.

The country has two deepwater ports: Chittagong, serving the eastern part of the country, and Mongla, serving the west, with a combined capacity of about 6 million tons. There are five main river ports—Dacca, Narayanganj, Chandpur, Barisal, and Khulna—and more than 1,500 smaller ports. The inland water system utilizes about 300,000 nonmotorized craft and several thousand motorized boats to provide essential communications facilities to the villages. According to estimates published in 1972, more than 25 million people were then dependent upon the inland water system for inland communications.

Road connections in Bangladesh are still inadequate. Although most of the large cities are connected by paved roads, there are only about 6,000 km of paved roads, and a large part of the highway system becomes submerged during the rainy season, rendering communications difficult. Bridges, ferries, embankments, and dikes are therefore necessary to the inland transportation system. Because of the difficulties of land travel, the number of motor vehicles is still small relative to the total population. In 1972 there were only about 60,000 private vehicles, 5,000 trucks, and 4,000 buses.

Bangladesh Biman is the national airline of Bangladesh. It has an extended network inside the country, connecting the main cities, and also operates some international flights from the airport in Dacca. Air India, BA, and Thai International Airlines also maintain regular service to Dacca.

10 COMMUNICATIONS

All postal and telecommunications services are controlled by the government. There are about 7,000 post and telegraph offices throughout Bangladesh. In 1972 there were an estimated 300,000 telephones, 296,000 radios, and 10,360 television sets. Radiotelegraph and radiotelephone services are available for domestic and international transmissions. There are four domestic radio stations and one television station, which broadcasts news and cultural and entertainment programs during evening hours. A foreign service, broadcasting in shortwave, offers programs in Bengali, English, Hindi, and Urdu.

11 HISTORY

In ancient times, the area of what is now Bangladesh was the eastern part of a region known as "Bang"; the region later became Bengal under the British rulers, who gradually obtained full control of the Indian subcontinent during the 18th century.

The recorded history of the region now called Bangladesh can be traced back to the 4th century B.C., when records provide evidence of a flourishing civilization with cities, palaces, temples, forts, and monasteries. The oldest surviving remains today are the ruins of the city of Mahasthan, the ancient Pundranagar, which flourished for more than 1,500 years, beginning around the 4th century B.C. The region was soon conquered by the Mauryan dynasty, a native Indian dynasty that reached its height under Asoka around 260 B.C.

During most of India's classical Hindu period (A.D. 320–1000), the region was a loosely incorporated outpost of empires centered in the Ganges Basin. Muslim invaders secured a foothold in the area around A.D. 1200, and after Turkish and Afghan invasions in the 13th and 14th centuries, Islam began to take firm hold. In 1576, the region was annexed by the Mughal Empire; under Akbar and his Muslim successors, during the 17th century, there was economic prosperity as well as political stability, with flourishing muslin- and silk-weaving industries and abundant rice harvests. After the death of the Emperor Aurangzeb in 1707, however, French and British trading companies struggled openly for control over trade. By the late 18th century, the British East Indian Company had control over the area. Machinery introduced by the British destroyed the traditional weaving industries, and by the early 19th century, Bengal was in a state of severe economic decline.

The Muslim aristocracy in Bengal long resisted British rule and refused to accept Western education until the turn of the century. As a result, the numerically dominant Muslims of Bengal remained backward in contrast to the Hindu middle class, which generally cooperated with the British, whose policies fostered a mutual antagonism between Hindus and Muslims which would dominate the political scene for years to come. To placate the Muslims, the British partitioned Bengal in 1905, creating a Muslim-dominated eastern sector, roughly corresponding to the territory of present-day Bangladesh. The move was at once denounced by the Hindus, and the decision was reversed in 1911. Enmities generated by the partition led to recurrent outbreaks of terrorism by both factions. In 1940, the All India Muslim League, founded earlier to promote Muslim interests, endorsed the ideal of a separate Muslim state, as propounded in 1930 by the philosopher-poet Muhammad Iqbal. A famine in 1943 led to as many as 2 million deaths in Bengal, and in 1946 there was virtual civil war between Hindus and Muslims. On 14/15 August 1947, as India became independent, Bengal was again partitioned, with the division of the subcontinent, in order to create the Muslim-majority state of Pakistan. Pakistan consisted of two distinct territories, about 1,000 miles apart and separated by India: West Pakistan, containing parts of

Punjab, Sind, Baluchistan, and North-West Frontier Province, and East Pakistan, containing the Muslim-majority districts of Bengal and the Sylhet District of Assam. In language, culture, and ethnic background, these two territories were totally disparate. The only real bond between them seemed to be their state religion—Islam. The territories also differed greatly in economic resources. East Pakistan proved totally unable to compete with the Western wing, and the resulting economic disparity was made an issue by Bengali nationalists, who wanted an autonomous East Pakistan.

Gen. Ayub Khan, who seized power in a military coup in 1958, established a strong centralized government in Pakistan, attempting to maintain tight control over the Bengali opposition. In 1969, the Ayub regime was overthrown, and Gen. Yahya Khan took power under martial law. The election of 7 December 1970 was fought on the issue of provincial autonomy; the Awami League, an offshoot of the original Muslim League, put forth a six-point program for maximum autonomy, and won 167 of 169 seats allotted to East Pakistan in the 313-seat National Assembly. But Yahya Khan postponed the opening of the Assembly session on the grounds that before the Assembly convened, differences would have to be ironed out between Sheikh Mujibur Rahman, the Awami League leader, and Zulfikar Ali Bhutto, leader of the Pakistan People's Party, the majority party in the West. The decision led to escalating violence, and on the evening of 25 March 1971, after a series of reconciliation attempts between Sheikh Mujib and the military government, Mujib was arrested and sent to West Pakistan, to be tried and imprisoned on treason charges. An army was sent to East Pakistan, and the Awami League was outlawed; meanwhile, Bengali nationalists declared an independent People's Republic of Bangladesh on 26 March. In the ensuing violence, the Mukhti Bahini (East Pakistan Liberation Army) launched attacks on public installations, and the regular Pakistani army attacked civilian centers of separatist sentiment. Millions of Bengalis fled over the border to seek refuge in India. Finally, on 4 December 1971, after numerous incursions, a large Indian army which was massed on the border of East Pakistan openly entered the conflict on the side of the Mukhti Bahini, and quickly brought about a separatist victory. The Pakistan army surrendered on 16 December, and the Bengali government-in-exile formally assumed responsibility.

Bangladesh never fully recovered from the devastation and socioeconomic disruption caused in 1971. Sheikh Mujib, who assumed power after he was released from prison in West Pakistan early in 1972, was a charismatic leader, but lacked the necessary administrative experience to deal with famine and economic crisis. Operating at first under a parliamentary system of government, he won a massive victory in the 1973 elections. But early in 1975 he rescinded the constitution, declared himself the president, and reserved all important power to himself, restricting political freedom and banning all opposition parties. Bengali opinion turned against the government for these new measures and for allegedly acquiescing to Indian hegemony in Bangladesh. Two seemingly contradictory opposition forces became prominent: the right-wing Islamic groups, which were opposed to secularism and Indian hegemony, and the pro-Peking radical factions, which were opposed both to Indian and to Soviet influence. On 15 August 1975, a group of young army officers staged a coup in which Sheikh Mujib was killed, along with members of his family. Martial law was declared, and a new cabinet was sworn in under the leadership of Khondakar Mushtaque Ahmed, the former commerce minister. There was a countercoup on 3 November 1975, and within four days power had reverted to military elements loyal to Maj.-Gen. Ziaur Rahman, formerly the army chief of staff, who ruled with the help of a 10-member Military Council, with former Chief Justice A. M. Sayem as president.

12 GOVERNMENT

Under the constitution of 16 December 1972, Bangladesh became a parliamentary democracy, with the president as nominal head of state and a prime minister as chief executive, responsible to a 315-member National Assembly (300 males elected, with 15 appointive seats reserved for women). The constitution incorporated four basic principles of state policy: nationalism, secularism, socialism, and democracy. On 25 January 1975, the prime minister, Sheikh Mujibur Rahman, secured passage of an amendment to the constitution that effectively abrogated most civil liberties, outlawed political opposi-

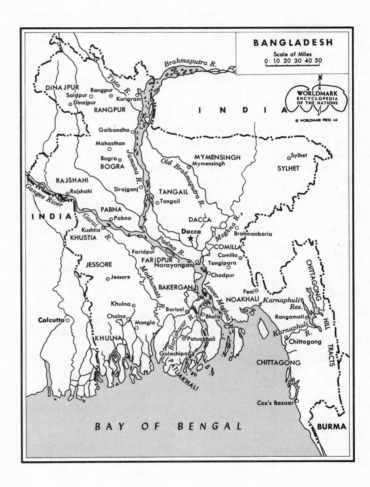

See continental political: front cover M7; physical: back cover M7
LOCATION: 20°35' to 26°38'N; 88°2' to 92°41'E. **BOUNDARY LENGTHS:** India, 2,583 km (1,605 mi); Burma, 233 km (145 mi); Bay of Bengal coastline, 574 km (357 mi). **TERRITORIAL SEA LIMIT:** 12 mi.

tion, and established a one-party state under presidential rule. The overthrow of Sheikh Mujib, on 15 August, and the countercoup of 3 November led to a military dictatorship under Maj.-Gen. Ziaur Rahman and a 10-member Military Council. The legislature remained dissolved, and political activities were banned under martial law. Subsequently, a Council of Advisers was formed, including teachers, physicians, and retired civil servants. Elections for a new National Assembly were promised for 1977.

13 POLITICAL PARTIES

From 1947 to 1971, when the region of East Bengal, now

Bangladesh, was part of Pakistan, there were numerous political parties. The Muslim League, a Muslim nationalist party that brought Pakistan into being, retained a predominant position until 1954, when it was defeated by the United Front, a coalition which included such parties as the right-wing Islamic Jama'at-i-Islam and Nizam-i-Islam, the Krishak Sramik (Peasants and Workers Party), the radical Ganatanri Dal Party, and the moderate-socialist Awami League. The Awami League, organized in the late 1940s as the Awami Muslim League, derived its strength and constituency from East Pakistan but had some representation in West Pakistan as well. It soon became the major opposition party to the Muslim League. The Communist Party of Pakistan, banned in 1954, continued to operate underground in both West and East Pakistan. The Pakistan National Congress, a Hindu party, and the Scheduled Castes Federation, a party of untouchables, were active in East Pakistan.

All parties were banned in 1958, but some were again allowed beginning in 1962. In the elections of March 1965, the Muslim League won a majority, but during the 1960s it splintered and lost influence. Ultimately, the left-wing Pakistan People's Party became the major party based in the West, while the Awami League gained continued strength in East Pakistan.

After the massive victory of the Awami League in the election of December 1970, when it won all but 2 of East Pakistan's 169 seats, it became, for all practical purposes, the sole spokesman for the Bengalis. The Awami League was the only party represented in the government-in-exile of 1971, although that government also enjoyed support from leftist forces, which advocated independence for East Pakistan. The right-wing parties did not support the secession movement, and after independence was achieved, these parties were banned and their leaders jailed for alleged collaboration with the Pakistani Army. In the elections of 7 March 1973, the Awami League won 293 seats out of 300.

On 25 January 1975, Sheikh Mujibur Rahman secured passage of a constitutional amendment making Bangladesh a one-party state. The only legally existent party, named the Bangladesh Krishak Sramik Awami League (BKSAL), was to be extended to provide links with workers, peasants, students, youth, and women, but these aims were not put into practice, and after the military coup of 15 August 1975, the new BKSAL was disbanded. It was expected that many of the old parties, including the right-wing parties hitherto banned by the government, would campaign for seats in a general election during 1977.

[14] LOCAL GOVERNMENT

Bangladesh is divided into 19 administrative districts, each governed by a senior civil servant known as the district magistrate or deputy commissioner. The district officer is responsible for tax collection, law and order, and development activities. The 19 districts are divided into 60 subsections, each headed by a subdivisional officer. The subsections are themselves split into 418 *thanas*, 4,351 union *parishads*, and 71,291 villages.

The future structure of local government in Bangladesh remains uncertain, but the new government has stressed the need for a strong rural police force, to protect villagers from terrorist violence, and also participates with local governments in programs for rural development and population control.

[15] JUDICIAL SYSTEM

The judicial system of Bangladesh is similar to that of neighboring countries, and it is modeled after the British tradition. Besides the 1972 constitution, which was the fundamental law of the land until it was abrogated in 1975 by martial law authorities, there are codes of civil and criminal laws. The civilian law incorporates certain Islamic and Hindu religious principles relating to marriage, inheritance, and other social matters.

The Supreme Court under the 1972 constitution had original, appellate, and advisory jurisdiction; there is also an elaborate network of subordinate courts. The constitution provided for an impartial and independent judiciary, but its provisions have been in suspension since early 1975.

[16] ARMED FORCES

In mid-1975, Bangladesh had an army of 30,000 men, a navy of 300, and an air force of 5,500 (most air force equipment was not operational). Paramilitary forces totaled 36,000. The military budget in 1973/74 was T470 million.

About 15,000 Bengali soldiers in the Pakistan army in 1971 defected to the liberation forces (Mukhti Bahini), and they formed the core of the Bangladesh army after independence. Another significant section of the armed forces consists of personnel stranded in Pakistan in 1971 who returned to Dacca only after the recognition of Bangladesh by Pakistan in 1974. A special security police force, called the Rakhhi Bahini, allegedly engaged in widespread terrorization of political dissenters under Sheikh Mujib. After the August 1975 coup, the Rakhhi Bahini was disbanded and absorbed into the regular army.

[17] MIGRATION

Since 1947, there has been a regular interchange of population between India and what is now Bangladesh, with Hindus migrating to India and Muslims emigrating from India. There has also been substantial migration between Bangladesh and West Pakistan. And since December 1971, several million refugees who fled to India during the war have returned, creating major resettlement problems.

[18] INTERNATIONAL COOPERATION

Bangladesh belongs to the UN and many of its member agencies. It is also a member of the IBRD and the Asian Development Bank, and is active in international Muslim organizations and conferences. Since independence, Bangladesh has received substantial amounts of economic aid from the US, India, and the oil-rich Muslim countries of the Middle East.

Bangladesh has declared itself to be nonaligned and has attempted to establish friendly relations in the region. Soon after independence, Bangladesh signed a friendship treaty with India, but the new leaders after the 1975 coup removed Bangladesh from the Indian orbit and instituted a policy of equal cooperation with other neighboring countries. Pakistan recognized Bangladesh in February 1974.

[19] ECONOMY

Bangladesh has essentially an agricultural economy. More than 75% of the population is engaged in farming, and nearly 62% of the land is cultivated. Methods are still traditional, and mechanized methods have not been widely introduced. The land is mostly fertile, and generally two or three crops are raised annually. But although agricultural output has increased, the growing population has created a perennial food shortage. Industrialization has also remained in a rudimentary stage.

The cyclone of November 1970 and the years of political unrest that culminated in the civil war of 1971 left the new nation of Bangladesh in a weak economic position. This position was further weakened by mismanagement and corruption, especially in the distribution of goods. With its highly unfavorable trade balance, chronic payments deficits, shortages of consumer goods, low productivity, and recent political instability, Bangladesh faced serious difficulties in the mid-1970s.

[20] INCOME

Real per capita income in Bangladesh has remained static since 1972, at about $60–70 per annum. The low per capita income has meant an average savings rate barely sufficient to maintain existing capital assets. The GDP in 1974/75 (in 1972/73 prices, at factor cost) was $6,325 million, of which agriculture contributed 58.7%; trade, 7.7%; industry, 7.4%; public administration, 4.9%; construction, 3.5%; power, 0.5%; and other sources, 17.3%.

21 LABOR

The estimated labor force is more than 26 million. More than 75% of all workers are employed in the rural sector.

Most industrial workers are unionized. Since 1972, the labor unions have become politicized, and radical parties have exerted substantial influence among union leaders. There are industrial tribunals to settle labor disputes. The government can impose labor settlements through arbitration, as well as by declaring a strike illegal. In 1969 there were 43 industrial disputes and 558,845 workdays were lost. Unemployment continues to be high, and agricultural workers are not protected by disability compensation.

22 AGRICULTURE

More than 90% of Bangladeshis live in the more than 70,000 rural villages where farming is the chief occupation. Most of the farmers own no more than 3 acres of land, and their holdings are badly fragmented. According to unofficial reports, landlessness among the peasants has increased from 20% to about 40% since 1972.

Rice dominates the production of about 80% of all cropped land in Bangladesh. Of the varieties grown, *aman* rice, which can be raised in inundated land and saline soil, occupies nearly 70% of the total land under rice. *Aus* rice, which cannot be grown in flooded fields, is raised mostly in higher areas of Bangladesh. *Boro* rice is grown in the winter, mainly in the swamps and marshy areas, but government-supported irrigation projects have encouraged its extension to other areas. To meet the challenge of the food shortage, the government of Bangladesh and international aid programs have introduced a high-yielding variety of rice called IRRI, with considerable success. Total rice production in 1975 was estimated at 13.3 million tons.

Jute is the main cash crop of Bangladesh, which produces as much as 50% of the total jute supply of the world. Jute is grown in most parts of the country; it is harvested from July to September. Its strong fibers are used to produce carpets, burlap bags, mats, upholstery, and other products. Jute is also being used to manufacture a new kind of textile for clothes. Raw jute and finished jute products account for about 85% of all foreign exchange earnings. Although tea is the second most important item among the agricultural exports, it accounts for only about 4% of foreign exchange earnings. Most of the tea plantations were started in the Sylhet District under British rule; about 90,000 acres of land in Sylhet and the Chittagong Hill Tracts are now in tea plantations. Most of the tea produced is consumed domestically.

The agricultural economy was greatly disrupted during the 1971 civil war. Agricultural inputs suffered badly in the border areas, transportation was severely affected, and water and land development projects were suspended. There was a substantial decline in the production of rice, jute, and tea, and stocks of food and seed became limited. By 1973/74, the output of many crops had still not returned to prewar levels; the government had to import about 2 million tons of food, part of which was purchased and part of which was received under various aid programs from the US and other countries. In 1973/74, production, in long tons, was sugarcane, 6,340,000; jute, 970,000; potatoes, 720,000; sweet potatoes, 630,000; oilseeds, 300,000; pulses, 210,000; wheat, 110,000; and tea, 27,100.

Policy toward agricultural development has been a subject of debate among government planners. The Integrated Rural Development Program of Bangladesh emphasizes efficient and widespread distribution of high-yielding seed varieties, fertilizers, insecticides, and irrigation pumps. The first stage of a large-scale irrigation scheme to pump water from the Ganges River to 1.8 million acres of land in the districts of Khustia, Jessore, and Khulna was completed in 1972. Smaller irrigation projects were under construction on the Teesta River in Rangpur and on tributaries of the Karnaful river in southeastern Bangladesh. A new project to provide extension, cooperative, and credit services to farmers was scheduled to be fully operative by 1981.

23 ANIMAL HUSBANDRY

The country continues to rely on buffalo and bullocks for draft power. Buffalo milk is an important item of consumption, especially in the form of clarified butter fat. Livestock quality is not high. There are about 26 million head of cattle and 700,000 sheep. In 1973/74, about 200,000 tons of meat and 250,000 tons of milk were produced.

24 FISHING

Fish is the staple food of Bangladesh, and the main source of protein. There are hundreds of varieties, including carp, salmon, pomfret, shrimp, catfish, and many local varieties. Dried fish is considered a delicacy in many parts of the country. About 800,000 tons of fish, mostly freshwater fish, are produced annually. While much of the fish is consumed domestically, Bangladesh exports a sizable quantity of freshwater fish to India and other neighboring countries, and freshwater shrimp and frogs' legs are exported overseas. Fishermen's cooperatives foster the use of modern fish-catching trawlers in the Bay of Bengal, and the government has established a fisheries corporation to stimulate production of freshwater fish for export.

25 FORESTRY

Bangladesh has about 2,243,000 hectares of forest, covering some 15.7% of the total area. In recent years, the pressure of population has led to enormous deforestation. The government-controlled Forest Industries Development Corporation supervises the development and exploitation of forest resources.

The main forest zone is the Sunderbans area in the southwest, mainly consisting of mangrove forests and covering about 752,200 hectares. Two principal species dominate the Sunderban forests: sundari trees, which grow about 50–60 feet high and are of tough timber, and gewa trees, a softer wood used for making newsprint. Teak and bamboo are grown in the central forests.

26 MINING

Natural gas is the only noteworthy mineral resource in Bangladesh. An estimated 20 million cu feet of natural gas has been found, and exploration is continuing. Natural gas is used for electricity generation and for fertilizers; the government controls the gas industry.

There are few other mineral resources. The Bay of Bengal area is being explored for oil, and in some offshore areas, drilling is being conducted by international companies. Bangladesh has reserves of good quality coal in the northern districts, but extraction is difficult since the deposits are located at a depth of more than 3,000 feet. Limestone is mined in the Sylhet and Chittagong districts. Bangladesh also has some copper reserves.

27 ENERGY AND POWER

A substantial portion of Bangladesh's electrical supply is met by the country's only hydroelectric plant at Kaptai; the rest of the country's power is produced by burning coal, gas, and oil. Except for a few private installations on the tea plantations and a few other industries, the power and energy sector is controlled by a government-managed corporation. Total power production was 1,172 million kwh in 1972, of which about 25% was hydroelectric. Installed capacity totaled 547,000 kw (15% hydroelectric).

28 INDUSTRY

Industrialization is relatively new in Bangladesh. Most of the manufacturing industries did not begin flourishing until after the 1947 partition. The jute industry is the single most important manufacturing industry in Bangladesh. More than 20,000 looms are now operating, and in 1973/74, an estimated 505,000 tons of jute goods were produced, a decline from earlier years and only 82% of the targeted goal. There are about 40 jute mills.

The cotton textile industry ranks second to jute. There are about 70 cotton mills, with more than 7,000 looms. Most of them produce yarn from imported cotton. In addition, hand looms meet one-fourth of the domestic need for cotton fabrics. In 1973/74, 93,300,000 pounds of yarn and 75,100,000 yards of cloth were produced—less than 80% of the targeted output.

Large-scale manufacturing includes several sugar mills in northwestern parts of the country, producing mostly for domestic consumption. There are two paper and two board mills capable of supplying domestic needs and of providing some surplus for export, and there are fertilizer factories near Dacca, Sylhet, and Comilla. There is also a steel mill in Chittagong, which was built in 1967 with Japanese help and for which iron has to be imported. Minor manufacturing includes matches, drugs, pharmaceuticals, glass products, ceramics, leather goods, and cigarettes. Most of the industries are controlled by the government.

Production in 1973/74 fell far short of government goals for most items, and actually showed a continuing decline from earlier years. In 1973/74, Bangladesh produced an estimated 273,619 tons of fertilizer, 84,000 tons of steel ingots, 26,500 tons of newsprint, 23,500 tons of paper, 80,000 tons of sugar, 16,500 tons of edible oils, and 1,500 tons of processed fish.

29 DOMESTIC TRADE

Except for jute, tea, paper, and a few other items, most of the commodities produced in Bangladesh are consumed inside the country. Normally, the farmers or fishermen sell to the wholesalers, and they in turn sell to distributors and retailers. Industrial commodities for domestic consumption are distributed through the same procedure. The middlemen in the distribution process have often benefited from excessive profits, creating hardships for farmers and consumers. To meet this situation, the government has introduced mechanisms by means of which farmers can sell directly to cooperative agencies acting on behalf of buyers. The government has also set up fair-price shops for consumers. Much domestic trade in rural areas continues to take place in the marketplaces, where farmers sell directly to consumers. Wholesalers from cities also bring some commodities to local markets.

Foreign products are imported by large commercial concerns located in the capital city of Dacca or in the ports, and are then distributed through wholesalers and retailers. Normal business hours are between 10 A.M. and 5 P.M., but most retail stores are open until 9 P.M. Limited advertising is done through newspapers, movie houses, handbills, and television.

30 FOREIGN TRADE

Since independence, Bangladesh has had a strongly negative trade balance. Imports have regularly been about double the value of exports, and the proportion was worsening in the mid-1970s. Exports of jute and jute goods, Bangladesh's sole significant earner of foreign exchange, have been stagnant, totaling T2,441.5 million in 1973/74 and T2,431.4 million in 1974/75. Other exports—including tea, hides and skins, hemp, bone meal, fresh and dried fish, chilies, wax, timber, oilcake, betel nuts, spices, and fresh vegetables—together account for less than 12% of the total. Major imports include food grains (2.3 million tons in 1974/75), petroleum products (1.2 million tons), fertilizers, cotton cloth and yarn, and capital goods of various types.

Principal exports in 1973/74 (in millions of taka) were:

Jute, processed	1,530.6
Jute, raw	910.9
Tea	99.3
Other exports	228.2
TOTAL	2,769.0

Principal imports in 1973/74 (in millions of taka) were:

Manufactured goods	1,928.9
Foodstuffs	1,386.4
Raw materials	1,383.3
Other imports	314.4
TOTAL	5,013.0

When Bangladesh was known as East Pakistan, much of its trade was with the western half of the country. Since 1971, however, Pakistan has played a negligible role in the foreign trade of Bangladesh. According to the IMF, in 1974 the principal export purchasers were the US (25% of total exports), the UK (12%), India (11%), and Australia (6%). Principal import suppliers were the US (29%), Australia (11%), Japan (9%), the Federal Republic of Germany (9%), and Canada (8%). Trade with the EEC accounted for 33% of exports and 18% of imports. A trade and tariff agreement on jute was reached with the EEC effective 30 June 1974.

31 BALANCE OF PAYMENTS

Declines in jute production and huge annual imports of food have generated a chronic balance-of-payments problem for Bangladesh. The net trade deficit for 1973 was $431.8 million, and in 1974 it was $641.4 million. Foreign aid and short-term borrowing were used to cover the balance.

The balance-of-payments situation may be summarized as follows (in millions of dollars):

	1973	1974
CURRENT ACCOUNTS		
Trade, net	-431.8	-641.4
Services, net	- 77.7	-100.7
Transfers, net	273.9	267.2
TOTALS	-235.6	-474.9
CAPITAL ACCOUNTS		
Long-term capital	115.1	380.1
Short-term capital	- 0.3	- 2.5
TOTALS	114.8	377.6
Errors and omissions	- 10.4	- 15.0
Net change	-131.2	-112.3

From 1972 through mid-1975, Bangladesh received an estimated $800 million in various types of US aid and at least $1,090 million from other sources. Drawings outstanding from the IMF totaled $249.8 million as of 31 January 1976, exceeding Bangladesh's combined international reserves of $190.8 million. Bangladesh's total foreign debt stood at about $675 million as of December 1974.

32 BANKING

Central banking is conducted by the Bangladesh Bank, which has its head office in Dacca. It is responsible for the circulation of money, supervision of commercial banks, and control of credit and foreign exchange. Total reserve money in December 1975 amounted to T5,033.1 million. Currency in circulation totaled T2,902 million in June 1975.

At the time of independence, there were 15 scheduled commercial banks, including 3 foreign banks, with 1,094 branches. Early in 1972, the government nationalized the domestic commercial banks, and they were subsequently merged into 6 commercial banks functioning under the general supervision of the Bangladesh Bank. In December 1975, total time and demand deposits of the commercial banks amounted to T11,147.1 million.

33 INSURANCE

The government nationalized the insurance business in 1972, creating an insurance corporation controlled by the government.

The insurance is mainly in the commercial and industrial fields. Life insurance is still limited to city dwellers and middle-class professionals.

34 SECURITIES

Most of the industrial sectors have been nationalized. As a result, the stock exchanges have only a limited role in speculative and profit-making aspects of trade and commerce. The Bangladesh Bank backs up securities in government-controlled industries.

35 PUBLIC FINANCE

The Bangladesh government prepares a budget with two sectors: current and development. The current budget for the year ending 30 June 1976 included the following sources of income (in millions of taka):

REVENUES

Import and export duties	2,400.0
Excise revenue	1,550.0
Sales tax	1,050.0
Income tax	650.8
Interest	636.6
State properties	213.6
Stamps and registration	175.0
Other sources	877.8
TOTAL	7,553.8

EXPENDITURES

Civil administration	1,346.1
Education	896.5
Defense	750.0
Railways	438.6
Interest payments	388.9
Emergencies	300.0
Health	246.5
Public works	216.3
Other expenditures	1,409.0
TOTAL	5,991.9

The development budget proposed to spend T9,500 million in various sectors for 1975/76. Of this amount, only T2,500 million was to be raised from internal resources; the rest was to be financed through foreign aid.

36 TAXATION

There is no agricultural income tax, but there are personal and corporate income taxes. A sales tax is levied on all important consumer goods. In the budget for 1975/76, however, essential agricultural implements and irrigation pumps were excluded from certain taxes.

Municipal and village councils are also empowered to levy minor taxes on property, ferry transit, roads, and marketplaces.

37 CUSTOMS AND DUTIES

Bangladesh gets a major portion of its revenue (an estimated 32% for 1975/76) from import and export duties. Automobiles and other items are heavily taxed, as are tobacco and alcohol. Dutiable items are subject to ad valorem taxes of up to 300% on some items. The government-controlled Tariff Commission makes recommendations about taxes to be levied on various items. Import licenses are controlled by the controller of imports and exports.

38 FOREIGN INVESTMENTS

Bangladesh nationalized most industries in 1972, and set up nine corporations to oversee them. Subsequently, the Bangladesh government relaxed its policy towards foreign investment and announced a program granting tax holidays to new foreign investors. Before establishing an industry, an investor must secure government permission, register his undertakings under the Companies Act, obtain the sanction of the controller of capital

issues, and secure a permit from the chief controller of import and export.

One of the largest sources of foreign capital investment in Bangladesh consists of the tea plantations owned by British planters. There are seven foreign companies exploring for oil in Bangladesh; they are expected to invest about $15 million by the early 1980s.

39 ECONOMIC POLICY

The Bangladesh constitution, in effect prior to the declaration of martial law in August 1975, emphasized socialism as a goal of state policy, and about 80% of the private sector was nationalized in the early 1970s. As the nationalized industries continued to flounder, the government began to change its policy in this regard. In the summer of 1974, the government promised that there would be no further nationalization of industry for about 15 years. Early in 1976, the government liberalized its economic policy further to provide new incentives for private investment.

Development planning has been used to achieve economic progress in Bangladesh. The major objectives of the planned development are increased national income, rural development, self-sufficiency in food, and increased industrial production. However, progress in achieving development goals has been slow, partly because of severe economic problems. A white paper released in September 1975 by the new government blamed the former regime of Sheikh Mujib for inadequate planning and for economic corruption. The document noted that despite a planned investment of more than $1 billion scheduled under the five-year plan introduced in 1973, overall industrial production had declined below 1969/70 levels. The underutilization of industrial capacity was blamed on lack of managerial expertise and, in particular, on the appointment of "inefficient, incompetent, and corrupt relatives" to high management posts.

40 HEALTH

There are about 90 government hospitals in Bangladesh, with more than 20,000 beds. There are only about 12,000 trained physicians (1.6 per 10,000 persons); the country also has more than 13,000 dispensaries to provide basic medical attention to villagers and others unable to obtain or afford private physicians. The country has about 1,000 registered nurses and 700 registered midwives.

Malaria, tuberculosis, and other serious diseases are endemic, and problems of public health are aggravated by widespread malnutrition and by periodic natural disasters. Maintaining the supply of pure drinking water is a very important public health problem. Approximately 200,000 tube wells have been constructed by the government, and there are also many private tube wells.

Average life expectancy for 1975 was estimated at 42.3 years.

41 SOCIAL WELFARE

Promotion of social welfare was a declared objective of public policy under the constitution of December 1972, and a major government department is devoted to social welfare tasks. There are also several hundred voluntary welfare organizations operating throughout the country. Private programs are coordinated and aided by the government. However, government funding for social welfare has not been large. In the 1975/76 current budget, the government allocated T35.9 million for social welfare, or only 0.6%. There is an additional allocation of T40 million for welfare programs in the development budget.

In recent years, the government has sought to utilize social welfare organizations to encourage family planning in an effort to curb the enormous growth of population in Bangladesh.

42 HOUSING

Public housing became a vital concern in 1972, when several million displaced persons returned from India. Their needs were met in part by providing temporary housing, but many displaced persons took shelter in the city slums. In 1975, the government cleared several slum areas in Dacca and resettled the inhabitants on the outskirts of the city.

The government maintains an urban housing program but does not have any housing development program for villages. The House Building Finance Corporation lends money for private as well as public housing. Dacca and Chittagong urban development is conducted under the guidance of town planning authorities, which develop land and allocate it for private dwelling and commercial purposes. In the 1975/76 budget, the government allocated T320 million for housing and land development, or 5.3% of ordinary expenditures. Substantial government funds are used to build public shelters in the cyclone-prone areas of the coastal districts. Most of the mills and factories have at least a partial housing program for workers and managerial staff.

⁴³EDUCATION

About 20% of the total population of Bangladesh is literate. The government, as a matter of policy, is attempting to broaden the educational base to remove mass illiteracy. In 1974/75 and 1975/76, the government allocated T823.7 million and T896.5 million, respectively, for education. The latter figure amounted to 15% of ordinary government expenditures for the fiscal year. Most of the educational institutions are supported by the government either fully or partially. The medium of instruction is Bengali.

More than 7 million students are enrolled in primary schools, 1.5 million in secondary schools, and more than 200,000 in higher institutions. There are six universities in Bangladesh. Bangladesh has seven medical colleges, with more than 3,000 students, and nine law colleges, with about 4,000 students. Research institutions include the Bangla Academy, the Atomic Energy Commission, the Asiatic Society, and the National Institute of Public Administration's Institute of Law and International Affairs.

⁴⁴LIBRARIES AND MUSEUMS

The largest library in Bangladesh is the Dacca University Library. It houses the University's collection and that of the former Public Library of East Pakistan. Other universities and colleges have their own libraries. The Bengali Academy has an excellent research collection.

The Dacca Museum contains a variety of sculptures and paintings from the Buddhist, Hindu, and Muslim periods. A museum at Comilla houses archaeological findings from 7th-century Mainamati, and the museum at Rajshahi contains many artifacts from the ruins of an 8th-century Buddhist monastery excavated nearby. There is a gallery of contemporary paintings as well as an ethnological museum in Chittagong.

⁴⁵ORGANIZATIONS

Bangladesh has numerous religious and cultural organizations. Various associations for the Muslim, Hindu, Christian, and Buddhist communities have long been active in organizing religious festivals and social activities. Every town also has several cultural groups, and stage dramas, musical soirees, dances, and other types of entertainment are put on from time to time.

The Bangladesh Women's Association, the Boy Scouts, and the Girl Guides are active in social life. There are also many philanthropic organizations in Bangladesh. Workers' associations are active in the industrial areas, and there are several national athletic organizations.

⁴⁶PRESS

The Bengali press during the Pakistani period up to 1971 was well known for its active role in championing Bengali nationalism and allied causes. In early 1975, Sheikh Mujibur Rahman nationalized all newspapers and allowed only a few to be published under official supervision. Later, after the August 1975 coup, government press policy was liberalized.

⁴⁷TOURISM

Tourism is a limited enterprise in Bangladesh, but the Bangladesh Tourist Bureau was active in the mid-1970s in promoting this industry, and the country has many real and potential tourist attractions.

Citizens of Commonwealth member nations need no visa to visit the country. Others can easily obtain visas for short visits. Cholera and yellow fever vaccinations are required. There is no restriction on the amount of foreign currency that can be brought into the country by tourists.

⁴⁸FAMOUS BANGLADESHIS

Many Bengalis distinguished themselves in political life during the long years prior to the creation of Bangladesh as an independent state. A. K. Fazlul Huq (d.1962), the former premier of Bengal Province, moved the Lahore Resolution of 1940, calling for an independent Pakistan, and dominated Bengali politics for half a century. H. S. Suhrawardy (1895–1964), another former premier of Bengal, served for a time as premier of Pakistan and was a mentor to the next generation of Bengali leaders. Sheikh Mujibur Rahman (1920–75), a leader of the Awami League, ultimately led the successful fight for the independence of East Pakistan, and after being released from prison in West Pakistan, returned to Bengal to become the first premier of Bangladesh on 12 January 1972. He was killed in the military coup of 15 August 1975.

⁴⁹DEPENDENCIES

Bangladesh has no territories or colonies.

⁵⁰BIBLIOGRAPHY

Ahmad, Nafis. *Economic Geography of East Pakistan.* London: Oxford University Press, 1968.

Ayoob, Mohammed. *India, Pakistan, and Bangladesh: Search for a New Relationship.* New Delhi: 1975.

Bangladesh Bureau of Statistics. *Statistical Digest of Bangladesh.* Dacca: 1972.

Brown, W. Norman. *United States and India, Pakistan, Bangladesh.* Cambridge: Harvard University Press, 1972.

Choudhury, G. W. *The Last Days of United Pakistan.* Bloomington: Indiana University Press, 1975.

Jackson, Robert. *South Asian Crisis: India, Pakistan, and Bangladesh.* New York: Praeger, 1975.

Kahn, A. R. *The Economy of Bangladesh.* London: Macmillan, 1972.

Robinson, E. A. G., and K. Griffin (eds.). *The Economic Development of Bangladesh within a Socialist Framework.* New York: Halsted Press, 1974.

Umar, Badruddin. *Politics and Society in East Pakistan and Bangladesh.* Dacca: 1974.

BHUTAN

Kingdom of Bhutan
Druk-Yul

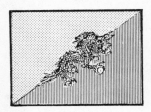

CAPITAL: Thimphu (Tashi Chho Dzong). **FLAG**: The flag is divided diagonally into an orange-yellow field above and a crimson field below. In the center is a wingless white dragon of the type known heraldically as the "Chinese Dragon." **ANTHEM**: *Gyelpo Tenjur*, beginning "In the Thunder Dragon Kingdom adorned with sandalwood." **MONETARY UNIT**: The Indian rupee (R) is the main basis of money transactions. Bhutanese coinage includes the gold sertum, divided into 100 nutams; 1 nutam is worth 100 chidams. The most common local coin is the tikchung, worth 50 chidams or R0.5; in addition, paper ngultram notes (equivalent to R1) were recently introduced. R1 = $0.1114 (or $1 = R8.9766). **WEIGHTS AND MEASURES**: Traditional units are used. **HOLIDAYS**: The King's Birthday, 11 November; National Day, 17 December. Buddhist holidays and festivals are observed. **TIME**: 5:30 P.M. = noon GMT.

¹LOCATION, SIZE, AND EXTENT
Bhutan, a landlocked country in the Himalaya Mountains, has an area of 46,620 sq km (18,000 sq mi), extending 306 km (190 mi) E–W and 145 km (90 mi) N–S. It is bordered on the E, S, and W by India and on the N and NW by China, with a total boundary length of 1,019 km (633 mi).

²TOPOGRAPHY
Bhutan is a mountainous country of extremely high altitudes and irregular, often precipitous terrain, which may vary in elevation by several thousand feet within a short distance. Elevation generally increases from south to north. The mountains are a series of parallel north-to-south ranges. The loftiest peaks, found in the Himalayan Mountain chain that stretches along the northern border, include Kula Kangri (24,780 feet) and Chomo Lhari (23,997 feet). Great spurs extend south from the main chain along the east and west borders. In the rest of the country are mainly ranges of steep hills separated by narrow valleys. Bhutan is drained by many rivers flowing south between these ranges and for the most part ultimately emptying into the Brahmaputra River. The Amo River drains the Chumbi Valley. The Wong with its tributaries drains the valleys of Paro Dzong and Thimphu (Tashi Chho Dzong); the Mo drains Punakha Valley. The largest river is the Manas.

³CLIMATE
Because of the irregular terrain, the climate varies greatly from place to place. In the outer foothills adjoining the Indian plains, rainfall averages from 200 to 250 inches a year; the jungles and forests are hot and steaming in the rainy season, while the higher hills are cold, wet, and misty. Violent Himalayan thunderstorms gave rise to Bhutan's name, which translates as "land of the thunder dragon." Rainfall is moderate in the central belt of flat valleys (3,500 to 10,000 feet). The uplands and high valleys (above 12,000 feet) are relatively dry. There is less rainfall in eastern Bhutan. In general, the mountainous areas are cold most of the year.

⁴FLORA AND FAUNA
Dense jungle growth is characteristic at altitudes below 5,000 feet. Above that height the mountain slopes are covered with forest, including beech, ash, birch, maple, cypress, and yew. At 8,000 to 9,000 feet are forests of oak and rhododendron. Above this level, firs and pines grow to the timber line. Primulas, poppies—including the rare blue variety—magnolias, and orchids abound.

The relative abundance of wild animals is attributed to the Buddhist reluctance to take life. In the lower parts of southern Bhutan, animals include cheetah, goral, sambar, bear, and rhinoceros. In the higher regions are snow deer, musk deer, and barking deer. Game birds include pheasants, partridges, pigeons, and quail. The encroachments of civilization have inevitably taken a toll, however, and in 1975, endangered species in Bhutan included the unique golden langur, wolf, Asiatic wild dog, clouded leopard, Indian tiger, leopard, snow leopard, Asian elephant, pygmy hog, Himalayan muskdeer, and shou.

⁵POPULATION
No census has ever been taken. The population in 1975 was estimated at 1,187,000, with an annual growth rate of 2.3% in the 1970s. Projected 1980 population is 1,325,000. Density is about 25 per sq km, and some 97% of the population is rural. The laboring population is not gathered into towns but lives in the countryside in the vicinity of fortresses called dzongs. A dzong, the official center of a region or district, often houses substantial numbers of Buddhist monks. Many place names incorporate the term "dzong," which means "castle-monastery."

⁶ETHNIC GROUPS
About 54% of the inhabitants are Bhutanese proper, members of Bhote tribal groups (known locally as Sharchops) who inhabit the eastern regions and have ethnic affinities with the people of Tibet. Direct descendants of Tibetan immigrants form about 32% of the population and live in western Bhutan. The two areas are roughly separated by the Sankosh River. Most of the remaining peoples are Nepalese settlers, living mostly in the south; Lepchas, originating in Sikkim; Paharias, who live in the southern foothills; and Santals, the descendants of migrants from India's Bihar State.

⁷LANGUAGE
Four main languages are spoken in Bhutan. The official language is Dzongkha, a Tibetan dialect spoken mainly in the northern and western parts of the country; Bumthangkha, also related to the Tibetan language, is spoken in central Bhutan, while Sarchopkha is spoken in eastern Bhutan. The Nepalese largely retain their own language.

⁸RELIGION
The religion of the Bhutanese is essentially the lamaistic Buddhism practiced in Tibet. It dominates the collective life of the Bhutanese through a large clerical body estimated at 4,000 to 5,000 monks or lamas centered in 8 major monasteries (called dzongs) and 200 smaller shrines (called gompas) scattered throughout the land. The lamas are of the Durk Kargue, or "Red

Hat," sect. The religion incorporates both the ideology of the classical Buddhist scriptures and the indigenous pre-Buddhist animistic beliefs called Bon. A large part of the male population and a lesser proportion of the female live in monasteries or nunneries. The custom of devoting at least one of the offspring in each family to a monastery is slowly eroding with time. About 25% of the population practices Buddhist-influenced Hinduism.

9 TRANSPORTATION
Traditionally, Bhutan's communications were mostly with Tibet. Most travelers continue to journey on foot or mounted on hardy ponies bred to withstand great altitudes and steep slopes. Goods are transported by porters or on pack animals, including yaks. Many of the rivers are still crossed by native cantilever bridges of excellent construction. The easiest access to the country traditionally was through two strategic Tibetan passes, the Natu La (14,000 feet) and the Jelep La (14,390 feet).

Prior to the 1961–66 development plan, there were no surfaced roads in Bhutan. Since then, a network of roads and about 20 suspension bridges have been built by India's Border Roads Organization. By 1975 there were approximately 830 miles of roads, including 260 miles of paved roads. Adequate mountain roads connect Bhutan with India.

There are airfields at Paro and Yong Phulta and commercial air links between Paro and Calcutta. There are bus services between Pucholing and Darrang in India and Paro and Tashi Gang in Bhutan. The government's Transport Department maintains a fleet of trucks and buses. Despite recent purchases, equipment remains grossly inadequate.

10 COMMUNICATIONS
An international postal service was inaugurated in 1963. There are direct postal and Telex links to India. In 1974 there were 51 post office branches and 480 km of telephone lines. An FM transmitter services some 6,000 radios. There is no television service.

11 HISTORY
Little is known of the history of Bhutan before the 18th century. The forebears of the Bhotes came from Tibet, probably in the 9th century when Tibetans invaded the area and met little resistance from the indigenous Tephu tribe. In modern history, the first recorded event occurred in 1772, when the British repelled a Bhutanese invasion of the princely state of Cooch Behar; peace was concluded in 1774. During the 18th century and most of the 19th, British efforts to open trade with Bhutan were futile. The Bhutanese frequently attacked the Duars (i.e., entrances), the relatively level areas of Assam and Bengal bordering their country. In 1866, following defeat at the hands of the British, the Bhutanese formally surrendered the Duars and accepted a British allowance of R50,000 a year, dependent upon keeping the peace. With British approval, in 1907, Ugyen Dorji Wangchuk became the first hereditary king. In 1910, the Punakha Treaty was concluded between the UK and Bhutan: the UK agreed explicitly not to interfere in Bhutanese internal affairs, while Bhutan accepted British guidance in handling external affairs.

The position occupied by the UK was assumed by India when it attained independence in 1948; the following year an India-Bhutan treaty was concluded that was an amplified version of the Punakha Treaty, with India replacing the UK in the text. Besides increasing Bhutan's annual subsidy to R500,000 and returning to Bhutan 32 sq mi of territory around Dewangiri (wrested by the British in 1866), the treaty made India responsible for Bhutan's defense and strategic communications. In 1959, China published maps that showed as Chinese part of the territory claimed by Bhutan; Chinese spokesmen also asserted that Bhutan belonged to a greater Tibet. The Indian prime minister, Jawaharlal Nehru, in response warned that an attack on Bhutan would be deemed an act of war against India. At about this time, India announced a specific road-building program, with a monetary allotment equivalent to $31.5 million.

On 5 April 1964, the prime minister, Jigme Dorji, was assassinated. The plotters, including the deputy commander of the army, were executed. In the 1960s, Bhutan's advance toward modernization and the end of its insularity were accelerated by economic plans prepared and underwritten by India. The king, Jigme Dorji Wangchuck (r.1952–72), had been a prime force behind a variety of social and political reforms that included the emancipation of some 5,000 slaves, a limitation on landholdings, and administrative changes in the direction of a constitutional monarchy. King Jigme Dorji's son, Jigme Singye Wangchuk, assumed leadership upon his father's death on 21 July 1972 and was crowned king on 2 June 1974.

12 GOVERNMENT
Until 1907, the Bhutanese government was a theocracy headed jointly by a supreme spiritual authority, the Dharma Raja, and a temporal ruler, the Deb Raja. The Dharma Raja, an incarnation of the Buddha, would manifest himself anew a year or two after the incumbent's death in an infant from a ranking family, who could be identified by certain sacred marks. The Deb Raja, nominally elected by a council, was in fact selected by the head of the most powerful family. In 1907, because of failure to locate the reincarnated Dharma Raja, the Deb Raja assumed his post also and thereupon retired. The government council, with the approval of the leading families and the chief lamas, then named Ugyen Dorji Wangchuk, penlop of Tongsa Dzong, as the first hereditary king. The present ruler, Jigme Singye Wangchuk, is the great-grandson of the first king.

Since 1969, Bhutan has functioned as a limited monarchy. The king is appointed from the royal hereditary line by the legislature and may be removed at any time by a two-thirds vote. The king is further subject to a legislative vote of confidence every three years.

The king appoints 4 ministers to a 12-member Royal Advisory Council, the country's chief administrative body. Most Council members are civil servants, but some are also representatives of the Buddhist hierarchy. A national assembly, known as the Tsongdu, consists of a maximum of 150 members, one-fourth of whom are appointed by the king. The others are elected by groups of village headmen who are in turn elected by a one-family one-vote system. The Tsongdu meets twice a year at Thimphu. Since 1969, it has been empowered to overrule bills proposed by the king or the Advisory Council.

13 POLITICAL PARTIES
All political parties are illegal. The only political party known in Bhutan was the Bhutan National Congress, which purported to represent the Nepalese in their opposition to government restrictions imposed upon them and which is said to have led several abortive revolts in Bhutan in the 1950s.

14 LOCAL GOVERNMENT
The country is divided into four regions—East, Central, West, and South—each administered by a governor appointed by the king. During the 19th century and in earlier periods, local officials known as penlops ruled their own territories and were powerful enough to defy the central government. Under the present system, there are 16 commissioners (dzongdas) of districts called dzongs, who are responsible for law and order. Popular elections are held in the villages at three-year intervals.

15 JUDICIAL SYSTEM
The legal system is based on English common law and Indian law. Local headmen and magistrates (thrimpon) hear cases in the first instance. Appeals may be made to a five-member High Court, established in 1968.

16 ARMED FORCES
The army consists of 4,000 lightly armed men, trained by Indian officers. India is responsible for Bhutan's defense.

[17] MIGRATION

Bhutan opposes immigration and forbids the entry of new settlers from Nepal. In 1962, however, about 4,000 Tibetan refugees entered Bhutan. Since then, the border with Tibet has been closed to immigration.

[18] INTERNATIONAL COOPERATION

Under the Indo-Bhutanese Treaty of 1949, the government of Bhutan agreed "to be guided by the advice of the Government of India in regard to its external relations." India provides an annual subsidy and an annual development grant. Following the 1962 Sino-Indian conflict, Bhutan closed its trade mission at Lhasa, Tibet.

Bhutan joined the Colombo Plan organization in 1962, the UPU in 1969, the UN in 1971, and ECAFE in 1973.

[19] ECONOMY

Operating on one of the most primitive levels yet found in the world, Bhutan's economy is substantially self-sustaining. Most of the inhabitants support themselves by a combination of small-scale farming and animal husbandry. There are also a number of craftsmen.

[20] INCOME

Bhutan's economy is not fully monetized, and statistical data for calculating the national income or GNP do not exist. Per capita income—estimated at well below $100—is among the world's lowest.

[21] LABOR

The work force was estimated at about 300,000 in the mid-1970s. About 99% of the Bhutanese are farmers or herdsmen. Serfdom, effectively a form of slavery in Bhutan, was declared illegal in 1958. In areas served by the development plan, every adult member of a family must contribute 23 days of labor per annum. Each adult may fulfill his own obligation, or one adult may fulfill it consecutively for the whole family.

[22] AGRICULTURE

Only about 9% of the land area is used for agriculture. Nonetheless, Bhutan is self-sufficient in food, with quantities of some crops available for export. Since there is little level space available for cultivation, fields are generally terraced. Stone aqueducts carry irrigation water. The low-lying areas raise a surplus of rice; in 1973, Bhutan's rice crop totaled 201,000 tons. Other crops are corn, wheat, barley, buckwheat, vegetables, cardamom, walnuts, and oranges. Part of the crop yield is used in making beer and chong, a potent liquor distilled from rice, barley, and millet. Paper is made from the daphne plant, which grows wild. Walnuts, citrus fruit, apples, and apricots are grown in government orchards. Holdings are restricted to 30 acres per family. Almost all farmers own their own land; tenancy is rare.

Since the mid-1960s, the government has established 11 demonstration farms, distributed more than 160,000 fruit plants, and completed minor irrigation schemes. High-yielding varieties of rice, wheat, and corn seeds have been introduced.

[23] ANIMAL HUSBANDRY

Yaks, cattle, and some sheep are put to graze in the lowland forests and, during the summer, in the uplands and high valleys. Yak butter is an important nutrient in the local diet. Food animals include hogs. By the early 1970s, the government had established eight livestock farms. Livestock totaled 590,000 in 1973. Wool has been in short supply since its import from Tibet was stopped by the government. Sheep breeding is, therefore, encouraged. A sericulture farm operates at Kanglung.

[24] FISHING

The government has established a hatchery and started a program of stocking Bhutan's rivers and lakes with brown trout. Freshwater fish are found in most rivers.

[25] FORESTRY

About 70% of Bhutan is covered with forests. Lack of transport facilities has hampered their exploitation. In the late 1960s, the government started forest management services for an area of 1,100 sq mi in southern Bhutan. Swedish interests have been exploring prospects for establishing a paper industry.

[26] MINING

For centuries, silver and iron have been mined in Bhutan for fabrication into craft articles. In recent years, Indian geologists have been prospecting for minerals and thus far have found deposits of copper, dolomite, gypsum, iron ore, mica, lead, zinc, limestone, and pyrite. There are deposits of coal, and production is about 30,000 tons per annum. Dolomite has constituted an important export to India since 1960. Extensive gypsum deposits in the east are to be developed with Indian collaboration.

[27] ENERGY AND POWER

Electricity was introduced in Bhutan in 1962. By the mid-1970s, three power stations adequate for local needs had been completed at Thimphu, Paro, and Wangdu Phodrang. By 1974, total capacity had reached 1,900 kw and production, 5 million kwh. The country's largest project, the 336-Mw Chhukha installation, was due to be completed in 1981.

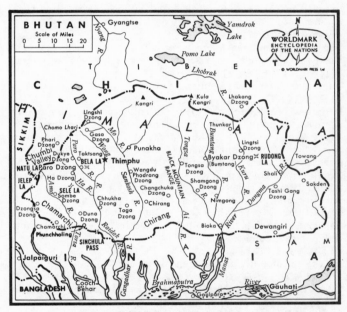

See continental political: front cover N7; physical: back cover N7

LOCATION: 26°42′ to 28°21′N; 88°45′ to 92°8′E. BOUNDARY LENGTHS: India, 607 km (377 mi); China, 412 km (256 mi).

[28] INDUSTRY

Craft manufacture is the predominant industrial occupation and homespun textiles—woven and embroidered cottons, wools, and silks—the most important products. Other Bhutanese handicrafts include paper; swords; wooden bowls; leather objects; copper, iron, brass, bronze, and silver work; wood carvings; and split-cane basketry.

In recent years, a cement factory and a match factory have been constructed. The government has set up two industrial estates at Phuntsholing and Gaylegphug, as well as a sawmill with a furniture-making unit at Thimphu. A large number of privately owned sawmills operate throughout the country. Bhutan also has two distilleries and a food-preservation factory.

[29] DOMESTIC TRADE

Except for small bazaars, there are few retail outlets. Bartering is common at the local level, with grains, butter, and cloth the principal commodities of exchange. By 1974, three cooperative marketing societies had been formed. Indian Brahmins sell imported articles and buy a number of handicraft items for export to India.

30 FOREIGN TRADE

Prior to 1953, Bhutan traded mainly with Tibet. In recent decades, virtually all trade activity has shifted to India. Bhutan exports vegetables, dolomite, coal, oranges, cardamom, timber, some preserved food, handicraft items, yak tails for fly whisks, and yak hair, which is used for theatrical wigs and Santa Claus beards. The chief imports from India are petroleum products (mainly kerosine), sugar, and cotton textiles. There is free trade, and India makes exchange available to finance imports. In the 1970s, annual exports averaged $1 million, while imports were estimated at $1.4 million.

31 BALANCE OF PAYMENTS

Statistics are not available. Trade deficits are thought to be largely made up through credits from the Indian government.

32 BANKING

Bhutan has recently been moving from a barter to a money economy. The Bank of Bhutan, established in 1968, is state-owned, and its reports reflect the growing volume of money transactions. The bank is scheduled eventually to become a bank of issue. The main office is at Phuntsholing, with a branch at Thimphu.

33 INSURANCE

The Royal Bhutan Insurance Corp., half state-owned, covers all classes of insurance. The use of insurance, however, is limited.

34 SECURITIES

There are no sales of securities.

35 PUBLIC FINANCE

In the 1968/69 budget, receipts were estimated at R11.87 million, current expenditure at R19.54 million, and development expenditure at R44.70 million. The sources of domestic revenue were excise taxes, R0.99 million; land revenue, R3.66 million; profits of public enterprises, R4.73 million; and other, R2.49 million. Nondevelopment expenditure comprised R7.85 million on administration and R11.69 million described as general expenditure but presumably devoted in part to the maintenance of monasteries. Most of the excess of expenditure over revenue is financed by India, the remainder raised from deposits and miscellaneous accounts.

36 TAXATION

Taxes—on income, animals, and land—are collected in cash.

37 CUSTOMS AND DUTIES

Under the Indo-Bhutanese Treaty of 1949, goods may pass from one country to another without payment of customs duties.

38 FOREIGN INVESTMENTS

There are few investments by foreigners in Bhutan.

39 ECONOMIC POLICY

The development of Bhutan's economy in 1961–76 has been achieved through three five-year plans at a cost of $87.1 million, with virtually all funding provided by India. Agriculture, education, and health have been stressed in each of the plans. In the third plan, 30% of outlays went to social services; 25.5% to transport and communications; 22.5% to agriculture; 11.6% to industry and power; and 10.4% to other sectors. A Planning Commission was established in 1972.

40 HEALTH

In 1974, Bhutan had 6 general hospitals and 45 dispensaries; there were also 4 special hospitals for leprosy. Beds numbered about 300. The country had 25 doctors, 51 nurses, and 161 other personnel. The government has undertaken BCG (bacillus Calmette-Guerin) and malaria eradication programs. Average life expectancy in 1975 was 46.1 years, among the lowest in Asia; in 1950, however, it had been 33.1 years.

41 SOCIAL WELFARE

There is no social welfare system. The sick, indigent, and aged are cared for by their families.

42 HOUSING

Houses are built of stone set in clay mixed with small stones and made into blocks or layers. Roofs are gently inclined and formed of pine shingles kept in place by heavy stones.

43 EDUCATION

Illiteracy is widespread, and education has been a major recipient of development funds. In 1971, R8.4 million was expended on education (compared with R1.4 million in 1962), of which R3 million was in capital outlays. In 1972 there were 468 teachers and 11,096 pupils in 89 primary and general-level secondary schools; 19 teachers and 285 students in 2 vocational schools; and 5 teachers and 39 students in a teacher-training institute. Each year, several hundred students are sent on government scholarships to study in India.

44 LIBRARIES AND MUSEUMS

A national museum has been established at Paro. A national library is to be established at Thimphu. Some monasteries have valuable collections of Buddhist manuscripts and art objects.

45 ORGANIZATIONS

There are no commercial, scholarly, or other organizations in the Western sense.

46 PRESS

There is one weekly newspaper, *Perkhang*, published by the government.

47 TOURISM

In September 1974, Bhutan opened its door to tourists. However, strict entry regulations, the remoteness of the country, and relatively limited transportation facilities preclude a large number of tourists. Entry is via India. Health requirements for entry include smallpox and cholera immunizations; tetanus, typhoid, and polio immunizations and gamma globulin are recommended.

48 FAMOUS BHUTANESE

There are no internationally famous Bhutanese.

49 DEPENDENCIES

Bhutan has no dependencies.

50 BIBLIOGRAPHY

Broun, Charles-Eudes. "Un état himalayan: le Bhoutan et son développement historique." *L'Asie française,* November 1910, pp. 468-81.

Casserly, Gordon. *Life in an Indian Outpost.* London: Laurie, 1914.

Coelho, V. H. *Sikkim and Bhutan.* New Delhi: Indian Council for Cultural Relations, 1967.

Davis, Samuel. "Remarks on the Religious and Social Institutions of the Bouteas, or Inhabitants of Boutan . . ." *Transactions of the Royal Asiatic Society of Great Britain and Ireland.* Vol. II. London: Parbury, Allen, 1830, pp. 491-517.

Karan, Pradyumna P. *Bhutan: A Physical and Cultural Geography.* Lexington: University of Kentucky Press, 1967.

Karan, Pradyumna P., and William M. Jenkins. *The Himalayan Kingdoms.* Princeton, N.J.: Princeton University Press, 1963.

Lamb, Alistair. *Britain and Chinese Central Asia.* London: Routledge and Kegan Paul, 1960.

Olschak, B. *Bhutan.* New York: Stein and Day, 1971.

Political Missions to Bootan, Comprising the Reports of the Hon'ble Ashley Eden, 1864; Capt. R[obert]. B[oileau]. Pemberton, 1837, 1838, with Dr. W[illiam]. Griffith's Journal; and the Account by Baboo Kishen Kant Bose. Calcutta: Bengal Secretariat Office, 1865.

Rennie, David Field. *Bhotan and the Story of the Dooar War . . .* London: Murray, 1866.

Singh, Madanjeet. *Himalayan Art.* New York: New York Graphic Society, 1968.

White, John Claude. *Sikkim & Bhutan: Twenty-one Years on the North-east Frontier, 1887-1908.* London: Arnold, 1909.

BURMA

Socialist Republic of the Union of Burma

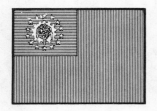

CAPITAL: Rangoon. **FLAG:** The national flag is red with 14 white stars encircling a rice stalk and industrial wheel against a blue background in the upper left corner. **ANTHEM:** *Kaba Makye (Our Free Homeland)*. **MONETARY UNIT:** The kyat (K) of 100 pyas is a nonconvertible paper currency. K1 = $0.1493 (or $1 = K6.6936). There are coins of 5, 10, 25, and 50 pyas and 1 kyat, and notes of 1, 5, 10, and 20 kyats. **WEIGHTS AND MEASURES:** Both British and metric weights and measures are in general use, but local units are also employed. **HOLIDAYS:** Peasants' Day, 1 January; Independence Day, 4 January; Union Day, 12 February; Resistance Day, 27 March; May Day, 1 May; Martyrs' Day, 19 July; Christmas, 25 December. Movable holidays include Full Moon of Tabaung, Thingyan (Water Festival), Burmese New Year's Days, Full Moon of Kason, Waso (Beginning of Buddhist Lent), End of Buddhist Lent, Tazaungdaing, and National Day. **TIME:** 6:30 P.M. = noon GMT.

¹LOCATION, SIZE, AND EXTENT

Situated in Southeast Asia, Burma has an area of 678,033 sq km (261,789 sq mi) extending *1,931* km (*1,200* mi) N–S and *925* km (*575* mi) E–W. It is bounded on the N and E by China, on the E by Laos, on the SE by Thailand, on the S by the Andaman Sea, and on the W by the Bay of Bengal, Bangladesh, and India, with a total boundary length of *8,134* km (*5,055* mi).

²TOPOGRAPHY

Burma is divided into four topographic regions: (1) a mountainous area in the north and west, ranging from 6,000 to over 20,000 feet in altitude, and including the Arakan coastal strip between the Arakan Yoma mountain range and the Bay of Bengal; (2) the Shan Highlands in the east, a deeply dissected plateau averaging 3,000 feet in height and extending southward into the Tenasserim Yoma, a narrow strip of land projecting 500 miles along the Malay Peninsula, in the southeast; (3) central Burma, a principal area of cultivation, bounded by the Salween River in the east and the Irrawaddy River and its tributary, the Chindwin, in the west; and (4) the fertile delta and lower valley regions of the Irrawaddy and Sittang rivers in the south, covering an area of about 25,900 sq km (10,000 sq mi) and forming one of the world's great rice granaries. Several good harbors are located along the long coastline and on some of the many islands.

³CLIMATE

Burma has a largely tropical climate with three seasons: the monsoon or rainy season, from the middle of May to mid-October; the hot season, generally from April through May and from October through November, immediately preceding and following the wet season; and the cool season, from December to March. Rainfall during the monsoon season totals more than 200 inches in upper Burma, particularly in the northern mountains and along the Arakan and Tenasserim coastal regions, and 100 inches in lower Burma and Rangoon. Central Burma, called the dry zone, in the lee of the Arakan Yoma, receives 25 to 45 inches, and Mandalay, the chief city in the area, about 30 inches. Temperatures from the cool to the hot seasons range from 15.5°C to 37.6°C (60°F to 100°F) in lower Burma; the extremes are greater in central Burma. The climate in upper Burma, particularly at altitudes ranging from 1,000 to 4,000 feet, is the most temperate throughout the year, while lower Burma, especially in the delta and coastal regions, is the most humid.

⁴FLORA AND FAUNA

Burma has a wide variety of animal and plant life. There are over 60 different species of wood alone. Teak, representing about 25% of the total forested area, thrives mainly in the mountainous regions; evergreen, bamboo, and palm in the freshwater delta swamps and along the coastlands; mangrove in the salty coastal marshes; mixed temperate forests and rolling grasslands in the Shan Highlands; and scrub vegetation in the dry central area. There are about 12 species of monkeys as well as tigers and leopards, and elephants and the half-wild pariah dogs are numerous. Several varieties of birds and insects are common, and fish abound along the coastline, in the tidal waters of the delta, and in the rivers and streams.

As of 1975, endangered species in Burma included the Asiatic wild dog, clouded leopard, Indian tiger, Indochinese tiger, dugong, Asian elephant, Malayan tapir, Javan rhinoceros, Sumatran rhinoceros, Himalayan musk deer, Fea's muntjac, Asiatic buffalo, gaur, white-winged wood duck, Sclater's monal, Hume's pheasant (western), Hume's pheasant (eastern), Blyth's tragopan, river terrapin, marsh crocodile, estuarine crocodile, gavial, and Burmese python.

⁵POPULATION

According to the census of 1973, Burma had a total population of 28,900,000. The estimate for January 1976 was 30,100,000, and population density was 115 per sq mi. A population of 35,195,000 was projected for 1980. At the end of 1975, Rangoon, the capital, had an estimated population of 2,200,000. The next largest cities are Mandalay, 417,000; Moulmein, 202,000; Bassein, 126,152; Akyab, 82,544; and Taunggyi, 80,678. Population growth is about 2.2% per year; the natural population increase averaged 22.9 per 1,000 annually for 1965–70. In 1973 there were 11,698,000 persons 14 and under, 15,469,000 aged 15–59, and 1,733,000 over 60. More than 80% of the population is rural.

⁶ETHNIC GROUPS

The Burmans, ethnically related to the Tibetans, comprise about 75% of Burma's total population. In remote times, the Burmans, migrants from the hills east of Tibet, descended the Irrawaddy Valley and intermarried with the previously settled Mon and Pyu peoples. Since then, however, many other migrant peoples from the northeast and northwest have settled in Burma: the Shans, Karens, Kachins, Kayahs, and Chins are among the more numerous. Although much ethnic fusion has taken place among these peoples and the Burmans, most of the later migrant groups continue to live as distinct cultural entities. There are about 2,410,000 Karens, 2,050,000 Shans, 780,000 Chins, 330,000

40   **Burma**   [7—11]

Kachins, and 65,000 Kayahs (formerly known as Karenni). An estimated 350,000 Indians and Pakistanis, 300,000 Chinese, and a small number of Europeans also reside in Burma.

7 LANGUAGE
Burmese, the official language, is spoken by 80% of the population. Some 20% speak other languages and dialects, and pronunciation varies greatly from area to area. Although Burmese is monosyllabic and tonal like other Tibeto-Chinese languages, its alphabet of 11 vowels and 32 consonants is derived from the Pahlavi script of South India; loan words from other languages are common. Burmese is the language of government, but according to the 1974 constitution, "if necessary the language of the national race concerned may be used."

8 RELIGION
The constitution guarantees freedom of religion. About 85% of the people are Hinayana or Theravada Buddhists. Under the government of former Premier U Nu (overthrown in 1962), Buddhism was the state religion. There is no longer any link between church and state.

Many Buddhists, including most of the people of the hill areas, are also animists, believing in powerful spirits called nats. The Chinese in Burma practice a traditional mixture of Mahayana Buddhism, Taoism, Confucianism, and ancestor worship; the Indians are Hindus, the Pakistanis are Muslims, and most of the Europeans are Christians. Although Christian missionaries had some success with peoples of the hill areas—the Karens, Kayahs, Kachins, and Chins—conversion among the Burmans and the Shans was negligible.

9 TRANSPORTATION
Because of Burma's near encirclement by mountain ranges, international land transportation is virtually nonexistent. Historically, Burma has been dependent on sea and river transport externally and internally, supplemented in modern times by the airplane. The Burma Road, connecting Lashio with Kunming in southern China, and the Ledo Road between Myitkyina and Ledo in Assam, northeastern India, are the only land ties between Burma and adjacent lands. There were 13,444 miles of roads in 1975; 500 miles were metaled, 2,539 were blacktopped, 3,700 were all-weather, and the rest were rural. Construction of a road between Rangoon and Bassein (about 100 miles) was completed in 1967. In addition, there are more than 8,000 miles of mule tracks, 4,700 miles of cart tracks, and 47,000 miles of village tracks. In 1973, an estimated 31,700 passenger cars and 34,300 commercial vehicles were registered.

The Burma railway system, a government monopoly, operates 2,677 miles of meter-gauge single-track railway. The main lines are from Rangoon to Prome (161 miles) and from Rangoon to Mandalay (386 miles) and then to Myitkyina (723 miles from Rangoon). In 1973, the passenger-mile figure was 1,887 million and net ton-miles were 388 million. A railway route opened· in 1964 operates from Pegu to Martaban in Karen State.

Inland waterways, including 5,543 miles of navigable passages, are the key to internal transportation, partly compensating for limited railroad and highway development. Some 500,000 small river craft ply the Irrawaddy (navigable for 400 miles), the Salween, the Sittang, and numerous tributaries and creeks. The Irrawaddy Delta, the focus of most water transportation, has some 1,700 miles of rivers and creeks and provides a seaboard for all types of craft. Inland water transportation registered 214 million passenger-miles and 376 million ton-miles in 1973. The state Water Transport Corporation (WTC) operates a fleet of about 800 vessels.

Ocean shipping, the traditional means of external transport, is controlled by the government, which operates coastal and oceangoing freighter-passenger lines. Rangoon, on the Rangoon River about 21 miles inland from the Andaman Sea, is the principal terminus for the highways, railroad, inland waterways, and airways; it is the chief port for ocean shipping, handling over 85% of the country's seaborne trade. In 1973, 751,000 tons of cargo were loaded at Rangoon, and 616,000 tons unloaded. The state-owned Burma Five Star Corporation had 10 ocean and 4 coastal ships in 1975.

The port of Rangoon was modernized in 1956 through a loan from the IBRD. Other ports include Akyab, serving western Burma; Bassein, serving the delta area; and Moulmein, Tavoy, and Mergui, which handle mineral and timber exports of the Tenasserim region. The WTC began a K115.5-million modernization program in 1974; the plan called for a new dockyard, 6 new coastal vessels, and 18 new smaller craft, among other improvements.

Burma is served by several foreign airlines, including Air France, BA, KLM, and Aeroflot; the government-owned Union of Burma Airways (UBA), established in 1948, is the main means of domestic air travel. The Department of Civil Aviation operates 4 major airports and 36 other landing fields throughout the country; Mingaladon, outside of Rangoon, is the principal airport. UBA's safety record is good under difficult operating conditions. In 1973, scheduled airlines flew 170 million passenger-km and 2.2 million ton-km of freight.

10 COMMUNICATIONS
The director-general of posts and telegraphs controls the telephone, telegraph, radio, and postal communications systems. In 1975 there were an estimated 25,000 telephones in use. Internal communication is mainly by wireless. Most external communications are routed through Sri Lanka and India. There is one broadcasting station, operated by the official Burma Broadcasting Service. There were 627,000 licensed radio receivers in 1973. A $21-million long-term loan for telecommunications development was approved by the IDA in May 1975.

11 HISTORY
The founding of a kingdom at Pagan in 1044 by Anawrahta marks the beginning of the history of Burma as a distinct political entity. The kingdom survived until 1287, when it was destroyed by the armies of Kublai Khan, and for the next five centuries disunity characterized Burma. In 1754, however, Alaungpaya defeated the Shan kingdom in northern Burma and the Mon kingdom in southern Burma and founded the last Burmese dynasty, which was in power until the advent of the British in the early 19th century.

The British conquest of Burma spanned 62 years: the first Anglo-Burmese War took place in 1824–26, when the British East India Co., acting for the crown, took possession of the Arakan and Tenasserim coastal regions; in 1852, at the end of the second war, the British acquired the remainder of lower Burma; and on 1 January 1886, following Burma's defeat in the third war, total annexation of Burma was announced. Incorporated into the British Indian Empire, Burma was administered as a province of· India until 1937, when it became a separate colony.

In 1897, Burma was given a legislative council consisting of nominated members with no real power, but in 1923 the Indian constitutional reforms popularly known as dyarchy were extended to Burma. The reforms divided the functions of government between the central government of India and the provincial government of Burma. In 1937, at the time of separation from India, Burma was permitted further steps toward responsible government; however, the British governor retained authority over foreign affairs, defense, currency, and the administration of frontier peoples.

From 1886 to 1948, the Burmese fought continuously for independence. The nationalists who finally gained freedom for Burma were a group of socialist-minded intellectuals, called the Thakins, from the University of Rangoon. They included Aung San, one of the founders of modern Burma; U Nu, independent Burma's first premier; Shu Maung, also known as Ne Win; and

Than Tun, a leader of the Communist revolt (1948) against the independent government. At the start of World War II, these anti-British nationalists collaborated with the Japanese, and with the aid of the Burma Independence Army, led by Aung San, Rangoon fell to Japan on 8 March 1943. They were soon disappointed with the Japanese occupation, however, and the Burma Independence Army was converted into an anti-Japanese guerrilla force called the Anti-Fascist People's Freedom League, which later assisted the British liberation of Burma.

On 17 October 1947, having assumed leadership of the Burmese nationalist movement following the assassination of Aung San and six of his associates, U Nu signed an agreement with British Prime Minister Clement Attlee covering economic and defense relationships between the two countries. On 4 January 1948, the sovereign Union of Burma came into being outside the Commonwealth of Nations.

A coup d'etat of 2 March 1962 overthrew the U Nu government, and a military government headed by a Revolutionary Council and led by Gen. Ne Win assumed control. Most major political figures in the democratic governments of the years 1948–62 were arrested but were released in 1966–68, including U Nu. An "internal unity advisory board" was created in 1968 with U Nu as a member; a majority of the board recommended a return to a multiparty parliamentary system—a proposal that Ne Win rejected. On 3 January 1974, the Socialist Republic of Burma was proclaimed; under a new constitution, Ne Win became president, and the government continued to be dominated by the military. In 1974, activities by insurgents loyal to U Nu intensified, and there were student riots following the death of former UN Secretary-General U Thant in November 1974. Another wave of strikes and demonstrations led to the closing of the University of Rangoon in June 1975.

12 GOVERNMENT
Burma began its independence in 1948 as a parliamentary democracy and as a quasi-federal state. Part of the country was divided into states with limited powers of local government, while the central part of the country (with the key cities of Rangoon and Mandalay and most of the population) was ruled directly by the central administration. The 1947 constitution, drawn up a half-year before independence, was overthrown on 2 March 1962, leading to the formation of an 18-officer Revolutionary Council headed by Gen. Ne Win. This Ne Win government, which had dissolved the sitting legislature, proclaimed the country a Socialist state, with Ne Win serving as both president and prime minister.

In 1972, Ne Win announced the first draft of a new basic law that would establish a Socialist republic in Burma, with the Burma Socialist Program Party, which had been transformed from an avowedly cadre-type party to a would-be mass party in 1969, the only party allowed. A December 1973 plebiscite endorsed the new constitution by 12,543,665 to 737,078, 91% of the eligible electorate taking part in the vote. Burma was officially proclaimed a Socialist republic on 3 January 1974, and the new basic law took immediate effect. Elections were held later in January and February 1974, followed by the convening of the new People's Assembly on 2 March 1974.

Under the 1974 constitution, the main governmental institutions include the 451-member unicameral People's Assembly (Pyithu Hluttaw), the president (chairman of the Council of State), the 29-member Council of State, the prime minister (a member of the Council of State), the Council of Ministers (18 members), the Council of People's Justices (5), the Council of People's Attorneys (5), the Council of People's Inspectors (5), and people's councils at the level of state (or division), township, and ward or village tract.

13 POLITICAL PARTIES
The Burmese party system was a democratic one, with several competing parties, before Ne Win took over in 1962. Ne Win sought to encourage the existing parties to combine into a single party in the first years of his rule, but when they failed to do so, he outlawed them altogether. The Burma Socialist Program Party

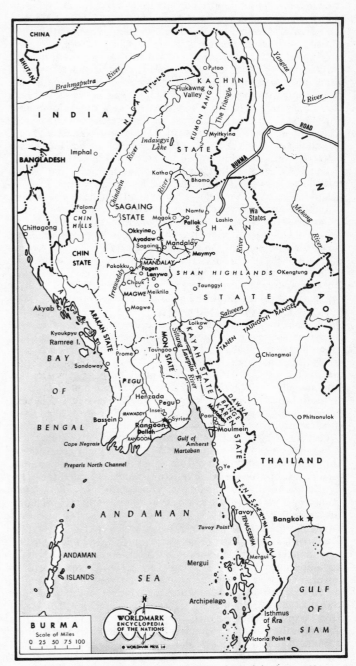

See continental political: front cover N7; physical: back cover N7

LOCATION: 92°10' to 101°11'E; 9°35' to 28°28'N. **BOUNDARY LENGTHS:** China, *2,185* km (*1,358* mi); Laos, *238* km (*148* mi); Thailand, *1,799* km (*1,118* mi); total coastline, *2,276* km (*1,414* mi); Bangladesh, *233* km (*145* mi); India, *1,403* km (*872* mi). **TERRITORIAL SEA LIMIT:** 12 mi.

(BSPP), created by Ne Win in 1962, was subsequently made the only legal party, a status sanctioned by the 1974 constitution.

Between 1948 and 1962, Burma's parties had been mostly socialist in economic orientation. The most important of these was the Anti-Fascist People's Freedom League (AFPFL), which gained independence for the country and which included within its ranks the distinct Burma Socialist Party. The AFPFL governed the country from 1948 to 1958, when a split between the Socialists and the more conservative independent members, led by U Nu, resulted in a temporary takeover by Gen. Ne Win. He voluntarily relinquished control of the government in 1960, when U Nu's new Union Party won a landslide victory.

Other parties before 1962 included two Communist movements, the "White Flags" and the "Red Flags," both of which took up arms early after independence and were later defeated by the government (the White Flags, however, were not completely eradicated until 1975). An above-ground Communist Party existed after 1949 and became the nucleus of the National United Front (NUF) in 1952. Both the Communists and the NUF, like all other parties except the BSPP, are now illegal, but several ex-NUF politicians hold key posts in the Ne Win government.

The BSPP is not, in fact, an autonomous institution, nor does it rule the state—as its models, the East European Communist parties, do. Brig. San Yu, one of Ne Win's top aides, is secretary-general of the party, which is dominated by the military.

On 27 May 1975, five ethnic organizations—the Karen National Union, Karenni (Kayah) National Progressive Party, New Mon State Party, Shan State Progress Party, and Arakan Liberation Party—formed the Federal National Democratic Front. They sought to overthrow the Ne Win government and establish a federal union based on national minorities. The army began an offensive against the insurgent groups in June.

14 LOCAL GOVERNMENT
Burma is a unitary Socialist republic comprising 14 states and divisions. The main distinction between the two kinds of units, which are functionally the same, is that the states represent an area where a national ethnic minority is the local majority, while the divisions have no such communal basis. The states are Arakan, Chin, Kachin, Karen, Kayah, Mon, and Shan. The divisions are Irrawaddy, Magwe, Mandalay, Pegu, Ragaing, Rangoon, and Tenasserim. States and divisions are broken down into townships, which include village tracts and towns. Village tracts consist of villages, and towns are divided into wards.

There are people's councils at all levels of local government. Their members are elected, but only the BSPP may nominate candidates. The local executive is the executive committee of the people's council. People's councils may refer questions to their counterparts at the next highest level of governmental organization.

15 JUDICIAL SYSTEM
The British-style judicial organs with which Burma began its independence, including a Supreme Court, were disbanded by the Revolutionary Council following Gen. Ne Win's 1962 return to power. The 1974 constitution provides for a five-member Council of People's Justices, state and divisional judges' committees, and township, ward, and village tract judges' committees. The Council of People's Justices is elected by the National Assembly from among its own members; nominations are made by the Council of State, which coordinates relations between central and local levels of government. Courts and other judicial organs that may be created by the judges' committees are coordinated by these committees at all levels of government.

The stated purpose of the judicial structure is to protect the Socialist system and to safeguard the interests of the working people. There is a separate system of military justice for members of the defense services.

16 ARMED FORCES
Burma's armed forces totaled an estimated 167,000 in mid-1975. The army had 153,000 men and women, with 3 infantry divisions and 84 independent infantry battalions organized into 9 regional commands. The army is organized chiefly for internal security duties, mainly against the various insurgent groups that have challenged successive Burmese governments almost from the start of independence. Military service is voluntary.

The navy and air force had 7,000 personnel each in mid-1975. The navy's responsibilities relate primarily to antismuggling and other coastal patrol duties; in 1975, its ships included 37 gunboats, 5 motor torpedo boats, and various support and patrol craft. The air force is also concerned mainly with internal security; in 1975, it had 11 combat aircraft, 28 transports, and 35 helicopters. Additional helicopters were received from the US in 1975 to help Burma combat the opium traffic (largely controlled by antigovernment insurgents, aided by the Chinese). There is also a 35,000-member People's Police Force. The military budget was K593.2 million in 1971/72.

The armed forces play a major role in Burmese politics. President Ne Win is an ex-general, and 15 of the 18 members of the Council of Ministers in 1975 were military men (2 active and 13 retired).

17 MIGRATION
Prior to World War II, Indians were the most significant Asian minority in Burma. In 1942, however, hundreds of thousands fled before the Japanese invasion; although many returned after the war, the Indian minority never achieved its prior proportions after 1945. Moreover, after independence the Burmese government instituted rigid restrictions on Indian migration. The Indian population was substantially reduced between April 1963 and June 1965, when 100,000 were repatriated as part of the government's program to increase the wealth and holdings of Burmese nationals. (Indians had dominated Burma's commerce.) The decline of both the Indians and the Chinese, Burma's second most important minority, continued through the mid-1970s.

18 INTERNATIONAL COOPERATION
Burma was admitted to UN membership in 1948 on the attainment of independence. It is a member of all the UN specialized agencies, including the IBRD, IMF, and IAEA. Regional bodies to which Burma belongs include the Asian Development Bank and the Colombo Plan. Through 1973, Burma had received foreign aid in excess of $735 million. China has been the chief single source ($114 million), but not all of these credits have been used. Other major donors have been Japan ($85 million), the US ($67 million), IBRD ($63 million), and the Federal Republic of Germany (FRG) ($57 million). Burma's foreign policy is neutralist, and the country belongs to no alliances.

19 ECONOMY
Burma has an agricultural economy. Rice, the major product, accounts for about 70% of the country's cultivated land. Forestry products (principally teak), mining production (mainly tin, tungsten, lead, and zinc concentrates), and fisheries contribute to the Burmese economy, but rice earns a major portion of total foreign exchange, and this dependence on a single export item places Burma in a vulnerable position. Although there is some industry—mainly silk weaving and dyeing, rice husking, oil refining, and wood carving—Burma's economy is insufficiently diversified and its industries are relatively undeveloped.

In the 12-year period 1962–74, GNP grew a fairly modest 42%, or about 3.5% annually, while population increased about 2.2% a year.

20 INCOME
In 1973/74, Burma's GDP was K14,852 million, as compared with K10,772 million in 1971/72. Per capita income rose from K378 in 1970/71 to over K490 in 1973/74. Inflation, however, prevented any increase in real income; consumer prices increased 26.4% in 1974 alone. Major contributors to the GDP in 1973/74 were agriculture, forestry, and fishing, 42.4%; commerce, 26.4%;

manufacturing, 8.4%; transport, storage, and communications, 4.1%; mining, 2.4%; and construction, 1.4%.

21 LABOR

In 1974, 70% of Burma's labor force of 11.6 million was engaged in agriculture, primarily rice cultivation. According to the government, a total of 829,388 were employed in manufacturing, 509,614 in government at various levels, 405,825 persons were employed in transportation, 173,865 in construction, 147,755 in forestry, and 61,010 in mining.

The Ministry for Housing and Labor is responsible for administering the labor laws. Burma was one of the first countries in Asia to enact a social security system, standards for agricultural salaries, a minimum industrial wage law, child labor legislation, and safety and sanitation standards. The 40-hour workweek is in effect in the modern sector of the economy, and industrial workers are entitled to a 10-day annual vacation, 14 days for religious and national holidays, 6 days of casual leave, and a maximum of 30 days of sick leave. However, much of this legislation and policy is not carried out in practice, particularly in the agricultural sector.

Trade unionism is limited. Under the Ne Win government, all labor is controlled by a single state-authorized labor organization. Workers' councils (and analogous peasants' councils) also have been created, but these are mainly means for government co-option of labor and the peasantry.

Wage levels are low and have been eroded by inflation. A senior official in 1975 earned only $300 a month. The lowest wage-earning group, unskilled workers, received about $20 a month; college graduates received $25–$30 a month if they could find employment, which most of them could not. Labor disruptions have troubled the Burmese economy during the 1970s.

22 AGRICULTURE

With 28% of the land under cultivation and approximately 70% of the total labor force engaged in farming, agriculture is the key to Burma's economy. Rice, by far the principal agricultural product, covers about 12.6 million acres of land in the fertile Irrawaddy delta region, the lower valleys of the Sittang and Salween rivers, and along the Arakan and Tenasserim coasts. Prior to World War II, Burma was the world's leading exporter of rice; annual production ranged between 6 million and 8 million tons, of which about 3 million tons were exported. However, after the war, which caused extensive damage to the economy, Burma did not achieve prewar levels of rice acreage and output until 1964.

Land under rice cultivation in 1940/41 totaled 12,832,000 acres, and production totaled 7,426,000 long tons, of which 3,120,000 long tons were exported; in 1973, 12,600,000 acres gave a harvest of 8,629,000 tons, a 17% increase over 1972. The government is officially the sole purchaser of the grain, reportedly buying half of what is produced. However, much rice is withheld by peasants because of the low level of government incentives. In 1974, the crop was about 8.6 million tons, of which only 17.4% was purchased by the government. In 1975, the government increased the price paid to rice growers by 50%.

Other crops in 1972, grown mainly in central Burma and the state of Shan, included 300,000 tons of pulses and beans and 44,000 tons of cotton. Wheat, sugar, tobacco, sesame, peanuts, and jute are among Burma's other agricultural products. Rubber is grown in small plantations in the Tenasserim and Irrawaddy delta regions. The amount of land under cultivation declined in the 1970s.

The government has tried to boost output through improved irrigation, land restoration projects, seed development and distribution, advances to farmers and agricultural banks, and nationalization of all lands not owned by active farmers. Between 1956 and 1965, land reclamation projects undertaken by the Land Reclamation Department of the Agricultural and Rural Development Corporation (ARDC) reclaimed 51,240 acres at a cost of K4.5 million.

The Ne Win government has initiated a number of irrigation projects since it came to power. Work on the Mu Valley Irrigation Project, which is being implemented under the UNDP, was begun in 1970. The cost is estimated to be K174.4 million. When completed, the project is expected to irrigate about 6 million acres of land.

In 1969, the practice of selling tractors and combined harvester threshers to village cooperatives was begun. Previously, the government had operated 6,838 tractors and harvesters stationed at 88 tractor stations. This system did not work out as well as expected, and the loss incurred by the government was K3.75 million.

In 1964, the Ne Win government assumed complete responsibility for the internal and external distribution of agricultural products. The Agricultural Marketing Board handles rice, tapioca, and tobacco; the ARDC controls jute, roselle, and cotton. The Ministry of Supply and Cooperatives deals with wheat.

23 ANIMAL HUSBANDRY

Despite Buddhist prohibitions against any kind of animal slaughter, the Burmese eat beef and other meats. Zebu (Indian) cattle and water buffalo are mainly raised as draft animals, however. Dairy farming, confined to the Shan and Kachin states, is negligible. Hogs and poultry are found in every village.

In 1975, Burma had an estimated 7,000,000 head of cattle, 1,300,000 hogs, and 200,000 sheep. Milk production was estimated at 365,000 tons in 1973; egg production in 1975 totaled about 500 million. The value in 1972/73 of livestock and fishery production was K804 million.

24 FISHING

Fishing is the most significant nonagricultural pursuit in Burma. Fish, which supply the main protein element in the Burmese diet, generally are dried and salted before marketing or consumed fresh or as fish paste. Traditionally, the Burmese have preferred fish from fresh or brackish water; although Burma has more than 1,400 miles of coastline, saltwater fishing is limited. To encourage a larger saltwater catch, the government has embarked on expanded deep-sea fishing operations and has erected a cold storage plant, a fish cannery, and a fish oil and meal factory. The total fish catch in 1973 was an estimated 463,400 tons, a 2.2% increase over 1972.

25 FORESTRY

Forests cover more than 55% of the country (145,300 sq mi); teak, the principal forest export, covers about 25% of the total forested area. As the world's leading exporter of teak, Burma supplies about 75% of the world market. The lumbering of teak, a 10-year process from the first girdling of the tree to its arrival at the sawmill, was disrupted by World War II; although postwar production has increased steadily, it has not reached prewar levels. The cut of other timber, however, has exceeded the prewar levels. Other forest products include lac, cutch, resin, and bamboo. All foreign timber concessions have been nationalized, and all forests are government-owned; the State Timber Board (STB) lumbers, mills, and markets forest products. The export of forest products increased in value from K140 million in 1971 to K211 million in 1973. The value of output from Burma's forests in 1972/73 was K331 million.

The STB has built sawmills at Dallah and Okkyin with a total conversion capacity of 390,000 tons annually. Round wood production was an estimated 21.2 million cu meters in 1973; sawn wood output was 410,000 cu meters. Wood production and processing industries employed 147,755 workers in 1974.

26 MINING

Mineral production contributed 2.4% to the GDP in 1973/74. Burma has rich and varied mineral deposits and resources. Lead, zinc, silver, copper, nickel, and cobalt are produced at the

Baldwin mine in Namtu; tin and tungsten at Mawchi mines in Kayah State and in the Tenasserim area; and petroleum at the Chauk and Lanywa fields. Jade, rubies, sapphires, and gold are mined, and deposits of iron ore, antimony, and coal have been discovered. Prior to World War II, Burma was a major minerals exporter. The war and subsequent internal strife lowered mineral production, however. In the 1950s, lacking funds and the necessary technical skills to rehabilitate and develop mines and mineral resources, the government entered into joint-ownership agreements with large foreign-owned mining enterprises and encouraged small private mining operations.

In 1963, the Burmese petroleum industry, under the British-operated Burma Oil Co., was completely nationalized, and in 1964 the Ne Win government nationalized all privately owned wells in Burma, as well as the Anglo-Burma Tin Co. The Petroleum and Mineral Development Corporation was formed in 1964 by the amalgamation of the Mineral Resources Development Corporation (founded in 1952), the Mines and Explosives Department, and the Burma Geological Development Corporation. The UN Special Fund made a grant of $1 million for extensive mineral exploitation, and the Burmese government matched these funds with an additional $1 million. Explorative work was begun in 1963, with special attention to petroleum, particularly in the Irrawaddy basin and delta. Natural gas was found at Ayadaw in the Palloku district, and iron ore near Taunggyi and in the Maymyo area. Coal deposits of 128 million tons have also been located. The Yadana Theingi Mine Development Project, begun in 1968, was designed to exploit lead and silver deposits. Burmese prospecting teams were engaged in the early 1970s in explorations for oil in the Sandoway and Akyab districts.

Contracts for oil exploration and production were awarded by the government to eight foreign companies in 1973. Strong efforts were also made in the first half of the 1970s to rehabilitate tin and tungsten mines completely or partly destroyed in World War II (and access to which was subsequently hindered by the Communist insurrection after independence). USSR, FRG, and Austrian financial and technical assistance supported these efforts.

In 1973, 968,000 tons of petroleum were produced; reserves were estimated at 6 million tons. An oil-exporting nation before World War II, Burma had to import 265,581 tons of crude petroleum in 1971 and 173,556 tons in 1972. Estimated output of ore concentrates in 1973 was zinc, 3,400 tons; tungsten, 667 tons; tin, 600 tons; antimony, 143 tons.

In 1974, 61,010 persons were engaged in mining activity; the value of mineral output was K192 million.

27 ENERGY AND POWER

In 1973, total installed capacity was 550,000 kw. Overall production increased from 545 million kwh in 1971 to 652 million kwh in 1973. Consumption increased from 395 million kwh in 1971 to 539 million kwh in 1973.

The Baluchaung station, at the Lawpita River dam near Loikaw, was completed in 1960 and was mainly financed by Japanese reparations. The installation of three additional generators at Lawpita in 1974 and a new natural-gas turbine plant at Kyunchaung doubled the country's installed electrical capacity. Lawpita feeds at least 53 towns, including Rangoon, and 145 villages; it is the main source of electric power in the national power grid.

28 INDUSTRY

Industry is geared largely to the processing of agricultural, mineral, and forest products. Rice milling remains the most important industry; other industrial activities include sawmilling, weaving of cotton textiles, petroleum refining at Syriam, and smelting at Namtu. Burma also has an exportable surplus of cement.

The gross value of industrial production reached K1,247

million in 1973/74. However, much of the real gain was in the period 1963–69; the increase from 1970 reflected a mounting inflationary spiral. Furthermore, according to government statistics, industry's share of the GDP has actually declined since the mid-1960s. Shortages of raw materials and spare parts, unqualified management, and an inadequately trained and motivated labor force largely accounted for this fall. Some industries did register output gains—principally those dealing with food, farm implements, and electrical products—but others suffered greater relative declines (such as clothing, mineral products, and bicycles).

The main industrial area is Pegu. In order to promote industrial expansion, the government established the Industrial Development Corporation in 1952. The Burma Economic Development Corporation (BEDC) was set up in 1961. In March 1963, the Ne Win government announced its decision to nationalize industries, and later that year it took over control of the BEDC, together with its 39 subsidiary firms. Transfer of these firms to appropriate government offices began early in 1964.

In 1974, Burma had 29,202 manufacturing establishments, mostly of modest size, of which 27,393 were privately owned. There were 1,476 state-controlled industries (including some of the country's largest), as well as 305 manufacturing cooperatives and 28 establishments that were privately owned but operated under government supervision.

Industrial products in 1973 included cement, 193,000 tons; nitrogenous fertilizers, 46,700 tons; refined sugar, 100 tons; cigarettes (1972/73), 1,811 million. Estimated petroleum refinery production in 1974 (in thousands of tons) included motor fuel, 217; kerosene, 245; distillate fuels, 284; residual fuel (1973), 378.

29 DOMESTIC TRADE

On 19 March 1964, the Ne Win government nationalized all wholesale businesses and the large private and cooperative shops in Rangoon. Small retail shops, hotels, and restaurants were exempted. On 9 April, these nationalization measures were extended throughout the country; village cooperatives were exempted. The Socialist Economy Construction Committee was set up to administer the nationalized businesses. The People's Stores Corporation, established in 1964, was initially responsible for the importation and distribution of essential foreign goods, the distribution of consumer goods produced in Burma, and the sale of Burmese products in foreign markets. The corporation was administered by a council headed by the Ministry of Supplies and Cooperatives. In 1970, the "people's stores," most of which had been unsuccessful, were replaced by consumer cooperatives.

Although significant marketing is done at Mandalay, Moulmein, Bassein, Henzada, Akyab, and Tavoy, Rangoon is Burma's most important business center. There are no commercial credit companies, and foreign firms selling to Burma customarily require a letter of credit on receipt of an order. The total value of all domestic trade in 1972/73 was put at K2,984 million.

Commercial advertising has declined sharply in recent years, but advertisements are still placed on a limited basis in various periodicals. Business customs are British-influenced, and English is widely used.

Usual business hours are from 9 A.M. to 5 P.M., Monday through Friday.

30 FOREIGN TRADE

After deficits in the late 1960s and early 1970s, Burma enjoyed foreign trade surpluses in 1973 and 1974. The 1973 surplus was the result of a 27.8% cutback in imports and only a slight decline in exports; in 1974, exports were up 48.9% while imports increased only 14.9%. Rice is Burma's principal export, generally accounting for one-third of export sales; rice exports declined sharply in 1973 but reached a record level in 1974. Teak is Burma's second leading export. Industrial products constitute Burma's leading imports.

Principal exports in 1972 (in thousands of dollars) were:

Rice	41,620
Wood, lumber, cork	31,895
Animal feed	12,145
Other exports	35,038
TOTAL	120,698

Principal imports in 1972 (in thousands of dollars) were:

Machinery	46,492
Textiles, yarns, fabrics	26,470
Transport equipment	17,660
Chemicals	14,692
Iron and steel	10,608
Crude petroleum	4,644
Milk and cream	3,797
Other imports	37,647
TOTAL	162,010

Japan is Burma's leading trade partner, supplying 27.4% of Burma's imports in 1972. In that same year, 50% of Burma's trade was with Asian countries and 25.5% with the EEC. Principal trade partners in 1972 (in thousands of dollars) were:

	EXPORTS	IMPORTS	BALANCE
Japan	14,835	44,377	−29,542
UK	11,256	17,198	− 5,942
FRG	5,654	14,497	− 8,843
Sri Lanka	17,541	92	17,449
China	4,223	12,711	− 8,488
Pakistan	9,697	6,090	3,607
India	4,823	10,462	− 5,639
Singapore	10,713	2,267	8,446
Other countries	41,956	54,316	−12,360
TOTALS	120,698	162,010	−41,312

31BALANCE OF PAYMENTS

Burma's balance of trade as a member of the sterling bloc was consistently favorable prior to World War II and was initially so in the postwar period. Foreign exchange reserves reached a postwar high of $266.81 million in June 1953 as a result of large receipts from rice exports. The price of rice on the world market subsequently declined, however, and Burmese foreign exchange holdings dropped to $108.5 million within the next two years. Stringent controls over consumer imports temporarily contributed to halting the decline, as did loans from abroad (from the US, India, the USSR, and the IBRD) and Japanese reparations payments. Burma also entered into a series of rice barter arrangements with Communist-bloc countries to ensure future disposition of large rice surpluses. As a result of favorable trade balances in the mid-1960s, Burma's foreign exchange reserves totaled $159 million at the end of 1968.

A decline in rice exports in the late 1960s and again in the early 1970s produced a serious balance of payments problem; however, a drastic cutback on imports and an infusion of long-term capital led to payments surpluses in 1973 and 1974. As a result of the improvement in its terms of trade, whatever its cause, Burma's international reserves increased to $100.3 million at the end of 1973 and $191 million as of 31 December 1974; however, by 31 October 1975, international reserves had dropped to $140.9 million.

The following is a summary of Burma's balance of payments for 1972 and 1973 (in millions of dollars):

	1972	1973
CURRENT ACCOUNTS		
Trade, net	−40.8	−55.1
Services, net	−24.4	−22.6
Transfers, net	18.8	17.7
TOTALS	−46.4	−60.0
CAPITAL ACCOUNTS		
Long-term capital	17.5	62.8
Short-term capital	0.2	0.1
TOTALS	17.7	62.9
Errors and omissions	11.2	31.3
Net change	−17.5	34.2

32BANKING

Effective 23 February 1963, all 24 commercial banks in Burma—10 foreign and 14 indigenously owned—were nationalized and amalgamated into 4 state banks. In addition to the Union of Burma Bank, which has a major impact on the government's fiscal policies, the other state banks were the State Agricultural Bank, the State Commercial Bank, and the Industrial Bank.

The People's Bank of Burma, which began functioning on 1 November 1969, resulted from the incorporation of the Central Bank, the Industrial Development Bank, three government financial agencies, and some of the people's banks (nationalized commercial banks). Incorporated into the People's Banks on 1 February 1970 were the State Commercial Bank, the State Agricultural Bank, and additional people's banks.

Bank deposits in August 1973 totaled K1,393.4 million (as compared with K1,124.4 million in September 1971). In August 1973, bank loans and advances amounted to K1,095.3 million (K1,449.6 million in September 1971). Burma's money supply in 1973 was K3,006.5 million (K2,093 million in 1971).

33INSURANCE

The Ministry of Commerce administers insurance laws, which mainly provide for guaranty deposits and reserve investment requirements. All the 78 foreign insurance companies registered in Burma were nationalized on 1 March 1963. All forms of insurance, including life, fire, marine, automobile, workmen's compensation, personal accident, and burglary are handled by the Insurance Division of the government-owned Union of Burma Bank. Life insurance coverage is compulsory for government employees.

In 1973, the total volume of premium income was K30,937,000 for life and K37,187,000 for non-life insurance. Total resources for life and general insurance were K424 million in 1973.

34SECURITIES

There are no stock or commodity exchanges in Burma.

35PUBLIC FINANCE

The government presents its budget in March. In 1974/75, total government receipts were estimated at K10,652 million and total public expenditures at K11,797 million, providing for a deficit for the 1 April–31 March fiscal year of K1,145 million. This was the ninth consecutive deficit budget for the Ne Win government. The government hoped to finance the deficit through various short- and long-term loans and foreign aid from international agencies and other countries, particularly Japan.

Major sources of government revenue from October 1973 through March 1974 (which totaled K4,502.6 million) were personal taxes, K216.9 million; import duties, K85.7 million; commercial taxes, K65.5 million; excise duties, K24.5 million; and other revenues (including sales and services by government departments and earnings from state business enterprises), κ4,110 million. During the same six-month period, the government spent κ5,284.2 million for various current operating expenses and κ429.5 million for capital investment. This compared with κ8,199.7 million for both current and capital purposes for the full 1972/73 fiscal year and κ8,722.8 million for 1971/72.

The government's public finance policies have dramatically reduced the value of the national currency. Between 1971/72 and 1972/73, for example, the Ne Win regime increased the amount of currency in circulation by almost 25% while the GDP was expanding by only 1.1%.

³⁶TAXATION

More than four-fifths of Burmese government revenues come from sources other than taxation. In 1972/73, 7.5% came from excise and state lottery taxes (7.1% in 1971/72), 5.2% from the income tax and surtax (7% in 1971/72), and 1.2% from taxes on land, forest products, minerals, and fisheries (1.3% in 1971/72).

³⁷CUSTOMS AND DUTIES

Burmese duties are primarily intended to raise revenue, although their financial importance is limited by the declining rate of imports and the fact that the government itself is by far the country's predominant importer. Import licenses are required for shipment of almost anything into the country. For most of the postindependence period, duties have been at the rate of 5% of the value of imported goods.

To preserve foreign exchange resources for essential imports (such as capital goods and industrial raw materials) as well as to provide nominal protection for local industries, the government has maintained a comprehensive system of quantitative restrictions for nearly all goods except such essential items as edible oils and tires and tubes. Sugar, soap, and cement imports have been restricted to protect domestic industries. There is a complete prohibition on imports of goods of which the government believes domestic production is sufficient.

³⁸FOREIGN INVESTMENTS

Foreign investment in Burma was heavy prior to World War II, but in the postwar period, and particularly after independence, a government policy of economic nationalism (and later socialism) strongly discouraged private foreign investment. After the nationalization of industry in 1963, private foreign investment in Burma was eliminated entirely. Foreign public assistance has been available, however, with Japan, China, and the FRG as Burma's principal suppliers. The cumulative total of US governmental aid to Burma through October 1973 was $112 million (approximately 49% in loans and 51% in grants); no new US-Burmese agreements have been signed since 1962. Burma's total external public debt was $417.4 million as of 31 December 1973.

In 1973, Burma agreed to production-sharing arrangements with foreign oil firms for offshore oil explorations. Eight foreign companies were involved in the arrangement for oil exploration and production in 13 offshore areas. Seismic and other surveys were commenced in late 1973 and drilling operations in 1975. This was one of several signs that Burma was relaxing its ban on foreign investment; with foreign reserves declining, the Ne Win government apparently felt that new sources of revenue were necessary, sources that required foreign capital and expertise.

³⁹ECONOMIC POLICY

The major aim of the present Burmese government is to rehabilitate, modernize, and diversify an economy that was extensively disrupted by World War II and that failed to develop between 1945 and 1975. To this end, all foreign companies, all banks, the entire transport system, all foreign and much domestic trade, and all the main branches of industry have been nationalized.

The second four-year development plan (1961–65)—drawn up before Gen. Ne Win's 1962 takeover—had as its chief aims the doubling of per capita income by 1973, the diversification of agriculture, the production of essential consumer goods, balanced regional development, compulsory primary education by 1969, the introduction of a free and adequate system of secondary education by 1979, and the establishment of rural health centers and hospitals. Total expenditures under the plan were to amount to κ2,628.9 million.

By the end of 1965, all major industrial establishments had been nationalized. In further nationalization measures, the government in 1968 took over 168 additional industrial enterprises in Rangoon and Mandalay. In January 1970, however, Gen. Ne Win announced that the managers of "people's stores" (established after the nationalization of retail trade in 1963) had proved inefficient, inexperienced, or corrupt. He therefore proposed that the stores be run as consumers' cooperatives, managed by members of the SPP or by ex-servicemen.

Despite the fact that the Ne Win government called itself Socialist, Burma had no economic plan between 1965 and 1971. In 1971, the government announced its first four-year economic development plan, but the plan's targets were not met, and it was revised in 1974 to coincide with Burma's formal proclamation as a Socialist republic. Between 1962 and 1974, Burma's GNP increased at a very modest rate, giving the country one of the lowest per capita incomes in the world (about $71 in 1974). Some nationalized industries showed declines in output, while others were hard pressed to hold their own. By 1974, the government had no choice but to modify some of its more rigid economic policies. The foreign investment ban, imposed in the 1960s, was relaxed, while foreign participation in mining was allowed for the first time in a dozen years. Privately owned businesses, to which the government had previously been opposed, were allowed in specified fields.

⁴⁰HEALTH

People in rural areas constitute more than 80% of Burma's population; until recently few of them had the benefit of modern medicine. Although the doctor-population ratio was 1 to 12,500 for the whole country, it was only 1 to 28,000 for the rural areas in 1967. To correct this imbalance, the country's health services were reorganized by sending more doctors to rural areas and increasing the number of rural health centers. Doctors in private practice were inducted for two years of national service.

The progress of the health services is reflected in the sharp rise in the number of hospitals and dispensaries from 185 and 46 in 1963 to 410 and 185 in 1973. Hospital care is free and uniform. The bed capacity of hospitals in 1973 was 20,871 (about 1 per 1,400 people). In 1973, Burma had 4,280 doctors, 8,621 nurses and midwives, and 924 health assistants. Rural health centers numbered 970.

To staff the new hospitals and dispensaries, the medical schools were expanded, nurse and midwife training courses were increased, an institute of paramedical science was established, and a new college of dentistry was opened.

A team of nutritionists conducts research on the Burmese diet and disseminates its findings and recommendations through the press, radio, and demonstrations in offices and factories. One result of these efforts has been that the height and weight of the average Burmese have increased. Smallpox, cholera, and plague have declined as health hazards, and programs are under way to eradicate malaria and tuberculosis.

In 1975, average estimated life expectancy was 51 years for males and 54.1 for females, compared with 46.1 and 49 years in 1965.

⁴¹SOCIAL WELFARE

Although considerable advances have been made in health services, Burma's aspirations toward a welfare state have been limited by lack of public funds. On 1 January 1956, the government inaugurated a social security program that compensates workers for wage losses arising from sickness, injury, and maternity leave, provides free medical care, and establishes survivor's benefits. The program is funded by contributions from employers, employees, and the government. As yet, Burma has neither unemployment insurance nor old age pensions.

Women have a high status in Burmese society and economic life. They may retain their maiden name after marriage, may obtain divorces without undue difficulty, and enjoy equal property and inheritance rights with men.

42HOUSING
Prewar housing in Burma compared favorably with that in other Southeast Asian nations, but largely because of World War II devastation, housing conditions have deteriorated. In 1970, the National Housing and Town and Country Development Board introduced a low-cost housing scheme for Rangoon aimed at providing apartments for 20,000 families. The cost of each apartment, measuring 20 feet by 23 feet, was to be K4,000. Occupants could either cover the full amount in cash and make a monthly payment of K9 for maintenance, or pay half in cash and K18 monthly for 25 years, plus K9 a month for maintenance.

In 1970/71 there were 29,044 public residential buildings with 96,558 rooms; by 1972/73 there were 33,436 structures with 106,032 rooms.

43EDUCATION
The system of education initiated by the Ne Win government in 1964 equates learning with livelihood. At that time, the government announced its intention of opening at least 1 agrarian high school and 1 technical high school in each district. By 1967 there were 6 agricultural high schools, 7 industrial trade schools, and 1 technical high school in the country; in addition, the government had taken over about 880 private schools.

Education is free but only primary education is compulsory. Burmese is the language of instruction, and English is taught in the secondary schools.

In 1972/73, Burma had 20,075 schools (13,794 in 1961/62), 10 technical institutes (5 in 1961/62), 6 intermediate colleges (4 in 1961/62), and 11 universities (2 in 1961/62). There were 4,226,895 students (1,961,741 in 1961/62) and 100,840 teachers (50,558 in 1961/62).

Burma's illiteracy rate was 45% in 1975; the Mass Education Council was attempting to increase literacy through special programs. Under the government's educational development program, a system of free and adequate secondary education was to be in existence by 1977.

44LIBRARIES AND MUSEUMS
The National Library in Rangoon, founded in 1952, has a collection of 49,000 volumes and is open to the general public. Other large libraries are the Arts and Science University Library in Mandalay, with 94,000 volumes, and the Universities' Central Library (formerly the University Library of Rangoon), with 110,000 volumes. Several small college libraries were opened in 1964, and three state libraries and museums were founded in 1955 at Kyaukpyu, Moulmein, and Mandalay. The National Museum of Art and Archæology in Rangoon was founded in 1952 and includes among its collection a replica of King Mindon's Mandalay Palace. Sometimes called the "land of golden pagodas," Burma also has thousands of Buddhist temples, many of which have been repaired and restored.

45ORGANIZATIONS
Although Burma has most common types of educational, religious, cultural, and social organizations, those associated with capitalist economic activity have all but disappeared; such organizations were formerly very numerous, active, and influential. The Rotary Clubs were forced by the government to disband in late 1975, as were numerous other Western-style organizations before them.

Cooperative and producers' societies, as well as consumer cooperatives, exist in substantial numbers, and there is a growing number of workers', peasants', women's, students', and other affiliates of the ruling BSPP.

46PRESS
The government professes to uphold the practice of freedom of the press, but there are no longer privately owned newspapers, and the print media are nearly completely government controlled. In 1963, the government established its own press agency, the News Agency of Burma, with a monopoly of internal news distribution. Chinese- and Indian-language newspapers are no longer allowed by the government, but three papers are still published in English. More than 95 periodicals of all types are published in Burma.

The seven daily newspapers published by the government in 1975 were:

	LANGUAGE	CIRCULATION
Mirror	English	90,000
Loketha Pyithu Nezin	Burmese	90,000
Botataung	Burmese	72,000
New Light of Burma	Burmese	30,000
Working People's Daily	English	20,000
Hanthawaddy	Burmese	18,500
The Guardian	English	13,000

The Rangoon Daily (circulation 18,000) was the last privately owned newspaper. It shut down when its publication permit was withdrawn in 1972.

There are some privately published magazines, but none have high circulations and none are of major influence. The government-published Forward has the highest circulation of any periodical (125,550 Burmese, 14,000 English). The Burmese-language International Affairs Journal has a circulation of 52,000. The English-language monthly Guardian circulates internationally; it has 8,000 subscribers.

47TOURISM
A visitor to Burma must have a passport, a visa, and certificates for smallpox vaccination and cholera inoculation. Seven-day tourist visas are easily obtainable. Visas for a longer period—from one month to three months—can also be obtained for valid business purposes, but special arrangements must be made with the government. Because of internal security problems, visitors are prohibited from traveling to the border states. Tourism is limited to the major cultural centers: Rangoon, Mandalay, Pagan, Pegu, and Taunggyi. Although the 1970s saw a relaxation in official policies toward foreigners, tourism is still not especially welcome.

48FAMOUS BURMESE
Anawrahta, who founded the early Burmese kingdom of Pagan in 1044 and established Hinayana Buddhism as the official religion, is a great figure in Burmese history, as are the Toungoo warrior-king Bayinnaung (1551–81) and Alaungpaya (1752–60), who established the dynasty that ruled Burma until 1886. Great writers of the Burmese past include Bhikkhu Ratthasara, author of the poem Hatthipala Pyo on the life of Gautama Buddha; Nawedegyi and Natshinnaung, poets of the Toungoo dynasties; and Binnyadala, who wrote of the long struggles of the Burmese king of Ava. In more recent times, U Ba Nyan and U Ba Zaw, well-known painters of the 1920s, introduced Western-style art into Burma; both died in the 1940s.

U Nu (b.1907) was independent Burma's first premier. Nu shares fame as a founder of modern Burma with Aung San (1916–47), called the Father of the Burmese Revolution. Other important modern figures are U Ba Swe (b.1915) and U Kyaw Nyein (b.1912), Socialist political leaders; Ne Win (Shu Maung, b.1910), premier after 2 March 1962 and president since 3 January 1974; and U Thant (1909–74), who served as UN secretary-general from 1961 through 1971.

[49] DEPENDENCIES
Burma has no territories or colonies.

[50] BIBLIOGRAPHY

American University. *Area Handbook for Burma*. Washington, D.C.: Government Printing Office, 1971.

Ba Maw. *Breakthrough in Burma*. New Haven, Conn.: Yale University Press, 1968.

Bingham, June. *Burma*. 3 vols. New Haven, Conn.: Human Relations Area Files, 1956.

Bixler, Norma. *Burma: A Profile*. New York: Praeger, 1971.

Butwell, Richard. *U Nu of Burma*. Stanford, Calif.: Stanford University Press, 1969.

Cady, John Frank. *A History of Modern Burma*. Ithaca, N.Y.: Cornell University Press, 1958.

Christian, John Leroy. *Modern Burma: A Survey of Political and Economic Development*. Berkeley: University of California Press, 1942.

Collins, Maurice. *Land of the Great Image*. New York: New Directions, 1959.

Donnison, F. S. V. *Burma*. New York: Praeger, 1970.

Furnivall, John Sydenham. *Colonial Policy and Practice: A Comparative Study of Burma and Netherlands India*. New York: New York University Press, 1956.

Furnivall, John Sydenham. *Governance of Modern Burma*. New York: Institute of Pacific Relations, 1958.

Furnivall, John Sydenham. *An Introduction to the Political Economy of Burma*. Rangoon: Burma Book Club, 1931.

Hagen, Everett Einar. *The Economic Development of Burma*. Washington, D. C.: National Planning Association, 1956.

Harvey, Godfrey Eric. *History of Burma*. New York: Octagon, 1967.

Johnstone, William C. *Burma's Foreign Policy: A Study in Neutralism*. Cambridge: Harvard University Press, 1963.

Kunstadter, Peter (ed.). *Southeast Asian Tribes, Minorities, and Nations*. Princeton, N. J.: Princeton University Press, 1967.

Leach, Edmund Ronald. *Political Systems of Highland Burma: A Study of Kachin Social Structure*. Cambridge: Harvard University Press, 1954.

Maung, Maung. *Aung San of Burma*. The Hague: Nijhoff, 1962.

Maung, Maung. *Burma and General Ne Win*. New York: Asia Publishing House, 1969.

Morehead, Frederick Thomas. *The Forests of Burma*. Calcutta: Longmans, Green, 1944.

Morgan, Kenneth William (ed.). *The Path of the Buddha: Buddhism Interpreted by Buddhists*. New York: Ronald, 1956.

Nash, Manning. *The Golden Road to Modernity*. New York: Wiley, 1965.

Nu, U. *Burma under the Japanese*. New York: St. Martin's Press, 1954.

Nu, U. *From Peace to Stability*. Rangoon: Ministry of Information, 1951.

Nu, U. *The People Win Through*. New York: Taplinger, 1957.

Nu, U. *Saturday's Son*. New Haven: Yale University Press, 1975.

Nu, U. *Towards Peace and Democracy*. Rangoon: Ministry of Information, 1949.

Orwell, George. *Burmese Days*. New York: Harcourt, Brace, 1935.

Pye, Lucien W. *Politics, Personality and Nation Building: Burma's Search for Identity*. New Haven: Yale University Press, 1962.

Smith, Donald E. *Religion and Politics in Burma*. Princeton, N. J.: Princeton University Press, 1965.

Stevenson, Henry Noel Cochran. *The Hill Peoples of Burma*. Calcutta: Longmans, Green, 1944.

Tinker, Hugh. *The Foundations of Local Self-Government in India, Pakistan, and Burma*. London: Athlone Press, 1954.

Tinker, Hugh. *The Union of Burma*. London: Oxford University Press, 1967.

Trager, Frank N. *Building a Welfare State in Burma, 1948–1956*. New York: Institute of Pacific Relations, 1958.

Trager, Frank N. *Burma—From Kingdom to Republic*. New York: Praeger, 1966.

Trager, Frank N., *et al. Annotated Bibliography of Burma*. New Haven, Conn.: Human Relations Area Files, 1956.

Trager, Helen. *Burma*. New York: Praeger, 1969.

Trager, Helen. *Burma through Alien Eyes*. New York: Praeger, 1966.

Walinsky, Louis J. *Economic Development in Burma, 1951–60*. New York: Twentieth Century Fund, 1962.

Woodman, Dorothy. *The Making of Burma*. London: Cresset Press, 1962.

Yoe, Shway. *The Burman: His Life and Notions*. London: Macmillan, 1896.

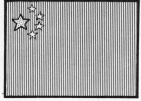

People's Republic of China
Chung-hua Jen-min Kung-ho-kuo

CAPITAL: Peking. **FLAG**: The flag is red with five gold stars in the upper left quadrant; one large star is near the hoist and four smaller ones are arranged in an arc to the right. **ANTHEM**: *Tung-fang Hung (The East Is Red)*. **MONETARY UNIT**: The renminbi (RMB—formerly called yüan) of 10 chiao or 100 fen is a nonconvertible paper currency. There are coins of 1, 2, and 5 fen, and notes of 1, 2, 5, 10, 20, and 50 fen and 1, 2, 3, 5, and 10 renminbi. Since August 1974, the government has listed buying and selling rates for the renminbi. During March 1976, the median exchange rate was RMB1=$0.509113 (or $1=RMB1.9642). **WEIGHTS AND MEASURES**: The metric system is the legal standard, but some Chinese units remain in common use, among them the catty or chin (0.5 kg or 1.1023 lb); mow or mou (1/15 hectare or 0.1647 acre); li (0.5 km or 0.3107 mile). **HOLIDAYS**: New Year's Day, 1 January; Spring Festival, from the first to the third day of the first moon of the lunar calendar, usually in February; May Day, 1 May; and National Day, 1 and 2 October. **TIME**: 8 P.M.=noon GMT; in Manchuria, 9 P.M.=noon GMT.

¹LOCATION, SIZE, AND EXTENT

The People's Republic of China (PRC), the third-largest country in the world after the USSR and Canada and the largest Asian country, has an area of 9,562,904 sq km (3,692,244 sq mi), extending 4,845 km (3,011 mi) ENE-WSW and 3,350 km (2,082 mi) SSE-NNW. Mainland China's 5,774-km (3,588-mi) coastline, extending from the mouth of the Yalu River in the northeast to the Gulf of Tonkin in the south, forms a great arc, with the Liaotung and Shantung peninsulas in the north protruding into the Yellow Sea and the Luichow Peninsula in the south protruding into the South China Sea. China's territory includes several islands, the largest of which is Hainan, off the south coast. Other islands include the reefs and islands of the South China Sea, extending as far as 4°N. These reefs and islands include Tungsha (Pratas) and the Sisha (Paracels), Spratly, Chungsha, and Nansha archipelagoes. China is bordered on the N by the Mongolian People's Republic (MPR) and the USSR; on the NE by the Democratic People's Republic of Korea (DRK); on the E by the Yellow and East China seas; on the S by Hong Kong, Macao, the South China Sea, Gulf of Tonkin, Socialist Republic of Viet-Nam (SRV) and Laos; on the SW by Burma, India, Bhutan, India (Sikkim), and Nepal; on the W by India, Jammu and Kashmir (disputed areas), Pakistan (west of Karakorum Pass), and Afghanistan; and on the NW by the USSR. China's total boundary length is 28,072.6 km (17,445 mi).

PROVINCES†	AREA (sq mi)	CAPITAL	POPULATION (1968 est.)
Anhwei	54,015	Hofei	35,000,000
Chekiang	39,305	Hangchow	31,000,000
Fukien	47,529	Foochow	17,000,000
Heilungkiang	178,996	Harbin	21,000,000
Honan	64,479	Chengchou	50,000,000
Hopei	79,979	Shihchiachuang	47,000,000
Hunan	81,274	Changsha	38,000,000
Hupei	72,394	Wuhan	32,000,000
Kansu	137,104	Lanchow	13,000,000
Kiangsi	63,629	Nanchang	22,000,000
Kiangsu	40,927	Nanking	47,000,000
Kirin	72,201	Changchun	17,000,000
Kwangtung	89,344	Canton	40,000,000

†Excluding Taiwan •1970 estimate *Approximate

Kweichow	67,181	Kweiyang	17,000,000
Liaoning	58,301	Shenyang	28,000,000
Shansi	60,656	Taiyüan	18,000,000
Shantung	59,189	Tsinan	57,000,000
Shensi	75,598	Sian	21,000,000
Szechwan	219,691	Chengtu	70,000,000
Tsinghai	278,378	Hsining	2,000,000
Yünnan	168,417	Kunming	23,000,000

AUTONOMOUS REGIONS

Inner Mongolia	454,633	Huhehot	13,000,000
Kwangsi-Chuang	85,096	Nanning	24,000,000
Ningsia-Hui	30,039	Yinchwan	2,000,000
Sinkiang-Uigur	635,829	Urumchi	8,000,000
Tibet	471,660	Lhasa	1,400,000

MUNICIPALITIES

Peking	3,386	—	7,600,000•
Shanghai	772	—	10,800,000•
Tientsin	1,500*	—	4,000,000•

²TOPOGRAPHY

China may be divided roughly into a lowland portion in the east, comprising about 20% of the total territory, and a larger section consisting of mountains and plateaus in the west. The principal lowlands are the Manchurian Plain, drained by the Sungari River, a tributary of the Amur (Heilongjiang), and by the Liao River, which flows to the Yellow Sea; the North China Plain, traversed by the lower course of the Yellow River (Huang Ho); the valley and delta of the Yangtze River (Ch'ang Chiang); and the delta of the (West) River Hsi surrounding Canton. West of these lowlands, the country's topography rises to plateaus of 4,000 to 5,000 feet: the Shansi and Shensi in the north, and the Mongolian Plateau in the northwest. Beyond lie the great mountain ranges and high plateaus of Tibet, with an average elevation of 15,000 feet. The highest mountains, which enclose the Tibetan high plateaus on the north and south, are the Kunlun mountain ranges and the Himalaya. North of Tibet are two plateau basins of Central Asia, the Tarim Basin and the Dzungarian Basin, which are separated from each other by the Tien Shan, another major mountain system. The Chinese portion of the Tien Shan, which also extends into the USSR, rises to 23,620 feet in the Khan Tengri peak.

From the Pamirs of Central Asia, the Altai, Tien Shan,

Kunlun, and Himalayan mountain systems extend toward China. Each consists of several parallel chains. Together, they form the chief watersheds of all the principal rivers in China. The Altai and Himalayan systems form the natural boundaries of China in the northwest and the southwest; the Tien Shan divides Sinkiang; the Kunlun system branches all over the country, forming the backbone of its topography.

All the great rivers flow eastward to the Pacific. In the northeast, the Amur (Heilongjiang) drains a great part of the Manchurian Basin as it winds along its 2,500-mile course. Other Manchurian rivers include the Liao Ho, the chief river in southern Manchuria, as well as the Tumen and the Yalu, which forms the boundary between China and the DRK. The main river of North China, and the second largest in the country, is the Yellow River (Huang Ho). From Kansu, it winds about 3,000 miles eastward to Shantung Province, where it empties into the Gulf of Chihli (Po Hai). The valley of the Yellow River includes an area of 600,000 sq mi.

Central China is drained mainly by the Yangtze (Ch'ang Chiang) and its tributaries. The largest river in China, the Yangtze travels more than 3,200 miles and drains more than 700,000 sq mi of land. As China's only long river with no natural outlet, the Hwai River, between the Yangtze and the Yellow, is subject to frequent flooding. The most important rivers of southern China are the Min and the Pearl (Chu). To the south are the upper courses of the Mekong (Lan-ts'ang) and Red (Yüan) rivers.

Northern China is in a major earthquake zone; on 28 July 1976, a major tremor (the largest in the world in 12 years) struck the city of Tangshan (90 miles east of Peking), causing widespread devastation.

³CLIMATE

Although most of China lies within the temperate zone, climate varies greatly with topography. Winter temperatures range from –27°C (–17°F) in northern Manchuria to –1°C (30°F) in the North China Plain and southern Manchuria to 4.4°C (40°F) along the middle and lower valleys of the Yangtze, to 15.6°C (60°F) south of the Nan Shan Range. Although summer temperatures are more nearly uniform in southern and central China, with a July mean of about 26.6°C (80°F), northern China has a shorter hot period and the nights are much cooler. Northern Manchuria has the greatest annual temperature range in China, from –27°C (–17°F) in January to 21°C (70°F) in July; winters last six months or more. In the extreme south, in tropical Hainan, the annual temperature range is only 8 centigrade degrees (15 Fahrenheit degrees).

Rain falls mostly in summer. The amount of precipitation ranges from 4 inches or less in the deserts of Central Asia to about 25 inches in Manchuria and North China, and increases to 80 inches or more in the valley of the Pearl River.

The principal climatic controls are a strong high-pressure system, centered in winter over Mongolia and Siberia, that produces dry, cold winters over most of China, and, in summer, the moisture-bearing monsoon winds, which originate over the Pacific and Indian oceans.

⁴FLORA AND FAUNA

The country may be divided into a number of regions, each with characteristic varieties of plants and animals. In the south, the Hsi (West) River Valley has tropical vegetation. Three grain crops or seven vegetable crops may be harvested each year. Rice, sugarcane, tobacco, and tropical fruits are grown. Large parts of Hainan are covered with luxuriant tropical forests. In the Yangtze Valley area of central China, the main grain crop is rice, as in the tropical south, and the region is renowned for tea and silk. Tung oil, citrus fruits, and bamboo are also grown. North China, including southern Manchuria, is a belt of depleted deciduous forest that has been largely replaced by wheat, cotton,

millet, and sorghum fields. Northern Manchuria is China's only region with rich black soils; the region once supported steppe grasslands but is now mainly under wheat and soybeans. Mountains enclosing these former steppes are covered with rich coniferous forests abounding in fur-bearing animals. In south China, the warm, wet lowlands resemble the country's far south, while the mountains are cold, covered with coniferous forest, and are the habitat of the giant panda. Western China, including Inner Mongolia and Central Asia, consists of semiarid grasslands and arid deserts with meager plant and animal life. Cotton and other crops are grown in irrigated oases. On the Tibetan plateaus, vegetation varies from alpine meadows in the east to virtually barren wastes in the west. Typical Tibetan animals are the yak and the Himalayan black bear.

As of 1975, endangered species in the southern regions of China (including Kwangsi-Chuang Autonomous Region and portions of Kwangtung and Yünnan provinces) included the Chinese egret, Japanese white stork, Sclater's monal, Elliot's pheasant, Cabot's tragopan, three species of crane (Japanese, Siberian white, and black-necked), Chinese crocodile lizard, and Burmese python. In the remaining Palaearctic region, endangered species included the snub-nosed langur, douc langur, wolf, Asiatic wild dog, giant panda, clouded leopard, four species of tiger (Indian, Siberian, Chinese, and Indochinese), leopard, amur leopard, snow leopard, Przewalski's horse, Asiatic wild ass, wild Bactrian camel, Himalayan musk deer, black muntjac, three species of sika (North China, Shansi, and South China), Thorold's deer, shou, yarkand deer, McNeill's deer, wild yak, Szechwan takin, golden takin, two species of white-eared pheasant, brown-eared pheasant, Chinese monal, Blyth's tragopan, Japanese crane, Siberian white crane, rufous-headed robin, Lower Yangtze Kiang crow-tit, Chinese giant salamander, and China alligator.

⁵POPULATION

By all available measures, China is the most populous nation in the world. In 1975, according to UN figures, 21.1% of the world's population (or about one in every five persons) lived in China. China's first modern census, taken on 30 June 1953, reported a total population of 601,938,035, including 7,591,298 in Taiwan and 11,743,320 Chinese residing or studying abroad. Thus, mainland China then had a population of 582,603,417. *Ten Great Years*, the government's statistical handbook issued in 1959, gave the following year-end population figures (excluding Hong Kong, Macao, and Chinese living abroad, but including 10.1 million persons in Taiwan): 548,770,000 (285,140,000 males) in 1949; 595,550,000 (308,850,000 males) in 1953; 656,630,000 (340,140,000 males) in 1957. Subsequent all-China nationwide population figures appearing in the Chinese press—700 million in August 1966; 750 million in February 1968—must be understood as rhetorical statements that are not intended as statistical releases of population data. Provinces and centrally governed cities gave figures for their own population in 1967/68, and these totaled 712 million. However, the China Cartographic Institute reported a total of 685,220,000 for 1970. The expression most widely used by Chinese officials in the mid-1970s was "nearly" 800,000,000.

The UN's median estimate for 1975 was 838,803,000; the population for 1980 was projected at 907,609,000, with the total expected to exceed 1 billion persons by about 1990. UN estimates yield an average density of 88 persons per sq km (227 persons per sq mi) in 1975. The greatest population density is found in the middle and lower Yangtze Valley, with a range of about 750 to 1,000 persons per sq km. Similarly high densities occur in the Hsi (West) River Delta near Canton. In the North China Plain, the average density is about 250 per sq km. Settlement decreases rapidly toward the western mountains and deserts.

In 1957 there were 124 cities with a population exceeding

100,000 persons, as compared with 105 such cities in 1952. Medium-sized cities (under 100,000 persons) totaled 52 in 1957, as compared with 54 in 1952. The largest cities are Shanghai (10.8 million estimated in 1970, 6.9 million reported in 1957); Peking, the capital (7.6 million in 1970, 4 million in 1957); Chungking, 4.4 million in 1968, 2.1 million in 1957); Tientsin (4 million in 1970, 3.22 million in 1957); Shenyang (formerly called Mukden—3 million in 1970, 2.4 million in 1957); and Wuhan (2.7 million in 1970, 2.15 million in 1957). Other large cities, with their 1957 populations (in millions), are Canton, 1.84; Harbin,

population. These non-Chinese peoples live mainly in sparsely populated western China, while the Chinese are concentrated in the heavily settled eastern lowlands. The ethnic groups, numbering 52, belong to two major linguistic families: the Indo-Chinese (or Sino-Tibetan) family, found primarily in southwest China, and the Altaic family, found mainly in the northwest. Major branches of the Sino-Tibetan family are the Chuang and the Tibetans, and of the Altaic family, the Uigurs and Mongols.

Ethnic minorities with more than 1 million persons as of the end of 1957 were Chuang (7,780,000), a Buddhist people of

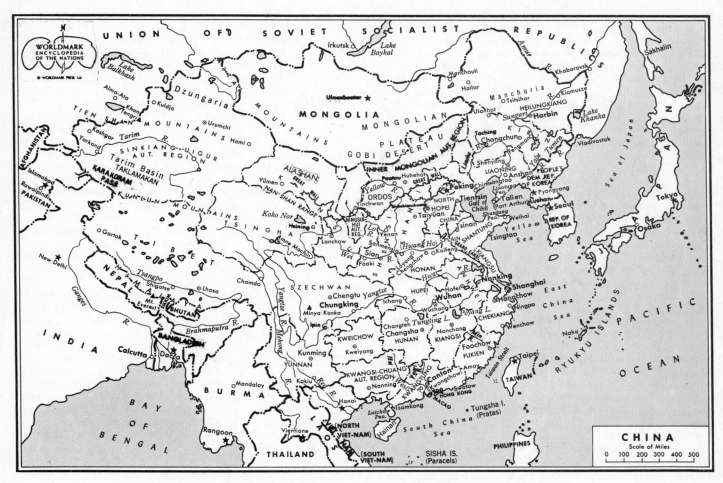

See continental political: front cover O6; physical back cover O6

LOCATION: (not including islands south of Hainan): 73°38′ to 135°5′E; 18°9′ to 53°34′N. **BOUNDARY LENGTHS**: MPR, *4,673 km (2,904 mi)*; USSR, *7,520 km (4,673 mi)*; DRK, *1,416 km (880 mi)*; Hong Kong, *84 km (52 mi)*; Macao, *1.6 km (1 mi)*; SRV, *1,281 km (796 mi)*; Laos, *425 km (264 mi)*; Burma, *2,185 km (1,358 mi)*; India (including Sikkim and excluding disputed portions of Jammu and Kashmir), *1,194 km (742 mi)*; Bhutan, *412 km (256 mi)*; Nepal, *1,078 km (670 mi)*; Jammu and Kashmir, *698 km (434 mi)*; Pakistan (west of Karakorum Pass), *523 km (325 mi)*;Afghanistan, *71 km (44 mi)*; total coastline (including Hainan), *6,511 km (4,046 mi)*. **TERRITORIAL SEA LIMIT**: *12 mi.*

1.55; Lushan/Talien (formerly called Port Arthur/Dairen), 1.51; Nanking, 1.42 (new figure of 1.7 in May 1968); Sian, 1.31; Tsingtao, 1.12; Chengtu, 1.1 (new figure of 1.6 in May 1968); and Taiyüan, 1.02.

The urban portion of the population was put at 23.5% in 1975. Some 25.3% of the population was under 15 years of age. The estimated 1975–80 average annual growth rate was put at 1.58%.

6 ETHNIC GROUPS
The population of ethnic minorities increased from 35 million in 1953 to 38 million at the end of 1957—about 5.8% of the total

Kwangsi related to the Thais; Uigurs (3,900,000), a Muslim Turkic people of Sinkiang; Hui (3,930,000), a Chinese-speaking Muslim people mainly of Kansu, Tsinghai, and other parts of northwest China; Yi, formerly called Lolo (3,260,000), a Buddhist people of southwest China related to the Tibetans; Tibetans (2,770,000), inhabiting Tibet and adjoining regions; Miao (2,680,000), a distinct ethnic group of the Sino-Tibetan family in south and southwest China; Mongols (1,640,000), mainly in Inner Mongolia; Puyi (1,310,000), a Buddhist people of southwest China related to the Thais; and Koreans (1,250,000), in areas adjoining the DRK. Some 2,430,000 Manchus claim descent from the Manchu conquerors of China, but they differ in no other respect from the Chinese. There are some 30 lesser ethnic groups, totaling 6,718,025 persons according to the 1953 census.

7 LANGUAGE

Chinese, a branch of the Sino-Tibetan linguistic family, is a monosyllabic tone language written by means of characters representing words. The script is nonphonetic and remains constant throughout China, but the spoken language has regional phonetic differences. Spoken Chinese falls into two major groups, separated roughly by a northeast-southeast line running from the mouth of the Yangtze River to the border of Viet-Nam. North and west of this line are the so-called Mandarin dialects, spoken by more than 450 million Chinese. These include the Peking dialect, spoken throughout north and northwest China and Manchuria, which the government is encouraging as a national spoken language; the Upper Yangtze dialect of southwest China; and the dialect of the Lower Yangtze Valley. The most important dialect south of the linguistic divide is that of Shanghai, spoken by more than 50 million people in the Yangtze River Delta. Cantonese, spoken by about 40 million people in China, is the language of the majority of Chinese emigrants. Thousands of Chinese characters must be memorized. In 1957, the government adopted a phonetic alphabet based on Latin letters and designed to help eliminate illiteracy. The new alphabet is used mostly for such purposes as writing some elementary textbooks and for denoting pronunciation of Chinese characters. Chinese publications continue to be written in Chinese characters.

Of the 52 minority peoples in China, only Hui, Manchus, and She use Chinese as a common language. More than 20 minority nationalities have their own written languages. The PRC government has assisted 13 minority peoples—Chuang, Puyi, Li, T'ung, Miao, Yi, Liau, Hani, Nasi, Kawa, T'ai, Lahu, and Chingpo—in creating or developing their own national languages and in learning Chinese.

8 RELIGION

Three faiths—Confucianism, Buddhism, and Taoism—have long been established in China. The practiced belief of the average Chinese traditionally was an eclectic mixture of all three. Confucianism has no religious organization but consists of a code of ethics and philosophy. Filial piety, benevolence, fidelity, and justice are among its principal virtues. Taoism, a native Chinese religion probably founded in the 6th century B.C. by Lao-tzu, and Buddhism, imported from India during the Han dynasty, both have elaborate rituals. Tradition-minded Chinese base their philosophy of life on Confucianism, but such "old habits" of thought came under strong attack during the mid-1960s and again in the mid-1970s, and have been replaced by aphorisms from the works of Mao Tse-tung. In the early 1950s, about 150 million Chinese were Buddhists and about 30 million Taoists. Muslims, formerly estimated at about 30 million, were reported to total 10 million by the 1953 census. The Roman Catholic Church, with about 2 million adherents in the mid-1970s, declared its independence of the Vatican in 1957; Catholics are now organized in the Patriotic Catholic Association. Protestants are believed to number less than 1 million. Under the Communist government, all Christian missionary activity ceased.

Religious institutions, activities, and beliefs were assaulted by the Red Guards at the beginning of the Cultural Revolution in mid-1966, and since then there has been little evidence of a restoration of religious life in any form.

9 TRANSPORTATION

Railways, roads, and inland waterways all play an important role in China's transport system, which has undergone major growth in the last three decades. China's rail network forms the backbone of the transport system. Chinese railways increased in length from 21,989 km in 1949 to about 44,000 km in 1975. In the rush to expand rail facilities during the Great Leap Forward, rails laid in 1958 totaled 3,500 km; 4,600 km were added in 1959. The construction pace slowed somewhat in the 1960s, but many major projects were completed in the first half of the 1970s, including double-tracking of major lines in the east; the electrification of lines in the west, including the 676-km Paoki-Chengtu link; and the addition of several new trunklines and spurs, many providing service to the country's more remote areas. Increased freight volumes have been achieved by loading freight cars up to 20% over their rated capacity and by using intermediate technology and equipment as an interim solution. Shortages of freight and tank cars continued into the 1970s, although the growth of freight traffic has continued to outpace the growth in rail capacity.

Road transport has become increasingly important. Motor roads grew from about 400,000 km in 1958 to 550,000 km in 1964 and to an estimated 700,000 km by 1973. In 1974, some 10,000 km of short-distance roads linking rural communities were completed. By the mid-1970s, however, no more than 2% of China's roads were paved, while only about one-fourth were improved, all-weather routes. Trucks are important in areas not served by railroads and waterways, especially rural districts not close to railroad stations or river ports. In 1973, annual truck production stood at about 110,000, as compared with 47,000 in 1966.

Inland waterways increased from 150,000 km in 1958 to about 170,000 in 1973, with much of the expansion occurring during the late 1960s. About 25% of the waterways are navigable by modern vessels; wooden junks are used on the remainder. The principal waterways are the Yangtze River, whose main ports are Chungking, Wuhan, Nanking, and Shanghai; the Sungari River in Manchuria, whose principal port is Harbin; and the lower Hsi (West) River, with the main port at Canton. The ancient Grand Canal, rendered impassable by deposits of silt for more than 100 years, has been dredged and rebuilt. By the mid-1970s, the Yangtze had been made navigable westward to Chungking for vessels up to 3,000 tons and for smaller craft as far as Ipin.

China's merchant fleet comprised a gross tonnage of 402,000 tons in 1960, 772,000 tons in 1967, and 2,285,000 tons in 1974 (the 1974 total does not include vessels under 1,000 tons). In 1974, the tanker tonnage was 350,000 tons, as compared with only 90,000 tons in 1967. During 1972-74 alone, China's shipping capacity more than doubled, with major expansions in shipbuilding capacity carried out at Shanghai (which built 12 ships of over 10,000 dwt in 1974), at Talien (an important tanker center), and in Kwangtung Province. China's 335 merchant ships can accommodate about one-third of the country's foreign trade; the balance is divided among ships leased from Hong Kong owners and from other foreign sources. The principal harbors are located at Talien, Tientsin, Shanghai, Tsingtao, and at Whampoa and Canton on the Pearl River. In addition, there are some 90 other secondary and minor ports. Port facilities are being expanded and improved, although shipping delays continue to occur due to the inadequate number of berths available to handle the rapid growth in overseas trade.

In the 1970s, pipelines were becoming increasingly important as a means of transporting oil. In January 1975, a 1,152-km line was completed, linking China's major oil field at Taching to the port of Chinwangtao on the Gulf of Chihli. However, the total length of pipelines in 1975, estimated at about 4,990 km, was far short of requirements.

The Civil Aviation Administration of China (CAAC) operates all domestic and international air services. Operations have grown significantly with the purchase, in the 1970s, of jet aircraft from the US, UK, and other Western sources. By the end of 1975, CAAC had direct flights to some 15 overseas destinations, including Hanoi, Kabul, Karachi, Moscow, Paris, Pyongyang, Rangoon, Tirana, Tehran, Tokyo, and Ulaanbaatar. More than

100 foreign airlines (representing about 30 nations) now serve China, with major service provided by Air France, Iran National Airways, JAL, PIA, and Swissair. International flights are handled at Peking, Shanghai, and Canton. In 1975 there were more than 100 domestic air routes. In 1973, China had a total of 380 civil and military airfields, of which 6 were major, 75 intermediate, and the rest smaller facilities.

10 COMMUNICATIONS

Most communications facilities fall under the authority of the Ministry of Posts and Telecommunications. China had 64,000 post and telegraph offices in 1959. Each county seat had a telegraph office and telephone exchange. By 1961, every rural commune had its own post office. The posts are responsible for the sale and distribution of newspapers and magazines, an important function in a country that relies heavily on these media for mass communications.

By 1975, China had about 1 million telephone outlets. At that time, some 98% of the country's communes were provided with telephone service. In addition, about 80% of the cities had automatic systems. The "telephone conference" is a vital and frequently used service of the telephone network in China, and it is particularly important because of the long distances in the country and relative lack of transport facilities. No attempt is made to provide individuals other than high government officials with telephones for their own personal use. In Canton there is a public telephone in each street serviced by messengers from 8 A.M. to midnight, and they summon the person called to the telephone (a fee of 4 fen is paid by the caller).

China had more than 150 broadcasting stations at the end of 1975 (as compared with only 1 station after World War II). The most important station is Peking's central People's Broadcasting Station; from there, programs are relayed by local stations. By 1974, the annual production of radios reached 12 million. In 1975, China had 37 television transmitting stations, as compared with 7 in 1965. Some 123 relay stations transmit programs originating from Peking to 23 of China's 26 provinces and regions. China produced 115,000 television sets in 1974; in 1975, an estimated 300,000 sets were in use, almost all of them installed in public meeting places, communes, and in government and economic enterprises.

Large segments of the rural population are as yet unreached by radio broadcasts; the government has thus been prompted to establish a massive wired broadcast network. The intensive development of small rural electric power stations made possible the expansion of the wired broadcast network in 1969. In 1974, about 65% of the rural population was linked to a system employing more than 141,000 loudspeakers.

In 1975, Radio Peking was broadcasting overseas via 62 shortwave transmitters in Peking and 3 in Tiranë, Albania. Broadcasts are beamed to virtually all major population regions of the world in more than 40 languages and dialects.

11 HISTORY

The original home of the Chinese people is probably the area of the Wei, Lo, and middle Yellow rivers. According to tradition, the Hsia dynasty (2200–1700 B.C.) constituted the first Chinese state. Its successor, the Shang dynasty (1700–1200 B.C.), which ruled over the valley of the Yellow River, left written records cast in bronze or inscribed on tortoise shell and bone. The Shang was probably conquered by the Western Chou dynasty (1200–800 B.C.), which ruled a prosperous feudal agricultural society. In 770 B.C., the Western Chou abandoned their capital on the site of Sian and established a new capital farther east at Loyang (770–249 B.C.). The new state, known as the Eastern Chou dynasty, produced the great Chinese philosophers K'ung Fu-tzu (Confucius) and Lao-tzu. Between 475 and 221 B.C., the Ch'in dynasty gradually emerged and unified China. Shih Huang Ti (r.246–210 B.C.), the first Ch'in emperor, ended the feudal

states and organized China into a system of prefectures and counties under central control. For defense against nomadic Mongolian tribes, Huang Ti built the first Great Wall. During the period of the Han dynasty (206 B.C.–A.D. 220), China expanded westward, the Huns in the Mongolian plateau were repelled, and contacts were made with Central Asia, the West, and even Rome. Under the later Han, Buddhism was introduced into China. After the Han period, three kingdoms (Wei, Shu, and Wu) contended for power, and nomadic tribes from the north and west raided northern China. From the 4th century on, a series of northern dynasties was set up by the invaders, while several southern dynasties succeeded one another in the Yangtze Valley, with their capital at Nanking. Buddhism flourished during this period, and the arts and sciences were developed in the Yangtze region. The empire was reunited, and work on the Grand Canal was begun under the Sui (581–618) and T'ang (618–907) dynasties.

Under the T'angs, especially under Emperor T'ai Tsung (627–49), China became powerful. Handicrafts and commerce flourished; a system of roads radiated from the capital (at the site of Sian); successful wars were fought in Central Asia and Korea; and China became the cultural and economic center of Asia. Poetry and painting flourished, particularly under Emperor Hsüan Tsung (712–56). A period of partition under the Five Dynasties (907–60) was followed by the Sung dynasty (960–1279), which is distinguished for literature, philosophy, and the invention of movable type, gunpowder, and the magnetic compass. However, Mongol and Tatar tribes forced the Sung to abandon their capital at Kaifeng in 1126 and move it to Hangchow. In the 13th century, the great Mongol hordes under Genghis Khan brought all of China under their control. Under Kublai Khan (1279–94), first ruler of the Mongols' Yüan dynasty (1279–1368), the Grand Canal was completed and a system of relay stations assured safe travel. European merchants, notably Marco Polo, and missionaries reached the Mongol capital of Cambaluc, on the site of Peking. The novel and the drama were promoted. After a long period of unrest, Mongol rule was succeeded by the native Chinese Ming dynasty (1368–1644), which established its capital at Nanking. During the reign of Cheng Tsu (1403–24), the zenith of the Ming empire, the capital was moved to Peking. The Portuguese reached China in 1516, the Spanish in 1557, the Dutch in 1606, and the English in 1637. The Ming dynasty was overthrown by the Manchus, invaders from the northeast, who established the last imperial dynasty, the Ching (1644–1911). The first century and a half of Manchu rule was a period of stability and expansion of power, with outstanding reigns by K'ang Hsi (1662–1722) and Ch'ien Lung (1736–96). The Manchus ruled as conquerors, but adopted Chinese culture, administrative machinery, and laws. Under Manchu rule, the Chinese empire included Manchuria, Mongolia, Tibet, Taiwan, and the Central Asian regions of Turkestan.

By the close of the 18th century, only one port, Canton, was open to merchants from abroad, and trade was greatly restricted. Demands by the British increased trade, and Chinese opposition to opium imports led to the Opium War (1839–42) and China's defeat. By the Treaty of Nanking (1842), the ports of Canton, Amoy, Foochow, Ningpo, and Shanghai were opened, and Hong Kong was ceded to Britain. The Taiping Rebellion (1850–64), aimed at the overthrow of the dynasty, ruined much of southern China. A second war (1856–60) with Britain, joined by France, resulted in the opening of Tientsin to foreign trade. Thereafter, the West dictated the terms to a moribund empire. Russia acquired (1858–60) its Far Eastern territories from China and later obtained Manchurian railroad rights and the lease of Port Arthur (now Lushan). In the Sino-Japanese War of 1895, Japan obtained Taiwan, the opening of additional ports, and the independence of Korea. In 1898, Britain, France, and Germany leased Weihai, Canton, and Chiaohsien (in Shantang Province), respectively. The Boxer Rebellion of 1900 was the last, unsuccessful effort to expel foreign influence. A revolution that finally overthrew Manchu rule began as a mutiny among troops in Wuchang on 10 October 1911. City after city repudiated the Manchus, and in February 1912, the dowager empress signed an abdication document for the infant emperor, Pu Yi. The Chinese republic, ruled first by Sun Yat-sen, followed by Yüan Shih-kai, entered upon a period of internal strife. Following Yüan's death in 1916, the Peking regime passed into the hands of warlords, while in Canton, Sun Yat-sen consolidated his Nationalist Party (Kuomintang). The Peking regime joined World War I on the Allied side in 1917. In 1919, refusal by the Versailles Peace Conference to accede to Chinese demands for the cancellation of various foreign privileges provoked widespread demonstrations throughout China. At the Washington Conference (1922), however, China obtained the abolition of certain foreign rights and the evacuation of the Shantung Peninsula by Japan and the UK.

But the Peking government was rapidly disintegrating. In the south, at Canton, the Kuomintang, in alliance with the Communists, built a strong, disciplined party. After Sun Yat-sen's death in 1925, his successor, Chiang Kai-shek, unified the country under Nationalist rule and made Nanking the capital in 1928. In 1927, a split developed between the Nationalists and the Communists, who sought refuge in southern Kiangsi Province. Their ranks severely depleted by Nationalist attacks, the Communists embarked on their arduous and now historic Long March during 1934–35. Gathering new recruits as they moved north, the Communists eventually reached Shensi Province in northwestern China, where—under the leadership of Mao Tse-tung—they set up headquarters at Yenan. Japan, taking advantage of Chinese dissension, occupied Manchuria in 1931. Increasing Japanese pressure against northern China led, in July 1937, to a Sino-Japanese war, which continued into World War II and saw Japanese forces occupy most of China's major economic areas. Nationalist China, established in the southwestern hinterland with its capital at Chungking, resisted with US and UK aid, while the Communists fought the Japanese in the northwest. Japan evacuated China in 1945, and both Communist and Nationalist forces moved into liberated areas. The rift between the two factions erupted into civil war. Although supported by the US, whose mediation efforts had failed, the Nationalists steadily lost ground through 1948 and 1949, were expelled from the mainland by early 1950, and took refuge on Taiwan. The Communists, under the leadership of Chinese Communist Party (CCP) Chairman Mao Tse-tung, proclaimed the People's Republic of China on 1 October 1949 at their new capital of Peking. A year later, China entered the Korean War (1950–53). In 1950, China invaded Tibet, which had asserted its independence after the overthrow of the Manchu dynasty. Tibet remained under nominal rule of the Dalai Lama while the Chinese delayed social changes designed to integrate Tibet with the People's Republic of China. In 1959, however, after the Dalai Lama's flight to India during a Tibetan revolt against Chinese rule, the Chinese government carried out the changes. Along the coast of Fukien Province, hostilities continued between the Communists and the Nationalists, who still hold, in addition to Taiwan, the Pescadores, Quemoy (near Amoy), and the Matsu Islands (near Foochow).

In domestic affairs, a rapid program of industrialization and socialization up to 1957 was followed in 1958–59 by the "Great Leap Forward," a crash program for drastic increases in output and the development of completely collectivized agricultural communes. The program ended in the "three bitter years" of economic crisis in 1960–62, followed by a period of restoration and retrenchment in economics and politics. After the economy

had recovered in 1965, Mao Tse-tung again started to steer the country into the revolutionary path, and gradually he built up momentum for the Cultural Revolution of 1966–69, the most dramatic and convulsive period in China since 1949. Major developments in the course of the Cultural Revolution were the "February Outline" of February 1966, a discussion sponsored by the subsequently deposed Peking CCP leader P'eng Chen, who attempted to shunt Mao's demands for revolutionization into purely academic and literary fields; the "16 Point Decision" of the CCP Central Committee issued in August 1966, laying down the line for the Cultural Revolution; the decision of January 1967 to request the military to intervene actively in political and civil affairs; the replacement of CCP and government organs by "revolutionary committees" in 1967–68, based on a "tripartite alliance"—comprising new revolutionary rebel organizations and the radical Red Guard youth movement, former officials willing to cooperate, and representatives from the army, whose officials generally were in charge; the removal from power of Liu Shao-ch'i, previously the second man after Mao in the Chinese hierarchy and chairman of the People's Republic, in 1966, and his formal dismissal from all CCP and government posts at a plenary session of the CCP's Central Committee in October 1968; the new CCP constitution drawn up by the Ninth CCP Congress in April 1969, naming Mao as chief and Lin Piao as deputy and as Mao's eventual successor; and the issuance of the new draft state constitution during a CCP Central Committee meeting in August–September 1970, also certifying Mao as the leader and Lin Piao as his deputy and successor. In early 1971, the government claimed that Lin had been killed in a plane crash, allegedly while fleeing to the USSR following an abortive coup. Lin was subsequently made the brunt of ideological attacks asserting he had tried to divert the orthodox reforms of the Cultural Revolution.

In the early 1960s, Chinese troops intermittently fought with Indian border patrols over conflicting territorial claims in Ladakh and the northeastern Indian state of Assam. Mediation attempts failed, but in 1963 the Chinese withdrew from the contested areas they had occupied and war prisoners were repatriated.

Growing discord between China and the Soviet Union became more open in 1960, when the USSR withdrew its scientific and technical advisers from China. Public polemics sharpened in intensity in the succeeding years, and the two powers competed for support in the world Communist movement. In 1969, Chinese and Soviet forces clashed briefly along the Ussuri River frontier in eastern Heilungkiang Province. Active struggles abated thereafter, with China holding that the border question should be settled through peaceful negotiation. Throughout the late 1960s and early 1970s, China played a major role in supporting the Democratic Republic of Viet-Nam (DRV) in the Indochinese conflict.

The first half of the 1970s witnessed dramatic shifts in the course of Chinese diplomacy. In November 1971, the PRC government replaced Taiwan's Nationalist government as China's representative at the UN and on the Security Council (the move followed a General Assembly vote of 76 to 35, with 17 abstentions). Following two preliminary visits by US Secretary of State Henry Kissinger, President Richard M. Nixon journeyed to China on 21 February 1972 for an unprecedented state visit. During the subsequent eight days of talks, the two countries took major steps toward normalization of relations. In a key step, the US announced its intention ultimately to withdraw all of its military forces and installations from Taiwan. In the period following the Nixon visit, US-China trade more than trebled, cultural exchanges were arranged, and (in May 1973) the two countries established liaison offices in each other's capital.

In the mid-1970s, China entered a second period of internal

turbulence. Factionalism reminiscent of the late 1960s reemerged on local levels during 1974 but these disputes did not seem to pierce the central government leadership. In January 1975, the fourth National People's Congress (the first such session since 1964) was convened in Peking and a new constitution—in essence a simplified version of the 1954 document—was adopted. But a period of rapid transition seemed imminent with the death in 1976 of China's two preeminent leaders, Mao and Chou En-lai. In October, Mao's position as Communist Party chairman was conferred on Hua Kuo-feng, a moderate who had served as acting premier since 7 February.

12 GOVERNMENT

In accordance with both the 1954 and 1975 constitutions, the highest organ of state power is the National People's Congress (NPC), in which legislative power is vested. The constitution stipulates, however, that the Congress is to function under the direction of the Chinese Communist Party (CCP). The NPC consists of deputies elected by provinces, cities under central government rule, the armed forces, and Chinese residents abroad. The provinces elect 1 deputy for every 400,000 persons, but at least 10 deputies from each province; cities under central government rule elect 1 deputy for every 50,000 persons. Ethnic minorities are represented by 300 deputies, the armed forces by 120 deputies, and overseas Chinese by 30 deputies. The 1975 constitution provides that the NPC be indirectly elected for a term of five years and meet at least once a year. The third Congress, elected in 1962, held only one session, ending in January 1965. The fourth Congress, with 2,885 deputies, convened in January 1975. Specific NPC functions are to amend the constitution, pass laws, and examine and approve the state budget and final accounts. The Standing Committee, the NPC's permanent working organ, appoints ambassadors, receives foreign ambassadors, and ratifies or nullifies treaties with other countries. Citizens over age 18 can vote and stand for election.

The 1975 constitution does not specifically provide for a head of state, although that function in effect falls to the chairman of the CCP, to whose offices was added that of commander-in-chief of the armed forces. The State Council, the executive organ of the NPC, consists of a premier, 12 deputy premiers, ministers, and heads of other major government agencies. The State Council issues administrative regulations and both formulates and executes the economic plan and the state budget.

Except for disruptions brought on during the Cultural Revolution, the CCP has played a decisive role in formulating broad and detailed government policies and supervising their implementation at all levels of administration. The actual performance of day-to-day government work by CCP organizations, however, has traditionally been opposed by most Chinese political theorists, although instances of this practice have occurred at different times in various localities. Party supervision of government is maintained not only through placement of CCP members in key posts, but also through specialized organs of the Central Committee of the CCP, which focus their attention on given subjects (e.g., propaganda, rural work). The CCP also forms branches within individual government units as well as in factories, communes, schools, shops, neighborhoods, and military units. The Cultural Revolution had a strong impact on central government ministries. By the early 1970s, 30 of the 49 State Council ministers and commissioners had lost their positions, and ultimately the 6 staff offices and 49 ministries and commissions of the State Council were reduced to 29 units. Overall supervision of the State Council was put under the "revolutionary leading group" composed of military representatives, government officials, and representatives of newly formed mass organizations.

13 POLITICAL PARTIES

The Chinese Communist Party (CCP) has been the ruling political organization in China since 1949. Eight other minor parties have existed, since 1949, as members of a United Front, but their existence has been purely nominal.

At its Ninth Congress in 1969, the CCP drew up a new party constitution, which stated that Mao Tse-tung was the leader of the CCP; the CCP itself was characterized as "the core of leadership of the Chinese people." At its Tenth Congress, held during August 1973, the CCP elected a new, enlarged Central Committee of 195 full members and 124 alternates.

In 1974, the CCP reported a membership of 28 million persons. Party membership is open to "revolutionary elements" such as workers, poor peasants, lower-middle peasants, and military personnel. Applicants must be recommended by two CCP members and approved by the local and next higher CCP branch. Party members are specifically permitted to "bypass the intermediate leadership and report directly to higher levels, up to and including the Central Committee and the Chairman." The top-level organization in the CCP is the 21-member Political Bureau (Politburo) of the Central Committee and the Bureau's five-man Standing Committee (the numbers are subject to change as the membership fluctuates). Triennial local congresses are called for at the county level and above and from People's Liberation Army (PLA) regimental unit levels and up. Party committees at all levels and in army units elect their own standing committees, secretaries, and deputy secretaries. CCP branches are formed in factories, mines, people's communes, offices, schools, neighborhoods, and other basic units.

During the Cultural Revolution of the late 1960s, the role of the revolutionary vanguard passed over to the Red Guards (since disbanded) and revolutionary rebels, and the role of ultimate arbiter of affairs to the PLA. The CCP organization was profoundly shaken, and the process of rebuilding under a shifting leadership was still under way in the mid-1970s.

14 LOCAL GOVERNMENT

China consists of 21 provinces, 5 autonomous regions, and 3 centrally administered cities. Provinces and autonomous regions, in turn, are divided into "special districts," counties (hsien), and cities under provincial jurisdiction, as well as into autonomous minor regions (chou) and autonomous counties, where non-Chinese minority groups reside. Counties, autonomous counties, and autonomous chou are divided into townships (hsiang), autonomous townships (for small minority groups), towns, and rural communes.

During the Cultural Revolution, local people's congresses were replaced by revolutionary committees. By the end of 1969, the task of transition had been completed in 95% of the local units from the subprovincial special districts down to the counties, communes, and the commune production brigades and teams. Accompanying this changeover was a stringent reduction in government personnel. The revolutionary committees were given permanent status by the 1975 constitution. The committees are to be elected by and responsible to the people's congress at the corresponding level, and they are also responsible to the next higher revolutionary committee and ultimately to the State Council in Peking.

15 JUDICIAL SYSTEM

According to the 1975 constitution, judicial authority is exercised by the Supreme People's Court, local people's courts at various levels, and special people's courts. Local courts are responsible and accountable to the legislature and the government unit on the corresponding level. The exercise of prosecution and trial authority must involve the general public in judicial processes. Mass discussion and criticism are to be conducted in "serious counterrevolutionary and criminal cases," and no citizen may be arrested except by decision of a people's court, or with the sanction of public security organs.

The president of the Supreme People's Court and other

members of the court are elected by the NPC for four-year terms. Local people's courts are elected by local bodies for four-year terms. The chief prosecutor, designated by the NPC for a four-year term, appoints prosecutors at local levels.

16 ARMED FORCES

Under the 1975 constitution, the military has been placed directly under the command of the chairman of the CCP. In 1955, China adopted a conscription law, subsequently modified to provide for 2–4 years' service in the army; 3–5 years' in the air force, coast guard, and seaborne security force; and 4–6 years' in the navy. The country is divided into 11 military regions, each region in turn divided into 2 or 3 military districts. In 1975, the army, officially called the People's Liberation Army (PLA), consisted of 197 divisions: 125 infantry, 20 artillery, 7 armored, 4 cavalry, and 41 engineers. PLA strength in 1975 was 2.8 million. In addition, there is a huge civilian militia, whose "basic members" total about 300 million.

The Chinese navy consists of 230,000 personnel (including 30,000 naval air personnel and 28,000 marines) and 1,145 vessels. Of these, 737 are military craft and 408 are miscellaneous boats (tugs, depot ships, oilers, supply ships). There are no aircraft carriers or heavy fighting ships. Lighter ships include 6 destroyers, 20 destroyer-escorts, 20 antisubmarine craft, and a fleet of 52 submarines. There is 1 long-range diesel-electric submarine capable of firing ballistic missiles with a 380-mile range. The naval air force has 600 combat aircraft, including 100 torpedo craft and light bombers. The air force in 1975 was estimated to have 220,000 personnel and 3,800 combat aircraft, mostly jet fighters, but also included a bomber fleet of more than 460 planes. Soviet-type fighters and transports have been manufactured under license in China.

By the mid-1970s, China had developed a sizable tactical nuclear capacity. China's first nuclear test occurred on 16 October 1964 and consisted of a 20-kiloton bomb exploded at the test site. A series of 15 tests followed, including a 3-megaton hydrogen bomb test in the atmosphere in October 1970; the last occurred in June 1974. On 24 April 1970, China orbited a 173-kg satellite which broadcast the Chinese national anthem; the satellite was twice the weight of the first Soviet Sputnik of 1957. China's nuclear stockpile in 1975 was thought to include 200–300 fission and fusion warheads, with a variety of missiles, including a multistage ICBM with an estimated range of 3,500 miles.

China pays great attention to militia training in schools, factories, and rural communes. In schools the emphasis is on basic theoretical training. In factories, the accent is on production, ideological education, and field camping during holidays. In rural areas militia work is active in agricultural production and construction.

In the absence of public budget figures since 1960, the International Institute of Strategic Studies estimated that China's defense expenditures were $6 billion in 1966 and $7.5 billion in 1968. Soviet reports put the totals higher: $6 billion in 1966, $8 billion in 1967, $10 billion in 1968. Western estimates of China's defense expenditures for 1973 ranged as high as $15 billion, but a decrease in arms expenditures during 1971–74 has been noted.

17 MIGRATION

The migration of millions of Chinese reached its peak in the 1920s, when thousands of farmers and fishermen from the southeastern coastal provinces settled in other countries of Southeast Asia. In 1949, after the Communist victory, some 2 million civilians and 700,000 military personnel were evacuated to Taiwan.

As of 1975, some 21,485,000 Chinese lived abroad: 20,400,000 in Asian countries and territories, 800,000 in the Americas, 152,000 in Europe, 67,000 in Australasia, and 66,000 in Africa. In Asia, Hong Kong had the largest number of overseas Chinese (hua-ch'iao), 4,300,000; Malaysia had about 4,000,000; Thailand,

3,000,000; Indonesia, 2,800,000; and Singapore, 1,700,000. Outside of Asia, the largest Chinese groups were in the US (450,000) and Canada (70,000). According to 1975 estimates, the proportion of Chinese in Singapore was 76%; in Malaysia, 33%; and in Thailand, 7%. Since in many places abroad the Chinese population has been growing at a rate faster than that of the local non-Chinese population, most countries have been trying to curtail the entrance of new Chinese immigrants. Emigration from China under the PRC government has been limited to refugees who reach Hong Kong.

Immigration is limited to the return of overseas Chinese. In 1958–62, more than 100,000 overseas Chinese returned to China (most of them returned from Indonesia in 1961) and were resettled on state farms especially set up for them.

Within China, the "down to the countryside" movement has removed tens of millions of students, officials, peasant migrants, and unemployed from cities and relocated them in rural areas, border regions, mountainous and hilly lands, and other less-developed and sparsely settled regions. Generally the movement is from the densely populated southeast to the west and north. An estimated 40 million persons were sent down before the Cultural Revolution and another 20 million from mid-1966 to 1970. Organizational streamlining during the Cultural Revolution may have reduced office staffs by 70% and sent 5 million officials down to the countryside to take part in production. Some officials were moved out as part of their redemption following criticism during the Cultural Revolution; others went on a temporary rotating basis for manual labor or on-the-spot observations. In the 1970s, bureaucrats, students, and other urban dwellers continued to be mobilized into production brigades for fixed periods of manual labor in the countryside. The goals of these programs have been to provide manpower to participate in agricultural production, to reclaim land in remote areas, to settle borderlands for economic and defense reasons, and, as has been the policy for three decades, to increase the proportion of Han Chinese in ethnic minority areas. Another purpose of this migration policy has been to relieve urban shortages of food, housing, and services, and reduce future urban population growth by removing large numbers of the 16–30-year age group.

18 INTERNATIONAL COOPERATION

In November 1971, the People's Republic of China replaced the Republic of China (Taiwan) as the representative of China in the UN. As of 1976, the PRC belonged to several specialized agencies, among them FAO, WHO, UNESCO, ICAO, and UPU. China is also a member of the Afro-Asian Solidarity Conference, the ICAI, ICMMP, IHB, IRU, the International Sugar Council, the International Union for the Publication of Custom Tariffs, and the PC of A.

Nearly since its inception, the PRC has maintained a varied and extensive program of overseas aid. From November 1950 to January 1952 (during the Korean conflict), Peking gave the DRK RMB18,285,000 ($7,430,000) as "comfort money." The extension of economic credits and grants to all countries from 1963 to 1965 totaled more than $2 billion. Of this amount, $815 million went to underdeveloped countries in Asia ($410 million), Africa ($264 million), and the Middle East ($141 million). The remainder went to Communist-aligned countries, including the DRV, $457 million; DRK, $330 million; Albania, $164 million; Cuba, $100 million; and Hungary, $57.5 million. During 1966–74, overseas aid totaled approximately $2 billion, with substantial amounts going to the DRV in the course of the Viet-Nam conflict. During the first half of the 1970s alone, China supplied the DRV with more than 1 million tons of rice, 500,000 tons of petroleum, and some $300 million in other forms of assistance. In 1975, China granted $1 billion in aid to the new government of Kampuchea (formerly Cambodia). Most aid from China has taken the form of direct supply of commodities and equipment. Loans are frequently provided interest-free and many have long-term repayment periods as well as long grace periods. China also sends large numbers of semiskilled Chinese workers and technical personnel to assist in public works projects abroad.

As of the end of 1970, the PRC had established diplomatic ties with 54 nations (66 countries recognized the Nationalist government on Taiwan and 10 maintained ties with neither government). By 1976, about 110 nations had extended full diplomatic recognition to the PRC, with a parallel drop to about 35 in the number recognizing Taiwan's government. Entering the second half of the decade, the PRC was approaching normal relations with nearly all of its Asian neighbors, including Japan, India, Pakistan, Malaysia, Thailand, and Singapore. Only the Republic of Korea appeared firmly detached from rapprochement.

China has accorded diplomatic or quasi-diplomatic status to representatives of the Palestine Liberation Organization, and the pro-Communist insurgency groups in Thailand and Malaysia. During the Viet-Nam conflict, the south Vietnamese Provisional Revolutionary Government maintained offices in Peking; in 1970, Kampuchea's Prince Sihanouk took up residence in China and established an exile Royal Government of National Union of Kampuchea in Peking.

[19] ECONOMY

Traditional China was predominantly agricultural. Adhering to farming patterns developed over a score of centuries, China could sustain a harsh level of self-sufficiency, given surcease from natural calamities. For almost three decades prior to 1949, the incessant ravages of civil disorder, foreign (principally Japanese) aggression, and gross economic neglect virtually decimated China's frail abilities to sustain itself. The first task of the new PRC government, thus, was restoration to prewar levels of the flow of natural resources. By the early 1950s, the government had succeeded in halting massive starvation. Virtually all means of production and distribution were brought under state control, and vast parcels of land were redistributed to the peasantry. During 1953–57, China's first five-year plan introduced a stress on heavy industry. Economic development was aided by imports of machinery and other industrial equipment from the USSR and East European countries. In return, China exported agricultural produce to them. A major geological prospecting drive resulted in the discovery of mineral deposits that provided a major thrust toward industrialization.

The "Great Leap Forward" of 1958–59 in industry and agriculture initially produced sharp gains, but the zeal for increased quotas quickly resulted in undue strain on resources and quality. The agricultural sector, its collectivization virtually completed by 1965, was reorganized in the late 1950s into larger commune units. The Great Leap was followed by "three bitter years" (1959/60–1961/62) of economic crisis brought on by bad harvests and the economic dislocation caused during the previous period. By 1961, the GNP had fallen to an estimated $81 billion, roughly the level reached in 1955. By 1965, however, a readjustment of expectations coupled with a careful program of industrial investment caused the economy to recover its former production pace. China's trade patterns, meanwhile, had shifted radically away from the USSR and toward Japan and Western Europe. China's proportion of trade with the Communist states fell from 69% in 1959 to 26% by 1966. Although aggregate agricultural output and yield per acre had gone up, the expansion in agriculture lagged behind that of industry, necessitating huge grain imports from the West. Beginning in 1961, China had to import 5 to 6 million tons of grains each year from Canada, Australia, and other countries at an annual cost of about $300–400 million. The economic impact of the Cultural Revolution of 1966–69 was first felt in transport, industry, and public services. Factional fighting and other disruptions resulted

in a drop in industrial production in 1967 estimated at between 10% and 20%. Good weather during 1966–68 prevented an agricultural slump but did not yield the abundance that might otherwise have occurred.

During the first half of the 1970s, China's economy registered solid gains in virtually all sectors. The country remained, by most measures, underdeveloped, and living standards were relatively spartan. Nonetheless, China was approaching levels of self-sufficiency—in food, primary industrial materials, and manufactured goods—far in excess of what had ever been achieved previously. Overall growth in trade and industry was spurred by dramatic increases in China's petroleum output. By 1975, the nation's oil fields—mostly located in remote northwest regions—were producing 1.5 million barrels a day (compared with 100,000 barrels daily in 1960), providing ample quantities for export to Japan and elsewhere. In 1974, GNP stood at $223 billion, reflecting a 120% increase in industrial production since 1970. Agriculture, which grew by only about 20% during the same period, was keeping pace—however marginally—with population expansion. China's ambitious fourth five-year plan (1971–75), which had aimed for an annual growth rate of 7.5% in national income, was pronounced successful, and the government subsequently set an annual growth rate of 15% for the remainder of the decade, a rate calculated to double the national income by 1980. With natural resources comparable to those of a major industrial power and the consumption levels of an underdeveloped country, China appeared capable of emerging from the last quarter of the century as one of the world's formidable economic entities.

[20] INCOME

During the first five-year plan (1953–57), GNP (at 1952 prices) increased from RMB67.86 billion ($28,275 million) in 1952 to RMB102.42 billion ($42,675 million) in 1957, a rise of 50.9%. In the same period, the value of industrial output rose more than 118%: from RMB34.32 billion ($14,300 million) to RMB74.94 billion ($31,225 million). This remarkable rate of growth was made possible only through the fullest exploitation of the existing capital stock and the maintenance of a high investment rate. Thus, capital accumulation rose by 101.3% from 1952 to 1956, its share in the total national income increasing from 18.2% in 1952 to 26.1% in 1956. Institutional changes under the five-year plan brought about a sharp redistribution in the sources of the national income. The state-owned sector's contribution to national income rose from 19% in 1952 to 33% in 1957; the cooperative sector rose from 1.4% to 55.9%, as a result mainly of the collectivization of private peasant households; the joint state-private sector rose from 0.6% to 8%, while the private sector dropped from 72% to 3%, and the so-called capitalist sector fell from 7% to 0.1%.

In 1960 it was reported that the major goals of the second five-year plan (1958–62) had been fulfilled three years ahead of schedule. The value of industrial and agricultural production in 1959 was said to have totaled RMB241.3 billion (about $96.5 billion), an increase of 31.1% over the 1958 total. Investment in capital construction totaled RMB26.7 billion (about $10.7 billion), an increase of 24.5% over 1958. The national income increased 21.6% and the state revenue amounted to RMB54 billion (about $21.6 billion), an increase of 29%.

Virtually no official national accounts statistics have been issued since 1960; thus, estimates of national income have been meaningful primarily to specialists who are able to evaluate the procedures by which the estimates are derived. Available indicators, however, provide general clues to the rate of growth of China's income, even in the absence of substantive official data. Western calculations (in 1973 dollars) placed the 1961 GNP at $82 billion; the total rose to $145 billion by 1966 and, after a slight decline during 1967–68, reached $179 billion in 1970. During 1970-74, the GNP grew at an average rate of more than 6% (compared with an annual average of 5.2% during 1958-74 overall), reaching an estimated $223 billion. In 1974, per capita GNP stood at $243, as compared with $118 in 1961 and $214 in 1970. In 1975, Western sources estimated the GDP to be distributed as follows: industry, 38%; agriculture, 37%; and transport and other services, 25%.

²¹LABOR

In 1974, China's economically active population was estimated at 350 million, or about 70% of the total population in the 15-64 age group. Upwards of 85% of the economically active sector was engaged in agricultural pursuits. Since 1957, the state has increasingly resorted to administrative allocation for job assignments, discarding prior reliance on incentives for attracting workers to certain sectors.

The government has conceded, for the present period, the need to maintain wage differentials in accordance with the dictum "to each according to his labor." The differentials remain quite low by Western standards, however: In the 1970s, the highest paid industrial employees (including management and technicians) earned an average of about five times the salary of the lowest-paid employee. Bonuses, an important production incentive prior to the Cultural Revolution, have since been eliminated in favor of "nonmaterial" incentives, such as rewarding outstanding workers with such honorific designations as "model worker" or "hero of labor." In 1971-74, the average wage for mining and industrial workers ranged from about RMB40 to RMB85 per month. The real income for agricultural workers has traditionally run 10-70% below that of industrial workers, although the gap has been narrowed somewhat by the improvement of benefits to farmers since the Cultural Revolution. Wages have been increased gradually over the years, the national average having grown by about 50% during 1952-71.

Although wage scales in China remain low, the range of benefits has been expanding. Male workers are eligible to retire between ages 55 and 60, female workers five years earlier. The state provides pensions at a rate of 60-70% of the last month's salary (70-85% in the case of government employees and cadres). Workers may receive six months' sick leave at 60-100% of salary. For work-related total disability, workers are entitled to lifetime compensation of 60% of their last salary. Maternity leave at full pay is provided for 56 days. In addition, numerous health, day-care, and educational benefits are provided free of charge. In urban areas, housing rentals rarely exceed 5% of the monthly wage.

On 27 December 1966, forces within the Cultural Revolution dissolved the All-China Federation of Trade Unions, previously the only nationwide labor organization. Some of its functions have been carried on by "revolutionary" organizations set up in factories, and by workers' congresses and trade unions organized on municipal and provincial levels. Strikes and lockouts are outlawed; they were, in fact, the exception until the advent of the Cultural Revolution, when they became widespread. Other labor problems encountered during the Cultural Revolution were "economism" among workers (i.e., emphasis on wages, bonuses, awards, and benefits, and appropriating factory funds and facilities under various pretexts); breakdowns in labor discipline (referred to as "anarchy"); disorders from fights between rival workers' factions (called "factionalism"); and slowness in developing sensitivity to nonmaterial incentives, as required by the current ideology. Signs of labor unrest stemming from low wages and many of these same issues reemerged during 1974, bringing on notable disruptions among railway workers; in 1975, labor clashes in Hangchow led to the calling in of the military.

²²AGRICULTURE

With some 85% of the population engaged in farming, agriculture forms the foundation of China's economy.

Limitations in topography, soil, and climate, however, have restricted cultivation to only about 11% of the total land area (107 million hectares). Despite recent advances—record grain crops totaling an officially estimated 259 million tons were produced in 1974—the enormous pressures of feeding and clothing China's vast and growing population remain among the country's most compelling concerns. Nevertheless, intensive methods have enabled China to become the world's leading producer of a variety of food crops, including rice, soybeans, millet, barley, sorghum, sweet potatoes, and peanuts.

The PRC government expropriated large landholdings in a land reform carried out in 1951-52 and redistributed the land among poor peasants. The land reform was followed by collectivization. In 1953 and 1954, mutual-aid teams were organized in rural areas. Subsequently, cooperatives were established. By the end of 1954, 11.5% of all peasant households had been collectivized; by 1955, 65%; and by 1965, 99%. The Chinese collective farms had virtually no mechanical equipment, but the peasants pooled their labor in various projects, such as water management, which had been beyond the capacity of individual peasants. In 1958, the collective farms were merged into larger units as people's communes. The communes are a type of rural production organization that is concerned not only with agricultural output, but also with subsidiary farm activities, such as light industry and handicrafts, usually produced for local consumption.

Far-reaching changes in the organization of communes took place during 1961-62. In 1961, the production brigade (the major division of a commune), of which there were about 750,000 in 1974, was regarded as the "basic accounting unit" and in 1962, the production team (the subdivision of a commune), of which there were 5 million in 1974, became the unit. This means that the teams, themselves consisting of a grouping of peasant households, operate the farms under the nominal supervision of the brigades. Production teams function as semiautonomous units making basic decisions on production and distribution of income. The commune mainly exercises the functions of a township government. By 1974 there were about 50,000 communes, each with an average of 14,700 persons on a farming area of 2,000 hectares. Each commune was subdivided into an average of about 15 production brigades, 100 production teams, and 3,300 households. Households, the final link in the system, are permitted the use of private plots, which comprise about 5% of the arable land assigned to a team. In the mid-1970s, these private holdings accounted for the bulk of the country's production of vegetables, fruits, and hogs, and were making important contributions in poultry and cash crops such as tobacco and oilseeds. Policy changes during 1961-63 reduced the size of the communes and thus increased their number from 26,000 to 74,000 by 1964. In the late 1960s, a number of mergers took place, so that there were about 50,000 communes in 1974.

The principal crops are grains (rice in the south and wheat in the north) and cotton. Paddy rice accounted for about 20% of croplands in grain and 44% of grain output as of 1973. Production of grain (including corn, wheat, sorghum, barley, oats, and millet) and sweet and white potatoes rose from 154.5 million tons in 1952 to an estimated 259 million tons in 1974. Significant growth was registered by wheat during the 1970s, with winter wheat now being grown in the south and central regions and in the North China Plain, while spring plantings are taking place in the northeast. The total wheat crop in 1973 was estimated at 35 million tons (compared with an annual average of 22 million during 1961-65), ranking China third in the world after the USSR and US. Ginned cotton production rose from 1.3 million tons in 1952 to 2.5 million in 1974. Other important crops are jute, kenaf tobacco, cane and beet sugar, peanuts (2.7 million tons in 1973), and rapeseed. The production of soybeans rose from 8.6 million tons in 1964 to 11.8 million tons in 1973. Sugar production is being expanded, having reached 1.8 million tons in 1974. Tea production has dropped sharply from its 1932 peak, when 225,000 tons were produced, but has been rising again in recent years. Silk production also has dropped from its 1931 peak of 220,800 tons of mulberry-grown silk and 93,500 tons of oak-grown tussah silk.

Although grain output during 1957 increased by about 40%, the total land area under cultivation is thought to have remained roughly at the same level, about 107 million hectares. Thus, land improvement apparently has taken priority over the clearing of new areas. In addition, gains in converting marginal lands are thought to have been offset by encroachments on farmlands by industry and mining. However, since the warm, moist climate in the southern part of China makes possible double or even triple cropping in the course of a year, the effective area actually sown in crops each year is much larger than the actual area suggests. Multiple cropping is facilitated by irrigation. The irrigated area is estimated to have increased from about 21 million hectares in 1952 to about 44 million hectares in 1973. In the north, about 10 million hectares have been irrigated in recent years, mainly in the North China Plain, through the use of tube wells. Despite massive labor campaigns, however, irrigation in the north remains far from adequate. In sharp contrast, the irrigation capacity in southern China—where irrigation systems have been operative for more than 1,000 years—was approaching its limits (through conventional means) by the 1970s.

Agricultural setbacks during the Great Leap, coupled with widespread drought, floods, and a combination of other natural calamities, severely reduced agricultural production during the 1959–61 period, when an estimated 65% of arable land was affected. During the last two decades, however, large-scale efforts in flood control have greatly reduced the threat of major destruction from that source. In addition, the use of rationing during lean periods has all but eliminated the likelihood of famine. Output resumed a slow but steady growth rate of 1.7% annually during 1967–74. The expansion of food production, however, still remains precariously close to the growth rate in population, compelling a program of imports. Since 1961, China has been forced to buy from 3 to 7 million tons of grain every year, chiefly from Canada, Australia, the US, France, and Argentina. Up to the end of 1975, these imports had totaled an estimated 78 million tons, with a peak of 7.7 million tons imported in 1973; in 1975, grain purchases totaled 4.4 million tons.

The expansion of fertilizer production is viewed as a key to major growth in the agricultural sector. Toward this end, China during 1972–74 contracted for the purchase of 13 large urea plants (at a total cost of $442 million) from Japan, the US, and Western Europe. It was expected that output from these plants could result in a 30% growth in grain output during 1974–80, with the effect of transforming China into a net exporter of food. In 1974, China produced 24.8 million tons of chemical fertilizers, while importing 5.7 million tons.

23 ANIMAL HUSBANDRY

Except in outlying areas, nearly all of China's arable land is devoted to crops. Most agricultural communes, however, also support the raising of large quantities of hogs and poultry. Pasture land for the grazing of sheep and cattle accounts for 3.24 million sq km, or 34% of China's total area; the four major pasture areas are Sinkiang, Kansu, Tsinghai, and Inner Mongolia. China had an estimated 63.3 million head of cattle and 72 million sheep in 1973, both relatively small numbers in view of the vast reaches of pasture land potentially available. Sheep are raised in the western grasslands by nomads. The nomads are being persuaded to form permanent settlements in order to increase livestock productivity.

China leads the world in swine production, the total number of

hogs reaching 235.8 million in 1973, as compared with 89.8 million in 1952. Hogs and pork products are becoming valuable export earners. In 1973, meat and live animal exports were valued at $485 million, comprising 10% of total exports.

24 FISHING

With a coastline of 5,774 km adjoining a broad continental shelf, China has excellent coastal fisheries. A vast number of inland lakes and ponds, covering a total area of about 260,000 sq km, adds to the fishing potential. The principal fisheries are located on the coast of southern and southeastern China, in the provinces of Kwangtung, Fukien, and Chekiang. The total catch of aquatic products was estimated at about 7 million tons in 1972. By mid-1961, the country's freshwater fish-breeding grounds had increased tenfold since 1949, to a total area of 20 million hectares.

25 FORESTRY

Centuries of dense habitation have virtually denuded the land mass of most of eastern China. As a direct result, flooding and soil erosion have traditionally wreaked havoc on Chinese agriculture. The forested area is now estimated at about 90 million hectares, or about 10% of the total territory of China. Total timber stands are estimated at 6 billion cu meters, but most of the forests are in remote regions, and lack of transportation has thwarted exploitation. Coniferous stands, which yield the most valuable commercial timber, are found mainly in Manchuria and adjoining parts of Inner Mongolia. Deciduous trees are felled in Szechwan and Yünnan. Total timber production in 1973 was estimated at 53 million cu meters, as compared with 11.2 million cu meters in 1952. Paper production rose from 603,000 tons in 1952 to 2 million tons in 1970. Paper production has benefited from the substitution of rice straw and other non-wood materials for wood pulp. Special forestry products originating in southwestern China include tung oil, cassia oil, and aniseed oil.

The government has, from the start of its first five-year plan in 1953, given high priority to campaigns for afforestation. By 1957, 11.29 million hectares had been planted. Many of the trees, however, were lost due to neglect after planting. Thus, while mass afforestation programs have continued in many regions, greater care is being taken to nurture trees through their early stages. Technical support is provided by a variety of forestry bureaus and by the staffs of state-owned tree plantations.

26 MINING

Intensive geologic exploration has yielded greatly expanded mineral reserves. This increase in known subsurface resources is reflected in production rises for China's most important mineral products, including coal, petroleum, oil shale, iron ore, copper, lead, zinc, tungsten, mercury, antimony, tin, and molybdenum. Virtually all provinces contain coal deposits, and production was said to have risen from 66.5 million tons in 1952 to 220 million tons in 1965 and to 389 million tons in 1974.

While coal production underwent a decline in the 1970s—with shortages reported in certain regions—oil output continued on a dramatic upward trend. Crude-oil production increased from 8.7 million tons in 1964 to 65.3 million tons in 1974, at which point China ranked as the world's thirteenth-largest producer. By 1980, production was expected to reach 200 million tons. Proven reserves have been put at 1.1 billion tons, with estimated potential reserves thought to range from 5.9 to 7.6 billion tons. About 30% of current volume is attributable to the recent exploitation of the vast Taching oil field in Manchuria's Sung-Liao Basin. The Taching fields have been publicized as the model of an industrial unit, combining the features of town and country in its layout and in its people's occupations and life-style. Other productive fields are in the western provinces of Kansu, Tsinghai, and Szechwan, and in the Singkiang-Uigur Autonomous Region. In addition, offshore deposits are now being explored in the Gulf of Chihli. By the mid-1970s, China no longer had to rely on oil imports; petroleum exports had, in fact, emerged as a major source of foreign exchange earnings. Domestic consumption of petroleum rose from 3.3 million tons in 1957 to 60 million tons in 1974; crude-oil exports, virtually nonexistent before 1973, exceeded 4 million tons in 1974, and were estimated at more than 8 million tons in 1975, earning some $700 million. By 1974, China's annual refining capacity was put at 47 million tons, sufficient to keep pace with local needs. Pipelines (more than 2,000 km added since 1970) and transport facilities are also being rapidly expanded.

Natural-gas output has also risen dramatically in recent years, owing largely to the discovery and exploitation of vast deposits in Szechwan Province during the late 1950s and early 1960s. By 1974, total national production had reached 60 billion cu meters, ranking China fifth in the world after the US, USSR, Canada, and the Netherlands. Some 87% of gas production comes from Szechwan, most of the remainder being oil-associated gas. In the 1970s, additional gas fields were being developed in Chekiang Province.

Iron ore production reached an estimated 17.7 million tons in 1957, 38.3 million tons in 1965, and 99.9 million tons in 1974, but the metal content of the ore is relatively low (less than 40% on the average) and requires concentration. Nevertheless, quantities have been sufficient to supply the country's sizable steel industry. Virtually all iron mining is presently carried out north of the Yangtze River. China is a major producer of tin (20,000 tons estimated in 1973), mined chiefly in Yünnan, tungsten (10,100 tons, mainly from Kiangsi), and antimony (12,000 tons, from Hunan).

Other important minerals and their estimated 1973 production were bauxite, 600,000 tons; manganese, 300,000 tons; lead, 100,000 tons; and copper, 100,000 tons. Phosphate rock production in 1973 was put at 3 million tons.

27 ENERGY AND POWER

Although the rivers provide a vast hydroelectric potential (an estimated 300 million kw), only a small part has been developed. Traditionally, coal has been the major primary-energy source in China, with auxiliary fuels provided by brushwood, rice husks, dung, and other noncommercial materials. China's recent emergence as a major oil and natural-gas producer, however, is producing significant changes in primary-energy patterns. In 1957, coal accounted for 94.6% of the nation's energy output, with hydroelectric plants taking up 2.5%, petroleum 1.9%, and natural gas 1%; by 1975, coal's proportion had fallen to 62.7% of the total, while natural gas made up 17.7%, petroleum 17%, and hydroelectric facilities 2.5%. Total energy output during the 1957–74 period increased from 102.2 million to 458.6 million coal-ton equivalents.

The abundance of coal continues to provide cheap thermal power for electric plants. Total production reached a peak of 47 billion kwh in 1960. After a decline in 1961–64, output recovered to 40 billion kwh in 1965; by 1974, production had soared to 108 billion kwh; of this total, some 85% was produced thermally. Large thermal power plants are situated in Manchuria and along the east coast of China, where industry is concentrated, as well as in new inland industrial centers, such as Chungking, Taiyüan, Sian, and Lanchow. In accord with the drive toward greater self-sufficiency in rural industrialization, some 50,000 small hydroelectric stations had been brought into operation by the mid-1970s, mainly owned and operated by communes. In 1965, 1,300 of China's 2,126 counties had electric power, and rural consumption was estimated to equal 25 times the 1957 total. A 220,000-volt power transmission line has been constructed in northeast China, tying in with the Peking power grid. Principal hydroelectric stations are situated on the Sungari River in Manchuria and on the Yalu River.

In the 1970s, China turned increasingly to foreign sources for the purchase of power-generating equipment. During 1972–75, China acquired three complete electrical plants from the US and 46 generators from Italy. Major individual acquisitions included Soviet equipment for construction of a series of 700-Mw power plants (1972); a 500-Mw thermal plant, purchased from Japan (1973) at a cost of $72 million; and a 650-Mw plant purchased from Italy (1974) and costing $86 million.

28 INDUSTRY

China has achieved a rapid increase in the gross value of industrial output. This value, which includes both heavy and light industries as well as handicraft production, rose by an annual average of 13% during the first 25 years (1949–74) of the People's Republic. The greatest surge in growth occurred during the first decade—the rate averaging 22% annually during 1949–60. During 1961–74, the yearly growth rate fell to about 6%, a function in part of the disruptions brought on by the collapse of the Great Leap (which accompanied the withdrawal of Soviet technicians in mid-1960;) and by work stoppages and transport disruptions during the Cultural Revolution. Although central planning resumed in the 1970s, industrial growth was hampered by the need to shift sizable resources to basic agricultural production. In 1974, industry expanded by only 4%, with further impediments brought on by work stoppages and absenteeism by workers complaining of low wages. Emphasis on the development of heavy industry and consumer goods has affected the total value of industrial output. While the value of producer goods in 1952 accounted for 39.7% of the total value of industry, and consumer goods for 60.3%, the ratio by 1958 had changed to 57% for producer goods and 43% for consumer goods. Throughout 1960–74, producer goods remained dominant, outstripping growth in the consumer-goods sector in virtually every year. By 1974, the gross value of industrial output stood at RMB369,256 million (RMB78,390 million in 1957), of which producer goods accounted for 61.7%, and consumer goods 38.3%.

Shanghai, traditionally the hub of China's industrial activity, remains the country's preeminent manufacturing center. Shanghai leads in the production of machine tools, diesel engines, steel, bicycles, computers, mining equipment, and a variety of consumer products. Throughout its initial three decades, the government has consistently held to a moderate program of industrial decentralization. By 1970, the traditionally dominant east and northeast regions together accounted for 48.2% of national output, as compared with 54.9% in 1952. Similarly, the northern region's share grew from 21.6% to 27.9% during the same period, while smaller gains were also registered in the central and northwest sectors. Coastal cities such as Tsingtao, Tientsin, and Talien, as well as Shenyang and Harbin in Manchuria, are being increasingly rivaled by new inland centers such as Peking, Taiyüan, Sian, Chengchou, Loyang, Lanchow, Wuhan, and Chungking.

Before the first five-year plan (1953–57), China had only one major steel center, Anshan in Manchuria, and several minor ones. All these produced 1.93 million tons of pig iron and 1.35 million tons of steel in 1952. By 1973, the annual capacity of the steelworks at Anshan was estimated at 5.9 million tons of crude steel. In September 1959, a new blast furnace at Paotou, one of the largest in the world, began operations. The Paotou complex was fully completed in 1961. Another large steel center at Wuhan, in central China, was started in 1958 and completed in 1961, with an annual capacity of 3 million tons. Soviet technicians had stayed on to complete the work at both Paotou and Wuhan. Wuhan's steel output was expected to be increased by 3 million tons with completion of a $430-million sheet-rolling and finishing mill in 1977. In 1973, China had at least eight modern steel plants, each producing more than 1 million tons annually. By 1974, total production of pig iron stood at 31.4 million tons (a peak of 33.7 million tons was reached in 1973); crude steel production in 1974 totaled 23.8 million tons (25.5 million tons in 1973). The encouragement of "backyard furnaces" during the Great Leap was quickly abandoned owing to extremely poor quality. The construction of smaller modernized plants has, however, continued throughout the country; by 1974, small- and medium-sized plants accounted for 28.3% of national pig iron output and for 12.6% of crude-steel output.

In 1974, China's textile mills produced an estimated 7,600 million meters of cotton cloth (5,050 million in 1957) and 65.2 million meters of wool cloth (18.2 million in 1957). In addition, China produced 401.3 million meters of silk cloth in 1971 (144.6 million in 1957). Average annual growth of synthetic fibers was reported at 15.7% during 1964-75; cotton yarn output grew by 6.3% during the same period.

China's petroleum-refining capacity has kept pace with the dramatic growth in crude-oil output during the past decade. By 1974, total refinery capacity was estimated at 47 million tons, sufficient to meet domestic requirements. As a consequence, synthetic petroleum, which had made up 35% of crude-oil production in 1963, fell to about 5% of the total by 1974. China's first modern refinery was completed with Soviet help at Lanchow in 1959. By 1974 there were at least 11 major refining facilities in the country, with the range of products having grown from about 10 in the 1950s to more than 160 in 1974.

Since 1961, industry has been providing agriculture with farm machines, chemical fertilizers, insecticides, means of transport, power, building materials, and other commodities in accordance with the policy of concentrating on agriculture. Handicraft cooperatives also have been busy making hand-operated or animal-drawn implements. In 1974, China produced an estimated 133,300 tractors (measured in 15-horsepower units), of which 90,300 were conventional tractors and 43,000 garden tractors. Production of powered irrigation equipment reached 5,984 1,000-horsepower units. Chemical-fertilizer production totaled 24,880,000 tons in 1974 (as compared with 803,000 tons in 1957). Of the 1974 total, 15,810,000 tons were nitrogen-based, 8,620,000 tons phosphorus-based, and 450,000 tons potassium-based. The construction of 13 of the world's largest ammonia-urea complexes by 1980 was expected to produce an even greater surge in the fertilizer growth rate.

Since 1963, great emphasis has been placed on transportation equipment, and China now produces varied lines of passenger cars, trucks, buses, and bicycles. In 1973, estimated output included 110,000 motor vehicles, 4,859,000 bicycles, 240 electric locomotives, 16,000 freight cars, and merchant vessels totaling 161,700 tons. Other consumer and industrial products in 1973 included 3,894,000 sewing machines, 75,000 television sets, and 8,064,000 radios. In 1974, China produced 31.6 million tons of cement.

29 DOMESTIC TRADE

Despite recent improvements, the inadequacy of China's land transportation system still dictates a domestic trade pattern in which most of the commerce is local and often dependent on human or animal transportation. Large-scale movement of goods between regions is confined largely to the rivers, particularly in central and southern China. Local trade is composed largely of vegetables, fish, meat, and handicraft products. Trade between regions consists chiefly of rice, cotton, salt, coal, and other essential commodities; specialty and luxury items such as silk, tea, herbs, chinaware, furs, and hides; handicraft products of high quality; and manufactured goods.

Three types of trade outlets—the periodic market, the peddler, and the urban shop—constituted the basis of the traditional commercial structure. In the last two decades, however, a number of state trading companies have been established for dealing in commodities such as food grains, cotton, textiles, coal, building materials, metals, machinery, and medicines. These companies, under the control of the Ministry of Commerce, have established branch offices and retail stores throughout the country. Periodic open markets still exist, although private traders have all but disappeared. Retail trade in rural areas is largely controlled by the All-China Federation of Supply and Marketing Cooperatives and its constituent organizations.

Wholesale trade is government-controlled. Organized state purchases of grains began in July 1953. In the fall of 1956, free markets were set up for products not covered by state purchases, including vegetables, poultry, fresh eggs, fresh fruit, canned fruit, bamboo articles, furniture, and charcoal. In 1959, however, the government began to require the communes to deliver fixed amounts of these products to the state. Retail trade, which amounted to RMB47 billion in 1957, was conducted in that year by state retail outlets, handling 38.5% of total retail turnover; cooperative outlets, 30%; joint stock-private outlets, 28.5%; and privately owned stores, 3%. Retail trade amounted to RMB63.8 billion in 1959.

The China Export Commodities Fair, usually held each spring and fall in Canton, has become an important point of contact for Westerners doing business with China. Attendance at recent Canton fairs has been put at 25,000.

30 FOREIGN TRADE

The government publishes trade figures only in terms of percentages and totals, but reasonably complete data by commodity and by country can be secured from the foreign trade data published by China's trading partners.

Despite its enormous size and vast productivity, China has yet to become a major trading nation. Total trade value comes to less than 6% of the GNP, while China's exports have never constituted more than 2% of the world export volume. Nonetheless, trade has performed functions within the economy, providing needed capital goods and technology to abet development, as well as primary commodities (such as grains) to supplement local supply in slack years.

Prior to 1949, some three-fourths of China's exports were agricultural products. This proportion fell to a low ebb of 13% during the agricultural crisis of 1961. During 1966-74, foodstuffs and crude agricultural materials held to an average of about 50% of exports. Textiles, which accounted for less than 4% of total exports in the early 1950s, rose appreciably to about 22% of the total in 1974. The dramatic rise in oil exports, reaching $450 million in 1974 and an estimated $800 million in 1975, has largely compensated for a recent lag in traditional exports; oil earnings in 1974 alone (with a total production of 65.3 million tons) constituted about 7% of total export value.

The composition of China's imports has changed markedly under the People's Republic. Imports of machinery and equipment rose from a pre-World War II ratio of 7% to 20% in 1952 and to a peak of 48% in 1959. By the 1970s, the proportion leveled off to about 20%. In the mid-1970s, metals constituted about 27% of imports (compared with 10% in the 1950s), while fuel imports fell from 10% of the 1950s' totals to negligible amounts since 1967. Food imports, however, which made up only about 2% of the import volume in the 1950s, averaged 20% of the total in 1973 and 1974. During 1961-66, annual grain imports (mainly wheat) averaged 5-6 million tons, at a cost of $400 million (averaging 26% of annual imports) yearly.

Since the early 1960s, imports have been held fairly much in balance with exports. Small deficits occurred in 1970 and 1973; in 1974, estimated exports totaled $6,305 million and imports $7,410 million, leaving a deficit of $1,105 million.

Principal exports in 1968 and 1973 (in millions of dollars) were as follows:

	1968	1973
Crude materials	415	870
Textile yarns and fabrics	270	795
Grains	130	535
Animals, meat, and fish	175	485
Clothing	180	275
Chemicals	85	245
Fruits and vegetables	140	225
Iron and steel	25	110
Other exports	525	1,355
TOTALS	1,945	4,895

Principal imports in 1968 and 1973 (in millions of dollars) were as follows:

	1968	1973
Iron and steel	265	930
Machinery and equipment	275	855
Grains	305	840
Chemicals	315	445
Textile fibers	100	400
Nonferrous metals	125	400
Rubber	85	165
Other imports	350	940
TOTALS	1,820	4,975

The direction of China's trade has followed three major patterns during the last five decades. Prior to World War II, Japan, Hong Kong, the US, and the UK together made up about three-fourths of the total trade volume. With the founding of the People's Republic in 1949, trade shifted radically in favor of the USSR and Eastern Europe. During 1952–55, more than 50% of China's trade was with the USSR; during 1956–60, the proportion averaged about 40%. As Sino-Soviet relations deteriorated during the 1960s, trade exchanges steadily declined, reaching a bare 1% of China's total volume in 1970. By the mid-1970s, six of China's seven leading trade partners were industrialized Western countries, and China's trade pattern overall reflected a high degree of multilateralism. Since 1973, Japan has ranked first as both importer (notably of oil and other raw materials) and exporter, and in 1974 accounted for 24.3% of China's total trade volume. The most dramatic change, perhaps, accompanied the emergence of the US as China's second-largest partner, with 7.9% of the total volume in 1974. During 1954–70, US trade with China was virtually nonexistent, most of that period having been marked by a US trade embargo with China. Foodstuffs (mainly grains), textiles, and nonferrous metals have led the surge in US exports to China; US imports from China remain marginal, although raw silk, printed cotton textiles, and animal bristles have begun to make inroads. Hong Kong continues to retain its important traditional role as an entrepôt and major source of foreign exchange; food makes up about half of China's exports to the colony. USSR trade, meanwhile, has recovered somewhat in recent years, ranking fifth in share of the 1972 volume and tenth in 1974. Of the other Socialist countries, Romania ranked second after the USSR.

China's principal trade partners in 1973 (in millions of dollars) were as follows:

	EXPORTS	IMPORTS	BALANCE
Japan	928	1,093	−165
US	64	812	−748
Hong Kong/Macao	825	10	815
FRG	130	357	−227
Malaysia/Singapore	325	135	190
Canada	53	356	−303
UK	102	238	−136
USSR	135	135	0
Australia/New Zealand	97	167	−70
France	128	103	25
Italy	112	84	28
Other countries	1,996	1,485	511
TOTALS	4,895	4,975	−80

31 BALANCE OF PAYMENTS

Both foreign trade and international financing in China are state monopolies, with policies and transactions administered by the People's Bank of China (PBC). Among its various functions, the PBC sets exchange rates for foreign currencies. The PBC releases foreign exchange to the Bank of China, which plays a major payments role through its branches in Hong Kong, Singapore, and London.

The government has, overall, maintained a record of financial stability, linked to a policy of stringent controls over its international transactions. Adhering generally to a principle of self-reliance, it has resorted to the use of commercial credit at certain junctures but has avoided falling into long-term indebtedness as a means of financing major development goals. In the period 1958–60, the Great Leap Forward and the succeeding years of economic crisis caused a sharp deterioration in China's international payments position. In 1960, large negative clearing account balances with Communist countries (−$625 million) were $210 million more than the foreign exchange reserves of $415 million. By the end of 1964, however, the negative balance with Communist nations had been reduced to $55 million, and China's net international financial resources stood at a surplus of $345 million owing to monetary gold holdings of $215 million and foreign exchange balances from trade with non-Communist countries amounting to $185 million. By 1965, the Chinese had completely cleared their long-term debt to the USSR and by 1968, as reported by Lin Piao in an address to the CCP congress in 1969, China had redeemed all national bonds and was free of all long-term external and internal debts.

Since the mid-1960s, China's trade with non-Communist states has expanded steadily, reaching about 85% of the trade volume by the mid-1970s. Until 1973, current-account payments within this sector are believed to have been kept in balance, with imports sharply cut back in response to deficit trade in the preceding years. During 1950–72, China's cumulative hard-currency commodity trade deficit of $1 billion was believed to have been offset by annual earnings of about $100 million from overseas remittances and invisibles and about $25 million from domestic gold production (and subsequent sales, mainly through Macao and Hong Kong). In the mid-1970s, China's foreign exchange reserves were put at anywhere from $1 billion to $5 billion, at all odds an adequate supply for several months of import purchases.

In 1975, China's repayment burden for short- and medium-term debts totaled $457.5 million (based on $275.7 million in payments for complete plants contracted for as of the end of 1974 and $200 million on an annual estimated $1 billion in five-year financing), all told a relatively modest burden even when measured against the conservative financial operations of other Socialist countries. Similar calculations place the repayment burden at $558.1 million in 1977, $1,032.4 million in 1980, and $1,271 million in 1982. In addition, projected average grain purchases during 1977–82 are expected to cost $700 million annually (as against about $1 billion each year in the mid-1970s).

32 BANKING

The People's Bank of China (PBC), the state bank with some 34,000 branches throughout the country, issues currency; makes loans to industrial, agricultural, and commercial enterprises; receives savings account deposits from government organizations, state and cooperative enterprises, and individuals; handles foreign currency and international settlements; and supervises the operations of specialized agencies such as the People's Construction Bank, the Bank of Communications, the Bank of China, and the Joint State-Private Bank. The People's Construction Bank, under the direction of the Ministry of Finance, makes payments for capital construction according to state plans and budgets. The Agricultural Bank of China, formerly a subsidized bank under the PBC but established as an independent agency in 1963, issues loans to state farms and communes, assists rural credit cooperatives, and receives savings deposits in rural areas. The Bank of Communications, under the Ministry of Finance, handles the state's investments in joint state-private enterprises.

The Bank of China (BOC) is a joint state-private banking corporation with 66% of its capital owned by the government; its general manager is a deputy director of the PBC. The BOC has branches throughout China as well as in Singapore, Hong Kong, and the UK. It handles foreign exchange and international settlements for the PBC. The BOC also controls 11 other commercial banks in Hong Kong and Singapore. In May 1969, the PBC/BOC began to encourage wider recognition for the renminbi as an international currency. In July 1969, the BOC's office in London began to quote forward exchange rates for renminbi against sterling, thus encouraging importers to hold Chinese currency rather than immediately convert it into another currency. As of 1976, the BOC had established correspondent relationships with some 20 banks in Japan and with more than 30 foreign bank branches in the US, although none had yet been established with a US bank; under these arrangements, the foreign banks open a renminbi account at the BOC's head office in Peking, and the BOC opens a hard currency account in its correspondent's bank. Thus, China remains unique among the Socialist countries in that it both uses its own currency in international transactions and permits Western interests to hold accounts in its currency. No foreign bank branches have been established in China. Foreign deposits on account with the BOC have been estimated at $500 million to $1 billion during the mid-1970s.

The Joint State-Private Bank is an amalgamation of 60 private banking houses; it handles savings deposit accounts for the PBC. At the commune level, banking and credit services are made available through credit cooperatives and through branches of the PBC, under the control of county PBC offices. The PBC branches monitor the finances of commune operations and assess the creditworthiness of these entities. Since 1966, credit cooperatives have been making loans to production brigades and teams as well as to households temporarily in need of cash. In 1974, the former type of transaction was reported to account for 88% of the cooperatives' loans. In the mid-1970s, the government mounted a campaign to increase bank deposits; savings in 1974 were reported to have increased by 12.5% over the previous year.

33 INSURANCE

The People's Insurance Company of China, formed in 1949 under the supervision of the PBC, is authorized to handle all kinds of insurance. Two additional state enterprises, the China Insurance Co. and the Tai Ping Insurance Co., are in operation. There are no private insurance firms in China.

34 SECURITIES

No private securities are traded.

35 PUBLIC FINANCE

The annual central-government budget is prepared by the Ministry of Finance and approved by the National People's Congress. The 1960 budget (the last to be published) was balanced at RMB70.02 billion. Industrial, commercial, and agricultural taxes comprised 34.8% of revenues; of expenditures, the largest outlays were listed for economic construction

(61.3%); social services, culture, and education (totaling 12.3%); and national defense (8.3%).

During its initial five-year plan (1953-57), the government followed the Soviet model of highly centralized economic management. During the second plan (1958-62), however, the Chinese leadership began a process of decentralization whereby both administrative and planning roles began gradually to be transferred to provincial authorities. In the post-1960 period, legal provisions stipulated enhanced authority for the provinces in taxation, price control, materials distribution management, and in the overall management of financial, commercial, and industrial activities. In the course of transition, the proportion of revenues collected directly by the central government fell from 40% to 20%.

China's national budget has thus come to reflect an amalgam of central- and provincial-government revenues and expenditures. The central government retains a principal role in national planning. Its budget continues to include defense expenditures; central government administration; and a relatively small number of health, education, and welfare projects directly controlled by Peking. The central government also maintains the key role in a national system of revenue sharing. Under this system, maximum levels of expenditure for each province, autonomous region, and centrally administered municipality are set by the central authorities. Where revenues exceed these limits, excess funds are transferred to the central government for remission as subsidies to less developed regions. Thus, in 1972, the most industrialized areas had the vast bulk of their revenues absorbed and redistributed elsewhere by the central government; for Shanghai, the proportion was 90%; for Liaoning, 82%; and for Kiangsu, 70%. The poorer units, including each of the five autonomous regions, retain all of their revenues; furthermore, more than 50% of Tibet's expenditures during 1960-73 are believed to have been subsidized by the central government.

36 TAXATION

The principal industrial tax used to be the turnover tax, an indirect sales tax levied on goods at the plant. In 1958, however, the turnover, commodity, and stamp taxes and part of the industrial and commercial tax were abolished and replaced by a consolidated tax on total sales. An agricultural tax is levied—frequently in kind—on the people's communes. Other taxes on collective enterprises include export duties, salt taxes, and various excise, business, and commerce taxes.

Wages and salaries are not subject to tax, but income taxes are applicable to the profits of business enterprises and interest derived from bank deposits. Progressive rates range from 5% to 30%.

37 CUSTOMS AND DUTIES

Import duties, a major source of revenue before 1949, are no longer important in China. Exports are ordinarily exempt from duties.

38 FOREIGN INVESTMENTS

There are no foreign investments per se in the PRC. During the last two decades—and especially in the 1970s—China has contracted for the construction of a substantial number of complete plants, notably for iron and steel manufacture and power generation. Such agreements, often made with private firms from Japan, the FRG, Italy, France, the UK, and Canada as well as with agencies of the Socialist states, have all called for the direct purchase of materials and services. Residual ownership by foreigners or remittance of profits from production are expressly disallowed.

Since the mid-1950s, the PRC has conducted an extensive program of assistance to underdeveloped countries. During the 1956-74 period, China is thought to have disbursed upwards of $5 billion in grants and economic credits. Such aid grew substantially in the 1970s, with commitments during 1970-74 totaling

$2.4 billion, or more than double the combined allocations of the previous two decades. Some two-thirds of funds in the 1970s went to Africa, with the Tan-Zam Railway the largest single investment project, absorbing more than $100 million annually in Chinese aid since 1970. Of the total distributed since 1956, 54.2% went to the underdeveloped countries of Africa, 21.1% to South Asia (mainly Pakistan), 10.8% to the Middle East, 8.8% to East Africa, 3.8% to Latin America, and 1.3% to Europe.

39 ECONOMIC POLICY

The profound restructuring of China's economy begun in 1949 at first adhered to orthodox models borrowed wholesale from the USSR. All major industrial, infrastructural, and financial enterprises were brought directly under the ownership of the state. Agriculture was collectivized. Management of the economy was closely controlled by central authorities, whose powers extended to the allocation of basic commodities and the basic division of resources into investment, consumption, and defense channels. Since the late 1950s, China has assiduously adapted Soviet forms to its own requirements, resulting in development of its unique commune system and of an evolving redistribution of economic authority, under which an important share in management and decision making has been assumed at provincial and local levels.

The use of long-range planning and growth targets continues to play an important role at least in periods of relative stability. Basic goals have been traditionally set forth by Chairman Mao, articulated in general terms by the Standing Committee of the Politburo of the CCP's Central Committee, and drafted into specific plans by the State Council. Administration is now largely the work of provincial and subprovincial levels of government.

In 1969, the government published a report on the future course for Socialist industrialization calling for a more open approach to foreign assistance and trade. Domestically, it confirmed the use of the "mass line"—the system of calling upon workers and peasants to take responsibility and initiative, and to work without material incentives; it stressed the "walking on the legs" policy—the simultaneous use of modern and traditional employment methods; and it reasserted the policy first enunciated during the Great Leap Forward: "take agriculture as the formulation and industry as the leading factor." Specifically, the program recommended expansion of industry through investment of profits derived from the sale of agricultural and light industrial products.

At the heart of the 1969 policy was a reversion to the commune system of 1958—a program to make the countryside self-sufficient, with every commune not only growing its own food but producing its own fertilizer and tools, generating its own electricity, and managing its own small handicrafts factories, health schemes, and primary schools. In contrast to the hastily organized communes of the Great Leap Forward period, the new units have frequently adhered to the traditional—and more manageable—structure of the Chinese countryside: Production teams, the basic unit for agricultural production, have been formed by the populations of villages; larger market villages have been made into headquarters for brigades; and former administrative towns have come to serve as focal points for communes. Reorganization, moreover, has been guided by principles of economic practicality and efficiency.

Long-range economic planning resumed in 1970 with the announcement of a fourth five-year plan for 1971-75. In late 1975, Premier Chou En-lai proclaimed the plan successful. Agricultural output was reported to have grown by 51% during the 1964-74 period, while gross industrial output was said to have increased by 190%. Specifically, the following growth rates (1964-74) for mining and industry were reported: petroleum, 660%; coal, 92%; steel, 120%; cotton yarn, 85.8%; tractors, 540%; chemical fertilizers, 350%; and electric power, 200%. In setting the goals for the 1976-80 plan, Chou called for continued expansion at a moderate pace of output and a sustained effort toward technological self-sufficiency. Industry continued to be cast in a major support role for agricultural development. Speaking of China's long-run future, Chou stated that the goal for 1980 was "to build an independent and relatively comprehensive industrial and economic system." The second stage, to be completed before the end of the 20th century, was "to accomplish the comprehensive modernization of agriculture, industry, national defense, and science and technology . . . so that our economy will be advancing in the front ranks of the world."

40 HEALTH

National health practices, including the provision of both Western and traditional Chinese health services, are under the supervision of the Ministry of Health. In 1959, the number of hospital beds was 570,000. Every county had a hospital, and many townships had clinics. Medical stations in industrial plants and shops serve factory workers and employees. By 1975, cooperative medical services had been established by some 90% of the country's production brigades. The services are supported by membership contributions and through welfare funds collected by the various communal divisions. Patients pay fees for consultation as well as for half of any resultant medical costs. Several major child and maternal health institutions have been established in Shanghai and Tientsin. In Peking there is the Central Maternal and Child Health Institute. Government employees receive free medical care (half cost for their dependents).

The government has placed major stress on preventive medicine and on general improvement of sanitary conditions in the country. Since the early 1950s, mass campaigns have been mounted to deal with major public health problems. These have included nationwide clean-up campaigns, mass educational programs in the sanitary preparation of food, the treatment of drinking water, personal hygiene, and waste disposal. The entire population was mobilized to eradicate the "four pests"—rats, sparrows, flies, and mosquitoes. Epidemic prevention centers were established to carry out massive immunizations, while parasitic diseases, affecting hundreds of millions in China, were also attacked. As a result, schistosomiasis, malaria, kala-azar, and hookworm are thought to have been largely brought under control. The high infant mortality rate was reduced from 20 per 1,000 (pre-1949) to 7.03 per 1,000 in 1957. Average life expectancy in 1975 was estimated at 63.6 years, as compared with about 45 years in 1950.

In 1958 there were about 80,000 physicians trained in Western methods and 470,000 doctors practicing traditional Chinese medicine, which relies heavily on acupuncture and medicinal herbs. Doctors were trained in 38 medical schools, of which 4 specialized in Chinese traditional methods and 4 in pharmacy. The total medical student body in 1956/57 was 46,218. In 1957, an Academy of Medical Science, which administers medical research, was established. Improved sanitation and health services have achieved major gains in controlling epidemic diseases.

In an effort to even out the disparity between rural and urban health services, medical personnel from hospitals—as much as 30-50% of the medical staffs—are being included in groups of people "sent down to the countryside." An expanding number of paramedical personnel, called barefoot doctors, now work in the rural areas. An increasingly important medical factor since the Cultural Revolution, these young peasants or middle-school graduates have been trained on the job by commune doctors or in two-month courses at commune health clinics. By 1975, there was estimated to be 1 barefoot doctor for every 700 persons in rural China, as compared with a ratio of 1 physician for every 8,000 persons (in rural areas) prior to the Cultural Revolution (1966-69).

41 SOCIAL WELFARE

In 1959, under terms of the labor insurance law of 1951, more than 16 million workers were provided with insurance against death, old age, illness, and disability. Workers' hospitals, sanatoriums, rest homes, and crèches also were established under the law.

In recent years, welfare funds paid out by collective enterprises have amounted to 12–13% of the cost of wages and salaries. Social welfare programs cover workers in state-operated enterprises and institutions, which include virtually all employees of government agencies, mining, manufacturing, industry, railroad, shipping, and construction units. Welfare in rural areas is administered by the communes, which provide clothing, shelter, and food for sick and disabled people, and place the aged in homes. Recreational and cultural services are also supported through welfare payments.

Population control and family planning have been given major stress at various junctures by the government. A massive birth-control campaign was initiated in the mid-1950s and resumed a decade later when stress was placed on postponing marriage and on mass distribution of contraceptives. Family planning was again receiving major emphasis in the mid-1970s, with birth control more fully integrated into public health programs. In 1973, the government reported that 200,000 female workers in Peking were given free gynecological examinations and birth-control information. Further, regulations were set forth for factories regarding the rights of women employees during pregnancy and early maternity.

42 HOUSING

The increase in the number of industrial workers, most of whom came from the countryside, produced a serious housing shortage. Government housing projects have gradually alleviated the overcrowding, which was also reduced in part by campaigns to mobilize urban dwellers for work—and frequently settlement —in rural areas. Rural households now provide most of their own housing construction, usually working after normal work hours and using whatever local materials are at hand. Housing construction amounted to 120.96 million sq meters of floor space during 1953–58.

43 EDUCATION

Prior to 1949, schools were available for less than 40% of school-age children; 85% of the people were illiterate. During 1949–59, school attendance increased nearly fourfold. In 1959, about 50 million children received preschool education; primary schooling was nearly universal, with some 92.6 million students (between 85% and 90% of all school-age children) in primary schools; 12 million were in secondary schools. By 1966, total school enrollment in China reached 116 million, with the average pupil receiving 5.5 years of formal schooling.

Tuition has traditionally been free in vocational secondary schools and in training schools for elementary teachers, as well as in colleges and universities, and students in need of food, clothing, and textbooks receive state grants-in-aid. Primary and general secondary-school students pay a nominal tuition fee. Part-time primary and secondary schools, evening universities, and correspondence schools exist for adult workers and peasants. In the late 1950s, an estimated 60 million people were enrolled in all types of spare-time schools, and more than 90 million adults attended study courses. Despite these advances, illiteracy remains a persistent problem in China, still affecting about half of the adult population.

In 1961 there were 761 institutions of higher learning in China, including 61 universities, 271 schools for technology and engineering, 113 agriculture and forestry schools, 142 medical schools, and 174 teacher-training colleges. The largest universities are Nanking University (founded 1888), Peking University (1898), Süchow University (in Kiangsu Province, 1900), the Polytechnic Tsinghua Institute and People's University in Peking, Futan and Tungchi universities in Shanghai, Sun Yat-sen and Nanfang universities in Canton, and Shantung University in Tsingtao. In 1957, the Academy of Sciences (established in 1949) consisted of 68 research institutes with a total staff of 17,335. In 1958, the Chinese University of Sciences and Technology was inaugurated in Hofei by the Academy of Sciences with an initial class of 1,600 students.

In 1965, 170,000 students were graduated from colleges and universities, one-third of them from engineering schools, one-third from teachers' colleges, and the rest from other colleges (28,000 from medical schools and 18,000 from agricultural colleges).

In 1957, education for minority nationalities was provided for 3,150,000 pupils in 23,890 primary schools and for 267,000 students in 363 secondary schools. Some 14,159 minority students attended colleges in 1957.

The Cultural Revolution affected education more than any other sector of Chinese society. China's schools were shut down in mid-1966 to give the student Red Guards the opportunity to "make revolution" on and off campus. Later the revolutionary activities dissolved into often violent factional struggles that kept the campuses in an uproar, destroyed some facilities, and made it impossible to resume new admissions or classes (except for political study sessions). More important, perhaps, the Cultural Revolution touched off wholesale purges within the educational establishment. Upper- and middle-level bureaucrats throughout the system were removed from office and virtually entire university faculties and staffs dispersed. Although many lower schools had begun to reopen during 1969, several universities remained closed through the early 1970s, as an estimated 10 million urban students were removed to the countryside to take part in labor campaigns.

The educational system that emerged in the Cultural Revolution's aftermath was in many respects distinct from the system that had preceded it. A key feature of the new system was decentralization: Major responsibility for the construction, administration, and financing of primary and secondary schools moved from the central Ministry of Education to the localities. In urban areas schools are run by factories or neighborhood CCP committees, while in the countryside schools are maintained by the communes and brigades. Salaries and outlays are guided by local norms and priorities. Revolutionary ideology and local conditions have become the principal determinants of curriculum. A 9-year program (compressed from 12 years) of universal schooling is to apply to youths 7–15 years of age. An important new type of school developed during the Cultural Revolution is the May 7 cadre school. Originally set up in remote areas, the May 7 schools now exist nationwide. Instruction relies heavily on discussion and self-criticism; students participate regularly in hard physical labor, and the schools often maintain small plants in line with the ideal of self-sufficiency. At age 16, nearly all graduates undertake work assignments.

Examinations for entry into higher education have been deemphasized; candidates between the ages of 18 and 25 are nominated by local CCP leaders, with the selection process based heavily on work records and political screening. Overall, the number of university places has been reduced, with an estimated 153,000 students enrolled in 1973 (compared with 1.5 million in 1965).

Some technical classes and experimental courses, emphasizing the "thoughts of Mao," combine education with production, compressing the period of baccalaureate study to three or even two years. Universities have established factories or set up liaisons with existing factories, and some industrial enterprises have set up their own schools. Students spend part of their time in the workshops; workers function as students; schools orient classwork around real production problems; and industry takes account of the pedagogical value when selecting schemes for plant operations and output diversity.

⁴⁴LIBRARIES AND MUSEUMS

The Peking Library (founded in 1912) is the national library and the largest in China, with more than 7.5 million volumes, including more than 200,000 rare ancient Chinese books and manuscripts. The Capital Library in Peking is the city's public library and operates lending, reference, and children's services. There are similar large municipal libraries in Chungking, Canton, Shenyang, Shanghai, and other large provincial cities. More than 1,000 public libraries are maintained at the county level. Small lending libraries and reading rooms can be found in factories and offices and on agricultural communes. The library of the University of Peking, with more than 2.7 million volumes, is the largest university library. Other important university collections are at Chungshan University in Canton (1.9 million volumes), Futan University in Shanghai (1.5 million), and Tsinghua University in Peking (1.3 million).

The Imperial Palace Museum in Peking houses collections of art, sculpture, silk fabric, and furniture and includes the celebrated Han-period jade clothes sewn with golden wire that were discovered in 1968. The Museum of the Revolution, also in Peking, has exhibits of the revolutionary movement in China from the Opium War to the founding of the People's Republic. Many museums are memorials to Chinese artists and writers, and house collections of their work. There are some 400 museums at the county level. In 1974, a lifesize army in pottery of 6,000 soldiers and horses was discovered in Shensi Province at the burial site of Shih Huang-ti, China's first emperor (221–206 B.C.) and founder of the Ch'in Dynasty.

⁴⁵ORGANIZATIONS

Prior to the Cultural Revolution, numerous and diverse organizations provided a carefully structured framework that encompassed all the common interests and purposes that normally draw people together into groups. These organizations were closely tied to the established regime and constituted a little-heralded but essential pillar of Communist society. Among these mass organizations were the Communist Youth League, the Women's Federation, the Federation of Literary and Art Circles, the Federation of Scientific Societies, and the Federation of Industry and Commerce.

At the beginning of the Cultural Revolution, most of them ceased to function, and a host of new organizations came into being. Red Guard organizations were set up in the schools, and "revolutionary rebel" organizations were set up in government ministries, offices, factories, and other units. As the Cultural Revolution progressed, these mass organizations coalesced, at the instigation of the central leadership, into Red Guard congresses, workers' congresses, and congresses of political officials. Combined with the dominant military element, they provided the organizational backdrop for the formation of revolutionary committees in 1967–68. With the effective if not nominal end of the Cultural Revolution in the early 1970s, many of the new mass organizations lost ground and appeared destined for gradual extinction. Meanwhile, local Communist Youth League organizations were clearly on the ascendancy in various provinces and municipalities.

⁴⁶PRESS

The press is controlled by the government, the CCP, or the various political and mass organizations associated with the CCP. In 1957 there were 358 national and provincial newspapers and 465 magazines. Minority newspapers are published in Mongolian, Uigur, Tibetan, Korean, and other languages.

The Cultural Revolution caused substantial upheaval among the press establishment in China. Many publications closed down, and others underwent purges of editorial staffs. Even the principal national newspaper, *Jen-min-jih pao (People's Daily)*, came under Red Guard fire. On 1 September 1966, the paper was reduced from six to four pages. During 1967–68, there were fewer editorials, and most of them were concerned with foreign rather than domestic affairs. Publication of *Hung ch'i (Red Flag)*, the most authoritative of the CCP publications, was suspended in November 1967 for eight months. When it reemerged in July 1968, it had an entirely new editorial staff (its troubles coincided with the paper's attacks on military elements). The editor of the intellectual newspaper *Kuang-ming jih pao (Kwangming Daily)* was sharply attacked for using the paper as a "tool of the anti-Party clique." The only national publication that survived unscathed was *Chieh-fang chun pao (Liberation Army Daily)*, the PLA's organ, which played a leading role in the Cultural Revolution and served as the chief newspaper during the first half of 1966, when other newspapers gave space to reprints of key articles from *Chieh-fang's* pages. Other large newspapers include *Wen hui pao* (Shanghai); *Chieh-fang pao (Liberation Daily,* Shanghai); and *Pei-ching jih pao (Peking Daily)*, formerly the organ of the Peking Communist Party Committee and an early focal point of purge.

Newspapers published in the various provinces and cities and publications directed specifically at workers include *Pei-ching kung-jen (Peking Worker)* and *Chiang-su kung-jen jih pao (Kiangsu Workers' Daily)*. The most authoritative publication for foreigners is the weekly *Peking Review*, distributed abroad in several languages. The *Ta Kung Pao* weekly supplement is distributed from Hong Kong.

Daily newspapers are subject to the careful control characteristic of all official media in China. An unprecedented development of the Cultural Revolution was the proliferation of uncensored Red Guard and revolutionary rebel newspapers, periodicals, pamphlets, leaflets, wall posters, graffiti, and documentary collections. The uncensored publications contained important documents that were never published in official media, including many statements made by Mao Tse-tung over the years but excluded from the standard collections of his works. News of factional fights, attacks against people who were not criticized by name in the regular media, details of the political crimes of purged leaders, and other material not published in the official media were made available. The phenomenon of "impromptu" news reports and critiques, often appearing on public bulletin boards, recurred during the political unrest of the mid-1970s.

⁴⁷TOURISM

Travel to China has increased sharply during the 1970s, although the volume remains low and facilities for visitors limited. Businessmen currently make up the largest proportion of foreign travelers, with most going to China to attend trade fairs, principally in Canton. The PRC also grants visas to journalists, scientists, physicians, educators, and others engaged in activities pertinent to China's development. The number of persons entering purely as tourists is still small, although the first visit of a foreign cruise ship was approved for the early 1970s.

Applications for visas are processed through PRC embassies. The China International Travel Service, the government's tourism and travel agency, offers a variety of tour arrangements through its Hong Kong agent, China Travel Service Ltd. Most visits are arranged for Peking, Shanghai, and Canton, with stops at the Great Wall and other major historical sites.

⁴⁸FAMOUS CHINESE

Confucius (K'ung Fu-tzu, 551–479 B.C.) is generally regarded as the most important historical figure as well as the greatest scholar of ancient China. His philosophy and social ideas include observance of filial piety, sanctity of the family, and social responsibility. Other early philosophers were Lao-tzu (c.604 B.C.), the reputed founder of Taoism; Mencius (Meng-tzu,

385–289 B.C.), who stressed the essential goodness of human nature and the right of subjects to revolt against unjust rulers; and Mo Ti (c.465–c.390 B.C.), who stressed the theme of universal love. Among the principal early poets was Chü Yüan (340–278 B.C.), whose *Li Sao*, an obscure melancholy rhapsody, is among the world's great poems. Ssü-ma Ch'ien (145–87 B.C.) produced the monumental *Shih-chi (Historical Memoirs)*, the first general history of China. Pan Ku (A.D. 32–92) wrote *Ch'ien-Han shu (History of the Former Han Dynasty)*, a continuation of Ssü-ma Ch'ien's work. Chang Heng (A.D. 78–139), an astronomer, is credited with having invented the first seismograph. Chang Chung-ching (152–219) was a celebrated physician. Tsu Chung-chih (429–500) calculated the figure 3.14159265 for π. Three brilliant poets of the T'ang dynasty period were Li Po (701–62), Tu Fu (712–70), and Po Chü-yi (772–846). Li Shi-chen (1518–93), an outstanding pharmacologist, wrote a monumental *Materia Medica*. Great authors of the Manchu dynasty period were Wu Ching-tzu (1701–54), who wrote *Ju-lin wai-shih (Unofficial History of the Scholars)*, a superb satire of the civil service system, and Ts'ao Hsüeh-ch'in (c.1715–63), who produced a remarkable novel, *Hung-lou meng (The Dream of the Red Chamber)*. Lusin, or Lu-hsün (Chou Shu-jen, 1881–1936), is generally regarded as China's greatest writer of the modern period. Mao Tun (Shen Yen-ping, b.1896) is a leading novelist.

Mao Tse-tung (1893–1976), the foremost figure of postrevolutionary China, became president of the Chinese Peasants Union (one of the precursors of the CCP) in 1927, took an active role with the Red Army in the war against Japan, and served as chairman of the Central Committee of the CCP from 1956–76. Other prominent Chinese Communist leaders include Chu Teh (1886–1976), the PRC's preeminent military figure, who became commander-in-chief of the Red Army in 1931 and chairman of the Standing Committee of the NPC; Chou En-lai (1898–1976), first premier of China's State Council; Liu Shao-ch'i (b.1898), who became China's head of state in 1959 but who was purged during the Cultural Revolution; and Lin Piao (1908–71), who became deputy premier and minister of defense in 1959 and who, prior to his death in a plane crash and subsequent political vilification, had been certified as Mao Tse-tung's successor in the new CCP constitution drawn up in April 1969. Women in the political hierarchy have included Soong Ching-ling, Sun Yat-sen's wife, and Chiang Ch'ing, Mao Tse-tung's wife, who emerged as a radical leader during the Cultural Revolution. Chiang, with other prominent radicals, was purged in the wake of the ascension of Hua Kuo-feng (b.1921) as CCP chairman in October 1976.

⁴⁹DEPENDENCIES
China has no territories or colonies.

⁵⁰BIBLIOGRAPHY

Barnett, A Doak. *Cadres, Bureaucracy and Political Power in Communist China*. New York: Columbia University Press, 1967.

Barnett, A. Doak. *Uncertain Passage: China's Transition to the Post-Mao Era*. Washington, D.C.: Brookings Institution, 1974.

Bianco, Lucien. *Origins of the Chinese Revolution, 1915–1949*. Stanford, Calif.: Stanford University Press, 1971.

Bloodworth, Dennis. *The Chinese Looking Glass*. New York: Farrar, Straus, and Giroux, 1967.

Boorman, Howard L. and Richard C. (eds.). *Biographical Dictionary of Republican China*. 4 vols. New York: Columbia University Press, 1967–71.

Buchanan, Keith. *The Transformation of the Chinese Earth*. New York: Praeger, 1970.

Chao, Kang. *Agricultural Production in Communist China, 1949–1965*. Madison: University of Wisconsin Press, 1970.

Ch'en, Jerome. *Mao and the Chinese Revolution*. New York: Oxford University Press, 1965.

Chen, Nai Ruenn (ed.). *Chinese Economic Statistics: A Handbook for Mainland China*. Chicago: Aldine, 1967.

Cheng, J. Chester. *The Politics of the Red Chinese Army*. Stanford, Calif.: Hoover Institution on War, Revolution, and Peace, 1966.

Cheng, Shih. *A Glance at China's Economy*. Peking: Foreign Languages Press, 1974.

Ch'ien, Tuang-sheng. *The Governmental and Politics of China, 1912–1949*. Stanford, Calif.: Stanford University Press, 1970.

China and U.S. Far East Policy, 1945–1966. Washington, D.C.: Congressional Quarterly Service, 1967.

China: A Reassessment of the Economy; A Compendium of Papers Submitted to the Joint Economic Committee, Congress of the United States. Washington, D.C.: Government Printing Office, 1975.

Clubb, O. Edmund. *Twentieth Century China*. New York: Columbia University Press, 1972.

Cohen, Jerome Alan (ed.). *Contemporary Chinese Law: Research Problems and Perspectives*. Cambridge: Harvard University Press, 1970.

Creel, Herrlee Glessner. *Chinese Thought from Confucius to Mao Tse-tung*. Chicago: University of Chicago Press, 1953.

Domes, Jürgen. *The Internal Politics of China, 1949–72*. London: Hurst, 1973.

Donnithorne, Audrey. *The Budget and the Plan in China: Central-Local Economic Relations*. Canberra: Australian National University Press, 1972.

Donnithorne, Audrey. *China's Economic System*. New York: Praeger, 1967.

Eckstein, Alexander (ed.). *China Trade Prospects and US Policy*. New York: Praeger, 1971.

Eckstein, Alexander. *Communist China's Economic Growth and Foreign Trade*. New York: McGraw-Hill, 1966.

Fairbank, John K. *China: The People's Middle Kingdom and the United States*. Cambridge: Harvard University Press, 1972.

Fairbank, John K. *The United States and China*. Cambridge: Harvard University Press, 1972.

Feuerwerker, Albert (ed.). *History in Communist China*. Cambridge: MIT Press, 1968.

Freedman, Maurice (ed.). *Family and Kinship in Chinese Society*. Stanford, Calif.: Stanford University Press, 1970.

Fung Yu-lan. *A Short History of Chinese Philosophy*. New York: Free Press, 1966.

Gittings, John. *Survey of the Sino-Soviet Dispute: A Commentary and Extracts from the Recent Polemics, 1963–67*. London: Oxford University Press, 1967.

Goldman, Merle. *Literary Dissent in Communist China*. Cambridge: Harvard University Press, 1967.

Griffith, William E. *The Sino-Soviet Rift*. Cambridge: MIT Press, 1964.

Halpern, A. M. (ed.). *Policies Towards China: Views from Six Continents*. New York: McGraw-Hill, 1965.

Herrmann, Albert (ed.). *Historical Atlas of China*. Chicago: Aldine, 1966.

Hinton, William. *Fanshen: A Documentary of Revolution in a Chinese Village*. New York: Vintage, 1968.

Hinton, William. *Iron Oxen: A Documentary of Revolution in Chinese Farming*. New York: Monthly Review Press, 1970.

Hommel, Rudolf P. *China at Work*. Cambridge: MIT Press, 1969.

Ho Ping-ti and Tang Tsou. *China's Heritage and the Chinese Political System*. Chicago: University of Chicago Press, 1968.

Hsieh, Chao-Min. *Atlas of China*. New York: McGraw-Hill, 1973.

Hsu, Immanuel C. Y. *The Rise of Modern China*. New York: Oxford University Press, 1970.

Hsueh, Chun-tu (ed.). *Revolutionary Leaders of Modern China*. New York: Oxford University Press, 1971.

Hucker, Charles O. *China's Imperial Past: An Introduction to Chinese History and Culture.* Stanford, Calif.: Stanford University Press, 1975.

Hummel, Arthur W. (ed.). *Eminent Chinese of the Ch'ing Period, 1644–1912.* New York: Paragon, 1964.

Hunter, Neale. *Shanghai Journal: An Eyewitness Account of the Cultural Revolution.* New York: Praeger, 1969.

Johnston, Douglas M., and Hungdah Chiu (eds.). *Agreements of the People's Republic of China: 1949–1967, A Calendar.* Cambridge: Harvard University Press, 1968.

Kirby, Edward Stuart (ed.). *Contemporary China: Economic and Social Studies: Documents, Bibliography, Chronology.* Hong Kong: Hong Kong University Press, 1956–date.

Klein, Donald W., and A. B. Clark. *Biographic Dictionary of Chinese Communism, 1921–1965.* Cambridge: Harvard University Press, 1971.

Lewis, John Wilson (ed.). *Party Leadership and Revolutionary Power in China.* London: Cambridge University Press, 1970.

Lindbeck, John M. (ed.). *China: Management of a Revolutionary Society.* Seattle: University of Washington Press, 1971.

Mu Fu-sheng. *The Wilting of the Hundred Flowers: The Chinese Intelligentsia under Mao.* New York: Praeger, 1963.

Myrdal, Jan. *Report from a Chinese Village.* New York: Pantheon, 1965.

Needham, Joseph. *Science and Civilization in China.* Cambridge: Cambridge University Press, 1954–date.

Oksenberg, Michael (ed.). *China's Developmental Experience.* New York: Praeger, 1973.

Orleans, Leo A. *Every Fifth Child: The Population of China.* Stanford, Calif.: Stanford University Press, 1972.

Perkins, Dwight H. (ed.). *China's Modern Economy in Historical Perspective.* Stanford, Calif.: Stanford University Press, 1975.

Perkins, Dwight H. *Market Control and Planning in Communist China.* Cambridge: Harvard University Press, 1966.

Price, R. F. *Education in Communist China.* New York: Praeger, 1970.

Pye, Lucian W. *China: An Introduction.* Boston: Little, Brown, 1972.

Pye, Lucian W. *The Spirit of Chinese Politics: A Psychocultural Study of the Authority Crisis in Political Development.* Cambridge: MIT Press, 1968.

Richman, Barry M. *Industrial Society in Communist China.* New York: Random House, 1969.

Rossabi, Morris. *China and Inner Asia.* New York: Universe, 1975.

Scalapino, Robert A. (ed.). *Elites in the People's Republic of China.* Seattle: University of Washington Press, 1972.

Schram, Stuart R. *The Political Thought of Mao Tse-tung.* New York: Praeger, 1969.

Shurmann, Franz. *Ideology and Organization in Communist China.* Berkeley: University of California Press, 1968.

Shurmann, Franz, and Orville Schell (eds.). *The China Reader.* 3 vols. New York: Vintage, 1967.

Seybolt, Peter J. *Revolutionary Education in China.* White Plains, N.Y.: International Arts and Sciences Press, 1973.

Sharfstein, Ben-ami. *The Mind of China.* New York: Basic Books, 1974.

Skinner, G. W. (ed.). *Modern Chinese Society: An Annotated Bibliography.* 3 vols. Stanford, Calif.: Stanford University Press, 1974.

Smith, Bradley, and Wan-go Weng. *China: A History in Art.* New York: Harper & Row, 1973.

Snellgrove, David, and Hugh Richardson. *A Cultural History of Tibet.* New York: Praeger, 1968.

Solomon, Richard H. *Mao's Revolution and the Chinese Political Culture.* Ann Arbor: University of Michigan Press, 1971.

Stavis, Benedict. *Making Green Revolution: The Politics of Agricultural Development in China.* Ithaca, N.Y.: Cornell University Press, 1974.

Stover, Leon E. *The Cultural Ecology of Chinese Civilization.* New York: Universe, 1974.

Sullivan, Michael. *The Arts of China: A Short History.* Berkeley: University of California Press, 1974.

Terrill, Ross. *Eight Hundred Million: The Real China.* Boston: Little, Brown, 1972.

Treadgold, Donald W. (ed.). *Soviet and Chinese Communism: Similarities and Differences.* Seattle: University of Washington Press, 1967.

Tregear, T. R. *Economic Geography of China.* New York: American Elsevier, 1970.

Tregear, T. R. *A Geography of China.* Chicago: Aldine, 1965.

Union Research Institute, Hong Kong. *CCP Documents of the Great Proletarian Cultural Revolution, 1966–1967.* Hong Kong: Union Research Institute, 1968.

U.S. Department of State. *The China White Paper, August 1949.* Stanford, Calif.: Stanford University Press, 1967.

U.S. Joint Economic Committee. *People's Republic of China: An Economic Assessment.* Washington, D.C.: Government Printing Office, 1972.

Vogel, Ezra F. *Canton under Communism: Programs and Politics in a Provincial Capital, 1949–1968.* Cambridge: Harvard University Press, 1969.

Wakeman, Frederic. *History and Will: Philosophical Perspectives of Mao Tse-tung's Thought.* Berkeley: University of California Press, 1973.

Watson, Francis. *The Frontiers of China: A Historical Guide.* New York: Praeger, 1966.

Whitson, William W., and Chen-Hsia Huang. *The Chinese High Command.* New York: Praeger, 1973.

Wu, Yuan-Li. (ed.). *China: A Handbook.* New York: Praeger, 1973.

Wu, Yuan-Li. *The Economy of Communist China.* New York: Praeger, 1965.

Yang, Ch'ing-k'un. *Religion in Chinese Society: A Study of Contemporary Social Functions of Religion and Some of Their Historical Factors.* Berkeley: University of California Press, 1961.

CYPRUS

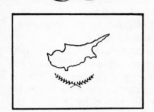

Republic of Cyprus
Kypriaki Dimokratia
Kıbrıs Türk Federe Devleti

CAPITAL: Nicosia. **FLAG**: The national flag consists of the map of Cyprus in gold set above two olive branches in green on a white field. **MONETARY UNIT**: The Cyprus pound (c£) of 1,000 mils is a nonconvertible paper currency. There are coins of 3, 5, 25, 50, and 100 mils, and notes of 250 and 500 mils and 1 and 5 Cyprus pounds. As of 29 February 1976, c£1=$2.5214 (or $1=c£0.3966). **WEIGHTS AND MEASURES**: Imperial weights and measures are widely used, but the use of the metric system is increasing. Local weights are also used. **HOLIDAYS**: New Year's Day, 1 January; Epiphany, 6 January; Greek Independence Day, 25 March; Cyprus Independence Day, 16 August; Greek Resistance Day, 28 October; Turkish Republic Day, 29 October; Christmas, 25 December; Boxing Day, 26 December. Movable Christian religious holidays include Good Friday, Holy Saturday, and Easter Monday. Movable Muslim religious holidays include ʿId al-Fitr, ʿId al-ʿAdhaʾ, and Milad al-Nabi. **TIME**: 2 P.M.=noon GMT.

¹LOCATION, SIZE, AND EXTENT

Cyprus is the largest Mediterranean island after Sicily and Sardinia. Including small island outposts of Cape Andreas known as the Klidhes, its area is 9,251 sq km (3,572 sq mi). The island is situated in the extreme northeast corner of the Mediterranean; it is 71 km (44 mi) s of Turkey, 105 km (65 mi) w of Syria, and 370 km (230 mi) N of Egypt. Cyprus extends 227 km (141 mi) ENE–WSW from Cape Andreas to Cape Drepanon and 97 km (60 mi) SSE–NNW. The average width is between 56 km and 72 km (35 mi and 45 mi); the narrow peninsula known as the Karpas, nowhere more than 16 km (10 mi) wide, extends 74 km (46 mi) northeastward to Cape Andreas, Cyprus has a coastline of 538 km (334 mi).

²TOPOGRAPHY

Two dissimilar mountain systems, flanking a central plain, occupy the greater part of the island. The Troodos Massif, in the southwest, attaining its highest point in Mt. Olympus (6,406 feet), sends out numerous spurs to the northwestern, northern, and southern coasts. In the north, a geologically older range, the Kyrenia Mountains, extends more than 100 miles along the coast in a series of rocky peaks, capped often by medieval castles. Between these principal formations lies the Mesaoria, a low plain extending from Famagusta Bay on the east to Morphou Bay on the west. Once forested, this treeless region, varying in width from 10 to 20 miles, now contains the bulk of the island's cultivable and pastoral area. There are few lakes or rivers; rivers are little more than rocky channels that carry away torrents during the thaw of spring and early summer.

³CLIMATE

Cyprus is for the most part dry, sunny, and healthful. The warm currents of the Mediterranean assure mild winters but bring humidity to the coastal area in the summer, when the central plain is hot and dry. On the hills, daily sunshine is interrupted only occasionally by a wet period rarely lasting more than a week. The mean annual temperature is about 20°C (68°F). A cool, rainy season lasts from October to March. In winter, snow covers the higher peaks of the Troodos; elsewhere the temperature seldom falls below freezing and conditions are mild and bracing. Rainfall is erratic and varies greatly in different parts of the island. The annual average precipitation ranges from below 12 inches in the west of the central lowlands to more than 45 inches in the higher parts of the southern massif. The main

agricultural areas receive rainfall of from 12 inches to 16 inches annually. Earthquakes are not uncommon.

⁴FLORA AND FAUNA

Except for some small lowland areas in which eucalyptus has been planted, the forests are natural growths of great antiquity, from which the Phoenician shipbuilders drew much of their timber. Forests consist principally of Aleppo pine. Other important conifers, locally dominant, are the stone pine, cedar (which is becoming rare), Mediterranean cypress, and juniper, the latter growing chiefly on the lower slopes of the Kyrenia Mountains. Oriental plane and alder are plentiful in the valleys, while on the hills Olympus dwarf oak mingles with pines of various species. Wild flowers grow in profusion, and herbs are numerous. Eagles are commonly seen in the mountains. The moufflon, a wild sheep, is found in diminishing numbers on the central plain and in the Stavros River Valley. The fauna as a whole is little different from that of the neighboring coastal region of Asia Minor.

⁵POPULATION

In 1975, the population of Cyprus was estimated at 673,000. This was an increase of 16.5% over the 1960 census figure of 577,615, and represents an average annual increase of 1.1%. A population of 714,000 was projected for 1980, based on a 1975 estimated crude birthrate of 21.9 per 1,000 people, a crude death rate of 7.1, and a net natural increase of 14.8. The population density was estimated at 72.7 per sq km (188.4 per sq mi). Nicosia, the capital, located in the center of the island in the Mesaoria plain, had a population of 116,100 in 1975. The 1975 population estimates for other chief centers—all seaports—were Limassol, 79,900; Famagusta, 39,100; Larnaca, 19,700; Paphos, 9,000; and Kyrenia, 3,900.

⁶ETHNIC GROUPS

Following the 1562 Turkish conquest, Cyprus received a substantial permanent influx of Ottoman Turks. Many soldiers became owners of feudal estates, and there was immigration from Anatolia and Rumelia. At times, the Turkish community was as large as the indigenous Greek community. There was virtually no intermarriage; each community preserved its own religion, language, dress, and other national characteristics. The 1973 war had the effect of further segregating the two communities, with most Turkish Cypriots living on the northern 40% of the island and most Greek Cypriots living in the south and west. In recent years, Greek Cypriots have outnumbered Turks more than four to one. Estimates in 1974 put the proportion of Greek and Turkish Cypriots at 80% and 18% respectively. The remainder are Maronites and Armenians.

7 LANGUAGE

Under British administration, English was the official language of the courts; English, Greek, and Turkish were languages of instruction in the schools. All three are now used in education, radio, and television. Many Turks speak fluent Greek, as well as Turkish, and English is widely spoken by both communities in the chief towns. Since independence in 1960, Greek and Turkish have become the official languages.

8 RELIGION

About four-fifths of the population is Greek Orthodox. Under the Cyprus ethnarch, Archbishop Makarios III, the church also has been the chief instrument of Greek Cypriot nationalism. As far back as A.D. 431, the independence of the Church of Cyprus was recognized by the Council of Ephesus and confirmed by Emperor Zeno in 478. The Church of Cyprus is one of the oldest "autocephalous and isotimous" constituent bodies of the Holy Orthodox Eastern Church, being senior by centuries to the Orthodox Church of Greece, and junior only to the four original patriarchates of Constantinople, Alexandria, Antioch, and Jerusalem. According to a 1973 estimate there were 488,200 Greek Orthodox Cypriots, 116,000 Sunni Muslim Turks, and 29,000 others.

9 TRANSPORTATION

More than 2,050 miles of asphalted highways provide all-weather communication between the principal towns and larger villages, and a 2,660-mile system of subsidiary roads connects all but a few remote villages. In addition to numerous taxicabs, the six chief towns are served by private buses, whose services are regulated by the Road Motor Transport Board. In 1973 there were 75,075 private motor cars, 17,500 motor trucks, 2,984 taxicabs, and 14,880 motorcycles. The roads are most significant, because internal transport is exclusively by road.

Because of motor transport competition, the government closed down its 71-mile railway in 1951; the only remaining lines are operated by mining companies.

Although off the main world shipping routes, Cyprus is served by passenger and cargo shipping lines. Famagusta on the east coast is the main port. Its harbor has been modernized since independence. The Limassol and Larnaca ports have been modernized and are now considered good deepwater harbors. Other ports are Karavostasi, Vasiliko, Limni, Boghaz, Kyrenia, and Paphos. In 1973, the net registered tonnage of vessels that entered and cleared Cyprus harbors was 5,152,000; total international cargoes loaded and unloaded amounted to 1,167,000 tons and 2,155,000 tons, respectively. Nearly half the trade passed through Famagusta. There are no inland waterways.

The civil airport at Nicosia was used by many international airlines until the 1973 war. Since the war, however, nearly all flights have been diverted to Larnaca or Ercan. Cyprus Airways has services to Middle Eastern countries, but there is no regular internal air service.

10 COMMUNICATIONS

In 1974 there were 30 main post offices and 837 postal agencies. The Cyprus Inland Telecommunications Authority operates the internal communications system. The telephone network is nearly wholly automatic. It includes all cities and 266 villages. In 1973 there were 62,000 telephones in use. A separate telephone network under the Forest Department serves a number of isolated places. Main towns and larger villages are served by 13 telegraph offices.

The Cyprus Broadcasting Corporation maintains regular service. The western part of the island is served by a new Limassol relay station. The number of radios was estimated as 205,000 in 1974. Television was inaugurated in 1957; two television relay stations were constructed in 1966. In 1974 there were more than 80,000 television sets in Cyprus. Radiotelephone and telegraph services to a number of countries are provided by a private company.

11 HISTORY

Numerous Stone Age settlements excavated in Cyprus indicate that as early as 4000 B.C. a considerable Neolithic population existed on the island. Living in circular huts, they produced decorated pottery of great individuality, and used vessels and tools ground from the close-grained rocks of the Troodos Mountains. Cyprus was famous in the ancient world for its copper, which, from about 2200 B.C., was used throughout the Aegean in the making of bronze. The island is believed either to have derived its name from or to have given it to this mineral through the Greek word kypros—copper. Although celebrated also for its cult of Aphrodite, Cyprus was at first only a far outpost of the Hellenic world. Greek colonizers came there in sizable numbers in 1400 B.C., and were followed soon afterward by Phoenician settlers. About 560 B.C., Cyprus was conquered by Egypt. Coveted by each rising civilization, it was taken in turn by Persia, Alexander the Great, Egypt again, Rome, and the Byzantine Empire. Its Christian history began with the visits of Paul, accompanied first (as described in the Acts) by Barnabas, and later by the apostle Mark. For several centuries after A.D.632, it underwent a series of Arab invasions. The island was wrested from its Byzantine ruler, Isaac Comnenus, in 1191 by Richard Coeur de Lion during the Third Crusade. Sold by the English king to the Knights Templar, it was transferred by that order to Guy de Lusignan, under whose dynasty the island experienced a brilliant period in its history, lasting some 300 years. Conquered in 1489 by Venice, Cyprus fell to the Turks 73 years later.

The administration of Cyprus by the UK began in 1878, under a convention with Turkey initiated by the British prime minister, Disraeli, at the Congress of Berlin and designed to establish Cyprus as a defensive base against further Russian aggression in the Middle East. Upon the entry of Turkey into World War I, Cyprus was annexed to the British crown. It was declared a crown colony and placed under a governor in 1925.

For centuries, Greek Cypriots have regarded Greece as their mother country and have sought union (enosis) with it as Greek nationals. In 1931, during the British occupation, enosis agitation, long held in check, broke into violence. Government House was burned amid widespread disturbances, and the administration applied severe repressive measures, including the deportation of clerical leaders. Agitation was dormant until the close of World War II, when it recommenced, and demands that the UK cede the island to Greece were renewed. A National Organization of Cypriot Fighters came into being, led by Col. George Grivas, a retired Greek army officer, and, in 1955, a campaign of terrorism was launched. Upward of 2,000 casualties were recorded. The unity of NATO was endangered by the opposing positions taken by Greece and Turkey, but efforts by NATO members to mediate the dispute proved unsuccessful.

Against this background, the prime ministers of Greece and Turkey met in Zürich, Switzerland, early in 1959 in a further attempt to reach a settlement. Unexpectedly, the Greek Cypriots set aside their demands for enosis and accepted instead proposals for an independent republic with representative government of Cyprus under a president. A formula for the island's future was drafted on 11 February. Approved by the governments of the UK, Greece, and Turkey, it received also the blessing of the Cyprus ethnarch, Archbishop Makarios III, who returned in triumph to the island from which he had been deported by the British government on charges of complicity with terrorism.

Besides determining Cyprus' legislative institutions, the

Zürich settlement provided for a number of instruments defining the island's future international status. Areas on Cyprus were set aside for the continuation of British military installations. The UK, Greece, and Turkey, the guarantor powers, had the right to act together or singly to prevent either enosis or partition. In addition, provision was made for Greek, Turkish, and Cypriot forces to be stationed together at a tripartite headquarters on the island. By 1 July 1960, agreement was reached on all outstanding differences. Independence was officially declared on 16 August 1960.

In December 1963, Turkish Cypriots, protesting a proposed constitutional change that would have strengthened the political power of the Greek Cypriot majority, clashed with Greek Cypriots and police. When fighting continued, Turkey appealed to the UN Security Council. On 4 March 1964, the Security Council voted to send in troops. On 10 August, Turkey and Cyprus agreed to accept a UN Security Council call for a cease-fire, but on 22 December, fighting again erupted in Nicosia and spread to other parts of the island. In March 1964, a UN force of about 7,000 men from 10 countries was stationed in Cyprus to keep the peace. In December 1965, the UN General Assembly passed a resolution calling on all states to "respect the sovereignty, unity, independence, and territorial integrity of the Republic of Cyprus, and to refrain from any intervention directed against it." The General Assembly requested the Security Council to continue UN mediation.

In 1967, violent clashes between Greek and Turkish Cypriots nearly precipitated war between Greece and Turkey, but the situation was stabilized by mutual reduction of their armed contingents on Cyprus. In January 1970, the United Nations peace-keeping force numbered some 3,500 troops from several foreign countries. Both the Greek Cypriot and Turkish Cypriot factions also maintained sizable national guards of their own. Although talks continued between the two communities, no agreement was reached on the two basic issues: Politically the Turks wanted full autonomy, while the Greeks demanded continued unitary majority rule; territorially the Turks wanted Cyprus divided into Greek- and Turkish-controlled zones. This again violated the Greek concept of a unitary state.

On 2 July 1974, Makarios accused the Greek government of seeking his overthrow and called for the immediate withdrawal of 650 Greek officers in the Cypriot National Guard. Less than two weeks later, the National Guard toppled the Makarios government, forcing the Archbishop into exile and installing Nikos Sampson as president. To counter the threat of Greek control over Cyprus, Turkish Cypriot leaders asked Turkey to intervene militarily. Turkish troops landed on 20 July, but within two days the UN force had been augmented and a UN Security Council cease-fire resolution had taken effect. Sampson resigned on 23 July, and Glafkos Clerides became acting president. While peace talks were conducted in Geneva, the Turkish military buildup continued, and when talks broke down in mid-August a full-scale Turkish offensive began. By August 16, when a second cease-fire was accepted, Turkish forces controlled about 40% of the island. Makarios returned to Cyprus and resumed the presidency in December. On 13 February 1975, in an action considered illegal by the Cyprus government, the Turkish-held area proclaimed itself the Turkish Cypriot Federated State; Rauf Denktaş, a former vice-president of Cyprus and the president of the interim Autonomous Turkish Cypriot Administration, became president. A Security Council resolution on 12 March regretted the proclamation of the new state and called for the resumption of intercommunal talks. During 1975, progress was made on refugee problems and the exchange of prisoners of war, but a political settlement appeared remote.

12 GOVERNMENT
The constitution of Cyprus respects the two existing ethnic communities, Greek and Turkish, by providing specifically for representation from each community in the government. The president must be Greek and the vice-president Turkish. These officers are elected for five years by universal suffrage by the Greek and Turkish communities respectively; each has the right of veto over legislation and over certain decisions of the Council of Ministers, a body composed of seven Greek and three Turkish ministers, designated by the president and vice-president jointly. Legislative authority is vested in the 50-member House of Representatives elected by the two chief communities in the proportion of 35 Greek and 15 Turkish. In January 1964, following the outbreak of fighting, Turkish representatives withdrew from the House of Representatives. Temporary constitutional provisions for administering the country were put into effect.

Archbishop Makarios was reelected president in the presidential elections of February 1968 and 1973; Rauf Denktaş was elected vice-president in 1973. No parliamentary elections were held from 1960 through mid-1976.

See continental political: front cover G6; physical: back cover G6
LOCATION: 34°33′ to 35°41′N; 32°20′ to 34°35′E. **TERRITORIAL SEA LIMIT:** 12 mi.

On 13 February 1975, subsequent to the Turkish invasion of Cyprus, the Turkish Cypriot Federated State was proclaimed in the northern part of the island, and Denktaş became its president. A draft constitution, approved by the State's Constituent Assembly on 25 April, was ratified by the Turkish Cypriot community in a referendum on 8 June. Establishment of the Federated State was described by Denktaş as "not a unilateral declaration of independence" but a preparation for the establishment of a federal system. The government of Cyprus considers the action illegal; both Cyprus and Greece protested before the UN Security Council. Treaties entered into at the time Cyprus became independent had precluded both enosis and federation.

13 POLITICAL PARTIES
Since 1970, the principal pro-Makarios party in the Greek community has been the Unified Front (Enieon), which supports Makarios, private property, and the Hellenic character of the Cypriot state. The Progressive Party of the Working Class (Anorthotikon Komma Ergazomenou Laou) is the Communist Party of Cyprus. The Progressive Front (Proodeftiki Parataxis) is a political party sponsored by the right-wing farmers' union. The United Democratic Union of the Center (Eniea Demokratiki Enosis Centrou) is a moderate left-wing party that favors nationalization of mining companies. The Democratic National Party (Demokratikon Ethnikon Komma) supports union with Greece.

The Turkish community has had few political organizations. Principal nationalist parties are the Republican Turkish Party (Cumhuryietçi Türk Partisi) and the National Solidarity Party (Ulusal Dayanisma).

14 LOCAL GOVERNMENT

Elected municipal corporations function in the chief towns and larger villages. The smaller villages are managed by commissions comprising a headman (mukhtar) and elders (azas). Voluntary district committees are responsible for activities outside the scope of the major government development projects.

The 1960 constitution provided for two communal chambers, these bodies having wide authority within the two main ethnic groups, including the power to draft laws, impose taxes, and determine all religious, educational, and cultural questions. The Greek Communal Chamber, however, was abolished in 1965, and its functions reverted to the Ministry of Education. The Turkish Communal Chamber embraces municipalities that are exclusively Turkish. Originally the duties of the Turkish Communal Chamber were to supervise Turkish cooperatives, sports organizations, and charitable institutions. But since about 1967, the Turkish communities have maintained strict administrative control of their own areas and have insisted on civil autonomy.

15 JUDICIAL SYSTEM

In the Greek Cypriot area, the Supreme Court is the final appellate court and has final authority in constitutional and administrative cases. It deals with appeals from assize and district courts, as well as from decisions by its own judges, acting singly in certain matters. There are six district courts and six assize courts, as well as seven Orthodox Church courts. The church courts have exclusive jurisdiction in matrimonial cases involving Greek Orthodox Church members. Appeals go from these courts to the appellate tribunal of the Church. The Supreme Council of Judicature appoints judges to the district and assize courts.

In the Turkish-held area, a Supreme Court acts as final appellate court, with powers similar to those of the Supreme Court in the Greek Cypriot area. In addition to district and assize courts, there are two Turkish communal courts as well as a communal appeals court.

16 ARMED FORCES

Under the Zürich agreement, Cyprus was to have an army of 2,000 men, of whom 60% were to be Greek and 40% Turkish; compulsory military service could be instituted only with the agreement of the president and vice-president of the republic. After the events of 19 December 1962, the government passed a military conscription law, enlisting men between the ages of 19 and 26. The Cypriot army, which is now wholly Greek, comprises some 15,000 men.

The Turkish community has its own police force of about 2,000 men; about 5,000 Turkish Cypriots are in the Fighters' Army. A sizable Turkish military presence on Cyprus (about 40,000 in November 1975) has complemented these native forces since the 1974 intervention. Peacekeeping units of the UN numbered more than 4,000. British forces are stationed on two British bases, Akrotiri and Dhekelia.

17 MIGRATION

The population has been diminished by annual emigration averaging from 2,500 to 3,500 in recent years. The emigrants are principally young agricultural workers, carpenters, tailors, dressmakers, laborers, barbers, waiters, and housekeepers. Emigration was high in the period from 1960 to 1964, averaging 8,470 persons annually. From 1965 to 1971 the annual rate declined to 2,830 and reached a new low of 1,312 in 1973. Immigration as such does not really exist. A substantial number of Cypriots return to take up permanent residence after years of living and working abroad.

The 1974 war on Cyprus made refugees of about one-third of the population; about 225,000 persons were listed by the UN as "displaced" on 29 August. About $22 million was spent under UN auspices for resettlement of and humanitarian assistance to refugees during 1974. During intercommunal talks in Vienna in 1975, it was agreed that 9,000 Turkish Cypriots would be allowed to migrate from the south to the Turkish-held area in the north, and that 10,000 Greek Cypriots who wished to stay in the north would be joined by 800 of their southern relatives.

18 INTERNATIONAL COOPERATION

Cyprus was admitted to UN membership on 20 September 1960 and has become a member of many of its specialized agencies. Cyprus is also a member of the Commonwealth of Nations. A cooperation agreement between Cyprus and the EEC became effective in June 1973.

19 ECONOMY

For ages, Cyprus has been an agricultural country. It has neither coal nor iron. Natural power resources are meager since the rivers are mere seasonal torrents.

Although the manufacturing and the service sectors have increased in importance, the largest sector of the Cypriot work force continues to be employed in agriculture, forestry, and fishing. Pastoral and agricultural acreage accounts for 66% of the land.

Agriculture is in transition from subsistence farming to production for local and export markets. Mechanization has reached an advanced stage, and primitive subsistence agriculture persists only in the form of fragmented small plots, affording part-time occupation to the holder. Full use is ingeniously made of an erratic water supply. Nearly half of the exports come from the agricultural sector, principally from citrus fruit, although manufacturing has been expanding steadily. A large deficit in past years was offset by tourism, expenditures of military bases, and remittances from Cypriots working abroad.

The 1974 coup against Makarios and the Turkish armed intervention have badly disrupted the economy. Physical destruction and the displacement of nearly a third of the population reduced the output of the manufacturing, agricultural, and service sectors. In 1975, the Ministry of Finance reported that the lands occupied by Turkish forces (about 40% of the total area) had accounted for about 70% of the country's gross output in 1972.

20 INCOME

The GDP rose from C£167.9 million in 1968 to C£302.5 million in 1973. The contributions of the individual sectors of the economy were commerce, 21.2%; mining, manufacturing, electricity, and gas, 20%; agriculture, forestry, and fishing, 13.4%; services, 12.4%; transport, storage, and communications, 9.5%; construction, 9.5%; ownership of dwellings, 7.7%; and others (including defense), 6.3%. National income increased from C£163.7 million in 1968 to C£296.5 million in 1973. Per capita GNP at constant 1967 market prices rose from C£303.3 in 1968 to C£400.2 in 1973. Per capita private consumption was C£328.5 in 1973. Per capita income rose from an equivalent of $494 in 1960 to $1,113 in 1973. Gross investment in 1973 was C£80.2 million, as compared with C£37.4 million in 1968. Most of the total investment is in machinery purchased abroad and in domestic housing. There is much less investment in agriculture and mining. Both GDP and national income declined in 1974 because of the war.

21 LABOR

In December 1973, the active labor force totaled 271,000. The largest group was employed in agriculture, followed by services and manufacturing. Unemployment, as measured by voluntary registration at labor exchanges, rose from 3,314 in 1973 to 11,207 in 1974.

Trade unions were legalized in 1937, and by 1973 there were 109 trade unions with 95,627 members. These unions represent employees in agriculture, forestry, fishing, mining, quarrying, building construction, utilities, governmental services, trade, and general labor. Registration of trade unions is compulsory. Workers of the Turkish community have their own organization, the Cyprus Turkish Unions Federation, which has 14 unions and more than 6,000 members.

Comprehensive labor legislation regulates employer-employee relations and provides for the health, safety, and welfare of workers. Wage rates are generally fixed by collective bargaining; overtime is recompensed at time and a half. Most industries have paid holidays, and a 44-hour workweek is the norm in most industries.

²²AGRICULTURE

Agricultural methods are adapted to the island's hot and dry summers and generally limited water supply. Spring and early summer growth is dependent on moisture stored in the soil from the winter rains, but summer cultivation is dependent on irrigation. In 1973, 11% of the land was irrigated and the remaining 89% was dry-farmed; the irrigated land provided 77% of total plant production in 1973 and 52% in 1974. In 1965, a government project was initiated to prevent excess loss of irrigation water.

Most farmers raise a variety of subsistence crops, ranging from grains and vegetables to fruits. Since 1960 there has been increased production of citrus fruits and potatoes. Principal crops in 1974 (in tons) included oranges, 155,000; potatoes, 150,000; grapes, 145,000; barley, 110,000; wheat, 95,000; grapefruit, 57,000; and lemons, 18,000. Tomatoes, carrots, olives, and other fruits and vegetables are also grown. Output of most export crops declined in 1974. Total agricultural income rose from c£34.7 million in 1968 to c£41.6 million in 1973.

The government's policy is to increase agricultural output, and it has established a number of agencies to carry out this objective. Special attention has been given to conservation and irrigation, mechanization, cooperatives, and experimentation under a broad extension program. The government requires that agricultural exports be of high quality, and it subsidizes the production of export crops, particularly cereals and grapes.

The areas that have been Turkish-held since 1974 include much of Cyprus' most fertile land.

²³ANIMAL HUSBANDRY

Animal husbandry has been receiving greater attention from the government, in order to increase meat production both for consumption and for export. The government's policy is to improve pasturage and control grazing. Sheep and goats, which feed upon rough grazing land unsuitable for cultivation, provide most of the meat and milk products. In 1973, goats numbered about 340,000, sheep about 430,000, and hogs about 163,000.

Indigenous cattle, kept primarily as draft animals, are decreasing with the advance of farm mechanization. There is no indigenous breed of dairy cattle, but near main towns, dairy stock, mostly shorthorns, are kept under stall-fed conditions, and Friesian cattle have been imported from the Netherlands and the UK. Cattle numbered about 17,500 head in 1973.

Livestock products in 1974 included 14,500 tons of pork, 7,900 tons of poultry meat, 67,000 tons of milk, and 93.6 million eggs. Output dropped below 1973 levels in virtually every category.

²⁴FISHING

The year-round fishing industry, which is carried on mostly in coastal waters not more than 2 miles from shore, employed 585 persons full- or part-time in 1974, including the owners of 393 rowboats, small sailing craft, small power-propelled vessels, and trawlers. The fish in Cyprus waters are small from the lack of nutrient salts, and the catches are meager. The 1974 catch was 23,750 cwt, which had a value of c£773,121. There is no deep-sea fishing. Sponges of good quality are taken, mostly by licensed fishermen from the Greek Dodecanese Islands. However, landings declined from 110 cwt in 1972 to 8 cwt in 1974, and the value of the catch correspondingly declined from c£35,200 to c£3,000.

²⁵FORESTRY

About 670 sq mi (18.7% of the island's total area) are forested; 532 sq mi are reserves managed by the Forest Department, the remainder being natural growths of poor scrub used by village communities as fuel and as grazing grounds. Besides furnishing commercial timber, the forests are of great importance as a protective cover for water catchment areas and in the prevention of soil erosion. Their value is also scenic, numerous holiday resorts being situated in the forest reserves. Most numerous by far among forest trees is the Aleppo pine. The stone pine is found on the highest slopes of the Troodos Massif; the cedar, once a flourishing tree, has become a rarity. In the lowlands, eucalyptus and other exotic hardwoods have been introduced. The demand for timber during World War I resulted in some overcutting, and in 1956 large fires further reduced the forests, particularly in Paphos, where 6 million cu feet of standing timber were destroyed. To offset these losses, all felling of fresh trees for timber was stopped and systematic reforestation begun. Cyprus' timber requirements average 3 million cu feet annually, approximately half of which must be imported. There are 5 large sawmills and 200 small band mills.

Timber cut amounts to about 1.1 million cu feet per year and brings an annual revenue of about c£200,000. A forestry college was opened at Prodhromos in 1951. The Cyprus Forest Industries Co. has been established to process large quantities of timber.

²⁶MINING

Mining grew between World War I and World War II but was halted during both wars. Production reached a peak in the mid-1950s, when minerals formed about 50% of total exports. In 1973, they fell to 19.4% of exports. The place of mining in the GDP similarly declined from 16.7% in 1952 to 3.8% in 1974. In 1973, 3,472 persons were employed in the mining industry.

Ownership and control of minerals and quarry materials are vested in the government, which may grant prospecting permits, mining leases, and quarrying licenses. The main mineral exports are copper, iron pyrites, chromium ores, asbestos, umber, bentonite, and gypsum. Copper pyrites are mined at Mavrovouni, Kinousa, and Limni. Asbestos (chrysotile) is produced from large quarries at Amiandos in the Troodos area; chromite (chrome iron ore) also is mined in the Troodos Massif. Gypsum, found near Kalavasos as well as in smaller quarries, is used locally.

Output of mines and quarries in 1974 (in tons) included iron pyrites, 171,910; copper concentrates, 49,804; marble, 38,900; chromium ore, 33,275; asbestos, 31,015; umber, 13,022; and raw gypsum, 11,150. Mineral production, especially of construction materials, declined markedly in 1974. Gross output declined from c£16,962,000 in 1973 to an estimated c£13,356,000 in 1974.

²⁷ENERGY AND POWER

The principal source of power is steam-generated electricity, which is distributed by the Electricity Authority of Cyprus from two generating stations at Dhekelia and Moni. These plants have an installed capacity of 204,000 kw. Production was 781.7 million kwh in 1973 and 693.3 million kwh in 1974. The grid system included all towns and 528 villages.

²⁸INDUSTRY

Industries are numerous and small in scale, most of them employing fewer than 10 workers. Working owners make up a large part of the industrial labor force. Manufacturing, encouraged by income tax concessions and protected by import tariffs, primarily involves the processing of local products for both export and the home market, or the production of consumer items such as canned fruits and vegetables; wine, beer, and soft drinks; confectionery products; dairy products, and other foods; footwear, hosiery, and other wearing apparel; quilts, pottery, and earthenware; plastic products; vegetable and essential oils; chemical products; and cigarettes and tobacco. Wines, leather handbags and luggage, canned fruits and vegetables, lithographed crown corks, and nails are made principally for export. Major plants include modern flour mills, tire-treading factories, knitting mills, ore-processing facilities, and a petroleum refinery. Furniture and carts are also manufactured. The requirements of the growing construction industry are met by two large cement factories and by plants supplying bricks, roofing tiles, mosaics, and gypsum.

In 1974, 27,264 persons were employed in manufacturing, a decline from 36,019 in 1973. Gross output totaled C£108,630,000, as compared with C£110,639,000 in 1973. In 1974, 338,400 tons of cement, 2,747,000 imperial gallons of beer for domestic consumption, and more than 271,000 proof gallons of other intoxicating beverages were produced.

Besides industries operated under factory conditions, there are a number of cottage industries; a large part of the olive crop is pressed for oil in small village presses, and lacemaking retains its traditional importance.

29 DOMESTIC TRADE

A flourishing cooperative movement provides facilities for marketing agricultural products. In 1972 there were more than 500 Greek cooperative societies, with more than 100,000 members. Since 1963, no data have been available on the Turkish cooperatives. Many towns and villages have cooperative stores.

In the towns there are small shops, general stores, and bazaars. Nicosia is the major commercial center and distribution point, and most importers and exporters have their main offices there. In 1973, domestic wholesale and retail trade was valued at C£26.3 million.

Advertising is mainly through newspapers and television; limited use is made of advertising agencies.

Business hours are from 8 A.M. to 1 P.M. and 2:30 P.M. to 6 P.M. in winter and from 7:30 A.M. to 1 P.M. and 4 P.M. to 7 P.M. in the summer. Shops are open only in the morning on Saturday.

30 FOREIGN TRADE

With limited natural resources, Cyprus is dependent on other countries for much of its needs. Other than minerals and some agricultural commodities, it has few surpluses; as a result, the balance of trade grows more unfavorable annually. In 1968, exports were 52.2% of imports, but in 1973, exports were 38.4% of imports. Principal export products are fruits and vegetables, copper ores and concentrates, wines, and apparel.

Imports reflect the heavy demand for machinery and other manufactured items, as well as for foods, fuels and lubricants, chemicals, and oils and fats. Trade was disrupted by the 1974 war, and exports declined from $154 million in 1973 to $129.4 million in 1974, as imports were declining from $447.8 million to $408.6 million.

Principal exports in 1974 (in millions of dollars) were:

Fruits and vegetables	61.8
Nonferrous metal ores	17.5
Alcoholic beverages	14.5
Clothing	6.1
Footwear	2.7
Other exports	26.8
TOTAL	129.4

Principal imports in 1974 (in millions of dollars) were:

Machinery	68.6
Petroleum and petroleum products	51.1
Textiles, yarns, fabrics	32.2
Chemicals	30.7
Cereals and preparations	29.3
Iron and steel	28.3
Transport equipment	22.0
Other imports	146.4
TOTAL	408.6

The UK is Cyprus' leading import supplier and export purchaser, accounting for 25.3% of total trade in 1974. Other EEC countries accounted for an additional 34%. Principal trade partners in 1974 (in millions of dollars) were:

	EXPORTS	IMPORTS	BALANCE
UK	51.8	84.1	− 32.3
FRG	8.1	37.8	− 29.7
Italy	2.3	31.8	− 29.5
Greece	2.5	26.9	− 24.4
France	1.1	26.9	− 25.8
US	0.9	25.9	− 25.0
USSR	10.8	15.9	− 5.1
Other countries	51.9	159.3	−107.4
TOTALS	129.4	408.6	−279.2

31 BALANCE OF PAYMENTS

During the 1950s, the annual trade deficit ranged from $40 million to $60 million, but this was generally overcome by UK Treasury transfers, by income from tourism, and by large remittances from overseas immigrants. The deficit, moreover, resulted principally from the cost of maintaining British military forces on the island and did not represent an actual difference between what Cypriots bought and sold abroad. By 1964, the annual trade deficit had been reduced, reaching a low of C£14.6 million. The Cyprus pound remained stable throughout the 1950s. After independence, however, reduced UK transfers and tourist income resulted in decreased monetary reserves.

In the late 1960s and early 1970s, invisible receipts increased substantially, and positive payments balances were recorded. In 1973 and 1974, however, increased trade deficits led to overall payments deficits. Following are summaries of Cyprus' balance of payments for 1973 and 1974 (in millions of Cyprus pounds):

	1973	1974
CURRENT ACCOUNTS		
Trade, net	−83.3	−86.3
Invisible receipts	97.4	104.3
Invisible payments	−42.3	−44.5
TOTALS	−28.2	−26.5
CAPITAL ACCOUNTS		
Short-term capital	7.3	1.9
Long-term capital	16.7	17.7
TOTALS	24.0	19.6
Errors and omissions	−0.3	− 3.7
Net change	−4.5	−10.6

International reserves, which reached a peak of $319.6 million at the end of 1972, declined to $214.1 million as of 31 March 1976.

32 BANKING

In 1963, the Ottoman Bank (since renamed the Bank of Cyprus) was designated as the government's banking and currency clearing agent. Central bank assets totaled C£109,592,000 as of 30 June 1975. There are 2 central cooperative banks, and in 1973 there were 804 cooperative banking societies, with 269,000 members, in the Greek cooperative movement. At the end of 1974, cooperative banks held demand deposits of C£6.18 million and time and savings deposits of C£23.4 million.

Principal overseas banks are Barclays Bank International (with its subsidiary, Barclays DCO, which provides medium-term financing on a commercial basis for development projects of all kinds), the Chartered Bank, the National Bank of Greece, the National and Grindlays Bank, and the Turkye Is Bankasi. Commercial local banks include the Bank of Cyprus, the Popular Bank of Cyprus, and the Turkish Bank of Nicosia. Specialized banking business is conducted by the Mortgage Bank of Cyprus, Lombard Banking (Cyprus), the Cyprus Development Bank, and the Cooperative Central Bank.

Currency in circulation totaled c£34,937,992 as of 30 June 1975.

³³INSURANCE
In 1973 there were 44 insurance companies, mostly British. Life, fire, marine, accident, burglary, and other types of insurance are available. As of 1974, all insurance companies had ceased operations because of political turmoil.

³⁴SECURITIES
There are no securities exchanges in Cyprus.

³⁵PUBLIC FINANCE
Import duties and income tax are the principal sources of government revenue. The principal ordinary expenditures are education, defense, and police and fire services. Following are summaries of central government revenues and expenditures for 1973 and 1974 (in millions of Cyprus pounds):

	1973	1974
REVENUES		
Direct taxes	15.6	13.7
Indirect taxes	28.7	22.7
Fees, charges, and reimbursements	7.7	6.5
Other receipts	11.6	10.8
TOTALS	63.6	53.7
EXPENDITURES		
Education	7.7	8.5
Defense	3.6	6.5
Police and fire services	5.0	6.0
Public health	3.8	4.5
Subsidies	6.3	8.0
Interest on public debt	2.6	2.3
Other ordinary expenditures	22.4	21.1
Development expenditures	17.7	13.5
TOTALS	69.1	70.4
Balance	−5.5	−16.7

The government debt as of 31 December 1974 was c£20 million, of which c£8 million was foreign.

³⁶TAXATION
Taxes on expenditure (customs, excise, etc.) and taxes on income are the main sources of government revenue.

Income tax was introduced in 1941. Individuals whose incomes do not exceed c£400 are exempt; for others, the tax ranges from 75 mils for every pound in excess of c£400 to 600 mils for every pound in excess of c£5,000. A withholding system, applying both to salaried employees and wage earners, has been in operation since 1953. Companies pay tax at the flat rate of 42.5% and deduct this from any dividends paid; in turn, shareholders may claim credit for the tax thus paid.

³⁷CUSTOMS AND DUTIES
Import duty is payable on a wide variety of commodities; highest rates are imposed on jewelry, caviar, furs, and other items listed as luxuries. Taxable at lower rates are liquors, cigarettes, spirits, motor vehicles, cotton and cotton piece goods, medicines, undressed hides and skins, paints, and iron and milled steel bars. Among some 175 items specifically exempt are wheat and barley, flour, butter, frozen meat, fresh fish, machinery, books and printed matter, and disinfectants and insecticides.

In May 1962, the government relaxed import restrictions and eliminated discriminatory treatment on imports from the dollar area. Following the decree, the minister of commerce and industry was granted additional legal powers to regulate imports, including authority to restrict or prohibit the import of any foreign product if such action would benefit the island's economy.

³⁸FOREIGN INVESTMENTS
The majority of factories are owned by domestic companies, but in most of the major industrial concerns there has been considerable British and Greek capital.

³⁹ECONOMIC POLICY
The first development plan (1962–66), designed to broaden the base of the economy and to raise the standard of living, was adopted in 1961. Plans called for an average annual growth rate of 5.5% (compound rate; the actual growth rate was 5.4%). The second development plan (1967–71) called for an annual growth rate of 7% in the GDP. Particular attention was to be paid to agriculture. Actual growth during this period was nearly 8% annually.

The third development plan (1972–76) envisaged an annual economic growth rate of 7.2%. However, a drought in 1973 and the war in 1974 badly disrupted development programs. Physical destruction, a massive refugee problem, and a collapse of production, services, and exports made it impossible for Cyprus to reach the targets of the 1974 development budget (c£17.3 million).

⁴⁰HEALTH
Cyprus had 482 doctors, 196 midwives, and 159 dentists in 1973. There were 129 hospitals, with 3,488 beds. In addition to six district hospitals there was a sanatorium. There are both public and private medical facilities, including a number of rural health centers. The island has a low incidence of infectious diseases, but hydatid disease (echinococcosis) is endemic. The infant mortality rate was 33.3 per 1,000 live births in 1973. The estimated average life expectancy in 1975 was 70.4 for males and 74.3 for females.

⁴¹SOCIAL WELFARE
In 1957, the colonial government introduced a comprehensive scheme of social insurance. This was amended in 1964 to include all working persons on the island, including farmers. Improvements in the scheme were made routinely up to 1974. It provides unemployment and sickness benefits; old age, widows', and orphans' pensions; maternity benefits; and death and marriage grants. Benefits are financed through contributions by employees (or the self-employed), employers, and the government.

In 1973, 183,000 persons were active contributors to social insurance programs. Total contributions to the system were c£5.9 million, and c£6.2 million was paid out in 1973.

⁴²HOUSING
Village homes in Cyprus are generally constructed of stone, sundried mud bricks, and other locally available material, but in some of the more prosperous rural centers there are houses of burnt brick or concrete.

In 1973 there were an estimated 164,000 occupied dwellings on Cyprus, of which 71,000 were urban dwellings. The growth rate for the urban housing stock was 3.7% in 1973. Density per room averaged 0.9 persons in 1973. A growing population has resulted in a shortage of dwellings, especially in urban areas. Housing problems were aggravated by the events of 1974, which resulted in the displacement of about 225,000 people.

⁴³EDUCATION
In 1959, the Greek and Turkish communities were made responsible for their own school systems. In 1965, the Greek Communal Chamber was abolished and its responsibilities placed in the Ministry of Education.

In the Greek educational system in 1974 there were 135 preprimary schools, with an enrollment of 6,320 pupils. Of these schools, only 13 were public. At the elementary level there were 558 public and 6 private schools, with an enrollment of 63,400. About 88% of eligible students go on to the secondary-level schools, of which 45 were public and 38 private in 1974. Enrollment reached 33,830 and 11,170, respectively. There were also 8 public secondary technical schools, with 4,670 students. At the third level, there were 7 institutions, with an enrollment of 850 students. Some 90% of Cypriot postsecondary students pursue their studies abroad. Cyprus also had 12 public special schools with an enrollment of 500 children in 1974. In 1974 there were 5,314 teachers in the educational system; 2,618 were attached to preprimary and primary schools, 2,525 served at the secondary level, 88 taught at the postsecondary institutions, and 83 were at special schools.

In 1973 there were 167 elementary schools in the Turkish area, with 16,014 pupils; 18 secondary schools, with 7,190 students; 6 vocational institutions, with 753 students; and 1 teacher-training institution, with 13 students.

44 LIBRARIES AND MUSEUMS

In 1973 there were 2 university, 649 secondary-school, 25 specialized, and 116 public libraries, with combined holdings in excess of 1.3 million volumes. The Ministry of Education Library in Nicosia (25,000 volumes) serves as a central public library for Cyprus. There are also municipal libraries in Famagusta, Limassol, Ktima, Larnaca, and Paphos, and a bookmobile service in the Nicosia environs. Among the most important specialized libraries are those of the Cyprus Museum (12,000 volumes), the Phaneromeni Library of the Eastern Orthodox Church (28,000), and the Pedagogical Academy (18,000).

The Department of Antiquities is responsible for a wide, continuing program of research at Neolithic and classical sites; on behalf of ecclesiastical authorities, it conserves the cathedrals, mosques, monasteries, and other monuments, and over a period of many years has cooperated with numerous scientific expeditions to investigate Cyprus antiquities. The entire range of archaeological discoveries from prehistoric to medieval times is displayed in the Cyprus Museum at Nicosia. Besides the central museum, important collections are preserved in museums at Paphos, Larnaca, and Limassol.

45 ORGANIZATIONS

The government encourages cooperative societies in many ways, including exemption from certain forms of taxation. In 1973 there were about 500 credit and savings societies; 300 consumer and supply cooperatives; and 50 producer, marketing, processing, and other societies.

The Carob Marketing Federation, whose members are the five Carob Marketing Unions, was established in 1953. There are a great number of youth organizations, particularly athletic clubs. In 1962, the island's commercial organizations, the Cyprus Chamber of Commerce, the Cyprus Federation of Trade and Industry, and the Union of Industrialists, combined to form the Cyprus Chamber of Commerce and Industry.

46 PRESS

Fifteen dailies, 12 weeklies, and 19 periodicals are published on Cyprus in English, Greek, or Turkish. Nicosia has traditionally been the publishing center for the island and the editorial headquarters of nearly all the daily newspapers and weeklies. Circulations are small, and few newspapers have trained editorial staffs. The following are the major daily newspapers (with estimated 1975 circulations):

	ORIENTATION	CIRCULATION
Phileleftheros (Greek)	Independent	15,000
Haravghi (Greek)	Democratic left-wing	13,500
Eleftheria (Greek)	National liberal	13,250
Agon (Greek)	Independent	12,000
Makhi (Greek)	Independent	12,000
Cyprus Bulletin (English)	Independent	8,000
Ethniki (Greek)	Enosis movement	8,000
Cyprus Mail (English)	Independent	5,700
Bozkurt (Turkish)	Independent	5,000
Halkin Sesi (Turkish)	Independent Turkish nationalist	5,000

47 TOURISM

Although Cyprus is situated off the main routes of travel and has few luxury hotels, the island's salubrious climate, its scenic beauties, extensive roads, and rich antiquarian interests have attracted numerous visitors. Of a total of more than 264,000 tourists in 1973, 116,000 came from the UK, 27,000 from the Federal Republic of Germany (FRG), 22,000 from Sweden, 15,000 from the US, and 15,000 from Greece. There were more than 100 hotels with 10,796 beds, primarily located in the larger towns on the coasts. The tourist trade was disrupted by the 1974 turmoil and was still below normal in 1975.

48 FAMOUS CYPRIOTS

Most widely known of Cypriots in the pre-Christian world was the philosopher Zeno (born about 336 B.C.), who expounded his philosophy of stoicism chiefly in the marketplace of Athens.

Makarios III (b.1913), archbishop and ethnarch since 1950 and a leader in the struggle for independence, was elected the first president of Cyprus in December 1959; reelected in 1968 and 1973, he was deposed in July 1974 but restored to power in December. Rauf Denktaş (b.1924), the leader of the Turkish Cypriot community, was elected vice-president in 1973, and became president of the Turkish Cypriot Federated State in February 1975.

49 DEPENDENCIES

Cyprus has no dependencies.

50 BIBLIOGRAPHY

Adams, Thomas W., and Alvin J. Cottrell. *Cyprus Between East and West.* Baltimore: Johns Hopkins Press, 1968.

Alastos, Doros. *Cyprus in History: A Survey of 5,000 Years.* London: Zeno, 1955.

Arnold, Percy. *Cyprus Challenge: A Colonial Island and Its Aspirations.* London: Hogarth Press, 1956.

Casson, Stanley. *Ancient Cyprus: Its Art and Archaeology.* London: Methuen, 1937.

Cyprus Chamber of Commerce and Industry Directory: A Guide to Commerce, Industry, Tourism, and Agriculture. New York: International Publications Service, 1969.

Durrell, Lawrence. *Bitter Lemons.* London: Faber & Faber, 1957.

Gunnis, Rupert. *Historic Cyprus: A Guide to Its Towns and Villages, Monasteries and Castles.* London: Methuen, 1937.

Henderson, Celia. *Cyprus.* Chester Springs, Pa.: Dufour, 1968.

Hill, Sir George Francis. *History of Cyprus.* Cambridge: Cambridge University Press, 1940-52.

Home, Gordon. *Cyprus Then and Now.* London: Dent, 1960.

Ioannides, Eudoros. *Cyprus Guerrilla: Grivas, Makarios, and the British.* London: Heinemann, 1960.

Karageorgis, Vassos. *Ancient Civilization of Cyprus.* New York: Cowles, 1964.

Kyriakides, Stanley. *Cyprus: Constitutionalism and Crisis Government.* Philadelphia: University of Pennsylvania Press, 1968.

Meyer, A. J., and S. Vassiliou. *The Economy of Cyprus.* Cambridge: Harvard University Press, 1962.

Nagel Travel Guide to Cyprus. New York: Cowles, 1964.

Newman, Philip. *A Short History of Cyprus.* London: Longmans, Green, 1956.

Purcell, H. D. *Cyprus.* New York: Praeger, 1968.

Republic of Cyprus. *The Second Five-Year Plan.* Nicosia: Planning Bureau, 1967.

Spyridakis, C. *Brief History of Cyprus.* Chicago: Argonaut, 1964.

FIJI

CAPITAL: Suva. **FLAG:** The national flag of Fiji consists of the red, white, and blue Union Jack at the upper left quadrant of a light blue field with the Fiji shield in the fly. **ANTHEM:** *God Save the Queen.* **MONETARY UNIT:** The Fijian dollar (F$) of 100 cents is a nonconvertible currency. There are coins of 1, 2, 5, 10, and 20 cents and notes of 50 cents and 1, 5, 10, and 20 Fijian dollars. F$1=US$1.1111 (or US$1=F$0.90). **WEIGHTS AND MEASURES:** British weights and measures are used, but conversion to the metric system is being considered. **HOLIDAYS:** New Year's Day, 1 January; (Independence) Cession Day, 10 October; Christmas Day, 25 December; Boxing Day, 26 December. Movable holidays are Good Friday, Holy Saturday, Easter Monday, Queen's Birthday, August Holiday, and Prince of Wales' Birthday. **TIME:** 12 midnight=noon GMT.

[1] LOCATION, SIZE, AND EXTENT

Fiji, in the South Pacific, comprises about 850 islands, of which only about 100 are inhabited. The island of Rotuma, added to Fiji in 1881, is geographically separate from the main archipelago and comprises an area of 44 sq km (17 sq mi). The total area (including Rotuma) is 18,272 sq km (7,055 sq mi). Fiji (not including Rotuma) extends 595 km (370 mi) SE–NW and 454 km (282 mi) NE–SW. The largest islands are Viti Levu, with an area of 10,386 sq km (4,010 sq mi), and Vanua Levu, with 5,535 sq km (2,137 sq mi). Fiji's total coastline is 2,601 km (1,616 mi).

[2] TOPOGRAPHY

The larger Fiji islands are volcanic, with rugged peaks, and flatland where rivers have built deltas. Coral reefs surround the islands. Viti Levu's highest point, Mt. Victoria, is 4,341 feet; 28 other peaks are over 3,000 feet. Its main river, the Rewa, is navigable by small boats for 70 miles.

[3] CLIMATE

Temperatures at sea level range from 15.6°C to 32°C (60°F to 90°F). The easterly trade winds blow throughout the greater part of the year. Annual rainfall is well distributed. In Suva it averages 123 inches. At sea level on the leeward sides of the islands there are well-defined wet and dry seasons, with mean annual totals of between 70 and 80 inches of rain.

[4] FLORA AND FAUNA

Almost half of Fiji is forested. The larger islands have forests on the windward side and grassland on the leeward slopes. Mangroves and coconut plantations fringe the coasts. Among indigenous fauna are bats, rats, snakes, frogs and lizards, and many species of birds. As of 1975, endangered species in the Fiji Islands included Macgillivray's petrel, masked parakeet, pink-billed parrot finch, Fiji iguana, and Fiji snake (*Ogmodon vitianus*).

[5] POPULATION

The 1975 population was estimated at 577,000, with a total of 635,000 projected for 1980. The average annual population growth rate is estimated at 1.91%, based on a crude birthrate of 23.2 per 1,000 inhabitants, a crude death rate of 4.1, and a net natural increase of 19.1. The estimated population density in 1975 was 31.6 per sq km (81.8 per sq mi). Suva, the capital, has a population of about 60,000, Lautoka, 12,000; Mba, 5,000; Nadi (Nandi), 2,800; Nausori, 2,100; Sigatoka, 1,200; and Savusavu, 1,000.

[6] ETHNIC GROUPS

The indigenous Fijian population is predominantly Melanesian, with a Polynesian admixture. In 1974, the population was estimated to be 51% of Indian origin, 44% indigenous Fijian, 1.7% part European, 1% Rotuman, 0.3% wholly European, and 2% other Pacific races.

[7] LANGUAGE

Fijian dialects belong to the Malayo-Polynesian group of languages. The Bau dialect is used almost throughout the archipelago, except on Rotuma Island, where the Polynesian Rotumans speak Rotuman. Hindustani is the lingua franca of the Indians of Fiji. English is the official language. Fijian and Hindi are also used in the Fiji parliament.

[8] RELIGION

Virtually all indigenous Fijians are Christians (about 83% Methodist and 13% Roman Catholic). Among the Indian Fijians, 80% are Hindu, 15.4% Muslim, and 1.3% Sikh.

[9] TRANSPORTATION

Fiji is extending its local roads, which are mostly gravel. In 1975, work on the new highway between Suva and Nadi (Nandi) was nearly completed. In 1972, some 22,000 vehicles were licensed; approximately 6,700 new vehicles were registered and licensed during 1973 and 1974. Since 1973, the number of cars brought into the dominion has been subject to quota restrictions. A private railroad of 362 miles from Tavua to Sigatoka serves most of the sugar-producing areas.

International airports at Nadi (Nandi) and Suva have regularly scheduled flights by eight international airlines, to and from Europe, Australia, New Zealand, Mexico, Canada, and the US. Fiji Airways links the islands and neighboring countries and territories.

[10] COMMUNICATIONS

Suva and the surrounding area are served by an automatic telephone exchange with more than 15,000 telephones. Fiji is a link in the world Commonwealth cable system and has radiotelephone circuits to other Pacific territories. The Fiji Broadcasting Commission has 10 medium-wave and 2 FM transmitters. Programs are broadcast in English, Hindustani, and Fijian.

[11] HISTORY

The Dutch navigator Abel Tasman sighted the Fiji group in 1643; Captain Cook visited it in 1774; and Charles Wilkes headed a US expedition there for three months in 1840.

Early in the 19th century, ships engaged in the profitable sandalwood trade. White men, armed deserters and shipwreck survivors, helped raise the chiefs of Bau to a dominant position. Then traders settled on the islands. Protestant missionaries from

Tonga arrived in 1835, and French Catholic priests in 1844. After a few chiefs had been converted, more and more Fijians became Christians. In the 1850s there was conflict between the districts of Bau and Rewa. Cakobau, the most powerful chief in Fiji at the time, was driven back to Bau. In 1855, he was joined by the king of Tonga, with 2,000 warriors. Their combined forces defeated the opposing chiefs at Kaba, and Cakobau became paramount chief of western Fiji. Following a period of administrative, economic, and financial difficulties, the chiefs appealed to the UK for assistance, and on 10 October 1874, Fiji was proclaimed a possession and dependency of the British crown.

Shortly after cession, indentured laborers from India entered Fiji. By 1916, when sponsored migration had virtually ceased, there were between 40,000 and 50,000 Indians. European settlers were granted elective representation in the Legislative Council in 1904, and Indians in 1929. Fijian representation was based on traditional lines until 1962, when the Council was reconstituted; the franchise was extended to women, and direct election of Fijian members was provided for. In 1966, the Council was enlarged and reconstituted, and Fiji was given virtual internal self-government. On 10 October 1970, Fiji became a sovereign and independent state within the Commonwealth of Nations.

12 GOVERNMENT
Fiji is a member of the Commonwealth, with the British queen as head of state and a governor-general acting on her behalf. The cabinet, responsible to the Fiji parliament, consists of a prime minister and ministers appointed by the governor-general. Parliament consists of an elected House of Representatives and an appointive Senate. The preindependence Legislative Council became the country's first House of Representatives. The 52-member House is apportioned as follows: 22 Fijian members (12 elected by voters on the Fijian common roll, 10 by voters on the national roll), 22 Indian members (12 elected by voters on the Indian common roll, 10 by voters on the national roll), and 8 general members—Chinese and European (3 elected by voters on the general common roll, 5 by voters on the national roll).

The Senate consists of 22 members: 8 nominated by the Council of Chiefs, 7 by the prime minister, 6 by the leader of the Opposition, and 1 by the Rotuman Council. The constitution provides for the appointment of an ombudsman to investigate complaints regarding the acts, omissions, decisions, and recommendations of specified governmental and other public bodies and offices.

13 POLITICAL PARTIES
The two major parties are the Alliance Party (AP) and the National Federation Party (NFP), formerly the Federation Party. The AP, formed in March 1966, is multiracial. It favored dominion status, with the British queen as constitutional monarch. The NFP, representing most of Fiji's Indians, favored a common roll and a republican form of government. In the April 1972 elections, the AP won 33 seats and the NFP 19.

Minor political parties include the National Political Organization of Fiji Indians, the Liberal Party, the Fijian Independent Party, and Muslim Political Organization. The Muslims seek proportional representation in the Senate.

14 LOCAL GOVERNMENT
Local government is organized under provincial and urban councils. Fiji is divided into 14 provinces, each with its own council. Some members are appointed, but each council has an elected majority. The councils have powers to make bylaws and to draw up their own budgets, subject to government approval. Suva has a city council, Lautoka a town council, and six other urban areas are administered by township boards. A few members of urban councils are appointed, but the majority of members are elected on a common roll of taxpayers and residents.

15 JUDICIAL SYSTEM
Fiji has a Supreme Court, a court of appeal, and magistrates' courts. The chief justice of the Supreme Court is appointed by the governor-general.

16 ARMED FORCES
Fiji has a regular force, a territorial force, and a reserve. The regular force has an infantry company of two platoons, and the territorial force one infantry battalion with supporting services.

17 MIGRATION
There is some migration to Fiji from neighboring Pacific islands.

18 INTERNATIONAL COOPERATION
Fiji joined the UN in 1970. It is a member of the SPC, the South Pacific Forum, the Asian Development Bank, ECAFE, and IDA, and is a signatory of the Lomé Convention.

19 ECONOMY
Fiji's economy is predominantly based on agriculture, gold mining, and tourism, and is heavily dependent on foreign trade. Major exports are sugar, coconut oil and copra, and gold; bananas, ginger, molasses, timber, and copper ore are also exported. Price, wage, rent, and other controls were instituted in 1973; despite these measures, consumer prices increased 14.4% in 1974 and 13.2% in 1975.

20 INCOME
The GDP in 1974 was F$302 million, which was 16% greater than the F$260 million GDP of 1973. Per capita income in 1974 was F$564.

21 LABOR
In 1975, Fiji had an estimated labor force of 162,400 persons, of whom 44,519 were wage earners and 26,344 salaried personnel.

Wages and conditions of employment are regulated by agreements between trade unions and employers. The average workweek ranges from 40 to 48 hours with time-and-a-half for overtime and doubletime for Sundays and holidays. There were 37 registered trade unions in 1975. Labor disruptions restricted productivity in the early 1970s.

22 AGRICULTURE
About 456,000 acres are under cultivation. In 1974, sugarcane was grown on 111,000 acres, producing 2,117,000 tons of cane and 269,000 tons of sugar, the lowest output in 10 years. The production of copra has fallen slightly. Sugar is a major export, coconut oil a lesser one. Rice production in 1973 was about 16,000 tons from 22,000 acres. Corn, tobacco, cocoa, pineapples, bananas, watermelons, and other fruits and vegetables are also cultivated.

23 ANIMAL HUSBANDRY
There were an estimated 130,000 head of cattle in 1973, down from 156,000 in 1972. Beef production has fallen steadily since 1971 and was about 1,400,000 lb in 1974. The decline is attributed to the excessive killing of female animals during 1969–70. Pork production has been rising and reached 286,000 tons in 1974. Milk production was about 45,000 tons in 1973.

24 FISHING
In 1972, 675 fishing vessels were registered. In 1974, 2,569,000 lb of fresh chilled or frozen fish, valued at F$658,000, and 1,148,000 lb of canned fish, valued at F$381,060, were exported. Export of pearl and trochus shells was increasing. Research on freshwater-fish breeding has progressed with the introduction of carp. A fish hatchery has been built.

25 FORESTRY
In 1972, forest lands in Fiji totaled 3,603 sq mi. The development of a national forestry policy in Fiji is hampered by the fact that most areas are owned by indigenous Fijians and administered by the Native Land Trust Board. Traditionally, logging and milling licenses have been issued for 12 months only, hence sawmill owners will not invest in machinery or development for so short a period. In the 1970s, however, the trend was toward long-term concessions.

26 MINING

Ownership of minerals is vested in the government, which grants mining and prospecting rights. Gold production was 2,488 kg in 1973, down from 3,301 kg in 1966. In 1973, about 1 ton of silver was produced, about half the 1968 total. In 1974, gold valued at F$6,139,895 and silver worth F$54,580 were mined. Manganese production, more than 6,000 tons in 1971, appears to have stopped. Prospecting is being carried out for oil, manganese, copper, bauxite, and phosphates.

27 ENERGY AND POWER

Electricity is generated by diesel-operated plants. The Fiji Electricity Authority, set up in 1966, is responsible for the generation and distribution of electricity throughout Fiji. Sugar mills generate their own power, as do hotels and other establishments outside town limits. Total installed electric capacity in 1973 was about 79,000 kw.

28 INDUSTRY

Fiji's industry is based primarily on processing of agricultural products, mainly sugarcane and coconut, and on mining and processing of minerals. Timber milling also has some export value. There are small industries supplying local needs, but expensive power, lack of trained labor, and small local markets inhibit growth.

29 DOMESTIC TRADE

Fiji has three large trading corporations and hundreds of small traders. The corporations own retail stores, interisland ships, plantations, hotels, travel services, copra crushing mills, and breweries. Small enterprises range from a single tailor or shopkeeper to larger family businesses. Most of these are operated by Indians or Chinese.

30 FOREIGN TRADE

Fijian exports in 1974 were valued at F$123,700,000. Sugar made up 70.5% of all domestic exports; coconut oil, 11.3%; gold, 9.1%; and others, 9.1%. Imports were valued at F$219,331,159, of which 27.2% were manufactured goods, 20.2% food and beverages, 16% machinery and transport equipment, 15.8% petroleum, and 20.8% other imports. The trade deficit was largely due to increased imports of goods for tourists. Principal trading partners in 1973 and their approximate percentages of Fiji's total trade were Australia, 25%; UK, 18%; Japan, 13%; New Zealand, 11%; US, 10%; and other countries, 23%. The UK and US were the leading export purchasers, while Australia, Japan, the UK, and New Zealand were the leading import suppliers.

31 BALANCE OF PAYMENTS

Fiji has an annual trade deficit and an annual deficit on current accounts. Long-term capital inflows, almost entirely from government sources, generally produce an overall payments surplus. In 1974, despite a trade deficit of US$92.3 million and a current accounts deficit of US$29.8 million, Fiji registered an overall payments surplus of $34.4 million. International reserves increased from US$27.4 million in 1970 to US$73.9 million in 1973 and US$109.5 million at the end of 1974.

32 BANKING

The Central Monetary Authority is the central bank facility in Fiji. Commercial banking facilities consist of branch offices of the Bank of New South Wales, the Bank of New Zealand, the Australia and New Zealand Bank, and the Bank of Baroda. Savings bank facilities are available at each bank, and, in addition, there are branches of the Post Office Savings Bank. Commercial and savings banks had reserves totaling F$25.2 million at the end·of 1975; demand deposits were F$51.8 million and time deposits F$69.4 million.

33 INSURANCE

In 1974 there were 17 insurance companies, of which 2 were domestically incorporated. Total assets stood at F$5 million at the end of 1974. Life insurance policies at the end of 1973 numbered 53,930, with a value of F$88,995,419. Gross premium income in the life sector totaled F$3,606,000; gross claims amounted to F$1,292,000.

In the non-life sector, gross premium income in 1974 totaled F$6,358,000; claims paid amounted to F$3,016,000. The largest class of insurance was fire (35%), followed by motor (28%) and marine cargo (15%). Third-party motor liability is compulsory.

34 SECURITIES

There are no securities exchanges in Fiji.

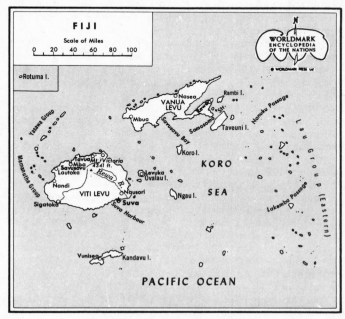

See Pacific Ocean map: front cover H7

LOCATION: 15°43′ to 21°2′s; 176°54′E to 178°28′w, not including Rotuma, which is at 12°30′s; 177°5′E. **TERRITORIAL SEA LIMIT**: 3 mi.

35 PUBLIC FINANCE

In 1974, Fiji's revenues and expenditures (in thousands of Fijian dollars) were:

REVENUES

Customs, duties, and port dues	37,016
Licenses, taxes, and internal revenue	35,260
Fees, sales, and reimbursements	3,935
Rents	791
Interest	310
Post office	96
Miscellaneous receipts	3,502
TOTAL	80,910

EXPENDITURES

Department emoluments and annual expenditures	57,825
Public debt service	7,430
Pensions, gratuities, and allowances	2,425
Other recurrent expenditures	7,713
Contributions to capital budget revenue	3,600
TOTAL	78,993

As of 31 December 1974, the domestic debt was F$55,029,646 and the overseas debt was F$31,999,122.

36 TAXATION

Local councils levy taxes to meet their own expenses. Dominion taxes include a nonresident dividend withholding tax, an interest withholding tax, and a dividend tax. On chargeable income the personal allowance has been abolished; instead, a rebate is deducted from the chargeable tax. Personal income tax is progressive to a maximum rate of 50%. The effective corporate tax rate in 1975 was 33.3% on chargeable resident income and 40% on profits of branches of foreign companies.

37 CUSTOMS AND DUTIES

Not quite half of Fiji's revenues is derived from customs duties. Customs revenues were F$35,873,208 in 1974, more than double the 1969 total. The port and customs service tax, previously chargeable at a rate of 5%, was abolished and incorporated within the tariff structure as a customs duty at the low rates of 7.5% on most items and 5% on selected items.

38 FOREIGN INVESTMENTS

The development of existing industries has largely been made possible by foreign investment. Fiji will continue to need overseas capital investment if employment is to be found for the large number of young people coming onto the labor market each year. The government made a determined effort to attract foreign capital with a development program for 1971–75.

39 ECONOMIC POLICY

The need to develop existing industries and establish new ones is a pressing problem in view of the expanding population. In the 1971–75 five-year development program, the government aimed to create employment opportunities by attracting more overseas investment and providing more manpower training programs. Development of tourism is a primary goal.

40 HEALTH

In 1972, Fiji had 186 doctors in government service and 30 in private practice. There were also 40 dentists and 675 nurses. Private dentistry was provided by 6 dentists in the main urban centers. Recurrent expenditure on health in 1972 was F$5,258,676. There are 2 main hospitals, 3 specialized hospitals, and 14 subdivisional hospitals.

Fiji is free of malaria. Some tropical diseases exist but are not considered a serious health threat. The average estimated life expectancy in 1975 was 73.2 years for females and 69.6 years for males. The infant mortality rate in 1973 was estimated at 21.5 per 1,000 live births.

41 SOCIAL WELFARE

General welfare work includes relief of destitution, maintenance of homes for the aged, free medical and legal aid to the needy, child care, and social casework to deal with delinquency.

42 HOUSING

The Fiji Housing Authority is a statutory body established to provide housing accomodations in urban areas for workers. It operates on the home ownership principle, although it does provide rental accomodation for very low income workers. It extends long-term credit for houses it builds and sells to workers.

43 EDUCATION

Education from primary to university level is available in Fiji, and although it is neither free nor compulsory, there is a high degree of literacy in the vernacular languages. There are government schools, and private schools operated by individual groups or by missions under government supervision.

The primary-school course covers eight years. Secondary schools offer a two-year course. Courses for foreign school certificates require an additional two to four years.

In 1973 there were 159,565 pupils in primary schools, with 4,147 teachers; 23,780 secondary pupils in 97 schools, with 993 teachers; and 2,966 pupils in technical and vocational schools, with 141 teachers.

The University of the South Pacific was opened near Suva in 1968. Its students are drawn from a number of Pacific countries.

44 LIBRARIES AND MUSEUMS

The Western Regional Library in Lautoka, which serves the western part of the island of Viti Levu, was established in 1964 with a grant from the British Council. Presently the collection exceeds 25,000 volumes. In 1970, the administrative offices of this library were moved to Suva and made part of the Library Service of Fiji, which helps maintain local libraries in several towns. Suva has its own public library of 40,000 volumes. The Library at the University of the South Pacific in Suva opened in 1968 and houses approximately 40,000 volumes.

The Fiji Museum, established in 1904, has a collection of Fijian artifacts that is considered the most complete in existence.

45 ORGANIZATIONS

A number of organizations provide forums for specialized cultural, commercial, or professional interests.

46 PRESS

The English-language *Fiji Times*, with a circulation of 20,200 in 1974, is the only daily newspaper. Periodicals and magazines include:

English—*Pacific Review*, triweekly; *Fiji Royal Gazette*, weekly; *News from Fiji*, weekly; *The Nation*, fortnightly; *News and Views*, fortnightly; *Fiji Farmer*, quarterly; and *Fiji Information*, annually.

Fiji—*Volagauna*, weekly; *Nai Lalakai*, weekly; *Vokalelewa ni Pasifika*, triweekly; *Tovata*, fortnightly; *Na Mata*, monthly.

Hindi—*Jagriti*, triweekly; *Shanti Dut*, weekly; *Fiji Samachar*, weekly; *Jai Fiji*, weekly; *Kisan Mitra*, weekly; *Fiji Sandesh*, weekly; *Prakash*, weekly.

Tamil—*Sangam*, monthly.

47 TOURISM

The development of the tourist industry has been recognized by the government as of great importance. In 1974, a total of 181,077 tourists visited Fiji. Most visitors were Australians (33%), New Zealanders (27%), or US citizens (16%). Gross receipts from tourism rose by F$11 million, or 23.2%, between 1973 and 1974, despite a 2.8% drop in the number of tourists.

Hotel accommodations, travel, and entertainment facilities for tourists have been increased. Persons arriving for a stay of not more than four months may be granted visitors' permits if they have valid passports.

48 FAMOUS FIJIANS

The best-known Fijians are Ratu Sir Lala Sukuna (d.1958), the first speaker of the Legislative Council in 1954; Ratu Sir George Cakobau (1912–73), the first Fijian to be governor-general; and Ratu Sir Kamisese K.T. Mara (b.1920), the prime minister since 1970.

49 DEPENDENCIES

Fiji has no dependencies.

50 BIBLIOGRAPHY

Brown, Stanley. *Men from Under the Sky*. Rutland, Vt.: Charles E. Tuttle, 1973.

Coulter, J. W. *The Drama of Fiji: A Contemporary History*. Melbourne: Flesh, 1967.

Derrick, R. A. *The Fiji Islands*. Suva: Government Printer, 1966.

Handbook of Fiji. Sydney: Pacific Publications (annual).

Legge, J. D. *Britain in Fiji, 1858–1888*. London: Macmillan, 1958.

Perkins, C. A. *Fiji: Many Flowering Islands*. London: Collins, 1967.

Reed, A. W., and I. Hames. *Myths and Legends of Fiji*. Wellington: Reed, 1967.

Snow, Philip A. *Bibliography of Fiji, Tonga, and Rotuma*. Miami: University of Miami Press, 1969.

Thomson, Basil. *The Fijians: A Study of the Decay of Custom*. London: Heinemann, 1908.

Ward, M. *The Role of Investment in the Development of Fiji*. Cambridge: Cambridge University Press, 1971.

FRENCH PACIFIC DEPENDENCIES

FRENCH POLYNESIA

The overseas territory of French Polynesia (Polynésie Française) in the South Pacific Ocean includes five island groups: (1) The Society Islands (Iles de la Société), discovered by the British in 1767 and named after the Royal Society, are the most important. They include Tahiti (at 17°40′s and about 149°20′w), the largest French Polynesian island, with an area of 1,042 sq km (402 sq mi); Moorea; and Raiatea. The French established a protectorate in 1844 and made the islands a colony in 1880. (2) The Marquesas Islands (Iles Marquises, between 8° and 11°s and 138° and 141°w), about 1,200 km (750 mi) NE of Tahiti, were discovered by Spaniards in 1595 and annexed by France in 1842. (3) The Tuamotu Islands, about 480 km (300 mi) s and sw of the Marquesas, were discovered by Spaniards in 1606 and annexed by France in 1881. (4) The Gambier Islands, SE of the Tuamotus, were discovered by the British in 1797 and annexed by France in 1881. Three of the islands, Mangareva, Taravai, and Akamaru, are inhabited. (5) The Tubuai or Austral Islands (Iles Australes), s of the Society Islands, were discovered in 1777 by James Cook and annexed by France in 1880. Clipperton Island (10°18′N and 109°12′w), an uninhabited atoll sw of Mexico and about 2,900 km (1,800 mi) w of Panama, was claimed by France in 1858 and given up by Mexico, which also had claimed it, in 1932. Total area of the territory is 3,673 sq km (1,418 sq mi).

The estimated mid-1974 population was 130,000, of which about 80% were Polynesian, 10% Asian, and 10% of European and mixed origin. Papeete, the capital city, on Tahiti, had a population of 47,744. About 55% of the population is Protestant and 30% is Roman Catholic; there are also small animist and Buddhist minorities. French, Tahitian, and English are spoken. As of 1975, endangered species included the Tahiti blue lory and Tahiti flycatcher in the Society Islands; the ultramarine lory and Marquesas ground dove on the Marquesas Islands; and the Henderson Island rail and Tahiti blue lory on the Tuamotus.

The territory is divided into four administrative areas (circumscriptions). A 30-member Territorial Assembly is elected every five years by universal suffrage. A Council of Government, consisting of six to eight members chosen by the Assembly, assists the French-appointed governor, who is the administrator for the whole territory of French Polynesia. A deputy and a senator represent the territory in the French parliament.

Tourism earns almost half as much as the visible exports. Five international airlines operate to and from French Polynesia. In 1972 there were one radio and one television station, and about 7,500 telephone subscribers.

Sugarcane, tropical fruit, vanilla, coffee, and coconuts are the principal products. Phosphate deposits, mined on Makatea in the Tuamotu Islands, were exhausted by 1966.

Currency is the Communauté Française de Pacifique franc (CFP Fr1=$0.0118, or $1=CFP Fr84.746). Exports in 1972 totaled CFP Fr1,341 million, and imports, CFP Fr14,270 million.

By 1974 there were 1 general hospital, 30 maternity centers, and 5 tuberculosis centers; the total number of hospital beds was 904. In 1972/73, 40,924 students attended 336 schools. There are 4 colleges and 7 technical schools.

FRENCH SOUTHERN AND ANTARCTIC TERRITORIES

These territories (Terres Australes et Antarctiques Françaises), an overseas territory of France, have a total area of 7,649 sq km (2,953 sq mi), not including Adélie Land, and are administered by an appointed administrator and consultative council from Paris. Most of the population of about 189 are researchers.

The Kerguelen Archipelago, situated at 48° to 50°s and 60° to 70°E, about 5,300 km (3,300 mi) SE of the Cape of Good Hope, consists of one large and about 300 small islands with a total area of 7,215 sq km (2,786 sq mi).

Crozet Archipelago, at 46°s and 50° to 52°E, consists of 5 main and 15 smaller uninhabited islands, with a total area of 327 sq km (126 sq mi).

Saint Paul, at about 38°25′s and 77°32′E, is an uninhabited island with an area of about 7 sq km (2.8 sq mi). Some 80 km (50 mi) to the N, at about 37°50′s and with an area of about 100 sq km (39 sq mi), is New Amsterdam (Nouvelle Amsterdam).

Adélie Land (Terre Adélie), comprising 432,000 sq km (166,796 sq mi) of Antarctica between 136° and 142°E, s of 60°s, was discovered in 1840 by Dumont d'Urville and claimed by him for France.

NEW CALEDONIA

New Caledonia (Nouvelle-Calédonie), a French overseas territory NE of Australia in the South Pacific Ocean, lies between 20° and 22°25′s and 164° and 167°E. It is about 400 km (250 mi) long and 50 km (30 mi) wide, with a land area of 18,997 sq km (7,335 sq mi). Mountainous and partly surrounded by coral reefs, the island is mostly forested or covered with low bush. With its dependencies and protectorates, it has an overall area of 19,103 sq km (7,376 sq mi). As of 1975, endangered species in New Caledonia included the dugong, kagu, cloven-feathered dove, giant imperial pigeon, and horned parakeet.

Total population in 1973 was 124,715; 52,736 were European. Nouméa, the capital city, had 57,000 inhabitants. In 1975, the territory had about 18,650 telephones and 4,490 km of roads.

New Caledonia was discovered in 1768 by Louis Antoine de Bougainville and was named by James Cook, who landed there in 1774. Local chiefs recognized France's title in 1844, and New Caledonia became a French possession in 1853. In 1946, it became a French overseas territory, and in 1958, its Assembly voted to maintain that status. Under a 1963 law, New Caledonia is administered by a governor and a Government Council composed of 5 elected councilors and a Territorial Assembly of 35 elected members. New Caledonia has one representative in the French National Assembly and one in the Senate.

The economy is based on agriculture and mining. Coffee, copra, cotton, cassava, tobacco, fruits, and niaouli essence (used in perfume making) are the principal crops, but agricultural production does not meet the domestic demand. Nickel represents about 98% of export value. Coffee, copra, iron, and chromium make up most of the other exports. Trade is mainly with France, Australia, Japan, and the US. In 1972, exports totaled CFP Fr17,415 million; imports totaled CFP Fr19.144 million.

Health facilities in 1974 included 1 hospital (500 beds), 2

private clinics (120 beds), and 17 medical centers. In 1972/73 there were 35,856 students in 240 primary schools, 14 secondary schools, and 1 private college.

Dependencies of New Caledonia include the Isle of Pines (150 sq km or 58 sq mi; 1974 pop., 1,175), 48 km (30 mi) to the SE; the Loyalty Islands (2,318 sq km or 895 sq mi; pop., 13,392), 97 km (60 mi) to the E; the Huon Islands, 274 km (170 mi) to the NW; the Bélep Islands, 50 km (31 mi) to the NW; the Chesterfield Islands, about 550 km (342 mi) to the W; and Walpole Island, about 145 km (90 mi) E of the Isle of Pines and SE of the Loyalty Islands. As of 1975, the Loyalty Islands parakeet was considered an endangered species.

NEW HEBRIDES

The New Hebrides (Nouvelles Hébrides), a group of islands 800 km (500 mi) w of Fiji and 400 km (250 mi) NE of New Caledonia, lying between 13° and 21°S and 166° and 170°E in the South Pacific, constitute an Anglo-French condominium. They comprise the New Hebrides group as well as the Banks and Torres islands. There are 9 large islands, of which Espiritu Santo is the largest, and some 60 small ones. The total area is 14,763 sq km (5,700 sq mi). Most of the islands are mountainous, with the highest peaks rising over 6,000 feet.

Total population at mid-1974 was estimated at 93,000. As of 1975, the estuarine crocodile was considered an endangered species.

The islands were discovered in 1606 by Pedro Fernandes de Quierós, and were visited by other Europeans during the next two centuries. In the 19th century, missionaries, traders, and planters settled on the islands, with the French and British predominating. In 1887, the UK and France signed a convention creating a joint naval commission to protect Anglo-French interests. In 1906, an Anglo-French convention established the Condominium of the New Hebrides, with a government under the authority of two high commissioners, the French governor of New Caledonia and the British governor of the Fiji Islands. A Franco-British accord of November 1974 called for establishment of a Representative Assembly with local authority.

Shipping services link the New Hebrides with Australia, the UK, and France. Air Pacific operates between Vila, Santo, Honiara in the Solomon Islands, and Suva in Fiji. A local airline, Air Mélanésie, provides services throughout the group of islands. In 1974, roads totaled 1,085 km; vehicles numbered about 3,000. There were 650 telephones in 1974. There is a radio station at Vila.

Main subsistence crops are bananas, manioc, taro, and yams. Copra, cocoa, nuts, and coffee are produced for export. Cattle, raised on large estates, and fishing are important. Manganese and timber are also exploited. Both the New Hebrides franc (NH Fr1=US$0.0118, or US$1=NH Fr84.746) and the Australian dollar (A$) are used as currency. In 1972, exports totaled A$13.6 million and imports A$26.8 million. The US, Japan, Australia, and France are major trade partners.

Pulmonary diseases and malaria are the main causes of death. French national government hospitals, staffed by French doctors, have been established at Vila, Santo, and Malekula. The UK maintains a hospital on Tanna. British and French national medical officers comprise a condominium medical service. In 1974, the New Hebrides had 17 doctors and 3 hospitals.

The condominium government has no education service, but it makes annual educational grants to each national administration. Both have their own schools and assist missions that run schools. In 1973/74 there were 80 French schools, with 7,817 students, and 132 British schools, with 12,517 students.

WALLIS AND FUTUNA

Wallis Island and the Futuna, or Hoorn, Islands in the Southwest Pacific were a French protectorate until recently. Lying about 400 km (250 mi) w of Samoa, at 13°22′S and 176°12′w, Wallis,

159 sq km (61 sq mi) in area, is surrounded by a coral reef with a single channel. The Futuna Islands are 190 km (120 mi) to the sw at 14°20′S and 179°w. They comprise two volcanic islands, Futuna and Alofi, which, together with a group of small islands, have a total area of about 116 sq km (45 sq mi).

The Futuna group was discovered by Dutch sailors in 1617, Wallis (at first called Uvea) by the English explorer Samuel Wallis in 1717. A French missionary established a Catholic mission on Wallis in 1837, and missions soon followed on the other islands. In 1842, the French established a protectorate, which was officially confirmed in 1887 for Wallis and in 1888 for Futuna. The islands had an estimated population of 9,000 in 1974, mainly Polynesians.

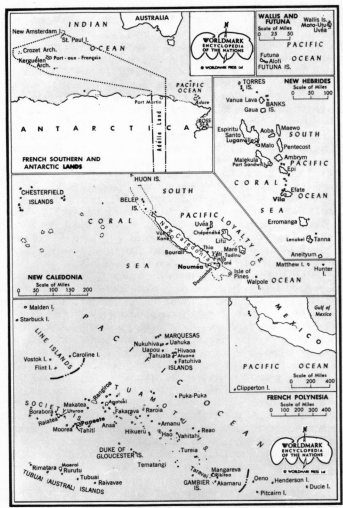

Fr. S. & Ant. Terr. See World Map Volume I: front cover C11
Wallis & Futuna Is. See Pacific Ocean map: front cover J7
N. Hebrides See Pacific Ocean map: front cover G7
N. Caledonia See Pacific Ocean map: front cover G8
Fr. Polynesia See Pacific Ocean map: front cover M7

In July 1961, the islands became a French overseas territory. A high administrator represents the French government; he is assisted by a Territorial Council. There is a Territorial Assembly.

Principal commercial activities are the production of copra and fishing for trochus. The chief food crops are yams, taro, bananas, and arrowroot.

In 1974 there were nine schools, with 2,540 students, run by Marist missionaries. Health facilities included three hospitals.

INDIA*

Republic of India
Bharat Ganarajya

CAPITAL: New Delhi. **FLAG**: The national flag, adopted in 1947, is a tricolor of deep saffron, white, and green horizontal stripes. In the center of the white stripe is a blue wheel representing the wheel (chakra) that appears on the abacus of Asoka's lion capital (c.250 B.C.) at Sarnath, Uttar Pradesh. **ANTHEM**: *Jana gana mana (Thou Art the Ruler of the Minds of All People)*. A national song of equal status is *Vande Mataram (I Bow to Thee, Mother)*. **MONETARY UNIT**: The rupee (R) of 100 paisa is a nonconvertible paper currency. There are coins of 1, 2, 3, 5, 10, 25, and 50 paisa, and notes of 1, 2, 5, 10, 100, 1,000, 5,000, and 10,000 rupees. As of 29 February 1976, R1 = $0.1121 (or $1 = R8.92061). **WEIGHTS AND MEASURES**: Metric weights and measures, introduced in 1958, replaced the British and local systems. Indian numerical units still in use include the lakh (equal to 100,000) and the crore (equal to 10 million). **HOLIDAYS**: Republic Day, 26 January; Independence Day, 15 August; Gandhi Jayanti, 2 October. Annual events—generally religious in nature or connotation—some national, others purely local, and each associated with one or more religious communities, number in the hundreds. The more important include Shivarati in February; Holi in March or April; Raksha Bandhan in August; Ganesh Chaturthi in August or September; Durga Puja in September or October; Dussehra in September or October; 'Id-ul-Fitr in September or October; Diwali in October or November; and Christmas, 25 December. **TIME**: 5:30 P.M. = noon GMT.

[1] LOCATION, SIZE, AND EXTENT

The Republic of India, Asia's second-largest country after China, fills the major part of the Indian subcontinent (which it shares with Pakistan, Nepal, Bhutan, and Bangladesh) and includes the Andaman and Nicobar Islands in the Bay of Bengal and Lakshadweep (formerly the Laccadive, Minicoy, and Amindivi Islands) in the Arabian Sea. The total area is 3,287,588 sq km (1,269,341 sq mi); the continental section extends 3,214 km (1,997 mi) N-S and 2,933 km (1,822 mi) E-W. India is bordered on the N by the disputed area of Jammu and Kashmir, west of the Karakoram Pass, China, Nepal, and Bhutan; on the E by Burma, Bangladesh, and the Bay of Bengal; on the S by the Indian Ocean; on the w by the Arabian Sea; and on the NW by Pakistan, with a total boundary length of 15,098 km (9,381 mi).

Internally, India is divided into 22 states and 9 territories. The major political divisions, their area, population, and capitals are:

STATES	AREA IN SQ KM	POPULATION 1971	CAPITAL
Andhra Pradesh	276,814	43,502,708	Hyderabad
Assam	78,523	14,625,152	Dispur
Bihar	173,876	56,353,369	Patna
Gujarat	195,984	26,697,475	Gandhinagar
Haryana	44,222	10,036,808	Chandigarh[1]
Himachal Pradesh	55,673	3,460,434	Simla
Jammu and Kashmir	222,236[2]	4,616,632	Srinagar (summer) Jammu (winter)
Karnataka[3]	191,773	29,299,014	Bangalore
Kerala	38,864	21,347,375	Trivandrum
Madhya Pradesh	442,841	41,654,119	Bhopal
Maharashtra	307,762	50,412,235	Bombay
Manipur	22,356	1,072,753	Imphal
Meghalaya	22,489	1,011,699	Shillong
Nagaland	16,527	516,449	Kohima
Orissa	155,782	21,944,615	Bhubaneswar
Punjab	50,362	13,551,060	Chandigarh[1]
Rajasthan	342,214	25,765,806	Jaipur
Sikkim[4]	7,105	209,843	Gangtok
Tamil Nadu	130,069	41,199,168	Madras
Tripura	10,477	1,556,342	Agartala
Uttar Pradesh	294,413	88,341,144	Lucknow
West Bengal	87,853	44,312,011	Calcutta
UNION TERRITORIES			
Andaman and Nicobar Islands	8,293	115,133	Port Blair
Arunachal Pradesh	83,578	467,511	Itanagar
Chandigarh[1]	114	257,251	Chandigarh[6]
Dadra and Nagar-Haveli	491	74,170	Silvassa[6]
Delhi	1,485	4,065,698	Delhi[6]
Goa, Daman, and Diu	3,813	857,771	Panaji
Lakshadweep[5]	32	31,810	Kavaratti[6]
Mizoram	21,087	332,390	Aizawl[6]
Pondicherry	480	471,707	Pondicherry
TOTALS	3,287,588[2]	548,159,652	

1. Chandigarh is a union territory as well as the capital of Haryana and Punjab.
2. Includes areas currently held by Pakistan and China.
3. Formerly Mysore.
4. Incorporated into Indian Union as of 26 April 1975.
5. Formerly Laccadive, Minicoy, and Amindivi Islands.
6. Headquarters.

[2] TOPOGRAPHY

Three major features fill the Indian landscape—the Himalaya and its associated ranges, a youthful mountain belt, folded, faulted, and uplifted, that marks the nation's northern boundary and effectively seals India climatically from other Asian countries; the Peninsula, a huge stable massif of ancient crystalline rock, long severely weathered and eroded; and the Ganges-Brahmaputra Lowland, a structural trough between the two rivers, now an alluvial plain carrying some of India's major rivers from the Peninsula and the Himalaya to the sea. These three features, plus a narrow coastal plain along the Arabian Sea and a wider one along the Bay of Bengal, effectively establish five major physical-economic zones in India.

Some of the world's highest peaks are found in the northern mountains: Godwin Austen (K2, 28,250 feet) is in Kashmir;

*All data for India as a whole exclude Sikkim, unless otherwise noted.

Kanchenjunga (28,166 feet) and Tent (24,088 feet) are in Sikkim-Nepal; Nanda Devi (25,643 feet), Trisul (23,360 feet), Badrinath (23,190 feet), and Dunagiri (23,184 feet) are in India; and Kamet (25,447 feet) is in India-Tibet.

The Peninsula consists of an abrupt 1,500-mile escarpment, the Western Ghats, facing the Arabian Sea; interior low, rolling hills seldom rising above 2,000 feet; an interior plateau, the Deccan, a vast lava bed; peripheral hills on the north, east, and south, which rise to 8,000 feet in the Nilgiris of Karnataka and Madras and the Cardamoms of Kerala and Tamil Nadu. The Peninsula holds the bulk of India's mineral wealth, and many of its great rivers, the Narbada, Tapti, Mahanadi, Godavari, Krishna, and Kaveri, flow through it to the sea. The great trench between the Peninsula and the Himalaya is the largest alluvial plain on earth—420,000 sq mi—and extends without noticeable interruption 2,000 miles from the Indus Delta (in Pakistan) to the Ganges-Brahmaputra Delta (shared by India and Bangladesh) at an average width of about 200 miles. Along this plain flow the Ganges, Brahmaputra, Son, Jumna, Chambal, Gogra, and many other major rivers, which provide India with its richest agricultural land.

³CLIMATE

Various climatic types exist in India. The lower east (Coromandel) and west (Malabar) coasts of the Peninsula and the Ganges Delta are humid tropical; most of the Peninsula and the Ganges-Brahmaputra Lowland are moist subtropical to temperate; and the semiarid steppe and dry desert of the far west are subtropical to temperate. The northern mountains display a zonal stratification from moist subtropical to dry arctic, depending upon altitude.

Extremes of weather are even more pronounced than the wide variety of climatic types would indicate. Thus, villages in western Rajasthan, in the Thar (Great Indian) Desert, may experience only a trace of rainfall yearly, while 1,500 miles eastward, in the Khasi Hills of Assam, Cherrapunji averages 426.1 inches yearly. Sections of the Malabar Coast and hill stations in the Himalaya regularly receive 100 to 300 inches yearly; many areas of the heavily populated Ganges-Brahmaputra Lowland and the Peninsula receive under 40 inches. Winter snowfall is normal for the northern mountains and Kashmir Valley, but for most of India, scorching spring dust storms and severe hailstorms are more common. The northern half of the country is subject to frost from November through February, but by May 49°C (120°F) in the shade may be recorded. The daily temperature range in humid, tropical Kerala often averages 2–3 centigrade degrees (4–5 Fahrenheit degrees) while in dry Rajasthan the range may be 33–39 centigrade degrees (60–70 Fahrenheit degrees). High relative humidity is general from April through September. Extratropical cyclones (similar to hurricanes) often strike the coastal areas between April and June and between September and December.

The monsoon is the predominant feature of Indian climate and helps to divide the year into four seasons: rainy, the southwest monsoon, June–September; moist, the retreating monsoon, October–November; dry cool, the northeast monsoon, December–March; hot, April–May. The southwest monsoon brings from the Indian Ocean the moisture upon which all Indian agriculture relies. Unfortunately, neither the times of its arrival and departure nor its duration and intensity can be predicted, and variations are great.

⁴FLORA AND FAUNA

About one-fourth of the land is forested. Valuable commercial forests, some of luxuriant tropical growth, are mainly restricted to the eastern Himalaya, the Western Ghats, and the Andaman Islands. Pine, oak, bamboo, juniper, deodar (*Cedna deodara*), and sal (*Shorea robusta*) are important species of the Himalaya; sandalwood, teak, rosewood, mango, and Indian mahogany are found in the southern Peninsula. Mid-latitude, subtropical, and tropical flowers all are grown widely in their appropriate climatic zones.

India has about 500 species of mammals, 2,000 species of birds, 30,000 species of insects, and a great variety of fish and reptiles. Wild animals, including deer, monkeys, and bears, live in the Himalayan foothills and the hilly section of Assam and the plateau. In the populated areas, many dogs and monkeys wander as wild or semiwild scavengers. Rare species are protected under the Wild Life Act of 1972. In 1974 there were 7 national parks and 130 designated wildlife sanctuaries.

As of 1975, endangered species in India included the lion-tailed macaque, three species of langur (John's, golden, and snub-nosed), Assam rabbit, Indus dolphin, wolf, Asiatic wild dog, Malabar large-spotted civet, clouded leopard (*Neofelis nebulosa*), Asiatic lion, Indian tiger, leopard, snow leopard, Asian elephant, dugong, Indian wild ass, great Indian rhinoceros, Sumatran rhinoceros, pygmy hog, swamp deer, Manipur brow-antlered deer, Kashmir stag or hangul, Asiatic buffalo, gaur, wild yak, Himalayan musk deer, Nilgiri tahr, markhor, white-winged wood duck, cheer pheasant, white-eared pheasant, Sclater's monal, three species of tragopan (Blyth's, Blyth's western, and western), Siberian white crane, great Indian bustard, river terrapin, marsh crocodile, estuarine crocodile, gavial, and Indian python. On the Andaman Islands, the Narcondam hornbill is an endangered species.

⁵POPULATION

India, the second most populous country in the world, had by the census of 1971 a population of 547,949,809 (including Sikkim, 548,159,652). The population had increased 24% since the previous decennial census, as compared with increases of 21.5% for 1951–61 and 13.3% for 1941–51. The 1975 population estimate was 613,217,000, with a projection of 694,309,000 in 1980, based on an annual growth rate of 2.48%. While birthrates remained almost stationary between 1940 and 1970, there was a rapid decline in death rates (about 15.2 per 1,000 in 1971–76, as compared with 27.4 in 1941–50 and 18.1 in 1961–70), resulting in a huge increase in total population. A decline in the birthrate to 29.6 per 1,000 by 1981 and to 24.8 per 1,000 by 1986 has been projected, largely because of India's aggressive promotion of family planning, contraception, and sterilization. The average density of population was estimated at 187 per sq km in 1975, but it varied in 1971 from 75 in Rajasthan to 504 in West Bengal and 549 in Kerala. The lowest density, 6 per sq km, was recorded in Arunachal Pradesh and the highest, 2,738 per sq km, in the union territory of Delhi (which is mainly urban).

In 1971, the population was 19.9% urban and 80.1% rural, and most of India's inhabitants lived in 575,721 villages with fewer than 10,000 residents. The majority of these villages had a population of less than 500. In 1971 there were 147 cities with a population of 100,000 or more. Those containing more than 1 million inhabitants each in the urban agglomeration were Calcutta (7,031,382), Bombay (5,970,575), Delhi (3,647,023), Madras (3,169,930), Hyderabad (1,796,339), Ahmadabad (1,741,522), Bangalore (1,653,779), Kanpur (1,275,242), and Poona (1,135,034).

⁶ETHNIC GROUPS

India's ethnic history is extremely complex, and racially distinct divisions between peoples generally cannot be drawn clearly.

LOCATION: 8°4' to 37°6'N; 68°7' to 97°25'E. BOUNDARY LENGTHS: China (not including the 523 km (325 mi) Pakistan-China boundary which is part of Jammu and Kashmir), 1,893 km (1,176 mi); Nepal, 1,508 km (937 mi); Bhutan, 573 km (356 mi); Burma, 1,403 km (872 mi); Bangladesh, 2,583 km (1,605 mi); total coastline, 5,110 km (3,175 mi); Pakistan, 2,028 km (1,260 mi). TERRITORIAL SEA LIMIT: 12 mi.

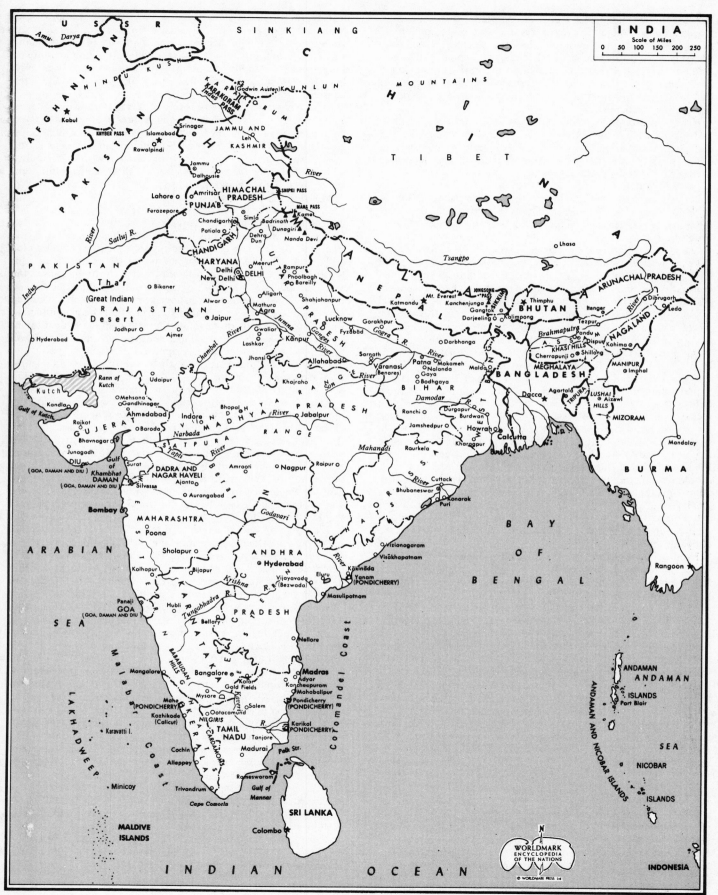

See continental political: front cover L7; physical: back cover L7

However, Negroid, Australoid, Mongoloid, and Caucasoid stocks are discernible. The first three are represented mainly by tribal peoples in the southern hills, the plateau, Assam, the Himalayas, and the Andaman Islands. The main Caucasoid elements are Mediterranean, including the dark-complexioned Dravidians of the south and other groups dominant in much of the north, and Indo-Aryan, a taller, fairer-skinned group dominant in the northwest.

Historical groupings result mainly in differences of languages and religion. The majority Hindu faith transcends language and racial stock affiliation, but Hinduism as a culture phenomenon differs widely among peoples of different social and economic classes, livelihoods, and geographic locations.

7LANGUAGE

A language survey was included in the 1971 census, but as late as 1976 no data had been released. The 1961 census recorded 1,652 different languages and dialects; one state alone, Madhya Pradesh, had 377. There are officially 211 separate, distinct languages, of which 14 are important enough to be recognized by the constitution. Nearly 90% of the population speaks 1 or more of the 14 regional languages. The most important speech family, culturally and numerically, is Indo-Aryan, which derives from Sanskrit. Hindi, spoken by 133,435,360 people (30.6% of the total population) in 1961, is the principal language in this family. Urdu, with 23,323,518 speakers (5.4%), differs from Hindi in being written in the Arabic-Persian script and containing a large admixture of Arabic and Persian words. Western Hindi, Eastern Hindi, Bihari, and Pahari are recognized as separate Hindi dialects. Other Indo-Aryan languages and their speakers (1961) include Bengali (7.8%), Marathi (7.6%), Gujarati (4.7%), Oriya (3.6%), Rajasthani (3.4%—with related local dialects of the area), Punjabi (2.5%), and Assamese (1.6%). Languages of Dravidian stock, largely derived from ancient Pali, are dominant in southern India and include Telugu (8.6%), Tamil (7%), Kannada (4%), and Malayalam (3.9%). A few tribal languages of eastern India, such as Ho and Santali, fit into the Munda speech family, an aboriginal tongue that predates Dravidian on the subcontinent. Smaller groups in Assam and the Himalayas speak languages of Mon-Khmer and Tibeto-Chinese origin. English is widely employed in government, education, science, communications, and industry, and is often a second language of the educated classes.

Hindi in Devanagari script is the official language. However, under the Official Languages Act of 1963, as amended, English is also recognized for official purposes. According to government policy, Hindi is eventually to become the national language, and for that purpose, Hindi instruction in non-Hindi areas is being rapidly increased and large numbers of scientific and other modern words are being added to its vocabulary. There is, however, very considerable resistance to the adoption of Hindi in the Dravidian-language areas of southern India, as well as in some of the Indo-Aryan-speaking areas, especially Bengal.

The importance of regional languages was well demonstrated in 1956 when the states were reorganized along linguistic boundaries. Thus, multilingual Hyderabad state was abolished by giving its Marathi-speaking sections to Bombay, its Telegu sections to Andhra Pradesh, and its Kannada sections to Mysore (now Karnataka). The Malayalam-speaking areas of Madras were united with Travancore-Cochin to form a single Malayalam state, Kerala. Madhya Bharat, Bhopal, and Vindhya Pradesh, three small Hindi-speaking states, were given to Madhya Pradesh, a large Hindi state, which, at the same time, lost its southern Marathi areas to Bombay state. Many other boundary changes occurred in this reorganization. Bombay State originally was to have been divided into Gujarati and Marathi linguistic sections but remained as one state largely because of disagreement over which group was to receive Bombay City. In 1960,

however, it too was split into two states, Gujarat and Maharashtra, based upon linguistic boundaries. In 1966 the government of India accepted the demand of the Punjabi-speaking people, mainly Sikhs, to divide the bilingual state of Punjab into two unilingual areas, the Hindi-speaking area to be known as Haryana and the Punjabi-speaking area to retain the name of Punjab.

India has almost as many forms of script as it has languages. Thus, each of the Dravidian and some of the Indo-Aryan languages have their own distinctive alphabets, which differ greatly in form and appearance. Some languages, such as Hindi, may be written in either of two different scripts. Konkani, a dialect of the west coast, is written in three entirely different scripts in different geographic areas.

8RELIGION

India is the cradle of two of the world's great religions, Hinduism and Buddhism. The classic texts of Hinduism—the *Rigveda* ("Songs of Spiritual Knowledge"), the *Upanishads*, and the *Bhagavad-Gita* ("Song of the Lord")—were written between 1500 and 400 B.C. Buddha lived in the 6th and 5th centuries B.C.; his teachings were first transmitted orally, then (beginning about the 1st century B.C.) variously systematized and conveyed throughout Asia. Jainism, a distinctive religion which developed contemporaneously with Buddhism, has largely been confined to India. The Sikh religion began in the 15th century as an attempt to reconcile Muslim and Hindu doctrine, but the Sikhs soon became a warrior sect bitterly opposed to Islam.

Freedom of worship is presently assured under the constitution. About 82.7% of the population adheres to Hinduism. Hindus have an absolute majority in all areas except Jammu, Nagaland, Kashmir, and the tribal areas of Assam. Sikhs are the majority group in the state of Punjab. Minor religious groups include Muslims (11.2%), Christians (2.6%), Sikhs (1.9%), Buddhists (0.7%), Jains (0.6%), and others (0.3%). Muslims comprise more than 10% of the population in Maharashtra, Bihar, Karnataka, and West Bengal, and more than 30% of the total population in Assam and Kerala. Christians, who form the majority in Nagaland, are a sizable minority in Kerala. The Jains are an important minority in Rajasthan and Gujarat, and the Parsees in Maharashtra.

The caste system is a distinct feature of Hinduism, wherein every person either is born into one of four groups—Brahmins (priests and scholars), Kshatriyas (warriors and rulers), Vaisyas (shopkeepers, artisans, and farmers), and Sudras (farm laborers and menial workers)—or is an untouchable (now known as Harijan, from the term used by Gandhi). Within the four major castes, there are 2,500 to 3,000 subcastes based upon occupation, geographic location, and other factors. The constitution outlaws caste distinctions, especially those applying to untouchability, but progress in changing customs is slow.

9TRANSPORTATION

The railway system is highly developed and is the major means of long-distance internal transport. By 1973, the length of the railways was 60,149 km, forming the largest system in Asia and the fourth longest in the world. In 1975, the IDA granted a credit of $110 million to support a five-year, $1-billion railway improvement program stressing electrification, track improvement, and expansion of a microwave signaling and communications system. Some 4,055 km of track were electrified in 1973. Except for 207 route km of narrow-gauge feeder lines, all railways are state-owned and divided into nine operating zones. Passenger traffic increased from 2,276 million in 1967/68 to 2,653 million in 1972/73, and freight traffic from 198 million to 201.3 million tons. Rolling stock in 1973 included 11,066 locomotives (8,963 steam), 35,840 passenger coaches, and 384,283 freight cars. The state-owned railways, the nation's largest public enterprise, brought in revenues of R11,660 million in 1972/73.

The road length in 1972 was about 1,129,915 km, of which 471,982 km were unsurfaced. There is a national highway system, and extensive construction work is in progress. In 1973, its length was 28,819 km and included 3,491 km and 195 bridges constructed since 1947. As of 31 March 1972 there were 2,032,000 motor vehicles, including 584,711 private automobiles, 363,916 trucks, and 645,608 motorcycles.

About 14,150 km of inland navigable waterways are in use, of which about 2,800 are navigable by mechanically propelled vessels. Most important are the Ganges, Brahmaputra, Godavari, and Krishna rivers, and the coastal plain canals of Kerala, Madras, Andhra Pradesh, and Orissa.

In 1974, the commercial fleet totaled 274 vessels of 3.09 million GRT, with another 2.1 million GRT on order; 48.8% of the tonnage was owned by central government enterprises. The tonnage is sufficient to handle all the country's coastal trade and about 40% of its trade with adjacent countries; the rest of India's trade is handled by foreign ships. Ten major ports handle the bulk of the import-export traffic; the leading ports are Bombay and Marmagao. There are another 160 intermediate and minor ports along the Indian coastline. Freight traffic handled at major ports in 1973/74 exceeded 64.3 million tons.

International airports are found at Bombay (Santa Cruz), Calcutta (Dum Dum), Delhi (Palam), and Madras (Meenambakkam). Some 84 other airfields are served by internal air transport. The Indian Airlines Corporation, a nationalized industry, operates all internal flights and services to neighboring countries. During 1973, it carried 2,790,973 passengers. Air India, also government-owned, operates long-distance services to 29 foreign countries on five continents. It carried 545,820 passengers in 1972/73. During 1973, all registered Indian aircraft carried about 66,000 tons of freight and mail.

10 COMMUNICATIONS

All postal and telegraph and most telephone services are owned and operated by the government. In 1973 there were 115,651 post offices (11,008 urban, 104,643 rural) in operation, as compared with 36,094 operating in 1951. There were 16,710 telegraph offices that handled telegrams in English as of 31 March 1973; 6,525 handled, in addition, messages in Hindi or any other Indian language written in the Devanagari script. National Telex service was inaugurated in 1963, and the first Devanagari Telex service began at New Delhi in 1969.

As of 1 April 1974 there were 1,629,000 telephones. International telephone services, radio and cable, are available between India and all major countries of the world through the Overseas Communications Service.

All India Radio (AIR), government-owned, operates short- and medium-wave transmission through 70 stations, and broadcasts in all major languages and about 125 dialects for home consumption. AIR also operates external services in 16 foreign and 8 Indian languages. The number of radios totaled about 14 million in 1973. In 1959, India's first television station was inaugurated in Delhi. By the end of 1973 there were nine television broadcasting centers and 163,446 licensed television sets. The School Television Section broadcasts regular in-school instruction programs on selected subjects.

11 HISTORY

India is one of the oldest continuously inhabited regions in the world. The earliest civilization that can be dated clearly is that of the Indus Valley, where, three to four millennia before Christ, scores of thriving cities and villages developed a distinct culture. About 1500 B.C., Aryan invaders began pouring through the Khyber Pass in quest of the lush plains of Hindustan and either destroyed or absorbed the Indus Valley civilization. Then followed a thousand years of instability, of petty states and larger kingdoms, as one invading group after another wrestled for power. During this period, the Indian village and family patterns and the caste system became well established and some distinguished literature evolved, including the *Ramayana* and the *Mahabharata*.

Alexander the Great invaded the Indus Valley in 326 B.C. His successors were absorbed by a new Aryan dynasty under the Maurya Empire. Chandragupta from his capital at Patna (Bihar) subdued most of northern India; his successor, Asoka (273-32 B.C.), placed all India under unified control. Asoka, converted to Buddhism, is remembered for his remarkable administrative, legal, and cultural achievements. Many of the Buddhist stupas, pillars, and elaborately carved cave temples found at Sarnath, Ajanta, Sanchi, Bodhgaya, and other locations date from Asoka and later Buddhist emperors. After Asoka, India was subdivided into a patchwork of kingdoms as other invaders from central and western Asia emerged through the northwestern passes. In the process, caste Hinduism prevailed over Buddhism, practically expelling it from the land of its origin.

True Hindu kingdoms first appeared in the Peninsula after the 4th century A.D., although states of Brahmanic origin long predated them. The Hindu Rajput princes reached their peak of power from A.D. 700 to 1000, although their descendants remained important dispensers of destiny well into British days. Remarkable Hindu architectural accomplishments, dating from long before Christ up to about the 16th century A.D., fill the Peninsula, among them the great temples of Konarak, Hampi, Tanjore, Mahabalipuram, Rameswaram, Conjeeveram, Madurai, Bhubaneswar, Puri, and Kharjaho. Most of these temples remain active centers of worship today.

In the 8th century, the first of several waves of Muslim invaders appeared at the traditional northwest portals; famed Mahmud of Ghazni (971-1030) made 17 forays into the subcontinent. The first Muslim sultan (king) of Delhi was Kutb-ud-din (13th century A.D.). Gradually, the Muslim power spread eastward and southward and reached its greatest territorial and cultural extent under the Mughals, descendants of the great Tatar leader Timur. Babur, who invaded Punjab in 1526, was the first Mughal to proclaim himself emperor of India after defeating the Afghan sultan of Delhi. However, it was only in 1560 that Akbar, Babur's grandson, established his authority over at least the Gangetic Valley. Akbar was also the first Muslim emperor to attempt the establishment of a national state in alliance with Hindu kings. Though illiterate, Akbar was a great patron of art and literature. There followed a galaxy of renowned emperors, including Shah Jahan and Aurangzeb; they and others left their imprint in massive palaces and mosques, superb fortresses, dazzling mausoleums, and elaborate formal gardens. The Taj Mahal, the deserted city of Fatehpur Sikri, and the Shalimar Gardens attest to the greatness of the Mughal culture. Under Aurangzeb (r.1658-1707), the Mughal empire reached its greatest extent, and its decline began. Aurangzeb's repressive policies resulted in armed upheavals. The Mahrattas in southwestern India, under Shivaji, the hero of much Mahratta folklore, fought the Mughals and later the British through much of the 17th, 18th, and 19th centuries.

Vasco da Gama reached Calicut (present-day Kozhikode) on the Malabar Coast in 1498, and for a century the Portuguese monopoly over Indian sea trade was disputed by no other European power. Portugal continued to hold Indian territory until 1961, but it lost its dominant position as early as 1612, when forces controlled by the British East India Company defeated the Portuguese and won concessions from the Mughal empire. The Company, which had been established in 1600, had permanent settlements in Madras, Bombay, and Calcutta by 1690. Its hegemony was threatened by the French East India Company, which was founded in 1664; by 1740, the trade volume of the French company was half that of its British counterpart. The two companies sought allies among rival Indian princes, and in 1746 the French forces captured Madras. Their triumph was short-lived, however, for in the Indian theater of the Seven Years' War (1756–63), the French and their allies suffered a disastrous defeat at Plassey (Palasi) in 1757, and by 1761 the French stronghold of Pondicherry had fallen. The architect of the British triumph, later known as the founder of British India, was Robert, Baron Clive, who became governor of Bengal in 1764. He and his successor, Warren Hastings, institutionalized British rule through the reformation of government service and the legal system. Eventually, the Maratha confederacy, the alliance of independent Indian states that had succeeded the Mughal empire, was reduced to a group of relatively weak and isolated principalities subordinate to the British. The British East India Company continued to rule India until 1858, when the British government assumed direct control during the Sepoy Mutiny (1857–59), a widespread rebellion initiated by Indian troops (sepoys) in the Company's service.

The succeeding decades were characterized by significant infrastructural developments, but also by a growing cultural gap between Indians and British, exacerbated by Hindu-Muslim rivalry. Indian troops supported the British in World War I, but even during the war years nationalism continued to rise. On 20 August 1917, the British secretary of state, Edwin Montagu, declared Britain's commitment to Indian self-government, and in 1918 the Montagu-Chelmsford report outlined a "dyarchy" of British and Indian administration. These plans were largely implemented between 1919 and 1921. At the same time, however, passage of the Rowlatt Bill in 1919, which permitted the imprisonment without trial of those suspected of sedition, aroused widespread opposition, led by Mohandas Karamchand Gandhi. His policy of noncooperation with the British swept the country; but in February 1922, alarmed by an outbreak of violence, he called a halt to the mass civil disobedience. During the succeeding decades, Gandhi initiated several other campaigns of mass actions, while stressing education, cottage industries, self-help, pacifism, and an end to the caste system. When, in March 1942, the British equivocated on the issue of Indian self-rule, Gandhi demanded immediate British withdrawal, and India refused to support the war against the Axis powers. In retaliation, Britain imprisoned most of India's political leadership. The victory of the British Labour Party in 1945 led to renewed negotiations between Britain and Hindu and Muslim leaders. When the Indian subcontinent finally attained independence on 15 August 1947, it was as two partitioned states based upon religious majority: India (Hindu) and Pakistan (Muslim). Independence brought a mass migration of 13 million Indians and an explosion of religious riots and murders; more than 6 million Hindus and Sikhs fled as refugees from Pakistan into northern India. A comparable number of Muslims fled to Pakistan. Gandhi, who opposed the partition, was assassinated by a Hindu extremist on 30 January 1948.

Adoption of a constitution on 26 January 1950 led to the establishment of a parliamentary government with Jawaharlal Nehru as prime minister. India's great size, growing population, and fragmented social structure, coupled with the refugee problems created by partition and the continuing tensions with Pakistan, posed unprecedented problems of development. By 1961, India had occupied all former French and Portuguese possessions on the subcontinent. In 1962, however, Chinese troops moved into disputed northern border areas, and Indian forces were badly defeated. Nehru died on 27 May 1964. His successor, Lal Bahadur Shastri, led India into war with Pakistan in August 1965 over the disputed state of Kashmir. The fighting was inconclusive, and the Tashkent agreement of January 1966 restored both sides to their prior positions. Shastri died on 11 January 1966, but his successor, Indira Gandhi, pledged to honor the Tashkent accords.

India again went to war with Pakistan in December 1971; the conflict resulted in the dismemberment of Pakistan and the creation of Bangladesh. Domestically, Mrs. Gandhi moved to consolidate her power within the ruling Congress Party and to suppress a wave of demonstrations and riots protesting food shortages. On 26 June 1975, after a new wave of dissidence and her conviction on minor election law violations that constitutionally required her resignation, she proclaimed a state of emergency; under the emergency decrees, press censorship was imposed and opposition political leaders were arrested. She then sponsored legislation that retroactively cleared her of the election law violations. The Supreme Court later upheld both that legislation and the government's right to imprison political dissidents without court hearings.

12 GOVERNMENT

India is an independent republic. Its constitution, which became effective on 26 January 1950, provides for a three-unit parliamentary form of government based on universal adult suffrage and headed by a president. It also contains a set of directive principles similar to the US Bill of Rights (but legislative acts and Supreme Court decisions in 1975–76 substantially weakened those guarantees). The parliament, or legislative branch of government, consists of the president, the Council of States (Rajya Sabha), and the House of the People (Lok Sabha). The Council of States has a maximum membership of 250, all but 12 of whom are elected by the state legislatures for six-year terms, with one-third elected every two years. Elected members represent the states and union territories, the other 12 are appointed by the president as experts in some field. The House of the People has a maximum membership of 525 (although the president may appoint members to represent the Anglo-Indian community and the union territories), with state representation based upon population. It has a maximum life of five years but can be dissolved earlier by the president; under the state of emergency proclaimed in June 1975, elections scheduled for early 1976 were postponed for at least one year.

The president is elected for a five-year term by an electoral college made up of the members of both parliamentary houses and the legislative assemblies of the states. Legally, all executive authority, including supreme command of the armed forces, is delegated to the president. He in turn appoints a Council of Ministers headed by a prime minister, who exercises de facto authority. This Council, which consists of cabinet members, ministers of state, and deputy ministers, formulates and executes the government program.

13 POLITICAL PARTIES

Although there are many active political parties, only a small number have attained parliamentary representation, and one, the Congress Party, has controlled the government by holding the vast majority of parliamentary seats. The Indian National Congress, founded in 1885, was the most powerful group fighting for independence in British India. It became the ruling party of a free India both by reason of its national popularity and by virtue of the fact that the major leaders of the independence movement were among its members.

The Congress Party's platform supports a democratic secular state with successive five-year plans of economic and social development. The Swatantra Party advocates the abolition of state participation in industry, decreased state control of private enterprise, and closer ties with the West. The Jan Sangh, similarly pro-West, aims to Hinduize Indian life and culture, eliminating Muslim and Christian elements. Communist parties have a long history in India but have suffered from schisms. There are now two major groups, one pro-Moscow and the other oriented toward Peking. The Maoist faction was further fragmented between 1971 and 1974. In November 1969, Indira Gandhi and her supporters formed a splinter group called the

New Congress Party, which favored a stronger socialist line than the opposition group. In December 1970, President V. V. Giri, on the advice of the Council of Ministers, dissolved the House of the People a year ahead of schedule, and in the elections held in early March 1971, the New Congress Party (which later resumed calling itself the Congress Party) won an overwhelming majority in the House of the People, with 350 of the 515 contested seats. The Marxist Communist Party of India (pro-Peking) won 25 seats; Dravidian Forward Party (Dravida Munnetra Kazhagan, based in Tamil Nadu), 23; the Communist Party of India (pro-Moscow), 23; Jan Sangh, 22; Opposition Congress, 16; Swatantra, 8; and other parties and independents, 48. By November 1974, the Congress Party controlled 363 seats.

The state elections of 1972, following India's victory over Pakistan in the war that created Bangladesh, resulted in a resounding victory for the Congress Party, which won 48% of the popular vote and more than 70% of the contested seats. By 1976, only two states, Tamil Nadu and Gujarat, did not have governments led by the Congress Party or its political allies. On 31 January 1976, Mrs. Gandhi requested the dismissal of the Tamil Nadu government; "president's rule" was imposed, under which the state was directly controlled by New Delhi. After the opposition government of Gujarat lost a confidence vote on 12 March, president's rule was invoked in that state until a Congress Party government could be formed.

¹⁴ LOCAL GOVERNMENT

The Republic of India is a union of states. The specific powers and spheres of influence of these states are set forth in the constitution, as are those of the central government. The central government has the power to set state boundaries and create and abolish states. The state governments are similar to the central government in form, with a chief minister and a cabinet responsible to the state legislature, which may be unicameral or bicameral. The governor of a state, appointed by the president of the union for a five-year term, acts only on the advice of the cabinet. The constitution, however, gives the president power—on the advice of the central government—to dissolve a state legislature and dismiss a state government, if no party commands the support of a majority. In such cases, the governor rules the state.

Under the States Reorganization Act of 1956, there were 14 states and 5 union territories. Through a gradual process of reorganization, incorporation, and annexation, India had 22 states and 9 union territories by the end of 1975. The most recent developments include the North-Eastern Areas Act of 1971, which created one new state (Meghalaya), gave statehood to two union territories (Manipur and Tripura), and established two new union territories (Mizoram and Arunachal Pradesh, formerly the North-East Frontier Agency). In 1975, Sikkim, formerly an Indian protectorate, became India's twenty-second state following the abolition of the monarchy by the Sikkim Assembly and ratification of the statehood proposal by Sikkimese voters.

Each state is divided into districts, districts into subdivisions, and subdivisions into taluks or tehsils. Local governments vary in organization and function, but all are based upon universal adult suffrage. Large towns are each governed by a corporation headed by a mayor; health, safety, education, and the maintenance of normal city facilities are under its jurisdiction. Smaller towns have municipal boards and committees similar to the corporations but with more limited powers. District boards in rural areas provide for road construction and maintenance, education, and public health. The constitution provided for the organization of village panchayats; nearly all the villages have been so organized. The panchayats are elected from among the villagers by all the adult population and have administrative functions and a judicial wing that enables them to handle minor offenses.

¹⁵ JUDICIAL SYSTEM

The laws and judiciary system of British India were continued after independence with only slight modifications. The Supreme Court consists of a chief justice and up to 13 judges appointed by the president to hold office until they reach the age of 65. The Court's duties include interpretation of the constitution, handling of all disputes between the union and a state or between states themselves, and judging appeals from lower courts.

In 1974 there were 17 high courts, subordinate to but not under the control of the Supreme Court. Each state's judicial system is headed by a high court (two high courts have jurisdiction over more than one state) whose judges are appointed by the president and over whom state legislatures have no control. Each state is divided into districts; within each district a hierarchy of civil courts is responsible to the principal civil courts, presided over by a district judge. The 1973 Code of Criminal Procedure, effective 1 April 1974, provides for the appointment of separate sets of magistrates for the performance of executive and judicial functions within the criminal court system. Executive magistrates are responsible to the state government; judicial magistrates are under the control of the high court in each state.

¹⁶ ARMED FORCES

The armed forces are entirely volunteer and consist of the regular army, navy, and air force; the territorial army (a reserve force); the Lok Sahayak Sena or national volunteer force; a national cadet corps; and an auxiliary cadet corps. The National Defense College at New Delhi trains senior officers of the three services. A national defense academy at Khadakvasla, near Poona, provides a three-year training program for officer cadets of all services.

In 1975, armed forces personnel totaled 956,000. The army had 826,000 men organized into 2 armored divisions, 15 infantry divisions, 10 mountain divisions, 5 independent armored brigades, 6 independent infantry brigades, 9 independent artillery brigades, and 2 parachute brigades. Armaments included 1,680 medium tanks and 120 light tanks. The navy (including the naval air force) had 30,000 men; naval vessels included 8 submarines, 1 aircraft carrier, 2 cruisers, 3 destroyers, 26 frigates, 8 fast patrol boats, 17 patrol boats, and 8 minesweepers. The naval air force had 1,500 personnel, organized into 1 attack squadron, 2 marine reconnaissance squadrons, 2 helicopter squadrons, 1 antisubmarine squadron, and 3 communications squadrons. The air force had 100,000 personnel and 725 combat aircraft; there were 3 light bomber squadrons, 14 fighter and ground attack squadrons, 18 interceptor squadrons, 1 reconnaissance squadron, 13 transport squadrons, and 8 helicopter squadrons. India was equipped with Soviet-made antiaircraft missiles; there were 20 missile sites in 1975. Budgeted defense expenditures in 1975/76 totaled R22,740 million (about $2,550 million). Arms imports between 1971 and 1974 totaled $749 million.

¹⁷ MIGRATION

Major migratory movements are to and from Sri Lanka, Malaysia, Burma, and Bangladesh. An estimated 5 million persons of Indian origin are domiciled abroad (excluding Pakistan), residing mainly in Sri Lanka, Malaysia, Burma, South Africa, Mauritius, Trinidad and Tobago, Guyana, the Fiji Islands, and the UK. Indian minority groups in foreign countries generally do not become assimilated with the local population but live as separate groups, intermarry, and retain their own distinctive culture even after a residence of several generations. Several black African states have either expelled or restricted the economic activities of their Indian residents.

¹⁸ INTERNATIONAL COOPERATION

India is a member of the Commonwealth of Nations. Even before its independence in 1947, India was already a member of the League of Nations and later of the UN. It belongs to most of the UN specialized agencies. New Delhi often has been a host for international conferences: ECAFE in 1956 and 1961; the International Red Cross and the Asian Regional Conference of the ILO in 1957; the annual meetings of the IBRD, the IMF, and the IFC in 1958; the International Eucharistic Congress, attended by Pope Paul VI, in 1964; and the UN Conference on Trade and Development in 1968. Indian armed forces and political missions have assisted in implementing truce and cease-fire agreements in Korea, Viet-Nam, Laos, Cambodia (now Kampuchea), the Middle East, Congo (now Zaire), and Cyprus.

19 ECONOMY

Agriculture is the largest sector of the Indian economy. It provides the livelihood of about 70% of the population and contributes more than 40% of the national income. The country is rich in mineral, forest, and power resources. Its ample reserves of iron ore and coal provide a substantial base for heavy industry. Coal is the principal source for generating electric power. But the development of the large potential for hydroelectric power supplies a rising proportion of India's power needs. Despite a twelvefold increase in petroleum production between 1961 and 1974, oil is still one of the main imports.

The need for planned economic growth was realized in India even before 1947; the urgency of stimulating it by public enterprise and social change was brought out in the five-year economic plans instituted since 1951. Outside the agricultural sector the Indian economy is a mixture of public, public-private, and private enterprises. But though the public sector provides the impetus for industrialization and for absorption of sophisticated technology, its quantitative contribution to the net domestic product is still small—10.8% in 1960/61 and 14.7% in 1970/71. A large proportion of the total manufacturing output is still contributed by small, unorganized industries.

Following the proclamation of a state of emergency in June 1975, a 20-point economic reform program was announced. Price regulations were toughened, and a moratorium on rural debts was declared. A new campaign was mounted against tax evaders, currency speculators, smugglers, and hoarders. The wholesale price index, which had increased to 178.4 by the end of 1974 (1970=100), dropped to 164.3 by December 1975, and the consumer price index declined from 178 at the close of 1974 to 170 by October 1975.

20 INCOME

In 1972/73, India's total national income in current prices was R389.2 billion, which came to R687.6 per capita, as compared with 1960/61 figures of R132.8 billion and R306, respectively. In constant prices, however, per capita income increased by only 10% during the period. The GNP in 1973/74 was R521.9 billion, and the net national product was R492.9 billion. Contributions to the net domestic product in 1972/73 included agriculture, 44.7%; manufacturing, 13.5%; commerce, 11.1%; finance and real estate, 4.6%; other sectors, 26.1%.

21 LABOR

At the time of the 1971 census, India's total labor force of 180.4 million was composed of 78.2 million cultivators; 47.5 million landless agricultural laborers; 4.3 million persons engaged in activities allied to agriculture (including forestry, fishing, hunting, and livestock tending); 10.7 million in large-scale manufacturing, servicing, and repair industries; 10 million in trade and commerce; 6.4 million workers in household industry; 4.4 million in transport, storage, and communications; 2.2 million in construction; 0.9 million in mining and quarrying; and 15.8 million in other services. Agriculture thus accounted for 130 million, or 72% of India's total working population. Unemployment and underemployment are high. As of 31 July 1975 there were more than 9 million people registered at 502 employment exchanges.

The total industrial work force in 1974 was 19.3 million, of whom 12.5 million were employed in the public sector and 6.8 million in the private sector. Employment on railways totaled 1.4 million in 1974; the textile industry had more than 1.5 million in 1972.

Plantations employed about 786,000 in 1972.

In 1972 there were 3,164,000 employees who earned less than R400 a month. Their average annual earnings were R3,011 per capita. Real wages increased only 3% between 1961 and 1972. The minimum wage for unskilled labor ranges from a low of R0.62 per hour in Tamil Nadu to a high of R6.50 in Punjab State. By law, earned income also includes a cost-of-living allowance and an annual bonus (applicable to all factories and all other establishments with 20 employees). Employers and employees contribute to the Employees State Insurance Scheme. The normal retirement age for wage earners is 58.

In 1972 there were 21,063 registered trade unions, with a combined membership of nearly 5 million. The leading trade union federations are the Indian National Trade Union Congress and the All India Trade Union Congress.

22 AGRICULTURE

In 1970/71, the total land area recorded for agricultural utilization was 306 million hectares. The net sown area was 141.2 million hectares (about 46%); the remaining area included 65.9 million hectares of forests, 46.2 million hectares of barren or built-up land, 17.3 million hectares of pastures or orchards, and 20.2 million hectares of fallow land. By 1974, the sown area had increased to 169 million hectares; the irrigated area had increased to 44.7 million hectares, or 26.4% of the cultivated area, as compared with 22.6 million hectares in 1951. At least 10 million hectares have been redistributed under land reform programs since 1951. Legislation has imposed ceilings on agricultural holdings that vary between states, regions, and classes of land.

The overwhelming preponderance of food crops, especially cereals, is a major feature of agricultural production. Rice leads all crops and, except in the northwest, is generally grown wherever the conditions are suitable. In 1973/74, 43,742,000 tons of rice were produced on 38,011,000 hectares. However, the acreage and production of other cereals, all to a large extent grown for human consumption, considerably exceed those of rice. These include jowar, a rich grain sorghum grown especially in the Deccan; wheat, grown in the northwest; and bajra, another grain sorghum grown in the drier areas of western India and the far south. A record wheat crop of 26,410,000 tons was harvested on 19,139,000 hectares in 1971/72; however, although plantings increased in 1972/73, the harvest decreased to 24,923,000 tons. Total production of food grains rose from 72,030,000 tons in the drought year of 1965/66 to 105,168,000 tons in 1971/72, leaving India nearly self-sufficient. But when the output dropped to 95,201,000 tons in 1972/73, massive grain imports and rationing had to be resumed. Vegetables, pulses, oilseeds, and sugarcane are the other main food crops. Nonfood crops are mainly linseed, cotton, jute, and tobacco; India is the world's third-largest producer of tobacco, producing 363,600 tons in 1972/73. Since World War II, it has been the world's largest producer of black pepper (26,000 tons in 1972/73). It also handles 70% of the world trade in cardamom, of which 2,950 tons were produced in 1973/74.

Tea, coffee, and rubber plantations contribute significantly to the economy, although they occupy less than 1% of the agricultural land (in hill areas generally unsuited to Indian indigenous agriculture). They are the largest agricultural enterprises in India. Tea, the most important plantation crop, is a large foreign exchange earner. It is grown mostly in Assam and northern Bengal, but also in southern India. Production in 1973 totaled a record 467.3 million kg. Coffee (90,000 tons in 1973/74) is produced in southern India, rubber (more than 107,000 tons in 1973) in Kerala.

An agricultural strategy aiming at the introduction of high-yielding varieties of seeds, multiple cropping, expansion of irrigation facilities through minor works, and enlarged supply of fertilizers has been adopted with some success.

Because of the ever-present danger of food shortages, the government tightly controls the grain trade. The government fixes minimum support and procurement prices and maintains buffer stocks. At the end of 1973, the Food Corporation of India, a government enterprise, owned or leased a storage capacity of 7.82 million tons.

23 ANIMAL HUSBANDRY

Although the livestock population of India is huge, animals as a whole play a relatively minor role in the agricultural economy. A very high percentage of domestic animals receive inadequate nourishment and consequently are of little milk or work value. Hindus do not eat beef, and most of them do not take meat in any form. However, there are more than 86 million Muslims, Christians, and Sikhs who do eat meat.

In 1973 there were an estimated 176.9 million head of cattle, 43.3 million sheep, 4.8 million hogs, 950,000 horses, and 980,000 asses. A 1966 livestock census also reported 52.9 million buffalo and 115 million poultry. Bullocks and water buffalo are important for draft purposes. Dairy animals are kept, but in spite of the large animal population, far too little milk is obtained. Milk output in 1973/74 was about 10.5 million hectoliters. During that year, India had 79 liquid milk plants, 12 factories for milk products, and 50 pilot milk schemes and rural dairy centers. About 12,350 tons of powdered milk were produced in 1973. Estimated egg production was 7.7 billion in 1973/74. Breeding experiments are under way in the dairy, hog, and poultry industries. A slaughterhouse modernization program was introduced toward the end of the fourth plan period.

The production of cattle and buffalo hides and goat- and sheepskins is a major industry, totaling some 60 to 70 million pieces yearly. About 35,000 tons of wool were produced in 1973/74.

24 FISHING

Fishing is an important secondary source of income to some farmers and a primary occupation in small fishing villages. Two-thirds of the catch consists of sea fish. The bulk is freshly marketed; of the remainder, more than half is sun-dried. Deep-sea fishing is not large-scale. Inland fishing is most developed in the deltaic channels of Bengal, an area where fish is an important ingredient of the diet. In recent years, the government has been encouraging ocean fishing through the establishment of processing plants and the introduction of deep-sea craft. In 1974, some 9,300 mechanized craft were in operation; 700 were introduced in 1973/74 alone. Fishing harbors have been built at 12 locations on the coasts of the Bay of Bengal and the Arabian Sea, with facilities under construction or planned for at least 7 other locations.

The Central Institute of Fisheries Education, Bombay, established in 1961, trains district fisheries officers, while the Central Institute of Fisheries Cooperatives at Cochin provides vocational training in fisheries. The Inland Fisheries Training Unit, north of Calcutta, and the Regional Training Center for Inland Fishery Operatives, at Agra, specialize in the development of commercial fish farming. By 1974, about 923 hectares were available for spawn rearing; in 1973/74, an estimated 188.8 million spawn and 48.3 million fingerlings were produced.

The total fish catch in 1973/74 was 2.27 million tons, of which marine fish accounted for 1.49 million tons. Fish exports, still only a fraction of the potential, have shown a steady gain in recent years and totaled 52,300 tons (valued at R895.1 million) in 1973/74.

25 FORESTRY

The major forest lands lie in the foothills of the Himalayas, the hills of Assam State, the northern highlands of the plateau, the Western Ghats, and the Andaman Islands. Other forest lands are generally scrub and poor secondary growth of restricted commercial potential. India's forests are mostly broad-leaved; only 5.6% are coniferous. In 1971/72 there were 746,000 sq km of forests. Exploitable forests covered 466,000 sq km (62.5%), 126,000 sq km (16.9%) were potentially exploitable, and 154,000 sq km (20.6%) were inaccessible. About 20,000 sq km have been planted under afforestation programs. Most forests (95.1%) are owned by state governments and are reserved or protected for the maintenance of permanent timber and water supplies. Forest products in 1973 included about 116.6 million cu meters of round wood and 2.8 million cu meters of sawn wood, as well as bamboos, canes, fibers, flosses, gums and resins, medicinal herbs, tanning barks, and lac.

26 MINING

India is well endowed with industrial minerals. Iron ore reserves, estimated at 8.18 billion tons of hematite ore and 2.03 billion tons of magnetite ore, are possibly the highest in the world. The best quality of mica comes from Bihar; India produced 13,475 tons of crude mica in 1973. India ranks third in the world in manganese deposits, which are estimated at 108 million tons. Bauxite deposits, estimated at 249 million tons, are exceeded only by those of Jamaica, but India's output of 1,270,000 tons in 1973 was less than one-tenth of Jamaica's. There are extensive workable reserves of fluorite, chromite, ilmenite (for titanium), monazite (for thorium), beach sands, magnesite, beryllium, copper, and a variety of other industrial and agricultural minerals. However, India lacks substantial reserves of some non-ferrous metals and special steel ingredients.

Principal iron ore output, mostly hematite of 55% to 75% metallic iron content, comes from the fabulously wealthy fields along the Bihar-Orissa border, which are close to all major existing iron and steel works. Smaller amounts are mined in the Bababudan Hills of Karnataka and elsewhere. Iron ore output totaled 35,210,000 tons in 1973. Manganese is mined in the Nagpur section of Maharashtra, northward in Madhya Pradesh, along the Bihar-Orissa border adjoining the iron ore deposits, along the Maharashtra-Madhya Pradesh-Rajasthan border, in central coastal Andhra, and in Karnataka. Production of manganese ore was 1,451,000 tons in 1973. Gold and silver come largely from the Kolar fields of southeastern Karnataka, where the gold mines have reached a depth of more than 2 miles. Diamonds, emeralds, and unpublished quantities of fissionable materials also are mined. In 1973, 3,320 kg of gold, 4,255 kg of silver, 21,017 carats of diamonds, and 3,195 carats of crude emeralds were produced.

Coal reserves, scattered through the central Peninsula and the northeast, are huge; the total is estimated at 80,950 million tons, of which more than 20,150 million tons are coking coal in the Gondwana coalfields in West Bengal. These reserves are among India's most important natural resources and have been the basis of the power, railway, and steel industries. The largest reserves are in the states of West Bengal and Bihar in the northeast. Almost the entire coal industry was nationalized by the government in 1972 and 1973. Coal output was about 77,088,000 tons in 1973.

Petroleum reserves are relatively small and were estimated at 118 million tons in 1973. From less than 100,000 tons in 1951, crude oil production rose to 7.2 million tons in 1973; nevertheless, 13.4 million tons were imported. Oil exploration and production are undertaken in joint ventures between government and private foreign companies. On 14 March 1974, Exxon's holdings in India were nationalized with compensation. Extraction of natural gas increased from 392 million cu meters in 1968 to 920 million cu meters in 1973; reserves are estimated at 70,000 billion cu meters.

Other mineral products in 1973 included 277,244 tons of chromite, 23,913 tons of zinc concentrates, 1,093,000 tons of copper ore, 39,793 tons of feldspar, and 15,098 tons of graphite. The total value of mineral output in 1973 (excluding nuclear materials) was R5,435,179,000.

27 ENERGY AND POWER

India supplies much of its own power requirements and, in addition, has a large development potential. Total installed electric capacity, which in 1947 was 1.4 million kw, reached 18.5 million kw in 1974, of which about 7 million kw was hydroelectric. Power production in 1973/74 totaled 71,050 million kwh, more than 90% of which was by public utilities. Industry accounts for about 70% of energy consumption. A 380-Mw nuclear power station, India's first, was completed in 1969 near Bombay. Another nuclear station, in Rajasthan, began partial operations in the early 1970s, and a third, near Madras, was under construction in 1975. Each will have a 420-Mw generating capacity. A fourth station has been planned for Narora in Uttar Pradesh. An IDA credit of $150 million was extended in 1976 to help India develop an integrated power generation and transmission system.

Rural electrification has grown steadily in recent years; in 1947 only 4,000 villages and towns had electricity, while by 31 March 1974, 154,786 villages (27.3% of the national total) had been electrified. Practically all major towns and cities have electricity.

28 INDUSTRY

Modern industry has advanced fairly rapidly since independence. Large modern steel mills, fertilizer plants, heavy-machinery plants, oil refineries, and locomotive works have been constructed. New plants are turning out a wide variety of consumer and producer goods, many never manufactured in India. Particularly active have been the heavy metallurgical and engineering, chemical, cement, and oil-refining industries. Yet, though the total industrial product is large, it is still far from sufficient, and the factories are unable to absorb more than a token of the unemployed millions. Nine states—Maharashtra, West Bengal, Tamil Nadu, Gujarat, Uttar Pradesh, Bihar, Andhra Pradesh, Karnataka, and Madhya Pradesh—together account for about 80% of Indian industry.

Textile industries dominate the industrial field. Full-time cottage workers (about 5 million) throughout the country handloom cotton, wool, silk, and rayon. Cotton and jute milling employ 25% of the nation's factory workers and command a sizable portion of the total productive industrial capital. Bombay, Ahmadabad, and the provincial cities in southern India lead in cotton milling; jute milling is localized at Calcutta, center of the jute agricultural area. Wool, silk, coir, and a growing rayon textile industry are important. In 1972/73, 1,168,000 tons of jute textiles, 7,924 million meters of cotton cloth, 918 million meters of silk fabric, and 113,000 tons of rayon yarn were produced. Sugar is the next most important agricultural processing industry, with 229 refineries in 1973/74; their combined output was 3,860,000 tons.

In 1972/73, output in the metallurgical industry included 6,820,000 tons of crude steel, 7,500,000 tons of pig iron, and 174,800 tons of virgin aluminum. Mechanical engineering industries produced 89,700 automobiles, 116,600 motorcycles, 2,383,000 bicycles, and 340,000 sewing machines. The electrical engineering industry showed especially remarkable growth, producing 1,821,000 radios (282,000 in 1960/61), 15,060,000 light bulbs (4,850,000 in 1960/61), and 2,430,000 electric fans (1,600,000 in 1972/73). Chemical fertilizer production grew from 938,000 tons in 1969/70 to 1,377,000 tons in 1973/74; however, substantial quantities of fertilizer must still be imported. In 1974 there were 51 cement factories, of which 9 were in the public sector; the total output for 1973/74 was 14.7 million tons. There were 9 oil refineries in 1973, processing 20.4 million tons of crude

oil. Refinery products in 1974 included 1,290,000 tons of motor fuel, 2,860,000 tons of kerosene, 7,118,000 tons of distillate fuel, and 4,240,000 tons of residual fuels.

According to the latest available survey (1970), 13,597 factories (employing 50 or more workers with the aid of power or 100 or more without) had a productive capital of R111,150 million and an output of R113,995 million. Although the public sector has been growing—from 77 plants on 31 March 1967 to 113 on 31 March 1973—it still accounted for only 14.7% of the net domestic product in 1970/71. However, the public-sector enterprises represented more than 50% of the value in large-scale manufacturing.

The Industrial Finance Corporation of India, established in 1948, gives long-term loans to industrial concerns. The National Industrial Development Corporation, established in 1954, promotes the development of India's heavy and medium industries. The Industrial Reconstruction Corporation of India was established in 1971 especially to help ailing industries. Eighteen state finance corporations assist medium- and small-scale regional industries.

29 DOMESTIC TRADE

Most commercial enterprises are small establishments owned and operated by a single person or a single family. Chain operations exist but are unusual. Retail outlets are often highly specialized in product and usually very small in both quarters and total stock. Indeed, often the Indian retail shop is large enough only to hold the proprietor and a small selection of stock; shutters fronting the store are opened during the business hours to allow customers to negotiate from the street or sidewalk. Fixed prices are rare, and customer-seller bargaining is the accepted means of purchase. In cities and larger towns similar stores tend to agglomerate in specialized bazaar areas. Clothing, jewelry, and furniture are often custom-made. Refrigeration and canning facilities are scarce. Principal foods marketed are cereals, dried vegetables, and a few fresh vegetables and fruits in season. Most food sales are from bulk. Imported, processed, and packaged foods are available in urban areas but are beyond the means of most persons.

Business operations are often characterized by a leisurely pace. Contracts are consummated only after protracted negotiations, generally on a personal basis. Aggressive sales promotion is noticeably absent, and business does not actively engage in creating or expanding product markets. Advertising, however, is growing apace in urban areas. Its media include, besides newspapers and magazines, movie slides and radio commercials (broadcast over the state-owned radio since 1967). Wall inscriptions and posters are ubiquitous in India's towns and villages.

India's internal trade is many times larger than its external trade. In addition to rail- and river-borne trade and some minor trade by air, there is also a coastal trade between the country's different maritime sections.

30 FOREIGN TRADE

Initially, India's foreign trade followed the pattern of that of all underdeveloped countries, exporting raw materials and food in exchange for manufactured goods. The only difference in India's case was that it also exported processed textiles, yarn, and jute goods. Industrialization, however, has resulted in the export of machine tools and industrial equipment even to Western countries. As a result, food exports, although increasing in absolute terms, have declined from 40% to about 8% of total export volume. In 1973/74, jute manufactures, cotton textile products, engineering goods, livestock and agricultural products, and minerals were the most important exports, while petroleum, machinery and vehicles, food grains, iron and steel, fertilizers, and nonferrous metals were the main imports. India was extremely hard hit by the high grain, petroleum, and fertilizer prices in 1973/74; its oil import bill more than doubled between 1972/73 and 1973/74, and grain imports increased sevenfold. India suffers from chronic trade deficits; a rare surplus was recorded in 1972. According to the IMF, exports in 1974 were R31,786 million and imports R40,872 million, for a deficit of R9,086 million; in 1975 the preliminary totals were R35,998 million in exports, R51,997 million in imports, and a deficit of R15,999 million.

Principal exports in 1973/74 (in millions of rupees) were:

Jute manufactures	3,889
Cotton textiles	2,353
Machinery, transport equipment, and metal products	1,731
Oil cake	1,706
Leather goods	1,659
Tea	1,420
Iron ore and concentrates	1,328
Pearls, precious and semi-precious stones	1,075
Other exports	9,671
TOTAL	24,832

Principal imports in 1973/74 (in millions of rupees) were:

Petroleum and petroleum products	5,603
Machinery	5,406
Wheat	3,461
Iron and steel	2,426
Fertilizers	1,622
Nonferrous metals	1,380
Other imports	9,266
TOTAL	29,164

The US is India's principal trade partner, accounting for 15.5% of total trade in 1973/74. Leading purchasers of Indian exports in 1973/74 were Japan, the US, the USSR, and the UK. Leading import suppliers were the US, Iran, Japan, the USSR, and the UK. The EEC annually accounts for about 25% of total trade, and Eastern Europe and the USSR about 15%. Principal trade partners in 1973/74 (in millions of rupees) were:

	EXPORTS	IMPORTS	BALANCE
US	3,428	4,934	−1,506
Japan	3,551	2,556	995
USSR	2,838	2,497	341
UK	2,584	2,448	136
Iran	427	2,676	−2,249
FRG	822	1,957	−1,135
France	486	698	− 212
Canada	308	1,154	− 846
Italy	684	491	193
Other countries	9,704	9,753	− 49
TOTALS	24,832	29,164	−4,332

31 BALANCE OF PAYMENTS

India has a chronic trade deficit. What bridges the gap between payments and receipts is mainly external aid, especially non-project assistance. Heavy imports of food grains and armament purchases caused a decline in India's foreign exchange reserves in the mid-1960s. From 1965 to 1968, these reserves stood below those of 1958. An economic recovery from 1968/69, however, eased the problem, and by 30 September 1970, foreign exchange reserves amounted to $616 million, as compared with $383 million on 31 December 1965. Foreign exchange reserves declined

to $566 million by the end of 1972 but actually increased to $841 million as of 31 December 1975, despite massive deficits on current accounts. During the same period, international reserves increased from $1,180 million to $1,373 million. The reason for this apparent stability is India's heavy use of IMF reserve funds. Outstanding IMF drawings at the end of 1975 totaled $907 million, of which $470 million was from the special Oil Facility.

The following are summaries of India's balance of payments for 1972 and 1973 (in millions of dollars):

	1972	1973
CURRENT ACCOUNTS		
Trade, net	75	−191
Services, net	−530	−607
Transfers, net	294	269
TOTALS	−161	−529
CAPITAL ACCOUNTS		
Long-term capital	360	478
Short-term capital	− 66	25
TOTALS	294	503
Errors and omissions	−267	− 51
Net change	−134	− 77

32 BANKING

A well-established banking system exists in India. On 31 December 1973 there were 73 scheduled commercial banks, all members of the reserve system, each with paid-up capital and reserves in excess of R500,000. Scheduled banks maintained a total of 16,503 branches as of December 1973, mainly in the major commercial and industrial centers of Maharashtra, West Bengal, Uttar Pradesh, Tamil Nadu states, and the Delhi territory. The scheduled banks included branches of 16 prominent UK, US, Dutch, and other foreign institutions. On 31 December 1973, aggregate deposits of all scheduled banks amounted to R100.63 billion, as compared with R46.46 billion in June 1969. Accounts of up to R10,000 per depositor are insured by the Deposit Insurance Corporation. As of 31 December 1973, 80 commercial banks and 411 cooperative societies were insured. In 1974, 8 Indian commercial banks with 56 branches were operating overseas, primarily in the UK, Fiji, Mauritius, and Singapore.

The Reserve Bank of India, nationalized in 1949, is the central banking and note-issuing authority. On 31 December 1975, its foreign assets amounted to R16 billion and foreign liabilities R7.28 billion, claims on government to R79.23 billion, and claims on commercial and cooperative banks to R13.77 billion. Reserve money totaled R75.61 billion and government deposits R1.86 billion. Currency in circulation on 31 December 1973 was R60,802 million.

The government follows a policy of social control over banks. Under a law that came into force on 9 August 1969, 14 major commercial banks with deposits of more than R500 million each were nationalized; the government has sought to use these public-sector commercial banks to extend banking services to undeveloped regions. The principal commercial bank is the State Bank of India, established in 1955.

Nonscheduled banks include all those that are incorporated but have less than R500,000 of paid-up capital and reserves. While their total number is high—500 to 600—they handle less than 10% of the country's total bank transactions. Both scheduled and nonscheduled banks adhere to a conservative lending policy and maintain high security requirements. Despite strict credit controls, total credit extended by all commercial banks increased from R36 billion in June 1969 to R70.4 billion in

December 1973, or from R68 to R122 per capita. A system of differential interest rates was introduced in 1972 to enable certain borrowers in backward districts to secure credit from public-sector banks.

In an attempt to regulate lending practices and interest rates, the government has encouraged the formation of cooperative credit societies. In 1971/72 there were 324,000 cooperative societies in India, with a total membership of more than 61.4 million. State cooperative banks numbered 26; they had a total working capital of R7,310.6 million and had advanced loans amounting to R9,316 million to agricultural and small-industrial borrowers.

In 1972/73 there were 157,775 agricultural credit societies with a membership of 31.9 million and a working capital of R12,257.2 million, which advanced loans amounting to R6,855.6 million during the year. In 1963, the government set up the Agriculture Refinance Corporation for granting medium- and long-term credit for the development of agriculture, animal husbandry, dairy farming, pisciculture, and poultry farming. Long-term credit is also provided by the cooperative land development banks. Nonagricultural credit societies and employees' credit societies supply urban credit.

On 1 July 1964 the Industrial Development Bank of India, a subsidiary of the Reserve Bank of India, was established to provide term finance to industry and also to serve as an agency to provide direct financial assistance to industrial units.

33 INSURANCE

The life insurance business was formally nationalized on 1 September 1956 by the establishment of the Life Insurance Corporation of India (LIC), which absorbed the life insurance business of 245 Indian and foreign companies. By 31 March 1973, LIC had 577 branches and 106 development centers throughout India. LIC also transacts business in certain African and Asian countries where there are large Indian populations. Total policies in force on 31 March 1973 numbered 16,792,000, and were valued at R92 billion. During 1972/73, LIC advanced R160 million to state governments to finance various housing schemes; another R337.5 million was advanced to cooperative housing finance societies and other housing authorities. LIC investments had a book value of R21.7 billion as of 31 March 1973. Restricted life insurance business is also handled by some state governments and the Post and Telegraphs Department of the national government.

The general insurance business was nationalized beginning in 1971. By 1973, all domestic and foreign insurers had been taken over. On 1 January 1974, all nationalized general insurance companies were merged into the General Insurance Corporation of India. Its paid-up capital as of 31 March 1974 was R321.9 million.

34 SECURITIES

The main stock exchanges are located in Calcutta, Bombay, and Madras, and there are secondary exchanges in Ahmadabad, Delhi, Kanpur, Nagpur, and other cities. Each exchange has its own regulations on membership and on security listings and transactions; outside Bombay and Ahmadabad these are not strict, and at times margin trading and other questionable practices have tended to produce wild speculations. Rules favor exchange members rather than public protection or benefit. Brokerage and jobbing are commonly combined.

The Industrial Credit and Investment Corporation of India (ICICI) is a privately owned and managed development bank established in 1955 with the advice and assistance of the IBRD to promote the growth of private industry. It makes long-term and medium-term loans and equity investments and engages in underwriting activities. Although its financial contribution represents only a small part of the total investment in the private sector, it is important as a source of foreign exchange for the private sector, as an agency for introducing new forms of term

financing and underwriting techniques, and as an intermediary for arranging participation by investors in the financing of Indian industrial enterprises. From 1955 through 31 December 1973, ICICI disbursed R3,088 million in development assistance.

As of 31 March 1974, India had 39,629 joint stock companies, of which 7,175 were in the public sector, 31,160 in the private sector, and 1,294 were registered nonprofit associations. The public-sector companies had a paid-up capital of R21,249 million; paid-up capital of private-sector companies totaled R56,597 million.

35 PUBLIC FINANCE

The government's financial year extends from 1 April to 31 March, and the budget is presented to the parliament on the last day of February. The executive branch has considerable control over public finance. Thus, while parliament can oversee and investigate public expenditures and may reduce the budget, it cannot expand the budget, and checks exist that prevent it from delaying passage. Recent budgets have reflected the needs of rapid economic development under rising expenditures of the five-year plans. Insufficient government receipts for financing this development have led to yearly deficits and a resulting increase of new tax measures and deficit financing.

Current central government revenues and expenditures for 1975/76 and 1976/77 (in millions of rupees) were:

	1975/76 (revised)	1976/77 (provisional)
REVENUES		
Income tax	10,600	9,570
Corporation tax	9,540	10,250
Wealth taxes	520	520
Union excise taxes	38,236	40,850
Customs receipts	13,570	14,700
Other taxes	2,229	2,479
States' share of taxes and duties	−15,990	−16,205
Nontax revenues	21,523	19,623
TOTALS	80,228	81,787
EXPENDITURES		
Defense	21,916	22,856
Interest payments	12,208	13,518
Other general services	8,180	8,730
Economic services	10,052	11,687
Social and community services	5,195	5,777
Grants-in-aid to states and union territories	12,986	13,672
Other grants and loans	630	656
TOTALS	71,167	76,896
Balance	9,061	4,891

The capital expense budget for 1976/77 totaled R52,800 million, of which R33,908 million consisted of loans and advances and R18,892 million constituted development expenditures, including R9,007 million for industry and minerals, R2,595 million for railways, and R2,548 million for defense. Capital receipts for 1976/77 totaled R44,225 million, including R14,970 million in recovered loans and advances, R5,351 million in domestic loans, and R8,149 million in external loans. Combined revenue and capital receipts for 1976/77 were R126,012 million and consolidated revenue and capital disbursements were R129,696 million, leaving a provisional net deficit of R3,684 million.

As of 31 March 1974, the central government had an outstanding debt of R170,580 million, of which R112,280 million was domestic. Of the R58,300 million in external debts, R19,480 million was owed to the US, R11,710 million to the IDA, R8,830 million to the UK, R4,850 million the the FRG, R2,670 million to the USSR, and R1,980 million to the IBRD.

Consolidated current state revenues budgeted for 1973/74 totaled R48,995 million, of which taxes contributed R31,599 million. Current expenditures totaled R52,140 million, of which R28,767 million went for programs in education (R11,520 million), health (R5,059 million), agriculture (R2,418 million), and community development (R1,755 million). Capital disbursements in 1973/74 were budgeted at R22,818 million.

36 TAXATION
Taxes are levied by the central government, the state governments, and the various municipal governments. The sources of central government tax revenue are union excise duties, customs duties, corporate and personal income (nonagricultural) taxes, wealth taxes, and gift taxes. State government sources, in general order of importance, are land taxes, sales taxes, excise duties, and registration and stamp duties. The states also share in central government income tax revenues and union excise duties. Municipal governments levy land and other property taxes and license fees. Many also levy terminal or octroi taxes, which are duties on goods entering the municipal limits. There is no uniformity in types or rates of state and municipal taxes. Because the lowest level of income subject to taxation (R6,000 for individuals) is above the income of most Indians, the federal personal tax is paid by only a fraction of the total households. The effective tax rates in 1974/75 (including a 10% tax surcharge) rose to 74.66% on earned income exceeding R10 million. Much of the total collected annually comes from 2,000 to 3,000 assessees whose incomes of more than R200,000 were taxed at 65.3% or more in 1974/75. For the tax year 1973/74, out of a population of more than 580 million, only 3,530,724 people paid income tax, 217,683 paid wealth tax, and 74,293 paid gift tax. Corporate tax in 1974/75 ranged from 45% for domestic companies in which the public held substantial interest and whose taxable income did not exceed R100,000, up to 70% for the least favored category; a 5% surcharge was also levied on all companies. A capital gains tax of 55% on buildings and land and 45% on other assets is also levied.

37 CUSTOMS AND DUTIES
The majority of imports and some exports are subject to tariffs. There are both revenue and protective tariffs, although the former are more important and have long been a major source of central government income. Most import duties run between 20% and 40% ad valorem, although some are as high as 90%. Protective tariffs designed to support home industries are newer and cover fewer imports; they average 20% to 50% ad valorem, although a few exceed 100%. While most tariffs are assessed ad valorem, a few imports have specific rates applicable. Tariffs may be waived on imports of capital goods for technological or export-oriented industries in designated free zones.

Excise duties are levied by both the central and the state governments and, like import tariffs, they are a major source of central government income.

38 FOREIGN INVESTMENTS
Economic expansion has depended heavily upon foreign participation in the form of direct grants and loans, technical assistance, and private business investment within the country. The governments and private agencies of the UK, US, USSR, the FRG, Canada, Australia, and other countries have contributed greatly, as have UN agencies and other international organizations. The IBRD has advanced large developmental loans to the government-owned railways, the Damodar Valley Corporation, and two private steel corporations; IBRD funds have also been allocated for river projects, port expansion, expansion of Tata Iron & Steel and Indian Iron and Steel, colliery development, and the Industrial Credit and Investment Corporation. By March 1974, authorized aid from the US cumulatively

totaled R58,940 million, including R2,860 million in grants and R34,430 million in loans. Aid from the IBRD and IDA totaled R28,320 million, of which R20,830 million had been utilized. Other main donors, with cumulative totals by March 1974, were UK, R13,280 million; FRG, R11,440 million; USSR, R10,330 million; and Japan, R5,160 million. All told, external assistance to India totaled R150,010 million, of which R132,020 million had been utilized by March 1974. New aid commitments of more than R16,000 million were announced in 1976. India's debts have been repeatedly postponed, rescheduled, and refinanced.

Foreign business investments in India as of 31 March 1969 amounted to R16,110 million, as against R5,112 million in 1960. The total included investments of R8,900 million in manufacturing; R2,240 million in construction, utilities, and transportation; R1,960 million in the petroleum industry; and R1,220 million in plantations. In the 1970s, several large enterprises in the mining and petroleum sectors were nationalized. The principal foreign investors as of 31 March 1969 were UK, R6,310 million; US, R4,300 million; FRG, R1,040 million; and Japan, R760 million. On 31 March 1974 there were 540 joint stock companies incorporated outside of India but having a place of business in India.

Under the Foreign Exchange Regulation Act of 1973, which came into force on 1 January 1974, all branches of foreign companies in which nonresident interest is more than 40% must reapply for permission to carry on business. Most companies were expected to reduce their holdings to no more than 40% by 1 January 1976, except that certain key export-oriented or technology-intensive industries were permitted to maintain up to 74% nonresident ownership. Tea plantations were also exempted from the 40% requirement. Although the government still officially welcomes foreign investments, collaboration and royalty arrangements are tightly controlled.

As of 31 March 1973, India had authorized assistance to other countries totaling R3,690 million, including R931 million in grants and R2,759 million in loans. The major recipients were Bangladesh, R1,677 million; Nepal, R1,010 million; Bhutan, R447 million; Burma, R200 million; and Sri Lanka, R174 million.

39 ECONOMIC POLICY
A socialistic pattern of society is the stated goal of the government. Envisaged is a mixed economy, private and public, with the responsibility of planned development and regulation in the government. Under the five-year plans, the government has become a participant in many industrial fields and has increased its regulation of existing private commerce and industry. Long the owner-operator of most railway facilities, all radio broadcasting, post, and telegraph facilities, arms and ammunition factories, and river development programs, the government has reserved for itself the right to nationalize any industries it deems necessary. Yet the government's approach is pragmatic, not doctrinaire, and agriculture and large segments of trade, finance, and industry still remain in private hands. Planning is supervised by a six-member Planning Commission, established in 1950.

In 1956, an industrial policy was announced in which two schedules of industries were specified: those in Schedule A were to be the exclusive responsibility of the state, those in Schedule B were to be progressively state-owned, although private enterprise was expected to supplement state efforts. Industries not listed specifically were, in general, to be left to private enterprise.

Schedule A: arms, ammunition, and allied defense equipment; atomic energy; iron and steel; heavy castings and forgings of iron and steel; heavy plant and machinery for steel production, mining, machine tool manufacture, and other basic industries; heavy electrical plants; coal and lignite; mineral oils; mining of iron ore, chrome ore, manganese ore, gypsum, sulfur, gold and diamonds; mining and processing of copper, lead, zinc, tin, molybdenum, tungsten, and atomic energy materials; aircraft; air transport; railway transport; shipbuilding; telephones and telephone cables; telegraph and wireless apparatus (excluding radio receiving sets); generation and distribution of electricity.

Schedule B: all other major minerals; aluminum and non-ferrous metals not included in Schedule A; machine tools; ferroalloys and tool steels; basic and intermediate products required by chemical industries; antibiotics and other essential drugs; dyestuffs and plastics; fertilizers; synthetic rubber; carbonization of coal; chemical pulp; road transport; sea transport.

India's first four five-year plans entailed a total public-sector outlay of R314.1 billion. The first plan (1951–56) accorded top priority to agriculture, especially irrigation and power projects. Of total expenditures of R19.6 billion, 22.2% went for irrigation and flood control, 14.8% for agriculture and allied sectors, and 26.4% for transport and communications. Domestic revenues provided 38.4% of the funds, domestic borrowings provided 52%, and external assistance 9.6%. The second plan (1956–61) was designed to implement the new industrial policy and to achieve a "socialist pattern of society." The plan stressed rapid industrialization, a 25% increase in national income (in fact, the achieved increase was only 20%), and reduction of inequalities in wealth and income. Of a total outlay of R46.7 billion (R25.9 billion by the central government, R20.8 billion by the states), 27% went for transport and communications, 20.1% for industry and minerals, and only 11.7% for agriculture. More than half the financing for the plan (51.2%) came from domestic borrowings; domestic revenues (26.3%) and external assistance (22.5%) made up the remainder. The third plan (1961–66) entailed total expenditures of R85.8 billion (R44.1 billion by the central government, R41.7 billion by the states). Industrialization was again the focus, with 24.6% spent on transport and communications and 20.1% on industry and minerals. Drought, inflation, and war with Pakistan made this plan a major disappointment; although considerable industrial diversification was achieved and national income rose by 8.2% annually, per capita income did not increase (because of population growth), and harvests were disastrously low. Because of the unsettled domestic situation, the fourth five-year plan did not take effect until 1969. The 1969–74 plan sought to control fluctuations in agricultural output and to promote equality and social justice. Total outlays rose to R162 billion (R85.5 billion by the central government, R76.5 billion by the states). Agriculture and allied sectors received 16.9%, more than in any previous plan, while industry and minerals received 18.5%, transport and communications 18.4%, and power development 17.8%, also more than in any previous plan. Financing through domestic borrowings increased to 53.2%, with domestic revenues providing 33.9% and external assistance 12.9%. Although the annual economic growth rate lagged far behind expectations, there was a major (if temporary) breakthrough in food-grain production.

The fifth five-year plan (1974–79) aimed at the removal of poverty and the attainment of self-reliance. A total outlay of R534.1 billion was envisaged, of which R161.6 billion was allocated to the private sector and R372.5 billion to the public. Once again, the emphasis was on industry, with mining and manufacturing taking 24%, transport and communications 19.1%, and agriculture 12.7%.

40 HEALTH

Great improvements have taken place in public health since independence. Nevertheless, the general health is far from satisfactory. Although the number of hospital beds increased from 113,000 in 1950/51 to 281,600 in 1973/74, hospital facilities and trained medical personnel are still far from adequate. Rural areas have seen the greatest progress: the number of rural health centers increased from 725 in 1956 to 5,250 in 1974.

A determined attack has been made on endemic diseases. The incidence of malaria was reduced by 98% between 1953/54 and September 1964. However, setbacks were reported after 1965, apparently because DDT-resistant strains of mosquitoes had developed. The death toll from smallpox was down from 57,000 in 1950 to 7,000 in 1963; a resurgence was reported in 1973, with 87,509 reported cases resulting in 5,457 deaths. A massive vaccination program helped contain the outbreak, and by 1976 smallpox was virtually eliminated. Between 1948 and 1973, 251 million people were tested for tuberculosis and 175.1 million received BCG, an anti-tuberculosis vaccine. There are 547 tuberculosis clinics, with nearly 39,000 beds. In 1974 there were also 251 leprosy control units, 313 venereal disease clinics, and 50 general hospitals with cancer treatment facilities. Many diseases remain, especially deficiency diseases such as goiter, kwashiorkor, rickets, and beriberi. Starvation is still known, and food shortages are frequent. The average life expectancy was estimated at 52.6 years for males and 51.5 years for females in 1975.

In 1974 there were 138,000 doctors, but there were many more unregistered practitioners and herb compounders, and a large number of registered practitioners following the Ayurvedic (ancient Hindu) and Unani (Persian for Greek, because the Arabs and Persians derived it from ancient Greece) systems. In 1974 there were about 88,000 nurses; there were an estimated 9,000 dentists and 51,000 pharmacists in 1970. In Western medicine in 1965 there were 100 medical colleges, 15 dental colleges, and 11 other training institutes. More than 100 colleges and schools teach the indigenous Ayurvedic and Unani systems of medicine, 74 teach homeopathy. New drugs and pharmaceutical plants, some assisted by the UN and some established by European and American firms, manufacture antibiotics, vaccines, germicides, and fungicides. However, patent medicines and other reputed curatives of dubious value still are widely marketed; medical advisers of the indigenous systems and their curatives probably are more widely followed than Western doctors and Western drugs and medical practices.

Family planning is a major social objective of the government. In 1974 there were 5,243 rural family planning centers, with 33,048 subcenters, and 1,919 urban centers. Between 1952 and 1974, more than 14,883,000 sterilization operations were performed, and insertions of a intrauterine device to prevent conception were made in 5 million cases. A factory has been set up by the government for manufacturing contraceptive devices, and their commercial distribution is encouraged. Condoms are also distributed free of charge at family planning centers.

41 SOCIAL WELFARE

Social welfare programs for children include supplementary nutrition for expectant mothers and for children under 7 years of age, immunization and health programs, holiday camps (2,200 in 1974) for low-income families, and prevocational training for adolescents. There are also services for the blind, deaf, mentally retarded, and orthopedically handicapped. Programs for women include welfare grants, women's adult education, and working women's hostels. Special measures are aimed at rehabilitating juvenile delinquents, prostitutes, and convicts. Begging in public places is forbidden by law in most states and localities. Other social welfare programs cover displaced persons (refugees from Pakistan), family planning and maternity care, rural community development, emergency relief programs for drought, flood, earthquake, and other disaster areas, untouchability (the scheduled castes or Harijans), and backward tribal peoples.

Labor legislation includes minimum wages for workers in large factories, railways, mines, and plantations. There are specific welfare funds for providing medical, educational, and recreational facilities for workers in coal mines, mica mines, plantations, and certain government enterprises. A limited state health insurance scheme applies to workers in large factories, and many government employees and their families in Bombay and New Delhi are covered under a contributory health scheme. Other limited insurance extends to employees of factories, mines, and plantations.

42 HOUSING

A small measure of progress has been seen in recent years toward improving the generally primitive, deplorable housing in which most Indians live. According to the 1971 census, the usable housing stock consisted of 82.5 million units (compared with 68.4 million in 1961); 66.4 million units were in rural areas and 16.1 million in urban areas. In 1974, the shortage of houses was estimated at 15.6 million. Under a number of housing schemes launched by the government, about 4 million houses were constructed between 1951 and 1966. The fifth five-year plan (1974–79) envisaged an expenditure of R3,430 million on housing from the state sector and R2,372 million from the central government, to be supplemented by R4,500 million from various central government and other public institutions for housing their low-income employees. Private-sector investment in housing was expected to total R36,400 million during the period.

The government began a slum-clearance scheme in 1956; control over the program was transferred to the states in 1969. A new central government program for improvement of slum areas was initiated in 10 cities in 1972; another 10 cities were added in 1973–74. This program, too, was transferred to the states in 1974. The fifth plan provided R1,055 million for slum improvements.

43 EDUCATION

According to the 1971 census, the population of India was 29.5% literate; male literacy was 39.5%, female 18.7%. In 1961, the literacy rate was 24%. The lowest literacy rate (below 20%) was ascribed to Rajasthan, Jammu and Kashmir, Bihar, Arunachal Pradesh, and Dadra and Nagar-Haveli. Kerala led all other states in literacy: 60.4% of the population, including 54.3% of the females and 66.6% of the males. The leader among the union territories was Chandigarh, with 61.6%, including 54.3% of the females and 67% of the males. Delhi followed with an overall rate of 56.6%.

Education in India always has been hampered by lack of funds and the insufficient resources of personnel, buildings, and instructional materials. Far fewer opportunities for education exist in rural than in urban areas; yet it is in rural areas that the bulk of the population resides. Another problem plaguing the government of independent India is that education beyond the beginning level has long depended upon English, as a remnant from the colonial era.

Since independence, public educational facilities have been expanded as rapidly as possible. The main goal has been primary education for children in the 6–11 age group. A new pedagogical approach, that of "basic education"—learning correlated with the physical and cultural environment and with domestic and commercial productive activities—has met with some success. In addition to primary education, there also has been marked expansion of educational facilities in secondary schools, colleges, universities, and technical institutes. An intensive development of adult education is under way in both urban and rural areas. Adult education programs have been undertaken through the Community Development movement. They include the Farmers' Functional Literacy Program and two institutes for industrial workers and their families.

Free and compulsory elementary education is a directive principle of the constitution. The percentage of the school-age population actually enrolled in primary school increased from 62.4% in 1960/61 to an estimated 83.9% in 1973/74. Progress in postprimary education has been less dramatic but still noteworthy. From 1960/61 to 1973/74, the enrollment percentage rose from 22.5% to 35.6% in middle schools and from 11.3% to 22% in secondary schools. In 1973/74 there were an estimated 63.8

million children enrolled in primary schools, 15 million in middle schools, and 8.5 million in secondary schools. In 1972, there were 1,096,561 primary-school teachers in 414,406 primary schools, 670,629 teachers in 94,199 middle schools, and 619,507 teachers in 38,488 secondary schools.

There has been a marked growth in the training of engineers and technicians since 1951. In that year there were 53 degree institutions and 89 diploma institutions. In 1973/74 there were 138 degree and 307 diploma institutions, with an annual enrollment of about 60,000.

Of the 95 universities in 1974, 77 had been established since independence. The older universities are in Calcutta, Bombay, and Madras, all established in 1857; Allahabad, 1877; Benares Hindu (in Varanasi) and Mysore (now Karnataka), both in 1916; Hyderabad (Osmania University), in 1918; and Aligarh and Lucknow, both in 1921. Most universities have attached and affiliated undergraduate colleges, some of which are in distant towns. Thus, Calcutta University has 218 affiliated colleges, Madras University has 157, Punjab University has 178, and Gujarat University has 136. Christian missions in India have organized more than three dozen college-rank institutions and hundreds of primary, secondary, and vocational schools. In addition to universities, there are nearly 3,000 arts and sciences colleges (including research institutes) and commercial colleges. In 1974 there were 12 rural institutes providing agricultural higher education. Among the more prominent technological higher schools are the Indian Institute of Science at Bangalore, the Indian Institute of Technology at Kharagpur and Madras, and the Indian Statistical Institute at Calcutta. The total enrollment in higher education was 2.93 million in 1972.

The autonomous University Grants Commission promotes university education and maintains standards in teaching and research. Many college students receive scholarships and stipends.

44 LIBRARIES AND MUSEUMS

In 1974 there were more than 10,000 libraries of all types in India. The National Library in Calcutta, with more than 1,400,000 volumes, is the largest in the country. Some of the other leading libraries are the Delhi Public Library in Delhi (500,000 volumes), the Central Secretariat Library in New Delhi (400,000 volumes), and the libraries of some of the larger universities. The Khuda Baksh Oriental Library in Patna, with a collection of rare manuscripts in Arabic, Urdu, and Persian, has been declared an "institution of national importance" by an act of parliament. Mobile libraries are also important in India; by 1970 there were 76 mobile libraries active in 10 states.

Most museums specialize in one or several aspects of Indian or South Asian culture; these include many minor museums devoted to the archaeological finds of a relatively small region. There are more than 200 museums in the country. Some of the more important museums are the India Museum in Calcutta, the Prince of Wales Museum in Bombay, and the National Museum and the National Gallery of Modern Art, both in New Delhi. Probably, however, the real museums of India are the thousands of architectural masterpieces of antiquity—the palaces, temples, mausoleums, fortresses, mosques, formal gardens, deserted cities, and rock-hewn monasteries—found in every section of the subcontinent.

Noted botanical gardens are located in Calcutta, Bombay, Lucknow, Ootacamund, Bangalore, Madras, and Darjeeling, and good zoological gardens are found in Calcutta, Bombay, Madras, Trivandrum, Hyderabad, Karnataka, and Jodhpur.

45 ORGANIZATIONS

Cultural activities, especially traditional arts and crafts, are promoted throughout India through the Academy of Art, the Academy of Dance and Music, and the Academy of Letters. Other state organizations for the furthering of cultural activities include the Ministry of Information and Broadcasting, the Indian Council for Cultural Relations, and the National Book Trust. There are a great many private cultural and institutional organizations based on religion and philosophy, language (including Sanskrit and Pali), drama, music and dancing, modern writing, the classics, and painting and sculpture. There are many political, commercial, industrial, and labor organizations, and rural cooperatives and recreational organizations are of some importance.

46 PRESS

The first newspaper in India, an English-language weekly issued in Calcutta in 1780, was followed by English-language papers in other cities. The first Indian-language newspaper (in Hindi) appeared in Varanasi (Benares) in 1845. In 1973 there were 12,653 newspapers published in 56 languages, led by Hindi (3,340), English (2,493), Urdu (990), Bengali (784), and Marathi (739). Bilingual newspapers are not uncommon. The newspapers included 830 dailies, 68 appearing two or three times a week, and 3,875 weeklies. In 1973, the combined circulation of all newspapers was 35.27 million, 33.5% of which was commanded by newspapers with individual circulations of more than 50,000 each. These newspapers themselves constituted less than 1% of the total number. The overwhelming majority (95.5%) had circulations of less than 15,000 each.

The principal national English-language newspapers are the *Indian Express*, with editions published in Ahmadabad, Bombay, Bangalore, Delhi, Madras, Madurai, and Vijayawada and a combined daily circulation of 412,492 in 1974; and the *Times of India*, published in Ahmadabad, Bombay, and Delhi, with a combined circulation of 255,641. Both are morning papers. Other principal dailies (with estimated 1974 circulation) are:

	LANGUAGE	CIRCULATION
BOMBAY		
Hindustan (m.)	Urdu	2,772,259
Lokasatta	Marathi	147,500
CALCUTTA		
Ananda Bazar Patrika (m.)	Bengali	305,750
Amrita Bazar Patrika (m.)	English	112,700
Jungantar (m.)	Bengali	187,000
CHANDIGARH		
Tribune (m.)	English	106,500
DELHI		
Hindustan	Hindi	162,500
Hindustan Times (m.)	English	141,000
Navbharat Times (m.)	Hindi	176,850
MADRAS		
Daily Thanthi (m.)	Tamil	308,181
Dinamani (m.)	Tamil	166,680
TRIVANDRUM		
Kerala Kaumundi	Malayalam and English	134,628
VIJAYAWADA		
Andhra Prabha	Telugu	115,419

On 1 February 1976, the four leading Indian news agencies—the Press Trust of India (English), United News of India (English), Hindustan Samachar (Hindi), and Samachar Bharati (Hindi)—merged to form Samachar, which means "news" in Hindi. The merger followed the cancellation by the government-owned All India Radio of subscriptions to all four services.

Freedom of the press has been nominally ensured by liberal court interpretations of the constitution, but the government has long held the right to impose "reasonable restrictions" in the interest of "public order, state security, decency, and morality." Under the state of emergency proclaimed in June 1975, stringent censorship was imposed. Early in 1976, the independent Press Council was abolished, and the government was permitted by law to prevent "the publication of objectionable matter" even after the state of emergency is lifted.

47 TOURISM

Foreign tourist travel has been gradually increasing in recent years; in 1951, India had 19,900 tourists; by 1973, the total had risen to 409,895. Foreign exchange earnings from tourism were R675 million in 1973. The government encourages tourism and maintains tourist information offices in 16 cities abroad, and in 11 Indian cities. There are also a number of state government tourist information offices, and major cities have privately owned travel bureaus. All Indian cities have comfortable Western-style hotels catering especially to foreign tourists. In 1974 there were 195 approved hotels with 12,190 rooms. The Department of Tourism has sponsored construction of youth hostels, forest lodges, and tourist bungalows.

A valid passport is required for entry into India; tourists from many countries need no visa. Inoculations against smallpox and cholera are recommended; inoculation against yellow fever is required if the tourist is coming from an area of infestation.

48 FAMOUS INDIANS

Unquestionably one of the greatest Indians was Siddartha Gautama (624?-544 B.C. according to Sinhalese tradition; 563?-483 B.C. according to most modern scholars), later known as Buddha ("the enlightened one"). Born along the northern edge of the Ganges Plain in what is politically Nepal today, he spent much of his life in eastern Uttar Pradesh and Bihar propounding the philosophical doctrines that were later to become Buddhism. Contemporary with Buddha was Vardhamana (599?-527 B.C.), also known as Mahavira ("great hero"), a saintly thinker of Bihar from whose teachings evolved Jainism. A great many later religious and political leaders left their indelible mark on the Indian scene. Some of the noteworthy were Asoka (d.238? B.C.); Chandragupta II (r. A.D. 380-415); Shivaji (1627?-80), hero of much Hindu folklore; Nanak (1469-1539), whose teachings are the basis of Sikhism; and Akbar (1542-1605), Aurangzeb (1618-1707), and Guru Govind Singh (1666-1708), who established Sikhism.

In modern times, the Bengali educator and reformer Rammohan Roy (1772-1833) has been called the "father of modern India." Swami Vivekananda (1863-1902), founder of the nonsectarian Ramakrishna Mission and a great traveler both in India and abroad, did much to explain the Hindu philosophy to the world and to India as well. Sarvepalli Radhakrishnan (1888-1975), a leading 20th-century Hindu scholar and philosopher, also served as president of India from 1962 to 1967. The rising position of India in science and industry is well exemplified by Jamshedji Nusserwanji Tata (1822-1904), founder of the nation's first modern iron and steel works, as well as many other key industries; the physicist Jagadis Chandra Bose (1858-1937), noted for his research in plant life; and Chandrasekhara Venkata Raman (1888-1970), who was awarded the 1930 Nobel Prize for research in physics.

In modern times no Indian so completely captured and so profoundly influenced the Indian masses, and imprinted such a deep spiritual effect on so many persons throughout the world, as Mohandas Karamchand Gandhi (1869-1948). Reverently referred to by millions of Indians as the Mahatma, the Great-Souled One, Gandhi is considered the greatest Indian since Buddha. As a political leader, his unifying ability and his unusual methods of nonviolence and passive resistance contributed materially to the liberation of India in 1947.

Gandhi's political heir, Jawaharlal Nehru (1889-1964), had almost an equally magnetic hold on the Indian people. Affectionately known as Chacha (Uncle) Nehru, he steered India through the communal riots that followed the partition of British India in 1947. His successor, Lal Bahadur Shastri (1904-66), a follower of Gandhi's, died shortly after signing a nonaggression pact with Pakistan. Indira Gandhi (b.1917), the daughter of Nehru, has been prime minister since 1966.

Modern India is the heir to a remarkable literary tradition which includes the classical Hindu texts and the anonymous Sanskrit epics *Ramayana* and *Mahabharata*. The greatest classical Sanskrit writer, and perhaps the greatest in Indian history, was the 5th-century poet and playwright Kalidasa; *Shakuntala* is his best-known work.

In modern times, Rabindranath Tagore (1861–1941), the great Bengali humanist, profoundly influenced Indian thought in his many songs and poems. Tagore received the Nobel Prize in literature in 1913 and through his lifetime wrote more than 50 dramas and about 150 books of verse, fiction, and philosophy. Another Bengali writer highly esteemed was the novelist Bankim Chandra Chatterjee (1838–94). They are the authors, respectively, of India's national anthem and national song. The novel in English is a thriving genre; notable modern practitioners include R. K. Narayan (b.1906), Bhabhani Bhattacharya (b.1906), and Raja Rao (b.1909). Influential poets of the last two centuries include the Bengalis Iswar Chandra Gupta (1812–59) and Sarojini Naidu (1879–1949), known as the "nightingale of India," a close associate of Gandhi and a political leader in her own right.

Modern interpreters of the rich Indian musical tradition include the composer and performer Ravi Shankar (b.1920) and the performer and educator Ali Akbar Khan (b.1922). Uday Shankar (b.1902?), a dancer and scholar, did much to stimulate Western interest in Indian dance. Preeminent in the Indian cinema is the director Satyajit Ray (b.1921).

⁴⁹DEPENDENCIES
Andaman and Nicobar Islands
The Andaman and Nicobar Islands are two groups of islands in the Indian Ocean, extending approximately 966 km (600 mi) N–S and lying about 644 km (400 mi) W of both the Tenasserim coast of Burma and peninsular Thailand. Their total area is 8,293 sq km (3,202 sq mi); their population was 115,133 in 1971. The Andamans were occupied by the British in 1858, the Nicobars in 1869; sporadic settlements by British, Danish, and other groups were known previously. These islands together form a union territory with its headquarters at Port Blair. The legal system is under the jurisdiction of the high court of Calcutta.

The Andaman Islands extend more than 354 km (220 mi) between 10° and 14°N and 92°12′ and 94°17′E. Of the 204 islands in the group, the three largest are North, Middle, and South Andaman; since these are separated only by narrow inlets, they are often referred to together as Great Andaman. Little Andaman lies to the south. The islands are hilly, rising in places to 2,400 feet. The climate is sultry and monotonous, with no dry season. Forests are the natural vegetation: lush tropical rain forest in the wettest sections, more jungle growth in the driest (but still moist) localities, and mangrove along the coast. The British used the islands as a penal colony from 1858 until well into the 1920s. Between 1953 and 1960, about 10,000 refugees from Pakistan resettled in the Andamans. Major crops of the Andamans are rice and coconuts; minor crops include rubber, tea, coffee, fruits, and vegetables. However, about 70% of the population is dependent upon forestry and related industries.

The Nicobars extend south from the Andamans between 10° and 6°N and 92°43′ and 93°57′E. Of the 19 islands, Car Nicobar, 121 km (75 mi) S of Little Andaman, holds more than half the total population; the largest, Great Nicobar, 146 km (91 mi) NW of Sumatra, is sparsely populated. The Nicobars are similar to the Andamans in topography and climate; their economy too is similar, although more primitive. Most of the population are Nicobarese, a people who probably belong to the Mon-Khmer group of South Asia; a few primitive aborigines inhabit Great Nicobar.

Lakshadweep
The union territory of Lakshadweep consists of the Laccadive, Minicoy, and Amindivi Islands, a scattered group of small coral atolls and reefs in the Arabian Sea between 10° and 13°N and 71°43′ and 73°43′E and about 322 km (200 mi) W of Kerala State. Their total area is about 32 sq km (12.4 sq mi). Minicoy, southernmost of the islands, is the largest. The Amindivi are the northern part of the group, but often the name Laccadives is used to refer to all of these islands. In 1971, the population of Lakshadweep was 31,810. The inhabitants of the Laccadives and Amindivis are Malayalam-speaking Muslims; those on Minicoy are also Muslim, but speak a language similar to Sinhalese. The islanders are skilled fishermen and trade their marine products and island-processed coir in the Malabar ports of Kerala. More than 110 mechanized fishing boats are in use. The main cottage industry is coir spinning. Politically, these islands were under the control of the state of Madras until 1956. The present territorial headquarters is at Kavaratti. Judicial affairs are under the jurisdiction of the high court of Kerala.

⁵⁰BIBLIOGRAPHY
Abid Husain, S. *The National Culture of India.* Bombay: Asia Publishing House, 1961.
Basham, A. L. *The Wonder That Was India.* New York: Taplinger, 1968.
Bauer, Peter Tamas. *Indian Economic Policy and Development.* New York: Praeger, 1961.
Bhatia, Krishan. *The Ordeal of Nationhood.* New York: Atheneum, 1971.
Bhatnagar, K. P., *et al. Transport in Modern India.* Kanpur: Kishore, 1955.
Bose, Nirmal Kumar. *Culture and Society in India.* Bombay: Asia Publishing House, 1962.
Bouglé, Célestin. *Essays on the Caste System.* Cambridge: Cambridge University Press, 1971.
Brass, Paul R. *Language, Religion, and Politics in North India.* Cambridge: Cambridge University Press, 1974.
Brecher, Michael. *Nehru's Mantle: The Politics of Succession in India.* New York: Praeger, 1966.
Davis, Kingsley. *The Population of India and Pakistan.* Princeton, N.J.: Princeton University Press, 1951.
De Bary, William Theodore, *et al.* (comps.). *Sources of Indian Tradition.* New York: Columbia University Press, 1958.
Directory and Yearbook. Bombay: Times of India (annual).
Dumont, Louis. *Homo Hierarchicus.* Chicago: University of Chicago Press, 1970.
Dutt, Romesh Chunder. *The Economic History of India.* 2 vols. London: Routledge & Kegan Paul, 1950.
Filliozat, Jean. *India: The Country and Its Traditions.* Englewood Cliffs, N.J.: Prentice-Hall, 1962.
Frankel, Francine R. *India's Green Revolution.* Princeton, N.J.: Princeton University Press, 1971.
Ginsburg, Norton Sydney (ed.). *The Pattern of Asia.* Englewood Cliffs, N.J.: Prentice-Hall, 1958.
Griffiths, Sir Percival Joseph. *Modern India.* New York: Praeger, 1965.
Harrison, Selig S. *India: The Most Dangerous Decades.* Princeton, N.J.: Princeton University Press, 1960.
Hutton, John Henry. *Caste in India: Its Nature, Function and Origins.* London: Oxford University Press, 1951.
Imperial Gazetteer of India. 26 vols. London: Clarendon Press, 1908.
Indian Railways. New Delhi: Ministry of Railways (annual).
Ishwaran, K. (ed.). *Change and Continuity in India's Villages.* New York: Columbia University Press, 1970.
Johnson, Gordon. *Provincial Politics and Indian Nationalism.* Cambridge: Cambridge University Press, 1974.
Kalaik-Kalanchiyam: The Tamil Encyclopaedia. Madras: The Academy for the Growth of Tamil. Distributed by Orient Longmans, 1958–date.
Keay, John. *Into India.* New York: Scribner, 1975.

Khan, N. A. *Problems of Growth of an Underdeveloped Economy: India.* Bombay: Asia Publishing House, 1961.

Kochanek, Stanley. *Business and Politics in India.* Berkeley: University of California Press, 1974.

Kumar, Ravinder (ed.). *Essays on Gandhian Politics: The Rowlatt Satyagraha of 1919.* Oxford: Clarendon Press, 1971.

Lamb, Beatrice Pitney. *India—A World in Transition.* New York: Praeger, 1966.

Lannoy, Richard. *The Speaking Tree: A Study of Indian Culture and Society.* London: Oxford University Press, 1971.

Majundar, Dhirendra Nath. *Races and Cultures of India.* Bombay: Asia Publishing House, 1961.

Marriott, McKim (ed.). *Village India: Studies in the Little Community.* Chicago: University of Chicago Press, 1955.

Menon, Vapal Pangunni. *The Transfer of Power in India.* Princeton, N.J.: Princeton University Press, 1957.

Merillat, H. C. L. *Land and Constitution in India.* New York: Columbia University Press, 1970.

Misra, B. B. *The Administrative History of India, 1834–1947.* London: Oxford University Press, 1970.

Moraes, Frank. *India Today.* New York: Macmillan, 1960.

Moraes, Frank. *Witness to an Era.* New York: Holt, Rinehart & Winston, 1973.

Mueller, M. *India, What It Can Teach Us.* Mystic, Conn.: Verry, 1961.

National Atlas of India. Dehru Dun: The National Atlas Organization, Ministry of Education & Scientific Research, 1957.

Nehru, Jawaharlal. *The Discovery of India.* London: Meridian, 1951.

Ostergaard, Geoffrey, and Melville Currell. *The Gentle Anarchists: A Study of the Leaders of the Sarvodaya Movement for Non-Violent Revolution in India.* Oxford: Clarendon Press, 1971.

Palmer, Norman Duncan. *The Indian Political System.* Boston: Houghton Mifflin, 1961.

Park, Richard Leonard. *India's Political Systems.* Englewood Cliffs, N.J.: Prentice-Hall, 1968.

Philips, C. H. (ed.). *Politics and Society in India.* London: Allen & Unwin, 1963.

Radcliffe-Brown, A. R. *The Andaman Islanders.* New York: Free Press, 1964.

Rawlinson, Hugh George. *India: A Short Cultural History.* New York: Praeger, 1952.

Raza, H. *Cultural Role of India.* Mystic, Conn.: Verry, 1968.

Reddaway, W. B. *The Development of the Indian Economy.* London: Allen & Unwin, 1962.

Rice, Edward. *Mother India's Children.* New York: Pantheon, 1971.

Sen, Sukumar. *History of Bengali Literature.* New Delhi: Sahitya Akademi, 1960.

Smith, Vincent Arthur. *The Oxford History of India.* Edited by Percival Spear. Oxford: Clarendon Press, 1958.

Spear, Percival. *India: A Modern History.* Ann Arbor: University of Michigan Press, 1972.

Statistical Abstract. New Delhi: Central Statistical Organization, 1949–date (annual).

Stebbing, Edward Percy. *The Forests of India.* London: John Lane The Bodley Head, 1922–26.

Tandon, Prakash. *Beyond Punjab, 1937–1960.* Berkeley: University of California Press, 1971.

Taylor, Carl C., et al. *India's Roots of Democracy: A Sociological Analysis of India's Experience in Planned Development.* New York: Praeger, 1966.

Tendulkar, Dinanath Gopal. *Mahatma: Life of Mohandas Karamchand Gandhi.* Bombay: Times of India, 1951–52.

Tinker, Hugh. *India and Pakistan: A Political Analysis.* New York: Praeger, 1966.

Tyson, Geoffrey. *Nehru: The Years of Power.* New York: Praeger, 1966.

Wadia, Darashaw Nosherwan. *Geology of India.* London: Macmillan, 1953.

The Wealth of India. 5 vols. New Delhi: Council of Scientific and Industrial Research, 1948–60.

Weber, Max. *The Religion of India: The Sociology of Hinduism and Buddhism.* Glencoe, Ill.: Free Press, 1958.

Woytinsky, Wladimir Savelyevich. *India: The Awakening Giant.* New York: Harper, 1957.

Yutang, Lin (ed.). *The Wisdom of India.* New York: Random House, 1942.

INDONESIA

Republic of Indonesia
Republik Indonesia

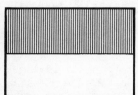

CAPITAL: Jakarta. **FLAG**: The national flag, adopted in 1949, consists of a red horizontal stripe above a white stripe. **ANTHEM**: *Indonesia Raya (Great Indonesia)*. **MONETARY UNIT**: The rupiah (Rp) of 100 sen is tied to the US dollar. There are coins of 5, 10, 25, 50, and 100 rupiahs and notes of 1, 2, 5, 10, 25, 50, and 100 rupiahs. Rp1 = $0.0024 (or $1 = Rp415). **WEIGHTS AND MEASURES**: The metric system is the legal standard, but some local units are used. **HOLIDAYS**: New Year's Day, 1 January; Independence Day, 17 August; Christmas, 25 December. Movable religious holidays include the Ascension of Muhammad, the end of Ramadan, the Descent of Nuzulul Qu'ran, Lebaran Puasa, Kartini Day, Lebaran Hadji, 'Id al-Fitr, 'Id al-'Adha', Mawlid al-Nabi, Good Friday, Easter Monday, and the First of Muharram. **TIME**: Western, 7 P.M. = noon GMT; Central, 8 P.M. = noon GMT; Eastern, 9 P.M. = noon GMT.

¹LOCATION, SIZE, AND EXTENT

The Republic of Indonesia consists of six large islands and 13,661 smaller islands forming an arc between Asia and Australia. With a land area of 1,904,345 sq km (735,270 sq mi), Indonesia is the fourth-largest Asian country, after China, India, and Sa'udi Arabia. It extends *5,271* km *(3,275* mi) E–W and *2,210* km *(1,373* mi) N–S. The principal island groups are Sumatra, 424,760 sq km (164,000 sq mi); the Greater Sunda Islands, comprising Java and Madura, with an area of 132,090 sq km (51,000 sq mi); Borneo, 72% of which belongs to Indonesia and is known as Kalimantan, 538,720 sq km (208,000 sq mi); Sulawesi, formerly called Celebes, 189,070 sq km (73,000 sq mi); the Lesser Sunda (Nusa Tenggara) Islands, 73,613 sq km (28,422 sq mi); the Maluku (Molucca) Islands, 74,504 sq km (28,766 sq mi); and West Irian (Irian Jaya), the western portion of the island of New Guinea, 412,781 sq km (159,375 sq mi). The eastern half of Timor, one of the Lesser Sunda group, is Portuguese Timor, an overseas province of Portugal. Indonesia has land boundaries with Malaysia (on Borneo), Papua New Guinea (on New Guinea), and Portuguese Timor. It is bounded on the N by the South China Sea, on the N and E by the Pacific Ocean, and on the S and W by the Indian Ocean. Indonesia's total boundary length is *39,111* km *(24,303* mi).

²TOPOGRAPHY

The large islands have a central mountain range rising from more or less extensive lowlands and coastal plains. Many inactive and scores of active volcanoes dot the islands, accounting for the predominantly rich volcanic soil that is carried down by the rivers to the plains and lowlands. The peaks rise to 12,000 feet in Java and Sumatra. Java, Bali, and Lombok have extensive lowland plains and gently sloping cultivable mountainsides. Extensive swamp forests and not very fertile hill country are found in Kalimantan. Sumatra's east coastline is bordered by morasses, floodplains, and alluvial terraces suitable for cultivation farther inland. Mountainous areas predominate in Sulawesi.

³CLIMATE

Straddling the Equator, Indonesia has a tropical climate characterized by heavy rainfall, high humidity, high temperature, and low winds. The wet season is from November to March, the dry season from June to October. Rainfall in lowland areas averages 70–125 inches annually, increasing with elevation to an average of 240 inches in some mountain areas. In the lowlands of Sumatra and Kalimantan, the rainfall range is 120–144 inches; the amount diminishes southward closer to the

Australian desert. Average humidity is 82%. Altitude rather than season affects the temperature in Indonesia. At sea level, the mean annual temperature is about 25° to 27°C (77° to 81°F). There is slight daily variation in temperature, with the greatest variation at inland points and at higher levels. The mean annual temperature at Jakarta is 25.6°C (78°F); average annual rainfall is 80 inches.

⁴FLORA AND FAUNA

The plant life of the archipelago reflects a mingling of Asiatic and Australian forms with endemic ones. Vegetation ranges from that of the tropical rain forest of the northern lowlands and the seasonal forests of the southern lowlands, through vegetation of the less luxuriant hill forests and mountain forests, to subalpine shrub vegetation. The bridge between Asia and Australia formed by the archipelago is reflected in the varieties of animal life. The fauna of Sumatra, Kalimantan, and Java is similar to that of Peninsular Malaysia, but each island has its peculiar types. The orangutan is found in Sumatra and Kalimantan but not in Java, the siamang only in Sumatra, the proboscis monkey only in Kalimantan, the elephant and tapir only in Sumatra, the wild ox in Java and Kalimantan but not in Sumatra. In Sulawesi, the Moluccas, and Timor, Australian types begin to occur; a marsupial is found in Timor. All the islands, especially the Moluccas, abound in great varieties of bird life, reptiles, and amphibians.

As of 1975, endangered species in western Indonesia included the pig-tailed langur, Kloss's gibbon, orangutan, Sumatra short-eared rabbit, Asiatic wild dog, clouded leopard, three species of tiger (Sumatran, Javan, and Bali), leopard, Asian elephant, Malayan tapir, Javan rhinoceros, Sumatran rhinoceros, Kuhl's deer, banteng, Sumatran serow, white-winged wood duck, Rothschild's starling, Rueck's blue flycatcher, river terrapin, estuarine crocodile, Siamese crocodile, false gavial, and Burmese python. In eastern Indonesia, endangered species included the lowland anoa, mountain anoa, maleo, Platen's Celebes rail, estuarine crocodile, New Guinean crocodile, and komodo dragon.

⁵POPULATION

Indonesia is the fifth most populous country in the world. As of th 1971 census, the population was 119,232,499, as compared with the 1961 census figure of 96,318,829. The estimated population in 1975 was 136,044,000; population for 1980 was projected at 154,869,000. The growth rate is high, estimated at over 2.6% annually in the mid-1970s. Of the 1971 population, about 64% (76 million) was concentrated on Java and Madura. The population of the other large islands was Sumatra, 20,800,000; Sulawesi,

8,500,000; Bali, Nusa Tenggara, and Irian Jaya, 8,600,000; and Kalimantan, 5,200,000. Overall density in 1975 was estimated at 71 persons per sq km (185 per sq mi). Java, with a density of about 618 per sq km, is among the world's most densely populated areas. In 1975, the Indonesian population was about 19% urban. Jakarta's population in 1974 was estimated at 4.7 million; Yogyakarta had 2.6 million; Surabaya, 1.6 million; Bandung, 1.3 million; and Medan, 1 million.

6 ETHNIC GROUPS

The indigenous peoples, ethnologically referred to as Malays or Indonesians, also are found on the neighboring islands of the Philippines, in Peninsular Malaysia, and even as far distant as Taiwan and Madagascar. Indonesians are characterized by smallness of stature, light to dark brown pigmentation, thick sleek black hair, broad formation of head, wide nose, and thick lips. The inhabitants of eastern Indonesia have Negroid features, the result of intermarriage with the Papuans of New Guinea.

Javanese constitute about 45% of the total population; Sundanese about 15%. There are about 20 smaller ethnic groups, such as The Madurese, Buganese, Balinese, Bataks, Dayaks, and Menangkabaus. Chinese number about 3 million.

7 LANGUAGE

Bahasa Indonesia, a product of the nationalist movement, is the official language, serving as a common vehicle of communication for the various language groups. Based primarily on Malay, it also contains many words from other Indonesian dialects as well as from Dutch, English, Arabic, Sanskrit, and other languages. English, now the second language of the country, is a compulsory subject in secondary schools. The rapid expansion of Bahasa Indonesia was accompanied by some confusion, but standards have developed and it is rapidly acquiring maturity. The Language Institute in the Ministry of Education stimulates and guides the new national language in its development.

8 RELIGION

About 90% of the inhabitants are adherents of Islam, but freedom of religion is guaranteed by the constitution. Hinduism was the religion of Java for several centuries, but when Islam swept over Indonesia in the 15th century Hinduism retreated to Bali, and more than 4 million Indonesians on Bali and elsewhere have remained Hindu in religion and culture. The religious faith of the Chinese in Indonesia may be characterized as Buddhist-Confucianist. About 70% of the 6 million or more Christians are Protestant. The chief Christian communities are found on Amboina (Ambon) and adjacent islands, northern Sulawesi, north-central Sumatra, and Timor and adjacent islands. In a few areas, as in central Kalimantan and Irian Jaya, the people are animist.

9 TRANSPORTATION

Indonesia is politically and economically dependent upon good communications and transportation among the islands. Transportation facilities suffered greatly from destruction and neglect during World War II and immediately thereafter. The revitalized and partially modernized system suffered an additional setback during 1957–58 as a result of the withdrawal of Dutch equipment and personnel.

Of the estimated 50,000 miles of public motor roads, about 18,000 miles are in Java and Madura and 18,000 miles are in Sumatra. The road network, which dates primarily from the 1930s, is in very bad condition. In the mid-1960s it was described as 45% "impassable," 41% bad, 9% "reasonable," and 5% good. The government has embarked on a road-building program that would almost double the present route mileage. In 1973, Indonesia had an estimated 306,700 passenger cars and 173,300 commercial vehicles.

Railways operate in Java, Madura, Sumatra, Sulawesi, Bangka, and Billiton, but only Java has anything approaching a complete network. The state owns almost all of the 4,530 miles in service. No new lines have been built in recent years.

Inland waterways form the most important means of transportation in Kalimantan and in parts of Sumatra. During recent years, numerous port and harbor improvements have been made. The principal ports of international trade are Tandjung Priok (near Jakarta) and Surabaya in Java and Belawan (near Medan), in Sumatra. Ports with less traffic but capable of handling sizable ships are Tjirebon and Semarang in Java; Palembang and Padang in Sumatra; Bandjarmasin, Balikpapan, and Pontianak in Kalimantan; Tandjungpinang in Bintan; and Makasar in Sulawesi. The vessels of more than 20 shipping lines call at Indonesian ports on regular or tramp service. The bulk of the cargoes has been carried in recent years by UK, Norwegian, and Japanese lines. In June 1960, Dutch ships, formerly important carriers, were forbidden to call at Indonesian ports. The ban was lifted in 1967. Shipping and port facilities are far short of the country's needs.

The center of domestic and international air routes is Jakarta's Kemajoran Airport. Aeroflot, Air Ceylon, Air India, Alitalia, BA, China Airlines, JAL, KLM, Lufthansa, Malaysian Airline System, Singapore Airlines, Pan Am, PIA, TWA, Qantas, SAS, Swissair, Thai International, and UTA provide international services. Garuda Indonesian Airways, government-owned, has services to Singapore, Bangkok, Manila, Japan, and Amsterdam, as well as interisland services. Domestic routes are also flown by Seulawah Mandala and Merpati Nusantara Airlines.

10 COMMUNICATIONS

The government owns and operates postal services and telecommunications facilities through Perumtel, a state enterprise. In 1974 there were 268,963 telephones in Indonesia. In July 1970, the IDA extended credits totaling almost $10 million for the improvement of telecommunications.

The government-owned Radio Republik Indonesia operates a network of 486 radio transmitters on shortwave and 100 on long- and medium-wave. Programs originating in Jakarta are in Indonesian; programs from regional stations are usually in local languages or dialects. Many schoolroom lessons for adults are by radio broadcasts. In 1972 there were about 6 million radios. The overseas service (Voice of Indonesia) broadcasts ten hours daily in Arabic, Chinese, Hindi and Urdu, English, Dutch, French, and Indonesian. Television service was inaugurated in 1963, and in 1970 there were an estimated 90,000 television sets. The construction of color-broadcasting facilities was contracted for in 1975.

11 HISTORY

The Indonesians are a racial mixture resulting from at least two waves of invasions from South China by way of the Malay Peninsula and some intermarriage of the Indonesians with later immigrants, especially with Indians. The important population groups of today are descended from the immigrants of the second wave, which occurred about two or three centuries B.C. They subjugated and absorbed most of the other inhabitants.

Indian immigration exerted strong influence in Java and Sumatra. Indonesia was under Buddhist influence for a time. Indian civilization last flourished on Java during the glorious century of the kingdom of Majapahit. This kingdom, founded in 1292 by King Vijaya, from its base in Java extended its control over the larger part of the area that is now Indonesia. Even before the empire of Majapahit had disintegrated, Muslim missionaries, probably Persian merchants, had begun to win much of the archipelago for Islam. About this time, also, the first Europeans arrived, and the first Chinese settlements were made. The Portuguese captured Malacca (now Melaka) on the west coast of the Malay Peninsula in 1511, and established control over the archipelago. Dutch ships visited Java in 1596. The Dutch came in increasing numbers and soon drove the Portuguese out of the archipelago except for the eastern half of the island of Timor, and began a rule that lasted nearly 350 years.

The States-General of the Dutch Republic in 1602 incorporated the East Indian traders as the United East Indian Company, and conferred upon it a monopoly of shipping and trade and the power to make alliances and contracts with the rulers of the East. Convinced that the only way to remove other European competitors was to obtain political control over the area, the Company shifted from a commercial to a territorial and political basis. By force and diplomacy, the Company became the supreme ruler of what became known as the Dutch East Indies. However, maladministration and corruption weakened the Company after its early years of prosperity, and the Dutch government nullified its charter in 1799 and took over its affairs in 1800.

exploitation replaced government exploitation; Dutch capital moved to the Indies in increasing amounts. At about the same time that the Indies government began to pay more attention to the welfare of the Indonesians, it became involved in a number of wars with tribal groups as it sought to extend and solidify its administration in outlying areas. These wars took huge sums badly needed for welfare purposes.

With the adoption of what was called the "ethical policy" at the beginning of the 20th century, the policy of native welfare was carried forward and the first steps were taken to give Indonesians participation in government. A central representative body, the Volksraad, was instituted in 1918. At first, it had only advisory powers, but in 1927 it was given colegislative powers.

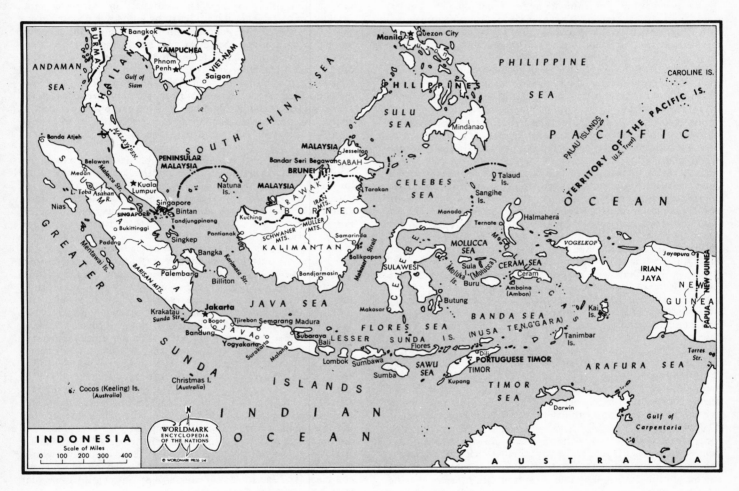

See continental political: front cover P10; physical: back cover P10
LOCATION (including Irian Jaya): 95°1′ to 141°2′E; 6°5′N to 11°S. **BOUNDARY LENGTHS**: Malaysia, *1,496* km (*930* mi); Papua New Guinea, *777* km (*483* mi); Portuguese Timor, *222* km (*138* mi); total coastline, *36,616* km (*22,752* mi). **TERRITORIAL SEA LIMIT**: 12 mi.

The British occupied the Indies during the Napoleonic wars, from 1811 to 1816. The Netherlands government, badly in need of money, instituted the "culture system" on Java, under which the Japanese, instead of paying a certain proportion of their crops as tax, were required to put at the disposal of the government a certain proportion of their land and labor and to grow crops for export under government direction. From a fiscal point of view the system was very successful, yielding millions of guilders for the Netherlands treasury, but this "net profit" or "favorable balance" policy fell under increasing moral attack in the Netherlands and was brought to an end about 1877. Private

An Indonesian nationalist movement began to develop during those years and steadily gained strength. The world economic depression, which was strongly felt in Indonesia, retarded the movement, but the Japanese occupation (1942–45) galvanized it. A group under the leadership of Sukarno and Hatta proclaimed an independent republic on 17 August 1945, formed a revolutionary government, and resisted Dutch reoccupation. After four years of intermittent negotiations and frequent hostilities, and after UN intervention, the Netherlands agreed to grant national independence to the Indonesians. The terms of separation were agreed upon at a round table conference at The

Hague in the autumn of 1949, and sovereignty was transferred to the new state on 27 December. A Netherlands-Indonesian union was established to assure cooperation between the two countries in defense, cultural, and economic matters, but it never developed any vitality and was dissolved on 10 August 1954.

Java has nearly two-thirds of the country's population, but the great sources of wealth are found on the the other, much less densely settled islands. Those living in the so-called Outer Islands believe too much governmental revenue is spent in Java and too little elsewhere. After Vice-President Hatta, a Sumatran, resigned in December 1956, many in the Outer Islands felt they had lost their chief and most effective spokesman in Jakarta. Territorial army commanders in Sumatra staged coups and defied the central government; other rebellious movements developed in Sulawesi. The government took measures providing for greater fiscal and administrative decentralization, but discontent remained, and the rebellion was put down by force.

The long dispute with the Netherlands over West New Guinea (now West Irian or Irian Jaya) was settled in 1962. In accordance with the agreement, the Netherlands in October 1962 transferred the administration of the territory to a UN administrator. On 1 May 1963, Indonesia took complete possession of West Irian, ending a seven-month interim administration by the UN, and immediately resumed diplomatic relations with the Netherlands.

On 17 August 1969, President Suharto announced that the people of West Irian, through eight consultative assemblies, had chosen to remain within Indonesia. UN observers were present at the exercise of choice, and on 19 November 1969, the General Assembly took note of the Secretary-General's report on the consultation in West Irian.

Indonesia opposed the formation of the Federation of Malaysia in September 1963, and announced a "crush Malaysia" policy. This policy was implemented by guerrilla raids into Malaysian territory that continued until August 1966, when a formal treaty was concluded between Indonesia and Malaysia. The treaty specified that a referendum would be held in Sabah and Sarawak to determine their future political affiliation.

Communist agitation within the country and secessionist uprisings in central and eastern Java came to a head in the 30th of September Movement under the leadership of Lt. Col. Untang. An attempted coup of 30 September 1965 was crushed immediately by the army, and in the ensuing anti-Communist purges more than 100,000 persons (mostly Indonesian Chinese) lost their lives. By mid-October, the army, under the command of Gen. Suharto, was in virtual control of the country. On 12 March 1966, following nearly three weeks of student riots, President Sukarno transferred to Suharto the authority to take in the president's name "all measures required for the safekeeping and stability of the government administration." In March 1967, the People's Consultative Congress voted unanimously to withdraw all governmental power granted to Sukarno under the 1945 constitution and appointed Gen. Suharto acting president. In March 1968, it conferred full presidential powers on Suharto, and he was sworn in as president for a five-year term. The Congress also agreed to postpone the general elections due in 1968 until 1971. Sukarno died in relative obscurity in June 1970.

On 3 July 1971, national and regional elections were held for the majority of seats in all legislative bodies. GOLKAR, a mass political front backed by Suharto, gained 60% of the popular vote and emerged in control of both the House of Representatives and the People's Consultative Assembly (PCA). In March 1973, the PCA elected Suharto to a second five-year term. Thus Suharto, with key backing from the military, approached a full decade of dominance over Indonesian politics. Under Suharto's "New Order," Indonesia has followed a conservative economic course stressing capital development and foreign investment. In foreign affairs, Suharto's government achieved vastly improved ties with the US, Japan, and Western Europe, while maintaining links with the USSR. While informal contacts with China resumed in the mid-1970s, Sino-Indonesian relations remained cool.

On 7 December 1975, Indonesian troops invaded Portuguese Timor and were shortly in full control of the territory. On 3 May 1976, the Suharto government announced its full integration of the territory as an Indonesian province, a step neither acknowledged nor acceded to by Portugal.

12 GOVERNMENT

A provisional constitution of 17 August 1950 provided for a unitary republic of Indonesia. The president and vice-president, "elected in accordance with rules to be laid down by law," were to be inviolable, but cabinet ministers were jointly and individually responsible. Sukarno and Hatta, the first president and vice-president, were elected by parliament. No term of office was stipulated by the constitution. The House of Representatives was to be a unicameral parliament of 260 members elected by a system of proportional representation for a four-year term, but it might be dissolved earlier by presidential decree. A constituent assembly of 514 members elected in 1955 to draft a permanent constitution began functioning in November 1956.

In practice, the government was not strictly parliamentary since President Sukarno played a role far greater than is usual for the head of state in a parliamentary system. He was the great national revolutionary hero and his popularity with the masses enabled him to exert great influence on government policy. Parliament was not strong enough to hold the president to the role prescribed by the constitution.

On 5 March 1960, Sukarno suspended parliament. He was to rule by decree until he created a People's Congress, composed of members of a new parliament and representatives of various regional groups and organizations (such as labor, women, youth, and the armed forces). In June 1960, he installed a new, self-appointed 283-member parliament drawn from 9 political parties and 14 "functional groups." In mid-August 1960, President Sukarno named 326 members who, with the 283 members of parliament, were to constitute the Provisional People's Congress. This Congress was to meet at least once every five years and to be responsible for drawing up the outlines of national policy and electing the president and vice-president.

In October 1967, Gen. Suharto, who had become Indonesia's effective ruler in March 1966, assumed the prime ministership and reorganized the cabinet, making all of its 12 ministers responsible to him. In February 1968, he dismissed 123 members of the People's Consultative Congress (PCC—an outgrowth of the Provisional People's Congress) and replaced them by his own nominees. In June 1968, following his appointment to a five-year term as president, Gen. Suharto formed a new cabinet, consisting of himself as prime minister and defense minister and 23 other ministers.

On 3 July 1971, general elections—the first since 1955—were held for portions of two reconstituted national bodies, a 460-seat House of Representatives and a 920-seat People's Consultative Assembly (PCA). Legislative responsibility was vested in the House, which consisted of 360 elective members and 100 members appointed by the president from the military and other groups. House members also sit as members of the PCA, two-thirds of whose total membership are elected officials. Under the Suharto government, the PCA has acted as a consultative body, setting guidelines for national policy. In March 1973, the PCA appointed President Suharto to a second five-year term.

Suffrage in Indonesia is universal: all citizens over 21 may vote in elections.

13 POLITICAL PARTIES

Indonesia has had a large number of political parties, owing chiefly to the system of proportional representation and Dutch example and influence. Before independence, Indonesian political elements formed, grouped, and regrouped in rapid succession, but after independence there was more cohesion and stability. Nevertheless, ministries under the unitary republic were coalitions in which the balance of power swung back and forth between left and right.

Until the autumn of 1955, when the first national elections were held, members of the House of Representatives were appointed by the president in consultation with party leaders. Of the 37,785,299 votes cast in the general election, six parties received more than 1 million votes each: the Indonesian Nationalist Party (Partai Nasional Indonesia—PNI), 22.3% of the total; Council of Muslim Organizations (Masjumi), 20.9%; the Orthodox Muslim Scholars (Nahdlatul Ulama—NU), 18.4%; the Indonesian Communist Party (Partai Komunis Indonesia—PKI), 16.4%; United Muslim Party, 2.9%; and Christian Party, 2.6%. Twenty-eight parties won 257 seats in the 273-member Parliament.

Almost all the political parties had socialist aims or tendencies. The PNI, many of whose prominent members were leaders in the prewar nationalist movement, represented a combination of nationalism and socialism. Government officials and employees had originally constituted its backbone, but subsequently it grew powerful among labor and farmer groups as well. The Masjumi was more evenly distributed throughout Indonesia than any other party. Although it contained a large percentage of the small middle class, its principles were markedly socialist, owing to the influence in the party of a religious socialist group. The NU, which broke away from the Masjumi largely because of differences in religious outlook, represented the orthodox but not strictly conservative views of the rural people and religious teachers. Before October 1965, the PKI, which did not depart from the orthodox Communist Party line, was strong in Indonesia, particularly in Java. The Christian Party was founded by Protestants; a smaller Roman Catholic Party was also formed. On 17 August 1960, Sukarno ordered the dissolution of the Masjumi and socialist parties on the grounds of disloyalty. A month later, 13 September, political action by all parties was barred. Early in 1961, notice was given that all political parties were required to apply for permission to function. On 15 April, parties certified to continue in existence included the PKI, PNI, NU, Catholic, Islamic Association, Indonesian, Indonesian Protestant Christian, Indonesian Islam Sarekat, and the League for Upholding Indonesian Independence. The PKI, which at the height of its power in 1965 had an estimated 3 million members and was the most powerful orthodox Communist Party outside the USSR, was banned by Gen. Suharto in March 1966. In a backlash of nationalism, more than 100,000 PKI members were estimated to have been killed in riots, assassinations, and purges. Since then, the party has operated underground and has become Chinese oriented. The Masjumi dissolved in 1960.

Under the Suharto government, political opposition in Indonesia has become increasingly quiescent. Prior to the 1971 elections, the government formed a mass organization known as the Joint Secretariat of Functional Groups (GOLKAR) as the political vanguard for its "New Order" program. GOLKAR drew upon elements outside of traditional party ranks—the civil service, labor, youth, cooperatives, and other groups—and succeeded in effectively circumventing the parties' ability to play a national role. Prior to the 1971 voting, a government-appointed election committee screened all prospective candidates, eliminating 735 from the initial list of 3,840; only 11 of those eliminated were from GOLKAR. Candidates were forbidden to criticize the government or to discuss religious issues. In the elections held on 3 July 1971, GOLKAR candidates received 60% of the vote, while winning 236 of the 360 contested seats in the House of Representatives. Apart from GOLKAR—which is not formally considered to be a political party—9 parties took part in the elections, as compared with 28 in 1955. The Orthodox Muslim NU placed second in the balloting, with 58 seats; the moderate Indonesian Muslim Party won 24 seats; and the PNI, Sukarno's former base, won only 20 seats. Four smaller groups—the Moslem Political Federation, the Protestant Christian Party, the Catholic Party, and the Islamic Party—divided the remaining 22 seats. The government announced that 54.6 million persons, or 94.2% of the electorate, had taken part in the voting. Following the elections, the traditional parties reorganized to form two groups—the Democratic Party and the Development Party. A Political Parties Bill, passed in 1975, encouraged the two-party structure while laying down a variety of restrictions on party activity. As a concession to Muslim groups, a Council of Religious Scholars (Majlis Ulama) was allowed to take form with permission for Islamic issues to be raised in political discussions.

14 LOCAL GOVERNMENT

Indonesia is divided into 26 provinces (not including Portuguese—or East—Timor). Each province is administered by a governor chosen by the central government from candidates proposed by the provincial assembly. Elections for the partially appointive provincial assemblies were conducted in 1971. The provinces are divided into 281 regencies (kabupaten), administered by regents appointed in the same manner as governors. Small towns and villages constitute the lowest units of administration.

15 JUDICIAL SYSTEM

Since 1951, the administration of justice has been unified. Government courts, each with a single judge, have competence in the first instance in civil and criminal cases. The High Court hears appeals in civil cases and reviews criminal cases. The Supreme Court is the highest court in the country; its primary function is judicial review. Judgment in civil cases involving Muslims is based on the principles of Muslim law. Judges are appointed by the central government. In the villages (desa), the old customary law (adat) justice procedures continue unchanged.

16 ARMED FORCES

The Indonesian armed forces, established on 5 October 1945, consist of an army, navy, and air force. A national military academy was opened in October 1957. The army numbers about 200,000, of whom about one-third are engaged in nonmilitary tasks. The air force, with a total complement of 28,000, has 47 combat aircraft and more than 125 other aircraft. The navy, with 38,000 personnel, includes 3 submarines, 9 frigates, 9 missile-armed motor torpedo boats, 38 patrol craft, 14 minesweepers, 10 amphibious attack vessels, and 3 support ships. Naval forces include a helicopter-equipped naval air wing and a marine brigade. Paramilitary forces include a police mobile brigade, with 12,000 personnel, and a militia of about 100,000.

17 MIGRATION

Formerly, there was considerable migration from and to China. Following the decree banning foreigners from participating in retail trade in rural Indonesia, some 120,000 Chinese left Indonesia in 1960 and the first six months of 1961. Following the attempted coup of 1965 and the resultant deterioration in relations between Indonesia and China, many more Chinese left Indonesia. Migration between the Netherlands and Indonesia has been greatly reduced. Nearly all the 250,000 Netherlands nationals in Indonesia in 1949 returned home. Probably several thousand Indonesians migrate to Singapore and Malaysia each year. In 1955, Indonesia and the Philippines made an agreement to control illegal migration between their bordering islands, and some Indonesians and Filipinos were repatriated.

To relieve the population pressure on Java and to develop the Outer Islands, the Dutch authorities encouraged migration from the former to the latter. The Indonesian government, resuming this policy, had hoped to move 2 million persons in the six-year period 1955–60, but only 163,559 persons transmigrated. Since the annual population increase of Java is about 2 million, the costly transmigration scheme can do little to relieve that island's human congestion.

[18] INTERNATIONAL COOPERATION

Indonesia was admitted to UN membership on 28 September 1950 and was a member of all the specialized agencies. Following the seating of Malaysia in the Security Council, Indonesia withdrew from the UN on 7 January 1965; it resumed its seat on 28 September 1966. Indonesia is also a member of the Colombo Plan, OPEC, IRC, IRSG, the International Tea Committee, the International Tin Council, the International Tin Study Group, the International Wheat Council, the IMF, Asian Development Bank, IBRD, and other intergovernmental organizations.

Indonesia became one of the founding members of ASEAN in 1967. In March 1970, a treaty of friendship was signed between Indonesia and Malaysia. The treaty also established the boundary between the two countries in the Strait of Malacca.

Foreign and multinational assistance has played a major role in Indonesia's development in recent decades. Prior to 1965, Indonesia received substantial assistance from the USSR and other Communist states; such funding included some $750 million in economic credits and more than $1 billion in military aid. Since 1966, the foreign-aid pattern has turned dramatically toward the West. A group of nations including the US, Netherlands, Japan, Belgium, France, Federal Republic of Germany (FRG), Italy, UK, Switzerland, Canada, and New Zealand joined to form the Inter-Governmental Group on Indonesia (IGGI) as a major funnel for aid. IGGI's estimated commitments for 1975 were more than $900 million. The US has taken up a major part of foreign-assistance funding, contributing $1.2 billion during 1966–73. During the 1970s, the IMF has taken a central part in reorganizing Indonesia's financial structure and methodologies. At the Indonesian government's invitation, the IMF has also provided the unique function of evaluating the country's economic programs for the purpose of advising donor nations. More recently, the IMF has expanded its role by advising the government on planning and foreign-aid allocation. In 1974/75, Indonesia was East Asia's largest single recipient of IBRD loans, with a total of $332 million allocated.

[19] ECONOMY

Indonesia's rich volcanic soils and abundant natural resources offer great potential even in view of the country's sizable population. Because of its great dependence upon the export of a relatively small range of primary commodities, however, Indonesia's economy remains predominantly "colonial" in nature. Even the substantial export gains of the past decade have failed to affect most Indonesians, who continue to lead an impoverished existence. In the 17th and 18th centuries, the basis of the economy was spices, in the 19th century it shifted to sugar and coffee, and in the 20th century, oil, tin, and rubber production became fundamental. Indonesia is the world's second-largest producer of natural rubber and the eleventh-largest producer of oil. The value of petroleum exports rose considerably following the oil crisis of the early 1970s; petroleum's share in Indonesia's total exports rose from 44.9% in 1969 to 72.7% in 1975. In 1972, timber surpassed rubber as the second-leading export. Most agricultural export commodities, such as rubber, tobacco, sugar, palm oil, and tea, have been produced on large holdings, partly held by foreigners. More than 70% of all exports are produced by Sumatra and about 14% by Java.

However important export commodities are for the economy, subsistence agriculture is the principal occupation of the vast majority of the population. Agriculture, forestry, and fishing account for more than half of the national income and provide more than two-thirds of total employment. Rice is the major staple food and the chief agricultural crop, but in spite of much planning and aid in increasing production, Indonesia has not yet been able to achieve self-sufficiency.

Industrial development is still small in relation to the size of the population and the national income. Most new industries being stressed are labor-intensive. In 1964, a vast array of foreign industries and plantations were expropriated. The country's infrastructure had deteriorated alarmingly, while foreign debts exceeding $2 billion had accumulated, prompting doubts over Indonesia's international credit standing. One of the most pressing tasks facing the new government of President Suharto was to restore the economy that was suffering from the effects of excessive imports and declining exports, extensive foreign borrowing for expenditure on nonproductive projects, and the crushing burden of foreign debt payments.

From early 1966, the government took steps to stimulate exports by allowing exporters to keep a larger proportion of their foreign exchange earnings. The government imposed strict controls on imports, encouraged foreign investments, returned many nationalized assets, ended nonproductive projects, and reduced government control of the economy.

By the end of 1968, the inflation rate, which had been 635% in 1966 and 120% in 1967, had fallen to 85%. The year 1969 marked a turning point in Indonesia's economy. Rapid inflation was brought under control, declining to 10% in 1971. The government successfully introduced fiscal and credit restraints, rescheduled internal debts, returned expropriated properties, liberalized foreign-investment laws, and actively sought assistance from overseas. By the mid-1970s, however, the economy began to experience difficulties brought on by world inflationary trends and increasing current-account payments deficits. IGGI, meeting in May 1975, went along with the government's anticipated requirements of at least $2 billion annually in bilateral aid and credits during the last half of the decade to offset the continuing drain from import purchases and debt payments. Indonesia's investment climate was severely shaken in 1975 by the near collapse of Pertamina, the giant government-backed oil conglomerate. An accumulation of debts and an overextended capital development program had led in March to the government's underwriting of Pertamina's obligations through the national Bank Indonesia. As of that time, Pertamina was in debt to the government for $3.2 billion in foreign loans and overdue oil payments, while some $113 million was owed to local firms. Overall, Pertamina owed more than the total debt amassed by the Sukarno government up to 1966.

[20] INCOME

In 1974/75, the GDP totaled Rp10,600 billion, as compared with Rp4,900 billion in 1972/73. For the 1973 calendar year, GDP was distributed as follows: agriculture, forestry, and fishing, 39.8%; commerce, 20.4%; mining, 9.3%; manufacturing, 8.6%; construction, 4%; transport and communications, 4%; and other activities, 13.9%. Per capita GDP in 1974/75 was about $190. Growth rate in per-capita income in the 1970s averaged about 2–3%, while GNP during the same period grew, at constant prices, by 6.7% yearly.

[21] LABOR

The 1971 census reported a labor force of 40.3 million (33.8% of the total population). Of the total number employed, 25.8 million (68.3%) were engaged in agriculture, forestry, and fishing; 3.3 million (8.7%) in other services; 3.1 million (8.2%) in commerce; 2 million (5.3%) in mining and industry; and 3.6 million (9.5%) in other sectors. Some 6.1% of the 1971 work force was unemployed.

Skilled workers and trained management personnel are few,

and labor productivity is low. The Ministry of Education and Culture, the Ministry of Labor, and the Industry Division of the Ministry of Economic Affairs have been training workers in various skills. Some of the larger industrial enterprises offer training programs and courses.

Since 1968, when the labor movement started, it has been linked with nationalist movements, and unions have been regarded as important functional groups in the revolution and in political life. SOBSI, the largest federation, was Communist-oriented and wielded great influence not only because of its large membership, but also because Indonesians identified it with anticolonialism and the struggle for independence. Following the 1965 coup, SOBSI was banned. The trade union movement is largely confined to Java and Sumatra. The percentage of organized workers is high among larger industrial firms, on estates, and in government services.

The Central Council of All Indonesia Trade Unions is the country's largest confederation, with a membership of about 3 million and some 28 national and 800 local unions. The second-largest is the All Indonesia Trades Union Congress, with a membership of about 400,000 in 24 national unions and 54 local unions. Other trade unions have a combined membership of about 300,000.

There is no minimum wage legislation, but in practice wages are regulated through arbitration awards that serve to set minimums for the industries. The 40-hour workweek and a basic 7-hour day are standard throughout Indonesia. The labor code of 1948 set standards regarding child labor, women and young persons in industry, hours of work, holidays, annual leave, and conditions of work. The code has been only partly implemented by ordinance and has chiefly come into effect through common practice. Under the labor accident law of 1951, in enterprises in which there are hazardous risks an employer is liable for medical care and full or partial wages for workers injured on the job, as well as for burial expenses and compensation to dependents in event of work-related death. Custom has extended these benefits to industrial workers not covered by this law.

22 AGRICULTURE

About 61% of Indonesian workers are engaged in agriculture, which also supports about 80% of the total population. Some 17 million hectares are under cultivation, with 35% to 40% of the cultivated land devoted to the production of export crops. Some 60% of the country's cultivated land is in Java.

The 1969–74 five-year development plan placed special emphasis on the development of agriculture. Rice production was to be increased, in part, through the construction and rehabilitation of irrigation works. Efforts were also being made to rehabilitate the government-owned estates producing rubber and palm oil. The IDA and Asian Development Bank have provided major assistance for both types of projects.

There are two main types of farming: small farms owned by Indonesians who engage in some rubber and other export crop production but chiefly in subsistence farming, and large foreign-owned or privately owned enterprises producing export crops. Small-scale farming is usually carried out on modest plots (those in Java average about 0.8 to 1 hectare) without benefit of modern tools and methods, good seed, or fertilizer. Although rice, vegetables, and fruit constitute the bulk of the small farmer's crops, about 20% of output is in cash crops for export, the chief of which is rubber.

Foreign management, indigenous laborers, single crops, large-scale operation, and progressive methods traditionally characterized estate agriculture. Of the estate-grown crops, rubber, tobacco, sugar, palm oil, hard fiber, coffee, tea, cocoa, and cinchona are the most important. Dutch, UK, US, French, and Belgian capital had financed estate agriculture, with the Dutch share being the largest until management of Dutch in-

terests was taken over by the Indonesian government in December 1957. Under the agrarian law passed in 1870, foreigners could not buy land; the estate lands were instead leased on a long-term basis. A foreign investment law of 1958 authorized leasing of lands for estate agriculture for periods generally of 30 years. In 1964, however, the 104 UK-operated plantations were confiscated without any compensation and Indonesian managers were appointed. In 1965, the US-operated plantations were expropriated, and all foreign enterprise was placed under the control and supervision of the Indonesian government. In 1967, some of the estates seized in 1965, including the US-leased rubber plantations, were returned. By 1970, the last of the tea and rubber plantations were restored to their original operators.

Pursuant to the agrarian reform law of 1960, President Sukarno issued a regulation to provide each farming family with at least 2 hectares of land. Indonesians were barred from owning more than 15 hectares of wet rice fields or 20 hectares of dry ground in sparsely settled areas; in thickly settled areas, the ceilings ranged from 5 to 10 hectares of wet fields and 6 to 12 hectares of dry ground.

Production of rice, the staple food, has been gradually increasing (15.4 million tons in 1974, as compared with 12.6 million tons in 1964), but production still fails to meet domestic requirements; 522,389 tons of rice had to be imported in 1973. Java raises about two-thirds of the domestic crop. Other important food crops are corn, cassava, sweet potatoes, peanuts, and soybeans.

With the increase in value of petroleum, forestry, and other products, the share of export crop earnings has declined steadily in recent years, accounting for only about 10.4% of the total export volume in 1973 (compared with more than 50% as late as the mid-1950s). Rubber and, since the early 1970s, coffee have been the most important export crops. Smallholders produce more than 50% of total export production, 60% of rubber, and the bulk of coconuts. About 885,800 tons of rubber were produced in 1973, as compared with about 648,400 in 1964. In 1973, some 174,000 tons of coffee were grown, as compared with a peak of 188,900 tons in 1972 and an annual average of 120,400 tons during 1960–65. Indonesia is the world's third-largest producer of palm oil; 290,000 tons were produced on estates in 1973, as compared with 160,900 tons in 1964. Tobacco (75,600 tons in 1973) and copra are also important export crops.

Because the population is rapidly increasing, the government seeks to achieve food self-sufficiency through expansion of arable acreage, improved farm techniques (especially the use of fertilizers and improved seeds), extension of irrigation facilities, and expanded training for farmers.

23 ANIMAL HUSBANDRY

In 1973, the livestock population was estimated at 6,250,000 head of cattle, 670,000 horses, 3,300,000 hogs, and 3,000,000 sheep. There are also about 3,000,000 buffalo in the country. The production of meat and dairy products (about 36,000 tons of milk in 1973) is secondary to the raising of draft animals for agricultural purposes and transportation. The government has established cattle-breeding stations and artificial insemination centers to improve the stock and has been carrying on research to improve pastures.

24 FISHING

Fish is the chief source of animal protein in the Indonesian diet. In 1973, the total catch was estimated at 1.3 million tons. Fishing is more important than statistics indicate because the catch of many part-time fishermen never enters trade channels. Commercial fishing is confined to a narrow band of inshore waters, especially off northern Java, but other fishing also takes place along the coast as well as in the rivers, lakes, coastal swamps, artificial ponds, and flooded rice fields. The government has stocked the inland waters, encouraged cooperatives to provide credit facilities, introduced improved fishing methods, and urged the motorizing of more boats.

25 FORESTRY

Forests represent a potentially vast source of wealth in Indonesia. Of the 100 million hectares of forests—53% of the land area of Indonesia—74% is in Kalimantan and eastern Indonesia, 24% in Sumatra, and 2% in Java and Madura. The more accessible forest areas of Sumatra and Kalimantan furnish the commercially cut timber for domestic consumption and export. Practically all forest lands belong to the state. In Java, all forests, and in the Outer Islands, extensive regions, particularly in the uplands, are in reserves. In Java, excessive cutting has caused soil erosion, aggravated floods, created water shortages, and damaged some irrigation facilities. Replanting and rehabilitation of the Javanese forests are slow, but reforestation in the Outer Islands is proceeding at a satisfactory pace. There is hope of obtaining wood pulp from pine and bamboo and commercial timber from new plantings of fir and pine. Reforestation has been undertaken on 43,000 hectares.

Total timber production in 1973 reached 126 million cu meters, as compared with 97.6 million cu meters in 1968. About half of the timber output is exported. Exports of timber doubled between 1968 and 1969, and since 1972 have comprised Indonesia's leading export earner after petroleum. In 1973/74, timber exports totaled $631 million ($720 million in 1974/75). This rise in production was due mainly to the increased investment in the timber industry in Kalimantan and central Sumatra by French, Japanese, US, and Philippine interests. In eastern Kalimantan alone, five concerns invested $40 million, setting a production target of 10 million cu meters. In 1970, some 57 foreign and local firms held concessions for a total of 6.9 million hectares of forest.

26 MINING

Petroleum grew to account for more than 70% of Indonesia's annual total export earnings in the mid-1970s. Indonesia ranked eleventh among petroleum-producing countries in 1975, with an estimated output of 63.3 million tons of crude oil (production in 1964 was 22.9 million tons). Known reserves in 1973 were put at 1,558 million tons, and untapped resources may be even larger. Sumatra, the richest oil area, produces about 70% of Indonesian oil; Kalimantan is the second-leading producer; Java and Madura have a scattering of smaller producing wells. Lesser amounts are also produced in Irian Jaya. In 1973, Indonesia produced 5,031 million cu meters of natural gas, nearly double the output of 1969.

Under the mining law of 1899 and the mining ordinance of 1930, the government can grant exploration licenses that carry the right to claim an exploitation concession except in the case of coal and oil. With respect to the latter, the government could contract with private companies for exploration and exploitation. Foreign oil companies operated under this arrangement with 40-year concessions. The foreign investment law of 27 October 1958 closed the mining of "vital minerals" to foreign capital but permitted special arrangements that could provide for exploitation by private corporations with Indonesian government participation. Prior to 1965, nearly 90% of Indonesia's petroleum was extracted by foreign companies and slightly more than 10% by state-owned companies. In March 1965, the government took over all foreign-owned oil companies, at the same time offering to allow the companies to continue operations under Indonesian control and supervision. The petroleum law of 1960 provided for foreign private enterprise to develop resources subject to contract agreements on a production-share basis. A public-sector enterprise, Pertamina, was set up to represent the government in all matters relating to the petroleum industry, including the negotiation and conclusion of contracts with foreign companies for exploration and production. Contracts signed with Pertamina during the 1970s included exploration and production-sharing agreements with UK, US, Japanese, Australian, and French concerns. The exploration areas have included 24,000 sq km of northeastern Kalimantan, 70,000 sq km between Java and Sulawesi, 74,000 sq km off the southern coast of Irian Jaya, 6,000 sq km on- and offshore north of Irian Jaya, 1 million hectares in southern Sumatra, and 14,200 sq km in central Sumatra. By the mid-1970s, Pertamina had grown into a huge consolidated conglomerate, assuming a dominant role in oil exploration and production, as well as expanding into other fields such as petrochemicals, fertilizers, and natural gas. In late 1974, however, Pertamina began to encounter serious financial difficulties leading in March 1975 to a severe curtailment of its autonomy, with the Bank Indonesia made the direct recipient of the national share in Pertamina's oil-export earnings.

Indonesia is the world's third-largest producer of tin. Production decreased from 34,365 tons in 1953 to a low of 12,727 tons in 1966. The decrease in production was due chiefly to the declining quality of the ore extracted in Bangka. Output began to increase gradually in the late 1960s, owing to increased investment, and by 1973 reached 22,492 tons. The chief deposits of tin are in Bangka, Billiton, and Singkep, three islands off the east coast of Sumatra. The government is the principal shareholder in tin production. A smelting plant began operations in Bangka in 1964, but most of the extracted tin ore is shipped abroad.

Indonesian deposits of high-grade bauxite were estimated before World War II to be one-fifth of the world's reserve. Production, which began in Bintan in 1935, rose to 648,000 tons in 1964 and nearly doubled in the course of the next decade, reaching 1,229,000 tons in 1973. The entire output is exported.

The railroads use much of the low-grade coal mined in Indonesia. Coal production decreased from 828,000 tons in 1956 to 448,000 tons in 1964 and to 149,000 tons in 1973. Iron ore is found in sizable quantities, but not commercially exploited; nickel exists in workable quantities in the iron ore of Sulawesi. There are fair to good reserves of manganese; small amounts of copper, gold, and silver; numerous minor metals in small quantities; iodine, diamonds, and phosphates; and considerable supplies of limestone, asphalt, clay, and kaolin.

The search for other minerals is being actively pursued. Surveys for tin are being carried out in the Bangka, Billiton, and Singkep areas: for manganese near Yogyakarta and near Halmahera Island; and for nickel in Sulawesi and Irian Jaya. US, Canadian, Dutch, and Japanese interests are participating. A consortium backed by FRG, Japanese, and US interests has completed plans for a $120-million copper ore project at Mt. Eistberg in Irian Jaya. With an estimated 33 million tons of copper, as well as small amounts of gold and silver, this field is reported to be the largest outcrop of base metal in the world.

27 ENERGY AND POWER

Power facilities are overtaxed, and demand for power is growing at a rate exceeding 15% annually. Total installed capacity in 1972 was 789,000 kw, as compared with 590,000 kw in 1967 and 343,000 kw in 1961. Production totaled 2,498 million kwh in 1972 and 2,932 million kwh in 1973. Of the total 1972 power production, hydroelectric plants produced 50.3% and diesel and steam plants the remainder. With the completion of the Jatiluhur project in August 1967, 700 million kwh were added to total power production.

Indonesia's per capita consumption rate for energy (146 kg of coal equivalent in 1973) is the lowest in East Asia. Past and present development plans call for greater producing facilities as well as for the nationalization of power through government purchase of private companies. In the 1970s, plans were under way for the wide-scale development of nuclear energy, to take advantage of the country's substantial uranium reserves.

²⁸INDUSTRY

Except for handicrafts and primary processing of agricultural products, industry has a small share (8.6% in 1973) in the GDP. Although less than 5% of gainfully occupied persons work in secondary industrial plants with 10 or more workers, the government regards industry as important, and industrial expansion is given a high priority in development plans.

Petroleum, sugar, rubber, tea, coconuts, palm kernels, sisal, kapok, rice, and cassava are among the primary products processed. Secondary industries produce consumer goods such as tires and tubes, rubber shoes, radios, batteries, soap, margarine, cigarettes, light bulbs, textiles, glass, and paper.

The most important industrial project of the 1970s, the $935-million P. T. Krakatau steel plant at Cilegon (in southwest Sumatra), entered the construction stage in 1975. Now owned by Pertamina, the project was initially conceived by Soviet advisers in the early 1960s. Krakatau's first construction stage is to result in an annual capacity of 500,000 tons of steel, with power supplied by two natural-gas-fed 80-Mw generators. Other newly established industries include cement works, spinning mills, a knitting plant, iron works, copper and other foundries, a ceramics plant, a leather-goods plant, a glass factory, an automobile assembly plant, a paper factory, a shipbuilding yard, and a urea fertilizer plant. There were 480,000 spindles in operation in 1970 with a capacity to produce 45,000 tons of yarn, but textiles still had to be imported in the 1970s. Cement production in 1973 was 730,000 tons. A paper factory and two shipyards, both built with Japanese assistance, began operations in the late 1960s. Indonesia's oil refineries, all owned by Pertamina, had a total capacity of 20,840,000 tons in the mid-1970s.

Despite the new industries, overall industrial growth has been small since World War II. Indonesian enterprises are handicapped by lack of capital and favorable financing arrangements, monetary instability, import and foreign exchange restrictions, power and transportation shortages, and a lack of experienced management and technical personnel.

Government policy to promote industrialization aims at reducing the need for mineral and agricultural imports and raising the standard of living by fuller employment and greater exploitation of Indonesian natural resources. The government plans, regulates, and implements industrialization, participates in new industrial enterprises, and has assumed both ownership and operation of enterprises formerly owned by foreigners.

²⁹DOMESTIC TRADE

Jakarta, the capital and chief commercial city, is Indonesia's main port of entry and distribution center. The principal business houses, shipping and transportation firms, and service agencies have their main offices there and branches in other cities.

Since the end of World War II, the government has sought to channel trade and business activities into Indonesian hands by a policy of granting special privileges to Indonesian firms: monopoly in export licenses, sole agency rights, exclusive import licenses to import and sell specific goods, preferences in trade, and making government purchases through Indonesians. Indonesians have been moving into every sector of marketing operations, particularly in the import business. In December 1957, Dutch interests were taken over by the government. In an attempt to break the Chinese grip on the rural economy and develop indigenous trade, regulations were adopted late in 1959 barring alien traders from operating in rural areas after 1 January 1960 and calling for the evacuation of aliens from rural areas in western Java to larger cities. About 300,000 Chinese merchants were affected.

The small farmer is aided in marketing his cash crops by the numerous marketing cooperatives.

Commercial business hours vary, but many are the same as those in government offices, usually 8 A.M. to 3 P.M. Retail stores and some other businesses are open from 8 A.M. to 4 P.M. Offices and most businesses close at 11 A.M. on Fridays.

Newspapers, magazines, posters, and billboards are the advertising media directed toward the literate; movie slides, portable loudspeakers, pictorial advertising, and "medicine shows" are directed toward the masses. There is little advertising by mail and none at all on the radio.

³⁰FOREIGN TRADE

Trade balances in the post-World War II period have invariably been favorable. Exports in 1974 totaled $7,426 million and imports, $3,754 million. Indonesia exports chiefly mineral, forestry, and agricultural products. In 1974, 80.3% of the total value of exports was provided by petroleum, rubber, tin, and coffee; these commodities had accounted for only about 55% in 1938. Imports consist mainly of raw materials and auxiliary goods for use in production, and consumption goods (including textiles and rice). Six state-owned trading companies, which handle about 80% of total trade, operate, two in the field of exports and four in the fields of imports and distribution. Import restrictions have been in effect since 1958. About three-fourths of the value of total exports is contributed by Sumatra and 12% by Java; but Java receives about 70% of the value of total imports and Sumatra only about 20%. Widespread dissatisfaction in the Outer Islands, particularly Sumatra, has given rise to smuggling.

Principal exports in 1970 and 1973 (in millions of dollars) were:

	1970	1973
Petroleum and petroleum products	346.3	1,608.7
Wood and lumber	105.4	580.9
Rubber	249.4	391.7
Basic manufactures	11.0	114.9
Coffee	66.3	77.6
Spices and pepper	14.5	65.6
Other exports	262.2	371.4
TOTALS	1,055.1	3,210.8

Principal imports in 1970 and 1973 (in millions of dollars) were:

	1970	1973
Machinery and transport equipment	305.4	941.9
Chemicals	113.8	290.4
Iron and steel	76.9	228.1
Food and live animals	128.4	226.9
Textile yarns and fabrics	104.9	171.7
Mineral fuels and lubricants	14.7	42.0
Other imports	148.0	394.1
TOTALS	892.1	2,295.1

In the 1970s, Japan became Indonesia's dominant trade partner, accounting for 53.1% of Indonesia's exports (mainly petroleum) in 1974, and supplying 30.3% of its imports. Other leading trade partners are now the US, Singapore, and the FRG. Trade with the Netherlands, which was of primary importance in the past, has been decreasing, especially since 1957. Trade with Malaysia, which ceased during the period of confrontation, was resumed after 1967.

Principal trade partners in 1973 (in millions of dollars) were:

	EXPORTS	IMPORTS	BALANCE
Japan	1,707.4	799.7	907.7
US	465.4	600.7	−135.3
Singapore	341.0	133.8	207.2
FRG	118.8	196.3	− 77.5
Australia	54.9	141.6	− 86.7

Netherlands	100.9	90.6	10.3
Hong Kong	14.0	166.2	-152.2
UK	32.1	103.1	- 71.0
China	0.4	48.8	- 48.4
Other countries	375.9	14.3	361.6
TOTALS	3,210.8	2,295.1	915.7

³¹ BALANCE OF PAYMENTS

Indonesia has had persistent balance-of-payments difficulties since independence, except in 1951, when the value of exports rose very high. Typically, surpluses on merchandise trade have been accomplished by restricting imports, but these surpluses have not provided sufficient exchange for debt repayments or other invisible payments such as profit remittances on foreign investments and interest payments on government loans from abroad. Balance-of-payments problems have worsened in recent years because expansion of the principal export industries, with the exception of petroleum, failed to keep pace with burgeoning import requirements for some consumer goods and machinery, equipment, and spare parts for development programs.

At the end of 1965, the economic and military debt of Indonesia totaled about $2.4 billion. When, by April 1966, Indonesia began to default on its foreign debt payments and the foreign exchange position became critical, emergency aid in the form of both money and food was offered by Australia, Belgium, France, Italy, Japan, Netherlands, FRG, UK, and US. Headed by Japan, these countries subsequently formed the IGGI aid consortium to grant systematic and coordinated long-term assistance. Indonesia's West European and Japanese creditors also formed a group, the "Paris Club," which, in 1969, agreed to cancel the interest on the outstanding debts and reschedule payment of the remaining principals over 30 years. In August 1970, Indonesia reached agreement with the USSR whereby its $750-million debt would also be repaid over 30 years on terms comparable to those arranged earlier with its West European and Japanese creditors.

Indonesia's balance-of-payments situation has improved during the early 1970s as a result of soaring petroleum earnings, increased foreign aid, and the imposition of fiscal restraints. By mid-decade, however, huge development costs again began to accumulate at a rate faster than could be compensated for by exports. Indonesia's international reserves fell sharply from a peak of $1,492 million at the end of 1974 to $586 million as of 31 December 1975 (as of 31 March 1976, they stood at $760 million). To help meet this erosion, Indonesia was granted over $900 million in bilateral aid and international-organization loans annually in 1974/75 and 1975/76.

³² BANKING

The government's Bank Negara Indonesia (BNI) was established in 1953 as the successor to the Java Bank. On 17 August 1965, all state banks with the exception of State Trading Bank were incorporated into the BNI as separate units. In January 1969, this policy was reversed and the integrated state banks were reorganized as individual banks. The former BNI, unit I, became the Bank Indonesia, which acts exclusively as a central bank. The export-import section of the former BNI, unit II, became the Bank Export Import Indonesia, with a capital of Rp200 million, and specializes in credits for the production, processing, and marketing of export products. The other section of BNI, unit II, became the Bank Rakjat Indonesia, with a capital of Rp300 million, and specializes in credits to agricultural cooperative societies and fishing and rural credit in general. BNI, unit III, became the Bank Negara Indonesia, with a capital of Rp500 million, and specializes in credits to the industrial sector. BNI, unit IV, became the Bank Bumi Daya, with a capital of Rp300 million, and specializes in credits to estates and for forestry operations. BNI, unit V, became the Bank Tabungan

Negara, with a capital of Rp100 million, and specializes in the promotion of savings among the general public. The State Trading Bank, which was not integrated, continues under the same name. It has a capital of Rp250 million and specializes in credits to the mining sector.

In 1967, as part of the new regime's policy of encouraging foreign investment, foreign banks were again permitted to operate in Indonesia. By legislation enacted in December 1967, foreign banks were allowed to operate in Jakarta on condition that they invest at least $1 million, of which at least $500,000 had to be brought into the country. The law also provided that foreign banks were to appoint Indonesian banks as their correspondents for any dealings outside Jakarta. In 1974 there were 10 foreign banks operating in Jakarta, most of them from the US and UK. In Java and Madura, there are village (desa) and village rice (lumbag desa) banks, and there are government-operated pawnshops as well as postal savings banks.

As of 29 February 1976, foreign assets of Bank Indonesia stood at Rp366.7 billion. Currency in circulation increased from Rp199.4 billion at the end of 1971 to Rp625.8 billion at the end of 1975. As of the end of 1974, deposit money banks held demand deposits totaling Rp416.2 billion (Rp81 billion at the end of 1970) and time and savings deposits of Rp412.2 billion (Rp145.3 billion in 1971). Domestic credits extended by deposit money banks amounted to Rp1,477.4 billion at the end of 1974, as compared with Rp287.4 billion at the end of 1969.

³³ INSURANCE

In 1975, 44 insurance companies handled non-life and 11 handled life. Many of the insurance companies operating in Indonesia are foreign; however, in the 1970s, efforts were being made to reduce foreign competition. A 1974 law requires all insurance companies to have a minimum working capital of Rp100 million.

Of the 11 life companies, 9 are domestically incorporated. In 1973, all life companies had fixed assets of Rp1,772.2 million, current assets of Rp2,014.9 million, and investment funds of Rp2,051.3 million. Policies in force numbered 724,518, with a value of Rp99,649.5 million. Gross premiums in 1974 amounted to Rp7,831 million; gross claims totaled Rp2,130 million.

In the non-life sector, gross premiums totaled Rp37,268 million in 1974; gross claims amounted to Rp16,678 million. Third-party motor liability insurance is compulsory.

³⁴ SECURITIES

The present Jakarta Stock Exchange came into operation in 1952. Until late 1957, most of the securities listed were those of Dutch firms, with a few Indonesian securities and Dutch certificates of US securities. There are few transactions on the exchange.

³⁵ PUBLIC FINANCE

Governmental expenditures have outrun public income by a considerable margin each year since 1952, and this cash deficit has been a major inflationary factor in the Indonesian economy. Current revenues and expenditures for 1970/71 and 1973/74 (in billions of rupiahs) are shown in the accompanying table:

	1970/71	1973/74
REVENUES		
Taxes on income	121.6	505.0
Import duties	70.6	128.2
Excise taxes	38.9	61.7
Other taxes	100.3	223.1
Other receipts	13.2	49.7
TOTALS	344.6	967.7
EXPENDITURES		
Agriculture and natural resources	40.7	101.7
Transport and communications	19.1	51.1

Other economic services	47.4	125.2
Education	7.8	35.4
Other social services	8.6	16.2
Interest on public debt	25.6	70.7
Defense	4.5	7.2
Other expenditures	304.2	756.8
TOTALS	457.9	1,164.3

As of 31 March 1974, Indonesia's domestic public debt stood at Rp7.9 billion (Rp4.7 billion in March 1970) and its foreign debt totaled Rp204 billion (Rp120.5 billion in March 1970).

36 TAXATION

Revisions undertaken since the early 1970s increased the contribution of direct and indirect taxes to 97.8% of central government revenues by 1974/75. Sales and excise taxes on domestic oil products were increased, as were income taxes on individuals, taxes on foreign oil companies, and taxes on imports. The corporation tax system was also simplified and some rates were lowered. In 1970, the maximum rate on taxable profits was lowered from 60% to 45%. The number of tax brackets was reduced to two; as of 30 June 1974, corporation profits up to Rp10 million are taxed at 20%, while profits exceeding that amount are taxed at 45%. Capital gains are taxed at 10% on the first Rp10 million in profits and 20% on amounts over that level. The maximum tax-holiday period has been extended from five to six years, but is restricted to new investments in priority areas. Smaller, existing enterprises undertaking investment for replacement or expansion became eligible for a 20% investment allowance.

37 CUSTOMS AND DUTIES

Trade and exchange controls, instituted in 1940 and frequently revised, have been used mainly as means of allocating foreign exchanges according to the government's judgment of the economy's needs and only to a small extent for protection purposes. Based on a system of exchange certificates linking export and import transactions, the regulations have applied to all commercial foreign trade except legalized barter between Sumatra and nearby ports and transactions by domestic producers of tin, petroleum, and bauxite executed under special agreements.

The deterioration in Indonesia's balance-of-payments position after 1961 led the government to modify its trade and foreign exchange regulations. To check the rising volume of less essential imports, higher effective exchange rates were required for such commodities, thus raising the costs of importing them. The government also resorted to increased licensing restrictions, virtually suspending the "free list" trade and reducing foreign exchange for many industrial goods. In 1964, imports were divided into five categories ranging from goods most essential to the economic life of the country to luxury manufactured goods, and levies were imposed at the rates of nil, 50%, 100%, 300%, and 800%, according to category. To stimulate exports, three categories (excluding petroleum) were established and a bonus assigned to each category. The first category (rubber, copper, tobacco, coffee, tin, pepper, tea, palm oil and kernels, and sisal) received a 20% bonus; the second category (primary produce), a 60% bonus; and the third category (handicrafts and light industrial products), a 100% bonus.

In the 1970s, import duties constituted the second-largest single source of government revenues after taxes on income. In 1974/75, import duties totaled Rp167.3 billion (compared with Rp57.7 billion in 1969/70), making up 12.3% of government receipts.

38 FOREIGN INVESTMENTS

Foreign investments have played a key role in the Indonesian economy since the turn of the 20th century.

The Dutch had been the principal foreign investors in Indonesia. They invested heavily in the production of sugar, cinchona, coffee, tobacco, rubber, and oil. UK investments were in oil, rubber, and manufacturing. Rubber estates, particularly those in northern Sumatra, had been operated by Belgian, UK, Danish, French, Norwegian, Swiss, and US individuals and companies. In the dispute with the Netherlands over Irian Jaya, the Indonesian government took over Dutch enterprises in the country and seized Dutch assets.

Although Indonesians have recognized that foreign capital is needed to develop their economy, government policies were ambiguous and hesitant throughout the 1950s and early 1960s. The foreign investment law of 1958 attempted to provide certain guarantees to foreign investors and to establish safeguards for Indonesian interests. At the same time, the government granted guarantees to some foreign-owned industrial enterprises that they would not be expropriated by the state or nationalized for a maximum period of 20 years, and to large agricultural enterprises, for 30 years. In November 1964, the government began to reverse this policy by nationalizing all British-owned commercial enterprises and placing them under direct Indonesian management and control. A decree of 25 February 1965 nationalized all US-owned rubber plantations in northern Sumatra and another decree of 19 March placed three oil companies—two of which were American—under the supervision and control of the government. Finally, on 24 April 1965, President Sukarno ordered the seizure of all remaining foreign property in Indonesia. This policy was again reversed after the ouster of Sukarno. During 1967-70, the confiscated estates were gradually returned to their former owners (except in cases where the owner opted to accept compensation).

To assist in the implementation of this new policy, the IGGI meets regularly to review Indonesia's foreign aid requirements. In 1969/70 it provided assistance totaling $365 million, which included food aid worth $135 million; it agreed to provide $600 million for 1970/71, of which $260 million was for development projects, $200 million was for nonfood aid, and $140 million for food aid. Total IGGI assistance reached $700 million in 1972/73; by 1975/76 the annual level of aid exceeded $900 million, including $500 million in loans from international organizations such as the IBRD, IDA, and Asian Development Bank.

The overall flow of private investments from overseas sources has been increasing during the 1970s, a response both to liberal terms offered under the Suharto government and to favorable world markets for Indonesian oil and other of its primary products. The annual flow of foreign investment funds approved by the government increased from $333 million in 1972 to $521 million in 1973 and to $1,050 million in 1974. US financing and participation have been dominant in the oil industry. Some 65 US firms invested more than $1 billion in petroleum enterprises during 1967-74, accounting for about 90% of the country's total production. In 1975 alone, an additional $1.2 billion was spent in the oil sector by US interests. During 1967-74, Japanese investments led all others in non-oil sectors, totaling $1.1 billion; US investors were second, supplying $507 million.

39 ECONOMIC POLICY

Indonesian levels of living are low. The economy is poorly balanced, being heavily dependent upon producing a few export commodities which, in turn, have materially benefited only a tiny minority of the population. Until the mid-1960s there had been few native large-scale or intermediate business undertakings. Since the late 1960s, the Suharto government has had to focus its main effort on financial stabilization, relying heavily on advice and assistance from the IMF, IBRD, and its IGGI backers. The results have been mixed: The fiscal crisis threatened by the accumulated debts of the Sukarno years was averted through debt rescheduling and improved economic management; nevertheless, the depth of Indonesia's continuing reliance on foreign aid remained apparent through the mid-1970s. Efforts to develop capital-intensive import-substitution industries have held out only marginal benefits to the vast majority of Indonesians, whose lives continue to remain entrenched at meager subsistence levels.

Public expenditures on the first five-year plan (1956–60) included 25% for mining and manufacturing, 25% for transport and communications, 15.4% for power projects, and 34.6% for all other categories. A new eight-year development plan was launched in January 1961. An estimated Rp240 billion was to be spent on 335 "A" projects, of which 25.1% was allocated for transport and communications, 21.7% for industry, 12.7% for special projects including the military, 12% for clothing, 10.5% for food, and 18% for all other categories. Eight "B" projects (petroleum, rubber, tin, and forestry) were to supply the financing for the "A" projects. Because of the lack of foreign financing, upon which most of the "B" projects depended, all "A" and some "B" projects were suspended in November 1964. For the period 1965–68, economic rehabilitation took precedence over development, and all official projects were evaluated on purely economic lines. A subsequent five-year plan (1969–74) placed emphasis on the development of agriculture. Aid to industries was encouraged for activities that support agricultural development, such as the production of fertilizers, cement, agricultural equipment, and machinery for processing agricultural products. Assistance was also given to industries that produced substitutes for imports such as textiles, paper, rubber tires, and housing materials. Total expenditures over the five-year period were put at Rp1,420 billion, with financing from both domestic and foreign sources.

In 1974, the government announced its 1975–79 five-year plan and indicated a shift from stabilizing policies to stepped-up development. The plan placed considerable focus on the rural economy, stressing labor-intensive industries along with improved provision of housing and education. In the program to aid farmers in increasing their output and marketing their commodities, emphasis is placed on encouraging farmers' cooperatives and banks. Labor unions have been encouraged to help improve the lot of the plantation and industrial workers.

⁴⁰ HEALTH
The Ministry of Health places emphasis on preventive work. Private initiative is encouraged in the curative field. The central government bears the major part of the expense of health work but expects autonomous local units to assume a greater financial share. Foreign enterprises have long spent considerable sums on medical care of their workers.

The campaign against malaria has been successful; yaws and trachoma are being successfully combated, but the plague and venereal disease are prevalent, especially in the cities. Overcrowded cities, poor sanitation, impure water supplies, substandard urban housing, and dietary deficiencies are contributing factors in the health situation. Average life expectancy in 1975 was estimated at 47.5 years.

Indonesia has received much help from the UN, particularly through WHO and UNICEF, in solving health problems. The Ministry of Health is seeking to build up a health service starting in the village with a hygiene officer, who is an official of the village, and working up through groups of villages with more facilities and better-trained personnel to the regional doctor, who is head of the curative-preventive work. So far this program has been confined to parts of Java. In 1971 there were 4,561 doctors, 547 dentists, 311 pharmacists, 15,008 nurses, and 6,977 trained midwives. The ratio of 1 doctor to every 26,142 persons, among the lowest in all of Asia, gives, moreover, an inflated picture in view of their uneven distribution: More than one-third of the country's doctors practice in Jakarta and other big cities, and many rural districts have no doctors at all.

In 1971, Indonesia had 1,199 hospitals, with a total of 86,022 beds. Under the 1970–75 plan, the government allocated Rp42,000 million for its health program, of which Rp36,000 million was for public health and Rp6,000 million for family planning.

⁴¹ SOCIAL WELFARE
The constitution enjoins the government to protect the family and to provide for the needs of the "poor and the waifs," but implementation of these principles has proceeded slowly because until recently Indonesia had virtually no persons with professional training to plan and put into effect a broad welfare program. A school of social work was set up in Surakarta in 1946. Various government departments are responsible for welfare activities: Juvenile delinquents are under the care of the Ministry of Justice; child care and maternal health programs are part of the public health program; the Ministry of Labor has responsibility for enforcement of labor welfare legislation; and the Ministry of Social Affairs is concerned with narcotics, traffic in women and children, prostitution, and people unable to provide for themselves (particularly demobilized soldiers). There is nothing approximating a general public assistance program or social security scheme in the Western sense, but the society is one where family and clan relationships are strong.

Many orphanages, homes for the aged, youth activities, and private volunteer organizations meet special needs. In some cases, they receive government subsidies for their programs.

In the 1970s, the government waged a huge campaign in the area of family planning and, by mid-decade, notable successes had been achieved. The National Family Planning Program, managed by the National Family Planning Coordination Board, allocated more than $40 million during 1970–75 in a campaign that enrolled some 4.5 million participants in Java and Bali. Some 150,000 residents of the Outer Islands were to be brought into the program in 1975/76.

⁴² HOUSING
Housing is an acute problem in both urban and rural areas. It is estimated that 300,000 additional houses each year are needed in the towns; however, only about 40,000 are being constructed annually. In the rural areas, housing falls below even the most modest standards. In the 1970s, about one-fifth of the country's housing consisted of one-room dwellings; in the countryside, about 52% had no piped water and 60% had no electricity.

Under the 1970–75 plan the government left construction of housing to private initiative and restricted itself to activities designed to stimulate house construction, such as town planning and the provision of water supplies and sanitation. The sum of Rp2,138 million was set aside for housing for low-income families and town and rural planning, and Rp9,305 million for the provision of water supplies and sanitation. The 1975–79 plan called for a sizable increase in direct government participation in rural housing development.

⁴³ EDUCATION
Vigorous efforts have been made to advance education and reduce illiteracy. In the mid-1970s, literacy was estimated at about 60%. Under the constitution, education must be nondiscriminatory and primary education is free and compulsory. Schools are coeducational, except for certain vocational and religious schools. Private schools receive government subsidies if they maintain government standards. Bahasa Indonesia is the medium of instruction, but local dialects may be used until the third level.

The school system includes a six-year primary or elementary school, a three-year junior secondary school, a three-year senior secondary school, and higher education given in universities, faculties, teacher-training colleges, and academies. The junior and senior technical schools have been brought into line with junior and senior secondary schools. Patterned after Dutch education, the system divides secondary-school students into groups according to curriculum. In the third year of the junior secondary school the students are separated into an A curriculum (languages) and a B curriculum (mathematics). In senior secondary school, the students normally continue in their previous curriculum, but B curriculum students may shift to an economics curriculum (C). Teacher-training schools range from the elementary teachers' training program of four years post-primary education up through teachers' colleges, academies, faculties, and universities. Upon entering institutions of higher learning, students must enter the appropriate division for which their curriculum has prepared them: thus, A curriculum students enter the language and philosophical faculties.

There has been a marked increase in the number of pupils in school. In 1972 there were 13,121,800 primary students in 66,240 schools, with 414,440 teachers; 1,440,445 general secondary students, with 103,687 teachers; and 594,721 vocational and technical students, with 156,512 teachers. In the same year there were 86,459 students at teacher-training institutions, with 8,618 teachers. In 1971, 251,870 students attended institutions of higher learning, including 175,500 in universities. There are 23 universities, the largest of which include the University of Indonesia (with branches in Jakarta and Yogyakarta) and the University of Gajah Mada (Yogyakarta). Most of the universities are new, having been established since the mid-1950s.

Education received added new stress in the 1975–79 national development plan. In 1975/76 alone, the government provided for the construction of 10,000 new primary schools, with another 10,000 to undergo renovations. A textbook program called for provision of 12.7 million new schoolbooks.

44 LIBRARIES AND MUSEUMS
The oldest library in Indonesia is the Central Museum Library, established in Jakarta in 1778. This library contains the country's largest collection in the social sciences and humanities—approximately 350,000 volumes. Another well-established library is the Bibliotheca Borgoriensis, founded in 1814 as a library associated with the botanical gardens in Bogor; it contains more than 200,000 volumes, and today is the national Central Library for Biology and Agriculture. Another national center is the National Scientific and Technical Documentation Center, founded in 1965 in Jakarta, with a collection of more than 17,000 volumes. The Library of the Indonesian Parliament, also in Jakarta, has 200,000 volumes. At present there is little coordination of public libraries, but there are state libraries and local reading rooms in almost every province. University libraries tend to be autonomous faculty or departmental libraries lacking central coordination.

The two outstanding museums in Indonesia are the Central Museum in Jakarta, which is a general museum of Indonesian history and culture, and the Bogor Zoological Museum in Java. There are also several regional historical museums throughout the provinces.

45 ORGANIZATIONS
The most successful cooperatives in Indonesia have been rural cooperatives designed to meet the small farmer's need for credit and aid in marketing cash crops.

Women in Indonesia enjoy a more favorable position than is customary in Muslim societies, a situation largely the result of the work of Princess Adjeng Kartini during the turn of the century in promoting the development of Javanese women. The movement for the emancipation of women preceded the nationalist movement by at least 10 years. Today, women are organized along religious lines as well as in broader groups and a federation. Among the organizations are the Association of Catholic Women, Association of Indonesian Housewives, Women Laborers' Association, Indonesian Young Women's Organization, and Association of Women in the Republic of Indonesia.

Many trade and business promotional organizations are concerned with individual sectors of the business world—exporters' organizations, sugar traders' associations, and so on. An Indonesian chamber of commerce and industries has connections with leading business organizations in the country. UK, Chinese, Indian, and Pakistani businessmen have national associations.

46 PRESS
The constitution declares that everyone has the "right to freedom of opinion and expression." Journalistic activities of foreigners, however, are limited in accordance with the policy that "freedom of expression" does not permit interference in domestic affairs or dissemination of "foreign ideologies" detrimental to the Indonesian system of government. Chinese papers were forced to close down in 1958 but later were permitted to reopen. Further curbs on the press were imposed during the period of confrontation with Malaysia and following the 1965 coup. In March 1966, the press was placed under the control of the chief of the army information center.

In 1973 there were 709 daily newspapers with a listed total circulation of 1,110,000. Most are published in Bahasa Indonesia, with a small number appearing in local dialects, English, and Chinese.

Leading dailies, with their 1975 circulations, are as follows:

	LANGUAGE	CIRCULATION
JAKARTA		
Duta Masjurakat	Bahasa Indonesia	618,000
Kompas	Bahasa Indonesia	150,000
Pos Kota	Bahasa Indonesia	150,000
Merdeka	Bahasa Indonesia	100,000
Sinar Havapan	Bahasa Indonesia	90,000
Indonesian Rze Rao	Chinese	30,000
Jakarta Times	English	30,000
OTHER CITIES		
Suara Merdeka (Semarang)	Bahasa Indonesia	50,000
Pikiran Rakjat (Bandung)	Bahasa Indonesia	40,000
Waspada (Medan)	Bahasa Indonesia	35,000
Kedaulatan Rakyat (Yogyakarta)	Bahasa Indonesia	30,000
Djawa Pos (Surabaya)	Bahasa Indonesia	22,500

47 TOURISM
A valid passport and an entry visa are required of every foreigner entering Indonesia. Passports issued by Israel and South Africa are not recognized. A tourist visa for visits of up to 30 days is obtainable only on proof of confirmed transportation into and out of Indonesia, or ticket and visa for next country to be visited; extended tourist visas for up to 90 days are available. The visitors must have a valid international health certificate of inoculation against smallpox, not older than three years, and cholera, not older than six months. Typhoid and paratyphoid inoculations not older than six months are not mandatory but are strongly recommended. An estimated 340,000 foreign tourists visited Indonesia in 1975, spending about $42.5 million.

48 FAMOUS INDONESIANS
Gadja Mada, prime minister and king of Hayam Wuruk from 1331 to 1365, brought many of the islands under one rule, the Majapahit Empire. Princess Adjeng Kartini (1879–1904), founder of a school for girls, led the movement for the emancipation of women. Her posthumously published letters, *Door duisternis tot licht*, occasioned considerable interest in the Western world. Many creative and performing artists have attained local prominence, but Indonesia's only internationally known artist is the painter Affandi (b.1910). Contemporary novelists of considerable local importance include Mochtar Lubis, Achdiat Karta Midhardja, Armijn Pane, and Utay Sontani. H. B. Jassin (b.1917) is an influential literary critic. Sukarno (1902?–70), a founder and leader of the nationalist movement, is the best-

known figure of modern Indonesia. President Suharto (b.1921), leader of Indonesia since Sukarno's overthrow, has since 1968 dominated Indonesia's political and economic life. Adam Malik (b.1917), foreign minister in the new regime, has established an international reputation as a negotiator in restoring and improving relations with Malaysia, the Philippines, the US, the UK, and the UN.

⁴⁹DEPENDENCIES
Indonesia has no territories or colonies.

⁵⁰BIBLIOGRAPHY

Alisjahbana, S. Takdier. *Indonesia: Social and Cultural Revolution*. New York: Oxford University Press, 1968.

American University. *Area Handbook for Indonesia*. Washington: Government Printing Office, 1970.

Anderson, Benedict R. O'G. *Java in a Time of Revolution*. Ithaca, N.Y.: Cornell University Press, 1972.

Boeke, Julius Herman. *Economics and Economic Policy of Dual Societies, as Exemplified by Indonesia*. New York: Institute of Pacific Relations, 1953.

Brackman, Arnold C. *The Communist Collapse in Indonesia*. New York: Norton, 1969.

Caldwell, Malcolm. *Indonesia*. New York: Oxford University Press, 1968.

Dahm, Bernhard. *History of Indonesia in the Twentieth Century*. New York: Praeger, 1971.

Dahm, Bernhard. *Sukarno and the Struggle for Indonesian Independence*. Ithaca, N.Y.: Cornell University Press, 1969.

Development of Education in Indonesia. Jakarta: Ministry of Education and Culture, Republic of Indonesia, 1956.

Emerson, Rupert. *Representative Government in South East Asia*. Cambridge: Harvard University Press, 1955.

Feith, Herbert. *The Decline of Constitutional Democracy in Indonesia*. Ithaca, N.Y.: Cornell University Press, 1962.

Feith, Herbert, and Lance Castles (eds.). *Indonesian Political Thinking, 1945–1965*. Ithaca, N.Y.: Cornell University Press, 1970.

Furnivall, John Sydenham. *Colonial Policy and Practice: A Comparative Study of Burma and Netherlands India*. New York: New York University Press, 1956.

Furnivall, John Sydenham. *Netherlands Indies: A Study of Plural Economy*. Cambridge: Cambridge University Press, 1967.

Geertz, Clifford. *Agricultural Involution: The Processes of Ecological Change in Indonesia*. Berkeley: University of California Press, 1963.

Geertz, Clifford. *Peddlers and Princes: Social Development and Change in Two Indonesian Towns*. Chicago: University of Chicago Press, 1963.

Geertz, Clifford. *The Religion of Java*. Glencoe, Ill.: Free Press, 1964

Geertz, Clifford. *Social History of an Indonesian Town*. Cambridge: MIT Press, 1963.

Goodfriend, Arthur. *Rice Roots*. New York: Simon and Schuster, 1958.

Grant, Bruce. *Indonesia*. Harmondsworth: Penguin, 1964.

Hanna, Willard A. *Bung Karno's Indonesia*. New York: American Universities Field Staff, 1961.

Holt, Claire. *Art in Indonesia: Continuities and Change*. Ithaca, N.Y.: Cornell University Press, 1967.

Holt, Claire (ed.). *Culture and Politics in Indonesia*. Ithaca, N.Y.: Cornell University Press, 1972.

The Indonesian Revolution: Basic Documents and the Idea of Guided Democracy. Jakarta: Department of Information, Republic of Indonesia, 1960.

Jones, Howard Palfrey. *Indonesia: The Possible Dream*. New York: Harcourt, Brace, Jovanovich, 1971.

Kahin, George McTurnan. *Nationalism and Revolution in Indonesia*. Ithaca, N.Y.: Cornell University Press, 1952.

Kartini, Raden Adjeng. *Letters of a Javanese Princess*. New York: Norton, 1964.

Kat Angelino, Arnold Dirk Adriaan de. *Colonial Policy*. Chicago: University of Chicago Press, 1931.

Legge, John D. *Indonesia*. Englewood Cliffs, N.J.: Prentice-Hall, 1964.

Legge, John D. *Sukarno*. New York: Praeger, 1972.

Leur, Jacob Cornelis van. *Indonesian Trade and Society: Essays in Asian Social and Economic History*. New York: Institute of Pacific Relations, 1955.

Liddle, R. William. *Ethnicity, Party, and National Integration*. New Haven, Conn.: Yale University Press, 1970.

Mackie, J. A. C. *Konfrontasi: The Indonesia-Malaysia Dispute, 1963–1966*. New York: Oxford University Press, 1974.

McVey, Ruth T. (ed.). *Indonesia: Its People, Its Society, Its Culture*. New York: Taplinger, 1968.

Mintz, Jeanne. *Mohammed, Marx, and Marhaen: The Roots of Indonesian Socialism*. New York: Praeger, 1965.

Neill, Wilfred T. *Twentieth Century Indonesia*. New York: Columbia University Press, 1973.

Nitisastro, Widjojo. *Population Trends in Indonesia*. Ithaca, N.Y.: Cornell University Press, 1970.

Noer, Deliar. *The Modernist Muslim Movement in Indonesia, 1900–1942*. New York: Oxford University Press, 1973.

Paauw, Douglas S. *Financing Economic Development: A Case Study of Indonesia*. Glencoe, Ill.: Free Press, 1959.

Purcell, Victor. *The Chinese in South East Asia*. New York: Oxford University Press, 1953.

Roeder, O. G. *The Smiling General: President Soeharto of Indonesia*. Jakarta: Gunung Agung, 1969.

Schiller, A. Arthur. *The Formation of Federal Indonesia, 1945–1949*. New York: Institute of Pacific Relations, 1955.

Statistical Pocket Book of Indonesia. Jakarta: Biro Pusat Statistik, 1963.

Sukarno. *Toward Freedom and the Dignity of Man. A Collection of Five Speeches*. Jakarta: Department of Foreign Affairs, Republic of Indonesia, 1961.

Van der Kroef, Justus Maria. *Indonesian Social Evolution*. Amsterdam: Van der Peet, 1958.

Vlekke, Bernard Hubertus Maria. *Nasantara: A History of Indonesia*. The Hague: Van Hoeve, 1959.

Wagner, Frits A. I. *Indonesia: The Art of an Island Group*. New York: McGraw-Hill, 1959.

Wallace, Alfred Russel. *The Malay Archipelago, the Land of the Orang Utan and the Bird of Paradise: A Narrative of Travel with Studies of Man and Nature*. New York: Macmillan, 1886.

Wertheim, Willem Frederik. *Indonesian Society in Transition: A Study of Social Change*. The Hague: Van Hoeve, 1956.

Wolf, Charles, Jr. *The Indonesian Story: The Birth, Growth and Structure of the Indonesian Republic*. New York: John Day, 1948.

Zainu'ddin, Ailsa. *A Short History of Indonesia*. New York: Praeger, 1971.

IRAN

Imperial Government of Iran
Keshvare Shahanshahiye Iran

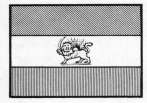

CAPITAL: Tehran. **FLAG:** The national flag is a tricolor of green, white, and red horizontal stripes. On the state flag, a golden lion and sun appear on the white stripe, the lion holding a sword in one raised paw, the sun over his back. **ANTHEM:** *Sorud-e-Shahanshahiye* (*National Anthem*) begins "Shahanshah-i-ma Zendah bada" ("Long life to our Shah"). **MONETARY UNIT:** The rial (R) of 100 dinars is a convertible paper currency. There are coins of 5, 10, 25, and 50 dinars and 1, 2, 5, and 10 rials, and notes of 20, 50, 100, 200, 500, 1,000, 5,000, and 10,000 rials. There are also $\frac{1}{4}$, $\frac{1}{2}$, 1, $2\frac{1}{2}$, and 5 Pahlavi gold coins; the Pahlavi contains 7.322 gm of fine gold. R1 = $0.0143 (or $1 = R69.825). **WEIGHTS AND MEASURES:** The metric system is the legal standard, but local units are widely used. **HOLIDAYS:** No Ruz (the New Year holiday) begins the 1st day of spring (21 March) and continues for three days; 13th Day of No Ruz, 2 April; Constitution Day, 5 August; Shah's Birthday, 26 October. Religious holidays (according to the lunar calendar) include Birthday of Imam Husayn; Birthday of the Twelfth Imam; Martyrdom of Imam ´Ali; Death of Imam Ja´afar Sadiq; ´Id-el-Fitr; Birthday of Imam Reza; ´Id-i-Qurban; ´Id-i-Qadir; Shab-i-Miraj; Martyrdom of Imam Husayn; 40th Day after the Death of Imam Husayn; Birthday of the Prophet; Birthday of Imam ´Ali. **TIME:** 3:30 P.M. = noon GMT.

¹LOCATION, SIZE, AND EXTENT

Situated in southwestern Asia, Iran covers an area of 1,648,195 sq km (636,370 sq mi) and extends 2,250 km (1,398 mi) SE–NW and 1,400 km (870 mi) NE–SW. Iran is bounded on the N by the USSR and the Caspian Sea, on the E by Afghanistan and Pakistan, on the S by the Gulf of Oman and the Persian Gulf, on the W by Iraq, and on the NW by Turkey, with a total boundary length of 7,680 km (4,772 mi). Iran's territory includes several islands in the Persian Gulf.

²TOPOGRAPHY

Most of the land area consists of a plateau some 4,000 feet above sea level and strewn with mountains. The Zagros and Elburz ranges stamp a V upon the plateau; the apex is in the northwest and within the lower area between the arms are to be found salt and barren deserts. Most of the drainage is from these two great ranges into the interior deserts, with limited drainage into the Caspian Sea and the Persian Gulf. The ranges run in parallel files, enclosing long valleys that provide most of the agricultural land. Mt. Demavend, northeast of Tehran, rises to 18,934 feet, while the Caspian littoral is below sea level and has a semitropical climate. Only the Karun River, emptying into the Persian Gulf, is navigable for any distance, but the rivers that rush down from high altitudes offer fine sources of power. Harbors of limited depth are found along the Persian Gulf, and the Caspian Sea has similar facilities for coastal fishing and trade with the USSR.

³CLIMATE

Iran has a continental type of climate, with cold winters and hot summers prevalent across the plateau. On the plateau, the annual rainfall does not exceed 12 inches, with the deserts and the Persian Gulf littoral receiving less than 5 inches. Snow falls heavily on the mountain peaks and is the principal source of water for irrigation in spring and early summer. The Caspian littoral is warm and humid throughout the year, and the annual rainfall is from 40 to 60 inches. Clear days are the rule, for the skies are cloudless more than half the days of each year. The seasons change abruptly. By the Persian New Year, the first day of spring, orchards are in bloom and wild flowers abound. The Tehran temperature ranges from 42°C (108°F) to −15°C (5°F).

⁴FLORA AND FAUNA

More than one-tenth of the country is forested. The most extensive growths are found on the mountain slopes rising from the Caspian Sea, with stands of oak, ash, elm, cypress, and other valuable trees. On the plateau proper, areas of shrub oak appear on the best-watered mountain slopes, and villagers cultivate orchards and grow the plane tree, poplar, willow, walnut, beech, maple, and mulberry. Wild plants and shrubs spring from the barren land in the spring and afford pasturage, but the summer sun burns them away. Bears in the mountains, wild sheep and goats, gazelles, wild asses, wild pigs, panthers, and foxes abound. Domestic animals include sheep, goats, cattle, horses, water buffalo, donkeys, and camels. Of the many birds common to other countries, the pheasant, partridge, stork, and falcon are favorites in Iran.

As of 1975, endangered species in Iran included the wolf, Baluchistan bear, leopard, Anatolian leopard, Caspian tiger, Asiatic cheetah, dugong, Asiatic wild ass, Persian fallow deer, marsh crocodile, and Central Asian grey monitor.

⁵POPULATION

According to the census of November 1966, the total population was 25,785,210. In November 1975, the estimated population was 33,707,541; the population for 1980 was projected at 38,492,000. The average population density was 20 per sq km (53 per sq mi), and the annual rate of increase 3%. The estimated crude birthrate in 1975 was 44.8 per 1,000 population, the crude death rate was 13.7, and the net natural increase 31.1. In 1975, about 43.5% was urban. The rural population (56.5%) included about 500,000 nomads. There were 20 cities with populations of more than 100,000. The largest, Tehran, the capital, had a population of 3,720,901 in 1974; Isfahan had 605,000; Mashhad, 592,000; Tabriz, 510,000; Shiraz, 373,000; Abadan, 312,000.

⁶ETHNIC GROUPS

Present-day Iranians, or Persians, are considered to be direct descendants of the Aryans who moved into the plateau in the second millennium B.C. They speak Persian, or Farsi, and number over half the total population. At various times after the 10th century A.D., Turkish tribes settled in the region, and Turkish-speaking groups are still found in several parts of the country. One-fifth of the total population dwells in Azerbaijan and areas to the east; these people speak a Turkish dialect known as Azari. Arab groups arrived during and after the 7th century A.D. Their descendants live in the southwest and in scattered colonies in the northeast.

In general, non-Iranian elements are to be found along the perimeter of the country. Of these, certain nomadic groups move back and forth across the actual frontiers. Tribal groups have been a conspicuous element in Iran for many centuries, migrating vertically in spring and fall between high mountain valleys and hot, lowland plains. In the Zagros range and its extensions are to be found the Kurds, Lurs, Bakhtiari, Qashqa'i, and Mamasani: the first three are said to be of stock similar to the Iranian element, and they speak languages that stem from ancient Indo-European languages. Other important migratory groups include the Khamseh, Shahsevans, Arabs, Baluchi, and Turkoman. The nomadic way of life is on the decline and the government of Iran looks forward to the day when all these groups are settled on good farmlands.

7 LANGUAGE
Farsi, called Persian by the West, is the official language of Iran; taught in all schools. Farsi is spoken by more than half the population. An Aryan language of the Indo-European group, it derives from ancient Persian, with an admixture of many Arabic words. Arabic characters and script are used in writing modern Persian. Dialects of Turkish, or Turki, are spoken throughout northwestern Iran, by the Qashqa'i tribe in the southwest, and in parts of the northeast by Turkoman tribes and others. Major groups of the Lurs, Kurds, and Bakhtiari have languages and dialects of their own that descend from earlier Indo-European languages, and the Baluchi language spoken in southeastern Iran also is of Indo-European origin. A small number of Brahui in the southeast speak a Dravidian language. Arabs, Assyrians, Armenians, and Jews retain their own languages.

8 RELIGION
About 98% of the people are Muslims, most members of the Shi'i sect. Iran is the only Muslim country where Muslims of the Sunni sect are in a minority. Shi'i Islam is the official religion of the country, and the ruler, prime minister, and cabinet ministers must be Muslims. The Christian population (429,000 in 1974) includes Armenians and, in the northwest, Nestorian Christians (Assyrians). Colonies of Parsis, or Zoroastrians, are to be found at Yezd, Kerman, and other large towns; in 1974, they numbered about 36,000. The Baha'is may number over 50,000; their faith sprang from the teachings of a 19th-century Muslim in Iran, but it has been denounced as heresy in Islam. There were 85,000 Jews in 1974.

9 TRANSPORTATION
In 1974, transport moved on 69,026 km of roads, ranging from caravan trails to 19,122 km of paved highways. The asphalting of major links in the highway system is proceeding rapidly. In 1974 there were 79,200 cars and 216,843 commercial vehicles. In 1966, Iran completed its section of the projected Asian highway that is to start from Bazargan on the Turkish border, run through Tabriz and Mashhad in Iran, cross the Afghan border, and eventually terminate in Thailand.

The 5,480 km of railroad are state-owned. The main line runs from the Persian Gulf to the Caspian Sea by way of Tehran. Branch lines extend out from Tehran: one to Mashhad in the northeast; one to Tabriz and Julfa in the northwest, which has been extended to the Turkish frontier; and one, still uncompleted in 1975, through Kashan in the direction of Kerman, Zahedan, and Pakistan. Under an agreement with France, a 103-km underground railway network is to be constructed in Tehran at a cost of at least $680 million.

Iran's main port is Khorramshahr on the Persian Gulf. Other ports on the Gulf are Bandar-e-Shahpur, Bandar 'Abbas, and Bushire. On the Caspian Sea, there are the ports of Bandar Pahlavi and Naushahr. In 1974, Khorramshahr handled 738 vessels, other Gulf ports 1,001, and the Caspian ports 434. In addition, there are the oil shipment ports of Kharg, Mashahr, and Abadan, from which 2,750 tankers sailed in 1974. The inland waterways are those of Lake Reza'iyeh and the Karun River. As of 31 December 1974, the Iranian merchant marine included 30 oceangoing vessels totaling 274,000 GRT.

The state-owned Iran Air maintains frequent service to 21 cities in Iran and is an international carrier. Twenty international airlines serve Tehran; Abadan also receives international traffic.

10 COMMUNICATIONS
Telegraph, telephone, and radio broadcasting services are state-owned. In 1974 there were about 600,000 telephones. Radio Tehran, the principal station, employs a maximum of 200,000 watts for sending programs over medium waves and 800,000 watts for shortwave broadcasting. Stations at Ahwaz, Zahedan, Tabriz, Rasht, Kermanshah, and Bandar-e-Lengeh are among those which also employ more than 100,000 watts each for regional broadcasts over medium waves. In addition, some 17 smaller stations employ a combined total of 115,000 watts for local programs over medium waves. In March 1974 there were about 6 million radio receivers. In 1956, Television of Iran, a privately owned station, began operation in Tehran and Abadan. The national radio organization and the government television network were merged in June 1971 to form National Iranian Radio and Television (NIRT). In March 1974, NIRT had 15 major television production and transmission centers. In addition, there were 11 intermediary (booster) stations and 70 microwave relay stations, giving Iran the most extensive television network coverage in Asia after Japan. The total number of television sets in Iran during 1974 was estimated at 1 million, of which 45% were in and around Tehran.

11 HISTORY
Excavations at sites of settlements and in caves have revealed valuable data about the prehistoric people of the Iranian plateau. As early as 6000 B.C., communities were carrying on agriculture, raising domestic animals, and producing pottery and polished stone implements. Sites datable to later than 3000 B.C. are numerous and offer quantities of bronze instruments and painted pottery of the finest types. In the second millennium B.C., masses of Aryans began to sweep westward across Asia: the Indo-Iranians crossed the plateau of Iran about 1500 B.C. and were followed about 900 B.C. by the Iranians, including groups of Medes, Persians, Parthians, Bactrians, and others. The Medes (Mada) settled in western Iran and established their capital at Ecbatana (modern Hamadan); the Persians (Parsa) settled to the south of them. The Medean king Cyaxares (625–585 B.C.) destroyed the power of neighboring Assyria. In the area of Parsa, the Achaemenid clan became overlords, and in 553 B.C. their leader, Cyrus, revolted against the Medes, formed a union of Medes and Persians, drove with armies both into Asia Minor and to the east of the Iranian plateau, and established the Achaemenid Empire. Cambyses, Darius, Xerxes I, and Artaxerxes I were notable rulers of this line who penetrated Greece, Egypt, and beyond the Oxus (now called the Amu Darya). The Achaemenid power centered at Susa and Persepolis; the ruined site of the latter is impressive even today. Zorastrianism was the religion of the rulers.

In his eastward sweep (334–330 B.C.), Alexander the Great defeated vast Achaemenid forces at Issus and Arbela, and went on to capture Susa and to burn Persepolis. In the following century (3d century B.C.), a nomadic Saka tribe (later known as the Parthians) moved into the area east of the Caspian and then into the Parthava of the Achaemenid Empire. The first three kings established and maintained the independence of the new Parthian kingdom; later rulers moved west to come in contact with and then to war with the Roman Empire. The Parthians considered themselves spiritual heirs of the Achaemenids and adopted Zoroastrianism as the official religion. Weakened by long wars with Rome, the Parthians were followed by a local dynasty, the Sassanian, which arose in the area of Fars in southwestern Iran. Wars with Rome continued and were followed by a struggle with the Byzantine Empire. The Sassanian period was one of cultural consolidation and was marked by economic prosperity and by a series of enlightened rulers.

Early in the 7th century A.D., Arab warriors burst out of the Arabian Peninsula to overwhelm the Sassanian Empire and to spread the teachings of the prophet Muhammad, embodied in

Malik Shah did much to promote cultural pursuits and enhance the character of Persian civilization. With the decline of the Seljuqs late in the 12th century, the Khwarazmshahs took over most of the region that had been under Seljuq rule.

In 1219, Mongol hordes under Genghis Khan began to move into Iran, and successive waves subdued and devastated the country. Hulagu, a grandson of Genghis, settled in Maragha in Azerbaijan and as Il-khan, or chief of the tribe, gave this title to the Il-khanid dynasty. His successors, such as Ghazan Khan and Oljaitu, ruled from Tabriz and Sultaniya, and once again untutored invaders became converts to Islam and patrons of Persian science, learning, and arts. Rivalries within the military

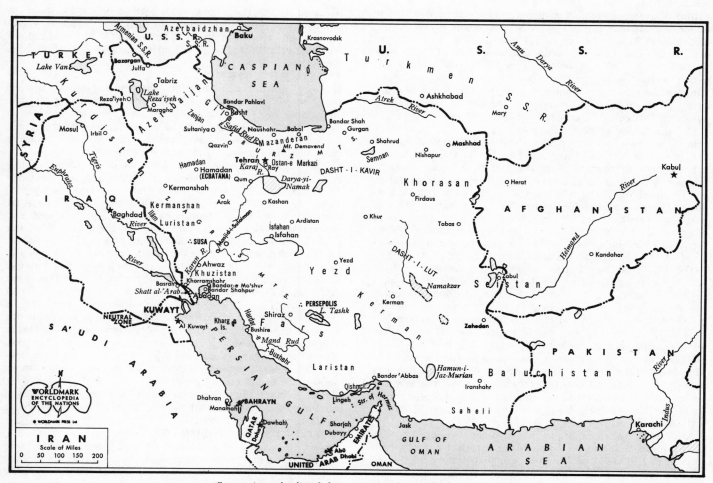

See continental political: front cover J6; physical: back cover J6

LOCATION: 25° to 40°N; 44° to 63°E. BOUNDARY LENGTHS: USSR, 1,740 km (1,081 mi); Caspian Sea coastline, 630 km (392 mi); Afghanistan, 850 km (528 mi); Pakistan, 830 km (516 mi); Gulf of Oman and Persian Gulf coastlines, 1,880 km (1,168 mi); Iraq, 1,280 km (795 mi); Turkey, 470 km (292 mi). TERRITORIAL SEA LIMIT: 12 mi.

Islam. By the opening of the 9th century, Islamic doctrine and precepts had spread over the plateau, and local dynasties faithful to the Muslim creed had begun to emerge. Early in the 11th century, the Turkish Ghaznavid dynasty held power from western Iran to the Indus. The greatest figure of this time was Mahmud of Ghazni, a renowned warrior and conqueror and a patron of the arts. The Ghaznavids were replaced by the Seljuqs, descended from Turkish nomad warriors enlisted in their service. The Seljuq kingdom had its capital at Ray, just south of Tehran, and stretched from the Bosporus to Chinese Turkestan. Of rude origins, such rulers as Tughril Beg, Alp Arslan, and

leadership brought about the breakdown of Il-khanid power in the second half of the 14th century.

In 1380, Timur (Tamerlane) began to move into the Iranian plateau from the east, and within a decade the entire area was in his power. The Timurid period saw a renaissance of culture at Herat and other towns, but the rulers lacked the force and ability to hold the empire together. Early in the 16th century a number of smaller, local dynasties emerged throughout Iran. Destined to become the most powerful was the Safavid dynasty, whose leaders, descendants of a spiritual head of the Shi'i sect, imposed this form of Islam on their subjects. The fourth and greatest of this line, Shah Abbas (r.1587–1628), moved the capital from Qazvin to Isfahan, where he had many splendid buildings constructed. The Safavid period, marked by the emergence of a truly native Iranian dynasty after the lapse of many centuries, was a period of military power and general prosperity. However, decline set in and, in 1722, Isfahan fell to invading forces from Afghanistan. Nadir Quli (better known as Nadir Shah), an Afshar tribesman from the north, rallied local elements to drive off the Afghans, and in 1736 established the Afshar dynasty. By the end of the 18th century, Zand rulers, dominant in the south, were replaced by the Qajars, elements of a Turkish tribe. Qajar rulers held power over all of Iran until the rise of Reza Khan, who became minister of war in 1921, prime minister in 1923, and (as Reza Shah) first sovereign of the Pahlavi dynasty in 1926. His authority was unchallenged until 1941 when, during World War II, UK and Russian forces entered Iran to counter the German threat. Reza Shah abdicated (1941) in favor of his son, Muhammad Reza Pahlavi. British forces evacuated Iran in April 1946. There was, however, a dispute with the USSR, which refused to withdraw its forces and supported the establishment of an autonomous republic in Iranian Azerbaijan. Soviet troops eventually withdrew from the country in December 1946, and the autonomist forces in Azerbaijan collapsed.

Oil, the source of nearly all Iran's national wealth, quickly came to dominate postwar politics. Muhammad Mossadeq, who as leader of the National Front in the National Assembly (Majlis) led the fight in 1947 to deny the USSR oil concessions in northern Iran, became chairman of the Majlis' oil committee. On 15 March 1951, the Majlis voted to nationalize the oil industry, which was dominated by the Anglo-Iranian Oil Co. (AIOC), a prewar concession to the UK; when the government of Prime Minister Hosein Ala took no immediate action against the AIOC, the Majlis demanded his resignation and the appointment of Mossadeq, who became prime minister in April. The AIOC was taken over, but its output rapidly declined, and the UK imposed an embargo on Iranian oil, as well as other economic sanctions. As Iran's economic situation worsened, Mossadeq sought to rally the people through fervent nationalistic appeals. An attempt by the shah to replace him failed in the summer of 1952, but by August 1953, Mossadeq had lost his parliamentary majority. Mossadeq dissolved the Majlis and then refused to resign when the shah again tried to oust him. The shah fled Iran for four days but returned triumphantly on 22 August, with solid backing from the military and the Western powers. A new conservative government issued an urgent appeal for aid; in September the US granted Iran $45 million. Mossadeq was convicted of high treason on 2 December 1953.

After 1953, the shah began to consolidate his power. New arrangements between the National Iranian Oil Co. and a consortium of US, UK, and Dutch oil companies were negotiated during April–September 1954 and ratified by the Majlis in October. The left-wing Masses (Tudeh) Party, which had been banned in 1949 but had resurfaced during the Mossadeq regime, was suppressed after a Tudeh organization was exposed in the armed forces. In 1957, the government sponsored two new parties, which contested parliamentary elections in 1960 and 1961. Meanwhile, Iran became affiliated with the Western alliance through the Baghdad Pact in 1955 and CENTO in 1958. Frontier demarcation agreements were signed with the USSR in April 1957.

Its foreign relations clarified, Iran turned to domestic reform. Under the "white revolution" of 1962–63, the shah encouraged an anticorruption campaign, land reform, electoral changes (including, for the first time, the rights of women to hold and vote for public office), and economic development. A referendum on domestic reform, held 26 January 1963, resulted in approval of the government's program by a vote of 5,598,711 to

4,115. Organized opposition to the program was suppressed, and the role of the political parties and the Majlis declined. In 1975, at the shah's order, Iran became a one-party state with the merger of all legal political parties into the National Resurgence Party.

Iran's relations with its Arab neighbors have not been completely harmonious. Iraq broke off diplomatic relations on 30 November 1971, after Iran occupied two islands in the Strait of Hormuz. Iraq subsequently charged that Iran was aiding the Kurdish rebellion by granting supplies and sanctuary to the secessionists. There were numerous border clashes in 1974, but on 6 March 1975, Iranian and Iraqi representatives reached agreement on the demarcation of their frontiers; as part of the accord, Iran closed its border to the Kurds, who were then defeated by the Iraqi army. As a member of OPEC, Iran encouraged and fully supported the quadrupling of crude oil prices in 1973; however, Iran does not belong to OAPEC and did not participate in the 1973–74 oil embargo against the US and the Netherlands.

12 GOVERNMENT

Iran is a constitutional monarchy, with the constitution of 1906 modified by a supplement of 1907 and amendments of 1925, 1949, and 1957. The shah is the chief of state, with wide prerogatives under the constitution. He commands the armed forces, names the prime minister, and may dissolve either or both legislative houses. The shah must be a Muslim.

The legislative branch is represented by the National Assembly (Majlis) and the Senate; the latter body was provided for in the constitution but not brought into legal being until February 1950. Members of the Majlis are elected for four-year terms from 268 constituencies by adults 20 years of age and older. Half of the 60 senators are named by the shah, and half are elected; the voting age for Senate elections is 25. The legislature receives proposed laws from the cabinet ministers and may also initiate bills. While both the Majlis and the Senate must approve most proposed legislation, the Majlis has exclusive rights in the realm of public finance. Parliament may call upon cabinet members to answer oral and written questions, and a prime minister must leave office if he receives a vote of no confidence from either body. Members of the Majlis represent all classes of the nation, including landowners, merchants, lawyers, professional groups, and so on, while the somewhat more conservative Senate consists of former cabinet ministers, former high officials, and retired generals.

The cabinet comprises the prime minister, departmental ministers, and ministers without portfolios. These numbered 21 and 7 respectively in 1975.

13 POLITICAL PARTIES

During the reign of Reza Shah (1926–41), political parties were not permitted to function. After 1941, parties sprang up, but, except for the Will of the People Party (Erade-yi-Melli) and the Masses (Tudeh) Party, most of them were of an ephemeral nature. The Communist-oriented Masses Party was better organized than the others and benefited from the services of devoted followers and foreign funds. In 1949, an unsuccessful attempt to assassinate the shah was traced to the Masses Party, and it was banned. However, it continued to work through almost a score of front groups, and its views were reflected in some newspapers and periodicals. From 1951 until August 1953, it supported Prime Minister Muhammad Mossadeq's policy of nationalism, but his ouster led to a decline of the party. In 1954, a Masses organization within the armed forces was exposed and broken up.

In 1957, the government itself decided to sponsor political parties. The first to appear (1957) was the Nationalist (Mellioun) Party, headed by Manochehr Eqbal, then prime minister. The second was the People's (Mardom) Party, headed by the former prime minister Asadullah Alam and intended to represent the loyal political opposition of the government in power. Its stated aims were to raise the living standards of farmers and laborers and to permit farmers to acquire their own land. These parties contested the parliamentary elections in 1960 and 1961, and then became less active. In December 1963, the New Iran (Iran-i-Novin) Party was founded by Hassan Ali Mansur, who had succeeded Alam as prime minister in March 1963. The New Iran Party commanded the majority in both legislative houses, and Amir Abbas Hoveyda, a member of this party, became prime minister in January 1965 after the assassination of Mansur.

On 2 March 1975, the shah ordered the formation of a single political organization, the Iran Resurgence (Rastakhiz) Party, into which were merged all existing legal parties. The new party aimed at mobilizing the country's human and material resources to the hilt and declared itself open to all Iranians who had attained maturity and were eligible to vote. Three cardinal principles were cited for membership in the party: faith in Iran's constitution, loyalty to the monarchical regime, and fidelity to the "white revolution." Amir Abbas Hoveyda, the prime minister and the incumbent secretary-general of the New Iran Party, was named secretary-general of the new political force for a period of two years. A party constitution was adopted on 2 May 1975 at a conference of 4,500 delegates. In the June 1975 parliamentary elections, about 750 candidates, all members of the Iran Resurgence Party, contested 268 seats in the Majlis and 30 Senate seats.

14 LOCAL GOVERNMENT

Iran is divided into 23 provinces (ostans), some of which correspond to ancient territorial divisions. The governor and district officials of each province are appointed by the central government. A percentage of taxes sent to Tehran is returned for local expenditures. In recent years the trend toward election of district and village councils to take over responsibility for local improvements and planning has been given support and extension through community programs. Provincial councils (anjumans) provided for in the supplementary laws of 1907 were first established in 1968 and have been developing rapidly since that time. Local government is under the authority of the Ministry of the Interior.

15 JUDICIAL SYSTEM

Legal and criminal codes now in use were enacted in 1925 and in the years immediately thereafter. During the reign of Reza Shah, laws were enacted doing away with traditional patterns of dress, the inferior position of women before the law, and capitulations in favor of foreigners. There are local courts, district courts, provincial courts, and a Court of Cassation or Supreme Court. The Ministry of Justice appoints judges; those of the high courts have permanent tenure.

16 ARMED FORCES

Military service is compulsory. All males are inducted into the armed services at age 21 for two years' training, during which time the government attempts to eradicate illiteracy among the recruits. In 1975, the army had 175,000 men, organized into 3 armored divisions, 4 infantry battalions, 2 independent brigades, and 1 Hawk missile battalion; reserves totaled 300,000. The navy had 15,000 men in 1975, the air force 60,000. A naval agreement is in force between Iran and Oman. More than 3,000 Iranian troops were on active duty in Oman early in 1976; ground, naval, and air units were supporting Omani government forces in the war against the Dhufar rebels.

Iran's defense budget increased from R54,954 million in 1971/72 to R693,000 million in 1975/76. Most of the increase was allocated to purchases of military hardware, and by the end of the decade Iran is expected to have one of the world's most modern military machines. The army had 1,160 medium tanks in 1975; 1,680 more were on order. The navy had 3 destroyers, 4 frigates, 25 patrol boats, and 6 minesweepers; 3 submarines, 6 destroyers, and 12 missile-equipped fast patrol boats were on order. The air force had 238 combat aircraft and 16 jet fighter squadrons; another 449 jet fighters were on order. Imports of armaments totaled $2,247 million during 1970-74.

17 MIGRATION

There is little immigration to Iran, with the exception of Shi'i Muslims coming from Iraq. There is some emigration to Europe and the US, particularly by Iranians who have studied overseas.

18 INTERNATIONAL COOPERATION

Iran is a member of the UN and all of its specialized agencies except GATT. It is a cofounder, with Turkey and Pakistan, of Regional Cooperation for Development, which has its headquarters in Tehran. In April 1976, the three nations agreed to establish a free trade zone and a joint development bank. Iran also is a member of CENTO. Iran is a founding member of OPEC and a leading supporter of higher petroleum prices.

19 ECONOMY

A country with a substantial economic potential, Iran witnessed a rapid economic growth averaging 9% annually in the late 1960s and reaching 42% in 1974/75. While its rich oil reserves have been developed, its extensive agricultural, mineral, and power resources largely await development, to be financed through oil revenues. The traditional land tenure system, under which farmers were sharecroppers, has been replaced through a land reform program inaugurated in 1962; by 1975, 4,025,680 farmers and members of their families had gained ownership of the land they tilled. In addition to carpets, Iran produces a variety of consumer goods and building materials. Oil, however, is still the lifeblood of the economy. It sustains Iran's favorable trade balance and contributes more than 80% of the foreign exchange receipts and an increasing share of budgetary revenues. With the astonishing growth of its oil revenues, Iran has become a major world economic power, whose investments helped several industrialized countries pay for their oil needs in 1974. However, Iran's $10.9-billion surplus on current accounts in 1974 helped fuel domestic inflation (consumer prices rose 18.4% in 1974/75), and that, coupled with a relative decline in oil revenues in 1975 (which remained high by pre-OPEC standards), forced Iran to cut back on foreign investments and domestic development.

20 INCOME

In 1975, Iran's GNP at current prices was estimated at $44.1 billion. National income at factor cost was $40.6 billion. In 1974, Iran's GNP was distributed as follows: oil, 50.6%; manufacturing and mining (excluding oil), 14.4%; agriculture, 9.4%; and other sectors, 25.6%.

21 LABOR

About 66% of Iran's total population in 1974 consisted of persons who were above the age of 10. Of these, 70.5% of the males and 13.5% of the females were economically active. The total labor force numbered about 9.2 million in 1974. The labor force in 1971 was distributed as follows: agriculture, 49%; manufacturing and mining, 30%; other sectors, 21%. About 8.5% of the workers were seasonal.

On 1 May 1974 there were 610 trade unions and 15 labor federations in Iran. The activity of labor unions has not generally been encouraged, except during 1942-49 and in 1952-53, when the Masses Party took the lead in organizing Iranian workers. After the Masses Party was suppressed in 1954, the Trade Union Congress of Iran was organized. Improvement of working conditions was one of the basic principles of the white revolution; in 1963, all trade unions were dissolved and syndicates of workers were required to be registered with the government. After new amendments to the labor laws of 1946 and 1959, factories employing more than 10 workers were required to give a share of their profit to their workers. By November 1974, at least 207,000 workers were participating in profit-sharing arrangements under

5,100 labor-management agreements. At that time, the Workers' Profit-Sharing Council required that all factories, regardless of size, must offer profit-sharing plans to their employees. Furthermore, workers have been allowed to buy shares in their factories under certain conditions.

The normal workweek is 48 hours: 8 hours a day, 6 days a week. Every worker is guaranteed 12 days' paid vacation a year. Men and women are entitled by law to receive equal pay for equal work.

22 AGRICULTURE

Of Iran's total area, 11.5% is agricultural land, 6.1% consists of pastures, and 11.5% is covered with forests. The remaining 70.9% consists of wasteland, built-up areas, lakes, mountains, and desert.

In 1974, the total land area under all kinds of agriculture was estimated at 15,330,000 hectares, or 9.3% of the total area. In that same year there were 37,940 tractors, most of which were produced in the tractor plant that began operating in Tabriz in 1971. Progress in Iranian agriculture was greatly stimulated by the land reform of 1962–63, under which 4,025,680 farmers and their family members had taken title to their land by 1975, after the old land tenure system was abolished.

However, with a rapidly increasing population and a sharply rising standard of living, Iran is no longer self-sufficient in its agricultural production. In October 1974, the government announced purchases of 2,500,000 tons of wheat, 300,000 tons of rice, and 220,000 tons of vegetable oils. In 1974, food imports were valued at $300 million.

In 1973/74, Iranian agricultural production, in tons, included wheat, 4,600,000; barley, 923,000; husked rice, 893,000; cotton, 650,000; and potatoes, 481,000. In addition there were sugar beets, 4,200,000; grapes, 804,000; sugarcane, 600,000; citrus fruits, 400,000; green tea, 100,000; and tobacco, 20,000. Almonds (49,000 tons) and pistachios (42,000 tons) were grown primarily for export.

As of March 1975, some 176,000 hectares were under irrigation. The fifth development plan (1973–78) envisaged an overall increase of 5.5% in agricultural production, but the revised plan raised the target to 8% annually, reflecting a shift in priorities toward agriculture. In 1974, a new policy of creating "agricultural poles" (intensive farm regions) was announced. The basic idea is to merge small and economically nonviable villages into larger units, and by redistributing land to create large and modern estates to which the latest mechanized methods can be applied.

23 ANIMAL HUSBANDRY

Animal husbandry is not only the major occupation of nomadic and seminomadic tribesmen scattered over Iran, but each farming village keeps flocks that graze on the less productive areas. In 1973/74 there were about 25 million sheep and 5.6 million head of cattle; donkeys, horses, and mules are also raised. Cattle are raised as draft animals and for milk and are not fattened for beef. Sheep produce many staple items: milk and butter, animal fat for cooking, meat, wool for carpet making, and skins and hides. Poor weather during the 1970s sharply reduced the domestic flocks, and Iran, which formerly exported 3,000 tons of wool annually, became an importer of wool during the 1970s. The output of agricultural products—1,845,000 tons of milk and 316,000 tons of meat in 1973—has not kept pace with population growth.

Serious efforts have been made since the mid-1950s to improve the quality of the domestic animals of Iran. The government carries on activities covering all aspects of breeding and care: the local production of vaccines; the introduction of selected types of sheep, cattle, donkeys, and hens; the grading and cleaning of wool in modern plants; and regional programs of artificial insemination. The poultry industry has grown rapidly in urban areas.

24 FISHING

The Caspian Sea provides a seemingly inexhaustible source of sturgeon, salmon, and other species of fish, some of which spawn in the chilly streams that flow into this sea from the high Elburz Mountains. In 1973, about 16,000 tons of fish and 3,000 tons of shrimp were caught by Iranian fishermen. Caviar of unrivaled quality is produced by the Iranian Fisheries Co., formerly a joint Russo-Iranian venture, but now wholly owned by the government of Iran. About 200,000 kg of caviar are sold per year, 94% of which is exported, providing a substantial share of the world's supply. Export sales in 1973/74 brought in about $7 million. The fishing grounds of the Persian Gulf were long neglected, but in recent years new fishing fleets and packing and conserving facilities have been established in the area. Here, too, export possibilities are promising.

25 FORESTRY

About 47 million acres (11.5% of the land area of Iran) are covered by forests. An estimated 5.4 million cu meters of round wood were produced in 1973. Along the northern slopes of the Elburz Mountains from near sea level to an altitude of 7,000 feet are dense stands of oak, ash, elm, beech, ironwood, cypress, walnut, and a number of other varieties. The deciduous forests on some 2 million acres in the Caspian littoral (6 million acres in all) are among the best in the world. The timber industry is controlled by the government. It produced about 97,000 cu meters of sawn wood in 1973, but its potential annual capacity is about 3 million cu meters.

The high plateau forests of Fars, Kurdistan, Luristan, and Khorasan comprise sparse stands of scrub oak, ash, maple, cedar, wild almond, and pistachio. Date palms, acacias, and tamarisks grow in the Persian Gulf area. Deforestation of the plateau has been going on for centuries, as nomads and villagers devastate wide areas in the production of charcoal and herds of goats swarm over new shoots. The basic law controlling the use of forests dates from 1943, and a forest range school was started in 1957 as an extension of the government's forest service. In 1962, the forests and pastures in Iran were nationalized to check trespassing deforestation. In 1963, a forestry college was established at Karaj, 23 miles west of Tehran, to train forestry engineers.

26 MINING

Iran possesses extensive and varied mineral resources. The copper deposits in Kerman, Azerbaijan, and other areas, not yet developed, are estimated at nearly 1 billion tons. Lead and zinc deposits are valued at more than $750 million. Modest quantities of coal, iron, antimony, chromium, lead, manganese, sulfur, salt, and magnesite are produced. Iron mining has developed rapidly; output of iron ore increased from 3,000 tons in 1970/71 to 50,000 tons in 1971/72 and 294,000 tons in 1973/74.

The mining law of 1957 divides all mineral resources into three categories. The first group—building materials on private lands—may be exploited by the owners. In the second group—metal ores, precious minerals and stones, salts, and solid fuels—the private owner must obtain a license for exploitation and pay the state 4% of the value of the product. The third category—petroleum deposits and radioactive materials—belongs to the government, wherever found, and the government, by act of Parliament, may grant concessions to foreign companies for the exploitations of these resources. Iran's mineral ores are generally finding their way into the world market, and the government is seriously assisting exploiters and exporters. In 1973/74, exports of important minerals were chromite, 200,000 tons; refined sulfur, 130,000 tons; lead, 108,000 tons; and zinc, 80,000 tons.

Iran's oil reserves, estimated at 9.3 billion tons, constituted 12.5% of the world's reserves in 1973 and are exceeded only by those of Sa'udi Arabia and Kuwayt. Iran was the fourth-largest oil producer in the world in 1973, with an output of 292,843,000 tons. The first oil concession was granted by the Iranian government in 1901, and the first well was brought in during 1908. Production was carried on by the Anglo-Iranian Oil Co. until the petroleum industry was nationalized in 1951, when the country's oil resources were placed under the management of the National Iranian Oil Co. (NIOC). Late in 1954, the active oil properties and facilities were awarded to a consortium of eight foreign companies, later joined by nine others. US, British, Dutch, and French interests are represented. In 1956, the Iranian Oil Co., another government enterprise, brought in a huge gusher at Qum, south of Tehran. In 1957, the legislature ratified an agreement with an Italian company covering an exploited area of Iran, and a joint Italo-Iranian company (SIRIP) was formed to explore and produce. In 1958, the Pan American Oil Co. acquired concession rights in the Persian Gulf and joined with the NIOC in a new mixed company, IPAC. By 1962, both SIRIP and IPAC were producing from wells in the Persian Gulf. Additional fields have been explored, and production has grown rapidly.

During the early 1970s, tremendous changes took place in the Iranian oil industry. The 1954 oil participation agreement was terminated, and on 31 July 1973 a new agreement was signed which replaced the concessionary arrangements with a buyer-seller relationship, the major Western oil companies agreeing to purchase crude petroleum under long-term contracts with the NIOC, which was given full control over the industry. Meanwhile, largely through the concerted action of OPEC, world oil prices were rising; the posted price of Iranian light crude oil increased from $1.79 a barrel in 1970 to $11.65 in 1974. There were indications, however, that oil had become overpriced on the world market, and by early 1976, Iran had dropped the posted price to $11.40. Oil revenues, though still remarkably high by pre-OPEC standards, dipped below expectations in 1975.

The natural gas industry has undergone rapid development. In 1973, Iran's natural gas reserves were estimated at 10.76 trillion cu meters, second highest in the world. Iran's output rose from 2,781 million cu meters in 1969 to 19,869 million in 1973, sixth highest in the world. Exploitation of natural gas is controlled by the National Iranian Gas Co. An agreement was concluded in 1966 for supplying natural gas to the USSR for 15 years from 1970, at an initial rate of 6,000 million cu meters a year and rising to 10,000 million in 1976 and eventually to 20,000 million. A 750-mile pipeline for this purpose was built in 1969. Inside Iran, a network of pipelines connecting Tehran, Qazvin, Isfahan, Shiraz, and Mashhad to Ahwaz and the gas fields is already under construction. In August 1974, Iran concluded an agreement with the Federal Republic of Germany (FRG) for the supply of natural gas to the FRG through the USSR.

27 ENERGY AND POWER

Although Iran is one of the world's leading oil-producing countries, Iranian industry formerly depended on other energy sources, such as electricity, coal, and charcoal. Recently, however, oil and especially gas are being increasingly employed. The country's hydroelectric resources are being exploited through 13 dams on major rivers; in addition there were 4 dams under construction and 3 under study at the end of 1975. In 1973/74, the total electricity output was 9,324 million kwh, as compared with 6,870 million kwh in 1972/73. Installed capacity was 4,117,000 kw, about twice the 1969 total; about 20% of capacity was hydroelectric. In 1974, Iran had two experimental nuclear plants; agreements concluded with France and the US call for the construction of a 2,400,000-kw plant, scheduled to come into operation in 1981.

28 INDUSTRY

There are three main groups of industry: oil refining and petrochemicals; transport equipment and electrical machinery; and cotton and woolen textiles.

There are five refineries—at Abadan, Masjid-i-Sulaiman, Tehran, Kermanshah, and Shiraz—with a total daily capacity of 664,880 barrels. In 1975, work was proceeding on the construction of a refinery at Tabriz, with a capacity of 80,000 barrels per day; in addition, there were plans on hand to build two more refineries, one at Isfahan (100,000 barrels a day) and the other at Neka in Mazandaran (130,000 barrels a day). A second refinery for Tehran (100,000 barrels a day) was also under consideration. Petroleum refinery products in 1973 included motor fuel, 3,165,000 tons; kerosene, 4,335,000 tons; distillate fuels, 5,457,000 tons; and residual fuel, 13,324,000 tons.

In 1964, the National Petrochemical Co. was created, and the NIOC began building a $26-million plant in Abadan for the production of plastics, detergents, and caustic soda. Since then, the petrochemical industry has undergone considerable expansion. By 1975, National Petrochemical was operating four plants, all of which were joint ventures with foreign investors. In 1973, these plants together produced more than 2 million tons of petrochemical products for export and local use.

Heavy metal industries in Iran began in 1966, when the USSR agreed to advance a credit of $286 million for a 600,000-ton steel mill at Isfahan. The installation, now called the Aryamehr Steel Mill, came to operation in 1972; in 1973/74 it produced 400,000 tons of cast iron and 250,000 tons of steel. Steel consumption in Iran, estimated at 2 million tons in the early 1970s, is expected to rise about 20% annually. To meet the need, seven more steel plants were to be built by 1985. The Arak Aluminum smelting plant, with an annual capacity of 45,000 tons, produced 38,000 tons in 1974. The Tabriz Machine Tool plant and Arak Machine Tools produced 25,000 and 6,000 tons of machine tools, respectively; two diesel engine plants produced 12,000 engines. In 1973/74, domestic manufacturers of motor vehicles produced 51,000 cars, 5,000 buses, and 6,000 trucks. In addition, 200,000 refrigerators, 240,000 gas ranges, 78,000 water heaters, 25,000 washing machines, 210,000 television sets, 181,000 electric fans, and 460,000 electric meters were manufactured.

The textile industry has prospered in recent years. In 1973/74, more than 520 million meters of cotton and synthetic fabrics and 14.5 million meters of woolen fabrics were produced. The making of handwoven carpets is a traditional industry in Iran that flourishes despite acute competition from machine-made products. In 1973/74, Iran exported 6.2 million sq meters of carpets, valued at $119.1 million. To promote self-sufficiency, Iran has encouraged development of the food-processing, shoemaking, paper and paper products, rubber, pharmaceutical, aircraft, and shipbuilding industries. Other industrial products in 1973 included cement, 3,489,000 tons; nitrogenous fertilizer, 142,800 tons; phosphate fertilizers, 73,600 tons; refined sugar, 650,000 tons; and cigarettes, 13,449 million.

29 DOMESTIC TRADE

Compared with the marketing systems of industrialized countries, Iran's is not well developed, and credit facilities are costly. Importers make use of irrevocable letters of credit covering their imports. The Bank for the Expansion of Exports offers credit facilities and an advisory service on grading, packing, and shipping to foreign markets. In summer, offices open as early as 7 A.M. and close at about 1 P.M.; during the rest of the year the hours are 8 A.M. until 4 P.M., with a rest period in the middle of the day. Since Friday is the official holiday, many establishments close early on Thursday afternoon. Most goods are sold in small shops or open-air markets, although Tehran has a few small supermarkets.

Within recent years there has been a great upsurge of advertising. The state-owned broadcasting system and the commercial television station accept advertising. Products are advertised in newspapers and motion picture theaters. Outdoor advertising is especially conspicuous in the capital city. Several advertising agencies in Tehran turn out artwork of high quality and conduct their own market surveys.

30 FOREIGN TRADE

Calculated on a balance-of-payments basis, Iran's trade surplus, steady throughout the 1960s, rose rapidly during the 1970s. The following is a summary of Iran's trade balance for 1970–74 (in millions of dollars):

	1970	1971	1972	1973	1974
Exports	2,417	3,735	4,298	7,154	24,805
Imports	1,658	2,075	2,591	3,833	7,087
Balance	759	1,660	1,707	3,321	17,718

The key element in this startling increase in Iran's trade surplus has been the price of crude oil. While the volume of crude oil exports increased 47% between 1970 and 1974, export prices for crude oil increased 38% between 1970 and 1972 and 378% between 1972 and 1974. The value of crude oil exports was estimated at more than $19 billion in 1975. In 1974, Iran exported 263.6 million tons of crude valued at more than $23 billion; the chief purchasers were Western Europe 44.5%, Japan 26.9%, North America 16.7%, and the remaining countries 11.9%.

Since crude oil is exported under complex licensing arrangements, the most recent Iranian commodity trade statistics do not include it. Since Iran has no monetarily significant exports aside from oil (the famed Persian carpets accounted for less than 1% of Iran's exports in 1974), official commodity figures show a multibillion-dollar annual deficit. Principal imports are basic manufactured goods and industrial equipment. The Iranian commodity trade year follows the Persian calendar, ending on 20 March.

Principal exports in 1973/74 (excluding petroleum, in millions of dollars) were:

Carpets	119.1
Cotton	85.3
Fresh and dried fruits	71.8
Nonferrous ores	32.8
Hides and leather	27.8
Fish and preparations (mostly caviar)	7.4
Vegetable oil	3.5
Other exports	233.8
TOTAL	581.5

Principal imports in 1973/74 (in millions of dollars) were:

Iron and steel	1,155
Machinery and equipment	1,137
Motor vehicles and parts	563
Textile yarns and fabrics	487
Electrical machinery and appliances	409
Chemicals and pharmaceuticals	117
Other imports	2,746
TOTAL	6,614

The FRG, US, Japan, UK, France, and Italy are Iran's principal suppliers of imports. The USSR is the chief purchaser of Iran's nonpetroleum exports. Trade with Communist countries is generally through barter arrangements. The distribution of trade in 1973/74 (excluding petroleum, in millions of dollars) was:

	EXPORTS	IMPORTS	BALANCE
EEC	175.2	2,511.9	-2,336.7
US	46.2	1,321.5	-1,275.3
Japan	31.6	999.4	- 967.8
Communist countries	139.1	422.3	- 283.2
Other countries	189.4	1,358.6	-1,169.2
TOTALS	581.5	6,613.7	-6,032.2

31 BALANCE OF PAYMENTS

The remarkable rise in Iran's oil income has had measurable impact on the country's balance of payments. Throughout the 1960s and early 1970s, Iran had a favorable trade balance, but substantial imports of services resulted in an annual deficit on current accounts. Long-term capital inflows from private sources reached a peak in 1965; between 1968 and 1973, capital from foreign governments played a prime role in Iranian development. Net long-term capital inflows from governmental sources reached $597 million in 1971 and $552 million in 1973, when, aided by rising oil prices, Iran registered its first surplus on current accounts and invested $343 million in foreign private enterprises. By 1974, with a net trade balance of $17,718 million and a current accounts balance of $10,893 million, Iran was one of the world's major exporters of capital, recording net long-term capital outflows of $2,155 million to foreign private enterprises and $2,443 million to other governments.

The reversal in Iran's payments position has been reflected in the country's accumulation of international reserves. Reserve holdings, which totaled $310 million at the end of 1969, reached $1,236 million in 1973 and $8,697 million in 1975. Foreign exchange reserves rose from $70 million at the end of 1970 to $7,652 million in 1974. During 1974 and 1975, Iran committed a total of $1,066 million to the IMF Oil Facility. Gold holdings have ranged between $129 million and $160 million throughout the 1960s and 1970s.

The following is a summary (in millions of dollars) of Iran's balance of payments for 1973 and 1974:

	1973	1974
CURRENT ACCOUNTS		
Trade, net	3,321	17,718
Services, net	-3,236	-6,801
Transfers, net	1	- 24
TOTALS	86	10,893
CAPITAL ACCOUNTS		
Long-term capital	125	-4,478
Short-term capital	49	57
TOTALS	174	-4,421
Errors and omissions	160	- 266
Net change	420	6,206

32 BANKING

The Central Bank of Iran, established by the Monetary and Banking Law of 1960, issues notes, controls foreign exchange, and supervises the banking sector. Law requires 40% of all notes issued to be covered by gold, convertible currencies, or subscription paid to international institutions in gold or convertible currencies. The remaining 60% is covered by government debts guaranteed by the value of the crown jewels, estimated at R25 billion. Currency in circulation increased from R64.1 billion in March 1973 to R71 billion in January 1974. During the same period, public deposits with banks rose from R165.1 billion to R218 billion, and private savings increased from R125.8 billion to R141.6 billion. Central Bank reserves reached R408.9 billion on 31 November 1975.

The rial became an international reserve currency on 19 September 1974, and the Central Bank announced on 6 October 1974 that all banks operating in Iran could thenceforth accept payment in rials for foreign orders of Iranian goods. On that occasion, special regulations were laid down for the import and export of raw (unworked) gold and silver. Similarly, the IMF was advised that it could freely convert the rial into foreign currencies.

In 1975 there were 30 banks operating in Iran. Of these, 8 were government-owned; the remainder were owned by local investors or were joint banks with foreign participation. The National Bank of Iran, founded by the state in 1927, is the largest commercial bank, with about 1,000 branches and a paid-up capital of R2 billion. The entire banking system included roughly 7,000 branch banks in January 1974. In April 1974, 5 leading European banks formally opened a joint office in Tehran.

Of the several specialized banks in Iran, the oldest, the Agricultural Credit Bank, established in 1933, has a paid-up capital of R825.1 million and provides short- and long-term credit for agricultural purposes. The Mortgage Bank, with a paid-up capital of R3,600 million, provides medium-term credit for house construction, and the Industrial Credit Bank caters to the credit requirements of small industries. The primary purpose of the Industrial and Mining Development Bank of Iran, established in 1959 by foreign and Iranian banking and industrial interests, is to extend long- and medium-term credit to industrial establishments in Iran, although in some instances it may participate directly in these enterprises. It also underwrites and distributes securities with a view to building up an Iranian capital market.

33 INSURANCE

The first domestic insurance firm in Iran, the Iran Insurance Co., incorporated in 1935, is entirely state-owned and has grown rapidly as the government agent for a variety of programs. As of mid-1975 there were 12 private companies and a state enterprise for reinsurance.

In December 1952, a government decree set forth stringent conditions on foreign insurance companies, limiting the amount a company may transfer abroad to $50,000 per year. Another statutory decree, issued in November 1962, required insurance companies to invest 50% of their life insurance premium income and 40% of their underwriting reserve for general branches in treasury bonds, which bear interest at 6% per annum. Consequently, there are only two foreign firms (UK and USSR) transacting insurance in Iran.

In June 1971, the Central Insurance Organization of Iran (CII) was created by an act of Parliament to oversee all insurance operations in the country. With a totally government-owned capital of R500 million, CII performs most of its functions through its authorized agency, the Iran Insurance Co. Under CII regulations, all organizations in which the government holds a majority of the shares must obtain their insurance exclusively from the Iran Insurance Co.

Direct gross premiums for 1974/75 totaled R16,565 million, of which 57% was for marine cargo insurance. Losses paid in 1974/75 amounted to R5,560 million.

Compulsory third-party motor insurance has been in effect since 1969.

34 SECURITIES

The Tehran Stock Exchange, locally known as the Bourse, was created in 1971. Its total turnover was R2,774 million in 1974, a very small amount when compared with the country's actual and potential wealth. In August 1974, two Iranian banks, the National Bank of Iran and the Industrial and Mining Development Bank of Iran, joined with the US firm of Merrill Lynch, Pierce, Fenner & Smith to begin international brokerage activities in Iran. Large government bond issues are a recent development in Iran, although some bonds were issued as early as 1920. The first large modern loan issue, valued at R200 million, was floated in 1951. Treasury bonds have been issued since 1962. These are short-term bonds bearing 6% interest; long-term

bonds carrying a maximum interest of 10.5% were floated in 1972. The total face value of government bonds floated through 1974 amounted to at least R268.9 billion.

35 PUBLIC FINANCE

Iran's fiscal year coincides with its calendar year, beginning on 21 March. The budget is submitted to Parliament on or before 21 January and approved by it by 6 March. The budget for 1974/75 showed revenues of R1,394.4 billion and expenditures of R1,143.6 billion, for a surplus of R250.8 billion. Sources of revenue were oil and gas, 86.4%; taxes, 11.7% (5.5% direct, 6.2% indirect); and other revenues 1.9%. Expenditures were 68.1% for current expenditures and 31.9% for development. Budget expenditures of more than R3,000 billion were forecast for 1976/77; because of a relative decline in oil revenues, a deficit exceeding R160 billion was projected.

The following is a summary of Iranian revenues and expenditures for 1972/73 and 1973/74 (in millions of rials):

	1972/73	1973/74
REVENUES		
Income taxes	38,849	48,008
Sales tax	17,068	10,957
Other taxes	64,942	84,581
Income from government enterprises	10,042	11,353
Oil revenue	178,196	311,251
Other receipts	210,333	308,183
TOTALS	519,430	774,333
EXPENDITURES		
Defense	91,060	134,929
Economic services	112,370	126,048
Social services	84,593	118,117
Public services	48,639	76,071
Other expenditures	182,768	276,587
TOTALS	519,430	731,752
BALANCE	—	42,581

36 TAXATION

About one-third of tax revenue comes from income taxes. The income tax law now in force dates from 1955. In its clauses, aspects of traditional practice are intermingled with the graduated scales of taxation in force in many other countries. Tax rates range from 10% on taxable income up to R300,000 to 55% on taxable income exceeding R50 million. All income is taxed separately; a husband and wife may not file jointly. All income taxes are withheld by employers, and wage earners need not file tax returns.

Companies organized to promote Iranian exports, to exploit, smelt, or refine mineral products, or to manufacture industrial products are exempt from the payment of income taxes for five years from the start of operations. There is a corporate profits tax of 10% of taxable income, a 15% tax on dividends, and additional taxes ranging from 15% to 60% on foreign branch income, royalty and interest payments to foreigners, and other dispositions of corporate income. Corporations must also pay a municipal tax of 3%. To curb speculation, high taxes and stringent restrictions have been imposed on all real estate transactions.

37 CUSTOMS AND DUTIES

Most goods entering Iran are subject to customs duties, the majority of which are on the c.i.f. value. In recent years, a number of govenment organizations and charitable institutions have been permitted to import their requirements free of duty. Some 10% by value of total imports is brought in by these organizations, which include the Plan Organization, the NIOC, and the Iranian State Railways. In April 1976, Iran, Pakistan, and Turkey agreed to establish a free trade zone.

38 FOREIGN INVESTMENTS
Up to the early 1970s, Iran rarely participated in foreign businesses. The NIOC, however, did invest in the construction of oil refineries in Madras, India, and other places, and it participated in several mixed ventures with foreign oil firms that held concessions for Iranian oil. But with the vast increase in oil revenues, Iran became in 1974 one of the world's leading creditor nations. In 1974 alone, bilateral agreements worth hundreds of billions of rials were signed with France, the FRG, Italy, and the UK. In July 1974, Iran agreed to purchase a 25% interest in the FRG steelmaking firm of Krupp Hüttenwerke; this is believed to be the largest single stake purchased by any oil-producing nation in a major European firm. In 1975, Iran began negotiating investments through the UNDP in developing nations.

Prior to World War II, foreign companies had important investments in Iranian banks, insurance companies, transport, and the oil industry. In 1955, Parliament enacted a law providing for withdrawal of invested capital in the currency that was brought into Iran, for the export of annual profits, and for adequate compensation in the event of nationalization of the industry or business. In 1957, the US and Iran exchanged notes recognizing that the US would guarantee its private investments in Iran against loss through actions by Iran. In 1958, the Majlis enacted a law protecting foreign capital investments. Foreign companies are moving into Iran to exploit mineral resources, to establish banks in partnership with Iranian capital, to build factories, and to carry out segments of the vast economic development program of Iran. The role of foreign capital in Iran's development program has been increasing; whereas the seven-year plan for 1949–56 involved foreign investments totaling $68 million, the five-year plan for 1973–78 calls for investments of $30 billion.

39 ECONOMIC POLICY
General economic policy is the concern of the High Council of the Plan Organization, which consists of the prime minister, the minister of economy, the minister of finance, director of the Central Bank, and the managing director of the Plan Organization. The Council has the task of maintaining efficient relations between the activities of the ministries and those of the Plan Organization. Execution of economic policy, as approved by both the High Council and Parliament, is in the hands of the ministries and agencies concerned. Iran carried out three development plans between 1949 and 1968. The first plan (1949–56) foundered because of the lack of oil revenues during the nationalization dispute and also because the IBRD refused to lend the hoped-for one-third of the projected development expenditures. The second plan (1956–63) also ran into financial difficulties when the domestic budget consumed a larger proportion of the oil revenues than expected. An austerity program from 1960, however, facilitated economic recovery. The third plan (1963–68) was successful, and the period witnessed rapid economic growth. It placed emphasis not only on the building of an infrastructure but also on quick-payoff projects making use of local resources. The private sector exceeded the target planned for investment. Substantial foreign aid, varied in its sources, was also forthcoming, and foreign investment in Iran totaled more than $2.7 billion. The fourth plan (1968–73) was far more successful than the previous ones, and most of its objectives were realized beyond expectation. The GNP rose during the fourth plan from R686 billion (at constant 1972/73 prices) to R1,165 billion, giving a mean annual GNP growth of 11.2%, as compared with the projected figure of 9%. Similarly, per capita GNP rose to about $560 ($300 had been the goal). In its revised form, the fifth plan (1973–78) provides for total fixed investments of R4,834 billion. Of this, the public sector will account for 66%,

the private sector for the remaining 34%. It is envisaged that at the end of the fifth planning period, the GNP will have risen to R3,686 billion, showing a real annual growth rate of 16.4%, and that per capita income will grow at 12.4% annually. Contributions to GNP in 1977/78 were expected to be oil, 48.7%; services, 27.2%; industries and mines, 16.1%; and agriculture, 8%.

40 HEALTH
Until recently, Iran was plagued by many health problems: high infant mortality, smallpox outbreaks, venereal disease, trachoma, typhoid fever, amoebic dysentery, malaria, tuberculosis, and the debilitating effects of smoking opium. However, national campaigns against such major diseases as malaria and smallpox have sharply reduced the death rate since the mid-1960s. The creation in 1964 of a health corps, consisting of physicians and high-school graduates who spend the period of their military service serving in semimobile medical units in rural areas, has been a main instrument of this progress. By January 1974, some 9,021 health corps members had served the rural areas. Roving health corps teams, comprising a doctor, a dentist, a pathologist, and (when possible) a nurse, may cover 30 to 50 villages and offer medical services to 10,000 to 15,000 rural inhabitants in the course of a year.

In February 1974 there were 11,774 physicians (1 per 2,800 inhabitants) and 1,489 dentists. In 1974/75 there were 45,000 beds in more than 500 hospitals. Another 20,000 hospital beds were to be added by 1977/78. At the same time, there were 2,800 clinics, 250 medical centers, 1,700 pharmacies, and 1,000 medical laboratories. It was announced in February 1975 that free medical care would be provided for low-income groups; initially R1,000 million was allocated by the government for the purpose. Estimated average life expectancy in 1975 was 53.5 years.

There are medical schools affiliated with universities in Tehran, Mashhad, Shiraz, Isfahan, Tabriz, and Ahwaz. Attempts are being made to encourage Iranian medical practitioners now serving outside the country to return to Iran; their number is believed to exceed 10,000.

41 SOCIAL WELFARE
Traditionally, the family and the tribe were supplemented by Islamic waqf (obligatory charity) institutions for the care of the infirm and the indigent. Iran's monarchical system has been slow to awaken to the responsibility of the state in this respect. In April 1974, the Ministry of Social Welfare was created with the object of coordinating and harmonizing the programs of social insurance organizations (previously affiliated with the Ministry of Labor) with those of the Social Services Organization, the Ministry of Health, and other government agencies engaged in social welfare. The Ministry has done a great deal in extending social insurance coverage in both rural and urban areas. It was anticipated that by the end of the fifth plan (1973–78), some 50% of the urban population would enjoy insurance coverage. Coverage for the whole country is not envisaged until the end of the 1980s. Social welfare programs in force in 1975 included workmen's compensation, disability benefits, maternity allowances, retirement benefits, death benefits, and family and marriage allowances.

Private charitable organizations date from as early as 1923, when the Iranian Red Lion and Sun Society (corresponding to the Red Cross) was established. Other charitable institutions include the Pahlavi Foundation, Farah Charity Society, Imperial Organization for Social Services, and Mother and Infant Protection Institute. Private organizations spend an estimated R20 billion annually for charitable purposes.

42 HOUSING
Rapid urbanization has made housing one of the country's most acute social problems. Although housing has always been given top priority in development plans, the gap between supply and demand for dwellings has grown increasingly wide. During the

fourth plan (1968–73), nearly 300,000 housing units were built; but because some 120,000 new families were added to the urban population during that period, the average density rose from 7.7 to 8.5 persons per house between 1968 and 1973. During the same period, the national urban housing deficit rose from 721,000 to 1,095,000 units. Under the fifth plan (1973–78), the housing target, originally set at 740,000 units, was increased to 810,000. Investment and credit for housing, R190 billion in the fourth plan, rose to more than R925 billion during the fifth. However, housing will be a problem for many years to come.

⁴³EDUCATION

Literacy training has been a prime concern in Iran. A literacy corps, established in 1963, sends educated conscripts to villages. During its first 10 years, the corps helped 2.2 million urban children and 600,000 adults become literate. A survey conducted in 1971 indicated that of the 22,320,000 Iranians of more than 6 years of age, 36.9% were literate. The proportion has further increased during the 1970s, although no official statistics are available.

Education is virtually free in Iran at all ages, from elementary school through university. At university level, however, every student is required to commit himself to serve the government for a number of years equivalent to those spent at the university. During the early 1970s, efforts were made to improve the educational system by updating school curricula, introducing modern textbooks, and training more efficient teachers. In addition, free midday food is distributed in all elementary shools. Teaching by television was introduced in October 1973, and plans call for the use of video cassettes and satellite television. Under the fifth plan (1973–78), some $8.2 billion was allocated for education. During the fourth plan (1968–73), 80% of urban and 40% of rural children went to school; this proportion was expected to rise to 100% and 80%, respectively, by the end of the fifth-plan period. In 1973 there were 22 kindergartens, 3,446 primary schools, 571 guidance (intermediate) schools, 617 general secondary schools, 64 technical schools, 115 higher schools, 31 vocational schools, and 8,250 adult education centers. Primary and secondary enrollment exceeded 4.7 million students.

The tradition of university education in Iran goes back to the early centuries of Islam. By the 20th century, however, the system had become antiquated and was remodeled along French lines. The University of Tehran, founded in 1935, had 17 faculties, 35 affiliated institutes (including 12 hospitals), and some 20,000 students in 1974/75. Other major universities are at Tehran, Tabriz, Mashhad, Ahwaz, Shiraz, Isfahan, and Reza'iyeh. In 1975 there were 235 institutions of higher learning, with a total student body of 123,114 and a combined faculty of 5,025 members.

⁴⁴LIBRARIES AND MUSEUMS

Public libraries and museums are fairly new in Iran. In 1974/75, Iran had 1,680 libraries with about 3.5 million books. The National Library at Tehran is forming a good general collection. The Library of Parliament, the largest in the country, has a very extensive collection of manuscripts and an unrivaled collection of documentary material in Persian, including files of all important newspapers since the inception of the press in Iran. The National Bank Library is especially strong in works on Iran in foreign languages. Several faculties of the University of Tehran have good libraries. Tehran has a fine building, which houses the Archaeological Museum, overflowing with fabulous treasures from the long cultural and artistic history of Iran, and the Ethnological Museum. The crown treasures of manuscripts, jeweled thrones, and a vast variety of other objects may be seen at the Gulistan Palace. The museums at Isfahan, Mashhad, Qum, and Shiraz feature antique carpets, faience, painted pottery, illuminated manuscripts, and fine craftsmanship in wood and metal; most of these objects date from the 12th to the 18th centuries.

⁴⁵ORGANIZATIONS

Long renowned for their individualism, the Iranians are now active in associating with modern public and private organizations. The government greatly encourages the growth of the cooperative movement; the first Workers' Consumers Society was established in 1948. Many villages have founded producers' cooperatives with official advice and support, and consumers' cooperatives exist among governmental employees and members of the larger industrial and service organizations. In 1974 there were 2,806 rural cooperative societies with 2,414,916 members and combined capital assets of more than R4 billion. There were also 1,068 workers' cooperatives and 747 urban cooperatives.

The Red Lion and Sun Society (the Iranian equivalent of the Red Cross) is active everywhere. The Society to Combat the Use of Opium has waged a campaign against use of the drug. The royal family operates and finances two charitable organizations: the Imperial Organization for Social Services and the Pahlavi Foundation.

The Boy Scout movement in Iran began before World War II. There are many sports and physical culture societies in Tehran and the provinces; emphasis is upon skiing and weight lifting. Iran also has an Olympic Association that trains and finances local athletes for Olympic and regional games. The Rotary International and the Lions Club are represented in Iran.

There are oganizations of journalists, physicians, and publishers. A book society is active, as is the Society of the Friends of Literature. Several institutions have excellent clubs for their employees, with full programs of sports, recreational activities, and publications; the National Bank and the Iranian State Railways were the pioneers in this field.

⁴⁶PRESS

The local press operates under a press law enacted by Parliament in 1955. To obtain licenses, newspaper owners must have a B.A. degree, good character, and funds adequate for publishing for a stated period. Suspension of publication, fines, and imprisonment may result from such violations of the law as printing false news or attacks on the royal family, revealing military secrets, and printing material injurious to Islam.

In 1972, 264 dailies and periodicals appeared in Tehran and the provinces, with circulations ranging from 2,000 to over 300,000. Several illustrated weeklies have circulations approaching 150,000. Technical and scientific publications each distribute about 2,000 copies. Most of the dailies appear in 4 pages, but *Kayhan* (with a 1974 circulation of 250,000) and *Ettela'at* (200,000), leading newspapers, have 20 to 40 pages. Weeklies and monthlies have between 36 and 120 pages. Two dailies, *Kayhan International* (10,000) and the *Tehran Journal* (8,000), appear in English; one, *Le Journal de Téhéran* (5,000), in French; and one, *Al-Akha'a*, in Arabic.

⁴⁷TOURISM

Visitors to Iran need a valid passport and a transit or entry visa. Visas are issued free of charge to nationals of some countries; a multiple entry visa obviates the need of an exit permit to leave Iran. Foreign exchange may be registered at the port of entry, and the visitor is allowed to take out up to the amount registered. Certificates of smallpox inoculation may have to be shown. Cholera and yellow fever vaccinations are required upon arrival from infected areas. Travel agencies make arrangements for travel by plane, rail, bus, or automobile within the country, and manage hotel accommodations. English is widely understood at Tehran and in provincial centers, French somewhat less so.

Not until 1963 did the Iranian government begin to pay attention to tourism as a potential industry. In that year, the Iranian National Tourist Organization was established. In 1974, this organization was absorbed by the Ministry of Information and Tourism, whose main task is to publicize Iran at home and abroad. In 1974, some 420,000 tourists visited Iran; tourist revenues totaled about $58 million.

48 FAMOUS IRANIANS

The long history of Iran has witnessed a brilliant galaxy of conquerors, wise rulers and statesmen, artists, poets, historians, and philosophers. In religion, there have been diverse figures. Zarathustra (Zoroaster), who may have lived in the 6th century B.C., founded the religion known as Mazdaism, with Ahura-Mazda as the god of good. In the 3d century A.D., Mani attempted a fusion of the tenets of Mazdaism, Judaism, and Christianity. The Bab (Sayyid 'Ali Muhammad of Shiraz, 1819–50) was the precursor of Baha'ism, founded by Baha'Allah (Mirza Husayn 'Ali Nuri, 1817–92).

Great Persian rulers of the pre-Christian era include Cyrus the Great (r.550–529 B.C.), Cambyses (r.529–522 B.C.), Darius the Great (r.521–486 B.C.), and Xerxes I (r.486–465 B.C.). Shah Abbas (r.1587–1628) expanded Persian territory and conquered Baghdad. Prominent political figures of modern times are Reza Pahlavi (1877–1944), who reigned as shah from 1925 to his abdication in 1941; and his son, Muhammad Reza Pahlavi (b.1919), who has been shah since 1941 and during whose reign Iran has recaptured some of its former glory.

The great epic poet Firdawsi (Abdul Qasim Hassan Ibn-i-Ishaq ibn-i Sharafshah, 940–1020), writing about A.D. 1000, produced the *Shahnama* (*Book of Kings*), dealing with four ancient dynasties and full of romantic and heroic tales that retain their popularity today. Omar Khayyam (d. c.1123), astronomer and poet, is known in the Western world for his *Rubáiyât*, a collection of quatrains freely translated by Edward FitzGerald. Important figures of the Seljuq period (11th and 12th centuries) include Muhammad bin Muhammad al-Ghazali (1058–1111), philosopher and mystic theologian, who exerted an enormous influence upon all later speculative thought in Islam; Farid al-Din 'Attar (Muhammad bin Ibrahim, 1119–1229), one of the greatest of mystic poets; and Nizami (Nizam al-Din Abu Muhammad, 1141–1202), noted for four romantic epic poems that were copied and recopied by hand and illuminated with splendid miniatures. In the 13th century, Jalal al-Din Rumi (1207–73) compiled his celebrated long mystic poem, the *Mathnavi*, in rhyming couplets; and Sa'di (Muslih ud-Din, 1184?–1291), possibly the most renowned Iranian poet within or outside of Iran, composed his *Gulistan* (*Rose Garden*) and *Bustan* (*Orchard*). About a hundred years later, in 1389, died another poet of Shiraz, Hafiz (Shamsud-Din Muhammad); his collected works comprise nearly 700 poems, all of them ghazals or lyrical odes.

Poets of the modern period include Iraj Mirza (1880–1926), Mirzadeh Eshqi (d.1924), Parveen Ettasami (d.1941), and the poet laureate Behar (Malik al-Shuara Bahar, d.1951). Preeminent among prose writers was Sadeq Hedayat (1903–51), author of the novel *Buf i kur* (*The Blind Owl*) and numerous other works. Other influential writers are Muhammad Hijazi (b.1900) and Sadiq Chubak (b.1916).

Miniature painting came to full flower in the second half of the 15th century. The greatest figure in this field was Bihzad, whose limited surviving work is highly prized. The School of Herat, composed of his followers, set the mode for all later work of this type.

49 DEPENDENCIES

Iran has no territories or colonies.

50 BIBLIOGRAPHY

Arberry, Arthur John (ed.). *The Legacy of Persia*. Oxford: Clarendon Press, 1953.

Armajani, Yahya. *Iran*. Englewood Cliffs, N.J.: Prentice-Hall, 1972.

Banani, Amin. *The Modernization of Iran, 1921–1941*. Stanford: Stanford University Press, 1961.

Bausani, Alessandro. *The Persians*. New York: St. Martin's Press, 1971.

Bharier, Julian. *Economic Development in Iran, 1900–1970*. New York: Oxford University Press, 1971.

Binder, Leonard. *Iran: Political Development in a Changing Society*. Berkeley: University of California Press, 1962.

Chubin, Shahram. *The Foreign Relations of Iran*. Berkeley: University of California Press, 1974.

Donaldson, Dwight M. *The Shi'ite Religion: A History of Islam in Persia and Irak*. London: Luzac, 1933.

Elwell-Sutton, Laurence Paul. *A Guide to Iranian Area Study*. Washington, D.C.: Educational Services, 1952.

Field, Henry. *Contributions to the Anthropology of Iran*. Chicago: Field Museum Press, 1939.

Ford, Alan Wayne. *The Anglo-Iranian Oil Dispute of 1951–52: A Study of the Role of Law in the Relations of States*. Berkeley: University of California Press, 1954.

Frye, Richard Nelson. *Iran*. London: Allen & Unwin, 1960.

Ghirshman, Roman. *Iran from the Earliest Times to the Islamic Conquest*. Harmondsworth: Penguin, 1954.

Herzfeld, Ernst Emil. *Iran in the Ancient East: Archaeological Studies*. . . . New York: Oxford University Press, 1941.

Jacobs, Norman. *Sociology of Development: Iran as an Asian Case Study*. New York: Praeger, 1966.

Lambton, Ann Katharine Wynford. *Landlord and Peasant in Persia*. London: Oxford University Press, 1953.

Lenczowski, George. *Russia and the West in Iran: A Study in Big-Power Rivalry*. Ithaca: Cornell University Press, 1953.

Olmstead, Albert Ten Eyck. *The History of the Persian Empire: Achaemenid Period*. Chicago: University of Chicago Press, 1948.

Pope, Arthur Upham. *A Survey of Persian Art from Prehistoric Times to the Present*. London: Oxford University Press, 1938–39. Index volume, 1958.

Ramazani, Rouhollah K. *The Persian Gulf*. Charlottesville: University Press of Virginia, 1972.

Sablier, Edouard. *From Persia to Iran: An Historical Journey*. New York: Viking, 1960

Statistical Yearbook of Iran, 1972/73. Tehran: Plan and Budget Organization, Statistical Center of Iran, 1975.

Sykes, Percy M. *History of Persia*. New York: Barnes & Noble, 1969.

Upton, Joseph M. *The History of Modern Iran: An Interpretation*. Cambridge: Harvard University Press, 1960.

Wilber, Donald Newton. *Contemporary Iran*. New York: Praeger, 1963.

IRAQ

The Republic of Iraq
Al-Jumhuriyah al-ʿIraqiyah

CAPITAL: Baghdad. **FLAG**: The national flag is a tricolor of red, white, and black horizontal stripes with three five-pointed stars in green in the center of the white stripe. **ANTHEM**: *Al-Salaam al-Jumhuriyah (Salute of the Republic)*. **MONETARY UNIT**: The Iraqi dinar (ID) of 1,000 fils is a nonconvertible paper currency. There are coins of 1, 5, 10, 25, 50, and 100 fils, and notes of 250 and 500 fils and 1, 5, and 10 dinars. ID1 = $3.377 (or $1 = ID0.296051). **WEIGHTS AND MEASURES**: The metric system is the legal standard, but weights and measures in general use vary, especially in domestic transactions. The unit of land is the dunam, which is equivalent to approximately 0.62 acre (0.25 hectare). **HOLIDAYS**: New Year's Day, 1 January; Army Day, 6 January; 14th Ramadan Revolution Day, 8 February; Spring Day, 21 March; Labor Day, 1 May; Declaration of the Republic, 14 July; and Peaceful Revolution Day, 17 July. Religious holidays include ʿId al-Fitr, ʿId al-ʿAdha', and Milad al-Nabi. **TIME**: 3 P.M. = noon GMT.

¹ LOCATION, SIZE, AND EXTENT

Present-day Iraq, comprising an area of 438,446 sq km (169,284 sq mi), corresponds roughly to the former Turkish provinces of Baghdad, Mosul (al-Mawsil), and Basrah (al-Basrah). It extends 984 km (611 mi) SSE–NNW and 730 km (454 mi) ENE–WSW. Iraq is bordered on the N by Turkey, on the E by Iran, on the SE by the Persian Gulf and Kuwayt, on the s by Saʿudi Arabia, on the w by Jordan, and on the NW by Syria, with a total boundary length of 3,738 km (2,323 mi). The Neutral Zone, administered jointly by Iraq and Saʿudi Arabia, was to be divided according to an agreement of 2 July 1975 which was subject to the ratification of the respective governments.

² TOPOGRAPHY

Iraq is divided into three distinct zones: the desert in the west and southwest; the plains; and the highlands in the northeast, which rise to 10,000 feet or more. Each zone has distinct geographic features that contribute to the variety of the country's demography, culture, and economics.

The desert is an upland region with altitudes of from 2,000 to 3,000 feet (between Damascus in Syria and al-Rutba in Iraq), but declines gently toward the Euphrates (al-Furat) River. The water supply comes from wells and wadis that at times carry torrential floods and that retain the winter rains.

Dominated by the river systems of the Tigris (Dijlah) and Euphrates, the plains area is composed of two regions divided by a ridge, some 250 feet above the flood plain, between al-Ramadi and a point south of Baghdad that marks the prehistoric coastline of the Persian Gulf. The lower valley, built up by the silt the two rivers carry, consists of marshland, crisscrossed by drainage channels. At Qarmat ʿAli, just above Basrah, the two rivers combine and form the Shatt al-ʿArab, a broad waterway through which oceangoing vessels enter Basrah.

In their upper valleys, the two streams form two basins, each with its own tributaries and separated by a broad stretch of upland plateau known as al-Jazirah. The narrow Wadi al-Tharthar receives streams from the north but it has no outlet and ends in a salt marsh. To the north is the Jabal (mountain) Sinjar.

The sources of the Euphrates and Tigris are in the Armenian Plateau. The Euphrates receives its main tributaries before entering Iraq, while the Tigris receives several streams on the eastern bank within the country. Among them are the eastern Khabur, the Great Zab (Zab al-Kabir) and Little Zab (Zab al-Saghir) rivers, the ʿUzaym River, which carries very fine silt, and, 20 miles below Baghdad, the Diyala. From earliest times to the present day, the peoples of Iraq have had to construct irrigation works and dams to control the rivers and the recurrent floods, for both the Euphrates and the Tigris often change their courses.

³ CLIMATE

Under the influence of the monsoons, Iraq in summer has a constant northwesterly wind (shamal), while in winter a strong southeasterly air current (sharqi) develops. The intensely hot and dry summers last from May to October, and during the hottest time of the day—often reaching 49°C (120°F) in the shade—people take refuge in underground shelters. Winters, lasting from December to March, are damp and comparatively cold with temperatures of about 10°C (50°F). Spring and autumn are short transition periods.

Normally, no rain falls from the end of May to the end of September. Mosul, in the north, has 13 inches of rainfall in 60 days; Baghdad, 5.5 inches in 28 days; Basrah, 5.7 inches in 21 days of the year. With annual rainfall of less than 15 inches, agriculture is dependent on irrigation.

⁴ FLORA AND FAUNA

In the lower regions of the Euphrates and Tigris and in the alluvial plains, papyrus, lotus, and tall reeds form a thick underbrush; willow, poplar, and alder trees abound. On the upper and middle Euphrates, the licorice bush yields a juice that is sold in Mosul and in Aleppo, Syria. Another bush growing wild in the semiarid steppe or desert yields gum tragacanth, which is used for manufacturing pharmaceutical products. On the higher and damp spots in the Zagros Mountains grows the valonia oak, the bark of which is used for tanning leather. About 30 million date palms produce one of Iraq's most important exports. For a short period in spring, the shrubs and grasses of the desert and steppes serve as pasture for sheep and goats.

Wild animals include the hyena, jackal, cheetah, fox, gazelle, antelope, jerboa, mole, porcupine, desert hare, and bat. Beaver, wild ass, and ostrich are rare. Wild ducks, geese, and partridge are the game birds. Vultures, owls, and ravens live near the Euphrates. Falcons are trained for hunting. In 1975, endangered species in Iraq included the wolf, leopard, Persian fallow deer, and Saʿudi Arabian dorcas gazelle.

⁵ POPULATION

According to the census of 1965, the population of Iraq was 8,097,230. By 1975, the number was officially estimated to have risen to 11,124,000; 1980 population was projected at 13,214,000.

The average population density in 1975 was 25.4 per sq km (65.7 per sq mi). Annual growth rate in the mid-1970s averaged about 3.4%. The nature of the country inevitably determines the distribution of population. Nomadic tribes roam the deserts south and west of the Euphrates and al-Jazirah, and Bedouins and seminomads graze their flocks on the pastures of the steppes and the highlands.

In 1975, about 38% of Iraq's inhabitants lived in villages, compared with about 50% a decade earlier. As of the 1970 census, Baghdad, the capital, and its suburbs had 1,984,142 inhabitants; Basrah, the main port, 333,684; Mosul (al-Mawsil), in an oil-producing region, 310,313; and Kirkuk, another oil center, 191,294.

⁶ETHNIC GROUPS

Arabs constitute about 80% of the total population. The Kurds, an Islamic non-Arab people, are the largest and most important minority group, comprising 15% of the national total. A seminomadic pastoral people, the Kurds live in the northwestern Zagros Mountains and in the highlands of eastern Anatolia (Turkey). They have occupied their present domicile and retained their identity since the 3d millennium B.C. About 1.7 million of the region's estimated 3.5 million Kurds live in Iraq, mostly in isolated villages in the mountain valleys near Turkey and Iran. Kurdish opposition to Iraqi political dominance continued into the 1970s, occasioning violent clashes with government forces.

Other minorities, together comprising about 5% of the total, include Turkomans, living in the north; Lurs in the east; Yazidis in Sinjar; Assyrians, south of Baghdad; Shabaks (Kurdish subdivision), south of Mosul; Sabaeans (Mandaeans); Sarlyas; and Armenians. Until the establishment of Israel, Iraq had about 100,000 Jews. They were one of the most ancient Jewish communities, and in the Middle Ages produced outstanding scholars. By 1973, their number was put at about 500.

⁷LANGUAGE

Arabic is the national language. Despite the prevalence of Arabic for 13 centuries, some minority languages and local dialects have survived. The languages of certain peoples (such as the Assyrians and Sabaeans) indicate an original connection with ancient, now extinct religious or ethnic groups not necessarily indigenous to Iraq. Kurdish, or a dialect of it, is spoken by the Kurds, Yazidis, Shabaks, and Sarlyas. The ancient Syriac dialect, although retained by the Assyrians, is gradually acquiring the character of a church language. Another Syriac dialect, Mandaean, is the liturgical language of the Sabaeans. A Persian dialect is spoken by the Lurs, while the Turkomans speak a Turkic dialect.

⁸RELIGION

Islam is the national religion of Iraq, adhered to by about 95% of the population. The principle of religious freedom guaranteed by the 1925 constitution was reaffirmed by the revolutionary government in its provisional constitution. The vast majority of Iraqis profess either Sunni or Shi'i Islam, but there are some heterodox Muslim sects. The Yazidis, numbering about 60,000, consider Satan a fallen angel, who will one day be reconciled with God. They propitiate him in their rites and regard the Old and New Testaments as well as the Qur'an as sacred.

Christianity claims some 250,000 adherents, belonging to various branches of Oriental Christianity. The Assyrians (who are not descended from the ancient Assyrians) are Nestorians. About 100,000 indigenous Christian "Chaldaeans," originally also Nestorians, joined, in the 19th century, under the influence of Roman Catholic missions, the Uniate churches, which are in communion with Rome. Their patriarch has his seat in Mosul. The Sabaeans, or Mandaeans, are often called Christians of St. John, but their religious belief and their liturgy contain elements of many creeds, including some of pre-Christian Oriental origin.

Since baptism is their main ritual, they always dwell near water and are concentrated on the river banks south of Baghdad. They number about 12,000.

There are some Monophysite Jacobites and about 25,000 Syrian Catholics; Roman Catholics and Orthodox Armenians together number about 4,000. Iraq's Jewish community, in sharp decline in recent decades, numbers about 500.

⁹TRANSPORTATION

Until the beginning of this century, the caravan was the main mode of transportation. Motor vehicles have superseded the camel, but still follow the caravan routes. In 1974, roads totaled 11,096 km, of which 4,441 km were paved. In that year, 137,087 motor vehicles were in use, including 61,062 private automobiles, 27,670 taxis, 12,591 buses, and 35,764 trucks.

Railroads are owned and operated by the Iraqi State Railways Administration. The standard-gauge railroad connects Iraq with Syria. The meter-gauge line connects Irbil in the north with Basrah by way of Kirkuk and Baghdad. In 1974 there were 2,218 km of railway lines.

Baghdad is an important air terminal; Basrah and Mosul (opened in 1973) also are international airports. Iraq Airways is the state-owned carrier. Some 20 other international airlines serve Iraq, including Aeroflot, Air France, Air India, BA, KLM, MEA, and SAS.

In 1974, Iraq had 13 merchant vessels (including 7 tankers) totaling 201,000 gross tons. Basrah, the major seaport, handles Iraq's international trade and is a transit point for overland transport to Iran. In 1974, 637 cargo vessels unloaded 2,715,000 tons of goods at the port. The new port of Umm Qasr handled 87,000 tons of cargo in 1974.

¹⁰COMMUNICATIONS

In 1974, Iraq had 348 post and telegraph offices. In that year, the country had 1,071 central telephone exchanges (compared with 483 in 1968) with 152,932 telephones, including 100,720 in Baghdad.

Radio and television broadcasting is operated by the government. Radio Baghdad, the only station, transmits in Arabic, on short- and medium-waves from 12 transmitters. It also has English and Kurdish broadcasts; some other foreign-language broadcasts have been added. A television station was opened in Baghdad in 1956, and by 1973, 6 television transmitters were in use. In 1973, there were 1,250,000 radios and 520,000 television sets in use in Iraq.

¹¹HISTORY

Iraq became a separate nation after the breakup of the defeated Ottoman Empire in 1918. The country, historically also called Mesopotamia, was assigned as a mandate to the UK; in 1932, it attained its independence and was admitted to the League of Nations.

Iraq's history, however, begins in ancient times. Some of man's earliest settlements from prehistoric times are found in present-day Iraq. Habitations, shrines, implements, and pottery found on various sites can be dated as early as the 5th millennium B.C. Some sites bear names that have been familiar from the Bible, which considered the "land between the two streams" the location of the Garden of Eden and "Ur of the Chaldees" the native land of the patriarch Abraham. Scientific exploration and archaelogical research have amplified, confirmed, and systematized the half-historical, half-legendary biblical reports.

Recorded history in Mesopotamia began with the Sumerians, whose original linguistic affinities have not yet been established with certainty. By the 3d millennium B.C. they had established city-states, and the records and accounts on clay tablets prove that they had a complex economic organization before 3200 B.C. The reign of Sumer was challenged by King Sargon of Akkad (c.2400 B.C.); but a Sumero-Akkadian culture continued in Erech (Tall al-Warka') and Ur (Tall al-Muqayyar) until it was superseded by the Semitic Babylonians (c.2000 B.C.) and Assyrians (beginning c.1800 B.C., but gaining chief importance only in the 1st millennium B.C.). The cultural height of Babylonian history is represented by Hammurabi (c.1792–1749 B.C.), who lent his name to a celebrated code of laws.

From Assur, their stronghold in the north, the Assyrians in turn challenged Babylon (c.1300 B.C.). Their great personalities figure as leaders, adversaries, or possible succor in the Old Testament. Their capital was Nineveh (Ninawa). At its height, Assyrian supremacy extended to Egypt. It had, however, to yield to the Scythians, who destroyed Nineveh in 606 B.C. Nebuchadnezzar rebuilt the city-state of Babylon (7th century B.C.), but it fell to Cyrus, the Achaemenian, in 539 B.C. Under his son Cambyses, the Persian Empire extended from the Oxus River to the Mediterranean, with its center in Mesopotamia. Its might, in turn, was challenged by the Greeks. Led by the Macedonian conqueror Alexander the Great, they defeated the Persians and penetrated deep into their lands. Alexander himself died in Babylon (323 B.C.) but the penetration of Greece into Asia endured.

The Seleucids, Alexander's successors in Syria, Mesopotamia, and Persia, built their capital, Seleucia, on the Tigris, just south of Baghdad. They had to yield power to the Parthians, who conquered Iraq in 138 B.C.

The Arabs conquered Iraq in A.D. 637. For a century, under the "Orthodox" and the Umayyad caliphs, Iraq remained a province of the Islamic Empire; but the 'Abbasids (750–1258) made it the focus of their power. In their new capital, Baghdad, their most illustrious member, Harun al-Rashid (r.787–809), a contemporary of Charlemagne, became, through the *Arabian Nights,* a legend for all times. Under Harun and his son al-Ma'mun, Baghdad was the center of brilliant intellectual and cultural life. Two centuries later, the Seljuq vizier Nizam al-Mulk established the famous Nizamiyah University, one of whose professors was the philosopher al-Ghazali (Ghazel, d.1111). A Mongol invasion in the early 13th century ended Iraq's flourishing economy and culture. In 1258, Genghis Khan's grandson Hulagu sacked Baghdad and destroyed the canal system on which the productivity of the region had always depended. Tamerlane conquered Baghdad and Iraq in 1393. Meanwhile, the Ottoman Turks had established themselves in Asia Minor and, by capturing Cairo (1517), their sultans claimed legitimate succession to the caliphate. In 1534, Süleyman the Magnificent conquered Baghdad and, except for a short period of Persian control in the 17th century, Iraq remained an Ottoman province.

Late in 1914, the Ottoman Empire entered World War I on the side of the Central Powers. A British expeditionary force landed in Iraq and occupied Basrah in November 1914. The long campaign that followed ended in 1918, when the whole of Iraq fell under British military occupation. The collapse of the Ottoman Empire stimulated Iraqi hopes for freedom and independence, but, in 1920, Iraq was declared a League of Nations mandate under UK administration. Riots and revolts led to the establishment of an Iraqi provisional government in October 1920. On 23 August 1921, Faysal, the son of Sharif Husayn bin 'Ali of Mecca, became king of Iraq. In successive stages, the last of which was a treaty of preferential alliance with the UK (June 1930), Iraq gained independence in 1932 and was admitted to membership in the League of Nations.

Faysal died in 1933. His young son and successor Ghazi was killed in an accident in 1939. Until the accession to the throne of Faysal II, on attaining his majority in 1953, his uncle 'Abdul Ilah, Ghazi's brother, acted as regent.

On 14 July 1958 the army rose under the leadership of Brig. 'Abd al-Karim al-Qasim (Kassim). Faysal II and Prime Minister Nuri al-Sa'id were killed. An agrarian reform law broke up the

great landholdings of feudal leaders and a new economic development program emphasized industrialization. Education and labor organizations were greatly expanded. In 1960, political parties were allowed to function again. In spite of some opposition from original supporters and political opponents, tribal uprisings, and several attempts at assassination, Qasim managed to remain the head of Iraq for four and a half years. On 9 February 1963, however, a military junta, led by Col. 'Abd al-Salam Muhammad al-'Arif, overthrew his regime and executed Qasim. The new regime followed a policy based on neutralism and aiming at cooperation with Syria and Egypt and improved relations with Turkey and Iran. These policies were continued after 'Arif was killed in an accident in 1966 and was succeeded by his brother, 'Abd al-Rahman al-'Arif. The 'Arif regime, however, was overthrown in July 1968 when Gen. (later, Marshal) Ahmad Hasan Bakr, heading a section of the Ba'th Party, staged a coup

See continental political: front cover H6; physical: back cover H6

LOCATION: 29° to 37°30'N; 39° to 48°E. **BOUNDARY LENGTHS:** Turkey, 305 km (190 mi); Iran, 1,515 km (941 mi); Persian Gulf coastline, 19 km (12 mi); Kuwayt, 254 km (158 mi); Sa'udi Arabia, 895 km (556 mi); Jordan 147 km (91 mi); Syria, 603 km (375 mi). **TERRITORIAL SEA LIMIT:** 12 mi.

and established a new government with himself as president. From the start, Bakr's policies were characterized by suppression of all opponents. In the 1970s, the Ba'th regime focused increasingly on economic problems, nationalizing the petroleum industry in 1972–73 and allocating large sums for capital development.

Since 1961, Iraq's Kurdish minority has frequently opposed with violence attempts by Baghdad to impose authority over its regions. In an attempt to cope with this opposition, the revolutionary government passed a constitutional amendment in July 1970 granting limited political, economic, and cultural autonomy to the Kurdish regions. But in March 1974, Kurdish insurgents, known as the Pesh Merga, again mounted a revolt, reportedly with Iranian military support. The Iraqi army countered with a major offensive against the Kurds during August. On 6 March 1975, Iraq and Iran concluded an agreement in which Iraq made certain border concessions in return for Iran's renunciation of its support for the Kurds. Kurdish resistance quickly collapsed and a cease-fire was arranged on 13 March.

¹²GOVERNMENT

The coup d'etat of 14 July 1958 established a regime surmounted by the military. Until his execution in February 1963, 'Abd al-Karim al-Qasim ruled Iraq, with a Council of State and a cabinet. On 27 July 1958, a fortnight after taking over, Qasim's regime issued a provisional constitution, which has remained in effect, although it was amended in 1966, 1970, and 1974 to accommodate changes in the status of the Kurdish regions. Under Marshal Bakr, the government was headed in 1975 by a Revolutionary Command Council and a cabinet composed of military and civilian leaders. Besides serving as president (head of state), Bakr was chairman of the Revolutionary Command Council and prime minister in the cabinet. He was also commander-in-chief of the armed forces and secretary-general of the Ba'th Party.

¹³POLITICAL PARTIES

Under the monarchy, Nuri al-Sa'id dominated Iraq with the support of the upper-middle and upper classes. Tribal, religious, and local loyalties took precedence over any attachments to Iraqi nationalism. The existing parties, recruited largely from the middle classes, were opposed to the entrenched interests of the rich; they were often labeled subversive even when they asked only for their democratic rights.

Some political parties had been created at the demand of Faysal I, who considered the existence of parties desirable for the political development of Iraq. During the decade 1935–45, however, they were ineffective as political factors. In 1946, the formation of parties was again permitted and five were founded. These had a wide range and included one that was Socialist (al-Hizb al-Watani al-Dimuqrati, or the National Democratic Party), one avowedly close to communism (al-Sha'b, or the People's Party), and one purely reformist (al-Ittihad al-Watani, or the National Union Party).

The response to these parties alarmed the conservative politicians. The Palestine War (1948) provided the pretext for suppression of the Sha'b and Ittihad parties. Only the National Democratic Party functioned uninterruptedly; in 1950, with the lifting of martial law, the others resumed work. Nuri al-Sa'id founded in 1949 the Constitutional Union Party (al-Ittihad al-Dusturi), with a pro-Western, liberal reform program to attract both the old and the young generations. In opposition, Salih Jabr, a former partisan of Nuri's turned rival, founded the Nation's Socialist Party (al-Ummah al-Ishtirakiyah), which advocated a democratic and nationalistic, pro-Western and pan-Arab policy. In 1954, however, Nuri al-Sa'id dissolved all parties, including his own Constitutional Union Party, on the ground that they had resorted to violence during the elections of that year.

After the coup of 1958, parties "voluntarily" discontinued their activities, but the Communists tried to form a National Union Party to include themselves, Kurdish sympathizers, and dissidents from the National Democratic Party. In January 1960, Premier Qasim issued a new law allowing political parties to operate again. Since that time, however, successive coups have thwarted their growth.

The Ba'thists, who first gained strength in Syria in the 1950s as a pan-Arab movement with strong nationalist and socialist leanings, had attracted a following among elements of the Syrian military. In February 1963, Qasim was overthrown and executed by officers affiliated with a conservative wing of Iraq's Ba'th movement. In November, a second coup was attempted by Ba'thist extremists from the left, who acted with complicity of the ruling Syrian wing of the party. 'Arif and the moderates survived the coup, and in the aftermath, Iraq's Ba'th organization receded from prominence. In July 1974, the government established the Iraqi Arab Socialist Union as the country's sole political party. With the 1968 coup, rightist elements of the Ba'th Party were installed in prominent positions by Gen. Bakr. Since then, the Ba'thists, organized as the Arab Ba'th Socialist Party, have been the ruling political group in Iraq.

A continuing source of internal instability in recent years has been the clamor of the large Kurdish minority for a separate state. Intermittent hostilities continued through the 1970s although, in 1966 and 1970, the government made far-reaching concessions to the Kurds to restore unity to the country. Following the Kurdish defeat in the 1974–75 war, the demands of the Democratic Party of Kurdistan—the political wing of the Kurdish movement—to participate in a negotiated settlement of the dispute were turned down by the Bakr government.

¹⁴LOCAL GOVERNMENT

Iraq is divided into 16 governorates (muhafazat; sing., muhafaza), each headed by a governor (mutasarrif) with a council. Governorates are subdivided into districts (aqdiya; sing., qada'), each under a deputy governor (qa'immaqam). A district consists of counties (nawahin; sing., nahiyah), the smallest units, each under a director (mudir). Towns and cities are administered by municipal councils (baladiyat; sing., baladiyah) each led by a mayor (ra'is al-baladiyah). Baghdad's municipality, the "governorate of the capital" (Amanat al-'Asimah) under its mayor or "guardian of the capital" (Amin al-'Asimah), serves as a model municipality. The settlement reached with the Kurds in 1970 provided for Kurdish autonomy in the muhafazat, aqdiya, and nawahin populated mainly by them. On 11 March 1974, the constitution was further amended to provide the Kurdistan region with an elected 80-member legislative council. However, the amendment provided for an appointed membership for an unspecified "transitional period."

The desert areas are under the administration of the Ministry of the Interior. They are divided into three separate districts or territories with a director for each: the Jazirah Desert (Badiyat al-Jazirah), Northern Desert (al-Badiyah al-Shamaliyah), and Southern Desert (al-Badiyah al-Janubiyah).

¹⁵JUDICIAL SYSTEM

The constitution provides for civil, religious, and special courts.

The civil courts have jurisdiction over civil, commercial, and criminal cases except for those that fall under the jursidiction of the religious courts. Those of the first instance have either limited (cases not exceeding ID500 in value) or general jurisdiction. Each category is presided over by a single judge. The limited courts sit at all governorate (muhafaza), district (qada'), and important county (nahiyah) headquarters. Courts of general jurisdiction are established at governorate headquarters and in the principal districts.

Magistrates' courts try criminal cases in the first instance but they cannot try cases involving punishment of more than seven years in prison. Such cases are tried in courts of sessions that are also appellate instances for magistrates' courts. Each judicial district (Baghdad, Kirkuk, Mosul, al-Hillah, Diyala, and Basrah) has courts of sessions presided over by a bench of three judges. There are no jury trials. The highest court of appeal is the Court of Cassation in Baghdad, with civil and criminal divisions. It is composed of 10 judges, including a president and two vice-presidents.

Cases involving the personal status of Sunni or Shi'i Muslims, Jews, Christians, and other religious sects are judged according to their own religious laws by religious courts. They also adminster the religious foundations (awqaf).

The sources for the legal system reflect the political history of the country as well as its religious diversity. Secular law is derived from Western patterns. The French legal thought of the Ottoman code of criminal law has been replaced by the British, with modifications of the codes established in Egypt (the Baghdad Penal Code) and the Sudan (the Baghdad Criminal Procedure Regulations). These codes have been amended but not superseded.

[16]ARMED FORCES
Military service is compulsory for men for two years. Women also serve in the armed forces. The total strength of the armed forces in 1974 was 135,000 (compared with 78,000 in 1969). The army had 120,000 men in three armored and four infantry divisions. In addition, army reserves numbered about 250,000. Equipment included some 1,290 tanks of Soviet origin. The navy, with a strength of about 3,000, had 29 motor torpedo and patrol boats. The air force had 12,000 men and 247 combat aircraft. Paramilitary forces included a 10,000-member national guard and about 9,000 others.

[17]MIGRATION
Immigration into Iraq comes mainly from Iran and other neighboring countries, but is not considerable. In the mid-1970s there were an estimated 30,000 resident aliens in Iraq, of whom about 40% were Iranians and the remainder mostly Jordanians, Syrians, other Arabs, and Pakistanis. Emigration is negligible, although an increasing number of young men, particularly from the depressed southern villages, migrate to the oil fields of Kuwayt. During the 1974–75 fighting in Kurdistan, some 130,000 Kurds, mostly women, children, and elderly people, fled to Iran to escape the conflict, and an additional 5,000 refugees entered Turkey. They were later joined by several Kurdish fighting contingents. Thousands subsequently returned to Iraq under an Iraqi government amnesty extended into April 1975.

A large wave of internal migration continues from the villages into the cities, especially Baghdad and Basrah, where the migrants form the unskilled labor force or swell the ranks of the unemployed. Much of this migration is seasonal.

[18]INTERNATIONAL COOPERATION
Iraq is a founding member of the UN and its specialized agencies and a charter member of the Arab League. Iraq also is a member of many other intergovernmental organizations, including OPEC. It was a member of the Baghdad Pact (later CENTO) but withdrew after the 1958 revolution when positive neutralism became the international policy of the new regime. Iraq has given both military and economic support to Arab parties to the conflict with Israel.

[19]ECONOMY
Oil is the most important sector of the economy, providing about one-fourth of the national income in the 1970s. Petroleum production, which began at Kirkuk in 1927, averaged 1,976,000 barrels daily in 1974, with a total of 719.3 million produced for the year. A nationalization program initiated during 1972–73 resulted in government control of virtually all national production by 1975, including full ownership of the predominant Iraqi Petroleum Co. Oil revenues provided 87% of the financing for the 1970–74 development plan. But agriculture remains the principal occupation, involving somewhat less than one-third of the total population.

Industry, apart from oil exploitation and refining, is a growing factor in the economy, although industrial development remains handicapped by lack of raw materials other than oil, insufficient private capital for investment, traditional preference for investing in land, lack of credit for the small entrepreneur and investor, and lack of skilled labor.

The greatest obstacle to the development of a stable economy and general prosperity is still the traditional imbalance between a relatively small number of large landholders or businessmen and the overwhelming majority of fallahin, with minute or no holdings of land, and small wage earners (government clerks or unskilled workmen). In addition, much of the domestic economy is based on barter or compensation in kind rather than cash. Recent reforms by the Ba'th regime have failed to come to grips fully with these traditional obstacles.

[20]INCOME
The national income for 1973 was estimated at ID1,802.3 million; per capita income was put at ID173.08. Between 1965 and 1972, the GNP rose from ID738.2 million to ID1,299.8 million. From 1965 to 1972, the average annual rate of growth of real GDP at factor cost was 8.2%. The 1972 GDP was distributed as follows: crude oil production, 25.3%; agriculture, forestry, and fishing, 21%; public administration and defense, 10.3%; industry, 9.9%; wholesale and retail trade, 8.1%; services, 6.9%; and other sectors, 18.5%. The 1970–74 development plan contemplated a 7.1% annual increase in national income. In 1974, domestic fixed capital formation at 1962 constant prices was estimated at ID305.6 million, compared with ID126 million in 1965.

[21]LABOR
Although, according to the 1965 census, the total labor force was 4.6 million, the active labor force was only a fraction of this total. Government estimates place the total work force at 2.7 million in 1970 and 3.3 million in 1975. Of the latter total, only about 9% were women; about 10% of the female population in the age 10–59 category were working in 1975, compared with a 52% rate for males in the same age group. Agriculture engages about half of the total manpower, but most of the work is seasonal, leaving the laborers unemployed for a large part of the year. Government service is the largest single employer; in 1972, the total number of persons working for government and semigovernment agencies was 385,978, of whom 12.5% were women. The shortage of skilled labor grows as industry increases. Child labor is prevalent, especially in traditional crafts. Children of 10 may work as apprentices, but may not constitute more than 20% of all workers employed in any one establishment. Women usually work in family enterprises or in agriculture.

Labor legislation regulates minimum wages, working hours, compensation for injuries, disease, and loss of life, and weekly and annual holidays. The minimum wage for skilled and unskilled labor is 270 fils ($0.76) a day. Children must be paid not less than 40% of the average pay for adults in the shop. Several social security laws have been enacted but they are so far enforceable only in the larger urban factories.

The organized labor movement in Iraq owes its existence and growth to the post-1958 regimes. In 1975, Iraq's General Federation of Trade Unions had 154 affiliated unions and branches, with a total of 859,639 workers. In addition, 418,863 agricultural workers were organized into 6,228 farmers' societies.

[22]AGRICULTURE
The large water supply from rainfall (in the north) and rivers, the rich alluvial soil of the lowlands, and an elaborate system of irrigation canals made Iraq a granary in ancient times and in the Middle Ages. After the irrigation works were destroyed in the Mongol invasion, agriculture decayed. Even in modern Iraq, about half of the population derive their income directly from cultivation and animal husbandry. However, only 46% of the area is arable, the rest desert and semidesert; only 29% of the arable land (5.75 million hectares) is cultivated, 48% by dry farming and 52% by irrigation.

Until the early 1960s, most of the land was owned by tribal shaykhs or large landowners, mostly urban absentee landlords. In 1953, an estimated 7,732 owners holding more than 97 hectares each controlled a major part of the land. Most peasants were sharecroppers who delivered up to 50% of their crops to their landlords. In 1959, the revolutionary government promulgated agrarian reform laws amending and amplifying previous attempts at agrarian reform. Various measures subsequently adopted led to the enactment in 1970 of a new agrarian reform law that limited permissible landholdings to 4 to 202 hectares, depending on location, fertility, and available irrigation facilities. A Supreme Agricultural Council administers or distributes confiscated landholdings. Up to 2,548,500 hectares of land were sequestrated, of which 1,465,700 hectares were distributed among 157,862 beneficiaries. Agrarian reform has been accompanied by irrigation and drainage works to increase the cultivable area, and by the establishment of cooperative societies for the provision of implements and machinery, irrigation facilities, and other services. By 1974, 1,386 agricultural cooperatives had been organized, with a combined membership of 217,723 and total area of 3.4 million hectares. In addition, 72 state-owned collective farms had been set up, with 11,253 members and 133,730 hectares. By 1975, irrigation was being aided by 12 dams and barrages, and strict water-use regulations. Among these, the Greater Mussayib project irrigates 83,750 hectares through three canals, and is designed to settle 2,800 farm families and to provide livelihood for about 50,000 persons.

While noteworthy, these reforms have thus far resulted in only marginal increases in agricultural production. In 1974, Iraq produced 1.34 million tons of wheat (compared with 1.18 million tons in 1969); 533,000 tons of barley; 68,000 tons of rice; and 40,000 tons of cotton. Iraq is the world's largest producer and exporter of dates; 385,000 tons were produced in 1973/74. Other crops included millet, durrah, lentils, beans, cucumbers, melons, figs, and nuts. Sugarcane, tobacco (government monopoly), and mulberries are grown mainly for domestic use.

23 ANIMAL HUSBANDRY
Animal husbandry is widespread. Sheep raising is most important; wool is exported, mainly to the UK, or used for weaving carpets and cloaks. In the mid-1970s there were about 5 million sheep; goats, raised mainly by nomads, numbered 1.5 million. Some 1.3 million head of cattle predominated in north and central Iraq. They were used for ploughing, transport, and operating irrigation wheels. There were also numerous donkeys, mules, camels, and horses. About 200,000 buffalo are the principal farm animals in the southern riverine areas. An occasional peasant owns an ox or a donkey as a draft animal; hogs are not raised in the country.

Iraq has a surplus in its meat supply; in 1974, 1.6 million sheep were slaughtered, 543,000 goats, 306,000 cows, 27,000 buffalo, and 20,000 camels. In addition, 3.1 million chickens and 83.1 million eggs were produced, with egg production concentrated on state farms.

24 FISHING
Centuries of overfishing without restocking have reduced the formerly plentiful supply of river fish. The 1974 catch of freshwater fish (including salmon that weigh up to 300 lb. and, especially in the Tigris, carp) was 9,443 tons. Iraq is making increased commercial use of Persian Gulf fish, with 6,200 tons caught in 1974.

25 FORESTRY
Forests of oak and Aleppo pine cover only 16,800 sq km (less than 4% of Iraq's entire area) in the northern governorates of Irbil, Nineveh, Diyala, al-Sulaymaniyah, and Kirkuk. They have been depleted by excessive cutting for fuel or charcoal, by fires and overgrazing. Since 1954, indiscriminate cutting has been prohibited, and charcoal production has ceased. The Ministry of Agriculture's forestry division has established tree nurseries, but lacks funds and trained personnel for adequate forest care and preservation. In 1974, some 9,900 hectares had been replanted with 1.66 million seedlings. In that year, a total of 3.87 million seedlings were produced and distributed nationally.

26 MINING
In 1974, Iraq was the eighth-largest producer of oil in the world. Accounting for 25% of national income, oil is the mainstay of the national economy. Oil revenues (ID364.1 million in 1972) help

balance the budget, stabilize the currency, establish a surplus balance of payments, and finance the development program through the Development Board and the Industrial Bank. Crude oil production in 1974 amounted to 719.3 million barrels, with more than 10 billion barrels produced during 1965-74. At the current rate of production, Iraq's current reserves are expected to near depletion by the 1990s.

The most important fields are at Kirkuk, with lesser fields at Naft Khaneh, 'Ayn Zalah, and Butmah in the Mosul area, and at al-Zubayr and Rumaylah near Basrah. From Kirkuk, the oil for export to the foreign market is piped to the Mediterranean. Until 1949, two 12-inch pipelines with an annual capacity of over 2 million tons each brought the oil to Tripoli in Lebanon and to Haifa in Palestine. In consequence of the war with Israel, the latter was shut down. In 1949, a new 16-inch line to Tripoli in Lebanon brought the output to 6 million tons. In 1952, a line to al-Baniyas in Syria was completed, with an annual capacity of 13.5 million tons. A new pipeline links wells of the Basrah Petroleum Co. with Iraq's oil terminal at al-Faw. In 1970, the contract for the construction of a 28-inch pipeline from the North Rumaylah field to al-Faw on the Gulf, a distance of about 90 miles, was awarded to a French company, and another pipeline from the field to the Mediterranean was projected.

Oil concessions were first granted in 1925 and the first production began two years later. The immense expansion is evident in its rise from 28,185,000 long tons in 1953 to 95,574,000 long tons in 1974.

In 1974, the three oil companies operating in Iraq controlled production as follows: 44,379,000 long tons by the Iraq Co. for Oil Operations (ICOO), 42,727,000 long tons by the Basrah Petroleum Co. (BPC), and 8,468,000 long tons by the Iraq National Oil Co. (INOC).

By 1975, as a result of nationalizations carried out since 1972, state-owned operations controlled 100% of national oil production. On 1 June 1972, ICOO, a national enterprise, took over the foreign-held Iraqi Petroleum Co., developer of the country's first field at Kirkuk. In March 1973, ICOO added the Mosul Petroleum Co. to its holdings. INOC, another government enterprise, began production at its North Rumaylah field in 1972, with annual production expected to reach 20 million tons. An agreement was signed with the USSR in 1969 for a $70-million loan to finance the exploitation of the North Rumaylah field directly by INOC, and drilling on the first well of the field was started in July 1970. In addition, INOC had by late 1973 acquired a 43% share of the BPC, taking over the 23.75% holding of US interests, the 14.25% Dutch holding, and the 5% held by the Gulbenkian Foundation. On 8 December 1975, the government completed the take-over of BPC. In 1974, oil companies also produced 328,963 million cu feet of natural gas.

Iraq's non-oil mineral resources are limited. Exploitation is rendered uneconomical by inadequate transport facilities and lack of coal for processing the ores. Geological surveys have indicated usable deposits of iron ore, copper, sulfur and sulfur compounds, gypsum, bitumen, dolomite, and marble; but so far, these resources have remained largely unexploited. In 1970, development of the sulfur deposits in Mishraq was begun in collaboration with Poland. In 1973, 395,000 tons were produced; the capacity of the field is expected eventually to reach 1 million tons a year. In the 1970s, about 50,000 tons of salt were also being produced annually.

27 ENERGY AND POWER
The development of both hydroelectric and thermal capacity has proceeded rapidly during the 1970s. In Baghdad, electricity is supplied by the Baghdad Light and Power Co. This thermoelectric fuel-oil plant was installed by British-Belgian firms, but was later nationalized and supplemented by a second plant. Other cities generate power in small municipal power stations.

Total electricity production in 1973 was 2,919 million kwh (1,914 million in 1969), of which Baghdad accounted for 2,289 million kwh (78.4%). Facilities owned by the National Electricity Administration accounted for 98.5% of the total amount of electricity produced in 1973.

28 INDUSTRY

Main industries are oil refining, food processing, textiles, leather goods, cement and other building materials, tobacco, paper, and sulfur extraction. In 1972, manufacturing comprised 9.9% of the GDP, as compared with 8% in 1965.

In 1974, Iraq had seven oil refineries, all managed by the government's Oil Refineries Administration. The oldest installation in Iraq is the Wand refinery at Kanaqin, built in 1931. The Daura refinery, built by the government in 1955, is the country's largest, with a daily capacity of 75,000 barrels. The government's Basrah refinery began production in 1974 with a capacity of 70,000 barrels. In 1973, 1,076 million gallons of petroleum products, including 226 million gallons of light fuel oil, were produced in Iraq.

In 1964, the government took over all establishments producing asbestos, cement, cigarettes, textiles, paper, tanned leather, and flour.

A cotton textile mill at al-Kut, completed in 1969, has an annual production capacity of 30.5 million meters of fabrics and 632 tons of cotton yarn. Other relatively new public sector industrial establishments include a sulfur plant at Kirkuk, a fertilizer plant at Basrah, an antibiotic factory at Samarra', an agricultural implements factory at Iskandariyah, an electric equipment factory near Baghdad, and a sugar mill at Maisan. In 1976, plans were announced for construction by US and Federal Republic of Germany firms of a $1-billion chemical complex at Basrah. The plant is expected to produce 150,000 tons annually of polyethylene and polyvinyl chloride, as well as 40,000 tons of caustic soda.

Expenditures on industry in execution of various economic plans during the 10 years ending in 1969 averaged 29% of the total spent on all sectors of the economy; during 1970–74 industry's share of these allocations fell to an annual average of 20%.

29 DOMESTIC TRADE

Two kinds of trading are practiced. The first consists of modern shops that serve almost exclusively a small group of well-to-do persons, mainly in the large cities. The second caters in the traditional ways of the bazaars to most of the population. Baghdad, Mosul, Basrah, and Kirkuk, being road and railway centers, serve as distribution points for the wholesale and import trade. Basrah is Iraq's only port of entry for foreign, ship-borne goods. The customer in the bazaar usually buys in very small quantities, and bargaining is common practice.

Baghdad leads in wholesale trade and in the number of retail shops. The modern department stores close on Sundays, while the bazaar shops are always open except on Muslim holidays and generally for an hour on Fridays during the noon prayer.

30 FOREIGN TRADE

Iraq's most valuable export article is oil, most of which goes to the European market. Between 1969 and 1974, the value of oil exports increased by 581%. In 1974, crude petroleum exports were valued at ID2,357 million, or 96% of the total export volume; these more than covered the trade deficit of ID576.5 million in all other items. Iraq is the world's greatest exporter of dates, the better varieties going to Western Europe, Australia, and North America. The UK, the USSR, Japan, Italy, France, and China were the principal suppliers of Iraq's imports in 1974. Iraq imports industrial machinery, vehicles and parts, and iron and steel. Imported consumer goods include tea, sugar, textiles, and dairy products.

Principal exports in 1974 (in millions of Iraqi dinars) were:

Petroleum	2,357.1
Dates, other fruits and vegetables	9.4
Petroleum products	8.3
Hides and skins	2.4
Crude animal and vegetable materials	1.6
Cement and nonmetallic mineral manufactures	1.3
Other exports	73.5
TOTAL	2,453.6

Principal imports in 1974 (in millions of Iraqi dinars) were:

Machinery and transport equipment	184.5
Iron and steel	123.7
Cereals	79.2
Sugar	59.5
Chemicals and fertilizers	42.3
Miscellaneous manufactures	16.5
Animal and vegetable oils	12.6
Dairy products	10.1
Other imports	144.6
TOTAL	673.0

Iraq's principal suppliers in 1974 included Japan (11.9% of total imports), FRG (8.4%), US (8.3%), France (7.7%), UK (5.6%), and USSR (4.8%). Iraq's oil exports, totaling ID2,357 million in 1974, are not reported by country of destination. In the mid-1970s, however, large quantities of Iraqi oil were known to have been sold to EEC countries and Japan.

31 BALANCE OF PAYMENTS

The foreign currency gained from oil exports covers the deficit in Iraq's trade balance. At the end of 1975, the international reserves of the Central Bank of Iraq amounted to $2,727.3 million, and the exchange holdings of the commercial banks totaled $89.8 million.

Following are balance-of-payments summaries for 1970 and 1974 (in millions of dollars):

	1970	1974
Merchandise balance	639	3,824
Services balance	−540	−1,433
Private transfers, net	1	—
Government transfers, net	1	− 13
Long-term capital	18	− 255
Short-term capital	1	37
Errors and omissions	−123	− 252
TOTALS	− 3	1,908

At the end of 1974, the Iraqi currency cover was as follows: foreign assets, 84.3% (32.7% in 1965); and gold bullion, 15.7% (37.3% in 1965).

32 BANKING

Since 1964, banking has been fully nationalized. The system comprises the Central Bank of Iraq, commercial banks, and a part of the accounts of sarrafs (moneylenders) who are licensed to engage in banking activities. The commercial banks include five specialized state-owned banks: the Agricultural Bank, the Industrial Bank, the Estate Bank, the Mortgage Bank, and the Cooperative Bank.

At the end of December 1974, private deposits amounted to ID224.1 million (including ID89.3 million in current accounts, ID112.9 million in savings accounts, and ID21.9 million in fixed deposits), as against ID100.2 million in 1969. Deposits in postal savings banks amounted to ID12.4 million, made by 222,309 individuals. Government and semigovernment deposits with commercial banks at the end of 1974 totaled ID199.6 million (including ID103.3 million in current accounts, ID751,000 in savings accounts, and ID95.6 million in fixed deposits).

Money supply as of 31 December 1974 totaled ID380.6 million (currency in circulation ID358.6 million, and demand deposits ID22.0 million).

33 INSURANCE
Insurance was nationalized in Iraq in 1964. The State Insurance Organization supervises and maintains three companies: the National Insurance Co., the Iraqi Life Insurance Co., and the Iraqi Reinsurance Co., with respective shares of 60.8%, 4.5%, and 34.7% of ID37,935,000, the total gross premium income in 1974. Non-life premium income in 1974 increased 120% over 1973, reinsurance 72%, and life 51%.

Third-party motor liability insurance is compulsory.

34 SECURITIES
Preference for investing savings in rural or urban real estate is common. Major private investments in industrial enterprises can be secured only by assurance of financial assistance from the government. There is as yet no developed capital market, and only the beginnings of a small market in stocks and shares traded through the banks.

35 PUBLIC FINANCE
There are several budgets, the ordinary budget under which the regular activities of the government are financed, and four separate budgets, those of the Iraqi State Railways, the Port of Basrah Authority, the al-Faw Dredging Scheme, and the tobacco monopoly. All are submitted at the same time and enacted under the same law. Municipal budgets require governmental approval; those of semi-independent government agencies require the approval only of the Minister of Finance. In addition there is a separate development budget.

Revenues and expenditures under the central government's ordinary budgets for 1972/73 (actual) and 1974/75 (estimated), in thousands of Iraqi dinars, were:

	1972/73	1974/75
REVENUES		
Oil revenues	109,303	497,100
Other direct taxes and duties	40,766	35,876
Indirect taxes	63,320	67,746
Revenues from government administrations	31,670	35,838
Other revenues	25,471	20,751
TOTALS	270,530	657,311
EXPENDITURES		
Education	71,451	122,656
Financial and economic affairs	39,100	84,012
Pensions and benefits	27,493	38,000
Health	17,635	32,733
Municipal affairs and works	13,637	32,183
Interior and justice	5,489	8,192
Other expenditures	170,554	339,535
TOTALS	345,359	657,311

The public debt is relatively small, since expenditures generally have been kept close to revenues. Several foreign loans were granted to Iraq, but most have been repaid. At the end of 1974, the public debt totaled ID251.98 million, of which ID107.92 million was domestic and ID144.06 million external.

36 TAXATION
Direct taxes are levied on income and on property. The rental value of dwellings, commercial buildings, and nonagricultural land is taxed at 10%, with a certain tax-free minimum. In 1939, graduated income tax rates were established on income from all sources except agriculture. An amendment in 1943 established a surtax on incomes, but exemptions were raised in 1952. Most agricultural income and inheritances are not taxed. In 1973/74, income tax revenues amounted to ID28.4 million, of which public-sector enterprises provided 73.8%; private sector, 14.9%; and other government sources, 11.3%. Legacy and inheritance taxes were collected from 500 persons.

Indirect taxation predominates. The land tax must be paid by all who farm government lands with or without a lease. Owners of freehold (lazimah) land pay no tax or rent. Much farm produce consumed on the farm or in the village is not taxed at all, but when marketed, farm products are taxed and the tax is collected from wholesalers who buy from the farmers. This tax is 10% on cereals and dates.

37 CUSTOMS AND DUTIES
Since about 1950, tariffs have been used primarily to protect Iraqi industry or to stimulate industries that might eventually reduce the need for foreign imports. This tariff system levies duties on luxury items but has reduced rates on cultural and industrial equipment and on certain raw materials and foodstuffs. It also protects the domestic leather, textile, jute, and cement industries. At times, duty has been lifted from various imported consumer goods, depending on local prices and supplies.

Customs duties are collected on weight, volume, or size. Customs receipts have increased through the growth in imports. Export duties of 5%, later lowered to 1%, were introduced in 1950, but many products remained exempt.

38 FOREIGN INVESTMENTS
Iraqi legislation considers the needs of foreign investors, who are entitled to take back the foreign capital invested. As yet, however, no legislation permits the export of Iraqi dinars earned while operating in the country. The decision is left to the discretion of the Central Bank of Iraq, which has usually authorized the export of dollars if it considered the business to be in the interest of the Iraqi national economy.

The oil industry traditionally comprised the largest and most important foreign investment in Iraq. The revolution of 1958 at first did not produce a change in Iraq's relations with the oil companies. But after continuous pressure and increasingly higher demands on the foreign-dominated Iraqi Petroleum Co., the revolutionary government revoked its concessions, and by the end of 1975 all oil production in Iraq had been brought under state control. Foreign interests, including firms from the US and other Western countries, continued to be active in various sectors of the Iraqi economy through 1976.

39 ECONOMIC POLICY
In order to raise the economic level, the government both controls and participates in petroleum, agriculture, commerce, banking, and industry. In the late 1960s, it made efforts to diversify Iraq's economic relations and to conserve foreign exchange. As an example, it was announced in 1970 that contracts for all planned projects would be awarded to companies willing to receive compensation in crude oil or petroleum products. The government has also undertaken to build an Iraqi tanker fleet to break the monopoly of foreign oil-transport companies. Imports of foreign products and luxury goods have been severely restricted. By the mid-1970s, nationalization had resulted in complete government control of petroleum production, while in agriculture farmers' cooperatives and state and collective farms were becoming increasingly prevalent.

Under the 1970–74 development plan, expenditures were ID1,932 million, with 87% of funding provided from oil revenues. The major categories of expenditures were agriculture, allocated 18% of the total; industry, 20.2%; transport and communications, 11.3%; and construction and services, 13.3%. The 1975 plan envisioned expenditures of ID1,076 million, with industry receiving 41.6% and agriculture 19.3%. While impressive, these statistics leave a margin of doubt in view of the underimplementation of previous plans. Frequent changes in the planning machinery and imbalance in sectoral expenditures compared to allocations have also hampered the fulfillment of planned targets.

40 HEALTH

Health standards are low. Except in the modern quarters of the large cities, sanitary conditions are poor and a high incidence of endemic illness prevails. Although the government has introduced measures for their eradication, hookworm, bilharziasis, and trachoma are still very common. Malaria, tuberculosis, trachoma, measles, and mumps kill thousands each year. Crowded housing conditions contribute to a high incidence of tuberculosis. Infant mortality in 1974 averaged 91.8 per 1,000 births. Average life expectancy in 1975 was estimated at 55.2 years.

Almost all medical facilities are controlled by the government. In 1973, the country had 3,842 physicians (1 for every 2,710 inhabitants), 604 dentists, 226 pharmacists, and 5,682 paramedical personnel. Most physicians prefer to practice in the large cities, and dentists and other specialists are almost unknown in rural districts. In 1973, 52% of the country's doctors practiced in Baghdad.

Social centers in rural districts service several villages and provide health and other social services.

In 1973 there were 160 hospitals of all kinds, with 20,907 beds (1 per 498 inhabitants). Of these hospitals, 13 with 430 beds were private. There were also 1,651 other health institutions, including 328 dispensaries.

41 SOCIAL WELFARE

A social security law passed in 1956 and revised in 1966 regulates working conditions, minimum wages, and age of employment and provides benefits or payments for disability, maternity, old age, unemployment, sickness, and funerals. This law applies to all establishments employing more than 30 people. One-fourth is paid by the insured person; three-fourths are shared by the government and the employer. The new law is based on enlarged insurance and puts less burden directly on the government. In 1974, 15,768 persons received old age, survivors', and disability pensions.

Traditionally, Middle Eastern society is based on the extended family, and its members are entitled to help, sustenance, and protection as a matter of right, not of charity, in illness, old age, or disability. Almsgiving is a religious duty. However, the incipient reorganization of the Iraqi social order through industrialization and migration to the cities is changing this traditional outlook and loosening family ties.

The traditional pious foundations (awqaf), established in perpetuity, have been brought under government control under a director general because of abuses in administration.

42 HOUSING

Living conditions for the sizable population that lives in villages and desert areas are still substandard. Most dwellings are one-room mud huts; better houses may be built partly of stone (in the north) and have more rooms, but are without sanitary facilities and electricity. Rural towns have a greater number of well-built houses with better furniture and sanitary installations; they may even have electricity and piped water; but electricity is expensive and water generally impure.

Though later statistics are not available, the housing situation has changed owing to considerable construction activity in the 1960s and 1970s. In 1974, permits were issued for the construction of 174 multiple dwellings and 27,201 houses.

Most new dwellings have piped water and electricity. In the working out of the state economic plans, construction absorbed a greater share than had been allocated to it, even at the expense of industry and agriculture.

43 EDUCATION

Illiteracy is still high despite increased government efforts to eradicate it. Most villages are served only by the traditional kuttab schools where children are taught the Qur'an and little else, but government schools are beginning to reach some villages. Even so, the average peasant child gets only a rudimentary education. Many children cannot attend school because they are needed for work in the fields. Education is centralized under the Ministry of Education, which appoints teachers, holds examinations, and controls curricula and organization. Education is compulsory on the primary level and free for both primary and secondary schools, but many areas lack both buildings and teachers. The number of government primary schools increased from 88 in 1920 to 6,659 in 1973/74. In that year there were 1,408,929 pupils, of whom 424,935 were girls, attending public and private schools at the primary level. Illiteracy is being combated in special schools for adults.

Primary schools provide a six-year course at the end of which the student must pass an examination to be admitted to secondary school. The curriculum is based on Western patterns but also includes religious teaching. The language of instruction is Arabic, in minority districts also that of the minority. Secondary schools have a three-year intermediate course followed by a two-year course in preparation for entrance to college. A national examination must be passed at its end. In 1973/74 there were 967 public and 126 private secondary schools with 274,445 students. In 1973/74 there were 64 vocational schools with 1,250 teachers and 15,639 students. Secondary education for girls dates from 1929; girls now make up about 29% of the total enrollment in secondary schools. A secondary-school certificate entitles the holder to a job as a government clerk; a normal school certificate, as a primary-school teacher. A university degree opens the door to the lower and a graduate degree to the higher ranks of the professions and government service.

In 1958, Baghdad's colleges were amalgamated into the University of Baghdad, the country's largest university, with 22,263 students in 1973/74. Other state universities (with 1973/74 enrollments) are al-Mustansiriyah (17,273), Mosul (5,850), Basrah (5,330), and al-Sulaymaniyah (2,044). Schools of law and of commerce charge tuition; all others are free. In exchange, the student must devote a specified number of years to government service. The number of students enrolled in all universities, 4 private colleges, and 8 technical institutes in 1973/74 was 58,351.

The government sends many students abroad, mainly to the UK, Lebanon, and other countries of the Middle East and Europe.

44 LIBRARIES AND MUSEUMS

The National Library in Baghdad, comprising a collection begun in 1924, was founded in 1963, and currently houses 52,000 volumes. The Ministry of Information, which is in charge of the Iraqi National Library, in the mid-1970s planned to open a new building for this library at a cost of about $2 million. The Central Library of the University of Baghdad has 190,000 volumes. One of the country's outstanding libraries is the Iraqi Museum Library, founded in 1934. It has modern research facilities and more than 50,000 volumes, many of them rare editions. In 1971 there were 110 public libraries in Iraq. Among the largest are the Mosul Public Library (66,000 volumes) and the al-Hillah Public Library (30,000). Other important public libraries are located in al-Kadisiyah, Basrah, Diyala, Karbala', Kirkuk, and al-Sulaymaniyah.

With the exception of the National History Museum and the National Museum of Modern Art, museums are under the control of the Department of the Directorate-General of Antiquities in Baghdad. Two of the most outstanding collections are at the Iraq Museum in Baghdad and the Mosul Museum. The Abbasid Palace Museum and the Museum of Arab Antiquities located in

Baghdad are housed in restored buildings from the 13th and 14th centuries, respectively.

45 ORGANIZATIONS

Chambers of commerce are active in Baghdad, Basrah, and Mosul. Cooperatives, first established in 1944, have come to play an increasingly important social role, especially under the post-1968 Ba'th government. In 1974, Iraq had 1,386 agricultural cooperatives, with 217,723 members, and in 1975, 6,298 farmers' societies, with 418,863 members. There were also 289 cooperatives active in other spheres (including 182 in housing), with membership in 26 registered societies totaling 5,170.

Youth organizations have been stressed by the current regime, and in 1974 there were 47 youth centers and 82 sports clubs for young people. The General Federation of Iraqi Youth and the General Federation of Iraqi Women are government-sponsored mass organizations. Red Crescent societies function in many cities and towns.

46 PRESS

Before World War I, there was little journalistic activity in Iraq. Many nationalistic papers were founded during the mandate, but the press still remains unimportant in Iraq's national life. Though a high illiteracy rate is evidently a factor, progress has been hampered by frequent changes of government and severe censorship under both the pre- and post-1958 regimes.

In 1975, the two leading newspapers were *Al-Thawra* (circulation 100,000) and *Al-Jumhuriyah* (25,000), both in Arabic. One daily, the *Baghdad Observer* (7,000), appeared in English.

47 TOURISM

A visa is required for entry into Iraq. There is a fee, unless the stay is for only two weeks or less.

In 1974, Iraq had 544,800 foreign visitors. More than half of these came from Syria, Jordan, Sa'udi Arabia, and other Arab states, mostly as pilgrims to Islam's holy shrines in Iraq. In 1974, the country had 901 hotels with 37,531 beds.

48 FAMOUS IRAQIS

Under the caliphs al-Ma'mun (r.813–33) and al-Mu'tasim (r.833–42), Baghdad was the center of the Arab scholarship that translated and modified Greek philosophy. A leading figure in this movement was Hunain ibn Ishaq (d.873), called Johannitius by Western scholastics. His contemporary was the great Arab philosopher Yaqub al-Kindi, whose catholicity assimilated both Greek philosophy and Indian mathematics. The founder of one of the four orthodox schools of Islamic law, which claims the largest number of adherents in the Muslim world, Abu Hanifa (d.767) was also a native Iraqi. Another celebrated figure in theology, 'Abd al-Hasan al-Ash'ari (c.913), who combated the rationalist Mu'tazila school, also lived in Baghdad; his influence still prevails in Islam. Al-Ghazali (Ghazel, d.1111), though Persian by birth, taught at the Nizamiyah University in Baghdad; he is one of the best-known Islamic philosopher-theologians. Iraq also produced famous mystics like Hasan al-Basri (642–728) and

'Abd al-Qadir al-Jilani (1077–1166); the latter's followers are numerous among Asian Muslims and his tomb in Baghdad draws many pilgrims. Modern Iraq has produced no artist or writer famous outside the Arabic-speaking world.

49 DEPENDENCIES

Iraq has no territories or colonies.

50 BIBLIOGRAPHY

Al-Marayati, Abid A. *A Diplomatic History of Modern Iraq*. New York: Speller, 1961.

Annual Abstract of Statistics. Baghdad: Central Statistical Organization, Ministry of Planning (annual).

Birdwood, Christopher Bromhead, Baron. *Nuri as-Said: A Study in Arab Leadership*. London: Cassell, 1959.

Dann, Uriel. *Iraq under Qassem: A Political History, 1958–63*. New York: Praeger, 1969.

Edmonds, Cecil John. *Kurds, Turks and Arabs: Politics, Travel and Research in North-Eastern Iraq*. London: Oxford University Press, 1957.

Field, Henry. *The Anthropology of Iraq*. Chicago: Chicago Natural History Museum, 1940–49; Cambridge, Mass.: Peabody Museum, 1951–52.

Harris, George Lawrence, *et. al. Iraq: Its People, Its Society, Its Culture*. New Haven, Conn.: HRAF Press, 1958.

Khadduri, Majid. *Independent Iraq, 1932–1958: A Study in Iraqi Politics*. London: Oxford University Press, 1960.

Kimball, Lorenzo Kent. *The Changing Pattern of Political Power in Iraq, 1958 to 1971*. New York: Speller, 1972.

Langley, Kathleen M. *The Industrialization of Iraq*. Cambridge: Harvard University Press, 1961.

Longrigg, Stephen Hemsley. *Iraq, 1900–1950: A Political, Social and Economic History*. London: Oxford University Press, 1953.

Longrigg, Stephen Hemsley, and Frank Stoakes. *Iraq*. New York: Praeger, 1958.

Lovejoy, Bahija. *Land and People of Iraq*. New York: Lippincott, 1964.

Maxwell, Gavin. *People of the Reeds*. New York: Harper, 1957.

O'Ballance, Edgar. *The Kurdish Revolt, 1961–1970*. Hamden, Conn.: Shoe String Press, 1973.

Qubain, Fahim I. *The Reconstruction of Iraq, 1950–1957*. New York: Praeger, 1958.

Safrastian, Arshak. *Kurds and Kurdistan*. London: Harvill, 1948.

Shwadran, Benjamin. *The Middle East: Oil and the Great Powers*. New York: Praeger, 1955.

Sousa, Ahmad. *Atlas of Iraq, Showing Administrative Boundaries, Areas & Population*. Baghdad: Surveys Press, 1953.

Warriner, Doreen. *Land Reform and Development in the Middle East: A Study of Egypt, Syria, and Iraq*. London: Royal Institute of International Affairs, 1962.

Zuwaylif, F. H. *Planning Development in Iraq, 1950–1960*. Ann Arbor, Mich.: University Microfilms, 1962.

ISRAEL*

State of Israel
Medinat Yisrael

CAPITAL: Jerusalem (Yerushalayim). **FLAG**: The flag, which was adopted at the First Zionist Congress in Basel in 1897, consists of a blue six-pointed Shield of David (Magen David) centered between two blue horizontal stripes on a white field. **ANTHEM**: *Hatikvah* (*The Hope*). **MONETARY UNIT**: The Israeli pound (IL) of 100 agorot is a nonconvertible paper currency. There are coins of 1, 5, 10, 25, and 50 agorot and 1 pound, and notes of 1, 5, 10, 50, and 100 pounds. IL1=US$0.1329 (or US$1=IL7.52). **WEIGHTS AND MEASURES**: The metric system is the legal standard, but some local units are used, notably the dunam (equivalent to 1,000 sq meters, or about 0.25 acre). **HOLIDAYS**: Israel officially uses both the Gregorian and the complex Jewish luni-solar calendar, but the latter determines the occurrence of national holidays: Rosh Hashanah (New Year), September or October; Yom Kippur (Day of Atonement), September or October; Succot (Tabernacles), September or October; Simchat Torah (Rejoicing in the Law), September or October; Chanukah (Feast of Lights), early winter; Purim (Feast of Lots), end of winter; Pesach (Passover), beginning of spring; Independence Day, May; Shavuot (Pentecost), late spring or early summer. **TIME**: 2 P.M.=noon GMT.

¹LOCATION, SIZE, AND EXTENT

Situated in southwestern Asia along the eastern end of the Mediterranean Sea, Israel has an area of 20,770 sq km (8,019 sq mi), extending *322 km (200 mi)* N–S and *111 km (69 mi)* E–W; at its narrowest, just north of Tel Aviv, it is 19 km (12 mi) across. In addition, Israel administers the areas taken in the Six-Day War (1967), which in 1976 totaled 60,830 sq km (23,487 sq mi), including the Golan Heights, 1,710 sq km (660 sq mi); Samaria and Judea (West Bank), 5,878 sq km (2,270 sq mi); and Sinai, 53,242 sq km (20,557 sq mi). Israel is bordered on the N by Lebanon, on the E by Syria and Jordan, on the s by the Gulf of Aqaba (Gulf of Elat), on the sw by Egypt, and on the w by the Mediterranean Sea. The total boundary length was 1,162.5 km (722.5 mi) following the 1949 armistice and *1,808 km (1,123 mi)* in June 1976, including the administered areas.

²TOPOGRAPHY

The country is divided into three major longitudinal strips: the coastal plain, which follows the Mediterranean shoreline in a southward widening band; the hill region, embracing the hills of Galilee in the north, Samaria and Judea in the center, and the Negev in the south; and the Jordan Valley. Except for the Bay of Acre, the sandy coastline is unindented for its entire length. The hill region, averaging 2,000 feet in elevation, reaches its highest point at Mt. Meron (3,963 feet). South of the Judean hills, the Negev desert, marked by cliffs and craters and covering about half the total area of Israel, extends down to the Gulf of Elat (Aqaba) on the Red Sea. The Jordan River—of its 156 miles, about half are in Israel—links the only bodies of water in the country: Lake Kinneret (Sea of Galilee) and the heavily saline Dead Sea—only one-half of its area in Israel—which, at 1,290 feet below sea level, is the lowest point on the earth's surface.

³CLIMATE

Although climatic conditions are varied across the country, the climate is generally temperate. The coldest month is January; the hottest, August. In winter, snow occasionally falls in the hills, where January temperatures normally fluctuate between 4.4°C and 10°C (40°–50°F) and August temperatures between 18.4°C and 29.4°C (65°–85°F). On the coastal plain, sea breezes temper the weather all year round, temperature variations ranging from 8.4°C to 18.4°C (47°–65°F) in January and 21°C to 29.4°C

(70°–85°F) in August. In the south, at Elat, January temperatures range between 10°C and 21°C (50°–70°F) and may reach 49°C (120°F) in August. The rainy season lasts from November until April, with rainfall averaging 42.5 inches annually in Upper Galilee and only 0.8 inch in Elat, although dewfall gives the south another several inches of water every year.

⁴FLORA AND FAUNA

The Bible describes the country as "a land of wheat and barley and vines and fig trees and pomegranates, a land of olive oil and honey," a description that still holds true. The original forests, evergreen and maquis, have largely been destroyed, but more than 100 million new trees have been planted over the last 50 years in a major reforestation program. Vegetation cover is generally thin, except in the coastal plain, where conditions are particularly favorable to the cultivation of citrus fruit, and in the Jordan Valley, with its plantations of tropical fruit. Among surviving animals, jackals and hyenas remain fairly numerous, and there are wild boar in the Hula region. With the growth of vegetation and water supplies, bird life and deer have recently increased. Invasions of desert locusts occur periodically.

As of 1975, endangered species in Israel included the wolf, Anatolian leopard, Sa'udi Arabian dorcas gazelle, Arabian gazelle, and Israel painted frog. On the Sinai Peninsula, endangered species included the Sinai leopard, dugong, and Arabian gazelle.

⁵POPULATION

According to the census of 20 May 1972, the population totaled 3,147,683. At the end of 1974, the estimated population was 3,408,900; a population of 3,898,000 was projected for 1980. In 1974, the crude birthrate was 27.7 per 1,000 population, the death rate was 7.2, and the net natural increase 20.5. Average density (excluding the administered territories) was 164 persons per sq km (425 per sq mi), with 85.6% living in urban localities. The largest city, Tel Aviv/Jaffa (founded in 1908), had an estimated population of 357,600 in 1974. Other large cities and their 1974 population are Jerusalem (the capital), 344,200 (based on jurisdiction as of 1974); Haifa, 225,000; and Ramat-Gan,

*Unless otherwise stated, data for Israel exclude the territories administered since 1967.

120,200. Besides the population of Israel (including East Jerusalem), 1,093,300 persons, as of 1974, lived in the territories administered by Israel since 1967. These included 674,500 in Judea and Samaria and 418,800 in the Gaza Strip and North Sinai.

⁶ETHNIC GROUPS

Of the estimated population of 3,408,900 at the end of 1974, 2,890,300 (84.8%) were Jews, 392,500 (11.5%) were Muslims, 84,500 (2.5%) were Christians, and 41,600 (1.2%) were Druzes or others. Of the Jewish population, 49.3% had been born in Israel, 10.9% in other parts of Asia, 12.3% in Africa, and 27.5% in Europe or the Americas. In 1948, 5.7% of the world Jewish population lived in Israel; by the end of 1973, Israel's share had risen to 20%.

The largest ethnic group is formed of Jews, drawn from many different countries and cultures. The traditional division of the Jews into Ashkenazim (Central and East Europeans) and Sephardim (South and West Europeans) is still given formal recognition in the choice of two chief rabbis, one for each community. A more meaningful division, however, would be that between Occidentals and Orientals, the latter forming the bulk of the population.

The minority non-Jewish population is overwhelmingly Arabic-speaking, but Israel's minorities are divided into a number of religious groups and include several small non-Arab national groups (Druzes, Circassians, Copts).

⁷LANGUAGE

The official languages are Hebrew and Arabic, the former being dominant. Modern Hebrew is the language of the Bible modified by absorption of elements from all historical forms of Hebrew and by development over the years. Arabic is used by Arabs in deliberations in the Knesset, in pleadings before the courts, and in dealings with governmental departments, and is the language of instruction in schools for Arab children. English is taught in all secondary schools and, along with Hebrew, is commonly used in foreign business correspondence and in advertising and labeling. Coins, postage stamps, and bank notes bear inscriptions in Hebrew, Arabic, and Latin characters.

⁸RELIGION

The land which is now Israel (and which the Romans called Palestine) is the cradle of two of the world's great religions, Judaism and Christianity. In the Old Testament, Jewish history begins with Abraham's journey into Canaan, to which the descendants of Abraham would later return after their deliverance by Moses from captivity in Egypt. Jerusalem is the historical site of the First Temple, built by King Solomon in the 10th century B.C. and destroyed by the Babylonians in 586 B.C., and the Second Temple, rebuilt about 70 years later and sacked by the Romans in A.D. 70. Belief in the life, teachings, crucifixion, and resurrection of Jesus of Nazareth (who, according to the New Testament, actually preached in that Temple) is the basis of the Christian religion. Spread through the proselytizing of St. Paul, the authors of the four Gospels, and other disciples, Christianity developed from a messianic Jewish sect to become, within three centuries, the established religion of the Roman Empire. Today, Christianity is the dominant religion of the Western world.

In present-day Israel, freedom of religion is guaranteed. The Ministry of Religious Affairs assists institutions of every affiliation and contributes to the preservation and repair of their holy shrines, which are protected by the government and made accessible to pilgrims. Supreme religious authority in the Jewish community is vested in the chief rabbinate, which also serves as the highest rabbinical court. Courts for the various religious communities are government supported; these have jurisdiction in matters of religion and personal status. The chief division among the Jews is between the Ashkenazic and Sephardic traditions, which are equally represented in the rabbinate. Most Arabs are Sunni Muslims. Christians are largely Greek Catholic or Greek Orthodox, but there are also Roman Catholics, Armenians, and Protestants. The Druzes, who split away from Islam in the 11th century, have the status of a separate religious community. The Baha'i world community has its central shrine in Haifa. There are some 5,000 synagogues, 100 mosques, and 160 churches and chapels in Israel.

⁹TRANSPORTATION

In 1974, the road network had a length of 10,657 km, of which 3,336 km were maintained by the government. With the building in 1957 of a highway extension from Beersheba to Elat, the Red Sea was linked to the Mediterranean. Trackage of the state-owned railway totaled 484 km in 1975. Railways, buses, and taxis constitute the principal means of passenger transport. In 1974 there were 408,280 motor vehicles, including 267,425 private cars and 104,698 trucks, taxis, and buses.

At the end of 1974, Israel had 106 merchant vessels, with a capacity of 2,304,253 GRT. Israeli vessels carry about 33% of incoming and outgoing cargoes, which totaled 9,970,000 tons in 1974. The main seaport, Haifa, can berth large passenger liners and has a 10,000-ton floating dock. Other ports include Ashdod (south of Tel Aviv) and Elat.

Israel Airlines (EL AL), among other airlines, operates international flights from Ben-Gurion (Lod) Airport. In 1974 the airport had 1,746,600 international passenger arrivals and departures. Israel Inland Airlines (Arkia) provides domestic service.

¹⁰COMMUNICATIONS

The state owns and operates the major communications services. The state radio stations include the government's Israel Broadcasting Authority (Shidurei Israel), the army's Defense Forces Waves (Galei Zahal), and the Jewish Agency's Zion's Voice to the Diaspora (Kol Zion la-Gola), aimed mostly at Jewish communities in Europe and the US. A radio-television station for Shidurei Israel was completed in 1969. In 1974, 52% of all families had telephones, 89% had radios, and 83% had television sets. There were 751,700 telephones in use in 1975.

¹¹HISTORY

The formative period of Israel, dominated at various times by judges, kings, prophets, and scribes, lasted from approximately 1200 B.C., when the Israelite tribes entered Canaan, to A.D. 70, when the Roman legions conquered Jerusalem, destroyed the Temple, exiled most Jews, and renamed the region Palestine. For the next two millennia there were successive waves of foreign conquerors—Byzantines, Persians, Arabs, Crusaders, Mongols, Turks, and Britons. Most Jews remained in dispersion, where many nourished messianic hopes for an eventual return to Zion; however, Jews in varying numbers continued to live in Palestine through the years.

Modern Zionism, the movement for the reestablishment of a Jewish nation, dates from the late 19th century and was given impetus by the founding of the World Zionist Organization in Basel, Switzerland, in 1897, under the leadership of Theodor Herzl. At the 1905 congress, a majority of delegates rejected the British offer of a Jewish homeland in Uganda and decided to seek a national home in Palestine. Zionist hopes were greatly bolstered when the British government pledged its support for

LOCATION (1949): 29°29' to 33°17'N; 34°16' to 35°41'E. **LENGTH OF 1949 ARMISTICE LINES:** Lebanon, 102 km (63 mi); Syria, 76 km (47 mi); Jordan, 531 km (330 mi); Gulf of Elat coastline, 10.5 km (6.5 mi); Egypt, 206 km (128 mi); Gaza Strip, 59 km (37 mi); Mediterranean coastline, 178 km (111 mi). **LENGTH OF LINES AS OF JUNE 1976:** Lebanon, 102 km (63 mi); Syria, *80 km (50 mi)*; Jordan, *480 km (298 mi)*; Sinai coastline, *399 km (248 mi)*; Egypt, *380 km (236 mi)*; Mediterranean coastline, *367 km (228 mi)*. **TERRITORIAL SEA LIMIT:** 6 mi.

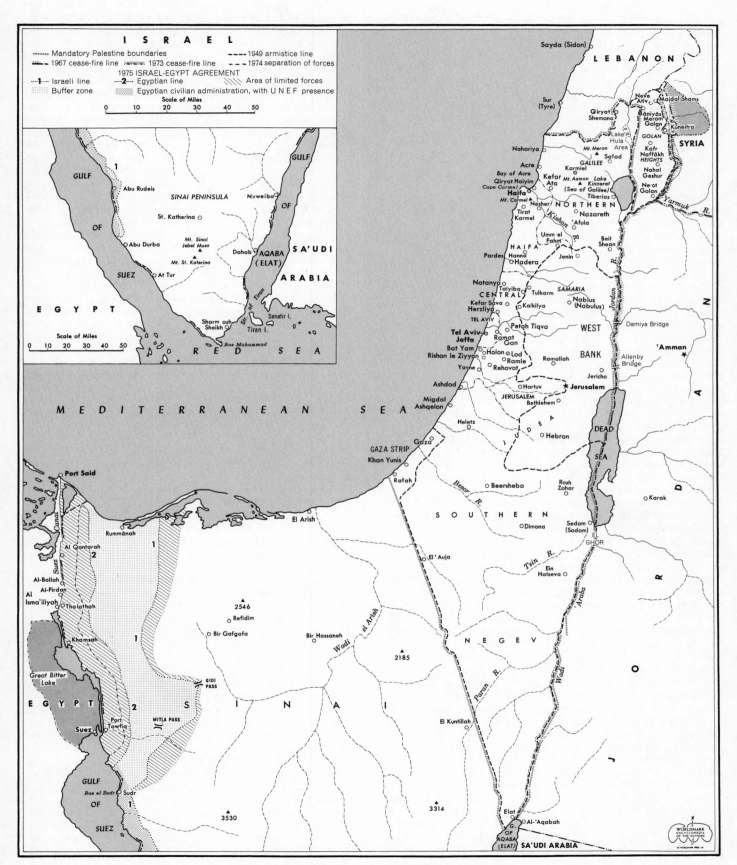

I S R A E L

○○○○○ Mandatory Palestine boundaries   – – – – 1949 armistice line
⌐⌐⌐⌐ 1967 cease-fire line   ⌐⌐⌐⌐ 1974 separation of forces
1973 cease-fire line
1975 ISRAEL-EGYPT AGREEMENT
···**1**··· Israeli line   ···**2**··· Egyptian line   ⫽⫽⫽ Area of limited forces
░░░ Buffer zone   ▒▒▒ Egyptian civilian administration, with U N E F presence

Scale of Miles
0   10   20   30   40   50

LEBANON

Sayda (Sidon)

Neve
Ativ
Majdal Shams

Qiryat
Shemona
Baniyas
Merom
Golan
Kuneitra

Sur
(Tyre)

GOLAN
HEIGHTS
Kafr
Naffakh

SYRIA

Nahariya   Lake
Hula
Area
Mt. Meron ▲ Safad

Nahal
Geshur

GALILEE
Acre   Karmiel
Bay of Acre
Qiryat Haiyim   Mt. Azmon ▲   Lake
Kinneret
(Sea of Galilee)
Cape Carmel/
Haifa   Tiberias   Ne'ot
Golan
Mt. Carmel
Nesher   Nazareth
Tirat
Karmel   'Afula

NORTHERN

Yarmuk R.

HAIFA   Umm el
Fahm   Beit
Shean
Pardes   Jenin
Hanna
Hadera

Natanya   Tulkarm   SAMARIA
CENTRAL   Nablus
Kefar Sava   Kalkilya   (Nablus)
Herzliya
TEL AVIV   Damiya Bridge
Petah Tiqva   WEST

**Tel Aviv-
Jaffa**   Ramat
Gan   BANK   'Amman ★
Bat Yam   Allenby
Rishon le Ziyyon   Holon Lod   Ramallah   Bridge
Yavne   Ramle
Rehovot   Jericho

Ashdod
○Hartuv   ★ Jerusalem
Migdal   JERUSALEM   DEAD
Ashqelon   Bethlehem   SEA

J
Heletz   U
D   O
E   Hebron
A

GAZA STRIP   Gaza   R
Khan Yunis   Rosh
Zohar   Karak   D

Rafah   Beersheba   A
Besor R.   Sedom
(Sodom)   N
El Arish   EL
GHOR

Dimona
SOUTHERN
R

El 'Auja   Tsin R.   Ein
Hatseva   A

Wadi el Arish   R
NEGEV   A
▲2546   B
Refidim   ▲2185   Wadi Araba   A

Bir Gafgafa   Bir Hassaneh   Paran R.   O

MEDITERRANEAN   SEA

Port Said

Suez Canal
Rummanah
Al Qantarah   1
2
Al-Ballah
Al-Firdan
Al
Isma'iliyah   Thalathah   1   GIDI
PASS

Khamsah   SINAI   El Kuntillah
1

Great Bitter
Lake   2   3314 ▲

EGYPT   S   I   N   A   I   J

MITLA PASS
2
Port   MITLA PASS   Elat
Suez   Tawfiq   Al-'Aqabah   G.
OF
AQABA   SA'UDI ARABIA
GULF   (ELAT)
OF   Ras el Sudr ○ Sudr   ▲3530
1
SUEZ

Inset map (top left):

GULF   GULF
OF
OF

Abu Rudeis   SINAI PENINSULA   Nuweiba   OF

St. Katherina ○   AQABA
(ELAT)
SA'UDI

Abu Durba   Mt. Sinai
Jebel Musa ▲   ARABIA
Mt. St. Katerina ▲
Dahab
SUEZ   At Tur   Str. of Tiran

EGYPT   Sanafir I.
Sharm ash
Sheikh   Tiran I.

Scale of Miles   Ras Muhammad   RED   SEA
0 10 20 30 40 50

WORLDMARK
ENCYCLOPEDIA
OF THE NATIONS
© WORLDMARK PRESS

this goal in 1917, in the Balfour Declaration, which was subsequently incorporated into the mandate over Palestine (originally including Transjordan) awarded to the UK by the League of Nations in 1922. The growth of the Jewish community under the mandate from 85,000 to 650,000, largely through immigration, on lands purchased from Arab owners was, however, attended by the rising hostility of the Arab community, which felt its majority status threatened by the Jewish influx. Shortly after the outbreak of World War II, British mandatory authorities issued a White Paper that decreed the virtual freezing of Jewish immigration and of land purchase and settlement. Armed Jewish resistance to this policy, as well as the growing international backing for the establishment of a Jewish state as a haven for the survivors of Nazi massacres, finally persuaded the British government to relinquish the mandate.

The Palestine problem was referred to the UN, whose General Assembly, on 29 November 1947, adopted a plan for the partition of Palestine into two economically united but politically sovereign states, one Jewish and the other Arab, with Jerusalem as an international city. The Arabs of Palestine, aided by brethren across the frontiers, at once rose up in arms to thwart partition. The Jews accepted the plan; on 14 May 1948, the last day of the mandate, they proclaimed the formation of the State of Israel. The next day, the Arab League states—Egypt, Iraq, Jordan, Lebanon, Sa'udi Arabia, and Syria—launched a concerted armed attack. There followed a mass flight of Palestinian Arabs abroad. The war left Israel in possession of a much larger territory than that awarded the Jews under the UN partition plan. Armistice agreements concluded in 1949 failed to provide the contemplated transition to peace, and sporadic Arab attacks along the borders were answered by Israeli reprisals. Tensions were exacerbated by Arab economic boycotts and by Egypt's nationalization of the Suez Canal on 26 July 1956. On 29 October 1956, Israel (with British and French support) invaded Egypt, soon gaining control of the Gaza Strip and the Sinai Peninsula. Fighting ended on 4 November; Israel, under UN pressure, withdrew from occupied areas and recognized borders consistent with its military position at the end of the 1948 war. UNEF personnel patrolled the armistice line.

Incidents persisted through the mid-1960s. Eventually, Egypt moved armaments and troops into the Sinai, ordering withdrawal of UNEF personnel from the armistice line, and closed the Strait of Tiran to Israeli shipping. On 5 June 1967, hostilities broke out between Israel, on the one hand, and Egypt, Syria, and Jordan, on the other. By 11 June, Israel had scored a decisive victory in the conflict, since termed the Six-Day War, and had taken control of the Sinai Peninsula, the Gaza Strip, the Golan Heights (in southern Syria), and the west bank of the Jordan River (including Jordanian-ruled East Jerusalem). The status of the territories captured by Israel during the 1967 war has repeatedly been the subject of UN debate. On 22 November 1967, the Security Council unanimously adopted the UK-sponsored Resolution 242 calling for the establishment of a just and lasting peace in the Middle East, the withdrawal of Israeli armed forces from territories occupied during the 1967 war, and acknowledgment of the "sovereignty, territorial integrity, and political independence of every State in the area and their right to live in peace within secure and recognized boundaries free from threats or acts of force." Israel indicated that return of the captured territories would have to be part of a general settlement guaranteeing peace, and in 1969 the Israeli government began allowing Jewish settlement in these areas.

Serious shooting incidents between Egypt and Israel resumed in June 1969, following Egypt's declaration of a war of attrition against Israel. In response to a US peace initiative, a cease-fire took effect in August 1970, but tensions continued, and Palestinian Arab guerrillas mounted an international campaign of terrorism, highlighted in September 1972 by the kidnap and murder of Israeli athletes at the Olympic Games in Munich.

On 6 October 1973, on Yom Kippur, Egypt and Syria simultaneously attacked Israeli-held territory in the Sinai Peninsula and the Golan Heights. The Arabs, aided by sophisticated Soviet weaponry, won initial victories, but by 24 October, when a UN cease-fire took effect, the Israelis had crossed the Suez Canal and were 101 km from Cairo and about 27 km from Damascus. The General Assembly on 8 December adopted Resolution 383 reaffirming the terms of the 1967 Security Council Resolution 242 and recommending that negotiations be undertaken. Under the impetus of the "shuttle diplomacy" exercised by US Secretary of State Henry Kissinger, formal first-stage disengagement agreements were signed with Egypt on 18 January 1974 and with Syria on 31 May 1974. On 4 September 1975, a second-stage disengagement pact was signed in Geneva, under which Israel relinquished some territory in the Sinai (including two oil fields) in return for Egyptian declarations of peaceful intent, free passage of nonmilitary cargoes to and from Israel through the Suez Canal, and the stationing of US civilians to monitor an early-warning system. A Sinai buffer zone was patrolled by UNEF personnel.

Since 1973, actions within the UN and its member agencies have made clear Israel's minority voting position. On 4 November 1974, UNESCO, by a vote of 35 to 23 with 26 abstentions, voted to impose sanctions and withdraw assistance from Israel for its alleged "persistence in altering historic features of Jerusalem"; Israel had annually contributed to UNESCO nine times as much as it had received. On 10 November 1975, by a 72–35 vote with 32 abstentions, the General Assembly adopted a draft resolution calling Zionism "a form of racism and racial discrimination." During debate on the resolution, the Israeli delegate charged that the UN was on its way to becoming "the world center of anti-Semitism." The US delegate called passage of the resolution an "infamous act."

Despite the persistence of serious external problems during its first quarter-century, Israel experienced an enormous expansion of its economic resources, and a steady stream of immigration quadrupled the Jewish population.

12 GOVERNMENT

Israel is a democratic republic. It has as yet no written constitution; the state has been guided by legislative enactments and official government programs. Legislative power is vested in the Knesset, executive power in the cabinet, and judicial power in the courts.

The 120 members of the unicameral Knesset are elected for four-year terms by universal secret vote of all citizens 18 years of age and over, under a system of proportional representation. The Knesset holds two ordinary sessions each year.

The head of the state is the president, elected by the Knesset for a five-year term. He appoints the prime minister, after consultation with political party leaders, and performs ceremonial duties. The cabinet, headed by the prime minister, is collectively responsible to the Knesset, whose confidence it must enjoy. A state comptroller appointed by the president for a five-year period is also responsible to the Knesset; he audits governmental financial transactions, makes recommendations for administrative efficiency, and investigates charges of governmental malfeasance.

13 POLITICAL PARTIES

Israel's multiple-party system reflects the diverse origins of the people and their long practice of party politics in Zionist organizations. In the elections of 31 December 1973, 22 parties or groups sought seats in the Knesset, but many were insignificant splinter groups, and only 9 elected any members. The first five Knessets were controlled by coalitions led by the Mapai (Israel Workers Party), mostly under David Ben-Gurion. The

Mapai is also the nucleus of the present Israel Labor Party, which in coalition with other parties has controlled Israel's governments since its formation from the Mapai and two other parties, in 1968. In elections on 31 December 1973, the Israel Labor Party, in alignment with the left-wing Mapam (United Workers Party) and with affiliated Arab lists, won 54 of the 120 seats. As of October 1974, the government, under Yitzhak Rabin, was composed of this alignment, in coalition with the Independent Liberals and the National Religious Party; the whole coalition commanded the support of 68 of the 120 Knesset seats.

The original Mapai, founded in 1930, was a moderate Zionist-socialist party calling for a directed welfare economy based on partnership between the General Federation of Labor (Histadrut), the government, and private enterprise. In 1968, it reunited with Achdut Ha'avoda (the Labor Unity Party), a left-wing faction that had broken away in 1954 and that stood for widespread agricultural settlement, an activist defense policy, and noninvolvement in the Cold War. Rafi (the Israel Labor List), founded in 1956 to support a constituency system and modernization of the economy, also was part of the merger, which, on 21 January 1968, produced the present Israel Labor Party. The merged party, like its components, is socialist, modernist, and democratic.

Left of the Israel Labor Party is Mapam, which calls for nationalization of natural resources and basic industries, Jewish-Arab working class solidarity, and neutrality in foreign relations. Since 1969, it has been part of the ruling coalition.

In September 1973, four right-wing nationalist parties combined to form the Likud, which thus became the major opposition bloc in the Knesset. Besides the State List and the Free Center, the Likud consists of the two parties that in 1965 had united to form the Gahal. One is the Herut (Freedom) Movement, founded in 1948 to support territorial integrity within Israel's historical boundaries and a greater economic role for private enterprise. The other is the Liberal Party, formed in 1961 out of the former General Zionist Party and the former Progressive Party; it supports private enterprise, a liberal welfare state, and electoral reform. The Likud advocates retention of all territories captured in the 1967 war as a safeguard to national security. It won 39 seats in the 1973 elections.

The Mizrachi-Hapoel Hamizrachi (National Religious Party), which won 10 seats in 1973, was founded in 1956; it favors the establishment of a society based on Jewish law, but otherwise follows the Mapai line. The Independent Liberal Party, with 4 seats, follows a moderate liberal platform. Both parties have frequently participated in coalition governments.

The ultraorthodox Agudat Israel and Poalei Agudat Israel parties (which together ran as the Torah Front and won 5 seats in 1973) urge the adoption of the Torah (the law of Moses) as the law of the state. Other parties include the Moked, an alliance of the Israel Communist Party (which supports a Jewish Communist state) and other left-wing factions (1 seat in 1973); the New Communist Party, which supports a non-Jewish Communist state (4 seats); and the Civil Rights List, a Labor splinter group that favors women's rights and legalization of civil marriage (3 seats).

14LOCAL GOVERNMENT

Israel is divided into six administrative districts: Jerusalem, Tel Aviv, Haifa, Northern (Tiberias), Central (Ramle), and Southern (Beersheba). Nine-tenths of the people are under local government jurisdiction, the remaining tenth living in new immigrant settlements or in Arab villages. In 1976 there were 33 municipalities, 117 local councils, 49 regional councils, and 38 settlements without municipal status. Most local governments are elected, both in Israel proper and in the administered territories.

15JUDICIAL SYSTEM

The law of Israel contains some features of Ottoman law, English common law, and other foreign law, but it is shaped largely by the provisions of the Knesset. Judges are appointed by the president on recommendation of independent committees. Magistrates' courts in all towns deal with most cases in the first instance, relatively small property claims, and lesser criminal charges. Three district courts, serving mainly as courts of appeal, have jurisdiction over all other actions except marriage and divorce cases, which are adjudicated, along with other personal and religious matters, in the religious courts of the Jewish (rabbinical), Muslim (Shari'ah), Druze, and Christian communities. Aside from its function as the court of last appeal, the nine-member Supreme Court also hears cases in the first instance brought by citizens against arbitrary government actions. There is no jury system. Capital punishment applies only for crimes of wartime treason or for collaboration with the Nazis, and has been employed only once in Israel's modern history, in the case of Adolf Eichmann.

16ARMED FORCES

The defense forces of Israel, land, sea, and air, grew out of the voluntary defense force (Haganah) created by the Jewish community in Palestine during the British mandate. Men and unmarried women between the ages of 18 and 26 are conscripted for 36 and 20 months, respectively, the women being trained for noncombat duties. Arabs may serve on a voluntary basis but are not encouraged to participate in combat. All men and childless women serve in the reserves until the ages of 55 and 34, respectively.

In 1975, the Israeli army had an estimated 15,000 regular troops, 120,000 conscripts, and 375,000 on mobilization; 5 armored brigades, 4 infantry brigades, and 2 parachute brigades were kept at full strength, with 25 other brigades partially mobilized. Armaments included at least 2,700 medium tanks and 3,600 armored vehicles. The navy had 4,000 regulars, 1,000 conscripts, and 6,000 on mobilization; vessels included 2 submarines (with 3 more on order) and 18 missile-equipped fast patrol boats. The air force had 15,000 regulars, 1,000 conscripts, and 20,000 on mobilization; there were 461 functional combat aircraft, with other aircraft in reserve. The combined reserve strength of all services was 450,000. The reserve force can be effectively mobilized for combat in 48–72 hours. Defense expenditures for 1975/76 were budgeted at IL22.3 billion, more than 30% of the GNP. Israeli arms purchases exceeded $3 billion between 1970 and 1974.

17MIGRATION

In 1948, 65% of Israel's Jewish population consisted of immigrants; many of these 463,000 immigrant Jews had fled from persecution in Russia and, especially during the Nazi period, Central and Eastern Europe. Israel's declaration of independence publicly opened the state "to the immigration of Jews from all countries of their dispersion," and the 1950 Law of Return granted every returning Jew the right to automatic citizenship. The Nationality Law specifies other ways—including birth, residence, and naturalization—that Israeli citizenship may be acquired. In the years 1948–74, Israel took in 1,492,482 Jewish immigrants. In 1948–51, the flow was at its heaviest, averaging 170,960 per year, about evenly divided between East European Jews, who were war refugees, and Oriental Jews from ancient centers of the Arab world. In the years 1952–56, most immigrants came from French North Africa; in 1957–58 there was a renewed inflow from Eastern Europe. After the lull of 1959–60, the flow of immigrants was renewed, reaching substantial proportions by 1963, when 63,364 Jews arrived. Jewish immigration fell to an annual average of 18,069 persons for 1965–68, and rose to an average of 38,523 per year for 1969–74. The proportion of Jewish immigrants from Europe and North America (as opposed to those from Asia and Africa) varied during the 1960s, but since 1969 it has risen steadily, from 56% in that year to 90% in 1974. In 1974, the Jewish immigrant population was 50.7% of all Israeli Jews and 43% of all Israelis. A certain amount of emigration has always taken place. In the period 1948–74, the total number of Jewish emigrants was estimated at 292,300.

Considerable Arab migration has also taken place, including an apparent wave of Arab immigration into Palestine between World War I and World War II. During the 1948 war there was massive Arab emigration; these emigrants have become known as the Palestinian refugees.

[18] INTERNATIONAL COOPERATION

Israel was admitted as the fifty-ninth UN member on 12 May 1949, and subsequently joined all the UN's affiliated agencies. It is also a member of many other international bodies. Israel has collaborated economically with many newly independent nations. Between 1958 and 1975, some 5,900 Israeli experts (not counting those in the service of international organizations) took their technical knowledge to more than 70 countries in Latin America, Asia, Africa, the Caribbean, and the Mediterranean areas, while more than 18,400 people came from these areas to study development methods in Israel. During that time, Israeli projects in developing countries enabled 12,000 families to be settled on the land. During the early 1970s, however, as Arab governments sought through the "oil weapon" to isolate Israel diplomatically and economically, relations with African and Asian nations cooled. The US is Israel's major political, economic, and military ally.

[19] ECONOMY

From the start, the economy has been faced with serious problems. Chief among these was the inflow of more than 1 million immigrants, most of them moneyless and unskilled, who had to be integrated into the country's economic life. The government makes large outlays for social welfare purposes, but is obliged to divert a considerable portion of its income to defense. In addition, traditional Middle Eastern sources of supply (e.g., of oil and wheat) and nearby markets for goods and services have been closed off. Israel must export on a large scale in order to maintain its relatively high standard of living; hence, it remains heavily dependent on a continuing flow of investment capital and public funds from abroad.

The economy is a mixture of private, state, and cooperative ownership and holdings of the labor movement. In the first 25 years of Israel's existence, the number of industrial enterprises more than doubled; some 740 agricultural settlements were established; and there were notable advances in housing, transportation, and the exploitation of natural resources. From 1969 to 1974, GNP grew at an annual rate of 8.9% (at constant prices), and reached IL25,261 million in 1974 (at 1970 prices). Per capita private consumption (at 1970 prices) has risen steadily, from IL1,655 in 1950 to IL3,808 in 1969 and IL4,548 in 1974. Inflation has increased in recent years; the consumer price index (1969=100) stood at 159 in June 1973, 219.4 in June 1974, and 307.1 in June 1975.

The administered territories have expanded Israel's economic base, but lower living standards in these areas have been a problem. The territories' combined GNP in 1973, at 1968 prices, was IL982 million, of which IL670 million derived from Judea and Samaria and IL312 million from Gaza and North Sinai. Per capita private consumption was IL1,031 in Judea and Samaria, IL770 in Gaza and Sinai. Agriculture dominates the economies of these regions. Large-scale imports of industrial products and agricultural commodities (mostly from Israel) resulted in a net trade imbalance of IL810.3 million and a payments deficit (goods and services) of IL282.7 million in 1974. The imbalance had to be met with IL163 million in transfer payments, which were obtained largely from Israel.

[20] INCOME

Israel's national income rose from IL11,192 million (at current prices) in 1968 to IL42,184 million in 1974. Per capita national income in 1974 was IL12,589 (about $2,800). The relative shares of the various branches of the economy in the net domestic product (at factor cost) for 1973 were industry, construction, and utilities, 35.5%; public services, 20.8%; trade, restaurants, and hotels, 10%; finance and business services, 9.2%; transport, storage, and communications, 8.1%; agriculture, forestry, and fishing, 5.9%; and other, 10.5%.

[21] LABOR

In 1974 there were 1,089,000 employed persons in Israel, of whom 34.3% were employed in industry, construction, and utilities; 26.1% in public services; 12.2% in trade, restaurants, and hotels; 7.7% in transport, storage, and communications; 6.5% in agriculture, forestry, and fishing; 6.5% in finance and business services; and 6.7% in other areas. The total represented an increase of 178,100 over the 1968 figure. The estimated number of unemployed persons in 1974 was 33,700, or 3% of the civilian labor force.

The majority of Israeli workers, including those in agriculture, are union members belonging to the General Federation of Labor (Histadrut), founded by Jewish farm workers in 1920), which has nearly 1.3 million members (including wives of male workers), some 250,000 members of cooperatives and others affiliated through the agricultural center, and more than 70,000 Arab members. The Histadrut also has an industrial corporation (Koor), which owns and operates many large factories, and a contracting corporation (Solel Boneh). It also manages an agricultural marketing society (Tnuva), a cooperative wholesale corporation (Hamashbir Hamerkazi), and a workers' bank. Other labor unions in Israel are relatively insignificant.

Wages and working conditions in the private sector are regulated by collective agreements between Histadrut and the Israel Manufacturers' Association. The law provides for a maximum 8-hour day and 47-hour week, establishes a compulsory weekly rest period of 36 hours, and lays down minimum rates for overtime. The wage structure itself provides relatively narrow differentials between the lowest and highest skills. The average annual wage of urban employees in 1974 was IL15,200. Wages rose more than 25% annually between 1970 and 1974.

[22] AGRICULTURE

Between 1948 and 1973, the cultivated area was expanded from 165,000 to 427,000 hectares. Agricultural production in 1973/74 was valued at IL5,402.7 million, almost double the value of output in 1970/71. Principal crops and their 1973/74 production totals (in tons) were citrus fruits, 1,698,000; other fruits, 347,300; vegetables, potatoes, melons, and pumpkins, 772,600; cereals and pulses for grain, 364,200; sugar beets and other industrial and oil crops, 289,100; and roughage, 1,849,000. Owing to the uniquely favorable soil and climatic conditions, Israel's citrus fruit has qualities of flavor and appearance commanding high prices on the world market. In 1974, citrus fruit exports earned more than $120 million.

The main forms of agricultural settlement are the kibbutz, moshav, moshav shitufi, and moshava. In the kibbutz all property is owned jointly by the settlement on land leased from the Jewish National Fund, and work assignments, services, and social activities are determined by elected officers. Although predominantly agricultural, many kibbutzim have taken on such industrial activities as food processing and the production of building materials. Numbering 235 in 1973, with a population of 102,654, the kibbutzim perform an important function in the colonization of arid and border areas. Devoted entirely to agriculture, the moshavim (workers' smallholder cooperatives) market produce and own heavy equipment, but their land is divided into separate units and worked by the members individually. This form of settlement has had special appeal to new immigrants. The moshavim shitufiyim are 28 collective villages that are similar in economic organization to the kibbutzim but whose living arrangements are more like the moshav. Their population has declined to about 5,800. There are 56 moshavot, rural colonies composed of independent farmers and based on private enterprise. They were the principal form of 19th-century settlement. Many have grown into urban communities.

New immigrants settling on the land are given wide-ranging assistance. The Jewish Agency, the executive arm of the World Zionist Organization, absorbs many of the initial costs, agricultural credits are extended on a preferential basis, and equipment, seeds, livestock, and work animals are supplied at low cost.

Israeli agriculture emphasizes maximum utilization of irrigation and the use of modern techniques to increase yields. An ever-expanding national irrigation system distributes water to 182,500 hectares, as compared with 30,000 in 1948. Water is transported via pipeline from Lake Kinneret to the northern Negev. More than 90% of Israel's subterranean water supply is being exploited.

[23] ANIMAL HUSBANDRY
There is little natural pasturage in most areas, and livestock is fed mainly on imported feeds and farm-grown forage. Livestock farmers are aided by subsidies. In 1973/74 there were 299,950 head of cattle (about nine times the number in 1948), 334,200 sheep and goats, and 11,750,000 poultry. About 1,489 million eggs, 591 million liters of milk, 164,000 tons of poultry meat, and 38,900 tons of cattle meat were produced.

[24] FISHING
Jewish settlers introduced the breeding of fish (mostly carp) into Palestine. The total fish catch has grown from 3,500 tons in 1948/49 to 22,700 tons in 1973/74. In addition to carp, important freshwater fish include catfish, barbel, and trout. The marine catch consists mainly of sardines, with lesser catches of gray and red mullet, red bream, bonito, sea pike, and hake.

[25] FORESTRY
There are small natural forests covering about 35,000 hectares, mostly in the north. Reforestation is regarded as vital to the conservation of water resources and the prevention of further soil erosion, and by 1974, 58,400 hectares were afforested, as compared with only 5,300 hectares in 1948. Of the 1974 total, 36,300 hectares were in coniferous trees, 12,500 in eucalyptus, and 9,600 in other trees, notably acacia. Forestry products in 1974 included 101,789 cu meters of plywood and 96,385 tons of paper, newsprint, and cardboard.

[26] MINING
Although Israel is not richly endowed with mineral resources, the Dead Sea is one of the world's richest sources of potassium chloride (potash), magnesium bromide, and other salts. Recent explorations, especially in the Negev, have also led to the discovery of deposits of phosphate, copper (low grade), glass sand, ceramic clays, gypsum, and granite. Most of the phosphate deposits, located in the northeastern Negev, are at best medium grade; they are extracted by open-pit mining. Commercially exploitable oil is found in small amounts at Helez and other locations. In 1974, Israel produced 950,000 tons of potash, 1,026,000 tons of phosphate rock, 9,500 tons of copper ore, and 45 million liters of crude oil. Imports of minerals and mineral fuels accounted for more than 35% of Israel's imports in 1974.

[27] ENERGY AND POWER
Nearly all electricity is supplied by the government-owned Israel Electric Corporation, which uses imported fuel oil. Electricity is generated principally by thermal power stations. Generating capacity has grown by more than 2,000% since 1948, reaching 1.6 million kw at the end of 1974; production in the latter year amounted to 8,837 million kwh. Consumption of electricity totaled 7,915.1 million kwh, of which 34.5% went for industry, 27.6% for household use, 16% for trade and public services, 13.4% for irrigation, and 8.5% for other uses. The number of electricity consumers in 1974 was 1,083,000 (compared with 179,000 in 1950). Because local fuel resources are scarce, the government is sponsoring intensive research in the generation of electricity by alternate sources. An Atomic Energy Commission, established in 1952, is laying the groundwork for a number of atomic power stations, the first of which is to be constructed in the early 1980s.

[28] INDUSTRY
More than half of the industrial establishments are in Tel Aviv, but a great deal of heavy industry is concentrated around Haifa. Most plants are privately owned. State enterprises are mainly devoted to exploitation of natural resources in the Negev; some other enterprises are controlled by the Histadrut.

Major expansion has taken place in textiles, machinery and transport equipment, metallurgy, mineral processing, electrical products, precision instruments, and chemicals. There were 6,600 industrial enterprises in 1972/73 employing 5 or more workers (for a total of 243,040 workers). Of these, only 813 firms (12% of the total) employed 50 or more workers. Total industrial employment of 270,900 persons (in 20,767 establishments) was 24% above the 1968 level. Industry still relies heavily on imported raw materials. Although production costs per unit have declined, industry remains handicapped by relatively high wage costs, low productivity, and shortage of bank credit. Incentive schemes and productivity councils, representing workers and management, have been set up in an attempt to increase work output.

Whereas in the past Israel's industry concentrated on consumer goods, it is advancing to the manufacture of capital goods. In 1972/73, industrial production by firms with five or more workers totaled IL7,217 million, as compared with IL2,518.6 million in 1965/66. Chief branches of industry contributing to this output included food, beverages, and tobacco, IL971.1 million in 1972/73; metal products, IL767.6 million; electrical and electronic equipment, IL673.6 million; textiles, IL634.4 million; chemical and oil products, IL552.2 million; and transport equipment, IL505.5 million. Industrial products in 1974 included cement, 1,428,000 tons; rubber tires, 1,650,000; superphosphates (16%), 220,000 tons; nitric acid (100%), 77,047 tons; ammonia, 67,693 tons; ammonium sulfate, 48,830 tons; polyethylene, 31,719 tons; cotton fabrics, 15,508 tons; beer, 340,910 hectoliters; wine, 163,910 hectoliters; cigarettes, 5,243 tons.

[29] DOMESTIC TRADE
Banks, commercial institutions, and the Histadrut have their headquarters in Tel Aviv, the business capital. Supermarkets and department stores are on the increase. Packaged goods are becoming more common, but many sales are still made from bulk. Cooperative societies market the agricultural produce of their affiliated settlements and farms. Tnuva, the Histadrut agricultural marketing society, sells more than 70% of Israel's farm products. Installment sales are becoming widespread. For importers, the customary terms of trade are cash against import licenses (which carry the allocation of the required foreign exchange rate in each case) or irrevocable letters of credit. Warehousing and cold storage facilities in port areas are generally adequate. Most banking and financial transactions are carried out in Tel Aviv. Advertising is used in newspapers, periodicals, posters, billboards, radio broadcasts, and at motion picture theaters.

In wholesale trade, 4,155 firms, employing 32,556 persons, had gross sales of IL18,206.7 million in 1972/73. In retail trade there were 36,333 establishments employing 80,355 persons during the same year. Large-scale retail sales (by cooperatives, chain stores, and department stores) totaled IL4.1 billion in 1974.

Saturday closing is the custom for all shops, offices, banks, public institutions, and transport services, except in the Arab areas. Shopping and office hours are Sunday to Thursday, 8 A.M. to 1 P.M. and 3 to 7 P.M. On Fridays and days preceding holidays, shops shut down about two hours before sunset, offices at 1 P.M. Banks are open 8:30 A.M. to 12:30 P.M. and close at noon on Fridays and on days before holidays.

30 FOREIGN TRADE

Polished diamonds, chemicals, machinery, transport equipment, and various other manufactures made up the bulk of Israel's exports in 1974; agricultural products, particularly fruits and vegetables, were also significant, and citrus fruits alone accounted for 7.6% of all exports. Export revenue rose from $29.7 million in 1949 to $1.8 billion in 1974, but the value of imports in the same period rose from $253.1 million to $4.2 billion, leaving substantial trade deficits. Israel must import nearly all of its petroleum and most of its raw materials for industry.

Principal exports in 1974 (in thousands of dollars) were:

Processed precious and semiprecious stones	645,876
Chemicals	263,900
Fruits and vegetables	231,996
Rubber, metal, and textile manufactures (including clothing)	230,077
Machinery and transport equipment	146,515
Other exports	306,495
TOTAL	1,824,859

Principal imports in 1974 (in thousands of dollars) were:

Petroleum and petroleum products	628,800
Machinery	600,858
Precious and semiprecious stones	465,294
Live animals, cereals, and other food	445,536
Transport equipment	423,451
Iron and steel	379,052
Chemicals	293,971
Crude materials, inedible	262,071
Other imports	737,618
TOTAL	4,236,651

In 1974, the chief buyers of Israeli products were the US, UK, the Netherlands, and the Federal Republic of Germany (FRG). The FRG moved to second place, after the US, as a supplier of Israel's imports. In 1974, the US provided 19% of Israel's imports and took 16% of its exports. Almost half of Israel's exports to the US were polished diamonds. Israel's trade with Common Market countries has been increasingly heavy, amounting in 1974 to 38% of its exports and 47% of its imports. Principal trade partners in 1974 (in thousands of dollars) were:

	EXPORTS	IMPORTS	BALANCE
US	300,616	789,090	-488,474
FRG	136,666	687,438	-550,772
UK	156,758	543,415	-386,657
Netherlands	138,621	223,317	- 84,696
Italy	69,166	225,560	-156,394
Belgium-Luxembourg	105,775	142,209	- 36,434
France	83,451	154,066	- 70,615
Switzerland	105,021	112,615	- 7,594
Japan	69,114	130,487	- 61,373
Hong Kong	118,580	5,925	112,655
Other countries	541,091	1,222,529	-681,438
TOTALS	1,824,859	4,236,651	-2,411,792

Israel reported the trade of administered areas in 1974 to total IL683.4 million in exports and IL1,493.7 million in imports. Most imports (89% by value) came from Israel; most exports (91%) went to Israel or Jordan.

31 BALANCE OF PAYMENTS

Israel's foreign trade has consistently shown an extremely adverse balance, owing mainly to the rapid rise in population and the expansion of the economy, which requires heavy imports of machinery and raw materials. The total trade deficit rose from less than $300 million in 1952 to more than $2 billion in 1974, although the percentage of imports covered by exports has increased (from less than 15% in the early 1950s to figures ranging from 40% to 70% in recent years). The deficit in goods and services rose from $306 million in 1952 to $3,355 million in 1974. The imbalance has been offset to some extent by the flow of funds from abroad. As of 1974, government obligations abroad amounted to $4,565 million. Summaries of Israel's balance of payments for 1973 and 1974 (in millions of dollars) are as follows:

	1973	1974
CURRENT ACCOUNTS		
Trade, net	-2,457	-3,026
Services, net	- 184	- 329
Transfers, net	2,171	1,674
TOTALS	- 470	-1,681
CAPITAL ACCOUNTS		
Long-term capital	974	635
Short-term capital	- 5	483
TOTALS	969	1,118
Errors and omissions	25	- 252
Net change	524	- 815

32 BANKING

The Bank of Israel, with headquarters in Jerusalem, began operations as the central state bank in December 1954. Its assets totaled IL82,522 million in 1974. The bank issues currency, accepts deposits from banking institutions in Israel, extends temporary advances to the government, acts as the government's sole banking and fiscal agent, and manages the public debt. At the end of 1969 there were eight commercial banks, the largest of which were the Bank Leumi, the Israel Discount Bank, and the Histadrut-controlled Bank Hapoalim. There were also 18 credit cooperatives and 22 other financial institutions. Among the subsidiaries of commercial banks are mortgage banks (some of which were also directly established by the government). The largest of these specialized institutions, the Tefahot Israel Mortgage Bank, provides many loans to home builders. The Israel Mortgage Bank, aided by the central government, handles many municipal loans for schools and other facilities.

Industrial development banks specialize in financing new manufacturing enterprises. The Industrial Bank of Israel, formed in 1957 by major commercial banks, the government, the Manufacturers' Association, and foreign investors, has received aid from the IBRD and has played a major role in the industrial development of the Negev area. The government-owned Bank of Agriculture is the largest lending institution in that sector. The Post Office Bank is concerned mainly with clearing operations, savings, sale of savings certificates, and postal orders.

The Bank of Israel's power to fix the liquidity ratio that banks must maintain against deposits has been an important instrument in governing both volume and types of loans. First put into effect in 1961, the liquidity ratio fluctuated between 62% in that year and 67% in 1966. Legal interest rate ceilings are 10% on loans to industry and agriculture and 11% for commercial loans. The Bank of Israel's rediscount rate on bills of Israeli currency was set at 6% at the end of 1965. Bank notes and coins in circulation totaled IL3,319 million at the end of 1974.

³³ INSURANCE

The State Insurance Controller's Office may grant or withhold insurance licenses and determine the valuation of assets, the form of balance sheets, computations of reserves, and investment composition. By the end of 1974 there were 28 Israeli insurance companies, and 53 foreign companies, including 19 Lloyd's of London brokers. At the end of 1974, domestic and foreign insurance firms combined had assets totaling IL2,970 million. During 1974, life insurance premiums received amounted to IL446.5 million. General insurance premiums totaled IL1,169 million, of which 77% was received by Israeli companies.

The most important category of general insurance is fire insurance. Automobile liability insurance is compulsory. War-damage insurance is compulsory on buildings and also on some personal property. A government insurance institute offers insurance against commercial and political risks arising from the granting of export credits.

³⁴ SECURITIES

Growing activity on the Israeli securities market made it necessary to convert the rather loosely organized Tel Aviv Securities Clearing House into the formally constituted Tel Aviv Stock Exchange in 1953. A further expansion took place in 1955, when debentures linked either to the US dollar or to the cost-of-living index—with special tax privileges—made their first appearance on the market. The market is largely devoted to loans of public and semipublic bodies, with provident funds and banks acquiring most of the securities placed. There is only one quotation daily for each security. The number of new issues reached a peak in 1963/64. By 1974 there were about 90 stocks traded; half were of banking and credit institutions, one-third were of commercial businesses, and the rest shares of utilities and land-development enterprises. Average marketable capital at the stock exchange grew from IL386.9 million in 1960 to IL4,024.9 million in 1970 and IL17,340.1 million in 1974. The annual turnover rate (ratio between trade volume and average marketable capital) was 19.7% in 1974.

³⁵ PUBLIC FINANCE

The proposed budget is submitted to the Knesset for approval each January and becomes effective for the fiscal year beginning 1 April. It consists of an ordinary budget, financed mainly by local taxation, and a development budget, financed largely from overseas funds, private contributions, State of Israel bonds, foreign loans, US grants and agricultural surpluses, and FRG reparations. There is also a budget covering state business enterprises.

The following table shows the 1974/75 and 1975/76 consolidated revenues and expenditures of the central government (in millions of Israeli pounds):

	1974/75	1975/76
REVENUES		
Income tax	8,446	10,060
Customs and duties	7,842	9,438
Purchase tax	2,812	3,740
Foreign loans and grants	8,918	13,350
Internal loans	4,100	5,900
Business enterprises	6,009	9,426
Other revenues	8,532	13,812
TOTALS	46,659	65,726
EXPENDITURES		
Defense	16,289	22,306
Education and culture	2,008	3,415
Health, welfare, housing	1,253	1,986
Price and export subsidies	2,900	4,300
Interest	3,466	5,000
Other ordinary expenses	6,008	7,513
Debt repayment	3,652	5,180
Other development expenses	5,074	6,600
Business enterprises	6,009	9,426
TOTALS	46,659	65,726

Of the ordinary expenditures in 1975/76, defense accounted for 50%; education and culture 8%; health, welfare, and housing 5%; price and export subsidies 10%; interest 11%; and the rest 16%.

The gross public debt of the national government increased from IL1,084 million as of 1 March 1956 to IL43,670 million by 31 March 1974. The domestic debt was 59.5% and the foreign debt 40.5%.

In 1973/74, local authorities of all types accounted for combined revenues of IL3,162.9 million and expenditures of IL3,237.7 million, for a deficit of IL74.8 million. Municipalities accounted for 72.4% of all expenditures, local councils for 14.9%, and regional councils for 12.7%. The combined public debt of local authorities as of 31 March 1974 was IL2,736.9 million.

³⁶ TAXATION

Israel's population is heavily taxed. Personal income tax rates for married persons in 1976 ranged from 25% on the first IL36,000 of taxable income to 60% on taxable income over IL102,000. The first IL14,400 of income is not taxed. Credits taken into account in tax computation are IL2,400 for a resident taxpayer and IL1,200 for a nonworking wife. For single taxpayers, the highest tax rate was 70%. There are tax allowances for certain payments for medical treatment, retirement funds, and life insurance. Special concessions are granted to residents in border settlements, new settlements, and the Negev. Taxes of salaried persons are deducted at source; self-empolyed persons make advance payments in 10 installments, subject to assessment.

There is a 40% corporate profits tax, as well as a 35% tax on corporate net income after payment of this tax. The two taxes are tantamount to a 61% corporate income tax. A value-added tax and a purchase tax are also levied.

Municipalities and local and regional councils levy several taxes and rates. There is an annual business tax on every enterprise, based on net worth, annual sales volume, number of employees, and other factors. A company is subject to this tax in each municipality in which it has a place of business. The maximum business tax levied on an enterprise situated within the boundaries of any particular local authority is IL7,500 per annum. General rates, a real estate tax (commonly based on the number of rooms and the location of the building), and water rates are paid by the tenants or occupiers rather than the owners.

³⁷ CUSTOMS AND DUTIES

Customs and duties contribute about 15% of government revenues. Israel has a single-column import tariff based on the Brussels nomenclature classification. Ad valorem rates predominate, although specific and compound rates are also used. Ad valorem duties are imposed at rates ranging from 3% to 150%, but the majority are between 10% and 50%. Most basic food commodities, raw materials, and machinery for agricultural or industrial purposes are exempt from customs duties. Highest rates are applied to nonessential foodstuffs, luxury items, and manufactured goods that are of a type produced in Israel.

A free-trade agreement between Israel and the EEC took effect on 1 July 1975. Under this agreement, EEC tariffs on Israel's industrial exports were immediately reduced by 60% and were to be completely phased out by 1977. Preferential treatment has also been extended to Israel's agricultural exports. In return, Israel has granted concessions to the EEC on many categories of industrial and agricultural imports. Under the agreement, Israel will gradually abolish its customs duties on imports from the EEC by 1989.

Goods of US origin are guaranteed most-favored-nation treatment under a treaty of friendship, commerce, and navigation between the US and Israel, in force since 1954. Under the US Generalized System of Preferences (GSP) effective 1 January 1976, Israel has been designated a beneficiary country. US customs duties have been eliminated on 2,700 articles under the GSP.

38 FOREIGN INVESTMENTS

Apart from reparations, capital imports are largely composed of long-term loans and grants designed for investment by the government or the Jewish Agency.

A law for the encouragement of capital investment (1951) was designed to encourage foreign investment in those industries and services most urgently required to reduce Israel's dependence on imports and to increase its export potential. Applying mainly to investments in industry and agriculture, and implemented by the Investment Center, which was established under the ministries of finance and commercial industry and which has offices in New York, the law offers such inducements as relief from property taxes during the first five years, special allowances for depreciation, exemption from customs and purchase tax on essential materials, and reductions in income tax rates. A nonresident foreign investor may transfer his profits in the same currency in which his investment was made.

Israeli investments abroad are not significant.

39 ECONOMIC POLICY

Economic policy is dictated by goals of national security, full utilization of resources, integration of immigrants, and the institution of a broad welfare program. The urgency of these goals imposes responsibilities on the government for planning, financing, and directly participating in productive activities. Government direct investment in enterprises totaled IL1,738.5 million as of 31 March 1974, and loans totaled IL8,024.4. Mining was the principal beneficiary of direct investments; more than half the loans were to the construction sector. In accordance with government plans, industry (mining and manufacturing) has increased its contribution to the net domestic product from IL1,051 million in 1968 to IL4,242 million in 1973. Its percentage contribution has remained relatively constant, however, at about 23–24%. Agriculture, forestry, and fishing have declined in importance, contributing about 6% in 1973.

The government has influenced the setting in which private capital functions through differential taxation, import and export licensing, subsidies, and high protective tariffs. The 1962 revaluation of the Israeli pound was accompanied by a new economic policy aimed at the reduction of protective tariffs, the continued support of development, the planning and implementation of long-range development, and the maximization of efficiency. Subsequently, the government has periodically decreed further monetary devaluations, new taxes, and other austerity measures designed to curb consumption and stimulate exports. On 5 October 1975, a 90-day freeze was imposed on the prices of all essential goods and services. However, on 24 February 1976, the government announced cuts in the price stabilization subsidies on bread, dairy products, and milk, measures that were expected to contribute to a 25% rise in the cost of living in 1976.

40 HEALTH

In 1974, the infant mortality rate was 23.5 per 1,000 and life expectancy was 70.5 years for Jewish males and 73.7 years for Jewish females (69.4 for non-Jewish males and 72.6 for non-Jewish females). There were 10,066 physicians (1 for every 339 persons; one of the world's highest ratios), 2,688 dental surgeons and practitioners, 2,173 pharmacists, and 714 licensed midwives. There were 126 hospitals, with a total of 23,077 beds, or 6.8 per 1,000 population. There were 48 general hospitals, 35 hospitals for chronic diseases, 40 mental hospitals, and 3 rehabilitation hospitals.

The Ministry of Health supervises all health matters and functions directly in the field of medical care. It maintains 35 hospitals (with 36% of Israel's hospital beds), in addition to infant welfare clinics, nursing schools, and laboratories. The largest medical organization in the country, the Workers' Sick Fund (Kupat Holim), the health insurance association of Histadrut, had a membership of 2.3 million members in 1973; it administers 14 hospitals, in addition to numerous clinics, convalescent homes, and mother-and-child welfare stations.

The Arab Department of the Ministry of Health recruits public health personnel from among the Arab population, and its mobile clinics extend medical aid to Bedouin tribes in the Negev.

41 SOCIAL WELFARE

The 1975/76 national budget for the Ministry of Social Welfare was about IL589 million. Aside from supervising a wide network of public and private social welfare agencies, the Ministry maintains special enterprises employing the blind and the handicapped, operates institutions for mentally and physically handicapped children, and administers a nationwide preventive service for problem children and youth.

Special legislation established the legal right to assistance of persons incapacitated for work, of survivors of those who died in the state service, and, under certain conditions, of persons whose claims antedated their immigration into Israel. Pensions have thus been paid to persons disabled while fighting with the Allied forces in World War II and to those invalided as a result of Nazi persecution. A national insurance law, which came into force in April 1954, provides insurance for the disabled and for survivors, maternity benefits, and monthly allowances for large families. Work-accident insurance provisions cover all employees, members of rural cooperatives, and, since 1957, all of the self-employed. In 1974/75, the National Insurance Institute insured 1,260,000 persons, and expended an estimated IL3,396 million. In 1974/75, 250,694 claimants received old age and survivors insurance (for a total expenditure of IL1,420 million), 187,605 families with three children or more received large-family allowances (IL941 million), and 93,501 birth grants were paid (IL908 million). The Institute is directly under the minister of labor and is governed by a 42-member council representing government, labor, and employers.

The Jewish Agency is primarily responsible for the initial phases of reception and absorption of immigrants. Hadassah provides vocational guidance and training to youth, and the Women's International Zionist Organization (WIZO) is active in family and child welfare.

Nonprofit institutions account for about one-fifth of all money spent on social welfare. Mo'etzet Hapo'alot (Women's Workers Council), a Histadrut affiliate, is active in this area, along with the private US-financed Malben agency, which helps handicapped immigrants, and Youth Aliyah, which operates a system of children's villages.

42 HOUSING

Israel suffered from a chronic housing shortage at its creation. Despite an extensive national building program and the initial allocation of some abandoned Arab dwellings to newcomers, nearly 100,000 immigrants were, in early 1958, still housed in the transit camps. By the mid-1960s, however, the extreme housing shortage had been overcome, and newcomers were immediately moved into permanent residences. From 1960 to 1974, a total of 543,760 housing units were constructed. At the end of 1974, about 44% of the residential buildings under construction were being built with public funds.

In 1971, 64.6% of Israeli families owned their own homes, 30.5% rented their dwellings, and 4.9% made other arrangements.

43 EDUCATION

Education is compulsory and free for all children between 5 and 15 years of age. A state education law of 1953 put an end to the separate elementary school systems affiliated to labor and religious groupings and established a unified state-administered system, within which provision was made for state religious schools. Four types of schools existed in 1975: public religious (Jewish) and public secular schools (the largest group); schools of the orthodox Agudat Israel (which operated outside the public-school system but were assisted with government funds); public schools for Arabs; and private schools, mainly operated by Catholic and Protestant organizations.

In 1974/75, educational institutions enrolled 1,014,414 pupils, of whom 795,937 were in Hebrew education and 146,377 in Arab education. There were 6,286 kindergartens and primary schools, 209 intermediate schools (grades 7–9), 569 postprimary schools, and 51 teacher-training colleges. Enrollment in Hebrew education included 574,504 pupils in kindergartens and primary schools, 50,882 in intermediate schools, 160,195 in postprimary schools, and 10,356 in teacher-training colleges. Enrollment in Arab education included 121,606 in kindergartens and primary schools; 8,929 in intermediate schools, 15,119 in postprimary schools, and 723 in teacher-training colleges. Arab school enrollment rose by more than 400% between 1950 and 1974. There were 48,187 teaching posts in Hebrew education in 1974/75, and 6,034 in Arab education. During 1974/75 there were also 342,693 pupils attending 1,253 educational institutions in the administered territories; kindergartens and primary schools accounted for a total of 241,718 pupils. About 29% of the pupils were enrolled in UNRWA-run schools. The official policy of the Israeli government is to minimize direct intervention in the schools of the administered territories, while insisting on the elimination of anti-Jewish and anti-Israel materials from textbooks.

The language of instruction in Jewish schools is Hebrew; in Arab schools it is Arabic. Arabic is taught as an optional language in Jewish schools, while Hebrew is taught in Arab schools from the fourth grade. In 1972, the literacy rate among Israelis aged 14 and over was 90.8% for Jews (87.9% in 1961) and 63.5% for non-Jews (48.3% in 1961).

There were seven institutions of higher learning in 1974/75, with a total enrollment of 53,100. The two most outstanding are the Hebrew University (founded in 1918) in Jerusalem and the Israel Institute of Technology (Technion, founded in 1912) in Haifa, both of which receive government subsidies of about 50% of their total budgets; the remaining funds are largely collected abroad. In 1974/75, more than 15,500 students were enrolled at the Hebrew University, whose faculty numbered 1,857. Technion's student enrollment in undergraduate and graduate programs totaled 8,550; the academic staff numbered 1,317. Tel Aviv University, formed in 1956, had an enrollment of 12,900 in 1974/75, and an academic staff of 2,403. Other institutions include the Bar Ilan University in Ramat-Gan, opened in 1955 under religious auspices; the Weizmann Institute of Science at Rehovot, notable for its research into specific technical, industrial, and scientific problems; and the university colleges of Haifa and Beersheba. National expenditure on education totaled

IL2,353.7 million in 1972/73, of which 28.2% came from the central government, 20.4% from local authorities, 46.7% from nonprofit institutions, and 4.7% from other sources.

44 LIBRARIES AND MUSEUMS

Israel's largest library, founded in 1924, is the privately endowed Jewish National and University Library in Jerusalem, with more than 1 million volumes. The original collection of 450,000 volumes, formerly located on nearby Mt. Scopus, access to which had been denied by Jordan after 1949, is now housed in Israel. An important collection of Arabic texts, numbering some 80,000 volumes, is housed in Jaffa. There are more than 700 libraries, and the Ministry of Education and Culture has provided basic libraries to some 480 rural settlements.

The most important museum is the Israel Museum, opened in 1965 in Jerusalem. Included in the museum are the Bezalel Museum, with its large collection of Jewish folk art; a Jewish antiquities exhibit; the Billy Rose Art Garden of Modern Sculpture; the Samuel Bronfman Biblical and Archaeological Museum; and the Shrine of the Book. The Palestine Museum, built in 1936, contains a rich collection of archaeological material illustrating the prehistory and early history of Palestine and Transjordan. The Tel Aviv Museum, founded in 1926, has more than 30,000 paintings, drawings, and sculpture. The country's 98 museums were visited by 5,151,800 persons during 1974/75.

45 ORGANIZATIONS

The World Zionist Organization (WZO) was founded by Theodor Herzl in 1897 for the purpose of creating "for the Jewish people a home in Palestine, secured by public law." The organization is composed of various international groupings represented in its supreme organ, the World Zionist Congress. The Jewish Agency, originally founded under the League of Nations mandate to promote Jewish interests in Palestine, comprises the executive arm of the WZO; since 1948, it has been responsible for the organization, training, and transportation to Israel of all Jews who wish to settle there. The United Israel Appeal (Keren Hayesod) is the financial instrument of the Jewish Agency; it recruits donations from world Jewry. The Jewish National Fund (Keren Kayemet le'Israel) is devoted to land acquisition, soil reclamation, and afforestation. Hadassah, the Women's Zionist Organization of America, is also active in Israel; it sponsors the Hadassah Medical Organization, which provides hospital and medical training facilities.

The main labor organization is the General Federation of Labor (Histadrut), a large economic complex whose interests include some of the largest factories in the country, an agricultural marketing society (Tnuva), a cooperative wholesale association (Hamashbir Hamerkazi), and a workers' bank. An important youth organization is Youth Aliyah, founded in 1934, which has helped to rehabilitate and educate more than 140,000 children from some 80 countries. First aid services in Israel are organized by the Red Shield of David (Magen David Adom), which cooperates with the International Red Cross.

There are numerous cultural, religious, business, and other societies and organizations.

46 PRESS

In 1974, 27 daily newspapers and some 714 other periodicals, 77 of them weeklies, appeared in 12 languages besides Hebrew. Most newspapers appear in 4–16 pages, but there are weekly supplements on subjects such as politics, economics, and the arts. Although there is no political censorship, restrictions are placed on coverage of national security matters. National daily newspapers (with their average 1974 circulation) include:

TEL AVIV	ORIENTATION	CIRCULATION
Ma'ariv (e.)	Independent	150,000
Yediot Acharonot (e.)	Independent	142,000

Ha'aretz (m.)	Independent Liberal	51,000
Davar (m.)	Histadrut	45,000
Viata-Noastra (m.; Romanian)	Independent	22,000
Al Hamishmar (m.)	Mapam	20,000
Uj Kelet (m.; Hungarian)	Independent	18,000
Yediot Hadashot (m.; German)	Independent	18,000
Letzte Neies (m.; Yiddish)	Independent	16,000
JERUSALEM		
Jerusalem Post (m.; English)	Independent	26,000
Al-Quds (m.; Arabic)	Independent	20,000

⁴⁷TOURISM

A passport, a visa (good for three months' residence), and a certificate of smallpox vaccination are required for entry. In the first decade after its founding, Israel was visited by some 335,000 tourists, who spent an average of $5 million annually; in 1974, 624,727 tourists visited Israel (more than double the number in 1965), and spent more than $100 million. The Tourist Industry Development Corporation fosters tourism by granting loans for hotel expansion and improvement. In 1974, Israel had 288 recommended hotels, with a total of 19,982 rooms.

⁴⁸FAMOUS ISRAELIS

Chaim Weizmann (b. Russia, 1874–1952), chief architect of the state, was leader of the Zionist movement for 25 years, as well as a distinguished chemist who discovered methods for synthesizing acetone and rubber. David Ben-Gurion (b. Poland, 1886–1973), an eloquent spokesman on labor and national affairs, served as Israel's first prime minister. Golda Meir (Myerson; b. Russia, 1898), like Ben-Gurion a former secretary-general of Histadrut, became well known as Israel's prime minister from 1970 to 1974. Other prominent contemporary figures include Abba Eban (b. South Africa, 1915), former foreign affairs minister and representative to the UN; Moshe Dayan (b.1915), military leader and political figure; Pinhas Sapir (b. Poland, 1907–75), labor leader and minister of finance.

Israel's foremost philosopher was Martin Buber (b. Vienna, 1878–1965), author of *I and Thou*. Outstanding scholars include the literary historian Joseph Klausner (1874–1958); the Bible researcher Ezekiel Kaufmann (b. Ukraine, 1890); the philologist Naphtali Hertz Tur-Sinai (Torczyner; b. Poland, 1886); the archaeologist Eliezer Sukenik (1889–1953); and the Kabbalah authority Gershom Gerhard Scholem (b. Germany, 1897).

The foremost poets are Uri Zvi Greenberg (b. Galicia, 1896), Avraham Shlonsky (b. Russia, 1900–73), and Nathan Alterman (b. Warsaw, 1910–70); and the leading novelists are Shmuel Yosef Halevi Agnon (b. Galicia, 1888–1970), a Nobel Prize winner in 1966, and Hayim Hazaz (b. Russia, 1897). Painters of note include Reuven Rubin (b. Romania, 1893–1975), Mane Katz (b. Russia, 1894–1962), Marcel Janco (b. Bucharest, 1895), and Moshe Mokady (b. Galicia, 1902). Paul Ben-Haim (Frankenburger; b. Munich, 1897), March Lavry (b. Riga, 1903–67), and Ödön Partos (b. Budapest, 1907) are well-known composers.

Significant contributions in other fields have been made by mathematician Abraham Halevi Fraenkel (b. Munich, 1891); botanist Hugo Boyko (b. Vienna, 1892); zoologist Shimon (Fritz) Bodenheimer (b. Cologne, 1897–1959); parasitologist Saul Aaron Adler (b. Russia, 1895–1966); physicist Giulio Raccah (b. Florence, 1909–65); rheologist Marcus Reiner (b. Czernowitz, 1886); and gynecologist Bernard Zondek (b. Germany, 1891–1966).

⁴⁹DEPENDENCIES

Israel has no dependencies or colonies.

⁵⁰BIBLIOGRAPHY

Albright, William Foxwell. *Archaeology of Palestine*. London: Penguin, 1949.

Appelbaum, Shimon. *Archaeology in Israel*. Jerusalem: Israeli Digest, 1967.

Area Handbook for Israel. Washington, D.C.: Government Printing Office, 1970.

Arendt, Hannah. *Eichmann in Jerusalem: A Report on the Banality of Evil*. New York: Viking Press, 1964.

Baker, Henry E. *The Legal Systems of Israel*. Jerusalem: Israel Universities Press, 1968.

Baratz, Joseph. *Village by the Jordan*. London: Marvill, 1954.

Ben Gurion, David. *Rebirth and Destiny of Israel*. New York: Philosophical Library, 1954.

Bentwich, Norman. *Israel Resurgent*. New York: Praeger, 1960.

Birnbaum, Ervin. *The Politics of Compromise: State and Religion in Israel*. Rutherford, N.J.: Fairleigh Dickinson University Press, 1970.

Brilliant, Moshe. *Portrait of Israel*. New York: American Heritage Press, 1970.

Eban, Abba. *The Voice of Israel*. New York: Horizon Press, 1957.

Encyclopaedia Hebraica. Tel Aviv: Massada, 1948–date.

Eisenstadt, Shmuel N. *Israel Society*. New York: Basic Books, 1967.

Fein, Leonard J. *Israel: Politics and People*. Boston: Little, Brown, 1968.

Freudenheim, Yehosua. *Government in Israel*. Dobbs Ferry, N.Y.: Oceana, 1967.

Frister, Roman. *Israel: Years of Crisis, Years of Hope*. New York: McGraw-Hill, 1973.

Halevi, Nadav, and Ruth Klinov-Malul. *The Economic Development of Israel*. New York: Praeger, 1968.

Halperin, Haim. *Changing Patterns in Israel Agriculture*. London: Routledge and Kegan Paul, 1957.

Herzl, Theodor. *The Jewish State*. New York: American Zionist Emergency Council, 1946.

Horowitz, David. *The Economics of Israel*. New York: Pergamon Press, 1967.

Hurewitz, J. C. *Middle East Politics: The Military Dimension*. New York: Praeger, 1969.

Hurewitz, J. C. *The Struggle for Palestine*. New York: Norton, 1950.

Israel. Department of Surveys. *Atlas of Israel*. 2d. ed. Jerusalem: Survey of Israel, Ministry of Labor, 1970.

Kallen, Horace Meyer. *Utopias at Bay*. New York: Herzl, 1958.

Kanovsky, Eliyahu. *The Economy of the Israeli Kibbutz*. Cambridge: Harvard University Press, 1966.

Koestler, Arthur. *Promise and Fulfillment: Palestine, 1917–1949*. New York: Macmillan, 1949.

Laufer, Leopold. *Israel and the Developing Countries*. New York: Twentieth Century Fund, 1967.

Learsi, Rufus (i.e., Israel Goldberg). *Fulfillment: The Epic Story of Zionism*. Cleveland: World, 1951.

Malkosh, N. *Co-operation in Israel*. Tel Aviv: Histadrut, 1954.

Marshall, Samuel Lyman Atwood. *Sinai Victory*. New York: Morrow, 1958.

Naamani, Israel T. *Israel*. New York: Praeger, 1972.

Parker, James. *A History of Palestine*. London: Gollancz, 1949.

Patai, Raphael (ed.). *Encyclopedia of Zionism and Israel*. 2 vols. New York: Herzl Press, 1971.

Pearlman, Moshe. *The Army of Israel*. New York: Philosophical Library, 1950.

Prittie, Terence. *Israel: Miracle in the Desert*. New York: Praeger, 1967.

Rosetti, Moshe. *The Knesset: Its Origins, Forms and Procedures*. Jerusalem: Israeli Government Press, 1966.

Sacher, Harry. *Israel: The Establishment of a State*. London: Weidenfeld and Nicolson, 1952.

Safran, Nadav. *From War to War: The Arab-Israel Confrontation 1948–1967*. New York: Pegasus Press, 1969.

Weizmann, Chaim. *Trial and Error: The Autobiography of Chaim Weizmann*. New York: Harper, 1949.

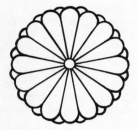

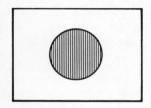

JAPAN

Nippon

CAPITAL: Tokyo. **FLAG**: The Sun-flag (Hi-no-Maru) consists of a red circle on a white background. **ANTHEM**: *Kimigayo (The Reign of Our Emperor)*, with words dating back to the 9th century. **MONETARY UNIT**: The yen (¥) of 100 sen is issued in coins of 1, 5, 10, 50, and 100 yen, and notes of 100, 500, 1,000, 5,000, and 10,000 yen. ¥1=0.0033366 (or $1=¥299.70). **WEIGHTS AND MEASURES**: The metric system is the legal standard. **HOLIDAYS**: New Year's Day, 1 January; Adults' Day, 15 January; Commemoration of the Founding of the Nation, 11 February; Vernal Equinox Day, 21 or 22 March; Emperor's Birthday, 29 April; Constitution Day, 3 May; Children's Day, 5 May; Respect for the Aged Day, 15 September; Autumnal Equinox Day, 23 or 24 September; Health-Sports Day, 10 October; Culture Day, 3 November; Labor-Thanksgiving Day, 23 November. **TIME**: 9 P.M.=noon GMT.

¹LOCATION, SIZE, AND EXTENT

Situated off the eastern edge of the Asian continent, the Japanese archipelago is bounded on the N by the Sea of Okhotsk, on the E and S by the Pacific Ocean, on the SW by the East China Sea, and on the W by the Sea of Japan. The total area of Japan is 377,483 sq km (145,747 sq mi). It extends *3,008* km (*1,869* mi) NE–SW and *1,645* km (*1,022* mi) SE–NW, and has a total coastline of *9,387* km (*5,833* mi).

The five main islands are Honshu, 230,862 sq km (89,136 sq mi); Hokkaido, 83,511 sq km (32,244 sq mi); Kyushu, 42,073 sq km (16,244 sq mi); Shikoku, 18,792 sq km (7,256 sq mi); and Okinawa, 2,245 sq km (867 sq mi). Each of the five main islands includes offshore islands in its area.

Of the thousands of other islands, four are of significance: Tsushima, 698 sq km (269 sq mi), in the straits between Korea and Japan; Amami-oshima, 709 sq km (274 sq mi), of the northern Ryukyu Islands off southern Japan; Sado Island, 857 sq km (331 sq mi), in the Sea of Japan off central Honshu; and Awaji Island, 593 sq km (229 sq mi), lying between Shikoku and Honshu. Two groups of islands, returned to Japan by the US in 1968, are located some 1,287 km (800 mi) due east of the Ryukyus: the Ogasawara (Bonin) Islands, about 885 km (550 mi) south of Tokyo, consist of 27 islands in three main groups—the Barley Islands, the Beechey Islands, and the Parry Islands—with a total area of 104 sq km (40 sq mi)—and the Kazan (Volcano) Islands, directly south of the Ogasawara group, a chain of islands extending 138 km (86 mi), with a total area of 28 sq km (11 sq mi).

Japan's principal island is Honshu, on which are located the capital city of Tokyo, the principal cities and plains, and the major industrial area. This island is divided into four unofficial regions: Tohoku, from north of Tokyo to Hokkaido; the Chubu or central region, from Tokyo south to the Nagoya area; the Kansai, including the important cities of Kyoto, Osaka, Kobe, and Nara; and the Chugoku, the narrow peninsula, thrusting westward from the Kansai between the Sea of Japan and the Inland Sea, a body of water running between southern Honshu and the island of Shikoku. The Tokyo-Yokohama region is called the Kanto.

²TOPOGRAPHY

The Japanese islands are the upper portions of vast mountains belonging to what is sometimes called the "Circum-Pacific Ring of Fire," which stretches from Southeast Asia to the Aleutian Islands. The first prominent feature of Japan is its mountainous structure. Landforms are steep and rugged, indicating that, geologically speaking, Japan is still a young area. Through the central part of Honshu, running in a north-south direction, are the two principal mountain ranges: the Hida (or Japan Alps) and the Akaishi Mountains, with heights ranging from 8,000 feet to 9,800 feet. There are more than 250 mountains with peaks of over 6,500 feet. The highest is the beautiful Mt. Fuji (Fujiyama in Japanese) at 12,389 feet.

A second major feature is the numerous volcanoes. Japan has 196 volcanoes, of which 30 remain active. Earthquakes occur continually, with an average of 1,500 minor shocks per year. Japan has seven major seismic zones. One of the world's greatest recorded natural disasters took place in the Kanto earthquake of 1923, when the Tokyo-Yokohama area was devastated and upward of 40,000 persons died.

The plains of Japan are few and small. Most plains are located along the seacoast and are composed of alluvial lowlands, diluvial uplands, and low hills. The largest is the Kanto Plain (Tokyo Bay region), about 2,500 sq mi. Others include the Kinai Plain (Osaka-Kyoto), Nobi (Nagoya), Echigo (northwestern Honshu), and Sendai (northeastern Honshu). There are four small plains in Hokkaido. Because of the very limited flat area, the population is heavily concentrated, and many Japanese regard their country as overpopulated.

Rivers tend to be short and swift. The longest is the Shinano-gawa (229 miles) in north-central Honshu, flowing into the Sea of Japan. The largest lake is Lake Biwa, near Kyoto, with an area of 260 sq mi. Lake Mashu in the Akan National Park of Hokkaido is considered the clearest lake in the world, having a transparency of 136 feet. Good harbors are limited because in most areas the land rises steeply out of the sea. Yokohama and Kobe are Japan's two most prominent harbors.

The Ryukyu Islands, among which Okinawa predominates, are the peaks of submerged mountain ranges. They are generally hilly or mountainous, with small alluvial plains.

³CLIMATE

Japan is located at the northeastern edge of the Asian monsoon climate belt, which brings much rain to the country. The weather is under the dual influence of the Siberian weather system and the patterns of the southern Pacific; it is affected by the Japan Current, a warm stream flowing from the southern Pacific along much of Japan's Pacific coast, tending to bring the area a milder and more temperate climate than is found in comparable areas elsewhere. Northern Japan is affected by the Okhotsk Current, a

149

cold stream flowing along the eastern coasts of Hokkaido and northern Honshu.

Throughout the year, there is fairly high humidity, with average rainfall ranging by area from 40 to 100 inches. Autumn weather is usually clear and bright. Winters tend to be warmer than in similar latitudes except in the north and west, where snowfalls are frequent and heavy. Spring is usually pleasant, and the summer hot and humid. There is a rainy season that moves from south to north during June and July. The frequent typhoons in the western Pacific at times cause severe damage in Japan.

Average temperature ranges from 16.6°C (62°F) in the southern portions to 9°C (48°F) in the extreme north. Hokkaido has long and severe winters with extensive snow, while the remainder of the country enjoys milder weather down to the southern regions, which are almost subtropical. The Ryukyus, although located in the temperate zone, are warmed by the Japan Current, giving them a subtropical climate. The typhoon season runs from May through October, and each year several storms usually sweep through the islands.

⁴FLORA AND FAUNA

Because of the variety and complexity in climate and land features, Japan's wildlife includes most varieties found elsewhere in the world.

Hokkaido flora is characterized by montane conifers (fir, spruce, and larch) at high elevations and mixed northern hardwoods (oak, maple, linden, birch, ash, elm, and walnut) at lower altitudes. The ground flora includes plants common to Eurasia and North America.

Honshu represents rich temperate flora. Common conifers are cypress, umbrella pine, hemlock, yew, and white pine. On the lowlands, there are live oak and camphor trees, and a great mixture of bamboo with the hardwoods. Black pine and red pine form the typical growth on the sandy lowlands and coastal area.

Shikoku and Kyushu are noted for their evergreen vegetation. Sugarcane, bananas, and citrus fruits are found throughout the limited areas, with broadleaf trees in the lower elevations and a mixture of evergreen and deciduous trees higher up. Throughout the region are luxuriant growths of bamboo.

About 140 species of fauna have been identified. The only primate is the Japanese macaque, a small monkey found in the north. There are 32 carnivores, including the brown bear, ermines, mink, raccoon dogs, foxes, wolves, walrus, and seals. There are 450 species of birds and 30 species of reptiles.

Japan's waters abound with crabs and shrimp; great migrations of fish are brought in by the Pacific Ocean currents. There are large numbers and varieties of insects. The Japanese beetle is not very destructive because of its many natural enemies.

As of 1975, endangered species in Japan included the Ryukyu rabbit, Ryukyu spiny rat, Kuril harbor seal, dugong, Ryukyu sika, short-tailed albatross, Japanese petrel, Japanese white stork, Japanese crested ibis, Aleutian Canada goose, Japanese crane, hooded crane, Japanese ancient murrelet, and Japanese giant salamander.

⁵POPULATION

The 1975 estimate of Japan's population was 111,120,000, ranking Japan sixth in population among the world's nations. According to the 1970 census the population was 103,720,060; 1980 population was projected at 117,546,000. In terms of density, Japan ranks fourth in the world, with 295 persons per sq km. In terms of density per unit of arable land, however, Japan ranks first in the world. The major concentrations are found in Honshu. The least densely populated major island is Hokkaido.

There are nine cities with populations of more than 1 million: Tokyo, Osaka, Nagoya, Kyoto, Yokohama, Kobe, Kitakyushu, Sapporo, and Kawasaki. The metropolis of Tokyo had an estimated population of more than 11 million as of January 1975.

The proportion of urban population to total area (about 75% in 1975) increased steadily from the end of World War II until about 1965. Since the 1965 census, however, net population flow into the center cities has decreased, while flow into the surrounding suburban areas has increased.

Japan's population pyramid shows that the population centers around the young adult age groups, the largest being the 25–30 group, a result of the postwar "baby boom" phenomenon. The number of births declined sharply thereafter, however. Japan is the only Asian country thus far to have brought its birthrate down to the level of industrial areas in other parts of the world. Japan's birthrate was estimated at 18.5 per 1,000 in 1975, as compared with about 24 in 1950. The sudden drop since 1950 is a result of government policy growing out of impoverished postwar living conditions and the desire to raise living standards.

⁶ETHNIC GROUPS

The Japanese are descended from many varied peoples of Asia. There is no agreement as to origins or specific ethnic strains. Archaeological and ethnological studies, prohibited just before and during World War II, are currently challenging many standard theories. In physical characteristics, the Japanese belong to the Mongoloid group, with faint admixtures of Malayan and Caucasoid strains. It is believed that waves of migration from the continental hinterland reached Japan during the end of the Paleolithic period. blending together into a complicated and diverse ethnic, linguistic, and cultural system. A major migration appears to have taken place in the 2d and 3d century A.D., and by the 4th century this group, called the Yamato clan, had established a monarchy in the present Nara prefecture. A well-organized group, it expanded its domain, mixing and merging with the existing farming and fishing peoples. Out of this dominance came the ruling class, or aristocracy. Early ethnic tracings indicate that migrations to Japan have come from such diverse areas as Indonesia and China in the south and such northern regions as Siberia and Alaska.

The one remaining distinct ethnic group in Japan is the Ainu, regarded as the aborigines of Japan. These people, living in the northern island of Hokkaido under state protection, are physically distinct from the contemporary Japanese, having Aryan-like features, including more pervasive facial and body hair. There is no agreement as to their origins. Through assimilation the pure Ainu is rapidly disappearing, together with his culture and language; the current population is about 16,000.

Aliens in Japan are mainly Koreans (643,096 in 1974) and Chinese (47,677) who have lived in Japan since 1945 or earlier; other aliens numbered 54,792 in 1974.

⁷LANGUAGE

Most linguists agree that Japanese is in a language class by itself, although there is some inconclusive evidence that traces it to the Malayo-Polynesian language family. In vocabulary, Japanese is rich in words denoting abstract ideas, natural phenomena, human emotions, ethics, and aesthetics, but poor in words for technical and scientific expression. For these latter purposes, foreign words are directly imported and written in a phonetic system (katakana). A distinct characteristic is the use of honorifics to show proper respect to the listener and his social station. There are, also, numerous words of the same meaning, their use differing according to the social relationship between the user and the listener.

Written Japanese owes its origin almost entirely to Chinese forms. Having no indigenous written style, Japanese since the 5th century have used Chinese characters, giving them both an approximate Chinese pronunciation and a Japanese pronunciation. In addition, the Japanese have invented phonetic symbols (kana) to represent grammatical devices unknown to the Chinese.

Attempts have been made to reduce the complexity of the

written language by limiting the number of Chinese characters used. The government has published a list of 1,850 characters for use in official communications. Newspapers adhere to this list.

8 RELIGION

The three principal religions in Japan today are Shinto, Buddhism, and Christianity. Religious identities are not mutually exclusive, and many Japanese maintain an affiliation with both a Buddhist temple and a Shinto shrine.

Shinto, originally concerned with the worship of spirits of nature, grew under the influence of Chinese Confucianism to include worship of family and imperial ancestors and thus provided the foundation of Japanese social structure. Shinto became an instrument of nationalism as the government, after 1868, officially sponsored and subsidized it, requiring that it be taught in the schools and that all Japanese belong to a state Shinto shrine. After World War II, Shinto was abolished as a state religion and the emperor issued an imperial rescript denying divine origin. Shinto exists as a private religious organization; its membership was 84,717,081 in 1972.

Buddhism is considered the most important religion in Japan; its various sects and denominations had a following of 83,646,509 in 1972. Introduced into Japan through China and Korea around A.D. 552, Buddhism spread rapidly throughout the country and has had considerable influence on the fine arts as well as the social institutions of the country. There are 13 sects (shu) and 56 denominations, the principal shu being Tendai, Shingon, Jodo, Zen, Soto, Obaku, and Nichiren. Japanese Buddhism was founded on the Mahayana school, which emphasizes the attainment of Buddhahood, whereas the Hinayana Buddhism of India emphasizes obedience to commandments and personal perfection. The great temples and gardens of Japan and the famous Japanese tea cermony (Cha-no-yu) owe their development to the influence of Buddhism. There are at present 12 universities in Japan connected with Buddhist organizations.

Christianity, introduced to Japan by the Jesuit St. Francis Xavier in 1549, was first encouraged by the feudal government, then placed under total prohibition in 1613 until the reopening of Japan to international intercourse in 1854. In 1972 there were 884,512 Christians in Japan.

Confucianism, an ethical rather than a religious system borrowed from China, became a philosophical cornerstone of Shinto inasmuch as it emphasized faithfulness to the emperor. In addition to the old-established religions there are modern cults known as Shinko Shukyo (New Religions). The Sokagakkai, a Buddhist offshoot, has become so popular that it controls a political party (Komeito), the third-strongest political group in Japan. The Risshokoseikai, another sect, claims more than 1.5 million adherents.

9 TRANSPORTATION

Despite its rugged terrain, Japan has a highly developed transportation system. In mid-1974, Japan had 26,866 km of railways. The Japan National Railways (JNR) had 21,099 km of main and branch lines in 1973; feeding into the main JNR system were 143 private company lines, comprising 5,794 km, of which 5,058 km were electrified. In 1973, 44.7% of all Japanese railroads were electrified. Like their counterparts elsewhere, Japan's railroads face many problems: increasing competition from automotive, sea, and air transport, as well as rising operator costs. High-speed lines, however, have been successful in partially meeting these problems; the most famous of these is the Tokaido Line, completed in October 1964, which operates between Tokyo and Osaka (515 km) in three hours. On 10 March 1975, the New Sanyo Line extension was completed from Tokyo through to Hakata in northern Kyushu, a distance of 1,069 km. Maximum speeds on the new line are 250 km per hour, and Sanyo now exceeds Tokaido as the fastest railway in the world.

Japan ranks first in the world in number of passengers carried by rail, with over 17 million transported in 1974. In that year, in the face of fierce competition, railways still handled 46.4% of Japan's passenger traffic volume.

Subway lines service six cities—Tokyo, Osaka, Nagoya, Kobe, Yokohama, and Sapporo; subways total 289 km of track, with 163 km in Tokyo's eight lines. Since October 1954, Tokyo has also been serviced by a commercial monorail transport system that connects it to the Tokyo International Airport at Haneda, 13 km away.

Roads have become the most important means of domestic transport, carrying 50% of total passenger traffic and 41.7% of freight traffic in 1974. Motor vehicles in 1973 included 14,473,000 passenger cars and 10,157,000 commercial vehicles. The number of passenger cars increased by some 600% during 1965–73. Tokyo, noted for its "traffic wars," has about 90% of the total registered automobiles. The length of paved roadway per motor car is 10 meters in Japan (there are 22 meters in the US and 23 in the UK).

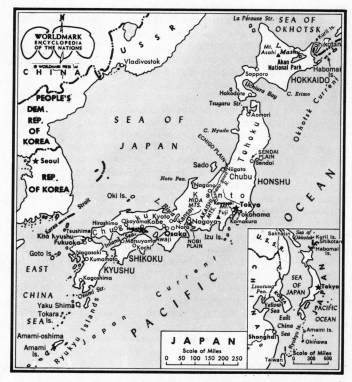

See continental political: front cover S6; physical: back cover R6

LOCATION: 122°56′ to 153°59′E; 20°25′ to 45°33′N. **TERRITORIAL SEA LIMIT:** 3 mi.

Bus travel expanded rapidly during the 1960s. Long-distance buses were introduced in 1964, and by 1973 there were 213,788 buses carrying 9.6 million passengers. There are about 1.1 million km of national and prefectural roads, of which 265,000 km are paved. Major road projects have been centered around Osaka, where several major expressways have been added. The recession of the mid-1970s forced a slowdown in many road projects, but in August 1975 a start was approved for the mammoth Honshu-Shikoku bridgeway project, scheduled for completion in 1988 at a total cost of ¥1.29 billion.

Japan is one of the world's greatest maritime nations. Eight ports and harbors that have a key bearing on the nation's economy are classified as important. Among them are

Kitakyushu and the Keihin harbor complex that serves the Tokyo and Yokohama area. In 1975, Japan ranked second in the world in gross tonnage of its merchant fleet, trailing Liberia. Its 2,143 merchant ships totaled 35,994,000 gross tons. In 1974, Japan's ships handled 19.5 million tons of exports and 259.3 million tons of imports. Since 1959, Japan has emerged as the world's leading shipbuilder and by 1975 was constructing nearly half of the world's ships, including giant supertankers (among them the *Nissei Maru*, the world's largest, at 484,337 deadweight tons).

JAL, the nation's major domestic and international airline, began operations in 1952 and inaugurated international flights in 1954. The All Nippon Airlines, established in 1957, is a domestic system serving smaller areas of the country and acting as a feeder line to JAL. Principal domestic airports include Haneda in Tokyo, Itami in Osaka, Itazuke in Fukuoka, and Chitose in Hokkaido. Tokyo International Airport (Haneda) is the only port of entry for international flights. In 1973, international services were to be transferred to a new facility at Narita, 50 km from Tokyo; built at a cost of $860 million and capable of handling 220 flights daily, Narita remained closed through mid-1976 in the wake of vehement protests from environmentalists and local residents. In 1973, Japan had a total of 763 registered commercial aircraft, accounting for 27,422 million passenger-km (11,997 passenger-km in international traffic) and 800.5 million ton-km of freight (669.4 ton-km in international).

10 COMMUNICATIONS

Japan had 21,679 post offices in 1973, handling the delivery of 12,937 million pieces of domestic mail and 191 million pieces of foreign mail. In that year, Japan had 35,274,000 telephones (about 10% of the world's total); there was 1 telephone for every 3.5 persons in Japan, as compared with 1 telephone per 1.6 in the US and 1 per 3.2 in the UK. Both telephone and telegraph services are administered by the Japan Telegraph and Telephone Public Corporation. Satellite communications are becoming important; the first Japanese-built satellite was launched in 1970.

A similar type of semigovernmental enterprise, the Japan Broadcasting Corporation (NHK) controls much of Japan's radio and television communications. As of 1973, NHK operated 738 radio stations. Commercial stations brought the number of radio stations to 906; many commercial stations are connected with large newspaper companies. Started in 1935, "Radio Japan" is also beamed by NHK throughout the world. Nearly every Japanese home has a radio.

NHK initiated television broadcasting in 1953. In 1974, Japan had 5,368 television stations, about 70% operated by NHK. Almost all television broadcasting is available in color. By 1970 there were about 25 million licensed television subscribers.

11 HISTORY

The origins of the Japanese nation are still unknown; mythology places the beginning in 660 B.C. with the ascendancy to the throne of the legendary Emperor Jimmu. It is generally agreed, however, that a clan known as the Yamato attained hegemony over southern Japan during the first three or four centuries of the Christian era and established the imperial family line. Earlier contacts with Korea were expanded in the 5th century to mainland China, and the great period of cultural borrowing began; industrial arts were imported; Chinese script was introduced, thereby permitting the study of medicine; the calendar was introduced, and eventually Buddhism also. Japanese leaders adopted Chinese governmental organization but based power upon hereditary position rather than merit. The first permanent capital was established at Nara in the early 8th century. In 784, it was removed to Kyoto, where it remained until 1868.

Chinese influence waned as native institutions took on particularly Japanese forms. Outside court circles, local clans gained strength, giving rise to military clan influence over a weakening imperial system. The leader of the powerful Minamoto clan, Yoritomo, established a military government at Kamakura in 1192 and forced the emperor to confer upon him the title of shogun, or generalissimo, thus giving rise to the shogunate form of government, a feudal system that lasted for nearly 700 years. This system operated in the name of the emperor, but all political power was in the hands of the dominant military clan, the emperors ruling in name only. Until the end of the 16th century, Japan was involved in almost continuous civil war. During this time, first contact with the Western world took place with the arrival of Portuguese traders in 1543 in southern Japan. A few years later, St. Francis Xavier arrived, introducing Christianity for the first time. Soon Spanish traders reached Japan.

By 1590, the country was pacified and unified by Hideyoshi Toyotomi, a peasant who had risen to a top military position. His work was consolidated by another great clan leader, Ieyasu Tokugawa. Appointed shogun in 1603, he established the Tokugawa shogunate, which was to rule Japan until the imperial restoration in 1868. The Tokugawas made Edo (modern Tokyo) their capital, closed Japan to intercourse with the outside world, and proscribed Christianity. For the next 250 years, Japan enjoyed peace, internal order, and a flowering of culture.

The arrival of Commodore Matthew C. Perry from the US in 1853—with his famous "black ships"—signaled the end of feudalism. The following year, Perry obtained a treaty of peace and friendship between the US and Japan, and similar pacts were signed with Russia, Britain, and the Netherlands. A decade of turmoil and confusion followed over the question of opening Japan to foreigners. A coalition of southern clans led by perspicacious young samurai (warriors) forced the abdication of the Tokugawa shogun and reestablished the emperor as head of the nation. In 1868, Emperor Meiji took over full sovereignty, signaling the entry of Japan into the modern era.

Intensive modernization and industrialization were initiated under the leadership of the samurai. A modern navy and army were established with universal military conscription, universal compulsory education was enforced, the government undertook the establishment of industry, technological assistance was imported, and the constitution of 1889 was promulgated. This constitution established a bicameral legislature, the upper house appointive, the lower house elective, with a civil cabinet headed by a prime minister responsible only to the emperor.

Japan became involved in two conflicts: the Sino-Japanese War of 1894–95 over the question of control of Korea, and the Russo-Japanese War of 1904–5 over the question of Russian expansion in Manchuria and influence in Korean affairs. Japan emerged victorious from both conflicts, its victory over the Russians marking the first triumph of an Asian country over a Western power. Japan received the territories of Taiwan and the southern half of Sakhalin Island as well as certain railway rights and concessions in Manchuria and recognition of paramount influence in Korea. In 1910, Japan formally established a protectorate over Korea.

During the reign of Emperor Taisho (1912–26), Japan participated in a limited way in World War I in line with the Anglo-Japanese Alliance of 1902. Japan was one of the Big Five powers at the Versailles Peace Conference, and in 1922 was recognized as the world's third leading naval power at the Washington Naval Conference. The domestic economy developed rapidly, and Japan was transformed from an agricultural nation into an industrially complex power. Economic power tended to be held by the industrial combines (zaibatsu), descendants of those families that had instituted the modernization of the country decades earlier. In 1925, universal manhood suffrage was enacted, and even military leaders found it necessary to take into consideration the growing influence of political parties.

In 1926, the present emperor, Hirohito, ascended the throne to begin the Showa era. The power of political parties was undermined, and the military became dominant. The military acted independently of the central government and started the invasion of Manchuria in 1931. By 1936, the army was supreme in politics, and party government was abandoned. Japan withdrew from the League of Nations, started a full-scale invasion of China, and signed the anti-Comintern Pact with Germany and Italy. The military leadership, viewing the USSR and the US as chief barriers to Japanese expansion, negotiated a nonaggression pact with the USSR in April 1941, thus setting the stage for the start of the Pacific war with the attack on Pearl Harbor on 7 December of that year.

Japan's military fortunes proceeded apace during the war's early years. With its capture of the Philippines on 2 January 1942, Japan had gained control of most of East Asia, including major portions of China, Indochina, and the southwest Pacific. Japan's forces, however, could not long hold out against the full onslaught of US military power. A series of costly naval campaigns—including the Battle of Leyte Gulf, the largest sea action ever fought—culminated in the recapture of the Philippines by Gen. Douglas MacArthur's forces during the winter of 1944/45. Japanese resistance in the Pacific was seriously curtailed by lack of manpower and equipment. US leadership, headed by President Harry S Truman, argued that a full invasion of Japan would prove too costly and decided thereupon on the use of atomic weapons. Thus, the first atomic bomb ever used in warfare was dropped on Hiroshima on 6 August 1945; a second bomb was dropped on Nagasaki on 9 August. Estimates of deaths—from both explosive force and radiation exposure—were put at 80,000–200,000 in Hiroshima and at 39,000–74,000 in Nagasaki.

In August 1945, Japan accepted the Potsdam Declaration for unconditional surrender. Formal surrender was signed aboard the USS *Missouri* on 2 September, within a month of the US atomic attack. The subsequent occupation, under the direction of Gen. Douglas MacArthur, Supreme Commander for the Allied Powers, began a series of ambitious reforms: a parliamentary system of government based on the sovereignty of the people, the legal prohibition of any political role for the emperor other than as titular head of state, land reform, dissolution of the industrial combines (zaibatsu), greater local political autonomy, and the establishment of a freer trade union movement. A new constitution was enacted and put into force on 3 May 1947.

The Japanese people participated with enthusiasm in the changes during this period of foreign importation, similar to the previous two great periods of borrowing in Japanese history. Under the stimulus of heavy economic aid from the US and of the boom produced by the Korean War of 1950, in which Japan became a major matériel supplier, and with the determination of the Japanese people to rebuild their country, the Japanese economy rapidly recovered and the standards of living have surpassed prewar levels by substantial margins. The state of war between the Western powers and Japan was formally ended by the San Francisco Peace Treaty, signed in September 1951 by 56 nations. The treaty went into effect in April 1952, but without the signatures of the USSR and China and some smaller countries. The state of war between Japan and the USSR was ended by mutual agreement, signed in 1956, following which Japan was elected to UN membership. A revision of the 1952 defense treaty with the US, under which a limited number of troops were to remain in Japan for defense purposes, was signed amid growing controversy in 1960 and forced the resignation of the prime minister.

On 22 June 1965, Japan signed a treaty with the Republic of Korea, (ROK) normalizing relations between the two countries. On 26 June 1968, Japan recovered sovereignty over the Bonin Islands, the Volcano Islands, and Marcus Island, which had been under US occupation since the end of World War II. In 1970, the US-Japanese security treaty was renewed, despite vigorous protest by the opposition parties and militant student organizations. On 15 May 1972, Okinawa and other Ryukyu Islands were returned by the US to Japan, although the US retained rights to essential military bases on the islands in conformity with a 1960 treaty. In November 1974, Gerald Ford visited Japan, the first US president to do so while in office, and in October 1975, Emperor Hirohito responded with a state visit to the US, also unprecedented.

In 1972, Japan also moved to restore full diplomatic relations with the People's Republic of China, thereby severing formal ties with the Nationalist Chinese government on Taiwan. Japan's economic and cultural links with Taiwan nonetheless survived virtually intact through the mid-1970s.

The majority Liberal-Democratic Party's (LDP) record of stable rule began to unravel in the 1970s, following the retirement from politics of Prime Minister Eisaku Sato in 1972. Sato's successor, Kakuei Tanaka, was forced to resign in December 1974 amid charges of improper use of his office for personal gain. Tanaka was succeeded by Takeo Miki, leader of a small LDP faction. The LDP government was further shaken by charges of officials' complicity in bribery transactions with US corporations.

12 GOVERNMENT

Japan follows the parliamentary system in accordance with the constitution of 1947. The most significant change has been the transfer of sovereign power from the emperor to the people. The emperor is now defined as "the symbol of the state and of the unity of the people." The constitution provides for the supremacy of the National Diet as the legislative branch of the government and for the separation of the legislative, executive, and judicial powers. It also provides the guarantee of civil liberties.

The executive branch is headed by a prime minister selected from among the Diet by its membership. The cabinet consists of the prime minister and from 11 to 20 state ministers, each heading a government ministry or agency. At least half of the ministers must be selected from the Diet, to which the cabinet is collectively responsible. Upon a vote of no confidence by the House of Representatives, the cabinet must resign en masse.

The National Diet is bicameral. The House of Representatives (the lower house) has a membership of 491, with terms of office for four years, except that all terms end upon dissolution of the House. Representatives are elected from 123 districts commonly called "medium constituencies," being neither local nor nationwide in extent. These are drawn up on a population basis. The House of Councillors (the upper house) has 252 members, 100 of whom are elected from a national constituency, the remainder from local districts. The term of office is six years, with one half elected every three years. The lower house holds primary power. In case of disagreement between the two houses, or if the upper house fails to take action within 60 days of receipt of legislation from the lower house, a bill becomes law if passed again by a two-thirds majority of the lower house.

Suffrage is universal, the voting age being 20 years with a three-month residence required. The 1947 constitution granted suffrage to women.

13 POLITICAL PARTIES

Although political parties have existed in Japan since 1874, their effectiveness was limited during the prewar period, when the principle of party responsibility in government was not generally accepted. There have always been two broad party divisions, the conservative and the progressive or proletarian, but the whole system suffered from two serious problems: government interference and suppression, which have disappeared in the postwar era; and the matter of personal loyalties rather than loyalty to a party and principle.

The Liberal-Democratic Party (LDP) represents the conservative elements of Japanese society. Formed in 1955 by the merger of the two leading conservative parties, this party has held the reins of government since its formation. Conservative parties have been in power since 1945, except for a period of Socialist ascendancy from May 1947 to October 1948.

The Japan Socialist Party (JSP) represents the reformative elements in the nation, but it also suffers from personality as well as ideological problems within its ranks. The JSP split into right and left wings over the ratification of the San Francisco Peace Treaty. In October 1955, however, the two factions reunited, preceding the unification of the conservative parties and actually forcing the conservative groups into a unified front, thus creating a formal two-party system in Japan.

The two parties are not far apart on social security and welfare programs. The LDP stands for the development of the economy through planning based upon freedom of enterprise and individual initiative, while the JSP calls for the nationalization of basic industries, support of small businesses, and the raising of the standard of living in the countryside.

On foreign policy and Japan's role in the international community, the two parties are far apart. The LDP supports close cooperation with the UN and the US and the establishment of an effective and expanded self-defense force, thereby reducing Japan's dependence upon outside military forces. On the specific issue of the Japan-US security treaty and relations with the People's Republic of China, the conservatives call for revision of the treaty to accommodate Japan's changed circumstances. In the 1970s, the LDP has supported accelerated normalization of Japan's relations with China as well as increased economic ties.

In January 1960, the weakened Socialists split once again, and the Democratic-Socialist Party (DSP), led by Suehiro Nishio, an anti-Communist Socialist, was formed. The JSP had called for the abrogation of the security treaty and its replacement by a collective security arrangement with the US, China, and the USSR. In the mid-1970s, major factions in the JSP formed around pro-Peking and pro-Moscow elements.

The Japanese Communist Party, legalized after World War II, has experienced major shifts in platforms, and its influence is considered to be waning. The party has traditionally sided with China in the Sino-Soviet ideological dispute, although in recent years the Japanese Communists have eschewed close identification with either side, focusing instead on social conditions at home.

The Komei (Clean Government) Party, the political wing of the Sokka-Gakkai Buddhist sect, gained considerable strength during the 1960s, but its strength appeared subsequently to be on the wane. Komei policies are conservative and anti-Communist, although in the Diet Komei members have voted with the liberal anti-LDP opposition.

Although the LDP continued to hold its majority in both houses through the mid-1970s, the party's rule became increasingly precarious, owing less to pressures from minority parties than to internal troubles. Traditionally, the LDP has functioned as a coalition of about 10 factions, each tightly organized and bound by personal loyalty to a factional leader. By mid-decade, policy differences among the factions and their leaders had become acute, with the pressured resignation of Prime Minister Tanaka in December 1974, accompanied by threats from his successor, Takeo Miki, to bolt the party and form a new group.

General elections for the House of Representatives were held on 10 December 1972, and for the House of Councillors on 7 July 1974. As of 31 March 1975, party distribution in both houses of the Diet was as follows:

PARTY	Representatives		Councillors	
	SEATS	PERCENTAGE	SEATS	PERCENTAGE
LDP	277	56.4	128	50.8
JSP	114	23.2	61	24.2
Communist	39	7.9	20	7.9
Komei	30	6.1	24	9.5
DSP	20	4.1	10	4.0
Other parties and independents	1	0.2	7	2.8
Vacancies	10	2.1	2	0.8
TOTALS	491	100.0	252	100.0

14 LOCAL GOVERNMENT

Local government throughout Japan was strengthened by the Local Autonomy Law of 1947. Administratively, Japan is divided into 47 local districts: 1 do (Hokkaido), 1 to (Tokyo), 2 fu (Osaka and Kyoto), and 43 ken. Within these districts there are cities, towns, and villages whose chief executives, mayors, village heads, together with local assembly members, are elected directly by the people within the respective community. Tokyo, as a metropolis, consists of 23 wards, called ku, 10 cities, 22 towns, and 10 villages.

Local public bodies have the right to administer their own affairs as well as to enact their own regulations within the law. The National Diet cannot enact legislation for a specific public entity without the consent of the voters of that district. Local governments control school affairs, levy emergency taxes, and carry out administrative functions.

15 JUDICIAL SYSTEM

The constitution provides for the complete independence of the judiciary. All judicial power is vested in the courts. The system consists of the Supreme Court, eight regional higher courts, district courts in each of the prefectures, and a number of summary courts. In addition, there are family courts, on the same level as the district courts, to adjudicate family conflicts and complaints such as partitions of estates, marriage annulments, and juvenile protection cases.

The Supreme Court consists of a chief justice and 14 other members. The chief justice is appointed by the emperor on designation by the cabinet; the other justices, by cabinet appointment. All appointments are subject to popular review at the first general election following appointment and then every 10 years thereafter in public referendum. Judges of the lesser courts also are appointed by the cabinet from lists of persons nominated by the Supreme Court. Their term of office is limited to 10 years, with the privilege of reappointment.

The Supreme Court is the court of last resort for determining the constitutionality of any law, order, regulation, or official act that is challenged during the regular hearing of a lawsuit. Abstract questioning of a law may not be instituted by the court. In April 1976, in what promised to develop as a major test of the court's authority, the justices ruled that Japan's electoral system was unconstitutional on the grounds that it did not provide equal representation for voters.

16 ARMED FORCES

The reestablishment of Japanese defense forces has been a subject of heated debate in the postwar period, especially in view of Article 9 of the constitution, through which Japan has renounced war as a sovereign right and the maintenance of "land, sea and air forces, as well as other war potential." However, under the threatening and unstable international conditions, especially the Korean War in 1950, Gen. MacArthur, Supreme Commander for the Allied Powers, recommended the establishment of a national police reserve to maintain domestic peace and order. Following the signing of the San Francisco Peace Treaty, the reserve force was reorganized into a national safety agency (1 August 1952).

On 1 July 1954, laws establishing a defense agency and a self-defense force became effective and the national safety force was divided into a ground self-defense force, a maritime self-defense force, and an air self-defense force. In 1956, the National Defense Council was created as a high-level advisory group.

The strength of Japan's armed forces in 1974 was 236,000. The army had 155,000 personnel, organized into 12 infantry and 1 mechanized divisions, and 4 combined brigades; there were also 39,000 men in reserve components. The navy, consisting of 39,000 personnel, had 138 vessels, including 29 destroyers and 15 submarines. Air force personnel numbered 42,000 men; combat aircraft totaled 445, including US-supplied jet fighters. Many units in the armed forces are understrength due to the siphoning off of young men to better-paying positions in industry. As a result of the war-renunciation clause of the constitution, Japan has armed itself with only defensive weapons; for example, it has no long-range bombers and no combat vessel bigger than a destroyer.

17 MIGRATION
Emigration was reinstituted in 1952. A sizable number of Japanese live in Brazil, most of whom had settled there before World War II. Persons of Japanese origin living in other countries included 591,290 in continental US and Hawaii and large communities in Canada, Peru, Argentina, and Bolivia. In 1974, the number of emigrating Japanese was 253,387, including 138,395 to Brazil, 62,921 to the US, 14,962 to Argentina, 11,455 to Peru, 6,461 to Canada, and 3,271 to Bolivia.

The government officially encourages emigration as a means of partially relieving population pressure within Japan. Government loans are available to emigrating persons, repayable within 12 years. In addition, the government provides machinery for screening and selecting applicants for emigration to ensure that they meet expectations of the recipient countries.

Immigration to Japan is small-scale, although the illegal entry of Koreans seeking work has become a problem. During 1970–74, the government deported 4,480 illegal ROK immigrants; at the end of 1975, however, from 40,000 to 100,000 were thought to be living covertly in Japan.

18 INTERNATIONAL COOPERATION
Japan was admitted to UN membership on 18 December 1956, and it holds membership in all of the specialized agencies. It is a signatory to GATT, participates in the Colombo Plan, and belongs to all major intergovernmental agencies. In 1963, Japan became a member of IMF and the OECD; it also belongs to the IDA. In June 1966, Japan was one of the nine nations to participate in the first meeting of the APC. Japan is also a charter member of the ADB, which went into operation in 1966; Japan furnished $200 million, a share equal to that of the US. Japan has been actively developing peaceful uses for nuclear energy, and in 1970, it signed the Geneva Protocol, which prohibits the use of poisonous and bacteriological weapons. In June 1976, Japan—the only nation to have suffered a nuclear attack—became the ninety-sixth signatory to the international Nuclear Nonproliferation Treaty.

In recent years, Japan has been extending technical and financial aid to many countries. Japan also was instrumental in establishing the Asian Productivity Organization, whose objective is to organize national productivity movements in various Asian countries into a more effective movement on a regional scale. Japan has entered into cultural agreements with many European and Asian nations and maintains an educational exchange program with the US. Through the Japan Overseas Cooperation Volunteers, Japan sends youths to work in developing countries.

In 1964, Tokyo was the site for the 18th Olympic Games and in 1972 the Winter Olympics were held in Sapporo. Expo '70, the first major international trade fair to be held in Asia, took place in Osaka.

19 ECONOMY
Japan's economy is the most advanced in Asia and, by the 1970s, the size and wealth of Japan's economic enterprises rivaled those of any nation in the world. Japan is the first Asian country to develop a large urban middle-class industrial society. It was also the first Asian country to achieve a sharp reduction in birthrates, thus setting the stage for notable further increases in per capita income.

The Japanese economy is primarily industrial. Although agriculture still employs a large proportion of the nation's work force, the number of farmers has been decreasing sharply in proportion to the expansion of industry.

Domestic raw material sources are far too limited to provide for the nation's needs, and imports are relied on for all raw cotton, raw wool, bauxite, and crude rubber used, as well as for varying proportions of other materials. To pay for these materials and for food, machinery, and other import needs, Japan exports mainly manufactured products. Its economic well-being has come to depend on continued expansion in exports.

After two decades of rapid expansion following World War II, the Japanese economy, beginning in late 1973, suffered an extremely long and intense recession, one that weakened the world economy as well. As a result of a $13-billion increase in oil costs in late 1973 and early 1974, the Japanese government and economy were forced to adopt a more restrictive demand management policy; for example, the government delayed public works programs and tightened the amount of money in circulation. This policy was also aimed at reducing the high inflation that had driven 1974 prices up by 20.8% and the cost of living up by 24.5% over the previous year. Consumers, frightened by higher prices, shorter working hours, and rising unemployment, increased their savings and lowered their demand for goods. Similarly, businesses were forced to decrease production (by 19% in 1974) and to decrease their real equipment investments (by 19.8%) as their inventories stockpiled to record heights. In 1974, for the first time since World War II, the GNP fell (by 1.8%). The recession was cushioned, however, by the nation's ability to improve its trade balance (by $11 billion) by increasing exports while reducing imports. The economy, aided by moderate government reflationary measures, began a slow recovery in 1975, and by early 1976 appeared to resume a growth pattern. In March 1976, Japan registered a record trade surplus of $1.35 billion, surpassing the previous peak reached in December 1972. The total balance-of-payments deficit for 1975/76 stood at $1,766 million, a marked improvement over the imbalance of $3,392 million in 1974/75 and $13,407 million in 1973/74.

20 INCOME
The GNP at current prices rose from ¥15,308 billion in 1960 to ¥131,682 billion in 1974, an increase of 760%. During the same period, total consumption rose from ¥9,849.4 billion to ¥132,886 billion. Private consumption rose from ¥7,626.2 billion in 1960 to ¥69,615 billion in 1968.

The GDP in 1974 stood at ¥132.7 billion (¥90.6 billion in 1972) and was distributed as follows: manufacturing, ¥29.8 billion (22.4% of the total); wholesale and retail trade, ¥20.4 billion (15.4%); construction, ¥9.4 billion (7.1%); agriculture, forestry, and fishing, ¥7 billion (5.3%); transport and communications, ¥7 billion (5.3%); and other sectors, ¥59.1 billion (44.5%).

In 1974, per capita income was estimated at $4,100, the highest in Asia. Personal savings, which had averaged 18% of personal disposable income during the 1957–61 period, rose to 25% of disposable income in 1974. Savings, as a percentage of personal disposable income, increased most sharply among lower-income groups, probably as a result of economic uncertainty. Since the lower-income groups usually spend a large share of their income, their reduced demand for consumer goods during this period further contributed to the recession.

21 LABOR

In 1974, the labor force comprised 52,740,000. In 1974, the distribution of employed workers was as follows: manufacturing, 27.2%; agriculture and forestry, 12.1%; commerce and finance, 24.1%; services, 15.9%; public utilities, 7%; construction, 8.8%; government, 3.7%; fishing and aquaculture, 0.9%; and mining, 0.3%. Females comprised 37.9% of the work force in 1974. The number of unemployed reached 1,050,000 in December 1975, the highest level in 16 years and a 26.1% increase over the previous December. Further, this figure did not account for the early retirements and reduced working hours (5.1%) common during the recessionary period.

Despite relatively low levels of unemployment prior to the mid-1970s, Japan has suffered a serious shortage of productive work for the labor force. Many who cannot find regular full-time employment accept temporary or part-time work at lower wages, and many others set up their own businesses, often using only family labor. Such petty enterprises and others of small scale are numerous in retail trade, manufacturing, services, and fishing, as well as in agriculture. The bankruptcy of many small businesses during the recent recession was a major source of unemployment. Employers tend toward traditional paternalistic, often authoritarian, control over their workers, but most regular workers in turn enjoy permanent status.

Unions have become a significant factor only since labor reforms were introduced by the US occupation. Union membership was always less than half a million before World War II, but jumped from virtually nothing at the time of surrender in 1945 to 5.7 million in 1947, and then to the 1973 figure of 12 million in 65,448 unions.

However, the rate of union membership has been decreasing in the past two decades, with 33% of all workers unionized in 1973 as against 53% in 1948. Union strength is greatest in transportation, among teachers, and in the fishing industry. Most members are organized in units called enterprise unions, which comprise the employees of a single firm.

22 AGRICULTURE

Agriculture is vital to Japan despite limited arable land (15.4% of the total area), dense population, and the highest degree of industrialization in Asia. Steep land (more than 20°) has been terraced for rice and other crops, carrying cultivation in tiny patches far up a mountainside. Japan has been able to develop intensive cultivation with the aid of a temperate climate, adequate rainfall, soil fertility built up and maintained over centuries, and such a large farm population that the average farm has an area of only 0.9 hectare. (At the end of 1974 there were some 5 million farms, a decline of 1 million from 1960.) Since World War II, modern methods, including commercial fertilizers, insecticides, and machinery, have been used so effectively that harvests increased substantially through the 1960s.

Japan now provides about 70% of its food domestically, as compared with about 90% in 1960. Imports have risen despite improved production and fertilization methods. A drain of agricultural manpower has held down agricultural production. The rice crop, however, has improved, having been increased about 40% in the 1950s. In 1974, Japan produced 12,292,000 tons of rice, supplying virtually all of the country's needs. In that year, rice accounted for 34% of the total value of agricultural output. About 60% of all arable land is devoted to rice cultivation. The consumption and importation of wheat have meanwhile fallen off sharply, with 232,000 tons produced in 1974, as compared with 1,631,000 tons in 1963.

One crop of major importance, silkworm cocoons, has declined sharply since before World War II. Production today is less than one-third of the prewar level as a result of the displacement of silk by nylon and other man-made fibers in the US and elsewhere. Japan nonetheless remains the world's largest producer of silk.

Other important crops and their annual production figures for 1973 (in thousands of tons) include: barley, 171,000; potatoes, 3,413; mandarin oranges, 3,389; soybeans, 118; sugar beets, 2,951; radishes, 2,679; Chinese cabbages, 1,779; tobacco, 157; and tea, 101.

Agricultural tenancy has declined markedly as a result of the US-occupation land reform, which began in late 1946. Nearly two-thirds of all farmland was purchased by the Japanese government at low prewar prices and resold to cultivators on easy terms. As a result, by the 1970s only about 4% of farm families were still tenants, as compared with 67% before reform. A more telling trend in recent years has been the sharp growth in part-time farm households. By 1975, about 88% of Japan's farm households had one or more persons earning income outside of agriculture. Although part-time farming has had the benefit of reducing the income disparity between farmers and nonfarmers, the practice has tended to keep farms smaller, less productive, and less responsive to market forces.

Okinawa, returned to Japanese control in 1972, supports semitropical farming, with sugarcane and pineapples providing about 45% of agricultural output.

23 ANIMAL HUSBANDRY

In the 1970s, only about 2.5% of the total land area was used for meadows and pastures. Several factors in Japan limit the availability of land for grazing: mountainous terrain, population pressure, and the relative inefficiency—in terms of food production—of using land for livestock rearing as compared with farming. The Buddhist injunction against eating the flesh of animals was another traditional factor limiting meat consumption, but horses and cattle have long been used as draft animals. Since 1945, however, the pattern of food consumption in Japan has altered dramatically, with meat, poultry, and milk coming into much greater demand. As a direct consequence, livestock production has been the fastest-growing sector in Japanese agriculture, accounting for about 27% of agricultural output in 1974, as compared with 15% in 1960.

In 1974 there were 3,650,000 head of cattle, 8,018,000 hogs, 124,000 sheep, 66,000 horses, and 250 million chickens. In 1973, beef production reached 245,769 tons (142,450 tons in 1960); pork, 970,520 tons (147,318 tons in 1960); milk, 4,908,359 tons (1,886,997 tons in 1960); and eggs, 1,800,186 tons. To meet the growing demand for beef, nearly half of the domestic supply is now derived from dairy cattle.

24 FISHING

Japan is the world's largest fishing nation, with a record catch of 10.7 million tons (excluding whaling) in 1973. The Japanese also consume more fish per capita than any other nation. The waters off Japan include cold and warm currents in which fish abound. More than 500,000 Japanese are engaged in the industry, both in nearby waters and in other fishing grounds in the Pacific Ocean, the South China Sea, and the Indian and Atlantic oceans. Whaling has declined in recent years, owing both to a rapid depletion of whales and to increased restrictions on whaling by international conventions. In 1973, 11,801 whales were caught, as compared with a peak of 26,986 in 1965; whales are still prized in Japan as a source of food and a variety of by-products. Salmon and crab are caught in the North Pacific, cod and tuna in the South Pacific.

Competition for fishing privileges in particular waters has brought Japan into conflict with the US and Canada over salmon, with the USSR over fishing in the sea of Okhotsk and other Soviet waters (between 1905 and 1945 Japan had special treaty privileges in these waters), with the ROK and China over the distance off their shores that may be prohibited to Japanese fishermen, with Australia over pearl fishing in the Arafura Sea, with Indonesia over fishing in what Indonesia regards as inland waters, and with the US, especially in north Pacific and Alaskan waters. As a result, Japan has explored and developed new fishing grounds and established joint enterprises with foreign countries.

Fish culture in freshwater pools as well as in rice paddies has long been practiced in Japan. Seaweed culture provides winter season activity for many fishermen. Pearl culture has for more than half a century been the foundation of a valuable export industry.

25 FORESTRY

Forests cover nearly 70% of the total land area of Japan and are a major source of fuel, lumber, pulp for paper and rayon, and a variety of wooden articles. Most houses are still built of wood. Of 25.2 million hectares of forests, the Japanese government owns 42%, which it maintains under strict regulations limiting overcutting. On private forest lands, cutting is less controlled. During World War II, cutting greatly exceeded growth, and overcutting continues today because of strong demand for forest products. Forest management and erosion control are urgent necessities in a land where gradients are very steep, where rainfall is heavy, and where flooding is frequent.

The Japanese cedar (sugi), which grows in most of Japan, is the most exploited species, followed by Japanese cypress (hinoki) and Japanese red pine (akamatsu). Total growing stock was 2,082.2 million cu meters in mid-1974; in 1973, total roundwood production was held to a limit of 41.6 million cu meters, as compared with 45.4 million in 1970 and 48.5 million in 1960. Sawn wood accounted for 62.8% of the total in 1973, and pulp 8.9%.

26 MINING

Japan is not rich in minerals, and mining is a relatively minor economic activity. In the mid-1970s, Japan was compelled to import more than 99% of its petroleum needs, 85% of its coking coal, 99% of its iron ore, 91% of its copper, and virtually all of its aluminum and nickel. Coal is the most important mineral product, accounting for more than half of all mineral production by value. Like most other mineral production in Japan, coal production has been undergoing steady decline in the last two decades. Other minerals are crude oil and lignite. The following figures give production in thousands of tons in 1974: coal, 20.3; iron ore, 542; pyrites, 1,959; metallic zinc, 240.8; and copper, 82.1. Natural gas, in contrast to most other resources, has been on the increase; total gas production (including petroleum gas and coal gas) in 1973 was 65.3 billion kilocalories, as compared with 16.4 billion kilocalories in 1960.

Japan produces virtually all of the steam coal consumed, but must import most of its coking coal. Domestic sources provide only a small percentage of needed iron ore and salt.

Imports must satisfy the remaining needs for these and most other minerals. Petroleum imports, now Japan's costliest, have increased rapidly. Offshore oil-drilling operations began in 1958, and by 1974 the yield supplied only about 0.3% of total demand.

27 ENERGY AND POWER

Japan ranks high among the nations of the world in electric power generated. Rivers are short and steep, making difficult the storage of water behind dams; nevertheless, hydroelectric power accounts for the bulk of electric power generated. Thermal electric power is necessary to supplement hydro power, especially in the winter dry season when power demand is at a peak. Japan's large waterpower resources have long been extensively exploited for generating electric power. From 1958 to 1973, hydroelectric power generation increased from 60.8 billion kwh to 71.6 billion kwh, but thermal electric power rose from 24.6 billion kwh to 388.8 billion kwh. In 1973, Japan's total production of 470.2 million kwh (including nuclear generation) ranked third

after that of the US and the USSR. Japan's per capita consumption of energy still lags behind that of other large industrial states; with the equivalent of 3,601 kg of coal consumed per capita in 1973, Japan ranked tenth in world energy use, amounting to 28% of the US total.

In October 1965, Japan's first commercial atomic reactor began supplying energy to the Tokyo-Yokohama-Chiba area. In 1969, the Japan Atomic Power Co. began construction of a second atomic power plant, the Tsuruga Plant; and in 1974, electric power companies were constructing four additional plants. In that year, Japan's total atomic power generating capacity reached 2.3 million kw, or about 2.4% of the national total of 96 million kw. By 1985, nuclear capacity was expected to reach 60 million kw.

28 INDUSTRY

Manufacturing has been a key element in Japan's economic expansion during three periods of phenomenal growth. First, during the 50-year rise of Japan from a feudal society in 1868 to a major world power in 1918, output in manufacturing rose more rapidly than that of other sectors. Second, during the 1930s, when Japan recovered from the world depression earlier and faster than any other country and embarked on an aggressive course in Asia, manufacturing, especially heavy industries, again had the highest rate of growth. Third, in the remarkable recovery since World War II, manufacturing, which had suffered severely during the latter stages of the war, was again a leader, although commerce and finance expanded even more rapidly.

In recent years, the rate of Japan's industrial growth has surpassed that of any other non-Communist industrialized country. In addition to spectacular expansion in the volume of output, Japanese industry has also achieved impressive diversity, with maximal application of efficiency standards and technological input. A brief economic recession forced production cutbacks in 1965; the longer and deeper recession of 1973–75 slowed Japan's economy more severely than any since the war. Japan's industrial production index (1960=100) had risen from 174.1 in 1965 to a peak of 482.2 in 1973, and fell back to 471.2 in 1974. Manufacturing is the source of the bulk of Japan's exports and the user of most imports. Japanese factories consume large amounts of imported raw materials and some imported semimanufactures and use much imported machinery, but manufactured goods for local consumer markets come from Japanese sources almost entirely.

The machinery industries, including electrical machinery and transportation equipment, stand first in value added by manufacture, accounting for about 20.3% of the total in 1973. Japan is the world's leading shipbuilder; it produced, for example, 14,734,000 gross tons of steel vessels in 1973. More than half the ships built are exported, including the world's largest oil tankers. Other transportation equipment includes passenger cars, trucks, buses, motorcycles and scooters, and bicycles, as well as locomotives and other railway equipment. In 1974, Japan was the world's largest producer of two-wheeled motor vehicles and second (after the US) in passenger car production; in that year, Japan produced 7,687,000 bicycles, 4,510,000 motorcycles, 3,931,800 passenger cars, and 2,574,200 trucks.

Japan's electronics industry has grown with extraordinary rapidity in recent years, and now leads the world. Radio and television sets and household appliances have been exported in large quantities in postwar years; in addition to generators, motors, transformers, and other heavy equipment, the industry now produces automatic devices, electronic computers, and communications and broadcasting equipment. Major electronic products in 1974 included 2.967 million transistors, 18.0 million radios, and 20.7 million television sets.

The metals industries come second in value added, with 17.4% of the total in 1973. Iron and steel industries occupy about half the value of this total. Nevertheless, Japan must import much of the iron ore and coking coal used, and sometimes also pig iron. As compared with the wartime peak of 7.7 million tons of crude steel output reached in 1943, postwar production beginning at 0.6 million tons in 1946 reached 12.1 million in 1958, 28 million in 1961, 66.9 million in 1968, and peaked at 119.3 million in 1973; in 1974, output fell back to 117.1 million tons.

Chemicals, the third-largest industrial grouping in Japan, have experienced rapid expansion in recent years. Products include industrial chemicals such as sulfuric acid, caustic soda, and fertilizers; plastics, dyestuffs, and paints and numerous other products used in Japan's advanced economy. The importance of the chemical industry has yet to be reflected in its exports, which accounted for only 7.3% of the total in 1974.

Textiles and apparel form the fourth-largest industrial grouping measured in value added. In terms of employment, however, the textile mill products industry is larger than either the chemical or the metals industry, although about half the size of the combined machinery industries. Despite a steady rise in volume of exports, the expansion of textile production has not kept pace with the rest of Japanese industry. The share of textiles in Japan's exports has dropped steadily from 30% in 1958 to 16.3% in 1967, and to 5.5% by 1974. Although synthetic fiber production has shown dramatic growth in recent years, cotton manufacturing continues to be dominant.

²⁹DOMESTIC TRADE
Marketing services and channels are complex and varied. In 1972, 8,112,153 persons were engaged in domestic, wholesale, and retail trade, accounting for 18.2% of the net domestic product. The number of wholesale and retail stores was 1,754,506; of these, 79.2% were small stores with fewer than four employees. Street hawkers and peddlers provide certain foods and small consumer items. Street stalls offer a wide range of food, clothing, household, and other items. Specialty shops exist in great profusion and about 100 associations of such shops represent common interests. Japan's first department store was opened in 1910. In 1957, there were 170 department stores; by 1974, the figure had risen to over 900, accounting for 13.2% of total retail sales. There are both chain stores owned and operated by a single management and voluntary chains of independent stores operating in association. There are also varied cooperatives, principally consumer, agricultural, and fishing.

In retail trade cash transactions have been traditional, but various forms of installment selling are being increasingly used, especially in the sale of durable goods, and the use of charge accounts is growing rapidly.

In wholesale trade, middlemen include jobbers, brokers, wholesalers, commercial agents, and cooperatives. Central wholesale markets are operated by a number of municipalities.

Promotion by displays, advertising, and other methods used in Western countries is growing rapidly in Japan. Advertising appears in the daily press, in the numerous weekly and monthly magazines, and in special publications of many kinds. Radio and television carry extensive advertising.

³⁰FOREIGN TRADE
Foreign trade is essential to the Japanese economy, and the government has concentrated on enlarging its foreign markets. Japan increased its share of world trade from 3.5% in 1961 to 13.2% in 1974. Imports consist mostly of foodstuffs, fuel, industrial raw materials, and industrial machinery. Exports are varied, but manufactures now account for about 95% of the total. The balance consists of food exports, mainly fish. During the 1973–75 recession, Japan's trade balance swung from a surplus of $0.7 billion in 1973 to an overall trade deficit in 1974 of $6.575 billion, due to the sharp rise of imported commodities, especially petroleum. But by early 1975, imports had dropped even faster than exports, markedly shrinking the trade deficit by the

year's end. In 1975, exports totaled $55,753 million and imports $57,863 million. By early 1976, record monthly surpluses had begun to accrue.

Principal exports in 1972 and 1974 (in thousands of dollars) were:

	1972	1974
Machinery and transport equipment	13,653,744	25,260,889
Manufactured goods	8,264,306	18,732,476
Chemicals	1,784,282	4,058,988
Crude materials, inedible	476,955	1,100,455
Food and live animals	646,909	820,929
Mineral fuels	73,925	248,199
Animal and vegetable oils and fats	26,827	87,332
Beverages and tobacco	18,798	25,336
Other exports	3,645,398	5,201,151
TOTALS	28,591,144	55,535,755

Principal imports in 1972 and 1974 (in thousands of dollars) were:

	1972	1974
Mineral fuels	5,715,134	24,895,218
Crude materials, inedible	7,114,309	14,136,021
Food and live animals	3,433,680	7,759,357
Manufactured goods	1,545,522	5,150,157
Machinery and transport equipment	2,376,239	4,290,789
Chemicals	1,148,000	2,668,114
Nonferrous metals	922,024	2,036,420
Other imports	1,215,802	1,174,380
TOTALS	23,470,710	62,110,456

The US retained its position as Japan's single most important trade partner through the mid-1970s; in 1974, the US accounted for 23% of Japan's exports and 20.4% of its imports. During the last decade, Asia has emerged as the leading trade region for Japan, taking about 30% of Japan's exports and providing 43% of imports (mostly petroleum and other raw materials for industry). Japan's leading Asian partners in 1974 included Sa'udi Arabia, Iran, China, ROK, Taiwan, and Hong Kong.

Distribution of trade by principal trade partners in 1974 (in thousands of dollars) was:

	EXPORTS	IMPORTS	BALANCE
US	12,799,350	12,682,206	117,144
Australia	1,998,101	4,024,962	−2,026,861
Sa'udi Arabia	676,954	5,238,315	−4,561,361
Iran	1,013,556	4,766,182	−3,752,626
Canada	1,587,263	2,675,681	−1,088,418
ROK	2,656,056	1,568,041	1,088,015
China	1,984,475	1,304,768	679,707
Taiwan	2,009,007	955,188	1,053,819
FRG	1,497,910	1,454,351	43,559
USSR	1,095,642	1,418,143	− 322,501
UK	1,529,741	877,738	652,003
Liberia	2,344,741	36,446	2,308,295
Philippines	911,212	1,104,819	− 193,607
Hong Kong	1,359,872	273,057	1,086,815
Other countries	22,071,875	23,730,559	−1,658,684
TOTALS	55,535,755	62,110,456	−6,574,701

³¹BALANCE OF PAYMENTS
Starting in 1960 the Japanese economy underwent a basic change. Import restrictions were lifted and, within three years, trade was 93% decontrolled. A heavy inflow of short- and long-

term capital followed the decontrol of exchange from 1960 on, and a surplus in capital transactions enabled Japan to improve its balance of payments considerably.

In the first half of the 1960s, Japanese sales abroad grew by 15.8% due to the competitiveness of Japanese commodities on the world markets. Though Japan made it a rule to offset deficits in the current account with the surplus in the capital account from 1960 to 1963, Japan's external economy underwent a structural change in 1964. A tremendous surplus in visible trade was offset by a number of factors, making the balance of payments unfavorable by an average of about $500 million.

Between 1968 and 1973 there was a favorable balance of trade but the balance in long-term capital transactions was unfavorable. A positive balance in short-term capital and trade transactions resulted in a dramatic increase in the overall surplus. This was maintained despite adoption of the floating yen and subsequent upward revaluations. During 1973–74, however, Japan's recession drove the balance of payments to a deficit of $6,839 million. The visible trade imbalance was $4,549 million in 1974, despite the fact that increased exports ($54,506 million) more than compensated for the rising cost of imports ($52,878 million). A deficit in the invisible trade balance also marked this period, with long-term capital showing a $3,953 million negative balance in 1974, while the inflow of short-term capital declined to $1,419 million. In 1975, the visible trade deficit was reduced to $2,110 million.

As of 29 February 1976, international reserves stood at $13,952 million (compared with $13,519 million at the end of 1974 and $18,365 million at the end of 1973), of which $11,675 million was in foreign exchange reserves and $864 million in gold.

32 BANKING

A highly sophisticated banking system continues to play a dominant role in Japan's financing of economic development. Banks provide not only short-term but also long-term credit, which often in effect becomes fixed capital in industry. As to sources of capital, 1973 figures show that of total industrial funds raised by Japanese enterprises from outside sources, financial institutions (both private and official) supplied 90.1%. Of this total, 92% came from private financial institutions.

The controlling national monetary institutions are the Bank of Japan (founded in 1882) and the Ministry of Finance. The Bank of Japan as central bank has power over note issue and audits financial institutions to provide guidance for improving banking and management practices. The National Banking Law of 1928 gives the finance minister large powers to supervise, investigate, and issue directives. Ceilings for interest rates are set by the Bank, while actual rates, commissions, and discounts are arranged by unofficial agreements among bankers and other financial institutions, including the National Bankers' Association.

As of the end of October 1975, reserve money of the national monetary authorities totaled ¥13,232 billion, with foreign assets of ¥4,063 billion. As of 30 June 1975, currency in circulation totaled ¥11,183 billion (compared with ¥10,111 billion in mid-1974 and ¥8,230 billion in mid-1973).

Thirteen important city banks, with branches throughout the country, account for about two-thirds of all commercial bank assets, the rest accruing to some 63 local banks and 7 trust banks that provide special services. As of October 1975, total deposits (demand plus savings accounts) stood at ¥107,645 billion.

The Bank of Tokyo, established by the Foreign Exchange Bank Law, finances about one-fourth of all Japanese foreign transactions. Other foreign exchange banks include the 13 city banks and the Industrial Bank of Japan, a special long-term credit bank. Commercial banks are closely related to industrial firms, which in turn depend heavily upon their banks for funds.

Japan's high rate of savings (total time deposits are greater than demand deposits) is facilitated by the fact that savings accounts are handled by all city and local banks throughout the country.

Specialized agencies include the Central Bank for Commercial and Industrial Cooperatives, mutual loan and savings banks, and credit associations.

33 INSURANCE

Insurance companies suffered greatly from the loss of overseas assets due to World War II and encountered difficulties in acquiring new contracts because of the progress of postwar inflation. However, as inflation subsided and the economy developed, the insurance companies recovered remarkably. Since the war, both agricultural cooperatives and the government have also become involved in the insurance business.

In Japan, firms may not engage in life and non-life insurance at the same time. In 1974 there were 40 Japanese insurance firms (20 life and 20 non-life) and 35 foreign companies (34 life and 1 non-life) transacting business. Both joint stock and mutual companies are permitted.

Life insurance is by far the most extensive of all classes of insurance; premium income is more than twice that of all non-life premium income. In 1974, life premium income totaled ¥2,859,137 million. In the same year there were 147,473,000 life policies (both individual and group) in force, valued at ¥205,035,343 million. Life insurance firms had total assets of ¥11,093,655 million as of 1974.

In the non-life field, automobile insurance is the largest sector, accounting for 29.2% of the business. Automobile liability insurance is compulsory. Fire insurance is next in importance with 28.5%, followed by automobile liability, 15.6%; cargo, 7.2%; marine, 6.5%; casualty, 4.5%; and others, 8.5%. Net premium income in 1974 for non-life totaled ¥1,415,939 million.

Total insurance reserves for 1974 amounted to ¥18,037 billion; claims on the private sector amounted to ¥18,763 billion, of which policy loans accounted for ¥595 billion.

34 SECURITIES

Major securities exchanges are in Tokyo, Hiroshima, Fukuoka, Nagoya, and Osaka; small regional exchanges are in Kyoto, Kobe, Niigata, and Sapporo. Although prior to World War II most stocks were held by large business firms (zaibatsu), stocks were subsequently released for public subscription.

The Tokyo Stock Exchange, the second largest in the world (after the New York Stock Exchange), is the most important in Japan. It has 83 members; most are "regular" and may act as both dealers and brokers; a smaller number of "saitori" members (12 members at the end of 1975) may serve only as middlemen in transactions between regular members. There were more than 1,400 listed companies on the Tokyo Exchange in 1975. On all Japanese exchanges at the end of 1975, a total of 1,713 companies was listed, with total capital stock listed of ¥10,146 billion and a calculated market value of ¥44,780 billion.

The number of private shareholders increased from 1.67 million at the end of World War II to 16.10 million in 1962 and 18.1 million as of 1974. Although 97.9% of the shareholders are individuals, as of 1974, only 33.5% of total listed securities were in private hands, the rest being held by institutions.

Activity on the Tokyo exchange fell off significantly as a result of the recession of the mid-1970s. Stock turnover in May 1975 was 5,136 million shares, valued at ¥1,771 billion (compared with 8,405 million shares at ¥2,002 billion as of May 1974).

35 PUBLIC FINANCE

Plans for the national budget usually begin in August, when various agencies submit their budget requests to the Ministry of Finance. On the basis of such requests, the Ministry, other government agencies, and the ruling party start negotiations. The government budget plan usually is approved by the Diet without difficulty, and the budget goes into effect each April.

Projected revenues for the general account budget for 1975/76 totaled ¥21,289 billion, an amount equal to total expenditures. Direct taxes are the most important source of government revenues, providing 62% of the 1975/76 total. Because of the size of Japan's military establishment, defense expenditures occupy a much smaller proportion of government outlays (6.2% in 1975) than in most other major industrial states. In an effort to combat recession in mid-1975, the government added ¥800 billion in public works projects to the budget, in addition to ¥560 billion in housing projects and ¥160 billion in antipollution investments.

Revenues and expenditures for the 1974/75 and 1975/76 (preliminary) general accounts budgets (in billions of yen) were as follows:

	1974/75	1975/76
REVENUES		
Taxes, of which	14,881	16,747
Personal income taxes	(5,542)	(6,605)
Corporation taxes	(5,755)	(6,141)
Liquor tax	(885)	(1,031)
Customs and duties	(417)	(445)
Other taxes	(2,282)	(2,525)
Stamp duties	493	593
Monopoly profits	316	478
Miscellaneous revenues	623	773
Public bonds	2,160	2,000
Surplus from previous year	725	698
TOTALS	19,198	21,289
EXPENDITURES		
Social security	3,129	3,927
Education and science	2,307	2,640
Pensions	597	756
Tax transfers to local authorities	4,199	4,430
Defense	1,226	1,327
Public works	2,965	2,910
Flood control	998	909
Other expenditures	3,777	4,390
TOTALS	19,198	21,289

In addition to general account outlays, the central government has, since 1973, disbursed funds under its Fiscal Investment and Loan Program. Total expenditures under this scheme increased from ¥6,925 billion in 1973/74 to ¥7,923 billion in 1974/75 and ¥9,310 billion in 1975/76. Investment and loan outlays (in billions of yen) in 1974/75 and 1975/76 (preliminary) were itemized as follows:

	1974/75	1975/76
Welfare, of which	3,301	4,175
Housing	(1,557)	(1,997)
Public amenities (e.g., water and sewage)	(1,300)	(1,557)
Agriculture and small industries	1,552	1,798
Roads, transport, and regional development	2,135	2,345
Basic industries and export promotion	935	992
TOTALS	7,923	9,310

36 TAXATION

In the postwar period, Japan adopted a tax system relying mainly on direct taxes, like those in the US and the UK. The most important taxes are the income tax, corporation tax, and liquor tax; receipts from these three taxes comprised 82.3% of all tax revenues in fiscal 1975.

The National Tax Administration Agency, a branch of the Ministry of Finance, administers income and corporation tax laws. National tax laws are augmented by an annual Special Taxation Measures Law which brings taxes in line with specific economic and social policies of the government and renders tax policies highly flexible in terms of changing fiscal conditions. Individuals are subject to a national income tax as well as local (prefectural and municipal) residence and business taxes. In 1975, income tax rates ranged from 10% on taxable income of ¥400,000 to 75% on income over ¥80 million. Corporations are subject to an income tax (40% in 1975), inhabitant's tax (a standard local tax, amounting to 6.92% of income), and a deductible standard enterprise tax (also local, at 12%); thus, the effective aggregate tax on corporations in 1975 was 52.61%, with a reduced rate of 40.88% available on income distributed as dividends. These rates are exclusive of temporary surtaxes and a capital gains tax.

Additional national taxes include customs duties; inheritance and gift taxes; a monopoly profits tax; a sugar excise tax; taxes on liquor, gasoline, and other commodities; and travel, admissions, and local road taxes.

37 CUSTOMS AND DUTIES

Policies affecting Japan's trade are overseen by the Ministry of International Trade and Industry. A new Japanese tariff schedule went into effect in June 1961, the first wholly new tariff since 1910. The new schedule raised import duties as an adjunct to the liberalization program announced in January 1960, a program that would lead to the modification or abolition of import restrictions on 440 items. By 1975, Japan had abolished quantitative restriction and licensing requirements for most imports. The exceptions were 81 items appearing on the negative list of GATT. Export restrictions are imposed on goods destined for Iran, Iraq, and Nigeria, as well as on commodities, such as minerals, deemed in short supply locally. All trade with Rhodesia is banned.

Duties are applied, with a few exceptions, on an ad valorem basis. Rates, as stipulated in the Customs Duty Law, vary depending on the product and country of origin. A variety of reductions or exemptions is provided through special legislation or through GATT. Raw materials, especially those used in the manufacture of important products, enter at preferential rates. Such items comprise the bulk of Japanese imports. Low rates also apply to foodstuffs and in particular to those produced in developing countries. Japan imposes a more favorable conventional import duty on merchandise from countries that grant Japanese products most-favored-nation treatment.

38 FOREIGN INVESTMENTS

Policies governing foreign investments in Japan have undergone steady liberalization since the mid-1960s. The Foreign Investment Law of 1950, still the cardinal body of legislation in this sector, was based on highly selective principles permitting entry of only such foreign capital as would help Japan expand its economy soundly. Foreign firms wishing to invest in Japanese industries usually had to go through lengthy preliminary negotiations with the Ministry of International Trade and Industry before filing a formal application. There were cases in which preliminary negotiations took several years. Upon joining the OECD in 1964, however, Japan committed itself to eventual free flow of foreign investments. In 1967, the government initiated a five-stage investment liberalization scheme, with the last stage completed during 1973–76. Although validation (or licensing) as required under the 1950 law is still necessary, as of 1 April 1976 most industries were made subject to automatic validation for up to 100% foreign acquisition. Individual screening procedures remain in effect for primary industries related to agriculture, forestry, and fishing; leather and leather products; petroleum refining and marketing; and large retail chains.

Total annual direct foreign investments in Japan grew from an estimated $550 million in 1968 to $1,778 million in 1974. Cumulative US investments in Japan totaled $3.3 billion, although a negative outflow of $918 million was recorded in 1974. UK, Federal Republic of Germany (FRG), French, and Canadian holdings are also important. The foreign investment flow declined in the mid-1970s as a result of the worldwide industrial slowdown; total funds approved declined from $5,583 million in 1972/73 to $2,926 million in 1973/74, but recovered to $4,914 million during 1974/75.

Japanese investments abroad grew to significant levels in the early 1970s, the result both of liberalizations on the outflow of capital and of the burgeoning prosperity of the Japanese economy. By 1974, total direct investments of Japan overseas reached $4.06 billion in long-term capital, with cumulative investments in the US estimated at $1.5–2 billion. Total foreign investment outflows increased from $2,337 million in 1972/73 to $3,497 million in 1973/74, but declined to $2,394 million in 1974/75. About 23% of the annual outflow has gone to the developing countries of Asia, 20% to the US, 17% to Latin America, and 15% to the UK.

Japan's financial assistance to developing countries and international agencies has also grown significantly in recent years. In 1974, official development aid totaled $1,126.2 million, as compared with $458 million in 1970. Of the 1974 total, $198.6 million was in bilateral grants and $681.8 million in bilateral loans. In addition, the government provided $798.5 million in direct investment financing. Private outflows to the same sources in 1974 totaled $1,042.2 million.

39 ECONOMIC POLICY

Japan's phenomenal economic growth in the 1960s was based on an efficient blend of two economic tendencies. First was government activism in national planning and implementation, with guidance of the largely free economy via sophisticated and powerful monetary and fiscal policies. Second was the unique Japanese way of coupling largely private ownership of assets with conservative, public-spirited management. In terms of GNP, Japan's mixed economy thus developed into the third largest in the world, after the US and the USSR.

Despite tremendous industrial achievements, much of the social infrastructure, such as roads, hospitals, and schools, has not been keeping pace. The spin-off of rapid industrial growth such as air, water, and noise pollution has presented a serious set of problems. Economic policy in Japan in the early 1970s began increasingly to contend with social as well as industrial infrastructure. The inflationary spiral that took hold in 1973 forced a curtailment of public-sector spending, but in mid-1975, the government undertook to spend ¥1,500 billion on public works and antipollution projects, with the hope that such projects could also serve to breathe life into the depressed economy.

Such problems as these, along with the objective of maintaining rapid GNP growth, have been the concern of the Economic Planning Agency. It produced the successful Ikeda plan (to double the national income between 1961 and 1970) and releases projections of key indicators at frequent intervals. In the main, the Ikeda plan consisted of no more than a series of projections of growth in a free market economy, with the basic assumption—the continued growth of Japan's overseas trade—largely outside of government control. During the plan's 10-year span, an annual growth of 11% in GNP was realized, as against the forecast rate of 7.2%. An economic and social development plan (1967–75) meanwhile witnessed GNP growth rate of 10.6%, as against 8.2% projected.

A second five-year economic and social plan (1970–75) projected a continued annual growth rate of 10.6%. But the 1973 world oil crisis and its aftermath severely shook Japan's trade-dependent economy; in 1974, the GNP actually shrank by 1.8%,

the first such negative growth in three decades. Actual growth for the plan period was put at 5.1% annually. In early 1973, the government seized upon inflation as the most critical aspect of the country's economic problems. As a result, Japan was led into the longest and most stringent period of restraint in its postwar history. A restrictive monetary policy was imposed, including successive increases in banking reserve ratios, as well as price controls and a variety of surveillance measures. Controls began gradually to be eased in late 1975 as the government looked toward a gradual restoration of growth trends, but planning continued to be an important policy mechanism. As a by-product of counterrecession policy, the government installed an energy-conservation program in December 1974 calling for substantial cutbacks in oil and electricity use at all levels; planners have projected the need to hold increases in Japan's energy supply to about 6–7% annually during 1970–85, as compared with the actual increase of 11.8% realized during 1960–70.

Although by mid-1976 government policies had sufficed to restore a healthy trend in the balance of payments as well as an unused inventory of resources, Japan still faced a host of long-range problems and choices. Economic activity and import volume rise and fall together in Japan, rendering the economy chronically vulnerable to upward trends in world prices. In addition, the government's continued commitment to an enlarged social policy (including improved health and old age benefits) may have the effect of an overall reallocation of resources, slowing investment volumes and, in turn, economic expansion.

40 HEALTH

Public concern with the health of the Japanese people has deepened considerably in the postwar period. Under the 1947 constitution, the Ministry of Welfare has become the central administrative agency responsible for maintaining and promoting public health, welfare, and sanitation. In addition to the immediate sections of the Ministry, there are attached agencies such as the Population Problems Research Institute, the National Institute of Public Health, regional offices of preventive medicine, quarantine stations, and national hospitals and sanatoriums. The Ministry of Labor is directly responsible for the welfare of the working population and the Ministry of Education superintends health programs for students and teachers. Health departments are maintained by each prefectural government and the larger municipal governments.

All hospitals and clinics are subject to government control with respect to their standards and spheres of responsibility. As of 1973 there were 8,188 hospitals (including mental institutions, tuberculosis sanatoriums, and leprosy hospitals), with a total of 1,125,606 beds (including only hospitals with 20 or more beds). In 1973 there were 71,927 general clinics and 31,163 dental clinics. Many country villages and isolated areas are without regular medical and dental services. In 1973, the total number of doctors in Japan was 124,684 (or 115 per 100,000 persons); dentists, 39,486; pharmacists, 71,569; and clinical nurses, 316,800. Every practitioner in the field of medicine or dentistry must receive a license from the Ministry of Welfare. In addition, the Ministry recognizes and authorizes certain quasi-medical practitioners as supplementary facilities to regular medical practice. Among these are included massage, acupuncture, moxa-cautery, and judo-orthopedics, practices based upon traditional professions in Japan.

The Tuberculosis Prevention Law requires health examinations for the entire population over 6 years of age. Expanded examination and treatment have brought about a decrease in the death rate as well as the infection rate in recent years. Infant mortality dropped to 11.3 per 1,000 in 1973, in contrast with the 1900 rate of 155 per 1,000. Average life expectancy rose from 45 years for men and 46 for women in 1930 to 71.5 for men and 77.3 for women in 1975, among the highest rates in all

Japan

of Asia. Cerebral hemorrhage, cancer, heart disease, respiratory illness, and old age are the chief causes of death in Japan.

41SOCIAL WELFARE

The present social insurance system includes national health insurance, welfare annuity insurance, unemployment insurance, workers' accident compensation insurance, seamen's insurance, a national government employees' mutual aid association, and day workers' health insurance. Per capita expenditure on social security programs remains low, however, in relation to expenditure in many other industrial nations.

Nearly the entire population receives benefits in one form or another from the health insurance system. Health insurance is compulsory for those employed at enterprises with five or more workers, and premiums are shared equally by the insured and their employers. In 1973, participants in the health insurance scheme totaled 44,125,000. Other sickness and health insurance is in force among farmers, fishermen, and their dependents.

Insurance systems for the aged, bereaved, and disabled exist for specific groups of workers and are operated by mutual aid associations. Unemployment insurance covered 23,364,000 persons in 1973, as compared with 18,550,000 in 1965. In April 1974, a new system was introduced, expanding maximum benefits from 60% to 80%, with the rate inversely proportional to earnings. Coverage is now obligatory for all enterprises regardless of size; under the previous system, agriculture, forestry, and fishing were excluded, as were firms with fewer than five employees, with the result that only 45% of the national work force was covered. Workmen's compensation must be provided by employers.

The Daily Life Security Law (1946) laid the groundwork for ever-growing social security. Out of this have come laws pertaining to child welfare, physically handicapped persons' welfare, social welfare service, welfare fund loans to mothers and children, aid to war-wounded and ill, and aid to families of deceased soldiers. The Daily Life Security Law provides direct aid for livelihood; education; housing; medical, maternity, and occupational disability, and funerals. In 1973, about 1.3 million persons were recipients of a living-expense relief system. More than a thousand welfare offices throughout the nation are staffed by full-time, salaried welfare secretaries and assisted by voluntary help. Institutions have been established to care for the aged, those on relief, and those needing rehabilitation. Children's welfare residences, by far the most numerous, numbered 23,979 in 1973, housing 1,525,025 children. Numerous private organizations assist government agencies.

The expanded social security and welfare programs have been beset with financial and administrative problems, and both national political parties agree that the social welfare system must be strengthened. In the 1970s, with many thousands of Japanese still in need, government priorities turned increasingly toward problems directly affecting the health and welfare of the population.

42HOUSING

An extremely severe housing shortage has been one of Japan's great postwar problems. It is estimated that in 1947, two years after the war's end, the need amounted to more than 4 million units. A construction program resulted in 9.7 million new units by the end of 1965. In 1966, the government undertook a five-year plan for the construction of 7.6 million houses by mid-1971; the plan was designed to fulfill the goal of "one house for each family."

Through the 1970s, the construction rate for new housing in Japan was exceeded only by that in the USSR and US. During 1971–74, 6,774,000 dwelling units were completed. It is estimated that 170,000 homes are needed annually merely to replace those destroyed by typhoons, floods, and fires. Most Japanese homes are constructed of wood; consequently superannuation is another factor in the need for new construction.

43EDUCATION

Japan's entire educational system was reorganized after World War II and the 6-3-3-4 plan prevalent in the US (6 years of primary school, 3 years of junior high school, 3 years of high school, and 4 years of college) was adopted. Education is compulsory and provided free of charge for 9 years, from the age of 6 through 14. Coeducation has become an accepted principle, and more women are entering institutions of higher learning. The literacy rate in Japan is now among the highest in the world, about 98%.

Entrance into high schools, the stage following the compulsory level, is by examination only, and most of these schools charge tuition. Most universities maintain a complete educational system from kindergarten through graduate school.

The senior high schools, junior colleges, and universities are divided into three types: private, public, and national, all of which receive prefectural and national support or annual subsidies. There are 76 national universities, with each prefectural capital having one school; the remainder are in the principal cities. The largest religious bodies, both Christian and Buddhist, maintain important universities and other educational institutions. There are many special schools for the handicapped.

Enrollment at the compulsory elementary and junior high school levels is very high, approaching 100%, with some 89% continuing into more advanced levels. In 1973, 24,592 primary schools had an enrollment of 9,817,000; 10,836 junior high schools, 4,779,000; 4,861 senior high schools, 4,199,000 (49.6% female); 63 technical colleges, 49,000; 500 junior colleges, 310,000; 405 colleges and universities, 1,597,000 (19.7% female). There were also 12,185 kindergartens, with a total enrollment of 2,129,000. The total teaching staff in primary and junior and senior high schools in 1973 was 886,000. The great emphasis on education, plus an expanding scholarship system, has caused overcrowding in most schools and universities. The number of university applicants is often 10 times as great as the number of available places.

Great stress is placed on social and adult education, especially in the rural areas, through the use of citizens' public halls, libraries, museums, athletic facilities, and the growing use of bookmobiles. Many universities have instituted correspondence courses for outlying areas.

The entire educational system is decentralized, with the Ministry of Education acting as coordinator and adviser to local educational agencies and administering national funds to be used in support of local educational endeavors. Prefectural and local boards of education are appointed by governors or mayors with the consent of their assemblies.

44LIBRARIES AND MUSEUMS

In 1948, the National Diet Library Law established the National Diet Library to provide reference service to the Diet, other libraries, and the general public. In 1950, this library absorbed the Ueno Library (the former national library) as one of its branches. The National Diet Library acts as a legal depository for Japanese publications and is also a depository library for the UN. In 1973 there were 2,657,649 volumes in the main library's collection.

Public libraries are beginning to find their place in Japanese life. Prior to the enactment of the Library Law of 1950, 70% of those who utilized libraries were students and scholars. Today, more and more libraries are becoming information centers, and increasing numbers of women are patronizing them. In 1971 there were 917 public libraries with total holdings of over 29.6 million volumes, and in 1972 there were 1,059 public and private college and university libraries, including branches and departmental libraries.

Museums in Japan are the oldest institutions for social education despite the fact that they have played only a minor role and have inadequate facilities. Except in large cities, typical Japanese museums take the form of the treasure halls of shrines or temples. In 1971 there were 375 museums, zoos, botanical gardens, and aquariums; 181 of them were privately owned.

45 ORGANIZATIONS

The Japanese people are notably organization-oriented and seem to have an almost ingrained habit of establishing organizations for action in all fields of endeavor. Individual action is not highly regarded, and individual responsibility traditionally has been avoided. The number of organizations in Japan is enormous.

There are such standard organizations as the Japan Red Cross, Japan Chamber of Commerce with regional and local branches, the General Council of Trade Unions, the Congress of Labor Unions, the Federation of Employers Associations, the Rotary Club, the Japan Medical Association, the Japan Actors' Society, the Motion Picture Association of Japan, the Japan Athletic Federation, the All-Japan Boy Scouts League and Girl Scouts League, the Japan YMCA and YWCA, and the Japan Youth Association.

The Japan Science Council, founded after the war to promote the scientific development of the nation, is a significant organization; it elects to life membership the 150 members of the Japan National Academy. The Japan Art Academy is important in the cultural field. The Society for International Cultural Relations, established in 1934, is active in the publishing field and in cultural exchange.

46 PRESS

The Japanese press is the world's third largest in terms of circulation; in ratio of copies to population, 534 per 1,000 in 1973, Japan is second only to the UK. Newspapers numbered more than 100, with a total circulation in 1974 of 40,006,000. The Japanese press is one the most vigorous and outspoken in the world. It operates under the constitutional provision of an absolute prohibition of censorship.

Leading Japanese dailies with their 1974 circulations are as follows:

	CIRCULATION	
TOKYO	MORNING	EVENING
Yomiuri Shimbun	3,816,387	2,467,508
Asahi Shimbun	3,214,516	2,338,530
Mainichi Shimbun	2,168,884	1,412,075
Nihon Keizai Shimbun	1,018,751	714,677
Sankei Shimbun	852,281	454,573
Tokyo Shimbun	512,875	355,471
OSAKA		
Asahi Shimbun	1,948,573	1,220,650
Yomiuri Shimbun	1,700,139	1,104,028
Mainichi Shimbun	1,669,728	1,024,485
Sankei Shimbun	1,033,269	619,571
OTHER CITIES		
Chunichi Shimbun (Nagoya)	1,672,539	918,184
Nishi Nippon Shimbun (Fukuoka)	606,466	264,881
Hokkaido Shimbun (Sapporo)	412,742	411,184
Kyoto Shimbun (Kyoto)	410,467	329,371

There are two domestic news agencies: the Kyodo News Service with 50 domestic bureaus and with foreign bureaus in every major overseas news center; and the Jiji Press, serving commercial and government circles.

47 TOURISM

Tourism in Japan is regarded as a major industry, since many foreign visitors as well as the Japanese themselves tour the country extensively. Since 1965, the number of foreign visitors has been rising at an annual rate of 10%. In 1975, 811,672 tourists

visited Japan; tourist receipts totaled $235 million in 1974. Accommodations include 298 first-class hotels, and numerous business hotels and ryokans or Japanese inns.

In April 1964, the Japanese government lifted restrictions on Japanese traveling overseas as tourists. In 1968, the number of Japanese traveling abroad exceeded that of foreign visitors for the first time. In 1974, 2,335,530 Japanese traveled overseas and spent $1,358 million.

Entry requirements call for a valid passport with the proper visa endorsement according to the purposes of the visitor's trip. Maximum period of stay for a traveler in transit is 15 days; for a tourist, 60 days; student or artist, one year; trader, educator, or correspondent, three years. Most European tourists are exempt from visa requirements, and visa fees are waived for US citizens visiting for less than a year. Vaccination or inoculation certificates are not required.

For tourists and transit travelers, it is necessary to have proof of entry into a country other than Japan and a ticket or guarantee of passage from Japan.

48 FAMOUS JAPANESE

The greatest classic of Japanese literature is the *Tale of Genji*, by Lady Murasaki (Murasaki Shikibu, 978–1031?). The foremost Japanese playwrights were Zeami (Motokiyo, 1363–1443) for the Noh Theater and Monzaemon Chikamatsu (1653–1725), who wrote for both the Bunraku and the Kabuki theater. Notable haiku poets were Matsuo Basho (1648–94), Buson Yosa (1716–81), and Issa Kabayashi (1763–1828). Ryunosuke Akutagawa (1892–1927) is best known for his story "Rashomon." Prominent modern novelists include Junichiro Tanizaki (1886–1965); Yasunari Kawabata (1899–1972), winner of the 1968 Nobel Prize for literature; Kobo Abe (b.1924) and Yukio Mishima (1925–70). A leading modern writer and Zen Buddhist scholar was Daisetz Teitaro Suzuki (1870–1966).

In the traditional Japanese arts, Kanaoka (fl. 9th century) was reputedly the first great Japanese painter, but none of his works survive. Sesshu (1420–1506) was the most famous landscape artist of his day. Ogata Korin (1659–1716) was a master painter of plants, animals, and people. The leader of the naturalist school was Maruyama Okyo (1733–95). The best-known painters and wood-block artists of the "ukiyo-e" style were Kitagawa Utamaro (1753–1806), Katsushika Hokusai (1760–1849), Saito Sharaku (fl. 1794–95), and Ando Hiragige (1797–1858). Three contemporary Japanese architects whose work is having a marked influence on international style are Kunio Mayekawa (b.1905), Hideo Kosaka (b.1912), and Kenzo Tange (b.1913).

Masters of the Japanese cinema include Kenju Mizoguchi (1898–1956), Yasujiro Ozu (1903–63), and Akira Kurosawa (b.1910). The leading film star is Toshiro Mifune (b.1920). Contemporary composers include Toshiro Mayuzumi (b.1929) and Toru Takemitsu (b.1930). Seiji Ozawa (b.1935) is a conductor of world renown.

Hideyo Noguchi (1876–1928), noted bacteriologist, is credited with the discovery of the cause of yellow fever and is famed for his studies on viruses, snake poisons, and toxins. Hideki Yukawa (b.1907), Japan's most noted physicist, in 1949 received the Nobel Prize for research on the meson. In 1965, Shinichiro Tomonaga (b.1906), a professor at Tokyo University of Education, became one of the year's three recipients of the Nobel Prize for physics, for work in the field of quantum electrodynamics. Leona Esaki (b.1925) won the Nobel Prize for physics in 1973.

Hirohito (b.1901) has been emperor of Japan since 1926. The leading statesman after World War II was Eisaku Sato (1901–75), prime minister from 1964 to 1972 and winner of the Nobel Peace Prize in 1974.

49 DEPENDENCIES

Under the terms of the San Francisco Peace Treaty of 1952, Japan renounced claims to many of its former overseas territories, including such major areas as Taiwan, Korea, the Kuril Islands, and southern Sakhalin.

The Amami island group, comprising the northern portion of the Ryukyu Islands, nearest to Kyushu Island, was returned to direct Japanese control by the US in December 1953. The remainder of the group, including Okinawa, was returned to full Japanese sovereignty in May 1972. The Ogasawara (Bonin) Islands and Kazan (Volcano) Islands were returned to Japanese sovereignty in June 1968.

In the northern area of Japan, the government maintains that the Habomai island group and Shikotan, lying just off Hokkaido and constituting fringe areas of the Kurils, belong to Japan and should be returned to Japanese administration. These islands are currently occupied by the USSR.

The Kuril Islands and southern Sakhalin are occupied by the USSR, and Japan claims no jurisdiction over them. However, the Japanese government has not formally recognized the Soviet claim to sovereignty over these areas.

⁵⁰BIBLIOGRAPHY

Abegglen, James C. *Management and Worker: The Japanese Solution.* New York: Harper & Row, 1973.

Allen, George C. *Japan's Economic Recovery.* London: Oxford University Press, 1965.

American University. *Area Handbook for Japan.* Washington, D.C.: Government Printing Office, 1974.

Allen, George Cyril. *A Short Economic History of Modern Japan, 1867–1937.* New York: Praeger, 1963.

Atlas of Japan: Physical, Economic and Social. Tokyo: International Society for Education and Information, 1974.

Axelbank, Albert. *Japan Destiny.* New York: Franklin Watts, 1973.

Baereald, Hans. *Japan's Parliament: An Introduction.* New York: Cambridge University Press, 1974.

Beasley, William G. *The Modern History of Japan.* New York: Praeger, 1974.

Benedict, Ruth. *The Chrysanthemum and the Sword.* Boston: Houghton Mifflin, 1946.

Borton, Hugh. *Japan's Modern Century.* 2d ed. New York: Ronald Press, 1971.

Bowers, Faubion. *Japanese Theatre.* New York: Nelson, 1952.

Brown, Delmer Myers. *Nationalism in Japan: An Introductory Historical Analysis.* Berkeley: University of California Press, 1955.

Brzezinski, Zbigniew K. *The Fragile Blossom: Crisis and Change in Japan.* New York: Harper & Row, 1971.

Bunce, William K. (ed.). *Religions in Japan: Buddhism, Shinto, Christianity.* Rutland, Vt.: Tuttle, 1959.

Cohen, Jerome (ed.). *Pacific Partnership: U.S.-Japan Trade.* Lexington, Mass.: Lexington Books, 1972.

Dore, Ronald P. (ed.). *Aspects of Social Change in Modern Japan.* Princeton, N.J.: Princeton University Press, 1967.

Dunn, C. J. *Everyday Life in Traditional Japan.* New York: Putnam, 1969.

Embree, John F. *Suye Mura: A Japanese Village.* Chicago: University of Chicago Press, 1939.

Gibney, Frank. *Japan: The Fragile Superpower.* New York: Norton, 1975.

Guillain, Robert. *The Japanese Challenge.* New York: Lippincott, 1970.

Hall, John Whitney. *Japan: From Prehistory to Modern Times.* New York: Dell, 1969.

Halloran, Robert. *Japan: Images and Realities.* New York: Knopf, 1969.

Hane, Mikiso. *Japan.* New York: Scribner, 1972.

Henderson, Harold G. *An Introduction to Haiku: An Anthology of Poems and Poets from Basho to Shiki.* New York: Doubleday, 1958.

Ike, Nobutaka. *Japan: The New Superstate.* San Francisco: Freeman, 1974.

Japan, Ministry of Transportation. *Japan: The Official Guide.* Tokyo: Japan Travel Bureau (annual).

Japan Biographical Encyclopedia and Who's Who. Tokyo: Rengo, 1958–date (irregular).

Japan Statistical Yearbook. Tokyo: Bureau of Statistics, Office of the Prime Minister (annual).

Japan Writers Society. *Japan Bibliographic Annual.* Tokyo: Hokuseido Press, 1956–date (annual).

Kawai, Kazuo. *Japan's American Interlude.* Chicago: University of Chicago Press, 1960.

Keene, Donald (ed.). *An Anthology of Japanese Literature, from the Earliest Era to the Mid-Nineteenth Century.* New York: Grove Press, 1955.

Langdon, Frank C. *Japan's Foreign Policy.* Vancouver: University of British Columbia Press, 1973.

Livingston, Jon (ed.). *The Japan Reader.* New York: Pantheon, 1974.

Matsumoto, Yoshiharu Scott. *Contemporary Japan: The Individual and the Group.* Philadelphia: American Philosophical Society, 1960.

Mainichi Newspapers. *Japan and the Japanese.* San Francisco: Japan Publications Trading Co., 1973.

Mason, Richard H. P., and John G. Caiger. *A History of Japan.* New York: Free Press, 1973.

Miller, Roy Andrew. *The Japanese Language.* Chicago: University of Chicago Press, 1967.

Minami, Hiroshi. *Psychology of the Japanese People.* Toronto: University of Toronto Press, 1972.

Monroe, Wilbur F. *Japan: Financial Markets and the World Economy.* New York: Praeger, 1973.

Morris, Ivan. *The World of the Shining Prince: Court Life in Ancient Japan.* New York: Knopf, 1964.

Ohkawa, Kazushi. *Japanese Economic Growth.* Stanford, Calif.: Stanford University Press, 1973.

Olson, Lawrence. *Japan in Postwar Asia.* New York: Praeger, 1970.

Paine, R. T., and Alexander Soper. *The Art and Architecture of Japan.* London: Penquin, 1955.

Reischauer, Edwin Oldfather. *Japan: The Story of a Nation.* New York: Knopf, 1970.

Sansom, Sir George Bailey. *A History of Japan.* 3 vols. Stanford, Calif.: Stanford University Press, 1958–63.

Sansom, Sir George Bailey. *Japan: A Short Cultural History.* New York: Appleton-Century-Crofts, 1962.

Seward, Jack. *The Japanese.* New York: Morrow, 1972.

Steiner, Kurt. *Local Government in Japan.* Stanford, Calif.: Stanford University Press, 1965.

Tanaka, Kakuei. *Building a New Japan.* Tokyo: Simul Press, 1973.

Tokyo News Service. *The Japan Who's Who.* Tokyo: Tokyo News Service (annual).

Toynbee, Arnold (ed.). *Half the World.* New York: Holt, Rinehart, & Winston, 1973.

Tsunoda, Ryusaku, *et al.* (eds.). *Sources of Japanese Tradition.* New York: Columbia University Press, 1958.

Varley, H. Paul. *Japanese Culture: A Short History.* New York: Praeger, 1973.

Webb, Herschel, and Marleigh Ryan. *Research in Japanese Studies: A Guide.* New York: Columbia University Press, 1965.

Yashiro, Yukio. *2000 Years of Japanese Art.* New York: Abrams, 1958.

JORDAN

The Hashimite Kingdom of Jordan
Al-Mamlaka al-Urdunniyya al-Hashimiyya

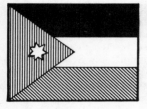

CAPITAL: ʿAmman. **FLAG:** The national flag is a tricolor of black, white, and green horizontal stripes with a seven-pointed white star on a red triangle at the hoist. **ANTHEM:** *Ash al-Malik (Long Live the King).* **MONETARY UNIT:** The Jordanian dinar (JD) of 1,000 fils is a nonconvertible paper currency. There are coins of 1, 5, 10, 20, 25, 50, 100, and 250 fils, and notes of 500 fils, and 1, 5, and 10 Jordanian dinars. As of 29 February 1976, JD1 = $3.03 (or $1 = JD0.33). **WEIGHTS AND MEASURES:** The metric system is the legal standard, but some local or Syrian units are still widely used, especially in the villages. **HOLIDAYS:** Arbor Day, 15 January; Arab League Day, 22 March; Labor Day, 1 May; Independence Day, 25 May; Accession of King Husayn, 11 August; King Husayn's Birthday, 14 November. Muslim religious holidays, fixed according to the Hijrah calendar, include the 1st of Muharram (Islamic New Year), ʿId al-Fitr, ʿId al-ʿAdhaʾ, Milad al-Nabi, and Laylat al-Miraj; Christmas and Easter are observed by sizable Christian minorities. **TIME:** 2 P.M. = noon GMT.

¹LOCATION, SIZE, AND EXTENT

Situated in southwest Asia, Jordan has an area of 97,740 sq km (37,738 sq mi), of which Samaria and Judea (West Bank), administered by Israel, comprise 5,878 sq km (2,270 sq mi). Jordan extends *562 km (349 mi)* NE–SW and *349 km (217 mi)* SE–NW. It is bounded on the N by Syria, on the NE by Iraq, on the E and S by Saʿudi Arabia, on the SW by the Gulf of Aqaba, and on the W by Israel, with a total boundary length of *1,805 km (1,121 mi)* following the 1949 armistice with Israel, and of *1,754 km (1,089 mi)* following the 1967 cease-fire.

²TOPOGRAPHY

The West Bank consists of the hill country of Judea and Samaria (elevation up to 3,300 feet). The Jordan Valley itself lies about 650 feet below sea level at its northern end, reaching a maximum depression of almost 1,300 feet at the Dead Sea; south of the Dead Sea the depression, called Wadi ʿAraba, slowly rises toward the south, reaching sea level about halfway to the Gulf of Aqaba. To the east of the Jordan River, the Transjordanian plateaus have an average altitude of 3,000 feet, with hills rising to more than 5,400 feet in the south. Farther eastward, the highlands slope down gently toward the desert, which comprises more than four-fifths of the East Bank. The Jordan River enters the country from Israel to the north and flows into the Dead Sea; its main tributary is the Yarmuk, which near its juncture forms the border between Jordan and Syria. The Dead Sea, 55 miles from north to south and about 10 miles wide, is the lowest area on earth. Its surface lies 1,290 feet below sea level, and its greatest depth is 2,598 feet below sea level. The Dead Sea has a mineral content of about 30%.

³CLIMATE

Most of the West Bank has a modified Mediterranean climate, with moderate winter rainfall and warm dry summers. The Jordan Valley has little rainfall, intense summer heat, and mild, pleasant winters. The hill country of the East Bank—ancient Moab, Edom, and Gilead—has a climate similar to that of Judea, with less rainfall and hotter summers. The desert regions are subject to great extremes of temperature. Rainfall varies from 30 inches per annum in the northern uplands to 20 inches in the East Bank uplands, 8 inches in the steppe region, 4 inches in the southern Jordan Valley, and virtually none in the eastern parts of the desert region. Temperatures at ʿAmman range from about −4°C (25°F) in winter to more than 38°C (100°F) in summer.

⁴FLORA AND FAUNA

Plants and animals are those common to the eastern Mediterranean and the Syrian Desert. The vegetation ranges from semitropical flora in the Jordan Valley and other regions to shrubs and drought-resistant bushes in the desert. Less than 2% of the land is forested. The wild fauna includes the jackal, hyena, fox, wild boar, wildcat, gazelle, and rabbit; vulture, sand grouse, skylark, sparrow, and goldfinch; viper, diced water snake, and Syrian black snake. As of 1975, endangered species in Jordan included the wolf, Anatolian leopard, three species of gazelle (Saʿudi Arabian dorcas, sand, and Arabian), and Arabian ostrich.

⁵POPULATION

The November 1961 census, the first ever taken in Jordan, showed a population of 1,706,226. Civil strife prevented a census planned for 1970. The total population in 1975, including that of the Israeli-held West Bank, was estimated at 2,688,000. A population of 3,177,000 was projected for 1980, based on an annual population growth of 3.3%; in 1975, the crude birthrate was estimated at 46.2 per 1,000 population, the crude death rate at 12.8, and the net natural increase at 33.4. The average population density in 1975 (including the West Bank) was about 28 per sq km (71 per sq mi). Nearly the entire population is concentrated in the northwestern 10% of the area. In 1972 ʿAmman, the capital, had an estimated population of 520,700; al-Zarqaʾ, 225,000; and Irbid, 115,000. The West Bank, held by Israel since 1967, contains Arab Jerusalem (al-Quds), Nablus, Hebron (al-Khalil), Jericho (al-Riha), and Bethlehem. In 1970 there were an estimated 273,000 refugees on the West Bank and 506,000 on the East Bank. About 45% of Jordan's population is urban, 50% lives in small rural villages, and 5% is nomadic or seminomadic.

⁶ETHNIC GROUPS

Ethnically, the Jordanians represent a mixed stock. The predominating single element is Arab, but except for the nomads and seminomads of the desert and steppe areas, this element is overlain by the numerous peoples that have been present in Jordan for millennia, including Greek, Egyptian, Persian, European, and Negro strains. The Circassians (about 12,000) constitute the largest distinctive non-Arab minority; there are also Druze and Turkoman minorities.

⁷LANGUAGE

Arabic is the language of the country and is spoken even by the ethnic minorities who maintain their own languages in their everyday lives. The spoken Arabic of the country is essentially a vernacular of classical Arabic; it is quite different from the spoken languages of Iraq and Egypt. There also are differences between the languages of the towns and the countryside and between those of the East and West banks. English is understood in the towns.

⁸RELIGION

Islam is the state religion, and most Jordanians (about 93%) are Sunni Muslims. Christians comprise about 6% of the population and live mainly in the towns; most are Greek Orthodox, Greek Catholic, Roman Catholic, or Protestant, and all are Arabic-speaking. Of the racial minorities, the Turkomans and Circassians are Sunni Muslims, the Druzes are a heterodox Muslim sect. The Baha'is are mainly of Persian stock. A tiny community of Samaritans maintains the faith of its ancestors, a heterodox form of the ancient Hebrew religion.

⁹TRANSPORTATION

Jordan's transportation facilities are underdeveloped, but improvements have been made in recent years. The 1973–75 development plan allotted JD35.8 million for transportation, more than for any other category. A good road network, scheduled for improvement in the late 1970s, links the principal towns and connects with Syria, Iraq, and Sa'udi Arabia. In 1975 there were 7,725 km of roadway in Jordan (including the West Bank), of which 75% was paved.

The rail system, some 480 km of narrow-gauge single track, is a section of the old Hijaz railway (Damascus to Medina) for Muslim pilgrims. It runs from the Syrian border through 'Amman to Ma'an, where it connects with a road to the port of al-'A-qabah. Its extension to al-'Aqabah is planned. Reconstruction of the section from Ma'an to Medina in Sa'udi Arabia, which had been destroyed in World War I, was undertaken in the early 1970s, as a joint venture by Jordan, Sa'udi Arabia, and Syria.

Al-'Aqabah, Jordan's only outlet to the sea, is situated at the head of the Gulf of Aqaba, an arm of the Red Sea. The port was initially developed after the 1948 Arab-Israeli war, which cut off Arab Palestine and Transjordan from Mediterranean ports; substantial development did not occur until 1959 and afterward. A phosphate berth to receive ships of up to 100,000 tons was completed in 1969. The port handled 1.5 million tons of goods in 1974.

The government-owned Royal Jordanian Airline operates domestic and international flights; other carriers with service to Jordan include KLM, Aeroflot, Middle East Airways, Egypt Air, Sa'udi Arabian Airways, and Kuwayt Airways. The major airport is at 'Amman; another major airport is being developed about 29 km south of the capital. An international airport north of Jerusalem is in Israeli hands. In 1975, civil aviation on the East Bank handled about 245,000 passengers and 4,000 tons of cargo.

¹⁰COMMUNICATIONS

Public communication and broadcasting facilities are government-controlled. Telephone and telegraph facilities were introduced soon after World War II. Telephone service, at first rudimentary, was expanded in the 1950s, and in 1975 there were more than 35,000 telephones on the East Bank, mostly in 'Amman and the larger towns. Cable traffic was expanded with the introduction of teleprinters in 1967 and commercial Telex services in 1969. In 1972, a satellite communications station was inaugurated at Baq'a; in 1974, it had 24 telephone channels and 48 cable channels, providing communications with most of the world. The only licensed broadcasting agencies are Radio Jordan and the Jordan Television Corporation. Radio Jordan, broadcasting daily over 10 transmitters, with a total output of 338,000 watts, reaches about 98% of the population. In 1976 there were more than 500,000 radios and about 200,000 television sets.

¹¹HISTORY

As part of the Fertile Crescent connecting Africa and Asia, the area now known as Jordan has long been a major transit zone and often an object of contention among rival powers. It has a relatively well-known prehistory and history. Neolithic remains from c.60000 B.C. have been found in Jericho. City-states were well developed in the Bronze Age (c.3200 to 2100 B.C.). In the 16th century B.C., the Egyptians first conquered Palestine, and in the 13th century B.C., Semitic-speaking peoples established kingdoms on both banks of the Jordan. In the 10th century B.C., the western part of the area of Jordan (on both banks of the Jordan River) formed part of the domain of the Hebrew kings David and Solomon, while subsequently the West Bank became part of the Kingdom of Judah. A succession of outside conquerors held sway in the area until, in the 4th century B.C., Palestine and Syria were conquered by Alexander the Great, beginning about 1,000 years of intermittent European rule. After the death of Alexander, the whole area was disputed among the Seleucids, the Ptolemies of Egypt, and native dynasties such as the Maccabees; in the 1st century B.C., it came under the domination of Rome. In Hellenistic and Roman times, a flourishing civilization developed on the East Bank; meanwhile, in southern Jordan, the Nabatean kingdom, a native Arab state in alliance with Rome, developed a distinctive culture, blending Arab and Greco-Roman elements. With the annexation of Nabatea by Trajan in the 2d century A.D., Palestine and Transjordan came under direct Roman rule. Christianity spread rapidly in Jordan and for 300 years was the dominant religion. The Byzantine phase of Jordan's history, from the establishment of Constantinople as the capital of the empire to the Arab conquest, was one of gradual decline. When the Muslim invaders appeared, little resistance was offered, and in 636, Arab rule was firmly established.

Soon thereafter, the area became thoroughly Arabized and Islamized, remaining so to this day despite the century-long domination by the Crusaders (12th century). In Ottoman times (1517–1917), Transjordan was part of the Damascus vilayet, while the West Bank formed part of the sanjak of Jerusalem within the vilayet of Beirut.

During World War I, Sharif Husayn bin 'Ali, Hashimite ruler of Mecca and the Hijaz, aided and incited by the UK (which somewhat hazily promised him an independent Arab state), touched off an Arab revolt against the Turks. After the defeat of the Turks, Palestine and Transjordan were placed under British mandate; in 1921, 'Abdallah, son of Sharif Husayn, was installed by the British as emir of Transjordan. In 1923, the independence of Transjordan was proclaimed with British tutelage. British control was partially relaxed under a 1928 treaty, and in 1939, a local cabinet government (Council of Ministers) was formed. In 1946, Transjordan attained full independence, and on 25 May, 'Abdallah was proclaimed king of the Hashimite Kingdom of Transjordan. After the Palestine war of 1948, King 'Abdallah annexed a butterfly-shaped area of Palestine bordering the Jordan (thereafter called the West Bank) which was controlled by his army, and which he contended was included in the area that had been promised to Sharif Husayn. On 24 April 1950, after general elections had been held in the East and West banks, an act of union joined Jordanian-occupied Palestine and the Kingdom of Transjordan, to form the state of Jordan. This action was recognized by the UK but condemned by some Arab states as evidence of inordinate Hashimite ambitions. Meanwhile, Jordan, since the 1948 war, had absorbed about 500,000 of some 1 million Palestinian Arab refugees, mostly sheltered in UN-administered camps, and another 500,000 nonrefugee Palestinians. Despite what was now a Palestinian majority, power remained with the Transjordanian elite loyal to the throne. On 20 July 1951 'Abdallah was assassinated, and his eldest son, Talal, was proclaimed king. Owing to mental illness, however, King Talal was declared unfit to rule (11 August 1952), and succession passed to his son Husayn, who was formally enthroned on 2 May 1953.

Between the accession of King Husayn and the war with Israel in 1967, Jordan was beset not only with problems of economic development, internal security, and confrontation with Israel, but also with difficulties stemming from its relations with the Western powers and the Arab world, which, since the overthrow of Egypt's King Faruk in July 1952, had become more strongly influenced by "Arab socialism" and aspirations to Arab unity (both for its own sake and as a precondition for defeating Israel). Notwithstanding the opposition of most Arabs, including many Jordanians, Jordan maintained a close association with the UK in an effort to preserve the kingdom as a separate, sovereign entity. Early in Husayn's reign, extreme nationalists stepped up their attempts to weaken the regime and its ties with the UK. The invasion of Egypt by Israel in October 1956, and the subsequent Anglo-French intervention at Suez, made it politically impossible to maintain cordial relations with the UK, and negotiations were begun to end the treaty with Britain, and thus the large military subsidies for which it provided. The end of the treaty also meant the end of British bases and of British troops in Jordan. The army remained loyal, and the king's position was bolstered when the US and Sa'udi Arabia indicated their intention of preserving Jordan against any attempt by Syria to occupy the country. After the formation of the UAR and the assassination of his cousin, King Faysal of Iraq, in a July 1958 coup, Husayn turned again to the West for support, and British troops were flown to Jordan from Cyprus.

When the crisis was over, a period of relative calm ensued. Husayn, while retaining Jordan's Western ties, gradually steadied his relations with other Arab states (except Syria), established relations with the USSR, and initiated several important measures of economic development. But even in years of comparative peace, relations with Israel remained the focus of Jordanian and Arab attention. Terrorist raids launched from within Jordan drew strong Israeli reprisals, and, in general, activities of the Palestine Liberation Organization (PLO) often impinged on Jordanian sovereignty, leading Husayn in July 1966, and again in early 1967, to suspend support for the PLO, thus drawing Arab enmity upon himself. On 5 June 1967 there was an outbreak of hostilities between Israel and Jordan, Syria, and the UAR. During that war, which lasted only six days, Israel occupied the Golan heights in Syria, the UAR's Sinai peninsula, and the Jordanian West Bank, including all of Jerusalem. Jordan suffered heavy casualties, and a large-scale exodus of Palestinians across the Jordan River to the East Bank swelled Jordan's refugee population, adding to the war's severe economic disruption.

After Husayn's acceptance of a cease-fire with Israel in August 1970, he tried to suppress various Palestinian guerrilla organizations, whose operations had brought retaliation upon Jordan. The imposition of military rule in September led to a 10-day civil war between Husayn's army and the Palestinian forces, ended by the mediation of other Arab governments. Subsequently, however, Husayn launched an offensive against Palestinian guerrillas in Jordan, ultimately driving them out in July 1971. The following September, Premier Wasfi al-Tal was assassinated by guerrilla commandos, and coup attempts, in which Libya was said to have been involved, were thwarted in November 1972 and February 1973.

Jordan did not open a third front against Israel in the October 1973 war, but sent an armored brigade of about 2,500 men to assist Syria. After the war, relations improved between Jordan and Syria. Husayn reluctantly endorsed the resolution passed by Arab nations on 28 October 1974, in Rabat, Morocco, recognizing the PLO as "sole legitimate representative of the Palestinian people on any liberated Palestinian territory"—including, implicitly, the Israeli-held West Bank. On 22 August 1975, Jordan announced that a Supreme Syrian-Jordanian Command Council would be formed to coordinate foreign and military policies.

12 GOVERNMENT

Jordan is a constitutional monarchy, with the king having wide powers over all branches of government. Legislative power is vested in the bicameral National Assembly, composed of a 30-member Senate and a 60-member lower house, the Chamber of Deputies. Senators are appointed by the king for renewable four-year terms; the Chamber of Deputies is elected by secret ballot for a four-year term, but the king may dissolve the Chamber and order new elections. There is universal suffrage, women having received the right to vote in April 1973. The National Assembly holds annual sessions and is convened and may be prorogued by the king, who also has veto power over legislation. The executive power of the king is administered by a cabinet or Council of Ministers. The king appoints the prime minister, who then selects the other ministers, subject to royal approval. The ministers need not be members of the Chamber of Deputies.

In the prolonged emergency created by the wars with Israel and by internal disorders, especially since 1968, King Husayn has wielded nearly absolute power.

See continental political: front cover G6; physical: back cover G6

LOCATION (1949): 29°17' to 33°20'N; 34°53' to 39°12'E. BOUNDARY LENGTHS: Syria, 356 km (221 mi). Iraq, 147 km (91 mi). Sa'udi Arabia, 744 km (462 mi). Gulf of Aqaba, 27 km (17 mi). Israel: 1949 armistice line, 531 km (330 mi); 1967 cease-fire line, 480 km (298 mi). TERRITORIAL SEA LIMIT: 3 mi.

13 POLITICAL PARTIES

Political parties were abolished on 25 April 1957, following an alleged attempted coup by pan-Arab militants. In subsequent elections, candidates qualified in a screening procedure by the Interior Ministry ran for office, in effect, as independents. The Jordanian National Union was formed in September 1971 as the official political organization of Jordan; renamed the Arab National Union in March 1972, it later became inactive.

14 LOCAL GOVERNMENT

Eastern Jordan is divided into five provinces (liwa's)— 'Ajlun, 'Amman, Balqa', Karak, and the Desert Area—each under a district commissioner appointed by the king on the recommendation of the interior minister. The West Bank is divided into three liwa's—Nablus, Jerusalem, and Hebron—which continue to function for local purposes despite Israeli administration. Each liwa' is subdivided into districts (aqdiya) under administrative councils, and each qada' into subdistricts (nawahin). The towns and larger villages are administered by municipal councils; the smaller villages are headed by a headman (mukhtar), who in most cases is elected informally.

15 JUDICIAL SYSTEM
There are six jurisdictions in the judiciary; four levels of civil and criminal jurisdiction, religious jurisdiction, and tribal courts. The Supreme Court, acting as a court of cassation, deals with appeals from lower courts. In some instances, as in actions against the government, it sits as a High Court of Justice. The courts of appeals hear appeals from all lower courts. Courts of first instance hear major civil and criminal cases. Magistrates' courts deal with cases not coming within the jurisdiction of courts of first instance. Religious courts have jurisdiction in matters concerning personal status (marriage, divorce, wills and testaments, orphans, etc.) where the laws of the different religious sects vary. The Shari'ah courts deal with the Muslim community, following the procedure laid down by the Ottoman Law of 1913. Christian sects have their own courts. Tribal courts, which have jurisdiction in most matters concerning tribesmen, are losing their importance as more individuals take their cases to the government courts instead.

16 ARMED FORCES
In 1975, the Jordanian army had some 75,000 men, organized into 2 infantry divisions, 2 armored divisions, 1 mechanized division, 2 air defense brigades, and 4 special forces battalions. The air force had at least 5,000 men and 42 combat aircraft. The navy had only about 250 men. Reserve manpower was estimated at 30,000, the militia at 15,000, and national police forces at 7,500. Expenditures for 1975 were estimated at at least $155 million, or about 22% of the national budget, excluding capital improvements from foreign aid.

17 MIGRATION
About one-half, or more, of the population consists of refugees from territory that became Israel. There is also considerable migration by nomadic groups across the Syrian, Iraqi, and Sa'udi Arabian borders. More than 100,000 Jordanians now live abroad, many attracted by job opportunities in oil-rich Arab states. Since June 1967 there has been a heavy influx of males from the West Bank to the East Bank, looking for work.

18 INTERNATIONAL COOPERATION
Jordan became a member of the UN on 14 December 1955 and belongs to all the specialized agencies except IAEA and IMCO. It is one of the founding members of the Arab League and also belongs to many intergovernmental organizations. Jordan has greatly benefited from the work of UNICEF and of the UNRWA, which helps the Palestinian refugees.

19 ECONOMY
Jordan's economy has been profoundly affected by the Arab-Israeli conflict. The incorporation of the West Bank after the war of 1948 and the first exodus of Palestinians from the territory that became Israel trebled the population, causing grave economic and social problems. The loss of the West Bank in 1967 resulted not only in a second exodus of Palestinians, but also in the loss of most of Jordan's richest agricultural land and a decline in the growing tourist industry. The 1970–71 civil war and the October 1973 war also brought setbacks to development plans. The steadying influence has been foreign aid. For the overall period from mid-1949 to mid-1973, the US was the major donor; total US economic assistance amounted to $650 million, despite a virtual cutoff from 1967 to 1970. US aid for 1976 alone was reported to be about $175 million, not including long-term credits for military sales. Arab loans and grants have also been important.

Jordan is traditionally an agricultural country, but it has to import about one-fourth of the food consumed. Agricultural production varies from year to year, depending on rainfall. Industry and mining are limited mainly to the production of phosphates and cement.

20 INCOME
Jordan's GDP in 1973 amounted to JD263.7 million, distributed as follows: trade and finance, 20.4%; public administration and defense, 18.2%; agriculture, 14.1%; manufacturing and mining, 12%; community and personal services, 11%; transportation and utilities, 10%; construction, 7.7%; and other sectors, 6.6%. Total available resources of JD349.8 million were expended as follows: government consumption, JD76.3 million; private consumption, JD220 million; and gross fixed capital formation, JD51.3 million. Increase in stocks was thus JD2.2 million. Per capita GDP at factor cost was an estimated JD83.6.

21 LABOR
The projected size of Jordan's labor force for 1976 (excluding the West Bank) was about 400,000. Based on data for the early 1970s, the force was distributed as follows: agriculture, 33%; public administration and defense, 23%; personal and social services, 10%; wholesale and retail trade, 7%; mining and manufacturing, 7%; transportation, 3%; construction, 2%; finance, 1%; other, 14%.

Unemployment and underemployment are serious problems. The unemployment rate reached a high of 14% of the labor force in 1970, declining to about 8% in 1972. Many workers have only seasonal agricultural employment, and many may be occupied in tasks of marginal economic value at minimum rates of pay. Hourly wage rates may be less than 90 fils ($0.30) for the lowest-paid manual workers, while a skilled bricklayer may earn 200 fils ($0.66). In 1953, the government enacted a trade union law that permitted the organization of unions subject to registration. The General Federation of Jordanian Trade Unions, formed in 1954, now has a membership of 33,000 in 25 unions. Independent unions include the Drivers' Union and the Union of Petroleum Workers and Employees. On 21 June 1960, a new labor code was instituted, regulating hours of work, minimum wage rates, procedures for the adjudication of labor disputes, and other labor matters.

22 AGRICULTURE
Agriculture still occupies an important position in Jordan's economy although 40% of the usable land consists of the West Bank under Israeli administration since 1967. Erosion is severe east of the Jordan River. On the whole, less than 1.3 million acres (excluding the West Bank) are planted in any given year. While the system of small owner-operated farms, peculiar to Jordan among the Arab countries and originating in the Land Settlement Law of 1933, limits the number of large landowners and share tenancy, miniscule holdings have inhibited development.

Irrigation schemes and soil and water conservation programs have received emphasis in Jordan's economic development. The 48-mile East Ghor Canal, substantially completed in 1966 and reconstructed in the early 1970s after heavy war damage, siphons water from the Yarmuk River and provided irrigation for about 34,000 acres by 1975. Further expansion was under way. The larger Yarmuk scheme, of which the East Ghor Canal is only the first stage, aims at harnessing the waters of the Yarmuk and Zarqa rivers to irrigate about 200,000 acres in the Jordan Valley. Water conservation in other areas has been undertaken with the rehabilitation of the old water system and the digging of wells.

The cooperative movement has made progress in the agricultural sector; there were 231 cooperatives in 1974. The Central Cooperative Union, established in 1959, provides seasonal loans and advice to local cooperatives. The Agricultural Credit Corporation, founded in 1960, provides low-cost loans to finance agricultural investments.

The main crops are wheat and barley, vegetables, fruits, and tobacco. Production fluctuates from year to year. In 1974, production (in tons, excluding the West Bank) was estimated as follows: wheat, 244,500 (50,400 in 1973, 211,400 in 1972); barley, 40,200 (5,900 in 1973, 34,000 in 1972); tomatoes, 133,500 (83,100 in 1973, 152,700 in 1972); other vegetables, 141,300 (65,000 in 1973, 93,400 in 1972); citrus fruits, 33,900 (15,400 in 1973, 20,900 in 1972); olives, 40,100 (5,200 in 1973, 35,000 in 1972); melons, grapes, and other fruits, 81,100 (83,500 in 1973, 97,000 in 1972); and tobacco, 900 (1,100 in 1973, 700 in 1972). As the production data make evident, the 1973 war seriously disrupted Jordanian agriculture.

23 ANIMAL HUSBANDRY

Animal husbandry is usually on a small scale and is often of the nomadic or seminomadic type indigenous to the area. The large nomadic tribes take their camels into the desert every winter, returning nearer to the cultivated area in summer. The camels provide transportation, food (milk and meat), shelter, and clothing (hair); the sale of surplus camels is a source of cash. Sheep and goat nomads make similar use of their animals. In 1974, Jordan's livestock on the East Bank consisted of 1,190,200 sheep and goats, 42,200 head of cattle, and 13,700 camels. Poultry is an important source of food; about 2.5 million chickens are raised annually.

24 FISHING

Fishing is unimportant as a source of food. The rivers are relatively poor in fish; there are no fish in the Dead Sea, and the short Gulf of Aqaba shoreline is not yet developed for fishing, though the quality of fish available there is excellent. Total fish catch reached 194.5 tons in 1966 but was only 150 tons in 1971 and 91.6 tons in 1974.

25 FORESTRY

Jordan has suffered from extensive deforestation, and most of the hillsides are bare. There once were fairly widespread forests of oak and Aleppo pine in the uplands of Judea and Transjordan, but felling was uncontrolled during World War I. Scrub forests and maquis growths are now fairly common. The olive, characteristic of the Mediterranean basin, is widely cultivated. The important forests are around 'Ajlun in the north and near Ma'an. In 1973-74, an area of 8,200 acres was newly planted with forest trees as part of a government program. The production of finished timber reached a peak of 5,695 cu meters in 1964 but fell to 568 cu meters in 1974.

26 MINING

Jordan's mineral resources consist chiefly of phosphate, potash from the Dead Sea, and limited iron ore, manganese, and copper deposits. Phosphate deposits at al-Rusayfah near 'Amman and at al-Hasa near the port of al-'Aqabah are estimated at more than 430 million tons. Phosphates in lower concentration cover about 60% of the East Bank and may total 1 billion tons. Production reached 1,156,297 tons in 1968—more than three times what it was in 1959—and, after declining in subsequent years revived to reach 1,680,000 tons in 1974. Plans call for production of 10 million tons a year under the 1976–80 development program, and a fertilizer factory with a 600,000-ton annual capacity is to be constructed at al-'Aqabah. Development of potash has been delayed by continued tensions with Israel. Plans for development of copper ores, estimated at 55 million tons in southern Jordan, were announced in 1975. Other potential for progress lies in the production of high-quality marble, at present produced in a modest quantity, and in the exploitation of high-grade iron ore deposits at 'Ajlun.

27 ENERGY AND POWER

Total electrical energy produced in 1974 on the East Bank amounted to somewhat more than 200 million kwh. All electric power generation was thermal, but hydroelectric power was expected to become available in 1976 with the completion of the first dam in the Yarmuk River project. The government elec-

trification plan calls for establishment of a national grid, linking the major cities.

The oil refinery at al-Zarqa', which began operation in 1960, produced almost all of Jordan's fuel requirements in the early 1970s, with a daily capacity of 15,000 barrels. Plans to build a second refinery in southern Jordan, with Romanian assistance, were announced in April 1975.

28 INDUSTRY

Industry is playing an increasingly important part in Jordan's economy under the pressure of an adverse balance of trade and with the encouragement of the government. In 1976, most plants were small operations involving assembly, processing, or handicrafts. However, most industrial income came from three heavy industries: phosphates, cement, and oil refining. Cement production rose from 381,210 tons in 1968 to 596,200 tons in 1974. The oil refinery at al-Zarqa' produced 748,400 tons of petroleum products in 1974. Phosphate production in 1974 reached 1,674,800 tons. Some other output totals in 1974 were 2,647,800 sq ft of leather, 1,973 tons of cigarettes, 3,288,000 liters of spirits and beer, and 47,000 batteries.

In 1974, Jordan had 1,487 industrial establishments, of which 118 were government enterprises. In 1965, the Industrial Development Bank was established with an authorized capital of JD3 million, of which JD1 million was subscribed by the government and JD2 million by private business. The bank extends medium- and long-term loans and provides technical advice.

29 DOMESTIC TRADE

Lack of proper storage facilities, inadequate transport service, and a lack of quality controls and product grading are handicaps to Jordanian trade. However, these deficiencies are being alleviated directly and indirectly, under the 1976–80 development plan. Traditional Arab forms of trade remain in evidence, particularly in villages, and farm products generally pass through a long chain of middlemen before reaching the consumer. In 'Amman, however, Westernized modes of distribution have developed, and there are supermarkets and department stores as well as small shops. Business hours are from 8 A.M. to 1 P.M. and from 3 to 6:30 P.M. six days a week. Shops close on either Friday for Muslims or on Sunday for Christians.

30 FOREIGN TRADE

Jordan exports mainly agricultural products and phosphates; imports consist mainly of manufactured products and foodstuffs. Exports rose from $34.1 million in 1968 to $154.7 million in 1974. Imports rose from $161 million to $486.6 million, bringing the trade deficit in 1974 to a total of $331.8 million.

Principal exports in 1974 (in thousands of dollars) were:

Phosphates ·	60,742
Food and live animals	32,130
Basic manufactures	22,340
Machinery and transport equipment	9,044
Chemicals	3,973
Miscellaneous manufactures	2,797
Beverages and tobacco	2,706
Other exports	20,998
TOTAL	154,730

Principal imports in 1974 (in thousands of dollars) were:

Food and live animals	132,922
Machinery and transport equipment	109,904
Basic manufactures	105,403
Miscellaneous manufactures	27,187
Chemicals	25,062
Mineral fuels	16,215
Other crude materials	13,635
Other imports	56,229
TOTAL	486,557

Jordan is a founding member of the Arab Common Market, and in 1974, Arab countries received 50.7% of Jordan's exports. EEC countries accounted for 29.4% of Jordan's imports in 1974. Leading purchasers of Jordanian exports were India, Sa'udi Arabia, Lebanon, Japan, and Syria. Major suppliers of Jordanian imports included the US, Federal Republic of Germany (FRG), UK, and Lebanon. Principal trading partners in 1974 (in thousands of dollars) were:

	EXPORTS	IMPORTS	BALANCE
US	947	54,682	− 53,735
Lebanon	14,924	35,751	− 20,827
FRG	457	45,136	− 44,679
UK	901	37,431	− 36,530
Japan	11,824	22,954	− 11,130
Syria	11,786	19,933	− 8,147
Sa'udi Arabia	19,633	11,884	7,749
India	22,601	9,231	13,370
Egypt	4,049	22,109	− 18,060
Other countries	67,608	227,446	−159,838
TOTAL	154,730	486,557	−331,827

31 BALANCE OF PAYMENTS

Jordan's chronically adverse trade balance has long been offset by payments from foreign governments and agencies, and especially from Jordan's oil-rich Arab allies. Nearly all Jordan's long-term capital receipts represent government rather than private investment. Balance-of-payments summaries for 1973 and 1974 (in millions of dollars) are as follows:

	1973	1974
CURRENT ACCOUNTS		
Trade, net	−224.7	−282.1
Services, net	37.4	20.5
Transfers, net	199.3	263.9
TOTAL	12.0	2.3
CAPITAL ACCOUNTS		
Long-term	22.5	32.1
Short-term	− 12.1	2.0
TOTALS	10.4	34.1
Errors and omissions	7.2	− 15.4
Net change	29.6	21.0

At the end of 1975, Jordan's reserve holdings included $32.7 million in gold and $438.1 million in foreign exchange. Jordan's total international reserves rose from $253.3 million in 1971 to $486.2 million at the end of 1975.

32 BANKING

The Central Bank of Jordan, founded in 1964 with a capital of JD2 million and reorganized in 1971, is in charge of note issue, foreign exchange control, and supervision of commercial banks, in cooperation with the Economic Security Council. Its total assets in late 1975 amounted to almost JD200 million. Money supply at the end of February 1975 totaled JD176.29 million. Currency in circulation at the end of 1974 amounted to JD115.49 million, as against JD30.24 million at the end of 1966.

The banking system includes, besides the Central Bank, five specialized credit institutions, with assets totaling JD41.2 million in late 1975, and nine commercial banks, five of them branches of large international banks, with total assets of about JD213 million in late 1975.

With credit available to farmers through the Jordan Development Board and the Agricultural Credit Corporation and with growth of the cooperative movement, usurious money-lending is in decline.

33 INSURANCE

The Clark Insurance Co. and the Jordan Insurance Co. offer commercial insurance of most kinds. In addition, several US and British insurance companies have branches or agents in Jordan.

34 SECURITIES

Establishment of a securities exchange in Jordan was in the planning stage as of early 1976.

35 PUBLIC FINANCE

Jordan has had to rely on foreign assistance for support of its budget, which has increased rapidly since the 1967 war. The budget estimates for 1974 (in millions of Jordanian dinars) were as follows:

REVENUES	
Direct taxes	7.2
Indirect taxes	21.6
Fees	9.2
Other receipts	18.0
Grants and loans	97.1
TOTAL	153.1

EXPENDITURES	
Defense	43.6
Education	10.9
Police	6.6
Health	3.9
Other current expenditures	28.1
Development expenditures	72.6
TOTAL	165.7
BALANCE	-12.6

Foreign grants and loans covered the deficit of JD115 million in 1973. The external public debt totaled JD150 million in mid-1975.

36 TAXATION

Direct taxes made up less than 5% of total revenue in 1974. Corporations are taxed at lower rates than individuals; incomes of cooperatives are tax exempt. Indirect taxes continue to account for a large share (45% in 1973) of all revenues. There are livestock taxes, various license fees, road transport fees, social welfare tax, national guard tax, and land taxes. Formerly, only about 60% of the tax forms were returned, but collection procedures and the operation of the system as a whole were modernized in 1973, producing improvements in this area. The traditional Muslim religious charity tax was replaced in 1973 with a new social welfare tax, used by the government for the support of mosques, religious schools, and charity institutions.

37 CUSTOMS AND DUTIES

On 5 February 1962, Jordan inaugurated a new customs and tariff system, in an attempt to protect and stimulate local industry, reduce the adverse balance of trade, and lower the cost of living. Duties are now assessed individually on particular items and vary generally from 10% to 70%; most items fall within the 10–30% category. There are ad valorem taxes on all imports amounting to 7.5%, except on alcohol, which is taxed at 25.5%. There is also an import license tax of 4%.

Jordan grants preferential treatment to imports from Arab League countries, under bilateral trade agreements that exempt certain items from duty, and under multilateral trade and transit agreements with Arab League countries. Goods assembled in Arab countries are granted 20% reduction if the assembly cost, including domestic labor and local raw material, is not less than 20% of total cost. All imports, except those originating in certain Arab countries, require an import license.

38 FOREIGN INVESTMENTS

Jordanians as of early 1976 were still prohibited from owning foreign securities, investing abroad without government permission, or holding bank balances in hard-currency countries.

In the past there has been little foreign investment in Jordan apart from the oil pipelines, but a series of tax inducements, including a six-year tax holiday for industry established in ʿAmman and a nine-year tax holiday for new industry outside the capital, was enacted starting in 1972. Jordan has received substantial capital assistance from other Arab governments. In addition, IDA development credits outstanding as of 30 June 1975 totaled $25,776,000 in disbursed funds. Foreign capital may be repatriated after 1 year over a period of four years.

³⁹ECONOMIC POLICY

Before the upheavals caused by the war of 1967, the government began to design its first comprehensive development plans. The Jordan Development Board was set up in 1952. It adopted a five-year program for 1961–65 and a seven-year program for 1964–70, which was interrupted by war. In 1971, a newly created National Planning Council, with wide responsibility for national planning, prepared the 1973–75 plan for the East Bank, with a planned total outlay of JD179 million. The main objectives were to reduce the trade deficit, to increase the GNP, to expand employment, and to reduce dependency on foreign aid. The plan allocated a total of JD179 million, including JD35.8 million (20%) for transportation, JD34.9 million (19.5%) for construction, JD27.6 million (15.4%) for agriculture and irrigation, JD26.1 million (14.6%) for mining and industry, JD14.8 million (8.3%) for municipal affairs, JD10.9 million (6.1%) for education, JD9.8 million (5.5%) for electricity, JD7.2 million (4%) for tourism and antiquities, and JD11.9 million (6.6%) for other purposes. The plan called for an investment of JD99.6 million (55.6%) by the public sector and JD79.4 million (44.4%) by the private sector. Foreign loans and assistance accounted for 42% of the public sector investment and 10% of the private sector investment. At least 60% of the planned projects were completed, and a new five-year plan, with a planned outlay of JD832 million, was instituted on 1 January 1976.

⁴⁰HEALTH

In 1974, Jordan (East Bank only) had 28 hospitals with 2,170 beds; 12 were government hospitals. There were 763 physicians in 1974, along with 123 dentists, 344 pharmacists, 318 nurses, and 173 midwives. UNRWA maintains its own hospitals and maternity centers. A medical faculty was opened at the University of Jordan in 1972.

Medical services are concentrated in the main towns, but in recent years the government has attempted to bring at least a minimum of modern medical care to rural areas. Village clinics are staffed by trained nurses, with regular visits by government physicians. As modern medicine has spread to the more remote areas and among the tribes, traditional methods have been dying out. The Ministry of Health, created in 1950, in cooperation with UNICEF, WHO, and UNRWA, has greatly reduced the incidence of malaria and tuberculosis. Trachoma, intestinal parasites, acute skin inflammations, and other endemic conditions remain common. In 1975, average life expectancy was estimated at 57.4 for females and 54.1 for males.

⁴¹SOCIAL WELFARE

Modern public welfare is still in its beginnings in Jordan. Recent labor legislation has covered working conditions, health and safety measures, sick leave, and provision of health services in outlying areas. The government's 1973–75 plan called for an outlay of JD1.46 million, or 0.8% of the total, for social welfare and labor, as well as an additional JD1.21 million, or 0.7%, for Muslim charitable and religious endowments. UNRWA conducts an extensive welfare program for the Palestine refugees. Many Christian sects maintain hospitals, orphanages, and schools, financed mainly from foreign sources.

⁴²HOUSING

Housing conditions are unsatisfactory, although some improve-

ment has been made since World War II. According to the last census taken, in 1961, 95,434 persons (5.6% of the total population) lived in tents: this, however, could be taken to indicate the persistence of the traditional dwelling pattern among the nomadic population rather than destitution.

A general housing shortage in the mid-1960s was aggravated by the influx of West Bank refugees after the 1967 war. Construction activity fell to 3.3% of GDP in 1971, but rose to 7.7% of GDP in 1973; 1,686 residential building permits were issued in the ʿAmman/al-Zarga' area in 1973, and 1,078 in 1974.

⁴³EDUCATION

Education is compulsory for nine years: six years for the elementary and three years for the preparatory, or lower secondary, stage. In 1973 there were 1,482 government schools and 213 private schools; 171 UNRWA schools in eastern Jordan had an enrollment of 14,418 pupils. According to Israeli statistics, in the Israeli-held areas of the West Bank in 1974/75 there were 213,684 pupils in 971 institutions, including 31,054 pupils in 87 UNRWA institutions.

In eastern Jordan in 1973 there were seven teacher-training schools, with 2,243 students; five industrial schools, with 1,177 students; three agricultural schools, with 366 students; a nursing, midwifery, and child-care school, with an enrollment of 206; and a social service institute, with an enrollment of 61. The Husayn Agricultural College, at Tul Karm, grants the B.S. degree. The University of Jordan, near ʿAmman, enrolled 3,589 students in 1973 in liberal arts, science, finance, law, and medicine. A second university, Yarmuk University, was scheduled to open in September 1976 in Irbid, with an initial enrollment of about 480.

An estimated 55% of the adult population of the East Bank is illiterate, but most of the children of school age now attend school. Since the mid-1960s, vocational and commercial training have been increasingly emphasized.

⁴⁴LIBRARIES AND MUSEUMS

The library at the University of Jordan has more than 100,000 volumes, and the Jordan Archæological Museum has a library of more than 30,000 volumes. Combined holdings of 8 public and 20 specialized libraries total more than 100,000 volumes. The al-Aqsa Mosque Library in Jerusalem is particularly noted for its rare Islamic manuscripts.

The most important museum in the territory occupied by Israel in 1967 is the Palestine Archæological Museum, built in 1936 outside the walls of the Old City of Jerusalem by the British mandatory government, under a grant from John D. Rockefeller, Jr. It contains a rich collection of archæological material illustrating the prehistory and early history of Palestine and Transjordan. Also located in the Old City of Jerusalem is the Museum of the Studium Biblicum Franciscanum. ʿAmman has two museums: The Jordan Archæological Museum run by the government's Department of Antiquities, and the Islamic Museum.

⁴⁵ORGANIZATIONS

Religious organizations still are of major importance, and membership in the hamula, the kinship group or lineage comprising several related families, also is of great significance as a framework for social organization. Literary and theatrical clubs have become popular, especially since World War II, but political organizations have died out since the 1957 ban on political parties. There are also chambers of commerce in ʿAmman and other large towns.

⁴⁶PRESS

In 1976 there were two dailies, *Al-Dustur* and *Al-Rai*, both published in Arabic in ʿAmman, with circulations of about 15,000 and 10,000, respectively. The latter is a government-controlled paper, founded after the 1970/71 civil war; the former is 25% government-owned. There are also six weeklies and several less frequent publications, all published in Arabic in ʿAmman. The press code, enacted in 1955, requires all newspapers to be licensed and prohibits the publishing of certain information—for example, about the royal family or concerning military affairs—unless taken directly from material released by the government.

⁴⁷TOURISM

Before the war in 1967, tourism was an important source of revenue and the major earner of foreign exchange. Large numbers of pilgrims and tourists came to visit the Holy Places of Christianity (the Church of the Nativity in Bethlehem, the Holy Sepulchre and the Stations of the Cross of Jerusalem, the Mount of Olives, and the Garden of Gethsemane outside the Holy City) and of Islam (the Dome of the Rock and al-Aqsa Mosque in Jerusalem, and the Tombs of the Patriarchs in Hebron), and the Old City of Jerusalem itself and other biblical sites in the country, such as Bethany, the River Jordan, and Jericho. The loss of the West Bank in 1967 caused a sharp decline in tourism. Tourist receipts dwindled from $32 million in 1966 to $13 million in 1968, as the number of visitors fell from 616,875 to 375,432. Foreign arrivals have, however, increased since 1968—from 301,800 in 1970 to 551,700 in 1974—and receipts from tourism increased from $9 million in 1971 to $31 million in 1973. Eastern Jordan is an area of immense historical interest, rich with tourist attractions. Notable among the Greco-Roman remains is Jarash (ancient Garasi), which was one of the major cities of the Dekapolis (the capital, 'Amman, was another, under the name of Philadelphia) and is archæologically one of the best preserved cities of its time in the Middle East. Petra (Batra), the ancient capital of Nabatea in southern Jordan, carved out of the red rock by the Nabataeans, is, after the Holy Places, probably Jordan's most famous historic site.

Eastern Jordan has modern hotel facilities in 'Amman and al-'Aqabah, and there are government-built rest houses at some of the remote points of interest. Tourists are permitted to bring in or out a maximum of JD100 in Jordanian currency and any amount in foreign currencies. Special authorization is needed for stocks, bonds, and gold coins. Passport and visa are required for entry.

⁴⁸FAMOUS JORDANIANS

As a separate Arab country, Jordan has had a relatively short history, during which only two men have become internationally known. The first of these was the founder of the kingdom, 'Abdallah (1882–1951), who, born in Hijaz and son of the sharif of Mecca, made 'Amman his headquarters. He was recognized as emir in 1921 and king in 1946. The second is his grandson, King Husayn (b.1935), who has ruled as king since 1953.

⁴⁹DEPENDENCIES

Jordan has no colonies or territories.

⁵⁰BIBLIOGRAPHY

'Abdallah, King of Jordan. *Memoirs of King 'Abdallah of Transjordan*. New York: Philosophical Library, 1950.

'Abdallah, King of Jordan. *My Memoirs Completed*. Washington: American Council of Learned Societies, 1954.

Abu-Lughod, Ibrahim (ed.). *The Transformation of Palestine*. Evanston, Ill.: Northwestern University Press, 1971.

Albright, William F. *Archæology of Palestine*. Gloucester, Mass.: Peter Smith, 1972.

Antown, Richard T. *Arab Village: A Social Structural Study of a Transjordanian Peasant Community*. Bloomington: Indiana University Press, 1972.

Bukhari, Najati al-. *Education in Jordan*. 'Amman: Ministry of Culture and Information, 1972.

Carr, Winifred. *Hussein's Kingdom*. London: Frewin, 1966.

Copeland, Paul W. *Land and People of Jordan*. New York: Lippincott, 1965.

Fisher, William B. *The Middle East: A Physical, Social and Regional Geography*. London: Methuen, 1971.

Gabbay, Rony E. *A Political Study of the Arab-Jewish Conflict: The Arab Refugee Problem*. Geneva: Droz, 1959.

Glubb, Sir John Bagot. *Britain and the Arabs*. London: Hodder & Stoughton, 1958.

Harris, George Lawrence (ed.). *Jordan: Its People, Its Society, Its Culture*. New Haven, Conn.: HRAF Press, 1958.

Hussein, King of Jordan. *My War with Israel*. As told to, and with additional material by, Vick Vance and Pierre Lauer. New York: Morrow, 1969.

Hussein, King of Jordan. *Uneasy Lies the Head*. New York: Geis, 1962.

IBRD. *The Economic Development of Jordan*. Baltimore: Johns Hopkins Press, 1957.

Khouri, Fred J. *The Arab-Israeli Dilemma*. Syracuse: Syracuse University Press, 1968.

Kurtzig, Michael E. *Jordan's Agricultural Economy in Brief*. Washington, D. C.: Government Printing Office, 1972.

Laqueur, Walter. *Confrontation: The Middle East and World Politics*. New York: Bantam, 1974.

Laqueur, Walter (ed.). *The Israeli-Arab Reader; A Documentary History of the Arab-Israeli Conflict*. New York: Bantam, 1971.

Lawrence, T. E. *The Seven Pillars of Wisdom*. Garden City, N. Y.: Doubleday, 1935.

Mansfield, Peter (ed.). *The Middle East: A Political and Economic Survey*. New York: Oxford University Press, 1973.

Morris, James. *The Hashemite Kings*. New York: Pantheon, 1959.

Nyrop, Richard F., *et al. Area Handbook for the Hashemite Kingdom of Jordan*. Washington, D. C.: Government Printing Office, 1974.

Odeh, Hanna S. *The Jordan Valley*. 'Amman: Jordan Development Board, 1968.

Peake, Frederick Gerard. *A History of Transjordan and Its Tribes*. Miami: University of Miami Press, 1958.

Smith, Sir George Adam. *Historical Geography of the Holy Land*. New York: Harper, 1931.

Pryce-Jones, David. *The Face of Defeat: Palestinian Refugees and Guerrillas*. New York: Holt, Rinehart, & Winston, 1972.

Snow, Peter. *Hussein: A Biography*. Washington, D.C.: Luce, 1972.

Vatikiotis, P. J. *Politics and the Military in Jordan*. New York: Praeger, 1967.

KAMPUCHEA

Democratic Kampuchea
Kampuchea Prachea Thipatay

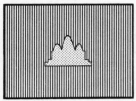

CAPITAL: Phnom-Penh. **FLAG**: The new national flag consists of a red banner with a representation of the temple of Angkor Wat in yellow at the center. **ANTHEM**: *Phleng Cheat (National Anthem)*. **MONETARY UNIT**: In March 1975, the revolutionary government announced issuance of a new riel (NR) to replace the riel (R) of the Lon Nol administration. However, as of June 1976, new currency had not appeared in the country and the economy was operating almost exclusively on a system of barter and government rationing. On 27 February 1975, R1 = $0.000606 (or $1 = R1,650). **WEIGHTS AND MEASURES**: Both the metric system and traditional weights and measures are in general use. **HOLIDAYS**: New Year Celebration, 13–15 April; Independence Day, 17 April; Plowing of the Holy Furrow, about 10 May; Entering of Buddha into Nirvana, about 14 May; and traditional monthly holidays. **TIME**: 7 P.M. = noon GMT.

¹LOCATION, SIZE, AND EXTENT
Situated in the southeast corner of Indochina, Kampuchea (formerly known as the Khmer Republic and as Cambodia) has an area of 181,035 sq km (69,898 sq mi), extending *730 km (454 mi)* NE–SW and *512 km (318 mi)* SE–NW. It is bounded on the NE by Laos, on the E and SE by Viet-Nam, on the SW by the Gulf of Siam, and on the W, NW, and N by Thailand, with a total boundary length of *2,715 km (1,687 mi)*.

²TOPOGRAPHY
Kampuchea is a country of forested mountains and well-watered plains. The central part of the country forms a gigantic basin for the Tonle Sap, or Great Lake, and the Mekong River, which flows down from Laos to the southern border with Viet-Nam. Between the Tonle Sap and the Gulf of Siam lie the Cardamom Mountains and the Elephant Chain, which rise abruptly from the sea and from the eastern plains. In the north, the 200-mile-long Dangrek Mountains, 1,000 to 2,500 feet high, mark the Thailand frontier. The short coastline has an important natural harbor, the Bay of Kompong Som, where the new port of Kompong Som (formerly Sihanoukville) is located.

The Mekong and the Tonle Sap dominate the life and economy of Kampuchea. The Mekong overflows during the rainy season, deposits vast quantities of alluvial soil, and, backing toward the Tonle Sap, causes that lake to increase in size from about 100 sq mi to almost 800 sq mi.

³CLIMATE
The climate is tropical, with a wet season from June through November and a dry season from December to June. Temperatures range from 20°C to 36°C (68°F to 97°F) and humidity is consistently high. The lowlands, which are inundated during the rainy season, receive about 80 inches of rainfall annually, but there is less precipitation in the western and northern portions of the country.

⁴FLORA AND FAUNA
Kampuchea, covered in its mountainous areas with dense virgin forests, has a wide variety of plant and animal life. There are palm, rubber, coconut, kapok, mango, banana, and orange trees, as well as the high sharp grass of the savannas. Birds, including cranes, pheasants, and wild ducks, and animals such as elephants, wild oxen, panthers, and bears abound throughout the country. Fish, snakes, and insects also are widespread.

As of 1975, endangered species in Kampuchea included the pileated gibbon, Asiatic wild dog, clouded leopard, Indochinese tiger, leopard (*Panthera pardus*), Asian elephant, Sumatran rhinoceros, Thailand brow-antlered deer, Asiatic buffalo, gaur, kouprey, giant ibis, river terrapin, Siamese crocodile, and Burmese python.

⁵POPULATION
In 1975, the population was 7,735,279, according to official government figures. Population growth is about 2.8% per annum. Although more than 75% of the land is arable, about 80% of the population is concentrated in less than one-third of the country. About 78% of the people live in rural areas, mostly along rivers. Phnom-Penh, the largest city, had about 600,000 inhabitants before the influx of refugees from the war that broke out in 1970. At the war's end, in April 1975, the city's population had swollen to nearly 3 million, creating conditions of severe deprivation and starvation. The new government immediately embarked on an evacuation of Phnom-Penh, and by March 1976, only 100,000–200,000 were thought to remain in the city. Upon consolidation of its control, the new government is thought to have set strict limits on the populations of towns and cities. Other cities include Battambang, Kompong Cham, Kampot, Siem Reap, Kompong Som, and Kratie.

⁶ETHNIC GROUPS
Over 85% of the Kampucheans are descendants of Khmers, with some mixture of Thai and Chinese elements. Approximately 6% of the population is Chinese. More than 200,000 Vietnamese were evacuated to the Republic of Viet-Nam (RVN) in 1970. Following the war's end in 1975, most of the 600,000 Vietnamese remaining in the country were reported to have emigrated to Viet-Nam. About 100,000 Cham-Malays, descendants of the old Kingdom of Champa, and tribes of Malayo-Polynesian origin are the other ethnic minorities. Prior to 1975, some 6,000 Europeans (mostly French) lived in Kampuchea, mainly in the cities. A Lao minority lives near Voeune Sai and some Burmese miners around Pailin.

⁷LANGUAGE
Khmer, the national language, is spoken by some seven million inhabitants. Unlike Thai or Vietnamese, Khmer is a nontonal language; most words are monosyllabic. French, the second language, has been in broad use in commercial and official circles. The Vietnamese and the Chinese use their own languages, as do the mountain tribes.

⁸RELIGION
Although Hinayana Buddhism is the religion of some 90% of the inhabitants, animism is adhered to by most persons as well. The Chinese and most Vietnamese practice a traditional mixture of

Mahayana Buddhism, Taoism, Confucianism, ancestor worship, and animism. Prior to 1975 there were some 100,000 Muslims (mostly Cham-Malays), 50,000 Roman Catholics (Europeans and Vietnamese), and a few Protestants. The mountain tribes are animists; in the post-World War II years, Christian missionaries made some converts among them. The 1976 constitution provided for freedom of religious practice except in cases where it proves inimical to national survival.

9 TRANSPORTATION

Land transport facilities suffered wholesale destruction during the 1970–75 war. By late 1975, however, the new government announced that all major roads had been reopened while major repairs to the railroads were under way. Kampuchea's first railway was a 385-km single track from Phnom-Penh to Paipet, which was badly damaged in the war. As a 262-km line from Phnom-Penh to Kompong Som was being finished, the war began, partly wrecking it. All major cities and towns are connected with Phnom-Penh by highway, and from there roads connect to Viet-Nam, Laos, and Thailand. The US-built 214-km Khmer-America Friendship Highway links Phnom-Penh with the port of Kompong Som on the Gulf of Siam. In 1970, before the onset of heavy fighting, there were 4,150 km of roads, about 70% of which were passable in all seasons. In 1972, Kampuchea had 27,200 passenger cars and 11,100 commercial vehicles.

The Mekong is the most important inland waterway. Total length of navigable waterways is 1,400 km during the rainy season, but only 600 km during the dry period. Phnom-Penh has facilities for ships up to 8,000 tons. Prior to 1975, Saigon was the major transshipment point for outgoing and incoming Kampuchean goods; the opening of the deepwater port of Kompong Som, with its berths for four 10,000-ton ships and good storage facilities, made Kampuchea largely independent of Viet-Nam for oceangoing shipping. In 1970, the port handled about 600,000 tons. Kep and Ream on the Gulf of Siam are ports of lesser importance. The first has been used as a fishing port, the second as a naval base.

Kampuchea's main airport is Pochentong at Phnom-Penh. Other landing fields are at Battambang and Siem Reap. Scheduled international air connections ceased in April 1975, following the coming to power of the Khmer Rouge government. In January 1976, a biweekly service between Phnom-Penh and Peking was inaugurated, the first instance of a regularly scheduled international flight under the new government.

10 COMMUNICATIONS

The communications system is government-operated. Prior to 1975, Phnom-Penh was linked by radiotelegraph to Saigon, Vientiane, Bangkok, Hong Kong, and France. In 1973 there were about 9,000 telephones, 1.1 million radios, and 10,000 television sets.

11 HISTORY

The Kampucheans are descendants of the Khmers, who in the 6th century overthrew the Indian-influenced Funan Empire, which for some 400 years had ruled Kampuchea. According to legends, the founder of the Khmer dynasty was Kambu Svayambhuva, and the name Kampuchea derives from his name.

From the 10th to the 14th century, after years of military expansion, the Khmers reached their apogee. Their empire extended over most of Southeast Asia (from central Viet-Nam southwest into the Malay Peninsula, and from Thailand north to the border of Burma). Angkor, the capital city, was a flourishing complex of great temples, palaces, and shrines. In the subsequent centuries, however, continuing attacks by the Thai (Angkor was captured by the Thai in 1431) and the Vietnamese weakened the empire, and by the end of the 18th century much of Kampuchea had become a Thai and Vietnamese condominium. In 1863, the king of Kampuchea placed the country under French protection. The French, joining what was then

known as Cambodia to Laos and Viet-Nam to form French Indochina, ruled the protectorate until the end of World War II.

Kampuchean nationalism received its greatest impetus during the Japanese control of Indochina in World War II and under the reign of King Norodom Sihanouk, who came to the throne in 1941. On 6 May 1947, Cambodia became a constitutional monarchy and was granted nominal independence within the French Union on 9 November 1949.

King Sihanouk, meanwhile, had assumed leadership of Cambodia's growing nationalist movement, and on 17 October 1953, during the height of the Franco-Indochinese war, was also granted full military control of his country by France. Sihanouk, a skilled politician, abdicated in March 1955 in favor of his father and mother, King Suramarit and Queen Kossamak, and then emerged as prime minister with unanimous support of the national legislature. King Suramarit died on 31 April 1960, but Prince Sihanouk, although retaining the title of chief of state, did not return to the throne.

During the Franco-Indochinese war, the Viet-Minh in Viet-Nam invaded Cambodia (1954), supported Communist bands of local Vietnamese, and sent aid to the Khmer Issaraks (Free Cambodians). The Geneva agreements of July 1954, which ended the Franco-Indochinese war, secured the withdrawal of French and Viet-Minh troops from Cambodia and the surrender of most of the Khmer Issaraks. During 1965–69, Prince Sihanouk suspended relations with the US, following an incident in which RVN troops pursued Vietcong elements into Cambodian territory.

On 18 March 1970, Marshal Lon Nol, prime minister and army chief, overthrew the chief of state, Prince Sihanouk, while the prince was on a visit to the USSR. The coup ended 1,168 years of rule by Khmer monarchs. Sihanouk thereupon took up residence in Peking, where, on 5 May 1970, he announced formation of the Royal Government of National Union of Kampuchea (GRUNK) under the political auspices of the National United Front of Kampuchea. In October, the Lon Nol government in Phnom-Penh abolished the monarchy and changed Cambodia's name to the Khmer Republic. The country, meanwhile, was being drawn inexorably into the widening conflict in Indochina. Upon assuming office, the Lon Nol government demanded, to no avail, a withdrawal of the estimated 40,000 Vietcong and Democratic Republic of Viet-Nam (DRV) troops from Cambodian territory. On 30 April, US President Richard Nixon announced an incursion into Cambodia of 30,000 US and 40,000 RVN troops with the object of destroying their opponents' strongholds along the Viet-Nam border. The operation was terminated on 30 June with uncertain results.

In elections held during June 1972, Lon Nol was elected president of the republic. Pressures from GRUNK insurgents continued to mount, especially following the conclusion of a ceasefire in Viet-Nam in January 1973 and the withdrawal of the last US troops from that country in March. US aid to the Lon Nol government had been substantial—during the peak period of assistance, from mid-1970 through 1972, US military aid totaled nearly $370 million and direct economic assistance an additional $150 million. With the reversal of US policy in Viet-Nam, however, support for the Khmer Republic began to taper off, and by the start of 1975, the Lon Nol government was plunged into a struggle for survival. In January, GRUNK forces (also referred to in the West as the Khmer Rouge) launched a major offensive aimed at gaining control of the Mekong River and isolating Phnom-Penh. Fierce and costly fighting ensued over the next three months, with the US undertaking a massive airlift to Phnom-Penh in February to fend off starvation and military collapse. On 1 April, the strategic Mekong ferry crossing at Neak Luang fell to the insurgents, clearing the way to a direct, final assault on Phnom-Penh. On that day, Lon Nol fled the country, to be followed by much of the ruling hierarchy. On 17 April, the Khmer Republic government officially capitulated to GRUNK forces, commanded by Khieu Samphan. The GRUNK government reported in March 1976 that the war had resulted in 1 million casualties, including 800,000 killed.

As an initial step, the new government ordered the near total evacuation of Phnom-Penh, where food, shelter, and medical resources had been stretched to the limit by the press of some 2.5 million refugees. The country was thereupon plunged into almost complete isolation, even from its neighbors in Vientiane, Saigon, and Hanoi, while massive reorganization of the country's economic, social, and political life was begun.

On 5 January 1976, a new constitution was promulgated and the country was officially renamed Democratic Kampuchea. On 20 March, the first general elections were held for a new 250-member People's Assembly. On 14 April, the Assembly named Khieu Samphan chairman of the State Presidium, replacing Prince Sihanouk, who had returned to the country in September 1975, as head of state. Sihanouk had formally resigned from the government on 5 April. Pol Pot was named prime minister, replacing Penn Nouth, who had lived in exile in China with Prince Sihanouk.

¹²GOVERNMENT
Kampuchea was a constitutional monarchy from 6 May 1947 until 9 October 1970, when Marshal Lon Nol formally established the Khmer Republic. On 30 April 1972, a new constitution was passed by a national referendum. It provided for a directly elected president and a bicameral legislature consisting of an elective 126-member National Assembly and 40-member Senate. Presidential elections took place on 4 June 1972, with Lon Nol emerging as victor (with 55% of the vote); legislative elections were held during the following August and September.

Upon the surrender of the Lon Nol government to the insurgent forces on 17 April 1975, rule by the Royal Government of National Union of Kampuchea (Gouvernement Royal de l'Union Nationale de Kampuchea—GRUNK) was effectively installed in Phnom Penh, with Prince Sihanouk as titular head of state. Effective rule over the country was initially provided by a small group of GRUNK officials who had remained clandestinely in the country to lead the insurgency through the 1970s. A new constitution approved in December 1975 by a 1,115-member national congress went into effect on 5 January 1976. The constitution provides for a unicameral, 250-member People's Assembly, elected for a five-year term by universal suffrage of citizens over age 18. Of the total membership, 150 are to be elected from the agricultural sector and 50 each from the armed forces and from the ranks of the workers. The Assembly is to meet only once a year, with ordinary legislative business managed by a standing committee. The first legislative elections under the new system were held on 20 March 1976.

The government's executive wing is selected by the People's Assembly. The principal executive body is the State Presidium, whose chairman is the chief of state. A nine-member cabinet is headed by a prime minister. In April 1976, Khieu Sampham was made chief of state, and Pol Pot was appointed prime minister.

¹³POLITICAL PARTIES
Under Sihanouk, the People's Social Community Party (Sangkum Reastr Niyum—PSCP) was the most important political group. In the 1955, 1958, 1962, and 1966 elections, with a platform of nonalignment, economic aid, and development, it captured all seats in the National Assembly. The extent to which Sihanouk had lost the confidence of PSCP legislators was evidenced in the 72-0 vote of no confidence in him in March 1970. Exiled in Peking following his overthrow by Lon Nol in March 1970, Sihanouk had allied himself with Cambodia's leftist insurgents under a group called the National United Front of Kampuchea (Front National Uni de Kampuchéa—FNUK).

Under the Khmer Republic government headed by Lon Nol, five political groups came to the fore. The Socio-Democratic Party (SDP), Lon Nol's own group, was quickly established as the most powerful group. Centrist opposition groups included the Republican Party, led by former acting prime minister Sisowath Sirik Matak; and the Democratic Party, headed by former National Assembly president, In Tam. Smaller groups included the Women's Party and the Pracheachon Party, representing a Marxist faction. In the presidential elections held in June 1972, Lon Nol, the SDP's candidate, defeated In Tam and lesser candidates by a relatively narrow margin of 55%. The legislative elections held in August–September were marred by a boycott by the minority parties, resulting in complete control of the legislature by the SDP.

With the victory of their forces in April 1975, leaders of the pro-Communist FNUK became the dominant political power in Kampuchea. Leadership of the party passed to Khieu Samphan. In the elections for the People's Assembly held on 20 March 1976, the 250 seats were contested by 515 candidates who had been screened politically by a government election committee. The government reported that 3,462,868 persons, or 98% of the electorate, had cast ballots. However, most prominent members of the GRUNK government—including Khieu Samphan, Pol Pot, and Ieng Sary (the foreign affairs minister)—did not stand for election to the Assembly.

See continental political: front cover O8; physical: back cover O8
LOCATION: 102°31′ to 108°E; 10° to 15°N. **BOUNDARY LENGTHS**: Laos, *541* km (*336* mi); Viet-Nam, *982* km (*610* mi); Gulf of Siam, *389* km (*242* mi); Thailand, *803* km (*499* mi). **TERRITORIAL SEA LIMIT**: *12* mi.

¹⁴LOCAL GOVERNMENT
Under the Lon Nol government, Kampuchea was divided into 20 provinces (khet), 7 subprovinces (anoukhet), 147 districts (srok), and more than 1,200 townships (sangkat or khum) and villages (phum). In addition, there were three autonomous municipalities: Phnom-Penh, Kirirom, and Kompong Som. During the 1970–75 war, most civilian governors were replaced by military officers.

Under the 1975 GRUNK government, administration of localities became largely decentralized. The country was redivided into some 41 new administrative districts. Within each district, the population has been organized into communes; cooperatives are the smallest socioeconomic units.

[15] JUDICIAL SYSTEM

Prior to 1975, conciliatory justices (sala lahouk) served as justices of the peace at the village or municipality level. One-man provincial tribunals (sala dambaung) had jurisdiction in all types of criminal and civil cases. Appeals jurisdiction in civil cases and most criminal cases was held by a court of appeals (sala outor). Another appeals court, the Court of Review (Sala Vinichhay), performed the role of a supreme court. The judicial system also included nationally administered criminal courts (sala okret) and a High Council of Magistracy, which judged government officials accused of improper actions.

In 1976, the judicial system was still undergoing reorganization by the GRUNK government. The constitution of January 1976 provided for a supreme judicial tribunal, whose members are to be appointed by the People's Assembly.

[16] ARMED FORCES

At the time of the Lon Nol coup in April 1970, the government's armed forces consisted of only 37,000 personnel. By September 1970, however, the army had been expanded to nearly 200,000 men and women and stood at about 175,000 in 1974. At that time, the navy had 11,300 personnel and some 180 small craft, including about 20 patrol boats. The air force, with about 7,000 personnel, operated approximately 60 piston-powered combat planes. Virtually all equipment supplied during the 1970–75 conflict was of US origin.

With the fall of the Lon Nol government in April 1975, the Khmer Republic's armed forces were disbanded. The GRUNK government's People's National Liberation Armed Forces of Kampuchea was thought to total about 80,000 personnel in 1975, organized into four divisions and three independent regiments. Equipment is of Soviet, Chinese, and US origin.

[17] MIGRATION

In the 1950s and 1960s, Prince Sihanouk permitted mainland Chinese to settle in the mountainous and wasteland areas and cultivate land that otherwise would have remained useless. Under the Lon Nol government, some 200,000 Vietnamese living in Kampuchea was repatriated to the RVN, ostensibly as a security measure. With the GRUNK victory in April 1975, most of the country's remaining 600,000 Vietnamese were reported to have emigrated to Viet-Nam. In addition, thousands of refugees, including several former officials and military personnel, fled across the Thai border or were evacuated by US aircraft. In mid-1976, some 10,000 Kampucheans were officially reported to be living in Thai refugee centers, with estimates of the total entering Thailand running as high as 50,000. In 1976, small numbers of Kampucheans, including persons who had gone to France and the US, began to return to the country.

Following its coming to power, the GRUNK government launched a sweeping nationwide resettlement program under which some 3 million persons were moved from Phnom-Penh and other cities into the countryside, where they were organized into work brigades. The food supply in rural areas was thought to be only slightly less critical than that in the cities, and widespread suffering was reported in the course of the transition.

[18] INTERNATIONAL COOPERATION

Kampuchea has been a member of the UN since December 1955 and has been a member of several of the specialized agencies. It has also been a member of the Columbo Plan Council, IPFC, IRC, IRSG, the UN Mekong Commission, and other intergovernmental organizations.

From the 1950s until the fall of Lon Nol's government in 1975, Kampuchea received economic aid at times from the Colombo Plan countries as well as, among others, from France, the US, the USSR, China, and Japan. US aid, discontinued at Sihanouk's request in 1963, was resumed in the spring of 1970 and totaled an estimated $1.8 billion (including an estimated $1.2 billion in military assistance) by the war's end.

During 1975–76, Kampuchea retained singularly strong ties with China, having received an estimated $1 billion to finance postwar reconstruction. Offers of assistance from other sources, including several Socialist countries, were reportedly rejected by the GRUNK government. The first governments to reopen their missions in Phnom-Penh were China, the Democratic People's Republic of Korea, and the DRV. Relations with Thailand were restored in October 1975, and in early 1976, Kampuchea moved to set up ties with three other ASEAN members—the Philippines, Malaysia, and Singapore—as well as with Burma. However, border clashes were reported in late 1975 with Saigon's Provisional Revolutionary Government and in early 1976 with Thailand. Ties with France remained severed, as did relations with the US, exacerbated since a May 1975 incident in which US marines attacked Kampuchean forces to win release of the US merchant ship *Mayaguez*, seized in the Gulf of Siam.

[19] ECONOMY

Kampuchea's economy has been based traditionally on agriculture. About 85% of the cultivated area is devoted to the production of rice, while rubber trees account for a major part of the remainder. Prior to the war years, Kampuchea's rice crop was usually ample enough to permit exports. The Tonle Sap, or Great Lake, is one of the major fishing reservoirs in Asia, and its products have played a key role in the Cambodian economy and diet. Cattle breeding is another important source of income.

During the 1970–75 period, Kampuchea's economy came to rely critically on US assistance. The GRUNK government was faced both with withdrawal of this aid and with wide-scale devastation—the country's richest areas bore the brunt of heavy US bombing attacks up to August 1973, while ground fighting led to massive destruction of transport and other facilities. The new government's reaction was to mobilize virtually the entire population in a mass labor campaign to rebuild the infrastructure while restoring agriculture to levels of self-sufficiency. In the industrial sector, the government claimed by early 1976 to have put into operation new textile mills, cement plants, sugar refineries, and iron smelters.

A profound reorganization of the country's economic structure was also under way during 1975–76. Private ownership of land (even small private plots as in China and the USSR) was disallowed, and landholdings were transferred to the state or state-organized cooperatives. All industrial enterprises were similarly transferred to state ownership. A remarkable feature of the newly structured economy was its apparent functioning (through June 1976) without benefit of an official currency. Most of the population was thought to be supported through a system of government food rationing and other forms of allotment. Officials did not preclude the eventual issuance of a currency, pending further evaluation of the present policy.

[20] INCOME

In the absence of both an official currency and a system of public accounts, national income statistics for postrevolutionary Kampuchea cannot be ascertained. National-accounts statistics have not, in fact, been published since the late 1960s. GDP, which stood at $875 million (at constant prices) in 1968, was estimated to have shrunk by at least one-third during the course of the 1970–75 war. Prior to the war, 38% of the GDP derived from agriculture, forestry, and fishing; commerce contributed 20% and industry 15%. Per capita GDP in 1969 was estimated at $100. Inflation reached dire proportions during the last years of the Lon Nol government, with annual rates exceeding 250% in 1973–74.

[21] LABOR

As before the war, the vast majority of Kampuchea's population (over 80%) in 1975 was thought to be engaged in agricultural pursuits. Many rural farmers also engage in part-time fishing or small-scale industrial undertakings. The government's mass-labor campaign, fully implemented during the last quarter of 1975, possibly mobilized more than 90% of the labor force (including many urban residents moved to the countryside) who were set to work farming rice, clearing land, and building and repairing dikes, irrigation canals, and roads. Workers were organized into state-owned enterprises, communes, and cooperatives, which also engaged in the provision of goods and services previously in the control of the private sector (prior to 1975, most commercial activities were in the hands of Kampuchea's Chinese minority). In the absence of a currency, workers received payments in rice; the annual allotment was reported at 250 kg (550 lb) in 1976.

22 AGRICULTURE

About 2.7 million hectares (about 15% of the total area) is suitable for agriculture. Some 85% to 90% of the cultivated land area has been devoted to rice, 3% to rubber, and the remainder to other crops. Rice provides the staple diet, and prior to the 1970–75 war, was Kampuchea's major export. Production peaked at 3.2 million tons in 1968, falling back to 2.7 million tons in 1970. In the course of the war, output fell off precipitously, declining from 2.1 million tons in 1971 to 953,000 tons in 1972, 655,000 tons in 1973, and an estimated 493,000 tons in 1974. Thus, Kampuchea, which had exported upward of 200,000 tons annually in the late 1960s, was compelled in 1974 to import 302,000 tons. Upon its coming to power in April 1975, the GRUNK government embarked on a major rice-production program, claiming a significant expansion of acreage and yields. As a result, the 1975 crop was reported as having reached 2.2 million tons, substantially above the annual need. The richest and principal region of rice cultivation is the Battambang area, where there are major irrigation works. Several large-scale irrigation projects were reported under way, many assisted by technicians from China. In 1976, 10,000 workers were reported working on a 63-km canal near Pursat that would eventually irrigate 90,000 hectares; an irrigation project in Kompong Cham was expected to provide water to 11,500 hectares; and in the vicinity of Prey Veng, 164 dikes, 60 ponds, and more than 30 canals were constructed.

Rubber has traditionally been the second most important agricultural crop. Rubber plantings, however, which covered 48,000 hectares in 1969, were almost completely destroyed by the end of 1971. Production, up to 51,100 tons in 1969, declined to virtually nil in 1971, recovering somewhat to about 16,000 tons in 1974. Most of the rubber estates are in the Kompong Cham area, where, prior to the 1970s, French-owned plantations accounted for 80% of the rubber trees; an estimated 60,000 hectares of rubber trees were growing in the mid-1970s. Most of the estates were nationalized in July 1974 by the Khmer Rouge.

Corn production dropped from 121,000 tons in 1970 to 15,000 tons in 1973, and yield per acre remained low. Other crops, with their respective 1970 and 1973 outputs in tons, included green beans: 20,000, 7,000; peanuts: 17,000, 1,000; sesame: 10,000, 2,000; and jute: 9,000, 4,000. Pepper is grown on the mountain slopes, primarily in Kampot and Takeo provinces. Tobacco (5,000 tons in 1972) is used almost entirely for local consumption. Cotton is planted on 6,000 hectares, primarily in Kompong Cham and Battambang provinces. Palm and cane sugar, soybeans, and sweet potatoes are also grown.

During the 1975–76 mass agricultural work campaign, self-sufficiency in food was given priority over cash crops; as an example, coffee plantations in Pailin were reported to have been replanted in bananas.

23 ANIMAL HUSBANDRY

Livestock, mainly raised by households, traditionally supplied an important supplement to the Kampuchean diet. Hogs were estimated at 1,150,000 in 1973. The Lon Nol government reported in early 1975 that more than 30% of the country's prewar cattle stocks (2,300,000, including oxen and domesticated buffalo in 1975) had been killed as a result of the fighting.

Following the war, the new government placed heavy stress on cattle and poultry breeding. Each family and work unit was instructed to raise chickens. The use of horses and buffalo as draft animals was also emphasized to offset the scarcity of mechanization.

24 FISHING

Production of freshwater fish, the main protein element in the Kampuchean diet, traditionally ranked next to rice and rubber in the country's economy. About half of Kampuchea's freshwater catch comes from Tonle Sap. The fishing season extends from October to February, when it reaches its height as the Tonle Sap contracts, thus concentrating the fish densely in a narrowing body of water. Offshore fishing grounds present a rich natural resource, as yet not fully exploited.

Freshwater fishing was one of the few economic activities that was not significantly curtailed by the war; the 1974 catch totaled an estimated 74,000 tons (67,000 tons in 1969), while the saltwater catch declined to 10,000 tons (20,000 tons in 1969).

25 FORESTRY

About 50% of the country (35,000 sq mi) is forested, but exploitation of forests has been limited because of transportation difficulties. There are about 19,000 sq mi of open forest, 12,000 sq mi of rain forest, and 4,000 sq mi of mangrove. The main products of the forest industry are timber, resins, wood oil, firewood, and charcoal. Production, averaging about 4 million cu meters of round wood in the late 1960s, fell off sharply as a result of the war; by 1974, timber output stood at 17% of the 1969 level, firewood at 13%, and charcoal at 8%.

26 MINING

Kampuchea's known mineral resources are for the most part limited. Iron deposits and traces of gold, coal, copper, and manganese have been reported in the Kompong Thom area. Substantial deposits of bauxite, discovered in the early 1960s north of Battambang and southeast of Phnom-Penh, have yet to be worked. Potter's clay is common, and deposits of jet, phosphates, and corundum are found. Zircons and jet have been exploited by a group of Kampucheans of Burmese descent in Stung Treng and Battambang provinces. Salt is found in the central provinces; production in 1974 was about 8,000 tons, or 10% of the prewar volume. Development of the two main phosphate deposits (of an estimated 350,000 tons each) was stressed in pre-1975 government planning.

Offshore oil was reportedly discovered by a French firm in August 1974 in the vicinity of the Wai Islands, located on the continental shelf in the Gulf of Siam. Both the GRUNK government and Viet-Nam laid claim to the islands.

27 ENERGY AND POWER

Wood is the most widely used fuel for transportation, industrial, and domestic purposes. Most of the few existing electric power plants must use imported diesel oil and natural gas. Several new power-generating facilities were installed in the mid-1960s, but progress slackened toward the decade's end. A 10,000-kw hydroelectric plant, built by Yugoslavia, was inaugurated on 11 March 1968 in the Kirirom Highlands. The country's total capacity was reduced by about one-third in the course of the war, reaching 41,000 kw by 1973/74; in that period, production stood at 150 million kwh.

28 INDUSTRY

Industrial activity has centered on the processing of agricultural and forestry products and, prior to 1975, on the small-scale manufacture of consumer goods. Rice milling has been the main food-processing industry. Up to the 1970–75 war, there were more than 1,000 mills with a daily capacity of 2 to 4 tons each. The first cement plant, with an annual capacity of 50,000 tons, was opened in 1964 at Chakray Ting (it was destroyed in January 1974). Other industries established during the 1960s include a sugar refinery with a capacity of 15,000 tons, a tire plant outside Phnom-Penh, and an assembly line for tractors. Also set up were a paper factory at Chhlong, with an annual capacity of 5,000 tons; a plywood factory at Dey Eth, with an annual output of 1 million board feet; and a textile factory at Kompong Cham, with an annual capacity of 1,500 tons of yarn and 5 million meters of cloth.

Industrial expansion came to a virtual halt in 1970 with the outbreak of war. The last major industrial facility, the Kompong Som oil refinery, became fully operational in late 1968 with an annual capacity of 500,000 tons, but ceased production in 1972. A few sectors (such as textiles and beverages) enjoyed a short wartime boom due to military orders, but by 1973, losses in territory and transport disruptions induced a rapid decline in activity.

The new government placed all industries under state control. By June 1975, the government announced that more than 80 industrial plants had been restored to a production footing, with food-processing enterprises, textile mills, and tire factories in Phnom-Penh all back at work supplying local demands.

29 DOMESTIC TRADE
Phnom-Penh was traditionally Kampuchea's principal commercial center. In the villages and smaller cities, food and other products were bought and sold in the marketplace. Formerly, the import business and the wholesale-retail business were largely in the hands of the French, Chinese, and Vietnamese.

In April 1975, all private shops in the country were closed, and virtually the entire system of domestic distribution and trade fell under control of the state. In the absence of any official currency, all commodity exchanges have taken the form of government rations or barter. Food distribution was placed largely under the control of the military.

30 FOREIGN TRADE
Kampuchea has traditionally been an exporter of primary products and an importer of finished goods. The country achieved a favorable balance of trade in the mid-1960s. In the late 1960s, however, an adverse balance reappeared, and in the early 1970s, normal trade patterns virtually disintegrated, the wartime economy being largely sustained by US-subsidized imports. By 1974, imports had soared to $263.3 million (compared with $52 million in 1970), while exports earned only $19 million ($38.2 million in 1970).

Rice, which made up about 40% of annual exports in the late 1960s, comprised fully 58.5% of Kampuchea's imports in 1973/74. Other major imports in 1973/74 were fuels (5.8% of the total), transport equipment (3.4%), chemicals (2.7%), and machinery (2.6%). Rubber (averaging about 20% of exports in the late 1960s) and other agricultural products comprised virtually all of the small export total in 1973/74.

In 1971, the US surpassed France as Kampuchea's chief source of imports. Principal trading partners in 1974 (in thousands of dollars) were:

	EXPORTS	IMPORTS	BALANCE
US	1,637	197,670	−196,033
Singapore	8,346	21,164	− 12,818
Thailand	1,299	24,782	− 23,483
Hong Kong	778	10,963	− 10,185
France	1,367	6,699	− 5,332
Japan	2,226	3,754	− 1,528
UK	567	2,214	− 1,647
Other countries	2,821	6,054	− 3,233
TOTALS	19,041	273,300	−254,259

Since March 1975, Kampuchea's trade patterns have undergone a dramatic restructuring, accompanied by what was viewed to be a drastic diminution in overall trade volume. The bulk of foreign trade appeared to be with China, as Kampuchea initially eschewed dealings with most of its former partners, including France and the US. In mid-1976, trade exchanges with both Thailand and Viet-Nam were increasing.

31 BALANCE OF PAYMENTS
Kampuchea's balance-of-payments position showed a deficit every year during the 1954–74 period. In the mid-1960s, the growth of industries producing import substitutes, the rising receipts from exports, and strict controls over import licensing temporarily decreased the overall deficit. However, with the onset of the war in 1970, the payments situation began to deteriorate rapidly. The trade deficits grew from 27.4 million SDRs in 1970 to 59.1 million SDRs in 1972, and 152.9 million SDRs in 1973; as of 31 October 1974, the imbalance stood at 144.9 million SDRs. At that time, foreign reserves stood at 25.6 million SDRs (compared with 54.1 million at the end of 1970). During 1971–74, foreign-aid payments (mainly from the US) offset these deficits, with annual provisions of 25.9 million SDRs in 1971, 66.6 million SDRs in 1972, 183.7 million SDRs in 1973, and 175.9 million SDRs through October 1974. Kampuchea is thought to have received a grant of $20 million from China to be applied to the country's reserves.

32 BANKING
All banking operations were nationalized by the Sihanouk government on 1 July 1964. The National Bank of Cambodia, a semiautonomous government agency functioning as the sole currency authority, was charged with central banking responsibilities, including the control of credit. The action of Premier Lon Nol in permitting foreign banks to do business in the country in early 1970 was a factor leading to his break with Prince Sihanouk and to the latter's overthrow in March 1970.

The Bank of Commerce financed import and export transactions and maintained control over foreign exchange allocations. The National Development Bank, established in 1956 to finance the development programs, financed projects under public ownership and management. The Office of Cooperatives was created in 1956 as an autonomous agency to extend short-term loans to farmers and artisans.

The money supply decreased from R6.7 billion at the end of 1962 to R6.3 billion at the end of 1963, but then increased to R6.6 billion in mid-1964. It dropped again by 1969 to R6.1 billion. By 1973, a severe inflationary pattern had set in; currency in circulation, amounting to R26 million in June 1973, soared to R44.2 million by June 1974.

By April 1975, the new government had assumed control of the National Bank, and virtually all banking operations in Kampuchea were suspended. In March, government officials had announced their intention of issuing a new currency through the National Bank, but the economy continued to function without benefit of a currency through mid-1976.

33 INSURANCE
All insurance companies were "Cambodianized" in 1960; 16 companies were in operation prior to the war. Under the new government, normal insurance operations have been suspended.

34 SECURITIES
Although stock exchanges did not exist in pre-1975 Kampuchea, stocks and bonds issued by local companies were sold in direct transactions between seller and buyer. Under the new government, all trading in securities was banned.

35 PUBLIC FINANCE
As of mid-1976, there was no evidence of a public budgetary system having been put into practice by the government. Prior to 1975, all government budgets of the preceding two decades had been marked by an excess of expenditures over internal revenues. Foreign aid and treasury reserves made up the difference.

In 1973/74, the last full fiscal year of the Lon Nol government, budgeted domestic revenues totaled R22,891 million, as compared with R11,892 million in 1972/73. Current expenditures for 1974 totaled R7,135 million (R43,154 million in 1973) and capital outlays, R500 million (R577 million in 1973). Offsetting US aid subsidies totaled R20,100 million in 1973 and R28,000 million in 1974.

[36] TAXATION

Prior to 1975, indirect taxes were the most profitable source of domestic revenue, especially monopoly excises, such as the sales tax on salt. Other indirect taxes include those on alcohol, tobacco, sugar, radios, and livestock. Income taxes, land taxes, and business license taxes were the principal direct taxes. Collection of taxes was a major problem for pre-1975 governments, the returns in some provinces being as low as 10% of estimated tax liabilities. During 1975–76, no centralized taxation was introduced.

[37] CUSTOMS AND DUTIES

During the 1960s and early 1970s, Kampuchea operated under a two-column tariff with minimum and general rates. Minimum rates applied to GATT contracting parties and other countries that had special agreements with Kampuchea. Goods of other countries were subject to the general rates, which were three times the minimum.

Much of the foreign trade after April 1975 is believed to have been contracted on a direct barter basis.

[38] FOREIGN INVESTMENTS

Although not prohibited, little private foreign capital was invested in pre-1975 Kampuchea. French capital in rubber plantations represented more than half of the total investment. US aid was resumed in 1970 and totaled an estimated $1.8 billion by the war's end. With the establishment of the GRUNK government, all foreign investment in the Kampuchean economy was expressly prohibited. In 1975, the government accepted some $1 billion in direct, unconditional grants from China, although it apparently rejected several offers of aid from other (including Socialist) countries.

[39] ECONOMIC POLICY

Prior to 1975, Kampuchean governments sought aid from foreign sources, both public and private, and attempted to improve the climate for private foreign capital investment. Both Sihanouk and Lon Nol also increased Kampuchean control of economic activities within the country. Aliens were prohibited from engaging in 18 professions or occupations, including those of rice merchants and shipping agents.

The Sihanouk government's approach to the problem of economic development was first outlined in a two-year development plan in 1955. There was particular emphasis on the development of education, transport facilities, communications, health, rural improvements, and small private enterprises. A five-year plan (1960–64) aimed at agricultural diversification; palm sugar refining; packaging of meats, vegetables, and fish; jute manufacturing; tire production; spinning and weaving; and tanning.

Main projects under the second five-year plan (1965–69) were a new cement plant capable of an annual production of 200,000 tons; a cane sugar mill at Battambang; a Phnom-Penh synthetic textile plant; an iron-scrap steel mill; a motor-pump factory; a urea plant at Kompong Som; and two oil mills. Progress was made on some projects but others lagged badly. Strained economic conditions and related discontent, primarily in Phnom-Penh, were factors leading to the overthrow of Prince Sihanouk in March 1970. The outbreak of war following the fall of Sihanouk brought almost all major projects to a halt. Most industrial projects completed in the 1960s were destroyed or badly damaged in the course of the war.

Although lacking in detailed articulation, the economic program enacted by the GRUNK government since April 1975 indicated a revolutionary restructuring of the country's economic life on a scale with few, if any, precedents. The government moved swiftly and decisively to disband virtually all vestiges of free enterprise in the country, including all private land ownership. Kampuchea, further, became the first contemporary state to abandon use of a currency (at least as of June 1976). The government has pursued a policy of total mobilization of the population and mass redeployment of labor.

The immediate goal of the GRUNK government's economic strategy appeared to be self-sufficiency in food. Aside from rice cultivation itself, significant labor was expended on the construction of irrigation networks to make possible two or three harvests annually. Meeting domestic needs for clothing was also stressed, with a repeated emphasis in all spheres of freeing Kampuchea's economy from the bonds of foreign assistance and participation. The government made it clear that once rice production was restored to an export footing, industrialization would be stressed along with the modernization of agriculture.

[40] HEALTH

Life expectancy in Kampuchea in the mid-1970s was estimated at 45.4 years, and some 50% of the children die before they are a year old. Dysentery, malaria, tuberculosis, trachoma, and yaws are widespread. The 1970–75 war exacerbated many of these problems, malnutrition becoming widespread among the millions driven to Phnom-Penh in the wake of the fighting. Tens of thousands are thought to have died owing to shortages of food, medical facilities, and supplies.

Prior to 1975 there were 3 hospitals, with 7,500 beds (about 1 bed for every 893 persons). There were 438 doctors in 1971 (1 physician for every 15,297 persons), as well as 71 dentists, 79 pharmacists, 3,639 nurses, and 1,426 midwives. It was not clear how many physicians remained in the country at the war's end, although virtually all foreign doctors and personnel—who had constituted a major segment of the health community—were reported to have left the country. The shortage of trained personnel, always a major problem, was thought to be among the major concerns facing the new government.

Prior to 1975, Phnom-Penh had a modern US-built hospital (for Buddhist bonzes), a French hospital built and staffed by the Calmette Foundation, and a Soviet-built hospital staffed by Soviet and local personnel, in addition to the Municipal Hospital and several private clinics staffed and operated by French physicians. The Pasteur Institute covered the country's need in vaccines. Each province had a hospital.

The Royal College of Medicine, opened in 1956, graduated its first doctors in 1960. A nursing school and a rural health training center were also functioning prior to 1975.

[41] SOCIAL WELFARE

The Sihanouk and Lon Nol governments enacted limited social legislation regulating hours of work, wages, and workmen's compensation. In 1955, a program of family allotments was inaugurated, under which employers contributed a monthly sum for the welfare of workers' families. There was also a pension system for orphans.

[42] HOUSING

Kampuchean housing traditionally compared favorably with that of other countries of Southeast Asia. The most common type of dwelling consists of one or more rooms raised on mangrove piles some 10 feet above the ground; it is generally crowded. Many houses in the cities are larger and of better quality. By mid-1976, mass emigration from the cities resulted in many dwellings being left vacant, in contrast to the dire overcrowding that occurred in the last years of the war. In the countryside, meanwhile, the waves of new migrants have placed inordinate pressures on existing facilities, with much of the transplanted population forced to reside in improvised shelters.

⁴³EDUCATION

About half of the Kampuchean population is thought to be literate. In 1972 there were 1,534 primary schools, with an enrollment of 479,616, and some 250 secondary schools, with an enrollment of about 104,000. Up to 1975, pagoda schools were still important in basic village education.

In 1972, higher institutions had 9,667 students. The Khmer University, a national institution of higher learning, founded in 1959, had schools of medicine, law, liberal arts, teacher education, science, architecture, and engineering. In addition, there was a Royal School of Administration and the School of Public Works. Monks received training at the Buddhist University in Phnom-Penh.

Prior to 1975, aid to education came from the US, France, and the USSR.

Under the GRUNK government, educational matters were placed under a newly created Ministry of Youth and Popular Education. As of mid-1976, however, all schools in Kampuchea remained closed, with formal educational activities among children reported to be confined to occasional gatherings for political instruction. The coming to power of the new government was accompanied by expressions of open hostility toward students, teachers, and intellectuals, as well as to the very concept of formal education as practiced under previous governments.

⁴⁴LIBRARIES AND MUSEUMS

Library facilities prior to the war were largely limited to the National Library (55,000 volumes, largely French) in Phnom-Penh. There were smaller libraries at the higher schools. The Khmer National Museum won repute as an excellent repository of Kampuchean art. The Ecole Française d'Extrême-Orient previously had charge of all archaeological research in the country and also had its own research library in Phnom-Penh.

The country in effect is a museum of the cultural achievements of the Khmer Empire. Surviving stone monuments, steles, temples, and statuary attest to a formidable and unique artistic heritage. Particularly imposing are the world-famous temple of Angkor Wat and the Bayon of Angkor Thom. Since the 1970–75 war, however, foreign access to historical sites in Kampuchea has been almost totally cut off.

⁴⁵ORGANIZATIONS

In 1975, cooperative organization became a central tenet of the GRUNK government's social and economic reorganization policy. By 1976, cooperative ownership was thought to have become a countrywide phenomenon, playing a major role—alongside state-owned enterprises—in both agriculture and industry.

Virtually all other social and commercial organizations, including chambers of commerce, were disbanded by mid-1975.

⁴⁶PRESS

Legislation passed in 1951 accorded anyone the right to publish in the country, provided the Ministry of Information was given notice. In 1956, however, the National Assembly enacted a censorship law affecting all publications not printed in the country. There were 16 periodicals published in Phnom-Penh after the March 1970 establishment of the Lon Nol government.

With the coming to power of the GRUNK government in April 1975, all vestiges of a mass-media daily press in Kampuchea disappeared. The government's radio station in Phnom-Penh has become the country's only daily organ of information.

⁴⁷TOURISM

Up until the encroachments of war in the late 1960s, Angkor Wat and other remains of the ancient Khmer Empire were the major attractions for visitors to Kampuchea. Under the GRUNK government, tourism has been nonexistent.

⁴⁸FAMOUS KAMPUCHEANS

Foremost among ancient heroes of Kampuchea were Fan Shihman, greatest ruler of the Funan Empire (150–550), and Jayavarman II and Jayavarman VII, monarchs of the Khmer Empire who ruled between the 10th and 13th centuries. Prince Norodom Sihanouk (b.1922), who resigned the kingship and won Kampuchea's independence from France, is the best-known living Kampuchean. In exile in China during 1970–75, he founded the GRUNK government, from which he resigned in April 1976. Khieu Samphan (b.1931), a former Marxist publisher and leader of the insurgency in Kampuchea, was named chairman of the State Presidium in the GRUNK government in April 1976, thus replacing Sihanouk as chief of state.

⁴⁹DEPENDENCIES

Kampuchea has no territories or colonies.

⁵⁰BIBLIOGRAPHY

American University. *Area Handbook for the Khmer Republic (Cambodia)*. Washington, D.C.: Government Printing Office, 1973.

Armstrong, John P. *Sihanouk Speaks*. New York: Walker, 1964.

Briggs, Lawrence Palmer. *Ancient Khmer Empire*. Philadelphia: American Philosophical Society, 1951.

Brodrick, Alan Houghton. *Little Vehicle: Cambodia & Laos*. London: Hutchinson, 1949.

Cady, John Frank. *The Roots of French Imperialism in Eastern Asia*. Ithaca, N.Y.: Cornell University Press, 1954.

Chatterji, Bijan Raj. *Indian Cultural Influence in Cambodia*. Calcutta: University of Calcutta, 1928.

Chemicais, L. *Le Cambodge*. Paris: Librairie d'Amérique et d'Orient, 1960.

Cole, Allan Burnett (ed.). *Conflict in Indochina and International Repercussions: A Documentary History, 1945–1955*. Ithaca, N.Y.: Cornell University Press, 1956.

Fifield, Russell Hunt. *The Diplomacy of Southeast Asia, 1945–1958*. New York: Harper, 1958.

Fifield, Russell H., and C. Hart Schaaf. *The Lower Mekong*. Princeton, N.J.: Van Nostrand, 1963.

Groslier, Bernard. *Angkor*. New York: Praeger, 1959.

Hammer, Ellen Joy. *The Struggle for Indochina*. Stanford, Calif.: Stanford University Press, 1966.

Herz, Martin Florian. *A Short History of Cambodia*. New York: Praeger, 1958.

Lancaster, Donald. *The Emancipation of French Indochina*. London: Oxford University Press, 1961.

LeMay, Reginald Stuart. *The Culture of Southeast Asia*. London: Allen & Unwin, 1954.

Matheson, Marion H. *Indo-China: A Geographical Appreciation*. Ottawa: Department of Mines and Technical Surveys, 1953.

Meyer, Charles. *Derriere le Sourire Khmer*. Paris: Plon, 1971.

Migot, André. *Les Khmers*. Paris: Presses de la Cité, 1961.

Monod, Guillaume Henri. *Le Cambodgien*. Paris: Larose, 1931.

Newnham, Thomas O. *Lake Village in Cambodia*. London: Longmans, 1967.

Osborne, Milton. *The French Presence in Cochin-China and Cambodia*. Ithaca, N.Y.: Cornell University Press, 1969.

Smith, Roger. *Cambodia's Foreign Policy*. Ithaca, N.Y.: Cornell University Press, 1965.

Steinberg, David J., et al. *Cambodia: Its People, Its Society, Its Culture*. New Haven, Conn.: Human Relations Area Files, 1959.

Thompson, Virginia, and Richard Adloff. *Minority Problems in Southeast Asia*. Stanford, Calif.: Stanford University Press, 1955.

Tong, André. *Le Dossier Sihanouk*. Paris: L'Association d'études et d'information politiques internationales, 1971.

Williams, Maslyn. *The Land in Between: The Cambodian Dilemma*. New York: Morrow, 1970.

Willmatt, William C. *The Chinese in Cambodia*. Vancouver: University of British Columbia, 1967.

DEMOCRATIC PEOPLE'S REPUBLIC OF KOREA

Choson Minjujuui Inmin Konghwa-guk

CAPITAL: P'yongyang. **FLAG**: A wide horizontal red stripe is bordered on top and bottom by narrow blue stripes, separated from the red by thin white stripes. The left half of the red stripe contains a red five-pointed star on a circular white field. **ANTHEM**: *The Song of General Kim Il Sung.* **MONETARY UNIT**: The won (w) of 100 ch'on is a convertible currency. There are coins of 1, 5, and 10 ch'on and notes of 50 ch'on and 1, 5, 10, 50, and 100 won. w1 = $1.06 (or $1 = w0.94). **WEIGHTS AND MEASURES**: The metric system and native Korean units of measurement are used. **HOLIDAYS**: New Year's Day, 1 January; May Day, 1 May; Liberation Day, 15 August; Founding of the Democratic People's Republic, 9 September. **TIME**: 9 P.M. = noon GMT.

¹LOCATION, SIZE, AND EXTENT

The Democratic People's Republic of Korea (DRK) occupies the northern part of the Korean Peninsula in East Asia. It has an area of 120,538 sq km (46,540 sq mi), extending 719 km (447 mi) NNE–SSW and 371 km (231 mi) ESE-WNW. It is bordered on the N by China, on the NE by the USSR, on the E by the Sea of Japan (including East Korea Bay), on the s by the Republic of Korea (ROK), and on the s and w by the Yellow Sea (including West Korea Bay), with a total boundary length of 2,702 km (1,679 mi). The ROK comprises the southern part of the Korean Peninsula.

²TOPOGRAPHY

The mountainous Korean Peninsula contains thousands of peaks, leaving only an estimated one-fifth of the peninsula as cultivable. Almost the whole of north-central Korea is occupied by a single mountain mass, dominated by the peninsula's highest peak, Mt. Paektu (9,003 feet), an extinct volcano with a scenic crater lake. From this mass, a chain of mountains with the Taebaek Range at its core runs parallel to the east coast down almost to Pusan in the ROK. About midway, the lesser Sobaek Range extends off to the southwest, in south-central ROK. Other peaks of note are Mt. Kwanmo (8,337 feet) in North Hamgyong, Korea's second highest; Mt. Myohyang (6,263 feet) in North P'yongan, rich in history and legend; and Mt. Kumgang ("Diamond Mountain," 5,374 feet), famed for the beauty of its vistas.

Principal rivers are the Tumen (323 miles) and Yalu (491 miles) along the northern border of the peninsula, both of which rise in Mt. Paektu; the Chongchon (123 miles) in the northwest corner of the peninsula; the Taedong (272 miles), which flows past P'yongyang; the Imjin (158 miles) near the 38th parallel in the west. Yellow Sea tides on the west coast rise to over 30 feet in some places; Sea of Japan tides on the east rise only some 3 feet.

³CLIMATE

The climatic range is greater than the limited size of the peninsula would suggest. The average January temperature is −16.6°C (−2°F) at Chunggang on the north-central border and −8°C (18°F) at P'yongyang. In the hottest part of the summer, however, the variation is not nearly so marked, average temperatures ranging from 24.4°C (76°F) in P'yongyang to 21°C (70°F) along the relatively cool northeast coast. Spring and fall are unusually pleasant, but winters are colder than the average for the latitude and summers are hot and humid. Precipitation is around 20 inches along the upper reaches of the Tumen, but more than half of the peninsula receives 30 to 40 inches per year. Unfortunately, nearly all of the rainfall occurs in the April-September period, especially during the late June to early August rainy season, creating major problems of flood and drought for Korean agriculture. Crops also may be damaged by typhoons in the early fall. Frostless days number about 180 in the northern part of the peninsula.

⁴FLORA AND FAUNA

Korea is rich in its varieties of plant life, which are typical of temperate regions. Over 3,000 species, some 500 of them unique to Korea, have been noted by botanists. There are few harmful plants. The animal life largely corresponds to that of nearby China and Siberia. Zoologists have identified over 500 fish, 400 birds, 100 mammals, and 40 reptiles and amphibians in Korea. Bears, wild boar, deer, snow leopards, and lynx are still to be found in the highlands, especially in the north. The shrinking of the forested area has reduced the animal population in recent years. Migratory water fowl, cranes, herons, and other birds are visible on the plains. Noxious insects and household pests infest the warmer regions and aquatic life is generally infected with parasites.

As of 1975, endangered species in the Korean Peninsula included the wolf, Asiatic wild dog, Siberian tiger, Amur leopard, Japanese sea lion, and several types of birds: the Chinese egret, the Japanese white stork, and Tristram's woodpecker.

⁵POPULATION

The population of the DRK in mid-1975 was estimated at 16,430,000, nearly double the post-Korean War low of 8,491,000 in 1953. The annual rate of population growth was estimated at 2.8%. The projected population for 1980 is 17,926,000. The population density varies greatly from region to region, with an average of 136 per sq km (353 per sq mi). The median age of the population in 1975 was 18.6 years. In 1975, 42.7% of the population was estimated to be urban (compared with 33.1% in 1965). Nine cities had populations in excess of 100,000; the largest, P'yongyang, had a population of perhaps 1.4 million. Other large cities include Hamhung, Ch'ongjin, Kim Ch'aek, and Wonsan; Hamhung was the only one of these cities with a population of more than 500,000.

⁶ETHNIC GROUPS

The Koreans are believed to be descended primarily from Tungusic peoples (Mongoloid race) who originated in the cold northern regions of Central Asia. There is scant evidence of non-Mongoloid admixture. Korea has no sizable ethnic minority. The total non-Korean resident population is probably about 50,000, nearly all of them Chinese. The former Japanese colonists in Korea, over 700,000 in 1944, were all repatriated after World War II.

[7]LANGUAGE

The Korean language is usually acknowledged to be a member of the Altaic family and is clearly related to other agglutinative tongues such as Turkic, Mongolian, and Japanese. Linguistic unification of the peninsula apparently followed political unification in the 7th century, and today the dialect differences are comparatively slight.

Korean is written with a remarkable and largely phonetic alphabet called han'gul. Created over 500 years ago (1446) under the great King Sejong, the Korean alphabet consists today of 14 basic consonants and ten simple vowels, all marvelously regular in shape. Han'gul letters are combined into syllables by clustering, in imitation of Chinese characters, rather than being written in the linear fashion of English, and this creates problems for modern typography. Before the invention of han'gul, Koreans wrote in Chinese, and indeed Chinese continued to be both the official language and the language of most literature until the beginning of the 20th century. With the beginning of the Japanese colonial administration in 1910, Japanese became the official language, and the use of Korean became highly restricted. Since 1949 the DRK has used only han'gul (calling it Choson muntcha) for writing, while ROK uses a mixed Sino-Korean script, necessitating knowledge of several thousand Chinese characters. North Korean linguists have studied han'gul extensively, publishing a six-volume dictionary in 1962. The traditional honorifics of the language, which vary according to the status of the speaker and the person spoken to, remain in use in both Koreas.

[8]RELIGION

Most Koreans are eclectic in their religious beliefs, the majority subscribing to varying mixtures of Confucian, Buddhist, Christian, Ch'ondogyo ("Religion of the Heavenly Way," an eclectic indigenous sect originating in the latter half of the 19th century), and animist beliefs. Native shamanism, especially its aspect of exorcism of evil spirits, traditionally was practiced by many Koreans in the rural areas. Geomancy also was widely followed and resorted to in such matters as the selection of auspicious building and tomb sites. Since the division of the peninsula, however, the practice of religion has been discouraged by the DRK government.

[9]TRANSPORTATION

Some 11,265 km (7,000 mi) of railroad track, of which about 70% is electrified, provide the principal means of transportation. The tracks run roughly parallel to the coastlines and river valleys. The principal rail lines are the Kyong-Ui line, running from Kaesong on the southern border through P'yongyang to Sinuiju on the northern Sino-Korean border and connecting with the Chinese rail system; the P'yongyang-Wonson line, the prime rail link connecting east and west; the P'yongyang-Hamhung-Ch'ongjin line; and the Wolla line connecting Wonsan and Najin on the east coast. There are several minor interior branch lines. Direct international passenger trains connect P'yongyang with Peking and Moscow.

Some 5,633 km (3,500 mi) of roads are in use, the major routes paralleling the rail lines. A new superhighway connects P'yongyang with Kaesong.

The most important rivers utilized for freight transportation are the Yalu, Taedong, and Chaeryong. Major ports in the east are Wonsan, Ch'ongjin, and Najin; in the west, Namp'o, Haeju, and Tasado. Air services have taken an increasingly important role in the country's domestic transportation. The air force controls civil air service between the major cities, while international services connect P'yongyang with China and the USSR.

[10]COMMUNICATIONS

Postal, telephone, and telegraph services are operated by the Ministry of Communications. International telephone lines operate between P'yongyang and Moscow, Peking, Prague, Warsaw, East Berlin, Budapest, Sofia, Bucharest, and Ulan Bator.

The central broadcasting station in P'yongyang has a 300-kw transmitter. Broadcasts reach to every corner of the country through a system of more than 1 million loudspeakers; the government said it reached 98% of communities by this means in the early 1970s. There were approximately 250,000 private radios in 1972. The national television network planned the production of 100,000 sets by 1976. The government makes widespread use of mobile film teams to reach people in the hinterlands. The film industry produced some 200 films in 1974, a few in wide-screen technicolor; the themes range from socialist realism to Korean War dramas and soap operas. Ubiquitous small-group meetings are used for reading and discussion of party and government newspapers, and for face-to-face communication.

[11]HISTORY

The history of the Korean people begins with the migration into the Korean Peninsula of Tungusic tribes from North China and Manchuria about 5,000 years ago. The archaelogical evidence indicates that these tribes already possessed neolithic (New Stone Age) culture and that it was not until about the 8th century B.C. that the art of working metal came to Korea from China. The recorded history of Korea, on the other hand, begins with the seizure of control over northwestern Korea in 194 B.C. by a military figure from China of unknown ethnic origin named Wiman. He usurped a throne that, according to legend, had been occupied by a descendant of a Chinese émigré nobleman (Kija, a historical figure) of the 12th century B.C. A popular Korean legend of much later origin asserts that Kija was preceded in his rule over the Korean Peninsula by the semidivine figure Tan-gun, offspring of the son of the divine creator and a "bear woman." Both Tan-gun and Kija still are widely revered.

The primitive state of Wiman fell victim to expanding Chinese power in 108 B.C. and there followed more than four centuries of Chinese colonial rule. During this period, the advanced Chinese culture slowly spread into nearly every corner of Korea, giving impetus to the coalescence of the loosely knit Korean tribes into statelike formations. By A.D. 313, when the Chinese power was destroyed, three Korean kingdoms had emerged. The three kingdoms had advanced cultures for the time, each having compiled a written history; this was also the period when Buddhism was introduced in Korea. Ultimately, one of the three, the Silla, crushed the other two and united all but the northernmost portion of the peninsula, ushering in the age of the Silla Unification (688-892). However, Korea again suffered threefold division until reunification was achieved under the leadership of Wang Kon, who proclaimed the new dynasty of Koryo.

Although Sinification of political and social institutions and of Korean thought went on at an accelerated pace, and there were some notable cultural achievements, the Koryo Dynasty (918-1392) was beset by foreign invasions: Beginning in 1231, the Mongol scourge fell upon Koryo, devastating the land and, from 1258, making puppets of the Korean kings. Following the collapse of the Mongol empire, Gen. Yi Song-gye assumed the throne of 1392, ushering in the long-lived Choson or Yi Dynasty.

The first hundred years of Yi Choson witnessed truly brilliant cultural achievements. The world's first authenticated casting of movable metal type was made in 1403. The Korean alphabet, han'gul, was developed. A rain gauge was invented and put into use throughout the peninsula. A spate of basic texts—histories, geographies, administrative codes, works on music—were compiled and issued under state auspices. Scholars competed for government posts through the civil service examination system. But by about 1500, the energies of Choson's hereditary ruling class began to be spent in internecine political struggles. Factional cleavage between Easterners and Westerners hardened, and Yi Choson was ill-prepared to meet the successive Japanese (1592-98) and Manchu (1627 and 1636) invasions. The brilliant naval victories of the revered Korean admiral Yi Sun-sin, with his ironclad "turtle ship," and the timely arrival of relief forces from Ming China, saved Choson from Japanese annihilation, but it was ultimately forced to become a tributary state of the Manchu Ch'ing empire.

In the 18th century, two energetic kings, Yongjo (1724–76) and Chongjo (1776–1800), were able to arrest somewhat the process of dynastic decline. But the intellectual and cultural revival, known as the Practical Learning Movement (Sirhak), they engendered was short-lived, and Choson's bitterest century followed.

The first half and more of the 19th century was marked by a succession of natural disasters, by mounting peasant unrest and insurrection, and by administrative relapse into hopeless corruption and inefficiency. Eventually a Korean figure came forward to attempt to rescue the dynasty from impending collapse. This was the Taewon'gun, father of the king, who held power during the decade 1864–73. But while his domestic reforms were generally enlightened and beneficial, he adopted an isolationist policy, including persecutions of the growing Catholic community in Korea. Such a policy was doomed to failure and soon after the Taewon'gun's downfall, the Kanghwa Treaty of 1876 with Japan opened Korea by force both to Japan and to the clamoring Western nations. During the last quarter of the 19th century, Korea was the prize in a complex rivalry for mastery of the peninsula among Japan, China, Western imperialist powers, and domestic political forces. During 1894–95, Japan seized upon the pretext of peasant uprisings in Korea's southern provinces (the Tonghak Rebellion, led by followers of what later came to be called the Ch'ondogyo religion) to destroy Chinese power in Korea in the Sino-Japanese War. A decade later, Japan turned back the Russian bid for supremacy in the Russo-Japanese War (1904–5), and in 1910, with the tacit blessing of the US and the European powers, the Yi Dynasty came to an end with the formal annexation of Korea by Japan.

For 35 years, Korea remained under the Japanese yoke, until liberated by US and Soviet troops at the end of World War II. Although Japanese colonial rule had brought Korea a considerable economic development along modern, Western lines, the benefits went primarily to the Japanese, and the process was accompanied by ever harsher political and cultural oppression. The Korean people staged a nationwide passive resistance movement in 1919 (the Samil or "March 1" Movement), only to have it swiftly and brutally crushed by their Japanese overlords. In the 1920s and 1930s, nationalist and Communist movements developed both within Korea and among Korean exiles in the USSR, Manchuria, and China proper, leading to sustained if periodic resistance to Japan. After the onset of Sino-Japanese hostilities in 1937, the Japanese aimed to eradicate Korean national identity; even the use of Korean was banned. Hence, when Japan was defeated and their country liberated in 1945, Koreans greeted the occupying forces of the US and the USSR with almost hysterical relief and joy.

Unfortunately, however, Korean rejoicing proved to be premature. In August 1945, as a result of US initiative, the 38th parallel was chosen as a line of demarcation between Soviet occupation forces (already in the north) and US occupation forces (introduced on 8 September). While the Americans set up a full military government allied with conservative Korean political forces, the Soviets allied their government with leftist and Communist Korean forces led by Kim Il Sung, who had been an anti-Japanese guerrilla leader in Manchuria. After a joint commission set up by the US and the USSR had failed to agree on plans for reunification of Korea, the problem was placed on the UN agenda in September 1947. In accordance with a UN resolution, elections were held on 10 May 1948 in South Korea alone: North Korea did not recognize UN competency to sponsor the elec-

tions. The newly elected National Assembly formulated a democratic constitution and chose Syngman Rhee, a long-time independence leader, to be the first president of the Republic of Korea (ROK) (15 August 1948). In December 1948, the ROK was acknowledged by the UN General Assembly as the only government in Korea to have been formed according to the original UN mandate.

In the north, the Soviet authorities aided Kim Il Sung in carrying out a thoroughgoing renovation of the political, social, and economic order. On 9 September 1948, the Democratic People's Republic of Korea was established. Like its southern counterpart, the DRK claimed to be the legitimate government of all Korea.

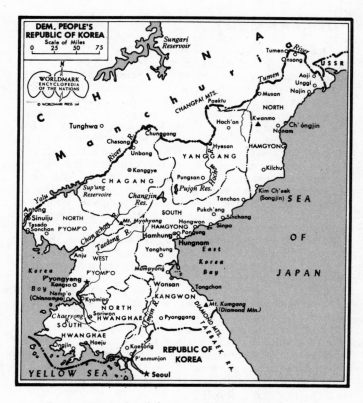

See continental political: front cover R5; physical: back cover Q5

LOCATION: 124°13′ to 130°39′E; 37°38′ to 43°1′N. **BOUNDARY LENGTHS:** China, *1,416* km (*880* mi); USSR, *18* km (*11* mi); ROK, *240* km (*149* mi); total coastline, *1,028* km (*639* mi). **TERRITORIAL SEA LIMIT:** 12 mi.

On 25 June 1950, the People's Army struck across the 38th parallel at dawn. The DRK forces advanced rapidly until the destruction of the ROK seemed imminent. At US urging, the UN Security Council branded the DRK an aggressor and asked the withdrawal of the attacking forces. On 27 June, President Truman ordered US forces into battle. A multinational UN Command was then created to join with and lead the South Koreans. An amphibious landing at Inchon (15 September) under Gen. Douglas MacArthur brought about the complete disintegration of the DRK's military position.

The UN forces, at MacArthur's urging, made a fateful decision to drive into the north. As they approached the Yalu River, China warned that it would not tolerate a unification of the peninsula under US/UN auspices. After several weeks of threats and feints, "volunteers" from the Chinese People's Liberation Army entered the fighting en masse, forcing MacArthur into a costly, pell-mell retreat back down the peninsula. The battle line stabilized nearly along the 38th parallel, where it remained for two years. On 27 July 1953, an armistice agreement finally was signed. The Korean War had brought incalculable destruction and human suffering to all of Korea, and it left the peninsula still more implacably divided. An international conference of April-June 1954 failed to reach an agreement on unification.

On 4 July 1972 came the revelation that representatives from both sides had met at the highest level and agreed to a joint communiqué providing for talks aimed at eventual unification. In 1974, however, the dialogue broke down amid recriminations and threats of a new war. In mid-1975, it appeared that the UN was on the verge of ending the UN Command apparatus, which for years had only token non-US contingents stationed in the ROK.

12GOVERNMENT
In the DRK, effective political authority is under the direction of the Korean Workers' (Communist) Party. The national legislature and constitutionally the highest organ of state power is the unicameral Supreme People's Assembly (SPA), elected on the basis of 1 deputy for every 50,000 persons. The first SPA, elected in August 1948 for a three-year term, actually lasted until 1956, the Korean War having forestalled new elections. The second SPA, elected in August 1957 for a term extended to four years by a constitutional amendment, had a membership of 215 deputies. Elections for the third SPA were held in October 1962 and the new Assembly, comprising 383 deputies, held its first session that same month. The third session of the fifth SPA met in March 1974, with 457 delegates chosen on the basis of 1 deputy for every 30,000 people. It decided on a complete abolition of taxation for citizens of the DRK, which its press hailed as the first such instance in the world.

To handle its functions between regular sessions, the SPA elects a presidium consisting of a president (who is the titular chief of state), several vice-presidents, a general secretary, and a number of regular members.

The SPA also names a cabinet, consisting of a premier, several vice-premiers, ministers, and heads of other major government agencies.

Suffrage extends to all men and women 18 years of age or older. Elections are on a single slate of Communist-approved candidates, on a yes or no basis. Following elections, it is usually asserted that nearly all those eligible had voted, and that their votes were unanimous in favor of the candidates.

13POLITICAL PARTIES
The Korean Workers' (Communist) Party, the ruling party of the DRK, was formed on 10 October 1945 through a merger of the Communist Party and the New Democratic Party. Party membership in 1972 was estimated to have risen to about 2 million. The principal party organ is the National Party Congress, which met for the fifth time in 1970. The Congress adopts the party program and approves the political line set by its Central Committee.

To guide the party between sessions of the National Party Congress, the Congress elects a Central Committee and a Central Auditing Commission, which looks after the party's financial affairs. The Central Committee (117 regular and 55 alternate members) elects a Political Committee (11 regulars and 9 alternates), which itself has a standing committee (6 members in 1966, later reduced to the current 4). A "united front" policy confers nominal status to two ostensibly non-Communist political parties: the Korean Democratic Party and the Friends Party (Chongu Party), for adherents of the Ch'ondogyo faith.

14LOCAL GOVERNMENT
Of Korea's 13 historic provinces, 6 were wholly or partly within the DRK after 1945. The Communist regime subsequently established two new provinces and divided a third into two sec-

tions, thus raising the number of provinces to nine. They are: North P'yongan, South P'yongan, Chagang, North Hwanghae, South Hwanghae, Kangwon, North Hamgyong, South Hamgyong, and Yanggang. In addition, there are three "special cities" (P'yongyang, Ch'ongjin, and Hamhung), and one "special region" (Kaesong), that are administered separately. The provinces were in turn divided into 15 cities and 163 counties (kun) as of 1975. There are some 4,200 wards and villages, the 3,700 or so villages corresponding for the most part with the agricultural cooperatives.

The DRK was a relatively unique system of people's assemblies and people's committees at all levels of administration. Members of the people's assemblies are elected for four-year terms at the provincial level, two-year terms at the county, township, and village levels. The assemblies supervise public, economic, and cultural activities. They also elect and recall people's committees, which are the permanent executive and administrative organs of the state at the local level.

15JUDICIAL SYSTEM
The DRK's judicial system consists of the Supreme Court, the procuracy, the courts of provinces, cities and counties, and special courts (courts-martial and transport courts). Most cases are tried in the first instance by people's courts at city or county levels. Provincial courts try important cases and examine appeals from lower court judgments. The Supreme Court is named by the Supreme People's Assembly. The lower courts are appointed by the people's assemblies at the corresponding level. A prosecutor-general, who is also appointed by the Supreme People's Assembly, is the country's chief law-enforcement officer. He appoints prosecutors at the provincial, city, and county levels.

Judges at the city and county level serve two-year terms and are usually Korean Workers' Party members. Supreme Court judges serve three-year terms; they hold plenary sessions once a year and represent the final appeal level. Courts are officially viewed as vehicles for instruction in the values of the state, with punishment often taking the form of "reeducation."

16ARMED FORCES
DRK citizens are subject to compulsory military service at the age of 18 in the People's Army (organized in 1948). The country maintains one of the largest and best-equipped military forces in the world, including some 1,000 heavy and medium tanks, 598 combat aircraft, and 20 SAM missile battalions. In 1975, the estimated total strength of the armed forces was 467,000, with 410,000 in the army, 17,000 in the navy, and 40,000 in the air force. An additional 40,000 are in the reserves, and some 1,260,000 citizens participate in a civilian militia.

The DRK's estimated defense expenditures in 1974 totaled $770 million, about 16% of the national budget.

17MIGRATION
During the generation of Japanese occupation (1910–45), some 3 million Koreans emigrated to Manchuria and parts of China, 700,000 to Siberia, some 3 million to Japan, and about 7,000 to the US (mostly to Hawaii). From the end of the war in 1945 through 1950, an estimated 3 to 4 million Koreans crossed the 38th parallel into the ROK, refugees either from communism or from the Korean War. Immigration has been limited to the small numbers of Koreans who freely or forcibly crossed to the north prior to 1953. Also, some 91,000 out of about 600,000 Koreans in Japan were repatriated to the DRK between December 1959 and the end of 1974.

18INTERNATIONAL COOPERATION
During the mid-1970s, the DRK came out of its relative isolation to pursue a vigorous international diplomacy. By 1975, it was recognized by 88 countries, a gain of 47 since 1972. Although not a member of the UN, the DRK now maintains an observer group at UN headquarters and is a member of several UN agencies, including the UPU and UNCTAD as well as WHO. The DRK has

become particularly active in third world diplomacy, and in August 1975 became the second Communist country to enter the League of Non-Aligned Nations. In addition, the DRK pursues a variety of exchanges with China, the USSR, and East European nations, and recently has opened exchanges with Japanese trade delegations, political parties, and journalists. The DRK retains treaties of friendship, cooperation, and mutual defense concluded with China and the USSR in 1961.

19 ECONOMY

The government's pursuit of a self-reliant economic policy has succeeded in transforming the DRK into one of the most autarkic economies in the world. Exceptions exist for certain heavy industrial and machine goods, and for commodities not available from its natural resources: oil, rubber, and coking coal. All the means of production are socialized except for small private farm plots and gardens.

The DRK was traditionally an agrarian country, although the Communist regime has used its rich mineral resources to promote industry, especially heavy industry. By 1965, industry accounted for 78% of the total output and agriculture 22%; the two sectors had thus reversed precisely the proportions reported in 1946. Since 1965, greater emphasis has been placed on agriculture and light industry, the latter stress owing to increasing demands for consumer goods. In the 1970s, industrial investments comprised 49% of total state investments, compared to 57% during the 1960s.

The Korean War devastated much of the DRK economy, but growth since the postwar reconstruction has been rapid. A generally accepted figure puts annual industrial growth during 1956-63 at about 25%. The rate slowed in the late 1960s to around 14%; in 1975, the government stated that the average annual rate for 1970–75 was 18.4%, with an increase of 25% in the last year. The official targets for the six-year plan (1971–76) were said to have been fulfilled by October 1975, one year in advance.

A State Planning Committee coordinates the economy, with corresponding committees at city, county, and province levels. Local and regional planning committees have been given greater latitude in planning since 1964.

20 INCOME

DRK national income figures, corresponding to Marxist economic usage, exclude services not directly related to production and distribution. Although national income figures in absolute money equivalents are not published, Kim Il Sung in 1966 disclosed a per capita income figure for the first time: w500 per household per year. Using that figure as a base, estimated national income in 1967 was 12.5 times that of 1946 and 8.6 times that of 1953. Total national income estimates by Western scholars suggested a figure of $4.1 billion in 1967, yielding a per-capita income of $316 (using purchasing-power parity exchange rates). This figure ranked the DRK favorably among developing economies. The government reported in 1975 that national income in 1974 had increased by 170% over that of 1970 (growth from 1967 to 1970 was probably minimal). Cooperative farmers were said to have received w2,360 per household in 1974. Western estimates put average household income at w1,212 for that year.

21 LABOR

Figures on occupational distribution have not been published since 1963. At that time, 40.1% of the labor force were classified as factory workers, 15.1% as office workers, 42.8% as agricultural cooperative members, 2% as cooperativized handicraftsmen. In 1946, only 12.5% of the work force were industrial laborers, indicating the great change in labor force composition. In another significant change, women now constitute half of all farm workers and one-third of all industrial workers. Total employment in 1974 was 7.8 million.

The DRK faces a constant labor shortage in virtually all sec-tors, but particularly in the technical professions. Recent plans have called for systematic increases in the number of technicians and specialists, toward a projected total of 1 million by 1976

Virtually all industrial and office workers belong to unions enrolled in the General Federation of Trade Unions. Salaries in the DRK range from w50 to w180 per month for factory and office workers to w300 to w350 for high officials.

22 AGRICULTURE

Most of the agricultural land is concentrated in the west-coast provinces of North and South P'yongan and North and South Hwanghae. Irrigation and flood-control projects are being carried out to increase output.

Because of its shorter and less rainy growing season and more severe winter, the DRK, unlike the ROK, has only one rice harvest per year. Thus, despite its prolific yield, irrigated rice gradually is being replaced by less productive crops such as corn, grain, sorghums, millet, potatoes, and rye, which are better suited to the country's shorter, drier cropping period. Rice, however, is still a principal crop.

The DRK claims to have become self-sufficient in grain production. Although it imports certain grain products, it also exports surpluses. The government stated in 1974 that total annual grain production had reached 7 million tons, thus fulfilling the goals of the six-year plan two years ahead of schedule. Per hectare yields of rice reached a high of 5.9 tons, with a record yield of 5 tons in corn production. Total rice production was put at 3.5 million tons, compared to 2.8 million tons in 1972. Kim Il Sung claimed in 1975 that the DRK had achieved the world's highest standard in per-unit-area yields of rice. Gains also have been achieved through the use of "miracle" rice strains, intensive application of fertilizer, and mechanization. It was announced that some 4 tractors are available for every 100 hectares of arable land, a 350% increase over 1970. With some 30,000 rice-transplanting machines, the claim is that 92% of the rice-transplanting process is now mechanized.

Double-cropping of grains other than rice has been maximized through the use of cold-bed seeding and new seed varieties, enabling an estimated half of total cultivated land to be double-cropped. Important crops besides rice include millet, corn, barley, wheat, soybeans, potatoes, cotton, and tobacco.

The country's farms were collectivized after the Korean War. The movement began late in 1953, and by the end of 1954, 32% of the peasants had become members of over 10,000 cooperatives and collectives. The process was completed by August 1958, when all of the DRK's 1,055,000 farm families had become members of over 16,000 cooperatives. In order to establish larger and more efficient operating units, the cooperatives were merged in the autumn of 1958 into approximately 3,800 units with about 300 families each; each farm comprised about 400 hectares. Produce is delivered to the government, which controls distribution through state stores. Most farm workers retain small private plots and can sell produce from them to the state or in peasant markets.

23 ANIMAL HUSBANDRY

Animal husbandry suffered from the aftereffects of the war, the poor harvests of 1954 and 1955, and a generally inferior feed supply. But a major effort has been made to increase corn and fodder supplies, to improve breeding practices, and to raise sharply numbers of livestock in all categories. By 1963, livestock production was 3.7 times that of 1946; in 1975, livestock totals were estimated as follows: cattle, 1.2 million; hogs, 2.2 million; sheep, 285,000; and horses, 43,000.

24 FISHING

Fisheries are one of the country's most important sources of both livelihood and food. A total catch in 1975 of 1.3 million tons included mackerel, anchovy, tuna, pollack, and shrimp, and represented nearly a threefold increase over the 1960 catch.

About 80% of fishing activity is concentrated in the Sea of Japan. Much of the annual catch is now used for export.

The fishing industry is entirely socialized, with some 230 maritime cooperatives. More than 10% of the estimated 35,000 fishing vessels in 1975 were fully automated factory ships.

25 FORESTRY

The DRK has rich stands of coniferous forest in its northern provinces of North P'yongan, Chagang, Yanggang, and North Hamgyong. The country had some 160 million cu meters of forest reserves in the early 1970s. Approximately 1% of the state budget is annually invested in afforestation, allowing for the planting of upward of 100,000 hectares each year. Predominant trees include oak, alder, larch, pine, spruce, and fir.

Timber production was estimated at 5.6 million cu meters in the early 1970s, an increase of 2 million cu meters over the 1960 figure. Lumber production was around 2 million cu meters. Important paper and pulp mills are at Kilchu near the east coast and at Sinuiju at the mouth of the Yalu.

26 MINING

Coal deposits include anthracite and lignite but are poor in bituminous coal, which must be imported for use as coke in the steel industry. Anthracite is mined chiefly along the middle course of the Taedong River (South P'yongan Province) and lignite in the Tumen River basin (North Hamgyong Province). The government reported a total coal production in 1975 of 53 million tons, a growth of 180% over the 1970 figure and more than triple the 1965 figure. Iron ore production (in tons) in 1973 was 8,900,000; tungsten, 2,750,000; magnesite crude ore, 1,900,000; zinc, 145,000; cadmium, 110,000; and lead, 95,000.

Much emphasis has been placed on the mechanization of the mining process, particularly in the few bituminous coal mines at Anju, Hakpo, and Aoji. In these mines, all production processes—from tunnelling to coal-cutting and carriage—are reportedly mechanized.

27 ENERGY AND POWER

Most of the DRK's electric power is derived from hydroelectric stations, although thermal power generating capacity has been increased recently and now constitutes 34% of total capacity. Total power output continues to rise significantly, standing at 5.1 billion kwh in 1956, 9.14 billion kwh in 1960, 16.5 billion kwh in 1970, and 28 billion kwh in 1975. In 1975, the country's production per capita was second only to Japan's in East Asia and four times as great as that of the ROK.

In 1973 there were some 1,500 electric power plants, 8 with capacities exceeding 100,000 kw and 24 in excess of 10,000 kw. The principal hydroelectric plants are the Sup'ung station on the Yalu, with a generating capacity of 700,000 kw; the Unbong plant at Chasong, also on the Yalu, with 400,000 kw; and stations on the Changjin, Hoch'on, and Pujon reservoirs, each with a capacity of about 200,000 kw. The first stage on the Sodu-su power plant has just been completed, with capacity projected at 400,000 kw. The largest thermal plant is at Pukch'ang with 800,000 kw; others at P'yongyang and Unggi have 500,000-kw and 100,000-kw capacities, respectively. Three additional thermal plants at Ch'ongjin, Hungnam, and Kim Ch'aek are planned for the late 1970s.

28 INDUSTRY

Under Japanese rule, northern Korea was designed mainly as a supplier of war materials, while manufacturing and processing branches were neglected. The Communist regime has emphasized the development of manufacturing industries, and by 1963 the metal-fabricating, textile, and food-processing industries accounted for 33.0%, 18.6%, and 13.7% of industrial output, respectively. Mining and metallurgy have grown quantitatively but not in terms of percentage of total output.

Instead, more sophisticated and consumer-oriented manufacturing industries have accounted for gradually increasing por-

tions of industrial output. Private enterprise in industry declined from 27.6% of total output in 1946 to only 2% in 1956, and the private sector was said to have disappeared by 1959. About 90% of all industry is state-owned and 10% is now owned by cooperatives.

The DRK's iron and steel industry produced 3,400,000 tons of pig and granulated iron and 5,850,000 tons of steel (including rolled steel) in 1975, representing increases over the 1970 figures of 70% and 50%, respectively. Major iron and steel works are located at Ch'ongjin, Kim Ch'aek, Kangso, and Kangson. DRK industry produced sophisticated machinery in 1974, including 50,000-kw generators, 300-hp bulldozers, 3,500-hp high-speed engines, and 2,500-hp diesel locomotives. Other plants produce aluminum, cement (7.2 million tons in 1974), magnesite, graphite, lead, zinc, machine tools, tractors, lorries, and trucks. The chemical industry produced 3 million tons of chemical fertilizer in 1974, doubling the 1970 figure, as well as a synthetic fiber, Vinalon, used widely in clothing. The petrochemical industry is centered in the Hungnam area.

29 DOMESTIC TRADE

Wholesale and retail trade is predominantly in state and cooperative hands; private merchants have gradually been eliminated. In 1946, private trade accounted for 96.5% of total business volume. By 1960, private trade had been entirely eliminated, with 78.8% conducted by the state, 20.4% by cooperatives, and 0.8% by farmers' markets.

Under the present domestic-pricing system, some commodities get a centrally determined price; some get regional prices; and some get extraordinary, short-term prices. Prices at farmers' markets for private-plot produce reflect local supply and demand fluctuations. In 1973, a bicycle cost about w160; a radio, w100; leather shoes, w18; a kg of chicken, w4.5; and a kg of fish, w2.

30 FOREIGN TRADE

The total value of the DRK's foreign trade in 1973 was $1.3 billion; the value of exports, $482 million, was nearly twice that of the 1966 level. Expanding exports, however, continue to be more than offset by rising import expenditures.

Foreign trade diversified substantially in recent years, lessening the country's dependency on the Communist bloc. Trade with Japan tripled from 1968 to 1973. About 30% of the DRK's exports in 1973 went to non-Communist countries, with more than half going to Japan. Imports fron non-Communist countries accounted for about 35% of the total volume. The USSR remains the DRK's main trading partner, accounting for about 35% of its total volume; China accounted for about 19% (compared with 6% for the USSR and 3% for China in 1962). The DRK's increased trade with West European countries in recent years was imperiled in 1974 by the DRK's inability to meet its international payments obligations.

The commodity structure of trade has shifted radically since the immediate post-Korean War era. Mineral exports have given way to fabricated metals (the former declined from 82% of trade in 1953 to 7% in 1969), while fuels have substantially replaced machinery and equipment as major import items. In 1973, principal exports included rice, fish, iron ore, pig iron, rolled steel, cement, and machinery of various types. Imports included petroleum, coking coal, rubber, wheat, cotton, base metals and manufactures, machinery, and transportation equipment.

31 BALANCE OF PAYMENTS

The DRK had a 1973 balance-of-payments deficit estimated at $296.2 million. This represented a sharp rise from trade balance figures in the 1960s, which ranged from deficits of up to $82 million to surpluses of up to $96 million. Much of the recent deficit is accounted for by substantial purchases of advanced technology, including complete factories, from non-Communist nations.

32 BANKING

The Central Bank, established in 1946, is the sole recipient of national revenues and the repository for all precious metals. It supplies basic operating funds to various sectors of the economy, and is subordinate to the Ministry of Finance. The Central Bank is an administrative organ that executes the fiscal policies of the State Planning Commission. It supervises the Foreign Trade Bank, established in 1959, and the Industrial Bank, established in 1964. The latter provides loans and credits to farm and fishery cooperatives and has an extensive system of branches which help to manage the financial operations of all cooperatives.

Savings facilities are brought close to the people by savings offices at all post offices, by special savings facilities established in industrial enterprises, and by "trust" sections in the agricultural cooperatives. Through this latter device, the new, larger farm and fishing cooperatives perform local banking functions, especially the raising and allocation of capital for local needs.

33 INSURANCE

The government provides various types of insurance services. State enterprises carry fire and natural disaster insurance and, as appropriate, livestock, marine, and passenger insurance on a compulsory basis. Individuals may take out various types of property, life, and travel insurance.

34 SECURITIES

By a cabinet decision of May 1950, government bonds were offered for public sale, with the proceeds to be used for economic construction. A lottery system was instituted to give bonus and preferred reimbursement to some bondholders.

35 PUBLIC FINANCE

The annual state budget is approved at regular sessions of the Supreme People's Assembly. State budgets generally show surpluses. The projected budget for 1975 was W11,517 million, more than double the 1968 figure of W5,234 million. In 1974, actual expenditures were W9,672 million, while revenues were W10,015 million, resulting in a surplus of W343 million.

36 TAXATION

All direct taxes were abolished in 1974. As a result, the socialist sector now contributes 100% of total budget revenue. The abolition, carried out with much fanfare, was said to have resulted in an increase of W28 per month in the purchasing power of the average household. Foreign aid, important after the Korean War, has not appeared as budgetary income since 1961.

37 CUSTOMS AND DUTIES

No information is available.

38 FOREIGN INVESTMENTS

The DRK neither makes nor permits foreign investments.

39 ECONOMIC POLICY

The economy is operated on a planned basis with the aim of giving priority to the development of industry, particularly heavy industry. Planning began in 1947, when the economy operated first under two consecutive one-year plans (1947 and 1948), followed by a two-year plan (1949–50), which was interrupted by the Korean War in June 1950. After the war, economic reconstruction followed the terms of a three-year plan (1954–56) and a five-year plan (1957–61). The industrial goals of the five-year plan were fulfilled in just half the allotted time, so 1960 was set aside as a year of adjustment. An ambitious seven-year plan then was launched in 1961, with the general objectives of a 220% increase in industrial output and a 150% rise in grain production. This plan had to be extended until 1970, however, before its targets were fulfilled. In 1975, the DRK announced completion of its six-year plan (1971–76) one year ahead of schedule, although certain outputs fall somewhat short of projected levels. Production targets included 30 billion kwh of electricity, 50 million tons of coal, 6.8 million tons of steel and rolled steel, and 2.8 million tons of synthetic fertilizer. The last two plans have emphasized agriculture and consumer goods, while continuing to give priority to heavy industry and improved technology.

40 HEALTH

In 1946, the country had 85 hospitals with 2,031 beds, and about 1 doctor for every 10,000 persons. In 1973 there were 2,671 hospitals with 106,000 beds, and about 20 doctors and paramedical personnel for every 10,000 persons.

The Ministry of Public Health is responsible for all national health services, including disease prevention and sanitation. A widespread system of immunization, with health committees for every block and street, combined with ubiquitous "people's clinics"—consisting of one paramedic and two nurses—have made health services available throughout the country. Western medicine is used alongside traditional Eastern medicine (tonguihak). Average life expectancy in 1975 was estimated at 62.8 years.

41 SOCIAL WELFARE

All citizens are entitled to free medical care, disability benefits, and retirement allowances. About 1% of workers' salaries is deducted for programs allowing paid vacations and paid maternity leaves, with the state making up the rest of the cost. The state runs about 400 rest centers and resorts providing free vacations to workers. Retirement pensions are roughly one-half of the annual average wage; those who continue working after retirement age receive both their salary and their pension.

42 HOUSING

A serious housing shortage was produced by the government's early stress on industrial construction rather than residential building. The housing deficit was severely aggravated by the destruction of the Korean War, which decimated about one-third of the country's housing. Since then, residential housing has received serious attention, and in the period from the war's end through 1960 some 24.6 million sq meters of housing floor space were built, half in the cities and towns.

In 1975, it was reported that 1 million new units had been built during the prior 15 years.

New houses and apartments tend to be of modular construction with indoor bathroom facilities. By 1975, all rural villages were said to have been electrified, with water supply facilities in 87% of all villages.

43 EDUCATION

Education is free and compulsory for 11 years. Children aged 1 to 5 are cared for in nursery schools, followed by a year of kindergarten, 5 years of primary school, and 5 years of secondary school. In 1972 there were 4,470 elementary schools, 4,980 secondary schools, and 140 higher institutions, with 1,590,000, 1,900,000, and 77,000 students, respectively.

Of the three universities, Kim Il Sung University (founded in 1946) is the largest, with about 15,000 full-time and part-time students in 1972. Admission to Kim Il Sung University is the highest educational honor; admission to all colleges is administered by the local people's committees. Criteria for admission include academic performance, political attitude, and economic class background. The other universities are Kim Ch'aek Technical University and P'yongyang Medical School. The Korean Academy of Sciences was founded in 1952. A widespread system of adult schools, correspondence courses, and work-place schools makes education available to all ages of the population. In 1974, fully one-half of the total population was enrolled in some manner of formal schooling.

44 LIBRARIES AND MUSEUMS

The DRK had only 7 libraries after World War II; by August 1949, the number had increased to 106 at province, town, and county levels. Wartime destruction has been repaired and in 1974 there were more than 200 public libraries. The largest is the State Central Library in P'yongyang with 1,500,000 volumes. In addition, there are research libraries at the academies of Sciences,

Social Sciences, Forestry, and Medicine, and at Kim Il Sung University.

The museums, numbering 17, include the Central Historical Museum, the National Liberation Struggle Museum, the Fine Arts Museum, the Ethnographic Museum, and the Korean Revolutionary Museum, all in P'yongyang.

45 ORGANIZATIONS

In addition to the Korean Workers' Party and the General Federation of Trade Unions, the DRK has a number of mass organizations brought into being for specialized political, economic, or cultural purposes. One of these (established May 1961) is the Committee for the Peaceful Unification of the Fatherland, which apparently has taken over the functions of the formerly powerful Democratic Front for the Unification of the Fatherland. Young adults are organized into the Democratic Youth Federation, an affiliate of the World Federation of Democratic Youth. Founded in 1946, it has a membership of about 2.3 million, while the Affiliated Young People's Corps has about 1.6 million members. The women's organization, the Democratic Women's Federation (founded 1945), has a membership of over 2 million.

46 PRESS

All newspapers and periodicals in the DRK are published by either government, party, or front organizations. The cabinet's Bureau of Publications subjects each edition to prepublication review and censorship. In 1975 there were some 30 newspapers with a total circulation for the year of well over 250 million copies. The leading national newspapers and their publishers were: *Nodong Sinmun* (Korean Workers' Party); *Minju Choson* (Presidium of the Supreme People's Assembly and the cabinet); *Choguk Tongil* (Committee for the Peaceful Unification of the Fatherland); *Nodongja Sinmun* (General Federation of Trade Unions); *Nongmin Sinmun* (Agriculture Ministry and the Farmers' Federation); *Minju Ch'ongnyon* (Democratic Youth Federation). In addition, each province has a newspaper and other mass organizations have their own organs. A state news agency, the Central News Service, is the sole organ for the gathering and dissemination of news information.

47 TOURISM

Tourist exchanges with Communist countries, especially China, are numerous. Since 1971, the government has welcomed touring delegations from numerous non-Communist nations, especially those from the underdeveloped nations. Japanese and Australian delegations have also been arriving in increasing numbers.

48 FAMOUS KOREANS OF THE DRK

The preeminent political figure of the DRK is Kim Il Sung, presi-dent and leader of the nation since 1948. Other influential figures are Kim Il, a prominent officeholder since 1954; Kim Yong-ju, Kim Il Sung's younger brother; O Chin-u, the minister of defense; and Nam Il (1914–76), former chief of staff, who became well known as an armistice negotiator at P'anmunjom (1951–53).

Some prominent cultural and scientific figures are Han Sor-ya (b.1900), novelist and short story writer; Yi Ki-yong (b.1895), novelist; Song Yong (b.1903), dramatist; Paek Nam-un (b.1895), economic historian and chairman of the Academy of Sciences; and Kye Ung-sang (b.1900), sericulture expert.

49 DEPENDENCIES

The DRK has no territories or colonies.

50 BIBLIOGRAPHY

The following books concern only the Democratic People's Republic of Korea of post-1945; for less specialized works on the history, geography, and culture of Korea see Bibliography for the Republic of Korea.

Choson chungana, nyongam 1961. [*Official Yearbook of Korea for 1961*.] P'yongyang: Central News Service of North Korea, 1962.

Chung, Joseph S. *The North Korean Economy*. Stanford: Hoover Institution, 1973.

Karshinov, L. N. *Koreyskaya narodno-demokraticheskaya respublika: Ekonomika i vneshyaya torgovlya*. [*Democratic People's Republic of Korea: Its Economy and Foreign Trade*.] Moscow: Vneshtorgizdat, 1958.

Kim Il Sung. *Selected Works*. 4 vols. P'yongyang: Foreign Languages Publishing House, 1972.

Koh, Byung Chul. *The Foreign Policy of North Korea*. New York: Praeger, 1969.

Paige, Glenn D. *The Korean People's Democratic Republic*. Stanford: Stanford University Press, 1966.

Post-War Reconstruction and Development of the National Economy in the Democratic People's Republic of Korea. P'yongyang: Foreign Languages Publishing House, 1957.

Pukhan Ch'onggam 1945–1968. [*General Survey of North Korea 1945–1968*.] Seoul: Kongsankwonmunje Yongguso, 1968.

Rudolph, Philip. *North Korea's Political and Economic Sturcture*. New York: Institute of Pacific Relations, 1959.

Scalapino, Robert A. *North Korea Today*. New York: Praeger, 1963.

Scalapino, Robert A., and Chong-sik Lee. *Communism in Korea*. 2 vols. Berkeley: University of California Press, 1973.

Suh, Dae-Sook. *The Korean Communist Movement 1918–1948*. Princeton: Princeton University Press, 1967.

REPUBLIC OF KOREA

Taehan Min-guk

CAPITAL: Seoul. **FLAG:** The flag, called the T'aegukki, utilizes ancient symbols, representing the paradox of eternal duality within absolute unity, which lend themselves to analogical illustration of most philosophical and ethical questions. On a white field, a central circle is divided into two parts, red on top and deep blue below, in the shape of Chinese yin and yang symbols. Broken and unbroken black bars in each of the four corners are variously arranged in sets of three, representing divination diagrams. **ANTHEM:** *Till Paektu Mountain Wears Away.* **MONETARY UNIT:** The won (w) is a nonconvertible paper currency with exchange rates fluctuating according to a floating system as recommended by the IMF. There are coins of 5, 10, and 100 won, and notes of 50, 100, 500, and 1,000 won. W1 = $0.00206 (or $1 = W484). **WEIGHTS AND MEASURES:** Both the metric system and ancient Korean units of measurement are used. **HOLIDAYS:** New Year's Days, 1–3 January; Independence Movement Day, 1 March; Memorial Day, 6 June; Liberation Day, 15 August; National Foundation Day, 3 October; UN Day, 24 October; Christmas, 25 December. **TIME:** 9 P.M. = noon GMT.

¹LOCATION, SIZE, AND EXTENT
Occupying the southern part of the Korean Peninsula in East Asia, the Republic of Korea (ROK) has an area of 98,485 sq km (38,025 sq mi), extending *642* km (*399* mi) NNE–SSW and *436* km (*271* mi) ESE–WNW. Bounded on the N by the Democratic People's Republic of Korea (DRK), on the E by the Sea of Japan, on the S by the Korea Strait, and on the W by the Yellow Sea, the ROK has a total boundary length of *1,558* km (*968* mi). The DRK comprises the northern part of the Korean Peninsula.

²TOPOGRAPHY
A land of mountains and valleys, the Korean Peninsula contains thousands of peaks. Almost the whole of north-central Korea is occupied by a single mountain mass, dominated by the peninsula's highest peak, Mt. Paektu (9,003 feet), an extinct volcano with a scenic crater lake. From this mass, a chain of mountains with the Taebaek Range at its core runs parallel to the east coast down almost to Pusan. About midway the lesser Sobaek Range extends off to the southwest, culminating in Mt. Chii (6,283 feet). Mt. Halla (6,398 feet) rises on volcanic Cheju Island.

Principal rivers are: the Tumen (323 miles) and Yalu (491 miles), along the northern border of the Peninsula, and in the ROK the Imjin (158 miles), near the 38th parallel in the west; the Han (320 miles), with Seoul near its mouth; the Kum (249 miles) and Yongsan (72 miles), which water the fertile plains areas of the southwest; the Somjin (132 miles), in the south; and the Naktong (326 miles), which waters the rich southeast region. Yellow Sea tides on the west coast rise to over 30 feet in some places, Japan Sea tides on the east rise only some 3 feet.

³CLIMATE
The peninsula's climatic range is great. The average January temperature of −20.5°C (−5°F) at Chunggang on the north-central border contrasts with averages of −5°C (28°F) at Seoul, −2°C (28°F) at Pusan, and 4.4°C (40°F) on Cheju Island. In the hottest part of the summer, however, the variation is not nearly so marked, average temperatures ranging from 25°C to 27°C (77°F to 80°F) in all southern areas to 21°C (70°F) along the relatively cool northeast coast. Precipitation varies from around 20 inches along the upper reaches of the Tumen to nearly 60 inches in the Somjin River estuary, with more than half of the peninsula receiving 30 to 40 inches per year. Unfortunately, nearly all of the rainfall occurs in the April-September period, es-

pecially during the late June to early August rainy season, creating major problems of flood and drought for Korean agriculture. Crops also may be damaged by typhoons in the early fall. Frostless days number about 240 in the southern regions.

⁴FLORA AND FAUNA
Korea is rich in varieties of plant life typical of temperate regions. More than 3,000 species, some 500 of them unique to Korea, have been noted by botanists. The animal life largely corresponds to that of nearby China and Siberia. Zoologists have identified more than 500 fishes, 400 birds, 100 mammals, and 40 reptiles and amphibians in Korea. Bear, wild boar, deer, and lynx still are found in the highlands, especially in the north, but the shrinking of the forested area has reduced the animal population in recent years. Migratory water fowl, cranes, herons, and other birds are visible on the plains. Noxious insects and household pests infest the warmer regions, and aquatic life is generally infected with parasites.

As of 1975, endangered species in the Korean Peninsula included the wolf, Asiatic wild dog, Siberian tiger, Amur leopard, Japanese sea lion, and 3 bird species (Chinese egret, Japanese white stork, and Tristram's woodpecker).

⁵POPULATION
The late-1975 ROK population estimate was 34,700,000, with a total of 37,444,000 projected for 1980. The 1970 census put the total at 31,469,132, an increase of 7.8% over the 1966 figure and about 20% above the 1960 total. The annual rate of population growth in 1975 was estimated at 2%; the median age was 20.4 years. The population density in 1975 was 352 persons per sq km, ranking third in the world. Seoul, the largest city, had a population of 6,884,000 in late 1975. The 1974 populations of other large cities were Pusan, 2,015,162; Taegu, 1,164,048; Inch'on, 689,793; Kwangju, 538,049; and Taejon, 452,402. Some 47.3% of the people lived in urban areas in 1975, as compared with 18.4% in 1950.

⁶ETHNIC GROUPS
The Koreans are believed to be descended primarily from Tungusic peoples (Mongoloid race) who originated in the cold northern regions of Central Asia. There is scant evidence of non-Mongoloid admixture. Korea has no sizable ethnic minority. The total non-Korean resident population is probably about 50,000, nearly all of them Chinese. The former Japanese colonists in Korea were all repatriated after the end of World War II.

7LANGUAGE

The Korean language is usually held to be a member of the Altaic family and is clearly related to other agglutinative tongues such as Turkic, Mongolian, and Japanese. Linguistic unification of the peninsula apparently followed political unification in the 7th century, and today there are only slight differences between the various dialects.

Korean is written with a remarkable and largely phonetic alphabet called han'gul. Created more than 500 years ago (1446) under the great King Sejong, the Korean alphabet consists of 14 basic consonants and 10 simple vowels, all regular in shape. Han'gul letters are combined into syllables by clustering, in imitation of Chinese characters, rather than in the linear fashion of English. Before the invention of han'gul, Koreans wrote in Chinese, and Chinese continued to be both the official language and the language of most literature until the beginning of the 20th century. With the start of the Japanese colonial administration in 1910, Japanese became the official language, and the use of Korean became highly restricted. Since 1949, the DRK has used only han'gul (referred to there as Choson muntcha) for writing, while the ROK has used a mixed Sino-Korean script, necessitating knowledge of several thousand Chinese characters. In the last few years, however, han'gul has been used increasingly in the ROK.

8RELIGION

Most Koreans are quite eclectic in their religious beliefs, the majority subscribing to varying mixtures of Confucian, Buddhist, Christian, Ch'ondogyo ("Religion of the Heavenly Way," an eclectic native sect originating in the 19th century), and local animist beliefs. Shamanism, especially its aspect of exorcism of evil spirits, survives among some Koreans in the rural areas. Geomancy is also used in matters such as the selection of auspicious building and tomb sites.

Christianity is the strongest organized religion in the ROK. In 1974 there were 13,900 churches of various sects, serving 4,253,468 followers. The other major organized religion, Ch'ondogyo, had 140 houses of worship and 718,000 followers. Although the practice of Buddhism and Confucianism is largely carried out without formal temple or shrine affiliation, some 7,986,000 Koreans in 1974 described themselves as followers of Buddhism, and 4,423,000 of Confucianism. Both belief systems came to Korea through China.

9TRANSPORTATION

With recent highway construction, road transportation has replaced railways as the most important means of passenger conveyance. Some 75% of all passenger traffic in 1975 was carried by motor vehicles, and 23% by the national railway system. The railways still carry the most freight, however—52%, compared to 21% for motor vehicles and 26% for ships. The bulk of ROK railroads, totaling 3,271 miles of track, are government-owned and -operated. The Seoul-Taejon-Mokp'o and Seoul-Pusan lines are the main trunk lines. In 1974 there were 184,603,000 railroad passengers.

A 265-mile superhighway connecting Seoul and Pusan was opened in 1970, permitting rapid modern bus service. Other completed or near-completed expressways in 1975 included the Mukho-Sokcho expressway on the east coast and roads connecting Seoul and Inch'on and Seoul-Wonju-Kangnung. Secondary roads connect all cities and large towns, although many are unpaved. In the rural areas, much transportation is still by oxcart and human labor. Bus transportation networks of varying quality serve most of the rural towns. There were 183,544 motor vehicles in operation in early 1975.

Maritime shipping is also important, with ships in 1975 totaling 1,401,159 gross tons, of which oceangoing vessels accounted for 1,205,322 tons and passenger-cargo ships (including ferries), 195,837 tons. Pusan is the largest port. In the last few years, ROK

shipbuilders have developed a capability for constructing oil-carrying supertankers.

Korean Air Lines has internal air service connections between Seoul, Pusan, Kangnung, Taegu, Kwangju, and Cheju Island, and international service to Tokyo and the US. Seoul's Kimp'o International Airport serves most international airlines operating in East Asia.

10COMMUNICATIONS

The Ministry of Communications operates the postal, telephone, and domestic telegraph services. A spot censorship system is in effect for both domestic and foreign mail, including publications entering the country. In early 1975, telephone subscribers totaled 877,000, an increase of 14.9% over the previous year. The government-operated Korean Broadcasting System (KBS) has stations in all major cities, but most programs originate in Seoul. There are 51 other radio broadcasting stations, including 5 FM stations, and 5.5 million receivers. Television broadcasting began in 1956; in 1961, the government set up KBS-TV as the first countrywide service. In 1975 there were 11 commercial television systems, plus a US Armed Forces-Korea network broadcasting in English. Koreans owned 1.5 million television sets in early 1975.

11HISTORY

(For information about Korean history prior to June 1950, see 11: History in the article on the Democratic People's Republic of Korea.)

At dawn on 25 June 1950, following two years of sporadic fighting, the People's Army of the DRK struck south across the 38th parallel. Proclaiming that the war was for national liberation and unification of the peninsula, the DRK forces advanced rapidly until the destruction of the ROK seemed imminent. US President Harry S Truman and his advisers, interpreting the attack as Soviet-sponsored, decided immediately to resist it. At US urging, the UN Security Council (with the Soviet delegate inexplicably absent) branded the DRK an aggressor and called for the withdrawal of the attacking forces. On 27 June, President Truman ordered US air and naval units into combat and on 30 June, US ground forces were sent into battle. The UK took similar action, and a multinational UN Command was created to join with and lead the ROK in its struggle against the invasion. Meanwhile, the city of Seoul had fallen, and the DRK troops had pushed into the southeast corner of the peninsula. At that juncture, however, UN lines held firm, and a daring amphibious landing at Inch'on (15 September 1950) under Gen. Douglas MacArthur brought about the complete disintegration of the DRK army. MacArthur, commanding the UN forces, made a fateful decision to drive north and destroy the aggressor in his home territory. As they approached the Yalu River, however, China warned that it would not tolerate a unification of the peninsula under US/UN auspices. After several weeks of threats and feints, "volunteers" from the Chinese People's Liberation Army entered the fighting en masse, forcing MacArthur into a costly, pell-mell retreat back down the peninsula. Seoul was lost again (4 January 1951) and then regained, before the battle line became stabilized very nearly along the 38th parallel. There it remained for two weary years, with bitter fighting but little change, while a cease-fire agreement was painfully negotiated. On 27 July 1953, an armistice agreement finally was signed. The Korean War was ended, but it had brought incalculable destruction and human suffering to all of Korea, and it left the peninsula still more implacably divided. An international conference envisioned in the armistice agreement was not held until mid-1954 and failed to reach an agreement on unification.

For 16 years thereafter, annual sessions of the UN General Assembly repeatedly discussed the Korean question, but achieved no progress. In 1971, the respective Red Cross organizations of the DRK and ROK began holding talks, and periodic negotiations ensued until 1974, when the dialogue broke down amid recriminations and threats of a new war. In late 1975, the UN appeared on the verge of ending the UN Command apparatus, which for years had retained only two or three token non-US contingents in the ROK.

Syngman Rhee, who became president of the ROK in 1948, ran the government until 1960. Rhee's authoritarian rule provoked the "April Revolution," the culmination of a series of increasingly violent student demonstrations that finally brought about his ouster. The Second Korean Republic, which followed Rhee, adopted a parliamentary system to replace the previous presidential system. The new government, however, was short-lived. Premier Chang Myon and his supporters were ousted after only 10 months by a military coup in May 1961 headed by Maj.-Gen. Park Chung Hee. The military junta dissolved the national assembly, placed the nation under martial law, and ruled by decree until late 1963 through the Supreme Council for National Reconstruction. Gen. Park created a well-organized political party—the Democratic-Republican Party (DRP)—designed to serve as a vehicle for the transition from military to civilian rule, and in October 1963, he easily won election as president of the Third Republic.

During the summer of 1965, riots erupted all over the ROK in protest against the ROK-Japan Normalization Treaty, which established diplomatic relations and replaced Korean war-reparation claims with Japanese promises to extend economic aid. The riots were met with harsh countermeasures, including another period of martial law and widespread arrests of demonstrators.

Park was elected to a second term in May 1967, and the DRP won a large majority in the National Assembly. In April 1971, Park ran for a third term, a move legalized by a 1969 constitutional amendment. Park defeated opposition candidate Kim Dae-jung by 946,000 votes in an election accompanied by opposition charges of fraud and corruption. In National Assembly elections held in May, the opposition New Democratic Party made major inroads, capturing 89 seats to the majority DRP's 113. Student demonstrations in the spring and fall of 1971 prompted Park to declare a state of national emergency in December 1971. In October 1972, Park proclaimed martial law, suspended the constitution, and dissolved the National Assembly. A national referendum in November approved the so-called "Yushin" ("Revitalizing") Constitution, inaugurating the Fourth Korean Republic. Among other provisions, the 1972 constitution permitted the president to run for an unlimited number of terms and reduced the National Assembly to a rubber-stamp organ. The new constitution led to more domestic unrest and the forcible abduction of Kim Dae-jung from Tokyo back to Seoul by the Korean Central Intelligence Agency. In March 1976, Kim and 17 others were indicted under an emergency decree that banned criticism of the 1972 constitution.

12 GOVERNMENT

The current ROK constitution, adopted in November 1972, represents a clear break with previous constitutions in its incorporation of nondemocratic procedures and provisions. It is presidential in form and authoritarian in effect. The president is indirectly elected by an electoral college, called the National Conference for Unification; the Conference's members, who numbered 2,359 in 1975, are themselves elected by universal suffrage. The presidential tenure is six years with no limit on reelection. The president has authority to take any issues he deems important directly to the public for national referendum. He is empowered to take emergency measures with regard to all state affairs in time of national emergency. He may dissolve the National Assembly at will. He may initiate amendments to the constitution and may have them directly approved in a national referendum. The ninth National Assembly (1973) had 219 members, 73 of them appointed by the president. Of the elected

members, 73 belonged to the ruling DRP and 52 to the opposition New Democratic Party. All citizens over age 20 may vote in national elections. The 1972 constitution reduced the number of constituencies from 157 to 73, thus enlarging the size of each electoral district. The term of office is six years for elected members, three years for appointed members. The National Assembly no longer has authority to conduct inspections and audits of government administrative agencies.

13 POLITICAL PARTIES

Until the mid-1960s, political parties in the ROK tended to follow the pattern of loosely organized factions or clubs, rather than modern political parties, with supporters clustering around one dominant leader or group of leaders. After the Korean War, a rudimentary party structure emerged. The Liberal Party was composed of followers of President Syngman Rhee and held clear majorities in the assemblies elected in 1954 and 1958; the opposition Democratic Party was headed by Chang Myon, who was narrowly elected vice-president in 1956; a third major party, the Progressives, was outlawed in February 1958 following the arrest of its leader, Cho Bongam, on charges of dealings with the

See continental political: front cover R6; physical: back cover Q6
LOCATION: 33°7' to 38°38'N; 124°36' to 130°56'E. BOUNDARY LENGHTHS: DRK, 240 km (149 mi); total coastline, 1,318 km (819 mi). TERRITORIAL SEA LIMIT: 3 mi.

DRK. With the overthrow of the Rhee government in April 1960, the Liberal Party was discredited and several new parties, including some of socialist coloration, were organized. In the subsequent national elections, the Democratic Party won an overwhelming victory and Chang Myon was named premier. The Democrats, however, were split into several factions and cliques and could not maintain enough cohesion to govern effectively. The military men who came to power on 16 May 1961 quickly dissolved all political parties and banned political activities. When the ban was lifted on 1 January 1963, three major political groupings emerged: the Democratic Republican Party (DRP), organized and backed by the military government; the Civil Rule

Party, led by former president Yun Po-sun; and the New Rule Party, whose spokesman was former Acting President Huh Chung.

In the parliamentary elections held in November 1963, the DRP received only 35% of the vote, but won a large majority in the National Assembly. Since that time, it has been able to dominate the various opposition parties. In 1973, the DRP won 39% of the national vote and 73 seats in the National Assembly.

In March 1965, Yun Po-sun, protesting the treaty with Japan, formed the New Korea Party. It subsequently merged with the Masses Party to become the New Democratic Party (NDP). In the 1973 general election, the NDP captured 52 seats in the National Assembly, and 33% of the vote. Although the NDP retains a core leadership of mostly elderly and ineffectual, if well-respected, politicians, in 1970 it nominated a young assembly-man, Kim Dae-jung, an energetic campaigner who breathed new life into the party. After his abduction in Tokyo in 1973, however, the NDP reverted to its previously docile posture. The Democratic Unification Party, an offshoot of the NDP, was formed in 1973 and has since won 3 seats in the National Assembly.

The 1972 constitution places various constraints on election campaigning, such as an 18-day limit on the campaign period, a 30-minute length on campaign speeches, and strict limits on campaign spending.

[14] LOCAL GOVERNMENT

The ROK has 11 administrative units: the 9 provinces of Kyonggi, Kangwon, North and South Ch'ungch'ong, North and South Cholla, North and South Kyongsang, Cheju Island, and 2 cities with special status, Seoul and Pusan. The provinces are divided into counties (kun), townships (myon), and villages (i or ri).

Administration is highly centralized, with all appointments down to the township level originating in Seoul. After the military coup of 1961, earlier systems allowing for some local autonomy and local election of officials and committees were done away with. The last local election was held in 1961.

[15] JUDICIAL SYSTEM

The highest judicial organ is the Supreme Court, under which is an appellate court. Lower courts consist of district and family courts. There has been increasing use of military courts to try civilians for martial-law and emergency-decree violations.

The 1972 constitution deprived the Supreme Court of its traditional power of judicial review; the president appoints, removes, and disciplines bench members on all levels. There is no jury system; a judge or panel of judges decides cases.

[16] ARMED FORCES

ROK citizens are subject to compulsory military service at the age of 18. In 1975, the estimated total strength of the armed forces was 625,000, with 560,000 in the army, 40,000 in the navy and marines, and 25,000 in the air force. An additional 1,128,000 are in the reserves, and some 2 million citizens participate in the Homeland Defense Reserve Force. An estimated 39,935 US soldiers aid in ROK defense.

The ROK's 1976 defense budget, proportionally one of the world's highest, was $1.4 billion, or 34.2% of the overall state budget. The ROK maintains one of the largest and best-equipped military forces in the world, with some 1,000 medium tanks, 40 artillery battalions, 3 missile battalions, and 230 combat and 117 support aircraft. The Korean force is supplemented by 3 US air force squadrons. US forces maintain an estimated 700 tactical nuclear weapons of all types on the ground in Korea. The Korean armed forces remain under the operational control of the UN military command in the ROK.

[17] MIGRATION

During the Japanese occupation (1910–45), some 3 million Koreans emigrated to Manchuria and other parts of China,

700,000 to Siberia, perhaps 3 million to Japan, and about 7,000 to the US (mostly to Hawaii). The great majority were from the populous southern provinces and large numbers of them returned home following the end of hostilities in 1945. In addition, from 1945 through 1950 an estimated 3 to 4 million Koreans crossed the 38th parallel into the ROK, refugees either from communism or from the Korean War. In recent years, the Korean government has encouraged emigration to South America (especially Brazil), the Federal Republic of Germany (FRG), and elsewhere. Most of the emigrants are workers who remit earnings back to Korea. Some 27,700 Koreans were employed abroad in 1975. In addition, Koreans have emigrated permanently to the US in large numbers since 1971, with the annual total exceeding 20,000 during 1973–75.

Migration within Korea, mainly from the rural areas to the cities, is substantial. In 1974 and 1975 alone, about 15% of the total Korean population changed its resident locality.

[18] INTERNATIONAL COOPERATION

The ROK is not a member of the UN, its most recent bid to join in the fall of 1975 having been defeated. It has observer status at the UN, however, and belongs to several UN agencies. It is a member of ASPAC, ECAFE, FAO, WHO, GATT, and other intergovernmental organizations. Although the UN Commission on the Unification and Rehabilitation of Korea (UNCURK) was dissolved in 1973, the UN Command originating from the Korean War continues to operate in the ROK.

The ROK pursues a vigorous international diplomacy, and in recent years has modified both its militant anti-Communist stance and its close alliance with the US. In mid-1975, the ROK was recognized by 93 nations. Since 1975, the ROK and Japan have drawn closer and pursue exchanges in many spheres. The ROK also has cultivated ties with neutral and underdeveloped countries in Africa and Asia in recent years. The ROK was a founding member of the Asian Nations' Anti-Communist League.

[19] ECONOMY

The ROK economy has greatly diversified and expanded since 1945, at which point 75% of the total population was engaged in agriculture, with rice production the major economic activity and heavy industry almost nonexistent. The economy stagnated after the Korean War, with annual growth rates never exceeding 7%. During the first five-year development plan (1962–66), the average annual growth rate was 8.3%; during the second plan (1967–71), 11.4%.

Although the rate of growth dropped to 8.2% in 1974 and to about 6% in 1975 due to high energy costs and inflation, in the mid-1970s the economy continued its steady transition from an agrarian to an industrial base. In 1973, industry's share of national income surpassed that of agriculture, culminating a 20-year trend. Heavy industry now accounts for about 30% of all industrial products in value, with annual growth rates of 15–20% sustained over the last decade. Much of the recent economic growth has been fueled by a rapidly expanding export sector, specializing in light consumer goods.

The energy crisis of 1973 set back the ROK's economic growth plans, since the country depends on oil imports for 60% of its domestic requirements. The discovery of oil in southeastern Yongil may alleviate Korea's energy dependence on outside sources. Fuel costs pushed inflation rates to 42% in 1974 and to an estimated 30% in 1975, raising doubts in late 1975 about the ROK's ability to meet its soaring burden in foreign-debt servicing. Outstanding public and private debts were estimated at $5,988.4 million in October 1975, or nearly one-third of that year's total GNP.

[20] INCOME

The GNP in 1975 was officially estimated at $18.3 billion, an increase of about 6% over the 1974 figure. This would yield a per capita GNP figure of $527, although independent sources placed per capita GNP at around $310. Gross national consumption rose at the rate of 10.5% in 1974 and by about 5% in 1975. The wage earner's share of the GDP slipped from 39% in 1970 to 36.8% in 1974. The average urban wage worker earned about $106 a month in 1974, compared to a high-school teacher's salary of $234, and an average farmer's income of perhaps $60 a month.

The 1974 GDP of ₩6,845 million derived from industry, 27.6%; agriculture, 25.1%; commerce, 18.5%; transport and communications, 5.7%; construction, 4.4%; and other sectors, 18.7%.

21 LABOR

Official ROK sources indicated that the economically active population (over age 14) stood at 13,543,000 in early 1975. Of the total employed of 13,144,000, 7,415,000 (57%) were engaged in agriculture, forestry, and fisheries. Although the unemployment rate was officially estimated at 3% in 1975, independent sources placed the actual rate at 8–10%, with significant underemployment.

The principal labor organization is the Federation of Korean Trade Unions, with a total membership of 530,900, distributed among 17 member unions. Collective bargaining has been restricted since the declaration of national emergency in late 1971; the statutory right to collective action has been suspended, and in practice strikes are prohibited. The few strikes that have occurred in the 1970s have been harshly suppressed. Despite a working standards law, child labor and workdays of 12–15 hours (with one day off per month) are common practices in the textile and transportation industries. Laborers' protection centers exist throughout the nation and, in 1974, handled 7,200 cases of illegal practices; however, their supervision is limited to enterprises of 30 or more employees.

22 AGRICULTURE

Some 23% of the ROK's land area is arable, and about 80% of the cultivated area is sown in grain. About half the population is currently engaged in agricultural activities, a sharp decrease since 1945. Rice makes up 40% of all farm production in value. Double cropping is common in the southern provinces.

The rice harvest in 1975 was 4,709,000 tons, a 5% increase over the 1974 figure of 4,445,000 tons. Wheat and barley production in 1974 stood at 1,851,000 tons. Potatoes, cereals, and pulses also are grown in substantial quantities.

Total grain production dropped in 1973 to 7,163,000 tons, as compared to the 1972 figure of 7,208,000 tons; in 1974, however, the total reached 7,304,000 tons, a 2% increase over the 1973 figure. Productivity is lower than in Japan, the DRK, and Taiwan; the average yield per acre of paddy fields is about 42 bushels.

The ROK runs a net deficit in food grains every year. Imports, mostly from the US, in 1974 totaled 2,732,000 tons of grain (wheat, rice, and corn), valued at $517.2 million.

Cotton, hemp, silk, ramie, and tobacco are the leading industrial crops. The orchards in the Taegu area are renowned for their apples, the prime fruit crop. Pears, peaches, persimmons, and melons also are grown in abundance. About two-thirds of vegetable production is made up of the mu (a large white radish) and Chinese cabbage, the main ingredients of the year-round staple kimchi or "Korean pickle."

Until the Korean War, tenancy was widespread in the ROK. The Land Reform Act of June 1949, interrupted by the war, was completed in 1953. It limited the arable land ownership to 3 hectares per household, with all lands in excess of this limit to be purchased by the government for distribution among farmers who had little or no land. Recent studies indicate that disguised tenancy may have returned in upwards of 20% of farming households. Although the typical Korean farmer owns the land he tills, his plot is often insufficient to support his household of

perhaps five members. The New Village Movement has attempted to increase productivity and modernize villages and farming practices since 1972. Application of inorganic fertilizer increased by 16% in 1974, but the average farmer still uses human nightsoil. Most agricultural labor is still human-intensive, with draft animals in short supply and mechanization limited.

23 ANIMAL HUSBANDRY

The raising of livestock has always been a supplementary occupation among ROK farmers. Very little land is set aside exclusively for this purpose except on Cheju Island, where horse grazing is fairly extensive. About 1.5 million head of cattle were raised in 1973; hogs totaled 1.6 million, an increase of 18% over 1972 and surpassing the 1966 peak of 1.45 million. Chickens and hogs are raised primarily for household consumption.

24 FISHING

With more than 1,400 miles of coastline, extensive continental shelves, and an interchange of warm and cold sea currents, Korean waters comprise some of the best fishing grounds in the world. In the 1930s, Korea ranked sixth among the world's exporters of fish, and fishing still accounts for a sizable 7% of total export earnings. Recent investments have led to rapid growth; the total catch in 1974 was 2,026,000 tons, tripling the 1968 figure and representing a 20% increase over 1973. Total fishery exports in 1974 stood at 257,415 tons, an 11.9% increase over the 1973 figure. Deep-sea fishing now constitutes 20% of the total catch, a remarkable growth since 1962, when the ROK had only five deep-sea vessels. New ships are large (usually over 100 tons), and many are mechanized.

25 FORESTRY

In 1910, 74.6% of the land area of Korea was listed as forest land, of which about one-third was classified as regular forest, just under one-third was denuded land, and the remainder was covered with brush. Since the Korean War, efforts have been made to restore the tree cover in the ROK, long ravaged by peasants in need of wood for fuel. In 1975, forests accounted for 67% of the total area.

About 74% of the forests are privately owned. Some 47% of the country's trees are coniferous. Although ₩67 billion in forestry products was exported in 1974, more than two-thirds of the domestic demand for lumber must be met by imports ($456.1 million in logs and pulp in 1974). In 1973, 9.5 million cu meters of round wood were produced, of which 6.6 million were coniferous.

26 MINING

The ROK has less than 30% of the Korean peninsula's estimated reserves of gold, silver, tungsten, molybdenum, and graphite and perhaps 10% of the deposits of coal and iron-bearing ores. Iron ore reserves have been estimated at 40 million tons and tungsten at 7.5 million tons.

The overall output of the mining industry has risen almost continuously since 1949. Since the oil crisis of 1973, priority has been given to the production of coal. Mineral production increased by 9.1% in 1974, a decline from the 16% rise in 1973. Coal production in 1974 rose by 12% to a total of 15 million tons. Although metallic-mineral mining expanded by 4.5% and nonmetallic-mineral mining by 9.3% during 1974, declines in earlier years offset this growth, yielding an overall increase since 1970 of only 6.4%. Gold, copper, and molybdenum production rose in 1974, but silver, lead, and zinc ore production decreased. Iron ore output was 493,000 tons in 1974, a rise of 27,000 tons over 1973, but a sharp drop from the 1969 figure of 734,000 tons. The ROK exported about $32 million worth of minerals in 1974.

The discovery of a major oil deposit in the coastal resort town of P'ohang was announced in November 1975. With reserves estimated at 6.3 billion barrels, the discovery was expected to alleviate the ROK's soaring fuel outlays, which reached $1.5 billion annually (about 130 million barrels) in the mid-1970s.

27 ENERGY AND POWER

Until 1948, more than half of the country's electricity was supplied from the great hydroelectric plants in the north, but in May of that year the DRK authorities cut off the flow of power. The ROK thus was forced to develop further its own inadequate hydroelectric sites and to build thermal power stations.

There was a fivefold increase in electric generating capacity during 1961–71. In early 1975, the country's total generating capacity was 3,925,000 kw. In 1975, a 250,000-kw generator was added to the Inch'on thermal power plant; and in 1973, a 200,000-kw hydraulic power plant began operating on the Soyang River, and an 80,000-kw hydraulic plant was completed for the Paldang dam. In late 1975, the ROK's first heavy-water nuclear power reactor began operating. Rural electrification is proceeding slowly, with 31% of the rural areas still without electricity in 1975.

28 INDUSTRY

Until the 1960s, manufacturing was chiefly confined to production for domestic consumption, and a substantial proportion of the output was produced by handicraft methods in homes and small factories. Since the beginning of the first five-year plan (1962–66), heavy industry has grown rapidly. Many concerns are built around former Japanese-owned enterprises that the government sold to private interests. However, considerable rehabilitation and expansion of manufacturing facilities, largely financed by US, Japanese, and UN economic aid, have taken place since the Korean War. As a result, the contribution of manufacturing to GNP rose to about 30% by the mid-1970s. Manufacturing achieved a 30.9% growth rate in 1973 and 16.1% in 1974. The textile industry remains the single most important industry in terms of value and employment, and is the leading export earner among manufactures.

In 1964, the first oil refinery opened at Ulsan with a daily capacity of 35,000 barrels; two other refineries are now in operation for a total refining capacity of 395,000 barrels a day. Nine petrochemical plants are in operation, producing 702,000 kl of gasoline, 2.1 million kl of naphtha, and 2.9 million kl of diesel oil. Production of basic metal products increased by 6% annually during 1970–74, and an integrated steel complex in P'ohang is now in operation, with an annual production capacity of 1,030,000 tons of crude steel. Four auto assembly plants produced 8,837 passenger sedans, 4,000 buses, and 19,000 trucks in 1974. Some 3.7 million radios and 1.4 million television sets were produced in 1974. The growing shipbuilding industry increased from a 250,000-gross-ton capacity in 1970 to 1.1 million gross tons in 1974.

29 DOMESTIC TRADE

Domestic trade is mostly in small, family-operated outlets. In the cities, such outlets are often concentrated in large markets. Several large, modern department stores now operate in Seoul and Pusan. Much trade in the rest of the country is still by itinerant peddlers or mobile sidewalk stands. In the rural areas, periodic market fairs continue to serve the farmers' needs. Black markets offering all manner of foreign goods are much in use. Haggling over prices is common.

Of late, an advertising industry has developed in the cities, utilizing radio, television, films, and billboards; handbills remain a favorite device of smaller tradesmen.

30 FOREIGN TRADE

The ROK's foreign trade expanded dramatically during the 1963–74 period, with foreign trade in 1974 accounting for fully 68% of the GDP. Exports climbed at an average rate approaching 40% in this period, with a spectacular rise of 98% in 1972/73. Total exports, which stood at $86 million in 1963, reached $4,460 million by 1974. However, the growth rate declined severely in 1974/75, with total exports at the end of the year standing at $5,064 million, a growth of only 14%. The government has focused on foreign-trade expansion as a principal means of securing the large amount of foreign capital necessary for economic development, with emphasis on export and import-substitute industries. Textiles, metallic products, electrical equipment, and plywood are the ROK's leading exports, as well as the fastest growing. Imports, however, have grown more rapidly than exports, with a growth rate of about 60% during 1972–74. With the slower export growth in 1975 came a slight diminution of imports, dropping from $6.8 billion in 1974 to $6.5 billion in 1975. The world recession struck hard at Korean trade in 1974, causing an 18% drop in total volume, one of the world's sharpest deteriorations. Wide trade deficits appeared consistently throughout the 1970s.

Exports and imports in 1974 (in thousands of dollars) were:

	EXPORTS	IMPORTS
Manufactured goods	1,475,543	1,000,236
Machinery and transport equipment	672,334	1,848,602
Miscellaneous manufactured articles	1,546,973	167,216
Food and live animals	299,735	818,246
Crude materials, except fuels	198,429	1,249,881
Mineral fuels, lubricants, related materials	107,731	1,054,494
Chemicals	91,833	630,887
Beverages and tobacco	47,514	10,659
Animal and vegetable oils, fats	1,776	54,407
Others	18,503	9,667
TOTALS	4,460,371	6,844,295

Principal trade partners in 1974 (in millions of dollars) were:

	EXPORTS	IMPORTS	BALANCE
Japan	1,380.2	2,620.6	− 1,240.4
US	1,492.2	1,201.9	290.3
Sa'udi Arabia	—	520.8	− 520.8
FRG	241.8	140.3	101.5
Canada	166.8	115.7	51.1
Indonesia	55.2	165.4	− 110.2
Other countries	1,124.2	2,079.6	− 955.4
TOTALS	4,460.4	6,844.3	− 2,383.9

Japan and the US are the ROK's chief markets; Western Europe is the other major market. Southeast Asia and, increasingly, the Middle East, constitute the minor marketing regions.

31 BALANCE OF PAYMENTS

The ROK's chronic trade deficits have had to be remedied by foreign aid and borrowing. The annual payments deficit jumped radically from $308.8 million in 1973 to $2,039.8 million in 1974. In 1975, the deficit stood at $1,845 million, necessitating a 96% increase in external borrowing during the year. The nation's total external debt stood at $5.9 billion at the end of 1975, compared to $2.3 billion in 1969. A total debt of $16 billion has been projected for 1981, if current rates of outflow are maintained.

The ROK's balance-of-payments accounts in 1970 and 1974 (in millions of dollars) are summarized as follows:

	1970	1974
Merchandise balance	−921	− 1,938
Services balance	119	− 310
Net transfers	180	221
TOTALS	−622	− 2,027

Long-term capital	458	1,079
Short-term capital	229	747
Errors and omissions	−8	29
CURRENT BALANCE	57	− 172

³²BANKING

The Bank of Korea, the central financial institution whose bank notes constitute the currency of the ROK, is a depository for government funds and is the only bank authorized to possess foreign exchange. Gold and foreign exchange reserves of the Bank of Korea stood at $1,550.1 million at the end of 1975, an increase of 50.7% over 1974. Other official banking functions are fulfilled by the Korea Exchange Bank, which handles import-export financing; the Korea Development Bank, which handles government financial and development funds; agricultural and fisheries cooperatives, which provide funds for rural development; the Medium Industry Bank; the Citizen's Bank; and the Korea Housing Bank.

In 1975 there were 15 commercial banks, including 5 based in Seoul and 1 in each of the provinces and in Pusan. As of 30 November 1975, deposits in all banking institutions totaled W1,910.4 billion, an increase of W425.9 billion since the end of 1974. In November 1975, the money supply stood at W1,136.8 billion.

³³INSURANCE

Standard forms of life, personal injury, endowment, and other insurance are issued by several private companies. There is also the government-owned National Life Insurance Company. Fire, marine, and damage insurance are offered by both domestic and foreign companies.

³⁴SECURITIES

The Korean Stock Exchange, a share-issuing private corporation, functions as the country's only stock exchange.

³⁵PUBLIC FINANCE

Estimated expenditure and revenue for fiscal 1975 (in billions of won) were:

EXPENDITURE	
General expenses	396.5
Investments, loans	385.4
National defense	353.1
Subsidies	156.8
Special account expenditures	561.2
TOTAL	1,853.0

REVENUE	
Domestic taxes	1,021.3
Trust income from foreign loans	94.6
Income from monopolies	88.0
Nontax income	33.5
Loans and grants	30.0
Trust fund income	24.6
TOTAL	1,292.0

³⁶TAXATION

Principal sources of tax revenue are customs duties, sales taxes, personal income taxes, and various excise taxes. As of 1975, two schedules for corporate taxation were in effect: for companies listed at the Korean Stock Exchange Commission, a reduced rate ranges from 16% on taxable income up to W1 million to 27% on income over W5 million; nonlisted companies are taxed at a rate of 20–40% at the same intervals. Tax relief is offered to new industries and corporations that are foreign exchange earners. The personal income tax is graduated from 30% on aggregate taxable income up to W3 million to a maximum rate of 65% on incomes over W45 million.

As taxes make up nearly 80% of revenue, the tax burden is by no means light. The total tax revenue is about 14% of GNP.

³⁷CUSTOMS AND DUTIES

Customs duties are levied upon imports on an ad valorem basis. The customs tax is primarily a source of revenue (it provides more than 11% of total tax revenue) and secondarily a means of differentiating between essential and nonessential imports.

³⁸FOREIGN INVESTMENTS

In a very real sense, the huge amounts of US and Japanese economic aid have constituted foreign investment in the ROK economy. No investment of foreign private capital occurred at all for some 15 years after the liberation of the country in 1945. Finally, in 1959, the government enacted a foreign investment encouragement law. In 1962, the government approved a plan to ensure reimbursement of specified foreign investors.

Economic aid funds from the US, Japan, and other countries, and from international organizations, totaled some $1.6 billion during the 1960s. Foreign public and commercial loans during 1970–74 totaled $3.4 billion, with $933 million received in 1974 alone. Private foreign investments totaled $124.1 million in 1974, off 13.4% from the previous year. Japanese investing has rapidly overcome early US predominance. During 1962–71, US sources invested $98.9 million in the ROK (57.3% of the total), compared to $50.5 billion from Japanese investors (29.3%). During 1972–74, however, Japanese investments totaled $301 million (85% of the total), as compared to $34 million from US investors (11%).

US aid to the ROK has remained important throughout the post-World War II era, totaling $12.1 billion during 1945–75—$5.7 billion in economic assistance and $6.4 billion in military aid. US aid was to be phased out after 1976. In 1975, it totaled $106 million, of which nearly 90% was in the form of surplus agricultural commodities.

³⁹ECONOMIC POLICY

The second five-year plan (1967–71) achieved an 11.7% annual growth rate, a rise in per capita GNP to $253, and an increase in the total value of exports to $1,130 million. The third five-year development plan (1972–76) emphasized economic stabilization and sustained economic growth. By 1976, the GNP was estimated to have grown by 80% and per capita income by 60% as compared with 1969.

⁴⁰HEALTH

Family planning has kept the birthrate down to around 2% in the last few years; major campaigns against typhoid and tuberculosis have been mounted, with typhoid cases down to 550 in 1974. By 1975, average life expectancy reached an estimated 62.8 years, as compared with 47.5 years in 1950.

In 1974, the ROK had 14,037 doctors (1 for every 2,370 persons), representing virtually no increase since 1968. About 40% of the country's medical personnel are in Seoul.

⁴¹SOCIAL WELFARE

Few countries have faced health and social welfare problems as acute as those caused in the ROK by the devastation of the Korean War. The war left a residue of 348,000 war widows, most of them with dependent children, and 100,000 war orphans. Some 595,260 homes were destroyed, 5,000 villages wiped out, and many large cities badly damaged. Relief services provided by the government have consisted mainly of financial support to veterans and their families; thus, by 1974, tht total number of people on the relief roll had diminished to only 137,068. Foreign-aid agencies, mostly private, established orphanages, hospitals, and vocational training programs after the devastation caused by the Korean War; many of them continue to function, although their services are much reduced.

⁴²HOUSING

After the liberation in 1945, southern Korea faced a housing shortage greatly compounded by high population growth rates. The third five-year plan called for the government to build 1 million housing units by 1976, but budget cuts precluded fulfillment. A housing shortage continues to plague the nation, with a deficit of 1,320,000 units in 1974, or about 21.5% of total housing requirements.

43 EDUCATION

The Education Law of 1949 provided for a centralized system under the control of the Ministry of Education and made the six-year elementary-school course compulsory. In 1974 there were 5,692,285 students in primary schools, 1,832,092 in middle schools, 839,318 in high schools, 178,650 in colleges and universities, and 10,236 in graduate schools. The leading government university is Seoul National University. Principal private institutions, all of them in Seoul, are Korea, Sung Kyun Kwan, Yonsei, Tongguk, Hanyang, Chungang, and Ewha universities. The last named is one of the largest women's universities in the world. The country had a total of 98 universities in 1975, of which 67 were private. The universities, which have become a principal focal point for antigovernment unrest, have been subject to increasing government scrutiny and closures. In 1976, a ruling by the Park government led to the removal of some 400–500 university professors.

44 LIBRARIES AND MUSEUMS

The National Central Library was founded in 1925 and has 400,000 volumes. Most sizable libraries in the ROK are found at universities. The largest collection is at the Seoul National University Library, which has 882,000 volumes and is especially rich in Yi dynasty materials.

The Korean National Museum, with centers in Seoul, Kyongju, Puyo, and Kongju, contains art objects reflecting more than 4,000 years of cultural history, including statuary pieces, ceramic ware, and paintings. The ROK also possesses, in its palaces and Buddhist temples and in university, college, and public libraries, collections of early printing, dynastic histories, and art objects.

45 ORGANIZATIONS

Clan and county associations are a conspicuous aspect of Korean social life. A traditional type of organization with a primarily economic function is the kye, a mutual loan association formed to provide funds for a specific and typically short-term purpose, such as to defray the expenses of a wedding or funeral.

A number of US-style organizations have taken root.

46 PRESS

The ROK press has been severely muzzled since the promulgation of the new constitution in 1972. Press censorship is in force, often with government agents in the pressrooms. The widely respected intellectual monthly, *Sasanggye (World of Thought)*, has not been allowed to publish for several years.

The leading newspapers, with their 1974 circulations, are:

SEOUL	CIRCULATION
Dong-A Ilbo	520,000
Chungang Ilbo	400,000
Choson Ilbo	350,000
Hankook Ilbo	350,000
Kyonghyang Sinmun	250,000
Sin-A Ilbo	130,000
PROVINCES	
Kook Che Sinbo (Pusan)	250,000
Chunnam Ilbo (South Cholla)	150,000
Maeil Sinmun (North Kyungsang)	105,000

47 TOURISM

The tourist industry has grown rapidly with more than 300,000 foreign visitors in 1975, as compared with 90,000 in 1967. The government has promoted the construction of tourist facilities. Tourist visas may be obtained through Korean consulates or embassies. Initial stays of up to 60 days are granted.

48 FAMOUS KOREANS

Among the many historical figures of Korea are Ulchi Mundok, victorious Koguryo general in the Sui China invasions of the early 7th century; Kim Yo-sin (595–673), warrior and folk hero in Silla's struggle to unify the peninsula; Wang Kon (877–943), founder and first ruler of the Koryo dynasty; Yun Kwan (?–1111), Koryo general who repulsed Jurched invaders; Kim Pu-sik (1075–1151), scholar-official who wrote the great *History of the Three Kingdoms*; Yi Song-gye (1335–1408), general and founder of the Yi dynasty; King Sejong (1397–1450), inventor of han'gul and Korea's greatest monarch; Yi Hwang (1501–70) and Yi I (1536–84), Neo-Confucianist philosophers and officials; Yi Sun-sin (1545–98), admiral who defeated the Japanese in every naval engagement of the Hideyoshi invasion; Chong Yag-yong (1762–1836), pragmatist scholar-official and prolific writer; and the Taewon'gun (1820–98), regent for his son and the central political figure of the late 19th century.

The two dominant political figures of the contemporary period have been Syngman Rhee (1875–1965), president of the ROK from 1948 to 1960, and Park Chung Hee (b.1917), the current president. Other well-known modern figures include Yun Po-sun (b.1897), political leader and former president (1960–62); Kim Chong-p'il, (b.1926), prime minister 1971–75; Kim Chi Ha (b.1942), the dissident poet; Kim Tae-jung (b.1925), New Democratic Party presidential candidate in 1971; and Bishop Chi Hak-sun (Daniel Chi, b.1921). The Rev. Mun Son-myong (b.1920), an evangelist, and Chung Kyung Wha (b.1943), a violinist, have both become well known internationally.

49 DEPENDENCIES

The ROK has no territories or colonies.

50 BIBLIOGRAPHY

Baldwin, Frank (ed.). *Without Parallel: Essays on the American-Korean Relationship since 1945*. New York: Pantheon, 1974.

Bartz, Patricia. *South Korea, A Descriptive Geography*. Oxford: Clarendon Press, 1972.

Bibliography of Korean Studies 1945–58. Seoul: Asiatic Research Center, Korea University, 1961.

Cole, David. *Korean Development: The Interplay of Politics and Economics*. Cambridge: Harvard University Press, 1971.

Conroy, Hilary. *The Japanese Seizure of Korea, 1868–1910*. Philadelphia: University of Pennsylvania Press, 1960.

Gale, James Scarth. *History of the Korean People*. New annotated ed. Seoul: Royal Asiatic Society, 1972.

Gordenker, Leon. *The United Nations and the Peaceful Unification of Korea*. The Hague: Nijhoff, 1959.

Hatada, Takashi. *A History of Korea*. Santa Barbara, Calif.: American Bibliographical Center, 1969.

Henderson, Gregory. *Korea: The Politics of the Vortex*. Cambridge: Harvard University Press, 1968.

Kim, C. I. Eugene, and Han-kyo Kim. *Korea and the Politics of Imperialism, 1876–1910*. Berkeley: University of California Press, 1967.

Korea: Its Land, People and Cultures of All Ages. Seoul: Hakwonsa, 1960.

Lee, Chong-sik. *The Politics of Korean Nationalism*. Berkeley: University of California Press, 1963.

McCune, Evelyn. *The Arts of Korea*. Tokyo: Tuttle, 1961.

McCune, George M. *Korea Today*. Cambridge: Harvard University Press, 1950.

McCune, Shannon. *Korea's Heritage: A Regional and Social Geography*. Rutland and Tokyo: Tuttle, 1956.

Paige, Glenn D. *The Korean Decision*. New York: Free Press, 1968.

Palais, James B. *Policy and Politics in Traditional Korea*. Cambridge: Harvard University Press, 1975.

Pihl, Marshall R. *Listening to Korea: A Korean Anthology*. New York: Praeger, 1973.

KUWAYT

State of Kuwayt
Dawlat al-Kuwayt

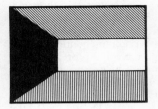

CAPITAL: Al-Kuwayt. **FLAG:** The flag adopted in 1961 is a rectangle, twice as long as high, divided equally into green, white, and red horizontal stripes, with a black trapezoid whose longer base is against the staff and is equal to the breadth of the flag, and whose shorter base is equal to the breadth of the white stripe. **ANTHEM:** National Anthem, melody only; no words. **MONETARY UNIT:** The Kuwayti dinar (KD) has 1,000 fils. There are coins of 1, 5, 10, 20, 50, and 100 fils and notes of 250 and 500 fils and of 1, 5, 10, and 100 Kuwayti dinars. KD 1=$3.41 (or $1=KD0.293). **WEIGHTS AND MEASURES:** The metric system is the legal standard, but imperial weights and measures also are in use, and some US measures are recognized. **HOLIDAYS:** New Year's Day, 1 January; the Amir's Accession Day, 25 February; National Day, 19 June. Movable religious holidays include 1 Muharram; Accession of the Prophet; Milad al-Nabi; 'Id al-Fitr; and 'Id al-'Adha'. **TIME:** 3 P.M.=noon GMT.

¹LOCATION, SIZE, AND EXTENT

Kuwayt is situated at the western head of the Persian Gulf. Its undemarcated borders preclude any definite figure for its area, which is estimated at about 17,818 sq km (6,880 sq mi). Kuwayt extends 205 km (127 mi) SE–NW and 176 km (109 mi) NE–SW. Islands that are a part of Kuwayt include Faylakah (an archaeological site, which is the only inhabited island), Bubiyan, Maskan, Auha, al-Warbah, al-Kubr, Umm al-Maradim, Umm al-Nami, Qaru, and al-Saghirah. Bounded on the E by the Persian Gulf, on the S and W by Sa'udi Arabia, and on the NW and N by Iraq, Kuwayt has a total boundary length (not including the islands) of 632 km (393 mi).

²TOPOGRAPHY

Kuwayt consists almost entirely of flat rolling desert and mud flats. There is a 400-foot ridge at Mina al-Ahmadi and a 900-foot prominence in the southwest corner. There are no streams.

³CLIMATE

During the summer, which lasts roughly from May to October, the air generally is dry, but southeasterly winds often bring daytime humidity to 90% for a few weeks in August or September. Between November and April, the climate is pleasant, with cool nights and warm sunny days. In December and January, night temperatures occasionally touch the freezing point. Summer temperatures range from 29.4°C (85°F) in the morning to more than 49°C (120°F) in the shade at noon. Frost, almost unknown on the coast, is common in the interior. Annual rainfall, totaling 1 to 7 inches, comes in the form of showers or storms between October and April. Cloudbursts have amounted to as much as 2.5 inches of rain in one day, and can partially destroy roads and houses. The prevailing northwest wind (shamal) is a cooling breeze in summer.

⁴FLORA AND FAUNA

Plants and animals are those common to the arid parts of Arabia. There is little vegetation except camel thorn in the desert and 'arfaj shrub along the coastal strip. Between October and March, however, when at intervals sufficient rain falls, the desert is transformed; grass and foliage are plentiful; flowers and plants appear in great variety; and in the spring truffles and mushrooms can be found. The fox and jackal are becoming increasingly uncommon and as of 1975, the sand gazelle and Sa'udi Arabian dorcas gazelle were considered endangered species. Fish are plentiful. Among the species of migratory birds are swallows, wagtails, chiffchaff, skylarks, and wrens.

⁵POPULATION

According to the 1970 census, Kuwayt had a total population of 738,662, representing an increase of more than 250% over the 1957 figure of 206,473 and 58.1% over the 1965 figure of 467,339. The preliminary estimate for May 1975 was 991,392; the UN projection for 1980 was 1,439,000. Al-Kuwayt, the capital, had an estimated population of 77,989 in 1975, with an additional population of 197,263 in the surrounding suburban area. Most of the rest of the population is located in the urban areas of Hawalli and al-Ahmadi. The average population density in May 1975 was estimated at 56 per sq km (144 per sq mi).

⁶ETHNIC GROUPS

Most Kuwaytis have their origin in the tribes of Najd. Kuwayt is unique among the nations of the world in that the majority of its population are foreign nationals. According to the 1970 census, 391,266 persons, of 53% of the total population, were non-Kuwaytis. The latter included 147,696 Jordanians and Palestinians, 39,129 Iranians, 39,066 Iraqis, 30,421 Egyptians, 27,217 Syrians, 25,387 Lebanese, 17,336 Indians, 14,712 Pakistanis, 14,670 Muscatans and Omanis, and 10,897 Sa'udi Arabians.

⁷LANGUAGE

Arabic is the official language. The Arabic spoken in Kuwayt is closer to classical Arabic than to the colloquial Arabic spoken in many other parts of the Middle East. English is used generally by businessmen, employees of oil companies, foreign residents, and students, and it is the second language taught in the schools.

⁸RELIGION

In 1970, Muslims numbered 699,798 (94.7%), and Christians 34,183 (4.6%). The Muslims, predominantly Sunni, include a substantial Shi'i minority.

⁹TRANSPORTATION

Kuwayt possesses a modern network of roads with all-weather highways running north to Iraq and south to Sa'udi Arabia. In 1974 there were 166,194 passenger cars, 8,000 taxis, 46,706 trucks, and 1,737 private and 1,151 public buses in use; a total of 35,653,026 passengers were transported by bus services in 1974. Land transport in 1973 accounted for 29.8% of Kuwayt's imports and exports. There are no railways.

In 1964, a cargo port was constructed at al-Shuwaikh in Kuwayt Bay. An oil port at Mina al-Ahmadi is equipped with the largest pier of its kind in the world, enabling eight large tankers to be loaded simultaneously. Kuwayt has regular calls from ocean shipping, and local sailing craft carry goods between Kuwayt and the neighboring shaykhdoms, Iraq, Sa'udi Arabia, and Iran. In 1974, 1,167 ships with a net registered tonnage of 5,039,451 entered al-Shuwaikh. Sea transport in 1973 accounted for 69.8% of Kuwayt's foreign trade.

Air transportation is highly advanced; more than 15 European, Asian, and Middle Eastern airlines have scheduled flights in and out of Kuwayt. Kuwayt Airways provides service to and from the Middle East and Europe. There were 8,481 flight arrivals at Kuwayt International Airport in 1974; passenger arrivals totaled 272,162.

10 COMMUNICATIONS
The government administers telephone, television, radio, postal, and telegraph services. In 1973, 95,000 telephones were operated from a fully automatic exchange. The Kuwayt broadcasting service has two short-wave and two medium-wave transmitters. One television station broadcasts daily. There were more than 125,000 television sets and 100,000 radios in 1973.

11 HISTORY
The historical records of the Arab coast of the Persian Gulf are meager. Archaeological discoveries on Faylakah Island dating back to 525 B.C. indicate that this part of the Gulf was a principal supply route for trade with India. There is evidence of early migrations to the East African coast by the seafaring inhabitants. The principal historical event was the conversion to Islam in the 7th century A.D. in the lifetime of Muhammad. In 636, Muslim armies under Khalid bin al-Walid participated in the Battle of the Chains just north of Kuwayt.

Kuwayt's recent history starts in 1716, when several clans of the tribe of Aniza migrated from the interior of the Arabian Desert to a tiny Gulf coastal locality, later to be called Kuwayt, a diminutive of the word *kut,* meaning "fort." In 1756, the settled tribesmen rallied around the al-Sabah family and chose as their ruler Shaykh Sabah Abdul Rahim, founder of the present ruling dynasty. During the latter part of the century, raids by land and by sea resulted in a decline of Kuwayt, but after the British suppression of piracy in the region, trading and shipbuilding prospered.

During the period in which Shaykh 'Abdallah al-Sabah ruled Kuwayt (1866–92), a dynastic battle raged in Arabia between the rival houses of al-Rashid and al-Sa'ud. The Turks supported Ibn Rashid and wanted to extend their control over the coastal area to the south of Kuwayt. Fearing that his territory would be annexed, Shaykh Mubarak al-Sabah (r.1896–1915) asked to be taken under British protection. The British were concerned not only because of Turkish claims but also because the Russians were seeking to set up a coaling station in Kuwayt, and both the Germans and the Turks had planned to make it a terminus of the Berlin-Baghdad railroad. In 1899, Shaykh Mubarak agreed not to alienate any of his territory or to receive representatives of any foreign power without British consent. In return, the British offered their services as well as an annual subsidy to support the shaykh and his heirs. Not until the outbreak of World War I, however, did Kuwayt receive the recognition of its independence and the pledge of British protection it had sought since 1899. On 19 June 1961, a treaty with the UK was terminated by mutual consent, and Kuwayt declared itself fully sovereign and independent.

The boundary with Sa'udi Arabia was settled by a treaty in 1922 that established a Neutral Zone, an area of approximately 2,500 sq mi in which each country was to have an undemarcated half interest. On 18 December 1969, the two countries signed an agreement formally dividing the Neutral Zone and establishing a new international boundary between the two countries.

Kuwayt's boundary with Iraq remains unsettled. Following Kuwayt's declaration of independence in June 1961, the amir requested UK assistance to ward off an Iraqi invasion. The British forces were later replaced by troops from the Arab League states. The UN upheld Kuwayt's sovereignty, and in October 1963, Iraq formally recognized Kuwayt's independence. In March 1973, however, there were armed clashes on the Iraq-Kuwayt border. A tentative settlement was announced in June 1975.

12 GOVERNMENT
According to the constitution of 29 January 1963, Kuwayt is an independent sovereign Arab state, and its people are part of the Arab nation. Succession is restricted to descendants of Mubarak al-Sabah; an heir apparent must be appointed within one year of accession of a new ruler. Executive power is vested in the amir, who exercises it through a Council of Ministers. The amir appoints a prime minister after traditional consultations and appoints ministers on the prime minister's recommendation.

The National Assembly consists of 50 elected representatives and 16 appointed ministers. Elections are held every four years among native-born literate adult males. Candidates must be native-born Kuwaytis at least 30 years of age. The Assembly may be dissolved at any time by the amir; a new election must take place within two months. The amir may ask for reconsideration of a bill passed by the Assembly, but a bill automatically becomes a law if, upon reconsideration, it is passed by a two-thirds majority, or by a simple majority in a subsequent session.

Women are not permitted to vote or hold office.

13 POLITICAL PARTIES
Although no political parties existed before 1962, some political activity did take place. Various groups, operating mainly as official or informal clubs, were affiliated with or included members of Ba'th, the Socialist party that advocates Arab unity, and there were a few active Communists. After the 1958 coup in Iraq, Kuwayt closed all clubs, almost without protest. No political parties were authorized in the 1975 elections.

14 LOCAL GOVERNMENT
Kuwayt does not have formal local governments comparable to those of other countries.

15 JUDICIAL SYSTEM
The system of Muslim law (the Shari'ah) was augmented by a 1959 law that established courts of law, regulated the judicial system, and adopted modern legal codes. A tribunal of first instance has jurisdiction over matters involving personal status, civil and commercial cases, and criminal cases, except those of a religious nature. The Court of Appeals, the highest in the land, is divided into two chambers, one with jurisdiction over appeals involving personal status and civil cases, the other over appeals involving commercial and criminal cases.

16 ARMED FORCES
Kuwayt's armed strength totaled 10,200 in mid-1975. The army had 8,000 men and 100 tanks; the air force, 2,000 men and 32 combat aircraft, with *Hawk* surface-to-air missiles on order; and the coast guard, 200 men and 29 naval craft. Budgeted defense expenditures in 1974 were KD41.7 million.

17 MIGRATION
With the discovery of oil and the consequent rise in living standards, Kuwayt has acquired a large immigrant population, attracted by work, free education for their children, and free medical care. The citizenship law requires Arabs to have 8 years of continuous residence before applying for Kuwayti citizenship; others, 15 years.

18 INTERNATIONAL COOPERATION
Kuwayt was admitted to UN membership on 14 May 1963 and is a member of all the specialized agencies. It is a member of the Arab League, OPEC, and OAPEC. Besides contributing regularly to the budget of UNRWA, Kuwayt has provided funds for young refugees to attend UNRWA vocational training centers. In the mid-1970s, Kuwayt became a principal contributor to the IMF Oil Facility, providing $313.2 million in loans in 1974.

In 1962, Kuwayt established the Kuwayt Fund for Arab Economic Development, patterned after Western and international lending agencies, to issue loans at low rates of interest for Arab economic development. By 1974, Kuwayt had approved loans amounting to KD136.2 million. In July 1975, the National Assembly widened the scope of the fund to include loans to non-Arab countries, particularly in Africa. In the period 1967-1970, Kuwayt made a yearly contribution of KD47.1 million to Egypt and Jordan to compensate for the loss of revenue resulting from the conflict with Israel.

19ECONOMY
In the past, Kuwayt depended on pearl fishing, but cultured-pearl production reduced this industry to negligible importance. Other forms of activity were entrepôt trade and boatbuilding.

The discovery of oil in 1934 transformed the economy. Kuwayt's enormous oil reserve and its virtually unlimited quantities of natural gas have provided the base for an economic presence of world-wide significance. Internally, the Kuwayti population had, by the mid-1970s, attained the highest living standard in the Middle East and one of the highest in the world. Oil wealth has stimulated trade, fishery development, agriculture, and service industries. The government has been carrying on a large construction program; it has modernized the infrastructure by building ports, roads, an international airport, a seawater distillation plant, and government and office buildings. The population has been directly affected through the establishment of wide-reaching welfare provisions, supported by large-scale construction of hospitals, schools, and low-income housing.

20INCOME
The bulk of national income (an estimated 95.8% in 1975) is derived directly or indirectly from oil concession revenues and royalties paid to the government. GDP in current prices increased from KD961.5 million in 1970/71 to KD3,229.5 million in 1974/75. During the same period, national disposable income increased from KD666.9 million to KD2,755.8 million. Per capita income in 1974/75 exceeded $9,000, the highest rate in the world at that time.

21LABOR
The government is the largest employer, followed by the Kuwayt National Petroleum Co. Wage scales distinguish between unskilled, skilled, and professional workers. The stability of the labor market attracts many workers from other Arab lands. They enjoy full equality and all benefits. The labor force included 242,197 persons, according to the 1970 census; of these, 176,828 (73% of the total) were non-Kuwaytis. In 1974, the government issued 22,929 labor permits to foreign nationals. In that year, there were 95,118 government employees.

The labor department controls organization of manpower, employment of foreign workers, unemployment problems, vocational training, enforcement of regulations, and industrial relations. The Labor Union of Kuwayt is sponsored by the government. In 1961, after it had been admitted to membership in ILO, Kuwayt ratified international labor conventions. In general, all workers are entitled to a 48-hour workweek, compensation for overtime, sick leave, termination pay, and access to machinery for settlement of disputes.

22AGRICULTURE
Despite scarcity of arable land, absence of rivers and streams, and paucity of rain, the development of agriculture has been actively pursued. Nevertheless, farming contributed only 0.03% to GDP in 1974. The government apportions arable land at nominal prices on a long-term basis among farmers to stimulate production of vegetables and other crops. It also provides farmers with long-term loans and low-cost irrigation. The state experimental farm, founded in 1953, is concerned with experimentation on vegetables and other plant life so that they can survive the rigors of the climate.

23ANIMAL HUSBANDRY
Bedouins raise camels, goats, and sheep for meat and milk. When the desert is green from the middle of March to the end of April, about a fourth of Kuwayt's meat supply is provided locally. At other times, the herds remain far from town in search of pasture. In 1974 there were 3,791 head of cattle, 6,863 sheep, 1,294 goats, and 1.5 million chickens. Locally produced poultry supplies 45% of domestic needs; eggs meet 20%; and milk, 6%.

24FISHING
Small boats catch enough fish to satisfy local demand. Species caught include sardines, mackerel, tuna, shark (for the fins exported to China), barracuda, and mullet. Crabs, crawfish, oysters, and shrimp are plentiful. Undik and zubaidi (butterfish) are tasty and very popular. The total fish catch in 1974 was valued at KD1.5 million.

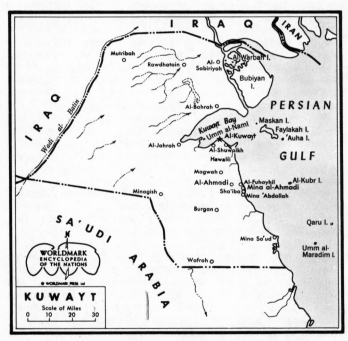

See continental political: front cover H7; physical: back cover H7

LOCATION: 28°32' to 30°6'N; 46°33' to 48°27'E. **BOUNDARY LENGTHS:** Persian Gulf shoreline, 212 km (132 mi); Sa'udi Arabia, 163 km (101 mi); Iraq, 257 km (160 mi). **TERRITORIAL SEA LIMIT:** 12 mi.

25FORESTRY
There are no natural forests in Kuwayt. The government has embarked on a program of planting more than 25,000 trees per year. Fruit and wood trees in 1974 occupied about 2,300 hectares.

26MINING
The Persian Gulf is a unique geologic area. Sedimentary deposits are combined with large, relatively unbroken folding that results in underground oil reservoirs 10 to 150 miles long, containing billions of barrels of oil. Kuwayt's known petroleum deposits outrank those of any other country except Sa'udi Arabia. With proven reserves of more than 10.5 billion tons, Kuwayt possesses over one-eighth of the known global resources of petroleum.

In 1974, Kuwayt was the world's seventh-largest oil producer and the fifth-largest oil exporter. The cost of production in Kuwayt is perhaps the lowest in the world. Kuwayt's vast pools of oil lie fairly close to the surface and conveniently near to tidewater. The oil rises to the surface under its own pressure and, owing to a natural gradient, flows downhill to dockside without pumping. In 1974, crude oil production in Kuwait totaled 929.3 million barrels, 804.8 million barrels of which were exported. In addition to oil, 466,939 million cu feet of natural gas were produced in 1974. In that year, the Kuwayt Oil Co. (KOC) produced 89.4% of the total output; the Arabian Oil Co., 7.4%; and the American Independent Oil Co. (Aminoil), 3.2%.

Oil was first discovered in commercial quantities in 1936, but only small amounts were produced prior to the end of World War II. In 1960, the Kuwait National Petroleum Co. (KNPC) was organized (60% government-owned and 40% privately owned) to participate in all phases of the oil industry from prospecting to final sales. KNPC has a monopoly on all petroleum sold domestically and, since 1968, has operated a refinery at Sha'iba.

KOC, originally owned in equal shares by British Petroleum Co. (BP) and Gulf Oil Corp. discovered commercial oil fields at Burgan, Magwa, Mina al-Ahmadi, and Minagish in southern Kuwayt and at Rawdhatain, al-Sabiriyah, and al-Bahrah in the north. Commercial production began in 1946 with nearly 6 million barrels (by 1973, annual production had increased to more than 1 billion barrels). From 1951 on, a 50-50 profit-sharing plan governed the split of revenue between the company and the amir. KOC's concession (which was to run to the year 2026) had covered all of Kuwait and its territorial waters, but in May 1962, it relinquished nearly half its area to the state.

With a 60-year concession for Kuwait's share of the Neutral Zone, dating from 1948, Aminoil is the operating company for the entire zone. Oil was discovered at Wafrah in 1953. Resources are estimated at 500 million barrels, and production rose from 14.7 million barrels in 1958 to over 35 million barrels in 1964, but dropped to about 30 million in 1974.

The Arabian Oil Co., owned by Japanese industrial interests, operates in the offshore region of the Neutral Zone. It obtained a concession from Sa'udi Arabia and Kuwait in 1958 and in 1974 about 68.7 million barrels were produced, of which Kuwait's share was 50%.

In the mid-1970s, government policy began pointing in the direction of an eventual state monopoly in the petroleum sector. On 7 April 1974, the government announced its intention to seek 100% control of KNPC. In May of that year, the National Assembly approved a plan whereby the Kuwayti government would acquire a 60% share in KOC, retroactive to 1 January 1974. As the government negotiated for increased participation in petroleum enterprises, it also concluded long-term agreements to permit those enterprises to extract crude oil under royalty arrangements highly favorable to the government. After the 1973 price increases, Kuwait repeatedly pressured oil producers to restrict petroleum output as a means of keeping crude oil prices high.

27 ENERGY AND POWER

All power is produced thermally from oil or natural gas. Installed capacity has grown dramatically during the past two decades, increasing from 30,000 kw in 1956 to 1,364,000 in 1974; capacity was expected to be 1,446,000 kw by 1975.

Domestic consumption was 3,632 million kwh in 1974. Most of the country is provided with electric current; electric refrigeration and air conditioning are widely available. An extensive diesel power generating system serves outlying villages.

28 INDUSTRY

Kuwait's two traditional industries, shipbuilding and pearl fishing, have been eclipsed by the technological age.

In the last two decades, however, the country has developed extensive refining operations, producing gasoline, aircraft fuel, kerosene, benzine, gas oil, diesel oil, fuel oil, and other petroleum products. Production in 1974 included (in thousand barrels): fuel oil, 62,113; naphtha, 13,936; diesel fuel, 12,434; gas

oil, 9,428; light distillates, 6,770; kerosene and light benzine, 4,460. Kuwait now also produces soap, flour, cleansers, detergents, asbestos, ammonia, fertilizer, and bricks. The construction industry is highly developed.

A complex seawater distillation plant is the largest of its kind in the world. Total installed distillation capacity in March 1973 was 52 million gallons per day.

29 DOMESTIC TRADE

Until the early 1960s, the traditional small shop or stall in the market dominated retail trade. During 1959–61, however, a modern business center with hundreds of new shops and offices was built, and some smaller villages developed retail stores with impressive stocks of foreign goods. Local terms of sale are cash or credit. Installment buying is becoming popular. Al-Kuwayt is the distribution center for the shaykhdom and serves the transit trade of nearby territories.

Usual business hours in summer (May to October) are from 6 A.M. to noon and from 4 to 6 P.M.; during the rest of the year, from 7 A.M. to noon and from 3 to 6 P.M. Stores are closed Fridays.

30 FOREIGN TRADE

Crude oil and oil products accounted for about 90% of the total value of exports in the mid-1970s. Of total petroleum exports in 1974, 48.14% went to the Far East; 12.64% to Western Europe; 6.29% to the Western Hemisphere; and 32.93% to the rest of the world, predominantly countries in the Middle East.

Principal imports are chemicals, construction materials, petroleum equipment, iron and steel commodities, cement, timber, foodstuffs, pumps, generators, electrical apparatus, power tools, household equipment, and motor vehicles. Per capita imports increased from about $200 in 1950 to more than $1,500 in 1974, when Kuwait imported goods worth more than $1.5 billion.

Principal exports in 1973 (in millions of dollars) were:

Crude petroleum	3,062
Petroleum products	394
Other exports	334
TOTAL	3,790

Principal imports in 1973 (in millions of dollars) were:

Machinery	200
Food and live animals	178
Transport equipment	158
Other imports	506
TOTAL	1,042

In 1973, the EEC accounted for 42.1% of Kuwait's total trade. The UK was formerly Kuwait's leading supplier of imports, but in 1973 Japan led in both imports and exports. An embargo on oil exports to the US and the Netherlands, imposed at the end of 1973, was lifted in March 1974. Principal trade partners in 1973 (in millions of dollars) were:

	EXPORTS	IMPORTS	BALANCE
Japan	716	186	530
UK	475	107	368
France	435	28	407
Netherlands	365	25	340
Italy	241	44	197
US	59	147	−88
Other countries	1,499	505	994
TOTALS	3,790	1,042	2,748

31 BALANCE OF PAYMENTS

The Kuwayti dinar is completely covered by the country's reserve fund, 50% of which must be in gold.

At the end of 1974, Kuwayt's international liquidity was as follows: gold holdings, $150.2 million; reserve position in IMF, $463.4 million (including $313.2 million in loans to the IMF Oil Facility); and foreign exchange, $936 million.

The balance of payments (in millions of Kuwayti dinars) for 1972/73 and 1973/74 was as follows:

	1972/73	1973/74
CURRENT ACCOUNTS		
Oil sector transactions	548.5	1,084.6
Other current transfers	− 99.7	−104.8
TOTALS	448.8	979.8
CAPITAL ACCOUNTS		
Capital transfers	−130.9	−244.7
Loans	− 9.6	0.7
TOTALS	−140.5	−244.0
Net change	308.3	735.8

32 BANKING

A branch of the British Bank of the Middle East has functioned in Kuwayt for many years. In 1952, Kuwayt's state bank, the National Bank of Kuwayt, opened as a private bank financed by local merchants. Since that time, other banks have been established; the Commercial Bank of Kuwayt in 1960, the Trust Bank in 1960, and the Gulf Bank in 1961.

A central bank was established in April 1969 (with a capital of KD2 million) to take over the functions of the former currency board, which established the measure and value of a new monetary system based on the Kuwayti dinar, the only legal tender since May 1960. On 31 March 1974, currency in circulation amounted to KD80.02 million; assets and liabilities of commercial banks totaled KD1,107.4 million. Savings deposits amounted to KD148 million; private demand deposits totaled KD127.5 million.

33 INSURANCE

Both domestic and foreign insurance companies operate in Kuwayt. Agents of foreign companies include those based in the UK, Lebanon, the US, Egypt, and India. Marine, fire, accident, and life insurance policies constitute about 99.5% of all policies issued. In 1973, these policies numbered 326,499, on which premiums totaling KD12.7 million were paid. Total value of insurance policies was KD1.6 billion at the close of 1973.

34 SECURITIES

There are no securities exchanges. The Kuwayt Investment Co. has been established to provide investors in Arab countries partnership with Kuwayti nationals. Its initial capital was fixed at KD15 million, of which the government of Kuwayt provided half, the rest subscribed by Kuwayti citizens. In 1968, Kuwayt Investment signed an agreement with the IBRD to place on the Kuwayt market IBRD bonds yielding 6½%, with an aggregate value of KD15 million.

35 PUBLIC FINANCE

Oil concession revenues and taxes on oil companies constitute the only significant source of government income. The budget, controlled by the Department of Finance, is presented to the National Assembly each year and allotments to various departments are made according to needs. The Department of Finance is required by law to show a budgetary surplus.

The following is a summary of government revenues and expenditures for 1973/74 and 1974/75 (in millions of Kuwayti dinars):

	1973/74	1974/75
REVENUES		
Royalties from oil companies	128.3	473.7
Income taxes from oil companies	402.8	446.0
Customs and duties	8.6	9.8
Other revenues	28.4	30.4
TOTALS	568.1	959.9
EXPENDITURES		
Education	54.4	62.1
Defense	39.0	41.7
Public health	26.7	31.4
Electricity and water	16.3	18.3
Finance and oil	14.5	16.5
Public works	14.8	16.0
Development projects	91.8	0.7
Transfers to attached and independent agencies	42.5	52.3
Other expenditures	174.3	213.5
TOTALS	474.3	452.5

36 TAXATION

Income from oil concessions is based on royalties, generally at the rate of 50% or higher. Individual or local company incomes are tax exempt. There are no local taxes on livestock or on small agricultural holdings.

37 CUSTOMS AND DUTIES

Customs duties are generally 4% ad valorem, but some goods are admitted duty-free. Imports of liquor are prohibited by law.

38 FOREIGN INVESTMENTS

UK, US, and Japanese interests in oil provide the bulk of the foreign capital invested in Kuwayt. Through tax concessions, Kuwayt welcomes foreign investment in heavy and light industries.

Because of inadequate opportunities for domestic investment, a sizable proportion of public and private savings in Kuwayt (74% in 1973/74) is held in the form of foreign assets. The external income which thus accrues comprises over 10% of the annual GNP.

39 ECONOMIC POLICY

A comprehensive development plan was launched in 1950 and revised in 1954. By 1962, most construction projects were completed and plans were advanced to establish industries that would assure continued prosperity when oil revenues declined.

In 1960, a Board of Construction and Economic Development was established to regulate and control economic and industrial projects. Kuwayt invited five leading international financial experts, including the former president of the IBRD, to devise a plan utilizing Kuwayt's surplus money. The plan, started in 1962/63, includes government-to-government loans, control and encouragement of private investments abroad, developments in Kuwayt, and foreign investments in Kuwayt. In 1974, the government approved loans totaling KD10,748,000, the bulk of which was meant for development of real estate.

40 HEALTH

Nearly all medical facilities and services are available free of charge to Kuwayt residents, citizen and noncitizen alike. In 1949, Kuwayt had 1 small hospital and 4 doctors. By 1974, there were 11 public hospitals and sanatoriums, 48 dental clinics, 286 small dispensaries (located in schools and other public facilities), 44 clinics, 27 maternity centers, and 12 health protection centers. There were 1,089 doctors (104 of them private), 70 dentists, 303 pharmacists, 1,918 nurses, and 258 midwives. A nurses' training school is conducted in conjunction with a 500-bed hospital. The ratios of 1 physician to every 891 persons and 1 bed to every 230 persons compare favorably with those of developed countries. Life expectancy in 1975 averaged 68.8 years.

41 SOCIAL WELFARE

Kuwayt has a widespread system of social welfare on a paternalistic basis, financed by the government's vast oil revenues. It has established welfare services for the poor and spent heavily for waterworks, public gardens, and other public facilities. Virtually all health services are available free of charge.

In 1974, 20,742 persons were receiving government welfare payments totaling KD5,403,000.

42 HOUSING

For centuries, housing in Kuwayt consisted of small cottages, mud houses, huts, and a few larger dwellings built of coral and plastered with cement and limestone. Improved housing for the general population has been a main government objective, as evidenced by the substantial allocation of funds to the Ministry of Public Works for large-scale construction development.

By the end of 1974, the government had built 13,569 standard housing units and allotted them to low-income families. Another government program set aside plots of land for low-income families to build houses with government-advanced loans.

43 EDUCATION

Kuwayt offers its students free education, including free food, clothing, books, stationery, and transportation, from kindergarten through the fourth year of college. In 1974/75, with an education budget of KD62 million, Kuwayt maintained 309 schools with 14,035 teachers and 182,778 students. There were 12,582 pupils and 1,001 teachers in 52 kindergartens; 83,581 students and 4,810 teachers in 111 primary schools; 55,238 students and 4,195 teachers in 90 intermediate schools; 28,520 students and 3,012 teachers in 35 secondary schools; and 2,857 students and 1,017 teachers in 21 vocational schools. Schools below university level are segregated by sex. The children of foreign residents enjoy the same privileges as Kuwayti children.

Kuwayt University was opened in 1966 with 866 students, and in 1973/74 had a teaching staff of 412 and a student enrollment of 4,446. Kuwayti nationals comprised 48.8% of the student body, while students from the Arabian Gulf states made up 18.3% of enrollment. Kuwayti students who complete their secondary-school science courses in the upper 80% of their class and arts courses in the upper 70% are eligible to study abroad at government expense. In 1974/75, 2,637 Kuwaytis were pursuing their higher education overseas, 1,446 of them supported by the Ministry of Education or Kuwayt University. In 1973/74, 446 Kuwayti students graduated from foreign universities.

The government has adopted a program to wipe out illiteracy by opening adult education centers, which, in 1974/75, numbered 125, with an enrollment of 26,075 men and women. The literacy rate, estimated at about 60%, is among the highest in the Arab world.

44 LIBRARIES AND MUSEUMS

The national library in al-Kuwayt has over 36,366 volumes, 27,633 of which are in Arabic; it has established 22 branches throughout the country. Some schools and oil companies maintain special libraries.

The Kuwayt Museum displays ancient Kuwayti artifacts (recovered from excavations on Faylakah Island which date back to 1000 B.C.) as well as plant, bird, and animal life. A collection of birds and reptiles is housed in a private zoo. The Kuwayt Oil Co. maintains a display center pertaining to the oil industry.

45 ORGANIZATIONS

The Ministry of Social Affairs and Labor encourages and supports cultural and recreational organizations and sponsors theatrical activities for youth. Boy Scouts are active. Cultural and recreational centers encourage hobbies and sports among youth.

There is a chamber of commerce in al-Kuwayt.

46 PRESS

In 1974, Kuwayt had 7 daily newspapers and 10 weekly newspapers. Several magazines were also published.

Major daily newspapers (with 1974 circulations) include *Ar-Rai al-ʿAmm* (Arabic, 8,000); *Akhbar al-Kuwait* (Arabic, 4,000); *As-Siyasah* (Arabic, 2,000); and the *Kuwait Times* (English, 2,000). The government's official gazette is the weekly *Al-Kuwait al-Yom* (*Kuwayt Today*). The popular monthly *Al ʿArabi,* similar to the *Reader's Digest,* is widely read in Kuwayt.

47 TOURISM

The government has launched a program designed to facilitate and encourage tourism. Owing to recent construction, al-Kuwayt has become one of the modernized capitals in the world. There are 2 luxury hotels (479 rooms) and 7 first-class hotels (772 rooms). In 1974, a total of 82,554 visitors spent 314,314 days in Kuwayt. Except for Arab or UK nationals, visitors must obtain visas in advance from Kuwayti embassies or consulates; smallpox vaccinations are required, and persons coming from cholera areas must be inoculated.

48 FAMOUS KUWAYTIS

During the reign of Amir Sir ʿAbdallah al-Salim al-Sabah (1870–1965), Kuwayt attained a prominent position among the great oil-producing nations of the world, and the state adopted a social welfare program founded on a unique patriarchal system. The Amir was revered as a man of simplicity, devotion, and deep concern for his people.

49 DEPENDENCIES

Kuwayt has no territories or colonies.

50 BIBLIOGRAPHY

Dickson, Harold Richard Patrick. *Kuwait and Her Neighbors.* Edited by Clifford Witting. London: Allen & Unwin, 1949.

El Mallakh, Ragaei. *Economic Development and Regional Cooperation: Kuwait.* Chicago: University of Chicago Press, 1968.

Freeth, Zahra, and Victor Winstone. *Kuwait: Prospect and Reality.* New York: Crane, Russak, 1972.

International Bank for Reconstruction and Development. *The Economic Development of Kuwait: Report of Missions Organized by the Bank at the Request of the Government of Kuwait.* Baltimore: Johns Hopkins Press, 1965.

Owen, Roderic. *The Golden Bubble: Arabian Gulf Documentary.* London: Collins, 1957.

Wilson, Sir Arnold Talbot. *The Persian Gulf: An Historical Sketch from the Earliest Times to the Beginning of the Twentieth Century.* London: Oxford University Press, 1928.

LAOS

People's Democratic Republic of Laos
Sataranalat Pasatepatay Pasason Lao

CAPITAL: Vientiane. **FLAG:** The new national flag, officially adopted in December 1975, is the former flag of the Pathet Lao; it consists of three horizontal stripes of red, dark blue, and red, with a white disc, representing the full moon, at the center. **ANTHEM:** *Pheng Sat Lao* (Hymn of the Lao People). **MONETARY UNIT:** The kip (K) of 100 cents is a nonconvertible paper currency. There are notes of 1, 5, 20, 50, and 100 kips. K1 = $0.000625 (or $1 = K1,600). It is expected that the currency of the Pathet Lao will gradually be brought into general use. **WEIGHTS AND MEASURES:** The metric system has been the legal standard, but older local units also are used. **HOLIDAYS:** Labor Day, 1 May; Independence Day, 19 July. Certain Buddhist festivals also are observed as national holidays: New Year (in April); Boun Bang-Fai, the celebration of the birth, enlightenment, and death of the Buddha (in May); the Water Holiday (in October); and the That Luang, a pagoda pilgrimage holiday (in November). A Lenten season for bonzes (Buddhist monks) lasts from July to October. **TIME:** 7 P.M. = noon GMT.

¹LOCATION, SIZE, AND EXTENT

Laos is a landlocked country in the Indochinese Peninsula near the eastern extremity of mainland Southeast Asia. Laos occupies an area of 236,800 sq km (91,429 sq mi), extending *1,162* km (*722* mi) SSE–NNW and *478* km (*297* mi) ENE–WSW. It is bordered on the N by China, on the E and SE by Viet-Nam, on the S by Kampuchea, on the W by Thailand, and on the NW by Burma, with a total boundary length of *4,513* km (*2,804* mi).

²TOPOGRAPHY

The terrain is rugged and mountainous, especially in the north, where jagged crests tower more than 8,000 feet. This mountainous northern region and the eastern part of the country bordering Viet-Nam are covered with thick forests. The Tran Ninh Plateau north of Xieng Khouang is a relatively low area, varying from 3,600 to 4,500 feet in height. From it flow rivers in three directions—east, south, and west. The highest point in Laos, Pou Bia (9,242 feet), is just south of this plateau. East of Pakse is the fertile Boloven Plateau, at about 3,500 feet. Toward the south are broad plains areas watered by many streams. Much of the country's rice is grown in these plains and low hills. Except for three passes, most of Laos is cut off from Viet-Nam by the Annamite Cordillera.

Except for Houa Phan Province and a relatively small area east of the main divide, most of Laos is dominated by the Mekong and its tributaries. The Mekong flows in a broad valley along the border with Thailand and through Laos for several hundred miles. In its low-water phase it is almost dry, but it rises more than 20 feet during the monsoon period. The river is wide but, except between Vientiane and Savannakhet, rapids are numerous, while below Savannakhet and at the extreme south there are large rapids and waterfalls. All the larger towns are situated on or near the Mekong.

³CLIMATE

Laos has a tropical climate with two main seasons, rainy and dry, each of five months' duration. From May through September, rainfall averages from 11 to 12 inches a month, but from November through March the monthly average is about half an inch. Humidity is high throughout the year, even during the season of drought. The hottest month is April. Temperatures fluctuate between 22°C and 34°C (72°F and 93°F). January is cool, with temperatures 14°C to 28.4°C (57°F to 83°F). In the spring strong winds blow from the south.

⁴FLORA AND FAUNA

Nearly two-thirds of Laos is covered by forests. Those of the lower part of the country are a northward extension of the Kampuchean type of vegetation, while the highland forests of the upper section are closer to central Viet-Nam in character, consisting of prairies interspersed with thickets. Bamboo, lianas, rattan, and palms are found throughout Laos.

Roaming the virgin forests are panthers and a dwindling number of tigers, elephants, and leopards. The elephant, until 1975 depicted on the national flag as the traditional symbol of Lao royalty, has been used throughout history as a beast of burden. A local breed of water buffalo also is universally used as a draft animal. Reptiles include cobras, geckos, kraits, and Siamese crocodiles. There are many varieties of birds, fish, and insects.

As of 1975, endangered species in Laos included the douc langur, Asiatic wild dog, leopard, clouded leopard, Indochinese tiger, Asian elephant, Sumatran rhinoceros, Thailand brow-antlered deer, Asiatic buffalo, gaur, kouprey, giant ibis, imperial pheasant, river terrapin, and Burmese python.

⁵POPULATION

A formal census has never been taken. The estimated population in 1975 was 3,303,000. The population is increasing at a rate of 2.4% per year; projected 1980 population is 3,721,000. The sparse population is unevenly spread, with the greatest concentration (up to 180 persons per sq mi) in the Mekong Valley. More than 89% of the population is rural, living in some 9,000 villages. The capital, Vientiane, had a population of about 181,000 in 1975. Other large towns include Savannakhet (52,000); Pakse (46,000); Luang Prabang, the former royal capital (45,000); Sayabouri (14,000); and Houei Sai (10,000).

⁶ETHNIC GROUPS

About 56% of the inhabitants are lowland Lao, comprising the Lao-lum (valley Lao, about 40% of the total) and Lao-tai (16%); both groups are ethnically related to the Thai. The remainder are Lao-theung and Lao-soung, or upland Lao, tribal groups in the highlands, most of whom are racially related to the Thai (though not as closely as the lowland Lao). The customs and religions of such tribes as the Ho, Kha, Kho, Lü, Man (Yao), and Meo are considerably different from those of the lowland Lao. The Man and the Meo, the Ho and the Kho, relatively recent immigrants, are strongly influenced by neighboring China.

About 50,000 foreign nationals, mainly Vietnamese and a smaller number of Chinese, live in Laos.

7 LANGUAGE

Lao, the official language, is closely related to the Thai language. It is monosyllabic and tonal, and contains words borrowed from Sanskrit, Pali, and Persian. Pali, a Sanskrit language, is used among the Buddhist priesthood.

The Lao-tai of the northern mountain valleys also speak a language closely related to Thai. The Kha, who live mainly in the mountains, speak various Mon-Khmer dialects akin to that spoken in Kampuchea. The northernmost groups are linguistically related to the Chinese. Some groups speak Lolo dialects.

French, the second language, is widely used in government and commerce. Many Laotians learned English during the last decade.

8 RELIGION

Nearly all the lowland Lao are adherents of Hinayana Buddhism, and a large part of their daily life is shaped by its rituals and precepts. Buddhist temples, found in every village, town, and city, serve as intellectual as well as religious centers. Vientiane and Luang Prabang are called "cities of thousands of temples." More than 70 pagodas were built in Vientiane alone in the 17th century, including the famous Vat Phra Kéo and the That Luang. Despite the major role that Buddhism, its temples, and its priests have played in Laotian life, the average lowland Lao regulates a large part of his day's activities in accordance with animistic concepts. Certain spirits (phi) are believed to have great power over the destinies of men and to be present throughout the material world as well as within nonmaterial realms. Thus, each of the four universal elements (earth, sky, fire, water) has its special phi; every road, stream, village, house, and person has a particular phi. Forests and jungles are inhabited by phi. Evil phi can cause disease and must be propitiated by sacrifices.

The upland tribes are almost exclusively animists and, although influenced to some extent by Buddhism, their indigenous beliefs predominate.

Christian missionaries have been active in Laos, but converts are comparatively few.

9 TRANSPORTATION

Lack of adequate transportation facilities has been a major deterrent to economic progress. Of the approximately 7,500 km of roads, fewer than 3,500 km are passable in the rainy season. Roadways have been improved with US, French, and Thai assistance; Nam Ca Dinh Highway was completed in 1965. Much work has been done on the 275-km road linking Vientiane and Luang Prabang, rendered inoperable by the war. In early 1975, the Democratic Republic of Viet-Nam (DRV) government agreed to reconstruct Viet-Nam's major links with Laos, including the road linking Pakane, on the Mekong, to Vinh, on the Gulf of Tonkin. China is now assisting in the construction of a road from Luang Prabang to Pak Bang, as part of a new network in the north that will lead into both Viet-Nam and China. In 1973, 14,910 motor vehicles were registered in the Vientiane zone. There are no railroads in Laos.

Major cities in Laos are connected by air services operated by several small airlines and by Air Laos, which also links Vientiane with Thailand, Kampuchea, Viet-Nam, and Hong Kong. Air France and Aeroflot also provide international service from Vientiane airport. In 1976, auxiliary domestic air services were being provided by Soviet personnel and equipment, in a role similar to that performed by Air America, a US enterprise financed by the CIA. There are 6 airports in the country, some 30 airstrips of more than 1,800 feet, and another 100 of lesser length.

A landlocked country, Laos has no water connection with the outside world except the Mekong, which forms a large part of the border with Thailand and flows through Kampuchea and Viet-Nam into the South China Sea. The Mekong is navigable for small transport craft and connects a 1,405-km inland waterway system, but rapids make necessary the transshipment of cargo. The recent war deprived Laos of its shortest link to the outside world by way of Viet-Nam to the Gulf of Tonkin, with the result that most goods have had to be shipped by way of Bangkok. Infrastructural work under way since 1975, however, promised to restore in part the shorter and cheaper outlet via Tonkin.

10 COMMUNICATIONS

All communications, including the radio network, are operated by the government's Telecommunications and Postal Service. In 1974 there were 5,500 telephones in the country. A direct telephone link to Bangkok was inaugurated in 1967, and connections with several other capitals were subsequently established. Regular radio broadcasts were begun from Vientiane in 1968; there were an estimated 102,000 radios in the country in 1973.

11 HISTORY

The lowland Laotians are descendants of Thai tribes that were pushed southward in the 13th century. In the mid-1300s, a powerful unified kingdom called Lan Xang was established by Fa-Ngoum, who is also credited with the introduction of Hinayana Buddhism in Laos. Lan Xang waged intermittent wars with the Khmers, Burmese, Vietnamese, and Thai and developed an effective administrative system, an elaborate military organization, and an active commerce with neighboring countries. In 1707, internal dissensions brought about a split of Lan Xang into two kingdoms: Luang Prabang in present-day upper, or northern, Laos and Vientiane in lower, or southern, Laos. Strong neighboring states took advantage of this split to invade the region. Vientiane was overrun and annexed by Siam (Thailand) in 1828. Luang Prabang became a vassal of both the Chinese and Vietnamese. This expansionism led to the establishment of a French protectorate over Laos in 1893.

The present boundaries of the kingdom of Laos follow those of the French protectorate over the kingdom of Luang Prabang. Siam abandoned its claims of suzerainty over Laos in 1893, and in the first decade of the 20th century concluded treaties with France whereby the borders of Laos were modified to the advantage of France. Although French control over Luang Prabang took the nominal form of a protectorate, the French colonial administration directly ruled the rest of Laos, legal justification being ultimately provided in the Lao-French convention of 1917. A new convention enlarged the kingdom of Luang Prabang to include two northern provinces in 1941, but the remainder of the country continued to be administered directly by France until 1945. Laos was one of five territories included within former French Indochina.

After the Japanese proclaimed on 10 March 1945 that "the colonial status of Indochina has ended," the king of Luang Prabang was compelled to issue a declaration of independence. On 27 August 1946, France concluded an agreement with the king of Luang Prabang, establishing him as king of Laos and reestablishing French domination over the country.

On 19 July 1949, Laos nominally became an independent sovereign state within the French Union. Additional conventions transferring full sovereignty to Laos were signed on 6 February 1950 and on 22 October 1953. All special economic ties with France and the other Indochinese states were abolished by the Paris pacts of 29 December 1954.

In the meantime, however, Vietnamese Communist (Viet-Minh) forces invaded Laos in the spring of 1953. A Laotian Communist movement, called the Pathet Lao (Lao State), led by Prince Souphanouvong, was created on 13 August 1950 and collaborated with the Viet-Minh during its Laos offensive. In the Geneva cease-fire of 21 July 1954, Laos lost control of the provinces of Samneua (now Houa Phan) and Phong Saly to the Pathet Lao. Reunification negotiations with Prince Souphanouvong were consummated on 2 November 1957, and the Pathet Lao transformed itself into a legal political party under the name of Neo Lao Hak Xat. A political swing to the right and refusal of the Pathet Lao forces to integrate into the Royal Lao Army led to an outbreak of fighting in May 1959.

A right-wing bloodless coup in January 1960 was answered in August by a coup led by paratroops, under the command of Capt. Kong Lê. It brought to power Prince Souvanna Phouma, who had been prime minister several times previously. Right-wing military elements under Gen. Phoumi Nosavan and Prince Boun Oum occupied the capital on 11 December, after a three-day artillery battle that destroyed much of the city. A new right-wing government under Prince Boun Oum was established, but further military reverses, despite a heavy influx of US aid and advisers, caused the government to ask for a cease-fire in May 1961. An international conference assembled in Geneva to guarantee the cease-fire. All three Laotian political factions agreed to accept Prince Souvanna Phouma as prime minister on 11 June 1962. On 23 July, the powers assembled at Geneva signed an agreement on the independence and neutrality of Laos which provided for the evacuation of all foreign forces by 7 October. The US announced full compliance, under supervision of the International Control Commission (ICC) set up in 1954. Communist forces were not withdrawn.

Fighting resumed in the spring of 1963. The ICC was unable to visit Communist-held territory because of Pathet Lao objections. As the 1960s advanced, Laos was steadily drawn into the role of a main theater in the escalating Viet-Nam war. The Laotian segment of the Ho Chi Minh trail emerged as a vital supply route for DRV troops and supplies moving south and was the target for heavy and persistent US bombing raids. While the Vientiane government was heavily bolstered by US military and economic support, the Pathet Lao received key support from the DRV, which was reported to have 20,000 troops stationed in Laos by 1974.

Efforts to negotiate a settlement in Laos began with US backing in 1971, but a settlement was not concluded until February 1973, a month after the US officially ended its direct military presence in Viet-Nam. On 5 April 1974, Laos' third coalition government was set up, with equal representation for Pathet Lao and non-Communist elements. Souvanna Phouma, 73 and in failing health, stayed on as prime minister, while Prince Souphanouvong was brought closer to the center of political authority as head of the newly created Joint National Political Council. The Pathet Lao had by this time asserted its control over three-fourths of the national territory and, following the fall of the US-backed regimes in Viet-Nam and Cambodia (now Kampuchea) in April 1975, the Laotian Communists embarked on a campaign to achieve complete military and political supremacy in Laos. Pro-Vientiane villages and strongholds fell to the new Pathet Lao advance, and in June 1975, Communist pressure forced the closure of the AID mission in Vientiane, a bulwark of US influence in the country. Rightist officials began fleeing Laos during the summer, and on 15 August the US announced termination of its Laotian military operations at Udon Thani (Udorn) airbase in northeast Thailand, thus signaling the end to more than two decades of US military presence in Laos. On 23 August, Vientiane was pronounced "liberated" by the Pathet Lao, whose effective control of Laos was thereupon secured.

On 2 December 1975, the establishment of the People's Democratic Republic of Laos was declared, with Prince Souphanouvong as president and Kaysone Phoumvihan as prime minister. King Savang Vatthana abdicated his throne, thus ending the monarchy that had survived in Laos for 622 years. Elec-

tions for a new National Assembly were called for April 1976; however, voting was put off amid reports of civil unrest and sabotage. A People's Supreme Council was convened meanwhile, with Prince Souphanouvong as chairman, and began the task of drafting a new constitution.

12 GOVERNMENT

According to the constitution of 1947 (amended in 1952 and 1956), Laos was a parliamentary democracy with a king as the nominal chief executive. The monarch was assisted by a prime minister (or president of the Council of Ministers), who was the executive and legislative leader in fact. The prime minister and cabinet were responsible to the National Assembly, the main repository of legislative authority. Its 59 members were elected every five years by universal adult suffrage.

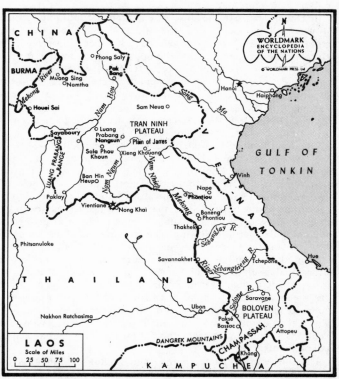

See continental political: front cover O8; physical: back cover O8

LOCATION: 100° to 107°E; 13°40′ to 22°40′N. BOUNDARY LENGTHS: China, 425 km (264 mi); Viet-Nam, 1,555 km (966 mi); Kampuchea, 541 km (336 mi); Thailand, 1,754 km (1,090 mi); Burma, 238 km (148 mi).

With the establishment of the People's Democratic Republic of Laos in December 1975, the Provisional Government and the Joint National Political Council—both executive organs of the coalition government of April 1974—resigned. On 29 November, King Savang Vatthana had abdicated, and governmental authority thus passed to a national congress made up of 264 delegates elected by newly appointed local authorities. The congress, meeting in Vientiane during 1–2 December, in turn appointed a 45-member People's Supreme Council (which included 9 members of the former Vientiane side of the civil war) to draw up a new constitution and named a new government headed by Kaysone Phoumvihan, a long-time Pathet Lao leader.

13 POLITICAL PARTIES

Elections to the National Assembly were first held in 1947. In the elections of 4 May 1958, the Pathet Lao's newly organized

National Political Front (Neo Lao Hak Xat—NPF) won 9 of the 21 seats in contention; 4 were won by the Santiphab faction, a neutralist group allied with them; and 8 were obtained by the Nationalist and Independent parties.

After the elections, the Nationalists and Independents combined to establish a new political party, the Rally of the Lao People (Lao Luam Lao—RLP), which held 36 of the 59 Assembly seats. The remaining 23 seats were divided among the NPF (9), the Santiphab grouping (7), the Democrats (3), the National Union (2), and 2 unaffiliated deputies. The leaders of the RLP, upon formation of that party, announced its purpose to be the defense of Laos against "an extremist ideology contrary to the customs and traditions of the Lao country" and the establishment of true unity and independence of the nation against "subversion from within and without." The NPF then and later called for a reduction in the size of the armed forces and of US military aid.

In December 1959, because of emergency conditions, Prime Minister Phoui postponed the election of new Assembly deputies until April 1960 and extended his special powers. This led to a split between him and the opposition Committee for the Defense of the National Interests (CDIN), which had urged earlier elections and the appointment of a caretaker government for the interim period. The resulting crisis forced Phoui's resignation.

The CDIN won a landslide victory in the elections of 24 April 1960, and Phoumi Nosavan, CDIN leader, formed a new political party, the Social Democrats (Paxa Sangkhom—SD). In August 1960, a coup led by Capt. Kong Lê brought down the government. Prince Souvanna Phouma became prime minister on 11 June 1962. In his 19-man cabinet, 4 posts were held by right-wing politicians, 11 by neutralists, and 4 others by Pathet Lao adherents. A Neutralist Party (Lao Pen Khang) had been set up by Souvanna Phouma in 1961, for the purpose of giving his side a popular-based following. The National Assembly came to the end of its five-year term in 1965. Political instability prevented the holding of national elections, and therefore a provisional assembly was convened to amend the constitution so as to provide a means for maintaining the legislature. The result was a general election held on 18 July and limited to civil servants, teachers, merchants, and village headmen. The new National Assembly was convened on 16 August, with the Neutralists retaining 13 seats, the SD 11, the RLP 8, and various independents 27.

The endorsement gained in the limited polling of 1965 was not sufficient to sustain Prime Minister Souvanna Phouma for long, and new voting—the first real and effective election in a decade —took place on 1 January 1967. About 60% of 800,000 eligible voters went to the polls in 1967, despite the Pathet Lao charge that the balloting was illegal. Souvanna Phouma's United Front took 32 of 59 seats in the National Assembly voting.

In the ensuing five years, the gulf between the Pathet Lao, on the one hand, and the enclave of rightists and neutralists that opposed them, on the other, widened appreciably. The pressures of war—both the civil strife within Laos and the larger conflict pressed by the external forces of the US and DRV—had thwarted the effectiveness of normal political processes. General elections held on 2 January 1972 were confined to government-controlled areas, with representatives for the Pathet Lao provinces elected by refugees from those regions. Despite the narrow range of political choices available to voters, only 20 of the 60 National Assembly deputies were reelected, reflecting a growing uneasiness with both the war and with the increasing evidence of corrupt practices among government officials. Despite right-wing pressures from within the Assembly, Souvanna Phouma—whose neutrality was favored by both the US and the DRV—retained the position of prime minister.

Through the mid-1970s, external events continued to presage developments in Laotian domestic politics. The withdrawal of US military support for the Thieu regime in Saigon was followed in April 1974 by the creation of a new coalition in Vientiane that gave equal political footing to the Pathet Lao. The National Assembly, which had become little more than a forum for disputes among right-wing factions, was dissolved by the king on 13 April 1975, an act that signaled the end of domestic political opposition to the inexorable progress of the Pathet Lao.

The formation of the Democratic People's Republic of Laos in December 1975 effectively established the Pathet Lao as the sole political force in Laos. Kaysone Phomvihan, general secretary of the Lao People's Revolutionary Party (the successor to the NFP that now forms the political core of the Pathet Lao) was named prime minister of the new government and Prince Souphanouvong, president of the country. Elections for a new National Assembly, called for April 1976, were subsequently postponed.

14 LOCAL GOVERNMENT

As of mid-1975, Laos was comprised of 16 provinces (khoueng). The provinces in turn were subdivided into districts (muong), each headed by a chaomuong. Districts were composed of townships (tasseng) and villages (ban). Under the Pathet Lao, local administration has been restructured, with elected people's committees in the villages functioning as basic units. During late August 1975, the Pathet Lao set up people's revolutionary committees to govern the provinces. Local police forces were replaced by workers' militia units. The Joint National Political Council, meeting in October, provided for elections to be held every three years for provincial and city councils, every two years for provincial capital councils, and annually for district capital councils. Both suffrage and candidacy were opened to all citizens 18 and over. The elections were to be organized and supervised by the Pathet Lao, with the stipulation that the number of candidates exceed the number of vacancies. In early November 1975, the first nationwide local elections under the new system were held.

15 JUDICIAL SYSTEM

Under the Pathet Lao, the Central Supreme Court in Vientiane has functioned as the highest court of the land. Under previous governments, jurisdiction over the constitutionality of legislation was reserved to the King's Council, the upper house of the National Assembly. The judicial system also included a court of appeals, 3 criminal courts (sitting at Vientiane, Pakse, and Luang Prabang), 1 provincial tribunal for each provincial capital, and 37 district justices of the peace. Reorganization of the judiciary was expected under the constitution being prepared in 1976.

16 ARMED FORCES

The Royal Lao Army in late 1974 numbered about 52,000 men. By the summer of 1975, most units had disbanded, and nearly all of the leadership had fled the country. The Lao People's Liberation Army (the Pathet Lao fighting forces) probably totaled no more than 35,000 (including neutralist defectors and DRV cadres and technical advisers) by mid-1975. As of early 1976, the DRV still maintained about 30,000 troops in Laos.

17 MIGRATION

There has been only limited population movement into Laos in modern times. During the last decade, under pressure of combat operations, Black Thai tribesmen moved southward into the Mekong Valley. From May 1975 until the final victory of the Pathet Lao, thousands of Lao refugees crossed into Thailand. In December 1975, the Thai government reported that 54,821 Lao refugees were living in the country. Illegal movements in both directions prompted the Thai government to close its Laos border on 17 November; after Laos assured the Thais that it would not interfere with Thai patrol boats on the Mekong, the border was reopened at two points on 1 January 1976.

[18] INTERNATIONAL COOPERATION

A member of the UN since 1955, Laos has participated in most of the specialized agencies. Laos has also been a member of the Colombo Plan Council and other intergovernmental organizations.

By terms of the 1954 Geneva agreements, Laos was barred from a military alliance with any country except France, but in February 1959 it denounced the Geneva accords. US aid to Laos began on 1 January 1955. Through the mid-1970s, US assistance averaged about $50 million annually, comprising about 70% of total external assistance. In mid-1975, following the closing down of the AID mission in Vientiane, US funding to Laos halted abruptly, although both sides of the government had argued that continued aid would be welcomed provided it was tendered without political conditions. Aid from France (totaling $6.3 million in 1975) nonetheless continued through 1976; by late 1975 assistance from other sources—including a $25-million loan from China—began to materialize.

In 1976, Laos' diplomatic relations with Thailand and the US remained intact, although severely strained. Recognition was quickly extended by the DRV, China, USSR, the Democratic People's Republic of Korea, Cuba, Iraq, and Pakistan, as well as by France, the UK, Australia, and other nations. Several economic and technical consultants from the Asian Development Bank, IBRD, and the Mekong Committee have remained working in the country.

[19] ECONOMY

Laos is overwhelmingly agricultural, with some 95% of the population engaged in farming. Because industrialization is limited, Laos imports nearly all the manufactured products it requires. Distribution of imports is limited almost entirely to Vientiane and a few other towns, and even there consumption is low. Economic progress has been impeded by the inaccessibility of potentially productive areas; the backward nature of agriculture; the absence of widely based skills, capital, and investment traditions; and the lack of coherent economic planning.

The hostilities of recent decades badly disrupted the economy, penetrating to the subsistence sector, which was since forced to depend on imports from Thailand to supplement its daily rice requirements. Since the mid-1960s, only the continuing flow of economic aid from the US, France, the UK, and Australia has managed to stave off total bankruptcy. In 1975, free rice shipments were received from the DRV (20,000 tons), China (10,000 tons), and Australia, although adequate replacements for US funding, cut off in midyear, had not yet been secured.

The mere presence of a unified political structure offered an immediate advantage to Laos' postwar recovery. With ample mineral resources and hydroelectric potential, the government began in late 1975 to pursue in earnest a variety of development projects to improve the infrastructure and thus gain better access to the country's prospective wealth. A five-year plan (1976–80) gave priority to gaining self-sufficiency in food.

[20] INCOME

The GNP for the Vientiane (e.g. non-Pathet Lao) zone was estimated at K36,700 million in 1974/75; per capita GNP was put at K35,000.

[21] LABOR

In the early 1970s, the work force totaled some 1,600,000, of whom about 80% were employed in agriculture, 15% in services, and 5% in industry.

Forced labor was abolished by the French, but prior to the Pathet Lao victory, a form of corvée was permitted in the Kha territory in northern Laos, and in some areas workers were requisitioned for porterage. In the former Vientiane zone, the only labor group of any kind was the Government Employees Association. Since late 1975, labor has been organized into the Pathet Lao's Labor Federation.

[22] AGRICULTURE

In 1972/73, Laos' cultivated area totaled 6,922 sq km, or only about 3% of the country's total area. Less than 300 sq km was irrigated. The main crop is rice, almost entirely of the glutinous variety. Except in northern Laos, where some farmers grow dry rice in forest clearings or on hillsides, most Lao are wet-rice farmers. The total rice crop area is estimated to be 550,000 hectares, and the yield is relatively low. Production, which averaged 609,000 tons annually during 1961–65, reached a peak of 904,000 tons in 1970, and fell back to 883,000 in 1973. Rice production is still insufficient to feed the population, and about 70,000 tons are imported annually. This deficit, however, is considered readily amenable to elimination through improved methods and extended irrigation. Vegetables are grown by most lowland farm families. Fruit and nut trees are extensively cultivated. Other agricultural commodities are corn, cardamom, coffee, tea, cotton, ramie, hemp, and tobacco. The mountain peoples have been known to grow large quantities of opium poppies, sold to dealers in the plains; this practice was the target of increased government sanctions in the mid-1970s.

The Pathet Lao government announced in late 1975 that the right of land ownership would be retained. The large holdings of absentee landlords were expropriated, however, and the land redistributed to peasant farmers. Plots were nevertheless set aside for the use of the landlords' families. The government offered assistance in the form of mechanized equipment to landlords who remained in Laos. Control of all water resources reverted to the government.

[23] ANIMAL HUSBANDRY

Cattle raising is important, especially in the southern plains and in the valleys of the Sebanghieng, Sedone, and Sebangfay rivers. Animal husbandry is primarily a household affair and has a profound effect on the social structure as well as the economic pattern of southern Laos. By 1964, increased production eliminated the need for cattle imports. In 1973 there were an estimated 450,000 head of cattle and 1,250 hogs in Laos. The war caused wholesale decimation of the livestock population. In 1976, teams of workers were being used in place of buffalo to pull plows.

[24] FISHING

Edible fish, found in the Mekong and other rivers, constitutes the main source of protein in the Laotian diet. The prize catch is the pa beuk, weighing 450 pounds and more. Despite the abundance of fish and their important contribution to the Laotian subsistence economy, there has been no systematic commercial development of the fishing areas.

[25] FORESTRY

About two-thirds of the total area is forested, and at least half of the forested area is commercially exploitable. Under pre-Pathet Lao governments, forests were part of the national domain, but they could be leased to private firms for exploitation. Lumbering is carried on in every region of Laos. The largest quantities come from Champassac, Savannakhet, Thakhek, and Vientiane. Paklay in western Laos is noted for its teak. Exploitation is easiest in areas near the Mekong River, which facilitates transportation. Elephants and oxen are used in most forestry operations. Aside from timber, firewood, and charcoal, other forestry products include benzoin and benzoin bark, bamboo, copra, kapok, palm oil, rattan, various resins, and sticklac.

[26] MINING

Although much of the country remains unprospected, the nature of the terrain has led to ardent speculation about future prospects for development. Such hopes were in part borne out by the discovery, in 1974, of a potash-rich sylvite field in the middle of the Vientiane plain; the deposit, which covers at least 30 sq km, is expected to yield 10 million cu meters per sq km. Exploitation of the sylvite, which can be used for the manufacture of fertilizers, soap, pharmaceuticals, and pesticides, was being sought by a variety of interests, including the USSR, German Democratic Republic, and Canada.

Tin and rock salt are the most important minerals now being exploited. The most accessible tin deposits are those at Phontiou and Nangsun; production totaled 1,300 tons in 1974 (1,230 tons in 1967), but utilization is well below full potential. Important iron deposits, with reserves of 68% ore estimated at 1 billion tons, have been discovered on the Plain of Jarres near Xieng Khouang. Traces of oil also have been found near Pakse and Vientiane, and an agreement has been signed with a French firm to explore the deposits. A substantial deposit of low-grade anthracite coal has been found at Saravane. Other mineral resources known to exist in Laos include antimony, copper, gold, gypsum, lead, manganese, pyrites, sulfur, and precious stones. Tungsten and copper deposits and gold-bearing alluvials produce a limited income for the local population, but have not been exploited by modern industrial methods.

27 ENERGY AND POWER

Laos' hydroelectric potential is vast, although development has begun only recently. Construction of the long-heralded Nam Ngum Dam 72 km north of Vientiane began in 1969, with the first stage completed in 1971. The power station will eventually have a capacity of 110,000 kw. The second stage of the project, which would also irrigate 5,000 hectares, was begun in 1975. In 1975, 76% of the electricity produced at Nam Ngum was exported to Thailand.

The overall output of electricity in Laos expanded by more than 1,300% in 1972 as a result of Nam Ngum entry into production. In 1973, total output was 245 million kwh (26 million kwh in 1968). Electricity is available in Vientiane, Luang Prabang, Savannakhet, Thakhek, Pakse, and Saravane, and is being introduced elsewhere. Aside from Nam Ngum, all electric power is generated thermally.

28 INDUSTRY

For lack of power and transport facilities, industry in Laos has been almost nonexistent. There are some small mining operations, charcoal ovens, about 30 sawmills, a cement plant, a few brick works, carpenter shops, a tobacco factory, rice mills, some furniture factories, and several construction projects. New industries projected are cotton spinning, brewing, coffee and tea processing, and plywood milling. New resource developments, including the Nam Ngum hydroelectric project and the Vientiane sylvite field, should provide significant impetus to industry.

Although handicraft products are produced mainly for home consumption, handicrafts account for an important part of the income of many Laotions. Some villages or areas specialize in certain types of products: silk fabrics, baskets, lacquerware, gold and silver jewelry and ornaments. Bricks, pottery, iron products, and distilled beverages are made in individual villages.

29 DOMESTIC TRADE

Prior to the coming to power of the Pathet Lao, there was a growing market in Laos for capital and consumer goods. Vientiane was the wholesale distributing point for much of the country. In late 1975, however, a large number of small traders and businessmen, many of them Chinese, Japanese, Pakistani, Thai, and Vietnamese, fled the country. The new government subsequently made it clear that the recent trend toward consumerism would be reversed in favor of a production-oriented society. In the early stages of reorganization, the Pathet Lao entered directly into the distribution and sale of essential commodities such as rice and sugar. As a result, the soaring prices of many items were brought under control.

In the countryside, markets are held at regular intervals, generally one day a week, at central villages or smaller towns. Once or twice a year lowland farmers barter cloth and handicraft products with the mountain peoples for cereals, deer and rhinoceros horns, and ivory. Certain items have been recognized as currency: brick tea, opium, tobacco, salt, silver, and gold.

Usual hours of business are from 9 A.M. until noon and from 3 to 6 P.M. There are no advertising agencies or commercial credit companies.

30 FOREIGN TRADE

Imports increased dramatically during 1967–70, but fell off sharply through 1974. Both trends in large measure followed the pattern of US funding, having been financed largely by US underwriting of the Foreign Exchange Operations Fund (FEOF), a stabilizing device. By mid-1975, in anticipation of the withdrawal of US financing, Laos had secured some $63 million in commodity aid support, with China the largest single source. Tin and wood are traditionally the most important commodity exports, together accounting for more than half of the country's sales abroad.

Principal exports in 1970 and 1973 for the Vientiane zone (in thousands of dollars) were:

	1970	1973
Wood	1,677	3,164
Tin	2,568	1,514
Food and live animals	395	41
Cotton	239	28
Coffee	370	25
Leather and hides	67	17
Other exports	1,878	302
TOTALS	7,194	5,091

Principal imports in 1970 and 1973 for the Vientiane zone (in thousands of dollars) were:

	1970	1973
Food	18,793	15,093
Machinery and transport equipment	21,105	12,223
Mineral fuels	25,844	10,625
Miscellaneous manufactured goods	5,573	1,953
Textiles	4,873	1,444
Cement	5,711	1,078
Other imports	31,972	12,298
TOTALS	113,871	54,714

The political transition of 1975 began to have an immediate impact on Laos' trade patterns, with the DRV, France, and China taking a more dominant role, and the US virtually disappearing as a factor. Principal trade partners of the Vientiane zone in 1973 (in thousands of dollars) were:

	EXPORTS	IMPORTS	BALANCE
Thailand	3,312	30,725	−27,413
Japan	86	6,432	− 6,346
Indonesia	1	5,376	− 5,375
US	3	2,942	− 2,939
Hong Kong	123	2,698	− 2,575
Singapore	20	1,577	− 1,557
Other countries	1,546	4,964	− 3,418
TOTALS	5,091	54,714	−49,623

31 BALANCE OF PAYMENTS

Laos has experienced severe trade deficits throughout the war-torn years of the 1960s and early 1970s. The trade balance in 1974 showed a deficit of more than $40 million ($88.6 million worth of exports as contrasted with $129 million worth of imports). From 1963 through mid-1975, however, substantial deficit financing was provided through the FEOF, an agency largely backed by the US, but also receiving funds from Japan, France, the UK, and Australia. FEOF holdings totaled $22 million in 1974, but fell to $12.5 million in 1975 (the agency was expected to be scrapped during 1976 by the Pathet Lao government). Foreign currency reserves meanwhile fell from $13.7 million at the end of 1974 to about $5.5 million in mid-1975. In June 1975, the flight of gold and hard currencies from the country forced the government to ban exports of gold and silver bullion. A devaluation of the kip (to K1,200 per $1) had the effect of further inflating its price, with the black market exchange rate soaring as high as K3,000 per $1. In late 1975, some measure of stability appeared to be returning.

³²BANKING
The National Bank of Laos, which began operations in 1955 in Vientiane, has had the exclusive right to issue currency and control foreign exchange. It has also had the authority to supervise and control the five commercial banks and to control credit. The first commercial bank was established in 1953, when the Bank of Indochina opened an agency in Vientiane that subsequently became a branch bank. Other commercial banks operating in early 1975 included the Lao-Vieng Bank, the Bank of Tokyo, the Lao Thai Bank, and the Lao Commercial Bank. The large-scale flight of foreign currency that accompanied the Pathet Lao's ascendency to power forced the new government to shut down Vientiane's banks in September 1975. Officials subsequently announced the expropriation of most private accounts, claiming they were the property of former rightists and "traitors." Foreign exchange reserves as of June 1975 stood at $5.5 million, as compared with $13.7 million at the end of 1974.

The supply of money in Laos increased in the mid-1960s and 1970s, rising from K4.1 billion in 1962 to K12.2 billion in 1964, K12.9 billion in 1969, and to K36.7 billion by the end of 1974. At that time, private bank deposits stood at K5.1 billion. Bank loans and advances stood at K6.9 billion as of June 1974, as compared with K5.1 billion in June 1973.

³³INSURANCE
As of mid-1975, regulations for insurance firms had not been enacted. Third-party liability insurance is compulsory for common carriers.

³⁴SECURITIES
There are no securities exchanges in Laos, but prior to mid-1975 Laotians were permitted to own foreign securities.

³⁵PUBLIC FINANCE
The civil war rendered normal budgetary procedures impossible, the budget having been covered largely by US aid and monetary inflation. The Laotian budget for fiscal 1975 (Vientiane zone only) showed estimated receipts of K19.6 million and expenditures of K37.6 million. Actual spending throughout the 1965–75 period is known to have exceeded expenditures in connection with the war effort against the Pathet Lao. Similarly, while budgeted income for 1974/75 was put at about $14 million, more than $50 million was known to have been received from US aid sources alone. Foreign aid and National Bank financing make up the deficit between budgeted revenues and expenditure. More than 60% of the wartime budget was devoted to the support of the armed forces.

Budgeted revenues and expenditures for 1969 and estimates for 1974 (in millions of kips) were as follows:

REVENUES	1969	1974
Import and customs duties	4,976.0	3,381.0
Direct taxes	597.0	865.0
Registration tax	184.0	280.0
Other indirect taxes	757.0	2,205.0
Income from services	450.0	2,131.2
Other revenues	140.0	4,923.3
TOTALS	7,104.0	13,785.5

EXPENDITURES		
Defense	8,494.0	14,142.5
State administration	2,544.6	3,069.5
Education and culture	1,364.7	2,564.0
Social security and health	495.7	892.9
Debt services	183.0	550.0
Transfers	154.4	486.5
Development expenditures	–	353.0
Other expenditures	2,728.1	6,727.1
TOTALS	15,964.5	28,785.5

Total budget figures for 1966, 1969, 1973, and estimates for 1974 (in millions of kips) were as follows:

	REVENUES	EXPENDITURES	DEFICIT
1966	4,570	14,072	– 9,502
1969	7,104	15,965	– 8,861
1973	8,008	22,807	–14,799
1974	13,786	28,786	–15,000

³⁶TAXATION
Because there is little commerce and most of the inhabitants remain outside the money sector of the economy, direct and indirect taxes have been of limited significance in Laos. Until 1974, customs duties (entirely on imports) provided more than half of total government revenues. Income taxes provided less than 10%, while indirect taxes contributed 13% in 1969 and 18% in 1974. Other levies are stamp duties, license fees, and registration fees.

³⁷CUSTOMS AND DUTIES
A simplified import schedule based on the nomenclature and groupings of the international, or Brussels, system was adopted in 1958. Duties on luxury goods ranged from 30% to 60%; lower duties were in effect for articles essential to the national economy. Compensatory duties were imposed on imports of commodities in competition with local goods. A general internal tax has been collected on the c.i.f.-plus-duties value of most imports. Certain commodities, including radios, alcoholic beverages, tobacco, and sugar, were subject to special excise taxes.

³⁸FOREIGN INVESTMENTS
There has been little foreign private investment. The development needs of Laos continue to be mainly infrastructural. Foreign aid and loans probably will constitute the primary source of capital in this regard. Aid from France was expected to increase in 1976, while new sources of funding were being sought, with some success, in the USSR, DRV, and China. Continued levels of activity through the mid-1970s were also expected among Japanese and Thai interests. In the past, Laotian foreign economic relations were particularly aided by the FEOF and the US Commodity Import Program, under which dollar exchange was provided to Laos, which in turn allocated dollars to local importers, who then made kip payments to the government for the purchase of foreign goods.

³⁹ECONOMIC POLICY
The National Plan and Foreign Aid Council was established in June 1956 to prepare a general plan for the development of Laos and to set up a series of five-year plans. In view of its limited capital resources, the government sought increased private foreign investment, continued US governmental economic assistance, and help from international monetary bodies and the Colombo Plan organization. An economic plan drafted by the Laotian government in 1962 could never be fully implemented, however, owing to internal instability. Little of the infrastructure work for public works, industry, and mining that was abandoned in 1961 has been resumed.

A long-range plan (1969–74) for economic and social development was launched in 1969, with projected expenditures of about

$110 million. Although a major project of the plan, completion of the Nam Ngum Dam, was fulfilled, a host of other targets had to be abandoned because of disruption stemming from the war. In late 1975, a second plan (1976–80) was prepared by the new Pathet Lao government with the aid of Asian Development Bank consultants. The plan made self-sufficiency in food its major interim target (1978), with overall stress on agriculture and related enterprises.

40 HEALTH

The use of Western medicine has improved health generally and reduced the incidence of malaria and smallpox specifically. But a high infant mortality rate and a variety of health problems remain. Most urban areas lack pure water and sanitary disposal systems. In parts of Laos, malaria—the most serious health threat—has been known to affect almost 70% of all children. Other health problems are acute upper respiratory infections (including pneumonia and influenza), diarrhea and dysentery, parasites, yaws, skin ailments, diseases of childhood, and tuberculosis. Life expectancy in 1975 was estimated at 43.5 years, among the lowest levels in Asia.

In 1972 there were 234 civilian and military physicians, (an average of 13,300 inhabitants for each doctor), 180 midwives, 880 nurses, and 18 dentists. Some 15 hospital establishments had 2,400 beds.

41 SOCIAL WELFARE

Assisted by the US, the government supplied rice and other forms of assistance to groups of refugees, mainly the Meo and the Lao-theung, who had been uprooted by the war.

42 HOUSING

The typical house is rectangular, built entirely of wooden planks and bamboo, with a thatched roof, and is raised off the ground on wooden pilings 1 or 2 meters in height. There is a critical housing shortage in the towns, and many dwellings are substandard. In 1965, a sizable program for the construction of private homes in urban areas was under way, with an eye toward renting new dwellings to the growing foreign community in Laos; in late 1975, these dwellings were appropriated by the Pathet Lao.

43 EDUCATION

The degree of literacy in Laos is not known precisely, but it is estimated at about 15%. In 1972, the public school system included 3,413 primary schools (about 750 Buddhist pagoda schools), with 7,340 teachers and a total enrollment of 274,067 pupils (41% female). In 1972, secondary schools had an enrollment of 20,819, including vocational schools with an enrollment of 2,273 and teacher-training schools with 3,913 students. In 1965, baccalaureate-level education was available for the first time in Laos with the addition of the fourteenth and fifteenth grades to the Ecole Supérieure de Pédagogie in Vientiane, which is maintained and staffed with French aid. Sisavong Vong University at Vientiane comprises a school of law and administration, a school of medicine, a school of vocational training, a school of agriculture, and a school of public works. In 1974, some 875 students were enrolled at the higher level.

44 LIBRARIES AND MUSEUMS

There are no large libraries or museums; however, a Buddhist institute owns a number of classical manuscripts, and many excellent traditional works of art and architecture may be seen in Vientiane and Luang Prabang. Of particular interest in Luang Prabang are the royal palace and the That Luang shrine.

45 ORGANIZATIONS

Prior to the installation of a Pathet Lao government in late 1975, there were chambers of commerce in Vientiane and Pakse. Boy Scout and Girl Scout organizations had long been active.

46 PRESS

There are small newspapers in Vientiane—in early 1975, these included *Lao-Presse, Siengsery Daily News, Say Kang, Xat Lao,* and *Vientiane Post.* The press is mostly government-controlled.

47 TOURISM

Past governments sought to promote tourism and took steps to publicize the country's natural and artistic attractions, but strife in the region has prevented tourists from visiting Laos.

48 FAMOUS LAOTIANS

One of the most cherished figures in Laotian history is Fa-Ngoum, who unified Lan Xang in the 14th century. Another dynastic personage still revered is the monarch Sett'at'irat, in whose reign (1534–71) the famous That Luang shrine was built. Chao Amou (1805–28) is remembered for having restored Vientiane to a glory it had not known since the 16th century. Important contemporary figures include Prince Souvanna Phouma (b.1901), former prime minister; and President Prince Souphanouvong (b.1902), leader of the Pathet Lao and a half-brother of Souvanna Phouma.

49 DEPENDENCIES

Laos has no territories or colonies.

50 BIBLIOGRAPHY

Adams, Nina S., and Alfred W. McCoy (eds.). *Laos: War and Revolution.* New York: Harper and Row, 1971.

Berval, René de (ed.). *Kingdom of Laos: The Land of the Million Elephants and of the White Parasol.* Saigon: France-Asie, 1959.

Cady, John Frank. *The Roots of French Imperialism in Eastern Asia.* Ithaca, N.Y.: Cornell University Press, 1954.

Champassak, Sisouk Na. *Storm over Laos.* New York: Praeger, 1961.

Cole, Allan Burnett (ed.). *Conflict in Indochina and International Repercussions: A Documentary History, 1945–1955.* Ithaca, N.Y.: Cornell University Press, 1956.

Dommen, Arthur J. *Conflict in Laos.* Rev. ed. New York: Praeger, 1971.

Dooley, Thomas A. *Tom Dooley's Three Great Books.* New York: Farrar, Straus and Giroux, 1960.

Fall, Bernard B. *Anatomy of a Crisis: The Laotian Crisis of 1960–61.* New York: Doubleday, 1969.

Halpern, Joel M. *Economy and Society of Laos.* New Haven: Southeast Asia Studies, Yale University Press, 1964.

Halpern, Joel M. *Government, Politics and Social Structure in Laos.* New Haven: Yale University Press, 1964.

Halpern, Joel M. *Some Reflections on the War in Laos.* Brussels: Centre d'étude du Sud-Est asiatique et de l'Extrême-Orient, 1970.

Kaufman, Howard K. *Lao Village Life.* Vientiane: US Operations Mission to Laos, 1957.

Kaufman, Howard K. *Village Life in Vientiane Province.* Vientiane: US Operations Mission to Laos, 1956.

Lancaster, Donald. *The Emancipation of French Indochina.* London: Oxford University Press, 1961.

Le Bar, Frank M., and Adrienne Suddard (eds.). *Laos: Its People, Its Society, Its Culture.* New Haven: HRAF Press, 1960.

Le Boulanger, Paul. *Histoire du Laos français: essai d'une étude chronologique des principautés laotiennes.* Paris: Plon, 1931.

Manich Jumsai, M. L. *History of Laos.* Bangkok: Chalermnit, 1967.

Matheson, Marion H. *Indo-China: A Geographical Appreciation.* Ottawa: Department of Mines and Technical Surveys, 1953.

Meeker, Oden. *The Little World of Laos.* New York: Scribner, 1959.

Modelski, George. *International Conference on the Settlement of the Laos Question.* Canberra: Australian National University, 1962.

Parmentier, Henri. *L'Art du Laos.* Hanoi: Ecole Française d'Extrême-Orient, 1954.

Sasorith, Katay Don. *Le Laos.* Paris: Berger-Levrault, 1953.

Viravong, Maha Sila. *History of Laos.* New York: US Joint Publications Research Service, 1958.

LEBANON

Republic of Lebanon
Al-Jumhuriyah al-Lubnaniyah

CAPITAL: Beirut (Bayrut). **FLAG:** The national flag, introduced in 1943, consists of two horizontal red stripes separated by a white stripe, which is twice as wide as either of the red stripes; at the center, in green and brown, is a cedar tree. **ANTHEM:** *Kulluna lil watan lil ʿula lil ʿalam (All of Us for the Country, Glory, Flag).* **MONETARY UNIT:** The Lebanese pound, or livre libanaise (LL), of 100 piasters is a convertible paper currency. There are coins of 1, 5, 10, 25, and 50 piasters and notes of 1, 5, 10, 25, 50, and 100 Lebanese pounds. The exchange rate declined from LL2.25 = $1 (or $1 = LL0.4444) in precrisis days to LL3 = $1 (or $1 = LL0.3333) in early 1976. **WEIGHTS AND MEASURES:** The metric system is the legal standard, but traditional weights and measures are still used. **HOLIDAYS:** Independence Day, 22 November; New Year's Day, 1 January; Easter, Christmas, and some other religious holidays are observed by Christians, and ʿId al-Fitr, ʿId al-ʿAdha', Milad al-Nabi, and other religious holidays by Muslims. **TIME:** 2 P.M. = noon GMT.

¹LOCATION, SIZE, AND EXTENT

Situated on the eastern coast of the Mediterranean Sea, Lebanon has an area of 10,400 sq km (4,015 sq mi), extending 217 km (135 mi) NE–SW and 56 km (35 mi) SE–NW. It is bordered on the N and E by Syria, on the S by Israel, and on the W by the Mediterranean Sea, with a total boundary length of 656 km (407 mi). The 1949 armistice line with Israel had not changed as of July 1976.

The Lebanon of today is the Greater Lebanon (Grand Liban) created by France in September 1920. It includes, besides the traditional area of Mount Lebanon (the hinterland of the coastal strip from Sidon to Tripoli), some coastal cities and districts formerly in the Ottoman Empire's Vilayet of Beirut, notably Saida, Beirut, and Tripoli, and the Biqaʿ Valley, which had been part of the Vilayet of Syria. This area is roughly four times that of Mount Lebanon itself.

²TOPOGRAPHY

The Mount Lebanon area is rugged; there is a rise from sea level to a parallel mountain range of about 2,000–3,000 meters (7,000 to nearly 10,000 feet) in less than 40 km (25 miles), and the soft rock and heavy downpour of winter rains have formed many deep clefts and valleys. The terrain has profoundly affected the country's history in that virtually the whole landscape is a series of superb natural fortresses from which guerrilla activities can render an unpopular government a costly and sporadic affair at best. East of the Mount Lebanon Range is the Biqaʿ Valley, an extremely fertile flatland about 16 km (10 miles) wide and 129 km (80 miles) from north to south. At the eastern flank of the Biqaʿ rise the Anti-Lebanon Range and the Hermon extension, in which stands Mount Hermon across the Syrian border. Lebanon contains few rivers, and its harbors are mostly shallow and small. Abundant springs, found to a height of 1,500 meters (5,000 feet) on the western slopes of the Lebanon Mountains, provide water for cultivation up to this height.

³CLIMATE

Lebanon has an extraordinarily varied climate. This is mainly the result of its range of elevation, and westerly winds make the Mediterranean side much wetter than the eastern hill- and mountainsides and the valleys. Within a 16-km (10-mile) radius of many villages there grow apples, olives, and bananas; within 45 minutes' drive in winter, spring, and fall, both skiing and swimming are possible. Rainfall is high by Middle Eastern standards, with about 35 inches yearly along the coast, about 50 inches in the mountains, and less than 15 inches in the Biqaʿ. About 80% of the rain falls from November to March, mostly in December, January, and February. Summer is a dry season, and humid along the coast. Average annual temperature in Beirut is 20.5°C (69°F), with a range from 13.4°C (56°F) in winter to 27.5°C (82°F) in summer.

⁴FLORA AND FAUNA

Olive and fig trees and grapevines are abundant on lower ground, while at higher altitudes there are cedar, maple, juniper, fir, cypress, valonia oak, and Aleppo pine trees. Vegetation types range from subtropical and desert to alpine. Hunting has killed off most wild animals. Jackals are still found in the wilder rural regions; in the south, gazelles and rabbits are numerous. Many varieties of rodents, including mice, squirrels, and gerbils, and many types of reptiles, including lizards, snakes, and a few poisonous species, may be found. Thrushes, nightingales, and other songbirds are native to Lebanon. There are also partridges, pigeons, vultures, and eagles. As of 1975, endangered species included the wolf, Anatolean leopard, and Mediterranean monk seal.

⁵POPULATION

No census has been taken since 1932. According to the Lebanese national population register, Lebanese population in November 1970 totaled 2,126,000, including those living outside the country and excluding registered Palestinian refugees. The latter numbered 188,000 on 30 July 1973. The mid-year UN estimate for 1972 was 2,963,000. Beirut, the capital, had an estimated population of 1,000,000 in 1975, and Tripoli (Tarabulus al-Sham), the second largest town, had 300,000. Other large towns include Zahlah, Saida (ancient Sidon), and Sur (Tyre).

⁶ETHNIC GROUPS

Ethnic mixtures dating back to various periods of immigration and invasion are represented, as are peoples of almost all Middle Eastern countries. A confusing factor is the religious basis of ethnic differentiation. Thus, while most Lebanese are Arabs, they are divided into Muslims and Christians, each in turn subdivided into a number of faiths or sects, most of them formed by historical development into separate ethnic groups. The Muslims are divided into Sunnis, Shiʿis, and Druzes. The Christians are mainly divided among Maronites, Greek Orthodox, and Greek Catholics.

Other ethnic groups include Armenians (most of them Armenian Orthodox, with some Armenian Catholics), almost all of whom arrived after World War I; and small numbers of Jews, Christian Syrians, and others.

7 LANGUAGE

Arabic is the official language, but other languages are spoken by the various religious minorities. About half of the population living in Lebanon is bilingual. French is spoken by some 40% of the population, English by about 15%, Armenian by about 5%, and Turkish by 1–2% of the population. The Arabic dialect of Lebanon contains various relics of the pre-Arabic languages and also shows considerable European influence in vocabulary.

8 RELIGION

Religious communities in the Ottoman Empire were largely autonomous in matters of personal status law and were at times treated as corporations for tax and public security matters. Membership in a millet, as these groups were called in Ottoman law, gave the individual his "citizenship," and this position, although somewhat modified, has given Lebanese politics its "confessional" nature. Religion is closely connected with civic affairs, and the size and competing influence of the various religious groups came to be a matter of overriding political importance. Under an agreement made at the time of the National Covenant of 1943, the president of Lebanon must be a Maronite Christian and the prime minister a Sunni Muslim, with a ratio of six Christians to every five Muslims in the legislature. But this arrangement subsequently ceased to reflect the strength of competing religious groups in the population. It is believed that Christians—estimated at 46% of the present population (compared with 54% in 1932)—are now outnumbered by Muslims; Sunni Muslims are estimated at 24.5% of the present total (22% in 1932) and Shi'is at 22% (18% in 1932). It was estimated in the mid-1970s that Lebanon has 500,000 Maronite Christians, 320,000 Greek Catholics, more than 300,000 Druzes, and several hundred thousand members of smaller religious groups. The imbalance of power between Christians and Muslims was a major factor contributing to the bitter civil war that began during 1975.

9 TRANSPORTATION

In 1972 there were 6,300 km of roads. Passenger cars and commercial motor vehicles numbered 276,660 in 1975. A plan to build some 700 km of new or modernized roads was introduced in the early 1970s, but was interrupted by the outbreak of civil war.

The 617-km state-owned railway consists of a narrow-gauge (1.05-meter) freight line from Beirut to Damascus in Syria, and a standard-gauge line, which runs along the coast from the south through Beirut to Tripoli and then inland to Homs in Syria, thus linking the Syrian, Turkish, and European networks.

Beirut is a major Mediterranean port. Other ports are Tripoli, Saida, and Juniyah. In 1973, the port of Beirut received 3,098 ships and handled 3,482,000 tons of freight. The Lebanese merchant fleet in 1973 numbered 131 vessels, with a capacity of 278,200 tons.

Beirut's airport handled 2,254,829 passengers in 1973. After fighting began in early 1975, traffic fell by at least 65%. Lebanon's two airlines, MEA and Trans-Mediterranean Airways (TMA), were both running at heavy losses.

10 COMMUNICATIONS

In January 1975 there were 227,000 telephones in Lebanon (as against 150,370 in 1968). An undersea cable linking Beirut with Marseille has been completed, and a new submarine telephone communication network linking Marseille to Beirut via Crete and Cyprus was inaugurated in December 1975. An earth satellite station in orbit over the Indian Ocean started operating in January 1971. Connections with Europe and the US, via satellite ground station and undersea telephone cables, are reasonably good.

The government radio station broadcasts in French and Arabic. The Lebanese Television Co. and Télé-Orient broadcast in Arabic, French, and English on two channels.

11 HISTORY

The geographical features of Lebanon have had a major effect on its history. Its mountains enabled the minority communities to survive the despotisms that submerged the surrounding areas. The sea provided trade routes in ancient times for exports from Lebanese cedar and spruce forests, and for commerce in copper and iron during the time of the Ptolemies and the Romans. Both Lebanon and Syria were historically associated from early times as part of Phoenicia (1200–1000 B.C.), and both were later swept up into the Roman Empire. In the 7th century A.D., the Arabs conquered part of Lebanon. Maronite Christians had long been established there; Islam gradually spread by conversion and migration, although the country remained predominantly Christian. In the 11th century, the Druzes established themselves in the south of Mount Lebanon as well as in Syria. Parts of Lebanon fell temporarily to the Crusaders; invasions by Mongols and others followed, and trade declined until the reunification of the Middle East under the Ottoman Empire.

For the most part, Ottoman officials of the surrounding areas left the Mount Lebanon districts to their own emirs and shaykhs. Fakhr' al-Din (1586–1635) of the Ma'an family set out to create an autonomous Lebanon, opened the country to Western Europe through commercial and military pacts, and encouraged Christian missionary activity. In 1697, the Shihab family acquired dominance, and from 1788 to 1840, except for a few intervals, Mount Lebanon was ruled by Bashir II of the Shihab family, who extended his power and was partially successful in building a strong state.

The Egyptian occupation of Syria (1832–40) opened the Levant to large-scale European penetration and tied Lebanese affairs to international politics, but it heightened hostility between Christians and Druzes, with the occupiers from time to time using armed groups of one against the other. The British invasion of 1840–41 served to deliver Lebanon from Egyptian rule and forced Bashir II into exile, but it also involved France and the UK in the problem of finding a modus vivendi for the religious factions. A partition of government did not work. Economic discontent was inflamed by religious antagonisms, and the Druzes, feeling their power dwindling, organized a major onslaught against the Christians in 1860. When the latter, fearing annihilation, requested European intervention, major powers sent fleets into Syrian waters and the French sent an army into Mount Lebanon. Under European pressure, the Ottoman government agreed to the establishment of an international commission to set up a new, pro-Christian government; an autonomous province of Mount Lebanon was created in 1864, with a Christian governor who, though the servant of the Ottoman state, relied upon European backing in disputes with his sovereign.

The entry of the Ottoman Empire into World War I led to an Allied blockade, widespread hunger, and the destruction of Lebanese prosperity. An Anglo-French force took the country in 1918, and in 1920, an Allied conference gave France a mandate over Syria, in which Mount Lebanon was included. The French separated from Syria the area they called Greater Lebanon (Grand Liban); it was four times as large as the traditional Mount Lebanon, and added a Muslim population almost as large as the Christian. The mandate years were a time of material growth and little political development.

Lebanon came under Vichy control in 1940, but in 1941, Lebanon and Syria were taken by a combined Anglo-Free French force. The Free French proclaimed Lebanese independence in November 1941, but when a strongly nationalistic government was created in 1943, the French intervened and arrested the new president, Bishara al-Khuri. An insurrection followed, prompting UK intervention and the restoration of the government. In 1945, agreement was achieved for the withdrawal of both UK and French forces, and in 1946, Lebanon assumed complete independence.

The 1950s and much of the 1960s were generally characterized by economic and political stability. Beginning in 1952, Lebanon received increased US aid and also benefited from an influx of Western commercial personnel and from growing oil royalties. It also seemed the calmest center of the Middle East, and the country, which had remained neutral in the Arab-Israeli war of 1948, also maintained neutrality in the wars of 1967 and 1973. In 1958, a reported attempt by President Camille Chamoun (Sha'mun) to seek a second term precipitated a civil war, and the US sent forces to help quell the insurrection. But the crisis was settled when Gen. Fu'ad Shihab (Chehab), who was supported by both government and opposition groups, was elected president in July. A compromise coalition cabinet appointed by him passed an electoral law adopting the secret ballot and raising the number of seats in the Chamber of Deputies from 66 to 99. By October, US forces were withdrawn, and public security was reestablished.

By the late 1960s, however, the country had entered a much more difficult period. Its economy was being disrupted by conflict in the Middle East, vividly brought home by the presence, near the border with Israel, of thousands of well-armed Palestinian guerrillas. The government seemed unable to prevent either guerrilla raids over the border into Israel or retaliatory acts by the Israelis, climaxed in April and May 1974 by a series of attacks on Lebanese villages in which scores of persons were killed and hundreds injured. Efforts to deal with the problem were denounced as insufficient by Christian rightists, while Muslim leftists defended the Palestinians, and both factions began to build private militias.

During the early months of 1975, sporadic violence between the two factions gradually erupted into full-scale civil war. For the period from 13 April to 6 July 1975 alone, according to one Beirut newspaper, more than 2,300 persons were killed and 16,300 injured. Despite sporadic lulls in the fighting, a series of changes in cabinets, and numerous paper truces (including a major "all-embracing" accord arrived at through Syrian mediation and announced on 22 January 1976), the violence dragged on. In April, as a concession to leftists, the Chamber of Deputies and President Suleiman Franjieh, who had been elected in August 1970, agreed to a constitutional amendment allowing him to be replaced. On 8 May 1976, Elias Sarkis was chosen to replace him; but Sarkis did not actually take office at that time. On 31 May and 1 June 1976, Syrian troops intervened openly in large numbers in an attempt to force the sides into a negotiated settlement. But as of midsummer, their efforts had proved unsuccessful.

12 GOVERNMENT

Lebanon is an independent republic. Executive power is vested in a president (elected by the legislature for six years) and a prime minister and cabinet, chosen by the president but responsible to the legislature. Legislative power is exercised by a 99-member Chamber of Deputies, elected for a four-year term of office by universal adult suffrage. The electoral reform law of 1960 determined the denominational composition of the legislature as follows: Maronites, 30; Sunni, 20; Shi'i, 19; Greek Orthodox, 11; Greek Catholics, 6; Druzes, 6; Armenian Orthodox, 4; Armenian Catholic, 1; Protestant, 1; and others, 1. Under special circumstances, the president may dissolve the Chamber and order new elections. Under an agreement dating back to the French mandate, the president must be a Maronite Christian, the prime minister a Sunni Muslim, and the president of the Chamber a Shi'i Muslim. However, the balance of power

among the various religious factions, and, indeed, the form of government as a whole, remained dependent upon the outcome of the civil war that began in 1975.

13 POLITICAL PARTIES

Political life in Lebanon is affected by the diversity of religious sects and the religious basis of social organization. Political groups that are mainly Christian, especially the Maronites, favor an independent course for Lebanon, stressing its ties to Europe and opposing the appeals of Islam and pan-Arabism. The Muslim groups favor closer ties with the surrounding Arab areas and are opposed to confessionalism (political division along religious lines). Principal political parties include the Parliamentary Democratic Bloc, a successor of the National Front Party, which organized the May 1958 insurrection and subsequently won the premiership; the Phalangist Party, National Liberation Party, and National Bloc, with a largely Christian Maronite membership; and various parties of the left, including the Progressive Socialist Party, the pro-Iraqi Arab Ba'th Socialist Party, and the Lebanese Communist Party. The various Palestinian guerrilla organizations grouped under the umbrella of the Palestine Liberation Organization have played an increasingly important role in the political life of Lebanon.

See continental political: front cover G6; physical: back cover G6

LOCATION: 35°6' to 36°36'E; 33°4' to 34°41'N. **BOUNDARY LENGTHS**: Syria, *359* km (*223* mi); Israel, *102* km (*63* mi); Mediterranean coastline, *195* km (*121* mi).

14 LOCAL GOVERNMENT

Lebanon is divided into the five provinces (muhafazat) of Beirut, North Lebanon, South Lebanon, Biqa', and Mount Lebanon, each with its district administration. The muhafazat are subdivided into 26 districts (aqdiya), municipalities, and villages. Provincial governors and district chiefs are appointed by presidential decree with cabinet approval. Municipalities are created by order of the Ministry of Interior, authenticating an approved application from the interested governor. Centralization is still the dominant principle, and local government, modeled somewhat on the French system in the early 19th century, continues to be administered largely by organs responsible to the central authorities. Some towns have elected municipal councils, but only in Beirut do the council and its president, the mayor, actually run municipal affairs. In most villages, councils of village elders or heads of families or clans still play a considerable role.

15 JUDICIAL SYSTEM

Ultimate supervisory power rests with the minister of justice, who appoints the magistrates. Courts of first instance, of which there are 56, are presided over by a single judge and deal with both civil and criminal cases. Appeals may be taken to 11 courts of appeal, each made up of three judges. Of the 4 courts of cassation, 3 hear civil cases and 1 hears criminal cases. A six-man Council of State handles administrative cases. Matters of state security are dealt with by a special nine-man Court of Justice. Religious courts—Islamic, Christian, and Jewish—deal with marriages, deaths, inheritances, and other matters of personal status.

16 ARMED FORCES

In 1975, and before it disintegrated, the Lebanese regular army numbered 18,000. It was Christian-dominated and aligned with the Phalangist Party.

Various political parties and organizations have their own militias: The Palestinian forces number 20,000 men; the Phalangist Party militia includes 6,000 men armed with various types of weapons and is backed by the Forces for the Protection of the Cedars (750 well-armed members). Many Christian deserters from the Lebanese army have joined the right-wing militias. The Syrian regime also maintains a force of several thousand men disguised as Palestinian guerrillas.

17 MIGRATION

The economic roots of emigration may be traced to the increase of crop specialization during the 19th century and to the subsequent setbacks of the silk market toward the end of the century. Political incentives also existed, and many Lebanese left their country for Egypt (then under British rule) or the Americas at the turn of the century. During the mandate period, internal migration from village communities to coastal cities was greatly accelerated. Since 1966, skilled Lebanese have been attracted by economic opportunities in the Persian Gulf countries.

The number of aliens living in Lebanon in 1975 has been estimated at more than 1,500,000—more than 50% of the population. This figure includes, among other groups, 350,000 Syrian residents, 315,000 visiting Syrians, 275,000 Palestinians living in refugee camps, and 95,000 living outside the camps. All applications for Lebanese citizenship were frozen for the last two decades for political reasons, most of the alien residents in Lebanon being Muslims.

More than 1,000,000 Lebanese live abroad, many in the US and Brazil. During the first nine months of the civil war, some 200,000 persons were displaced; many of these fled to France, Syria, Jordan, Egypt, and the Gulf countries.

18 INTERNATIONAL COOPERATION

Lebanon has been a member of the UN since its foundation and of the specialized agencies, except IMCO and GATT. It is the host to UNRWA and is one of the founding members of the AL. Syria and other AL states took part in efforts to bring about a negotiated end to the civil war during 1975 and 1976.

19 ECONOMY

Lebanon is traditionally a trading country, with a relatively large agricultural sector and a small but well-developed industry. Until the civil war, it had always figured prominently as a center of tourist trade. The per capita income is relatively high, due in part to investment in industry and the formation of sizable gold and foreign exchange reserves (LL4,662 million at the end of March 1975), continued receipt of remittances from Lebanese nationals living abroad, and percolation of part of the new oil wealth from the Middle Eastern oil-producing countries. A policy of free enterprise and free transfer of capital and foreign exchange profits from financial transactions increased and encouraged the transfer of large funds to Lebanon for safekeeping and investment. Higher profits were reinvested in extensive building construction and in agricultural improvements, notably in fruit cultivation and poultry farming. The economy revolves around service industries, which in recent years have accounted for about 70% of the GDP. Commerce alone has contributed more than 30%. Agriculture has supplied less than 10% of the GDP, with industry providing 13–15%, and the remainder originating from power, construction, transport, and communications.

The Arab-Israeli conflict from 1967 onward and a banking crisis in 1966 had the effect of arresting development in some sectors. The restoration of internal stability and confidence in 1970 sparked a temporary recovery, but in 1973, economic activity slowed as a result of a new round of domestic political disturbances and the October Arab-Israeli war. The civil war that erupted in April 1975 seriously affected the economy. Before the end of a year's fighting, 70 of the country's major industrial plants had been destroyed, more than 3,500 businesses had been destroyed, burnt, or looted, and a number of international banks and companies had moved their Middle East operations from Beirut.

20 INCOME

In 1972, the GDP was LL6,365 million. The distribution of the GDP by sectors (in millions of Lebanese pounds) was as follows: trade, 2,007; industry, 884; agriculture, 631; energy and power, 129; real estate and construction, 290; transportation and communications, 478; other sectors, 1,946. National income per capita in 1972 was about LL2,000. Lebanon forfeited about half of its GNP for the year 1975 during 150 days of hostilities. The 1974 GNP amounted to an estimated LL7,000–8,000 million.

21 LABOR

In February 1976, the labor force was estimated at about 500,000, 19% of whom were engaged in agriculture. Before the fighting there were 130,000 workers in industry, 18,000 in the tourism sector, and the remainder in commerce, transport, and communications. One-quarter of the Lebanese working population is employed in the oil states, while unskilled labor is drawn to Lebanon from Syria. About 70,000 to 80,000 jobs were affected directly or indirectly during the first year of civil war. Estimates in February 1976 put the figure of those out of work at about 40,000. Underemployment is widespread, and unemployment resulting from the seasonal nature of agriculture and tourism is considerable. Labor productivity is low compared with the US and Western Europe, but higher than in most other developing countries.

Organization of labor is recent and has grown rather slowly, partly because of the small number of industrial workers, but also because of the availability of a large pool of unemployed. Agricultural and most trade workers are not organized. In March 1962, the Lebanese Confederation of Trade Unions was founded in Beirut, following the merger of several federations of trade unions. These trade unions numbered 115 in 1968, with a total membership of about 35,000.

22 AGRICULTURE

Only 19% of the working population is engaged in agricultural activity. Lebanon's agricultural sector could be easily stimulated by a policy of land irrigation, but since agriculture makes up only about 10% of the national income, the tendency has been to develop the more profitable trading and service sectors. Expansion of cultivated areas is limited by the arid and rugged nature of the land. The most important crop is citrus fruits, of which 306,735 tons were produced in 1973. About 116,177 tons of apples were harvested; other fruit crops included grapes, 107,490 tons; bananas, 43,900 tons; olives, 32,250 tons; and pears, 12,181 tons. In 1973, Lebanon produced 55,138 tons of wheat, 6,511 tons of barley, 14,643 tons of pulses, 59,127 tons of tomatoes, 29,827 tons of cucumbers, 24,285 tons of watermelons, 139,431 tons of sugar beets, and 9,876 tons of tobacco. Lebanon does not produce enough food for its own needs. The total value of agricultural production in 1973 was LL578 million.

The Verdure Plan, carried on from 1964 to 1973 in an effort to increase Lebanon's agricultural output, concentrated on the conservation and improvement of soil, the provision of farm equipment to small farmers, the training of supervisory personnel, and the provision of financial aid to farmers. The Litani River irrigation project, designed to utilize Lebanon's most important water resources, was initially to have been completed in 1976. But the program was delayed, mainly for fear of Israeli expansion in that area.

23 ANIMAL HUSBANDRY

The livestock population in 1973 was estimated at 226,000 sheep and 84,000 head of cattle (including 48,000 cows). As part of the Verdure Plan, the government purchases dairy products at support prices in order to guarantee a regular monthly income to each smallholder owning two or more cows. In an effort to increase dairy production, the Ministry of Agriculture bought 1,000 cows in March 1973. Its final aim is to replace 330,000 goats with 50,000 cows. As Lebanon's own meat and milk production is below consumption needs, 141,126 head of cattle, 348,771 sheep, 6,000 tons of frozen meat, and 5,257 tons of powdered milk were imported in 1972. In 1972, Lebanon exported 4,010,000 chickens and 366 million eggs, mainly to Arab markets.

24 FISHING

The fishing industry has not progressed significantly, mainly because of the lack of modern fishing boats, insufficient refrigeration facilities, and the illegal use of explosives, which severely cut catch potentials. A five-year fisheries plan (1965–69), designed to reduce fish imports and provide employment in the canned-fish industry, achieved little success. In 1973, locally caught fish was valued at LL7,747,000.

25 FORESTRY

It is estimated that the present 134,000 hectares of forests could be expanded to 200,000 hectares (about 20% of the total land area). Most of the forests are in the central part of the country; pine and oak trees predominate. Few of the famous ancient cedars have survived; small cedar forests have been planted in high altitudes since World War I. Overgrazing by goats, which was the prime cause of erosion, is being combated, and reforestation efforts are under way. Income from forestry in 1973 was LL4.6 million, as compared with LL1.4 million in 1972.

26 MINING

Mining activity is slight. Small quantities of bitumen, iron ore, lime, and salt have been produced, but with the exception of iron ore, the quality of these minerals is generally poor. However, important deposits of oil shale were discovered in April 1973. The reserves were estimated at 500,000 million tons of bituminous shale, containing 17.5% oil on the average. In 1975, the government was considering moves to set up a national oil company, which would be in charge of all exploration, production, transport, and refining activities; at least 14 oil companies were said to be interested in seeking oil exploration licenses.

27 ENERGY AND POWER

Electric power production rose from 1,036 million kwh in 1968 to 1,790.8 million kwh in 1973, of which 1,312.4 million kwh were produced hydroelectrically. Production of electric power in 1968–73 increased by 73%. Installed capacity in 1972 totaled 538,000 kw, of which 46% was hydroelectric. By November 1974, electricity was available to 99.2% of the population.

28 INDUSTRY

A small but competitive industrial sector concentrates primarily on light consumer goods, but in recent years has tended to move into lines that require greater specialization. Food processing, textiles, cement, oil refining, and the processing or manufacturing of nonmetallic mineral products are the leading industries.

In 1973, investment in industry reached LL2,000 million, the value of production totaled LL2,150 million, and the number of workers employed reached 120,000. Light manufacturing industries experienced a 30% annual increase in value of exports up to 1973, in which year industrial exports totaled LL446.3 million. Damage to industrial installations during the early months of the civil war was estimated conservatively at around $160 million by February 1976.

Crude oil is pumped from Sa'udi Arabia and Iraq through pipelines operated, respectively, by the Trans-Arabian Pipeline Co. (Tapline) and the Iraq Petroleum Co. (IPC). IPC assets and installations were taken over by the Lebanese government after IPC stopped its operations in Iraq. Lebanese refineries received 2,039,400 tons of crude oil in 1972, as compared with 2,001,100 tons the previous year. Plans were being made for a third oil refinery with a capacity of at least 7 million tons per year, directed mainly to export markets. The country's two refineries suspended operations on 27 August 1975, but Tapline subsequently resumed pumping Sa'udi crude oil to Lebanon at a rate of 50,000 barrels a day.

29 DOMESTIC TRADE

Trade is by far the most important sector of the Lebanese economy, accounting in recent years for about one-third of the national income. The main trading activity is related to the importation of goods and their distribution in the local market. The distribution is generally handled by traders who acquire sole right of import and sale of specific trademarks, and although competition is keen, the markup tends to be high. Distribution of local products is more widely spread among traders. The smallness and competitiveness of the market has discouraged the development of wholesale houses, but has fostered the growth of small shops dealing directly with local and foreign suppliers.

Government offices and the larger banks are generally open from 8 or 8:30 A.M. to 2 P.M. (to 1 P.M. in summer), and commercial offices, from 8 or 8:30 A.M. to 1 P.M. (to 1 or 2 P.M. in summer) and from 3 to 6 or 7 P.M., but shops stay open long hours.

There is no single price level for the same item; the actual price charged generally depends on the short-term condition of the market and on the result of bargaining. Retail credit is common, and advertising has developed rapidly in motion picture theaters and the press. The Beirut price index showed a rise of 11.1% in 1974, from 121.7 to 135.2 (1966 base=100). The food index went up 16.6%, and the clothing index 13.8%.

During the first year of civil violence, 3,600 commercial establishments were destroyed, burned, or looted.

30 FOREIGN TRADE

Foreign trade plays an important role in the economic life of Lebanon as a source of both income and employment. The trade deficit in 1973 was LL1,738.4 million, as compared with LL1,629.6 million in 1972; a 37% increase in exports failed to offset substantial increases in imports. Machinery and equipment, including electrical goods, were the chief imports; a considerable portion of the nation's food supply also had to be imported. The Federal Republic of Germany (FRG) was the largest importer, followed by the US. Lebanon's main clients (accounting for nearly half of all exports by value) were Arab states, led by Sa'udi Arabia. Precious metals and stones, and related products, were the chief exports by value.

Principal exports in 1973 (in millions of Lebanese pounds) were:

Precious stones, metals, coins	333.4
Machinery and transport equipment	318.1
Agricultural, livestock, and food products	284.7
Textiles and textile products	172.2
Other exports	489.1
TOTAL	**1,597.5**

Principal imports in 1973 (in millions of Lebanese pounds) were:

Machinery and transport equipment	798.0
Minerals and mineral products	738.4
Agricultural, livestock, and food products	568.3
Textiles and textile products	411.8
Chemicals and pharmaceuticals	259.8
Other imports	559.6
TOTAL	**3,335.9**

Principal trading partners in 1973 (in millions of Lebanese pounds) were:

	EXPORTS	IMPORTS	BALANCE
France	161.9	361.4	−199.5
US	71.9	376.3	−304.4
UK	148.3	259.5	−111.2
FRG	19.3	379.7	−360.4
Sa'udi Arabia	260.7	69.5	191.2
Italy	22.7	292.9	−270.2
Switzerland	68.0	145.2	− 77.2
Iraq	50.1	119.8	− 69.7
Japan	4.2	125.8	−121.6
Syria	77.2	49.3	27.9
Libya	118.9	6.5	112.4
Other countries	594.3	1,150.0	−555.7
TOTALS	**1,597.5**	**3,335.9**	**−1,738.4**

31 BALANCE OF PAYMENTS

The balance of payments has generally been positive, with a rising merchandise-trade deficit more than offset by buoyant net earnings from services and substantial net receipts of foreign capital and unrequited transfers. The surplus in balance of payments rose from LL122 million in 1968 to LL839 million in 1972. However, a sharp rise in imports, a slowing of the demand for services, and a reduced level of capital inflow, brought about by internal disturbances and the October 1973 Middle East war, produced a deterioration in 1973.

Summaries of the balance of payments in 1972 and 1973 (in millions of Lebanese pounds) are shown in the following table:

	1972	1973
CURRENT ACCOUNTS		
Trade, net	−1,401	−1,742
Total services, net	1,249	1,295
Travel and tourism, net	(380)	(330)
Transportation, net	(220)	(250)
Investment income, net	(175)	(200)
Other services	(474)	(515)
Transfers, net	105	130
TOTALS	**− 47**	**− 317**
Nonmonetary-sector capital movements	886	725
TOTAL BALANCE	**839**	**408**

Capital inflow has mainly been from other Middle East nations and from Lebanese emigrants whose investments abroad were being curtailed. Heavy tourism has been a major factor in the surplus in service accounts. These and other sources of earnings were seriously affected by the outbreak of civil war in 1975.

32 BANKING

The Bank of Lebanon, established on 1 April 1964, is now the sole bank of issue. Its powers to regulate and control commercial banks and other institutions and to implement monetary policy were expanded by amendments to the Code of Money and Credit promulgated in October 1973. The Bank of Lebanon reported assets and liabilities balanced at LL4,174.8 million as of 30 September 1975. Liabilities included LL1,970.4 million in demand deposits, LL1,746.5 million currency in circulation, and LL205.8 million in other deposits. Assets included LL1,402.5 million in gold reserves, LL98.8 million in loans to the private sector, and LL16.4 million in public-sector loans. Gold reserves and foreign exchange reserves have traditionally been virtually equal to total banking deposits. Total foreign exchange holdings of Lebanese banks rose from LL3,980 million on 31 December 1974 to LL4,662 million on 31 March 1975. Total bank deposits, including nonresident accounts, rose by 6.4% to LL10,901 million. Advances to the private sector totaled LL5,787 million on 31 March 1975, as compared with LL5,649 million as of 31 December 1974. Financing foreign trade and discounting trade bills make up most banking transactions; exchange and transfer of capital in the international market are substantial. To encourage the movement and deposit of foreign capital in Lebanon, a bank secrecy law of 1956 forbids banks to disclose details of a client's business even to judicial authorities.

In 1968, several banks were seized, liquidated, or merged; as a result, the number of commercial banks operating in Lebanon was reduced from 93 to 74. At the end of 1974, 18 wholly owned branches of foreign banks accounted for 38% of total assets, and 24 banks with majority participation by overseas interests accounted for another 39%. Foreign banks operating in Lebanon included Chase Manhattan, Moscow Narodny, Banco di Roma, First National of Chicago, Société Générale, Grindlay's Bank, and Chemical Bank. The middle of 1974 saw the start of reductions in the 7% reserve requirement on deposits in foreign currencies, and in March 1975, the cabinet approved a bill in effect exempting foreign-currency deposits by nonresidents from local taxes on interest.

During the first year of civil conflict in 1975/76, more than LL2.5 billion was withdrawn from Lebanese banks, mostly for transfer abroad. By injecting foreign currency, mainly dollars, into the system from its ample reserves, the Central Bank attempted to maintain the value of the Lebanese pound. More than a dozen foreign-controlled banks moved their staffs to other financial centers, such as Athens, Bahrayn, and Cairo; and at least three Lebanese banks applied for permission to set up branches in Paris, where many affluent Lebanese had taken up residence and purchased property.

33 INSURANCE

Activities of insurance companies are regulated by the National Insurance Council. All insurance companies must deposit a specific amount of money or real investments in an approved bank and must retain in Lebanon reserves commensurate with their volume of business. In 1974, 13 Lebanese and 55 foreign insurance companies operated in the country. Non-life premiums written in 1973 were valued at LL55,037,610, of which accident insurance accounted for 61%. Life insurance premiums in 1972 totaled LL16.5 million; life policies in force numbered 115,000.

34 SECURITIES

The Beirut Stock Exchange was officially opened in 1952 as a center in which the few available company shares can be traded.

35 PUBLIC FINANCE

The annual ordinary budget of the central government must be approved by the Chamber of Deputies. In addition to the ordinary budget, there are several autonomous budgets (customs, tourism, national economy, telephones, lottery, water services, etc.), an extraordinary budget covering capital expenditures of the central government, and special expenditures of sums received from loans. Municipalities also have independent budgets.

Estimated ordinary expenditures for 1975 and those proposed for 1976 (in millions of Lebanese pounds) were as follows:

	1975	1976
National defense	314.9	326.9
National education	263.5	279.3
Public works	233.2	216.9
Hydraulic resources	48.3	64.2
Health	47.9	52.6
Agriculture	42.7	44.2
Tourism	30.8	29.3
Payments on debts	88.9	100.5
Reserves	40.9	32.6
Other expenditures	525.7	570.0
TOTALS	1,636.8	1,716.5

In February 1976, the Lebanese Council of Ministers allocated $200 million on a program to reconstruct the country's war-shattered economy. Of the total, $20 million was to go for emergency relief operations, $40 million for loans to repair damaged housing, and the balance for assisting tourism and other key sectors of the economy adversely affected in the civil war.

The Lebanese government faced the formidable problem of financing a massive deficit resulting from heavy financial obligations and from huge shortfalls in revenues. Income from customs was estimated to have fallen from LL469 million in 1974 to LL259 million in 1975. Declines were also expected in income and property taxes (an estimated LL105 million was received in 1974) and in petroleum pipeline royalties (from an estimated LL65 million collected in 1974).

³⁶TAXATION
In 1973, indirect taxation yielded LL408 million, while direct taxation yielded LL287.3 million. Tax evasion is acknowledged to be a major problem; economists estimate that as little as 20% of all direct taxes due are actually collected. Income tax is progressive and ranges from 4% to 42% on establishments and from 2% to 10% on wages and salaries. Income from agriculture is subject to a graduated land tax ranging from 2% to 35% of net income. Dividends are not taxed but there is a 10% tax on interest, excluding interest on savings accounts. Excise duties are levied on petroleum products, tobacco products, and cement.

³⁷CUSTOMS AND DUTIES
There are no export duties. Import duties, however, are levied on most goods. Some agricultural and industrial products are protected by a 30% to 50% ad valorem duty, and in February 1975, duties were increased on a number of luxury items, including cars (raised to 38%), spare parts (to 7%), tires (to 14%), alcoholic beverages (to 20%), and whiskey (to 50%).

Preferential duties are applicable to imports from Arab countries and from Common Market countries. A free zone in Beirut is widely used as a point of entrepôt trade.

³⁸FOREIGN INVESTMENTS
Foreign investment is principally from Kuwayt, Sa'udi Arabia, the UAE, Syria, France, and the UK; US investments are mainly in oil transportation, storage facilities, and a fertilizer plant. Syrian investments in 1970 were estimated at LL400 million. In 1970, the Intra Investment Co., with a capital of LL280 million, was formed by Lebanon, Qatar, Kuwayt, and the US Commodity Credit Corporation to administer assets of the Intra Bank, which closed in 1966.

To encourage foreign investment, major new enterprises are exempt from income tax for six years after their establishment. There are no limitations on the entry and transfer of capital at the free rate of exchange and no registration, taxes, or fees on such capital movement.

³⁹ECONOMIC POLICY
Since World War II, Lebanon has followed free-enterprise and free-trade policies. The government operates only certain public utilities and the tobacco monopoly. The country's favorable geographical position as a transit point and the traditional importance of the trading and banking sectors of the economy are at the root of this policy.

The aim of making Lebanon a center of trade, finance, and tourism has been supported by stable currency backed largely by gold, by a conservative fiscal policy, by various incentives to foreign investors, and by minimization of banking regulations. A bill to establish a banking free zone was approved in March 1975.

The government planned to allocate $2,200 million over five years to improve internal security, and a housing bank was to be established to provide long-term financial aid for the reconstruction of war-damaged property. About $1,500 million was to be sought from the US, Europe, and Arab oil-exporting states to help finance the rebuilding of the economy.

⁴⁰HEALTH
In 1972, Lebanon had 143 hospitals, with 11,370 beds, excluding mental institutions. The hospitals were supplemented by mobile medical units that reached villages in remote areas of the country. There were 2,200 physicians, 1,551 nurses; and 442 midwives. Average life expectancy in 1975 was estimated at 65.2 years.

⁴¹SOCIAL WELFARE
A government social security plan, not yet fully implemented, is intended to provide sickness and maternity insurance, accident and disability insurance, family allowances, and end-of-service indemnity payments. Monthly contributions to the plan are from the employer, 86%; government, 10%; and employee, 4%. Under its provisions, every eligible employee receives coverage of 70% of all medical expenses, sickness-benefit payments lasting up to 26 weeks, and a lump-sum retirement payment equal to 20 times his last monthly salary. The first stage, covering industrial workers, went into effect in 1965. These benefits were subsequently extended to cover about 50% of the labor force. Foreigners employed in Lebanon are entitled to benefits if similar rights are available for Lebanese in their home countries. The 1975 budget for the National Social Security Fund, was LL240.5 million, a rise of about 28% over the 1974 figure. Voluntary social work societies also conduct relief and welfare activities.

⁴²HOUSING
Despite substantial construction activity since World War II and a boom in construction during the 1960s, there was a shortage, especially of low-cost residential units, in the early 1970s. The situation was aggravated by the subsequent civil war, during the first 10 months of which an estimated 10–20% of all dwellings in the Beirut area were severely damaged or destroyed.

⁴³EDUCATION
Lebanon's literacy rate is relatively high, over 80%. Free primary education was introduced in 1960. In 1972/73 there were 2,486 schools (1,354 public and 1,132 private), with 665,301 pupils, of whom 497,723 were at the preprimary or primary level and 167,578 were at the secondary level. Universities in 1973/74 included the American University of Beirut, with 4,600 students; the Arab University of Beirut, with 25,000; and the Lebanese University, with 15,000. There were also 12 technical schools, with a combined enrollment of about 5,000. A teacher-training school is planned for the end of 1976.

44 LIBRARIES AND MUSEUMS

Lebanon has about 15 sizable libraries with specialized collections of books, manuscripts, and documents. Most libraries are in Beirut, but there are also collections at Saida and Harissa. The National Library of Lebanon, founded in 1921, has more than 100,000 volumes, but the largest library is that of the American University in Beirut, with 380,000 volumes. The Université Saint Joseph has several specialized libraries, including the Bibliothèque Orientale, with 150,000 volumes. The library of the St. John Monastery in Khonchara, founded in 1696, contains the first known printing press in the Middle East.

The National Museum of Lebanon, in Beirut, has a collection of historical documents and many notable antiquities, including the sarcophagus of King Ahiram (13th century B.C.), with the first known alphabetical inscriptions. The American University Museum also has an extensive collection of ancient artifacts.

45 ORGANIZATIONS

There are chambers of commerce and industry in the four principal cities (Beirut, Tripoli, Saida, and Zahlah) and a Rotary Club in Beirut. Lebanon has an Automobile and Touring Club, a French Chamber of Commerce, an Association of Lebanese Industries, and several voluntary social welfare agencies. Intellectual and cultural societies in Lebanon include the Cenacle Libanais, the Institute of Developmental Studies, the Lebanese Association of University Professors, the November 22 Club, and the Lebanese Student League.

46 PRESS

In 1976, 40 daily newspapers, 45 political weeklies, 115 nonpolitical weeklies, and 150 monthlies were published in Beirut. The leading Arabic newspaper is *Al-Nahar*, which commands about 57% of all daily newspapers sales in Lebanon. *L'Orient-le jour* (French) and the *Daily Star* (English) are among the other major papers.

47 TOURISM

Lebanon's antiquities, notably at Sidon, Byblos, and Ba'albek, combine with a pleasant climate and scenery to attract increasing numbers of tourists, especially from other Arab countries. In 1973, 1,904,495 tourists visited Lebanon, 1,019,498 of whom were Syrians and 533,641 were other Arab nationals. More than 594,000 tourists visited Lebanon in the first quarter of 1975, a 10% increase over the first quarter of 1974.

During the civil war of 1975/76, however, fighting heavily damaged major hotels in Beirut and deterred tourist activity. Trade lost by Lebanese hotels in 1975 as a whole was estimated at LL50–60 million, and about 16,000 jobs were lost in the tourism sector.

Tourists who are not Arab nationals require visas to enter Lebanon. Exit visas are required for tourists who stay more than three months.

48 FAMOUS LEBANESE

Khalil Jibran (Gibran, 1883–1931), a native of Lebanon, achieved international renown through his paintings and literary works. He is best known for his long poem *The Prophet*. Dr. Charles Habib Malik (b.1906), for many years Lebanon's leading diplomat, was president of the 13th UN General Assembly in 1958/59.

49 DEPENDENCIES

Lebanon has no territories or colonies.

50 BIBLIOGRAPHY

Abu-Izzeddin, H. S. *Lebanon and Its Provinces: A Study by the Governors of the Five Provinces.* Mystic, Conn.: Verry, 1963.

American University, Washington, D.C. *Area Handbook for Lebanon.* Washington, D.C.: Government Printing Office, 1969.

Binder, Leonard. *Politics in Lebanon.* New York: Wiley, 1966.

Bouron, Narcisse. *Les Druses: histoire du Liban et de la montagne haouranaise.* Paris: Berger-Levrault, 1930.

Christopher, John B. *Lebanon.* New York: Holt, 1966.

Fadel, H. A., et al. *Lebanon: Its Treaties and Agreements.* Dobbs Ferry, N.Y.: Oceana, 1967.

Gulick, John. *Social Structure and Culture Change in a Lebanese Village.* New York: Wenner-Gren Foundation for Anthropological Research, 1955.

Haddad, George Meri. *Fifty Years of Modern Syria and Lebanon.* Beirut: Dar-al-Hayat, 1950.

Harfouche, J. K. *Social Structure of Low-Income Families in Lebanon.* Mystic, Conn.: Verry, 1965.

Harik, Ilya F. *Politics and Change in a Traditional Society: Lebanon 1711–1845.* Princeton, N.J.: Princeton University Press, 1967.

Hitti, Philip K. *Lebanon in History, from the Earliest Times to the Present.* London: Macmillan, 1957.

Hourani, Albert. *Syria and Lebanon: A Political Essay.* London: Oxford University Press, 1946.

Hudson, Michael C. *Precarious Republic: Political Modernization in Lebanon.* New York: Random House, 1968.

Lammens, Henri. *La Syrie: précis historique.* 2 vols. Beirut: Catholic Press, 1924.

Longrigg, Stephen Hemsley. *Syria and Lebanon under French Mandate.* London: Oxford University Press, 1958.

Meo, Leila T. *Lebanon, Improbable Nation.* Bloomington: Indiana University Press, 1965.

Patai, Raphael (ed.). *The Republic of Lebanon.* 2 vols. New Haven, Conn.: Human Relations Area Files, 1956.

Polk, William R. *The Opening of South Lebanon, 1788–1840.* Cambridge: Harvard University Press, 1963.

Qubain, Fahim I. *Crisis in Lebanon.* Washington: The Middle East Institute, 1961.

Rondot, Pierre. *Les Institutions politiques du Liban: des communautés traditionnelles à l'état moderne.* Paris: Institut d'études de l'Orient contemporain, 1947.

Salem, Elie Adib. *Modernization Without Revolution.* Bloomington: Indiana University Press, 1973.

Salibi, K. S. *The Modern History of Lebanon.* New York: Praeger, 1965.

Sayigh, Yusif. *Entrepreneurs of Lebanon.* Cambridge: Harvard University Press, 1962.

Stewart, Desmond Sterling. *Turmoil in Beirut: A Personal Account.* London: Wingate, 1958.

Suleiman, Michael W. *Political Parties in Lebanon: The Challenge of a Fragmented Political Culture.* Ithaca, N.Y.: Cornell University Press, 1967.

Sykes, John. *Mountain Arabs.* Philadelphia: Chilton, 1968.

Thubron, Colin. *Hills of Adonis: A Quest in Lebanon.* Boston: Little, Brown, 1969.

Ziadeh, Nicola A. *Syria and Lebanon.* New York: Praeger, 1957.

MALAYSIA

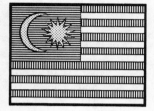

CAPITAL: Kuala Lumpur. **FLAG**: The national flag consists of 14 alternating horizontal stripes of which 7 are red and 7 white; a gold 14-pointed star and crescent appear on a blue field in the upper left corner. **ANTHEM**: *Negara Ku (My Country)*. **MONETARY UNIT**: The Malaysian ringgit (M$) is divided into 100 sen (¢). There are coins of 1, 5, 10, 20, and 50 sen, and notes of 1, 5, 10, 50, 100, and 1,000 Malaysian ringgit. M$1=$0.39143 (or $1=M$2.5547). **WEIGHTS AND MEASURES**: British weights and measures are generally used, but some local units also are found. **HOLIDAYS**: Wesak Day, 19 May; Birthday of His Majesty the Yang di-Pertuan Agong, 5 June; National Day, 31 August; Christmas, 25 December. Movable holidays include Hari Raya Puasa, Hari Raya Haji, the First of Muharram, Milad al-Nabi, Diwali, and the Chinese New Year. Individual states celebrate the birthdays of their rulers and other holidays observed by ethnic groups. **TIME**: 7:30 P.M.=noon GMT.

¹LOCATION, SIZE, AND EXTENT

Situated in Southeast Asia, Malaysia, with an area of 329,745 sq km (127,315 sq mi), consists of two noncontiguous areas: Peninsular Malaysia (formerly West Malaysia), on the Asian mainland, and Sarawak and Sabah, known together as East Malaysia, on the island of Borneo. Peninsular Malaysia, protruding southward from the mainland of Asia, comprises an area of 131,587 sq km (50,806 sq mi), extending 748 km (465 mi) SSE–NNW and 322 km (200 mi) ENE–WSW. It is bordered on the N by Thailand, on the E by the South China Sea, on the S by the Strait of Johore, and on the W by the Strait of Malacca and the Andaman Sea, with a total boundary length of 2,507 km (1,558 mi). Sarawak, covering an area of 124,447 sq km (48,049 sq mi), on the northwest coast of Borneo, extends 679 km (422 mi) NNE–SSW and 254 km (158 mi) ESE–WNW. It is bounded by Brunei on the N, Sabah on the NE, Indonesia on the E and S, and the South China Sea on the W. Sarawak's total boundary length is 2,621 km (1,629 mi). Situated at the northern end of Borneo, Sabah's area is 73,711 sq km (28,460 sq mi), with a length of 412 km (256 mi) E–W and a width of 328 km (204 mi) N–S. To the N is the Balabac Strait, to the NE the Sulu Sea, to the SE the Celebes Sea, to the S Indonesia, to the SW Sarawak, and to the W the South China Sea, with a total boundary length of 2,008 km (1,248 mi).

Malaysia consists of 13 states: Johor, 18,985 sq km (7,330 sq mi); Kedah, 9,425 sq km (3,639 sq mi); Kelantan, 14,931 sq km (5,765 sq mi); Melaka (formerly known as Malacca), 1,650 sq km (637 sq mi); Negri Sembilan, 6,643 sq km (2,565 sq mi); Pahang, 35,965 sq km (13,886 sq mi); Pulau Pinang, including Seberang Prai (formerly known as Penang and Province Wellesley, respectively), 1,033 sq km (399 sq mi); Perak, 21,005 sq km (8,110 sq mi); Perlis, 795 sq km (307 sq mi); Selangor, 8,200 sq km (3,166 sq mi); and Trengganu, 12,955 sq km (5,002 sq mi), all in Peninsular Malaysia; and Sabah and Sarawak in East Malaysia. It also includes numerous small islands.

²TOPOGRAPHY

Four-fifths of peninsular Malaysia is covered by jungle and swamp. The northern regions are divided by a series of mountain ranges that rise abruptly from the wide flat coastal plains. The highest peaks, Gunong Tahan (7,186 feet) and Gunong Korbu (7,163 feet) are in the north-central area. The main watershed follows a mountain range about 50 miles inland, roughly parallel to the west coast and reaching from the Thai border to Melaka.

The rivers flowing to the east, south, and west of this range are swift and have cut some deep gorges, but on reaching the coastal plains they become sluggish. The western coastal plain, barely above sea level and thickly covered with mangrove, contains most of the country's population and the main seaports, Pinang (actually an offshore island) and Kelang (formerly Port Swettenham). These and other Peninsular ports are subject to silting. The eastern coastal plain has a gradual slope but is mostly jungle and lightly settled. It is subject to heavy storms from the South China Sea and lacks natural harbors.

Sarawak consists of an alluvial and swampy coastal plain, an area of rolling country interspersed with mountain ranges, and a mountainous interior. Rain forests cover the greater part of Sarawak. Many of the rivers are navigable.

Sabah is split in two by the Crocker range, which extends north and south some 30 miles inland from the west coast, rising to over 13,450 feet at Mount Kinabalu. Most of the interior is covered with tropical forest, while the western coastal area consists of alluvial flats making up the main rubber and rice land. There are many rivers, which, in the eastern part of the country, often form the only means of transportation.

³CLIMATE

The climate of Peninsular Malaysia is equatorial, characterized by fairly high but uniform temperature—ranging from 23.4° to 30.6°C (74° to 87°F)—throughout the year, high humidity, and copious rainfall (averaging about 100 inches annually). There are seasonal variations in rainfall, with heaviest rains from October to December or January; except for a few mountain areas, the most abundant rainfall is in the eastern coastal region, where it averages over 120 inches per year. Elsewhere the annual average is 80 to 120 inches, the northwestern and southwestern regions having the least rainfall. The nights are usually cool because of the nearby seas. The climate of East Malaysia is relatively cool for an area so near the equator.

⁴FLORA AND FAUNA

Plants and animals of Peninsular Malaysia are those common to the tropical evergreen rain-forest regions of South Asia. Camphor, ebony, sandalwood, teak, and many varieties of palm trees abound. The jungle fauna includes seladang (Malayan bison), deer, wild pigs, tree shrews, honey bears, forest cats, civets, monkeys, crocodiles, huge lizards, and snakes. The seladang is considered the largest wild ox in the world. It weighs a ton and is vicious when injured or cornered. An immense variety of insects, particularly butterflies, and some 575 species of birds are found.

Due to the mingling of Southeast Asian and Australian forms of life, a great wealth of species (although not genuses) exists in Sabah and Sarawak, resulting in a complex evolution influenced by geological developments. Wide belts of coastal forests consist of mangroves and the white-barked Myrtacea. Sandy stretches are covered by stiff, bluish grass and black filaos (resembling cypress). Lowland forests contain some 400 species of tall dipterocarps (hardwoods) and semihardwoods; fig trees abound, attracting small mammals and birds, and groves are formed by the extensive aerial roots of warangen (a sacred tree to indigenous peoples). As altitude increases, herbaceous plants become more numerous—buttercups, violets, and valerian—until moss-covered evergreen forests are reached between 5,000 and 6,000 feet.

East Malaysia's insect and bird life is the richest in species in the world, including the gigantic beetle Brupestes, longicorns, large butterflies, and many brilliantly colored birds of paradise. The great swampy forests of Sabah and Sarawak are one of the last natural habitats of the endangered orangutan; they are also inhabited by the seladang, hornbill, and the endangered two-horned Sumatran rhinoceros.

As of 1975, other endangered species in Malaysia included the four-striped ground squirrel, Asiatic wild dog, clouded leopard (*Neofelis nebulosa*), Indochinese tiger, leopard, Asian elephant, Malayan tapir, Asiatic buffalo, gaur, white-winged wood duck, Malaysian peacock pheasant, rufous-headed robin, Rueck's blue flycatcher, river terrapin, false gavial, and two species of crocodile (estuarine and Siamese). The tapir, tiger, and two species of rhinoceros are totally protected by the government.

5 POPULATION

The total population of Malaysia at the end of 1972 was officially estimated at 11,149,768, of which 9,379,927 were in Peninsular Malaysia, 1,033,157 in Sarawak, and 736,684 in Sabah.

The population of Malaysia in 1975 was estimated at 12,093,000. Population for 1980 was projected at 13,998,000. The population density in 1975 was 37 per sq km and the annual rate of increase during 1970–75 was estimated at 2.89%. The crude birthrate was 38.7 per 1,000 and the death rate 9.9 per 1,000. Approximately 43.9% of the total population was under 15 years of age. The population is concentrated in the western coastal plain; since the end of World War II there has been a heavy migration to the urban centers.

The 1970 census populations of the major cities were Kuala Lumpur, 451,728; George Town, 270,019; Ipoh, 247,689; Johor Baharu, 135,936; Melaka, 86,357; and Seremban, 79,915.

6 ETHNIC GROUPS

The population of Malaysia consists of three main racial groups—Malays, Chinese, and peoples of the Indian subcontinent. Official estimates at the end of 1972 reported the following distribution for Peninsular Malaysia: Malays, 4,991,405 (53.2%); Chinese, 3,325,595 (35.5%); Indians and Pakistanis, 989,679 (10.5%); and other groups, 73,248 (0.8%). The Semang and Sakai, aborigines numbering about 50,000, are the remnants of early peninsular migrations. The Semang tribes live mainly in the northern jungles, while the seminomadic Sakai dwell in mountainous country. Small enclaves of Thai, Ceylonese, and Europeans comprise the remaining minority groups. British nationals play a key role in the commerce of Peninsular Malaysia, especially in the tin, rubber, and palm oil industries. The Malays predominate in the rural areas; the Chinese are concentrated in the rural, agricultural, and mining areas; Indians and Pakistanis are either town dwellers or workers on rubber plantations. Enmity between Chinese and Malay communities has occasionally erupted into violence in recent decades.

Indigenous tribes constitute about half of Sarawak's population; the largest indigenous group are the Sea Dayaks, or Ibans,

(30.2% of the total population), followed by the Land Dayaks (8.7%), Melanaus (5.4%), and 53,320 other indigenous peoples (5.2%). The balance of Sarawak's population includes 315,947 Chinese (30.6%), 195,625 Malays (18.9%), and 10,276 others (1%). Some 61.8% of Sabah's population comprises indigenous peoples, principally Kadazans (26.9%), Bajaus (11.4%), and Muruts (4.5%). The balance is dominated by Chinese (21.5%), Malays (4.1%), and others (12.6%).

7 LANGUAGE

Malay is the national language and the lingua franca of all Malaysia. Because the Malaysian culture developed no written language of its own, Malay is transcribed using the Roman alphabet, Rumi (used widely in official circles), or Arabic (called Jawi) script. Known locally as Bahasa Malaysia, Malay became the sole official language in September 1967. Up to that time, English had also been an official language; English is still widely used in government and business. Chinese (notably Hokkien, Cantonese, and Hakka dialects), Arabic, Tamil, Hindustani, Punjabi, Kadazan, and many other languages and dialects are spoken.

8 RELIGION

Islam is the official religion of Malaysia, and more than half the people of Peninsular Malaysia are Muslims. The head of state, the yang di-pertuan agong, is also the national leader of the Islamic faith. The constitution, however, guarantees freedom to profess, practice, and propagate other religions. Religious lines generally follow ethnic lines: almost all Malays are Muslims; most Indians are Hindus, with a substantial minority of Muslims, Sikhs, and Parsees; and most Chinese are Confucian-Buddhists. Some Chinese are Muslims. Christianity also has won adherents among the Chinese and Indians.

The indigenous peoples of East Malaysia are still largely animist, although many have become Christian.

9 TRANSPORTATION

The north-south mountain range down the center of the peninsula has set the transportation pattern of Peninsular Malaysia. Main transport lines run north and south, while east-west connections are few. Most of the main arteries lie west of the range. In 1974, the highway system in Malaysia consisted of about 11,500 miles of roads, of which some 9,200 miles were permanently surfaced. In Sabah and Sarawak there were 2,080 and 2,100 miles of road, respectively. The main road system is well constructed and maintained; the government has built a system of feeder roads from rural points and industrial sites to railway stations. At the end of 1974, vehicles registered in the country included 368,169 private passenger cars, 107,538 commercial vehicles, and 8,378 buses. Preference is given to Malay-speaking applicants for permits to operate commercial vehicles.

The government-owned Malayan Railway operates some 1,036 miles of meter-gauge running lines. In equipment, engineering service, and maintenance, the railway is of high standard. A modern air-conditioned train operates between Singapore and Bangkok, the Malaysian line linking up with the Thai line. In East Malaysia, Sabah Railways serves the west coast and parts of the interior.

Peninsular Malaysia has international airports at Sabang, 12 miles from Kuala Lumpur, Pinang, Kuchins, and Kota Kinabalu; there are also 14 domestic airports and numerous landing strips throughout the country. Some 15 international airlines provide direct flights from Hong Kong and more than 30 cities in Australia, Thailand, India, the Middle East, and Europe to Kuala Lumpur. The Malaysian Airline System (MAS), the country's national airline, links Peninsular and East Malaysia with the rest of the world.

Singapore handles about three-fourths of Peninsular Malaysia's international shipments and, through 41 steamship lines, connects it with every part of the world. In Malaysia, the principal seaports are Kelang and Pinang (170 miles apart), with subsidiary port facilities at Melaka, Port Dickson, and Telok Anson on the west coast, Dungun and Tumpat on the east coast. Pinang (a free port) and Kelang both offer firm anchorage in deep sheltered waters but lack sufficient berthing docks. New deepwater berths and transit and storage godowns have been constructed at Kelang. Melaka is primarily a lighterage port; Telok Anson and Port Dickson are coastal oil ports. Heavy tonnages of iron ore have in recent years been loaded and transshipped from Dungun and Tumpat, but Dungun is inoperative during the severe monsoon season. A total of 13,940,000 tons of cargo was handled in Malaysian ports in 1972.

The sea and the rivers are the chief means of transport in Sarawak. Local shipping companies, mainly Chinese, ply the main rivers and between coastal ports.

augurated in 1963, operated more than 48 transmitters in 1974; service was extended to Sabah in late 1971. In 1973 there were 359,000 television subscribers (compared with 26,000 in 1968). Subscribers receive a two-network program.

¹¹HISTORY

The ancestors of the Malays came down from South China and settled in the Malay Peninsula about 2000 B.C. Sri Vijaya, a strong Indo-Malay empire with headquarters at Palembang in southern Sumatra, rose about A.D. 600 and came to dominate both sides of the Strait of Malacca, levying tribute and tolls on the ships faring between China and India. In the 11th century, however, Sri Vijaya fell before the attacks of a new empire in Java. About 1400, a fugitive ruler from Tumasik (now Singapore) founded a principality at Malacca (now Melaka), a port on the Strait about 100 miles north of Singapore. From it, Muslim In-

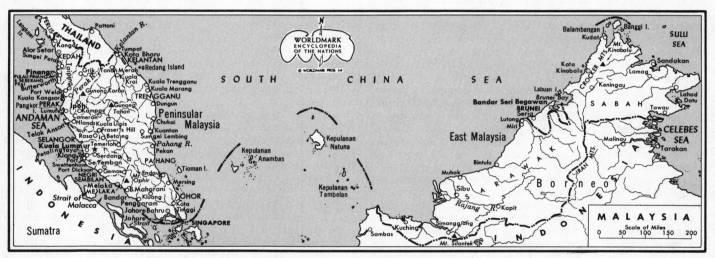

See continental political: front cover O9, P9; physical: back cover O9, P9

LOCATION: Peninsular Malaysia; 1°17′ to 6°43′N; 99°38′ to 104°39′E. Sarawak: 0°52′ to 4°59′N; 109°38′ to 155°43′E. Sabah: 4°6′ to 7°22′N; 115°7′ to 119°17′E. **BOUNDARY LENGTHS**: Peninsular Malaysia: Thailand, 576 km (358 mi); total coastline, 1,931 km (1,200 mi). Sarawak: Brunei, 418 km (260 mi); Sabah, 135 km (84 mi); coastline, 888 km (552 mi). Sabah: Sarawak, 135 km (84 mi); total coastline, 1,558 km (968 mi). Total boundary length of Indonesia with Sarawak and Sabah, 1,496 km (930 mi). **TERRITORIAL SEA LIMIT**: 12 mi.

¹⁰COMMUNICATIONS

The government owns and operates a well-developed and well-equipped telecommunications system. A heavy volume of communications traffic exists between Malaysia and Singapore. At the end of 1973, Malaysia had about 234,000 telephones, including private wire and public coin stations. Automatic dialing for the majority of exchanges is provided by a very high frequency (VHF) radio circuit. There are about 21 telephones per 1,000 population, a high ratio for an Asian country. Telegraph and radiotelephone connections link Peninsular Malaysia with most foreign countries.

The government operates special radio circuits for the broadcasting, civil aviation, and meteorological departments and the Malayan Railway, as well as circuits for military and police authorities. Radio Malaysia broadcasts in English, Malay, Iban, Biatan, Kadazan, Murut, Bajau, five Chinese dialects, and Tamil. Programs are currently carried over 31 shortwave and 66 medium-wave transmitters in various parts of the country that are linked by microwave circuits. In 1973, licensed radios numbered 462,000; actual sets in use, however, are probably double the official figures. In 1962, Radio Malaysia accepted limited advertising for the first time. Television Malaysia, in-

dian and Arab missionaries carried Islam to the Malay Peninsula and the Indonesian archipelago.

It was at Malacca that the West obtained its first foothold on the peninsula. At the height of its glory and power, the principality fell to Portugal in 1511. In their turn, the Portuguese were driven out by the Dutch in 1641.

The British East India Company laid the groundwork for British control of Malaya in 1786 by the lease from the sultan of Kedah of Penang, an island off the west coast of Malaya about 500 miles north of Singapore. Fourteen years later, it obtained from him a small area on the mainland opposite Penang (now Pulau Pinang) which the company named Province Wellesley (now Seberang Prai). In 1819, a farsighted British colonial administrator, Sir Thomas Stamford Raffles, having seen the potentialities of Singapore as a naval base and trading center, obtained permission to establish a settlement there; and in 1824, by agreement and financial settlement, the island was ceded to the British East India Company. In 1825, the Dutch settlement at Malacca was ceded to Great Britain. Penang, Singapore, and Malacca were combined in 1829 to form the Straits Settlements. They were administered from India until 1867 and from the Colonial Office in London thereafter.

For 50 years after the acquisition of Singapore, the British did not interfere with the Malay states, in spite of civil war, anarchy, piracy, and slavery. The states of Perak and Selangor in 1874 secured treaties of protection from the British. Similar treaties were subsequently made with the sultans of Negri Sembilan (1874–89) and Pahang (1888). In 1895, these four states became a federation (the Federated Malay States), with a British resident-general and a system of centralized government. In 1909, under the Bangkok Treaty, Siam ceded the four northern states of Kelantan, Trengganu, Perlis, and Kedah to the UK, and in 1914 Johore became a British protectorate, but these entities remained outside the federation.

The establishment of law and order, the development of the rubber industry, and the growth of tin mining brought prosperity to Malaya and attracted large numbers of Chinese and Indians to the country.

Japanese forces invaded Malaya in December 1941 and occupied it throughout World War II. A year after their return in September 1945, the British formed the Malayan Union. It was succeeded by the Federation of Malaya on 1 February 1948. During the next eight years, rapid progress was made toward responsible government and independence in spite of a Communist insurrection in 1948, which kept the country in a state of emergency for over a decade.

The Federation of Malaya agreement was signed on 5 August 1957; on 31 August, Malaya became an independent country with membership in the Commonwealth of Nations. On 1 August 1962, Britain and Malaya agreed in principle on the formation of the new state of Malaysia—a political merger of Singapore and the British Borneo territories (Sarawak, Brunei, and North Borneo) with the Federation—by 31 August 1963. On 1 September 1962, Singapore in a 70% plurality referendum voted for incorporation in the proposed Malaysia. An abortive revolt staged by Brunei's ultranationalistic Partai Rak'yat in December 1962 obscured this sultanate's future in Malaysia. On 16 September 1963, the Federation of Malaya, the State of Singapore, and the newly independent British colonies of Sarawak and North Borneo (renamed Sabah) formed the Federation of Malaysia, subsequently renamed simply as Malaysia. (Brunei opted not to join the Federation and has remained a UK dependency.) Under the Malaysia plan, internal security and external defense and affairs became the responsibility of the central Malaysian government; autonomy in domestic and economic matters was retained by other member areas.

On 7 August 1965, the Singapore government seceded from the Malaysian Federation and established an independent republic. Internal disorder stemming from hostilities between Chinese and Malay communities in Kuala Lumpur disrupted the 1969 national elections and prompted the declaration of a state of emergency lasting from mid-1969 to February 1971. Communist insurgency activities, largely dormant for more than two decades, resumed in the mid-1970s in the wake of the US military withdrawal from Southeast Asia. In 1975, guerrilla attacks occurred both in the northern peninsula and in Sarawak. Throughout the decade, however, the government succeeded in sustaining both political stability and the nation's high rate of economic growth.

12 GOVERNMENT

Malaysia is a constitutional monarchy consisting of 13 states, 9 of which were formerly principalities under British protection and 4 of which (Melaka, Pulau Pinang, Sarawak, and Sabah) were former British settlements ruled by appointed governors. The present constitution, promulgated on 16 September 1963, is based on the 1957 constitution of the former Federation of Malaya with provisions for the special interests of Sabah and Sarawak. It provides for the election of a head of state, the yang di-pertuan agong, or paramount ruler, for a single term of five years by and from the conference of the nine sultans of Peninsular Malaysia. The constitution also provides for a deputy head of state, chosen in the same manner and for the same term. On 19 June 1975, Tuanka Yahya Putra, the sultan of Kelantan, was elected as Malaysia's sixth supreme head of state.

The Conference of Rulers, which consists of the sultans of the individual states, has limited legislative but considerable advisory power. Its consent must be obtained for any law that alters state boundaries, affects the rulers' privileges, honors, or dignities, or extends any religious acts, observances, or ceremonies to the country as a whole. The conference must be consulted on proposed changes of administrative policy affecting the special position of the Malays or the vital interests of other communities.

The head of state appoints the prime minister, leader of the majority party or coalition in the House of Representatives, who then chooses his cabinet; executive power rests in the prime minister and cabinet.

Parliament consists of two houses. The 58-member Senate (Dewan Negara) consists of 26 elected members (2 from each state) and 32 members appointed by the paramount ruler on the basis of distinguished public service or their eligibility to represent the racial minorities. Senators must be at least 30 years old; they hold office for six years and have overlapping terms. Members of the House of Representatives (Dewan Ra'ayat) must be at least 21 years old. They are elected by universal adult suffrage from 154 single-member constituencies (114 from Peninsular Malaysia and 40 from East Malaysia) determined by a population count. Their term is five years unless the House is dissolved earlier.

13 POLITICAL PARTIES

Prior to World War II, there was limited political activity in Malaya, but the Japanese occupation and its aftermath brought a new political awareness. Postwar political parties sought independence, and although the Malays feared domination by the populous minorities, particularly the economically stronger Chinese, the United Malays National Organization (UMNO), the leading Malay party, and the Malaysian Chinese Association formed the Alliance Party in 1952. This party was later joined by the Malayan Indian Congress. In the general elections of July 1955, the Alliance won 51 of the 52 seats in the legislative council, and Tunku Abdul Rahman, a Malay prince, was appointed chief minister. When the Alliance achieved Malayan independence in 1957, Tunku Abdul Rahman became prime minister and retained the post after the formation of the Federation of Malaysia in 1963. The Alliance is mainly pro-Western, and the UMNO, in particular, is a conservative party with Western-trained leaders friendly toward European economic interests.

In August 1965, a loose coalition, known as the Malaysian Solidarity Convention (MSC), was formed to protest the policies of the Alliance Party, which the MSC claimed had led to the secession of Singapore. The MSC is composed of five minor parties: the United Democratic Party, the People's Progressive Party, the People's Action Party, the Sarawak United People's Party, and the Party Machinda.

The Malayan Communist party, a powerful and well-organized group after the war, penetrated and dominated the trade unions. In 1948, however, after the Communists had resorted to arms, they were outlawed, and martial law was declared. The struggle against the Communists—never more than a few thousand and mainly Chinese—disrupted the Malayan economy and retarded political integration. After more than 10 years of conflict, the Communist threat was greatly reduced, although in the mid-1970s it was showing signs of a resurgence.

In the elections of April 1964, the Alliance Party won a majority of 89 of the 154 House seats. Malaysia's third general election since independence was held in Peninsular Malaysia on 10 May 1969. This was followed by communal rioting, mainly between Malays and Chinese, resulting in much loss of life and damage to property. The government suspended parliament and declared a state of emergency. A National Operations Council was created to combat terrorism and maintain order. The government postponed elections in East Malaysia until July 1970.

In the May 1969 Peninsular elections, the ruling Alliance Party suffered a setback, winning only 66 seats, as compared with 89 in the 1964 elections. By the time parliament was reconvened on 22 February 1971, the Alliance had achieved a two-thirds majority (required for the passage of constitutional amendments) with the addition of 10 unopposed seats from Sabah and through a coalition with the 12-member Sarawak United People's Party. The elections for state assemblies had also resulted in a setback for the Alliance party, which before the elections had controlled 10 of the 13 state assemblies, but after the elections only 7. In September 1970, Tunku Abdul Rahman retired as prime minister and was replaced by the deputy prime minister, Tun Abdul Razak.

In 1973, the Alliance party formed a broad coalition known as the National Front (Barisan Nasional) and comprising 11 minority parties, including 6 from the peninsula and 5 from East Malaysia. The National Front succeeded in winning 135 seats in national elections held on 24 August 1974. The largest opposition group to emerge from the elections was the militant Democratic Action Party, which polled more than half of the Chinese popular vote but won only 9 seats, owing to a legislative apportionment that heavily favored Malay voters. Unlike the previous elections, the 1974 balloting proceeded calmly and without disturbance. Tun Abdul Razak, who was retained as prime minister, died in office on 14 January 1976. He was replaced by former deputy prime minister Datuk Hussein bin Onn, the son of the founder of the UMNO, Dato Onn bin Ja'afar.

¹⁴LOCAL GOVERNMENT

Of the 11 Peninsular states, 9 are headed by sultans, who act as titular rulers and as leaders of the Islamic faith in their respective states. Pinang and Melaka are headed by federally appointed governors. State governments are parliamentary in form and share legislative powers with the federal parliament. Effective executive authority in each state is vested in a chief minister, selected by the majority party in the state legislature. The legislative assembly, composed of elected members, legislates in conformity with the Malaysian and state constitutions, subject to the sultan's assent.

There are five main types of local government authorities: (1) The City Council of George Town is fully elective and presided over by a mayor; the City Hall of the Federal Territory of Kuala Lumpur has an advisory board comprising nominated members and presided over by a mayor. The City Hall of the Federal Territory is the direct responsibility of the federal government. (2) Municipal councils in Melaka and Ipoh have nominated members. (3) Town councils in larger towns have an elected majority and an administrative officer appointed by the state government. (4) Finally, there are appointed town councils and town boards, and (5) elected local councils in rural areas. Financial autonomy and administrative responsibility are not uniform, but there is a trend toward autonomy in local matters.

Upon incorporation into the Federation of Malaysia in 1963, both Sabah and Sarawak adopted separate constitutions for their local self-government. Each government is headed by a chief minister, appointed by the majority party of the elective legislature. Virtually the entire leadership of Sabah, including the chief minister, Fuad Stephens, was killed in a plane crash near Kota Kinabalu in June 1976.

¹⁵JUDICIAL SYSTEM

Malaysia has a unified judicial system and all courts take cognizance of both federal and state laws. The legal system is founded in British common law. Most cases come before magistrates and sessions courts, although there are local courts (Penghulus' courts) with limited and local jurisdiction. Religious courts for Muslim issues and juvenile courts also exist. The Federal Court, the highest court in Malaysia, reviews decisions referred from the High Court of Peninsular Malaysia, the High Court of East Malaysia, and subordinate courts. The Federal Court has original jurisdiction in disputes among states or between a state and the federal government. The supreme head is the lord president of the Federal Court. A Ministry of Law and Attorney-General was established in August 1974.

¹⁶ARMED FORCES

The Malaysian armed forces consist of the army, navy, and air force, together with volunteer and auxiliary forces for each arm. The minister of defense, chairman of the Armed Forces Council, is responsible for the armed forces.

As a result of consultations between Malaysia, the UK, Australia, New Zealand, and Singapore, the Five Power Defence Arrangements came into force in 1971, replacing the Anglo-Malaysia Defence Treaty. The new arrangements provided for consultation between Malaysia and its partners in the event of external aggression or threat of such aggression. The Malaysian government announced that it viewed the new accord as a transitional arrangement that would be abolished once the neutralization of Southeast Asia, as envisaged in the ASEAN Kuala Lumpur Declaration of 1970, is achieved.

In 1975, the armed forces totaled 61,100 personnel. The total strength of the army was 51,000. It had 29 infantry battalions, 3 reconnaissance regiments, 3 artillery regiments, and supporting air defense, signal, engineer, and administrative units. Contingents of the Malaysian army patrol the Malaysian-Thailand border against Communist guerrillas. The army contributed a force to the UN operations in the Congo (now Zaire) from October 1960 to March 1963.

The Malaysian navy, in 1975, had 4,800 personnel, 2 frigates, 6 coastal minesweepers, and 32 patrol boats. The air force had about 5,300 personnel and 40 combat aircraft.

Introducing the 1974 budget, the prime minister and minister of defense announced that the expenditure on defense and security for the year would be M$747 million, or 14% of the country's estimated revenue; in 1975, expenditure for defense and security was M$1,018 million, or 9.5% of the total.

¹⁷MIGRATION

Not until British economic enterprise first attracted foreign labor after 1800 did large-scale Chinese, Indian, and Malaysian migration (nonnative Indonesians and Borneans) take place. The early migrants were transients: in 1921, only 20.3% of the Chinese and 11.9% of the Indians were Malaya-born. However, migration data for subsequent years shows a general tendency to permanent settlement by these nonindigenous portions of the population. The percentages of the total Chinese population reporting Peninsular Malaysia as their birthplace were 29.1%, 62.5%, and 74.4% for the years 1931, 1947, and 1957, respectively. The percentages of Indians reporting their birthplace as Peninsular Malaysia were 21.1%, 51.4%, and 64.6% for the years 1931, 1947, and 1957, respectively. By 1953, the Malays were a minority in their own territory. The government enacted restrictive legislation against further immigration, and by 1968, the Malays formed slightly more than 50% of the population. To control immigration, regulations came into effect in 1968 concerning passports and border crossings between Malaysia and Indonesia and between Malaysia and the Philippines. By 1970, a large proportion of the Chinese (approximately 86.4%) and Indians (about 81.7%) were born in Peninsular Malaysia.

[18]INTERNATIONAL COOPERATION

Malaysia is a member of the UN and its specialized agencies, of the British Commonwealth, the Colombo Plan, and ASEAN. Malaysia is a signatory to the Five Power Defence Treaty (with the UK, Australia, New Zealand, and Singapore). Prior to the 1970s, Malaysia pursued a pro-Western policy of alignment, but in recent years has promoted the neutralization of Southeast Asia while concurrently establishing ties with China, the Democratic Republic of Viet-Nam (DRV), the Democratic People's Republic of Korea, and Cuba, and strengthening relations with the USSR and other East European states. Links with its traditional allies, including the UK and US, have remained strong in the course of this transition.

[19]ECONOMY

Malaysia enjoys one of the most stable and prosperous economies in East Asia. Economic development has resulted in an export-oriented economy, with exports accounting for about 52% of the GNP in the mid-1970s. In 1974, the level of economic activity resulted in the GNP's reaching US$8.7 billion. The growth rate was 6%, as against 3.9% in 1967. Per capita income in 1974 stood at US$715.5, a 4% increase over the previous year.

Peninsular Malaysia's economy is based chiefly on its plantation and mining activities, which produce one-third of the world's rubber and tin. Rubber accounts for about 30% by value of Malaysia's total exports, and tin for 15% to 20%. Malaysia is the world's largest exporter of palm oil, contributing one-third of world exports since 1966. The government has sought to counter world fluctuations in tin and rubber prices through an active policy of industrialization and agricultural diversification.

About 50% of the economically active population is engaged in agriculture. A peasant subsistence economy of rice and fish and mixed farms is situated mainly in the north and east of the peninsula and along the fringe of the jungle. As a result of price support and production subsidies, Peninsular Malaysia now supplies 80% or more of its rice requirements.

Sarawak's basic economy is subsistence agriculture supplemented by the collection of forest produce and by fishing, and by the cultivation of cash crops, primarily rubber and pepper. More than two-thirds of the inhabitants are engaged in agriculture, which earns well over half the national income. Nevertheless, much of the region's annual rice needs must still be imported. The basis of Sabah's economy is agriculture, with timber and rubber of prime importance.

[20]INCOME

Malaysia has the third highest per capita income in Asia, after Japan and Singapore. In 1974 it reached US715.5, as compared with US$322 in 1968. Malaysia's GDP in 1974 (at factor cost) was M$17,014 million. It was distributed (in millions of ringgit) as follows: agriculture, M$4,108 (24.1%); manufacturing, M$2,875 (16.9%); forestry and fishing, M$1,414 (8.3%); mining and quarrying, M$954 (5.6%); construction, M$863 (5.1%); electricity and water resources, M$388 (2.3%); and commerce, finance, and other services, M$6,412 (37.7%).

[21]LABOR

In 1974, Malaysia's work force was estimated at 3.8 million. At the end of 1970, Malaysia had an active labor force of 3,597,000 out of a population of 5,880,000 in the 15–64 age range. Males constituted 67.7% of the labor force and females 32.3%; 32.4% of the work force consisted of persons in the 15–24 age group. Of the 3,328,000 who were employed, 1,749,000 (52.6%) were in agriculture, forestry, and fishing; 321,000 (9.6%) in services; 318,000 (9.6%) in manufacturing; 309,000 (9.3%) in wholesale and retail trade; 284,000 (8.5%) in public administration and defense; 129,000 (3.9%) in transport, storage, and communications; 91,000 (2.7%) in construction; 87,000 (2.6%) in mining and quarrying; and 40,000 (1.2%) in other sectors. Malays comprise the bulk of the agriculturalists, cultivating most of the rice paddies or working on self-owned rubber smallholdings. The Chinese, Indians, and Pakistanis are mainly urban, with the exception of a nominal number employed on the rubber estates.

Unemployment has been serious since 1965. The rapid population increase, wider educational opportunities, and the migration to the towns have accentuated the problem. In 1974, the unemployment rate stood at 7%. The rate of unemployment in the major towns exceeded 10%. Underemployment is the major problem in rural areas. Since 1965, the government has fostered a youth training program. Malaysians are given preference when job openings occur. Non-Malaysians are required to register when they need employment. Development of new industries and work projects that create more job opportunities is encouraged by the government. While there has been an increase in unemployment in Peninsular Malaysia, East Malaysia has experienced a general shortage of labor.

By 1974, the country had a total of 344 registered unions (industrial, civil service, and employer), with a total membership of 459,070. Peninsular Malaysia had 264 unions, with 432,149 members; Sabah, 23 unions, with 8,571 members; and Sarawak, 57 unions, with 18,350 members. Plantation workers and mining employees make up the two largest unions. The trade-union movement is generally organized along ethnic lines. Indians have tended to dominate the central labor organization, the Malaysian Trades Union Congress, and the constituent unions.

Commerce and industry operate on a 46-hour week. Protective labor legislation in Malaysia is more extensive than in most Asian countries. New employment and labor legislation was enacted in 1957, ensuring fair contracts and safe working conditions; regulating the employment of children, minors, and women; and establishing rest days as well as housing and medical care. The Employees' Social Security Act of 1969 comprises an Employment Injury Insurance Scheme and an Invalidity Pension Scheme. Coverage extends mostly to urban industrial workers and was expanded to include Sabah and Sarawak in March 1974.

[22]AGRICULTURE

Agriculture is the most important sector of the Malaysian economy, contributing about one-fourth of the GDP, employing about half of the work force, and providing about 55% of the country's exports. Five-sixths of East Malaysia is dense jungle and its topography and climate are not conducive to farming. Peninsular Malaysia, however, is predominantly an agricultural region. Cultivation is carried out on the coastal plains, river valleys, and foothills. Of the 7.7 million acres cultivated in 1974, about 4.2 million were in rubber, 1.5 million in rice, and 1.1 million in palm oil. The rest of the cultivated area was in coconut, tea, and spices. About two-thirds of the farms are less than 5 acres. Most large plantation holdings are owned by Europeans, Chinese, and Indians.

The Malay peasant is predominantly a subsistence farmer, although in some areas rice is raised as a cash crop. Rubber and oil palm are chiefly large-scale plantation industries. Coconuts, however, are cultivated by small landholders. Domestic rice furnishes Peninsular Malaysia with about 82% of its requirements; most of East Malaysia's rice supply, however, must be imported. Rice production for 1974 totaled 1,341,000 tons. Rubber is the major single commodity in the Malaysian economy, accounting for 17% of the GNP and 30% of exports in 1974. The government, through the Rubber Research Institute of Malaya, has concentrated on improving production, and in the 1970s Malaysian natural rubber was competing successfully with synthetics. Malaysian rubber production in 1974 was estimated at 1,499,900 tons, with Peninsular Malaysia accounting for 97.5%; palm oil, 968,300 tons; fresh pineapples, 241,500 tons; copra, 133,000 tons; and pepper, almost entirely produced in Sarawak, 29,800 tons.

To ensure a less vulnerable agricultural economy, the government is promoting diversification of agriculture; increased production of crops such as pineapple and cocoa; improved methods of cultivating, marketing, and storing; and expanded research and agricultural education. Some of the measures that have been taken since the mid-1970s are the implementation of drainage and irrigation schemes, extension of irrigation projects, improvement in the quality and quantity of agriculture instructors, institution of research programs, and the correction of shortcomings in the fields of land tenure, credit, and marketing facilities. Marked success has been achieved in palm-oil development; during 1966–74, the area of palm-oil estates tripled while production increased more than fivefold. A national council for food and agriculture was formed in 1966 to advise the government on agricultural programs.

23 ANIMAL HUSBANDRY

Peninsular Malaysia is free of most of the infectious and contagious diseases that plague livestock in the tropical zone, but the livestock industry is limited by unfavorable climate and lack of natural pastures. The livestock population on the peninsula in 1973 included 805,000 hogs, 326,000 head of cattle, and 41,000 sheep. The Malayan swamp buffalo and indigenous breeds of cattle are used mainly as draft animals. Hog raising and export are handled mainly by non-Muslim Chinese. Slaughter is religiously prescribed in Muslim communities.

24 FISHING

Offshore, local estuary, and pond fishing are under the control of the Department of Fisheries. Although fishing has not been fully developed, it contributes 15% of the value of domestic food and provides a primary source of protein in the country's diet. The total catch in 1973 was 444,700 tons, as compared with 296,300 tons in 1966; the increase has been largely the result of increased adoption and acceptance of trawling.

Inshore fishing with hand-operated gear from nonpowered boats remains common, but a government training program in navigation and engine care is accelerating the use of powered boats that can fish in offshore waters. Freshwater fishing in paddy fields and irrigation ditches is integrated with rice farming and hog production.

The government encourages the development of credit and marketing cooperatives for fishermen and is introducing mechanized techniques, researching fish resources, and promoting canneries. A marine extension section was set up in 1968 to help bridge the gap between research and the fishermen and to give technical advice and assistance to fishermen. Fisheries technicians for oceangoing vessels are being trained at the Fishermen's Training Institute in Pinang, under UN sponsorship; two Marine Fisheries Training Centers are located in Pinang and Kuala Trengganu.

Malaysia entered the tuna fishing industry in 1959 with the incorporation of the Malayan Marine Industries Limited, a joint Malaysian-Japanese venture. A second wholly Malaysian-owned tuna fishing company was formed in 1967.

25 FORESTRY

Almost 75% of Peninsular Malaysia is forested, with 13,375 sq mi in forest reserves (8,561 sq mi are permanent production forests; 4,814 sq mi are protected forests). Average quality of timber is low and most forests are inaccessible. Almost all commercial cutting is carried on below 500 feet. The sawmilling industry is the third largest in Peninsular Malaysia, after tin and rubber. Sawmills are chiefly Chinese-owned. In 1973, Malaysia's forests yielded 32 million cu meters of round wood. Hardwood timber has become a major export earner.

Of Sabah's total area, about 80%, or 23,000 sq mi, is forested; the accessible timber areas are situated on the east and southeast coasts. It is estimated that about 11,600 sq mi are a potential source of timber.

26 MINING

Mining, after rubber production, is the chief source of Malaysia's wealth. Peninsular Malaysia possesses vast unexploited and untapped mineral deposits, rich reserves of tin, iron, and bauxite ores, and substantial deposits of other minerals as indicated by an aeromagnetic mapping survey as far back as 1956/57.

Malaysia is the world's largest tin producer, supplying 37% of the world's output in 1974. In that year, some 1,000 mines processed 67,048 tons of tin metal and concentrates, a decrease from the 1968 total of 75,069 tons. Tin mining employment of 44,050 as of December 1974 showed a downward swing from the 1968 total of 53,499. Fluctuations in world tin demand are an important determinant of output.

Small amounts of low-grade bituminous coal are mined for local consumption. Iron ore production increased markedly since World War II under stimulus of Japanese demand, but production has dwindled rapidly, from a peak of 3,899,000 tons in 1965 to 472,998 tons in 1974. The output of bauxite, all of which is exported, rose from 60,000 tons in 1940 to 799,000 tons in 1968 and to 932,500 tons in 1974. Other minerals extracted include gold, columbite, monazite, tungsten, manganese, kaolin, and ilmenite. Offshore mining is still in the preliminary stages, but there are indications of great promise for this type of mining for tin and other minerals.

Although Europeans, Chinese, and a few Japanese own and operate most of the mines, subsoil resources are public property of the states, which grant prospecting licenses and mining leases. Royalties on coal and gold accrue to the states, and export duties are levied on other minerals by the government, which returns part to the states.

There are known deposits of iron ore, chromite, copper, nickel, dolomite, gold, manganese, and phosphates in Sabah. Prospecting for chromite and iron ore is under way. Copper reserves, estimated at 70 million tons, were located in 1961. Reserves of phosphates are estimated at 12,000 tons.

Sarawak's mineral resources include oil, bauxite, phosphates, coal, antimony, mercury, and aluminum ore. Sarawak produced 29.3 million barrels of petroleum in 1974.

In 1968, Malaysia signed agreements with two US companies for oil prospecting off the east coast of Peninsular Malaysia. Preliminary drilling was begun in 1968. Prospects for large-scale commercial production increased markedly during the 1970s, and in 1975 the government authorized the National Petroleum Co. (PETRONAS) to acquire control of foreign petroleum operations. Take-over negotiations in 1975 led to a shutdown of production facilities.

27 ENERGY AND POWER

Malaysia's total generating capacity in 1974 stood at 1,120,627 kw, of which 88.5% was in Peninsular Malaysia, 5.8% in Sabah, and 5.7% in Sarawak. In the period 1963–74 there was rapid expansion in the supply of power in Peninsular Malaysia. Electrical energy increased from 1,621.6 million kwh in 1963 to 2,641.5 million kwh in 1967; by 1974, production reached 4,971.4 million kwh, of which 24% was used by the tin industry. In that year, national production stood at 5,308.1 million kwh, of which about 24% was hydro-generated. In 1974, the National Electricity Board, a state-owned corporation, supplied about 98% of the inflow power.

Since local coal is an inferior grade and fuel oil has to be brought in by sea, the government in the past decade has greatly expanded the country's hydroelectric network. The first stage of the M$54-million hydroelectric project in Cameron Highlands was completed in 1963, adding more than 300 million kwh to total generating output. The second stage, completed in 1968, added another 400 million kwh. The Temenggor hydroelectric scheme in Perak was due for completion in 1977.

In 1963, the IBRD made a loan equivalent to US$51.9 million to the National Electricity Board to assist in the financing of the second stage of the Cameron Highlands scheme and for the construction of several thermal plants with a combined capacity of 162,800 kw. In 1966, the IBRD approved another loan equivalent to US$37 million to the National Electricity Board to assist in financing the construction of plants that will add an additional 231,400 kw to generating capacity. The Board completed the 60-Mw Prai thermal power station in 1968; with the aid of a US$35-million IBRD loan, the Prai facility was to be extended to three 120-Mw generators by 1980. With the completion of transmission lines, bulk power is now available in the northern and southern parts of Peninsular Malaysia.

In 1968, work was begun on the South Malaya power development scheme which involved the construction of the Port Dickson thermal power station on the west coast of the peninsula, with two 60-Mw generators, and the extension of two 30-Mw generators in Johor Baharu, at the southern end of the peninsula.

28 INDUSTRY

The most important industries in Malaysia are processing (rubber milling and packing, tin concentrating and smelting, sawmilling, fish curing, milling of rice, coconut, and palm oil, production of beverages and tobacco), engineering (railway and vehicle workshops, dockyards, foundries, and forges), and handicrafts (weaving, goldsmithing, and the making of attap and rattan ware). Miscellaneous manufactures include cement, soap, rubber goods, and furniture.

Although manufacturing is not yet a large sector in the country's economy, its importance in terms of employment and output is increasing. In 1974, manufacturing contributed 16.9% of the GDP, as compared with 11.4% in 1968. Manufacturing output increased from M$995 million in 1968 to M$2,875 million in 1974; in 1974, industrial production increased by 11.3%. The manufacturing sector has been given higher priority by the Capital Investment Committee created in 1969, and the government is giving more attractive incentives to employment-creating projects.

The government of Malaysia remains generally committed to a policy of free private enterprise. It is rapidly building the physical and institutional infrastructure necessary for industrial growth. It has embarked on a program of urban and rural economic development in order to raise the living standard and the purchasing power of the population.

The Investment Incentive Act of 1968, intended to speed up the industrialization of Malaysia, offers three broad categories of incentives: it gives pioneer status grants and tax holidays to companies establishing new industries; to companies that do not qualify for pioneer status, it gives investment tax credits in the form of deductions not less than 25% of capital expenditure. The act gives additional incentives to companies that participate in Malaysia's export drive in the form of tax deductions and accelerated depreciation allowances. Apart from the incentives offered in the law, the government's declared policy is the use of tariff protection as a means to encourage industrialization. Manufacturing incentives are also granted in the form of partial or total exemption from import duties on capital equipment for initial equipment or expansion and on raw materials.

29 DOMESTIC TRADE

Imported goods are channeled into the Malaysian market through local branches of large European mercantile firms; by local importers with buying agents abroad; through branch offices and representatives of foreign manufacturers; by local Chinese, Indian, and Arab merchants who import directly; and by commission agents. Chinese businessmen occupy an important place in the marketing structure and control a large share of the direct import trade.

For warehousing of imported goods, the facilities of the port of Singapore are used, while rubber for export is warehoused mainly on plantations. There is no regular system of commercial credit, but business firms generally quote bank references on their letterheads.

Quotations for imports are preferred c.i.f. port of destination, and US imports are usually paid for by letter of credit. Time drafts are not customary for imports from the dollar area but are often used, up to 90 days, for imports from Commonwealth countries. Export sales are usually invoiced in foreign currency, not necessarily that of the country of destination.

Usual business hours of European firms are from 9 A.M. to 4:30 or 5 P.M., Monday through Friday, with generally a half-day on Saturday. Chinese and Indian firms are open longer hours and seven days a week for family businesses.

Newspaper and motion picture advertising is directed toward the higher-income consumer, while radio advertising, outdoor displays, and screen slides are used for the lower-income consumer, who is less likely to be literate. Trade fairs are supervised by the Ministry of Commerce and Industry.

30 FOREIGN TRADE

Malaysia is primarily an exporter of agricultural and mineral raw materials and an importer of food and finished products. Of the two principal exports, rubber accounted for 30.1% of the total value of exports in 1974, and tin 14.7%. Nonferrous metals, coconut products, palm oil and kernels, timber, and fruits and vegetables comprise most of the remainder. The principal imports for domestic consumption are foodstuffs, textiles, metal goods, machinery, petroleum products, and chemicals.

Principal exports in 1969 and 1972 (in thousands of dollars) were:

	1969	1972
Rubber	663,488	424,322
Nonferrous metals	304,474	304,879
Tin	304,473	302,697
Wood, lumber, and cork	253,770	287,500
Palm oil	53,909	118,484
Petroleum products	116,961	108,590
Other exports	13,505	39,349
TOTALS	1,710,580	1,585,821

Principal imports in 1969 and 1972 (in thousands of dollars) were:

	1969	1972
Machinery and transport equipment	278,215	482,447
Basic manufactures	216,352	278,012
Foodstuffs	248,400	264,243
Chemicals	96,363	123,226
Mineral fuels, lubricants	165,754	120,329
Crude materials	100,566	101,360
Miscellaneous manufactured goods	66,774	72,321
Other imports	68,935	52,245
TOTALS	1,241,359	1,494,183

Malaysia's principal trade partners in 1972 (in thousands of dollars) were:

	EXPORTS	IMPORTS	BALANCE
Japan	271,967	304,727	-32,760
Singapore	369,343	129,223	240,120
US	218,893	133,227	85,666
UK	111,533	186,083	-74,550
Australia	29,154	111,148	-81,994
FRG	49,912	66,829	-16,917
China	24,979	63,574	-38,595

Other countries	510,040	499,372	10,668
TOTALS	1,585,821	1,494,183	91,638

Malaysia has sustained a favorable trade balance throughout the 1960s and 1970s. In 1974, exports totaled US$4.5 billion and imports US$4.37 billion.

31 BALANCE OF PAYMENTS

Despite current-account deficits registered in 1971, 1972, and 1974, Malaysia's financial posture remained sound through the mid-1970s. Surpluses in merchandise trade were sustained throughout the period, despite generally adverse world economic conditions. Further, annual debt service on foreign borrowing has been kept low relative to export costs. Foreign exchange reserves have been held at levels sufficient to finance five months' worth of imports. As of 31 March 1976, international reserves stood at a peak level of US$1,672 million (foreign exchange reserves, US$1,472 million), as compared with US$1,618 million at the end of 1974 and US$664 million in 1970.

Malaysia's balance of payments for 1972 and 1974 (in millions of ringgit) is summarized as follows:

	1972	1974
CURRENT ACCOUNT		
Merchandise balance	380	939
Nonmonetary gold	− 15	− 9
Freight and insurance	−309	−760
Other transportation	− 35	− 30
Travel	−101	− 80
Investment income	−378	−500
Government transactions	25	25
Other services	−108	−100
Private transfers	−176	−177
Government transfers	19	32
CURRENT TOTALS	−698	−660
CAPITAL ACCOUNT		
Private long-term capital	531	914
Official long-term capital	646	220
Net errors and omissions	− 75	− 87
Deposit money banks	− 15	65
CAPITAL TOTALS	1,087	1,112
TOTAL BALANCE	389	452

32 BANKING

In 1958, foreign state-owned banks were banned and the Bank Negara Malaysia was created as the central banking institution. During 1959–75, the Bank's foreign assets grew from M$1,020 million to M$3,943 million. Malaysian currency in circulation amounted to M$2,496 million at the end of January 1976, as compared with M$2,030 million at the end of 1974.

At the end of 1974, Malaysia had 35 licensed commercial banks, with 386 branch offices throughout the country. Nine foreign banks were represented in the country. As of 31 January 1976, demand deposits in commercial banks totaled M$2,109 million (M$1,982 million at the end of 1974), and time and savings deposits, M$5,661 million (M$4,551 million in 1974). In January 1976, the banks held M$814 million in foreign assets. International trade is financed mainly by the commercial banks.

33 INSURANCE

The volume of insurance business written in 1974 was higher than that of any previous year. The number of insurance companies registered in Malaysia in January 1975, however, had declined to 92 from 122 in 1960. Of these, 69 conducted general insurance business, 8 life, 13 both life and general, and 2 reinsurance. Of the total, only 19 were locally incorporated; 75% of the 1973 business was transacted through foreign-owned companies, the majority of which were UK-based. Total assets of all insurance companies were valued at M$694.7 million as of September 1974, as compared with M$336.8 million at the end of 1968. The life insurance sector has been growing rapidly, with funds totaling M$565 million in September 1974. The law requires insurance firms to maintain a minimum of 75% of their assets in authorized Malaysian holdings, including 20% in government securities and Treasury bills. Third-party motor liability insurance is compulsory; motor insurance accounts for 45% of general insurance.

34 SECURITIES

In July 1973, the Kuala Lumpur Stock Exchange became an independent entity, having broken off from the joint Stock Exchange of Malaysia and Singapore. Since 1 September 1974, a second, smaller exchange has operated as the Malay Stock Exchange Division of the Komplek Kewangan Malaysia Berhad. Trading on the Kuala Lumpur exchange fell off sharply in 1974, in reaction to both domestic inflation and depressed overseas markets. At the end of 1974, the market value of shares listed on the exchange fell to M$8,085 million, a 39% decrease from 1973. The volume of shares traded in 1974 totaled 391 million units valued at M$722 million, as compared with the 1973 totals of 262 million shares, valued at M$707 million. Industrials have attracted the bulk of activity on the exchange, with turnover exceeding the combined value of real estate, commodities, and hotel issues during 1973–74.

Net funds raised through government securities transactions totaled M$717 million in 1974, as compared with M$885.5 million in 1973 and M$786.2 million in 1972. Domestic loan issues financed 45.7% of government development outlays in 1974 (78.6% in 1973).

35 PUBLIC FINANCE

Deficit spending was commonly practiced by the government in the 1970s. The budget for 1976 called for current revenues of M$5,100 million, while current expenditures totaled M$5,340 million and development outlays M$1,980 million. The deficit was to be financed principally through M$1,350 million in domestic borrowing and M$785 million in overseas borrowing.

Government revenues and expenditures for 1972 and those estimated for 1974 (in millions of ringgit) were:

	1972	1974
REVENUES		
Income tax	740.6	1,017.3
Sales tax	115.9	223.0
Export duties	231.8	270.1
Import duties	588.9	747.4
Excise duties	366.0	452.8
Licenses and registration	196.5	226.0
Income from property and government enterprises	220.9	219.0
Other revenues	458.1	378.8
TOTALS	2,918.7	3,534.4
EXPENDITURES		
Education, youth, and sports	770.3	1,050.3
Defense	590.9	747.1
General administration	300.8	483.2
Natural-resource development	443.1	701.6
Transport	267.3	426.0
Health	249.1	356.5
Internal security	284.2	345.1
Public debt service	388.0	482.9
Transfer payments	226.8	135.0
Other expenditures	508.9	636.5
TOTALS	4,029.4	5,364.2

As of 31 December 1974, the domestic public debt stood at M$7,544 million (M$4,272 million at the end of 1970) and the foreign-currency debt at M$1,497 million (M$745 million in 1970).

36 TAXATION

Direct taxes emerged as the largest single source of government revenue in recent years with rates having been raised significantly in the 1970s.

Income tax is levied on incomes of all persons (including companies) accrued in the country in the previous year. The income of residents is taxed at rates ranging from 6% on the first M$2,500 to 50% on income exceeding M$50,000. Nonresidents, executors, trustees, and companies are charged a flat rate of 40% on taxable income. A 5% development tax is also assessed for corporate income. Incentives are available for pioneer industries and for certain capital investments. Export incentives and allowances are also in force. Capital gains over M$200,000 are assessed at a flat rate of 50%. A 10% surtax is applied to tin profits.

Indirect taxes include a sales tax, stamp duties, and license and registration fees.

37 CUSTOMS AND DUTIES

Customs and duties are administered under the Ministry of Finance by the Royal Customs and Excise, Malaysia. Duties function both as revenue raisers and as regulatory instruments. Import tariffs on textiles are applied ad valorem and provided M$56.5 million in revenues in 1974. In that year, measures taken to counter inflation and stimulate the economy included exemption from import duties for nitrogenous fertilizers, fuel oil, kerosine, sugar, and plywood; a ban on a variety of food exports; and increased progressivity in the rubber export surcharge rate, as well as imposition of progressive export surcharges on rubber and tin.

38 FOREIGN INVESTMENTS

The government encourages foreign investors with a tax holiday of 2–8 years for investments in new industries and assurance of convertibility and repatriation of capital and profits. In 1975, the Industrial Coordination Act established new equity participation guidelines that required a substantial majority of Malaysian ownership of new import-substitution industries catering to the domestic market and using local technology; 45–70% Malaysian ownership is now stipulated for export industries using "nondepleting local raw materials" and at least 70% for those using "depleting" raw materials. Export industries using imported raw materials may be as much as 100% foreign-owned.

Foreign interests, mostly from the UK, own about two-thirds of the rubber acreage and one-sixth of tin enterprises. As of 1976, more than 500 foreign companies had invested more than US$8 billion in Malaysia. The annual foreign-investment inflow reached US$162.8 million in 1974 and US$191.6 million in 1975; the largest investment sources are Singapore, the UK, Japan, and the US. The US has emerged as an important investment source in recent years, with private investments totaling US$461 million by 1975.

39 ECONOMIC POLICY

Government policy since 1969 has focused on the economic improvement of the Malay segment of the population. The government remains generally committed to a policy of free enterprise, although it owns and operates the railway and communications systems. In the 1970s, the government undertook a variety of measures to ensure greater Malaysian participation in the economy. In 1970, a government holding company, Pernas, was created to encourage Malay-controlled businesses; in 1975, the government attempted, through Pernas, to strengthen Malaysian interests in the tin-mining sector. Also in 1975, the government established Petrobas with the overall aim of acquiring majority control of the country's petroleum operations. The Industrial Coordination Act of 1975 attempted to secure a stronger influence for government policies by requiring the licensing of small local enterprises and by setting limits on foreign participation in the processing, domestic distribution, and export of local raw materials.

In the 1970s, development expenditures of the public sector were increased substantially in order to establish directions for capital investment and economic growth. Overall investment strategies are set forth through long-range development plans. Annual investment under the Second Malaysia Plan (1971–74) exceeded M$1.6 billion, with 72% devoted to economic projects, 14% to social infrastructure, 10% to defense and security, and 4% for general administration. Transport, communications, and utilities received 33% of total outlays, while agriculture and rural development took 23%. Central economic goals included the development of higher-yield rubber, agricultural diversification, and uplifting of rural sectors into the economic mainstream. The Third Malaysia Plan (1976–80) contemplated a continuation of the policies set forth in the first half of the decade. Annual development outlays in the mid-1970s were stepped up to an average of about M$2 billion.

40 HEALTH

Malaysia enjoys a comparatively high level of health, the consequence of long-established health and medical services. Average life expectancy in 1975 was 61.8 years, as compared with 48.5 years in 1950. Under the tuberculosis control campaign, begun in 1961, more than 2 million persons have been X-rayed and another 2 million given BCG vaccinations. As a result of the yaws elimination campaign, begun in 1954, the disease had been virtually eliminated in the late 1960s. Work on the systematic eradication of filariasis was carried on by trained teams. A malaria eradication program was begun in 1967.

The country faces an acute shortage of medical doctors, dentists, and pharmaceutical chemists. A faculty of medicine was established in the University of Malaya in 1963; and in 1969 it produced, as its first group of graduates, 61 doctors. In 1972 there was a total of 2,482 physicians (of whom 2,299 were in Peninsular Malaysia), 823 dentists (1973), 6,845 nurses, and 3,772 midwives (1973). Some 89 hospitals provided about 32,883 beds in 1973. For the care of the rural population, the government maintains about 1,400 health clinics, approximately 200 of which are mobile. A number of rural hospitals are also run by the states. The government has developed rural health centers throughout the country, each staffed with a team consisting of a nurse, a midwife, and a sanitary inspector. The government also supports the Institute for Medical Research in Kuala Lumpur, with branch laboratories in Ipoh and Pinang. Government expenditures for health services in 1974 totaled M$356.5 million, as compared with M$186.2 million in 1970.

41 SOCIAL WELFARE

Public financial assistance is to be considered within the framework of Malayan society with its highly developed sense of family and clan responsibility. The government has generally encouraged volunteer social welfare activities and has subsidized programs of private groups. The Department of Social Welfare, under the Ministry of Welfare Services, administers and coordinates programs. The government's program of public assistance takes the form of cash, commodities, and institutional care. Children's services, begun in 1952, render casework services and administer children's homes. A probation service provides care and assistance for juvenile delinquents and dependents and a handicapped persons service aids the deaf, mute, and blind. In addition, care is provided for the aged and chronically ill.

In 1969, a social security scheme was enacted to provide injury insurance and disability pensions. By early 1974, injury coverage was provided to 537,657 workers and 16,489 employers in Peninsular Malaysia's 31 centers and to 24,750 workers and 16,489 employers in Kota Kinabalu and Kuching. In 1975, the Social

Security Organization was seeking international assistance to allow extension of coverage to farmers and fishermen.

42 HOUSING

Some 40% of the country's dwelling units consist of one room; about one-fourth are equipped with internal plumbing and electricity. With the urban population expanding rapidly, the government established a housing trust in 1950 to plan and build low-cost housing. Under a program begun in 1968, units can be bought on an installment purchase system at not more than M$30 a month for each unit at an interest rate of 3% for 17 years.

The Malaya-Borneo Building Society is the leading source of funds for private housing in Malaysia. Emphasis in housing trust plans has changed from dwellings constructed for outright sale to low-cost rental housing. Private enterprises and cooperative building societies are also active in the urban construction field.

43 EDUCATION

While expenditure on education continued to increase, government policy in the 1970s laid particular emphasis on technical and vocational training. The aim was to produce qualified personnel who could contribute to the development of the country in an era of rapid technological and scientific advancement. The estimated expenditure on education and youth programs in 1974 was M$1,050.3 million, as compared with M$556.8 million in 1970.

Six years of free primary education is given to all children in Malay, English, Chinese, and Tamil medium schools. This is followed by three years of comprehensive general and prevocational education. A further two years of education at the postcomprehensive level, either in a vocational or an academic program, is offered. A two-year preuniversity course prepares students for admission to the universities.

The government intends to make Malay the medium of instruction in primary and secondary schools by the end of 1980. English will be retained as a compulsory second language. Muslim religious instruction is compulsory for all Muslim children, while private Christian schools offer religious training to their students.

School enrollment in Peninsular Malaysia in mid-1974 included 1,554,611 pupils in 4,381 primary schools, and 705,825 students in 984 secondary schools and 96 technical and vocational schools. Sabah had 123,419 pupils in 775 primary schools and 43,257 students in 88 secondary schools. Sarawak's enrollment included 165,484 in 1,214 primary schools and 50,202 in 107 secondary schools.

In 1972/73, 23,617 students were enrolled at institutions of higher education. Institutions of higher learning include the University Kebangsaan Malaysia (the national university), the University of Malaya, and the Technological University of Malaysia, all in Kuala Lumpur; the University of Agriculture; University Sains Malaysia (formerly the University of Penang); and MARA Institute of Technology. The universities had an enrollment of 11,488 students for the 1972/73 academic year. The University of Malaya is the largest, with 8,918 students in 1973/74. The Muslim College is a higher educational institution for Muslim religious education. In 1972/73, Malaysia also had 18 teacher-training colleges (3,856 students) and a number of agricultural and technical colleges (combined enrollment, 8,273 students). There are no universities in East Malaysia. Sarawak has a vocational school and three teacher-training colleges.

44 LIBRARIES AND MUSEUMS

The National Archives and Library of Malaysia, with 51,253 volumes, was established in 1971 and has been charged with wide responsibilities under the National Library Act. Various other university, special, and public libraries also exist in the country. The University of Malaya library, with 452,177 volumes as of July 1974, is still the largest library in Malaysia. Other important libraries include those at the University Sains Malaysia, with 115,036 volumes; the University Kebangsaan Malaysia, 123,476 volumes; the University of Agriculture, 45,000 volumes; the Technological University of Malaysia, 41,723 volumes; The MARA Institute of Technology, 60,305 volumes; the Rubber Research Institute, 50,000 volumes; the Institute of Medical Research, 15,000 volumes; the Forest Research Institute, 11,000 volumes; and the Malaysian Agricultural Research and Development Institute, 3,035 volumes. Pinang has a public and a university library. Public library services are also increasingly being provided in almost all states of Malaysia; the largest are in Ipoh (60,000 volumes) and Kuala Lumpur (45,000). There are information centers and reading rooms throughout the country—even in some villages—which are supplied with literature by the Department of Information. The Ministry of Agriculture's library in Kuala Lumpur has 70,000 volumes.

The National Museum of Malaysia, constructed on the site of the former Selangor museum (destroyed in World War II), houses extensive collections of Malayan archaeology, ethnography, and zoology. The Perak Museum has a varied collection and a library specializing in archival, ethnographic, and zoologic materials. The Museum of Asian Art was opened in 1974 in the University of Malaya.

45 ORGANIZATIONS

The Malaysian government promotes thrift, credit, processing, marketing, farming, consumer, and housing cooperatives. The cooperative movement was introduced in Malaya in 1922. In 1974 there were 794,934 Malaysians in 1,562 registered cooperative societies. The Chinese are organized along clan, common dialect, or occupational lines into rural credit associations. These local associations set up and maintain schools, build temples, and provide burial, relief, and employment services.

In the larger cities, chambers of commerce, organized along racial lines, promote the economic welfare of the group.

46 PRESS

Malaysia enjoys a large measure of press freedom. Journalism and printing standards are comparatively high. While the press is normally moderate and objective, it has adopted certain tacit measures to protect Malaysia's plural ethnic and cultural foundations, a role that was especially evident during the 1969 emergency. In 1973, Malaysia had 37 daily newspapers, with an estimated total circulation of 1,097,000. The Chinese-language press is the largest segment, followed by English, Malay, Tamil, Punjabi, and Kadazan. The *Straits Times*, the country's largest daily, is published in English with both Kuala Lumpur and Singapore editions.

Leading Malaysian dailies (with their 1975 circulations) were:

	LANGUAGE	CIRCULATION
KUALA LUMPUR		
Straits Times	English	130,000
Shin Min	Chinese	86,000
Sin Chew Jit Pao	Chinese	81,500
Nanyang Siang Pao	Chinese	76,000
Minguan Malaysia	Malay (Rumi)	75,000
Utusan Zaman	Malay (Jawi script)	69,000
Malayan Thung Pao	Chinese	50,000
Utusan Melayu	Malay (Jawi script)	50,000
Berita Minggu	Malay (Romanized)	46,000
Utusan Malaysia	Malay (Rumi)	44,000
Chung Kuo Pao	Chinese	36,000
Berita Harian	Malay (Rumi)	32,000
Malay Mail	English	26,000
Tamil Nesan	Tamil	12,500
GEORGE TOWN (Pinang)		
Kwong Wah Yit Poh	Chinese	40,000
Sing Pin Jih Pao	Chinese	39,900
Star	English	20,000
Straits Echo	English	10,000

KOTA KINABALU (Sabah)
Overseas Chinese

Daily News	Chinese	22,670
Daily Express	English and Romanized Malay	15,000
Kinabalu Sabah Times	Chinese	12,000
Kinabalu Sabah Times	English, Malay, and Kadazan	12,000

KUCHING (Sarawak)

Sarawak Vanguard	Chinese	9,500
See Hwa Daily News	Chinese	9,500
International Times	Chinese	8,200
Sarawak Tribune	English	5,500
The Vanguard	English	5,500

OTHER TOWNS

Miri Daily News (Miri, Sarawak)	Chinese	14,000
Tamil Muraso (Petaling, Jaya)	Tamil	13,000
Malaysia Daily News (Sibu, Sarawak)	Chinese	12,000

47 TOURISM

Passports are required of all entrants, although Malaysia has visa abolition agreements with all Commonwealth countries, the US, and some 15 other countries. Smallpox vaccination certificates are required for all visitors; cholera and yellow fever inoculations are necessary for those arriving from infected areas.

In 1974, Malaysia had 114 hotels of international standard, with 7,300 rooms. Most large hotels are in Kuala Lumpur and Pinang. The best-known hill resort areas are Cameron Highlands, Frazer's Hill, and Pinang Hill. Island resorts off the coast of the peninsula are Langkawi and Pangkor. Tourists numbered 907,000 in 1974.

48 FAMOUS MALAYSIANS

Among the foremost Malaysian leaders of the past was Sultan Mahmud, 16th-century ruler of Malacca. A great figure in Malay culture was 'Abdallah bin 'Abd al-Kabir (surnamed Munshi', 1796–1854), sometimes referred to as the "greatest innovator in Malay letters." Best-known figure in the political life of modern Malaysia is Tunku Abdul Rahman Putra bin Abdul Hamid Halimshah (b.1903), first prime minister of the Federation of Malaysia. Other political leaders are Tun Abdul Razak (1922–76), the nation's second prime minister (1970–76); Dato Onn bin Ja'afar (1895–1962), a founder of the United Malays National Organizaton (UMNO); and Sir Cheng-lock Tan (1883–1960), leader of the Malaysian Chinese Association (MCA).

49 DEPENDENCIES

Malaysia has no dependencies.

50 BIBLIOGRAPHY

Allen, D. F. *Report on the Major Ports of Malaya*. Kuala Lumpur: Government Press, 1951.

Allen, D. F. *Report on the Minor Ports of Malaya*. Kuala Lumpur: Government Press, 1953.

Allen, Richard. *Malaysia, Prospect and Retrospect: The Impact and Aftermath of Colonial Rule*. New York: Oxford University Press, 1968.

American University. *Area Handbook for Malaysia*. Washington, D.C.: Government Printing Office, 1970.

Clutterbuck, Richard. *The Long, Long War: Counterinsurgency in Malaya and Vietnam*. New York: Praeger, 1966.

Das's Year Book of Malaya. Kuala Lumpur: Das (annual).

Edmonds, I. G. *The New Malaysia*. Indianapolis: Bobbs-Merrill, 1973.

Esman, Milton J. *Administration and Development in Malaysia*. Ithaca, N.Y.: Cornell University Press, 1972.

Ginsburg, Norton Sydney, and Chester F. Roberts, Jr. *Malaya*. Seattle: University of Washington Press, 1958.

Gullick, J. M. *Malaysia*. New York: Praeger, 1964.

Hall, Daniel George Edward. *A History of South-East Asia*. New York: Macmillan, 1962.

Hodder, Bramwell William. *Man in Malaya*. London: University of London Press, 1959.

IBRD. *The Economic Development of Malaya*. Baltimore: Johns Hopkins Press, 1955.

Kahin, George. *Government and Politics of Southeast Asia*. Ithaca, N.Y.: Cornell University Press, 1976.

Kennedy, Joseph. *A History of Malaysia, A.D. 1400–1959*. London: Macmillan, 1970.

Mackie, J. A. C. *Konfrontasi: The Indonesia—Malaysia Dispute, 1963–1966*. New York: Oxford University Press, 1974.

McKie, Ronald C. *The Emergence of Malaysia*. Westport, Conn.: Greenwood, 1973.

Mason, Frederic. *Schools of Malaya*. Singapore: Moore, 1957.

Means, Gordon P. *Malaysian Politics*. New York: New York University Press, 1970.

Miller, Harry. *A Short History of Malaysia*. New York: Praeger, 1966.

Milne, R. S. *Government and Politics in Malaysia*. Boston: Houghton Mifflin, 1967.

Milne, R. S., and K. J. Ratnam. *Malaysia—New States in a New Nation*. London: Cass, 1974.

Moore, Joanna. *The Land and People of Malaya and Singapore*. London: Black, 1957.

Ness, Gayl D. *Bureaucracy and Rural Development in Malaysia*. Berkeley: University of California Press, 1967.

Ongkili, James P. *Modernization in East Malaysia, 1960–1970*. London: Oxford University Press, 1972.

Parkinson, Cyril Northcote. *A Short History of Malaya*. Singapore: Moore, 1956.

Purcell, Victor. *The Chinese in Malaya*. New York: Oxford University Press, 1968.

Purcell, Victor. *Malaysia*. New York: Walker, 1965.

Robinson, John Bradstreet Parry. *Transformation in Malaya*. London: Secker & Warburg, 1956.

Roff, William R. (ed.). *Kelantan: Religion, Society and Politics in a Malay State*. Kuala Lumpur: Oxford University Press, 1974.

Roff, William R. *The Origins of Malay Nationalism*. New Haven, Conn.: Yale University Press, 1967.

Runciman, Steven. *The White Rajahs*. Cambridge: Cambridge University Press, 1960.

Ryan, N. J. *The Making of Modern Malaysia and Singapore*. London: Oxford University Press, 1969.

Ryan, N. J. *Malaya through Four Centuries: An Anthology, 1500–1900*. London: Oxford University Press, 1959.

Silcock, T. H. *Towards a Malayan Nation*. Singapore: Eastern Universities Press, 1961.

Tarling, Nicholas. *Britain, the Brookes and Brunei*. London: Oxford University Press, 1972.

Thompson, Sir Robert. *Defeating Communist Insurgency: The Lessons of Malaya and Vietnam*. New York: Praeger, 1966.

Tweedie, Michael Wilmer Forbes. *Prehistoric Malaya*. Singapore: Moore, 1955.

Tweedie, Michael Wilmer Forbes, and J. L. Harrison. *Malayan Animal Life*. New York: Longmans, Green, 1954.

Wang Gungwu (ed.). *Malaysia: A Survey*. New York: Praeger, 1964.

West, Albert John Frederick, and John Rose. *Practical Geography of Malaya*. London: University of London Press, 1959.

Williams-Hunt, P. D. R. *An Introduction to the Malayan Aborigines*. Kuala Lumpur: Government Press, 1952.

Winstedt, Sir Richard Olof. *Malaya and Its History*. New York: Longmans, Green, 1966.

Winstedt, Sir Richard Olof. *The Malays: A Cultural History*. London: Routledge & Kegan Paul, 1950.

MALDIVES

Republic of Maldives

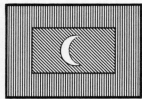

CAPITAL: Malé. **FLAG**: The national flag consists of a white crescent at the center of a green field which, in turn, is at the center of a red field. **MONETARY UNIT**: As of 29 February 1976, the Maldivian rupee (MR) of 100 larees equals $0.1296; $1=MR7.7130. **WEIGHTS AND MEASURES**: The metric system has been adopted, although some local units remain in use. **HOLIDAYS**: National Day, 26 July; Republic Day, 11 November. 'Id al-Fitr, 'Id al-'Adha', and Milad al-Nabi are some of the Muslim religious holidays observed. **TIME**: 5:00 P.M.=noon GMT.

¹LOCATION, SIZE, AND EXTENT

The Maldive Islands are an archipelago in the Indian Ocean to the southwest of India and Sri Lanka, with an area of 298 sq km (115 sq mi), extending 795 km (494 mi) N–S and 159 km (99 mi) E–W. The second-smallest country in Asia, the Maldives consists of about 1,087 islands in 19 atolls, with a total coastline of 2,393 km (1,487 mi). Only about 200 of the islands are inhabited. The northernmost atoll is about 483 km (300 mi) southwest of Cape Comorin and 644 km (400 mi) from Sri Lanka. To the north is Minicoy atoll, about 113 km (70 mi) from the nearest of the Maldives and separated from them by Eight Degree Channel; Minicoy belongs to India.

The name Maldive is said to be derived from the two words *mahal*, meaning "palace," and *diva*, meaning "island."

²TOPOGRAPHY

The islands vary from tiny banks nearly awash to real islets. Gan in the Addu Atoll is 5 miles long. Some of the islands are in process of formation and are constantly increasing in size; others are gradually washing away. The islands are level and extremely low-lying, with elevations rarely exceeding 8 feet above sea level. Many contain freshwater lagoons. Some atolls have encircling reefs, while others are made up of many small ring-shaped reefs.

Four main channels divide the atoll groups: Kardiva, or Five Degree, Channel (Kaharidu Kadu), about 24 miles wide; Veimandu, or Kolumadula, Channel, 15 miles wide; One and a Half Degree Channel, 50 miles wide; and Equatorial Channel, 46 miles wide.

³CLIMATE

The Maldives' equatorial climate is hot and humid, with a mean temperature of about 27°C (81°F). The December range is from 26.6°C to 29°C (80°F to 84°F), and in March and April the range is from 29.4°C to 32°C (85°F to 90°F), with about 26.6°C (80°F) at night. The weather during the northeast monsoon (November-March) is mild and pleasant; the southwest monsoon (June-August) is violent and very rainy. The northern atolls are subject to more violent storms than those in the south. Annual rainfall in the south averages 150 inches and in the north, 100 inches.

⁴FLORA AND FAUNA

The islands are covered with a dense scrub. The northern and southern islands are more fertile than those in the central group, and the eastern islands generally are more fertile than the western. Plantain, papaya, mango, and banyan trees flourish. Shrubs and flowers are widespread. Rats, rabbits, and flying foxes are the only mammals. Birds include ducks, bitterns, curlews, snipes, and various sea birds. Small scorpions, beetles, and land crabs are common. The surrounding waters contain sharks, swordfish, and porpoises.

⁵POPULATION

According to the 1974 census, the population was 128,697. Most islands of any size are inhabited, depending on water, soil, and available anchorage. Malé, the largest town, is on Malé Island at the southern extreme of the Malé Atoll; it had a population of 16,731 in 1974.

⁶ETHNIC GROUPS

The original inhabitants of the Maldives are thought to have been of Dravidian origin. The people of the northern atolls have to some extent intermarried with peoples from western India, Arabia, and North Africa. Inhabitants of the southern islands show stronger physical affinities with the Sinhalese of Sri Lanka. Black African slaves imported from Zanzibar and Arabia married Maldivians. There are some Caucasian and Malayan elements.

⁷LANGUAGE

The Maldivian language, called Divehi, is similar to the old Sinhala, or Elu of Ceylon. It has contributed the word *atoll* to international terminology. In recent years, the language has been influenced by Arabic and Urdu. Some Maldivians speak English.

⁸RELIGION

There is evidence that the early Maldivians were Buddhists. Their conversion to Islam dates from 1153. With few exceptions, the people are Sunni Muslims.

⁹TRANSPORTATION

Malé, the capital, and some other more important islands have fairly good roads. The number of motor vehicles in Malé and in Addu Atoll has increased considerably in the last few years. Interatoll transportation still depends mostly on local sailing boats, called batheli and odi. Although some mechanized boats carry cargo and, occasionally, passengers between Malé and other atolls, interisland transport is mainly by means of dhonis (small boats). Oceangoing shipping has been increasing and, at the end of 1974, the Maldives had 34 ships of 91,000 gross tons. Shipping is controlled by Malship Shipping Ltd. A modern airstrip on the island of Hululule, across the Malé harbor, was completed in 1966 with assistance provided by the government of Sri Lanka under the Colombo Plan. A national airline, Air Maldives, was established in 1974; the only international link is to Colombo, Sri Lanka, also served by Air Ceylon.

¹⁰COMMUNICATIONS

Malé has a 60-kw radio station which broadcasts local as well as foreign programs from 6 A.M. to 11 P.M. All of the atolls are connected by radiotelephone to Malé. Within the atolls, most of the inhabited islands maintain contact with Malé by means of walkie-talkies. Communication with the rest of the world is maintained largely through Sri Lanka and India.

¹¹HISTORY

The Maldive Islands were first known to the West through Ptolemy c. A.D. 160. They may have been ruled in ancient times by the Chinese. Later, they paid an annual tribute to principalities of western India. The people were converted to Islam in 1153. From that year, an unbroken line of 92 sultans served as local rulers until 1953. In 1343, Ibn Battutah, the Arab traveler and historian, visited the islands and served for a time as a qadi.

For a century or more after their discovery by the Portuguese traveler Dom Lourenço de Alameida in 1507, the Maldives were occupied by Portuguese garrisons and forced to pay a tribute to Goa. In the 17th century, the Dutch, who were then in control of Ceylon (now Sri Lanka), concluded a treaty with the sultan, and thereafter the Maldivian sultans sent tribute to the rulers of Ceylon and claimed their protection.

British protection of the islands was formally recorded in 1887. By terms of the compact, the sultan recognized the suzerainty of the British sovereign and disclaimed all right or intention to enter into negotiations or treaty with any foreign state except through the ruler of Ceylon. When Ceylon became a sovereign state in 1948, a new agreement was signed with the UK government, providing for the islands to remain under the protection of the crown, for external affairs to be conducted by or in accordance with the advice of the UK government, for the UK to refrain from interfering in the internal affairs of the islands, and for the sultan to afford such facilities for UK forces as were necessary for the defense of the islands or the Commonwealth. No tribute was to be paid by Maldives. New agreements reaffirming these provisions were signed in 1953, 1956, and 1960.

The sultanate, dominated by the Didi family since 1759, was abolished in 1953, and the islands were declared a republic. The first president, Amin Didi, ordered the emancipation of women and other reforms that were resented by more conservative elements among the people, and nine months later he was overthrown. His cousins Muhammad Farid Didi and Ibrahim Ali Didi became co-presidents in September 1953, and a month later the National Assembly voted to turn the islands back into a sultanate. The new sultan, Muhammad Didi, was installed at Malé on 7 March 1954 and Ibrahim Ali Didi, the prime minister, formed a new government.

Public reaction against a new agreement of 1956 allowing the UK to reestablish its air base on Gan Island was so strong that, in December 1957, Prime Minister Ibrahim was forced to resign, and Ibrahim Nasir, who succeeded him, began to insist that the UK base would violate Maldivian neutrality. When the government sent a representative to Gan to tell the islanders to stop working for the British, they attacked him. Early in 1959, the people of the Addu Atoll declared their independence.

In January 1959, a rebellion broke out in the three southernmost atolls. The rebel headmen declared the formation of a United Suvadiva Republic (with a population of 20,000) and demanded recognition from the UK. Although the UK refused recognition, the Nasir government made public its suspicions that the UK had engineered the coup. Central government forces crushed the rebels in two of the atolls but made no attempt to interfere on Gan or any of the other seven main islands in the Addu group. By March 1960, the Suvadiva Republic was declared dissolved, and a committee ruling under the sovereign control of the sultan was set up, including among its members ʿAbdallah Afif, leader of the rebellion.

In February 1960, the Maldivian government made a free gift to the UK government of the use of Gan Island and other facilities in Addu Atoll for 30 years, and a fresh agreement was drawn up between the governments. The UK agreed to bring about a reconciliation between the Maldivian government and the dissident inhabitants of the southern islands. By 1962,

however, inhabitants of the central and northern islands apparently lost patience at the UK's failure to implement the agreement successfully. Anti-British resentment took overt forms, and in late 1962 the UK sent a frigate to Malé to protect UK citizens. The British evacuated ʿAbdallah Afif to the Seychelles.

The Sultanate of the Maldive Islands achieved independence on 26 July 1965 and became a member of the UN the same year. The UK retained the facilities on Gan and agreed to pay the Maldivian government $2,380,000; $2,100,000 to be spent over a period of years for economic development.

In March 1968, a referendum resulted in an 81% vote to abolish the sultanate and to reestablish a republic. A new republican constitution came into force on 11 November 1968, establishing the country as the Republic of Maldives.

¹²GOVERNMENT

In 1932, Sultan Muhammad Shams al-Din Iskandar III granted Maldives its first constitution, providing for a People's Assembly of 47 members elected annually from and by literate male residents. A Legislative Council of 28 members (17 selected by the People's Assembly) was to serve for five years. The sultan appointed a prime minister in consultation with the Legislative Council from among its members. A second constitution, prepared by the eminent British authority Sir Ivor Jennings, was adopted by the new republic in 1953, but it was abandoned in 1954 when the sultanate was restored. According to the constitution adopted in 1954, the government was to be headed by a sultan elected for life. A referendum held in September 1968 appointed a president under a revived republican system. By a vote of 97.16%, the prime minister, Ibrahim Nasir, was elected president. On 11 November 1968, President Nasir assumed office, and a new constitution, largely a revised version of the 1954 document, went into effect.

The president, elected by the Majlis (parliament) to a four-year term, must be confirmed in office by popular referendum. The president heads the executive branch and appoints the cabinet, fixed at nine members by a 1975 referendum. The constitution allows as many vice-presidents as the president desires.

The unicameral Majlis is a body of 54 members, 46 of whom are directly elected (2 from each of the 19 atolls and 8 from Malé) by universal adult suffrage of citizens over 21. Eight members are appointed by the president. Elections to the Majlis are held individually and do not necessarily coincide with its sessions. The Majlis drafts legislation that becomes law after ratification by the president.

¹³POLITICAL PARTIES

There are no organized political parties. Candidates stand for election as independents and campaign on personal stature.

¹⁴LOCAL GOVERNMENT

The Maldives is divided administratively into 19 atolls, each headed by a government-appointed verin, or chief. On each inhabited island a kateeb, or headman, also appointed by the government, supervises and carries out the orders of the government under the supervision of the atoll verin.

¹⁵JUDICIAL SYSTEM

Justice is meted out according to traditional Islamic law (Shariʿah) by a body appointed for that purpose by the president.

¹⁶ARMED FORCES

The armed forces of Maldives consist of lascoreen, or militia, and police guards. Armed boats patrol the territorial waters to protect the local fishing industry.

The Gan Island airfield, built during World War II, is now used by the UK as a staging and refueling area.

¹⁷MIGRATION

Migration is negligible.

¹⁸INTERNATIONAL COOPERATION

The Maldives was admitted to UN membership on 21 September

1965, but it does not maintain a permanent mission at UN headquarters. It is a member of UNDP, FAO, UNICEF, WHO, UPU, ITU, and IMCO. In 1963, the Maldives became a member of the Colombo Plan Organization. The country's only permanent overseas representation is an embassy in Sri Lanka.

19 ECONOMY
The Maldives economy is among the least developed in the world. The staple foods are local fish and rice, which must be imported. Fish alone accounts for more than 90% of total exports. Coconuts, copra, rope (made from dried coconut fibers), shells, tortoise shell, bone dust, red stone, ambergris, and handicrafts are also produced locally and exported in small quantities. The government is seeking to reduce reliance on fishing through promotion of processing industries and tourism.

20 INCOME
Precise data do not exist, there being no system of national accounts. Most of the islands' income derives from fishing. Per capita income is estimated at less than $100 per annum.

21 LABOR
More than half the male population is engaged in fishing. Weaving is mainly performed by women. The shortage of both skilled and unskilled labor is a major problem.

22 AGRICULTURE
Millet, corn, pumpkins, sweet potatoes, pineapples, sugarcane, almonds, and many kinds of tropical vegetables and fruits are successfully cultivated. Coconut palms provide copra and coir, the most important exports after fish. Maldivian mangoes and coconuts are reputed to be particularly delicious. Virtually all rice, a staple food for the population, must be imported; an FAO expert began tests in 1970 on the feasibility of growing rice in the islands.

23 ANIMAL HUSBANDRY
Fodder is insufficient for more than a few head of cattle, but there are many goats and chickens.

24 FISHING
Fishing is the chief industry, although the surrounding seas are rough and Maldivians are not equipped to go deep-sea fishing. About a dozen fishermen go out in a large sailing boat (masodi); four to six men use a smaller type of craft (masdhoni). Thousands of such boats are used, built by local craftsmen. Live sardines are thrown out as bait, and unbaited hooks and lines are used to pull in the fish.

The main catch, a species of tuna or bonito, ranges from about 3 to 10 lb in weight. The fish are cut up, boiled, and smoked on open bamboo racks over coconut-wood fires. After being dried and cut up into smaller pieces resembling black or brown hardwood, they are put in gunny sacks and exported, mainly to Sri Lanka. This dried "Maldive fish" (which the Maldivians call kalubila mas or kadu mas and the Sri Lankans call umbalakada) is considered a delicacy in Sri Lanka and India and is used mainly as a condiment. Annual export value of Maldive fish in 1974 was MR11.9 million, while fresh fish earned MR2.7 million.

Shell gathering is a relatively important activity in the Maldives, with large quantities of cowries exported for use as ornaments. Several rare shell species are also collected.

25 FORESTRY
There are no forests as such. Coconut wood, however, is used in the building of boats and the construction of houses. Some teak is imported for use in the building of larger bungalows.

26 MINING
There are no mineral resources.

27 ENERGY AND POWER
The power plant in Malé provides electricity and power for the island. A smaller plant on the island of Hulele supplies power for the airstrip on that island.

28 INDUSTRY
After the dried-fish industry, the manufacture of coir, a rope made from dried coconut fibers, is the most important. Maldivian coir has been highly regarded for centuries for its light color, strength, and fineness. Lacemaking (handmade pillow lace), introduced by the Dutch in the 17th century, provides another well-known product. Some lace is made with gold and silver thread imported from India. Maldivian lacquerwork and finely woven mats are famed for their quality and design. Carpenters, masons, goldsmiths and silversmiths, stoneworkers, cloth weavers, netmakers, and sail weavers also produce handicraft products of excellence and artistic quality.

29 DOMESTIC TRADE
Malé Island is the chief commercial center. Sri Lankan and Indian merchants in Malé act as their own importers, exporters, and wholesalers. The importing of rice and exporting of ambergris are government monopolies.

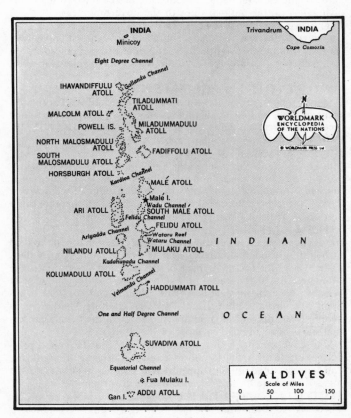

See continental political: front cover L9; physical: back cover L9
LOCATION: 7°7'N to 0°43'S; 72°31' to 73°46'E. **TERRITORIAL SEA LIMIT:** 2.77–55 mi.

30 FOREIGN TRADE
Fish is the leading export product, traditionally accounting for more than 90% of the total export value. Also exported are coconuts, copra, coir, cowrie shell, tortoise shell, and some local handicraft products. Rice, wheat flour, and salt are imported, as are kerosine, oil, sugar, cotton piece goods, and a few manufactured products. Most trade is with Sri Lanka, with much of the balance going to India and Burma.

In 1974, exports were valued at MR15,567,800 (compared with MR12,362,477 in 1973 and MR15,063,915 in 1972); imports in 1973 totaled MR16,882,063 (MR21,205,198 in 1972). Of 1974 exports, Maldive fish and related products accounted for 76.4% of the total value; fresh fish, 17.3%; copra, 1.6%; and other exports, 4.7%.

³¹BALANCE OF PAYMENTS
Although precise data are not available, trade deficits are known to be common. Tourist receipts began making a minor contribution in the 1970s.

³²BANKING
In 1974, the State Bank of India opened a branch office in Malé, providing the country with its first bank. Foreign trade transactions have been conducted through the Central Bank of Ceylon.

³³INSURANCE
Insurance facilities are not available.

³⁴SECURITIES
There is no dealing in securities.

³⁵PUBLIC FINANCE
Information is not available.

³⁶TAXATION
There is no income tax. License fees are charged for boats and motor vehicles. Uninhabited islands are leased for farming to individuals who pay annual dues to the government.

³⁷CUSTOMS AND DUTIES
Customs duties are a primary source of government revenues. Imports of liquor, pork products, and dogs are prohibited. Malé is a free port, as are a few other islands being developed as tourist areas.

³⁸FOREIGN INVESTMENTS
Under a 1969 agreement with the UK, the Maldives received a grant of $1.2 million to finance economic development. Other forms of assistance have been received from WHO, UNDP, UNICEF, the Colombo Plan, and CARE.

³⁹ECONOMIC POLICY
The government has a series of development programs to improve and expand fishing and related industries, food processing, tourism, communications, and health and education services. Part of the economic thrust has been to broaden the economic base away from its overwhelming reliance on fishing.

⁴⁰HEALTH
In recent years, considerable progress has been made in the field of health, although the needs remain great. There is a modern 42-bed hospital in Malé, part of the UK aid program to the Maldives. As of the early 1970s, there were only a handful of Western-trained physicians on the islands, and surgical treatment was virtually nonexistent. WHO is training Maldivians as health assistants and nursing aides to work in the health centers that have been opened in most of the atolls.

The government, with the help of WHO, has launched projects to eradicate malaria and to control filariasis, tuberculosis, and leprosy. Inadequate transport and communications are the major impediments to adequate health coverage.

⁴¹SOCIAL WELFARE
There is no organized social welfare system. Assistance is traditionally provided through the extended family. Family pride dictates care to the ill, handicapped, widows, and orphans.

⁴²HOUSING
Some of the houses on Malé are built in imitation of those in Colombo. Most, however, have coral or coconut-wood walls; the roofs are tiled or made of corrugated galvanized iron. The poorer houses are walled from the street with mats, called cadjan, or palm leaves.

⁴³EDUCATION
Somewhat less than two-thirds of the population is thought to be literate. The government operates three middle schools in Malé, each using English as the medium of instruction. In addition, there are some 240 private schools, of which 43 are in Malé. In 1971/72 there were 32 preprimary teachers, with 805 pupils; 35 primary-school teachers, with 925 students; and 26 secondary-school teachers, with 336 students.

Maldivians must go abroad for higher education; about 75 study overseas annually with WHO or Colombo Plan assistance.

⁴⁴LIBRARIES AND MUSEUMS
Malé has a public library and a museum housing a collection on Maldives history.

⁴⁵ORGANIZATIONS
There are a number of sports clubs in Maldives, including six in Malé, and a Muslim religious organization in Malé.

⁴⁶PRESS
There are two newspapers, a daily published in Divehi and a biweekly in English.

⁴⁷TOURISM
The government is encouraging rapid expansion of tourist facilities. Natural attractions are crystal-clear lagoons and white beaches that are ideal for swimming, fishing, and surfing. Modern tourist facilities have opened in the Malé Atoll. Two travel agencies began operations in Malé in late 1972.

⁴⁸FAMOUS MALDIVIANS
Ibn Battutah (Muhammad bin ʿAbdallah bin Battutah, b. Tangier; 1304–77), the remarkable Arab traveler and geographer, lived in the Maldives for several years, served as a qadi there, and married the daughter of a Maldivian vizier.

Sultan Iskandar Ibrahim I, who reigned for nearly 40 years during the 17th century, built the Hukuru Miskit, the principal mosque on Malé Island, in 1674.

⁴⁹DEPENDENCIES
Maldives has no dependencies.

⁵⁰BIBLIOGRAPHY
Agassiz, Alexander. *The Coral Reefs of the Maldives*. Cambridge: Harvard University Museum of Comparative Zoology, 1903.

American University. *Area Handbook for the Indian Ocean Territories*. Washington, D.C.: Government Printing Office, 1971.

Bell, Harry Charles Purvis. *The Maldive Islands: Monograph on the History, Archeology, Epigraphy*. Colombo: Ceylon Government Press, 1940.

Bernini, Francesco, and George Corbin. *Maldive*. Turin, Italy: R. Aprile, 1973.

Blood, Sir Hilary Rudolph Robert. "Memories of the Maldive Islands." *Contemporary Review*, February 1957, 73–76.

Gardiner, J. Stanley (ed.). *The Fauna and Geography of the Maldive and Laccadive Archipelagoes . . .* 2 vols. Cambridge: Cambridge University Press, 1901–6.

Hockley, T. W. *The Two Thousand Isles: A Short Account of the People, History and Customs of the Maldive Archipelago*. London: Witherby, 1935.

Ibn Battutah. *Ibn Battutah in the Maldives and Ceylon*. Translated by Albert Gray. Journal of the Royal Asiatic Society. Extra No. 1882.

Ibn Battutah. *The Rehla*. Translated by Mahdi Husain. Baroda, India: Oriental Institute, 1953.

Maldives Ministry of External Affairs. *The Maldive Islands*. Colombo: Gunasena, 1952.

Progress of the Colombo Plan, 1968. Colombo: Colombo Plan Bureau, 1968.

Pyrard de Laval, François. *The Voyage of François Pyrard of Laval to the East Indies, the Maldives, the Moluccas and Brazil*. Vols. 76, 77, 80. London: Hakluyt Society, 1887–90.

MONGOLIA

Mongolian People's Republic
Bügd Nayramdah Mongol Ard Uls

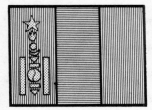

CAPITAL: Ulaanbaatar. **FLAG**: The national flag, adopted in 1946, contains a light blue vertical stripe between two red stripes; in gold, on the stripe nearest the hoist, is a five-pointed star surmounting the soyombo, Mongolia's independence emblem. **ANTHEM**: *Bügd Nayramdah mongol ard ulsyn, ulsyn suld duulal (Anthem of Our Country, or Our Free Revolutionary Land)*. **MONETARY UNIT**: The tugrik (T) of 100 mungges is theoretically at parity with the Soviet ruble. There are coins of 1, 2, 3, 5, 10, and 20 mungges, and notes of 1, 3, 5, 10, 25, 50, and 100 tugriks. T1 = $0.298 (or $1 = T3.3555). **WEIGHTS AND MEASURES**: The metric system is the legal standard. **HOLIDAYS**: New Year's Day, 1 January; May Day, 1 May; Constitution Day, 30 June; Mongol Revolution Day, 11 July; Naadam, three days in summer; Bolshevik (Soviet) Revolution Day, 7 November. Movable holidays include Mongol New Year's Day. **TIME**: 8 P.M.=noon GMT.

¹LOCATION, SIZE, AND EXTENT

Situated in east-central Asia, the Mongolian People's Republic (MPR) has an area of 1,565,000 sq km (604,248 sq mi), extending 2,368 km (1,471 mi) E–W and 1,260 km (783 mi) N–S. A landlocked country, Mongolia is bordered on the N by the USSR and on the E, S, and W by China, with a total boundary length of 7,678 km (4,771 mi).

²TOPOGRAPHY

Mongolia is essentially a vast plateau with an average elevation of 1,580 meters. The MPR comprises a mountainous section in the extreme west, where the peak of the Mönh Hayrhan of the Mongolian Altay Mountains rises to a height of 4,362 meters. Other mountain ranges are the Hentiy along the Soviet border and the Hangay in west-central Mongolia. The southern part of the country is occupied by the Gobi, a rocky desert with a thin veneer of shifting sand. Recent explorations have uncovered large reservoirs of water two to three meters beneath the desert surface.

³CLIMATE

Mongolia has an arid continental climate with a wide seasonal range of temperature and low precipitation. In winter, it is the site of the great Siberian high, which governs the climate of a large part of Asia and gives Mongolia average January temperatures of –33°C to –15°C (–27°F to 5°F) and dry, virtually snowless winters. In summer, remnants of the southeasterly monsoon bring most of the year's precipitation. Total annual precipitation ranges from 10 to 15 inches in mountain areas to less than 5 inches in the Gobi Desert.

⁴FLORA AND FAUNA

Mongolia is divided into several natural regions, each with its characteristic plant and animal life. These regions are the mountain forests near the Soviet Siberian border; the mountain steppe and hilly forest farther south, followed by the lowland steppe grasslands; the semidesert; and finally the true desert. Larch and Siberian stone pine are characteristic trees of the northern forests, which are inhabited by bear, Manchurian red deer, snow panther, wild boar, and elk. The saiga antelope and the wild horse are typical steppe dwellers. As of 1975, endangered species in Mongolia included the wolf, Menzbier's marmot, snow leopard, Przewalski's horse, Asiatic wild ass, and wild bactrian camel.

⁵POPULATION

As of 1 January 1976, the population of the MPR totaled 1,468,600. Projected 1980 population is 1,669,000. In 1975, about 51% of the people lived in urban areas, in sharp contrast to the 22% urban total in 1950. At the end of 1973, the population of Ulaanbaatar, the principal city, came to 303,000 and that of Darhan to 27,300. In 1969, Selenge Province had an urban population of 22,300; Dornod Province, 21,000; Dzavhan Province, 18,400; Dorngovĭ Province, 15,900; and Höcaföl Province, 15,800. At the beginning of 1973, average density was only 0.86 person per sq km. The average rate of population increase in the mid-1970s was about 2.8% per annum.

⁶ETHNIC GROUPS

In 1969, 75.3% of the population was Khalkha. The Kazakhs, the largest minority group, represented 5.2% of the total population. There are also small numbers of peoples of Soviet and Chinese origin.

⁷LANGUAGE

Khalkha Mongolian, the official language, is one of the large dialect groups of the Mongolian branch of the Altaic language family. Early in the 13th century, the Mongols adopted a perpendicular, left-to-right alphabet from the Turkic Uigurs, and retained that script until modern times. The literary language differed increasingly from the living spoken language, and in 1941 the Mongolian government decided to introduce a new phonetic alphabet that would accurately reflect modern spoken Mongolian. The new alphabet consists of the Cyrillic letters used in Russian, exept for two special characters needed to render the Mongol vowels *ö* and *ü*. After a period of preparation (1941–45), the new alphabet was introduced in 1946 in all publications, and in 1950 in all business transactions. Differences between the Khalkha language spoken in the MPR, the Buryat language spoken in Buryat Autonomous Soviet Socialist Republic of the USSR, the Chahar and Ordos languages of China's Inner Mongolian Autonomous Region, and other Mongol dialects are comparatively small and chiefly phonetic. A characteristic phonetic feature of Mongolian is the law of vowel harmony, which requires that a word contain either the so-called back vowels, *a, o, u,* or the front vowels, *e(ā), ö, ü,* but not an association of the two types of vowels. Kazakh, Russian, and Chinese are also spoken in the MPR.

⁸RELIGION

The Mongols are of the Lamaist Buddhist religion, which has been strongly influenced by native shamanism. Prior to the government's campaign against the monasteries in the 1930s, there were nearly 100,000 lamas (theoretically celibate) in Mongolia. In 1937–39, the Communist regime closed virtually all monasteries, confiscated their livestock and landholdings, tried the higher lamas for counterrevolutionary activities, and induced thousands of lower lamas to adopt a secular mode of life. In 1918 there were 700 monasteries, with about 100,000 lamas. In the 1970s, only about 80 lamas remained. In current practice, historical figures such as Genghis Khan are revered ceremonially.

⁹TRANSPORTATION

The Trans-Mongolian Railway, about 1,500 km in length, connects Mongolia with both China and the USSR. Ulaanbaatar has been connected to the Trans-Siberian Railway via Bayantümen since 1939, via Sühbaatar since 1950, and to the Chinese Railways via Dzamïn üüd since the end of 1955. Choybalsan is also connected to the Trans-Siberian system via Ereentsav. The Ulaanbaatar Railways has been linked to Nalayh since 1938 and to Darhan and Tamsagbulag since 1964. The Sharïn Gol Open-Pit Coal Mining Industry was connected to the Darhan industrial center during the third five-year plan (1961–65) by a 60-km rail line. Work on the 200-km railroad line between Salhit and Erdenet-ovoo, the new copper-molybdenum mining and industrial center in Bulgan Province, began in 1973.

Mongolia has more than 5,000 miles of hard-surfaced roads. In addition, there are about 50,000 miles of unpaved roads. Freight and passenger traffic are carried on the Selenge River and across Hövsgöl Lake.

Mongolia's first air service began operating between Ulaanbaatar and Verkhneudinsk in eastern Siberia in 1926. Regular flights now link Ulaanbaatar to Moscow, Irkutsk, and Peking as well as to all the province (aymag) centers. In 1974, almost 50% of all the counties (somons) were provided with air service.

¹⁰COMMUNICATIONS

In 1972 there were 392 post offices throughout the MPR and 141 telephone exchanges; 22,600 telephones were in use, and the length of telephone and telegraph lines amounted to 17,400 km. On 1 September 1934, radio broadcasting began in the MPR. Radio Ulaanbaatar presently broadcasts programs in Mongolian, Russian, Chinese, English, and Kazakh. In 1972 there were 101,400 radio receivers. A television station that transmits locally produced programs and a satellite station are located in Ulaanbaatar. In 1974, Ulaanbaatar, Dzuunmod, Darhan, and Choybalsan, as well as settlements and county cooperatives near Ulaanbaatar, received television broadcasts.

¹¹HISTORY

Mongols played no important historic role before the end of the 12th century. The Mongol tribes united under the leadership of Genghis Khan early in the 13th century, set up their capital at Karakorum, and established a vast empire extending from the northern Siberian forest to Tibet and from the Caspian Sea to the Pacific. After the death of Genghis in 1227, his empire was divided among his followers into Mongol states: the Yüan dynasty of China, which reached its peak under Kublai Khan (1260–94); the Hulagid state, founded by Hulagu in Iran; and the Golden Horde in southern Russia, founded by Batu, the grandson of Genghis Khan.

In the 14th century, the great Mongol states disintegrated, and the Yüan dynasty in China collapsed in 1368, to be replaced by the Ming dynasty. Hulagu's Persian empire disintegrated in 1370, and the Golden Horde was attacked and shaken by the forces of Prince Dmitry Donskoy in Russia, in 1380. In 1369, at the age of 33, Tamerlane proclaimed himself ruler of all the land lying between the Tien Shan and the Hindu Kush mountain ranges. The Mongols retired to their original steppe homelands, splitting into three major groups: the northern Khalkha Mongols, north of the Gobi Desert; the southern Chahar Mongols, south of the Gobi; and the western Mongols (Oirats). (The Kalmyk Mongols of European Russia constitute a branch of the Oirats. Buryat Mongols live north of the Khalkhas, around Lake Baykal, in the USSR.)

A cleavage developed between the northern (outer) Mongols and the southern (inner) Mongols, who had been more closely associated with Mongol rule in China. On their way to conquer China, the Manchus subdued the southern Mongols in 1636, thus placing them under the rule of China's Manchu dynasty (1644–1911). Northern Mongols, who had been fighting with western Mongols for supremacy, sought Manchu aid against their foes and accepted Manchu suzerainty in 1691. Finally, Manchus destroyed the western Mongols as a historic force in 1758. The Russian-Chinese border treaties of Nerchinsk (1689) and Kyakhta (1727) confirmed Chinese rule over both southern and northern (Khalkha) Mongols, but assigned the Buryats to Russia.

Following the overthrow of the Manchu dynasty by the Chinese revolution in 1911, northern Mongol princes proclaimed an autonomous Outer Mongolia under the rule of the Jebtsun Damba Khutukhtu (Bogdo Gegen, or the Living Buddha of Urga). A treaty with the tsar's government pledged Russian assistance for the autonomous state. After the Bolshevik Revolution, the Chinese exploited Russia's weakness, reoccupied Outer Mongolia in 1919, and ended its autonomy. In early 1921, the Chinese were driven out by Russian counterrevolutionary forces under Baron von Ungern-Sternberg. He in turn was overcome in July 1921 by the Mongol revolutionary leaders Sukhe Bator and Choibalsan, assisted by the Soviet Red Army.

Under Soviet influence, a nominally independent state headed by the Jebtsun Damba Khutukhtu was proclaimed on 11 July 1921 and lasted as a constitutional monarchy until the Living Buddha's death in 1924.

The Mongolian People's Republic was proclaimed on 26 November 1924. With the support of the USSR, Communist rule was gradually consolidated. Large landholdings of feudal lords were confiscated starting in 1929, and those of lamaseries in 1938. A mutual assistance treaty in 1936 formalized the close relations between the USSR and the MPR. After a virtually unanimous plebiscite in favor of Mongolian independence, Nationalist China formally recognized the MPR in 1946.

On 14 February 1950, China and the USSR signed a treaty that guaranteed the MPR's independence. Conflicting boundary claims between the MPR and China were settled by treaty on 26 December 1962, and on 15 January 1966 the MPR and the USSR concluded a 20-year treaty of friendship, cooperation, and mutual assistance. The MPR was admitted to the UN in October 1961 and became a member of COMECON in June 1962.

In June 1974, Marshal Yumjaagiin Tsendenbal, first secretary since 1940 of the Mongolian People's Revolutionary Party, was elected chairman of the Presidium by the legislature, and hence president of the MPR, succeeding Jamsarangin Sambuu, who died in 1972.

¹²GOVERNMENT

According to the 1960 constitution, the supreme organ of government is the People's Great Hural, a national legislature elected by universal suffrage of citizens 18 years of age and over. In 1973, 336 deputies, including 65 from Ulaanbaatar districts, were elected to the People's Great Hural. Each deputy serves a four-year term. The Hural approves major laws and decrees submitted by the government; amends articles of the constitution; confirms the annual economic plans; approves the budget and oversees its implementation; elects its Presidium from its own members; and appoints the state procurator and the members of the Council of Ministers and the Supreme Court.

The Presidium, which represents the Hural between sessions, consists of a chairman who serves as the chief of state, a first deputy chairman, a deputy chairman, a secretary, and six other members. The Presidium is responsible for the organization and agenda of the Hural, and has the authority to convene regular and unscheduled meetings and to call for elections; it possesses all powers related to foreign relations and national defense, including the declaration of war when the Hural is not in session.

The Council of Ministers is the supreme executive organ of the government. It is responsible to the Presidium and, by extension, to the Hural, and consists of a chairman, two first deputy chairmen, five deputy chairmen, ministers, and heads of special offices and committees. Control of the MPR government is effectively in the hands of the Mongolian People's Revolutionary Party, whose first secretary, Yumjaagiin Tsendenbal, is also chairman of the Presidium.

13 POLITICAL PARTIES

The Mongolian People's Revolutionary Party (MPRP), founded as Mongolia's Communist Party in 1921, is the only political organization in the MPR. In 1971, the MPRP had 58,048 members and candidate members. Its program calls for realization of a people's democracy based on the working people; equal rights of all nationalities, and of men and women; antireligious propaganda while respecting the religious feelings of individuals; improved social and working conditions; development of the economic potential through mechanization of agriculture, exploitation of natural resources, and industrialization. The Central Committee of the MPRP, which in 1971 consisted of 83 members and 55 candidate members, guides party affairs between sessions of the party congresses, convened every four years. The Central Committee has a secretariat composed of the first secretary, who is the actual party leader, the secretary of the Central Committee, and three other secretaries. It elects its Political Bureau, comprising seven members and two candidate-members. The Political Bureau, also known as the Politburo, is a policy-making body comprising the highest party leadership.

The next level of party committees is that of provinces (aymags) and cities. Party committees also exist at county (somon) and town levels, as well as in agricultural cooperatives, state farms, offices, schools, hospitals, and other enterprises. Party cells exist when the size or membership is not sufficiently large to justify the establishment of a committee. A section is the smallest unit but requires no fewer than three members.

14 LOCAL GOVERNMENT

In January 1973, the MPR administratively consisted of 18 provinces (aymags) and 304 counties (somons). Ulaanbaatar and Darhan are separate administrative units, which in turn are divided into districts. Each level of local administration has its own assembly of people's deputies, elected every three years. In June 1972, 14,216 deputies were elected to the province, city, town, county, and various district assemblies.

15 JUDICIAL SYSTEM

Justice is administered through the Supreme Court elected by the People's Great Hural; province and city courts elected by the corresponding assemblies of people's deputies; and other, lower courts. All citizens aged 23 or over may be elected as judges or people's assessors to lower courts. The state procurator is appointed by the Hural, and sees to the correct implementation of all laws by government officials and ordinary citizens.

16 ARMED FORCES

The Mongolian People's Army is under the jurisdiction of the Ministry of Defense and has a civilian administration. The army oversees units of construction troops. Two years' service is compulsory for all males. In 1974, the armed forces totaled 30,000. The army had 28,000 personnel and a reserve strength of 30,000. The air force had 2,000 personnel and is equipped exclusively with transport and other support aircraft. Virtually all military equipment is of Soviet origin. The militia, consisting of about 18,000 frontier guards and security police, is under the jurisdic-

tion of the Ministry of Security. The MPR budget allocated T373 million for defense in 1975.

17 MIGRATION

Few MPR nationals live outside of the country, but more than 3 million persons of Mongol extraction live in China—in Inner Mongolia, Manchuria, Tsinghai, Kansu, and Sinkiang-Uigur. Between 1955 and 1962, some 20,000 Chinese laborers entered Mongolia to work on construction projects, but in 1964 the MPR expelled them. Following their expulsion, some 10,000 Soviet engineers, technicians, and laborers came to Mongolia to undertake various industrial projects.

18 INTERNATIONAL COOPERATION

The MPR was admitted to the UN in 1961 and currently participates in ESCAP, FAO, IAEA, ICJ, ILO, ITU, UNCTAD, UNESCO, UPU, WHO, and WMO. The MPR is a member of COMECON, the JINR, and the Organization for Railway Cooperation among the Socialist Countries. In June 1972, it became a member of CEMA and in that year established diplomatic relations with Japan.

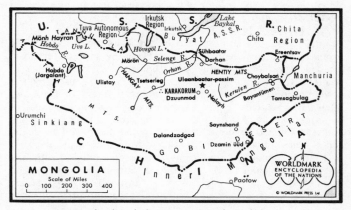

See continental political: front cover O5; physical: back cover O5

LOCATION: 87°47′ to 119°54′E; 41°31′ to 52°16′N. **BOUNDARY LENGTHS**: USSR, 3,005 km (1,867 mi); China, 4,673 km (2,904 mi).

19 ECONOMY

The dominant sector of the economy is animal husbandry, now almost entirely socialized in cooperatives. In 1972, livestock raising accounted for 83.4% of the total agricultural output. In spite of the arid climate, farming has been playing an increasingly important role in the economy. In 1972, raw materials for food cultivation and food products represented 43.6% of Mongolia's total exports, while these categories accounted for 13.7% of total imports. The government has been promoting industrialization through the exploitation of mineral resources and the development of light industry, focusing especially on those sectors that utilize raw materials derived from animal husbandry. The state owns virtually all machinery and equipment, and regulates the entire distribution and marketing system.

20 INCOME

The estimated GNP in 1974 was $2.8 billion.

21 LABOR

A majority of the population are engaged in livestock production and farming, and most of these are organized in collective farms. In 1972, the number of persons employed elsewhere in state sectors of the economy totaled 214,500, including 47,000 in industry, 26,000 in commerce, 21,600 in communications, 20,200 in agriculture, and 17,700 in capital construction work. In that year, the number of female workers and employees in the national economy came to 89,700, or 41.8% of the total. A serious shortage of skilled labor has required the procurement of a large supplementary work force from the USSR and Eastern Europe.

All workers are members of Mongolian trade unions. According to the labor code, the working day is fixed at eight hours, and in occupations that are harmful to health, at six to seven hours. Industrial workers and office employees are entitled to paid annual vacations.

22 AGRICULTURE

The total cultivated area in 1972 amounted to 475,300 hectares, 74.9% of which belonged to state farms and 25.1% to agricultural cooperatives. During that year, grain was grown on 88.4% of the total cultivated land, vegetables on 0.3%, potatoes on 0.6%, and fodder crops on 10.7%. In 1972, 205,000 tons of grain (including 169,700 tons of wheat, 17,300 tons of barley, and 16,700 tons of oats), 10,200 tons of potatoes, 10,900 tons of vegetables, and 59,800 tons of fodder crops (including 2,600 tons of silage) were harvested in both state and cooperative sectors. Some 645,700 tons of hay, including 142,900 tons on state farms and 370,700 tons on cooperatives, were also produced.

Farm machinery available to agriculture in 1972 included 6,300 tractors, 2,600 tractor plows, 700 tractor cultivators, 3,100 tractor drills, and 2,000 grain combines.

23 ANIMAL HUSBANDRY

Animal husbandry continues to be the backbone of the MPR economy. Pastures comprise about 85% of the national territory. In 1972, 74.8% of all the livestock belonged to 272 agricultural cooperatives, and 4.7% to the state farms; 20.5% constituted the private property of cooperative members, workers, officials, and other citizens. That same year there were 23,109,100 head of livestock in the MPR, including 625,100 camels, 2,239,300 horses, 2,189,400 head of cattle, 13,716,900 sheep, and 4,338,400 goats. Some 13,700 hogs and 123,000 fowl were also raised.

Hunting remains an important commercial activity, with furs and skins the chief products. In 1972, output included 845,400 marmot skins, 34,300 squirrel skins, 29,100 fox skins, 21,200 steppe fox skins, 4,300 wolf skins, and T219,000 worth of other pelts.

24 FISHING

In 1972, the output of the MPR's inland fishing industry amounted to some 188 tons.

25 FORESTRY

Forests cover about 10% of the total territory of the MPR, mainly in the area around Hövsgöl Lake. It is estimated that the country's total timber resources represent no less than 1.25 billion cu meters. Birch, cedar, larch, and fir trees predominate.

In 1972, the lumber industry yielded 692,900 cu meters of commercial timber and 363,900 cu meters of sawn timber. Lumber and woodworking industries accounted for 14.3% of the total industrial output of the MPR in 1972.

26 MINING

The MPR is self-sufficient in coal and possesses about 3 billion tons of coal reserves. In 1972, the MPR mined 2,252,600 tons of coal, representing 4.3% of the country's total industrial output. It also mined 79,400 tons of fluorspar and 30,400 tons of lime. The MPR also produces petroleum in Saynshand, as well as gold, tungsten, and uranium. The state is currently developing the Erdenet Copper-Molybdenum Mine in cooperation with the USSR.

27 ENERGY AND POWER

In 1972, the installed capacity of the electric power stations in the MPR amounted to 226,200 kw, with an output of 631.1 million kwh. Three major power plants are located in Ulaanbaatar, one in Darhan, and smaller facilities are in Sühbaatar and Choibalsan.

28 INDUSTRY

Most industry remains small-scale and is engaged in the processing of livestock and agricultural products. Cement and textiles are also important. The production of industrial commodities represented 47.1% of the gross industrial output in 1972 and the production of consumer goods, 52.9%. State-owned industry accounted for about 97% of industrial output, with 3% produced by the cooperative sector. The MPR presently has three large industrial centers, located in Ulaanbaatar, Darhan, and Choybalsan. In 1973, the light industry sector produced 50.9% of total industrial output and provided 41% of exports.

29 DOMESTIC TRADE

Consumer goods produced at Ulaanbaatar or imported from abroad are distributed by state marketing agencies to retail outlets in local administrative centers. In 1972, the total value of the retail trade turnover was T2,117.7 million. Some of the main retail trade commodities are flour, rice, green tea, fruit, milk, milk products, meat, meat products, tobacco, cotton, wool and silk fabrics, sewing machines, bicycles, radios, watches, and clocks.

30 FOREIGN TRADE

Mongolia's chief trading partner is the USSR. Socialist countries, including China, accounted for 99.1% of the MPR's exports and 98.8% of its imports in 1972. Other trade partners include Japan (since 1972) and the UK. In 1972, non-foodstuff raw materials and processed goods accounted for 43.7% of the MPR's exports; raw materials (for food production), 28.8%; and food products, 14.8%. Machinery and equipment accounted for 26.5% of its imports; manufactured consumer goods, 34.8%; fuels, minerals, and metals, 12.3%; food products, 11.8%; and raw materials (for food production), 1.9%.

31 BALANCE OF PAYMENTS

Mongolia consistently imports more than it exports. The imbalance is covered by USSR gifts and cancellations of accrued debt.

32 BANKING

The principal banking institution is the Mongolian State Bank, which until 1954 was a joint USSR-Mongolian enterprise known as Mongolbank. It has branches and savings branch offices throughout the country. The State Bank is the official bank of issue and handles all accounts of state and cooperative organizations. It also grants short-term and long-term loans for economic development in industry, agriculture, and animal husbandry.

33 INSURANCE

There is no private insurance system.

34 SECURITIES

No private securities are sold.

35 PUBLIC FINANCE

The annual budget is submitted to the People's Great Hural for approval. In 1974, the budget of the MPR called for revenues in the amount of T2,620 million and expenditures of T2,610 million. About 90% of revenues are derived from state-owned and cooperative enterprises by means of turnover taxes and profit-withholding taxes. Budget expenditures for 1972 were broken down as follows: 43.2% (T936.3 million) for development of the national economy; 41.3% (T894.7 million) for social and cultural endeavors; and 15.5% (T334.1 million) for administrative and other expenses.

36 TAXATION

The turnover tax, accounting in 1972 for 66.5% of all the revenue, is an indirect sales tax levied at the production stage on all manufactured commodities. Personal taxes consist of income taxes paid by salaried industrial workers and office employees, and livestock taxes on private herders, based on the number of livestock owned.

37 CUSTOMS AND DUTIES

Customs duties are insignificant, yielding less than 1% of total state revenues.

38 FOREIGN INVESTMENTS

There are no private investments. The USSR and allied countries extend loans and gifts to the Mongolian government. In recent years, technical aid has been supplied by various UN agencies.

39 ECONOMIC POLICY

The MPR operates on the basis of a planned economy. The first annual economic plan, promulgated in 1941, was followed by six additional annual plans. The financing of these plans was assisted by loans totaling about T1.7 billion from the USSR and about T300 million from China. The fourth five-year plan (1966–70) envisioned the receipt of 550 million rubles in loans, 90% supplied by the USSR.

During these periods of planned economic development, the rate and value of capital investment increased rapidly. The investment amounted to T203.7 million during the first five-year plan (1947–51); T673.2 million during the second five-year plan (1952–57); T1,476.8 million during the subsequent three-year plan (1958–60); and T3,862.4 million during the third five-year plan (1961–65). The fourth five-year plan (1966–70), which called for capital investments of T5,290.2 million, failed to achieve projected growth levels in livestock. The 1971–75 plan, as did its recent predecessors, stressed the development of permanently settled agricultural and livestock enterprises as well as light industry. In 1972, T1,146.5 million was allocated for economic development; of this, 61.2% was earmarked for construction and installation work, 30.9% for machinery and equipment, and 7.9% for other types of investment.

40 HEALTH

Health care is administered under state auspices and all medical and hospital services are free. In 1972 there were 2,578 physicians, or 19.2 physicians for each 10,000 persons. At the end of 1972, 1,285 physicians were located in Ulaanbaatar and 75 in Darhan. Medical personnel also included 9,041 physician's assistants, 421 pharmacists, 4,628 nurses, and 48 dental technicians. Facilities in 1972 included 114 hospitals, with 9,851 beds; 216 physician-staffed medical stations; 846 stations staffed with medical assistants; 25 hygiene stations; 315 nurseries; 11 rest centers; and 315 pharmacies. The government is giving special priority to increasing the number of physicians and other health personnel and expanding facilities in rural areas. Each province has at least two hospitals, and each agricultural cooperative and state farm has a medical station staffed either by a physician or by medical assistants.

In 1975, the birthrate was estimated at 36.7 and the death rate 8.1 per 1,000 (compared with 43.2 and 10.5, respectively, in 1960). Average life expectancy in 1975 was 62.8 years (45 years in 1950). Pulmonary and bronchial infections, including tuberculosis and brucellosis, are widespread but are being brought under control through the use of ayrag, an indigenous drink brewed from horse's milk with demonstrated healing qualities. Cholera, smallpox, typhus, and other epidemic diseases have been virtually eliminated. Health services account for 10% of the MPR's annual budget expenditures.

41 SOCIAL WELFARE

The social insurance program provides for free medical services, benefits for temporary disability, and pensions for permanent disability and old age. Expectant mothers are granted paid maternity leaves, and state aid is provided for mothers with large families.

42 HOUSING

Although there are many stone and wood buildings in Ulaanbaatar and some of the larger provincial centers, the standard housing of the nomadic herders, as well as of many city dwellers, is the yurt, a light, movable, dome-shaped tent consisting of skin or felt covering stretched over a lattice frame. However, more permanent housing facilities have been appearing in rural areas throughout the country. Large apartment-house complexes with stores, services, and cultural facilities are rising in Ulaanbaatar as well as in various other cities and towns. In 1972, the state and cooperative housing fund provided 1,792,500 sq meters of living space.

43 EDUCATION

In 1947, literacy was made compulsory, and by 1970 more than 80% of the population was literate. In early 1975, 35,961 children were enrolled at 535 kindergartens. In 1974 there were 163 primary schools, 336 eight-year schools, and 56 ten-year schools; 289,295 students attended general-education schools at all levels. In addition, some 18,500 youths studied by means of 130 short-term general education courses for workers, 103 seasonal courses, 51 evening courses, and 49 correspondence sections. Furthermore, more than 36,800 students attended 6 higher institutes, 21 specialized secondary schools, and 29 schools for technological training. At present, more than 47,800 students from rural areas reside in dormitories adjoining schools.

The Mongolian State University was founded in 1942. The University cooperates with the Joint Nuclear Research Institute at Dubna, as well as with other institutes and universities located in the USSR and the German Democratic Republic. Research is also undertaken in conjunction with MPR government ministries in fields of agriculture, fuel, power, and geology, and with the State Construction Research Institute in pursuit of various problems related to nuclear physics, biophysics, national resources, and mineral studies as well as to research concerned with energy, communications, and construction. During 1974/75, more than 1,000 students were scheduled to attend higher and specialized schools in the USSR and other Socialist countries.

The scope of work of the MPR Academy of Sciences, founded in May 1961, includes the administration of libraries, museums, and archives; the preparation of textbooks and maps; the coordination of research in agriculture, animal breeding, economics, geography, geology, and natural history and in the history, language, and literature of the Mongolian people; the recording of traditional songs and legends; and the maintenance of agricultural experimental stations, a hydrometeorological service, a seismological station, and an astronomical observatory. The Academy has its own publishing house.

44 LIBRARIES AND MUSEUMS

The Mongolian State University has a library of 300,000 volumes. The State Public Library, which is under the jurisdiction of the Academy of Sciences, contains 1 million volumes in Mongolian, Chinese, English, French, German, Manchu, Russian, Tibetan, and other languages. It also has a collection of valuable Buddhist manuscripts. In 1972 there were 421 public libraries, with 5.7 million volumes, and 628 reading rooms, with 214,000 volumes, distributed throughout Mongolia. The State Museum, located in Ulaanbaatar, containing art treasures and antiquities, the Revolutionary Museum, the Sukhe Bator and Choybalsan Museum, the Ulaanbaatar Museum, and the museum of religion are all under the jurisdiction of the Academy of Sciences.

45 ORGANIZATIONS

Mongolia's mass organizations, all of which work closely with the MPRP, include the Mongolian Revolutionary Youth League (founded in 1922), the Mongolian Pioneers' Organization, the Organization of Working Women (founded in 1933), and the Mongolian-Soviet Friendship Society (founded in 1947). Professional and cultural organizations include the Union of Mongolian Artists, the Union of Mongolian Composers, the Mongolian Association for Lawyers, the Union of Mongolian Journalists, the Union of Mongolian Students, the Union of Mongolian Writers, and the Union of Philatelists. Other organizations are the Mongolian Committee for Afro-Asian Solidarity, Mongolian Union for Peace and Friendship

Organizations, and the Mongolian Committee for the Defense of Peace.

46 PRESS

In 1972 there were 37 newspapers in the MPR, with a combined annual circulation of 83,487,700. These included *Unen*, the organ of the Central Committee of the MPRP and the MPR government; *Hodolmor*, the organ of the trade unions; *Dzaluuchuudyn Unen*, organ of the Central Committee of the Mongolian Revolutionary Youth League; *Shine Hodoo*, organ of the Ministry of Agricultural and the Supreme Council of the Federation of Agriculture Cooperatives; *Utga Dzohiol Urlag*, organ of the Union of Mongolian Writers; and *Ulaan Od*, offical publication of the armed forces. Also published were 3,834,100 copies of 38 periodicals, including *Namyn am'dral*, journal of the Central Committee of the MPRP, and *Shinjleh Uhaan*, bimonthly publication of the Academy of Sciences.

47 TOURISM

In 1972, 1,037 travelers visited the MPR from abroad. The numbers of travelers from non-Socialist countries, although small, has been increasing steadily, and totaled 467 in 1972.

Visitors require passports, visas, and certificates of vaccination against smallpox. Ulaanbaatar has one tourist hotel, with 300 rooms. There is a Mongolian Tourist Bureau.

48 FAMOUS MONGOLS

A long line of Mongol khans have left their mark on history ever since Genghis Khan (r.1206–27) set up the first Mongol empire. Outstanding among them were Kublai Khan (1216–94), a grandson of Genghis, who conquered most of China; Hulagu Khan (1217–60), a brother of Kublai, who conquered Persia and Syria; Batu Khan (d.1255), Kublai's cousin, who overran Russia, Poland, and Hungary; and Timur, also known as Tamerlane (1336?–1405), who pushed his military power for short periods into southern Russia, India, and the Levant.

In recent times, two national leaders were Sukhe Bator (1894–1923) and Khorloin Choibalsan (1895–1952). Yumjaagiin Tsendenbal (b.1917), intermittently first secretary of the Central Committee of the MPRP since 1940, and chairman of the Council of Ministers since 1952, was elected chairman of the Presidium of the People's Great Hural in June 1974.

The founder of modern Mongolian literature is Tsendyn Damdinsuren (b.1908). Rinchen (b.1905) is one of the most important authors. Leading playwrights are Ch. Oydov (1917–63) and E. Oyuun (b.1918). Other prominent writers are D. Natsagdorj (1906–37), D. Namdag (b.1911), U. Ulambayar (b.1911), and Ch. Lodoydamba (1917–70). B. Damdinsuren and L. Murdorzh are noted composers.

49 DEPENDENCIES

The MPR has no territories or colonies.

50 BIBLIOGRAPHY

Ballis, William Belcher. "Political Evolution of a Soviet Satellite: The Mongolian People's Republic." *Western Political Quarterly*, June 1956, pp. 293–328.

Ballis, William Belcher, *et al. Mongolian People's Republic (Outer Mongolia).* New Haven: HRAF Press, 1956.

Barnett, Doak. *Communist China and Asia.* New York: Harper, 1960.

Bawden, C. R. *A Modern History of Mongolia.* New York: Praeger, 1968.

"A Bibliography of Books and Articles on Mongolia." *Journal of the Royal Central Asian Society*, April 1950, pp. 186–201; July–October 1950, pp. 298–330.

Bibliography of the Mongolian People's Republic. New Haven: HRAF Press, 1956.

Central Statistical Board of the Council of Ministers of the MPR. *50 Years of the MPR, Statistical Collection.* Ulaanbaatar: 1971.

Cheney, G. A. *The Culture of Outer Mongolia.* Bloomington, Ind.: Mongolia Society, 1969.

Chumichev, D. A. *Mongol'skaya Narodnaya Respublika.* [*Mongolian People's Republic.*] Moscow: 1966.

Friters, Gerard M. *Outer Mongolia and Its International Position.* Baltimore: Johns Hopkins Press, 1949.

Ginsburg, George. "Local Government in the MPR, 1940–1960." *Journal of Asian Studies*, August 1961, pp. 489–508.

Ginsburg, George. "Mongolia's 'Socialist' Constitution." *Pacific Affairs*, Summer 1961, pp. 141–56.

Jackson, W. A. Douglas. *The Russo-Chinese Borderlands.* Princeton, N.J.: Van Nostrand, 1962.

Knutson, Jean Nickell. *Outer Mongolia: A Study in Soviet Colonialism.* Kowloon: Union Research Institute, 1961.

Kolarz, Walter. *Peoples of the Soviet Far East.* New York: Harper, 1954.

Lattimore, Owen. *Inner Asian Frontiers of China.* Boston: Beacon Press, 1940.

Lattimore, Owen. *Mongol Journeys.* New York: Doubleday, Doran, 1941.

Lattimore, Owen. *Nationalism and Revolution in Mongolia.* With a translation from the Mongol of Sh. Nachukdorji's *Life of Sukebatur.* New York: Oxford University Press, 1955.

Lattimore, Owen. *Nomads and Commissars: Mongolia Revisited.* New York: Oxford University Press, 1962.

MacLean, Fitzroy. *To the Back of Beyond: An Illustrated Companion to Central Asia and Mongolia.* Boston: Little, Brown, 1975.

Maslennikov, Vasili A. *Contemporary Mongolia.* Bloomington, Ind.: Mongolia Society, 1964.

Micheli, Silvio. *Mongolia: In Search of Marco Polo and Other Adventures.* New York: Harcourt, Brace & World, 1967.

Montagu, Ivor G. S. *Land of Blue Sky: A Portrait of Modern Mongolia.* London: Dobson, 1956.

Murphy, George G. S. *Soviet Mongolia: A Study of the Oldest Political Satellite.* Berkeley: University of California Press, 1966.

Ovdienko, Ivan. Kh. *Economic-Geographical Sketch of the Mongolian People's Republic.* Bloomington, Ind.: Mongolia Society, 1965.

Ovdienko, Ivan. Kh. *Sovremennaya Mongoliya.* [*Modern Mongolia.*] Moscow: 1964.

Petrov, Victor P. *Mongolia: A Profile.* New York: Praeger, 1970.

Rupen, Robert A. *Mongols of the Twentieth Century.* Bloomington: Indiana University Press, 1964.

Sandag, Sh. *The Mongolian Struggle for National Independence and the Building of a New Life.* Ulaanbaatar: State Publishing House, 1966.

Sanders, Alan J. K. *The People's Republic of Mongolia: A General Reference Guide.* New York: Oxford University Press, 1968.

Shirendev, B., and M. Sanjdorj (eds.). *The History of the Mongolian People's Republic.* Cambridge: Harvard University Press, 1976.

Tsegmid, Sh. *BNMAU-yn gazar zui.* [*Geography of the Mongolian People's Republic.*] Ulaanbaatar: Publishing House of the Ministry of Education, 1957.

Vreeland, Herbert Harold, III. *Mongol Community and Kinship Structure.* New Haven: HRAF Press, 1957.

Zhukov, E. M., *et al.* (eds.). *History of the Mongolian People's Republic.* Moscow: 1973.

NAURU

Republic of Nauru

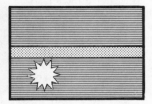

CAPITAL: There is no formal capital. The seat of government is in the district of Uaboe. **FLAG:** The flag has a blue background divided horizontally by a narrow gold band, symbolizing the equator. Below the band is a white 12-pointed star, representing the island's 12 traditional tribes. **ANTHEM:** *Anibare Bay* is taken from a popular local song but the formal words have not yet been written. **MONETARY UNIT:** The Australian dollar (A$) of 100 cents is the legal currency. There are coins of 1, 2, 5, 10, 20, and 50 cents, and notes of 1, 2, 5, 10, 20, and 50 dollars. A$1 = US$1.25 (or US$1 = A$0.80). **WEIGHTS AND MEASURES:** Imperial weights and measures are used. **HOLIDAYS:** Independence Day, 31 January; Good Friday; Constitution Day, 17 May; Angam Day, 23 October (a celebration of the day on which the population of Nauru reached the pre-World War II level); Christmas Day, 25 December; and Boxing Day, 26 December. **TIME:** 11 P.M. = noon GMT.

¹LOCATION, SIZE, AND EXTENT

Situated in the western Pacific, Nauru is the smallest Asian country, with an area of 21 sq km (8.2 sq mi), extending 5.6 km (3.5 mi) NNE–SSW and 4 km (2.5 mi) ESE–WNW. It lies between two island groups, the Solomons and the Gilberts. Its nearest neighbor is Ocean Island, 306 km (190 mi) to the E. Nauru has a coastline of 19 km (12 mi).

²TOPOGRAPHY

The island is oval-shaped and is fringed by a wide coral reef. It has no natural harbor or anchorage. A relatively fertile belt varying in width from 150 to 300 yards encircles the island. From this belt a coral cliff rises to a central plateau about 200 feet above sea level. Buada Lagoon, a permanent, often brackish lake, covers some 300 acres in the southeastern end of the plateau. Apart from the water of some brackish ponds and of an underground lake, all water has to be collected after rain.

³CLIMATE

Nauru has a dry season marked by easterly trade winds and a wet season with westerly monsoons extending from November to February. The average annual rainfall is about 81 inches, but great variations are recorded and long droughts have been a recurrent feature. Temperatures remain steady at between 21°C and 26°C (70–79°F) the year round, and relative humidity is also constant at about 80%.

⁴FLORA AND FAUNA

The plateau area contains large phosphate deposits which almost completely inhibit any useful natural growth. Large areas of scrub and creeper with occasional coconut and tamanu trees grow here. On the coastal belt, coconut palms and pandanus (a type of screw pine) thrive. Some hibiscus, frangipani, and other tropical flowers grow, but do not abound here as on other of the Pacific islands. Bird life is not plentiful, although noddies, terns, and frigate birds frequent the island. There are no indigenous animals; however, hogs and poultry were introduced many years ago. Fish life is abundant in the seas encircling Nauru, and good catches of tuna and bonito are taken. As of 1975, the Nauru nightingale warbler was classified as an endangered species.

⁵POPULATION

As of 30 June 1972, the population of Nauru was 6,768, including 3,471 Nauruans, 883 Chinese, 627 Europeans, and 1,787 other Pacific islanders. The Nauruan population had increased 9.4% since January 1968. Most Nauruans live around the coastal fringes, in their traditional districts. Most Chinese as well as most immigrants from the Gilbert Islands and Ellice Islands (Tuvalu) are settled in communities near the phosphate works.

⁶ETHNIC GROUPS

The Nauruan people are the only indigenous ethnic group on the island. They are of mixed Micronesian, Melanesian, and Polynesian origin and resemble the last strain most closely. Their origins are unexplored. They are divided into 12 clans or tribes in which descent is matrilineal, although kinship and inheritance rules have some patrilineal features. The 12 clans are Eamwit, Eamwidumwit, Deboe, Eoaru, Emea, Eano, Emangum, Ranibok, Eamwidara, Iruwa, Irutsi (extinct), and Iwi (extinct). Admixtures of Caucasian and Negroid blood in the 19th century and frequent intermarriage with other Pacific islanders have changed the present-day features of Nauruans from those of their forebears. The Caucasians on the island are almost all Australians employed in administrative or teaching posts, or in the phosphate industry. The Chinese and immigrants from the Gilbert Islands and Tuvalu come to the island as laborers in the phosphate industry and a small proportion are accompanied by their families.

⁷LANGUAGE

English is used in the schools, in government, and in all business transactions on the island. The Nauruan language is distinct from other Pacific tongues. Most Nauruans are bilingual but use Nauruan in everyday life.

⁸RELIGION

The Nauruans have accepted Christianity since the end of the 19th century. About two-thirds of them are Protestants and the remainder are Roman Catholic.

⁹TRANSPORTATION

Transport to and from Nauru has always been by ships calling at the island to unload freight and pick up phosphates for delivery to Australia, New Zealand, and other countries. Nauru has a fleet of six ships (Nauru Pacific Line) and three more under charter. Air Nauru flies regular air services to the Pacific islands, Japan, and Australia. Air Pacific maintains weekly service to Fiji.

On the island itself there is only one major ring road. There were 1,534 motor vehicles registered in 1972. Apart from a small railway (used to carry phosphates) and a school bus service, there is no other local transport.

¹⁰COMMUNICATIONS

Communication with the outside world is maintained by a radio link that has been important in cross-Pacific communication for many years. A small telephone exchange provides on-island communication. Shortwave radio reception from overseas is poor because of the island's isolation. The government-owned Radio Nauru broadcasts in English and Nauruan to an estimated audience of 6,500 people.

11 HISTORY

The first recorded discovery of Nauru was made by Captain John Fearn of the whaling ship *Hunter* in November 1798. He named the island Pleasant Island. From the 1830s to the 1880s the Nauruans had a succession of visitors—runaway convicts, deserters from whaling ships, and other men who can be classed as beachcombers. The beachcombers provided the Nauruans with their first real contact with Western civilization and introduced them to firearms and alcohol. The beachcombers acted as a buffer between two cultures but they were often a bad influence on the Nauruans. Several times beachcombers and Nauruans attempted to cut off and capture visiting ships, so that eventually Nauru came to be avoided as a watering place by ships whaling in the area. The advent of firearms also disturbed the balance of power between the tribes on the island; sporadic tribal warfare culminated in a 10-year civil war from 1878 to 1888. At about the same time the British and German imperial governments had agreed to the partition of the Western Pacific in 1886. Their purely arbitrary line of demarcation left Nauru in the German sphere of influence quite accidentally. It was not until 1888, on the petition of the beachcombers turned traders, that the German government decided to proclaim Nauru a protectorate. Thus the island was annexed in October 1888, and the people were disarmed, some 765 weapons being confiscated. The missionaries arrived at about the same time, but they had a greater impact on the Nauruan culture than did the German administration.

In 1901, Albert Ellis, a New Zealand geologist, discovered that there were large deposits of phosphate on both Nauru and Ocean Island. Ocean Island, a British possession, began to be mined immediately, but it was not until 1907 that phosphate was mined on Nauru, after the German government had granted a concession to the British Pacific Phosphate Co. Laborers from the German Caroline Islands were hired because the Nauruans had no interest in working in the mines.

Nauru was occupied by the Australian Expeditionary Force in 1914, and phosphate continued to be shipped all through World War I. After that war Nauru was made a League of Nations Mandate of the British Empire, and the governments of Australia, New Zealand, and Great Britain agreed to administer the island jointly through an administrator to be appointed by Australia. At the same time that the three governments obtained the mandate, they jointly purchased the Pacific Phosphate Co.'s rights to Nauru phosphate for UK£3.5 million and began to work the deposits through a three-man board called the British Phosphate Commissioners (BPC).

The phosphate industry expanded greatly in the years between the wars. Australian and New Zealand farmers enjoyed substantial savings, for Nauru phosphate was sold at a much lower price than phosphate from other countries. As for the Nauruans, with their small royalty of 8d a ton in 1939, they opted out of the industry completely and turned in on their own culture.

War came to Nauru in December 1940 when the island was shelled by a roving German raider and four phosphate ships were sunk. The Japanese occupied the island from August 1942 until the end of the war three years later. Twelve hundred Nauruans were deported to Truk, a small atoll 1,000 miles northwest of Nauru, and many died there. Nauru itself was flattened, and all the industrial plant and housing facilities destroyed. The Nauru population fell from 1,848 in 1940 to 1,369 in 1946. Australian forces reoccupied Nauru in September 1945,

and the remaining Truk Nauruans were repatriated in January 1946.

The three mandatory governments placed the Mandate of Nauru before the UN, which on 1 November 1947 approved a trusteeship agreement for Nauru in which the island became a Trust Territory administered jointly by Australia, New Zealand, and Great Britain, who were to share the sacred trust of developing self-government for the island. The Nauruans had had a Council of Chiefs to represent them since 1927, but the Council had advisory powers only. Dissatisfied Nauruans made a number of complaints to the Administering Authority and to the Trusteeship Council, with the result that a Nauru local government council was set up in 1951. The first elections for the council were held in December 1951, and 9 members were elected from constituencies drawn on traditional district lines. But since control of the council was exercised by the administrator, the Nauruans continued to press for further political power. They asked for positions of importance in the administration and an increase of royalty payments, and expressed concern about the future of the island because the increased rate of phosphate exportation would, it was feared, exhaust the deposits by the year 2000.

By constant negotiations the Nauruans forced the BPC to pay royalties on a rights rather than needs basis, and with the establishment of a world price in 1964 royalties were raised. The Nauruans achieved control of the industry in 1967 by purchasing the plant and machinery owned by the BPC preliminary to taking over the industry completely in 1970.

Australia attempted to resettle the Nauruans in 1964 on Curtis Island, off the coast of Queensland. The Nauruans, although in principle not averse to resettlement, refused it because of political considerations. They wanted to own the island and to maintain their identity by political independence. Australia would not agree to this, and the plan therefore failed.

This failure reinforced the Nauruans' desire for political independence. With the support of the Trusteeship Council, they established an elected Legislative Council in 1966. With achievement of the control of phosphate in 1967, the way was clear to complete independence, and although Australia attempted to keep control of Nauru's defense and external affairs, the Nauruans insisted on complete self-determination. Thus, on 31 January 1968, the twenty second anniversary of the return of the Nauruan survivors from Truk, Nauru became the smallest independent republic in the world.

12 GOVERNMENT

The constitution of the Republic of Nauru, adopted for the proclamation of independence on 31 January 1968 and amended on 17 May, provides that the Republic shall have a parliamentary type of government. It contains provisions for the protection of fundamental rights and freedoms—a subject of particular importance because about half the inhabitants are short-term migrants ineligible for citizenship. Legislative power is vested in a parliament of 18 members elected for a three-year term by Nauruan citizens who have attained the age of 20 years. Executive power is exercised by the president, who also fulfills the residual duties of head of state; he is elected by parliament and is assisted by a five-member cabinet, which he appoints.

The island's 14 districts are divided into 8 constituencies, as follows: Boe; Aiwo; Anabar, Ijuw, and Anibare; Anetan and Ewa; Buada; Denigomodu, Nibok, Uaboe, and Baiti; Meneng; and Yaren. Seven of the eight constituencies return two members each. The constituency of Ubenide, which is a contraction of Denigomodu, Nibok, Uaboe and Baiti, returns 4 members, making a total of 18 members of parliament.

Suffrage is universal for Nauruan citizens only. Citizenship is defined in the constitution as being restricted to those of Nauruan or of Nauruan and Pacific islander parentage.

The most recent legislative elections were held in December 1973. Hammer DeRoburt became president at independence in 1968 and was reelected in 1971 and 1974.

13 POLITICAL PARTIES
No political parties exist on Nauru.

14 LOCAL GOVERNMENT
The Nauru local government council is elected from the same constituencies as is the parliament, except that seven of the eight constituencies return one member and Ubenide returns two members, making nine in all. The council elects a chairman (formerly the head chief), a treasurer, and a secretary. It meets in the *Domaneab*, a Nauruan meetinghouse.

15 JUDICIAL SYSTEM
The constitution of Nauru provides for a Supreme Court with a chief justice presiding. Cases are heard in the district courts, and appeals made in the first instance to the central court. The Supreme Court is also the supreme authority on the interpretation of the constitution.

16 ARMED FORCES
Nauru has no armed forces.

17 MIGRATION
Immigration to Nauru is strictly controlled by the government. Nauruans are free to travel abroad.

18 INTERNATIONAL COOPERATION
Nauru is a member of the South Pacific Forum, ITU, and UPU. It is also a "special" member of the Commonwealth of Nations. Nauru does not belong to the UN.

19 ECONOMY
The economy of Nauru has long been dependent on phosphates. About two-thirds of the original deposits of 100 million tons have been extracted and exported, and it is expected that the deposits will be exhausted by the end of the century. Revenue from phosphates has been used to diversify the island's economy, mainly through overseas investment and the development of a national airline and a national shipping line. Aside from phosphates, Nauru has few domestic resources, and many food products and virtually all consumer manufactures must be imported.

20 INCOME
In 1971, the GNP was estimated at us$25 million. Per capita GNP was more than us$4,000, among the highest in the world.

21 LABOR
In 1972, the total work force was 2,473; 1,408 workers were employed in the phosphates industry, 845 were employed by the government, and 220 had other employers. There is only one trade union, the Nauruan Workers' Organization.

22 AGRICULTURE
There is no commercial agriculture on the island. However, some market gardening is carried on by the Chinese.

23 ANIMAL HUSBANDRY
Pigs and chickens roam uncontrolled on the island; hence, there is no organized production.

24 FISHING
There is as yet no fishing industry on Nauru, although fish are generally plentiful. Fish consumption is high, since meat has to be imported from Australia.

25 FORESTRY
There are no forests on Nauru, and all building timber has to be imported.

26 MINING
Phosphate extraction, the only mining on the island, is done mainly by mechanical shovels from between the coral pinnacles. It is trucked to a central storage pile and transported to storage hoppers by rail. After being crushed and dried, the rock is placed on conveyor belts to pass to the arms of the two cantilevers, about 200 feet long, that project out over the reef to waiting ships. About 2 million tons are exported annually.

27 ENERGY AND POWER
Power requirements on the island are met by a diesel oil generator. Nearly all buildings are connected to this supply.

28 INDUSTRY
The phosphate industry is the only industry on the island. It is under the control of the Nauru Phosphate Corporation, a statutory corporation which is responsible to the president of the Republic in his capacity as minister for island development and industry.

29 DOMESTIC TRADE
The Nauruan-owned Nauru Cooperative Society operates two stores on the island. A Nauruan-owned supermarket, some small private stores, and an open-air Chinese market make up the rest of retail trading. The island is completely dependent on imported goods; foodstuffs come mainly from Australia and electrical goods from Hong Kong.

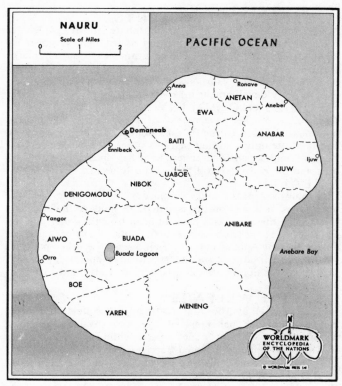

See Pacific Ocean map: front cover G6
LOCATION: 0°31's and 166°56'E. TERRITORIAL SEA LIMIT: 12 mi.

30 FOREIGN TRADE
Nauru's only export is phosphate rock. The value of exports rose from us$19.2 million in 1972 to us$63.9 million in 1974, as world phosphate prices increased. More than 57% of Nauru's phosphate exports were to Australia, 23% to Japan, and nearly 18% to New Zealand. Imports increased from us$6 million in 1972 to us$19.6 million in 1974. Nearly 58% of imports came from Australia, and more than 30% came from the Netherlands. Many foodstuffs and virtually all manufactured goods must be imported.

31 BALANCE OF PAYMENTS
Nauru has a strong favorable balance of trade, and investments abroad are substantial.

32 BANKING
The Commonwealth Savings Bank of Australia and the Bank of

New South Wales have branches in Nauru. Most of the income from phosphates is invested in long-term funds overseas.

³³INSURANCE
Third-party motor insurance is written with an Australian company, and ships of the Nauru Pacific Line are insured with Lloyds of London.

³⁴SECURITIES
There is no stock exchange in Nauru.

³⁵PUBLIC FINANCE
Administrative costs in Nauru are met from the proceeds of phosphate sales. The Nauruan budget for 1972/73 included A$10,355,172 in expenditures and A$11,034,642 in revenues. The fiscal year extends from 1 July to 30 June.

³⁶TAXATION
There is no income tax in Nauru, although the parliament has power to impose such taxes.

³⁷CUSTOMS AND DUTIES
Duties are payable only on imported cigarettes, tobacco, and alcohol.

³⁸FOREIGN INVESTMENTS
Apart from the investment in the phosphate industry, which has been purchased by the government of Nauru, there has been little investment on the island. The government of Nauru has large investments overseas in long-term funds financed from phosphate royalties. Nauru also has invested heavily in commercial property development in Australia.

³⁹ECONOMIC POLICY
The policy of the government of Nauru is to exploit the phosphate deposits to the fullest extent for the highest returns, and it is attempting to find markets other than Australia, New Zealand, and Japan. The government has diversified into shipping and hopes to develop fishing and tourism.

⁴⁰HEALTH
Tuberculosis, leprosy, and vitamin deficiencies have been the main types of illness on the island. With modern facilities and treatments, these diseases have all been brought under control. There were 2 modern hospitals, with a total of 207 beds in 1971. One serves phosphate industry employees; the other provides free medical treatment for the rest of the population. In 1971 there were 10 doctors, 2 dentists, 1 pharmacist, and 61 nurses and midwives.

⁴¹SOCIAL WELFARE
Medical, dental, and hospital treatment and education are free in Nauru. Other benefits—old age and invalid's pensions, widow's and sickness benefits and child endowment—are provided for under the Social Services Ordinance of 1956-65. This ordinance is administered by the Nauru local government.

⁴²HOUSING
Ownership of houses built for Nauruans under a housing scheme is vested in the Nauru local government council, but some Nauruan homes are privately owned. Nearly all houses have electricity connected, and the standard of the newer houses has improved greatly in the number of facilities provided.

⁴³EDUCATION
Attendance at school is compulsory for Nauruan children from 6 to 16 years. Two types of schools are available, both coeducational: those run by the government and those conducted by the Roman Catholic Church. Education on Nauru is to intermediate standard; higher education overseas, mainly in Australia, is assisted by the government in the form of competitive scholarships. Schools are conducted also for the children of laborers in the phosphate industry.

In 1973 there were 88 teachers and 1,450 students in nine primary schools, and 33 teachers and 433 students in two secondary schools.

⁴⁴LIBRARIES AND MUSEUMS
Nauru has one small lending library but no museums.

⁴⁵ORGANIZATIONS
The Boy Scouts, Girl Guides, and similar organizations function on the island. One community organization and several Nauruan district organizations are also active.

⁴⁶PRESS
Apart from some district newssheets in Nauruan, and two regular English newssheets, people on Nauru have to rely on imported newspapers. The government issues a gazette and a bulletin (circulation: 1,000) that prints local and foreign news.

⁴⁷TOURISM
There is at present no tourism on Nauru, and entry for visitors is restricted. However, a modern hotel has been constructed on the island, and the government is seeking to develop the tourist industry.

⁴⁸FAMOUS NAURUANS
The best-known Nauruan is its first and only president, Hammer DeRoburt (b.1922), who, with his election to the Nauru local government council in 1956, began a long battle to obtain economic and political independence for the Nauruan people. He assumed the presidency in 1968 and was reelected in 1971 and 1974.

⁴⁹DEPENDENCIES
Nauru has no dependencies.

⁵⁰BIBLIOGRAPHY
American University. *Area Handbook for Oceania*. Washington, D.C.: Government Printing Office, 1971.

Armfield, Hugh. "Nauru: The Island and Its People," *Australian Territories VI*, no. 3 (1966), 14–22.

Davidson, J. W. "Republic of Nauru," *Journal of Pacific History*, III (1968), 145–50.

Ellis, A. F. *Ocean Island and Nauru*. Sydney: Angus and Robertson, 1935.

Hambruch, P. *Nauru*. Hamburg: Friedrichsen, 1914.

Hughes, H. "The Political Economy of Nauru," *The Economic Record*, December 1964. Melbourne University Press.

Packett, C. Neville. *Guide to the Republic of Nauru*. Bradford, Yorkshire: C.N. Pickett (Lloyds Bank Chambers), 1971.

Viviani, N. M. *Nauru—Phosphate and Political Progress*. Canberra: Australian National University Press, 1970.

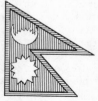

CAPITAL: Kathmandu. **FLAG**: The national flag consists of two red adjoining triangles, outlined in blue and merging at the center; the points are at the fly. On the upper triangle, in white, is a symbolic representation of the moon; on the lower triangle, that of the sun. **ANTHEM**: The national anthem begins: "May His Nepali Majesty, solemn and supremely valiant, be the King prosperous forever." **MONETARY UNIT**: The Nepal rupee (NR) of 100 paisa is a nonconvertible paper currency. There are coins of 1, 2, 5, 10, 20, 25, and 50 paisa, and notes of 1, 5, 10, and 100 Nepal rupees. NR1 = $0.07968 (or $1 = NR12.55). **WEIGHTS AND MEASURES**: Indian standards are followed, including the maund (480 pounds), used principally for agricultural products. **HOLIDAYS**: National Day, 18 February; King's Birthday, 28 December. Hindu and Buddhist religious holidays, based on the lunisolar calendar, change from year to year. Saturdays rather than Sundays are general holidays. **TIME**: 5:40 P.M. = noon GMT.

¹LOCATION, SIZE, AND EXTENT

A comparatively narrow strip of territory dividing India from China, landlocked Nepal has an area of 141,499 sq km (54,633 sq mi), extending *885* km (*550* mi) SE–NW and *201* km (*125* mi) NE–SW. In its length lie some 800 km (500 mi) of the Himalayan chain. Nepal is bounded on the N by China and on the E, S, and W by India, with a total boundary length of *2,671* km (*1,660* mi).

²TOPOGRAPHY

Nepal is made up of three strikingly contrasted areas. Southern Nepal has much of the character of the great plains of India, from which it extends. Known as the Terai, this region comprises both cultivable land and dense jungle, the latter being for the most part a game preserve inhabited by the wild elephant, tiger, and other typically Indian fauna. Besides being a hunting ground, the forests are worked for their valuable timber. The Terai contains one-third of Nepal's population and makes up about one-fourth of the total area. The second and by far the larger part of Nepal is formed by the Churia, Mahabharat, and Himalayan mountain ranges, extending from east to west. Their altitude increases toward the north, culminating on the Tibetan border in Mount Everest (29,028 feet), standing amid other noble peaks. These cross ranges account for the direction of the rivers. Three principal streams rise in Tibet, break southward through deep Himalayan gorges, and enter respectively the Karnali, Gandak, and Kosi basins. Flowing toward India, they become tributaries (as are all Nepal's rivers) of the Ganges system. A high central region, some 230 sq mi in extent between the main Himalayan range and the Mahabharat range, is known as Kathmandu Valley, or the Valley of Nepal. Overlooked by mountains rising on the north to 9,000 feet, the valley with its fertile soil and temperate climate contains a thriving agriculture. Here is situated Kathmandu, the capital, at an elevation of 4,300 feet, with the foothill towns of Bhatgaon and Patan nearby, this being the only region of the kingdom having any considerable density of population.

Triangulated in 1850, Mount Everest was officially given the status of the world's highest peak in 1859. In November 1954, the summit was officially declared to be 29,028 feet. The summit was reached for the first time on 29 May 1953 by Edmund Hillary, a New Zealander, and Tenzing Norgay, a Sherpa guide.

³CLIMATE

Below the Kathmandu Valley and throughout the Terai, the climate is subtropical and, in the swamps and forests, extremely humid. The valley itself enjoys the temperate conditions generally found between 4,000 feet and 11,000 feet altitude. At 4,300 feet (the elevation of Kathmandu above sea level), a rainy season lasts from June to October. Colder weather follows, lasting until the middle of March, when the warm season begins and increases in intensity until broken by the rains, which accounts for precipitation of about 60 inches annually. Even at the height of summer, temperatures rarely exceed 32°C (90°F) in the shade. Northward of the valley, a subalpine zone continues to altitudes of about 14,000 feet; above that elevation, the country is covered with thick snow during the long winter, and extreme cold is experienced in the upper Himalaya. Thunderstorms are common throughout Nepal.

⁴FLORA AND FAUNA

The wide range of climate accounts for correspondingly marked contrasts between both flora and fauna in different regions of the country. In the south, the sal (the wood of which is used for railroad ties), sisu, and other subtropical trees are abundant in forests; in the extreme north, junipers are seen even at the altitude of the glacial moraines. Many kinds of conifers also exist in the alpine zone, along with the yew, various hollies, birch, dwarf rhododendrons, and other alpine flora. At temperate altitudes are found the oak and maple. Dominant in the Langtang Valley are the cheer pine, willow, alder, and evergreen oak. Blue pine and silver fir are frequent in the subalpine zone, where also grow tree rhododendrons—magnificent plants often reaching a growth of 40 feet. Ground orchids, lilies, yellow and blue poppies, and crimson anemones are prevalent in central Nepal. The profusion of wild flowers extends to very high altitudes; at 17,000 feet, several varieties of primula, pink and white cotoneaster, and white erica have been gathered, along with many kinds of alpine mosses and ferns.

The hyena and jackal still exist in southern Nepal, although in decreasing numbers. Rhesus monkeys and a variety of other small jungle animals remain common. At middle altitudes are found the black bear (*Ursus tibetanus*), several species of cats, squirrel, hare, deer, and antelope. Higher in the mountains, wild sheep and goats, marmots, and a species of tailless mouse-hare are numerous. Small black spiders were found at 22,500 feet on rocky ledges traversed by the Mt. Everest expedition of 1952. Birds of Nepal include the green finch, dove, woodpecker, nuthatch, warbler, flycatcher, bulbul, and other familiar species. At about 9,000 feet are found the hill partridge, pheasant, yellow-backed sunbird, minivet, and many of the flowerpeckers; the redstart, pipit, wagtail, snow pigeon, snowcock, and golden eagle thrive in both the alpine and subalpine zones.

As of 1975, endangered species in Nepal included the wolf, Asiatic wild dog, Indian tiger, Asian elephant, pygmy hog, great Indian rhinoceros, Asiatic buffalo, gaur, wild yak, Cheer pheasant, Indian python, two species of deer (Himalayan musk and swamp), and two species of leopard (common and clouded).

5 POPULATION

According to the 1971 census, Nepal had a population of 11,555,983. In 1975, the population was estimated at 12,572,000, with an average annual growth rate in the mid-1970s of 2.25%, and the population for 1980 was projected at 14,231,000. Average density in 1975 was 89 persons per sq km. Population distribution is uneven, with about two-thirds of the people concentrated in the hilly, central region. The rural population far outnumbers the urban, with only 4.8% of the people living in cities and towns. Kathmandu, the capital, has an estimated population of about 200,000, while Patan and Bhatgaon (the other chief towns of Nepal) have about 140,000 and 85,000 respectively. Only three other towns have populations of more than 10,000: Biratnagar, Nepalganj, and Birganj.

6 ETHNIC GROUPS

Nepal consists of two primary ethnic elements: Mongolians who migrated to Nepal by way of Tibet, Sikkim, Assam, and northern Bengal; and Indo-Aryans from the Indian plains and from the sub-Himalayan hill areas to the west of Nepal. There are also small remnants of Dravidian tribes, but their influence on the ethnic composition of the Nepalese is negligible. The racial influence of the Gurkhas (or Gorkhas) is found in all parts of Nepal, the result of intermarriage between Indian tribes and Nepal's aboriginal Mongolian stock after the successive waves of migrations from India dating back as far as the 14th century. Bhotias, of Tibetan origin, are the principal occupants of northern Nepal. In the central valley, Newars and Murmis predominate, the former being responsible for most of the agriculture and trade. Less numerous groups include Gurungs and Magars in the west and Kiratis and Lepchas in the east. Classed as Aoulias are several tribes living in malarious regions of southern Nepal, their collective name being that of the strain of malaria prevalent in that area.

The term Gurkha, loosely applied to any inhabitant of Nepal, was originally restricted to the royal family of the small kingdom of Gurkha and their followers the Gurungs, Khas, Magars, and Thakurs.

7 LANGUAGE

There are three basic language groups: (1) Munda, a division of the Austroasiatic group, includes Khambu, Yakha, Hayu, Limbu, and Thami; (2) Tibeto-Burman languages include Gurung, Magar, Newari, Sunwar, and Murmi; (3) Indo-Aryan languages, a division of the Indo-European group, include Nepali (also called Gurkhali, Khaskura, or Parbatiya) and various dialects of Hindi spoken in the Terai—Bhojpuri, Kumaoni, Mithili, and others. Tibetan is spoken and written by the Bhotias in the north. Newari, although in large part Tibetan, shows Sanskrit influences. The western tribes speak a version of Pahari (language of the mountains) that contains Sanskrit elements. Hindi is spoken along the Indian border.

Nepali is the official language. It is the mother tongue of 55% of the population and is understood by another 30%. It is the language for most intertribal communication; it is used in government publications and has been the language of most of the written literature since the Gurkha conquest. Except in primary schools, where children are taught in their own languages, Nepali is the medium of instruction. English is taught as a second language in secondary schools and colleges and is widely understood in business and government circles.

8 RELIGION

Although the royal family is Hindu, as is, nominally, about 95% of the population, Hinduism and Buddhism exist side by side in Nepal and to some extent are intermingled. The importance of both in the national life is everywhere manifest; 2,733 temples and shrines have been counted in the Kathmandu Valley alone, while innumerable others are scattered along trails and roads extending to the most distant mountain passes, where Hinduism merges almost completely with Buddhism as the northern border is reached. Also extremely numerous are wayside religious monuments in which seats are provided for the refreshment of foot passengers. Bodhnath and Shambunath are famous Buddhist temples. The ancient temple of Chandrigiri is dedicated to both religions. The Baghmati River, flowing through central Nepal, is sacred and is an objective of pilgrims, as are certain mountains and lakes, including the legendary lake near Gosainkund. Unlike those of Tibet, the religious communities of northernmost Nepal are poor; frescoes in the monasteries have for the most part been painted by visiting lamas passing through the country from Tibet. Butter has important ceremonial uses, being burned in altar lamps and also molded into objects of veneration.

In some areas, both Hinduism and Buddhism are blended with a variety of animism. Christians and Muslims comprise about 2% of the population.

9 TRANSPORTATION

In 1950, Nepal had only about 200 miles of mostly unpaved roads, and overland travel into the country was almost exclusively by foot. By 1976, Nepal maintained some 2,000 miles of motorable roads, about one-third of which were paved. Nevertheless, Nepal's ratios of road mileage to area and to population remain the lowest in the world. The principal highways are the 72-mile road that penetrates the Kathmandu Valley, connecting it with Thankot at the Indian border; the 67-mile road between Kathmandu and Kodari on the Tibetan border; the 650-mile east-west Mahendra highway, still partially under construction; and the 131-mile Sunauli-Pokhara highway. Construction extending the 112-mile Kathmandu-Pokhara highway to Surkhet is in progress, with Chinese aid valued at $75 million.

A narrow-gauge railway, opened in 1927, runs from Raxaul, India, to Amlekhganj, a distance of 29 miles, entering the Terai at the frontier town of Birganj. An electrically driven ropeway, inaugurated in 1925 and improved with US aid in 1962, carries 25 tons an hour a distance of 27 miles and to a height of 4,500 feet in the Kathmandu Valley.

Most of Nepal, however, is traversable only by mountain passes and bridle paths; pack animals, including sheep and goats, assist men and women porters in the transfer of freight. In the absence of many roads, civil aviation has become important. Several fair-weather (DC-3) airstrips are in use in addition to the Tribhuwan airport at Kathmandu, which, with a 7,500-foot runway, can handle medium-sized jets. Domestic flights are operated by the Royal Nepal Airlines Corp. The airline schedules flights to important cities in India, Thailand, and Bangladesh. Services with India, Burma, and Thailand are also provided by national airlines of those countries.

10 COMMUNICATIONS

Postal, telephone, and telegraph services are operated by the government. Telephone service connects Kathmandu with Birganj on the Indian frontier, and another line links the capital with foothill towns in the eastern Terai. A telecommunications network includes a 1,500-telephone automatic exchange and a network of 91 radio relay stations. In 1974, there were 9,200 telephones in use.

Radio Nepal broadcasts in Nepali, Hindi, Newari, and English on both shortwave and medium-wave lengths. Radios are common even in remote villages, but there is no television.

11 HISTORY

Myth and legend largely enter Nepal's historical literature, which (in the *Vamavali*) traces the origins of the country in the distant past. According to this account, Nepal was founded by the Gupta dynasty of Ne-Muni and derived its name from this source. Early dates are generalized and uncertain. Reliable chronology is reached only after the conquest of Nepal by Harisinha-deva, rajah of Simraun, recorded in 1324. Under the Malla dynasty, Nepal was administered in four separate states: Banepa, Bhatgaon, Kantipur (modern Kathmandu), and Lalitpur (now Patan). Prithwi Narayan Shah, the ruler of Gorkha, a small principality in the hills west of Kathmandu, established the modern kingdom of Nepal in 1769 by incorporating the Kathmandu Valley in his kingdom. Before this, the entire region of what is now called Nepal was divided into as many as 46 small principalities and states that were sovereign and independent for all practical purposes. Descendants of Prithwi Narayan continued his rule, introduced Hinduism as the official religion, and established most of the present boundaries.

Nepal's freedom from the influence of larger powers was broken with the British occupation of India and also by involvement with China as the result of a Nepalese invasion of Tibet. A dictated peace followed in 1792, after the Chinese forces had advanced into Nepal. In the same year a second commercial treaty was ratified between Great Britain and Nepal. For some time, relations with British India remained peaceful, but in 1814 Britain warred on Nepal as a result of Indo-Nepalese border disputes. Fighting continued 17 months; at its conclusion in March 1816, Nepal yielded some of its territory and agreed to a permanent British residency at Kathmandu. Thereafter, except for a short period during the First Afghan War (1839–42), friendship grew between Nepal and the UK and endured throughout the period of the Indian Mutiny (1857), during which the prime minister, Jung Bahadur, sent some 12,000 Nepalese troops to the support of the British garrisons. This established a pattern of internal government and foreign relations for Nepal that lasted for nearly a century. In the latter part of the 19th century, Jung Bahadur became the country's virtual ruler; he banished the king and queen, placed the minor heir on the throne, and instituted the office of hereditary prime minister, which remained in his family—the Ranas—until 1951. Externally, Nepal became a supplier of soldiers to Britain. The Gurkha regiments serving in the British and Indian armies won fame and laurels through their power and endurance, first in 1857, then in Britain's war with Tibet in 1904 and, finally, in the two world wars. It was through these occurrences that Nepal, otherwise isolationist, maintained a link with events outside her borders. In 1923, the Treaty of Sagauli (1816) between Nepal and the UK was replaced by a treaty of friendship that recognized Nepal's complete independence.

Following the end of the World War II, the termination of British rule in the subcontinent caused deep stirrings of change in Nepal. Resentment began to be felt against the aristocratic, military despotism of the Ranas, who permitted the king merely nominal powers. In 1946, the Nepali Congress Party was formed by the brothers Koirala. In 1950 there were disturbances that caused King Tribhuvana Bir Bikram to take refuge for a time in India. The rising influence of popular political parties proved decisive. On 15 February 1951, a new government took office with a 12-member cabinet. The century-old rule of the Rana family thus ended, with its authority reduced to the holding of two minor posts. Unstable conditions continued, however, during a struggle for power lasting several years under the new order. Although 4,000,000 potential voters had enrolled by 1953, demands for the creation of a constituent assembly and the holding of free elections remained unsatisfied.

Six different cabinets, lacking popular support and riddled with internal dissension, held office in rapid succession between 1951 and 1957. For several months (1957–58), King Mahendra, who had succeeded his father, King Tribhuvana (d.1955), ruled without a cabinet. Nepal's first democratic constitution, promulgated 12 February 1959, provided for constitutional monarchy with two houses of parliament and a cabinet and prime minister responsible to the lower house. The first parliament was inaugurated on 24 July 1959. In December 1960, the king dismissed his cabinet and dissolved parliament, charging them with misuse of power. He governed the country through a Council of Ministers. During most of 1962, rebels conducted guerrilla action under Gen. Subarna Shamsher. The resistance movement had been set up against King Mahendra following dissolution of parliament in 1960. When the Sino-Indian conflict erupted in October 1962, guerrilla action was temporarily suspended.

See continental political: front cover M7; physical: back cover M7
LOCATION: 26°20′ to 30°16′N; 80°15′ to 88°15′E. **BOUNDARY LENGTHS**: China, *1,078* km (*670* mi); India, *1,593* km (*990* mi).

On 18 April 1963, King Mahendra promulgated a new constitution based on a four-tiered panchayat (council) system, culminating in the National Panchayat. In January 1967, he ordered a series of amendments, thus introducing a gradual liberalization process. Meanwhile, Nepal succeeded in maintaining equally friendly relations with each of its giant neighbors, China and India. In 1961, Nepal signed an agreement with China defining the boundaries between the two countries. In 1969, Nepal secured the withdrawal of the Indian military mission in Kathmandu while avoiding rupture in relations with India. Road communications with both India and China and air links with India, Burma, and Thailand reflect Nepal's emergence into a nonsatellite status in relation to its neighbors.

In January 1972, King Mahendra died and was succeeded by his 27-year-old son Birendra Bir Bikram Shah Dev. King Birendra has kept Nepal on the course of moderate political and social reform set by his father.

12 GOVERNMENT

The 1963 constitution declares the king to be the sole source of authority for all governmental institutions in Nepal. The constitution provides for a tiered panchayat (council) system. There are panchayats at the village, town, district, and zonal levels. The National Panchayat (parliament), which completes the administrative structure, has a single chamber with 125 members—90 elected by the zonal panchayats, 15 representing government-sponsored mass organizations, 4 from a university graduates' constituency, and 16 nominated by the king. The first national parliamentary elections under the new constitution were held in 1967. The king appoints the Council of Ministers, which includes a prime minister, from the members of the National Panchayat; the Council is responsible both to him and to the National Panchayat.

13 POLITICAL PARTIES

The 1963 constitution prohibited the formation of political parties and associations. Political parties first appeared in Nepal in 1950 when the Nepali Congress Party was formed and led the rebellion against the Ranas. In the elections of 1959, the Congress Party won 73 of the 109 seats. The second largest party was the Conservative Gurkha Parishad with 19 seats. Other parties were the Praja Parishad, left-wing and Socialist, the Communist Party, and the National Democratic Party, a splinter group of the Congress Party. Since 1967, the government has pursued various steps toward accommodation of former political groups, including encouragement of some leaders to join the government ranks. At the end of 1975, imprisoned members of the Nepali Congress Party were freed by order of the king.

14 LOCAL GOVERNMENT

For centuries, the heads of petty principalities within Nepal exercised judicial, police, and other powers over people under their control. Under the panchayat reforms introduced in 1963, the country is now divided into 14 zones, in turn divided into 75 districts. The zones are directly administered by commissioners appointed by the central government. Zonal assemblies are formed out of the 11-member district panchayats. The panchayats are executive bodies elected from the district assemblies, whose members are selected from village and town panchayats. Each of the 3,600 villages and 14 towns also have 11-member panchayats as well as local assemblies. All Nepalese citizens aged 21 or older are members of the assembly of the locality in which they reside, and all vote in the selection of their local panchayat representatives. Most Nepalese live in villages (grams) or towns (nagars), the former division applying to villages or village groups with 2,000 or more persons; towns have a population of 5,000 or more. The panchayat system is in part derived from local government forms long in practice in some areas of Nepal.

15 JUDICIAL SYSTEM

There is a court of first instance, civil and criminal, at each district headquarters and also a court of appeal. There are three high courts—at Kathmandu, Biratnagar, and Nepalganj—to which further appeals may be taken. At the apex is the Supreme Court in Kathmandu: it is empowered to issue writs of habeas corpus and decide on constitutionality of laws. The court is composed of a chief justice, assisted usually by two other judges, and with seven additional judges in reserve.

16 ARMED FORCES

Nepal's small standing army is formidable by the criteria of conventional warfare because of its large proportion of well-trained troops (generally known as Gurkhas), who have distinguished themselves in two world wars. Gurkhas account for 16,000 of a total of some 20,000 regulars. Gurkhas also are preponderant in the militia of about 26,000 men. With such trained reserves, Nepal is capable in an emergency of rapidly expanding its army. The army maintains a small number of air transports and helicopters. In 1973/74, Nepal spent NR83.2 million on defense.

17 MIGRATION

Since the border with India has no guards or checkpoints, people move from one country to the other without restrictions. Hundreds of thousands of Nepalese work in India. As a result of the Tibetan revolt of 1959, some 7,000 Tibetan refugees have settled in Nepal.

18 INTERNATIONAL COOPERATION

Nepal was admitted to UN membership in 1955 and is a member of ESCAP, FAO, UNESCO, UPU, IBRD, IMF, ITC, ICAO, ITU, and WHO. It joined the Colombo Plan group in 1952.

During 1952–73, Nepal received some $410 million in international assistance, with slightly less than half coming from the US.

19 ECONOMY

Despite reforms begun in the 1950s, general living standards have remained at a subsistence level and agricultural development has been impeded by the overpopulation of the cultivable areas and the concentration of landownership. Nepal thus remains one of the least developed countries in Asia. Until 1968, the meager transportation facilities were mainly in the north-south direction, with the result that much of the country remained dependent for the movement of goods on mountain trails. The opening of an east-west highway, expected to be completed by the early 1980s, promises to integrate the nation economically. Most of the foreign-trade volume is accounted for by India, although the proportion has been declining in recent decades. The industrial sector is small. However, the country's economic potential is by no means insignificant. Kathmandu Valley and the Terai zone are fertile areas. There is great forest wealth, which includes not only valuable timber trees but also medicinal herbs that grow on the Himalayan slopes, and several other products. Deposits of several minerals are known to exist. Swift Himalayan rivers have a vast potential for development of hydroelectric power.

20 INCOME

In 1973/74, Nepal's GDP at market prices was valued at NR13,128 million. An estimated two-thirds of national income is derived from agriculture. Per capita income, about $90, was among the lowest in the world. In the early 1970s, the annual rate of growth in the GDP was 2.1%.

21 LABOR

Agriculture provides a livelihood for about 93% of the population, while handicrafts, porterage, trade, military service, and government work account for the other 7%. A few thousand factory workers are employed in Biratnagar. Most agriculturists are peasant farmers, and there are many wage laborers, but only in the peak seasons. Among some tribes, women do most of the farm work, while in others, especially among strict Hindus, they do no farming at all. Many occupations are effectively restricted to certain castes, although the practice has been declared illegal.

22 AGRICULTURE

About 93% of Nepal's population derives its livelihood from agriculture. Arable land accounts for about 30% of the total area, with some 12 million acres actually cultivated. There is a regional imbalance and lack of integration in Nepal's agriculture. Although the country produces an overall exportable surplus of food grains, some areas of the country, particularly Kathmandu Valley and the hill areas, have a food deficit. Lack of transportation and storage facilities prevents the movement of food grains from the Terai to the hills; the result is that Nepal both exports and imports the same items of food.

Some of the arable land is still held free of taxation by a few large landowners and farmed by tenants, and productivity is low. The government has officially abolished tax-free estates (birta), eliminated the feudal form of land tenure (jagira), set a limit on landholdings, and redistributed the extra land to farm tenants. Its economic plans include also the use of improved seeds, fertilizers, insecticides, and better implements; the extension of irrigation; and the construction of transportation and storage facilities. Under the second and third plans for economic development (1962–70), some 500,000 acres of land were brought under irrigation through various projects at a cost of over NR150 million.

Rice, Nepal's most important cereal, is grown on some 2.7 million acres, mainly in the Terai but also on every available piece of ground in the Kathmandu Valley during the monsoon season. In 1974/75 rice production totaled 2,453,000 tons, reflecting only a slight gain over average levels during the past two decades. Production of corn, grown on the carefully terraced hillsides, was about 827,000 tons in 1974/75; the area under cultivation for this crop was roughly estimated at more than 1 million acres. The production of millet, another crop in the hill regions, totaled 143,000 tons. Production of wheat—a winter crop—is limited by the scarcity of water. In the 1970s, it was cultivated on some 800,000 acres, but it was estimated that it could be grown on 3.5 million acres after extensive irrigation. In 1974/75, production totaled 331,000 tons, as against 175,000 tons in 1966. The cash crops are potatoes, sugarcane, oilseeds, jute, and tobacco, of which 307,000 tons, 251,000 tons, 65,000 tons, 45,000 tons, and 5,000 tons, respectively, were produced in 1974/75. Sugarcane, jute and tobacco are the major raw materials for Nepal's own industries. Potatoes are grown in Ilam and fruit mainly in Dharan, Dhankuta, and Pokhara. There are also some tea gardens found in Ilam and Soktim.

23 ANIMAL HUSBANDRY

Livestock, adapted to many uses, forms an essential part of the economy. In farm work, oxen and asses are largely employed. Herds of yaks, cows, and their hybrids, zobos, are grazed in the central valley and to some extent along the borders of the foothill jungles. A few hogs usually are kept on the larger farms. Sheep and goats are used for food and also as pack animals, particularly in the distribution of salt over the trade routes; the sheep flocks in addition supply a valuable type of wool.

In 1973, Nepal had an estimated 6,450,000 head of cattle, 2,250,000 sheep, and 300,000 hogs. Poultry are kept principally by the Newars, who carry on most of the agriculture in the Kathmandu Valley. The number of poultry farms has been increasing steadily; in 1973 there were some 14 million chickens, and an estimated 12,200 tons of eggs were produced. Butter and cheese are traditionally among Nepal's leading exports, and Nepali cheese has a good reputation in foreign markets. There is a cheese-processing plant at Kathmandu, with eight more cheese factories due to be established in the 1970s.

24 FISHING

Until recently, fishing in Nepal was unrestricted and fish were taken from the streams with the use of dynamite. From 1962 to 1965, annual fish production was about 100 tons. The third plan (1965–70) contemplated annual fish production of 285 tons from commercial fish farming.

25 FORESTRY

Forests cover about one-third of Nepal's total area. Sal, sisu, and other commercially valuable trees flourish in the Terai and are to some extent exploited. In northern zones are large areas in which oak, maple, juniper, silver fir, and many other types of conifer grow unused because of Nepal's lack of capital, power supplies, transportation, and other commercial facilities. Overcutting and grazing have not yet depleted Nepal's considerable forest resources. To prevent their wasteful exploitation, forests were nationalized in 1957 and there are now more than 11 million acres of state-owned forest land. In 1973, 9.1 million cu meters of round wood were produced, most of it exported.

In 1961, the government established a Department of Medicinal Plants to encourage Nepal's commercially important herb exports. There are seven regional herbals farms, herbal trading centers at Kathmandu and Nepalganj, and a botanical garden at Godavari for the demonstration of various plants. There is also a royal research laboratory, with regional branches, for drug analysis.

26 MINING

Although mining is an ancient occupation, the country's mineral resources have been little exploited. Cobalt, copper, and gold were once mined. There are known deposits of iron, lead, zinc, lignite, graphite, nickel, manganese, mica, limestone, marble, talc, quartz, ceramic clays, slate, silver, and, possibly, petroleum.

Development plans include the encouragement of small-scale mining and provide for continuing mineral surveys. In 1963, a Bureau of Mines was established at Kathmandu to coordinate tests on mineral deposits. Mica is mined in small quantities and exported to India, where it is dressed and trimmed. There have been some trial shipments of talc. In the 1970s, development of iron, coal, and copper deposits had begun.

27 ENERGY AND POWER

Although the hydroelectric potential is great and has been estimated at 10 million kw, as a whole the kingdom lacks an adequate power supply. In 1972, total installed capacity was 53,000 kw, of which 42,000 kw were hydroelectric. Production in 1972 totaled 101 million kwh, compared with 14 million in 1964. India has joined with Nepal in the construction of hydroelectric and irrigation projects on the Kosi River, where China has helped build a 10,000-kw plant, and on the Gandak. At mid-decade, discussion were under way for development of the vast potential of the Karnali River in the west. In 1969, new generators were installed at the Trisuli Hydel Project, which supplies electricity to Kathmandu, to increase its capacity to 21,000 kw. In that year, an integrated grid system was first established in central Nepal.

28 INDUSTRY

Until recently, modern industry was almost nonexistent. Only 0.66% of Nepal's GDP derived from industry in 1964/65. In the ensuing 10 years, however, industrial development was given emphasis in economic planning. There is now a fair amount of light industry, largely concentrated in southeastern Nepal. There are sawmills, as well as jute, sugar, cigarette, match, cotton and synthetic fabrics, wool, footwear, tanned leather, stainless steel, cement, agricultural tool, and tea factories. Processed jute is a major foreign exchange earner; production amounted to 12,265 tons in 1974/75. Sugar production rose from 1,836 tons in 1960/61 to 11,926 tons in 1974/75. A similar growth in output has been achieved in other industries. Cigarette production amounted to 2,265 million in 1974/75, as against 250 million in 1960/61. Textile plants were first established in 1964 and produced 200,000 meters of cotton fabric in 1974/75. A steel-rolling mill, established in 1965, uses imported materials and produces over 2,000 tons of stainless steel annually. In recent years, the government has given priority to such industries as lumber, plywood, paper, sugar, cement, lime, and mica that utilize domestic raw materials and reduce the need for imports. Plans were under way in the 1970s for cement, lime, and mica factories. Foreign technicians provide training in cottage industries, and local workers are trained at the Cottage Industry Center in Kathmandu. The Nepalese Industrial Development Corporation provides loans and technical advice to new enterprises.

29 DOMESTIC TRADE

For many Nepalese, local trade is part-time activity and is, in general, limited to such products as cigarettes, salt, kerosine, and cloth. Marketing centers are along the main trails and are supplemented by small local markets. Poor communications facilities make domestic trade impractical.

Most shops are open from 9 A.M. to 8 P.M. and government offices from 10 A.M. to 5 P.M. Saturdays are weekly holidays.

30 FOREIGN TRADE

Traditionally, Nepal's foreign trade was limited to Tibet and India. Since 24 September 1956, Nepalese trading agencies have been confined in Tibet to Shigatse, Kyerong, and Nyalam, with Lhasa, Shigatse, Gyantse, and Yatung specified as markets for trade; treaty arrangements signed on that date with China strictly regulated the passage of both traders and pilgrims in either direction across the border. Trade with India, however, is unrestricted and accounts for most of Nepal's foreign trade (although the proportion has been declining in recent decades). In 1953, India agreed to remit levies on most goods intended for Nepal, subject to export controls being tightened by the

Nepalese government to prevent such imports from leaking back into India for sale at lower than market rates. Facilities for trade are afforded by a number of markets on the frontier, which serve also as customs posts.

In 1974, Nepal's exports were valued at $32.4 million and imports at $81.8 million. The recorded trade statistics of Nepal, however, are to be interpreted cautiously in view of a long open border with India. Exports consist chiefly of rice, jute and jute products, oilseeds, timber, and herbs. Imports are dominated by heavy machinery, transport equipment, textiles, chemicals, fertilizers, metal manufactures, and petroleum products.

Principal trade partners in 1974 (in millions of dollars) were:

	EXPORTS	IMPORTS	BALANCE
India	22.4	45.0	–22.6
Japan	2.3	15.2	–12.9
US	3.2	2.4	0.8
UK	1.1	3.9	– 2.8
Hong Kong	0.1	4.6	– 4.5
Other countries	3.3	10.7	– 7.4
TOTALS	32.4	81.8	–49.4

³¹BALANCE OF PAYMENTS

Nepal does not publish statements of balance of payments. However, there are records of the receipts and expenditures of convertible foreign exchange that indicate a fairly consistent surplus, despite perennial deficits in merchandise trade. A principal source of foreign exchange comes from Nepalese civil servants and soldiers in Indian and British employ and from pensions earned by Nepalese British army veterans. Important earnings are also derived from jute exports and, increasingly, from tourism.

Foreign exchange holdings increased fairly steadily in the early 1970s, moving from $78 million in 1969 to a peak of $124 million in September 1974; by June 1975, however, these holdings had slipped to $101 million, the lowest point since late 1972. As of August 1975, total international reserves stood at $107.8 million, as compared with a peak of $135.6 million in September 1974.

Nepal's international liquidity began to lose ground in late 1974, a reflection of increased costs for fuels and other imports. This trend, coupled with a projected decline in the use of Gurkhas by the British army, threatened difficulties for the country's future balance-of-payments posture.

³²BANKING

Nepal's banking system consists of the Rashtra Bank of Nepal, the central bank, with a commercial subsidiary, the Rastriya Banijya Bank; the Nepal Bank, another commercial bank; and state-owned banks for industrial and agricultural development.

The Rashtra Bank was inaugurated by King Mahendra in 1956 as the central banking institution with a capital of NR10 million. Besides regulating the national currency, it issues notes of various denominations and assists in preparation of the government budget. Unlike most central banks, the Rashtra Bank may advance loans to industry if both the government and the bank consider the loan sound.

On 31 August 1975, total foreign assets of government monetary authorities were NR1,100.6 million, of which NR778 million was in claims on the government and official entities. On that date, currency in circulation totaled NR858.2 million. A vast expansion of paper currency resulted from the progressive monetization of the Nepalese economy and from the decree making Nepalese currency the only legal tender, thus abolishing the old dual currency system under which both Indian and Nepalese rupees circulated freely.

The Nepal Bank was established in 1938 as a joint venture of the government and private shareholders with an authorized capital of NR10 million. It has 47 offices in Nepal and is the chief source for financing trade. The Nepalese Industrial Development Corporation, founded in 1958, partly finances most new ventures in manufacturing. The Department of Cottage Industries also gives industrial loans. The Agricultural Development Bank is the principal institution granting financial assistance to farmers.

On 31 August 1975, the foreign assets of Nepal's commercial banks totaled NR311.1 million. Time and savings deposits totaled NR782 million.

³³INSURANCE

There exists a Nepal Insurance Co., with capital confined to the country and necessary funds available for development work.

³⁴SECURITIES

There is no stock exchange in Nepal. Since 1964 the government has issued several series of 6% and 7% development bonds with maturity periods of 5 to 10 years. About one-third of the bonds are owned by individuals.

³⁵PUBLIC FINANCE

Government revenue was derived for many years chiefly from privately owned land (amounting to about 30% of the country's area), from customs duties, and from forest and mining royalties. In 1955, however, because of increasing costs of development projects and of administration, the government discarded the practice of adjusting the budgetary deficit by drawing on reserves in favor of raising additional revenue through taxation. Subsequently, a progressive income tax was introduced.

Budget deficits grew steadily during 1971–74, increasing from NR39.1 million to NR237.3 million. In 1973–74, revenues totaled NR766.4 million and expenditures NR1,226.3 million. The deficit was offset by NR222.6 million in foreign grants, NR103.5 million in domestic borrowings, NR87.9 million in foreign exchange borrowings, and NR45.9 million in transfers. The government's spending on development projects is funded mainly by aid from India, China, and the US.

Government revenues and expenditures for 1973/74 and estimates for 1974/75 (in millions of Nepalese rupees) were as follows:

	1973/74	1974/75
REVENUES		
Sales tax	98.5	187.8
Import duties	143.8	185.0
Excise duties	77.4	120.9
Land revenue	96.9	95.0
Income tax	32.6	40.0
Other taxes and receipts	317.2	379.8
TOTALS	766.4	1,008.5
EXPENDITURES		
Current expenditures		
Social services	85.8	129.2
General administration	77.2	105.7
Defense	81.3	97.3
Economic services	52.1	76.8
Interest on public debt	22.6	34.1
Other current expenditures	155.8	133.2
Capital expenditures		
Transportation	261.7	328.0
Agriculture	86.0	91.1
Education	75.3	86.2
Industry and mining	73.3	84.0
Irrigation	78.4	69.7
Other capital expenditures	176.8	266.9
TOTALS	1,226.3	1,502.2

As of 15 July 1974, the public debt stood at NR502.1 million (compared with NR115.5 million in 1970); of the 1974 total, NR219 million was foreign.

36 TAXATION

In 1955, a progressive income tax was imposed. It is levied on incomes over NR7,000, with a 25% maximum on incomes exceeding NR50,000. Income for industrial undertakings is taxed at 5%. Rent-free land is taxed on a modest scale. Income from land revenue in 1974/75 was estimated at NR95 million. Since 1958, taxes have been levied on urban houses and on water and vehicles. There are various excise taxes. A 2% sales tax and several new excise duties were added in 1965. Income from sales tax in 1974/75 was estimated at NR187.8 million. The rural population still carries by far the major tax burden.

37 CUSTOMS AND DUTIES

Exports and imports are subject to tariffs and surcharges, which combine to form the most important single source of revenue. Much potential revenue is lost, however, because of the open borders and untrained customs service officers in the 157 customs checkpoints. Indian imports receive preferential tariff treatment.

38 FOREIGN INVESTMENTS

Nepal welcomes foreign investment, especially in large-scale industry. In 1961, the government adopted the Industrial Enterprises Act, which ensures nondiscriminatory treatment for foreign investors, repatriation of capital profits, tax exemptions, and foreign exchange facilities. Most foreign private capital invested in Nepal comes from India.

In the public sphere, India now provides more than $14 million annually in economic assistance. US aid has also become important, with AID alone contributing about $8 million a year in the 1970s. Both China and the USSR, as well as the Federal Republic of Germany and the UK, have provided grants and assistance for various transportation and industrial projects.

39 ECONOMIC POLICY

Economic development activities began in 1953. Roads and airfields were constructed, community development projects were launched, dairy factory and cheese manufacturing centers were established, and irrigation projects were undertaken to bring more acreage under cultivation. In 1956, all these projects were integrated into a five-year plan (1956–61) for economic development. Principal aims for the plan were to assist existing industries, revive and expand cottage industries, encourage private investments, and foster technological training.

A second three-year plan (1962–65), costing NR596.81 million, was declared a comparative success. On 15 September 1965, a new five-year plan (1965–70) was launched. Designed to raise the national income by 19%, the plan was the first to be drawn up within the context of the panchayat system, which was to be an important medium in the administration of projects. Of the plan's total outlay of NR2,500 million, about 10% was to be spent through the panchayat sector. Since 1965, projects have been given priority on the basis of their relative contribution to agricultural development. A plan announced for 1975–80 called for NR11,404 million in outlays. The emphasis in all the economic plans has been on infrastructure projects, primarily for the development of transportation, communications, electricity, irrigation, and manpower development.

Since 1972, King Birendra has undertaken a number of administrative changes to promote development, including the establishment of a broadly representative National Development Council to advise the National Planning Commission on needs and priorities. The king has also set up four regional development centers—at Dhankuta, Kathmandu, Pokhara, and Surkhet—to act as focal points for local development.

40 HEALTH

Although protected by a barrier of foothills, Nepal is in frequent danger from epidemics, notably cholera. Other common diseases are malaria, black fever (kala-azar), amoebic dysentery, eye diseases, tuberculosis, typhoid, and venereal diseases.

The average life expectancy in 1975 was estimated at 46.1 years. In 1975 there were 62 hospitals with about 2,400 beds (1 per 5,238 inhabitants); and 370 physicians (1 per 33,978 inhabitants), and about 10 dentists, 10 pharmacists, 175 nurses, and 100 midwives. Most of the medical personnel work in the Kathmandu Valley, and few or no health services exist in many parts of the country. A medical college is planned for Kathmandu.

41 SOCIAL WELFARE

There is a countrywide village development service initiated by the government in 1952, which endeavors to meet the villagers' need for food, clothing, shelter, roads, communications, health, and education. The village development workers demonstrate better methods of production, sanitation, and health and teach the villagers to read and write.

42 HOUSING

In the Kathmandu Valley, village houses are made of stone or mud bricks, with thatched roofs and raised eaves. Elsewhere, houses often are made of bamboo and reeds. Most houses have two stories, but some contain only two rooms, a sleeping room and a room for cooking. The well-constructed houses of the Sherpas are generally built of stone and timber, roofed with wooden slats. About four out of five urban dwellings in Nepal are owner occupied.

43 EDUCATION

The proportion of literate persons, although small, is rising and was estimated in 1975 at about 14%, an advance of 10% from the 1954 census. Education facilities have been expanding rapidly as a result of government action. In the mid-1970s, about one-third of primary-age schoolchildren were receiving an education, as compared with 15% in 1961. In 1973/74, 9,925 primary and secondary schools had a total enrollment of 622,617.

Traditional schools (pathshalas) provide a classical education emphasizing languages. Gompas along the northern border train boys and men to become Buddhist religious leaders. English schools are modeled after those in India. Under a 1954 plan, a national school system with a single curriculum has been replacing the traditional schools, although English schools have been increasing.

Tribhuwan University was established in 1959 at Kathmandu. In 1961, it granted its first degrees to 150 students. Three-fourths of the students are in liberal arts and sciences. Others take law, commerce, and education. Of the 34 colleges, 9 are junior colleges, 22 liberal arts colleges, and 3 provide professional and graduate education. In 1973/74, 19,314 students were enrolled in higher education. Women make up about 15% of the college enrollment.

44 LIBRARIES AND MUSEUMS

Kathmandu, the repository of the country's historical literature, has public libraries and a museum. Several private and college libraries and the Nepal Museum have good book collections. Major libraries are the Singh Darbar, Secretariat Library; Lal Darbar, Central Library; National Library; the Ranipolhari, Bir Library; Indian Library; British Reading Room; and the USIA Library.

45 ORGANIZATIONS

The leading commercial organization is the Nepal Chamber of Commerce. Professional organizations include the Nepal Medical Association and the Nepal Drivers' Association. Social organizations include Paropkar, Nepal Women's Organization, Nepal Youth Organization, Nepal Peasants' Organization, Nepal Children's Organization, an organization for ex-servicemen, and several scholarly organizations.

46 PRESS

Freedom of the press is guaranteed by the constitution. Dailies, weeklies, and monthlies in Nepali, Newari, Hindi, and English are published mainly in Kathmandu. In 1975, the country had 24 dailies with a total circulation of about 100,000. There were also several weeklies and monthlies.

The major dailies, with their 1975 circulations, are:

	LANGUAGE	CIRCULATION
Gorkha Patra	Nepali	25,000
Rising Nepal	English	20,000
Samaya	Nepali	18,000
Nepali	Hindi	9,500
Commoner	English	7,000
Naya Samaj	Nepali	3,000
Sahi Aawaj	Nepali	2,100
Samaj	Nepali	2,100

47 TOURISM

Reversing a policy enforced for centuries, the Nepal government now encourages visitors, a result of worldwide publicity given to the achievements of mountain climbers, whose expeditions until 1949 were permitted into the country only under severe official scrutiny and restraining regulations. Tourism was officially included for the first time in 1956 among the country's potential large assets. Since then, tourist traffic has exceeded even the expectations of the state economic planners. The 1965–70 plan anticipated 20,000 tourists annually by 1970; in 1968 there were already 24,200 and in 1974, 72,601. About 25% of the tourists were from the US. As of 1975, there were 15 hotels with 1,291 beds. New facilities include three international-standard hotels in Kathmandu and a tree-top resort in the Terai. In 1973/74, tourist receipts totaled NR97.7 million, as compared with NR53.2 million in 1972/73 and NR13.2 million in 1969/70.

Tourist visas are valid for the Kathmandu Valley, Pokhara, and Chitwan; special permits are required for other areas as well as for climbing expeditions. Cholera and smallpox immunizations are required, while DPT inoculations (for children) and inoculations against diphtheria, tetanus, yellow fever, poliomyelitis, rabies, typhoid, and typhus are recommended.

48 FAMOUS NEPALESE

Buddhism one of the world's great religions, is based on the teachings of Siddhartha Gautama, the Buddha, who was born about 563 B.C. near Kapilavastu in the Terai and died about 483 B.C. at Kusinagara. Amar Singh Thapa, Nepali military leader of the 19th century and rival of Gen. David Ochterlony in the war between British India and Nepal, is a national hero. The two best-known Rana prime ministers were Sir Jung Bahadur Rana (1817–77) and Sir Chandra Shamsher Jang Rana (1863–1929). Two highly regarded authors are Bhanubhakta, a great poet of the 19th century, and the dramatist Bala Krishna Sama (Shamsher, b.1903), known as the Shakespeare of Nepal.

Far wider renown was gained for Nepal by a Sherpa porter and mountaineer, Tenzing Norgay (Namgyal Wangdi, b.1914), who, with Edmund Hillary, a New Zealander, ascended to the summit of Mt. Everest in 1953. Already eminent among Sherpa guides, Tenzing was chosen by Sir John Hunt, leader of the British expedition, "as a matter of course" for the ultimate stage

of the assault and became, with its success, the idol of his fellow countrymen.

49 DEPENDENCIES

Nepal has no territories or colonies.

50 BIBLIOGRAPHY

Bista, Dor Bahadur. *People of Nepal*. Kathmandu: Government of Nepal, 1967.

Caplan, Lionel. *Land and Social Change in East Nepal: A Study in Hindu-Tribal Relations*. Berkeley: University of California Press, 1969.

Chatterji, B. *Study of Recent Nepalese Politics*. Mystic, Conn.: Verry, 1967.

Eskelund, Karl. *The Forgotten Valley*. London: Redman, 1960.

Hagen, Toni. *Nepal: The Kingdom in the Himalayas*. New Delhi: Oxford Book and Stationery, 1960.

Hornbein, Thomas. *Everest, the West Ridge*. New York: Ballantine, 1966.

Joshi, Bhuwanlal, and Leo E. Rose. *Democratic Innovations in Nepal*. Berkeley: University of California Press, 1966.

Karan, Pradyumna P., and William M. Jenkins. *The Himalayan Kingdoms: Bhutan, Sikkim, and Nepal*. Princeton, N.J.: Van Nostrand, 1963.

Karan, Pradyumna P., and William M. Jenkins. *Nepal: A Physical and Cultural Geography*. Lexington: University of Kentucky Press, 1960.

Kazami, Takehide. *The Himalayas: A Journey to Nepal*. Tokyo: Kodansha, 1968.

The Kingdom of Nepal. Washington: Royal Nepalese Embassy, 1959.

Maron, Stanley, Leo E. Rose, and Juliane Marion Heyman. *A Survey of Nepal Society*. New Haven, Conn.: HRAF, 1956.

Northey, William Brook. *The Land of the Gurkhas*. Cambridge: Heffer, 1937.

Regmi, Mahesh C. *Land Tenure and Taxation in Nepal*. Berkeley: University of California Press, 1963–67.

Ripley, Dillon. *Search for the Spiny Babbler: An Adventure in Nepal*. Boston: Houghton Mifflin, 1952.

Rose, Leo E. *Nepal: Strategy for Survival*. Berkeley: University of California Press, 1971.

Rose, Leo E., and Margaret W. Fisher. *Politics of Nepal: Persistence and Change in an Asian Monarchy*. Ithaca, N.Y.: Cornell University Press, 1970.

Sekelj, Tibor. *Window on Nepal*. London: Hale, 1960.

Shaha, Rishikesh. *Heroes and Builders of Nepal*. London: Oxford University Press, 1965.

Singh, Madanjeet. *Himalayan Art*. New York: New York Graphic Society, 1968.

Tenzing Norgay and James Ramsey Ullman. *Tiger of the Snows*. New York: Putnam, 1955.

Tuker, Sir Francis Ivan Simms. *Gorkha: The Story of the Gurkhas of Nepal*. London: Constable, 1957.

Wood, Hugh B. *Nepal Bibliography*. Eugene, Ore.: The American-Nepal Education Foundation, 1959.

NEW ZEALAND

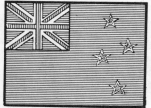

CAPITAL: Wellington. **FLAG**: The flag has two main features: the red, white, and blue Union Jack in the upper left quarter and the four-star Southern Cross in the right half. On the blue state flag the stars are red outlined in white; on the red national flag, used by individuals or commercial institutions at sea, the stars are red. **ANTHEM**: *God Save the Queen*. **MONETARY UNIT**: The New Zealand dollar (NZ$) of 100 cents is a nonconvertible currency; it replaced the New Zealand pound on 10 July 1967. There are coins of 1, 2, 5, 10, 20, and 50 cents, and notes of 1, 2, 5, 10, 20, and 100 dollars. NZ$1 = US$1.0473 (or US$1 = NZ$0.9548). **WEIGHTS AND MEASURES**: Metric weights and measures are used. **HOLIDAYS**: New Year's Day, 1 January; Anzac Day, 25 April; Queen's Birthday, 1st Monday in June; Labor Day, last Monday in October; Christmas Day, 25 December; Boxing Day, 26 December. Movable holidays are Good Friday and Easter Monday. Each province has a holiday on its own anniversary day. **TIME**: 12 midnight = noon GMT.

¹LOCATION, SIZE, AND EXTENT

Situated in the southwest Pacific Ocean, New Zealand proper, with a total area of 268,704 sq km (103,746 sq mi), consists of the North Island, covering 114,453 sq km (44,190 sq mi); the South Island, 150,718 sq km (58,192 sq mi); Stewart Island, 1,746 sq km (674 sq mi); the Chatham Islands, 963 sq km (372 sq mi); and several minor, outlying island groups—the Kermadec Islands, 34 sq km (13 sq mi), Campbell Island, 114 sq km (44 sq mi), and uninhabited Auckland Island and other offshore islands, 676 sq km (261 sq mi). New Zealand extends 1,600 km (994 mi) NNE–SSW and 450 km (280 mi) ESE–WNW. It has a total coastline of 9,173 km (5,700 mi).

²TOPOGRAPHY

Less than one-fourth of the land surface of New Zealand lies below the 650-foot contour. The mountain ranges in the North Island do not exceed 6,000 feet in height, with the exception of the volcanic peaks of Egmont (8,260 feet), Ruapehu (9,175 feet), Ngauruhoe (7,515 feet), and Tongariro (6,458 feet), the last three of which are still active. This volcanic system gives rise to many hot springs and geysers. The South Island is much more mountainous than the North Island, but is without recent volcanic activity. The Southern Alps, running almost the entire length of the South Island from north to south, contain 17 peaks of 10,000 feet or above, of which the highest is Mount Cook or Aorangi (12,349 feet). There are also several glaciers in the Southern Alps, the largest being the Tasman Glacier, 18 miles long and 1.25 miles wide. The rivers are mostly swift-flowing and shallow, few being navigable. There are many lakes, those in the South Island being particularly noted for their magnificent mountain scenery.

³CLIMATE

New Zealand has a temperate, moist ocean climate without marked seasonal variations in temperature or rainfall. The prevailing winds are westerly, with a concentration of strong winds in the Cook Strait area. The generally mountainous nature of the country, however, causes considerable variations in rainfall, e.g., between the eastern and western sides of the Southern Alps, and, by preventing stratification of air into layers of different density, results in an absence of extensive cloud sheets and a consequent high percentage of sunshine. Mean annual temperatures at sea level range from about 14.4°C (58°F), with a total rainfall of 39 inches, in Auckland in the northern part of the North Island, to about 10°C (50°F) and rainfall of 47 inches at

Invercargill in the southern part of the South Island. Highest annual rainfall (260 inches) occurs at Milford Sound on the west coast of the South Island.

⁴FLORA AND FAUNA

Like other regions separated from the rest of the world for a long period, New Zealand has developed a distinct flora. About 75% of the native flora is unique, and it includes some of the world's oldest plant forms. However, the flowering plants, conifers, ferns, lycopods, and other vascular tracheophytes that constitute much of the land vegetation do show affinities with plants of the Malayan region, supporting the theory of an ancient land bridge between the two regions. More than 250 species are common to both Australia and New Zealand. The Antarctic element, comprising over 70 species related to forms in the flora of South America and the Southern Ocean islands, is of great interest to botanists.

The kauri pine, now found only in parts of the North Island, for more than a century has had world fame for its timber. The rimu and the totara also are timber trees. Other handsome trees include the pohutukawa and other species of rata and kowhai. New Zealand flax, formerly of great importance in the Maori economy, is found in swampy places. Undergrowth in the damp forests consists largely of ferns, of which there are 145 species. They clothe most of the tree trunks and branches, and tree ferns form part of the foliage. Tussock grass occurs on all mountains above the scrub line and over large areas in the South Island.

Apart from seals and two species of bats, New Zealand has no indigenous land mammals. Sea mammals include whales and dolphins.

There is a great diversity of birds, some 250 species in all. Among the flightless birds the most interesting is the kiwi, the only known bird with nostrils at the tip of the bill instead of at the base. Other characteristic birds are the kea, a bird of prey; and the tui, a beautiful songbird. All but one of the genera of penguins are represented in New Zealand. Several species of birds, the most famous being the Pacific godwit, migrate from breeding grounds in the Arctic Circle to spend spring and summer in New Zealand.

Many species of birds and mammals have been introduced. Some of them have become pests, such as the rabbit, the deer, the pig (now wild), and the North American opossum.

As of 1975, endangered species in New Zealand included the

king shag, New Zealand brown teal, takahe, New Zealand snipe, Kakapo parrot, New Zealand laughing owl, stitchbird, two species of parakeet (Forbes' and orange-fronted), three species of the New Zealand bush wren (North Island, South Island, and Big South Cape Island), two species of kokako (South Island and North Island), two species of saddleback (South Island, North Island), two species of piopio (North Island, South Island), three species of leiopelma (Coromandel, Stephen's Island, and North Island), and the tuatara, a lizardlike creature, the only surviving representative of the order Rhynchocephalia, unique to New Zealand.

5 POPULATION

The estimated population on 31 March 1975 was 3,105,400, an 8.5% increase over the March 1971 census total of 2,862,631. The average annual growth rate in 1973 and 1974 was above 2%. Although immigration is a significant factor in population, most of the population growth was due to natural increase; in 1974, the crude birthrate was 19.5 per 1,000 population, the death rate was 8.3, and the net natural increase 11.2. The projected population for 1980 is 3,263,000. The population density in 1975 was 11.6 per sq km (29.9 per sq mi), with about 72% of the population living on the North Island and 28% on the South Island. More than 80% of New Zealand's inhabitants live in urban areas. The seven major urban areas, known officially as statistical divisions, are Auckland (796,600 in March 1975); Wellington, the capital (354,660); Christchurch (326,410); Hamilton (152,740); Dunedin (120,890); Napier-Hastings (109,360); and Palmerston North (87,000).

6 ETHNIC GROUPS

About 90% of the population is classified as European; the overwhelming majority is of British descent. There are small groups of Dutch, Chinese, Indians, Arabs, Yugoslavs, Greeks, and Poles.

The most significant minority group is the indigenous Maori people, Polynesians with a distinctive culture and a well-ordered social system.

Although the Treaty of Waitangi (1840) guaranteed to the Maori people all the rights and privileges of British subjects and full and undisturbed possession of their lands, these guarantees were often overlooked. As a result of war and disease, the Maori population declined to less than 42,000 by 1896. At the turn of the century, however, a group calling itself the Young Maori Party began to devote itself to the promotion of Maori welfare and status. In the 20th century, and especially after World War II, a more enlightened government policy prevailed.

In March 1974, there were 246,200 Maoris or part-Maoris, an increase of 2.7% over 1973; at that time, Maoris represented about 8% of the population. More than two-thirds were unskilled wage earners and most were landless. Although Maori acquisition and development of land have been promoted, there is not enough land to afford a livelihood to more than about 25% of the Maori population. Thus, many Maoris leave their tribal villages to seek job opportunities in the towns and cities. In 1974, nearly 59% of the Maori population lived in urban areas, with the largest Maori concentration in the South Auckland area.

During recent years, increasing numbers of migrants from New Zealand's former colonies and from other Pacific islands have come to New Zealand. Many of these, especially the Cook Islanders, are Polynesians having ethnic and linguistic ties with the Maoris. The non-Maori Polynesian population in 1971 was 45,413.

7 LANGUAGE

English is the universal language, although Maori, a language of the Polynesian group, still is spoken among the Maori population and is taught in the Maori schools.

8 RELIGION

New Zealand has no state church. The bulk of the population in 1971 belonged to one of four main churches: the Church of England, 895,839 (31%); the Presbyterian Church, 583,701 (20%); the Roman Catholic Church, 449,974 (16%); and the Methodist Church, 182,727 (6%). There are numerous other Protestant denominations, two Christian sects (Ratana and Ringatu) that are indigenous to New Zealand, and a small Hindu community. In 1973 there were 4,200 Jews.

9 TRANSPORTATION

The mountainous nature of New Zealand has made the development of rail and road communications difficult and expensive, particularly on South Island. In 1974, 4,797 km of railways (all state-owned) were operative. In 1971, New Zealand drew a $4.13-million loan from the IBRD for a six-year railway development program.

Capital investment in roads exceeds that for all other forms of transport service. Total length of roadways as of 31 March 1973 was 92,380 km; almost all roads were hard surfaced. As of 31 March 1975, registered motor vehicles included 1,142,326 private automobiles, 206,776 trucks, 3,130 buses and service vehicles, and 67,136 motorcycles.

With a gross registered merchant marine of only 203,472 tons in 1975, New Zealand is largely dependent on UK shipping for its overseas trade. In 1974, a government-owned shipping corporation was set up to operate shipping services. Its ships serve the coastal and Pacific island trade; its subsidiary, the New Zealand Shipping Line, carries New Zealand-UK trade. Auckland and Wellington, the two main ports, have good natural harbors with deep-water facilities and modern port equipment. Other ports capable of efficiently handling overseas shipping include Whangarei, Tauranga, Lyttleton (serving Christchurch), Bluff, Napier, Nelson, Taranaki, Otago, and Timaru. Total tonnage in New Zealand ports has more than doubled since 1962. In 1974, 20,502,000 tons of cargo were unloaded and 15,749,000 tons loaded at New Zealand ports. Almost 1 of every 10 New Zealanders owns one or more pleasure boats.

International air service is provided by Pan Am, Qantas, BA, UTA, and Air Pacific. Air New Zealand Ltd., which is owned by the New Zealand government, operates air services throughout the Pacific islands to Australia, Singapore, Hong Kong, Honolulu, and Los Angeles. There are 13 major airports, of which Mangere (Auckland), Harewood (Christchurch), and Rongotai (Wellington) are international airports. Internal air services are operated almost entirely by the New Zealand National Airways Corp., a government enterprise.

10 COMMUNICATIONS

Postal, telegraph, cable, and telephone services are operated by the New Zealand government. In 1974, New Zealand ranked fifth in the world in number of telephones per person—49 per 100. The total number of telephones as of 31 March 1974 was 1,437,344, with more than 650 telephone exchanges, nearly 92% of them automatic.

In a government reorganization of radio and television broadcasting completed in 1975, the former New Zealand Broadcasting Corp. was decentralized into three independent publicly owned corporations—two competing nationwide television channels and one radio network. The Broadcasting Council of New Zealand was established to oversee standards and avoid duplication of services. All three corporations and the Council are responsible to the public through the House of Representatives. TV-1 operates out of Wellington and Dunedin. TV-2, with separate studios, staff, and revenues, operates competing services out of Auckland and Christchurch. Films purchased overseas make up about 70% of television programming. Commercial advertising is broadcast five days a week. More than 85% of New Zealand homes have television sets. Color television, using the German PAL system, was introduced in October 1973, but only 10% of households had color television sets in 1975. There were 730,316 black-and-white and 33,379 color sets licensed as of August 1975.

Radio New Zealand provides programs for 51 medium-wave stations and 2 short-wave transmitters. Of these, 31 stations broadcast advertising material. A number of private commercial radio broadcasting stations have been licensed since 1970. An estimated 2.7 million radios were in use in 1973.

11 HISTORY

The first European to discover New Zealand was Abel Tasman, a navigator of the Dutch East India Co., who sighted the west coast of the South Island in 1642. He did not land because of the hostility of the Maori inhabitants. Owing to the absence of written records, it is impossible to give any accurate date for the settlement of the Maoris in New Zealand. According to their oral traditions, they migrated from other Pacific islands to New Zealand several centuries before Tasman's discovery, the chief migration having taken place about 1350. No other Europeans are known to have visited New Zealand after Tasman until Capt. James Cook of the British Royal Navy made his four voyages in 1769, 1773, 1774, and 1777. In this period, he circumnavigated both islands and mapped the coastline.

In the 1790s, small European whaling settlements sprang up around the coast, and in 1814 the first mission station was set up in the Bay of Islands by Samuel Marsden, chaplain to the governor of New South Wales. In 1840, the Maori chieftains entered into a compact, the Treaty of Waitangi, whereby they ceded sovereignty to Queen Victoria while retaining territorial rights. In the same year, the first organized attempt at colonization from Britain was made by the New Zealand Co. The first group of British migrants arrived at Port Nicholson and founded the city of Wellington. Further settlements were made in the South Island by the New Zealand Co.—in Nelson in 1842, in Dunedin in 1848 (with the cooperation of the Presbyterian Church of Scotland), and in Canterbury in 1850 (with the cooperation of the Church of England). After the Maori Wars (between 1860 and 1870), resulting largely from discontent with the official land policy, the colony of New Zealand rapidly increased in wealth and population. Discovery of gold in 1861 resulted in a large influx of settlers. The introduction of refrigerated shipping in 1882 enabled New Zealand to become one of the world's greatest exporters of dairy produce and meat. The depression of the early 1930s revealed to New Zealand the extent of its dependence on this export trade and led to the establishment of more local light industry. New Zealand entered World Wars I and II at the side of the UK, New Zealand troops serving in Europe in both wars and in the Pacific in World War II.

Representative institutions were granted to the colony by the British Parliament in 1852. In 1907, New Zealand was made a dominion; and in 1947, the New Zealand government formally claimed the complete autonomy that had been available to self-governing members of the British Commonwealth under the Statute of Westminster, enacted by the British Parliament in 1931.

After World War II, New Zealand and US foreign and defense policies were increasingly intertwined. New Zealand signed the ANZUS Pact in 1951 and was a founding member of SEATO in 1954. New Zealand troops fought with UN forces in the Korea conflict and with US forces in South Viet-Nam. The involvement in Viet-Nam touched off a national debate on foreign policy, however, and all New Zealand troops were withdrawn from Viet-Nam by the end of 1971; New Zealand's military participation in SEATO was subsequently terminated. In December 1972, New Zealand established diplomatic relations with China and severed official contacts with Taiwan.

12 GOVERNMENT

New Zealand is an independent member of the Commonwealth of Nations. Like the UK, it is a constitutional monarchy, the head of state being the representative of the crown, the governor-general, who is appointed for a five-year term.

Government is democratic and modeled on that of the UK. The single-chamber legislature, the House of Representatives, has 87 members, elected by universal adult suffrage for a term of three years. Adult male suffrage dates from 1879; adult women received the right to vote in 1893. The voting age was lowered to 18 in November 1974. Since 1867, the House has included four representatives of the Maoris. Persons of at least half Maori ancestry may register either in a Maori electoral district or a European district. Members are elected by simple majority. Although there have been coalition governments, the two-party system usually operates. The party with a majority of members elected to the House of Representatives forms the government, the other party becoming the opposition.

See Pacific Ocean map: front cover H9

LOCATION: 33° to 53°S; 162°E to 173°W. **TERRITORIAL SEA LIMIT:** 3 mi.

On his appointment, the prime minister, leader of the government party, chooses some 20 other ministers to form the cabinet. Each minister usually controls several government departments, for which he is responsible to the House of Representatives. Ministers also are members of the Executive Council, which advises the governor-general. Although the cabinet is the de facto governing body, it has no legal status. Members of the cabinet and the governor-general form the Executive Council, the highest executive body.

An act of 1962 established the post of ombudsman, whose principal function is to inquire into complaints from the public relating to administrative decisions of government departments and related organizations. Between October 1962 and March 1974, the ombudsman processed 9,600 complaints.

13 POLITICAL PARTIES

Although the New Zealand legislature began to function in 1854 under an act of 1852, it was not until near the end of the century that political parties with a national outlook began to be formed. This development was hastened by abolition of the provincial parliaments in 1876.

From 1890 to 1912, the Liberal Party was in power. It drew its strength from small farmers and from the rapidly increasing working class in the towns. It enacted advanced legislation on minimum wages, working conditions, and old age pensions, and established the world's first compulsory system of state arbitration.

The Liberals were replaced as the government by the Reform Party in 1912; the main items in the Reform platform were the "freehold" for certain types of farmers (i.e., the right to purchase on favorable terms the land they leased from the crown) and the eradication of patronage in the public service. During part of World War I, there was a coalition of the Reform and Liberal parties. In the meantime the Labour Party had been formed in 1916, when several rival labor groups finally came together. This party derived partly from old Liberal tradition, but its platform on socialization and social welfare was more radical.

The Reform Party continued in office until 1928 and was then succeeded by the United Party, a revival of the old Liberal Party. In 1931, these two parties came together and governed as a coalition until 1935. In that year, after a severe economic depression, a Labour government was returned to power. Labour remained the government until 1949, although for periods during World War II a coalition war cabinet and later a war administration were created in addition to the Labour cabinet. During its term of office, Labour inaugurated an extensive system of social security and a limited degree of nationalization.

After their defeat in 1935, the old coalition parties joined to form the National Party. It came to power in 1949, and held office until 1957, when it was replaced by the Labour Party. The National Party was returned to power at the 1960 election, and maintained its majority in the elections of 1963, 1966, and 1969; in the 1969 election, however, it won only 45.2% of the vote, compared with 44.25% for Labour (minor parties captured the remaining 10.55%). In 1972, a Labour government was elected, but in 1975 the National Party reversed the tide, winning 55 seats and 47.2% of the total vote, compared with Labour's 32 seats and 39.5% of the vote. A National Party cabinet was formed on 12 December 1975, with Robert Muldoon as prime minister and minister of finance.

Although more than 25 other parties and political groups contested the 1975 election, their direct political impact has not been significant. The largest of the minor parties, the Social Credit Political League, put up candidates in every constituency in 1975 but took only 7.9% of the vote and won no seats in the House; it has held no seats since 1969. The Values Party, which campaigned on a platform of youth and conservation, increased its share of the vote from 2% in 1972 to 5.1% in 1975 but won no seats either.

14 LOCAL GOVERNMENT

There are two main types of local government authorities, territorial and special purpose. As of November 1974 there were 543 local authorities functioning, including 105 county councils, 136 borough (including city) councils, and a wide variety of special purpose authorities dealing with the administration of harbors, hospitals, electricity and water distribution, and other public services. Boroughs provide for the needs of population concentrations of at least 1,500, while counties cater to the primary needs of rural areas. Most units of local government are elected at three-year intervals. In boroughs the mayor is elected directly by the voters. The chairman of a county council is elected by the council itself.

The Local Government Act of 1974 provides for the phasing out of this system. The act empowered the Local Government Commission to establish regional councils throughout New Zealand by 1979. District councils will eventually replace the borough-county system; several community councils will be elected within each district to give residents greater participation in local government.

15 JUDICIAL SYSTEM

In most civil and criminal cases, heard first in magistrates' courts, there is the right of appeal to the supreme court, which is the court of first hearing for cases where a major crime or an important civil action is involved. The highest court, the Court of Appeals, exercises an appellate jurisdiction only. Its decisions are final unless leave is granted to appeal to the Privy Council in London. There are also several special courts, such as the court of arbitration, the Maori land court, the land valuation court, the compensation court, and the children's and young persons' courts.

16 ARMED FORCES

Service in the New Zealand armed forces is now voluntary. Under the National Service Act of 1961, however, male British subjects between the ages of 18 and 21 may be required to undergo a short period of full-time military service followed by three years of part-time service. Volunteers serving on this basis now constitute a territorial force which supplements the regular forces. In 1975, the army had a regular force of 5,525 and an active territorial force of 5,618. The navy had 2,850 regulars and 3,235 reserves, 4 missile-equipped frigates, and 14 patrol craft. The air force had 4,310 regulars, 1,360 reserves, and 36 combat aircraft.

17 MIGRATION

New policy guidelines for immigration were issued by the government in May 1974. Immigrants are now selected according to specific criteria, such as job skills, health, character, age, and family size. British subjects possessing valid passports may take up permanent residence without restriction, and special exceptions are made for immigrants from the South Pacific. The government also maintains an assisted-passage scheme for immigrants from the UK, the US, and West European nations. The subsidy scheme operates without quota, and prospective employers contribute to the fare and resettlement of immigrants. Out of a total of 59,518 immigrants and long-term visitors in 1973/74, 6,755 were assisted. Of the total, 31,811 immigrants came from the UK and 20,319 from Australia. During 1973/74, the New Zealanders departing permanently numbered 9,591, while another 26,832 residents departed for 12 months or more. A majority of emigrants depart for Australia.

18 INTERNATIONAL COOPERATION

New Zealand is a member of the UN and its specialized agencies, as well as of the Asian Development Bank, Commonwealth of Nations, ANZUS, ECAFE, SPC, and the Colombo Plan. In 1973/74, New Zealand contributed a total of NZ$29.1 million in technical assistance, capital assistance, and direct aid or loans to developing nations, amounting to 0.3% of the estimated GNP. The major recipients were the Cook Islands (NZ$3.9 million), Indonesia (NZ$2 million), Niue (NZ$1.6 million), Western Samoa (NZ$1.4 million), and Malaysia (NZ$1.1 million). By 1975/76, New Zealand expected to be spending 1% of its GNP on foreign aid, including private flows and grants from voluntary agencies. New Zealand became a full member of the OECD in May 1973 and of the IDA in January 1975.

¹⁹ECONOMY

New Zealand's economy has traditionally been based on pastoral farming. The last few years, however, have seen the beginnings of heavy industry, and there has been a large expansion in light industries such as plastics, textiles, and footwear, mostly to supply the home market. In recent years there has been a trend toward the development of resource-based industries, and the forest industry has greatly expanded. Pulp, log, and paper products are now a major earner of overseas exchange. As of the 1971 census, 11.5% of the work force was employed in farming and 25.1% in manufacturing. In 1972–73, the value of all farm produce rose 36.2%; during the same period, the value of factory production rose 15.3%. On the negative side, the inflation rate increased steadily from 7% in 1972 to 11.1% in 1974 and an estimated 15% in 1975.

For financing both the imports of raw materials and the high proportion of manufactured goods, New Zealand has traditionally relied on the receipts from the export (principally to the UK) of its restricted range of primary products (mainly wool, meat, dairy products). This dependence on the income from so few commodities makes the economy vulnerable to fluctuations in their world prices and a fall in these prices, as in 1958 and 1974, inevitably results in the restriction of imports or a substantial trade deficit.

²⁰INCOME

In 1973/74, the GNP was NZ$8,593 million. Of the total national income of NZ$7,521 million, NZ$4,821 million was distributed in wages and salaries, an increase of 21.9% over 1972/73. Personal expenditures accounted for NZ$5,163 million of the GNP; government-provided goods and services, NZ$1,257 million; and investments, both private and government, NZ$1,869. Between 1969/70 and 1973/74, the GDP increased 79.9% in current prices but only 16.6% in constant prices.

Contributions to the GDP by sector in 1972/73 were services, about 51%; manufacturing, 24%; agriculture, forestry, and fishing, 14.2%; and other industries (including mining, construction, and public utilities), 10.8%.

²¹LABOR

In April 1974, the labor force totaled an estimated 1,191,300 men and women. As of the 1971 census, 54.9% of the male population and 23.3% of the female population were employed. Of the total 1971 work force, 134,159 (12%) were employed in primary production, including agriculture; 388,071 (34.7%) in secondary industry; and 596,605 (53.3%) in services. The registered unemployment figure has been negligible; it averaged 4,556 for 1974, or less than 1% of the labor force. However, in 1975, the real unemployment rate was estimated at more than 3%.

Compulsory unionization during the 1936–61 period resulted in the creation of many small unions; the law was modified in 1962. Since most unions are occupational or craft-based, industrial agreements generally require the cooperation of numerous unions. As of the 1971 census, 39% of wage earners were unionized, and in 1973 there were 305 unions with 427,692 members.

The Industrial Relations Act of 1973 restructured New Zealand's industrial legislation and institutions, setting up three bodies to aid in the settlement of disputes: the Industrial Mediation Service, the Industrial Conciliation Service, and the Industrial Commission. The Commission is involved only if conciliation fails, and its arbitration is binding. The 1973 act also provides for the right to strike, although there are restrictions once a dispute is before conciliation. In 1974 there were 380 strikes involving 70,904 workers.

In January 1975, minimum wages were raised to NZ$54.88 per week for males and NZ$46.65 for females. These wage rates, however, are set at a rate lower than the standard rate for unskilled labor, and the average wage for males in 1974 was NZ$86.36. Regulations issued in 1974 set guidelines for the adjustment of wages in both public and private employment. By law, employees in most occupations have a 40-hour workweek, 8 hours a day, 5 days a week. Excess hours are generally paid at overtime rates. Legislation or industrial contracts secure sick leave, paid holidays, and accident compensation for all workers.

²²AGRICULTURE

Two-thirds of the total area of New Zealand is devoted to agriculture and animal husbandry, 56% of the farmlands being in holdings of 40.5 hectares or over. About two-fifths of occupied land is crown land, leased to farming tenants by the state: about half is held in freehold by individuals; and the remaining portion is held in leasehold. Capital investment in land improvement and mechanization has contributed greatly to the steady growth in agricultural production which occurred without an increase in the farm labor force. More than 96,000 tractors and 11,000 harvesters are in use.

Cereal cultivation, 92% of which takes place on the South Island plains and downlands, fluctuates in terms of both acreage and size of crop. In 1972/73, hectares sown to wheat totaled 107,690, with a yield of 376,111 tons; 15,079 hectares yielded 44,965 tons of oats; and 73,750 hectares yielded 285,261 tons of barley. Grain and field crops earned an estimated 6% of the total gross farm income in 1972/73.

New Zealand is largely self-sufficient in horticultural products and exports some of these, such as apples and honey. In 1973, 143,500 tons of apples, 24,850 tons of peaches, and 20,800 tons of pears were produced. Other food crops, in tons, included onions, 36,984; cabbage, 28,449; carrots, 27,443; cauliflower, 23,369; tomatoes, 22,780.

The Department of Agriculture and the Department of Scientific and Industrial Research provide farmers and horticulturalists with advice and encouragement on new farming methods, elimination of plant diseases, and improvement of unproductive land. Constant research is going on in all these aspects of agriculture. Government subsidies assist in improving and bringing under cultivation marginal and hitherto unused scrub land. In 1975, 26 new farms were planned for settlement, 35 in 1976, and 50 in 1977.

Agricultural aviation is a large and growing industry. About half the total fertilizer and lime applied to farms in New Zealand is spread by means of aircraft, and aircraft used in agriculture comprised 30% of the civil aircraft in 1974.

²³ANIMAL HUSBANDRY

The combination of relatively warm temperatures and adequate rainfall makes New Zealand one of the richest pastoral areas in the world. Even in the south, where quite severe winters occur, farm animals need not be housed. In 1971/72, 5,058,100 hectares of tussock and native grasses were used for grazing. In 1974 there were 7,275,000 head of beef cattle, 2,140,000 head of dairy cattle, 55,883,000 sheep (including 40,366,000 breeding ewes), and 507,000 hogs. Dairying and beef production are concentrated in the North Island, which has 83% of the total cattle and 92% of the dairy stock. Sheep farming is more evenly distributed between the North and South islands. The natural tussock land in the mountainous areas of the South Island and the surface-sown grassland in the less steep parts of the North Island are used to raise sheep for wool. The extensive use of aircraft for the spread of top dressing has greatly improved hill pasture, most of which is not readily accessible to normal top dressing with fertilizers.

Products of animal origin average annually over 75% of the total value of New Zealand's exports. New Zealand is the world's largest exporter of butter and is a leading exporter of meat, wool, and cheese. The wool clip, which has increased steadily since 1948, was 285,000 tons in 1974, slightly lower than the previous year. Meat production also dropped slightly in 1973/74 (the first decline in nine years) to 900,000 tons from 1,097,000 tons in 1972/73. Butter production in 1973/74 totaled about 219,000 tons; the cheese output was 89,000 tons. Wool accounted for 23% of total gross farm income, mutton and lamb 21%, dairy products, 21%, beef 19%, and hogs 2%.

The wholesale distribution of milk and some agricultural produce is the responsibility of the milk boards and other producers' boards, on which the government is represented. These boards regulate the marketing and standards of the various commodities and in most cases guarantee a minimum price to the farmer for his products. The export of dairy products is in the hands of the Dairy Products Marketing Commission, which regulates sales and standards and controls payments to producers. A Meat Producers Board serves an analogous function for the export meat industry.

24 FISHING

Although many kinds of edible fish are readily obtainable in New Zealand waters, the fishing fleet remains small, and little fish processing is done. The amount of fish landed has increased steadily, however, from 6,488 tons in 1936 to 66,400 tons in 1971; the number of fishing vessels nearly doubled from 1,570 in 1962 to 3,100 in 1971; and the number of commercial fishermen increased from 2,761 in 1962 to 5,275 in 1971.

In the 1950s there was an increase in the catch of rock lobster (crayfish), stimulated by a thriving export trade to the US of frozen rock lobster tails; however, after reaching a peak in 1968, when 10,910 tons were produced, the rock lobster catch declined to 4,771 tons in 1973.

In 1966, New Zealand introduced a 9-mile fishing zone beyond the 3-mile territorial limit.

25 FORESTRY

At the time Europeans began coming to New Zealand, about 70% of the land was forest. This has been reduced by settlement, farming, and exploitation to about 23%. Much of the remaining natural forest is reserved in national parks, or as protection forest on mountain land. In 1974, about 70% of the total forest area was crown-owned and administered by government departments. The Kaingaroa State Forest in the Rotorua district covers 149,735 hectares and is the largest planted forest in the world.

For wood production, New Zealand now relies heavily on its planted forests of quick-growing exotic species, mainly radiata pine, which can be harvested every 25–30 years. These provide about 90% of the wood for production of sawn timber, wood panel products, pulp, paper, and paperboard. In 1974 there were 651,000 hectares of exotic forests, 343,000 hectares of which were in state ownership and 308,000 hectares in private ownership. Planting is continuing at a rate of 28,000 hectares annually to cope with expansion of forest-based industries.

Total sawn timber production in 1974 was 2,054,000 cu meters. Total paper and paperboard production in 1974 was about 534,000 tons, including 218,000 tons of newsprint, 31,000 tons of printing and writing paper, and 285,000 tons of other paper and paperboard. Wood pulp production has expanded greatly since 1965, reaching a high of 857,989 tons in 1974.

26 MINING

Many different minerals are found in New Zealand, but few have been extensively exploited. In 1973, mineral production was valued at NZ$75 million. The Maui offshore natural gas field, one of the 20 largest gas fields in the world, was discovered in 1969 off the Taraniki coast and is now being developed and will be exploited mainly for electricity generation; 419.8 million cu meters of natural gas were produced in 1973. A small amount of crude petroleum is also extracted. Coal production is sufficient for domestic consumption and a small amount is exported; 1973 coal output was 2,468,000 tons. Estimated recoverable coal reserves amount to over 800 million tons. The once important

gold deposits of the South Island, discovered in 1861, are largely exhausted; only 343.5 kg were mined in 1973. Large quantities of iron-bearing sands are present, especially on North Island beaches; 2,181,000 tons of iron sands were extracted in 1973. Titanomagnetite concentrates are produced for Japanese use from iron sand deposits on the North Island's west coast. In 1973, about 1 million tons were exported. Uranium-bearing minerals have been located in an area of the South Island, but as yet no serious testing has been attempted.

Output of building materials in 1973 included 41,048 tons of building stone and 22,592 tons of road sand, rock, and gravel.

27 ENERGY AND POWER

New Zealand's per capita consumption of electricity is among the highest in the world. A network of transmission lines links all major power stations, bringing electricity to 99% of the population. Of the 18,352 million kwh generated for public supply in 1974/75, 77% was produced from hydroelectric resources and 7% from geothermal steam. Future hydroelectric potential is limited, however, and thermal power based primarily on coal and natural gas is becoming increasingly important.

New Zealand now meets some 41% of its total energy requirements from indigenous resources, the balance coming from imports of crude oil and refined petroleum products. Natural gas from the Kapuni field supplied nine North Island towns, some large industries, and the 600-Mw New Plymouth power station in 1975. Gas from the Maui offshore natural gas and condensate field was due onshore by October 1978 and was expected to halve New Zealand's present dependence on imported petroleum by 1985.

28 INDUSTRY

Industrial production has increased rapidly since the end of World War II, stimulated by intermittent import controls that often enabled domestic industry to increase output without competition. A most significant feature of New Zealand industry in recent years has been the establishment of heavy industry with Commonwealth and US capital. Plants include metal and petroleum processing, motor vehicle assembly, textiles and footwear, and a wide range of consumer appliances. Manufacturing is still mainly on a small scale. In 1974, the average number of employees per factory was 32. Almost one-third of all registered factories employed 5 or fewer workers, and only 5% had more than 100 employees.

Food processing is still the most important industry, and although it fell from a 50% to a 30% total output value between 1969 and 1974, it still employs more workers than any other industry. Second in importance is the textile industry, which accounts for nearly 8% of the total value of industrial output. Other industries, in decreasing order of output value, are metal products, transport equipment, machinery, wood and cork products, and paper products.

Selected industrial products in 1972/73, included 72,389 automobiles, 13,228 trucks and vans, 67,104 refrigerators, 77,455 home freezers, 114,000 radios, 33,739 television sets, 7,230,000 gallons of wine, 78,857,000 gallons of beer and stout, 5,708 million cigarettes, and 230,000 short tons of flour.

29 DOMESTIC TRADE

Most retail firms are small by US standards. The 1972/73 business census revealed aggregate retail sales of NZ$4,314 million, amounting to an average turnover of NZ$128,000 for each of the 33,700 retail stores. However, many smaller retailers are being supplanted by small supermarkets and shopping centers; others have converted to self-service operations. There is very little retail mail-order trade. Automobiles and large appliances are increasingly being sold on the installment (hire-purchase) plan.

General and trade papers, regional publications, and television and radio are used extensively as advertising media.

Business hours vary, especially since the introduction of staggered work hours, known as "glide time." Offices open as early as 7:30 A.M. and remain open until about 6 P.M. Stores open at 8:30 or 9 A.M. and close generally at 5 or 5:30 P.M. Some stores remain open until 9 P.M. on Thursday or Friday. Saturday trading is becoming more prevalent at popular beach resorts near the larger urban areas. Sunday trading is confined to "dairy shops" permitted by law to sell a restricted range of foodstuffs. All offices and banks are closed on Saturdays, Sundays, and statutory holidays.

30 FOREIGN TRADE

New Zealand's trade per capita is one of the highest in the world; total trade averages about 40% of the GNP. More than 70% of export receipts is derived from meat, dairy, wool, and other agricultural and livestock products; manufactured goods are slowly taking an increasing share of the total. Imports consist mainly of manufactured goods and raw materials for industry. Foreign trade more than doubled in value between 1970 and 1975. In 1973, exports reached a record total of US$2,559.4 million, and imports were US$2,186.4 million; but in 1974, as export prices declined, the value of exports dropped to about US$2,400 million, while imports increased to more than US$3,600 million, producing trade and balance-of-payments deficits for the year.

Principal exports in 1973 (in millions of US dollars) were:

Wool and animal hair	586.4
Dairy products and eggs	439.6
Mutton and lamb	384.0
Beef and veal	352.2
Hides, skins, and furs	128.4
Other exports	668.8
TOTAL	2,559.4

Principal imports in 1973 (in millions of US dollars) were:

Machinery	429.5
Transport equipment	301.1
Chemicals	296.7
Textile yarns and fabrics	201.4
Petroleum and petroleum products	156.4
Iron and steel	147.8
Foodstuffs	115.7
Other imports	537.8
TOTAL	2,186.4

The UK is New Zealand's principal trade partner, accounting for 22.9% of total trade in 1973. Australia ranked next with 15.5%, the US with 14%, and Japan 13.2%. The UK's entry into the EEC on 1 January 1973 had considerable impact on New Zealand's trade patterns. In 1970, nearly 34% of New Zealand's exports went to the UK; by 1973, however, the British share had declined to 24.5%, with a further decline registered in 1974. Trade with all nine EEC members declined from 40% of New Zealand's total trade in 1970 to 33.7% in 1973. Principal trade partners in 1973 (in millions of US dollars) were:

	EXPORTS	IMPORTS	BALANCE
UK	627.1	459.4	167.7
Australia	198.8	537.2	-338.4
US	401.8	263.5	138.3
Japan	337.3	290.9	46.4
FRG	69.2	97.3	- 28.1
Canada	70.2	58.4	11.8
Other countries	855.0	479.7	375.3
TOTALS	2,559.4	2,186.4	373.0

31 BALANCE OF PAYMENTS

Since New Zealand's foreign trade depends on agricultural and livestock products, and since prices for these commodities are volatile, New Zealand's balance of payments may swing sharply from one year to the next. Generally, deficits outweighed surpluses during the 1950s and 1960s. Consistent surpluses were recorded between 1969 and 1973, when international reserves increased from US$210 million to US$893 million. However, a poor trade performance in 1974 contributed to a current accounts deficit of more than US$1,131 million. International reserves declined to US$640 million in 1974 and closed out 1975 at US$428 million, indicating that another payments deficit had been recorded.

The following are summaries of New Zealand's balance of payments for 1973 and 1974 (in millions of US dollars):

	1973	1974
CURRENT ACCOUNTS		
Trade, net	575.8	- 487.1
Services, net	-447.0	- 706.7
Transfers, net	85.9	62.6
TOTALS	214.7	-1,131.2
CAPITAL ACCOUNTS		
Long-term capital	-79.9	543.8
Short-term capital	40.5	40.9
TOTALS	-39.4	584.7
Errors and omissions	-99.0	93.9
Net change	76.3	- 452.6

To meet rising costs, New Zealand drew US$105 million from the IMF Oil Facility in 1974 and US$224 million in 1975.

32 BANKING

The Reserve Bank of New Zealand, established in 1933, exercises control over monetary circulation and credit. It is the bank of issue, handles all central government banking transactions, manages the public debt, and administers exchange control regulations. The Reserve Bank of New Zealand Amendment Act (1973) empowered the Bank to regulate credit from all sources, and required it to make loans as the minister of finance may determine in order to ensure continued full employment. Notes in circulation during 1974 (weekly average) amounted to NZ$305.8 million, as compared with NZ$262.3 million in 1973 and NZ$173.9 million in 1969.

There are five commercial banks in New Zealand, one of which, the Bank of New Zealand, is state-owned. Total deposits in the commercial banks for 1974 (weekly average) were NZ$2,063.7 million, as compared with NZ$809.3 million in 1969.

There are 12 trustee savings banks. The Post Office Savings Bank (established in 1865) has about 1,200 branches throughout New Zealand. Private deposits in trustee savings banks in March 1974 were NZ$711.6 million, and in the Post Office Savings Bank NZ$1,139.8 million.

33 INSURANCE

There were 26 life insurance companies conducting business in New Zealand in 1973/74 (9 of them purely New Zealand concerns), 64 accident insurance companies (mainly New Zealand- and UK-based), and 51 fire insurance companies. The government provides insurance through the Government Life Insurance Office and the State Insurance Office, which undertakes accident, fire, and marine insurance.

Growth in life insurance assets averaged more than NZ$100 million annually in recent years, totaling NZ$1,970.9 million at the end of 1974. New Zealand ranks fifth behind Canada, the US, Japan, and Sweden in its ratio of the value of life insurance policies to national income; annual premiums paid for life insurance amount to about 3% of national income.

Premium payments in 1973 included NZ$221.8 million for 2,533,000 life insurance policies, NZ$60.8 million for 2,149,598 fire insurance policies, and NZ$137.4 million for accident insurance policies.

34 SECURITIES

The stock exchanges in Auckland, Wellington, Christchurch, Dunedin, and Invercargill are members of the Stock Exchange Association of New Zealand, with headquarters in Wellington. Official listing is granted to companies that comply with the Association's requirements. These do not impose qualifications as to share capital but provide that the company must be of sufficient magnitude and its shareholding sufficiently well distributed to ensure a free market for its shares.

Subject to the recommendation and approval of the stock exchange nearest to the registered offices, companies may secure unofficial listing for their shares. All transactions in shares quoted in the unofficial list are subject to special brokerage rates.

35 PUBLIC FINANCE

The House of Representatives usually meets at the end of every June, and votes supplies from month to month until the estimated expenditure for the year ending the next 31 March has been approved and the annual appropriation act passed. The following are consolidated central government revenues and expenditures budgeted for 1972/73 and 1973/74 (in millions of New Zealand dollars):

	1972/73	1973/74
REVENUES		
Direct taxes	1,346.5	1,735.2
Indirect taxes	484.5	556.4
Interest	119.0	127.5
Other receipts	185.8	93.1
TOTALS	2,135.8	2,512.2
EXPENDITURES		
Social services	520.6	639.9
Education	379.4	442.7
Health	339.6	399.0
Defense and foreign relations	152.3	173.0
Industrial development	153.0	141.9
Price stabilization	36.2	112.2
Other expenditures	559.9	601.1
TOTALS	2,141.0	2,509.8
BALANCE	-5.2	2.4

For 1975/76, gross government expenditures were budgeted at NZ$4,939.4 million; tax revenues were budgeted at NZ$3,197 million, of which 76.6% was direct taxation. The gross central government debt as of 31 March 1974 was NZ$3,734.5 million, or NZ$1,227.32 per capita. More than 87% of the debt was domestic.

For the year ending 31 March 1973, receipts of local authorities totaled NZ$696 million and expenditures NZ$674.2 million. The gross public debt of local authorities as of 31 March 1973 was NZ$722.4 million, or NZ$242.86 per capita.

36 TAXATION

Earnings are taxed in one combined general income and social security tax introduced on 1 April 1969. For wage and salary earners, the income and social security tax is deducted by the employer on a pay-as-you-earn basis (called PAYE), with annual adjustments. The graduated scale for income-social security tax payments for 1976 ranged from a minimum of 19.5% of the first NZ$2,000 of taxable income to a maximum of 57.2% on taxable

income in excess of NZ$20,001. Under a new system of special exemptions and rebates introduced on 1 April 1974, tax rebates for the taxpayer, spouse, dependents, relatives, and housekeeper are allowed as deductions from the actual tax assessed. In addition, there are special exemptions for donations to charities and for school fees, not to exceed NZ$200; a standard deduction for wage and salary earners of NZ$50 for out-of-pocket employment expenses; and other deductions for life insurance premiums and contributions to retirement funds.

Actual tax receipts in 1973/74 from all sources totaled NZ$2,395.1 million or NZ$799.58 per person (the per capita figure was NZ$427.93 in 1969/70). Of this, income and social security tax receipts totaled NZ$1,697.9 million.

A sales tax, usually 20% or more, is assessed on many imported articles as well as on some domestically produced items; many types of goods are exempted. Excise taxes are imposed on sugar, tobacco products, and alcoholic beverages.

Local authorities are largely dependent on property taxes. There are three main systems of rating: (1) capital (land improvements) value; (2) annual value; (3) unimproved value. The actual amount of the rate is fixed by each local authority. In 1973/74, the central government contributed 62.5% of the revenues of local authorities through transfers; rates and license fees accounted for 32.4%; and trading profits, 5.1%.

37 CUSTOMS AND DUTIES

Customs taxation is based principally on an ad valorem scale, but specific duties are applied to some goods. Rates of duty payable depend upon the country of origin. The rates were revised 1 July 1974, after the UK entered the Common Market. The new tariff provided separate preferential rate scales for Great Britain, Northern Ireland, and the Irish Republic; for Australia, Canada, other Commonwealth countries, and (for certain items) Malaysia; and for a limited range of goods from developing countries.

In the year ending 31 March 1975, customs and excise duties accounted for nearly 10% of the central government's total tax revenue.

38 FOREIGN INVESTMENTS

Investment in New Zealand's economy by overseas companies through New Zealand subsidiaries has increased steadily, with the largest contribution from UK sources. Total overseas investment reached a high of more than NZ$181.7 million in 1973/74. Of this total, NZ$84.2 million was from the UK, NZ$54.9 million from the US and Canada, NZ$42.2 million from Australia. Overseas investment assets held by the Reserve Bank reached a peak of NZ$407.6 million at the end of 1973 but declined to NZ$222.3 million as of 31 December 1974. Gross private overseas investment by New Zealand companies totaled at least NZ$15.9 million in 1973/74, of which the UK received NZ$9 million and Australia NZ$6.9 million.

39 ECONOMIC POLICY

Economic policy is established and directed by the government through taxation, Reserve Bank interest rates, price and monopoly controls, and import and export licensing. Import controls, introduced early in 1958, were further tightened in 1961 and 1973 to correct deficits in the balance of payments. About 30% of imports, by value, in 1974 came under import licensing control, including automobiles and most consumer goods.

In 1961, the Monetary and Economic Council was established to report and make recommendations on the stability of prices, economic growth, rate of employment, and the standard of living. The Council's first reports dealt with long-term problems of slow growth and instability; more recent reports have treated the current situation. In March 1974, a top cabinet committee became responsible for long-term economic planning, a function formerly assumed by the National Development Council, which was established in 1969. The government sought to improve New

Zealand's economic performance by more intensive use of modern technology and marketing practices, particularly in the agriculture, forestry, and manufacturing sectors.

To help maintain economic stability, the government assists, and in some cases controls, various economic enterprises (agricultural distribution and marketing, commercial banking, and some insurance).

40 HEALTH

In 1974 there were 3,182 active medical practitioners (1 physician for every 976 persons). There were also 1,061 dentists (916 in private practice, the remainder employed by the government) and 2,608 registered pharmacists. New Zealand has more than 19,000 nurses and midwives. Most physicians practice under the National Health Service, established by the Social Security Act of 1938, but private practice outside the scheme is permitted.

The Health Service provides hospital treatment, maternity services from a general practitioner, most prescribed drugs, laboratory diagnostic services, dental care, routine immunizations for children under 16, and some health appliances free of charge. Partial benefits are paid for private hospitalization, X-ray services, physiotherapy, and hearing aids.

The number of public hospitals in 1974 was 196, including 78 general hospitals, 72 maternity hospitals, 27 special hospitals, and 19 old persons' homes, with a total of 28,191 beds. In addition, there were 153 licensed private hospitals, with a total of 4,430 beds. Public hospitals are managed under the supervision of the minister of health by local hospital boards, whose members are elected. The Mental Health Division of the Department of Health operates 15 public mental hospitals, and there is 1 private mental hospital. There is free, voluntary immunization against poliomyelitis both for schoolchildren and for adults. Voluntary welfare organizations make valuable contributions to public health, and are assisted by grants from public funds. The infant mortality rate in 1974 was 18.8 per 1,000 live births for the total population, one of the lowest rates in the world. The rate for the Maori population was 19.4 per 1,000 live births, a significant improvement over the 1967 rate of 29.7. Life expectancy at birth was 69.09 years for non-Maori males and 75.16 years for non-Maori females during 1970–72, but 60.96 years for Maori males and 64.96 years for Maori females. Estimated average life expectancy in 1975 was 72.4 years. The principal causes of death are heart disease, cancer, and cerebrovascular diseases.

For the year ending 31 March 1975, NZ$111 million was spent on medical benefits, more than double the 1969/70 total.

41 SOCIAL WELFARE

The Social Security Act of 1964 consolidated and advanced existing social legislation. By a system of monetary benefits on a compulsory contributory basis and a system of medical and hospital benefits, all persons in New Zealand are now protected economically from disabilities arising from age, sickness, unemployment, and widowhood. The former separate social security tax was combined, as of 1 April 1969, with the graduated general income tax applicable to all wage earners. Monetary benefits under the Social Security Act are paid for retirement, old age, unemployment, sickness, and emergencies; and to widows, orphans, families, invalids, and miners. Medical benefits include medical, hospital, and pharmaceutical payments.

Retirement and family benefits are paid irrespective of income and property. A revised accident compensation plan enacted in 1972 and effective as of 1 July 1974 provides continuous coverage for all persons in regular employment, whether at work or not. The plan is financed by a levy on employers and by a contribution from general revenue; and compensation is 80% of average earnings. The plan also insures against injury or death by motor vehicle accident, regardless of blame; the plan is financed by levies on motor vehicle owners.

The safety, health and welfare benefits, holiday provisions, hours of work, and overtime of all workers are closely regulated. Much valuable social welfare work in the public health field, notably in infant care, is carried out by voluntary organizations which are assisted by grants from public funds. During 1974/75, a total of NZ$735.1 million was distributed in social security benefits, including NZ$224.9 million in old age benefits; NZ$141 million to pensioners; NZ$111 million for medical care; NZ$28 million for widows' benefits; NZ$13.7 million for disability; NZ$15.9 million for sickness; and NZ$5.1 million for unemployment compensation.

42 HOUSING

The number of houses and apartments built in New Zealand has increased steadily since 1965, reaching a peak in 1974/75, when 34,000 new houses and flats were built. Nearly half of the total housing stock—850,000 dwellings—has been constructed since 1953. Since that year, the government has introduced measures designed to assist the financing of housing by contractors and private owners. These include increases in the maximum housing loans advanced by the State Advances Corporation, low-interest loans for families with low incomes, and the establishment of a home savings scheme through the Post Office Savings Bank. Interest rates on loans from the government Housing Corp. start at 3% for low-income families. The agency also has a stock of approximately 53,000 houses and flats available for rental, with preference given to low-income families. Since 1950, the government has generously subsidized local authorities to provide pensioners' housing.

The average cost of a home unit was about NZ$23,000 in 1974; the average bank loan to homeowners was about NZ$14,000. Most families own their own homes. The average dwelling has about 1,000 to 1,500 sq ft, with three bedrooms, living room, dining room, kitchen, laundry, bathroom, toilet, and garage. Most units are built of wood and have sheet-iron or tiled roofs. In 1971 there were 801,686 inhabited dwellings, of which about 26% were rented, 41% owned with mortgages, and 26.5% owned outright without mortgages.

43 EDUCATION

Education in New Zealand is free, secular, and compulsory for children between 6 and 15, although most children attend school from the age of 5. Primary and secondary schools are administered by district education boards (or boards of governors) and school committees (the latter elected by householders), under the authority of the Ministry of Education. Kindergartens are run either by private persons or by voluntary organizations with partial state subsidies. Primary education is given at primary and intermediate schools (the latter giving the last two years of primary education), and postprimary education at either secondary schools, technical high schools, or consolidated schools for pupils who live in rural areas. Evening classes, particularly in practical and vocational subjects, are given by technical and secondary schools, and adult education classes in wider cultural subjects are given by the universities. Most state schools are coeducational. In 1974 there were 473,099 students in public primary schools and 177,582 students in public secondary schools.

There are special schools for physically and mentally handicapped or maladjusted children; in 1973, such schools had 14,434 pupils. For children in isolated areas, there is a public correspondence school, which had 7,805 pupils in 1974. In some regions there are special state primary and secondary schools for Maori children, but more than 60% of Maori children attend public schools. In 1974 there were 76,994 Maori students in state primary schools and 2,974 in private schools; the number of Maori students in state secondary schools was 20,797, with 1,846 in private schools.

Private primary and secondary schools are operated by individuals and religious bodies; in 1974 there were 50,574 students in private primary schools (most of them run by the Roman Catholic Church) and 31,014 students in private secondary schools.

There are six universities: the University of Auckland, University of Waikato (at Hamilton), Massey University (at Palmerston North), Victoria University of Wellington, University of Canterbury (at Christchurch), and University of Otago (at Dunedin). An agricultural institution, Lincoln College, is associated with the University of Canterbury. University tuition fees are low, and financial assistance is given to applicants who have passed special qualifying examinations. In 1973 there were 38,772 students in the university system. Practical tertiary education is provided by 11 technical institutes, which had 3,378 full-time and 100,581 part-time pupils in 1973; a technical correspondence institute, with 17,679 students in 1973; and a community college. The 9 teacher-training colleges had 7,616 students, and there were 388 students in 4 teacher-training centers for kindergarten.

Government expenditure on education for 1973/74 was NZ$442.7 million. As a percentage of the total budget, education expenditures increased from 6% in 1945/46 to 17.6% in 1973/74. There has been a marked increase in school enrollment since World War II, only partly accounted for by the rise in population. A more important factor is the increased number of pupils going on to secondary education—60% in 1936, 80% in 1945, and over 95% in 1974.

44 LIBRARIES AND MUSEUMS

The National Library of New Zealand was founded in 1966 by the amalgamation of several state libraries and service divisions. It is composed of the National Library, with 415,000 volumes; the Alexander Turnbull Library, with 157,000 volumes; the General Assembly Library, with 370,000 volumes; the Extension Division, which provides services to public and school libraries throughout the country; and the Library School, which offers courses for the training and certification of librarians. The 1969 library census recorded a total of 445 libraries, including 266 public libraries supported by local authorities, the largest being in Auckland, Christchurch, Dunedin, and Wellington.

Outstanding art galleries and museums are the Auckland City Art Gallery (European and New Zealand paintings); the Canterbury Museum, Christchurch (ornithology, anthropology, and history); the Dunedin Public Art Gallery (paintings, period furniture, and china); the Otago Museum, Dunedin (ethnography, classical antiquities, ceramics); the National Museum, Wellington (botany, ethnology, history); and the National Art Gallery, Wellington (paintings, sculpture, etchings, engravings). In 1971 there were 87 public and private museums.

45 ORGANIZATIONS

Almost all aspects of New Zealand life have their appropriate organizations, commercial, agricultural, labor, cultural, or welfare, as the case may be. A few of the more important ones in different spheres are the Federated Farmers of New Zealand, the New Zealand Fruitgrowers' Association, the New Zealand Employers' Federation, the Chamber of Commerce (represented in almost every large town), the Returned Servicemen's Association, the New Zealand Federation of Labour, the Plunket Society (which deals with child welfare), the Royal Society of New Zealand, "Heritage" (devoted to the assistance of children deprived of one parent), the New Zealand Red Cross Society, the New Zealand Press Association, the New Zealand Institute of Public Administration, and the New Zealand Public Service Association. Important cultural organizations are the National Orchestra, the New Zealand Opera Company, the New Zealand Ballet Company, the Queen Elizabeth II Arts Council, and the New Zealand Music Federation.

46 PRESS

Aside from the usual British legal limits for libel, there is com-

plete freedom of the press in New Zealand. The 8 daily newspapers in the 4 main metropolitan areas had a total daily circulation of 747,850 in 1974. In smaller towns and cities, 33 daily newspapers had a total circulation of about 317,000. Most nondaily newspapers are rural. New Zealand's first two Sunday newspapers began publishing in 1965.

The largest newspapers and their 1974 circulation figures are:

New Zealand Herald (m.)	Auckland	229,000
Auckland Star (e.)	Auckland	133,000
Evening Post	Wellington	100,359
The Dominion (m.)	Wellington	74,000
The Press (m.)	Christchurch	74,000
Christchurch Star (e.)	Christchurch	69,000
Otago Daily Times (m.)	Dunedin	43,500
Evening Star	Dunedin	30,000

47 TOURISM

New Zealand draws many thousands of tourists to its shores because of the beauty, diversity, and compactness of its natural attractions and its varied sporting facilities. The number of tourists increased from 82,000 in 1964/65 to 361,000 in 1974/75; most came from Australia. Despite the downturn in world economic conditions, tourism increased 13.5% over 1973/74. Receipts from tourism in 1973/74 totaled NZ$78.5 million. As of 31 March 1973 there were 20,547 rooms in licensed hotels and motels.

All overseas visitors (except British subjects who are permanent residents in Australia) need passports valid for at least six months beyond their intended stay in New Zealand. No visas are required for persons who are traveling on valid British passports; for citizens of Belgium, Denmark, Finland, metropolitan France, the Federal Republic of Germany (FRG), Iceland, Liechtenstein, Luxembourg, Monaco, the Netherlands, Norway, Sweden, or Switzerland; or for US or Japanese nationals not planning to stay in New Zealand more than 30 days.

Apart from certain health and similar regulations, there are few bars to temporary admission into New Zealand. Visitors must comply with an entry permit system, although British-born and US citizens of European origin are relieved of this formality. Broadly speaking, to qualify for permits, applicants must be in good physical and mental health and have return passages already arranged. Aliens staying longer than three months in New Zealand must register with the police on arrival and should have three passport-sized photographs.

48 FAMOUS NEW ZEALANDERS

Among New Zealand's best-known statesmen are Sir George Grey (1812-98), governor and later prime minister; Richard John Seddon (1845-1906), prime minister responsible for much social legislation; William Ferguson Massey (1856-1925); and Peter Fraser (1884-1950), World War II prime minister. Sir John Salmond (1862-1924) was an eminent jurist. William Pember Reeves (1857-1932), outstanding journalist, politician, and political economist, was director of the London School of Economics. Frances Hodgkins (1869-1947) was a highly regarded painter. Katherine Mansfield (Kathleen Beauchamp Murry, 1888-1923), author of many evocative stories, was a master of the short-story form. New Zealand's best-known living authors are Maurice Shadbolt (b.1932) and Sylvia Ashton-Warner. Two outstanding leaders of the Maori people were Sir Apirana Ngata (1874-1950) and Sir Peter Buck (1880-1951). Lord Ernest Rutherford (1871-1937), pioneer in atomic research and 1908 Nobel Prize winner for chemistry, was born in New Zealand. Sir Truby King (1858-1938) pioneered in the field of child care. Other scientists include Sir Harold Gillies (1882-1960) and Sir Archibald McIndoe (1900-62), whose plastic surgery methods did much to rehabilitate war victims; Sir Brian G. Barratt-Boyes (b.1924), a researcher in cardiac-thoracic surgery; and Albert W. Liley (b.1929), a researcher in perinatal psychology. Prominent in the arts have been ballet dancers Alexander Grant (b.1925) and Rowena Jackson (b.1926); the singer and actor Inia Watene Te Wiata (1915–71); and the soprano Kiri Te Kanawa (b.1944). Sir Edmund Percival Hillary (b.1919) was the conqueror of Mt. Everest. The celebrated political cartoonist David Low (1891–1963) was born in New Zealand.

⁴⁹DEPENDENCIES
Cook Islands
The Cook Islands, part of New Zealand since 1901, became internally self-governing on 4 August 1965. The Cook Islands Constitution Act of 1964 established the island group as wholly self-ruling but possessed of common citizenship with New Zealand as well as of a common head of state (the Queen). New Zealand remains, however, responsible for the defense and external affairs of the islands. There is a similarity between the Cook Islands–New Zealand relationship and that between Puerto Rico and the United States.

A parliamentary type of government, like New Zealand's, characterizes the new political relationship, with a cabinet composed of a prime minister and five other ministers. The former resident commissioner on New Zealand's behalf became the New Zealand high commissioner (after the Commonwealth fashion) with the coming of autonomy. Cook Islands products continue to enter New Zealand freely, and the level of subsidies to the islands from the New Zealand government has persisted.

The Cook Islands, 15 islands lying between 8° and 23°s and 156° and 167°w, more than 3,220 km (2,000 mi) northeast of New Zealand, were discovered by James Cook in 1773. They became a British protectorate in 1888 and were annexed to New Zealand in 1901. They consist of the Southern Group, 8 islands the largest of which are Rarotonga (6,666 hectares) and Mangaia (5,191 hectares), and the Northern Group, 7 islands varying in size from Penrhyn (984 hectares) to Nassau (121 hectares). The total area is 241 sq km (93 sq mi). The northern islands are low-lying coral atolls, while the southern islands, including Rarotonga, the administrative seat, are elevated and fertile, and have the greater population. Except for Rarotonga, the islands suffer from lack of streams and wells, and water must be conserved. The islands lie within the hurricane area, and sometimes experience destructive storms. The population (19,522 in 1974, almost entirely Maori) is Polynesian and close in language and tradition to the New Zealand Maori. They are converts to Christianity. The islands are visited by government and freight vessels, and interisland shipping services are provided by commercially owned boats. An international airport opened for full services in December 1973. Each permanently inhabited island has a radio station.

The economy is based on agriculture, with the main exports being citrus fruits and juices, tomatoes, bananas, and pineapples. Other exports are copra, pearl shell, and manufactured goods. In 1974, exports amounted to NZ$109.7 million. The main imports are foodstuffs, piece goods, oils, gasoline, tobacco, vehicles and parts, timber, and cement. In 1974, imports amounted to NZ$400,000.

Revenue for public finances is derived mainly from import duties and income tax. In 1970/71, revenue and subsidy receipts and expenditures totaled NZ$1.2 million. The New Zealand government provides triennial grants and subsidies for capital development in health, education, other social services, economic development, and other purposes (NZ$7.45 million for 1971–74).

Free, compulsory education is provided by the government at primary and secondary levels for all children between the ages of 6 and 15, and thereafter for about 40% to New Zealand School Certificate level (after 3 years of secondary education). In 1974,

6,785 students attended government schools, with 88 additional students receiving education or vocational training under the New Zealand Training Scheme. All Cook Islanders receive free medical and surgical treatment, and schoolchildren receive free dental care.

The 22-member Legislative Assembly—to which the prime minister and other cabinet members are responsible—is elected by the adult population of the islands and can void the applicability of New Zealand laws to the territory under its jurisdiction. The constitution of the autonomous islands also allows a declaration of independence if ever this should be the wish of the political leadership.

Niue
An isolated coral island, Niue is 966 km (600 mi) from the southern Cook Islands, and located at 19°02′s and 169°52′w. Niue became a British protectorate in 1900 and was annexed to New Zealand in 1901. Although Niue forms part of the Cook Islands, because of its remoteness and cultural and linguistic differences it has been separately administered. Niue has an area of 259 sq km (100 sq mi). Its population (of Polynesian stock) was estimated to be 4,142 at 31 December 1973 and is continuing to decline, principally because of emigration to New Zealand; in 1973, 1,010 Niueans left and 533 returned, for a loss of 477.

Niue became self-governing on 19 October 1974, in free association with New Zealand. Under the constitution, the former leader of government became the premier. An assembly of 20 members is elected by universal suffrage; 14 members representing village constituencies and 6 at large are elected. According to the constitution, New Zealand will continue to be responsible for the external affairs and defense of Niue and for providing economic and administrative assistance.

Niue's soil, although fertile, is not plentiful; arable land is confined to small pockets of soil among the coral rocks, making agriculture difficult. Since there are no running streams, the island is dependent on rainwater. The economy is based mainly on agriculture. Copra, bananas, and kumaras (sweet potatoes) are exported. There are 77 miles of all-weather roads. A steamship company maintains monthly service to New Zealand. A telephone system connects the villages. An airport became fully operational in 1971. Budget deficits are met by the New Zealand government, which also makes grants for capital development. In 1973/74, Niue government income totaled NZ$1.1 million; expenditures, NZ$2.4 million; and grants and loans from New Zealand, NZ$1.6 million. Health services and education are free. Education is compulsory for children 6 to 14 years of age. In 1973, 1,503 children were enrolled, and there were 51 Niueans attending school in New Zealand.

Tokelau Islands
The Tokelau Islands, situated between 8° and 10°s and 171° and 173°w, about 483 km (300 mi) north of Western Samoa, consist of three atolls, Fakaofo, Nukunono, and Atafu. Total area is about 10 sq km (4 sq mi). Each atoll has a lagoon encircled by a number of reef-bound islets varying in length from 100 yards to 4 miles, in width from 100 to 400 yards, and extending more than 10 feet above sea level. All villages are on the leeward side, close to passages through the reefs. Lying in the hurricane belt, the islands have a mean annual rainfall of 120 inches. The inhabitants, of Polynesian origin, are British subjects and New Zealand citizens. Their language, which is dying out, resembles Samoan, the official language. Total population in 1973 was 1,587. Formerly part of the Gilbert and Ellice Islands group, the Tokelaus were transferred to New Zealand jurisdiction in 1925 and became part of New Zealand at the beginning of 1949. There is no resident European staff; executive functions are carried out on each atoll by appointed Tokelau mayors, magistrates, clerks, and other officials. An administrative officer based in Western Samoa coordinates administrative services for the islands.

Subsistence farming and the production of copra for export are the main occupations. Visits are made regularly by New Zealand Air Force planes, and a chartered vessel makes regular trading visits. Sources of revenue are an export duty on copra, customs dues, postage stamps, and trading profits.

Total government revenues for 1973/74 were NZ$42,274, and expenditures for the same period were NZ$393,671. Expenditure is devoted mainly to agriculture, the provision of social services, and administrative costs. Annual deficits are met by New Zealand government subsidies. Nutrition and health are reasonably high.

Ross Dependency
The Ross Dependency (between 160°E and 150°W and south of 60°S) is a section of the Antarctic continent that was brought under the jurisdiction of New Zealand in 1923. Its area is estimated at 414,400 sq km (160,000 sq mi). It is virtually entirely covered by ice and is normally uninhabited. New Zealand activities in the Dependency are coordinated and supervised by the Ross Dependency Research Committee (a government agency) and implemented by the Antarctic division of the Department of Scientific and Industrial Research. Exploitation of the region, apart from scientific expeditions, has been confined to whaling. A joint US-New Zealand scientific station established at Cape Hallett in 1957 for participation in the International Geophysical Year continues to operate for purposes of scientific research.

50 BIBLIOGRAPHY
Beaglehole, Ernest. *Mental Health in New Zealand.* Wellington: New Zealand University Press, 1950.

Beaglehole, John Cawte. *The Discovery of New Zealand.* London: Oxford University Press, 1961.

Beaglehole, John Cawte. *New Zealand: A Short History.* London: Allen & Unwin, 1936.

Best, Elsdon. *The Maori As He Was: A Brief Account of Maori Life As It Was in Pre-European Days.* Wellington: Government Printer, 1953.

Buck, Sir Peter Henry. *The Coming of the Maori.* Wellington: Maori Purposes Fund Board, 1949.

Condliffe, John Bell. *New Zealand in the Making: A Study of Economic and Social Development.* London: Allen & Unwin, 1959.

Condliffe, John Bell. *The Welfare State in New Zealand.* London: Allen & Unwin, 1959.

Condliffe, John Bell, and W. G. T. Airey. *A Short History of New Zealand.* Wellington: Whitcombe and Tombs, 1957.

Cumberland, K. B., and J. W. Fox. *New Zealand: A Regional View.* Wellington: Whitcombe and Tombs, 1963.

Cumberland, Kenneth Bradley. *South West Pacific: A Geography of Australia, New Zealand and Their Pacific Island Neighborhoods.* New York: Praeger, 1968.

Firth, Raymond William. *Economics of the New Zealand Maori.* Atlantic Highlands, N. J.: Humanities Press, 1959.

Fong, Ng Bickleen. *The Chinese in New Zealand.* Hong Kong: Hong Kong University Press, 1959.

Goldblatt, David. *Democracy at Ease: A New Zealand Profile.* London: Pall Mall Press, 1957.

Gordon, B. K. *New Zealand Becomes a Pacific Power.* Chicago: University of Chicago Press, 1960.

Hare, Anthony Edward Christian. *Report on Industrial Relations in New Zealand.* Christchurch: Whitcombe and Tombs, 1946.

Hoag, Malcolm W. *Political and Strategic Relations (Australia, New Zealand, United States): The View from Washington.* Santa Monica, Calif.: RAND Corporation, 1970.

Jackson, Keith, and John Harré. *New Zealand.* New York: Walker, 1969.

Larkin, T. C. *New Zealand External Relations.* London: Oxford University Press, 1962.

Lipson, Leslie. *The Politics of Equality: New Zealand's Adventures in Democracy.* Chicago: University of Chicago Press, 1948.

McClymont, William Graham. *Exploration of New Zealand.* London: Oxford University Press, 1959.

Miller, Harold Gladstone. *New Zealand.* London: Hutchison, 1950.

Milne, Robert Stephen (ed.). *Bureaucracy in New Zealand.* Wellington: New Zealand Institute of Public Administration, 1957.

New Zealand Business Who's Who. Wellington: Watkins Press, 1955.

New Zealand Government Economic Survey. Wellington: Government Printer, 1952–date (annual).

New Zealand Journal of History. Auckland: Department of History, University of Auckland (semiannual).

New Zealand Official Year Book. Wellington: Government Printer, 1896–date (annual).

Oliver, William Hosking. *The Story of New Zealand.* London: Faber and Faber, 1960.

Osborne, Charles (ed.). *Australia, New Zealand and the South Pacific: A Handbook.* New York: Praeger, 1970.

Oxford New Zealand Encyclopedia. London: Oxford University Press, 1965.

Padovan, Renzo. *The Maori as an Artist.* Wellington: Reed, 1957.

Parker, Robert Stewart. *Economic Stability in New Zealand.* Wellington: New Zealand Institute of Public Administration, 1953.

Polaschek, Raymond Joseph. *Government Administration in New Zealand.* Wellington: New Zealand Institute of Public Administration, 1958.

Polaschek, Joseph (ed.). *Local Government in New Zealand.* Wellington: New Zealand Institute of Public Administration, 1956.

Reeves, William Pember. *The Long White Cloud.* London: Allen & Unwin, 1950.

Robson, John Lochiel (ed.). *New Zealand: The Development of Its Laws and Constitution.* London: Stevens, 1954.

Ross, Angus (ed.). *New Zealand's Record in the Pacific Islands in the Twentieth Century.* New York: Humanities Press, 1969.

Scott, Kenneth John. *The New Zealand Constitution.* Oxford: Clarendon Press, 1962.

Scott, Kenneth John (ed.). *Welfare in New Zealand.* Wellington: New Zealand Institute of Public Administration, 1955.

Siegfried, André. *Democracy in New Zealand.* London: Bell, 1914.

Sinclair, Keith. *A History of New Zealand.* Harmondsworth: Pelican, 1959.

Sinclair, Keith. *Origins of the Maori Wars.* Wellington: New Zealand University Press, 1957.

Stevens, J. *The New Zealand Novel, 1860–1965.* Wellington: Reed, 1966.

Sutch, William Bell. *Poverty and Progress in New Zealand.* Wellington: Co-operative Publishing Co., 1941.

Sutch, William Bell. *The Quest for Security in New Zealand.* New York: Oxford University Press, 1958.

Tapp, Edwin John. *Early New Zealand.* Melbourne: Melbourne University Press, 1958.

Webb, Leicester. *Government in New Zealand.* Wellington: Department of Internal Affairs, 1940.

Who's Who in New Zealand. Wellington: Reed (annual).

Wood, Frederick Lloyd Whitfield. *New Zealand in the World.* Wellington: Department of Internal Affairs, 1940.

Wood, Frederick Lloyd Whitfield. *The New Zealand People at War.* Wellington: Department of Internal Affairs, 1958.

Wright, Harrison Morris. *New Zealand, 1769–1840: Early Years of Western Contact.* Cambridge: Harvard University Press, 1959.

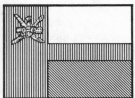

OMAN

Sultanate of Oman
Sultanat Uman

CAPITAL: Muscat (Masqat). **FLAG**: A new national flag, officially adopted on 17 December 1970, replaced the former simple red banner. The flag is red with a broad stripe of white at the upper fly and green at the lower fly; in the canton, white crossed swords overlay a ceremonial dagger. **ANTHEM**:*Nashid al-Salaam al-Sutani (Sultan's National Anthem)*. **MONETARY UNIT**: The Omani riyal (RO) of 1,000 baizas, established in November 1972, is a convertible paper currency. Both the Indian rupee and Maria Theresa thaler had previously been in use. There are coins of 2, 5, 10, 25, 50, and 100 baizas, and notes of 100, 250, and 500 baizas and 1, 5, and 10 riyals. RO1 = $2.8951 (or $1 = RO0.3454). **WEIGHTS AND MEASURES**:Official conversion to the metric system was completed on 15 November 1974. Both imperial and local systems had been used previously. **HOLIDAYS**: Accession of the Sultan, 23–24 July; the Sultan's Birthday, 19 November. Movable Muslim religious holidays include 'Id al-Fitr, 'Id al-'Adha', Milad al-Nabi, and al-Hijra. **TIME**: 4 P.M. = noon GMT. Solar time is also observed in the Sultanate.

¹LOCATION, SIZE, AND EXTENT

The Sultanate of Oman is the second-largest country after Sa'udi Arabia on the Arabian Peninsula, with an area estimated at 212,457 sq km (82,030 sq mi). Oman's territory includes the tip of the strategically important Musandam Peninsula, which juts into the Strait of Hormuz. Oman's part of the peninsula is separated from the rest of the country by the territory of the United Arab Emirates (UAE). Oman proper extends *972* km (*604* mi) NE–SW and *513* km (*319* mi) SE–NW. It is bordered on the N by the Strait of Hormuz, on the NE by the Gulf of Oman, on the E and S by the Arabian Sea, on the SW by the People's Democratic Republic of Yemen (PDRY), on the W by the Rub' al-Khali (Empty Quarter) and Sa'udi Arabia, and on the NW by the UAE. Oman's boundaries are only partially delineated; its estimated total boundary length is *3,234* km (*2,010* mi).

²TOPOGRAPHY

Physically, Oman, except for the province of Dhufar, consists of three divisions: a coastal plain, a mountain range, and a plateau. The coastal plain varies in width from 10 miles to practically nothing near Muscat, where the hills descend abruptly to the sea. The mountain range reaches its greatest height in the Jabal Akhdar at about 9,900 feet. The plateau has an average height of about 1,000 feet and is mostly stony and waterless, extending to the sands of the Rub' al-Khali, or Empty Quarter. The coastline southward to Dhufar is barren and forbidding. From Salalah, a semicircular fertile plain extends to the foot of a steep line of hills, some 2,000 to 3,000 feet high, and forms the edge of a stony plateau also extending to the sands of the Rub' al-Khali.

³CLIMATE

Annual rainfall in Muscat averages 4 inches. The rain falls mostly in January. Dhufar is subject to the southwest monsoon, and rainfall up to 25 inches has been recorded in the rainy season from late June to October. While the mountain areas receive more plentiful rainfall, some parts of the coast, particularly near Masirah Island, sometimes receive no rain at all within the course of a year. The climate generally is very hot, with temperatures reaching 54.4°C (130°F) in the hot season, from May to October. They seldom drop below 12°C (54°F) in the cold season.

⁴FLORA AND FAUNA

Desert shrub and desert grass, common to southern Arabia, are found. Vegetation is sparse in the interior plateau, which is large-

ly gravel desert. The greater rainfall in Dhufar and the mountains makes the growth there more luxuriant. Coconut palms grow plentifully in Dhufar, and frankincense grows in the hills. Oleander and varieties of acacia abound.

Animals include cheetah, hyena, fox, wolf, and hare. Birds include the Arabian see-see partridge, redleg chukor partridge, and the Muscat bee-eater. As of 1975, endangered species in Oman included the South Arabian leopard, dugong, Arabian oryx, Arabian gazelle, and Arabian tahr.

⁵POPULATION

In 1974, the total population was estimated at 740,000, with a density of 3.5 persons per sq km. The greatest concentrations are around Muscat and on the Batinah coast. Muscat and its environs have undergone a population explosion, growing from 25,000 to 80,000 during 1970–75. Salalah is the principal town of the south. About 85% of the population remains rural, including some 100,000 nomadic and seminomadic peoples. Average annual growth rate in the 1970s was 3.1%.

⁶ETHNIC GROUPS

The population is predominantly Arab except on the Batinah coast, where there are Baluchi, Iranian, and black elements, and in Muscat and Mutrah, where there are Khojas and other Indians, Baluchis and Pakistanis, and few Arabs. Tribal groups are estimated to number over 200.

⁷LANGUAGE

The language is Arabic. Urdu, Farsi, and several Indian dialects are also spoken, especially in the cities of Muscat aand Matrah.

⁸RELIGION

The religion is Islam. Approximately half of the population belongs to the Ibadhi sect. Tribes in the north are mainly Sunni Muslims of the Hanbali, Shafai, and Wahhabi rites. Pre-Islamic beliefs and practices survive among the nominally Wahhabi Shihuh tribe of the Musandam Peninsula.

⁹TRANSPORTATION

Until relatively recently there was only one road in Oman, a 10-km stretch linking Muscat with Matrah. By mid-1974 there were 400 km of first-class asphalt roads and a further 4,020 km of roads with maintained natural surfaces. A main coastal road has been laid from Muscat to Suhar, a distance of 240 km, and the first link in a road from Muscat to Buraymi on the UAE/Sa'udi Arabia border has been completed. In 1974 there were about 14,500 registered motor vehicles, as compared with 840 in 1970.

An international airport near Sib, 30 km northwest of Muscat, opened in October 1973; it is served by BA, Gulfair, MEA, Pan Am, and five other airlines.

A fully operative deepwater port at Matrah can handle 1.5 million tons of cargo per year. Salalah has a new port outlet at Raysut to handle an increasing trade in agricultural produce.

10 COMMUNICATIONS

In 1975 there were 15 post offices in Oman, as compared with 2 in 1970. Cable and Wireless operates a telegraph and telephone service at Muscat. In November 1975, the entire country was connected to a 12,000-line telephone network.

Recently developed radio and television facilities are government-owned. A 10-kw radio transmitter, built in 1972, broadcasts from Bait al-Falaj, and there are also transmitters at Sib and Salalah. A color-television station in Muscat was supplemented in February 1976 by a new station in Dhufar.

11 HISTORY

Oman's history can be traced to very early times. The descendants of Joktan (mentioned in the tenth chapter of Genesis) migrated as far as Dhufar (Sephar). Phoenicians probably visited the coastal region. Other groups that probably came to the area include the long extinct Baida and Ariba, Semitic tribes from northern Arabia; the first Himyar dynasty from Yemen, which fell to the Persians in the time of Cyrus, about 550 B.C.; ancient Greek navigators; and the Parthians (174–136 B.C.).

The entire population was converted to Islam during the lifetime of Muhammad, but Oman soon became the center of the Ibadhi sect, which maintained that any pious Muslim could become caliph or imam, and that the imam should be elected. The Oman tribes have elected their imams since the second half of the 8th century.

The first contact with Europe was in 1508, when the Portuguese overran Muscat. They maintained control until they were driven out with Persian aid in 1650. During the next 75 years, Oman conquered Mombasa, Mogadishu, the island of Zanzibar, and the Portuguese possessions in East Africa.

The first sultanate was established in Muscat about 1775. In 1798, Britain concluded its first treaty with Muscat. Sa'id bin Sultan (r.1804–56) became dependent on British support. Having rejected the Ibadhi tenet that the imam be elected, Muscat lost control of the interior, which was not regained until 1955.

In 1920, the Treaty of Sib was signed between the sultan of Muscat and the imam of Oman, acknowledging the independence of the imamate of Oman. From 1920 to 1954, there was comparative peace. On the death of the imam in 1954, Sultan Sa'id bin Taymur tried unsuccessfully to succeed him.

In 1954, Sa'id bin Taymur concluded a new agreement with the Petroleum Development (Oman) Ltd., an internationally owned but British-managed oil company that had the oil concession for Oman. By this agreement, the company maintained a small army, the Muscat and Oman Field Force (MOFF), raised and officered by the British. In early 1955, it subdued the area up to and including the town of 'Ibri. When the British occupied Buraymi, the MOFF occupied the rest of Oman and expelled the imam. In 1959, the last of the insurgents supporting the imam were defeated, whereupon the sultan voided the office and declared the Treaty of Sib terminated. The imam, exiled in Sa'udi Arabia, tried vainly to muster Arab support for his return.

The change of regime did not affect the controversy over the political status of the territory. The Anglo-French declaration of 10 March 1962 has been cited as the basis of the recognition of the Sultanate as independent in international law. The Arab states, however, have asserted that the UK was maintaining a colonial regime in the Imamate of Oman. In January 1970 and April 1971, the UN Assembly session reaffirmed Oman's right to independence. In late 1971, Oman joined the UN and has since retained close military and administrative links with the UK.

On 23 July 1970, Sultan Sa'id bin Taymur was ousted by his son, Qabus bin Sa'id. The new ruler changed the name of Muscat and Oman to the Sultanate of Oman.

Tribal unrest in Dhufar continues to plague the Omani government. Following the outbreak of a separatist tribal revolt in Dhufar in 1964, the rebels formed a group that later became known as the Popular Front for the Liberation of Oman and the Arab Gulf (PFLOAG). The insurgents received support from the PDRY and arms and equipment from the USSR and other Communist-allied nations. In February 1975, the PFLOAG's name was changed to the Popular Front for the Liberation of Oman and its aim reduced to the liberation of Oman alone. To curb the insurgency in Dhufar, Sultan Qabus expanded and reequipped the armed forces. In 1972, the first Iranian "task force" troops were sent to Oman at the sultan's request. During the next three years, with the help of Iranian troops and new armaments purchases, the government intensified its military operations against the guerrillas.

12 GOVERNMENT

Oman's sultan is an absolute monarch. The sultanate has no constitution, legislature, or legal political parties. In 1970, Sultan Qabus appointed a cabinet of ministers responsible for various government departments and functions. As of 1976, however, there was no collective responsibility.

13 POLITICAL PARTIES

There are no legal political parties.

14 LOCAL GOVERNMENT

The country is divided into 40 wilayats, governed by walis appointed by and responsible to the national government. The area of Muscat is administered by a governor. A system of rural municipalities was being organized in the 1970s, with responsibilities for land use, public health, and sanitation. By 1975, 11 rural municipalities had been established.

15 JUDICIAL SYSTEM

Shari'ah courts based on Qur'anic law administer justice, with the chief court at Muscat. Qadis or religious judges are appointed by the sultan, and function within each wilayat. There is also a foreigners' court at Muscat. Appeals from the chief court are made to the sultan, who exercises powers of clemency. The UK retains limited jurisdiction over British subjects.

16 ARMED FORCES

During 1970–75, Oman increased its regular armed forces from 3,000 to 14,100 men. The army had 12,900 personnel, the air force 1,000, and the navy 200. Another 1,500 men (Jebalis or mountain dwellers) are organized into paid home guard units (Firqat) in their tribal areas. All military service is voluntary. In addition to Omani forces, there were in 1975 some 300 British officers in service in Oman, an estimated 3,500 Iranian troops, and some 6,000 Baluchi tribesmen.

17 MIGRATION

There is frequent movement of workers between Oman and neighboring states. In the 1960s, an estimated 20,000 persons emigrated for political reasons. Many migrants have returned to Oman to work in its oil fields. In 1975, nearly 40,000 expatriates worked in Oman.

18 INTERNATIONAL COOPERATION

In 1971, Oman gained membership in both the Arab League and the UN. Oman is also a member of IBRD, WHO, IMF, IFC, and IDA. It has not, however, been admitted to membership in OPEC or OAPEC.

19 ECONOMY

Oman's location at the entrance to the Persian Gulf for centuries made it an entrepôt for trade, including a substantial traffic in arms and slaves. Its prosperity declined when, as a result of Western dominance in Asia, traditional trade patterns and communications routes were radically changed in the 19th century. Oman's economy became predominantly agricultural.

The situation changed with the discovery of oil in 1964. Production began in August 1967 and by the mid-1970s, most of the economy revolved around oil. Oil production provided about $1 billion annually, or about 90% of the government's total revenues and all of the country's foreign exchange. Present reserves, however, are not expected to last much beyond 1990.

20 INCOME
The GNP at factor cost rose from RO85.9 million in 1970 to RO132.7 million in 1973. The GDP at market prices stood at RO175.1 million in 1973. Per capita GNP, among the lowest in the world prior to the 1960s, stood at $566 in 1973.

21 LABOR
Unskilled labor is plentiful. More than 80% of the population is occupied in agriculture. The skilled local labor force is small, and many of the larger industries depend on expatriates from India and Pakistan. The nonrural labor force now numbers about 56,000 workers, of which Omanis account for only 20,000.

22 AGRICULTURE
The potential for expanding agriculture in Oman is good. Land use is determined primarily by the availability of water. There is extensive cultivation along the Batinah and Shumailiyah coasts. In the interior, cultivation is confined to areas near wadis where water is taken off by a system of water channels (fallaj). Motor pumps are coming into increasing use. The total area under cultivation is estimated at about 36,000 hectares.

The principal agricultural product is the date. On the Baunah coast, date groves form a strip 150 miles along and 25 miles wide. Fruits grown in Dhufar include bananas, plums, and coconuts. Citrus fruits (notably limes), nuts, and tobacco are grown in Oman. Along the Batinah coast, a wide variety of produce is grown, including fruits, wheat, rice, and durra. Agricultural production was valued at RO6.9 million in 1973.

23 ANIMAL HUSBANDRY
Goats, sheep, donkeys, and camels are widely raised. There is a relatively large-scale cattle-raising industry in Dhufar. The camels of Oman are famous for their fine riding qualities.

24 FISHING
The waters of the Gulf of Oman are rich in sardines, mackerel, crustaceans, tuna, marlin, parrot fish, and sharks. In 1972, the Ministry of Development engaged a US company to undertake onshore and offshore research with a view to setting up processing plants and improving fishing techniques.

25 FORESTRY
The use of wood as the sole fuel and overgrazing by goats have partially destroyed the forests of Oman, but the interior of the country is fairly well wooded.

26 MINING
Oil, discovered in 1964 in western Oman, has transformed economic life in Oman. Annual production during 1970–74 averaged 106.9 million barrels, and the estimate for 1975 approached 130 million barrels. Reserves are estimated at 5,250 million barrels. When production began in 1967, several foreign interests combined to form a majority backing in Petroleum Development (Oman). In July 1974, Shell participation dropped from 85% to 34%, Compagnie Française des Pétroles from 10% to 4%, and Partex (C. S. Gulbenkian Estate) from 5% to 2%; the remaining 60% is now owned by the government.

Copper deposits have recently been discovered northwest of Muscat. Chromite and manganese have also been found.

27 ENERGY AND POWER
In 1973, government-owned facilities had a total capacity of 21.4 Mw, with 17.1 Mw in the Muscat area. Production was 38.9 million kwh. The Ghubra desalination plant and attached power-generating station were completed in February 1976, at a cost of $54 million. The complex produces 6 million gallons of fresh water daily; the generating station was to have a 77-Mw capacity by the end of 1976.

28 INDUSTRY
Besides oil, industry in Oman still consists largely of small-scale food-processing enterprises. In 1975, industry and construction employed about 15% of the work force. In the mid-1970s, several new ventures were under way, including a cement plant, a flour mill, a natural gas fertilizer plant, and a gas liquefaction plant.

29 DOMESTIC TRADE
In Muscat and Mutrah, almost all business is carried on by long-established and settled Khoja and Hindu merchants. Normal business hours are 8 A.M.–1 P.M. and 3:30–6:30 P.M. from Saturday through Wednesday. Businesses close at 1 P.M. Thursday and remain closed Friday. Business hours are reduced during the Ramadan fast.

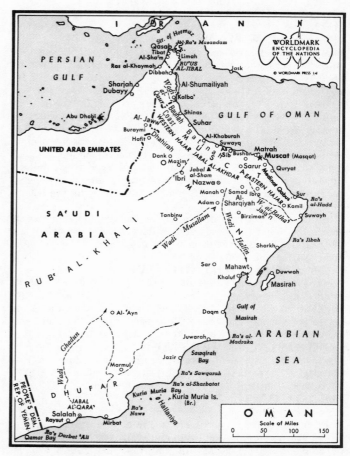

See continental political: front cover J7; physical: back cover J7
LOCATION: 53° to 60°E; 16° to 25°N. **BOUNDARY LENGTHS**: Total coastline, 1,860 km (1,156 mi); PDRY, 288 km (179 mi); Sa'udi Arabia, 676 km (420 mi); UAE, 410 km (255 mi). **TERRITORIAL SEA LIMIT**: 12 mi.

30 FOREIGN TRADE
Since 1967, oil has been the chief export. The main imports are food, machinery, textiles, cement, petroleum products, and motor vehicles; exports, aside from oil, consist chiefly of dates, dried limes, dried fish, tobacco, and hides.

In 1974, exports totaled $904.5 million, of which all but $1.2 million was from oil; imports were worth $711.1 million. Since 1972, the Gulf states have replaced the UK as Oman's principal source of imports, mostly transshipments. The UK remains the principal source of direct imports, followed by the Netherlands, Japan, India, and Pakistan.

31 BALANCE OF PAYMENTS

Slumping oil production led to a record payments deficit of $81.8 million in 1973. But this sum was reduced in 1974 when net receipts from the oil sector rose fourfold to $750 million. The 1975 balance was expected to show an even greater improvement. Reserves as of 31 December 1974 stood at $186 million.

32 BANKING

The Oman Currency Board, a central bank set up in April 1975, has powers to regulate credit and is authorized to make temporary advances to the government. The commercial banking sector expanded rapidly in 1974, with the number of commercial banks reaching 12 in 1975. Foreign assets of commercial banks showed a net increase of $103.9 million in 1974.

33 INSURANCE

In 1974, seven foreign insurance firms had outlets in Oman.

34 SECURITIES

There is no stock exchange.

35 PUBLIC FINANCE

The 1975 budget envisaged a drop in budgetary deficit from RO60 million in 1974 to RO38 million. However, the 1974 deficit was artificially high, as a result of the government's purchase for RO36.6 million of a 60% share in Petroleum Development (Oman). Capital expenditures on other projects in 1975 rose by about 23%, roughly paralleling the rise in oil revenues, which increased from RO298 million ($865 million) to RO387 million ($1,222 million). In 1975, defense expenditures absorbed more than capital development. The 1975 defense allocation of RO208 million represented about 45% of total outlays of RO461 million. In May 1975, the sultan decided to decrease nonmilitary spending further and to devote $800 million to financing the war.

36 TAXATION

Introduced in 1971, a corporate income tax on commercial enterprises other than individual traders remains the only tax in the country. Rates range from 5% on RO5,000 to 50% on incomes of RO500,000 and over.

37 CUSTOMS AND DUTIES

As of August 1974, the government abolished customs duties on imports of cement, rice, wheat and wheatflour, milk, cooking oils, sugar, meat, fresh fruits, and tea. Customs duties on cigarettes and tobacco are 77% and 37%, respectively, and vary from 1% to 17% on all other items except liquor.

38 FOREIGN INVESTMENTS

The principal foreign investments remain those in Petroleum Development (Oman). Foreign private investment is officially encouraged through an initial five-year tax holiday.

39 ECONOMIC POLICY

With the quintupling of government oil revenues in 1974 and a projected increase of 33% in 1975, the government planned to embark on an ambitious effort to modernize the economy. While development expenditures in the first half of the 1970s emphasized infrastructure and social services, the strategy at mid-decade turned increasingly toward income-generating projects, with emphasis on agriculture and fishing. A national development plan for the 1976–80 period is being prepared with IBRD assistance.

40 HEALTH

In 1975, there were 15 hospitals, with more than 1,200 beds. Facilities are grossly overburdened; some hospitals see as many as 1,000 outpatients a day. The shortage of locally trained personnel remains dire. Of the 2,500 people employed by the Ministry of Health, about 1,500 are expatriates, mainly from India, Pakistan, and Egypt. Average life expectancy in 1975 was estimated at about 49 years.

41 SOCIAL WELFARE

There is no public social welfare system.

42 HOUSING

In May 1973, Sultan Qabus approved the Law of People's Housing to make housing loans to people in low income groups. By 1975, 1,000 low-income units had been built. A new residential town, Medinat Qabus, containing 950 units, was to be completed in 1978.

43 EDUCATION

Only about 5% of the total population was literate in 1975. There were 176 schools, 6 of which offered postprimary instruction. In 1974 there were 1,225 teachers, including 225 women, and 34,830 pupils, of whom 7,658 (22%) were girls.

During 1975, two teacher-training colleges were to be opened and plans were begun for the first stage of an education project involving the construction of a primary teacher-training institute for 300 students, and a basic education and skill-training center for 280 female students in Muscat.

44 LIBRARIES AND MUSEUMS

A British Council library of 5,000 volumes was founded in 1972 in Muscat. In 1975, the construction of a national museum of archaeology and ethnology was under way at the Bait Nadir in Muscat; a temporary museum was opened in 1974 in Qurum.

45 ORGANIZATIONS

Social and cultural organizations in the Western sense do not exist in Oman.

46 PRESS

The only publication issued in the Sultanate is *Oman*, published weekly since 1972 by the government information service.

47 TOURISM

Tourists are discouraged, but it is expected that once development has reached sufficient levels vistors will be welcomed. Muscat's only hotel of international standard was completed in 1975. Two new hotels at Qurum were to be completed in 1976.

48 FAMOUS OMANIS

Oman's great religious leader, whose followers are called Ibadhis, was 'Abdallah bin Ibad (699–?). His teachings are still followed in Oman. Ahmad iban Sa'id (r.1741–83), founder of the present dynasty, freed Muscat from Persian rule. Sultan Qabus bin Sa'id (b.1940) has ruled Oman since his removal of Sa'id bin Taymur, his father, in 1970.

49 DEPENDENCIES

The Sultanate has no territories or colonies.

50 BIBLIOGRAPHY

American University. *Area Handbook for the Peripheral States of the Arabian Peninsula.* Washington, D.C.: Government Printing Office, 1971.

Kelly, J. B. *Sultanate and Imamate in Oman.* London: Oxford University Press, 1959.

Landen, Robert G. *Oman since 1856.* Princeton, N.J.: Princeton University Press, 1967.

Miles, Samuel Barrett. *The Countries and Tribes of the Persian Gulf.* London: Harrison, 1919.

Phillips, Wendell. *Oman: A History.* New York: Reynal, 1969.

Salil ibn Ruzaik. *History of the Imâms and Seyyids of 'Omâ, from A.D. 661–1856. . . .Continuing the History down to 1870,* by George Percy Badger. London: The Hakluyt Society, 1871.

Skeet, Ian. *Muscat and Oman.* Levittown, N.Y.: Transatlantic Arts, 1974.

PAKISTAN

Islamic Republic of Pakistan
Islami Jamhooria Pakistan

CAPITAL: Islamabad. **FLAG**: The national flag is dark green with a white vertical stripe at the hoist and a white crescent and five-pointed star in the center. **ANTHEM**: The opening lines of the national anthem, sung in Urdu, are "Blessed be the sacred land, Happy be the bounteous realm, Symbol of high resolve, land of Pakistan, Blessed be thou citadel of faith." **MONETARY UNIT**: The rupee (R) of 100 paisa is a nonconvertible paper currency. There are coins of 1, 2, 5, 10, 25, and 50 paisa, and notes of 1, 5, 10, 50, 100, and 500 rupees. R1=$0.10 (or $1=R9.93). **WEIGHTS AND MEASURES**: The metric system was introduced in 1966. **HOLIDAYS**: Pakistan Day, 23 March; May Day, 1 May; Independence Day, 14 August; Defense of Pakistan Day, 6 September; Anniversary of Death of the Quaid-e-Azam, Mohammad Ali Jinnah, 11 September; Christmas and Birthday of the Quaid-e-Azam, 25 December. Religious holidays, following the lunar Hegira, include Eid-ul-Fitr, Eid-ul-Azha, Jumat-ul-Wida, Muharram, and Eid-e-Milad-un-Nabi. Several holidays are local for the provinces. **TIME**: 5 P.M.=noon GMT.

¹LOCATION, SIZE, AND EXTENT

Situated in southern Asia, Pakistan has an area of 803,943 sq km (310,403 sq mi), extending *1,875* km (*1,165* mi) NE–SW from the ranges of the Hindu Kush and the Himalaya to the Arabian Sea and *1,006* km (*625* mi) SE–NW. The enclave of Junagadh, claimed by Pakistan, and Jammu and Kashmir, the final status of which has not yet been determined, are not included in the area. Pakistan is bordered on the NE by China, on the E by Jammu and Kashmir to the Karakoram Pass, on the E and SE by India, on the S by the Arabian Sea, on the SW by Iran, and on the W and NW by Afghanistan, with a total boundary length of *6,661* km (*4,139* mi).

²TOPOGRAPHY

More than two-thirds of Pakistan is arid or semiarid. The west is dominated by the Baluchistan plateau, consisting of arid plains and ridges. Rivers, streams, and lakes exist only seasonally. The arid south ends at the rugged Makron coast and rises to the east into a series of rock-strewn ranges, the Kirthar, and, northwards of the Bolan Pass, the Quetta, Bugti, and Sulaiman ranges, that extend to the Indus plains. A semiwatered plateau surrounds Rawalpindi, bounded to the south by the salt range. Southward, the extensive Punjab plains support a large population.

In the northern areas of Pakistan, the forest-clad hills give way to lofty ranges, including 60 peaks over 22,000 feet high. The principal ranges, trending NW-SE, include three Himalayan ranges—Pir Panjal, Pangi, and Zaskar—leading into the Muztagh and Karakoram mountains.

The Indus is the principal river of Pakistan. Its major tributaries are the Jehlum, Chenab, Ravi, and Sutlej.

³CLIMATE

Pakistan's climate is dry and hot near the coast, becoming progressively cooler towards the northeastern uplands. The winter season is generally cold and dry. The hot season begins in April and by the end of June the temperature may reach 49°C (120°F). Between July and September, the monsoon provides an average rainfall of about 15 inches in the river basins, and up to about 60 inches in the northern areas. Rainfall can vary radically from year to year, and successive patterns of flooding and drought are not uncommon.

⁴FLORA AND FAUNA

Forests cover only about 3.6% of Pakistan. The mangrove forests of the coastal region give way to the mulberry, acacia, and date palms of the sparsely vegetated south; the foothills support phulai, kao, chinar, and wild olive, and the northern forests have stands of oak, chestnut, walnut, pine, ash, spruce, yew, and fir. Above 10,000 feet, birch, dwarf willow, and juniper are also found.

Pakistan's wide range of animal life includes the Siberian ibex, sheep, bear, jackal, fox, wild cat, muskcat, hyena, porcupine, gazelle, peacock, python, and boar.

As of 1975, endangered species in Pakistan included the Indus dolphin, wolf, Baluchistan bear, Asiatic cheetah, Indian wild ass, Himalayan musk deer, river terrapin, marsh crocodile, gavial, Indian python, two species of leopard (common and snow), and four species of markhor (common, Kabul, straight-horned, and Chiltan).

⁵POPULATION

According to the 1972 census, the population of Pakistan was 64,892,000. The estimated population in 1975 was 70,560,000, and a total of 82,952,000 was projected for 1980. With the acquisition of independence by Bangladesh (formerly East Pakistan) in 1972, Pakistan's national population was reduced by about 70,000,000, or about 52% of the total. Prior to the separation, Pakistan had ranked as the sixth-largest nation in the world; in 1975, it ranked tenth.

Population growth averaged about 3.2% annually between 1970 and 1975. Nearly 45% of the population is under 15 years of age. The population density was about 88 per sq km in 1975. There was an increase of 27.1% between 1951 and 1961. Urban areas accounted for 19.8% of the population in 1951; the proportion rose to 22.5% in 1961, to 25.5% in 1972, and reached 26.9% by 1975. The following cities had over 100,000 inhabitants according to the 1972 census: Karachi, 3,469,000; Lahore, 2,148,000; Lyallpur, 820,000; Hyderabad, 624,000; Rawalpindi, 615,000; Multan, 544,000; Gujra–wala, 366,000; Peshawar, 273,000; Sialkot, 212,000; Sargodha, 203,000. The recently constructed national capital, Islamabad, had grown from a small village to a city of 77,000.

⁶ETHNIC GROUPS

In the western section of Pakistan are to be found the Baluchi, divided into 12 major tribes, some of them purportedly of Dravidian origin. In the area of the delta and the lower course of the Indus River are Sindhi peasant tribesmen and just to their north an isolated area of Brahui, of Dravidian origin. In the east-central region are the Rajputs and the Jats, elements of Indo-

Aryan origin who were converted to Islam many centuries ago. In the north and northwest are the hardy, warlike, nomadic and seminomadic Pathans. A number of Pakistanis trace their origin to the Arabian Peninsula.

7 LANGUAGE

Urdu is the national language, but English remains the common medium of government, law, commerce, higher education, and the upper middle class. During the Mughal period, a fusion of local dialects and Persian produced Urdu, a "language of the camp" (zaban-i-urdu). Although regional languages and dialects persist, Urdu is the main language of Pakistan; while it is spoken by only about half the population, it is understood everywhere except in the rural or mountainous areas on the western frontier. Punjabi, Pushtu, Gujarati, and Sindhi are important regional languages. Many other languages, including representatives of the Austric, Dravidian, Indo-European, Indo-Aryan, Iranian, Central Asian, and Tibeto-Chinese families, are spoken by small groups.

8 RELIGION

Pakistan is an Islamic state. In 1974, about 68 million people, some 97% of the population, were Muslim, giving Pakistan one of the largest Islamic communities in the world. Most of the Muslims are of the Sunni sect, although there is a substantial number of Shi'is. Members of the Isma'ili sect are concentrated at Karachi. Ahmadiyas, not accepted as orthodox by other Muslim groups, are mostly in Punjab Province.

Important minority groups include about 1 million Hindus and 700,000 Christians. A colony of Parsis (about 5,000), believers in Zoroastrianism, has long been established at Karachi.

9 TRANSPORTATION

Railways are the chief carrier of passenger and freight traffic. In recent years, the government has undertaken an extensive program to improve service. In 1974, Pakistan Railways operated 8,811 km of track and owned 92 locomotives, 3,174 coaches, and 37,256 freight cars. During 1973/74, the volume of passenger traffic was 7,200 million passenger-km.

In 1973/74, Pakistan's road system included 19,899 km of all-weather roads. The Karachi-Hyderabad superhighway was opened to passenger traffic in April 1970. There were 177,300 passenger cars and 79,100 commercial vehicles in use in 1973.

The natural harbor of Karachi, which provides Pakistan with its major port and serves also as the principal port for Afghanistan, covers an area of 6.5 sq km and handles over 10.5 million tons annually. Port Qasim is being developed 22 km south of Karachi to help handle the increased shipping traffic. In 1974, the government nationalized the shipping industry; in that year, the 58 oceangoing vessels under the Pakistani flag (7 passenger-cargo ships and 51 cargo vessels) constituted a total GRT of 667,000.

International airlines serving Karachi include Air France, Alitalia, BA, JAL, KLM, Lufthansa, Pan Am, SAS, Swissair, and Iran Air. The government-run Pakistan International Airlines (PIA) maintains domestic services as well as flights to Europe, the US, and the Far East. There is also an important airport at Islamabad.

10 COMMUNICATIONS

Postal, telegraph, and telephone services are owned and operated by the state. As of March 1975, there were 8,549 post offices. The number of telephones then in use totaled 221,000. Automatic telephone service has been installed in most cities and large towns. Radiotelephone and radiotelegraph services are available within the country and to foreign countries.

The government-owned Radio Pakistan operates shortwave and medium-wave transmitters. Karachi is the broadcasting center, and there are important transmitters at Hyderabad, Quetta, Lahore, Rawalpindi, Peshawar, Multan, Bahawalpur, and Islamabad. There are three television stations. In 1974 there were

about 1.3 million licensed radios and 130,000 television receivers.

Pakistan's Indian Ocean Intelsat communications stations began service in 1971 near Karachi.

11 HISTORY

Islam arrived in the Indian subcontinent in the 8th century A.D., following the invasion of Sind by an Arab general, Mohammad Bin Qasim, of the Umayyad Caliphate. In the 10th century, Muslims swept from the northwest through the Khyber Pass and established Muslim sovereignty over the northern areas of India as far as what is now Bangladesh.

Muslim power and culture reached a climax under the rulers of the Mughal Empire during the 16th and 17th centuries. Local Muslim figures continued to control much of India until well after the coming of the British in the first decade of the 18th century.

British power in India was gradually threatened by the steady growth of Indian nationalism, leading to the establishment of the Indian National Congress in 1886. When the Congress showed signs of becoming a vehicle of Hindu nationalism, the Muslims founded the All-India Muslim League in 1906 to safeguard Muslim interests. In 1930, Mohammad Iqbal, philosopher and poet of a striking Muslim renaissance, called for the creation of a separate, independent Muslim state. This goal was endorsed by the Muslim League in 1940. Another prominent Muslim leader was Mohammad Ali Jinnah, known as Quaid-e-Azam, or "the Great Leader." In his early life, Jinnah had been a member of the Indian National Congress. He led the movement for a separate Muslim state with such vigor and skill that all opposition was overcome.

Pakistan came into existence on 14 August 1947, when, in accordance with the terms of the Indian Independence Act as enacted by the British parliament, the vast subcontinent was partitioned into the dominions of Pakistan and India on the basis of Muslim and non-Muslim majority areas. Chaudhuri Rahmat Ali coined the name Pakistan in 1933 by taking the initials P.A.K. from Punjab, Afghan (for the Pathans of the Northwest Frontier Province), and Kashmir, and adding the remainder for Baluchistan. (Additionally, the word "Pakistan" means "the land of the[religiously] pure.")

Besides the effort to build a viable national economy and the continuing search for a form of government that would have broad acceptance, relations with India have been a dominant factor in the first three decades of Pakistan's independent existence. These have been influenced by disputes over the former princely state of Jammu and Kashmir and the division of the waters of the Indus and Ganges rivers. An Indus water basin treaty was signed in 1960.

However, the dispute over Jammu and Kashmir, which led to fighting in 1947–48 and a brief but all-out war in 1965, proved less tractable. In 1949, the UN secured from both parties acceptance of its recommendation that the status of this territory be determined by an impartial plebiscite, but they disagreed violently over the conditions for the vote. In 1965, Pakistan and India signed a declaration in Tashkent under which they agreed to withdraw their troops to the positions existing on 5 August 1965, prior to the outbreak of hostilities. When Indian forces joined the civil war in East Pakistan in December 1971, open hostilities also broke out in Kashmir. While Pakistani forces were routed in the East, fighting on the Kashmir front was inconclusive. A cease-fire line was agreed to on 17 December. Following the war, the Simla Summit Conference, convened on 28 June 1972, recognized the cease-fire line as a line of control to "be respected by both sides without prejudice to the recognized position of either side." The Simla Agreement held through the mid-1970s, although a political solution to the dispute remained in abeyance.

In the elections held in December 1970, the Awami League won all but one or two of East Pakistan's seats in the Constituent

Assembly, thus assuring itself a majority. The Pakistan People's Party (PPP) won a majority of West Pakistan's seats. The election was the first direct universal vote in the 23 years of Pakistan's independence. The inaugural session of the Assembly, convened by President Yahya Khan on 3 March 1971, failed to agree on a constitution redefining the status of the country's two divisions. Following the postponement of the session for party talks, the Awami League set up a parallel government in Dacca and all links with West Pakistan were severed.

Following the breakdown of further talks, tensions in the East reached an alarming pitch. In August 1971, East Pakistan's Mukti Bahini (Liberation Army) stepped up its guerrilla attacks on public installations and the regular army. As insurgent attacks intensified through the fall, the army responded with increasing severity, frequently indulging in bloody reprisals against the civilian population. On 4 December, following numerous incursions, massed Indian armed forces entered the conflict on the side of the Bengali insurgents. The battle quickly turned against the Yahya Khan government. On the afternoon of 16 December, Pakistani forces submitted to an unconditional surrender, and the secession of East Pakistan had become reality.

On 10 January 1972, Sheikh Mujibur Rahman, the long-time leader of the separatist movement in East Pakistan, arrived in Dacca following his release from prison by the Pakistan government. On 11 January, Sheikh Mujib, acting as president of the newly-declared independent nation of Bangladesh, issued a provisional constitution. India's formal recognition of the Bangladesh government was soon followed by that of the USSR and the UK. On 30 January 1972, Pakistan withdrew from the British Commonwealth.

Thus, with the formal and de facto succession of East Pakistan to the status of an independent state, the nation of Pakistan became coterminous with what had previously been the region of West Pakistan. The country had thus, in effect, lost 15% of its territory and 52% of its population to Bangladesh.

On 20 December 1971, President Yahya Khan resigned and was succeeded by Zulfikar Ali Bhutto, leader of the PPP. A new constitution that had the effect of strengthening the office of prime minister was adopted in a tense atmosphere on 10 April 1973. The constitution was brought into force on 14 August 1973, after which Bhutto assumed the office of prime minister. In parliamentary elections held on 10 August, Chaudhri Fazal Elahi was named the new president.

On 22 February 1974, Pakistan announced its formal recognition of Bangladesh; in April, a constitutional amendment terminating the claim to East Pakistan was adopted. In January 1976, Bangladesh opened an embassy in Islamabad. The mid-1970s also witnessed a gradual easing of tensions with India, as underscored by the resumption of trade between the two countries after a protocol signed on 26 November 1974. Tensions at home continued, however, as the government dispatched troops to Baluchistan in 1974 to quell a guerrilla uprising in the territory. On 10 February 1975, the Bhutto government dissolved the National Awami Party, the nation's largest opposition party, confiscated its property, and arrested over 300 of its members. The state of emergency proclaimed in 1971 was extended for six months on 4 March 1974 and again on 26 August. As of early 1976, however, the stern measures of the Bhutto regime appeared to be achieving a modicum of stability.

12 GOVERNMENT

The constitution that took effect on 14 August 1973 replaced that of 1962, under which the country comprised the two provinces of East and West Pakistan. It carries over the 1962 precept whereby Islam is the state religion and all existing as well as future laws are to be brought within the purview of the Qur'an and the Sunnah. The president is head of state, but the powers of chief executive are vested in a prime minister. The Parliament, a bicameral

legislature consisting of a National Assembly and Senate, jointly elects the president, who must be a Muslim over 45 years of age. The prime minister, whose advice to the president is binding, is elected by the National Assembly, of which he must be a member.

The National Assembly consists of 210 members, 200 of whom are elected directly by universal adult suffrage; in addition, until 1982, 10 seats are reserved for women, to be elected by members of the Assembly. The Senate has 45 members—10 members elected by each of the four provincial legislatures, 3 from the federally administered tribal areas, and 2 from the Federal Capital Territory (Islamabad). The voting age in Pakistan is 18.

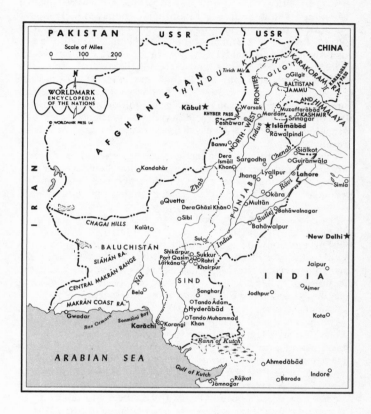

See continental political: front cover L6; physical: back cover L6

LOCATION: 23°41' to 37°5'N ; 60°52' to 77°49'E. **BOUNDARY LENGTHS:** China, *523* km (*325* mi), including boundary of Jammu and Kashmir to the Karakoram Pass; India, *2,028* km (*1,260* mi); Arabian Sea Coastline, *814* km (*506* mi); Iran, *830* km (*516* mi); Afghanistan, *2,466* km (*1,532* mi). **TERRITORIAL SEA LIMIT:** 12 mi.

13 POLITICAL PARTIES

Political life in independent Pakistan never succeeded in bridging the profound gap that separated the eastern and western wings of the country. Among the parties that brought Pakistan into being in 1947, the Muslim League emerged as preeminent, owing largely to its identification with the cause of Islamic nationalism. Initially composed of an aggregation of diverse political elements, the party in time became rent with internal rivalries. In provincial elections in East Pakistan in 1954, the Muslim League was defeated by a coalition called the United Front. Elements of the United Front included the Awami League and the Krishak Sramik Party. The Krishak Sramik, or Peasants and Workers Party, stood for the autonomy of East Bengal. The Awami League, originally the Awami Muslim League, collected adherents from those dissatisfied with the progress of the province under the Muslim League. The United Front broke up not long after the 1954 elections with its elements cast in opposition to each other. The Communist Party of Pakistan, banned by the government in 1954, continued to function underground. The Azad Pakistan Party appeared in West Pakistan in 1952 and established the reputation of being Communist-inspired if not Communist-controlled. In 1958, it apparently merged with a new radical grouping, the National Awami Party. In West Pakistan, the Republican Party was brought into being in 1956, originally to take over leadership from the declining Muslim League.

On 8 October 1958, the activities of all political parties were suspended by President Ayub. In 1962, the National Assembly legalized political activity but banned parties that worked against "the integrity and security" of Pakistan, or behaved in a manner "prejudicial to Islamic ideology," or received foreign aid. A new Muslim League was organized in 1962. Parties forming the opposition in the National Assembly were the National Democratic Front, the Awami League, and the Council Muslim League. In the March 1965 election, the Muslim League won 126 of the 155 seats in the Assembly. On 25 March 1969, amid civil disorder in both East and West arising from opposition demands for direct elections and parliamentary rule, Ayub Khan resigned in favor of Maj. Gen. Mohammad Yahya Khan, who proceeded to rule as president under martial law.

Numerous political realignments during the 1960s produced a new array of groupings contesting the national elections held in December 1970. Three wings of the reconstituted Muslim League of 1962 emerged to back separate slates of candidates in 1970. While the Muslim League's power had grown diffuse, the Awami League, led by Sheikh Mujibur Rahman, had consolidated its strength in the East. The political vacuum in the West was meanwhile becoming filled by the left-wing Pakistan People's Party (PPP), founded in 1967 by Zulfikar Ali Bhutto, a former foreign minister. A total of 291 seats were contested in the elections of 7 December 1970. The results gave the Awami League 151 seats; the PPP, 81; various other parties, 37; and independents, 16.

The new National Assembly was convened on 3 March 1971. The Assembly's legal existence, however, had been predicated on its task of promulgating a new constitution. On the grounds that a common course could not be agreed to by the Awami League and the PPP, President Yahya Khan ordered a postponement of the Assembly. The action was bitterly opposed by the Awami League, which moved swiftly to begin forming an independent polity in the East. During the evening of 25/26 March, Sheikh Mujib was arrested and taken to West Pakistan, where he was tried on charges of treason and imprisoned. As the crisis deteriorated into civil war, Yahya Khan announced on 26 March the outlawing of the Awami League.

Following the war, which resulted in the victory of Indian-backed secessionist forces in the East and the establishment of the independent state of Bangladesh, Yahya Khan resigned on 20 December 1971 and was replaced as president by the PPP leader, Ali Bhutto. During April 1973, the National Assembly was reconvened to draft the new constitution, which came into force on 14 August 1973. In elections for the newly created Senate held during 4-10 July, the PPP won a majority of 33 of the 45 seats; the National Awami Party (NAP) took 8 seats and formed the major opposition; the remaining parties and independents held 4 seats. Ali Bhutto acceded to the office of prime minister on 14 August. The NAP, which drew its major strength from Northwest Frontier Province and Baluchistan, became increasingly outspoken in its attacks on the Bhutto government's use of military force to quell insurgent activity in Baluchistan. On 10 February 1975, the government banned the NAP and arrested over 300 of its members, thus effectively eliminating the only serious political opposition to the Bhutto regime.

14 LOCAL GOVERNMENT

Pakistan is divided into four provinces—Punjab (with its capital at Lahore), Sind (Karachi), Northwest Frontier (Peshawar), and Baluchistan (Quetta). Each province has a popularly elected provincial assembly and a governor appointed by the president. The governor acts on the advice of a chief minister who is elected by the local assembly. In addition to the provinces, there are 10 federally administered tribal areas and the Federal Capital of Islamabad. The provinces, tribal areas, and Federal Capital are all represented in the federal Senate. There are also 11 tribal areas directly administered by provincial governments. The Pakistani-controlled segment of Jammu and Kashmir, referred to as Azad Kashmir, is administered by an appointed president and council of ministers; the seat of government is Muzaffarabad.

A Council of Common Interests, comprising the four provincial chief ministers and four members nominated by the prime minister to represent the federal government, formulates and manages policies largely affecting economic and infrastructural development in the provinces.

The Basic Democracies Order of 26 October 1959 provided for a pyramidal structure of basic democracies that has at the lowest level the union councils in rural areas and town committees in urban areas. Just above are tahsil councils, for areas larger than villages or urban areas, but smaller than districts, then district councils, and, finally, division councils.

15 JUDICIAL SYSTEM

The judicial system comes directly from the system that was used in British India. The Supreme Court of Pakistan has original, appellate, and advisory jurisdictions. The president of Pakistan appoints the justices. Each province has a high court, the judges of which are also named by the president. Immediately below the high courts are district and session courts, and below these are subordinate courts and village courts on the civil side and magistrates on the criminal side.

Emphasis has been placed upon the British tradition of an independent, impartial judiciary. The 1973 constitution sought to strengthen this independence by providing for removal of judges only by the Supreme Judicial Council, consisting of the chief justice and two ranking judges from both the Supreme Court and high courts. An attorney general, appointed by the president, has a right of hearing in all cases.

16 ARMED FORCES

In 1975/76, Pakistan's armed forces totaled 392,000. The army's strength of 365,000 was composed of 4 armored brigades, 13 infantry divisions, and 1 air defense brigade. The navy, with a manpower of 10,000, had 3 submarines, 6 40-ton midget submarines, 4 destroyers, 4 frigates, and 14 patrol boats. The air force, with a total strength of 17,000 men, had 278 combat aircraft. Paramilitary forces, including frontier corps, armed tribal levies, and local defense units, totaled 55,000. Military service is voluntary. Defense expenditures in 1975/76 were estimated at R7,020 million.

17 MIGRATION

Prior to the 1971 civil war, migration was largely limited to Hindus moving to India, particularly from East Pakistan. A number of Muslims continue to migrate from India to Pakistan.

According to government estimates, about 60,000 Pakistanis (mostly professional and skilled workers) emigrate each year to accept better paying jobs. As of 1976, an estimated 100,000 Pakistanis were living in the UK, 50,000 in the United Arab Emirates, and 30,000 in Kuwayt. The government has taken restrictive measures to curb the flow of emigration.

18 INTERNATIONAL COOPERATION

Pakistan became a member of the UN in 1947, and is a member of its specialized agencies and of CENTO, a regional defense alliance. As an Islamic state, Pakistan is an active member of the Islamic Conference and participates in various Muslim Afro-

Asian organizations. Following the establishment of Bangladesh, Pakistan withdrew from both the British Commonwealth and SEATO in 1972. During the civil war, China rallied to the support of Pakistan, while the USSR, an offtime supplier of economic and military assistance to Pakistan, supported Bangladesh and India.

In 1960, Pakistan and India signed the Indus water basin treaty opening the way to the peaceful use and development of water resources.

Major funding for the Indus projects has been provided by the IBRD and IDA, as well as by the Asian Development Bank, Japan, the US, Canada, France, Italy, the Federal Republic of Germany (FRG), and the UK. Both India and Pakistan have contributed heavily to the Indus Basin Development Fund, which directs the project.

Since the early years of independence through 1975, Pakistan is estimated to have received more than $9.4 billion in economic aid, making it one of the largest such recipients in the underdeveloped world. As of 1974, the IBRD and IDA had lent Pakistan more than $1 billion, including $286 million devoted to agriculture alone. During the mid-1970s Pakistan also received nearly $1 billion in aid from Iran and the Arab states. In the period 1972–75, the US contributed more than $200 million to Pakistan in the form of relief and economic assistance for a variety of projects.

19 ECONOMY

Pakistan is essentially an agricultural country. About one-fourth of the land is farmed or used for grazing; 57.3% of the labor force is engaged in agriculture; in 1974, 33% of the GNP derived from agriculture. Per capita income is low (about $110 in 1974/75) and most farming remains at primitive levels. Most of the cultivated area is in food crops for domestic consumption. Total agricultural production, which showed no rise in earlier years, began to increase remarkably in the late 1960s.

When the country was created, there were few industries, banks, or mercantile firms. Since that time, industrial production has risen significantly. By 1974, industry accounted for about 15% of the GNP and employed about 12% of the work force. Production growth has been aided by significant expansion of power facilities, largely in the Indus Basin. The most important sectors now include cotton textiles, fertilizers, cement, iron and steel, and electrical goods. Pakistan is generally poor in natural resources, although extensive reserves of natural gas are being uncovered. Small amounts of iron ore, petroleum, and low-quality coal are mined.

Despite the economic disruptions of the 1971 war, Pakistan's economy during the 1970s displayed notable resilience. Economic growth was about 5% annually, with the most significant gains coming in agriculture. During 1972–73, the government undertook large-scale nationalization of industrial and infrastructure facilities. Despite a 110% devaluation by the Bhutto government, inflation continues to be a major problem, averaging about 25% annually in the mid-1970s.

20 INCOME

The GNP increased from R32.3 billion in 1969/70 to an estimated R37.7 billion in 1974/75, representing an average annual increase of 3.3%. This growth rate, however, subsumed two countervailing factors, the severance of East Pakistan from the national economy in 1972, and inflationary pressures experienced throughout the period. Taking these elements into account, the GNP is calculated to have undergone a real growth of about 5% annually during the period. Due to the country's high birthrate, however, per capita income (at constant prices) remained virtually stable during the period, reported at R541 in 1969/70 and R544 in 1974/75.

The accompanying table lists the distribution of the GNP, by percentage, for 1971/72 and 1973/74:

	1971/73	1973/74
Agriculture, forestry, and fishing	33.3	32.6
Wholesale and retail trade	13.2	14.2
Manufacturing	14.1	14.3
Transportation and communications	6.0	6.5
Utilities	1.5	1.4
Construction	3.2	3.6
Other sectors	28.7	27.4

21 LABOR

In 1975, the total labor force was estimated at 20.5 million, compared with 12.7 million (in West Pakistan) in 1965. In the 1970s, the labor force was being joined by an additional 600,000 persons yearly. The low proportion of the labor force to the population of the country (about 29%) is in part attributable to the limited participation of women in the work force, thought to be no more than about 6% of the total. A labor census for 1971/72 showed that agriculture accounted for 57.3% of the total work force; industry, 12.5%; wholesale and retail trade, 9.9%; community and social services, 7.3%; transportation and storage, 4.8%; construction, 3.4%; and other sectors, 4.8%. In rural areas, some 70% of the population are engaged in agricultural pursuits. Underemployment and seasonal unemployment are major problems; in urban areas, unemployment has frequently gone as high as 15% in recent years. The Ministry of Labour operates employment exchanges.

Although the trade union movement is of recent origin, by 1974 there were 7,172 unions, with a membership of 741,174; most unions belonged to the All-Pakistan Confederation of Labour, with about 370,000 members, or the All-Pakistan Federation of Trade Unions (255,000 members as of mid-1974). Both groups are affiliated with the ICFTU. Labor-management differences are handled by the central conciliation machinery, established under the provisions of the Industrial Disputes Act of 1947. Disputes not resolved by this organization are referred to special industrial tribunals.

Labor unrest has been a continuing problem. The government has created a National Industrial Relations Council to promote the growth of national trade unions and to adjudicate disputes with nationwide impact. Benefits such as bonuses, paid holidays, and job security regulations are set forth in the basic West Pakistan Industrial and Commercial Employment Ordinance of 1968. A social security scheme introduced in 1967 covered some 449,000 industrial workers as of March 1975. Workmen's compensation (the basic law passed in 1923) and child labor provisions (1972) are also in force. By mid-1975, 49 local labor courts had been established to hear grievances and preside over disputes.

22 AGRICULTURE

Agriculture occupies the vast majority of Pakistan's population and is the largest single contributor to the GNP (32.6% in 1973/74, including forestry and fishing). Total cultivated area in 1974 was somewhat over 10 million hectares. The development of a huge irrigation network—by 1975, covering two-thirds of the total cultivated area—together with massive land reclamation projects, has made possible the farming of vast tracts of previously barren and unusable land. Grains constitute the most important food crops, with wheat, rice, and corn the major products. Cotton, the most important cash crop, generates more foreign trade income than any other export item. Sugarcane, tobacco, rope, and mustard, and—as a recent development—rice are also large export earners.

Wheat is the staple food. Pakistan was practically self-sufficient in wheat immediately following partition, and in 1950 exported some 140,000 tons. Mainly because of water shortages and deterioration of soil fertility, however, production fell below its prewar level in 1951/52 and tended thereafter to recover only gradually. In 1952–54, emergency imports of wheat were obtained. Since then, owing largely to the implementation of Indus Basin irrigation schemes, wheat production has risen from an annual yield of about 3.1 million tons to an annual average of 6.9 million tons during 1970–74. In 1974/75, 5.8 million hectares were sown in wheat. In 1974/75, 2.2 million tons of rice were produced on 1.6 million hectares, and in 1973/74 substantial quantities of rice (valued at $212 million) were made available for export. In 1973/74, 695,000 tons of corn were produced on 608,000 hectares.

Pakistan is a leading cotton exporter. The bulk of the crop covering a total of 2,031,000 hectares in 1974/75 is grown in the Indus Valley; output was 3,567,000 bales (of 392 lb each). Production totals for other major export crops in 1973/74 were sugarcane, 22.7 million tons; rope and mustard, 282,000 tons; and tobacco, 62,000 tons.

Farming production remains limited by primitive methods, and mechanization is uncommon. The introduction of improved wheat and rice varieties has met with some success, although the greatest impact on agriculture has derived from the Indus Basin irrigation schemes, which had, by the 1970s, provided Pakistan with the largest irrigated network in the world. When completed in the 1980s, the project is expected to transform Pakistan's agricultural capacity. The increased availability of water has made possible increased use of chemical fertilizers; in 1974/75, 427,000 tons were consumed, with the most intensive consumption occurring in cotton production. The government has instituted soil conservation, farm mechanization, land reclamation, and plant protection programs. The FAO has conducted soil fertility surveys along with a program to increase the use of fertilizers.

To increase smallholders' equity and provide further incentives for agricultural improvement, the government decreed in 1959 that the maximum holding for any person should be 500 acres of irrigated land or 1,000 unirrigated acres. Land in excess of these amounts was acquired by the government and paid for in interest-bearing 30-year bonds. In March 1972, the maximum permissible size of a holding, measured in terms of production index units, was reduced by two-thirds, with the government empowered to confiscate without payment all excess land for free redistribution to landless peasants and small tenants. As of 31 March 1975, 361,000 hectares were so confiscated, with 175,000 hectares redistributed in subsistence parcels among 53,458 impoverished farmers. To help the new landowners, the government provides loans for purchase of seed, feed, and bullocks.

23 ANIMAL HUSBANDRY

Camels are used for transport throughout the more barren south and west, bullocks and donkeys elsewhere. Sheep range widely over the grazing lands of middle and northern Pakistan and yield up to 20,000 tons of wool, the bulk of which is exported. Among local breeds of cattle, the Red Sindh and the Sahiwal are renowned for milk, and the Bhagnari and Dhanni for draft purposes.

In 1973/74 there were 12.7 million head of cattle, 17.5 million sheep, 400,000 horses, 900,000 asses, 90,000 hogs, and 5 million goats.

During 1973/74, exports of hides, skins, and leather were valued at R442 million; wool exports were worth R60.2 million. During the mid-1970s, special programs were instituted to develop egg and poultry exports, as well as to improve milk productivity.

24 FISHING

With a coastline of 814 km, Pakistan has considerable fisheries resources that are as yet not fully developed. Production in 1975 was estimated at 230,000 tons of fresh fish, most landed off coastal waters. Fisheries installations in Sind and Punjab were seriously damaged during the 1973 floods. Species include salmon, mullet, pomfret, mackerel, shrimp, and local varieties.

To exploit the potential fisheries resources, the government has undertaken such projects as a modern harbor for fishing vessels at Karachi, the procurement of diesel-powered vessels, cold storage and marketing facilities, the export of frozen shrimp, and the encouragement of cooperative fish marketing societies. It also promotes fish as a diet supplement among poorer Pakistanis.

25 FORESTRY

Only 3.6% of Pakistan's total land area (about 2.9 million hectares) can be considered as forest land. Of this total, however, only about 19,000 hectares are classified as commercial or productive forests.

Under Pakistan's dry climate, shrub jungle is more conspicuous than extensive forests. The acacia predominates and sal trees are highly regarded. In the submountainous regions of the north, there are extensive pine forests. Firewood is obtained from the forests of the Indus Basin. Some of the finest forests in the subcontinent are in the disputed state of Jammu and Kashmir.

In 1973, 8.8 million cu meters of round wood were produced (as compared with 18.4 million cu meters cut in 1970).

Protection and extension of the forest areas are the responsibility of several organizations of the state, including a forest college and research institute, and the Forestry Department. During 1973–75, 11,500 new hectares were forested, and some 230,000 trees were planted annually in the mid-1970s.

26 MINING

The prospecting and exploitation of mineral resources are subject to government planning and regulation. The Mineral Development Corporation and the Resource Development Corporation (RDC), both established in 1974, direct development of the mining sector and manage government-owned mining enterprises.

The mining sector contributes only about 1% to the GNP. Natural gas is by far the most valuable resource, with reserves estimated at 474 billion cu meters at the end of 1974. During 1973/74, 4.79 million cu meters of gas were produced. The government's Oil and Gas Development Corporation (OGDC), established in 1961, has carried out extensive aeromagnetic surveys which recently resulted in the discovery of three new gas fields, including one near Karachi. The fuller exploitation of natural gas reserves is expected to go far in offsetting Pakistan's lack of petroleum and coal for industrial uses. The OGDC has also had primary responsibility for petroleum exploration and development, although by 1974, private concessions were granted to private firms, several of US origin. Known reserves remain small; in 1973/74, 2.3 million barrels were produced.

Mineral reserves are meager and of poor quality. In 1973/74, production included limestone, 2,941,000 tons; rock salt, 369,000 tons; and gypsum, 214,000 tons. Local coal is of inferior types and the demand requires massive imports; coal production stood at 1,039,000 tons in 1973/74. Chromite is one of the few valuable minerals available in commercial quantities; in 1973/74, production totaled 13,000 tons. Smaller quantities of antimony, fire clays, iron ore, silica sand, and sulfur are produced. In 1974, the RDC began a large copper-mining operation in northern Baluchistan.

27 ENERGY AND POWER

During the past decade, energy consumption has expanded at an average rate of about 12% yearly. By 1974/75, total installed capacity was 3,150 Mw, of which 46.5% was from thermal sources, 46.2% hydroelectric, and 7.3% nuclear. Public utilities accounted for over 99% of the total. Production in 1974/75 reached 12,200 million kwh, compared with a national total of 6,700 million kwh in 1969/70. Some 44% of output is consumed by the agricultural sector, 32% by industry, and 24% by other commercial and domestic users.

Two factors have contributed to the recent growth of the power sector: the initial harnessing of the vast hydroelectric potential of the Indus Basin (estimated at 25,000 Mw), and the increased availability of natural gas as a fuel for thermal generators. The Indus Basin Development Fund built the Mangla Dam, completed in 1967 at a cost of $520 million; the dam produces 1 million kw of energy, and has a potential of 3 million kw. The Tarbela Dam, the world's largest earth- and rock-filled dam, completed in 1976 at a cost of $1.1 billion, will eventually generate 2.1 million kw of hydroelectric power. A Canadian-built nuclear plant at Karachi with a capacity of 137,000 kw began production in 1972.

During the period 1964–75, the number of villages receiving electrical service increased from about 2,500 to 3,500, and the number of consumers increased from 838,000 to 2,230,000.

28 INDUSTRY

The area from which Pakistan was formed was underdeveloped industrially, and since 1947 the government has given the highest priority to industrial development. During the late 1950s and 1960s, light industry expanded rapidly—especially textiles, fertilizers, and other manufactures derived from local raw materials. By 1974/75, industry's share of the GNP was 15.9%, compared with only 7% in 1950. Small-scale and cottage industries employ about three-fourths of Pakistan's industrial workers and account for about one-third of industrial production.

In November 1973, 10 basic industries were wholly nationalized and separate holding companies were established to oversee their operations. They produce chemicals, fertilizers, engineering products, petroleum products, cement, automobiles, and other industrial products requiring a high level of capital investment.

At the time of partition, Pakistan was producing 40% of the cotton output of undivided India but owned only 4% of the total number of textile mills. In recent years, many cotton textile plants have been built (there were 155 in mid-1955), and Pakistan has become self-sufficient in coarse and medium varieties of cotton cloth, and exports substantial quantities. Factories also have been established for the production of synthetic fabrics and woolen worsted yarn. Textiles, especially cotton yarn and cloth, now lead all other industrial products by value of output. Nearly 50% of the industrial work force are employed in textiles.

Highly mechanized establishments produce machines and machine parts, machine tools, electrical equipment, foundry components, rerolled steel products, soap, paints, varnish, bricks, ceramics and glass, sports goods, and surgical instruments. Chemical fertilizers have been given special impetus by the government, and in 1976, six large plants were in production and another eight were planned or under construction. In 1973/74, the country produced 566,400 tons of urea, 89,000 tons of ammonium sulfate, and 22,300 tons of superphosphate. Other important industrial products in 1973/74 were cement, 3,095,000 tons; refined sugar, 589,000 tons; vegetable ghee, 220,900 tons; and soda ash, 79,900 tons.

Government efforts to develop heavy industry began to bear new results in the mid-1970s. In 1974/75, fully 50% of federal public-sector investments went toward iron and steel and related industries. A shipbuilding works at Karachi is now capable of constructing five 15,000-dwt ships annually. Three oil refineries are in operation, two at Karachi and one at Rawalpindi, with a fourth under construction at Multan. The total 1975 capacity of 3.65 million tons was expected to be doubled by 1978.

With IDA credit assistance, the Pakistan Industrial Development Corporation is developing industrial estates for small- and medium-scale industries, is assisting the occupants in financing machinery and equipment, is providing technical and managerial assistance and certain common production facilities, and is assisting the occupants in obtaining credit and raw materials and in marketing their products. The Pakistan Industrial and Technical Advisory Center provides technical advice and administers programs to upgrade the skills of industrial workers. The Investment Advisory Center counsels both private and public industrial investment policies.

29 DOMESTIC TRADE

Nearly 15% of the national income of Pakistan derives from wholesale and retail trade, and many steps have been taken to improve marketing and distribution facilities. In the mid-1970s, the government began more actively supervising the supply and pricing of essential commodities, including fruits, vegetables, livestock, and dairy products.

Consumers' cooperatives were traditionally confined to employees of the government and of industrial enterprises. The government has established several cooperative marketing and distribution organizations.

Foreign goods are brought in by large importing concerns, centered at Karachi, and distributed to retailers through many intermediaries. There are several produce exchanges at Karachi, and the trade organizations are represented by the Federation of Chambers of Commerce and Industry.

Normal business hours are from 10 A.M. to 5 P.M. Friday is the day of rest.

Advertising remains small in scope, in part because of the high illiteracy. Outlets include newspapers, posters, handbills, and color slides shown in the motion picture houses. There is no advertising on Radio Pakistan.

30 FOREIGN TRADE

Pakistan's principal exports originally were only primary raw materials destined to be processed elsewhere, but there is a growing capacity to export manufactured goods, which during 1972–74 comprised 60.6% of all exports.

Principal exports in 1969/70 (for former West Pakistan) and in 1973/74 (in millions of rupees) were:

	1969/70	1973/74
Cotton manufactures	512	3,280
Rice	9	2,098
Leather	109	419
Raw cotton	210	376
Fish and fish products	83	276
Petroleum products	49	176
Other exports	637	3,536
TOTALS	1,609	10,161

Principal imports in 1969/70 (for former West Pakistan) and 1973/74 (in millions of rupees) were:

	1969/70	1973/74
Food grains	56	1,555
Machinery	709	1,196
Iron and steel	361	1,107
Transport equipment	340	1,078
Electrical goods	219	598
Chemicals	91	352
Tea	1	343
Pharmaceuticals	62	184
Other imports	1,446	7,157
TOTALS	3,285	13,570

Principal trade partners in 1973/74 (in millions of rupees) were:

	EXPORTS	IMPORTS	BALANCE
US	541	3,452	−2,911
Japan	633	1,126	− 493
UK	687	950	− 263

FRG	465	1,051	− 586
Sa'udi Arabia	397	893	− 496
Italy	491	300	191
Netherlands	159	515	− 356
China	39	571	− 532
France	266	343	− 77
Iran	329	221	108
USSR	256	181	75
Other countries	5,898	3,967	1,931
TOTALS	10,161	13,570	−3,409

The UK, traditionally Pakistan's most important partner, has slipped to third position in recent years behind the US and Japan. In the past decade, the US has come to account for between one-sixth and one-fourth of Pakistan's annual imports; a sizable proportion of US imports are financed by AID loans. The EEC countries constitute the largest bloc of trade partners, accounting for 22.5% of Pakistan's exports and 25.5% of imports in 1973/74.

31 BALANCE OF PAYMENTS
During the first decade after independence, Pakistan's foreign exchange earnings were concentrated in raw jute (produced in East Pakistan) and raw cotton. Exports of these two commodities were, however, exposed to frequent and sharp fluctuations in world prices.

The performance of exports did not show any significant improvement until the government introduced an export bonus scheme in January 1959. The scheme provided incentives to exporters through making a part of exchange earnings available to them in the form of bonus vouchers freely disposable in the market. Mainly as a result of the operation of this scheme, foreign exchange earnings increased at an impressive rate of 8% per year during 1960–69. During the 1970–74 period, exports increased in value by 129% overall, mainly because of inflation, but a high rate of real growth was sustained through mid-1973 and resumed in 1975.

The levels of imports doubled, however, during 1960–65, largely because of a notable increase in aid flows. Efforts to rationalize the imports were continued during the succeeding five years. In 1972/73, following the breakaway of East Pakistan, the government began import regulation on an annual (rather than five-year) basis. In general, purchases of consumer goods have been held down, while imports of agricultural and industrial raw materials have been liberalized.

Following several successive years of deficits, an overall surplus of $92.9 million was realized during 1968/69. A poor showing in export commodities incurred a sharp deficit in 1969/70, which widened further in 1970/71, a year wracked by economic chaos and war. In 1971/72, the government began a series of stern measures to restore confidence; a major devaluation of the rupee accompanied by an assiduous program of export promotion and import control produced a notable payments balance of $152.5 million in 1972/73. Thereafter, unfavorable world conditions combined with adverse crop conditions at home to produce rapidly widening shortfalls through the mid-1970s. However, a $580-million loan for 1975–77 and debt reschedulings in the amount of $650 million were expected to enable Pakistan to weather the period. As of 31 March 1975, reserves of the State Bank held firm at $409 million, a slight increase over holdings of $403 million at the end of June 1974.

32 BANKING
The State Bank of Pakistan, established in 1948 at Karachi, with branches in the larger cities, is the central banking institution. The government holds 51% of the bank's paid-up capital; 49% is held by corporations, societies, and individuals. The State Bank has exclusive responsibility for the issuance of currency; it is the financial agent of the central and provincial governments, is responsible for the flotation and management of the public debt, and has other defined functions. On 31 March 1975, currency in circulation amounted to R11,767.4 million, and the State Bank held R4,768 million in foreign assets. Of a total of R14,418 million in reserve money, R3,531 million involved foreign liabilities.

On 1 January 1974, 15 of the nation's largest commercial banks (classified as "scheduled banks") were nationalized and regrouped under 5 state banking institutions: the National Bank of Pakistan, Habib Bank, United Bank, Muslim Commercial Bank, and Allied Bank of Pakistan. By March 1975, the government-controlled banking system thus came to comprise all but 36 of the nation's 4,485 bank branches, accounting for 91.8% of total bank deposits and 92.5% of outstanding domestic credit. Shareholders of the scheduled banks were compensated in the form of State Bank bonds. The Pakistan Banking Council has been established to review organizational and operational questions pertaining to the new banks.

Cooperative banks and smaller commercial banks, some with foreign backing, continue to function. At the end of March 1975, cooperative banks held R198.9 million in demand deposits and R285 million in time and savings deposits. The post office savings system reported R1,420 million in deposits as of 28 February 1975. The state also provides credit through the Agricultural Development Bank of Pakistan and the House Building Finance Corporation; industrial loans are made available through the Pakistan Industrial Credit and Investment Corporation (established in 1957), the Industrial Development Bank of Pakistan (1961), and the National Development Finance Corporation (1973), which functions in the public sector.

33 INSURANCE
Pakistan's life insurance sector was nationalized in 1972 and placed under the aegis of the State Life Insurance Corporation of Pakistan (SLIC). One of SLIC's first steps was to standardize and reduce premium rates and to encourage coverage among a wider segment of the population. During 1974, the total life investment portfolio rose from R1,401 million to R1,576 million; ordinary life premiums increased by 6.5%, and group life premiums by 18.8%. The total value of life insurance in force in 1974 was about R17 billion.

At the end of 1973, there were 28 domestic and 22 foreign (mostly UK) companies covering general insurance. Total volume of gross non-life premiums in that year amounted to R319.9 million; the two largest classes of non-life insurance were marine, 52% of the premiums, and fire, 27%.

34 SECURITIES
There are stock exchanges at Lahore and Karachi, with the latter (founded in 1949) accounting for a major share of the business. The Securities and Exchange Authority of Pakistan regulates the securities market and supervises the activities of listed companies. Speculation and profit taking are prevalent, and there are wide fluctuations in many stocks of local enterprises. Rules passed since 1971 have aimed at fuller disclosure of accounts to shareholders and a closer accounting of the activities of major shareholders. Government securities remain fairly stable, benefiting from price support by the State Bank of Pakistan. The State Bank can exercise certain protective functions. Between June 1974 and April 1975, the number of companies listed on the Karachi exchange grew from 264 to 283; the turnover of shares increased from 110.5 million to 365.2 million and the aggregate market value of shares rose from R35.5 million to R45.4 million.

The government-sponsored Investment Corporation of Pakistan (established in 1966) provides a mechanism for wide distribution of the equities of public limited-liability companies and offers services for the management of investors' portfolios. As of March 1975, the corporation had floated six mutual funds worth R70 million.

35 PUBLIC FINANCE

The fiscal year extends from 1 July to 30 June. The federal government frames two separate budgets: revenue (current account) and capital. Deficits have appeared annually since 1971/72, a combined result of the loss of revenues from East Pakistan and stepped-up defense expenditures, which, by 1973/74, accounted for a weighty 41.5% of current outlays. Interest payments on the public debt have become the second largest expenditure. The federal revenue budgets (in millions of rupees) for 1970/71 and 1973/74 were as follows:

	1970/71	1973/74
REVENUES		
Excise duties	1,736.9	3,872.0
Customs duties	2,099.9	2,528.0
Income and corporation taxes	222.1	757.2
Sales tax	164.7	427.4
Other revenues	22.8	344.5
TOTAL	4,246.4	7,929.1
EXPENDITURES		
National defense	3,201.5	4,741.5
Debt services	923.5	2,124.0
Civil administration	806.5	1,217.5
Development expenditure	253.0	534.0
Transfers to provincial governments	244.7	253.7
Other expenditures	322.1	2,556.1
TOTAL	5,751.3	11,426.8

Capital budget expenditures more than doubled between 1970/71 and 1974/75, rising from R5,540.4 million to R11,728.2 million. Of the 1974/75 total, 60.2% was earmarked for economic development. Financing from domestic resources accounted for R4,901.0 million (46.8% of the total); funds from external resources (loans and grants from foreign governments for projects and commodities) accounted for R5,567.9 million (53.2%). Gross disbursements of external resources to Pakistan from developed market economies and multilateral agencies in 1974/75 was $1,022 million; of the total, $254 million was expended on debt service, leaving $768 million in net transfers.

Since July 1970, the four provinces have framed their own budgets, which provide the main support for education and health. Revenue (current-account) budget totals for the provincial governments for 1974/75 (in millions of rupees) were as follows:

	REVENUES	EXPENDITURES
Baluchistan	316.2	380.4
Northwest Frontier	381.7	557.2
Punjab	2,034.0	2,429.3
Sind	895.4	1,100.6

As of 30 June 1974, Pakistan's total external debt stood at $5,581.5 million, of which $4,395.2 million was in outstanding or disbursed obligations. Massive short-term debt rescheduling was arranged by Pakistan's Western aid sources following the civil war. During 1974/75, following further arrangements for rescheduling, Pakistan was allotted a total of $1,743.7 million, of which $896.1 million was pledged from new agreements with Iran and other Muslim countries.

36 TAXATION

Pakistan lives predominantly by foreign trade, and its import tariff is essentially revenue-producing. Customs and excise duties amounted to 61.8% of total revenues in 1974/75, while income and corporation taxes provided only 5.6%.

The national government does not levy income tax on agricultural income, and personal and noncorporate business incomes below $1,260 a year are also exempt from income tax. Rates are progressive, rising from 2.5% in the lower category to 80% in the higher, the latter rate including a surtax. Total tax payable, however, may not exceed 70% of income.

The basic corporation tax is an income tax on total taxable income at a flat rate equivalent to 30%. In addition there is a 30% surtax (35% for banks) on which rebates are available for public companies (5%), food-processing industries (10%), and exporters (up to 25%), among other categories. A capital gains tax ranges from 5% to 20% and a 20% tax is applied to stock dividends of non-public companies.

Other important federal tax sources are a single-point sales tax, payable only once by importers, and a salt tax.

Established proportions of the various taxes levied by the federal government are distributed to the provincial governments. In addition, the provinces collect for their exclusive use taxes on land revenue, immovable property, vehicles, professions and services, mineral rights, and excise taxes. Municipalities and other local governments also levy taxes.

37 CUSTOMS AND DUTIES

Pakistan's customs tariff brings in the major share of national revenue. Of the nearly 600 categories of tariff items listed, just over 100 are duty-free. Most dutiable items are subject to ad valorem duties that range from 3% to 300% (such as on certain classes of automobiles), with the average about 30%. The use of a tariff for protection now covers more than 15 developing local industries. Tariffs are levied on major items of export, but these rates are subject to change as measures are taken to encourage or discourage the export of raw materials. A tariff commission makes recommendations in a number of related fields and these suggestions are usually implemented by the government.

Import customs receipts increased from R1,736.9 million in 1970/71 to R2,750 million in 1974/75.

38 FOREIGN INVESTMENTS

Foreign aid and investments have played a critical role in Pakistan's economic development since the first years of independence. Since 1954, the government has tried to attract foreign investment to maintain economic development, provide specialized technical knowledge, and bring in much-needed foreign exchange. Incentives for private investments include guarantees for the repatriation of capital invested in approved industries, facilities for remittance of profits, and guarantees for equitable compensation in the event of nationalization of an industry. In addition, special tax concessions available to certain local industries also are available to foreign investors. In 1958, in order further to attract foreign investment, the government waived an existing requirement that a fixed percentage of local capital, usually 40%, must be associated in foreign-supported enterprises.

At the end of 1960, the UK provided the bulk of private foreign investment ($170 million), followed by India ($90 million) and the US ($60 million). Such investments from mid-1965 to March 1970 amounted to $333.3 million. The largest investment came from the US ($143 million), followed by the UK ($24 million) and Japan ($9.4 million). The total comprised investments from about 24 countries. Foreign investments in 1974/75 amounted to $300 million, of which $100 million came from US sources.

Commitments of assistance from governmental and intergovernmental sources, which began in 1950, reached $10.6 billion by mid-1975 (excluding $874 million allocated through the Indus Basin Development Fund). Of the total, $8 billion was in the form of loans repayable in foreign exchange and $2.6 billion was in grants.

39 ECONOMIC POLICY

The government's economic policy has concentrated attention on achieving self-sufficiency in food, developing the export industry, and, in the 1970s, expanding the scope of nationalization. Policy making was previously the province of the National Economic Council, but, since enactment of the 1973 constitution, major policy changes have been orchestrated through direct authority of the central government.

In 1971/72, following the secession of East Pakistan, multiyear planning was discarded in favor of yearly projections. Under the Bhutto government, radically new programs have been launched, largely with the purpose of transforming the public sector into a dominant and controlling force within the national economy, while reducing the size and potency of the private sector's economic role.

A major new land reform program introduced in March 1972 had, by March 1975, resulted in the confiscation (for eventual redistribution) of 45.3% of all privately cultivated farmland. By September 1973, the government had nationalized industries in 11 major categories of production: iron and steel; basic metals; heavy engineering works; heavy electrical equipment; motor vehicle assembly and manufacture; tractor assembly and manufacture; basic chemicals; petrochemicals; cement; public utilities, including electricity generation and oil and gas transportation and distribution; and vegetable ghee production. Shipping and life insurance also were brought under government control. In a third major step, most of the commercial banks were nationalized on 1 January 1974, resulting in control of more than 90% of all banking business by the State Bank and the five newly created banking units.

In the mid-1970s, considerable efforts were being made to redress the adverse balance-of-payments situation which was leading the economy further into overseas debt obligations. The level of investments was raised significantly, with private-sector development outlays reaching R5.8 billion and public outlays R850 million in 1974/75; in that year, investments were expected to comprise 19% of GNP, compared with 13% in 1972/73. The government thus sought to sustain an annual growth rate of 6% through the 1970s, the minimum rate necessary to effect real changes in living standards among a population that is expanding at a rate of 3% annually.

40 HEALTH

In 1947, all of Pakistan had only 3,000 physicians and 2 medical schools. By 1975 there were about 10,000 doctors, about one-third of whom were women, and the 14 medical schools were graduating about 1,000 physicians a year, a figure expected to rise to 3,500 by 1980. Many medical students are sent abroad under a higher medical training program. Special attention is given to the training of nurses, and several training centers are in operation. In 1975, there were about 4,000 nurses and female health aides. The country had 38,835 hospital beds in 1975, the vast majority located in urban areas. About 160 health centers and 400 lesser facilities serve the rural population.

Despite notable advances in health-care provision, more than 85% of the population is without modern medical care. Medical personnel ratios remain alarmingly low: 1 doctor per 7,056 persons and 1 nurse per 17,640. The general level of sanitation is poor. The government has made a continuing effort to deal with the specific health problems of Pakistan: malaria, tuberculosis, intestinal diseases, venereal diseases, and skin diseases. Average life expectancy in 1975 was estimated at 52.3 years. A smallpox eradication program undertaken with WHO was pronounced successful as of November 1974.

A people's health scheme, announced in March 1972, envisioned the gradual extension of basic health care and low-cost medicines to the mass of the population, but the scheme was soon dropped, ostensibly because of poor organization. A nationwide health survey, later undertaken with UNDP/WHO assistance, was expected to provide the basis for a new effort in national health care.

41 SOCIAL WELFARE

Although traditionally described by its leaders and politicians as an Islamic social welfare state, Pakistan has been slow in taking over major responsibility for such welfare problems as unemployment, sickness, handicaps, and old age.

Until the 1970s, the full scope of social welfare programs remained to be acknowledged and implemented in Pakistan. Some modest improvements were effected through the setting up of service units in rural communities, the institution of pilot projects to overcome extreme poverty, the opening of centers for the vocational training of the handicapped, and the inclusion of instruction in local welfare in the schools. A social security scheme enacted in 1967 covered only about 449,000 workers, or 17% of the industrial work force by March 1975. Some 225 social security medical-care units are maintained around the country. Since 1973, cost-of-living allowances have been paid to workers earning less than R1,000 monthly (as of mid-1975). In 1976, the ILO was assisting the government in completing an old age pension scheme.

The dangers of overpopulation shook the government out of its apathy toward social welfare. The third five-year plan (1965–70) allocated R284 million for implementing a population planning program, the objective of which was to reduce the annual birthrate from 50 to 40 per 1,000, aiming ultimately (by 1985) to reduce it to 35. A population planning council, assisted by provincial planning boards, supplies contraceptives. By early 1976, when the new program of "contraceptive inundation" began to show clear results, an estimated 20% of Pakistan's fertile couples were using contraception and live births had fallen to about 44 per 1,000 population.

In 1950, the National Council of Social Welfare was established to coordinate voluntary social welfare organizations. Programs concerned with the welfare of women are coordinated under the All-Pakistan Women's Association. Several other nongovernmental organizations continue to be active.

42 HOUSING

In the field of housing, major attention focused on care for the 10.5 million urban displaced persons who migrated from India to Pakistan following partition in 1947. By 1958, satellite towns and colonies had been established in West Pakistan to house 136,000 displaced families, and 42,000 dwelling units had been provided in Karachi for poor and destitute displaced persons. Financing was derived from the Rehabilitation Tax Fund and from US aid.

Demands for low-cost housing are met in part through the government's House Building Finance Corporation, whose activities are largely confined to the provision of sites and services, with construction undertaken by the private sector. Attention has focused on housing developments in Karachi and Lahore. Expenditures on housing provided for by the three five-year plans were R861 million in 1956–60, R850 million in 1960–65, and R2,477 million in 1965–70. Housing outlays in the 1974/75 development budget reached R728 million, a 544% increase over the 1971/72 allocation; the provision of 23,200 residential plots was called for during the year. Increases in drinking-water supplies for rural and urban dwellers and new sewerage systems for cities have also been major targets in the mid-1970s. However, the rapid increase in urbanization, coupled with the rising population, has added to the housing shortage in urban areas.

43 EDUCATION

Pakistan has one of the lowest literacy rates in the world. In 1975, only about 21% of the population over age 5 could read or write.

A massive educational reform announced on 15 March 1972 aimed ultimately to provide free and universal education through the tenth year of formal schooling. As an initial step, private educational institutions at all levels—numbering 3,181 in 1972—were nationalized. Additional goals included a reform of the curriculum away from general education and in favor of agricultural and technical subjects; equality of access to formal schooling for low-income groups and females; financial aid programs for poor students; and broad expansion and improvement of higher-level facilities. Curriculum bureaus have been set up at federal and provincial levels and a National Council of Education was established to formulate and evaluate educational development policy.

As of March 1975 there were 50,400 primary schools (an increase of 13,200 over the West Pakistan total in 1969/70) with 4,730,000 pupils; and 7,600 secondary schools with 1,509,000 students. There were 59 vocational and technical schools with a total enrollment of about 9,000. From 1970 to 1975, 52,000 primary school teachers were trained. Girls attend separate schools at both primary and secondary levels.

In 1975, about 66,000 students were enrolled at 214 degree-granting colleges and an additional 156,000 attended 145 intermediate-level institutions. Arts and sciences colleges are affiliated with the universities of the Punjab (at Lahore, established 1882), Sind (at Hyderabad, 1947; at Karachi, 1951), Peshawar (1950), and Karachi (1951). Construction of a Baluchistan University campus was under way in 1976 and plans were announced for establishment of Multan University in the Punjab. An agricultural university was established in 1961 at Lyallpur. Two engineering and technological universities have been established at Lahore (1961) and Islamabad (1966). Research institutions include the Institute of Islamic Studies at Lahore, the Iqbal Academy at Karachi, and the Pakistan Institute of International Affairs at Karachi. Urdu as well as English is used for instruction. In colleges and universities only English is used.

More than 16,000 adult literacy centers have been established in recent years, the majority in Sind. In addition, the People's Open University was established to provide mass adult education via correspondence and the communications media.

44 LIBRARIES AND MUSEUMS
The largest library in Pakistan is that of the Punjab University at Lahore, with a collection of about 265,000 volumes, including about 18,000 manuscripts. Other sizable collections are at the University of Karachi (200,000 volumes) and the University of Sind (105,000 volumes). Other important libraries are the Punjab Public Library in Lahore (200,000 volumes); the Liaquat Memorial Library (100,000 volumes), the Central Secretariat Library (15,000 volumes), and the National Archives (7,000 volumes), all in Karachi. A new National Library of Pakistan at Islamabad was under construction in 1976.

Interesting museums are more widely dispersed. The National Museum of Pakistan contains prehistoric material from the Indus Valley civilization, Buddhist statues and carvings, and material from the Islamic centuries, including the renowned Mughal period. The Peshawar Museum has a splendid collection of Buddhist sculpture of the Gandhara style. The Lahore Museum has an outstanding collection of Greco-Buddhist sculpture. Fine mosques, shrines, and mausoleums of the Islamic centuries are to be found, and among the best of the surviving gardens of the Mughal period are those at Lahore, including the Shalimar gardens.

45 ORGANIZATIONS
Numerous organizations advance a considerable variety of interests—cultural, welfare, religious, educational, and athletic. The Islamic community is represented by several flourishing organizations. Other religious communities, such as the Zoroastrians, have their own organizations. Within the Village Agricultural Industrial Development program, a number of service organizations are active: the Chand Tara Youth Clubs, development area councils, and village councils. The National Council of Social Welfare, established in 1956, displays a

proprietary interest in a number of welfare societies. The All-Pakistan Women's Association has been active for two decades. There is a Pakistan Boy Scouts Association and a Pakistan Girl Guides Association.

46 PRESS
In 1973 there were 102 dailies—most of them with a very small circulation—printed in Urdu, English, and a few other languages, and about 1,100 other periodicals. Most papers and magazines are published in the Punjab and in Karachi. Several Karachi papers publish editions in other cities.

Pakistan's leading daily newspapers (with their language and 1975 circulations, where available) are:

	LANGUAGE	CIRCULATION
KARACHI		
Dawn	English	22,800
Dawn	Gujarati	7,000
Daily News	English	12,000
Vatan	Gujarati	12,000
Star	English	n.a.
Daily Jang	Urdu	n.a.
Mashriq	Urdu	n.a.
Musawat	Urdu	n.a.
Morning News	English	n.a.
LAHORE		
Mashriq	Urdu	75,000
Imroze	Urdu	40,000
Pakistan Times	English	40,000
Nawa-i-Waqt	Urdu	24,000
Musawat	Urdu	n.a.
RAWALPINDI		
Ta'meer	Urdu	15,000
Nawa-i-Waqt	Urdu	3,000
Jang	Urdu	n.a.
Pakistan Times	English	n.a.
PESHAWAR		
Khyber Mail	English	5,000
Al Fala	Urdu and Pushtu	n.a.
Al-Jamiat-e-Sarhad	Urdu and Pushtu	n.a.

While freedom of the press has always been provided for constitutionally, severe restrictions were imposed on the press between 1958 and 1969.

47 TOURISM
Most visitors to Pakistan are required to have a visa and a valid passport. Tourist visas are valid for stays up to 30 days and transit visas for 15 days. However, visas are not required for up to 30 days from citizens of Commonwealth countries or from European countries that have concluded visa agreements with Pakistan. Road permits are available for land crossings into India at Wagah (between Lahore and Amritsar in India). There are no health restrictions on visitors entering Pakistan except in regard to smallpox immunization. Visitors are permitted to export foreign currencies up to the amount registered when they entered the country; personal effects are allowed free entry.

A Department of Tourism, under the Ministry of Communications, furnishes a variety of services. In 1974, 153,133 tourists visited the country, an increase of 8.8% over 1973, and tourist receipts were valued at $20.75 million.

48 FAMOUS PAKISTANIS
Several figures of monumental stature are associated with the creation and establishment of Pakistan. The poet and philosopher of a revitalized Islam, Mohammad Iqbal (1873–1938), who wrote in Urdu, Persian, and English, first called for the establishment of a Muslim state on the subcontinent in a statement made in 1930. Mohammad Ali Jinnah (1876–1948), the

Quaid-e-Azam, or "Great Leader," rallied the Muslims to this cause and became the first governor-general of the Commonwealth of Pakistan. His "right hand," Liaqat Ali Khan (1896–1951), was the first prime minister of the nation until his assassination. Chaudhury Mohammad Ali (b. 1905), a former prime minister, played a key role in the organization of the new government in 1947. Field Marshal Mohammad Ayub Khan (1908–74) served as commander-in-chief of the Pakistani army, as minister of defense in 1954–55, and as president of Pakistan from October 1958 to March 1969. Sir Mohammad Zafrulla Khan (b. 1893), a distinguished jurist, was several times minister of foreign affairs and later a member of the World Court at The Hague; in 1962, he served as president of the 17th UN General Assembly. Zulfikar Ali Bhutto (b. 1928), who rose to prominence as founder and leader of the socialist-leaning Pakistan People's Party, became prime minister in 1973 and guided the country's political and economic transformation following the loss of East Pakistan.

In literature, the paramount position is still held by the great Urdu writers who lived before the establishment of Pakistan. Ghalib (1796–1869) and Iqbal are recognized as the two greatest Urdu poets. Contemporary writers who have won fame include the Urdu poet Faiz Ahmad Faiz (b. 1911), imbued with a strongly socialist spirit, and the Urdu short story writer Saadat Hasan Manto (1912–55), who challenged many accepted values.

Foremost among Pakistan's painters is Abdur Rahman Chughtai (1899–1975), with works that seem to blend the Mughal heritage with modern technical devices.

⁴⁹DEPENDENCIES

Pakistan has no territories or colonies.

⁵⁰BIBLIOGRAPHY

Abbott, Freeland. *Islam and Pakistan.* Ithaca: Cornell University Press, 1968.

Ahmad, K.S. *Geography of Pakistan.* London: Oxford University Press, 1964.

Ali, Chaudri Mohammad. *The Emergence of Pakistan.* New York: Columbia University Press, 1967.

Andrus, James Russell, and Azizali F. Mohammed. *The Economy of Pakistan.* Stanford: Stanford University Press, 1966.

Area Handbook for Pakistan. Washington, D.C.: Government Printing Office, 1971.

Bhutto, Zulfikar Ali. *The Myth of Independence.* Karachi: Oxford University Press, 1969.

Binder, Leonard. *Religion and Politics in Pakistan.* Berkeley: University of California Press, 1961.

Biographical Encyclopedia of Pakistan. Lahore: International Publishers, 1955.

Bolitho, Hector. *Jinnah, Creator of Pakistan.* New York: Macmillan, 1955.

Brines, Russell. *The Indo-Pakistani Conflict.* London: Pall Mall, 1967.

Brown, W. Norman. *The United States and India, Pakistan, Bangladesh.* Cambridge: Harvard University Press, 1972.

Burke, S. M. *Mainsprings of Indian and Pakistani Foreign Policies.* Minneapolis: University of Minnesota Press, 1974.

Caroe, Sir Olaf. *The Pathans: 550 B.C.–A.D. 1957.* New York: St. Martin's Press, 1959.

Chaudhri, Mohammed Asan. *Pakistan and the Great Powers.* Karachi: Council for Pakistan Studies, 1970.

Choudhury, G.W. *Pakistan's Relations with India, 1947–1966.* New York: Praeger, 1968.

Crescent and Green (A Miscellany of Writings on Pakistan). New York: Philosophical Library, 1956.

Feldman, Herbert. *From Crisis to Crisis: Pakistan, 1962–69.* London: Oxford University Press, 1972.

Feldman, Herbert. *Pakistan: An Introduction.* New York: Oxford University Press, 1968.

Feldman, Herbert. *Revolution in Pakistan: A Study of the Martial Law Administration.* London: Oxford University Press, 1967.

Hasan, K. Sarwar. *Pakistan and the United Nations.* New York: Manhattan, 1961.

Husain, A. F. A. *Human and Social Impact of Technological Change in Pakistan.* 2 vols. Dacca: Oxford University Press, 1956.

Ikran, Sheikh Mohammad, and Percival Spear. *The Cultural Heritage of Pakistan.* Karachi: Oxford University Press, 1955.

Jahan, Rounaq. *Pakistan: Failure in National Integration.* New York: Columbia University Press, 1972.

Lamb, Alastair. *The Kashmir Conflict: A Historical Survey.* New York: Praeger, 1967.

Maron, Stanley (ed.). *Pakistan: Society and Culture.* New Haven: Human Relations Area Files, 1957.

Mayne, Peter. *The Narrow Smile.* London: Murray, 1955.

Pakistan, Ministry of the Interior. *Central Statistical Yearbook.* Karachi: Manager of Publications, 1952–date.

The Pakistan Year Book and Who's Who. Karachi: Kitabistan, 1949–date.

[Pakistan Yearbooks.] Karachi: Pakistan Publications, 1948–date. (Various titles.)

Papanek, Gustav F. *Pakistan's Development, Social Goals and Private Incentives.* Cambridge: Harvard University Press, 1967.

Sayeed, Khalid B. *Pakistan: The Formative Phase, 1857–1948.* London: Oxford University Press, 1968.

Siddiqui, Kalim. *Conflict, Crisis and War.* New York: Praeger, 1972.

Spate, Oskar Hermann Khristian, and A. T. A. Learmouth. *India and Pakistan: A General and Regional Geography.* New York: Barnes & Noble, 1967.

Stern, Joseph, and Walter Falcon. *Growth and Development in Pakistan: 1955–1969.* Cambridge: Harvard University Press, 1970.

Tinker, Hugh. *India and Pakistan: A Political Analysis.* New York: Praeger, 1967.

Wilber, Donald N. *Pakistan Yesterday and Today.* New York: Holt, Rinehart and Winston, 1964.

Wilcox, Wayne Ayres. *Pakistan: The Consolidation of a Nation.* New York: Columbia University Press, 1963.

Ziring, Lawrence. *The Ayub Khan Era.* Syracuse: Syracuse University Press, 1971.

PAPUA NEW GUINEA

CAPITAL: Port Moresby. FLAG: The flag is a rectangle, divided diagonally. The upper segment is scarlet with a yellow bird of paradise imposed; the lower segment is black with five white stars representing the Southern Cross. ANTHEM: No decision on a national anthem has yet been made. MONETARY UNIT: The kina (K) of 100 toea (t) is linked in parity with the Australian dollar. There are coins of 1, 2, 5, 10, and 20 toea and notes of 1, 2, 5, 10, and 20 kina. K1 = US$1.25 (or US$1 = K0.80). WEIGHTS AND MEASURES: Conversion to the metric system is now complete. HOLIDAYS: New Year's Day, 1 January; Independence Day, 16 September; Christmas, 25 December; Boxing Day, 26 December; and movable religious holidays such as Easter. TIME: 10 P.M. = noon GMT.

¹LOCATION, SIZE, AND EXTENT

Situated to the north of Australia, Papua New Guinea has a total land area of 475,368 sq km (183,540 sq mi), including the large islands of New Britain, New Ireland, and Bougainville, and hundreds of small islands. The country extends 2,082 km (1,294 mi) NNE–SSW and 1,156 km (718 mi) ESE–WNW. Mainland Papua New Guinea shares the island of New Guinea, the second-largest island in the world, with Irian Jaya, a province of Indonesia. To the N is the Trust Territory of the Pacific Islands (US); to the E are the Solomon Islands; to the W, Papua New Guinea shares a border with Irian Jaya; and to the S, its nearest neighbor is Australia. Papua New Guinea has a total boundary length of 4,572 km (2,841 mi).

²TOPOGRAPHY

Papua New Guinea is situated between the stable continental mass of Australia and the deep ocean basin of the Pacific. The largest section is the eastern half of the island of New Guinea, which is dominated by a massive central cordillera, or system of mountain ranges, extending from Indonesia's Irian Jaya to East Cape in Papua New Guinea at the termination of the Owen Stanley Range, and including the nation's highest peak, Mt. Wilhelm (14,793 feet). A second mountain chain fringes the north coast and runs parallel to the central cordillera. Active and recently active volcanoes are prominent features of New Guinea landscapes, but there are no glaciers or snowfields. In the lowlands are many swamps and flood plains. Important rivers are the Sepik, flowing 700 miles to the north, and the Fly, for a similar distance to the south.

The smaller islands of Papua New Guinea are also areas of extreme topographic contrast and generally feature mountain ranges rising directly from the sea or from narrow coastal plains. Volcanic landforms dominate the northern part of New Britain and Bougainville, and some of the smaller islands are extremely volcanic. The Bougainville-New Ireland area comprises Bougainville and Buka islands, the Gazelle Peninsula of New Britain, New Ireland, New Hanover, the St. Matthias group, and the Admiralty Islands.

³CLIMATE

The climate of Papua New Guinea is chiefly influenced by altitude and by the monsoons. The northwest or wet monsoon prevails from December to March, and the southeast or dry trade winds from May to October. Annual rainfall varies widely with the monsoon pattern, ranging from as little as 40 inches at Port Moresby to as much as 300 inches in other coastal regions. Most of the lowland and island areas have daily mean temperatures of about 27°C (81°F), while in the highlands temperatures may fall to 4.4°C (40°F) at night and rise to 32°C (90°F) in the daytime. Relative humidity is uniformly high in the lowlands at about 80%.

⁴FLORA AND FAUNA

The flora of Papua New Guinea is rich and varied, with habitats ranging from tidal swamps at sea level to alpine conditions. In low-lying coastal areas, various species of mangroves form the main vegetation, together with the beautiful casuarina, sago, and palm. There are large areas of tropical and savanna rain forest in which valuable trees such as kwila and cedar are found. Orchids, lilies, ferns, and creepers abound in the rain forests. At elevations of 3,000 to 4,000 feet there are large stands of varieties of pine. At the highest altitudes, mosses, lichens, and other alpine flora prevail.

Papua New Guinea has one of the most varied bird faunas in the world. About 850 species have been recognized, as compared with about 650 known in Australia and 500 in North America. Papua New Guinea is the major center for a number of bird families, particularly the bird of paradise, the bower bird, the cassowary, the kingfish, and parrot.

There are about 200 species of mammals, many nocturnal, of which rodent and marsupial orders predominate. Butterflies of Papua New Guinea are world famous for their size and vivid coloring.

As of 1975, endangered species in Papua New Guinea included the long-beaked echidna, dugong, watut leaf warbler, estuarine crocodile, and New Guinean crocodile.

⁵POPULATION

The estimated population in 1975 was 2,757,521, of whom 2,719,290 were indigenous Papua New Guineans and 38,231 were nonindigenous. The population growth rate was estimated in 1975 at about 2.5%, based on a crude birthrate of 40.8 per 1,000 and a death rate of 15.5 per 1,000 for a natural rate of increase of 25.3. Average population density in 1975 was 5.8 per sq km (15 per sq mi).

The population is predominantly rural; only 276,318 persons lived in urban areas in 1971. The major areas of population are in the highlands and eastern coastal areas of the island of New Guinea, and on the island of New Britain. Major cities and their estimated populations in 1973 were Port Moresby, the capital, 91,761; Rabaul, 62,329; and Lae, 50,834.

⁶ETHNIC GROUPS

Indigenous Papua New Guineans vary considerably in their ethnic origins, physical appearance, and spoken languages. The major ethnic groups are Papuans, highlanders, Micronesians, Melanesians, and some Polynesians.

In the 1971 census, 47,157 Europeans were identified, mostly of Australian origin; 2,760 Chinese; and 3,768 persons of mixed race.

7 LANGUAGE

Under the Australian administration of the former Territory of Papua and New Guinea, English was the official language. However, it was the mother language of only some 72,000 people, although there were some 364,000 speakers of English. Pidgin, a Melanesian lingua franca with roots primarily in English and German, is used by some 734,000 people, and Police Motu by 153,000 people. Since there are more than 700 indigenous languages in Papua New Guinea, the lingua francas have been necessary as a means of communication between different ethnic and tribal groups.

8 RELIGION

Indigenous religions, varying widely in ritual and belief, remain important in tribal societies in Papua New Guinea. More than half of the population is nominally Christian, with about 400,000 Catholics and 320,000 Lutherans. There are European missionaries of the Anglican, Roman Catholic, Lutheran, Methodist, and Seventh-day Adventist churches in Papua New Guinea.

9 TRANSPORTATION

Transportation is a major problem in Papua New Guinea because of the difficult terrain. Major population centers are linked chiefly by air and sea, although road construction is increasing to supplement these expensive means of transport. No natural road network exists, although the road connecting Lae to the highlands and the regional highlands road network are of national significance. In 1972 there were about 16,460 km (10,228 mi) of roads in Papua New Guinea. An estimated 19,000 passenger cars and 17,000 commercial vehicles were registered in 1972. A loan of K7.9 million from the Asian Development Bank is to be used to extend the Hiritano highway west along the coast from Port Moresby. There are no railroads.

The government has about 70 coastal work boats, none more than 30 feet long, operating along the coast. In 1975, K1.5 million was allocated for their replacement. International cargo cleared in 1973/74 was estimated at 4,385,000 tons.

Papua New Guinea's national air carrier, Air Niugini, established in 1973, has undertaken most of the services previously provided by Australian lines. International service is also provided by Qantas and domestic services by Air Pacific and Melanesian Airlines. In 1974/75, 184 commercial aircraft and 34 private aircraft were in operation. In 1971/72, 206,755 passengers embarked on overseas air travel, while internal scheduled and charter services carried 706,000 persons, reflecting the high rate of domestic air travel. Upgrading of Port Moresby's airport at a cost of K9 million, to be completed in 1976, was funded by the Australian Department of Civil Aviation.

10 COMMUNICATIONS

Telephone facilities consist of 36 automatic exchanges and 7 manual exchanges, with 14,748 telephones in use on 30 June 1973. There are 16 cable and 15 radio international channels. A coastal radio service provides communications between land-based stations and ships at sea.

The Papua New Guinea Broadcasting Commission was formed in 1973 from facilities of the Australian Broadcasting Commission and the Administration of Papua and New Guinea. It operates 2 medium- and 20 short-wave transmitters and broadcasts 130 hours weekly in English, pidgin English, Police Motu, and other vernaculars. In 1974 there were about 150,000 radios in use.

11 HISTORY

Papua New Guinea appears to have been settled before 8000

B.C., with migrations first of hunters and later of agriculturalists probably coming from Asia by way of Indonesia. Early communities had little contact with each other because of rough terrain, and so maintained their independence, as well as their individual languages and customs.

New Guinea was first sighted by Spanish and Portuguese sailors in the early 16th century and was known prophetically as *Isla del Oro* (Island of Gold). The western part of the island was claimed by Spain in 1545, and named New Guinea for a fancied resemblance of the people to those on the West African coast. Traders began to appear in the islands in the 1850s, and the Germans sought the coconut oil trade in northern New Guinea about that time. The Dutch and the British had earlier agreed on a division of their interests in the island, and from 1828, the Dutch began to colonize the western part of the island.

Although the British flag was hoisted on various parts of eastern New Guinea, annexation was not ratified by the British government. Some Australian colonists were eager to see New Guinea become a British possession, for trade, labor, gold mining, and missionary reasons; however, it was not until 1884, after an abortive Australian annexation attempt and under fear of German ambitions in the area, that Britain established a protectorate over the southern coast of New Guinea and adjacent islands. The Germans followed by laying claim to three different parts of northern New Guinea. British and German spheres of influence were delineated by the Anglo-German Agreement of 1885. Germany took control of the northeastern portion of the island, as well as New Britain, New Ireland, and Bougainville, while Britain took possession of the southern portion and the adjacent islands.

German New Guinea remained intact until the outbreak of war in 1914, when it was seized by Australian forces. In 1921, it was placed under a League of Nations mandate administered by Australia, and in 1947, it became the Trust Territory of New Guinea, still administered by Australia, but subject to surveillance of the UN Trusteeship Council.

British New Guinea passed to Australian control in 1901 and was renamed the Territory of Papua in 1906. Though the territories retained their separate identities and status, they were administered jointly by Australia from headquarters at Port Moresby.

In 1972, the territory was renamed Papua New Guinea, and on 1 December 1973, it was granted self-government. Separatist movements in Papua in 1973 and secessionist activities on the island of Bougainville in 1975 have died out, though debates over citizenship and land-reform provisions were vigorous until the 1975 passage of the constitution. Papua New Guinea achieved complete independence on 16 September 1975.

12 GOVERNMENT

Papua New Guinea is an independent, parliamentary democracy in the British Commonwealth, with a governor-general representing the head of state, Queen Elizabeth II.

Under the 1975 constitution, legislative power is vested in the National Parliament (formerly the House of Assembly) of 108 members, including 18 representing provincial electorates and others elected from open electorates. Suffrage is universal and voting compulsory for adults in elections held every four years. The party, or coalition of parties, with a majority in the National Parliament forms the government, and executive power is undertaken by the National Executive Council selected from the government parties and chaired by the prime minister. On Independence Day there were 17 ministers handling 20 ministries.

13 POLITICAL PARTIES

Several parties have emerged in Papua New Guinean politics. In the House of Assembly elected in 1973, the Pangu Pati formed a coalition government with the People's Progressive Party, led by

Prime Minister Michael Somare. Opposition parties were dominated by the United Party which, under Tei Abal, is supported by a strong following in the highlands. At the time of constitutional discussions from 1973 to 1975, the Nationalist Pressure Group, led by Father John Momis, became allied with the Country Party, to urge more radical policies on citizenship and on providing a provincial government for any district that requests it. Party allegiances have been somewhat fluid, and regional and tribal politics have an important impact on political outcomes. The Papua Besena Party, which stands for the secession of Papua from Papua New Guinea, has had fluctuating support even on its home ground and had one member in the 1973 Parliament. Several Bougainville members of the Parliament resigned in 1975 in order to prosecute the cause of Bougainville secession led by Josephine Abaijah. On 1 September 1975, they staged a unilateral declaration of independence for what they called the Republic of North Solomons. However, unity was restored for the 16 September 1975 independence ceremonies. In February 1976, Bougainville secessionists again made a show of strength, burning government property and blocking roads. They dispersed following an airlift of government police and appeals from Prime Minister Somare.

14 LOCAL GOVERNMENT
Papua New Guinea is divided into 19 districts. Provincial government was proposed but not included in the constitution ratified in 1975, and only Bougainville maintained a provincial assembly in 1975. Most districts have local authorities who administer development projects and the distribution of central government funds. In addition, there are numerous locally elected government councils.

15 JUDICIAL SYSTEM
The Supreme Court is the highest judicial authority and final court of appeal in the country. Other courts are the national court; district courts which deal with summary and nonindictable offenses; and local courts established to deal with minor offenses, including matters regulated by local customs.

The Papua New Guinea government has undertaken a process of legal reform under which village courts have been established to conserve and reactivate traditional legal methods.

16 ARMED FORCES
The main armed force is the Papua New Guinea Defence Force, which on 26 January 1973 was formed from the territory's army, navy, and air force. It consists of about 3,500 personnel, and was formerly officered only by Australians, although Papua New Guineans are gradually assuming control. Equipment includes 5 patrol boats and 4 DC-3s for air transport. The Papua New Guinea Police Force is an armed constabulary with a strength of about 5,000. Australia contributes to the upkeep of the military forces.

17 MIGRATION
The government review of migration found major trends toward a net outflow of nonindigenous residents, principally Australians and some Chinese, as Papua New Guinea moved toward independence in 1975. This emigration may have been influenced by constitutional provisions that restricted eligibility for naturalization of nonindigenous residents to those with eight years' residency, but limited their tax and business rights to the same status as those of aliens. There has been some migration of Filipinos to Papua New Guinea to work in its administration.

18 INTERNATIONAL COOPERATION
Papua New Guinea became a member of the UN in 1975, and belongs to the British Commonwealth, South Pacific Forum, Asian Development Bank, IBRD, FAO, and ESCAP. It is a signatory of the Lomé Convention.

19 ECONOMY
Economic activity is concentrated in two sectors, agriculture and mining. The subsistence sector produces livestock, fruit, and vegetables for local consumption. Agricultural products for export include coffee, copra, cocoa, tea, rubber, palm oil, and pyrethrum. The agricultural export sector was once dominated by Australian interests, but Papua New Guinean producers are playing an increasing role.

Copper exports from the rich Bougainville mine make a large contribution to the country's balance of payments and government revenues, and have become the significant feature of the economy.

Papua New Guinea's economy, both through administration and expansion of productive services, depends to a large extent on the inflow of Australian aid. In 1974/75, aid amounted to K225 million (excluding colonial pensions) and made up more than one-half of the nation's revenue.

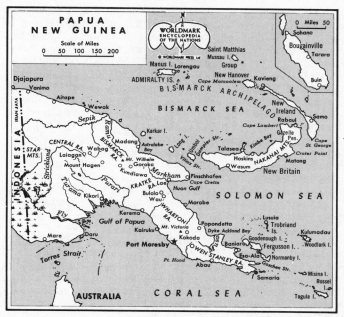

See continental political: front cover E6; physical: back cover H1

LOCATION: 140°51' to 160°E; 0° to 12°S. **BOUNDARY LENGTHS:** Total coastline, 3,795 km (2,358 mi); Indonesia, 777 km (483 mi). **TERRITORIAL SEA LIMIT:** 3 mi.

20 INCOME
GDP in current prices grew from K786 million in 1972/73 to K1,004 million in 1973/74, an increase of 27.7%. Real growth in GDP was 12%. The GDP was expected to decline in 1974/75 due to the collapse of copper prices and a drop in the prices of other export commodities. Estimated contributions to the GDP in 1971/72 were agriculture, forestry, and fishing, 34%; construction, 15%; wholesale and retail trade, 7%; manufacturing, gas, electricity, and water services, 6%; transport and communications, 6%; financing, insurance, and real estate, 4%; mining and quarrying, 3%; and other, 25%.

Per capita income in 1973/74 was about K320.4, up from K259.7 in 1972/73. However, the distribution of income is distorted by the presence of highly paid foreign workers in the public and private sectors. Excluding these, the per capita household disposable income of Papua New Guineans is estimated to have been K157 in 1971/72.

21 LABOR
Although most of the adult population is involved in productive

activity, only about 20% were involved in monetary-sector activity in 1971. As of 30 June 1972, wage and salary earners in Papua New Guinea numbered 139,426, of whom 120,014 were indigenous. An overwhelming majority of indigenous wage earners were male, and significantly more worked in rural areas than in urban areas. Wage and salary earners were concentrated in agriculture, including fishing and forestry; commerce; and government and public authority employment. Legislation covers working conditions and wages, especially for rural workers, and provides for collective bargaining negotiations of wage and other disputes. An employment ordinance placed the onus on employers to train and use only indigenous employees in certain office jobs by mid-1975.

In 1972, there were 35 industrial associations with more than 32,000 members.

22 AGRICULTURE

Agriculture in Papua New Guinea is divided into a large subsistence sector and a small monetary sector for export. Subsistence crops include yams, taro, and other staple vegetables.

Cash crops are increasing in rural areas, stimulated by government-financed development programs. An import replacement program in livestock, fruits, vegetables, rice, sugar, and tobacco has been undertaken. Production by small farmers of coffee, copra, cocoa, tea, rubber, and oil palm is important for export, although production on plantations, which are usually foreign-owned, is also significant. Such plantations, which in 1974 accounted for only about 0.9% of the arable land, are gradually being sold back to nationals. Total smallholder production in 1974/75 was about K26 million worth of coffee, K15 million of copra, and K15 million of cocoa, while total exports of these commodities were about K37 million worth of coffee, K30 million of copra, and K40 million of cocoa.

Land areas under production in 1970/71 included copra, 137,594 hectares; cocoa, 19,425 hectares; coffee, 22,258 hectares; and rubber, 2,023 hectares.

23 ANIMAL HUSBANDRY

A total of 47,000 head of cattle was owned by local farmers in June 1975, and production was being encouraged with the aim of achieving self-sufficiency in meat supplies. Hog and poultry production was also increasing, and a buffalo industry was established in the Sepik River Valley. The farming of crocodiles, whose hides are exported, has also been growing.

24 FISHING

In many coastal parts of Papua New Guinea fishing is of great economic importance to the people. The government is involved in the development of fishing through supply of freezers, transport, and research. The total value of fish catches is not known, although K4.3 million worth of tuna, crayfish, and prawns was exported, chiefly to Japan, in 1972/73.

25 FORESTRY

Forest land covers between 32 and 36 million hectares, or roughly 70% of the total land area, of which more than half is estimated to be commercially exploitable, including a great variety of hardwood and soft wood species.

The total log harvest in 1974/75 was 860,000 cu meters, as compared with 1,080,000 cu meters in 1973/74. The decline was due to a fall in demand in Japan for logs, and in Australia for sawn timber because of the worldwide economic recession. In 1972/73, export of timber logs was valued at K5.6 million; sawn timber, K2.7 million; and plywood, K2.4 million; by 1973/74, total timber exports reached K20.3 million.

26 MINING

Prior to World War II, gold mining contributed 75% of Papua New Guinea's export earnings. This proportion declined greatly in following years, contributing an average of about K1 million per year. Production in the year ending 30 June 1973 was about 18,685 kg.

In 1971/72, the Bougainville copper mine, one of the richest in the world, began to export copper ores and concentrates which reached the value of K125.6 million in 1972/73. By 1973/74, exports reached K311.9 million, more than double the 1972/73 figure. This mine has become by far the largest export earner for Papua New Guinea, although the downturn in world copper prices in 1974 somewhat reduced returns. The Papua New Guinea government renegotiated the original agreement with Bougainville Copper Ltd. so as to gain a greater share of the profits accruing from sales. Further, the government has set up the Mineral Resources Stabilization Fund to reduce the impact of fluctuations in copper revenues on the economy.

Mineral exploration has been expanded. The government has taken over the drilling program in the Star Mountains at the OK Tedi site, which has a proven deposit of more than 150 million tons of copper but was abandoned by Kennecott Ltd. when the company was unable to agree with the government on plans for the nearly inaccessible deposit. Further exploration is proceeding at other sites. In addition, there has been exploration for oil and gas in the Gulf of Papua, on the Turana River, and off Bougainville.

27 ENERGY AND POWER

As of 30 June 1973, Papua New Guinea had an installed electricity capacity of 71.4 Mw. Of the total production of 66.3 million kwh, 31.2 million kwh came from hydroelectric facilities, 23.1 million kwh from thermal plants, and 12 million kwh were purchased from Bougainville Copper.

28 INDUSTRY

The industrial sector is largely undeveloped. As of 30 June 1972 there were about 700 factories employing a total of 15,539 persons. Industries are concentrated in industrial metals, timber processing, machinery, food, drinks, and tobacco. The annual value of their output at the end of June 1972 was K111 million.

Handicraft and cottage industries have been expanding. A government-sponsored program assists Papua New Guineans in setting up businesses and purchases equity in existing businesses. It is also encouraging small-scale import-substitute operations.

29 DOMESTIC TRADE

Trade in rural areas is mostly informal, and cash is used in transactions. The local market, particularly in fruit and vegetables, is an important feature of life in the country. Domestic trade in urban centers is dominated by large Australian-owned stores with multiple outlets.

30 FOREIGN TRADE

In 1973/74, Papua New Guinea's exports totaled K531 million and imports K301 million. This was the first year that there had been a substantial surplus in balance of trade after years of trade deficits. This surplus was due to the rapidly increasing value of copper exports, but it disappeared in 1975 when copper prices fell.

Principal exports in 1972/73 (in millions of kina) were:

Copper ore and concentrates	125.6
Coffee	23.4
Copra and coconut products	15.1
Cocoa	11.3
Timber and plywood	11.0
Fish and shellfish	4.3
Tea	2.0
Rubber	2.0
Gold	1.0
Other exports	4.7
Reexports	29.0
TOTAL	229.4

Principal imports in 1972/73 (in millions of kina) were:

Machinery and transport equipment	73.5
Food, drink, and tobacco	52.8
Manufactured goods	39.2
Chemicals and chemical products	12.4
Minerals, fuels, and lubricants	11.1
Other imports	21.8
TOTAL	210.8

Through most of the period when Papua New Guinea was a territory administered by Australia, the two were also major trading partners. In the 1970s, Papua New Guinea's trade with other countries, especially Japan, increased. In 1972/73, Australia supplied 59% of the imports and Japan received more than 35% of the exports from Papua New Guinea.

Principal trading partners in 1972/73 (in millions of kina) were:

	EXPORTS	IMPORTS	BALANCE
Australia	46.0	123.5	−77.5
Japan	81.4	35.6	45.8
FRG	53.4	−	53.4
US	11.5	21.0	− 9.5
UK	11.4	9.0	2.4
Others	25.7	21.7	4.0
TOTALS	229.4	210.8	18.6

³¹BALANCE OF PAYMENTS
Papua New Guinea's trade balance was significantly in deficit from 1969 through 30 June 1972, and only a small surplus was recorded in 1972/73. A significant surplus of K230 million was recorded in 1973/74. This surplus was due primarily to rising copper exports, while the earlier trade deficit was due in large part to imports of equipment needed for the establishment of the Bougainville copper mine.

Transfers of aid funds from Australia and capital inflow for the Bougainville copper mine were major influences on the current account balance. Property income payments abroad increased substantially from 1969/70 to 1973/74, so that the balance of current account in the latter year was K279 million. In 1973/74, capital transfers from abroad were K62 million.

³²BANKING
The Bank of Papua New Guinea, the country's central bank, was established in 1973, and the currency, the kina, was first issued in April 1975. The kina is backed by a standby arrangement with Australia, and the value of the kina is tied to the Australian dollar. The net operating profit of the bank in 1974/75 was about K500,000.

The Papua New Guinea Banking Corporation was set up in 1973 to take over the savings and trading business of the former Australian-government-owned bank operating in Papua New Guinea. It competes with private commercial banks, most of which are branches of Australian banks. The Corporation has 14 branches, 12 subbranches, and 200 agencies in all parts of Papua New Guinea. The Papua New Guinea Development Bank loaned K10 million in 1974/75 for development of small businesses in the country.

Commercial bank deposits on 30 June 1975 were K229 million, up from K100.8 million on 30 June 1973.

³³INSURANCE
In 1974, one domestic and five foreign companies transacted insurance in the country. As of 30 June 1973, total sums insured by life companies were K189.2 million.

³⁴SECURITIES
There is no securities exchange in Papua New Guinea.

³⁵PUBLIC FINANCE
The government relies heavily on Australian aid and on revenues from the Bougainville copper mine, although the domestic tax base has been expanded quite rapidly. Government revenues and expenditures for 1974/75 (in thousands of kina) were:

REVENUES	
Direct taxation	81,016
Customs and duties and other indirect taxes	96,569
Australian government grants and loans	225,348
TOTAL	402,933

EXPENDITURES	
Commodity-producing sector	39,308
Economic overhead	83,426
Social services	94,565
General administration, law, and order	82,229
Public works and miscellaneous	29,050
Transfer of government functions	71,711
TOTAL	400,289

Estimated revenues for 1975/76 were K400,136,000, while estimated expenditures were K408,136,000.

³⁶TAXATION
Company incomes were taxed in 1975 at a rate of 35%, and an added dividend withholding tax of 15% was also levied. In addition, progressive tax rates were applied to individuals' income. In 1971/72, 32,263 individuals were taxed K16 million on a total taxable income of K128 million; 1,088 companies, with a total taxable income of K66 million, were assessed taxes of K13.5 million. Direct taxes in 1973/74 amounted to K58.2 million and increased by almost 40% in 1974/75. Other taxes include land and property taxes, estate and death taxes, gift taxes, and stamp duties.

³⁷CUSTOMS AND DUTIES
A general levy is charged on all imports, with higher excises on luxury items, ranging up to 45% on household electrical appliances and 50% on vehicle registrations. In 1974/75, import duties and charges raised K29.7 million, while excises raised K20.3 million. An export tax on agricultural exports raised K1 million.

³⁸FOREIGN INVESTMENTS
In 1969/70, total inflow of private overseas investment was K110.7 million, the bulk of it in the mining sector. Most of this investment came from Australia. Since that time, with the completion of the bulk of the investment in the Bougainville copper mine, Australian investment in Papua New Guinea has declined, and a net outflow of capital was recorded in 1974/75. However, direct investments from Japan, China, Malaysia, Singapore, and other countries have been increasing in the oil, minerals, timber, fishing, and livestock sectors.

In 1974, Papua New Guinea established the National Investment and Development Authority to coordinate foreign investment, register all new foreign investment, and establish priorities for foreign investment.

³⁹ECONOMIC POLICY
The fundamental purposes of Papua New Guinea's economic strategy have been distilled into the nation's eight aims: a rapid increase in the proportion of the economy under the control of Papua New Guineans; a more equal distribution of economic benefits; decentralization of economic activity; an emphasis on small-scale artisan, service, and business activity; a more self-reliant economy; an increasing capacity for meeting government

spending from locally raised revenue; a rapid increase in the equal and active participation of women in the economy; and governmental control and involvement in those sections of the economy where control is necessary to achieve the desired kind of development.

Taxation, increased trade, and the attraction of new foreign investments are being used to achieve these national goals. A central policy aim of the government is to increase its self-reliance; that is, to reduce dependence on Australian aid, which in 1974/75 amounted to K225 million. This is gradually being achieved, although Papua New Guinea will continue to rely on large amounts of Australian aid pending further development of natural resources.

As Papua New Guinea's population is overwhelmingly rural, agricultural development policies, together with government-supported social welfare policies, are of major economic importance. The gradual shift from the subsistence sector to the cash economy has provided opportunities for more revenue, but it has also brought with it desires for more government services.

There are important inequalities in income distribution in Papua New Guinea, both between the indigenous and nonindigenous populations, and also among different geographic regions, because of their varied resources. The government aims to ameliorate these inequalities, principally through taxation and the distribution of government development grants.

40HEALTH
The Department of Public Health provides a comprehensive health service, both preventive and curative. In 1971 there were 456 hospitals, with a total of 16,664 beds. In that year, the country had 233 doctors, 33 dentists, 33 pharmacists, and 1,541 nurses. The main health problems are malaria, tuberculosis, leprosy, and venereal disease. Significant malnutrition occurs in some areas, and pneumonia and related respiratory infections are major risks. In 1974/75 there was a campaign to spray for protection against malaria, and special efforts were made to detect leprosy and diagnose venereal diseases. The number of tuberculosis patients under treatment declined. Rural infant mortality at 170 per 1,000 in 1974/75 was significantly higher than urban infant mortality at 100 per 1,000. In 1975, average life expectancy was estimated at 50.2 years.

41SOCIAL WELFARE
Health and education programs are provided in all parts of the country; however, Papua New Guinea does not have a system of public social welfare payments. Rural communities traditionally assume communal obligations to those in need.

42HOUSING
Traditional housing in rural areas appears to be adequate; but in urban areas there are some acute shortages of housing due to increased urban immigration. In most urban areas, squatter settlements have been established. In 1973/74, only 1,486 new houses and flats were completed in urban areas, sorely failing to meet the demand.

43EDUCATION
The overall literacy rate in 1975 was 13.3%. In 1975, 238,000 pupils, about 56% of primary-school-age children, were in primary schools. Primary school attendance has been growing by about 3% per year in the 1970s. Pupil-teacher ratios are about 1:32, but availability of education varies in different regions of the country. In 1975 there were 30,000 students in 80 high schools, 3,600 students in technical colleges, and 2,100 students in teacher-training colleges. There are two universities, the University of Papua New Guinea at Port Moresby, founded in 1966, and the University of Technology at Lae.

44LIBRARIES AND MUSEUMS
Libraries exist at the universities, and local libraries are well established in urban centers. The Papua New Guinea Museum and Art Gallery in Port Moresby has a good collection of art and general ethnography. The government is attempting to conserve what remains of traditional art and artifacts and has imposed restrictions on the export of such goods.

45ORGANIZATIONS
Chambers of commerce, service clubs, farmers' associations, the Employers Federation, and various trade unions form the nucleus of formal organizations in Papua New Guinea. Various youth and church groups also operate.

There are important local and regional associations which fulfill both political and economic aims. The Mataungan Association of New Britain is one, and others are established in Bougainville and the Trobriand Islands.

46PRESS
The major newspaper is the *Papua New Guinea Post-Courier*, which is published daily in English with a circulation of about 18,000. Other local news sheets are published, many in pidgin. The twice-monthly *Our News*, published by the Department of Information, circulates about 27,000 copies in English and 15,000 in pidgin. There are more than 85 periodicals, with a combined circulation of 339,500, published in English, the lingua francas, and various vernaculars.

47TOURISM
Tourists must have a valid passport, obtain an entry visa to Papua New Guinea, and hold an onward ticket and a health certificate. In 1973/74, 20,797 tourists visited Papua New Guinea, spending about K11 million.

48FAMOUS PAPUA NEW GUINEANS
The best known Papua New Guineans are Michael Somare (b.1936), chief minister during colonial rule and the nation's first prime minister; Albert Maori Kiki (b.1931), author of *Kiki: Ten Thousand Years in a Lifetime*; and Vincent Eri, author of *The Crocodile*.

49DEPENDENCIES
Papua New Guinea has no dependencies.

50BIBLIOGRAPHY
Berndt, Ronald M., and Peter Lawrence (eds.). *Politics in New Guinea*. Nedlands, West Elm, Australia: University of West Australia Press, 1971, or Seattle, Washington: University of Washington Press, 1971.

Brookfield, H. C. *Melanesia: A Geographical Interpretation of an Island World*. London: Methuen, 1971.

Bureau of Statistics. *Summary of Statistics, 1972–73*. Port Moresby: 1975.

The Encyclopedia of Papua and New Guinea. Melbourne: 1972.

Griffin, James. *A Foreign Policy for an Independent Papua New Guinea*. Sydney: Australian Institute of International Affairs, Angus and Robertson, 1974.

Hastings, Peter. *New Guinea Problems and Prospects*. Melbourne: Australian Institute of International Affairs, Chesire, 1973.

Howlett, Diana. *Papua New Guinea: Geography and Change*. Melbourne: Thomas Nelson, 1973.

National Planning Committee. *Programmes and Performance 1975–76*. Port Moresby: 1975.

National Planning Committee. *Strategies for Nationhood*. Port Moresby: 1974.

Nelson, Hank N. *Papua New Guinea—Black Unity or Black Chaos?* Bingwood, Victoria: Penguin, 1972.

Ross, A. Clunies, and S. Langmore. *Alternative Strategies for Papua New Guinea*. Melbourne: Oxford University Press, 1973.

Shand, Richard T., and M. L. Thradgold. *The Economy of Papua New Guinea: Projections and Policy Issues*. Canberra: Australian National University, 1971.

Stephen, David. *A History of Political Parties in Papua New Guinea*. Lansdowne Press, 1972.

Tudor, Judy. *Papua New Guinea Handbook*. Sydney: Pacific Publications, 1974.

PHILIPPINES

Republic of the Philippines
Republika ñg Pilipinas

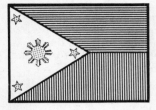

CAPITAL: Manila. **FLAG:** The national flag consists of a white equilateral triangle at the hoist with a blue stripe extending from its upper side and a red stripe extending from its lower side. Inside each angle of the triangle is a yellow five-pointed star, and in its center is a yellow sun with eight rays. **ANTHEM:** *Bayang Magiliw (Nation Beloved).* **MONETARY UNIT:** The peso (₱) is divided into 100 centavos. There are coins of 1, 5, 10, 25, and 50 centavos and 1 peso, and notes of 5, 10, 20, 50, and 100 pesos. ₱1=$0.1342 (or $1=₱7.4500). **WEIGHTS AND MEASURES:** The metric system is the legal standard, but some local measures are also used. **HOLIDAYS:** New Year's Day, 1 January; Bataan Day, 9 April; Labor Day, 1 May; Independence Day, 12 June; Philippine-American Friendship Day, 4 July; National Heroes Day, 30 November; Christmas, 25 December; and Rizal Day, 30 December. Movable religious holidays include Holy Thursday and Good Friday. **TIME:** 8 P.M.=noon GMT.

¹LOCATION, SIZE, AND EXTENT

The Republic of the Philippines consists of an archipelago of approximately 7,100 islands situated SE of mainland Asia and separated from it by the South China Sea. The total land area is approximately 299,404 sq km (115,600 sq mi), 93% of which is contained within the 11 largest islands: Luzon, 105,708 sq km (40,814 sq mi); Mindanao, 95,586 sq km (36,906 sq mi); Samar, 13,079 sq km (5,050 sq mi); Negros, 12,704 sq km (4,905 sq mi); Palawan, 11,784 sq km (4,550 sq mi); Panay, 11,515 sq km (4,446 sq mi); Mindoro, 9,736 sq km (3,759 sq mi); Leyte, 7,213 sq km (2,785 sq mi); Cebu, 4,411 sq km (1,703 sq mi); Bohol, 3,864 sq km (1,492 sq mi); and Masbate, 3,269 sq km (1,262 sq mi). Only 357 islands have areas that exceed 2.59 sq km (1 sq mi). The Philippine archipelago includes all the islands located therein except Palmas, which was ceded to the Netherlands (later, to Indonesia) in 1928. The Philippines' length is *1,851* km (*1,150* mi) SSE-NNW, and its width is *1,062* km (660 mi) ENE-WSW; Palawan and the Sulu Archipelago extend from the main group SW toward Borneo, separated from it by the Balabac Strait and the Sibutu Passage, respectively. The Philippines is bounded on the N by the Bashi Channel, on the E by the Pacific Ocean, on the S by the Celebes Sea, on the SW by the Sulu Sea, and on the W by the South China Sea, with a total coastline of *12,958* km (8,052 mi).

²TOPOGRAPHY

The topography is extremely varied, with volcanic mountain masses forming the cores of most of the larger islands. The range culminates in northern Luzon in Mount Pulog (elevation 2,931 meters, or 9,613 feet), and in Mindanao in Mount Apo, the highest point in the Philippines (elevation 2,954 meters, or 9,690 feet). A number of volcanoes are active, and the islands have been subject to destructive earthquakes. Lowlands are generally narrow coastal strips except for larger plains in Luzon (Cagayan Valley and Central Plains), Mindanao (Cotabato and Davao-Agusan valleys), and others in Negros and Panay. Rivers are short, generally seasonal in flow. Important ones are the Rio Grande de Cagayan, Agno, Abra, Bicol, and Pampanga on Luzon, and the Cotabato and Agusan on Mindanao. Flooding is a frequent hazard, with recent disastrous floods occurring in 1972 and 1976. The shores of many of the islands are embayed (Manila Bay is one of the finest harbors in East Asia); however, several islands lack adequate harbors and require offshore lightering for sea transport. The only two inland water bodies of significant size are Laguna de Bay (Luzon) and Lake Lanao (Mindanao). Sheltered inland seas occur between the islands.

³CLIMATE

The Philippine Islands, in general, have a maritime tropical climate and, except in the higher mountains, temperatures remain warm, the annual average ranging from about 26°C to 28°C (79° to 82°F) throughout the archipelago. Rainfall and seasonality differ markedly throughout the islands owing to varying exposures to the two major wind streams, northeast trades or monsoon (winter) and southwest monsoon (summer). Generally, the east coasts receive heavy winter maximum rainfall (80–120 inches), the west coasts heavy summer maximum (80–140 inches); intermediate and southern locales receive lesser amounts more equally distributed (40–80 inches). Baguio, in the mountains of northern Luzon, recorded the world's heaviest 24-hour rainfall (in 1911, 45.99 inches). Violent tropical storms (baguios), or typhoons, are frequent. The average annual rainfall in the Philippines is 100 inches.

⁴FLORA AND FAUNA

The Philippines supports a rich and varied flora with close botanic connections to Indonesia and mainland Southeast Asia. Forests are typically tropical, mixed in composition, with the dominant family, Dipterocarpaceae, representing 75% of the stands. The forest also has many vines, epiphytes, and climbers. A large part of the open grasslands, ranging up to eight feet in height, are man-made, the aftermath of the shifting, fire-clearing agricultural system. Most contain tropical savanna grasses, harsh, nonnutritious, and difficult to eradicate.

Common mammals include the wild hog, deer, wild carabao, monkey, civet cat, and various rodents. There are about 1,000 species and subspecies of birds, among the more numerous being the megapodes (turkeylike wildfowl), button quail, jungle fowl, peacock pheasant, dove, pigeon, parrot, and hornbill. Reptilian life is sparse; there are crocodiles, and the larger snakes include the python and several varieties of cobra.

As of 1975, endangered species in the Philippines included the Mindanao gymnure, dugong, Asiatic buffalo, tamarau, monkey-eating eagle, Palawan peacock pheasant, Mindoro imperial pigeon, giant scops owl, Koch's pitta, Cebu black shama, ashy ground thrush, sail-fin lizard, and two species of crocodile (Mindoro and estuarine).

⁵POPULATION

The 1970 census reported the population at 36,684,000, an increase of 9,596,000 over the 1960 census count. In mid-1975, the population was estimated at 43,048,000; projected 1980 population is 52,203,000. In the 1970s, the annual growth rate was about 3.1%, one of the highest in the world. The population is essentially rural (about 64% in 1975), with one major urban concentration—Manila (estimated at 1.5 million in 1975). Important lesser cities (with populations reported in the 1970 census) are Quezon City, part of greater Manila (754,452), Davao (392,473), Cebu (347,116), Iloilo (209,738), Pasay (206,283), Zamboanga (199,901), and Basilan (143,829).

Average population density in 1975 was estimated at 144 per sq km. The population is unevenly distributed, being concentrated in Luzon (45.7%) and the Visayan Sea islands (21%). Population densities range from 15.9 persons per sq km in Palawan to 34,746 persons per sq km in Manila.

6 ETHNIC GROUPS
Ethnic Filipinos (Malayan and Indonesian racial stock) constituted about 99% of the total population. Minority groups include Chinese, Indians and Negritos, and Caucasians, mainly of Spanish and US origin.

The Chinese, European, and US groups have an economic and social status of considerably greater importance than their small proportion would indicate. The Negritos have generally remained outside Filipino society, living in a seminomadic state in relatively inaccessible mountain areas. Religious rather than ethnic differences account for two important minority cultural groups—Muslims in the southwestern part of the archipelago, and the mountain people of northern Luzon (generally animists of Indonesian stock).

In 1971, the Tasaday, a Stone Age tribe of about 24 people, were found in Mindanao. Isolated for perhaps thousands of years, the Tasaday exist at the earliest stages of human social development, having no leadership hierarchy and living as food gatherers with no agriculture or domesticated animals.

7 LANGUAGE
According to the 1973 constitution, there are two official languages: English, spoken by 44.7% of the population; and Pilipino, based on Tagalog, the national language adopted in 1946 and understood by 55.2% of the Filipinos. Spanish, introduced in the 16th century and an official language until 1973, is now spoken by only 3.6% of the population. Some 66 native dialects (basically of Malay-Indonesian origin) are spoken. Besides Tagalog, which provides the mother tongue for 24.5% of the population, eight of the other dialects can be considered major tongues: Cebuano (spoken as a mother tongue by 24% of the population), Iloko (17.3%), and Panay-Hiligaynon (10.2%); the majority of the remaining 24% speak Bikol, Samar-Leyte, Pampango, Pangasinan, and Moro-Maguindanao. English is the language of intercommunication. The teaching of Pilipino is mandatory in public and private primary schools, and its use is encouraged by the government.

8 RELIGION
The Philippines is the only predominantly Christian country in Asia. Freedom of religion is provided by the constitution. Most of the population (85%) belongs to the Roman Catholic Church. Members of the Filipino Independent Church (Aglipayan), founded in 1902 in protest against the dominance of foreign clergy in the Catholic Church, constitute 4% of the population. Muslims (representing 4%) are concentrated in Mindanao and the Sulus. Various Protestant churches represent about 3%. Animists, mainly in the more inaccessible mountainous areas of Luzon and Mindanao, constitute about 3% and Buddhists less than 1%.

9 TRANSPORTATION
The total length of roads and highways in 1975 was 80,000 km, of which about one-fourth was paved. Luzon contains about half of the total roads and the Visayan islands about one-third. During 1966–75, some 30,000 km of roads were constructed as part of an infrastructure program of the Marcos government. There were 362,500 passenger cars and 252,500 commercial vehicles in 1973, nearly half of which were registered in Manila.

There are 1,354 km of railways, 1,140 km on Luzon and 214 km on Panay; both lines are operated by the Philippine government, the latter under government receivership. On Luzon, Bacnotan and San Fernando (La Union) are connected with Legaspi (Albay) through Manila, and on Panay the capital city, Iloilo, is connected with Roxas.

Water transport is of paramount importance for interisland and intraisland transportation. A small offshore fleet registered under the Philippine flag is engaged in international commerce, but most ocean freight is carried to and from the Philippines by ships of foreign registry. Of the 351 public ports, 20 are ports of entry for vessels engaged in foreign trade. Manila is the busiest Philippine port in international shipping, especially for imports and transshipment, followed by Cebu and Iloilo.

Four airlines have domestic routes: PAL, Air Manila, Filipinas Orient Airways (Fairways), and Fleming Air Service Transport (FAST). PAL has international routes throughout Asia and to Australia, the US, and Europe. International airlines serving Manila include Air France, BA, China Airlines, JAL, KLM, NWA, Pan Am, and Qantas. The Philippine Civil Aeronautics Administration maintains 74 civil airports and 39 private airfields; air transport provides important links to outlying areas.

10 COMMUNICATIONS
All islands and the more important towns and cities are interconnected by wire and radio. One cable company and three private foreign radio companies maintain overseas communications. In 1974 there were 410,290 telephones (282,561 of which were in Manila) serviced by the Philippine Long Distance Telephone Co. and about 30 smaller systems, including a government-owned facility. In 1973, radio transmitting stations numbered 327 and licensed radios totaled 1.8 million, or 45 per 1,000 inhabitants. There were 15 television broadcasting stations and 450,000 licensed television sets in 1973.

11 HISTORY
The Philippine Islands are thought to have been first settled by Negritos, who crossed then existing land bridges from Borneo and Sumatra some 30,000 years ago. These peoples were later outnumbered by successive waves of Malays, who arrived from the south, at first by land and later on boats called barangays, a name also applied to their communities. By the 14th century, Arab traders made contact with the southern islands and introduced Islam to the local populace. Commercial and political ties also linked various enclaves in the archipelago with Indonesia, Southeast Asia, India, China, and Japan.

Ferdinand Magellan, the Portuguese-born navigator, landed on Cebu on 7 April 1521 and claimed the Philippines for Spain. The spirit of freedom of the Filipinos, however, led to continued resistance to Spanish rule. Magellan himself was killed by the Filipino chieftain Lapulapu. The Spanish renamed the islands in honor of King Philip II, and an invasion, under Miguel López de Legaspi, soon followed. The Spanish conquest, facilitated by the almost complete conversion of the natives to Christianity, proceeded quickly, and by 1572, except for the Moros—Muslim converts in Mindanao and the Sulu islands—it was concluded. The archipelago, as a province of New Spain, was administered from Mexico. Trade became a monopoly of the Spanish government. Galleons transshipped Oriental goods sent to Manila to Acapulco in Mexico, and thence to Spain.

Although Spain governed the islands until the end of the 19th century, its rule was constantly threatened by the Portuguese, the Dutch, the English (who, in 1762, captured and occupied Manila), the Chinese, and the Filipinos themselves. After the

1820s, which saw the successful revolts of the Spanish colonies in the Americas, the Filipinos openly agitated against the government trade monopoly, the exactions of the clergy, and the imposition of forced labor. This agitation brought a relaxation of government controls: ports were opened to world shipping, and the production of such typical Philippine exports as sugar, coconuts, and hemp began.

Filipino aspirations for independence, suppressed by conservative Spanish rule, climaxed in the unsuccessful rebellion of 1896. José Rizal (1861–96), the most revered Filipino patriot, was executed, but Gen. Emilio Aguinaldo and his forces continued the war. When the Spanish-American War (1898) ended Spanish rule, the Philippine nationalists did not accept US rule in its place. When the short-lived formal warfare between US forces and Filipino troops ended with the fall of Tarlac Province, Gen. Aguinaldo continued guerrilla resistance in the mountains of northern Luzon.

In the face of continued agitation for independence, the US Congress passed a series of bills that ensured a degree of Philippine autonomy. The Tydings-McDuffie Independence Law of 1934 instituted Commonwealth government and further stipulated complete independence in 1944. Manuel L. Quezon was elected first president of the Commonwealth of the Philippines.

On 8 December 1941, the Japanese invaded the Philippines. The Philippines and its surrounding waters became the focal points of the most bitter and decisive battles fought in the Pacific during World War II. By May 1942, the Japanese had achieved full possession of the islands. US forces, led by Gen. Douglas MacArthur, recaptured the Philippines in early 1945, following their success in the Battle of Leyte Gulf, the largest naval engagement in history. On 4 July 1946, 10 months after the surrender of the Japanese, the Republic of the Philippines was inaugurated, with Manuel A. Roxas as its first president.

Both casualties and war damage wreaked on the Philippines were extensive, and rehabilitation was the major problem of the new state. Communist guerrillas, called Hukbalahaps, were threatening the Republic. Their revolutionary demands were countered by land reforms and by pacification operations in which Ramón Magsaysay distinguished himself. He was elected to the presidency in 1953, and died in an airplane crash in 1957. Magsaysay was succeeded by Carlos P. García, who was subsequently confirmed in office by elections in 1958. Diosdado Macapagal was elected president in November 1961. He was succeeded by Ferdinand E. Marcos, following the 1965 elections. Marcos, reelected in 1969 by a record majority of 62%, became the first president to serve two terms.

On 21 September 1972, President Marcos placed the entire country under martial law, charging that the nation was threatened by a "full-scale armed insurrection and rebellion," ostensibly led by a Communist force called the New People's Army. Marcos arrested many of his more vehement political opponents, some of whom remained in detention for several years. With the state of emergency in force, Marcos proceeded to implement his "New Society" plan, a sweeping reform program that provided for major land redistribution, administrative reorganization, and an attack on crime and official corruption. In January 1973, a new constitution was promulgated, incorporating many of the previously announced reforms. Three national referendums held during 1973–75 to confirm the continuance of martial law were overwhelmingly approved amid scattered charges of tampering and coercion. In September 1975, President Marcos announced a massive new purge of the bureaucracy, involving the initial firing of about 2,000 civil servants and officials. By the end of that year, there were an estimated 6,000 political prisoners still being held by the Marcos government; an estimated 52,000 political arrests had been made since 1971.

Muslim insurrectionist activity in the south intensified during 1974–75, with large battles against government troops occurring in Cotabato and on Jolo and Basilan islands in the early months of 1975. By the end of 1975, government losses had reached an estimated 2,500–3,000. By mid-1976, open fighting had subsided into stalemate, with rebel forces—dominated by the Moro National Liberation Front—shifting their tactics to a campaign of kidnapping and hijacking.

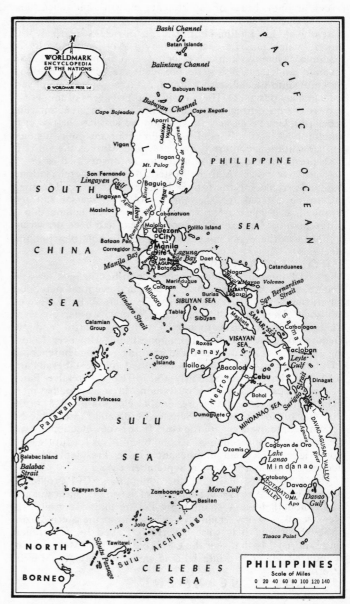

See continental political: front cover R8; physical: back cover Q8
LOCATION: 4°23′ to 21°25′N; 116° to 127°E. **TERRITORIAL SEA LIMIT:** 0–300 mi.

¹²GOVERNMENT

Since 1972, the government has operated under martial law declared by President Marcos. In November 1972, a constitutional convention completed the draft of a new constitution, which went into effect on 17 January 1973, replacing the prior 1935 document. The 1973 constitution is parliamentary in form and democratic in principle. The constitution permits the president to issue legislation under conditions of martial law, pending the convening of a National Assembly at the president's discretion.

The head of state is the president, elected for a six-year term by a majority of the National Assembly (the president was previously elected by direct popular vote). The 1973 constitution also vested broad powers in the office of the prime minister, who controls executive departments, exercises general supervision over local governments, is commander-in-chief of the armed forces, appoints heads of departments, bureaus, and offices, and can conclude treaties subject to ratification by the National Assembly. The Philippine president possesses general veto power (which may be overridden by a two-thirds vote in the National Assembly) and can disapprove items in appropriation, revenue, and tariff bills. The president may call the National Assembly into special session, limiting it to consideration of subjects he may designate. He may suspend privileges of the writ of habeas corpus during emergencies (invasion, insurrection, and rebellion). Under the new constitution, he also has the power to initiate most legislation and to appoint supreme court justices. The constitution conferred on Ferdinand Marcos the posts of both president and prime minister for an unspecified term.

Legislative power is to be vested in a unicameral National Assembly, replacing the former bicameral Congress. Members are to be elected for six-year terms by universal suffrage, although, as of mid-1976, no details of the size of membership or of the plan for legislative reapportionment had been drawn up. Neither was there any indication of plans to hold new national elections.

13 POLITICAL PARTIES

The first Philippine political party, established in 1900, was the Federal Party, which advocated peace and eventual statehood. Later, the Nationalist Party and the Democratic Party were established. They did not produce an actual two-party system, since the Nationalists retained exclusive control and the Democrats functioned as a "loyal opposition." However, following Japanese occupation and the granting of independence, an effective two-party system was instituted by the Liberal Party (LP) and the Nationalist Party (NP). The Progressive Party, formed in 1957 by adherents of Ramón Magsaysay, polled more than 1 million votes in the presidential election of 1958. In the elections of November 1965, Senator Ferdinand Marcos, the NP candidate, received 55% of the vote. In the 1969 election, he was elected to an unprecedented second term. Plans for future elections have been held in abeyance since President Marcos' declaration of martial law in September 1972.

The Communist Party of the Philippines (CPP), officially banned by the Anti-Subversion Act of July 1957, has remained active nonetheless. A splinter pro-Peking guerrilla group, the New People's Army, maintains a base in northeastern Luzon, although its activities were severely checked by government forces in 1975. In that year the CPP's old-line, pro-Moscow wing renounced violence while lending open support for Marcos' reforms.

14 LOCAL GOVERNMENT

Under the constitutions of 1935 and 1973, the country has been divided into provinces, municipalities, and chartered cities, each enjoying a certain degree of autonomy. Each of the 74 provinces elects a governor, a vice-governor, and two provincial board members for terms of four years. Other provincial offices (treasurer, assessor, etc.) are appointive and administratively under the corresponding department of the national government.

Local elections were last held in 1971, with most officeholders retained in office following the invocation of martial law in 1972. Authority of these officials gradually eroded, however. In 1975, the Marcos government began a significant reorganization of

local-government structure. On 27 February 1975, a referendum was approved granting Marcos the power to appoint all governors, vice-governors, and provincial board members. In a more momentous development, the government has begun to strengthen the status of the country's 12 regional councils as governing bodies. Created as administrative units for regional economic development, the councils began to be augmented in late 1975; regional commissioners were provided with sizable budgets by the central government. The councils were encouraged to discover and to implement the programs best suited to their localities.

Municipalities, of which each province is composed, are public corporations governed by municipal law. Within each municipality are villages (barrios), each with a barrio-captain as its head.

There are 61 chartered cities created by special law that only the National Assembly can repeal or amend. Under a 1975 referendum, all city mayors are appointed by the president.

15 JUDICIAL SYSTEM

Under the 1973 constitution, the Supreme Court, composed of a chief justice and 14 associate justices, is the highest judicial body of the state, with supervisory authority over the lower courts. Under martial law, civilian courts have shared jurisdiction with military courts in certain cases. The court of appeals, composed of a presiding justice and 17 associate justices, sitting in divisions of 3 members, relieves the Supreme Court of most cases involving questions of fact. Courts of first instance are trial courts of record. The Philippines is divided into 16 judicial districts subdivided into 212 branches, each court with one or more judges of first instance. There is a municipal court for each city and a justice of the peace for each municipality. Additional special courts include juvenile and domestic relations (Manila), courts of tax appeal, industrial relations, and agrarian relations.

Justices of all lower courts are appointed by the president, generally for life. Philippine courts function without juries.

16 ARMED FORCES

The total armed forces numbered 67,000 in 1975 (excluding the constabulary), virtually double the total for 1969. Defense estimates for 1975/76 totaled ₱2.9 billion ($407 million). The army (39,000 personnel) had 3 light combat infantry divisions and 2 infantry brigades. In 1975, 41 combat battalions were committed to anti-insurgency operations in the south. Navy personnel totaled 14,000. The navy had 1 destroyer escort, 46 patrol craft, 4 minesweepers, and 11 landing ships. In 1975, the Philippines had 10 engineer-construction battalions. The air force had a strength of 14,000. Its equipment consisted of 52 combat aircraft and some 65 transport planes. The Philippine constabulary totaled 34,900; paramilitary forces numbered 59,900; and a local self-defense force, 25,000. Total armed forces reserves in 1975 stood at 218,500.

In 1966, the Philippines concluded a pact with the US under which US base leases were reduced from 99 years to 25 years.

17 MIGRATION

Since political independence, both immigration and emigration have become insignificant. In recent years, immigration has leveled off at approximately 3,000 persons annually, approximately double the number of emigrants.

The rapid growth of the Philippine population has led to considerable internal migration. On Luzon, frontierlike settlements have pushed into the more remote areas. The Cagayan Valley in northern Luzon has received some 100,000 Filipino migrants, mainly since 1956. Mindoro and Palawan islands also have attracted numerous settlers. There also has been a massive movement to metropolitan Manila.

18 INTERNATIONAL COOPERATION

The Philippines is a charter member of the UN and the specialized agencies. It participates in the International Sugar

Agreement and the International Wheat Agreement. The SEATO charter, to which the Philippines is a signatory, was concluded in Manila. In 1966, the Philippines became a member of ASPAC. It led in the formation of the Asian Development Bank, which opened its headquarters in Manila in 1966. In 1973, the Philippines acceded to GATT as a provisional member.

The Philippines has availed itself of various UN agencies for financial and technical assistance.

On 9 June 1975, the Philippines accorded recognition to China in the course of a state visit to Peking by President Marcos, the first such trip by an ASEAN head of state.

19ECONOMY

The Philippines is primarily an agricultural nation, raising crops for subsistence and export. It is the world's largest producer of coconuts and manila hemp (abacá). Manufacturing, which has expanded and diversified since political independence, depends on imported raw materials and cannot supply internal needs. Mining, once centered on gold, is now diversified, with chromite, copper, and iron providing important earnings. The economy is heavily dependent on foreign trade. Exports of primary products fail to balance imports (primarily manufactures) and the government has attempted to restrict imports.

Although Philippine economic productivity is rising (in terms of hours worked, numbers of employed, and capital expansion) and the natural resource base is good (minerals, water, arable land), low living standards and the low purchasing power of the domestic market, plus international competition in export commodities, have restricted growth. In the 1970s, significant gains were made under the Marcos government's infrastructure projects. Transport, electricity, and water-resource development have received primary attention. Well over $1 billion in international loans has been granted in support of this program.

20INCOME

The GNP at market prices reached ₱105,891 million in 1974/75, as compared with ₱84,483 million in 1973/74 and ₱61,118 million in 1972/73. Per capita GNP stood at ₱2,491 in 1974/75, a 19% increase over the previous year, although most of the gain was absorbed by inflation. As of June 1975, GNP was distributed as follows: agriculture, forestry, and fishing, 32.5%; industry, 24.7%; services, 17.5%; commerce, 16.4%; transport and communications, 3.6%; construction, 2.9%; and mining, 2.4%.

21LABOR

The Philippines had an employed labor force of 14,244,000 in mid-1974. About 53% were engaged in agriculture, forestry, and fishing (compared with 58% in 1968); 14.7% in commerce; 13.3% in industry; 8.3% in government and public services; and 10.7% in other sectors. Unemployment fluctuates seasonally, varying between 500,000 and 2 million. In August 1974, the number of unemployed was 578,000.

The Industrial Peace Act of 1953 protects the right of workers to form unions and bargain collectively. In May 1974, the government passed a new labor code that restructured the trade union movement on a one-industry, one-union basis. Strikes, lockouts, and pickets are prohibited. Most trade unions are small; many have been united in the Philippine Trade Union Council or in other national confederations. Government services are provided by the Bureau of Labor Relations and labor arbiters of the Department of Labor.

A minimum wage law provides for a minimum hourly wage of ₱8 for industrial workers and ₱4.75 for agricultural workers. Most small farms, retail stores, and service enterprises are exempt from coverage. Workmen's compensation and social security benefits are available. There has been a basic eight-hour workday since 1939 in industry, with 160% rate of pay for overtime and for Sundays and legal holidays. Labor by women and children is regulated, with employment prohibited for those under age 14.

22AGRICULTURE

About 38% of the total land area is under cultivation, and an additional 25% is considered potentially arable. Three-fourths of the cultivated area is devoted to subsistence crops and one-fourth to commercial crops, mainly for export. Farms average 3.27 hectares in size, but almost half of the farms are less than 2 hectares. Soils are generally fertile, but 30% of the agricultural land is suffering pronounced erosion.

In 1973, the Marcos government's land-reform program undertook to transfer landownership to about half of the country's 900,000 tenant farmers. Under the plan, tenants on farms of 7 hectares or more are entitled to purchase land at terms arrived at with the landlord; landlords can be reimbursed directly by the tenant in 15 annual payments or through government bonds. By mid-1975, 183,600 certificates for land purchase had been issued to tenants; resistance from owners has been strong, however, and only about 15,000 tenants had become amortizing owners by that time.

Roughly half the cultivated land is devoted to the two principal subsistence crops: 60% (3.4 million hectares in 1973) to rice alone and the remainder (2.3 million hectares) to corn. Rice production in 1974 was 3.6 million tons of paddy. With annual requirements of 3.9 million tons, however, the Philippines had to import rice. Corn output in 1973 was 2,342,000 tons. Lesser food crops include sweet potatoes, beans, cassava, peanuts, and various fruits and vegetables. Commercial agriculture, dominated by large plantations, centers around coconuts and copra, sugarcane, tobacco, and pineapples. Copra production, in which the Philippines leads the world, rose from 1,470,900 tons in 1965 to an estimated 1,820,000 tons in 1975. Sugarcane production exceeded 2.6 million tons in 1975, providing the country's single largest export item.

In 1973/74, the government launched a food production drive designed to triple the average rice yield. The key feature of the program was the government's provision of no-collateral credit of up to ₱1,200 per hectare at low interest rates. These loans carried a proviso, however, that they be spent on seed, fertilizer, and pesticide in ratios prescribed by government technicians. The results by the end of 1975 were judged disappointing, however, in part due to farmers' reluctance to purchase fertilizer, which had increased in cost by some 300% during 1974. Further, loan repayment has been lax, prompting the government to use troops to arrest those in default. In 1975, the government began a 10-year irrigation program that called for the expansion of irrigated land from 1 million to 2.3 million hectares.

23ANIMAL HUSBANDRY

Animal husbandry never has been important, meat consumption being very low (an average of 22 lb, including carabao meat, beef, horse meat, pork, and poultry, per person annually). Carabao (4,973,000 in 1973) are the principal draft animals, particularly in the rice paddies; hogs (8,627,000 in 1973) are the chief meat animals (except in Muslim sections). In 1973 there were 2,099,000 head of cattle and about 310,000 horses. Large numbers of goats and a few sheep are also raised. Dairying is insignificant. In 1973 there were 49,964,600 chickens.

24FISHING

Fish is the primary source of protein in the Filipino diet. Some 2,000 species abound in Philippine waters. Despite a doubling in output in the past decade, the fishing industry remains relatively undeveloped, and large quantities of fish are imported. In 1973, the catch totaled 1,248,500 tons (about 15% from fish ponds).

Anchovy, mackerel, sea bass, red snapper, sardines, herring, mullet, barracuda, pompano, tuna, bonito, and shark are most plentiful. Principal commercial fishing grounds are off Palawan, north of Panay and Negros, and to the south and west of Mindanao. These waters are fished by larger ships (40–100 gross tons) operating out of Manila, Iloilo, and Cebu, which account for about one-third of the total catch. Subsistence fishing is conducted throughout the archipelago. Fish ponds, chiefly for cultivation of bangos or milkfish, are principally in the swampy coastal areas of western Panay and around Manila Bay. Fish are generally preserved by sun-drying and salting.

Pearl shells, sponges, sea cucumbers (trepang), shark fins, and sea turtles are exported.

25 FORESTRY

Forests are an important economic resource in the Philippines. Approximately 44% of the Philippines is covered by commercial forests, some 98% of which is owned by the government and managed through the forestry and land bureaus. Major commercial forest reserves are located in Mindanao, Luzon, Samar, Negros, and Palawan. Dipterocarps represent 90% of the salable timber, of which white lauan, red lauan, tangile, apitong, yakal, and guijo contribute 70% of the annual cut (all marketed as Philippine mahogany). In 1973, the production of round wood totaled 35.1 million cu meters.

Local plywood and veneer manufacturing has expanded rapidly in recent years. Among other forest products are bamboo, rattan, resins, tannin, and firewood. Rubber output totaled 23,100 tons in 1973. The total value of forest exports declined to $150 million in 1975 ($337 million in 1973), owing largely to an adverse world market for plywood and logs (in response, the government subsequently banned the export of logs).

26 MINING

Minerals constitute an important sector of the economy, second only to agricultural products in export value. Copper (221,200 tons produced in 1973, from northern Luzon, Cebu, Negros, and Samar) is the leading mineral, followed by gold (17,801 kg from northern Luzon and Cebu) and iron ore (1,414,000 tons from southeastern Luzon, southern and northern Mindanao). The Philippines is the world's leading producer of refractory chromite (from Masinloc) and produces sizable quantities of metallurgic chromite (from western Luzon); chromium ore production in 1973 totaled 232,300 tons. Manganese, mercury, silver, lead, and zinc also are produced for export. The US is the main purchaser of refractory chromite; Japan is the only market for iron ore. With the opening of a refinery in April 1975, the Philippines became Asia's first nickel producer. Clays, limestone, pyrites, guano, silica sands, and salt are produced for local consumption. Coal deposits are small, scattered, and of low quality; however, there is some coking coal on Mindanao. Extensive exploration for petroleum is being conducted by some 16 consortia on Luzon and the Visayas, and in 1961 US and Philippine companies began development of productive oil wells on Cebu. Six offshore and two onshore wells entered production in 1975.

The government has retained mineral rights and leases land to producers.

27 ENERGY AND POWER

Installed electric capacity at the end of 1972 totaled 2,449,000 kw, of which hydroelectric plants contributed 849,000 kw. The total capacity of enterprises generating primarily for public use was 1,770,000 kw. The Philippines' vast hydroelectric potential, estimated at 6,000,000 kw, has thus been only marginally tapped. Large hydroelectric plants have been installed on the Agno and Angat rivers on Luzon and at Maria Cristina Falls on the Agusan River in Mindanao. Thermal plants, mostly burning imported crude oil, contribute the remainder of the electric capacity. A geothermal potential of 1,330,000 kw is presently being developed in Albay, Laguna, and Leyte. Total electric production in 1972 was 10,398 million kwh.

The National Power Corporation (NPC), an autonomous government-owned corporation, supplies bulk power to some 124 franchise holders serving about 200 cities and municipalities. NPC embarked on a program designed to add 946,000 kw to the grid by the end of 1972. In 1975, a US firm contracted to build the country's first nuclear power plant.

28 INDUSTRY

Manufacturing, which accounted for about 24.7% of the GNP in 1975 and employed about 13.3% of the labor force, is limited in spite of notable diversification and expansion in the postwar period. Of the total net domestic production of ₱40,655 million in 1974, 20.8% was derived from processing and manufacturing industries. Industry is concentrated in the Manila area. Despite growing attention to export potential, manufacturing is still conducted primarily for domestic consumption. The leading manufactures (by value) are foods, tobacco products, chemicals and drugs, beverages, wood products, and wearing apparel. There is considerable production of other producer goods (building materials, textile yarns) and consumer goods (textiles, rubber products, metal products). In the past decade, stress has been placed on import substitution, with automobile assembly and manufacture, cement, and shipbuilding showing notable progress in the 1970s. Mineral processing has gained greatly in significance, refined products having clear advantages over raw materials in export markets. Three large ferrous-metal plants have been built since the mid-1960s: A $100-million integrated steel mill with an annual capacity of 250,000 tons of steel products was constructed in 1967 in Mindanao; a second integrated steel mill in Rizal Province, with an annual capacity of 250,000 tons of billets, was completed in 1970; and a Japanese-owned iron sinter plant, with an annual capacity of 5 million tons, was to begin production in 1977. In April 1975, a $270-million nickel refinery began production on Nonoc Island; by 1976, the plant was to attain its full annual capacity of 7.5 million lb of refined metal, accounting for 8% of total world output and placing the Philippines fifth among the world's nickel producers.

In recent years, foreign-owned oil companies have been building refineries in the Philippines, and in 1973, refineries had an annual output of 1,935,000 tons of gasoline, 1,916,000 tons of distillate fuel oil, and 3,715,000 tons of residual fuel oil. Ownership of industrial enterprises is to a large extent in private (usually foreign) hands (US, Chinese, UK, Spanish, and, increasingly, Japanese), owing largely to the reluctance of Filipinos to invest capital in anything but land. The Private Development Corporation, founded in 1963, finances local industrial projects.

29 DOMESTIC TRADE

The archipelagic structure of Philippine marketing requires establishment of regional centers and adds considerably to distribution costs, alien domination of much of marketing, direct government participation, and the proliferation of small firms. Warehousing facilities are available at most ports. Formerly, aliens (chiefly Chinese) controlled about 57% of Philippine retail trade. Under the Retail Trade Nationalization Act of 1954, only Philippine nationals and entities may engage in retail trade. The ruling applies not only to sales to consumers, but also to sales of capital goods to manufacturers and processors. US citizens and entities are exempt.

Small stores typify retail trade. Installment purchasing is little developed. Generally, sales are for cash or on open account. Retailing is conducted on a high markup, low turnover basis. A law provides for price-tagging on retail items.

Business is generally conducted from 8 A.M. to noon and from 1 or 2 P.M. to 5 P.M. Monday through Friday, with Saturday a half day in an increasing number of firms. English is the general language of commercial correspondence.

Most advertising is local. The chief media are newspapers, radio, posters, billboards, and sound trucks.

30 FOREIGN TRADE

The Philippines' foreign trade largely consists of exports of primary commodities and raw materials (agricultural and forest products, minerals) and imports of manufactured items, raw materials, and fuels.

Principal exports in 1968 and 1974 (in thousands of dollars) were:

	1968	1974
Sugar	144,323	759,132
Copper concentrates	79,858	382,239
Crude coconut oil	76,972	358,182
Logs/lumber	217,446	232,551
Copra	123,155	130,997
Other exports	320,396	809,919
TOTALS	962,150	2,673,000

Principal imports in 1968 and 1974 (in thousands of dollars) were:

	1968	1974
Mineral fuels and lubricants	105,169	681,912
Machinery other than electric	237,825	458,052
Base metals	109,949	320,292
Transport equipment	143,412	289,296
Chemical elements and compounds	33,463	230,748
Cereals	40,633	161,868
Explosives and miscellaneous chemicals	38,243	123,984
Electrical machinery and appliances	60,950	113,652
Textile fibers	48,999	96,432
Dairy products	34,658	82,656
Other imports	341,799	885,108
TOTALS	1,195,100	3,444,000

The US and Japan continued in 1974 as the Philippines' primary trading partners, the US taking 42.4% of exports (Japan, 34.9%) and supplying 24.1% of imports (Japan, 26.8%). Between 1968 and the first quarter of 1975, OPEC's share of imports increased from 4.3% to 19.3%, due primarily to the increased cost and demand for petroleum. During the same period the US's share of exports declined from 45.6% to 24.5%.

Principal trade partners in 1974 (in millions of dollars) were:

	EXPORTS	IMPORTS	BALANCE
US	1,133.1	828.8	304.3
Japan	932.4	923.9	8.5
Sa'udi Arabia	7.2	370.0	−362.8
FRG	68.2	135.4	− 67.2
Netherlands	158.0	44.1	113.9
UK	56.3	137.7	− 81.4
Australia	29.5	152.2	−122.7
Kuwayt	.8	161.0	−160.2
Taiwan	27.3	81.1	− 53.8
Hong Kong	31.6	28.6	3.0
Other countries	228.6	581.2	−352.6
TOTALS	2,673.0	3,444.0	−771.0

31 BALANCE OF PAYMENTS

The Philippine economy is greatly dependent upon international payments and receipts because the nation is essentially a producer of raw materials and an importer of manufactures. Throughout most of the postwar period, the Philippines has experienced frequent trade deficits, aggravated by inflationary pressures. Deficits have been counterbalanced by US government expenditures, domestic gold production, transfer of payments from abroad, official loans (US Export-Import Bank,

IBRD, private US banks), net inflow of private investment, tourist receipts, and contributions from the IMF. By terms of a reparations agreement with Japan (1956), the Philippines was to receive the equivalent of ₱1,110 million in services and capital goods over a 20-year period. By 1975, the US had paid the Philippines $708 million for war damage claims and rehabilitation.

Pressures on the balance of payments continued through the 1970s, with trade deficits occurring annually except for 1973, when a payments surplus of $665 million was recorded. Since 1974, however, trade deficits have resumed, prompted by a 350% increase in oil costs; the situation improved somewhat in 1974 with an 87% increase in export prices, but the Philippines remained vulnerable to changes in world market conditions.

Despite adverse trade conditions, international reserves grew at an annual rate of 43.5% during 1968–74, with a jump of 210.8% registered for 1973. As of February 1976, reserves stood at $1,461 million, as compared with $1,505 million at the end of 1974, and $121 million in 1969.

Summaries of the balance of payments for mid-1973 and mid-1975 (in millions of dollars) are given in the following table:

	Mid-1973	Mid-1975
Goods, freight, and insurance on merchandise	256	−465
Other services and private unrequited transfers	112	162
Central government unrequited transfers	− 1	31
Long-term capital		
Direct investment	54	52
Other government capital	− 41	98
Other private capital	−166	22
Short-term capital		
Deposit-money banks	− 80	124
Other institutions	− 87	154
Net errors and omissions	8	− 57

32 BANKING

The Philippine banking structure consists of the government-owned Central Bank (created in 1949), which acts as the government's fiscal agent and administers the monetary and banking system, and of some 36 commercial banks, of which 30 are private domestic banks, 2 government-affiliated, and 4 foreign. Other institutions include about 700 rural banks, 25 private development banks, and 7 savings banks. The largest commercial bank, the Philippine National Bank, is a government institution with about 100 provincial branches and agencies. It supplies about half the commercial credit, basically as agricultural loans. As of 31 August 1975, commercial banks had reserves of ₱1,636 million; demand deposits stood at ₱4,801 million and time and savings deposits at ₱8,293 million. The government operates about 1,500 postal savings banks and the Development Bank of the Philippines, capitalized at ₱500 million.

The money supply as of 31 March 1975 stood at ₱9,606.9 million, an 18.5% increase over the end of 1974, and 29% over 1973. Of the March 1975 total, 53.2% was of external origin.

33 INSURANCE

Some 146 private insurance companies operate in the Philippines, of which 23 are foreign. In 1975, 23 firms were engaged in life insurance, 123 in nonlife, and 4 in reinsurance. Total investments by insurance companies amounted to ₱674 million in 1975.

The Government Service Insurance System, a government organization set up in 1936, provides life insurance, permanent disability, accident, old-age pension, and burial insurance, and salary and real estate loan benefits. Compulsory third party motor liability insurance came into effect on 1 January 1976.

34 SECURITIES

Philippine stock exchanges are self-governing, although the Philippine Securities and Exchange Commission, established in 1936, has supervisory power over registrants. As of the end of 1975, the Philippines had three stock exchanges: the Makati Stock Exchange, carrying the largest number of transactions; the Manila Stock Exchange; and the Metropolitan Stock Exchange, established in February 1975. The volume of transactions remains small, although it is on the increase. Between 1972 and 1974, the trading volume expanded from 23.6 billion shares valued at ₱500 million to 148 billion shares at ₱5.9 billion. Of the 1974 total value, 79.7% was invested in mining concerns, traditionally the most heavily traded sector; 14.1% went into petroleum; and only 6.2% into commerce and industry.

35 PUBLIC FINANCE

Even prior to the 1972 declaration of martial law, the president of the Philippines had considerable authority over the national budget. Since 1972, legislative review has been dispensed with, the budgets being issued by presidential decree. Historically, the budget balanced until the postwar years, which were marked by large deficits. Despite an improved tax structure and fiscal restraints, deficits have continued through the 1970s. In recent years, the government has looked increasingly to domestic sources for financing its investment projects. During 1968–74, the internal debt expanded by an average annual rate of 24.9%, reaching ₱19.1 billion as of March 1975; the external debt rose by an average of 15.4% during the same period, standing at ₱1.8 billion in March 1975.

Economic development has accounted for the largest single share of government expenditures in recent years, accounting for an annual average of 37.9% of total outlay during 1968–76; social development has averaged 26.6% of annual expenditures; and defense has taken an average of 15.8%.

The following table summarizes (in millions of pesos) government revenues and expenditures for 1972/73 and estimates for 1974/75:

	1972/73	1974/75
REVENUES		
Income taxes	1,749.6	2,928.0
Import duties	1,438.1	3,228.7
Excise taxes	62,.7	1,454.5
Other taxes	2,808.8	3,790.4
Other revenues (net)	516.6	3,366.9
TOTALS	7,140.8	14,768.5
EXPENDITURES		
Agriculture and natural resources	1,294.4	4,043.4
Transport and communications	1,293.3	3,173.4
Other economic services	995.0	2,200.7
Education	1,558.2	2,532.7
Other social services	483.6	865.7
Defense	854.5	1,608.1
Debt service	295.3	579.4
Other expenditures	1,799.9	2,838.4
TOTALS	8,574.2	17,841.8

36 TAXATION

The Philippine tax system includes personal and corporate income taxes, excise taxes, license and business taxes, and import duties. The individual income tax is graduated; as of 1975, tax rates varied from 3% on net taxable income of ₱2,000 or less to 70% levied on incomes in excess of ₱500,000. Corporate income taxes are 25% of net income up to ₱100,000 and 35% on amounts exceeding the first ₱100,000. New and necessary industries are wholly tax exempt or subject to reduced taxation.

Other taxes are levied on business enterprises. Specific (excise) taxes are imposed on selected commodities such as alcoholic beverages, tobacco products, and petroleum products. In addition, the government levies a variety of other taxes, including mining and petroleum taxes, stamp taxes, residence taxes, and estate and gift taxes; sales taxes range from 7% (on sawn lumber or locally manufactured appliances) to over 300% on large imported automobiles. Some cities, such as Manila, levy wholesale and retail sales taxes.

37 CUSTOMS AND DUTIES

A new tariff and customs code became effective 1 July 1957. A new classification system based on the Brussels Nomenclature was adopted and new rate structures were enforced. Most imported goods are subject to ad valorem duties based on market values. Most imported products, as well as goods locally produced, are subject to percentage sales taxes at rates ranging from 320% to 7%, varying with classification of commodity (highest for luxuries). Since 1973, the president has been empowered to raise or lower duties (within the 10–100% range), set import quotas, and ban the import of any commodity.

Export duties, based on gross f.o.b. value at time of shipment have been variously applied to shipments of raw materials, namely wood, mineral, vegetable, and animal products.

Although special trading relations exist with the US, many of the privileges are being gradually reduced.

Recent governments have acknowledged severe problems caused by smuggling and corrupt practices of customs officials.

38 FOREIGN INVESTMENTS

In 1974, new foreign investments registered with the government's Board of Investment (BOI, established in 1967) totaled $207.6 million. In 1974, Japan surpassed the US as the leading source of foreign investment; during the first half of 1975, Japanese investors accounted for 30% of total investments placed through BOI, while US interests supplied 24%. By 1974, cumulative US investments in the Philippines were estimated to exceed $1 billion. Investments have been concentrated in trade, utilities, mining, petroleum, refining, and export agriculture. Investment is affected by import controls, exchange controls, and requirements that Filipinos (and US nationals prior to 4 July 1974) exercise a majority control of industries exploiting natural resources. The pace of foreign investment increased following the declaration of martial law and especially after March 1973, when the Central Bank allowed the repatriation of new foreign capital and the unrestricted remittance of profits. Special encouragement is given to pioneer manufacturing endeavors and to joint ventures with a minimum of 60% Filipino capitalization.

Filipino capital investment in foreign countries is negligible. The Philippines has been the recipient of a substantial flow of international economic assistance, especially in the early postwar years. During 1946–73, US assistance alone amounted to $2.7 billion, of which $736 million was in direct economic aid, and $279 million in Eximbank credits. By the end of 1973, debts to multilateral agencies totaled $478.9 million. Since April 1971, international foreign-assistance programs have been coordinated through an IBRD-sponsored International Consultation Group.

39 ECONOMIC POLICY

Although the Philippine economy is based on a private enterprise system, the government owns and operates mills and manufacturing plants. In the mid-1970s, the government implemented a "socialized pricing" policy as well as other control mechanisms that had the effect of strengthening its hand as a determinant in the economy.

Since 1972, the main tenets of the Marcos government's economic policies, as articulated through the National Economic Development Authority, have included the more equitable distribution of income and wealth, substantial development of the infrastructure, and a shift in export emphasis from raw materials (e.g., logs, copra, and copper ore) to finished and semifinished commodities. In line with these goals, the government has sought to strike a balance between long-term, capital-intensive projects and smaller-sized labor-intensive projects. In mid-1975, President Marcos decreed a shift from capital-intensive (i.e., mechanized) to labor-intensive methods for all infrastructural projects, providing cost increases could be held below 10%.

Long-range planning during the past decade has functioned almost exclusively as an expression of President Marcos' policies. The development program (1967–70) aimed to increase the growth rate of per capita income from the 0.9% level in 1961–65 to 2.4%; to increase national income by 5.7% a year during the plan period; and to reduce the unemployment rate from 13% (1965) to 7.2% (1970). The government invested $3.5 billion (19% of total capital formation) in integrating the traditional and modern sectors of the economy. Marcos' first long-range plan following the 1972 declaration of martial law was a four-year (1974–77) infrastructural development program calling for a total outlay of ₱21,500 million, with a foreign exchange component of 42% of the total; 35% was to be expended on transportation, 33% on energy and power, 20% on water resources, 10% on education, health, and welfare, and 2% on telecommunications. A 1976–79 plan, announced in late 1975, envisioned a total outlay of ₱38,000 million (after inflation, a lower figure than the previous plan's), with 42% derived from foreign exchange. Energy and power was to be the major focus of the new plan, with 34% of expenditures, followed by transportation, 30%; water resources, 23%; social programs, 7%; and other sectors, 6%. Major external backing for the plan was to be derived from the IBRD, the Asian Development Bank, the US, and Japan.

40 HEALTH
In 1972 there were 14,425 public and private health establishments in the Philippines, with a combined bed capacity of 35,676. Approximately half of the total bed capacity is in the Manila metropolitan area. In 1972, public and private hospital personnel included 3,544 physicians and 5,895 nurses; private hospital personnel included 117 dentists, 99 midwives, and 222 pharmacists. Pulmonary infections (tuberculosis, pneumonia, bronchitis) are prevalent, but malaria is virtually unknown in larger cities and is being eradicated in the countryside. Average life expectancy in 1975 was estimated at 59.1 years.

41 SOCIAL WELFARE
The government program includes the purchase and subdivision of big estates for resale on installment plans, the settlement of landless families in new areas, building of rural roads, schools, and medical clinics, and the distribution of relief supplies to the needy.

The social security system established in 1957 covers employees of private firms in industrial and agricultural production. Membership for employers is compulsory. The system's benefits include compensation for confinement due to injury or illness, pensions for temporary incapacity, indemnities to families in case of death, old age pensions, and benefits to widows and orphans. Charges to cover the system are paid jointly by employers and employees. A Medical Care Act is now compulsory for social security participants and provides hospital, surgical, and medical-expense benefits to members and their dependents.

42 HOUSING
Manila suffers from severe overcrowding, with more than one-third of its population living as squatters without benefit of running water, sewerage, or electricity. In 1975, the government spent about $8 million for low-cost housing in the city, an amount far below that required to make appreciable inroads on the problem. A major construction boom under way in the 1970s was primarily in nonresidential projects. Accessoria, or wooden row houses with galvanized roofs, characterize Filipino city housing. The typical rural dwelling consists of nipa, cogon, or split bamboo walls, a nipa or cogon roof, a bamboo floor, and open windows; 2.6 rooms (31 sq meters) house an average of six persons.

43 EDUCATION
Education is free and compulsory in the primary schools and is coeducational. English is the main medium of instruction, although Pilipino or local vernacular languages are used for instruction in the lower primary grades. About 83% of the population 10 years of age and over is literate.

Government expenditure on education in 1974/75 was ₱2,532.7 million, or about 14% of the budget. In 1972, primary schools had an attendance of 7,622,424, with a total teaching staff of 247,551. Secondary schools had a total enrollment of 1,791,176, including 1,631,363 in general education and 159,813 in vocational education.

The low level of technical expertise among the work force has prompted the government to encourage high-school graduates to pursue vocational training and to limit the number of places available in liberal arts colleges. In 1972, total enrollment in higher education was 678,343. The University of the Philippines, founded in 1908, is the leading institution of higher learning, with some 25,000 students. In addition, there are some 27 private universities.

44 LIBRARIES AND MUSEUMS
The Philippines has about 400 public libraries and reading rooms. The National Library in Manila (now the Bureau of Public Libraries) suffered severe damage during World War II. Larger libraries are at the universities, notably at the University of the Philippines (more than 700,000 volumes), the University of Santo Tomás (more than 200,000 volumes), Silliman University (more than 116,000 volumes), and the Far Eastern University (more than 117,000).

The National Museum in Manila collects and exhibits materials and conducts research in natural history, ethnography, painting, sculpture, photography, history, and maps. The Santo Tomás Museum contains an art gallery and archaeology and anthropology collections. Government projects in the mid-1970s included the construction of the Folk Arts Center in Manila and the National Arts Center at Makiling, Los Banos.

45 ORGANIZATIONS
Between 1939 and 1949, some 1,370 cooperative associations with 260,134 members had been organized. In general, however, consumer cooperatives were ineffectual before 1952. That year, the first effective cooperative movement, the Agricultural Credit Cooperative Finance Administration, was established with an authorized capital of ₱100 million; its general aims were to promote organization of small farmers, assist in obtaining credit, establish orderly and systematic marketing, and upgrade agriculture.

The Chamber of Commerce of the Philippines has branches in Manila and other important towns, and there are associations of producers and industrial firms in many areas.

The Philippine Academy is the oldest and best-known scholarly organization. There are many associations of persons active in such fields as agriculture, architecture, art, biology, chemistry, economics, library service, literature, engineering, medicine, nutrition, veterinary service, and the press.

46 PRESS
Although freedom of the press is guaranteed by the constitution, censorship was imposed by the Marcos government through its Media Advisory Council. Although disbanded in early 1975, the Council was replaced by a self-censoring publishers' board. Later in the year the Philippines was expelled from membership in the International Press Institute. The following were among the leading dailies published in the Philippines in 1975:

MANILA	LANGUAGE	CIRCULATION
Philippines Daily Express	English	269,163
The Bulletin Today	English	200,000
Balita Ng Maynila	Pilipino	115,350
United Daily News	Chinese and English	16,000

OTHER CITIES		
Times-Journal (Pasig)	English	89,717
Business Day (Quezon City)	English	25,000
The Republic (Cebu)	English	20,000

An underground press movement became increasingly active in 1975, including *Ang Bayan*, the Communist Party organ; the pro-New People's Army *Liberation*; and *Signs of the Times*, a frequently antigovernment weekly published by the Association of Major Religious Superiors, containing provincial news supplied by parish priests.

47 TOURISM

In 1951, the government undertook the development of tourism as an income-earning industry with the establishment of the Bureau of Tourist and Travel Industry and its semiprivate subsidiary, the Philippine Tourist and Travel Association. In 1975, an estimated 500,000 tourists visited the Philippines. Tourist spending increased from $38.3 million in 1972/73 to $124.2 million in 1974/75.

A tourist requires a passport and a 59-day tourist visa; no visa is required for a stay of less than 15 days. Visas are renewable. Transients are allowed a stay of 72 hours. Smallpox inoculation certificates are required and cholera inoculations for those arriving from an infected area. Typhoid, tetanus-diphtheria, and poliomyelitis vaccinations are recommended.

Hotels in Manila meet international standards. A convention center and several major new hotels were added in Manila in the mid-1970s. In recent years, hotels with good accommodations have been constructed in some provincial cities.

48 FAMOUS FILIPINOS

Filipinos have made the most important marks in the political arena. Foremost are José Rizal (1861–96), distinguished novelist, poet, physician, linguist, statesman, and national hero; Andrés Bonifacio (1863–97), leader of the secret Katipunan movement against Spain; and Emilio Aguinaldo y Famy (1869–1964), commander of the revolutionary forces and president of the revolutionary First Philippine Republic (1899). Notable Filipinos of this century include Manuel Luiz Quezon y Molina (1878–1944), first Commonwealth president; Ramón Magsaysay (1907–57), distinguished leader in the struggle with the Hukbalahaps; and Carlos Peña Rómulo (b.1899), Pulitzer Prize-winning author, diplomat, and president of the fourth UN General Assembly. Ferdinand E. Marcos (b.1917), who won distinction as a guerrilla fighter during the Japanese occupation, has been the dominant political figure in the Philippines since his first election to the presidency in November 1965. His wife, Imelda Romualde Marcos (b.1930), emerged as a powerful force within her husband's government during the 1970s.

Fernando Ma. Guerrero (1873–1929) was the greatest Philippine poet in Spanish. Two painters of note were Juan Luna y Novicio (1857–99) and Félix Resurrección Hidalgo y Padilla (1853–1913). Contemporary writers who have won recognition include Claro M. Recto (1890–1960), José García Villa (b.1914), and Carlos Bulosan (b.1914). José A. Estella (1870–1945) is the best-known Filipino composer. Filipino prizefighters have included two world's champions, Pancho Villa and Ceferino García.

49 DEPENDENCIES

The government of the Philippines claims former British North Borneo (now the Malaysian states of Sabah and Sarawak and the UK protectorate of Brunei), basing its claims on actions of the sultan of Sulu, in whom original sovereignty resided. The government insists that the Sulu sultan leased North Borneo to representatives of the British North Borneo Company and that he did not and was not empowered to sell outright sovereignty rights to private persons or firms.

50 BIBLIOGRAPHY

American University. *Area Handbook for the Philippines.* Washington, D.C.: Government Printing Office, 1969.

Averch, H. A., F. H. Denton, and J. E. Koehler. *A Crisis of Ambiguity: Political and Economic Development in the Philippines.* Santa Monica, Calif.: Rand, 1970.

Benitez, Conrado. *History of the Philippines, Economic, Social, Political.* Boston: Ginn, 1940.

Berstein, David. *The Philippine Story.* New York: Farrar, Straus, 1947.

Blair, Emma Helen, and James Alexander Robertson. *The Philippine Islands, 1493–1898.* 55 vols. Cleveland: Clark, 1903–9.

Carlson, Sevinc, and Robert A. Kilmarx (eds.). *U.S.-Philippines Economic Relations.* Washington, D.C.: Georgetown University Center for Strategic and International Studies, 1971.

Corpuz Onofre. *Philippines.* New York: Cambridge University Press, 1965.

Eggan, Frederick Russell, et al. *Selected Bibliography of the Philippines.* New Haven, Conn.: Human Relations Area Files, 1956.

Farwell, George. *Mask of Asia: The Philippines Today.* New York: Praeger, 1967.

Forbes, William Cameron. *The Philippine Islands.* Cambridge: Harvard University Press, 1945.

Golay, Frank H. (ed.). *The Philippines: Problems and Prospects.* New York: Asia Society, 1971.

Golay, Frank H. (ed.). *The United States and the Philippines.* Englewood Cliffs, N.J.: Prentice-Hall, 1966.

Henderson, William (ed.). *Southeast Asia: Problems of United States Policy.* Cambridge: MIT Press, 1964.

Jocano, F. L. *Growing Up in a Philippine Barrio.* New York: Holt, 1969.

Keesing, Felix Maxwell. *The Ethnohistory of Northern Luzon.* Stanford, Calif.: Stanford University Press, 1962.

Krieger, Herbert William. *Peoples of the Philippines.* Washington, D.C.: Smithsonian Institution, 1942.

Landé, Carl H. *Leaders, Factions and Parties: The Structure of Philippine Politics.* New Haven, Conn.: Yale University Press, 1965.

Meyer, Milton W. *A Diplomatic History of the Philippine Republic.* Honolulu: University of Hawaii Press, 1965.

Mineral Resources of the Philippines. Manila: Bureau of Mines, Department of Agriculture and Natural Resources, Republic of the Philippines, 1955.

Phelan, John L. *The Hispanization of the Philippines: Spanish Aims and Filipino Responses, 1565–1700.* Madison: University of Wisconsin Press, 1959.

Roland, Albert. *Philippines.* New York: Macmillan, 1967.

Rómulo, Carlos Peña. *Crusade in Asia: Philippine Victory.* New York: Day, 1955.

Smith, Robert Aura. *Philippine Freedom, 1946–1958.* New York: Columbia University Press, 1958.

Spencer, Joseph Earle. *Land and People in the Philippines: Geographic Problems in a Rural Economy.* Berkeley: University of California Press, 1952.

Wernstedt, Frederick L., and Joseph Earle Spencer. *The Philippine Island World: A Physical, Cultural, and Regional Geography.* Berkeley: University of California Press, 1967.

Wolff, Leon. *Little Brown Brother: How the United States Purchased and Pacified the Philippine Islands at the Century's Turn.* New York: Doubleday, 1961.

Yen, Y. C. James. *Rural Reconstruction and Development.* New York: Praeger, 1967.

PORTUGUESE ASIAN DEPENDENCIES

MACAO

Macao (Macau) is situated on the south coast of China, on the west side of the Canton River, almost directly opposite Hong Kong, which is 56 km (35 mi) away. Located between 22°6' and 22°13'N and 113°33' and 113°37'E, it consists of a peninsula, about 5 km (3 mi) long and 1.6 km (1 mi) wide, and two small islands, Taipa and Coloane, with a total area of about 16 sq km (6 sq mi). The total coastline is 41 km (25 mi).

The estimated population in 1975 was 320,000. The population density of about 53,300 per sq mi was one of the highest in the world. Chinese, many of them refugees from China, comprise about 99% of the total. Large-scale movement of Chinese in and out of Macao has inevitably affected the economic and social life of the territory.

In 1973 there were 19 miles of paved roads and about 5,000 motor vehicles. A causeway links Taipa and Coloane islands, and a 1.7-mile bridge between Macao and Taipa was completed in 1974. Macao's main asset is its harbor. In 1974, 6,960,000 gross tons of shipping entered the port. Macao has six postal stations and two telephone and two telegraph stations. The number of telephones in 1974 was about 13,000. A government and a private radio station both broadcast in Portuguese and Chinese.

The first Portuguese attempts to establish relations with China were made in the early 16th century. In 1557, the Chinese authorities agreed to Portuguese settlement of Macao, with leasehold rights. The Portuguese, however, treated Macao as their possession and established a municipal government in the form of a senate of the local inhabitants. Disputes concerning jurisdiction and administration developed. In 1833, Macao together with Timor became an overseas province of Portugal under the control of the governor-general of Goa, and in 1849, Portugal succeeded in having Macao declared a free port. On 26 March 1887, China confirmed perpetual occupation and government of Macao and its dependencies by Portugal, but the question of the delimitation of the boundaries was left unsettled.

As the only neutral port on the South China Sea during World War II, Macao enjoyed a modicum of prosperity. In 1949, the government of the People's Republic of China renounced the "unequal treaty" granting Portuguese suzerainty over Macao but has refrained from upsetting the status quo. Civil disturbances in late 1966 between Macao police and Chinese leftist groups resulted in concessions to the territory's pro-China elements. The 1974 military coup in Portugal led to a constitutional change in Macao's status from a Portuguese province to a "special territory." In changes enacted in 1976, Macao continued to be ruled by a Portugal-appointed governor, although the territory is now empowered to make its own laws, appoint and control its own civil service, and contract directly for foreign loans. A new 17-member Legislative Council was, for the first time, to include 6 popularly elected delegates. In January 1976, Portugal's remaining few hundred troops were withdrawn from Macao.

The unit of currency is the Macao pataca (P); Hong Kong dollars circulate freely. P1 = US$0.03408 (or US$1 = P29.343). In 1974, government revenues totaled P129.6 million, with cor-

porate taxes and import duties important sources; expenditures were P87.8 million. At the end of 1974, currency in circulation stood at P112 million, as compared with P80.8 million in 1972.

Macao's is primarily a consumer economy. There is little agriculture, and the territory is almost entirely dependent on imports for its food. Fishing is the most important primary activity. Industries, which employed 35,200 persons in 1974, consist mainly of small- or medium-scale enterprises concerned especially with the finishing of imported semimanufactured goods, in particular the manufacture of clothing, ceramics, matches, and fireworks, and the printing and dyeing of cloth and yarn. With the aura of a quiet Mediterranean seaport and a variety of gambling facilities, Macao now looks to tourism as its chief source of income, although in recent years the volume of non-Hong Kong visitors has been declining. In 1974, 2.13 million tourists (including 1.7 million from Hong Kong) spent P735.1 million in Macao. In 1975, large-scale development of tourist facilities and infrastructure was under way on Taipa and Coloane islands.

Macao's historic role has been that of a gateway for south China, from which it still imports most of its food. It has close trade relations with neighboring Hong Kong, another free port, which serves as a point of transshipment for Macao's exports and imports. Gold trading, formerly a major facet in Macao's economy, virtually came to a halt in 1974–75 following the Hong Kong government's decision to lift its own restrictions on gold trading. During 1960–73, some 347 tons of gold were imported into Macao.

Total exports in 1974 were valued at P551.2 million. The principal exports are textiles, clothing, ceramics, optical equipment, and fish; 43% of exports went to EEC countries; 9.2% to the US; 9% to Hong Kong; and 8.3% to Portugal. The principal imports for domestic use are rice, fuels, and chemicals. Total imports in 1974 were valued at P648.7 million, with China, Hong Kong, Portugal, and the US the main suppliers. Transit trade still dominates the flow in and out of Macao.

In 1974, primary schools had 20,205 pupils and secondary schools, 16,479 students. Government schools are operated mainly for the children of civil servants and wealthier families. Poor Chinese students are educated in schools indirectly supported by China. The Medical and Health Department, critically understaffed, had only 14 physicians and 94 nurses in 1974; it operates a 400-bed hospital. The 800-bed Kiang Vu Hospital has a largely China-trained staff. Major reforms in education, health, housing, and welfare services were being studied by the government in 1976.

PORTUGUESE TIMOR

The overseas province of Portuguese Timor, lying between 8°7' and 9°28's and 124°2' and 127°22'E, consists of the northeastern part of the island of Timor (one of the Lesser Sunda Islands of Indonesia), the small enclave of Okussi Ambeno on the northwest coast of Indonesian Timor, and two smaller islands, Atauro and Jaco, with a total area of 14,925 sq km (5,763 sq mi). A central chain of mountains has its highest points in the western part of the territory. The coastal areas are generally very hot, but the mountain regions have a more moderate climate. The Asian monsoon brings rain all over the island from December to May, while the Australian monsoon brings rain over the south coast and the central region between June and August.

In 1975, the estimated population was 672,000. Indigenous Malayo-Polynesian inhabitants totaled about 86%, Chinese 6%, and mestizos 6%. The rest were of European and other origins. The population density is 45 per sq km. Díli, seat of government and the only important port, has about 25,000 inhabitants.

Non-Indonesian languages exhibiting features of Papuan (Dagada, Makasai, Kairui, and Bunak) are spoken in the mountainous areas. Indonesian languages with a Melanesian structure, including Membai, Tukodeda, Galoli, and Idate, are spoken in the rest of the territory; Tetum is the official and most widely used language. Portuguese has also been important as a lingua franca.

The territory has neither railroads nor inland water transport, but there is a good road system of 2,896 km. Small coastal sailing vessels are the chief means of transport. Aerial services are maintained between the major centers, and there is weekly air service with Kupang, capital of the Indonesian part of the island. Díli has an international airfield. The territory has 59 telephone stations (794 instruments in 1972) and 4 radio stations at Díli.

The first Portuguese arrived at Okussi in the mid-16th century. After many conflicts with the Dutch, the present boundaries were finally fixed around 1850, but there was considerable continued local resistance, and military campaigns were fought until 1913. Timor was occupied by the Japanese in 1942, but in 1945 it was retaken by Allied forces and returned to Portuguese administration.

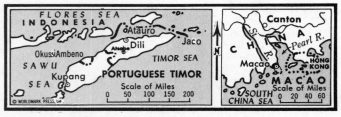

Port. Timor See cont'l pol.: front cover R10; phys.: back cover Q10
Macao See cont'l pol.: front cover P7; phys.: back cover P7

Following the Portuguese military coup in August 1974, representatives of Portugal, Indonesia, and Australia met during September–October to discuss the territory's future. A decolonization program was set in motion with an attempt to distribute authority among the three leading Timorese political factions—the Timorese Democratic Union (UDT), a moderate group initially favoring continued association with Portugal; the Revolutionary Front for Independent East Timor (Fretilin), founded from a nucleus of leftist intellectuals and favoring a graduated course toward full independence; and the Popular Democratic Association of Timor (Apodeti), which advocated merger with Indonesia. Rivalry among these groups erupted into armed conflict in August 1975. Following an attempt by the UDT to mount a coup against Portuguese authorities, Fretilin forces, with support of local troops, emerged victorious in the first round of fighting, occupying Díli and eventually winning

control of most of the territory, including the former Apodeti stronghold of Atsabe. Remnants of the UDT fled in disarray toward the Indonesian border along with some 40,000 refugees. UDT leaders thereupon shifted their policy to integration with Indonesia. On 6 October, UDT and Apodeti forces launched a counterattack, apparently with the support of Indonesian equipment and personnel.

On 7 December 1975, a force of 1,000 Indonesian paratroopers invaded the territory and seized the capital. Portugal thereupon broke off relations with Indonesia, while the UN General Assembly and Security Council subsequently voted to condemn the attack and called for Indonesia's withdrawal. Most major resistance meanwhile collapsed amid reports of civilian massacres carried out by all of the major parties to the crisis. On 3 May 1976, Indonesia announced its official integration of the territory as Indonesia's 27th province, in accord with the resolution of a 37-member People's Assembly meeting in Díli.

Portuguese Timor's economy is highly primitive and undeveloped. Although both soil and climate are favorable for agriculture, there has been no significant progress in economic development. About 90% of the population is engaged in subsistence agriculture, which accounts for three-fourths of the GNP. Corn and rice are the important grains; sweet potatoes, beans, cassava, and a variety of other food crops are also grown. Coffee provides about 90% of the territory's foreign exchange and has been grown mostly on large Portuguese-owned estates.

In 1972 there was more livestock than population; livestock plays an important part in the economy. Livestock included 83,000 head of cattle, 197,000 goats, 133,000 buffalo, and 120,000 horses. There are many valuable woods, but except for sandalwood most of them have not yet been commercialized. Industrial production is limited to a few small-scale factories and a sawmill.

Coffee of excellent quality is the principal export, followed, in terms of value, by copra and rubber. A substantial amount of imports, which include foodstuffs, textiles, machinery, and metal products, originate in Portugal, Singapore, Australia, Macao, and Taiwan. In 1974/75, exports were valued at 140 million escudos (162 million in 1973/74) and imports at 310 million escudos (252 million escudos in 1973/74). Normally self-sufficient in food, Portuguese Timor was compelled to import 84 million escudos' worth of foodstuffs in 1974/75 as a result of the civil war.

In 1974, government revenues of 215.7 million escudos were balanced by expenditures. Large government deficits were traditionally offset by subsidies from Portugal. Under a Portuguese development plan (1968–73), 187.7 million escudos in investments were approved for the territory. Prior to the civil war, plans were under way to develop a tourist industry; 12,783 tourists visited Portuguese Timor in 1972.

In 1971, health facilities included 74 hospitals and clinics, with 1,590 beds; there were only 24 physicians (about one for every 25,000 persons), 1 dentist, 3 pharmacists, 138 nurses, and 14 midwives. Malaria is the most prevalent disease, and dietary-deficiency diseases are common. Average life expectancy in 1975 was estimated at 40 years.

Education has been mainly concentrated in the Roman Catholic missions. In 1971/72, the territory had 339 primary schools, with 33,655 pupils, and 1 secondary school, with 197 students. In addition, Timor has 5 technical schools, with 930 students, and a teacher-training school, with 108 pupils.

QATAR

State of Qatar
Dawlat Qatar

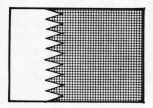

CAPITAL: Doha (Al-Dawhah). **FLAG**: Maroon with white serrated border at the hoist. **ANTHEM**: *Qatar National Anthem*. **MONETARY UNIT**: The Qatar riyal (QR) of 100 dirhams was introduced on 13 May 1973. There are coins of 5, 10, 25, and 50 dirhams, and notes of 1, 5, 10, 50, and 100 riyals. QR 1 = $0.2527 (or $1 = QR3.957). **WEIGHTS AND MEASURES**: Both the British and metric systems are used; however, it is the government's intention to convert fully to the metric system in the future. **HOLIDAYS**: New Year's Day, 1 January; Independence Day, 3 September; Christmas, 25 December; Boxing Day, 26 December. Muslim religious holidays include 'Id al-Fitr, 'Id al-'Adha', and Milad al-Nabi. **TIME**: 4 P.M.=noon GMT.

¹LOCATION, SIZE, AND EXTENT
Comprising an area of 11,000 sq km (4,247 sq mi), the State of Qatar consists of a peninsula projecting northward into the Persian Gulf, extending *161* km (*100* mi) N–S and *89* km (*55* mi) E–W. It is bordered on the s by the United Arab Emirates (UAE) and Sa'udi Arabia and has a total boundary length of *490* km (*305* mi). Qatar also includes a number of islands, of which the most important is Halul.

²TOPOGRAPHY
The terrain is generally flat and sandy, rising gradually from the east to a central limestone plateau. The Dukhan anticline rises from the west coast as a chain of hills of up to 325 feet and is about 56 km (35 miles) long. Some low cliffs mark the northern end of the east coast. Extensive salt flats at the base of the peninsula support the theory that Qatar was once an island.

³CLIMATE
Qatar's summer, from May to October, is extremely hot. Mean temperatures in June are 42°C (108°F), dropping to 15°C (59°F) in winter. Humidity is high along the coast. Rainfall is minimal.

⁴FLORA AND FAUNA
Vegetation is sparse and typical of Gulf desert regions. The gazelle, once common in Qatar, is now rarely seen. Protection is afforded to a herd of rare white oryx. Jerboas (desert rats) and an occasional fox are found. Birds include flamingo, cormorant, osprey, kestrel, plover, lark, and other migrants. Reptiles include monitors, other lizards, and land snakes. Life in the seas around Qatar is considerable and varied, including prawn, king mackerel, shark, grouper, and swordfish.

⁵POPULATION
In 1975, the population was estimated at 180,000, with some 80% residing on the eastern coast in the vicinity of Doha. Two other towns have grown up around the oil industry: Dukhan and the port of Umm Sa'ud. Average density is about 16 persons per sq km (42 per sq mi).

⁶ETHNIC GROUPS
Only about half of the population are indigenous Qataris, who are of Bedouin Arab stock. Nomadic Bedouin tribes occupy the interior. An additional 20% of the population comprises Arab immigrants from Egypt, Iraq, the United Arab Emirates (UAE), and Oman, as well as a large group of Palestinians. Iranians comprise about 23% of the total, and Indians and Pakistanis about 7%. About 1,000 Europeans live in Doha.

⁷LANGUAGE
Arabic is the language of Qatar, spoken in a form akin to the Arabic of Bahrayn and other parts of the Gulf. Thus, Qatar's colloquial Arabic is rich in Persian words, but is closer to the classical than the spoken Arabic of the Levant. English is widely spoken, and Farsi is used by smaller groups in Doha.

⁸RELIGION
Islam is the official religion of Qatar and is practiced by the great majority of the people. The Qataris are mainly Sunni of the Wahhabi sect.

⁹TRANSPORTATION
The modern road system dates from 1967. The first priority was to construct a highway to the Sa'udi border and link up with the main roads to Kuwayt, Jordan, Syria, and the West. By 1975, a network of more than 800 km (500 miles), including 354 km (220 miles) of first-class roads, linked the various parts of Qatar.

Doha airport's 15,000-foot runway is the second-longest civil runway in the world. About 20 international airlines, including BA, Gulfair, and MEA, regularly serve Doha.

The new port of Doha, opened in 1972, can accommodate four vessels. A dock with facilities for ships drawing up to 18 feet was completed in 1973. Qatar's port facilities remain grossly inadequate, however, and further expansion is urgently being undertaken. An industrial port is being constructed at Umm Sa'id, currently the major outlet for crude oil.

¹⁰COMMUNICATIONS
Qatar's telephone, cable, and Telex services are operated by Cable and Wireless in partnership with the Qatar government. A 5,000-line telephone switchboard was installed in Doha in mid-1976, with stations at Khor, Ruwais, and Umm Sa'id to be added by the end of 1977. In 1976, Doha's fully automatic telephone exchange had a total of 17,000 lines. The rate of telephone ownership—about 13 instruments per 100 persons—is the highest in the Arab world. International telecommunications are channeled through Bahrayn, but Qatar is developing its own international telecommunications lines, and work on an earth station for beaming on the internationally owned Indian Ocean satellite is nearing completion.

The government's domestic radio broadcasts, until 1975 carried by 100-kw high-frequency and 50-kw and 10-kw medium-frequency equipment, currently average 12 hours daily. In September 1975, the government added a 750-kw medium-frequency transmitter at al-Arish, on the northern coast. Color television is broadcast from two transmitters totaling 200 kw.

¹¹HISTORY
Archaeological evidence shows that human habitation existed in Qatar for many centuries prior to the modern age; however, little is known of Qatar's history until the 18th century. The al-Thani family, forebears of the present rulers, arrived in Qatar then from what is now Sa'udi Arabia. During the same century,

the al-Khalifah family, who currently rule Bahrayn, arrived from Kuwayt.

In 1868, Britain intervened in behalf of the Qatari nobles and negotiated the Perpetual Maritime Truce, signed by Muhammad bin Thani, an accord that terminated the Bahrayni claim to Qatar in exchange for a tribute payment. In 1872, however, Qatar fell under Ottoman occupation and Jasim bin Muhammad bin Thani became Turkish deputy-governor of Qatar. Turkish dominion prevailed until the outbreak of World War I and the subsequent withdrawal of the Turks from the Arabian Peninsula. Qatar thereupon established its independence and, in 1916, Shaykh 'Abdallah bin Jasim al-Thani signed a treaty with the UK granting British protection in exchange for a central role for the UK in Qatar's foreign affairs. A 1934 treaty further strengthened this relationship. Commercial quantities of high-quality oil were discovered at Dukhan in 1940, but full-scale exploitation did not begin until 1949.

In 1960, Shaykh Ahmad bin 'Ali al-Thani succeeded his father, who had become too old to rule effectively. Nonetheless, social and economic development during the subsequent decade was disappointing, especially in view of the increasing availability of oil revenues. In January 1968, the UK announced its intention to withdraw its forces from the Persian Gulf States by the end of 1971. Discussions took place among the Trucial States, Bahrayn, and Qatar, with a view to forming a federation. The Trucial States formed the United Arab Emirates, but Qatar could not agree to the terms of the union. On 1 September 1971, the independent State of Qatar was declared. A new treaty of friendship and cooperation was signed with the UK, and Qatar was soon admitted to membership in the Arab League and the UN.

On 22 February 1972, Shaykh Khalifah bin Hamid al-Thani, the deputy amir and prime minister, seized power in a peaceful coup, deposing his cousin, Shaykh Ahmad. Since his accession, Shaykh Khalifah has led a vigorous program of economic and social reform, including the transfer of royal income to the state.

12 GOVERNMENT
Qatar is a monarchy ruled by an amir. In 1970, in anticipation of independence, Qatar promulgated a Basic Law, including a bill of rights, that provides for an executive Council of Ministers (Cabinet) and a legislative Advisory Council, members of which are to serve three-year terms. The Council of Ministers, appointed by the amir and led by a prime minister (the head of government), formulates public policy and directs the ministries. Shaykh Khalifah has served as acting prime minister since the 1972 coup, and the 20-member Advisory Council has had little effective power. All government posts have remained appointive. No electoral system has been instituted and no provisions for suffrage have been established.

13 POLITICAL PARTIES
There are no organized political parties, but the influx of numerous expatriate Arabs has begun to introduce progressive and nationalist ideas into traditional Qatari society.

14 LOCAL GOVERNMENT
Government reform has been active most notably in the decentralization of administrative authority. Since 1968, six municipal councils (Doha, al-Wakrah, Khor, Takhira, Rayyan, and Umm Salal) have been functioning in Qatar. The councils manage their own planning and development programs, but they remain directly accountable to the Ministry of Municipal Affairs. The Doha Municipal Council has 15 elected members and 4 appointed by the amir, generally the pattern in the other municipalities.

15 JUDICIAL SYSTEM
The legal system is based on the shari'ah (canonical Muslim law). The judiciary consists of the Qatar municipal court, the traffic and labor court, and the court of justice. The Basic Law of 1970 provided for the creation of an independent judiciary.

16 ARMED FORCES
The Quatar Security Force is composed of 2,200 personnel, organized into a 1,600-man army and small naval and air force units. Military equipment in use includes 13 UK-supplied combat aircraft and 4 coastal patrol boats. The police force, numbering around 1,300, has responsibility for internal security, criminal investigations, traffic, and marine patrols.

17 MIGRATION
By the mid-1970s, an influx of Arab and non-Arab workers comprised half of Qatar's total population. Since 1972, the government has exerted greater control over this influx with a view to providing more employment opportunities for Qataris.

18 INTERNATIONAL COOPERATION
Following independence in 1971, Qatar joined both the UN and the Arab League. The new state has since established diplomatic relations with most Arab and many non-Arab countries, including the US, UK, USSR, France, and Japan. Qatar is a member of OAPEC and OPEC, as well as UNESCO, FAO, IMF, and IBRD.

19 ECONOMY
Until recent decades, the Qatar peninsula was an undeveloped, impoverished area, with a scant living provided by the traditional occupations of pearl diving, fishing, and nomadic herding. In 1940, a major oil discovery was made at Dukhan and, in the ensuing decades, oil has been the dominant factor in the Qatari economy. Oil exports in 1974 earned $1.5 billion, as compared with $25 million for all other exports and reexports. Other economic activities remain limited, but agriculture has received considerable stress in recent years, resulting in quantities of fruits and vegetables becoming available for export in the 1970s.

20 INCOME
Qatar's 1974 GNP was put at $1.5 billion, of which some 90% was derived from oil. Per capita income, estimated at about $4,000 in 1974, was growing at an average annual rate of 12% in the mid-1970s.

21 LABOR
About 70% of the economically active population is engaged in industry (largely oil-related) and services. Most of the remaining 30% work in small-scale farming, grazing, and fishing. The oil companies directly employ around 2,000 workers.

Working conditions are governed by labor laws of 1972, which provide for a 48-hour week, annual leave, severance notice, and holiday and sickness allowances. There are no trade unions. Consultative bodies of workers have been set up in the oil companies.

22 AGRICULTURE
Despite its dry climate, Qatar has sufficient land and water (from 1,400 natural wells) to feed its population and, at current levels of expansion, is expected to achieve self-sufficiency in food by 1980. By the mid-1970s, development sufficed to provide small surpluses for export, amounting, in 1974, to 1,000 tons of vegetables—including carrots, tomatoes, and eggplants—to other Gulf states. In 1974, 25,520 tons of fodder (mainly alfalfa) and 18,342 tons of vegetables were produced.

23 ANIMAL HUSBANDRY
A 1974 census of Qatar's livestock population showed 5,616 head of cattle, 36,380 sheep, 42,315 goats, 8,148 camels, 297 horses, and 68,600 poultry.

24 FISHING
The Qatar National Fishing Co., a Qatar-UK partnership begun in 1966, exports Gulf prawns, mainly to Japan and the US. In 1974, it exported 290,000 kg, valued at QR1,232 million. Pearl fishing, once important in Qatar, has virtually disappeared.

25 FORESTRY
There are no forests in Qatar.

26 MINING
Qatar's substantial oil reserves, estimated at 6 billion barrels,

dominate the country's economy. Production averaged 420,000 barrels per day in 1975 (600,000 in 1974), and oil revenues have approached $1.5 billion annually in the 1970s. The Qatar Petroleum Co. (QPC) controls the Dukhan oil field on the west coast, and Shell Qatar exploits three seabed fields between 80 km and 120 km off the east coast. Qatar Oil Co. (Japan) was due to begin production in the waters between Qatar and Abu Dhabi in 1976; under a marine agreement, Abu Dhabi and Qatar will share the proceeds.

A huge new offshore gas field being developed in 1976 promised to become the largest venture ever undertaken in Qatar. Gas reserves estimated in the range of 40,000 billion cu feet placing the field among the world's largest, ranking with Hassi R'Mel in Algeria and Gröningen in the Netherlands.

In 1974, QPC and Shell agreed to terms for a 60% transfer of their shares to the government. Early in 1975, the government began negotiations with both companies on the terms of an eventual complete take-over of the industry. In anticipation of achieving full ownership, the government formed the Qatar General Petroleum Corporation (QGPC) in September 1974 as a holding company and as the operational arm of the Ministry of Petroleum. QGPC has a capital of QR1 billion and will eventually extend its sphere from oil to gas and all related industries.

27 ENERGY AND POWER
Qatar's electrical capacity was 160 Mw in 1975, as compared with 70 Mw in 1970. The capacity of the 10-turbine power station at Ra's Abu Abbud was increased by 17 Mw in 1975. Additional generators are located at Umm Sa'id, Umm Bab, Dukhan, and central Doha.

The government is taking vigorous action to ensure the long-term reliability and quality of its water and electricity supply services. Two major projects in 1975 were the construction of a gas-fueled QR900-million complex at Ra's Abu Futas, with ultimate generating and distillation capacities of 200 Mw and 30 million gallons per day; and the development of a master plan for water supply and distribution to meet consumption demands through 1990.

28 INDUSTRY
Apart from oil-exporting enterprises, there are only four industrial plants of any size in Qatar: a cement works, a small local refinery, a fertilizer plant, and a natural gas liquefaction plant. In 1976, Shell was constructing a second and much larger liquefaction plant (expected to be operational in 1978) to utilize an anticipated daily supply of some 240 million cu feet of gas from its offshore fields. To carry out the project, with a cost put at $200 million, the Qatar Gas Co. was formed.

The government also hoped to complete a petrochemical complex, with anticipated capacity of 200,000 tons a year of ethylene and 145,000 tons a year of polyethylene. A $150-million iron and steel complex being built by Kobe Steel of Japan at the Umm Sa'id industrial estate was expected to produce 400,000 tons of steel products a year by mid-1977. Iron bars for use in reinforcing concrete in building were to be the major product.

29 DOMESTIC TRADE
As elsewhere in the Gulf, wholesale and retail operations in Qatar are frequently combined in the same enterprise. Local laws require that commercial agents be of Qatari nationality.

Business hours are from 8 A.M. to 12:30 P.M. and from 3 to 6 P.M. Government offices are open in the mornings only, as are some of the larger companies. Consumer advertising can be undertaken in motion picture theaters, the press, and on billboards. Radio and television services do not accept advertising.

30 FOREIGN TRADE
In the mid-1970s, crude oil supplied more than 98% of Qatar's annual exports. Exports, traditionally far in excess of imports, rose from QR2,946.4 million in 1973 to QR9,092 million in 1974. Principal non-oil products are fertilizers, shrimp, agricultural commodities, and cement. Exports and reexports, exclusive of petroleum, totaled QR145.7 million in 1974, as compared with QR67.2 million in 1973. The main destinations were Sa'udi Arabia, the Philippines, Brazil, Iran, and Sweden.

Qatar's imports totaled QR1,068.9 million in 1974, an increase of QR290.5 million over 1973 and QR763 million over 1970. Main imports are oil and gas recovery equipment, steel bars and pipes, motor vehicles, woven synthetic fabrics, foodstuffs, machinery, electrical goods, air-conditioning equipment, spare parts, and radio and television receivers. Three industrialized countries provided 41.9% of Qatar's 1974 imports: Japan, QR190.9 million; the UK, QR147.7 million; and the US, QR109.5 million. Other significant suppliers were Lebanon and the Federal Republic of Germany.

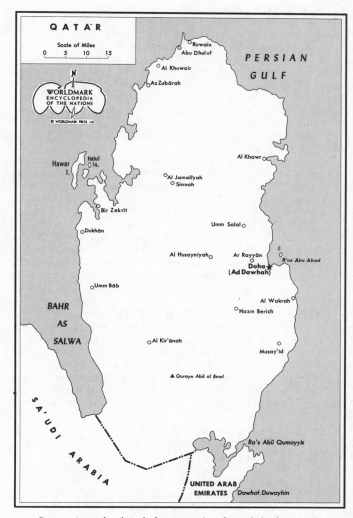

See continental political: front over J7; physical: back cover J7
LOCATION: 26°23′ to 24°31′N; 50°43′ to 51°41′E. **BOUNDARY LENGTHS:** Persian Gulf coastline, *378* km (*235* mi); UAE, *45* km (*28* mi); Sa'udi Arabia, *67* km (*42* mi). **TERRITORIAL SEA LIMIT:** 3 mi.

31 BALANCE OF PAYMENTS
In recent years, Qatar has had a persistent balance-of-payments surplus, induced primarily by sharply higher foreign exchange receipts from transactions of the oil sector. The surplus in the

balance of payments averaged 65 million SDRs during 1970–73 and was projected at more than 1 billion SDRs for 1974.

32 BANKING

Qatar's monetary and banking system comprises the recently established Qatar Monetary Agency and 11 commercial banks. The Qatar National Bank, the country's largest, and the newly opened Commercial Bank of Qatar are the only wholly-owned Qatari commercial banks. As of 31 September 1975, foreign assets of government authorities stood at QR402.5 million, while foreign holdings of the commercial banks totaled QR620.1 million.

33 INSURANCE

The Qatar National Insurance Co. is among the 12 insurance companies represented in Qatar.

34 SECURITIES

There is no stock exchange. Shares in Qatari public companies are traded through the banks.

35 PUBLIC FINANCE

Revenues, of which about 98% derive from oil, have more than doubled outlays in the 1970s. The state's budget for the Muslim year AH 1395 (which commenced on 12 January 1975) provided for a 60% increase in capital allocations, with current expenditures of QR1,000.7 million; receipts for that year reached QR5,496.6 million. Major development expenditures were for heavy industry, QR305 million; housing, water supply, and electricity, QR602 million; transport, communications, and agriculture, QR477 million; education, health, and information, QR275 million; and justice and security, QR144 million.

36 TAXATION

The major tax is an income tax levied on companies producing oil. Locally registered companies are liable to a corporation tax of 5–50%. No corporate liability is applied to foreign firms operating through a Qatari agent. There is no personal tax liability in Qatar for either foreigners or nationals.

37 CUSTOMS AND DUTIES

Import licenses are not required except for liquor (whose consumption is limited to non-Muslims), firearms, ammunition, and dangerous drugs. Customs duties are 2.5% on all commodities except for tobacco and cigarettes (10%), records and musical instruments (15%), and cement (40%). There is a 1.5% duty on goods in transit.

38 FOREIGN INVESTMENTS

The Qatar government encourages overseas investment in Qatar conditioned on a majority Qatari interest. In addition to the 40% share held by foreign interests (mainly UK, Dutch, French, and US) in oil companies, there is a 27% foreign investment in the Qatar Fertilizer Co., the Qatar share having been transferred to the Qatar National Petroleum Co.; a 40% foreign interest in the national shrimp-exporting enterprise; and a share in the Qatar Hotels Co.

The Qatar Investment Board, established in February 1972, develops both incoming and outgoing investments.

39 ECONOMIC POLICY

Qatar follows a policy of diversifying and extending its industrial and commercial activities to reduce the current dependence on oil. Infrastructure, heavy and light industry, agriculture, and fishing have all been development targets in the 1970s.

40 HEALTH

Free public health services are extended to all residents of Qatar, regardless of nationality. The Ministry of Health has tried with some success to keep pace with a rapidly expanding population. A 648-bed hospital was under construction in Doha in 1976 to supplement the 400 beds available at the city's Rumaillah Hospital. With five small "cottage" hospitals and several specialist and general clinics located in Doha and the interior, Qatar in 1975 could muster 700 beds attended by about 100 specialists and doctors. A school for nurses was opened in 1970.

41 SOCIAL WELFARE

Public health services and education are provided free by the state through the Ministry of Labor and Social Affairs, which also provides help to orphans, widows, and others in need of assistance.

42 HOUSING

A "popular housing" scheme provides dwellings through interest-free loans and installment repayments on easy terms. Occupants are required to pay only 70% of the cost of their houses during a 20–25 year period. The 1975 budget allocated QR130 million for state homeownership schemes. During the 1970s, over 650 units were provided free of charge, and 640 out of 890 being built in 1976 were similarly earmarked.

43 EDUCATION

Literacy in 1975 stood at about 20%, but was increasing rapidly. The long-term goal of the Ministry of Education, Culture, and Youth Care is free compulsory education for boys and girls at all levels. A 100% attendance rate for primary levels is the immediate target. Four major schools (secondary and preparatory for boys, preparatory and primary for girls), with 4,000 places, were scheduled for completion in 1976.

The school population increased from 1,000 in 1955 to 31,166 pupils in 1975, with 1,971 teachers. All children receive free books, meals, transport, clothing, and boarding facilities if required. Scholarships for higher education abroad are given to all who qualify. In 1975, 789 Qataris, of whom 137 were women, were studying abroad.

In 1973, with the cooperation of UNDP and UNESCO, a teacher-training college was opened with an enrollment of 161 students (including 98 women). In 1976, the college was being expanded into a University of the Lower Gulf, with additional faculties for civil aviation, science, engineering, and administration.

44 LIBRARIES AND MUSEUMS

There is a large public library in Doha. A National and Marine Museum, with an aquarium and displays devoted to the life of Qatar's pearl fishers, was due to open in 1976.

45 ORGANIZATIONS

The Qatar Chamber of Commerce was founded in Doha in 1963. There are a number of social and sporting clubs, including the Beacon Club and the Doha Sailing Association.

46 PRESS

Qatar has an Arabic daily, al-Arab; a weekly, al-Aruba; a monthly, al-Dawhah; and house publications of the various oil companies.

47 TOURISM

Plans to attract international tourists have been set aside until more hotel accommodations become available. Both smallpox and cholera immunizations are required.

48 FAMOUS QATARIS

There are no internationally famous persons in Qatar.

49 DEPENDENCIES

The State of Qatar has no territories or colonies.

50 BIBLIOGRAPHY

Abu Hakima. *History of Eastern Arabia*. Beirut: Khayyats, 1965.

American University. *Area Handbook for the Peripheral States of the Arabian Peninsula*. Washington, D.C.: Government Printing Office, 1971.

Anthony, John Duke. *Arab States of the Lower Gulf*. Washington, D.C.: Capitol Hill Press, 1975.

The Gulf: Implications of British Withdrawal. Washington, D.C.: Center for Strategic and International Studies, 1969.

Kelly, John B. *Britain and the Persian Gulf, 1795–1880*. Oxford: Oxford University Press, 1968.

Marlowe, John. *The Persian Gulf in the Twentieth Century*. London: Cresset, 1962.

Qatar, 1970. Doha: Government of Qatar, 1971.

SA'UDI ARABIA

The Kingdom of Sa'udi Arabia
Al-Mamlakah al-'Arabiyah al-Sa'udiyah

CAPITAL: Riyadh. **FLAG**: The national flag bears in white on a green field the inscription, in Arabic, "There is no god but Allah and Muhammad is the Messenger of Allah." There is a long white sword beneath the inscription; the sword handle is toward the fly. **ANTHEM**: The Sa'udi Arabian National Anthem is a short instrumental selection. **MONETARY UNIT**: The Sa'udi riyal (SR) is divided into 20 qirsh, in turn divided into 5 halal. There are coins of 1, 2, and 4 qirsh and (since December 1972) 5, 10, 25, and 50 halal, and notes of 1, 5, 10, 50, and 100 riyals. SR1 = $0.28328 (or $1 = SR3.53). **WEIGHTS AND MEASURES**: The metric system has been officially adopted in Sa'udi Arabia. **HOLIDAYS**: National Day, 23 September. Muslim religious holidays include 'Id al-Fitr and 'Id al-'Adha'. **TIME**: Solar time is observed. 3 P.M.=noon GMT.

¹LOCATION, SIZE, AND EXTENT

Sa'udi Arabia comprises the bulk of the Arabian Peninsula in Southwest Asia. The third-largest country on the continent after China and India, it has an area of 2,149,690 sq km (829,997 sq mi), extending 2,295 km *(1,426* mi) ESE-WNW and *1,423* km *(884* mi) NNE-SSW. Sa'udi Arabia is bounded on the N by Jordan and Iraq, and on the NE by Kuwayt, on the E by the Persian Gulf, Qatar, and the United Arab Emirates (UAE), on the SE and S by Oman, on the S by the People's Democratic Republic of Yemen (PDRY), on the SW by the Yemen Arab Republic (YAR), and on the W by the Red Sea and the Gulf of Aqaba, with a total boundary length of 7,027 km *(4,336* mi). The Neutral Zone, administered jointly by Sa'udi Arabia and Iraq, was to be divided according to an agreement of 2 July 1975 which was subject to the ratification of the respective governments.

²TOPOGRAPHY

A narrow plain, the Tihamah, parallels the Red Sea coast. Inland, in the north, the Hijaz Mountains (with elevations of 3,000 to 9,000 feet) rise sharply, but the highest mountains (over 9,000 feet) are in 'Asir in the south. 'Asir is an area extending about 230 miles along the Red Sea and perhaps 180 to 200 miles inland. East of the Hijaz, the slope is more gentle, and the mountains give way to the central uplands (Najd), a large plateau varying from about 5,000 feet in the west to about 2,000 feet in the east. The Dahna, a desert with an average width of 35 miles and an average altitude of 1,500 feet, separates Najd from the low plateau (Hasa) to the east (average width, 100 miles; average altitude, 800 feet). This in turn gives way to the low-lying Gulf coastal region.

At least one-third of the total area is sandy desert. The largest of the deserts is the famed Empty Quarter (Rub' al-Khali) in the south with an area of roughly 250,000 sq mi. Nafud, its northern counterpart, has an area of about 22,000 sq mi. There are no lakes. With the exception of artesian wells in the eastern oases, there is no perennially flowing water.

³CLIMATE

The climate is very dry and very hot; dust storms and sandstorms are frequent. Day and night temperatures vary greatly. From May to September, the hottest period, daytime temperatures reach 54.4°C (130°F) in the interior, and are among the highest recorded anywhere in the world. Temperatures are slightly lower along the coasts, but humidity is higher, especially in the east, which is noted for heavy fogs. From October to May, the climate is more moderate, with evening temperatures between 15.6°C and 21°C (60°F and 70°F). Average rainfall over most of the country is 4 inches, most rain falling between November and May.

Between 10 and 20 inches fall in the mountainous 'Asir area, where there is a summer monsoon.

⁴FLORA AND FAUNA

Vegetation is sparse owing to aridity and soil salinity. The date palm tree, the tamarisk, and acacia are prevalent. Wild animals include the oryx, jerboa, fox, lynx, wildcat, monkey, panther, and jackal. The favorite game bird is the bustard. The camel and Arab stallion are renowned, as is the white donkey of Hasa. Fish abound in the coastal waters and insects, scorpions, lizards, and snakes are numerous.

As of 1975, endangered species in Sa'udi Arabia included the wolf, Asiatic cheetah, dugong, two species of leopard (South Arabian and Sinai), and three species of gazelle (sand, Sa'udi Arabian dorcas, and Arabian).

⁵POPULATION

Preliminary results from Sa'udi Arabia's first census, taken in mid-1974, indicated a population of 5.6 million. Previous estimates had run as high as 8 million. The annual rate of increase during the mid-1970s was about 3%; the population density was 2.6 per sq km. There are no official estimates of the population of major cities, but reasonable estimates are Jiddah, the principal port, 500,000; Riyadh, 450,000; Mecca (Makkah), containing Islam's holiest shrine, 250,000. In addition, al-Hasa oasis (including the town of al-Hufuf) may contain 200,000; Medina, the second-holiest city of Islam, 150,000; and al-Ta'if and al-Dammam, 100,000 each. In 1975, about 21% of the population was urban; in recent decades, the proportion of nomadic peoples has declined from about 50% to 20%.

⁶ETHNIC GROUPS

The great majority of the Sa'udis have a common Arabian ancestry and the population is homogeneous in both religion and language. Divisions are based mainly on tribal affiliation, the primary division being between groups that are sedentary agriculturalists or traders and the Bedouins, who are nomadic pastoralists. The two groups traditionally have been antagonistic. Admixtures of Turks, Iranians, Indonesians, Pakistanis, Indians, various African groups, and other non-Arab Muslim peoples appear in the Hijaz, mostly descendants of pilgrims to Mecca.

⁷LANGUAGE

Arabic, the native language of the indigenous population, is a Semitic language related to Hebrew and Aramaic. Local variations in pronunciation do not prevent oral communication between people from opposite sections of the Arabian Peninsula. The language is written in a cursive script from right to left. The 28 letters of the alphabet have initial, medial, and terminal forms.

Short vowels are seldom indicated. English is now understood in oil-producing areas and commercial centers.

8 RELIGION

The overwhelming majority of the people of Sa'udi Arabia are orthodox, or Sunni, Muslims. The dominant interpretation is that of Wahhabism, a fundamentalist Muslim reform movement first preached by the 18th-century religious leader Muhammad bin 'Abd al-Wahhab. He urged a return to the true faith. Only the worship of God was true worship. There also is a small Shi'i minority. The holy city of Mecca is the center of Islam and the site of the sacred Ka'bah sanctuary, toward which all Muslims face at prayer. An annual pilgrimage (hajj) brings hundreds of thousands to Mecca and Medina from all corners of the Muslim world.

There are several thousand foreign Christian employees—Arab, US, and European. Jews have not been allowed to enter the country since 1948 except under unusual circumstances. Non-Muslims may not enter the cities of Mecca and Medina.

9 TRANSPORTATION

Until recently, the camel was the chief means of transportation. In 1972 there were an estimated 166,000 registered motor vehicles, of which some 90,100 were passenger cars. Sa'udi Arabia had 8,614 miles of main roads and 4,601 miles classified as agricultural roads in 1972. Paved roads link Jiddah, Mecca, Medina, al-Ta'ifi, and Riyadh. The Sa'udi Government Railroad (350 miles) operates between al-Damman on the Gulf and Riyadh. A line connecting Medina to Damascus is under construction. The Hijaz Railway, destroyed by T. E. Lawrence during World War I, has not yet been restored.

Government-owned Sa'udi Arabian Airlines (SAUDIA) serves the capitals of most Arab countries as well as Istanbul, Karachi, Bombay, and London. There are major airports at Dhahran, Jiddah, and Riyadh and 19 other airports. TWA maintains SAUDIA aircraft and the training of its personnel; by 1973, 120 of the 170 pilots were Sa'udis.

Jiddah and Yanbu' (opened 1966) on the Red Sea and al-Damman on the Persian Gulf are the main ports. Sixteen vessels (77,000 tons) operated under Sa'udi registry in 1974. The traditional dhow is still used for coastal trade.

10 COMMUNICATIONS

Postal, telephone, cable, and wireless services are regulated by the Ministry of Communications. The country is directly connected by radiotelephone with the US, other Arab countries, and Western Europe. Automatic internal lines now connect most of the major cities. In 1974 there were some 84,700 telephones. Radio broadcasts emanate from more than 20 stations of the government-owned Radio Mecca. By 1974, 7 government television stations were in operation. In 1974, an agreement was signed with France to introduce color broadcasting. The number of radios was estimated at 87,000 and television sets at 120,000 in 1972.

11 HISTORY

For several thousand years, Arabia has been inhabited by nomadic Semitic tribes. Towns were established at various oases and along caravan routes. Followers of Muhammad (c.570–632), imbued with religious zeal, expanded beyond the Mecca-Medina area and within a century conquered most of the area east and south of the Mediterranean Sea between Persia on the east and Spain on the west. Although Arabs were dominant in many parts of the Muslim world, and there was a great medieval flowering of Arab civilization, the Peninsula itself (except for the holy cities of Mecca and Medina) declined in importance and remained virtually isolated for almost a thousand years. As a province of successive Islamic caliphates that established their capitals in Damascus, Baghdad, Cairo, and Istanbul, its rulers claimed no more than a local autonomy.

The foundations of the kingdom of Sa'udi Arabia were laid in the 18th century by the fusion of the military power of the Sa'udi family and Wahhabism, an Islamic puritan doctrine preached by Muhammad bin 'Abd al-Wahhab. Muhammad ibn Sa'ud (r.1744–65) and his son 'Abd al-'Aziz (r.1765–1803) gave the religious reformer refuge in their center al-Dar'iyah in central Arabia, and together they embarked upon a program of religious reform and territorial expansion. By 1801, Najd and Hasa were occupied. Abd al-'Aziz's son and successor, Sa'ud (r.1803–14), brought the Hijaz under Sa'udi control and took the holy city of Mecca. The Ottomans called upon their governor of Egypt, Muhammad 'Ali, to put down the Sa'udis. A long struggle (1811–18) finally resulted in Sa'udi defeat. Sa'ud had died in 1814, and his son 'Abdallah (r.1814–18) was captured and beheaded.

When international conditions forced Muhammad 'Ali to withdraw his occupation forces in 1840, the Sa'udis embarked upon a policy of reconquest. Under Faysal (r.1843–67), Wahhabi control was reasserted over Najd, al-Hasa, and Oman, with Riyadh as the new capital. Hijaz, however, remained under the control of the sharifs of Mecca until 1925. After Faysal's death, conflict between his sons led to a decline in the family's fortunes. Taking advantage of these quarrels, the Ibn Rashids, a former Sa'udi vassal family, gained control of Najd and conquered Riyadh. The Sa'udi family fled to Kuwayt in 1891.

In January 1902, 'Abd al-'Aziz, a grandson of Faysal, who was to gain fame under the name Ibn Sa'ud, succeeded in driving the Ibn Rashid garrison out of Riyadh. At a decisive battle in 1906, the Rashidi power was broken. In 1913, the Sa'udis again brought Hasa under their control.

In December 1915, Ibn Sa'ud signed a treaty with the British that placed Sa'udi foreign relations under British control in return for a sizable subsidy.

Warfare broke out again in Arabia in 1919 when Husayn, the sharif of Mecca, who had become an independent king, attacked the Sa'udis. Husayn was defeated and Ibn Sa'ud annexed 'Asir. In 1921, he finally rid Arabia of the Rashids and, by 1923, he had consolidated his kingdom by occupying the districts west and north of Ha'il.

Husayn of Mecca provoked another conflict with Ibn Sa'ud in March 1924 by proclaiming himself caliph. War broke out and the Sa'udis captured al-Ta'if, Mecca, and Medina (5 December 1925). 'Ali, who had replaced Husayn as king, abdicated and on 23 November 1925, Ibn Sa'ud entered Jiddah. This increase in Ibn Sa'ud's territory was acknowledged by the British in a treaty of 20 May 1927 that annulled the 1915 agreement and recognized his independence. On 22 September 1932, the various parts of the realm were amalgamated into the kingdom of Sa'udi Arabia within much the same boundaries that exist today.

With the discovery of oil in the 1930s, the history of Sa'udi Arabia became irrevocably altered. Reserves have proved vast—about one-fourth of the world's total—and production, begun in earnest after World War II, has provided a huge income, much of it expended on infrastructure and social services. Sa'udi Arabia's petroleum-derived wealth has considerably enhanced the country's influence in world economic and political forums. Following the 1967 Arab-Israeli war, the Sa'udi government undertook a vast aid program in support of Egypt and Jordan, initiated with an annual subsidy of $140 million. Sa'udi Arabia joined the 1973 Arab boycott against the US and the Netherlands and, as a key member of OPEC, lent its support to the postwar rise in oil prices, a move that had stunning consequences on the world economy as well as causing a dramatic upsurge in Sa'udi Arabia's wealth and power.

Political life in Sa'udi Arabia during the 1960s and 1970s remained stable, despite two abrupt changes of national rulers. On 2 November 1964, Crown Prince Faysal ibn 'Abd al- 'Aziz became king and prime minister following the abdication of his brother King Sa'ud. His first act as prime minister was to announce a sweeping reorganization of the government, and his major social reform was the abolition of slavery. On 25 March 1975, King Faysal was assassinated by a nephew in an apparently isolated act. Faysal was immediately succeeded by former Crown Prince Khalid ibn 'Abd al-'Aziz al-Sa'ud. King Khalid embarked on an expanded development program, including a plan for 1976–80 involving $144 billion in expenditures.

12GOVERNMENT

Sa'udi Arabia is a monarchy in which the sovereign's dominant powers are regulated according to Muslim law (Shari'ah), tribal law, and custom. There is no law of succession in Sa'udi Arabia; the ruler is selected in family council. The Council of Ministers was first designated by Ibn Sa'ud in 1953, and in 1958 a body of regulations was promulgated. Under this document, which approximates a constitution, the king appoints a prime minister and, on the recommendation of the prime minister, a deputy prime minister and other ministers. In practice, however, the post of prime minister has been reserved to the king. Although there is provision for establishment of a consultative Legislative Assembly in Mecca, Sa'udi kings have continued to legislate and administer by royal decree.

Recently enacted reforms include an unemployment compensation law; additions to the free medical and educational benefits already established; and social security regulations for the old, disabled, orphans, and women having no means of support. Economic, commercial, and social regulations to constitute a complete body of laws are being developed.

13POLITICAL PARTIES

Although there are no political parties in Sa'udi Arabia, various groups constitute political power groups, such as the 'ulama (religious scholars) and the supporters of the Wahhabi doctrine. Other alliances, among merchants and businessmen, for example, are concerned with economic matters. There is also a small middle class whose political sympathies are with the Arab nationalist movement. Each group makes its influence felt in the policy-making bodies of the government and with the king, whose leadership is upheld as long as he adheres to Islamic law, tradition, and the collective decision of the 'ulama.

14LOCAL GOVERNMENT

The kingdom consists of 18 provinces, of which 6—including Eastern Province and the principal cities—are designated as major provinces. Since 1963, all provinces have been headed by crown-appointed governors, most of whom have been princes or members of the royal household. The oil wells are located in Eastern Province, formerly known as Hasa and incorporating the oasis of al-Hasa.

Various local government councils were set up under the municipality laws of 1938, 1949, and 1963. The cities of Mecca, Medina, Jiddah, and some other large cities have elected municipal governments.

Tribal and village leaders report directly to district governors, thus giving the government some control in outlying districts. Each shaykh traditionally rules in consultation with a council. A large segment of the population remains tribally organized. Tribes, headed by paramount shaykhs, are divided into subtribes headed by shaykhs. Local decisions are made by tribal shaykhs, amirs, or other chief officials and their councils (majalis).

15JUDICIAL SYSTEM

The judiciary is composed of lower courts that handle misdemeanors and minor civil cases; high courts of Islamic law located in Mecca and Jiddah; and courts of appeal. A judicial supervisory committee of three members and a president appointed by the king supervises all courts. Islamic law (the Shari'ah) prevails in Sa'udi Arabia, but justice is also based on tribal and customary law ('urf). Government decisions approved by the king regulate finance and labor relations.

16ARMED FORCES

Sa'udi Arabia's armed forces totaled 47,000 men in 1974. Military service is voluntary. In 1974/75, the budget allocation for defense and national guards was SR2,418 million. Total army strength in 1974 was 40,000. The army had a number of tanks and antitank missiles, and 10 batteries of surface-to-air missiles. The navy's strength was about 1,500 men. It had 4 patrol vessels. The air force, with 5,500 men, had 95 combat aircraft. Armed tribal levies numbered 16,000. They are used chiefly for internal security.

See continental political: front cover H7; physical: back cover H7

LOCATION: 16°23' to 32°14'N; 34°30' to 56°22'W. BOUNDARY LENGTHS: Jordan, 744 km (462 mi); Iraq, 895 km (556 mi); Kuwayt, 163 km (101 mi); Persian Gulf coastline, 549 km (341 mi); Qatar, 67 km (42 mi); UAE, 586 km (364 mi); Oman, 676 km (420 mi); PDRY, 830 km (516 mi); YAR, 628 km (390 mi); Red Sea and Gulf of Aqaba coastlines, 1,889 km (1,174 mi). TERRITORIAL SEA LIMIT: 12 mi.

17MIGRATION

Emigration is limited. Immigration of professionals, technicians, and others from the surrounding Arab states and growing numbers from outside the region has been spurred by the development of the oil industry and by the lack of adequately trained and educated Sa'udi personnel. Palestinian Arabs, displaced by the establishment of the State of Israel, are the chief immigrant group.

18INTERNATIONAL COOPERATION

Sa'udi Arabia has been a member of the UN since its inception and participates in its specialized agencies except ILO, IMCO, and GATT. It is a founding member of the Arab League and participates in the activities of a number of other intergovernmental organizations. In January 1968, it concluded an agreement with Kuwayt and Libya for the establishment of OPEC and of the parallel Arab group, OAPEC. Jiddah is the temporary headquarters for the Arab Secretariat, established in 1969.

19ECONOMY

Prior to the discovery of oil, the greatest source of income in the country was the levies imposed on pilgrims to Mecca. Although the levies have been abolished, more than 600,000 pilgrims brought $263 million in foreign exchange to Sa'udi Arabia in 1973. It is estimated that in 1974/75 oil revenues in royalties and taxes produced 96.1% of the total budget of SR98,247 million. Further, while the specter of depletion loomed increasingly for many of the world's oil producers in the 1970s, Sa'udi Arabia's known reserves actually increased significantly during the decade, raising the prospect of expanding production through the 20th century.

However, the government is trying to diversify its economy; it has undertaken an intensive mineral exploration project; it is also promoting development of industries utilizing petroleum, including steel and petrochemical manufacture. At present, Sa'udi Arabia has little industry other than oil, and must import manufactured goods and foodstuffs. In 1974/75, SR26,397 million, or 57.7% of the total current expenditures, was allocated to development projects, with added emphasis on desalination, electricity, irrigation, and refining for export. Nearly half of the population in the 1970s remains tied to the traditional forms of herding and oasis agriculture.

20 INCOME

The GNP was estimated at SR87,773 million in 1973/74, a dramatic increase over the SR12,727 million earned in 1968/69 and a direct result of the sharp increase in oil prices. The GDP in 1973/74 was estimated at SR100,965 million, an increase of 149% over 1972/73. Per capita GDP, at SR18,029, rivaled levels in many developed nations. Oil royalties and income tax on oil companies account for most of the national income. Although about half of the inhabitants are engaged in agriculture, they produce less than 5% of the GNP.

21 LABOR

The concept of a hired labor force came to Sa'udi Arabia with the arrival of the Arabian American Oil Co. (Aramco) and other industrial ventures connected with the exploitation of oil. By the mid-1970s, nearly 1 million foreigners worked in Sa'udi Arabia, mostly in the oil sector. Industry and mining overall employed about 8% of the available indigenous labor force. About 46% of the population and 75% of the work force, however, is still engaged in the traditional occupations of farming and animal husbandry. The oil industry originally recruited workers through village and tribal leaders. However, Aramco now provides on-the-job training at all levels, and the number of skilled and semiskilled workers is increasing.

No labor unions exist, but there are professional and trade guilds. Labor-industry relations are prescribed by law. The Ministry of Labor and Social Affairs supervises both labor and industry, arbitrates labor disputes, and supervises vocational and trade schools. Traditional values continue to hinder the entry of women into the industrial work force.

A 1969 royal decree instituted a series of social insurance provisions that provide compensation for work-related disability, old age, and death. Coverage for temporary disability and unemployment is contemplated. Working hours are set at a maximum of 11 per day, although an 8-hour day and 48-hour week are the norms. Paid holidays and vacations (15 days per year) are provided.

22 AGRICULTURE

Although agriculture engaged about three-fourths of the adult labor force in the mid-1970s, less than 5% of the GNP derived from agricultural activity. About 40% of Sa'udi Arabia's land area is suitable for grazing, but only about 1% of the total is under permanent cultivation. Small owner-operated farms characterize Sa'udi Arabia's land-tenure system. About 96% of the farm area is owned, and only 4% rented. Less than 3% of the agricultural holdings are of 20 acres or more and 45% are 1 acre or less in size. Two-thirds of the cropped land is used for cereals, about 18% for vegetables, and 13% for fruit and dates. Although Sa'udi Arabia

is one of the world's leading date producers, with an annual yield estimated at nearly 200,000 tons, the growing of dates has declined in the past few years in favor of wheat, corn, alfalfa, rice, grapes, and a variety of fruits and vegetables. Nevertheless, dates remain the only major staple food crop whose production is sufficient to meet local demand. Nearly half of Sa'udi Arabia's food is imported. In 1973, an estimated 150,000 tons of wheat were produced.

The capital budget for 1974/75 allocated $305.5 million (SR1,053.5 million) to water and agriculture. By 1975, six large desalination plants were installed or under construction. Moreover, the government set up an agricultural bank in 1975 to advance loans on easy terms to farmers for agricultural improvement. Improved irrigation has been a prime target for many regions. Since 1967, three dams have been completed in Diriyyah, one in Huraimilah, and a large dam in Wadi Jizan in southern 'Asir. Plans were announced in 1974 for the construction of two dams in the Sudair and Riyadh areas.

FAO assists irrigation projects, advising on better crop practices and soil restoration. The International Locust Mission is also active.

23 ANIMAL HUSBANDRY

In 1972, official sources reported 1,237,770 sheep, 755,210 goats, 185,920 cows, 99,076 donkeys, 58,652 camels, 1,030 horses, and 331,315 poultry in Sa'udi Arabia. Camels as a source of food have steadily declined in importance as imports of animal foodstuffs have increased and as greater varieties of agricultural products are produced locally. The importance of the Arabian horse as an export item is declining. Donkeys and mules are still valued as pack animals and the white donkeys of Hasa are well known. Sheep are found in all parts of Sa'udi Arabia where pasturage is available and are raised for milk as well as for meat and wool or hair. Goats are kept for milk. Their hair is used in rugs and tents, and their skins serve as water bags. Cattle are unsuited to the conditions in most of Sa'udi Arabia. Poultry, which provide a variation to the limited diet, are increasing. There is no hog raising since pork is banned as unclean by Islamic law.

24 FISHING

Fishing is an important occupation along both Sa'udi coasts and, with few exceptions, traditional techniques are used. In view of the inadequate domestic food supply, however, attention is being given to more scientific methods of fishing. The export of Gulf shrimp has become a relatively significant activity in recent years. An FAO team has surveyed the Red Sea coastal area. Under the supervision of the Ministry of Agriculture, a company was formed in 1952 to exploit Red Sea fisheries; it is equipped with modern fishing vessels, an ice plant, a 200-ton storehouse, and other facilities.

25 FORESTRY

The only forest growth is found in the mountainous area that extends from southern Hijaz to 'Asir. The principal varieties—acacia, date, juniper, wild olive, sidr, tamarind, and tamarisk—are generally not useful for timber, but some wood from date palms is used for construction.

26 MINING

Oil was first discovered in Sa'udi Arabia in 1938. By 1975, Sa'udi Arabia had become the world's third-leading producer (after the US and USSR) and the largest exporter of crude oil, with an average daily production of 7.5–8 million barrels estimated in 1976 (compared with a 3-million-barrel average in 1969). About 85% is exported. In 1974, the total crude oil production (including Sa'udi Arabia's share in the Sa'udi Arabia-Kuwayt Neutral Zone) was 3,095 million barrels, with export earning estimated at $29 billion.

In 1976, Sa'udi Arabia had 32 known oil fields (21 onshore), of which 13 were in production. Total reserves were estimated at 180 billion barrels—more than one-fourth of the world's known supply—including 7 billion barrels in three fields discovered in 1975. Of the total reserves, 98% fell under the onshore holdings of Aramco, originally a US-dominated company now 60% owned by the Sa˚udi government (negotiations for a complete takeover were under way in 1976). Three joint ventures of Sa˚udi Arabia's Petroleum and Minerals Organization (Petromin) and several French, Italian, Japanese, and other firms have been engaged in exploration in the offshore areas. Natural gas reserves are also substantial, put at about 45 billion cu feet.

A modern mining firm, the Sa˚udi Arabian Mining Syndicate, was founded in 1934 to exploit the mineral resources of Hijaz. Only one mine has been worked—the ancient gold and silver mine of Mahad al-Dhahab (the cradle of gold), which is located southeast of Medina and probably dates from the time of King Solomon. Recent surveys have discovered more than 20 minerals in 300 areas of the country. The al-˚Amar-al-Rayn quadrangle, among other sites, is believed to contain gold, silver, copper, zinc, lead, iron, and pyrites. An intensive search for additional mineral deposits is being carried on by more than 70 Sa˚udi, French, Japanese, and US firms. A modern mining code encourages foreign participation, although majority holdings by national interests have increasingly been stressed.

27 ENERGY AND POWER

Sa˚udi Arabia has limited waterpower resources. In rural areas, animals are still the main source of power. Increasingly, however, the oil-powered diesel engine is being used to run generators (the major cities have electricity), to pump water, and for many new purposes. In 1974, the electric power generated by the major plants (in millions of kwh) was as follows: Jiddah, 451.8; Riyadh, 419.0; Dharan, 323.6; Mecca, 180.3; Medina, 55.2. Additional generating plants are scheduled to be built in the al-Qunfudah, al-Neeriyyah, and Masda areas. The addition of these plants will increase the availability of electricity in rural areas. Total installed capacity of electric energy in 1972 was 341,000 kw (compared to 28,600 in 1960); in 1973, 1,182.6 million kwh were produced, a 21% increase over the previous year.

A combined electric power and water desalination plant at Jiddah was completed with US help in 1969, with a capacity of 5 million gallons of water per day and 50,000 kw. A similar plant, scheduled for construction at al-Jubail, would have a capacity of 20 million gallons of water per day and 200,000 kw when in operation. Six desalination plants were expected to be in operation by the end of 1976.

28 INDUSTRY

Industry in Sa˚udi Arabia in the 1970s remained virtually synonymous with oil. The country now has four refineries, the largest of which is owned by Aramco. The government's Petromin operates a refinery at Jiddah. Two other refineries are owned by Getty and the Arabian Oil Co. of Japan. In 1974, exports of refined oil totaled 194 million barrels valued at $1,969 million (138 million in 1968, valued at $283 million). The country's refinery capacity was being expanded in the mid-1970s, as was the production of petroleum by-products, notably fertilizer and sulfuric acid. The Sa˚udi Arabian Fertilizer Co. doubled its production of urea during 1972–73 to 150,000 tons.

The only other local industry of any size is cement, of which 1,063,700 tons (about 80% of domestic consumption) were produced in 1974. A steel-rolling mill at Jiddah was being expanded to a capacity of 100,000 tons in 1976. In that year, two flour mills and a textile plant were under construction and discussions were under way for a 140,000-ton-capacity aluminum plant.

The glut of oil proceeds in recent years has been a boon to light industries producing consumer goods for the local market. With the exception of a date-syrup plant and a few others, most manufacturers rely on imported raw materials. The most notable growth has occurred among food processors, and recent additions include a meat-packing plant; processing plants for ice cream, yogurt, and other dairy products; a vegetable cannery; and a biscuit factory. Other firms now produce canvas cloth, surgical supplies, paper products, plastic pipes, electric appliances, paints, detergents, and pharmaceuticals.

29 DOMESTIC TRADE

Barter is the traditional means by which nomads and farmers have obtained each other's products. Weekly markets are held in villages and small towns. But the economy is being progressively monetized and is now completely so in the larger towns and cities. Newspapers, magazines, and billboards are the principal means of advertising.

Normal business hours are from 8 A.M. to 1 P.M. and 5 P.M. to 8 P.M. on Saturday through Wednesday and from 8 A.M. to 1 P.M. Thursday. During the month of Ramadan, the workday is limited to six hours. Friday is a holiday in Sa˚udi Arabia.

30 FOREIGN TRADE

Before the oil industry developed there was very little foreign trade. However, in 1973 total exports were valued at SR33,501.5 million, virtually all of which constituted oil exports. By 1974, total exports were estimated at SR110,360 million, with oil exports constituting SR110,250 million. Oil earnings have traditionally produced vast trade surpluses, with the value of exports running more than fourfold the cost of imports in the mid-1970s. Non-oil exports included dates, pearls, jewelry, mineral products, and hides and skins. About 80% of oil exports go to Western Europe, Asia, and Oceania. Total imports in 1973 were valued at SR7,352 million; the major categories of imports were machinery, electric appliances, and transport equipment, SR2,523 million; food grain and other foodstuffs, SR1,875 million; textiles and clothing, SR657 million; and building materials, SR534 million.

In 1973, principal trade partners (in millions of Sa˚udi riyals) were:

	EXPORTS	IMPORTS	BALANCE
Japan	4,938.5	1,132.6	3,805.9
Italy	3,321.8	197.4	3,124.4
Netherlands	3,111.2	316.2	2,795.0
France	3,060.7	156.3	2,904.4
UK	2,657.2	525.5	2,131.7
US	1,609.2	1,407.0	202.2
Spain	2,040.1	13.1	2,027.0
FRG	1,101.5	507.5	594.0
Bahrayn	770.3	40.6	729.7
India	343.4	87.3	256.1
Others	10,547.6	2,968.2	7,579.4
TOTALS	33,501.5	7,351.7	26,149.8

31 BALANCE OF PAYMENTS

Prior to the 1970s, government development spending, special payments to Arab countries, and import costs combined to offset Sa˚udi Arabia's oil income. The payments situation altered radically in the mid-1970s, however, owing to the dramatic jump in world oil prices and, hence, in Sa˚udi Arabia's oil income. By the end of March 1976, gold, foreign investments, and convertible foreign exchange earnings held by the Sa˚udi Arabian Monetary Agency, the country's central banking institution, rose to an estimated $45 billion. International reserves alone stood at $23.7 billion in February 1976, placing Sa˚udi Arabia second in the world in that category behind the Federal Republic of Germany (FRG). Projected oil revenues for 1976 were put at $30 billion, an amount far in excess of planned government outlays for the year.

Sa˚udi Arabia's balance of payments for 1969 and 1974 (in millions of dollars) is summarized as follows:

	1969	1974
Merchandise, net	960	34,562
Services, net	−819	−11,128
Private transfers	−134	− 518
Government transfers	− 93	− 847
Long-term capital	14	− 3,773
Short-term capital	− 3	− 319
Errors and omissions	− 52	− 97
TOTALS	−127	17,880

32 BANKING

The Sa'udi Arabian Monetary Agency was established by royal decree in 1952 to maintain the internal and external value of currency. This Agency issues notes and coins with 100% cover in gold and convertible foreign exchange and regulates all banks and exchange dealers. It maintains 10 branches.

There are 12 banking houses with 77 branch offices, of which 64 belong to 5 domestic banks (the largest of them the Sa'udi National Commercial Bank and the Riyadh Bank) plus 13 branches of 7 foreign banks. Three clearing houses were inaugurated in the late 1960s at Jiddah, Riyadh, and al-Damman.

In 1974, total currency in circulation was SR3,620 million and deposits SR2,992 million. Much gold and silver is privately hoarded. Bank advances and loans to the private sector stood at SR4,896 million by the end of March 1975. Deposits in commercial banks stood at SR7,156 million. At the end of 1975, official gold holdings were valued at $126 million ($119 million at the end of 1969), foreign exchange at $20,832 million ($465 million in 1969), and reserve position in IMF at $2,430 million ($23 million in 1969).

33 INSURANCE

There are several insurance firms operating in Sa'udi Arabia, but no statistics concerning their operation are available.

34 SECURITIES

There is no stock exchange in Sa'udi Arabia.

35 PUBLIC FINANCE

In 1974/75, Sa'udi Arabia had a record budget of SR98,247 million, 96.1% of the revenues being derived from oil. The rest was derived mainly from communications and customs duties. Current expenditures amounted to SR45,743 million, of which 57.7% was allocated to development projects, 7% to the Ministry of Finance and National Economy, 5.5% to the Ministry of Education, 5.3% to the Ministry of Defense and national guards, 4.2% to the Ministry of the Interior, and 1.6% to the Ministry of Health. Capital expenditures amounted to SR52,504 million, or 53% of the total budget. Of the SR26,397 million allocated to development projects, 15.9% was for the development of transport and communications, 14% for the interior, 4.8% for education, 4.4% for civil aviation, 4% for water resources and agriculture, and 1.7% for health.

36 TAXATION

The taxing authority in Sa'udi Arabia is the Department of Zakat and Income Tax. The first income tax, decreed in November 1950, taxed all personal income in excess of SR5,000 at the rate of 5% and imposed a tax upon corporation profits. A new income tax law of 1956 substantially increased government revenues, but did not affect Sa'udis or wholly Sa'udi-owned corporations. By the mid-1970s, three separate forms of taxation had evolved—the income tax, applied to foreigners in the self-employed or professional categories; the zakat, an Islamic tax derived from the Shari'ah and applied directly to income and property of Sa'udi Arabians (and resident Gulf state nationals); and the jihad (Holy War) tax, an emergency tax applied to citizens since 1970. Income of members of the royal family is tax exempt. The zakat rate is 2.5%, half of which is paid into the government, with the other 1.25% being directly distributed by citizens to the poor.

In 1976, petroleum companies paid income tax at a flat rate of 85% of net income. All other companies were taxed at rates ranging from 25% of taxable income up to SR100,000 to 45% on amounts over SR365,000. Personal income-tax rates for foreigners ranged from 5% to 30%. A pilgrimage tax, which called for foreigners to pay a fee upon entering the country, was abolished in 1974.

37 CUSTOMS AND DUTIES

Specific duties are levied on certain imported items. For other items there is an ad valorem rate that fluctuates considerably. Aramco does not pay duty on items imported for use in its operations. Liquor, firearms, ammunition, and narcotics may not be imported.

38 FOREIGN INVESTMENTS

A small group of upper-class Sa'udis has traditionally held substantial investments overseas. This group has large demand deposits in US and West European banks and considerable investments in commercial ventures, especially in real estate, in Lebanon, Egypt, and other Middle Eastern countries. In the mid-1970s, the Sa'udi government substantially increased its overseas activities and by March 1976, the Sa'udi Arabian Monetary Agency was estimated to have placed about $28 billion in foreign investments, with about half invested in the US (including some $12 billion in US treasury bills, government bonds, and short-term deposits) and the remaining proportion in Western Europe and Japan. In addition, some $5 billion was thought to be invested with the IMF.

US capital, especially Aramco money, invested in Sa'udi Arabia amounted to more than $1.5 billion in 1975 and, despite recent moves by the Sa'udi government to secure majority control of the oil industry, has been increasing as the search for and production of oil continues. Considerable Japanese capital is also invested in the oil industry. A five-year tax holiday is offered to new foreign firms with a minimum 25% Sa'udi ownership.

39 ECONOMIC POLICY

The government's economic policies in the 1970s were characterized by a notably more assertive role in its management both of oil revenues and of the nation's economic development. In a sharp departure from the laissez-faire approach of the 1950s and 1960s, the government moved to acquire a 60% interest in Aramco, the country's major petroleum enterprise and, in 1976, entered negotiations for a full take-over. Since 1970, the government has stepped up oil production while achieving, through OPEC, a sharp increase in oil prices. As a result, vast new sums became available for expenditure on development and defense, as well as for increased aid to other Arab countries. The 1975/76 budget called for $31.5 billion in expenditures, of which some $4.7 billion was earmarked for defense purposes. In May 1975, the Council of Ministers approved a new five-year development plan (1976–80), calling for $144 billion in capital outlays. Projects to be financed under the plan included natural gas extraction and processing; petrochemical production; export refining; production of fertilizers, steel and aluminum, and electricity; and desalination. In the infrastructural sector, large outlays were planned for housing, education, roads, and telecommunications.

40 HEALTH

The main health problem is undernourishment, which results in widespread scurvy, rickets, night blindness, anemia, and a low resistance to tuberculosis. Dysentery attacks all ages and classes and an incidence of close to 100% of trachoma is suspected. A government campaign to eradicate malaria mosquitoes had good results. Typhoid is endemic, but acquired immunity prevents serious outbreaks of this disease. Sewage disposal and other health facilities are inadequate, but progress is being made in providing better medical care. In 1975, average life expectancy was estimated at 47.8 years, as compared with 37.2 years in 1955.

The government has accomplished excellent results in preventing epidemics among the yearly influx of pilgrims. A modern quarantine station built at a cost of $3 million was opened at Jiddah in April 1956. Large hospitals have been established at Riyadh, Jiddah, Mecca, al-Ta'if, and al-Damman, and almost all towns have some kind of medical facility. At the end of 1972 there were 51 hospitals under the supervision of the Ministry of Health, with a total of 8,132 beds, and 533 health centers and health clinics. The budget of the Ministry of Health for the fiscal year 1974/75 was SR727 million, or 1.6% of the total budget, with additional funds of SR435 million allocated under the development projects budget. The country had about 2,000 physicians in 1973, or about 1 doctor for every 2,800 inhabitants.

41 SOCIAL WELFARE
Social welfare in Sa'udi Arabia is traditionally provided through the family or tribe. Those with no family or tribal ties have recourse to the traditional Islamic pious foundations or they may request government relief, which is supported from the collection of Islamic taxes. The Social Security Department grants annual stipends to orphans, widows, divorcees, invalids, and indigent families, as well as assistance in cash to persons partially disabled or afflicted by natural calamities.

In 1975, more than 195,000 workers were covered by the government's pension plan, which covers employees of all private firms as well as public companies employing 20 or more workers.

Aramco has a welfare plan for its employees that includes pension funds, accident compensation, and free medical care. Several of the oil companies provide medical and educational services.

42 HOUSING
Sedentary Sa'udis ordinarily live in traditional housing and nomads live in tents. The recent influx of rural people to towns and cities, coupled with the rise in levels of expectation among the urban population, has created a serious housing problem. Improvement in urban housing is one of Sa'udi Arabia's foremost economic needs. Since 1973, contracts have been awarded for the construction of more than 25,000 new housing units. Plans are also being discussed for the construction of an additional 100,000 housing units. Under the 1976–80 development plan, construction is projected for desert areas.

In the oil districts, Aramco, through loans and other assistance, has encouraged private home construction and has built accommodations for its unmarried Sa'udi staff.

43 EDUCATION
Although the educational system is still inadequate, steady progress has been made. Literacy is low (estimated at under 25% in the mid-1970s) and varies according to location—town, village, or rural—but there is a highly developed oral culture. Both religious and secular schools are supported by the government, and education is free to all at all levels, including college and postgraduate study.

In 1973/74 there were 2,604 elementary schools, with 577,736 pupils (including 687 schools for girls with 192,057 pupils) and 26,612 teachers; 440 intermediate schools, with 100,544 pupils and 5,950 teachers; 77 secondary schools, with 27,268 pupils and 1,628 teachers; and 6 colleges and universities, with 11,025 students.

The budget of the Ministry of Education for the fiscal year 1974/75 was SR2,515 million, or 5.5% of the total budget, plus an additional SR1,265.6 million allocated under the development projects budget. The shortage of Sa'udi teachers is so acute that many of the secular schools are largely staffed from neighboring Arabic-speaking countries, especially Egypt. In 1968, the old teacher-training institute system was overhauled: 7 institutes for elementary education with 1,163 students and 4 institutes for secondary education with 155 students were set up. A vocational

institute, established at Riyadh with help from the UNDP, trains technicians for a variety of professions.

The Riyadh University, established in 1957, has seven colleges: arts, science, pharmacy, agriculture, engineering, education, and commerce. A college of medicine was added in 1970. In 1972/73, 4,369 students were enrolled. In addition, there is the Islamic University at Medina, founded in 1961, nd King 'Abdul 'Aziz University in Jiddah, established in 1967 as a school of economics and business administration; the College of Petroleum and Minerals in Dhahran trains specialists for the petroleum industry. There are some 32 institutes and 2 colleges of religious studies, with a total enrollment of about 8,000 students. In 1972/73, 1,839 students, sent by the government, were receiving higher education abroad (943 in the US and 466 in other Arab countries).

In 1975, the government announced its support of an international school system to serve the children of Western advisers and contractors. Enrollment is expected to reach 10,000 by 1980.

In the area of its operations, Aramco has built primary schools and provided funds for their operation and maintenance under government direction. Aramco also operates training programs for its Sa'udi employees.

44 LIBRARIES AND MUSEUMS
The National Library in Riyadh was founded in 1968 and has 16,000 volumes. Larger libraries, however, are found at Riyadh University (65,000 volumes); Islamic University (30,000); and King 'Abdul 'Aziz University (25,000). The library of the College of Petroleum and Minerals in Dhahran, with 100,000 volumes, is the largest specialized collection in the country. There are 10 public libraries; the largest, at Riyadh, contains 15,000 volumes. There are no museums.

45 ORGANIZATIONS
Sa'udi social tradition, which emphasizes the exclusiveness of family, clan, and tribe, militates against the formation of any other social organizations. The absence of political and economic organizations also is a result of the prevalence of tradition. There is a semiofficial chamber of commerce.

46 PRESS
The first newspaper in what is now Sa'udi Arabia was Al-Qiblah, the official publication of King Husayn of Hijaz, founded in 1915. With the end of the short-lived Hijaz kingdom in 1925, a Sa'udi-sponsored paper, called Umm al-Qura (The Mother of Towns, i.e., Mecca), was established and continues on a weekly basis as an official paper. In 1964, the new National Press Institutions took over from private firms the operation and control of newspapers and periodicals. The dailies and their circulations in 1975 were Al-Bilad, Jiddah, 30,000; Al-Nadwah, Mecca, 11,000; Al-Riyadh, Riyadh, 10,000; Al-Madinah al-Munwarah, Jiddah, 5,500; Okadh, Jiddah, 1,200; Al-Jazirah, Riyadh, no figures given; and Riyadh Daily Newsletter, Riyadh, 1,400 (1972). Weeklies and their circulations are Ummal-Qura, Mecca, 25,000; Al-Dawah, Riyadh, 7,000; Al-Yawn, al-Damman, 6,000; and Al-Yamamah, Riyadh, 6,000. There are three periodicals devoted to commerce and two, Hajj, Mecca, and Al-Manhal, Jiddah, of general interest. Several periodicals formerly published by the government were suspended in 1964. Aramco publishes two English-language weeklies, Oil Caravan Weekly and Sun and Flare.

47 TOURISM
Tourism in the normal sense is unknown and not encouraged. Every year, however, there is a great influx of foreign pilgrims, for pilgrimage to Mecca, one of the five basic obligations of Islam, is incumbent on every Muslim who is financially and physically able to perform it. In 1974, 918,777 foreign Muslims, an increase of 51.2% over 1973, went on the pilgrimage. These included, apart from pilgrims from Arab countries, 106,686 from Turkey, 66,534 from Pakistan, 57,314 from Iran, 68,872 from Indonesia, 21,874 from India, 51,764 from Nigeria, 15,366 from

Malaysia, and 6,299 from Afghanistan. The government has spent a considerable sum on the renovation and expansion of the holy mosques in Mecca and Medina.

Requirements for a visa include a certificate of religion and a statement of financial responsibility from an employer. Persons of Jewish faith, barring extraordinary exceptions, are denied entry. Cholera and smallpox inoculations are also required.

48 FAMOUS SA'UDIS

The Sa'udi who has gained greatest renown outside the kingdom is 'Abd al-'Aziz ibn 'Abd al-Rahman al-Faysal al-Sa'ud, better known as Ibn Sa'ud (1880–1953), the father of his country. Forced into exile with his family at a young age, he reconquered his patrimony and left behind him the state of Sa'udi Arabia.

On 2 November 1964, Faysal 'Abd al-'Aziz al-Sa'ud (1906–75) was proclaimed king. Assassinated by a nephew on 25 March 1975, Faysal in his role as prime minister instituted many economic and social reforms, including the abolition of slavery. King Faysal was immediately succeeded as king and prime minister by Khalid ibn 'Abd al-Aziz (b.1913), who, together with Crown Prince Fahd ibn 'Abd al-'Aziz (b.1920), both continued and broadened his predecessor's development policies.

49 DEPENDENCIES

Sa'udi Arabia has no territories or colonies. Some borders, however, remain undefined and are the subject of conflicting claims. The possible presence of oil adds importance to these disputes. Five of these disputes, however, were settled in recent years. An agreement was reached in 1971 whereby the Neutral Zone separating Sa'udi Arabia from Kuwayt was divided administratively between the two countries. A dispute between Sa'udi Arabia and the Sultanate of Oman over control of the Buraymi oasis was settled by an agreement in 1974. In that year, Sa'udi Arabia and the newly formed United Arab Emirates reached an accord fixing their border. The Neutral Zone between Sa'udi Arabia and Iraq was similarly settled in 1975.

50 BIBLIOGRAPHY

American University. *Area Handbook for Sa'udi Arabia.* Washington, D.C.: Government Printing Office, 1971.

De Gaury, Gerald. *Arabia Phoenix.* London: Harrap, 1946.

De Gaury, Gerald. *Rulers of Mecca.* London: Harrap, 1951.

Doughty, Charles Montagu. *Travels in Arabia Deserta.* London: Cape, 1936.

El Wassie, A. *Education in Sa'udi Arabia.* London: Macmillan, 1970.

Hitti, Philip K. *History of the Arabs.* New York: St. Martin's Press, 1956.

Holm, Henrietta M. *The Agricultural Resources of the Arabian Peninsula.* Washington, D.C.: Foreign Agriculture Service, Department of Agriculture, April 1955.

Kheirallah, George. *Arabia Reborn.* Albuquerque: University of New Mexico Press, 1952.

Lateef, N. A. *Characteristics and Problems of Agriculture in Saudi Arabia.* Background Country Studies, No. 4. New York: Program Analysis Service, Agriculture Division, FAO, October 1956.

Lebkicher, Roy, George Rentz, and Max Steineke. *The Arabia of Ibn Saud.* New York: Moore, 1952.

Lebkicher, Roy, et al. *Aramco Handbook.* New York: Arabian American Oil Company, 1960.

Lipsky, George Arthur. *Saudi Arabia: Its People, Its Society, Its Culture.* New Haven, Conn.: HRAF Press, 1959.

Macro, Eric. *Bibliography of the Arabian Peninsula.* Coral Gables: University of Miami Press, 1958.

Margoliouth, David Samuel. "Wahhabiyya." *Shorter Encyclopaedia of Islam.* Edited by H. A. R. Gibb and J. H. Kramers. Ithaca, N.Y.: Cornell University Press, 1953.

Meulen, Daniël Van der. *The Wells of Ibn Sa'ud.* New York: Praeger, 1957.

Musil, Alois. *The Manners and Customs of the Ruwala Bedouins.* New York: American Geographical Society, 1928.

Nicholson, Reynold Alleyne. *A Library History of the Arabs.* Cambridge: Cambridge University Press, 1956.

Owen, Roderic. *The Golden Bubble: Arabian Gulf Documentary.* London: Collins, 1957.

Philby, Harry St. John Bridger. *Arabia.* London: Benn, 1930.

Philby, Harry St. John Bridger. *Arabian Days: An Autobiography.* London: Hale, 1948.

Philby, Harry St. John Bridger. *Arabian Highlands.* Ithaca, N.Y.: Cornell University Press, 1952.

Philby, Harry St. John Bridger. *Arabian Jubilee.* London: Hale, 1952.

Philby, Harry St. John Bridger. *Arabia of the Wahhabis.* London: Constable, 1928.

Philby, Harry St. John Bridger. *The Background of Islam, Being a Sketch of Arabian History in Pre-Islamic Times.* Alexandria: Whitehead, Morris, 1947.

Philby, Harry St. John Bridger. *The Empty Quarter, Being a Description of the Great South Desert of Arabia Known as Rub' al Khali.* London: Constable, 1933.

Philby, Harry St. John Bridger. *Forty Years in the Wilderness.* London: Hale, 1957.

Philby, Harry St. John Bridger. *The Heart of Arabia: Record of Travel and Exploration.* London: Constable, 1922.

Philby, Harry St. John Bridger. *The Land of Midian.* London: Benn, 1957.

Philby, Harry St. John Bridger. *Sa'udi Arabia.* London: Benn, 1955.

Philby, Harry St. John Bridger. *Sheba's Daughter: Being a Record of Travel in Southern Arabia.* London: Methuen, 1939.

Riley, Carroll L. *Historical and Cultural Dictionary of Saudi Arabia.* Metuchen, N.J.: Scarecrow Press, 1972.

Rutter, Eldon. *The Holy Cities of Arabia.* New York: Putnam, 1928.

Sanger, Richard H. *The Arabian Peninsula.* Ithaca, N.Y.: Cornell University Press, 1954.

Saudi Arabian Monetary Authority. *Statistical Summary, 1974/75.* Jiddah (annual).

Shaffer, Robert. *Tents and Towers of Arabia.* New York: Dodd, Mead, 1952.

Thomas, Bertram. *Arabia Felix.* New York: Scribner, 1932.

Twitchell, Karl Saren, and Edward Jabra Jurji. *Saudi Arabia: With an Account of the Development of Its Natural Resources.* Princeton, N.J.: Princeton University Press, 1953.

Vidal, F. S. *The Oasis of Al-Hasa.* New York: Local Government Relations, Arabian Research Division, Arabian American Oil Company, 1955.

Winder, R. Bayly. *Saudi Arabia in the Nineteenth Century.* New York: St. Martin's Press, 1965.

SINGAPORE

Republic of Singapore

CAPITAL: Singapore. **FLAG:** The flag consists of a red stripe at the top and a white stripe on the bottom. On the red stripe, at the hoist, are a white crescent opening to the fly and five white stars. **ANTHEM:** *Long Live Singapore.* **MONETARY UNIT:** The Singapore dollar (s$) is divided into 100 cents. There are notes of 1, 5, 10, 20, and 50 cents and 1, 5, 10, 50, 100, and 1,000 dollars, as well as coins of various fractions of a dollar. s$1 = US$0.4027 (or US$1 = s$2.483). **WEIGHTS AND MEASURES:** Imperial weights and measures and some local measures are used. **HOLIDAYS:** Major Western, Chinese, Malay, Muslim, and Indian holidays are celebrated, many of which fall on annually variable dates because of the calendars used. Major holidays include New Year's Day, 1 January; Thaipusam (Hindu festival); Chinese New Year; Good Friday; Holy Saturday; Easter Monday; Hari Raya Puasa (Muslim festival); Wesak Day (Buddhist festival); Labour Day, 1 May; National Day, 9 August; Hari Raya Haji (Malay Muslim festival); Bank holidays, 1 and 2 July; Milad al-Nabi (birthday of Muhammad); Deepavali; Christmas, 25 December. **TIME:** 7:30 P.M. = noon GMT.

¹LOCATION, SIZE, AND EXTENT

The Republic of Singapore, the third-smallest country in Asia, consists of Singapore Island and several smaller adjacent islets. Situated in the Indian Ocean off the southern tip of the Malay Peninsula, Singapore has an area of 581.4 sq km (224.5 sq mi), of which Singapore Island comprises 542.6 sq km (209.5 sq mi) and the islets 38.8 sq km (15 sq mi). Singapore Island extends 50.7 km (31.5 mi) ENE–WSW and 31.4 km (19.5 mi) SSE–NNW, and has a coastline of 135 km (84 mi), of which 84 km (52 mi) are along the water channel between the Island and the Malay Peninsula. Singapore is connected to the nearby western portion of Malaysia by a causeway 1.2 km (0.75 mi) in length across the narrow Johore Strait. Singapore's position at the eastern end of the Strait of Malacca, which separates western Malaysia and the Indonesian island of Sumatra, has given it economic and strategic importance out of proportion to its small size.

²TOPOGRAPHY

Singapore Island is mostly low-lying green undulating country with a small range of hills at the center. The highest point of the island is Bukit Timah (581 feet). There are sections of rain forest in the center and large mangrove swamps along the coast, which has many inlets, particularly in the north and west. Singapore's harbor is wide, deep, and well-protected.

³CLIMATE

The climate is tropical, with heavy rainfall and high humidity. The range of temperature is slight; the average annual maximum is 30.6°C (87°F), and the average minimum 24°C (75°F). The annual rainfall of about 95 inches is distributed fairly evenly throughout the year, ranging from 10 inches in December to 7 inches in May. It rains about one day in two.

⁴FLORA AND FAUNA

Singapore Island is in the main denuded, the dense tropical forest that originally covered it being mostly cleared. There is some rain forest in the central area of the island, however, as well as extensive mangrove swamps along the coast. Urban development has limited animal life. As of 1975, endangered species in Singapore included the river terrapin and false gavial.

⁵POPULATION

In 1975, Singapore's estimated population was 2,248,000 (as contrasted with 1,864,900 in 1965). Population for 1980 was projected at 2,437,000. About one-third of the population is under 15 years

of age, and half is under 21. The government has pressed a vigorous birth control campaign, and as of the mid-1970s the rate of population increase had declined to an annual rate of 1.4%, having been as high as 4.3% in the period 1947–57.

A virtual city-state, fully 90.2% of Singapore's 1975 population was urban. The population density, at 3,867 persons per sq km (10,013 per sq mi), was the highest of any nation in the world.

⁶ETHNIC GROUPS

The people of Singapore are predominantly of Chinese origin. Of an estimated 1974 population of 2,219,100, 1,689,500 (76.1%) were ethnic Chinese (most of them born, however, in Singapore or in neighboring Malaysia). Some 334,100 (15.1%) were Malays (including Indonesians); 153,500 (6.9%) were Indians (including Sri Lankans); and 42,000 (1.9%) were Europeans, Eurasians, and others.

⁷LANGUAGE

There are four official languages: Chinese (Cantonese dialect), Malay, English, and Tamil. English is the principal medium of government and is widely used in commerce and education.

⁸RELIGION

There is complete separation of state and religion in Singapore. Freedom of religion is both constitutionally guaranteed and honored in practice. Precise figures on religious affiliation are not available. The Chinese (except for an estimated 2% who are Christian) practice Buddhism, Taoism, and Confucianism to a varying degree. Malays and persons with origins in the Pakistani and Bangladeshi portions of the Indian subcontinent—or about 17% of the population—are almost exclusively Muslims. Most of the Indian minority are Hindus. In 1973 there were 500 Jews.

⁹TRANSPORTATION

Singapore's history is partly the history of the island-country's important regional role as a transportation link between East and West, North and South, and the mainland and insular portions of Southeast Asia. As long ago as 1822—only three years after the establishment of a British colonial presence on the island—1,575 ships called at the new port of Singapore from nearby islands, Europe, India, and China. It was a pattern that has continued down to the present time. With a natural deepwater harbor that is open the full year, Singapore now ranks as the fourth-largest port in the world. Its anchorage facilities can accommodate supertankers. Ships of some 250 shipping lines, flying the flags of 63

311

countries, regularly call at Singapore, about 200 of them arriving every day. In 1974, Singapore itself had 1,083 ships registered, totaling 3,392,000 gross tons. In that year, 36,187 ships discharged 37,713,600 tons of freight and loaded 22,738,900 tons.

Commercial air service was inaugurated in Singapore in 1930. Singapore's international airport at Paya Lebar, 7.5 miles from the business center of the city, was constructed in 1953 and is one of the best-equipped in Southeast Asia. In 1974, some 28 international airlines operated more than 50,000 scheduled flights through Singapore. More than 2,014,250 passengers and 33,843,000 kg of freight were landed in that year. Singapore's own flag carrier is Singapore Airlines, which uses jumbo jets on scheduled services to Tokyo, London, and Sydney, among other destinations.

The first automobile was driven in Singapore as early as 1896, and within a decade this mode of transport began to have a major impact on the island. In 1976, there were about 319,000 private motor cars in the country, or 142 cars per 1,000 inhabitants. Increases in registration and license fees in 1972, designed to slow the growth in ownership of motor vehicles, failed to have the desired result. There are 1,188 miles of roads.

Singapore's sole rail facility is a 16-mile section of the Malayan Railways, which links Singapore to Kuala Lumpur.

10 COMMUNICATIONS

Postal, telephone, and telegraph services in Singapore are among the most efficient in Southeast Asia. There are 48 post offices and 31 postal agencies. Local one-day delivery is routine, and transit time from Singapore to overseas destinations is the fastest in the region.

Telecommunications services are administered by the Telecommunication Authority of Singapore. Service is available on a 24-hour basis for worldwide telegraph, telephone, and Telex communication. Domestic telephone service is provided by the Singapore Telephone Board. There were about 61,600 telephones in 1974.

The Broadcasting Division of the Ministry of Culture operates radio and television services. Radio programs are broadcast in Chinese, Malay, English, and Tamil. Television Singapore, inaugurated in 1963, operates daily on two channels. There were about 700,000 radios and 55,000 television sets in the country in 1974.

11 HISTORY

The early history of Singapore is obscure. There appears to have been a reference to an island at the tip of the Malay Peninsula by a Chinese explorer as early as A.D. 231. Some historians believe a city was founded on the island as early as the 7th century, while other sources claim that "Singapura" (Lion City) was established by an Indian prince in 1299. It was thought to be a thriving trading center in 13th and 14th centuries, until it was devastated by a Javanese attack in 1377.

Singapore, however, was an almost uninhabited island when Sir Stamford Raffles, in 1819, established a trading station of the British East India Company on the island. In 1824, the island was ceded outright to the Company by the Sultan of Johore, the Malay state at the extreme southern end of the Peninsula, and in 1826 it was incorporated with Malacca and Penang (now Pinang) to form the Straits Settlements (which was the form of its legal status and administration up to World War II). The trading center grew into the city of Singapore and attracted large numbers of Chinese, many of whom became merchants, until it became a largely Chinese-populated community. With its excellent harbor, Singapore also became a flourishing commercial center and the leading seaport of Southeast Asia, handling the vast export trade in tin and rubber from British-ruled Malaya.

In 1938, the British completed construction of a large naval base on the island, which the Japanese captured in February 1942 during World War II, following a land-based attack from the Malay Peninsula to the north. Recaptured by the UK in 1945, Singapore was detached from the Straits Settlements to become a separate crown colony in 1946.

Under a new constitution, on 3 June 1959, Singapore became a self-governing state, and on 16 September 1963, it joined the new Federation of Malaysia (formed by bringing together the previously independent Malaya, Singapore, and the formerly British-ruled northern Borneo territories of Sarawak and Sabah). However, Singapore, with its predominantly urban, Chinese population and highly commercial economy, began to find itself at odds with the Malay-dominated central government of Malaysia. Frictions mounted, and on 9 August 1965, Singapore separated from Malaysia to become wholly independent in its own right as the Republic of Singapore. Lee Kuan Yew, a major figure in the move toward independence, has served as the country's prime minister since 1965.

12 GOVERNMENT

The constitution of the Republic of Singapore, as amended in 1965, provides for a parliamentary form of government, with a president serving as titular head of state.

The legislature consists of a 65-member Parliament. The prime minister, selected by a majority of the Parliament, acts as effective head of government. The prime minister appoints a cabinet which, in 1976, consisted of a deputy prime minister and 14 other ministers. The maximum term for parliamentary sessions is five years, although elections may be called at any time within that period. The president of the Republic is elected by the Parliament for a term of four years.

Singapore practices universal suffrage, and voting has been compulsory for all citizens over 21 since 1959.

13 POLITICAL PARTIES

Singapore in 1976 was effectively a single-party state. There were five legal opposition parties, but the ruling People's Action Party (PAP) of Prime Minister Lee Kuan Yew held all the seats in Parliament. In the 1972 elections, the PAP won only 69% of the votes, but the distribution of the opposition's support was sufficiently diffuse to permit PAP victories in all of the contested seats.

The PAP itself came into being in 1955, when it won 3 seats out of 25 for the Legislative Assembly. The PAP was a strongly socialist party at its start and combined both moderate and extreme leftist elements (with Lee Kuan Yew belonging to the former faction). In 1959, the party won 43 of 51 seats in an enlarged Assembly, receiving 54% of the 525,000 votes cast in the election. Lee Kuan Yew was subsequently named prime minister in June 1959.

In 1961, the radical wing of the PAP split from Lee's majority faction. The former PAP leftists formed a new party of their own, the Socialist Front (SF) and comprised the strongest opposition party in the Parliament until 1966. In 1966, 11 SF members resigned their seats in Parliament, and 2 others joined the underground opposition to the Lee government. Led by pro-Peking Lee Siew Choh, the SF won only 4.5% of the vote in the 1972 elections.

The strongest showing by an opposition party in the 1972 voting was made by the Workers Party (WP), whose leader is J. B. Jeyaretnam. The WP, which captured 11.9% of the 1972 vote, has been critical of undemocratic practices within the PAP government. Although the PAP has itself advocated close relations with neighboring Malaysia, the WP is even stronger in its espousal of ties with the adjacent country. This contrasts sharply with the position of the SF, which is anti-Malaysian and voiced the strongest opposition to Singapore's inclusion in the Federation of Malaysia in 1963.

Smaller minority parties are the United National Front, which is also critical of antidemocratic dimensions of Lee's rule and is pro-Malaysian (it won 7.2% of the vote in 1972); the Chinese-dominated People's Front (which took 3% of the 1972 balloting); and the Singapore Malays National Organization (SMNO), an affiliate of the ranking political organization in neighboring Malaysia, the United Malays National Organization (SMNO won 1.3% of the 1972 vote). The illegal Malayan Communist Party and the underground Malayan National Liberation Front are pro-Peking parties that advocate overthrow of the governments of both Singapore and adjacent Malaysia and operate, albeit clandestinely, within a single Malaysian-Singaporean polity.

14 LOCAL GOVERNMENT

Singapore, veritably a city-state, has no local government divisions. The former city council and rural board have been integrated into departments of the central government.

15 JUDICIAL SYSTEM

Singapore's legal system is based on British common law. The judiciary includes a Supreme Court as well as district, magistrate's, and special courts. Minor cases are heard in the country's ten magistrate's courts and in district courts (two civil and four criminal), each presided over by a district judge. The Supreme Court is headed by a chief justice and is divided into the High Court, the Court of Appeal, and the Court of Criminal Appeal. The High Court has unlimited original jurisdiction in both criminal and civil cases but ordinarily chooses to exercise such jurisdictional authority only in major cases. In its appellate jurisdiction, the High Court hears criminal and civil appeals from the magistrate's and district courts. Appeal in a civil case heard by the High Court in its original jurisdiction is to the Court of Appeal, and in a criminal case, to the Court of Criminal Appeal.

16 ARMED FORCES

Singapore has made major efforts since 1965 to develop its own armed forces. Compulsory national service has been in effect since 1967. Male citizens are called up for 24–36 months' full-time military service at age 18.

Singapore's armed forces are small, but they are well trained and equipped, and their reserve strength (25,000 in 1975) is substantial. In 1975, the army had an estimated 25,000 personnel, including one armored brigade. The navy had 2,000 personnel and was equipped with 7 patrol craft and 6 missile gunboats. The air force, established in 1969, had 3,000 personnel and 95 combat aircraft. Paramilitary forces included 7,500 police and a home guard of 30,000.

17 MIGRATION

Singapore had only a few Malay fishermen as inhabitants at the time of its founding as a British trading post in 1819. It was subsequently, and quite rapidly, populated by immigrant peoples, primarily Chinese but also Malays (from Sumatra as well as adjacent Malaya) and Indians (who took advantage of common British governance to migrate to Singapore in search of better employment). Thus, immigration, rather than natural increase, was the major factor in Singapore's fast population growth through the mid-20th century.

In November 1965, following separation from Malaysia, Singapore's newly independent government introduced measures to restrict the flow of Malaysians entering the country in search of work. These immigrants, who averaged 10,000 a year up to 1964, had to establish residence for several years to qualify for citizenship. In addition, all noncitizens were required to apply for a work permit. In 1973, the government issued 3,809 entry permits for permanent residence, 64,604 employment passes, and 9,085 dependents' passes.

18 INTERNATIONAL COOPERATION

Singapore follows an active policy of cooperation with international bodies and the community of nations. A member of the Commonwealth of Nations, Singapore also belongs to the UN and its various specialized agencies. It is a participant in the Asian Development Bank and has acceded since 1973 to GATT. Probably its most important international association, however, is its membership—along with Malaysia, Indonesia, Thailand, and the Philippines—in ASEAN, which it joined at the time of its founding in 1967. Singapore has played a leading part in the important regional grouping, which has sought to maximize international economic cooperation among its member-states, to regularize political consultation on the part of the constituent governments, and to limit foreign political and military interference in the area.

Under Premier Lee Kuan Yew, Singapore has had particularly close relations with the US, although relations with the USSR have also been cordial. Because of its large ethnic Chinese majority, however, Singapore has been reluctant to seek out direct diplomatic ties with China, although there have been a variety of indirect economic and other exchanges with Peking.

19 ECONOMY

Historically, Singapore's economy was based primarily on its role as an entrepôt for neighboring countries. It did not have minerals or other primary products of its own to export, but it served a major economic function by processing and transshipping the goods of nearby lands. As a result, Singapore became highly active in shipbuilding and repair, tin smelting, and rubber and copra milling. Until about 1960, however, its economy was frequently shaken by major fluctuations in its export earnings (particularly from rubber and tin) as a consequence of often adverse commodity and price trends.

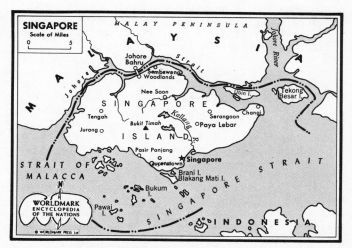

See continental political: front cover 09; physical: back cover 09

LOCATION: 1°9′ to 1°29′N; 103°32′ to 104°6′E. TERRITORIAL SEA LIMIT: 3 mi.

Since the early 1960s, Singapore has attempted to break away from the economic patterns that had developed and prevailed during the previous 140-odd years. Its government embarked on an ambitious and largely successful program of promoting industrial investment (both from abroad and locally), developing industrial estates, and providing industrial financing and technical services. By the mid-1970s, Singapore had built a much more diversified economy, with its own manufactured goods taking a place in world trade. Singapore still engages in the processing of other countries' primary products and transshipping, but its own high-skill industries are coming to the forefront as the main basis of its economy.

Singapore must still import most of its foodstuffs. In the 1960s and 1970s, Singapore achieved self-sufficiency in eggs, poultry, and pork, often producing surpluses for export.

[20] INCOME

Singapore's per capita income, the highest in Asia after Japan's, reached US$2,376 in 1974. The GDP in 1974 was s$12,927.5 million (as compared with s$10,387.8 million in 1973 and s$8,155.8 million in 1972). The 1974 GDP was distributed as follows: wholesale and retail trade, 28.4%; manufacturing, 25.1%; transport, storage, and communications, 10.3%; construction, 7.4%; utilities, 1.9%; agriculture and fishing, 1.7%; and other sectors, 25.2%.

[21] LABOR

In 1975, Singapore's work force totaled 644,349. Of this number, 234,231 (36.3%) were employed in manufacturing; 195,136 (30.3%) in services; 172,650 (26.8%) in commerce; 21,709 (3.4%) in farming and fishing; and 20,623 (3.2%) in other sectors. Although there are occasional lags, Singapore has achieved virtually full employment, with workers frequently brought in from Malaysia to ease shortages. Continued growth of the work force from the mid-1960s through the mid-1970s was largely the result of the government's successful industrialization program. Half of the increase in employment (61,576) between 1972 and 1973, for example, was in the manufacturing sector of the economy.

The Industrial Relations Act of 1968 controls relations between management (public as well as private) and labor. The Industrial Relations and Conciliation Section of the Ministry of Labour seeks to assist the parties in the event of the outbreak of serious differences. Of 997 labor disputes in 1973, 720 were amicably settled with the assistance of the Ministry.

There are 144 registered trade unions in Singapore, including 92 employee unions, 51 employer unions, and 1 trade-union federation. Total membership is about 191,500. Some 41 of the unions are affiliated with Singapore's National Trade Unions Congress (which represents, as a result, about 87% of the country's unionized workers). The government generally asserts a strong influence over labor-union policies.

[22] AGRICULTURE

Urbanization and industrialization have taken ever larger amounts of land away from agricultural activity in post-World War II Singapore. Many of the rubber and coconut plantations that dominated Singapore's landscape before the war have disappeared altogether. Housing for a growing population—and factories for its employment—today stand where rubber and coconut trees used to grow. Nonetheless, agriculture remains an important part of Singapore's total economic activity, growing methods on the island being the most intensive in all of Southeast Asia. Vegetables and a specialized Singapore product, the orchid, remain significant sources of income. Remarkably, through the decade of the 1960s, Singapore was able to increase its primary produce annually through intensification. The total value of farm produce in 1973 was estimated at s$395 million, while exports of orchids alone earned the nation s$3 million. Production of fresh vegetables in 1973, which totaled 55,950 tons, met 43% of the consumption needs of Singapore's generally well-nourished population.

[23] ANIMAL HUSBANDRY

Singapore has been self-sufficient in pork, poultry, and eggs since 1964, a notable achievement considering the modest amount of land available and the demands of growing urbanization and industrialization. Hog and poultry farming, indeed, together comprise Singapore's largest primary industry, affording frequent surpluses exported to neighboring Malaysia. In 1973, 1.2 million hogs, 24 million chickens, 3.5 million ducks, and 405 million eggs were produced.

The Pig and Poultry Research and Training Institute at Sembawang conducts research on feeding, housing, breeding, management, and disease control.

[24] FISHING

Local fishermen operate chiefly in inshore waters, but some venture into the South China Sea and the Indian Ocean. Traditional fishing methods are in use along coastal waters, but there is a trend toward mechanization in both offshore and deep-sea fishing. In 1974, Singapore's fishermen caught 18,556 tons of fish, about one-third of which was exported. However, 51,057 tons of fish had to be imported.

Since 1969, when the Jurong Central Fish Market was opened, all fresh fish have been auctioned at a central location. The 40-acre Jurong facility provides modern shore-support assistance and processing plants. Training in offshore and deep-sea fishing techniques is provided by the Fishery Training Center at Changi. The Marine Fisheries Research Department of the Southeast Asian Fisheries Development Center, a regional project, engages in the search for new fishing grounds.

[25] FORESTRY

There is little productive forestry left on the island, but Singapore continues to have a fairly sizable sawmilling industry, processing timber imported largely from Malaysia (with some additional imports from Indonesia). Both Malaysia and Indonesia are expanding their processing capacities, however, and Singapore may find itself in a fairly competitive relationship with these two neighbors in the near future. As recently as 1973, however, timber and woodworking industries on the island turned out s$431 million worth of products, a 50% increase over 1972. Improved prices for timber on world markets was a factor in this increase.

[26] MINING

There is no mining in Singapore.

[27] ENERGY AND POWER

Installed capacity in 1972 was 727,000 kw; all power was generated thermally. Electricity generated in 1974 totaled 3,864.3 million kwh, more than twice the 1969 total of 1,876.1 million kwh. High-tension transmission of 1,236.1 million kwh to industrial consumers represented the largest type of usage, and in large part accounted for the extraordinary expansion of Singapore's manufacturing sector during 1969–74. Gas consumption in 1974 was the equivalent of 391.1 million kwh, of which 156.6 million kwh were sold to the Housing and Development Board.

[28] INDUSTRY

When Singapore's industrial activity was largely confined to processing of goods for its complex entrepôt trade, rubber milling and tin smelting were the major industries. Political and economic factors combined to change this situation, however. Economically, the rubber milling industry steadily declined as a result of a drop in demand, supply problems, and other factors. Singapore's separation from Malaysia in 1965 prompted the latter country to develop its own tin-smelting facilities.

The modern industrialization of Singapore began in 1961 with the creation of the Economic Development Board to formulate and implement an ambitious manufacturing scheme. Most of the first factories set up under this program were of an import-substitute nature requiring tariff protection, but many of such protective tariffs were subsequently withdrawn. Large-scale foreign manufacturing operations in Singapore commenced in 1967 with the establishment of plants of several major multinational electronic corporations.

The Jurong Town Corporation was established under the Jurong Town Corporation Act of 1968 to develop and manage industrial estates and sites in Singapore. All industrial sites and estates, including Jurong Town, were taken over by the corporation from the Economic Development Board in June 1968. During the 1962–74 period, the manufacturing sector grew by an average annual rate of about 20%, while industry's share of the GDP rose from 9.8% to 25.1%. By 1973, foreign investments in the manufacturing sector alone had reached s$2,659 million, creating more than 110,000 jobs in a five-year period and more than doubling the industrial labor force. Such dramatic achievements were in large measure made possible by the existence in Singapore even before the 1960s of one of the most developed economic infrastructures in Southeast Asia, as well as by the country's traditionally skilled, disciplined, and highly motivated work force.

In 1976, Singapore's main industrial activity was contained in metals and engineering, shipbuilding and repairing, petroleum, chemicals and plastics, electronic and electrical products, precision equipment and optical products, timber and woodworking, food and beverages, and textiles.

²⁹DOMESTIC TRADE

Marketing has always been an activity in which Singapore's Chinese have played a major role, and their participation has increased in recent years as local branches of European firms have become less important. Indian and Arab merchants are also prominent. Warehousing, packaging, freight forwarding, and related services are of a high standard.

Usual business hours for Western firms are 9 A.M. to 4:30 or 5 P.M., with many businesses closed from 1 to 2 (or 2:30) P.M. Most major enterprises and foreign firms operate Monday through Friday and are open a half day on Saturday. A number of Chinese and Indian businesses maintain longer hours, with some open seven days a week.

Advertising is done by radio and television, outdoor displays, slides in motion picture theaters, and in newspapers. There are several advertising agencies. Consumers are highly brand-conscious, and advertising concentrates considerably on product trademarks.

³⁰FOREIGN TRADE

Singapore's trade patterns have changed significantly in the period since World War II and, more recently, since the end of its status as a UK dependency. Formerly functioning largely as an entrepôt center for the incoming and outgoing traffic of its neighbors in Southeast Asia, Singapore has become an exporting country in its own right, particularly since the advent of its accelerated industrialization in the early 1960s. The leading exports of the mid-1960s—rubber, coffee, pepper, and palm oil—had been replaced in the mid-1970s by a variety of capital-intensive manufactures.

The value of exports increased by 44.9% in 1973, and exceeded imports for only the second time since 1966. Exports in 1974 stood at s$14,154.6 million, a 58.9% advance over the previous year. Imports, however, grew by 63.1%, totaling s$20,404.9 million.

Principal exports in 1974 (in millions of Singapore dollars) were:

Minerals, fuels, and lubricants	3,693.0
Machinery and transport equipment	2,918.6
Inedible crude materials	2,506.2
Manufactured goods	1,069.9
Chemicals	917.1
Food and live animals	814.0
Miscellaneous manufactured articles	807.5
Other exports	1,428.3
TOTAL	**14,154.6**

Principal imports in 1974 (in millions of Singapore dollars) were:

Machinery and transport equipment	5,405.8
Minerals, fuels, and lubricants	4,897.9
Manufactured goods	3,591.8
Inedible crude materials except fuels	1,648.7
Food and live animals	1,551.2
Miscellaneous manufactured articles	1,345.9
Chemicals	1,220.6
Other imports	743.0
TOTAL	**20,404.9**

Singapore's allies within the ASEAN group—principally Malaysia and Thailand—now account for the largest single part of its foreign market, having comprised 17.9% of the total trade volume in 1974. Japan was second as a major trading partner, followed by the US, the UK, and the EEC countries.

Principal trade partners in 1974 (in millions of Singapore dollars) were:

	EXPORTS	IMPORTS	BALANCE
Japan	1,610.5	3,653.9	−2,043.4
Malaysia	2,347.4	2,686.1	− 338.7
US	2,100.7	2,858.1	− 757.4
UK	574.5	996.3	− 421.8
Hong Kong	901.4	470.9	430.5
Australia	687.7	571.0	116.7
FRG	428.2	712.3	− 284.1
Thailand	343.2	542.6	− 199.4
China	125.8	643.9	− 518.1
Netherlands	231.7	274.6	− 42.9
France	262.9	234.2	28.7
Italy	177.8	237.1	− 59.3
USSR	236.4	25.7	210.7
Other countries	4,126.4	6,498.2	−2,371.8
TOTALS	**14,154.6**	**20,404.9**	**−6,250.3**

³¹BALANCE OF PAYMENTS

Singapore's foreign trade is characterized by a near-continuous deficit, although there have been individual years in the 1960s and 1970s when Singapore exported more than it imported. Trade deficits are ordinarily balanced by income from services in connection with transshipments (primarily to and from other Southeast Asian countries), tourism (which has increased steadily in recent years), insurance, financing, and capital investments from abroad.

Singapore's balance-of-payments position in 1970 and 1974 (in millions of US dollars) is summarized as follows:

	1970	1974
Merchandise balance	−855	−2,352
Services balance	291	1,178
Private transfers	− 21	− 36
Government transfers	13	2
CURRENT BALANCE	**−572**	**−1,208**
Long-term capital	140	715
Short-term capital	33	− 172
Errors and omissions	583	954
TOTALS	**184**	**289**

³²BANKING

Singapore's 54 banks have a total of 212 banking offices. Some 12 banks are locally incorporated; the remainder are branches of various overseas banks. Since 1971, the government has pursued a policy of seeking variety of representation among foreign banks in terms of countries and geographical regions. Most of the new foreign banks allowed into Singapore in the 1970s have been offshore banks that have concentrated on foreign-exchange transactions. As of 31 January 1976, reserves of the commercial banking sector stood at s$557 million; demand deposits totaled s$1,840 million, and time and savings deposits, s$4,192 million.

Currency is issued by the Singapore Board of Commissioners of Currency. As of 1975, currency in circulation amounted to s$1,546 million (as compared with s$1,143 million at the end of 1973).

³³INSURANCE

At the end of 1974 there were 74 insurance companies, of which

58 provided non-life, 8 life, and 8 both life and non-life coverage. Most insurance firms are branches or agencies of UK (or other Commonwealth), European, and US companies, although local participation in insurance activity—particularly business insurance—is increasing. Marine and warehouse insurance constitutes most of the business insurance, but almost all types of commercial insurance are available.

At the start of 1974, total assets of life insurance funds were s$247 million and of general insurance, s$161 million. Life insurance policies numbered 111,509. Life insurance companies are required to invest a minimum of 75% of their insurance funds in authorized assets and 20% in Singapore government securities; for general insurance companies the comparable requirements are 55% and 15% respectively.

Third-party motor liability insurance has been compulsory in Singapore since 1958.

³⁴SECURITIES

There is an active curb market for securities, handled on a commission basis through brokers who are members of the Singapore Stock Exchange. Government bonds are generally purchased by banks and other institutional investors. Brokers, operating through correspondents, also deal in securities on Australian, Hong Kong, London, and other exchanges.

³⁵PUBLIC FINANCE

Since 1971, Singapore's fiscal years have ended 31 March. Current government accounts, which have shown surpluses throughout the 1970s, do not reflect revenues and expenditures of the Development Fund. The principal categories of government revenues and expenditures for 1973/74 and estimated for 1974/75 (in millions of Singapore dollars) were broken down as follows:

	1973/74	1974/75
REVENUES		
Income taxes	585.7	700.0
Import duties	312.6	336.9
Excise taxes	163.4	184.6
Other taxes	399.4	436.2
Other revenues	758.1	665.3
TOTALS	2,219.2	2,323.0
EXPENDITURES		
Defense	524.8	637.7
Education	261.4	288.9
Social and community services	221.8	284.5
Transport and communications	35.9	48.4
Agriculture, manufacturing, and construction	12.9	40.7
Other economic services	18.8	33.9
Interest on public debt	177.7	244.7
Other expenditures	854.1	720.7
TOTALS	2,107.4	2,299.5

³⁶TAXATION

Individual and commercial incomes are taxed whether derived in Singapore or from outside sources. Types of direct taxation include income, property, estate duty, and payroll taxes; the Inland Revenue Department is responsible for the assessment and collection of all such levies. Individuals pay income taxes on a sliding scale that ranges from 6% on the first s$2,500 to 55% on income exceeding s$100,000; companies are charged at a fixed rate of 40% on taxable income. A married man earning s$5,000 annually pays only s$60 in income tax, and no tax at all if he has two children. Industrial establishments, companies, and various other businesses are eligible to deduct from their gross profits varying and usually generous depreciation allowances for building, plants, and machinery.

³⁷CUSTOMS AND DUTIES

Prior to 1966, Singapore was essentially a free port with import duties levied only on alcoholic beverages, tobacco and tobacco products, petroleum products, and certain soaps. In 1959, however, a law was passed empowering the government to levy import duties on other products to protect local industries. In the mid- and late 1960s, many new tariffs were established with the primary aim of helping local manufacturing firms get on their feet. In the early 1970s, many items were withdrawn from the tariff list, and by the end of 1973 there were only 197 items on the list, as compared with 349 in 1972. In 1973, all protective tariffs were lifted as an anti-inflationary move.

Singapore has two free-trade zones, in Teluk Ayer Basin and the main Port of Singapore. Free-trade provisions also apply to the Jurong Town Corporation, in cases where traders repack dutiable goods for transshipment.

³⁸FOREIGN INVESTMENTS

Legislation to attract new foreign investments (the Economic Incentives Act) was passed in 1967; it granted exemption from taxation for a five-year period to investors for export development and other types of activity and provided inducements and guarantees with respect to repatriation of profits and capital. Overseas offices to promote such foreign investment have been set up in New York, Chicago, San Francisco, London, Paris, Frankfurt, Zürich, Tokyo, Hong Kong, Stockholm, and Melbourne. The Capital Participation Scheme, adopted in 1973, permits high-technology industries to set up branches in Singapore with 50% equity participation by the government.

With resultant changes in Singapore's industrial development, there have also been alterations in incentives. In the mid-1970s, the main criteria for granting tax incentives were capital investment ratios (including training costs) per worker, value added per worker, and the ratio of technical personnel and skilled workers to the total work force. In recent years, major investment activity has focused on petroleum refining, general manufacturing, electronics, and hotel construction, as well as on traditional endeavors such as shipping, banking, insurance, and external trade. By 1975, total US private investments in Singapore totaled more than US$575 million.

³⁹ECONOMIC POLICY

Historically, Singapore's economic role was that of a trading and primary product-processing center for much of the Southeast Asian region. Technological change and political considerations in the post-World War II period—not least of all the nationalism that accompanied the quest for independence among the region's European colonies—have combined to alter dramatically the economic self-perception and public policies of this diminutive island-state. By the late 1950s, it was obvious that prospects for economic growth would be severely limited if Singapore remained bound by its old economic role as entrepôt. The decision to industrialize—and to do so rapidly—was a conscious policy decision of a government determined to keep pace with technological and economic changes elsewhere in the world.

Initial emphasis in the government's economic development program was upon employment. The increasing trend toward economic self-sufficiency in neighboring Indonesia and Malaysia—and the steady retreat of the UK from defense responsibilities in the region as a whole (centered on its large Singapore naval and air facilities)—prompted the government to go all-out in its effort to find alternate employment for the island's highly skilled and disciplined work population. By the end of the 1960s, this problem was effectively solved, with Singapore boasting one of the lowest unemployment rates in all of Asia.

Emphasis in the mid-1970s has been on labor skills and technology, especially as these are identified with such modern industries as machine tools, petrochemicals, electronics, and other precision work. A high level of participation by private foreign capital continues to provide an important cornerstone to this development.

40 HEALTH

Singapore's population enjoys one of the highest health levels in all of Southeast Asia. This achievement is largely attributed to good housing, sanitation, and water supply, as well as the best hospital and other medical facilities in the region. The crude mortality rate in 1975 was 5.3 per 1,000, while average life expectancy was estimated at 70.8 years.

Despite marked progress in upgrading the quality and efficiency of health services, shortages remain in both facilities and personnel. In 1975, Singapore had 17 government hospitals, with 8,031 beds, and 7 additional private hospitals, with 986 beds, yielding a ratio of 4 beds to every 1,000 people. To handle increasing demands for health services, the government began in the 1960s to create a network of outpatient dispensaries, which totaled 26 by 1974. Primary medical care through these dispensaries and through 46 maternal and child health clinics is supplemented by a relatively large number of general practitioners located throughout Singapore Island. In 1974 there were 1,565 registered physicians, of whom 709 (including 109 employed by the University of Singapore) participated in the government's medical service. The physician-to-population ratio stood at about 1 per 1,436 persons.

The Dental Health Branch maintains a comprehensive clinical and preventive dentistry service, operating 95 dental clinics.

41 SOCIAL WELFARE

Government-provided social welfare services are directed by the Social Welfare Department, which is often assisted by various voluntary organizations, most of them affiliated with the Singapore Council of Social Service. Public assistance is available to persons 55 years of age and older, although younger people may benefit from it if they are medically unfit for work. In 1973, a monthly average of 7,407 families received such aid at a cost to the government of s$3,041,523. Besides institutionalized care, the Social Welfare Department also administers fostering and homemakers' service schemes for needy children and young persons. The government operates 13 social welfare homes, 5 for boys, 5 for girls and women, 2 for destitute persons, and 1 for the aged. Social welfare assistance is also provided by mutual-benefit organizations (of which there are 427 with a combined membership of 191,367) and voluntary services.

The Family Planning and Population Board, created in 1965, has responsibility for implementation of the government's family planning and population program. From 1966 to 1973, 211,073 women registered with the Board for advice and assistance, while 24,575 women and 828 men were surgically sterilized.

42 HOUSING

Sustained rapid population growth in the years preceding and following World War II provided Singapore with an acute housing shortage. In 1947, a housing committee determined that, with a squatter problem worsening each year, 250,000 persons required immediate housing, while another 250,000 people would need new housing by the late 1950s. In 1960, the Housing and Development Board was established by the new PAP government. During its first five-year building program (1960–65), the Board spent s$230 million to construct 53,000 dwelling units for more than 250,000 people. It was in this period that Queenstown, Singapore's first satellite community, was developed; by the mid-1970s, Queenstown had a total of 27,000 living units in seven neighborhood complexes, housing upward of 150,000 people.

In the second five-year building program (1966–70), 67,000 additional units, accommodating 350,000 persons and costing s$305 million, were built. About 125,000 more units—more than in the first two programs combined—were erected by the Board in the third building period (1970–75). In 1975, as a result of these government-sponsored efforts, 940,000 persons—or 41.8% of the total population of Singapore—lived in facilities built by the Housing and Development Board.

43 EDUCATION

Approximately 75% of the population of Singapore is literate, a percentage that has been increasing annually. A comprehensive public-education policy is designed to produce a literate as well as technically qualified population. All children who are Singapore citizens are entitled to six years of free primary education. Primary schooling is available in all four official languages.

In 1973 there were 557 schools in Singapore, including 265 government schools, 228 government-aided schools, and 64 private schools. The total school population was 523,708, with 350,599 at primary and 173,109 at secondary levels. Of the students in the upper levels of secondary school, 67,110 were receiving an academic education, 15,645 technical, and 2,414 commercial. Seven vocational institutes offered training courses in the metal, woodworking, electrical, electronic, and building trades. There were 18,631 teachers in government and government-aided schools in 1973, 11,700 in primary schools and 6,931 in secondary schools. The teacher-student ratio was 1 to 30 at the primary level and 1 to 25 at the secondary level.

Five institutions of higher education exist in Singapore. The most comprehensive of these, the University of Singapore, had 5,356 students and 965 instructors in 1974. Nanyang University had 2,483 students and an instructional staff of 199. Besides these two universities, there are the Singapore Technical Institute, Ngee Ann Technical College, and Singapore Polytechnic.

44 LIBRARIES AND MUSEUMS

There are two main libraries in Singapore. The National Library of Singapore (founded in 1844 and known, until 1960, as Raffles National Library) contained 738,185 items in 1975, including 702,696 books in the four official languages. Of the total collection of books, 406,072 were for adults, 51,914 for young people, and 244,710 for children. The National Library houses the government archives and serves as a repository for official publications printed in Singapore since 1946. The library has four urban branches, as well as a mobile unit serving the rural portions of the island. The University of Singapore Library contained nearly 500,000 volumes in 1976, including 135,000 volumes in Chinese and an extensive medical collection of about 81,000 volumes.

The National Museum (formerly Raffles Museum), established in 1887 on its present site, has collections of natural history, ethnology, and archaeology. Since 1965, it has also specialized in the art, culture, and way of life of Singapore's multiracial communities. An art gallery, established in 1974 by the Ministry of Culture, features works by the peoples of Southeast Asia as a whole. The Art Museum and Exhibition Gallery of the University of Singapore includes in its collections Asian art objects, contemporary Singaporean and Malayan painting and textiles, and facsimiles of Western sculpture.

45 ORGANIZATIONS

Singapore has a wide variety of organizations, some of these private in their origin and direction and others essentially government-controlled. Its hot and humid climate notwithstanding, Singapore has many sports clubs and associations, notably in the areas of badminton (in which Singaporeans have distinguished themselves internationally), basketball, boxing, cricket, cycling, golf, hockey, horse racing, motoring, polo, swimming, tennis, and yachting. There are also service clubs belonging to international associations; YMCA's and YWCA's; Chinese, Indian, and Malay chambers of commerce; and a multicommunal Singapore chamber of commerce.

In addition to such largely private organizations, the government established in 1960 a People's Association to organize and promote mass participation in social, cultural, educational, and recreational activities. There was in the mid-1970s, accordingly, a comprehensive network of community centers throughout the country set up by the People's Association. Management, women's, and youth subcommittees exist as active units of the Association.

A Singapore Sports Council, designed to develop and promote competitive and recreational sports in the country, was created in 1973. By 1976, all 65 constituencies of Singapore's government had their own sports associations.

46 PRESS

Singapore has nine daily newspapers, with at least one printed in each of the four main languages. The total circulation of daily papers in 1975 was 536,775. The oldest and most widely circulated daily is the English-language *Straits Times*, founded in 1845. More than 200 periodicals are published in various languages.

Although freedom of the press is guaranteed by law, the government has taken various actions against newspapers with which it has been at odds in recent years. The International Press Institute has on different occasions cited Singapore for interference with press freedom.

In 1975, Singapore's newspapers, with their daily circulations, were:

NEWSPAPER	LANGUAGE	CIRCULATION
Straits Times (m.)	English	235,000
Sin Chew Jit Poh (m.)	Chinese	86,318
Nanyang Siang Pau (m.)	Chinese	63,308
Shin Min Daily News (m.)	Chinese	45,750
Min Pao Daily (m.)	Chinese	25,000
New Nation (e.)	English	17,000
Berita Harian (m.)	Romanized Malay	11,600
Tamil Malar (m.)	Tamil	9,222
Tamil Murasu (m.)	Tamil	5,254

47 TOURISM

Tourists wishing to enter or visit Singapore must have a valid passport or other internationally recognized travel document. Visas are required for aliens (including those in transit) except for nationals of the UK and the British Commonwealth, Liechtenstein, the Netherlands, San Marino, Switzerland, and the US. Nationals of Belgium, Denmark, Finland, France, Iceland, Italy, Luxembourg, the Federal Republic of Germany (FRG), and Sweden do not need visas for stays of less than three months. Both smallpox and cholera inoculations are required.

Singapore's tourist volume has been increasing steadily in recent years. In 1974, 652,827 tourists visited Singapore, as compared with 298,535 in 1968. Another 102,483 persons visited the country for a combination of business and pleasure. In 1973, Singapore earned a record s$528.3 million from tourism, accounting for 5% of the GNP. In 1975 there were 71 hotels in the country, with a total of 9,153 rooms. Seven more hotels were completed in 1976, bringing the total number of available rooms to 11,750.

48 FAMOUS SINGAPOREANS

Sir Thomas Stamford Bingley Raffles (1781–1826) played the major role in the establishment of a British presence on Singapore Island in 1819; he introduced policies that greatly enhanced Singapore's wealth, and he suppressed the slave trade. Raffles also distinguished himself as a collector of historical and scientific information. The English writer and educator Cyril Northcote Parkinson (b.1909), formerly Raffles Professor of Political Theory at the University of Singapore, became internationally known as the originator of Parkinson's Law.

Singapore's dominant contemporary figure is Lee Kuan Yew (b.1923), prime minister since 1959.

49 DEPENDENCIES

Singapore has no territories or colonies.

50 BIBLIOGRAPHY

Abdul Rahman, Tengku, and Lee Kuan Yew. *Malaysian Situation*. Singapore: Ministry of Culture, 1964.

Buchanan, Iain. *Singapore in Southeast Asia: An Economic and Political Appraisal*. London: Bell, 1972.

Buckley, Charles B. *An Anecdotal History of Old Times in Singapore*. Kuala Lumpur: University of Malaya Press, 1965.

Chan, Heng Chee. *Singapore: The Politics of Survival, 1965–67*. Singapore: Oxford University Press, 1971.

Chatfield, G. A. *A History of Singapore*. Singapore: Moore, 1962.

Chua, Peng Chye. *Planning in Singapore: Selected Aspects and Issues*. Singapore: Chopmen, 1973.

Chuang, S. H. *Animal Life and Nature in Singapore*. Singapore: University of Singapore Press, 1973.

Fletcher, Nancy McHenry. *The Separation of Singapore from Malaysia*. Ithaca, N.Y.: Southeast Asia Program, Cornell University, 1969.

Gamer, Robert E. *The Politics of Urban Development in Singapore*. Ithaca, N.Y.: Cornell University Press, 1972.

George, T. J. S. *Lee Kuan Yew's Singapore*. London: Deutsch, 1973.

Hughes, Helen, and Poh Sing You. *Foreign Investment and Industrialization in Singapore*. Madison: University of Wisconsin Press, 1969.

Johnson, Desmond S. *An Introduction to the Natural History of Singapore*. Singapore: University of Singapore Press, 1973.

Josey, Alex. *Lee Kuan Yew*. Singapore: Moore, 1968.

Josey, Alex. *The Singapore General Elections, 1972*. Singapore: Eastern Universities Press, 1972.

Kirby, Stanley W., et al. *The Loss of Singapore*. London: HMSO, 1957.

McKie, Ronald. *Singapore*. Sydney: Angus & Robertson, 1972.

Makepeace, Walter (ed.). *One Hundred Years of Singapore*. London: Murray, 1921.

Mills, Lennox A. *British Malaya, 1824–67*. New ed. Singapore: Malayan Branch of the Royal Asiatic Society, 1961.

Pang, Cheng Lian. *Singapore's People's Action Party: Its History, Organization and Leadership*. New York: Oxford University Press, 1971.

Ramachandra, S. *Singapore Landmarks, Past and Present*. Singapore: Eastern Universities Press, 1961.

Saw, Swee-hock. *Singapore: Population in Transition*. Philadelphia: University of Pennsylvania Press, 1970.

Seah, Chee Meow. *Community Centres in Singapore: Their Political Involvement*. Singapore: University of Singapore Press, 1973.

Singapore Year Book. Singapore: Government Publications Bureau (annual).

Smith, T. S. *Background to Malaysia*. London: Royal Institute of International Affairs, 1963.

Wilson, Dick. *The Future Role of Singapore*. London: Royal Institute of International Affairs, 1972.

Wong, Francis Hoy Kee. *Perspectives: The Development of Education in Malaysia and Singapore*. Singapore: Heinemann Educational Books, 1972.

Wong, Kum Poh (ed.). *Singapore in the International Economy*. Singapore: University of Singapore Press, 1972.

Wurtzburg, Charles E. *Raffles of the Eastern Isles*. London: Hodder and Stoughton, 1954.

Yeo, Kim Wah. *Political Development in Singapore, 1945–55*. Singapore: University of Singapore Press, 1973.

SOLOMON ISLANDS

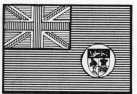

CAPITAL: Honiara. **FLAG**: The flag is blue with the Union Jack at the upper left quarter and the seal of the Solomon Islands in a white disk at the center of the fly. **ANTHEM**: *God Save the Queen*. **MONETARY UNIT**: The Australian dollar (A$) has been the traditional unit of currency. A Solomon Islands currency was expected to be introduced in late 1976. **WEIGHTS AND MEASURES**: Imperial weights and measures are in use. **HOLIDAYS**: New Year's Day, 1 January; Christmas, 25 December; Boxing Day, 26 December; and movable religious holidays. **TIME**: 10 P.M. = noon GMT.

¹LOCATION, SIZE, AND EXTENT
The Solomon Islands comprises a chain of six large and numerous small islands situated in the South Pacific, N of Australia and about 485 km (300 mi) E of New Guinea. Extending *1,688* km (*1,049* mi) ESE–WNW and *468* km (*291* mi) NNE–SSW, the Solomon Islands has an area of 28,446 sq km (10,983 sq mi). The largest island is Guadalcanal, covering about 6,475 sq km (2,500 sq mi); other major islands are Malaita, San Cristobal, Vella Lavella, Choiseul, Rennell, New Georgia, and the Santa Cruz Islands. The total coastline of the Solomon Islands is *4,197* km (*2,608* mi).

²TOPOGRAPHY
The topography varies from the 7,000-foot volcanic peaks of Guadalcanal to low-lying coral atolls. Densely forested mountain ranges are intersected by precipitous, narrow valleys. The highest peak is Mt. Popomanishu (7,647 feet) on Guadalcanal, an island that also contains the country's most extensive alluvial grass plains. Rivers are narrow and impassable except by canoe. Extensive coral reefs and lagoons surround the island coasts.

³CLIMATE
The Solomon Islands have a tropical climate. From December to March, northwest equatorial winds bring hot weather and heavy rainfall; from April to November, the islands are cooled by drier southeast trade winds. Damaging cyclones have occurred during rainy seasons. Annual temperatures in Honiara range from 20°C (68°F) to 33.4°C (92°F). Annual mean rainfall is 120 inches (about 90 inches in Honiara); humidity averages about 80%.

⁴FLORA AND FAUNA
Most islands are covered by dense rain forests, with extensive mangrove swamps along the coasts. The islands abound in small reptiles and mammals, and in insect life. Most of the coral reefs surrounding the Solomon Islands are dead or dying. The UK's Royal Society sent an expedition to study the problem in 1965.

. As of 1975, endangered species in the Solomon Islands included the dugong, San Cristobal mountain rail, and estuarine crocodile.

⁵POPULATION
The 1970 census had reported a population of 160,998. Most mountainous and heavily wooded areas are inaccessible (except to tribal groups of the interior), and most of the population is concentrated in the coastal areas. Malaita, the most populous island, had about 60,000 inhabitants. Honiara, on Guadalcanal, the largest town and chief port, had about 18,900 inhabitants. The total population in 1974 was estimated at 185,000. Average density was about 7 persons per sq km.

⁶ETHNIC GROUPS
According to the 1970 census, Melanesians numbered 149,667,

or 93% of the total population. Other groups included 6,399 Polynesians, 2,362 Micronesians, 1,280 Europeans, 577 Chinese, and 713 others. Melanesians live mainly on the larger islands (including about 54,000 on Malaita), while Polynesians inhabit the smaller islands and atolls.

⁷LANGUAGE
Pidgin English is used as a lingua franca, but English is the official language. More than 60 local languages and dialects are spoken, each within a very restricted geographical area.

⁸RELIGION
Christianity, introduced by missionaries, is the largest organized religion. Most Christians adhere to the Anglican Church. Indigenous animist beliefs are held by a sizable segment of the population.

⁹TRANSPORTATION
Interisland communications are poor, and roads are few. In 1974 there were about 180 miles of main roads and 400 miles of secondary roads in the Solomons. About 1,000 miles of new roads were expected to be added by 1980.

Regular shipping services link the Solomons with other Pacific islands, Australia, Japan, and Europe. Honiara is the principal port. A fleet of government vessels provides interisland connections; vessels in operation at the end of 1974 numbered 40. Henderson's Field is the site of Honiara's civil airport. Biweekly flights of Air Pacific connect the Solomons with Fiji and Brisbane, Australia. Solair, a small private airline, offers interisland services.

¹⁰COMMUNICATIONS
A radiotelephone service provides overseas links. In 1973 there were some 1,400 telephones on the islands. A government-owned radio service broadcasts 66 hours weekly, including educational programming. Equipment includes three 6,000-watt transmitters. There were about 12,000 radios in 1973.

¹¹HISTORY
The Solomon Islands were thought to have been originally inhabited by Melanesians, whose language has affinities with Malay. Their precise origin, however, is not known. The first European contact with the Solomons in 1567 was the sighting of Santa Isabel Island by the Spanish explorer Alvaro de Mendaña. In 1568, Mendaña and another Spaniard, Pedro de Queirós, explored some of the islands. Mendaña named the islands Islas de Salomon, thinking that the gold source for King Solomon's riches was located there. European contact with the Solomons was cut off for nearly two centuries until they were visited by the English navigator Philip Carteret in 1767. Following Carteret's visit, the British navy began to make periodic calls at the islands. During the period 1845–93, the Solomons were frequently visited by mis-

319

sionaries and traders. Indigenous peoples were also subjected to exploitation by blackbirders, in effect kidnappers who would impress their captives into forced labor, often on colonial sugar estates in Fiji or Queensland, Australia. The brutality of this practice provoked reprisals on the part of the islanders, resulting in mass slayings of both Europeans and local peoples. In 1893, the British government stepped in and established a protectorate over islands in the southern Solomons, including Guadalcanal, Savo, Malaita, San Cristobal, and the New Georgia group. The remainder of the Solomons had fallen under German dominion, and some of these—including Choiseul, Santa Isabel, and Ontong Java—were transferred by treaty to Britain in 1900, thus completing the polity that has survived to the present day. The British Solomon Islands Protectorate, as the group came to be known, initially fell under the jurisdiction of the High Commissioner for the Western Pacific, an office that had been created in 1877.

During World War II, the Solomons provided the theater for some of the most bitter fighting of the Pacific War. Japanese troops invaded and occupied Guadalcanal in 1942. A Japanese airfield on the island's northern coast—later known as Henderson's Field—was captured by US marines on 7 August 1942, the opening foray in the Battle of Guadalcanal. Guadalcanal was evacuated by Japan in February 1943, although Japanese forces remained elsewhere in the Solomons until 1945. Widespread destruction and loss of life were visited on the local peoples during the war, leaving a strong residue of anti-European sentiment that lasted well into the postwar period. One of the outgrowths was the development of a pro-independence political movement in Malaita known as the "Marching Rule."

In 1953, local advisory councils were set up in Malaita, eventually spreading to other islands of the protectorate. In 1960, the government established central nominated Executive and Legislative councils. These were granted their first elected minority in 1964. A new constitution promulgated in April 1970 provided for replacement of the two councils by a unitary Governing Council, the majority of whose members were to be elected. During May and June, the Solomon Islands' first general election was held, with voters selecting 17 of the Council's 26 members. On 21 August 1974, a new constitution introduced a ministerial system of government headed by a Council of Ministers. A Legislative Assembly subsequently chose Solomon Mamaloni as the Solomons' first chief minister. In May 1975, a delegation from the Solomon Islands, led by Mamaloni, met with UK officials in London and set up a timetable for internal self-government and for full independence. On 22 June 1975, the territory's name was officially changed from the British Solomon Islands Protectorate to Solomon Islands.

On 2 January 1976, the Solomon Islands achieved internal self-government, with a UK-appointed governor retaining responsibility for defense, external affairs, internal security, and public service. In all other matters, the governor was to act on the advice of the chief minister and the Council of Ministers. Following new general elections in late 1976, the granting of complete independence was scheduled to occur in 1977.

12 GOVERNMENT
The constitution promulgated on 24 March 1970 created a unitary Governing Council, the first legislative body in the Solomons to have an elected majority, chosen by universal adult suffrage. General elections were again held in 1973 for all members of a newly constituted Council, which in 1974 was transformed into the Legislative Assembly, empowered to select a chief minister heading an executive Council of Ministers.

On 2 January, internal self-government was proclaimed, with a UK-appointed governor retaining responsibility in foreign affairs and defense until the Solomon Islands will have attained full independence in 1977.

13 POLITICAL PARTIES
In the early 1970s, two political parties emerged to contest the preindependence elections for the territory's new legislative body: the People's Progress Party (PPP), led by Solomon Mamaloni, and the United Solomon Islands Party (USIP), headed by Jonathan Fifi'i. In August 1974, the 24-member Legislative Assembly elected Mamaloni as chief minister. Mamaloni resigned his office in November 1975 over an internal dispute but was reelected in the following month. His new coalition cabinet contained a five-member USIP majority. As of early 1976, the USIP held 9 seats in the Assembly; the PPP, 7; and independents, 8.

14 LOCAL GOVERNMENT
The islands are divided into four administrative districts, headed by district commissioners. Within each district, elected local councils in virtually all areas administer a variety of services, supported through local taxes. In outlying areas, village headmen undertake various duties under supervision of the district commissioners.

15 JUDICIAL SYSTEM
Since 1961, jurisdiction has been vested in the High Court of the Western Pacific, magistrate's courts, and native courts. Appeals from magistrate's courts go to the High Court and, if necessary, to the Fiji Court of Appeal in Suva. Final appeal is to the Judicial Committee of the UK Privy Council in London. Appeals from native courts are heard by the district commission; in the case of land disputes, appeals are to the High Court.

16 ARMED FORCES
Pending independence, defense of the Solomon Islands falls under the sole authority of the UK, with direct responsibility vested in the crown-appointed governor in Honiara.

17 MIGRATION
Since 1955, immigrants from the Gilbert Islands have settled in underpopulated areas. Movements from the countryside to Honiara and other towns have begun to create problems of overcrowding.

18 INTERNATIONAL COOPERATION
The Solomon Islands is a member of the British Commonwealth of Nations and was expected to apply for UN membership following full independence in 1977. The Solomons is an associate member of the EEC.

19 ECONOMY
Most of the population is tied to subsistence agriculture. Although the monetary sector is making steady inroads, the subsistence segment of the economy still accounted for about 47% of the GDP in the mid-1970s. The capital sector is dependent on the production of copra, timber, and fish for export. To broaden the basis of the economy, the production of other cash commodities, particularly cocoa, spices, and palm oil, is being encouraged. The development of large-scale lumbering operations has increased timber production considerably during the past two decades. The islands are believed to hold considerable mineral wealth and, in the 1970s, exploitation of bauxite reserves was begun, along with continued prospecting for copper and nickel.

20 INCOME
Monetary incomes increased by an average annual rate of 6% during the 1960s. In 1975, the GDP totaled A$33.4 million as compared with A$16.9 million in 1963. Per capita GDP in 1973 was A$185.

21 LABOR
The vast majority of Solomon Islanders are supported by subsistence farming. The employed work force in 1975 totaled 12,693, of whom 840 were foreigners (mostly from Australia, New Zealand, and the UK). Some 34% of the work force was employed by the government. The country suffers an acute shortage of skilled workers, and an estimated 80% of professional and

technical employees are recruited from overseas. Unskilled salaried positions, on the other hand, are in short supply.

In 1975, the Solomons had one trade union and three employers' associations. On 1 January 1975, a basic minimum wage of A$0.15 per hour (for a 45-hour workweek) was set for Honiara. Most employed persons work a 5-5½-hour day, six-day week, with overtime bringing the average workweek to 45 hours. Government regulations require employers to provide housing to workers whose jobs do not permit them to travel to and from home each day. The law requires provision of medical attention in the case of illness; the payment of wages during sickness is customary rather than mandatory.

²²AGRICULTURE

Aside from copra—the dominant export and the economic lifeline of the Solomons—most crops are raised for local consumption. The major food crops are coconuts, yams, taro, sweet potatoes, cassava, and green vegetables. The government has encouraged the cultivation of rice—rotated with soybeans—in the Guadalcanal Plains. In the mid-1970s, about 500 acres of land were irrigated for rice growing.

Most copra is produced in large estates, located principally on Guadalcanal, Choiseul, the Russell Islands, San Cristobal, Santa Isabel, and Vella Lavella. The major producer is Lever Pacific Plantations. Production reached a record 26,192 tons in 1971, and export earnings have been increasing steadily, rising from A$3,634,031 in 1970, to A$9,012,532 in 1974, when copra supplied about half of the Solomons' export earnings. Development plans call for the expansion of production to 45,000 tons by 1985, making viable the construction of a copra mill on the islands. The overseas marketing of copra is a monopoly of the government's Solomon Islands Copra Board. Much stress has been given by the Commonwealth Development Corporation to the establishment of an 8,000-acre oil palm plantation on Guadalcanal; its first commercial crop was expected in 1975, with an anticipated annual output at 17,000–20,000 tons.

²³ANIMAL HUSBANDRY

Cattle were traditionally kept on coconut plantations as a means of controlling the growth of grass. In recent years, many large copra estates have been turning to cattle raising as a commercial endeavor. There were 13,619 head of cattle on the islands in 1970. Since then, the Lever enterprise has introduced a 9,000-head experimental herd on Guadalcanal.

²⁴FISHING

Fish are an important element in the local diet. Recently, however, fishing has been growing rapidly as a commercial activity. In 1970, the islands shipped their first exports of crayfish, and by 1974, fish exports totaled A$3,716,964, virtually triple the 1971 figure of A$1,237,839. By mid-decade, plans were under way for the construction of a tuna cannery.

²⁵FORESTRY

Timber is an important resource in the Solomons. Forests cover about 90% of the total area, with 1,000 sq mi of timber stands presently accessible to commercial exploitation. In the mid-1970s, about 550 sq mi of timberland were being cut by commercial enterprises. Important forest timbers are kuari, balsa, teak, Honduras and African mahoganies, Queensland maple, silky oak, and black bean. In 1973, timber production was 8.9 million cu feet, down from 14.6 million cu feet in 1972.

²⁶MINING

A UN-sponsored aerogeophysical survey, completed in 1968, led to an upsurge in activity in mineral exploration. The major discovery was of an estimated 30 million tons in bauxite reserves on Rennell Island. In 1971, Japan's Mitsui Mining and Smelting Co. signed an agreement with the government to begin trial mining of the reserves, which are both high grade and easy to extract. Alluvial gold miners on Guadalcanal were producing some 400 troy ounces of gold annually in the 1970s.

²⁷ENERGY AND POWER

Most electric power is supplied by the government-controlled Solomon Islands Electricity Authority. Major generating facilities are maintained at Honiara, Auki, Gizo, and Kirakira. Many private undertakings produce their own electricity. During the 1970s, production was increasing at an average rate of 17% annually. In 1973, installed capacity totaled about 6,000 kw and production reached 11.5 million kwh.

²⁸INDUSTRY

Industrial activity in the Solomons is minor, and is lacking in both the capital and skilled labor necessary for significant development. Small firms produce a limited array of goods for the local market: biscuits, tobacco products, rattan furniture, baskets and mats, concrete blocks, and metal manufactures.

See Pacific Ocean map: front cover F6
LOCATION: 5° to 12°30′S; 155° to 170°E. **TERRITORIAL SEA LIMIT:** 3 mi.

²⁹DOMESTIC TRADE

Honiara is the commercial center. A large segment of the population still relies on bartering. Most commercial enterprises are in the hands of Chinese or Europeans.

³⁰FOREIGN TRADE

The Solomon Islands' overseas trade volume has expanded rapidly in recent years, although the cost of imports continues to outpace export growth. While exports doubled in the 1960s, import outlays more than tripled. Exports rose from US$7,771,000 in 1970 to US$12,619,000 in 1973, while imports increased from US$11,223,000 to about US$16,000,000 in the same period. World market conditions plus a series of damaging cyclones during the past decade combined to cause wide fluctuations in the composition of exports in the 1970s. Copra, which traditionally accounted for 90% of the export value and averaged about half of the total volume, accounted for only 32.1% of the total in 1973; in that year, wood and lumber made up 43.4%, and fish 18.2%. Machinery and transport equipment made up 23.4% of imports in 1973. Foodstuffs continue to comprise the second-largest import category, making up 21% of the import volume in 1973.

The direction of the Solomon Islands' trade continues to be limited by the huge distances to potential export markets. In 1971, Japan surpassed Australia as the Solomons' most important trade partner. By 1973, Japan took 53.8% of exports and provided 11.9% of imports. Other important trade partners are the UK, Federal Republic of Germany, American Samoa, Singapore, and New Zealand.

31BALANCE OF PAYMENTS
Continuing deficits in the visible trade balance have been offset by payments from the UK to both current and capital accounts.

32BANKING
The Solomon Islands has two banks, both foreign: the Commonwealth Banking Corporation of Australia and the Australia and New Zealand Banking Group Ltd. Both have offices in Honiara, with the latter maintaining savings branches throughout the islands.

33INSURANCE
A variety of insurance coverage is available through representatives of foreign companies.

34SECURITIES
There is no securities market in the Solomon Islands.

35PUBLIC FINANCE
The 1974 budget was balanced at A\$12,493,680. Locally derived revenues have been insufficient to cover expenditures; in 1974, the UK provided some A\$1.5 million in support of recurrent outlays, amounting to 17% of current expenditures for the year.

36TAXATION
Indirect taxes provide the bulk of current government revenues. The most important of these are import taxes and taxes on major exports. Income taxes are as yet not major revenue producers. Individual incomes are taxed on a graduated scale ranging from 5% on the first A\$600 of taxable income to 35% on incomes exceeding A\$8,100; in no case may the tax exceed 25% of total income. Companies are taxed at a fixed rate of 25%.

37CUSTOMS AND DUTIES
All products imported into the Solomons are subject to customs duties. Concessionary rates or duty-free status are granted to manufacturing machinery and equipment, raw materials, chemicals, and building materials.

38FOREIGN INVESTMENTS
The government encourages direct foreign investment through tax concessions, remission of customs duties, and other forms of assistance. Foreigners may repatriate profits (after taxes) and, under most conditions, capital investments. A primary role in the development of resources is reserved to the government. The Exchange Control Ordinance requires the approval of the finance minister for all foreign-currency transactions in excess of A\$25,000. Japanese interests have been the major new source of private foreign investment in the 1970s.

39ECONOMIC POLICY
In the 1970s, the government has sought to speed development with an eye toward reducing financial and economic dependence on the UK. The Solomon Islands' sixth national development plan (1971-73) called for capital expenditures of A\$17.5 million, of which A\$5.1 million was devoted to economic infrastructure, A\$4.7 million to health and education, A\$4.5 million to natural-resource development, A\$2 million to government services, and A\$1.2 million to commerce and industry. During 1971-74, the UK provided an annual average of about A\$4 million in capital development assistance. The seventh national development plan (1975-79) emphasized rural development.

40HEALTH
Poor standards of general hygiene and inadequate sanitation continue to produce outbreaks of endemic diseases. The government operates the 171-bed Central Hospital in Honiara, as well as 6 district and rural hospitals, a leprosarium, and several maternity and child-care clinics. A variety of medical services is also provided by the missions, which operate three hospitals.

41SOCIAL WELFARE
The bulk of organized welfare services is provided by church missions. In small villages and outlying areas, assistance is traditionally provided through the extended family.

42HOUSING
The government has built low-cost housing projects in Honiara to help ease congestion. Outside of Honiara, housing is primitive, with overcrowding becoming a problem even in smaller villages.

43EDUCATION
Education is not compulsory, and most schools charge fees. The government did not directly participate in formal education until 1957, and in the mid-1970s, its activities were largely confined to secondary schools. Christian missions (mainly Anglican), supported by government grants, are the sole providers of primary schooling. In 1972, 25,570 pupils (38% female) attended 365 primary schools, with 1,088 teachers; 1,303 students attended general secondary schools (including 1 government school); and 554 students were in technical and vocational programs. Some 86 teacher-training students attended the Solomon Islands Training College. There are no facilities for higher education.

44LIBRARIES AND MUSEUMS
There is a national library in Honiara with two branches, and small libraries at the teacher-training college and Honiara Technical Institute, both in Honiara. There are also 8 school libraries. At present there are no museums.

45ORGANIZATIONS
Cooperative societies are important in rural areas for the distribution of locally produced goods. In 1971 there were 158 primary and 4 secondary cooperatives, with a total of 8,240 members. Honiara has a Chamber of Commerce.

46PRESS
There are no daily newspapers in the Solomon Islands. The government issues a fortnightly newssheet; a monthly, the *Kakamora Reporter*, is published independently.

47TOURISM
Tourism, although encouraged through the government's Tourist Authority, is not seen as a major growth area, owing to lack of investment. In the 1970s, an average of about 7,000 persons (including 5,000 cruise-ship passengers) visited the Solomon Islands annually.

48FAMOUS SOLOMON ISLANDERS
There are no internationally famous Solomon Islanders.

49DEPENDENCIES
The Solomon Islands has no dependencies.

50BIBLIOGRAPHY
Corris, Peter. *Passage, Port and Plantation*. Parkville, Victoria: Melbourne University Press, 1973.

Grattan, C. Hartley. *The Southwest Pacific to 1900: A Modern History*. Ann Arbor: University of Michigan Press, 1963.

Horton, D. C. *Fire over the Islands: Coast Watchers of the Solomons*. Sydney: Reed, 1970.

Jack-Hinton, Colin. *Search for the Islands of Solomon 1567-1838*. Oxford: Clarendon Press, 1969.

Jones, Muriel. *Married to Melanesia*. London: Allen and Unwin, 1974.

Kent, Janet. *The Solomon Islands*. Harrisburg, Pa.: Stackpole, 1973.

Laracy, High. *Marists and Melanesians: A History of Catholic Missions in the Solomon Islands*. Honolulu: University of Hawaii Press, 1975.

Ross, Harold M. *Baegu: Social and Ecological Organization in Malaita, Solomon Islands*. Urbana: University of Illinois Press, 1973.

SRI LANKA

Republic of Sri Lanka
Sri Lanka Janarajaya

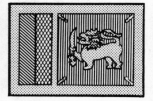

CAPITAL: Colombo. **FLAG**: The national flag contains, at the hoist, vertical stripes of green and saffron and, to the right, a maroon rectangle with yellow bo leaves in the corners and a yellow lion symbol in the center. The entire flag is bordered in yellow, and a yellow narrow vertical area separates the saffron stripe from the dark maroon rectangle **ANTHEM**: *Sri Lanka Matha (Mother Sri Lanka)*. **MONETARY UNIT**: The Sri Lanka rupee (R) of 100 cents is a nonconvertible paper currency with one official rate. There are coins of 1, 2, 5, 10, 25, and 50 cents and 1 rupee, and notes of 2, 5, 10, 50, and 100 rupees. R1 = $0.1296 (or $1 = R7.713). **WEIGHTS AND MEASURES**: British weights and measures are the legal standard, but some local units are also used. **HOLIDAYS**: Tamil Thai Pongal Day, 14 January; Day before Sinhala and Tamil New Year's Day, 13 April; Sinhala and Tamil New Year's Day, 14 April; May Day, 1 May; Republic Day, 22 May; Bank Holiday, 30 June; Bandaranaike Commemoration Day, 26 September; Christmas Day, 25 December; Bank Holiday, 31 December. Movable holidays include Maha Sivarathri Day, Milad-un-Nabi, Good Friday, 'Id-ul-Fitr, Deepavali Festival Day, and 'Id-ul-Azha'; in addition, the full moon of every month of the Buddhist calendar, called a Poya day, is a public holiday. **TIME**: 5:30 P.M. = noon GMT.

¹LOCATION, SIZE, AND EXTENT

Sri Lanka (formerly Ceylon) is an island in the Indian Ocean situated S and slightly E of the southernmost point of India, separated from that subcontinent by a narrow strip of shallow water, Palk Strait. It has an area of 65,610 sq km (25,332 sq mi), extending 435 km (270 mi) N-S and 225 km (140 mi) E-W. Sri Lanka's total coastline is *1,204 km (748 mi)*.

²TOPOGRAPHY

The south-central part of Sri Lanka is a rough plateau cut by a range of mountains with peaks from 7,000 to 8,000 feet high. The highest point is Pidurutalagala (8,282 feet). Narrow coastal plains skirt the mountainous section on the east, south, and west, but in the north the extensive coastal plain fans out, reaching from the eastern to the western shores of the island. Five-sixths of the land is less than 1,000 feet in elevation. Numerous rivers and streams flow seaward in all directions from the central mountain area.

³CLIMATE

The climate, although tropical, varies from warm in the coastal plains and lowlands to temperate in the hill and mountain regions. The wet zone in the southwest receives an average rainfall of from 75 inches in the lowlands to over 200 inches in the hill country, most of the rain coming during the southwest monsoon season. In the remaining three-fourths of the island, lying to the north and east of the range, average rainfall varies from 25 to 75 inches. Located near the equator, Sri Lanka has neither summer nor winter, only rainy and dry seasons. Average temperature is 26.6°C (80°F).

⁴FLORA AND FAUNA

Most plants and animals are those common to southern India, but there are additional varieties. The plant life ranges from that of the equatorial rain forest type to that of the dry zone and the more temperate climate of the highlands. Tree ferns, bamboo, palm, satinwood, ebony, and jak trees abound. The wide range of mammals, birds, and reptiles once found in Sri Lanka has been reduced by the conversion of forests into rice fields, but water buffalo, deer, monkeys, and leopards are among the larger animals still present. The elephant herds were reduced from about 10,000 at the turn of the century to about 1,500 in 1970. The Ceylon elk (sambhur) and the polonga snake are peculiar to Sri Lanka. Birds are numerous, many varieties from colder coun-

tries wintering on the island. Sri Lanka has well-organized game and bird sanctuaries. Insects abound. Numerous fish are found in the shallow offshore waters.

As of 1975, endangered species in Sri Lanka included the Asian elephant, dugong, Asiatic buffalo, red-faced malkoha, Ceylon crocodile, estuarine crocodile, and Indian python.

⁵POPULATION

The 1971 census total, based on a 10 % sampling, was 12,711,000, a 20.1% increase over the 1963 census figure; of the 1971 population, 50.1% was 19 years of age or under. The annual birthrate steadily declined from 39.7 per 1,000 in 1950 to 27.8 per 1,000 in 1973. With the death rate also declining from 12.4 to 7.7 during the same period, net annual natural increase was reduced from 27.3 to 20.1. The mid-1975 population estimate was 13,986,000; the projection for 1980 was 15,465,000. The average population density in mid-1975 was 213 per sq km (552 per sq mi), one of the highest among nonindustrial countries. About three-fourths of the population is concentrated in the southwestern quarter of the island, giving this area a density above 300 per sq km.

About 22.4% of the population was urban in 1971, compared with 15.3% in 1953. According to the 1971 census, Colombo, the capital and chief city, had a population of 585,000. Other urban centers (with their 1971 populations) are Dehiwala–Mt. Lavinia, 131,000; Jaffna, 108,000; Moratuwa, 91,000; Kotte, 87,000; Kandy, 83,000.

⁶ETHNIC GROUPS

According to the 1971 census, Sinhalese constitute the largest population group, numbering 9,147,000 (72% of the total population). Sri Lanka Tamils (descendants of medieval invaders) totaled 1,416,000 (11.1%); Indian Tamils, 1,195,000 (9.4%); Sri Lanka and Indian Moors and Malays (mostly of Arab extraction), 853,000 (6.7%); Burghers (descended from the Dutch) and Eurasians totaled 44,000 (0.3%). There is a small group of perhaps 4,000 to 5,000 Veddas, an aboriginal tribe, in the most inaccessible forest regions of southeastern Sri Lanka; together with other scattered groups, they made up the remaining 0.5%. Tamil autonomist sentiment remained active in the mid-1970s.

⁷LANGUAGE

English was the official language under the British and remained so until 7 July 1957, when a new law made Sinhala the one official

323

language of Sri Lanka. This measure was bitterly opposed by the Tamil minority. Riots, disorders, and dissension grew, leading to a Tamil civil disobedience campaign and a temporary state of emergency. The 1972 constitution recognized Sinhala as the official language, but all laws must be translated into Tamil; the use of Tamil is specified in the Tamil Language (Special Provisions) Act. Sinhala is an Indo-Aryan language related to Pali. Tamil is a Dravidian language spoken in northern Sri Lanka and in southern India.

8 RELIGION
According to the 1971 census, Buddhists constituted 67.4% of the total population; Hindus, 17.6%; Christians, 7.7%; and Muslims, 7.1%. Nearly four-fifths of the Christians are Roman Catholic. Religious and ethnic lines are somewhat parallel. Most Sinhalese are Hinayana Buddhists, the Indian Tamils are largely Hindu, the Moors and Malays are predominantly Muslim, and the Eurasians are Christian. Although the constitution of 22 May 1972 guarantees freedom of religion and establishes Sri Lanka as a secular state, it stipulates that "it shall be the duty of the State to protect and foster Buddhism."

9 TRANSPORTATION
In 1973, the government maintained 16,290 miles of roads. In 1973, registered motor vehicles numbered 187,671, including 89,771 cars and cabs, 38,787 trucks, and 12,192 buses.

In 1971, all but 87 of the 954 miles of railway were broad-gauge (5½ feet). The railway is state-owned and state-operated. The railway system carried 89,336,000 passengers and 1,805,000 tons of freight in 1973.

Colombo, one of the great commercial seaports of Asia, formerly was an open roadstead, but the construction of breakwaters has made it one of the world's greatest artificial harbors. Situated near the production center of the island, it handles more than 95% of Sri Lanka's international shipping; in 1974, it handled 2,318,000 tons of goods. Ports of the open roadstead type are Trincomalee, Galle, Batticaloa, Kankesanturai, Kayts, and Jaffna. The central government maintains 146 miles of inland waterways.

Four civil airports are available for use by international services: Ratmalana (near Colombo), Kankesanturai (near Jaffna), Amparai (in Gal Oya Valley), and Katunayaka (24 miles north of Colombo). Air Ceylon, Sri Lanka's only airline, maintains a daily service between Colombo, Jaffna, and Madras. In 1973, Air Ceylon handled about 28.1% of Sri Lanka's international passenger air traffic, with 29,390 passengers arriving and 39,859 departing; 15,492 passengers were carried on domestic services, less than one-fourth the 1971 total. Aeroflot, BA, KLM, Qantas, Singapore Airlines, Pakistan International, and Swissair operate foreign services through Colombo.

10 COMMUNICATIONS
The central government owns and operates all telephone, telegraph, cable, and radio facilities, except in a few rural districts, which are served by private exchanges.

In 1973 there were 39,600 direct telephone lines, more than half of which were in Colombo. The government operates both commercial and noncommercial radio broadcasting services in Sinhala, Tamil, and English. There were 505,290 licensed radio sets in 1973. No television broadcasting currently originates in Sri Lanka.

11 HISTORY
Sri Lanka's location, south of India, yet separated from it by a narrow strait, exposed the island to frequent invasions from the mainland but also enabled it to maintain an independent existence. The first Aryan settlers, the Sinhalese, came late in the 6th century B.C., probably from northern India, and later groups of Sinhalese followed. At Anuradhapura, Polonnaruwa, and elsewhere, they developed a great civilization, which was destroyed by civil wars and by the incursions of Tamils who in-

vaded Ceylon from across the straits and set up a kingdom in the northern part of the island.

When the Portuguese arrived in 1505, there were several Sinhalese kingdoms and a Tamil kingdom at Jaffna. The Portuguese eventually conquered all these kingdoms, except that of Kandy in the mountains, and introduced Christianity. They were driven out by the Dutch, who captured Colombo in 1656 and Jaffna two years later. The Dutch established an efficient administration, built up trade, and left a legacy in the form of Roman-Dutch law. They in turn were driven out by the British when the Netherlands fell under the control of French Revolutionary forces. In 1796, the Dutch governor of Ceylon surrendered all territory under his control. For two years Ceylon was administered by the East India Co. from its offices in Madras, but this arrangement proved unpopular and led to a Sinhalese revolt. In 1798, Ceylon was removed from company control and made a British crown colony. When the Kandyan chiefs ceded their territory in 1815, the island was united under British rule.

Under the British administration, first coffee, then tea, and finally rubber were introduced and developed. A series of constitutions were promulgated (1798, 1801, 1831-33, 1910). With the development of a nationalist movement in the 20th century, demands for democratic political reforms became steadily more insistent. The 1920 constitution provided for a partially elective legislative council. The constitution of 1924 provided for the election of a majority of the council members, but left wide powers with the governor. Universal adult suffrage and a large measure of self-government were granted by the constitution of 1931. Finally, in 1948, Ceylon was granted "fully responsible" government, and became a self-governing dominion of the Commonwealth of Nations.

On 19 July 1970, Ceylon took the first step toward severing all constitutional links with the British crown and Parliament. Under a new constitution, approved 22 May 1972, Ceylon officially became Sri Lanka, an independent republic within the Commonwealth of Nations. Following an abortive insurrection attempt in 1971, political developments in Sri Lanka have been marked by increasing restrictions of civil liberties and progressive accumulation of power by Prime Minister Sirimavo R. D. Bandaranaike and her Sri Lanka Freedom Party.

12 GOVERNMENT
Under the constitution of 22 May 1972, Sri Lanka is an independent republic within the Commonwealth of Nations. The new constitution abolished the bicameral system of government, which had consisted of a Senate and House of Representatives, and vested all legislative power in a National Assembly. As of 1975, the Assembly consisted of 157 members; 151 were elected in 1970 by universal adult suffrage, and 6 had been previously appointed by the governor-general, a position abolished under the new constitution. (William Gopallawa, who had been governor-general in 1972, became the nation's first president.) Originally the 151 had been elected for five-year terms, but their tenure was extended to 1977 by the new constitution, which mandates six-year terms for future Assembly members. The prime minister and cabinet ministers are chosen from the membership of the Assembly. The cabinet is collectively responsible to the National Assembly; when it ceases to enjoy the confidence of a majority of that body, it must either resign or ask the president to dissolve the Assembly and call a new election. The president, who is head of state, head of the executive, and commander-in-chief of the armed forces, is appointed by the prime minister and acts on the prime minister's advice.

All citizens 18 years of age or older may vote in national and local elections.

13 POLITICAL PARTIES
The first prime minister of independent Ceylon was Don Stephen Senanayake, leader of the independence movement. His cabinet,

which came to power in 1946, represented a coalition of which his own United National Party (UNP) constituted the chief unit. The UNP itself was the product of a union made just before the 1946 elections of the Sinhalese Party, the Ceylon Muslim League, and the Ceylon National Congress. Other members of the coalition were the Tamil Congress, the Labour Party, and some independents. In the general election of 1947, the UNP gained 42 out of the 95 seats to which members could be elected. The opposition could not agree on a leader until 1951, when S. W. R. D. Bandaranaike left the UNP and formed the Sri Lanka Freedom Party (SLFP).

Disagreements over financial and linguistic problems led to the dissolution of parliament in February 1956. Shortly before the election campaign began, Bandaranaike formed the People's United Front (Mahajana Eksath Peramuna—MEP), composed of his own SLFP, the Trotskyite faction of the Lanka Sama Samaja Party (LSSP), and a group of independents; the MEP called for the extension of state control, nationalization of tea and rubber plantations, termination of British military bases, and a foreign policy of nonalignment. In the elections of 1956, the UNP led by Kotelawala retained only 8 seats in the House of Representatives, while the MEP won 51 seats.

In September 1959, Prime Minister Bandaranaike was assassinated by a Buddhist monk, and Wijayananda Dahanayake, his successor, was unable to retain the MEP's slender parliamentary majority. On 5 December 1959, the parliament was dissolved. In the elections of March 1960, the UNP obtained 50 of the 151 seats at stake, and its leader, Dudley Senanayake, who became the new prime minister, chose a cabinet consisting only of UNP members. The SLFP obtained 46 seats, and all other parties received a total of 55 seats. Since Senanayake could not command a parliamentary majority, he resigned in April 1960 and new elections were held on 20 July. The SLFP, now led by Sirimavo R. D. Bandaranaike, widow of the former prime minister, won 75 seats to 30 for the UNP, although the latter received more votes than the SLFP. On 21 July 1960, Mrs. Bandaranaike became prime minister, the first woman in the world to achieve that distinction. She announced a program of nationalization of enterprises. In the general elections held in March 1965, Dudley Senanayake of the UNP succeeded Mrs. Bandaranaike as prime minister; the UNP won 66 seats of the 151 elected seats in the legislature.

At the general election held on 27 May 1970, the SLFP, led by Mrs. Bandaranaike, won 90 seats out of a total of 151. The following were the party positions: SLFP, 90; LSSP, 19; UNP, 17; Federal Party, 13; Communist Party (CP), 6; Tamil Congress, 3; independent, 2. Mrs. Bandaranaike revived the United Front, including the SLFP, LSSP, and CP. This coalition drafted the new constitution, which was opposed by the UNP as vesting too much power in the prime minister. The United Front broke up in 1975, when three ministers from the LSSP were expelled from the cabinet by Mrs. Bandaranaike and the CP minister subsequently resigned. As of late 1975, Mrs. Bandaranaike held the portfolios of prime minister, foreign affairs, defense, planning and economic affairs, and plan implementation.

14LOCAL GOVERNMENT

Sri Lanka is divided into nine provinces and 22 administrative districts in the charge of officers appointed by the central government and subject to the control of the Ministry of Home Affairs. The administrative districts are in turn divided into 139 divisions. There are four types of local authorities: in 1971 there were 542 village committees, 83 town councils, 37 urban councils, and 12 municipal councils. Rural areas are supervised by district revenue officers, aided by local headmen. Local governing groups are popularly elected.

15JUDICIAL SYSTEM

Civil law is based on Roman-Dutch law introduced during the period of Dutch rule, but in the area around Kandy an indigenous type of law prevails. Criminal law is British. Tamils and Muslims have their own laws governing property disposition and certain observances. There are 28 district courts, 34 magistrates' courts, 30 courts of request (restricted to civil cases), and 45 rural courts.

In criminal cases, the Supreme Court (composed of a chief justice and eight associate justices) has appellate jurisdiction. A special court of appeal was established in 1971 to replace the appellate role of the Privy Council in London. Under the 1972 constitution, jurisdiction over legislation passed by the National Assembly is restricted to a special constitution court, appointed by the president on the advice of the prime minister. Sinhala is the official language of the courts.

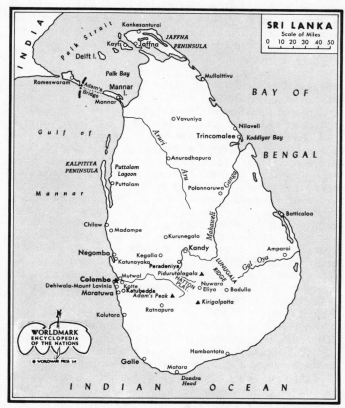

See continental political: front cover M9; physical: back cover M9
LOCATION: 5°55′ to 9°50′N; 79°42′ to 81°53′E. **TERRITORIAL SEA LIMIT:** 12 mi.

16ARMED FORCES

Service in the military forces is voluntary. Total armed strength in mid-1975 was 13,600; budgeted defense expenditures for 1975 were R170.1 million. The Army Act, which became operative in 1949, provides for a small, conventional army. In 1975, the army had 8,900 personnel organized into 1 brigade of 3 battalions, 1 reconnaissance regiment, and 1 artillery regiment; reserves totaled 12,000. The navy, founded in 1950, had 2,400 personnel in 1975; naval craft included 1 frigate, 5 fast gunboats, and 24 coastal patrol craft. The air force, organized in 1951, had 2,300 men and 12 combat aircraft in 1975; its primary responsibilities were to combat illegal immigration, engage in air-sea rescue operations, and perform air surveys. Paramilitary forces in 1975 totaled 16,300.

[17]MIGRATION

Migration is almost exclusively between Sri Lanka and India. Negotiations were begun in 1954 over Ceylon's demands for the repatriation of Indians resident in Ceylon. An agreement signed in 1964 stated that India would repatriate 525,000 of the 975,000 persons of Indian origin, while Ceylon would absorb 300,000 and grant them Ceylonese citizenship; the future of the remaining 150,000 was to be the subject of a separate agreement. By January 1974, 106,423 Indians had been repatriated, and 60,813 had officially become citizens of Sri Lanka.

Otherwise, migration to Sri Lanka is sparse. Ceylonese emigrated to Australia, Canada, the US, UK, and Commonwealth countries in Africa in the 1960s. Most of these emigrants were from the minority communities.

[18]INTERNATIONAL COOPERATION

The government of Sri Lanka is opposed to all military defense alliances but actively participates in other forms of international cooperation. On 14 December 1955, Ceylon was admitted to membership in the UN. Sri Lanka is a member of all the specialized agencies, the Commonwealth of Nations, the Colombo Plan, and other intergovernmental organizations.

[19]ECONOMY

Sri Lanka long concentrated on the production of three agricultural commodities—tea, rubber, and coconuts—at the expense of food production. These three commodities formerly accounted for three-fourths of the country's total agricultural production and about 90% of its exports by value. Thus, Sri Lanka had to import more than half its food requirements and nearly all its manufactured goods. In the 1970s, food plantings have increased, but Sri Lanka's exports are still dominated by the three plantation crops, which made up 72% of the export earnings in 1974. Thus, the economy remains highly sensitive to the fluctuation of world market prices and economic conditions. Although more acreage is devoted to rice growing than to the production of any of the three great export crops, Sri Lanka produces only about 60% of its consumption of this staple food.

Sri Lanka was one of the countries most seriously affected by the rise in oil and fertilizer prices in 1973 and 1974. Rising unemployment, a heavy debt burden, drought in the 1974/75 growing season, and inefficiency in state-run enterprises dimmed Sri Lanka's economic prospects in the mid-1970s.

[20]INCOME

During the period 1958-64, the average rate of growth in the GDP at constant prices was about 3.4%, resulting in a per capita rise in GDP of about 0.7% per annum. The rate of gross domestic capital formation at current prices, which during the 1950s had more than doubled and reached R923.6 million in 1960, slowed down considerably in 1961-64. Since 1964, the GDP in current prices has increased by 163%, but in constant 1959 prices the increase has been only 42.1%. It is estimated that during the period 1965-74, real national income increased from R7,241.7 million to R9,587.1 million. Government estimates put GNP per capita in 1972 at $164.

In 1974, the GDP in current prices was R19,694.4 million. Agriculture, forestry, hunting, and fishing contributed 42.4%; wholesale and retail trade, 13%; manufacturing, 12.6%; services, 10%; transport, storage, and communications, 8.5%; construction, 5.1%; and all other activities, 8.4%.

[21]LABOR

According to the 1971 census, the economically active population totaled 3,622,000 (22.5% women). The agricultural sector employed 49.4%; 24.6% held jobs as laborers, as transport equipment operators, or in agriculture-related occupations; and 12.9% were sales and service workers. Trained personnel are in short supply. Unemployment has been rising since the late 1960s, and underemployment among agricultural workers is marked. In 1973, 505,935 workers registered as unemployed or un-

deremployed, a 23.1% increase over 1970; about half were classified as unskilled. Only 1,278 persons were placed in new jobs by employment exchanges in 1974.

An employer is liable for compensation to workmen hurt, disabled, or incurring occupational diseases while on the job, but he is not obligated to carry insurance. Sri Lanka has minimum wage, safety, health, and welfare laws, and legislation dealing with women, young persons, and children in industry, but adequate staff to enforce the labor laws is needed.

At the end of 1973 there were 1,644 active labor unions, with a total membership of 1,217,740. The largest trade union federations are the Ceylon National Trade Union Confederation, the Ceylon Workers' Congress, the Ceylon Federation of Labor, and the Democratic Workers' Congress.

[22]AGRICULTURE

Agriculture, the mainstay of the economy, employs nearly half the working population: three-fourths of those working in agriculture are engaged in the production of tea, rubber, and coconuts, the three crops that comprised about 72% of Sri Lanka's export earnings in 1974. Tea production in 1973 was 465.8 million pounds, considerably below the 1962-72 average; plantings were 598,740 acres. Rubber production in 1973 was 340 million pounds on 564,824 acres. The coconut tree acreage was estimated at 1,152,428 in 1962; no later estimate has been offered by the government. Coconut production in 1973 was 1,957 million nuts. A new government emphasis on self-sufficiency in food production resulted in substantially increased 1973 plantings of sweet potatoes, potatoes, corn, and manioc. However, soaring fertilizer prices and a drought lasting through the summer of 1975 adversely affected food production in 1974/75 and forced the government to import food on an emergency basis. Rice production increased from 62.9 million bushels in 1972/73 to 76.8 million bushels in 1973/74, of which 27.2% was purchased under the government's guaranteed price scheme. Rising rice production is largely the result of increased acreage; yield per acre has declined since 1967/68.

The government reported on 26 August 1974 that the first phase of its land reform program was complete. Under the Land Reform Law of 1972, all property holdings exceeding 50 acres (except for property controlled by publicly owned companies) were vested in the Land Reform Commission for redistribution; a total of 559,377 acres were redistributed, including one-fifth of the land under tea. Under the Land Reform Amendment Bill of 11 October 1975, all publicly owned estates (including the major British-owned tea and rubber plantations) were nationalized, with compensation to be determined by the government. About 415,000 acres on 396 estates were affected by the measure.

[23]ANIMAL HUSBANDRY

Sri Lanka's livestock population is comparatively small: in 1973 there were 1,673,415 head of cattle, 715,896 water buffalo, 91,010 hogs, 576,690 sheep and goats, and 7,528,473 chickens. Furthermore, animals are not of high quality, the consequence partly of religious considerations and primitive agricultural conditions. The natural pasturage lacks both nutritional value and palatability, and prospects for new pastures are not promising. Meat production in 1973 was estimated at 25,000 tons; milk production was 35,541,000 gallons, and 466,812,000 eggs were produced.

[24]FISHING

Fishing produces less than the country's needs and yields a meager income to approximately 120,000 fishermen, most of whom use primitive boats and gear in the shallow waters that surround the island. In 1973, the total fish catch was estimated at 100,700 tons, compared with 96,100 tons in 1964.

[25]FORESTRY

About 44.2% (7,164,710 acres) of the total land area consists of woodland; proclaimed reserves and state forests totaled 5,521,224 acres in 1973.

In 1973, 658,973 cu feet of soft timber logs were cut, and 3,033,806 cu feet of other logs. Forestry products included 719,414 cu feet of sawn timber and 136,718 cu yards of firewood for domestic use.

26 MINING
Sri Lanka leads the world in the production of high-grade graphite; in 1974, 10,262 tons were produced, of which 9,622 tons were exported. Graphite production is now a state monopoly. The island's gem industry is world famous. In the Ratnapura district there are considerable deposits of sapphire, ruby, chrysoberyl, beryl, topaz, spinel, garnet, zircon, tourmaline, quartz, and moonstone. Rare earth minerals of the cerium, yttrium, zirconium, niobium, tantalum, thorium, and uranium groups have been found. Thorianite appears to be widely distributed in promising quantities. Large quantities of kaolin near the surface are found in many areas, particularly near Colombo and along the coast near Galle. There are large surface deposits of quartz sand. Miocene limestone from the Jaffna peninsula is used in the manufacture of cement. The beach sands contain large quantities of ilmenite, rutile, monazite, and zircon. In the dry zone coastal areas the manufacture of salt by solar evaporation of seawater is a flourishing government monopoly. Production of salt in 1974 amounted to 113,387 tons. Aided by long-term credits from the USSR, oil explorations have been conducted in the northern regions.

27 ENERGY AND POWER
The Sri Lanka Electricity Board, a state enterprise, supervises the generation and transmission of electric power in Sri Lanka. Installed capacity in 1974 was 365,000 kw, of which more than three-fourths was hydroelectric; power generation totaled 1,101.6 million kwh. Sales of electricity totaling 888.1 million kwh in 1974 included 459.4 million kwh (42%) for industrial use, 202.4 million kwh (18%) for local authorities, 117.1 million kwh (11%) for commercial use, and 79.9 million kwh (7%) for domestic use.

28 INDUSTRY
Except for the processing of tea, rubber, and coconut, and the milling of rice, there is little large-scale industrial activity. Since 1956, the government has placed great emphasis on industrial development, chiefly by means of state ownership and control of basic industries. State-owned industries are operated by corporations with boards appointed by the government. In 1975, at least 26 such corporations were engaged in industrial activity.

Total cement production increased 19.1% between 1972 and 1974. Two new cement plants came into production in 1966 and 1967 and a plant for the production of rolled steel and wire products was commissioned in 1965. Output of rolled steel declined 36.2% between 1972 and 1974, but the 1974 output of wire products was up 68% over 1973. State refinery output rose steadily through 1973 but declined in 1974 because of higher prices for crude oil; 1974 output included 351,740 tons of diesel fuel, 198,986 tons of kerosene, and 98,613 tons of gasoline.

29 DOMESTIC TRADE
Most retail stores are small and unspecialized. Marketing and distribution are dominated by the strong and well-developed cooperative movement. The government assists the movement with loans, price guarantees, and supervision. Since 1970, government monopolies have taken a major role in the wholesale distribution of imported goods as well as many domestic commodities.

Usual business hours are from 9 A.M. to 1 P.M. and 2 to 5 P.M. Credit is extended in local trade, bills being payable late in the following month.

Products are advertised in newspapers, trade journals, and annuals, motion picture theaters, and on the commercial radio. There are several advertising firms in Colombo, some with connections abroad.

30 FOREIGN TRADE
Sri Lanka's principal exports are tea, natural rubber, and coconut products, especially desiccated coconut and coconut oils. Despite production declines in all three commodity classifications, Sri Lanka's export earnings increased by 32.7% in 1974, largely because of improved world prices. Food and beverages accounted for 45.9% of imports in 1973 and 42.8% in 1974; the most important comestibles were flour, rice, and refined sugar. Petroleum products, which had accounted for only 1.8% of imports in 1972, made up 10.9% of import costs in 1973 and 19.9% in 1974. Although the volume of imports actually declined in 1974, import costs rose from R2,715 million in 1973 to R4,554 million in 1974, largely because of much higher prices for petroleum products and fertilizers. Thus, Sri Lanka's trade balance, which has been negative since 1966, registered a record deficit of R1,082 million in 1974.

Principal exports in 1974 (in millions of rupees) were:

Tea	1,360
Rubber	738
Coconut products	397
Precious and semiprecious stones	109
Other exports	868
TOTAL	3,472

Principal imports in 1974 (in millions of rupees) were:

Petroleum products	905
Flour	857
Rice	720
Chemicals	232
Fertilizer	221
Sugar, refined	190
Machinery	186
Construction materials	147
Other imports	1,096
TOTAL	4,554

In 1974, 22.1% of Sri Lanka's total trade was with Commonwealth countries, 17.9% with the EEC (excluding the UK), 8.2% with EFTA, and 7.7% with Eastern Europe (including the USSR). China is Sri Lanka's leading trade partner; although the total volume of trade between the two countries rose from R541 million in 1970 to R626 million in 1974, China's share of Sri Lanka's trade declined from 12.4% to 7.8% during the same period.

Principal trade partners in 1974 (in millions of rupees) were:

	EXPORTS	IMPORTS	BALANCE
China	267.2	358.7	− 91.5
UK	367.1	170.3	196.8
Pakistan	267.1	278.9	− 11.8
US	242.7	145.3	97.4
USSR	99.3	145.5	− 46.2
India	8.8	218.9	− 210.2
Other countries	2,219.8	3,236.4	−1,016.5
TOTALS	3,472.0	4,554.0	−1,082.0

31 BALANCE OF PAYMENTS
Sri Lanka's balance-of-payments position is highly sensitive to price changes in the world market because it depends upon a few export crops to pay for its imports. During the early 1950s, exter-

nal factors were fairly favorable; in the late 1950s and the 1960s, however, the payments balance was chronically unfavorable. Gold and foreign exchange reserves held by the Central Bank and the government declined from $176 million in 1958 to $51 million at the end of 1964, while foreign assets of the Central Bank decreased from $113 million to $29 million over the same period. By 1969, reserve holdings were down to $40 million, $28 million of which was in foreign assets held by the Central Bank.

Because the drain of foreign reserves was becoming severe, the government adopted a series of corrective measures. These produced gradual improvements in the payments balance and actually produced surpluses in 1972 and 1973. In 1974, however, a sharp increase in the current accounts deficit required extensive short-term trade credits, emergency grants from foreign governments, and drawings from the IMF Oil Facility. International reserves, which had peaked at $114 million as of March 1974, stood at $70 million in October 1974. Of the total, $55 million was in foreign-exchange holdings of the Central Bank. The following is a summary of Sri Lanka's current accounts balance (in millions of rupees) in 1973 and 1974 (provisional):

	1973	1974
Trade balance, net	−298	−1,227
Services, net	52	76
Transfers, net	85	252
TOTALS	−161	− 899

At the end of 1974, Sri Lanka's total external debt (excluding short-term trade credits) was R4,333.8 million, of which R627.7 million was to the IMF.

32 BANKING
The Central Bank of Ceylon, established in 1949, began operations in 1950 with a capital of R15 million contributed by the government. The sole bank of issue, it administers and regulates the country's monetary and banking systems. At the end of 1974, foreign assets of the Central Bank amounted to R420.1 million, or 13.9% of total assets. Total currency in circulation in 1974 was R1,829 million.

Other statutory banks are the Development Finance Corporation of Ceylon, the Agricultural and Industrial Credit Corporation, and the State Mortgage Bank (established in 1931 to provide long-term credit primarily for agriculture). Total loans outstanding from these three institutions were R171,418,000 by the end of 1974.

Demand deposits of the commercial banks totaled R1,377 million at the end of 1974; time and savings deposits were R1,582 million. As of 31 December 1974, 366,203 savings deposits in 1,271 rural banks totaled R61,549,118.

33 INSURANCE
Until 1962, insurance was almost wholly a foreign enterprise; on 1 January 1962, the life insurance business was nationalized, and the state-owned Insurance Corporation of Sri Lanka was granted a monopoly on new life insurance. By 1964, the monopoly was extended to life and all other insurance. There are 20 branches of the Corporation throughout the country.

In 1974, the number of life policies in force was estimated at 171,335. In 1974, the premium income for life insurance was R72,619,000 and for fire, motor, accident, and marine insurance, R85,900,000.

34 SECURITIES
The Colombo Brokers' Association operates an organized stock market handling both stocks and commodities, most of the shares being in plantation (tea and rubber) companies.

35 PUBLIC FINANCE
The approved budget estimate for 1975 called for revenues of R4,881 million and expenditures of R6,941 million, for an overall

budget deficit of R2,060 million and a net cash deficit of R1,476 million. Budget deficits, which are chronic, are financed largely through domestic and foreign borrowing.

Central government budgets for 1964 and 1974 (in millions of rupees) were:

REVENUES	1964	1974
Import duties	481.5	293.6
Taxes on income	312.6	506.8
Export duties	217.8	400.0
Other indirect taxes	376.1	2,234.8
Sales and charges	57.1	70.6
Other revenues	80.1	303.6
TOTALS	1,525.2	3,809.4

EXPENDITURES	1964	1974
Current expenditure on goods and services	825.3	1,785.8
Gross fixed capital formation	452.7	932.1
Food subsidies	375.4	584.0
Interest on public debt	113.7	601.9
Current transfers to local governments	39.8	66.8
Other transfer payments	171.3	541.6
Loans granted	24.5	85.8
Other items (net)	− 16.1	548.5
TOTALS	1,986.6	5,146.5
Of which:		
Education	357.8	632.9
Agriculture and irrigation	192.8	431.4
Health	159.4	340.7
Manufacture and mining	94.3	43.5
Communication	70.5	349.8
Defense	59.3	128.7
Housing	37.5	42.7
BALANCE	− 461.4	−1,337.1

As of 31 December 1974, the gross public debt stood at R12,380.1 million, of which R9,406.4 million was domestic and R2,973.7 million was foreign.

36 TAXATION
In 1974, income taxes represented 13.3% of total government revenue. Income tax rates have been adjusted to benefit those individuals with family responsibilities. The highest marginal rate of income for individuals is 45%; in addition, a surtax of 20% and 35% has been imposed together with a scheme of rebate for savings in order to promote savings and investments. Company tax has been reduced from 57% to 50%, but for nonresident companies there is a further tax of 6% in lieu of estate duty and 5% in lieu of wealth tax. Capital expenditure for land development and planting may be deducted from the income tax.

37 CUSTOMS AND DUTIES
In 1965/66, import and export duties yielded 27.4% of the government's revenue, but in 1974 only 18.2%. The importance of duty revenue has been eclipsed in recent years by revenues from the sale of foreign exchange entitlement certificates (FEECs), which every importer and exporter must purchase from the Central Bank of Ceylon. Receipts from the sale of FEECs increased from R673.7 million in 1973 to R964.1 million in 1974.

Preferential rates are levied on imports from Commonwealth nations, Ireland, and Burma. Sri Lanka is a member of GATT.

With few exceptions, imported goods are subject to regulation, but many commodities are governed by open general licenses and may be imported freely without individual license. For commodities that are produced in Sri Lanka, and for certain others, no licenses are issued. Some essential items, such as sugar, flour, and rice, are imported only on government account.

³⁸ FOREIGN INVESTMENTS

The great agricultural enterprises, insurance companies, and banks were developed originally by foreign capital. In 1959, foreigners owned almost 36% of the country's rubber acreage and 6% of the tea plantations; 80% of the insurance business was written by foreign companies, and the banking business was largely a monopoly of British and Indian firms.

Since 1961, when nationalization became widespread, private investors have been reluctant to place new funds in Sri Lanka. Consequently, the country has had to depend almost entirely on loans and short-term credits. New debts have exceeded repayments in every year since 1964, and outstanding liabilities reached R2,973.7 million by 31 December 1974. Of this total, R2,047.1 million was in nonproject commodity loans, about one-third of which were from the US. Project loans outstanding as of 31 December 1974 totaled R848.6 million, including R135.8 million from IDA and R119.5 million from IBRD. Project and nonproject loans from China totaled R377.9 million by the end of 1974.

³⁹ ECONOMIC POLICY

Like many other ex-colonial, less-developed countries, Sri Lanka follows a socialist policy. The government owns factories and mills and operates the salt industry as a monopoly. The government-established Ceylon Development Corporation extends medium- and long-term loans to agricultural and industrial enterprises.

Government intervention increased during Mrs. Bandaranaike's first administration (1960–65). In 1962, the government seized the major installations of three Western oil companies that for 40 years had sold their products in Ceylon, and it formed a government-owned Ceylon Petroleum Corporation. The corporation was empowered to act as importer, supplier, and distributor of petroleum products and was given authority to requisition or compulsorily acquire property and to control and regulate the prices of oil products.

In June 1970, the government announced that it would put an end to policies of "economic dependence and neocolonialism" followed by the previous government; a national plan would be prepared to create a socialist society; the importation of all essential commodities would be handled by the state; the share of the state in export trade would be progressively expanded; and government agencies would be established to direct the plantation industry. This program was largely implemented by October 1975, when the large rubber and tea plantations were nationalized.

Specific economic goals were incorporated in the five-year plan for 1972-76, announced 9 November 1971. The plan emphasized agricultural development, especially food production. An overall economic growth rate of 6% annually was projected, and per capita income was to increase from R910 to R1,150 in real terms. New government projects were to create 810,000 new jobs and thereby ameliorate the unemployment problem. It was evident by late 1975 that a combination of factors, including increased import costs, inflation, and a disappointing harvest in 1974/75, had made these goals unreachable.

⁴⁰ HEALTH

The government provides medical service free or at a nominal cost to almost everyone, but its health program is hampered by a worsening shortage of trained personnel and hospital beds. At the end of 1973, the Department of Health Services had 2,164 physicians (1 for every 6,090 persons), 1,178 assistant medical practitioners, and 6,348 nurses. In 1972, the department had 338 hospital establishments, with 38,443 beds (1 per 343 persons). There is a limited number of private hospitals and medical practitioners.

Malaria, smallpox, cholera, and plague have been virtually eliminated. Malnutrition, tuberculosis, and the gastrointestinal group of infectious diseases are the chief medical problems. With the present trend of population growth (for example, 25.9 births and 5.8 deaths per 1,000 in 1975), the prospects are poor for the relief of inadequate housing, overcrowding, and vitamin-deficient diets. Average life expectancy in 1975, however, was 69.3 years, a relatively high level for South Asia. In 1966, a family-planning project for the whole country was introduced by the government. The importance of population control was reemphasized by Prime Minister Bandaranaike at a 1974 conference sponsored by Sri Lanka's Family Planning Association.

⁴¹ SOCIAL WELFARE

The government announced in June 1970 that a comprehensive scheme for social insurance, including old age benefits and a national pension, would be introduced in the near future. By 1973, however, only 158,792 persons received monthly public assistance allowances, totaling R18,206,000. Colombo, Kandy, and Galle administer their own programs of public assistance within a scheme set up by the Poor Law of 1939. Elsewhere, the government pays monthly allotments to the aged, sick and disabled, to destitute widows, and to wives of imprisoned or disabled men.

To stimulate private efforts, the government makes grants to supplement the funds of volunteer agencies engaged in various welfare activities, particularly orphanages, homes for the aged, and day nurseries.

⁴² HOUSING

The rapid population increase, coupled with a lag in construction during and immediately following World War II, created an acute housing shortage, high rents, high building costs, and many unsanitary and unfit houses.

The 1971 census showed a total of 2,217,478 housing units, of which 1,558,765 were rural, 421,155 urban, and 237,558 situated on agricultural estates. While 34.5% of urban units and 7% of estate units were supplied with electricity, only 2.8% of rural dwellings were; 45.3% of urban units and 74.8% of estate dwellings were supplied with piped water, compared with only 4.8% of rural dwellings.

According to housing ministry estimates, 28-30,000 houses a year were built between 1970 and 1975, compared with 18-19,000 annually during the previous five-year period. From May 1970 to April 1975, the housing ministry built or provided aid for a total of 28,872 units.

⁴³ EDUCATION

According to the 1971 census, 78.1% of the population over 10 years of age is literate. All education from kindergarten up to and including professional training at the University of Sri Lanka is free. Education is compulsory for children between the ages of 6 and 14, except when schools are not within reasonable distance of the pupil's home. Nearly 90% of school-age children attend classes.

The public educational system was consolidated in 1970 into elementary, secondary, and higher levels. In 1973 there were 6,288 elementary schools, 3,102 secondary schools, and 270 government-supervised Buddhist temple schools (pirivenas); the total student enrollment was 2,596,970. A total of 98,925 teachers taught in schools operated or authorized by the government in 1973; the estimated government expenditure on education in 1974 was R632.9 million.

The University of Sri Lanka, consolidated in 1972, has five campuses—Peradeniya, Colombo, Vidyadaya, Vidyalankara, and Katubedda—and a law college. Included in the consolidated university system are the former Vidyalankara University (established 1959), formerly known as the Vidyalankara Pirivena (established 1875), a celebrated seat of learning for Oriental studies and Buddhist culture; the former Vidyadaya University (established 1959); and the former University of Ceylon (founded 1942). In 1973, the University enrolled 12,395 students and had a faculty of 1,450. The government sponsors some 26 teacher-training schools.

⁴⁴LIBRARIES AND MUSEUMS

The Public Library in Colombo, with 132,000 volumes and 11 branches, is the largest public library in the country. Apart from the libraries in Anuradhapura, Jaffna, Kandy, and a few other towns, most public libraries have only small collections of books. The University of Sri Lanka in Peradeniya has holdings of 300,000 volumes, while the Colombo campus has 80,000. There are several special libraries in Colombo, including the National Museum Library, which has been a depository for Ceylonese publications since 1885.

The four national museums, at Colombo, Kandy, Ratnapura, and Jaffna, contain collections pertaining to paleontology, zoology, prehistory, archaeology, and ancient art. One of Asia's finest zoological collections, as well as the largest known collection of Sinhala palm-leaf manuscripts, is in the Colombo museum. Three national botanic gardens located at three different elevations above sea level represent Sri Lanka's three distinct zones of vegetation.

⁴⁵ORGANIZATIONS

At the end of 1973 there were 7,985 primary cooperative societies in the island, with a membership of 1,682,148 and a total working capital of R559,572,000. In addition, there were 6,674 rural development societies spending a total of R2,091,000 on public works projects.

Chambers of commerce include the National Chamber of Commerce of Sri Lanka, the Ceylon Chamber of Commerce, the Indian Chamber of Commerce, and the Moor Chamber of Commerce. There are numerous trade and industrial organizations.

⁴⁶PRESS

In 1972, a five-member national Press Council with extensive powers over the press was established; members are appointed to three-year terms by the president on the advice of the prime minister. In 1973, the government took over Associated Newspapers of Ceylon, which had controlled 60% of the country's papers; the lone remaining opposition chain, the Independent Newspapers Group, was severely restricted in 1974.

In 1971, there were 25 dailies, with a combined circulation of 536,000. The principal morning and evening dailies published in Sri Lanka (with their 1974 circulations) are:

	LANGUAGE	CIRCULATION
COLOMBO		
Dinamina (m.)	Sinhala	82,000
Davasa (m.)	Sinhala	65,000
Daily News (m.)	English	52,000
Lankadipa (m.)	Sinhala	21,000
Thinapathi (m.)	Tamil	19,000
Virakesari (m.)	Tamil	18,500
Aththa (m.)	Sinhala	17,500
Thinakaran (m.)	Tamil	15,000
Mithiran (e.)	Tamil	13,000
Janatha (e.)	Sinhala	11,000
Daily Mirror (e.)	English	10,500
JAFFNA		
Eelanadu (m.)	Tamil	8,700

In 1971, Sri Lanka had 120 nondaily journals with a combined circulation of 961,000; 46 of these were published one to three times a week.

⁴⁷TOURISM

All visitors other than nationals of the UK and dependencies, Canada, Ireland, and Pakistan must have a valid passport with a visa. Passengers traveling through infected areas must also possess valid certificates of vaccination and inoculation. In 1973, 77,888 tourists visited Sri Lanka for an average stay of 10 days;

estimated receipts from tourism were R58.6 million. By nationality, tourists in 1973 included visitors from France, 12,147; Federal Republic of Germany, 10,286; Scandinavia, 9,041; India, 7,794; UK, 7,464; and US, 5,109. An estimated 85,000 tourist arrivals were recorded in 1974.

The ruins of Anuradhapura, one of the world's great centers of Buddhist art and civilization, attract visitors from all over the world. There were 2,468 hotel rooms in 1973; 5,460 rooms were projected for 1977. Extensive tourist development is planned for the beach resort off Trincomalee.

⁴⁸FAMOUS CEYLONESE

One of the great rulers of the Anuradhapura period was Dutugemunu (reigned about 100 B.C.), who is famous for having saved Ceylon and its religion from conquest by Indian invaders. Mahasen, king of the 3d century A.D., built many fine dagobas and other monuments that delight and amaze visiting art lovers. The classic period of Ceylonese art flourished under Kassapa, a king of the 5th century. The great figure of the Polonnaruva period was Parakramabahu I the Great (1153–86), who unified the government of Ceylon, built many magnificent structures, and organized the economy. Most famous in modern Ceylon was Don Stephen Senanayake (1884–1952), leader of the independence movement and first prime minister of independent Ceylon. Solomon West Ridgway Dias Bandaranaike (1899–1959), prime minister from 1956 to 1959, is regarded as the founder of Ceylon as a socialist state. His widow, Sirimavo R. D. Bandaranaike (b.1916), has been prime minister in her present term since 1970.

⁴⁹DEPENDENCIES

Sri Lanka has no territories or colonies.

⁵⁰BIBLIOGRAPHY

Ceylon Year Book. Colombo: Government Publications Bureau (annual).

Cook, Elsie Kathleen. *Ceylon: Its Geography, Its Resources and Its People.* London: Macmillan, 1953.

De Silva, S. F. *A Regional Geography of Ceylon.* Colombo: Colombo Apothecaries, 1954.

The Economic Development of Ceylon. Report of a Mission Organized by the IBRD at the Request of the Government of Ceylon. Baltimore: Johns Hopkins Press, 1953.

Ferguson's Ceylon Directory. London: Ceylon Observer (annual).

Jennings, Sir William Ivor. *The Constitution of Ceylon.* London: Oxford, 1951.

Jennings, Sir William Ivor, and Henry Wijayakone Tambiah. *The Dominion of Ceylon: The Development of Its Laws and Constitution.* London: Stevens, 1952.

Kearney, Robert N. *Communalism and Language in the Politics of Ceylon.* Chapel Hill, N.C.: Duke University Press, 1967.

Kearney, Robert N. *The Politics of Ceylon (Sri Lanka).* Ithaca: Cornell University Press, 1973.

Kearney, Robert N. *Trade Unions and Politics in Ceylon.* Berkeley: University of California Press, 1971.

Ludowyk, E. F. C. *A Modern History of Ceylon.* New York: Praeger, 1967.

Lydowyk, E. F. C. *Short History of Ceylon.* New York: Praeger, 1967.

Mills, Lennox A. *Britain and Ceylon.* London: Longmans, Green, 1945.

Mills, Lennox A. *Ceylon Under British Rule, 1795–1932.* New York: Barnes and Noble, 1965.

Pakeman, S. A. *Ceylon.* New York: Praeger, 1964.

Snodgrass, Donald R. *Ceylon: An Export Economy in Transition.* Homewood, Ill.: Irwin, 1966.

Wilson, A. Jeyaratnam. *Politics in Sri Lanka, 1947–1973.* New York: St. Martin's Press, 1974.

Woodward, Calvin A. *The Growth of a Party System in Ceylon.* Providence: Brown University Press, 1969.

SYRIA

Syrian Arab Republic

Al-Jumhuriyah al- 'Arabiyah al-Suriyah

CAPITAL: Damascus (Dimishq). **FLAG**: The national flag is a horizontal tricolor of red, white, and black stripes; in the white center stripe, stretching horizontally, is a golden eagle. **ANTHEM**: *Al-Nashid al-Suri* (*The Syrian National Anthem*) begins "Protectors of the nation, peace be upon you." **MONETARY UNIT**: The Syrian pound (s£) of 100 piasters is a nonconvertible paper currency. There are coins of 1, 5, 10, 25, and 50 piasters, and notes of 1, 5, 10, 25, 50, 100, and 500 Syrian pounds. s£1 = $0.2703 (or $1 = s£3.7). **WEIGHTS AND MEASURES**: The metric system is the legal standard, but local units are widely used. One rotl equals 449 gm (0.9905 lb); 100 artal equal 1 kantar (99.05 lb). One faddan, consisting of 333.3 kassabah, equals 1,038 acres. **HOLIDAYS**: New Year's Day, 1 January; National Day, 8 March; Arab League Day, 22 March; Independence Day, 17 April; Martyrs' Day, 6 May. Muslim religious holidays are fixed according to the lunar Hijra calendar and include 'Id al-Fitr, 'Id al- 'Adha', Milad al-Nabi, and Laylat al-Miraj; Christian religious holidays include Christmas, 25 December; Easter (Catholic); and Easter (Orthodox). **TIME**: 2 P.M. = noon GMT.

¹LOCATION, SIZE, AND EXTENT

Situated in southwest Asia, at the east end of the Mediterranean Sea, the Syrian Arab Republic has an area of 185,180 sq km (71,498 sq mi), of which 1,150 sq km (444 sq mi) are administered by Israel in the Golan Heights. Syria extends 793 km (493 mi) ENE-WSW and 431 km (268 mi) SSE-NNW. It is bounded on the N by Turkey, on the E and SE by Iraq, on the S by Jordan, on the SW by Israel, and on the W by Lebanon and the Mediterranean Sea, with a total boundary length of 2,415 km (1,500 mi) following the 1949 armistice with Israel, and of 2,419 km (1,503 mi) according to the 1974 line.

²TOPOGRAPHY

There are four main geographic zones: (1) the narrow coastal plain along the Mediterranean shore; (2) the hill and mountain regions—the Ansariyah (Alawite) Mountains in the northwest paralleling the coast, the eastern slopes of the Anti-Lebanon Mountains, and the Jabal Druz; (3) the steppe and desert region, traversed by the Euphrates River; and (4) the Jazirah in the northeast, steppe country with low rolling hills.

The Anti-Lebanon Mountains, extending southward along the Lebanese border, serve as a catchment for the rainfall of central Syria. To the north of this range, the Ansariyah Mountains slope westward to the Mediterranean. Between these two ranges in northwestern Syria lie small mountain valleys irrigated by the Orontes River. The highest peaks in the Ansariyah Mountains reach over 5,000 feet; at the head of the Euphrates River in the north, the elevation is 1,000 feet. One of the world's largest basaltic outcroppings, the Jabal Druz, about 13,000 sq mi, is situated in the southeast.

³CLIMATE

The climate varies from the Mediterranean type in the west to extremely arid desert conditions in the east. The coastal regions have hot summers and mild winters; in the mountains, summer heat is moderated according to elevation and the winters are more severe. The steppe and desert areas have extremely hot, arid summers and greatly varying winter temperatures ranging from 21°C (70°F) to below freezing. Average temperatures for Damascus range from about 21°C to 43.4°C (70°–110°F) in August and from about -4°C to 15.6 °C (25°–60°F) in January. Rainfall averages 40 inches on the coast, 50 inches in some mountain areas, from 10 to 20 inches east of the mountains in the

region from Aleppo to Damascus, and 5 to 10 inches in the steppe areas; the desert may get as little as half an inch annually. In dry years, rainfall may be reduced by half. The rainy season is from November to March.

⁴FLORA AND FAUNA

The coastal plain is highly cultivated, and the little wild growth found is mainly of the brushwood type, such as tamarisk. On the northern slopes of the Ansariyah range are fairly extensive pine forests, while oak and scrub oak are common in the less well-watered central portion. Terebinth is predominant in the low hill country of the steppes, and wormwood grows on the plains. Some sections of the Jabal Druz are covered with a dense maquis.

The wildlife of Syria includes types common to the eastern Mediterranean region, together with typical desert species. There is a diminishing number of bears in the mountains; gazelle and antelope are found wherever grazing is available and human competition not too severe; there are also deer in some sections. Smaller animals include squirrel, wildcat, otter, and hare. In the desert, viper, lizard, and chameleon are found in relatively large numbers. Native birds include flamingo and pelican, as well as the various ducks, snipe, and other game birds. Syria is on one of the main north-south routes of migrant birds, and many species are found there in season.

As of 1975, endangered species in Syria included the wolf, Anatolian leopard, Syrian wild ass, and Sa'udi Arabian dorcas gazelle.

⁵POPULATION

According to the 1970 census, Syria's population was 6,304,685. In 1973, it was estimated at 7,259,000, including Palestinian refugees (who numbered 155,723 at the end of 1970). With an estimated crude birthrate of 45.4 per 1,000 population and a crude death rate of 15.4 in 1970–75, the net natural increase was 30; the overall rate of population increase was estimated at 3% annually. The population density was estimated at 39.2 per sq km, but most of it was concentrated in a small area. In 1975, an estimated 45.5% of the population was urban. Damascus (Dimishq), the capital, perhaps the oldest continuously inhabited city in the world, had a population of 1,457,934 in 1970. The population of Aleppo (Halab), a northern trading and agricultural center, was 1,316,872. Other main cities are Homs (Hims), 546,167; Hama (Hamah), 514,748; and Latakia (al-Ladhiquiya), 389,552.

6 ETHNIC GROUPS

Racially, the Syrians are varied, and, except where ethnic distinctions have found religious expression, racial types are generally intermixed among the inhabitants. However, the nomads of the interior desert are pure specimens of the Mediterranean type. Armenian communities in the cities, along with the Kurds and the Turkish-speaking communities in the north, are Armenoids. The Druzes, most of whom live in the Jabal Druz, show an affinity to the tribes of the Persian Zagros. There is also an Assyrian minority and a small Jewish community. According to the 1970 census, there were 6,094,389 Syrian nationals, 155,723 Palestinians, 44,369 people from other Arab states, and 10,204 others.

7 LANGUAGE

The language of the majority is Arabic. Dialect variations are pronounced from region to region and even from town to town. The written language, classical Arabic, based on the Qur'an, is common to all Arabic-speaking countries and is the basis of the standard spoken form. Kurdish and Armenian are the minority languages. Aramaic, the language of Christ, is still spoken in some villages.

8 RELIGION

Islam is the religion of the vast majority. Most of the Muslims are Sunnis; some are Shi'is or Isma'ilis.

The Alawis constitute an important minority in Syria. Although they consider themselves Muslims, they combine their avowed creed with Christian rituals and esoteric cults. Also important are the Druzes, whose religion is an amalgamation of Shi'ite Islam and Christianity. Muslims, Alawis, and Druzes together comprise more than 86% of the population. The Christian population, including Greek Orthodox, Armenian Catholic, Armenian Orthodox (Gregorian), Syrian Catholic, Syrian Orthodox, Maronite Christian-Protestant, and Nestorian, make up most of the remainder. Other religious minorities are Chaldeans, Jews (4,000 in 1973), and Yezidis.

Under the 1973 constitution, Islam is no longer declared to be the religion of the state, but the president of Syria must still be a Muslim and Islamic law remains recognized as a major source of legislation. Freedom of worship is guaranteed by the constitution.

9 TRANSPORTATION

Syria is served by three railroads: the Northern Line, the Syrian section of the old Baghdad Railway, 248 km of standard-gauge track; the Southern Line, including the Aleppo-Qasir, Homs-Akkari, Akkari-Tartus, and Aleppo-Tabka sections, 484 km of standard-gauge track; and the Hijaz Railway from Damascus to the Jordan border, with 299 km of narrow-gauge track. The construction of a 756-km railway linking Latakia, Alleppo, and Qamishli was expected to be complete by mid-1976. Syria is connected with Turkey (hence, with Europe) and Iraq by rail links.

Although the road system grew 25% in 1970–73, it still is inadequate, particularly in view of demands imposed by increased economic activity. There were 14,459 km of motorable roadway in 1974, of which 10,578 km were asphalted, 1,527 km were paved but not asphalted, and 2,354 km were dirt. There are road connections with Iraq, Jordan, Lebanon, and Turkey; roads to Israel are not in use. In 1970, construction of two sections of the Damascus-Baghdad international motorway up to Tanaf on the border was completed. In 1974 there were 21,370 private automobiles, 9,519 taxis, 5,838 government automobiles, 2,826 buses, 20,913 trucks, 10,066 motorcycles, and 551 jeeps.

Latakia is the main port and handles most of the oceangoing trade. Other ports are Erwad, Jablah, Tartus, and al-Baniyas. In 1973, 3,430 ships entered and left Syrian ports; 34,751 tons of international cargoes were loaded and 2,211 tons unloaded.

Damascus is a connecting point for a number of major airlines, and a new international airport was completed in 1970. A total of 1,535 tons of imports and 1,079 tons of exports passed through Syrian airports in 1973. Passenger arrivals and departures totaled 376,076. Syrian Arab Airlines provides service to Aleppo, Qamishli, Latakia, and other smaller airports; it also flies to some other Arab and non-Arab capitals.

10 COMMUNICATIONS

All communications facilities are owned and operated by the government, including postal service, telegraph, telephone, radio, and television. A microwave telephone link between Damascus and Beirut was completed in 1961. In 1975, a new communications network was completed, which includes cables linking Damascus with other major towns and with Beirut, and improved links with Turkey and Western Europe. There were 143,320 telephones in use in 1973, including 128,120 automatic lines.

The Syrian Broadcasting Service transmits on medium and short waves, and broadcasts in Arabic, English, French, German, Hebrew, Portuguese, and Spanish. There were 2.5 million radios and about 150,000 television sets in use in 1972.

11 HISTORY

Syria's capital, Damascus, is one of the world's oldest cities. Along the Syrian and Lebanese coastlands, an advanced civilization was developed under the Phoenicians, and trade, industry, and seafaring flourished. The wealth of the land attracted many conquerors, and Syria was invaded successively by Hittites, Egyptians, Assyrians, Persians, and others. In the 4th century B.C., Syria fell to Alexander the Great, first in a long line of European conquerors. After the breakup of his empire, dominion over Syria was disputed by the Seleucid and Ptolemid successor states, and Persians invaded when the opportunity arose; eventually the Seleucids gained control. In the 1st century B.C., all of Syria, Lebanon, Palestine, and Transjordan was conquered by the Romans and organized as the Province of Syria, although in the more remote and less wealthy areas control was exercised through native rulers until A.D. 105, when the whole region came under direct Roman rule. Christianity spread throughout the land, particularly after it became the official Roman religion under Constantine the Great.

In 637, Damascus fell to the Arabs. Most Syrians were converted to Islam, and Arabic gradually became the language of the area. Under the Ummayad caliphs, Damascus became the capital of the Islamic world, and a base for Arab conquests. Under the 'Abbasids, the caliphate was centered at Baghdad, and Syria was reduced to provincial status. Thereafter, Syria fell prey to a succession of invaders, including Byzantines and Crusaders from Western Europe. Some parts of Syria came under the sway of Seljuqs and 'Ayyubids, a Kurdish dynasty, eventually under their leader Saladin (Salah al-Din). During the 13th century, Mongol hordes frequently invaded Syria, and for 200 years parts of Syria were controlled by Mamluks, who ruled it from Egypt through local governors. In 1516, the Ottoman forces of Sultan Selim I defeated the Mamluks, and for the next four centuries Syria was a province of the Ottoman Empire.

During World War I, Sharif Husayn of Mecca threw in his lot with the Allies and revolted against Ottoman rule. After the war, with British forces in control, the formal entry of Allied troops into Damascus was made by Arab forces under Amir Faysal, Husayn's son, on 30 October 1918. Faysal and the Arab nationalists, whose number had been growing since 1912, opposed French aspirations to Syria and claimed independence under the terms of agreements between the British government and Husayn. In March 1920, Faysal was proclaimed king of Syria by a congress representing Syria, Lebanon, and Palestine. In June, however, the French, who had been allotted a mandate for Syria and Lebanon by the Agreement of San Remo (April 1920), ejected Faysal and installed local administrations of their own choosing. Arab nationalist sentiment resented French rule, and unrest persisted until the outbreak of World War II. In 1941, Free French and British forces wrested control of Syria from Vichy France. In 1943, under pressure from the UK and the US, the French permitted elections and the formation of a nationalist government in August. The UK and the US recognized Syria's independence in 1944, but French troops were removed only after armed British intervention in May 1945 and pressure from the US.

Two parties that had led the struggle for independence, the Nationalist Party and the People's Party, dominated Syrian political life after 1944. The Palestine War of 1948, however, which resulted in the defeat of the Arab armies and the loss of most of Palestine to Israel, discredited the Syrian leadership. In December 1948, riots against the government were put down by the army; and from 30 March 1949 to September 1950, several army factions struggled to gain control of the state. Col. Adib Shishakli ruled Syria from 1950 to 1954, when he was ousted by another army coup.

The years from 1954 to 1958 were marked by an increasing military and economic dependence on the Soviet bloc. Anti-Western feeling, with its roots in the mandate period, had been sharply aggravated by the creation of Israel with the support of the West. Closer relations with Egypt, already receiving Soviet support, were developed. The growth of the Ba'th Party, a socialist group, matched these developments. The Suez crisis of 1956 also fanned anger against the West. But there were elements in both Syria and Egypt that did not want to see Western influence in the Middle East replaced with Soviet influence. In February 1958, therefore, the Nasir regime in Egypt and Syrian anti-Communist nationalists joined in proclaiming a union of Syria and Egypt, the United Arab Republic (UAR). The Egyptians exercised political domination, with regional power placed in the hands of a Syrian military junta, and a socialist program was introduced. In September 1961, after a military coup, Syria seceded from the UAR. A conservative government, elected in December, began a process of desocialization, but it was turned out in March 1962 by another army coup. Civilian government was again reinstated, but it too was overthrown on 8 March 1963 by the National Council of the Revolutionary Command, and a radical socialist government dominated by the Ba'th Party was formed.

Succeeding years were marked by internal struggles between moderate and leftist factions of the Ba'th Party and by military conflict with Israel. The moderates, under Amin al-Hafiz, were overthrown in February 1966, but regained power under Gen. Hafiz al-Asad, who became chief of state on 16 November 1970. He assumed the presidency, a newly created office, for a seven-year term beginning in March 1971, and a permanent constitution was ratified by popular referendum on 12 March 1973.

In the June 1967 war between Israel, on one side, and Syria, Egypt, and Jordan on the other, Israel gained control of the Golan Heights in Syria. After the war, Israel refused to withdraw, Syria rejected Western-sponsored peace plans, and sporadic violence continued. Syria's support for Palestinian guerrillas operating from Lebanon and in Jordan also strained relations with those countries. On 6 October 1973, Syrian troops launched a full-scale attack against Israeli forces in the Golan Heights, as the Egyptians attacked in the Suez Canal area. After the UN cease-fire of 24 October, Israel remained in control of the Golan Heights, and Syria boycotted peace negotiations in Geneva. However, on 31 May 1974, Syria signed a US-mediated disengagement accord with Israel, restoring part of the Golan Heights to Syria and creating a buffer zone, manned by UN Disengagement Observation Force (UNDOF) troops. In 1974, 1975, and 1976, Syria renewed the UNDOF mandate at six-month intervals.

In recent years, Syria has intervened militarily in neighboring Arab states to secure political ends. In September 1970, Syrian armored forces crossed the border into Jordan to support the Palestinians during the Jordanian civil war; the Syrians were routed by troops loyal to King Husayn. In 1976, Syrian troops entered Lebanon to enforce a cease-fire between Christian and Muslim forces.

12 GOVERNMENT

Since independence, Syria has made several attempts at constitution making. The constitution of 1950 was revived in amended form in 1962 and then abrogated. A provisional constitution adopted in April 1964 was suspended in 1966 and replaced to some extent by a continuing series of edicts. The fundamental law that thus emerged considered Syria to be a socialist republic forming part of the Arab homeland, required that the head of state be a Muslim, recognized Islamic law as a main source of legislation, ordained collective ownership of the means of production, and permitted private ownership on condition that it did not conflict with the building of a socialist economy. In 1971, a People's Council was nominated by the president as a transition toward a republican form of government.

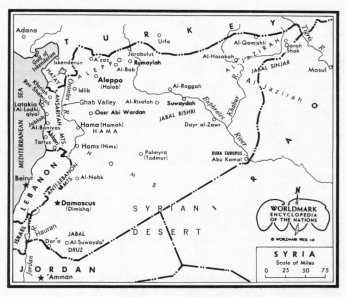

See continental political: front cover G6; physical: back cover G6

LOCATION (1949): 32°30' to 37°30'N; 35°50' to 42°E. BOUNDARY LENGTHS: Turkey, 845 km (525 mi). Iraq, 596 km (370 mi). Jordan, 356 km (221 mi). Israel: 1949 armistice line, 76 km (47 mi); 1974 line, 80 km (50 mi). Lebanon, 359 km (223 mi). Mediterranean coastline, 183 km (114 mi). TERRITORIAL SEA LIMIT: 12 mi.

On 12 March 1973, a new constitution, embodying socialist principles, was ratified in a popular referendum. Strong executive power is vested in the president, who serves a seven-year term; he appoints the cabinet, headed by a prime minister. The choice of president is made by party officials, approved by the unicameral People's Council, and ratified by referendum. Elections for the 186-member People's Council, Syria's first national elections since 1962, were held in March 1973. Suffrage is universal, beginning at age 18.

13 POLITICAL PARTIES

Prior to 1963, the main parties were the National Party and the People's Party (Sha'b), both outgrowths of the National Bloc, which was active during the French mandate period (1920 through World War II). The National and People's parties were conservative and nationalistic, and represented the substantial landowning and property-owning classes, although the Sha'b was somewhat more reformist. The Syrian Popular Party (Hizb al-Qawmi al-Suri), anti-Marxist and nationalistic, had as its main principle the reunification of Greater Syria, including Lebanon, Jordan, and Palestine, and the establishment of a single Arab state in the fertile crescent. The left-wing Ba'th Party, formed in 1953 by the union of the original Ba'th, once moderately nationalist and socialist, and the Arab Socialist Party, supported Arab unity and independence and the achievement of socialism in the Arab world; it has branches in other Arab countries as well. The Syrian Communist Party, originally an underground movement, was allowed legal status during and after World War II, but was outlawed in 1947, when it supported the partition of Palestine, and remained outlawed until 1954, when it began to attract support from minority groups and intellectuals.

The Ba'th and the Syrian Popular parties lost much of their strength in the political life of the Arab world after 1958. The former was too closely connected with the rise of Soviet influence in Syria, and its being swept aside during the union with Egypt (1958–61) did not enhance its prestige. The Syrian Popular Party never recovered from the failure of its coup attempt in Lebanon in 1962. The Communists lost much support when they were outlawed under the union, lost even more as the Suez crisis dimmed in Arab memories, and were seriously compromised by their violence in Iraq.

Through its association with the successful revolts in Iraq and Syria early in 1963, the Ba'th made a dramatic comeback from the low point of 1958. Standing as it did for the two most powerful ideas in the Arab world—Arab unity and the achievement of social justice through state action—it was the natural beneficiary of the failures of past governments to fulfill their promises and of their ever-increasing concern with their own power and interests at the expense of Arab unity. The gains of the Ba'th were rather by default than by positive action, however, and it owed more to the military than the military owed to the Ba'th.

The civil war in neighboring Jordan in September 1970 had repercussions in Syria. It caused a crisis in the conflict between the civilian ("progressive") wing of the Syrian Ba'th Party and the military ("nationalist") wing. Earlier friction between the two Ba'thist groups in 1968 and 1969 had led to a compromise settlement. The nationalist group had become powerful, and Gen. Hafiz al-Asad had removed progressives from key posts in the armed forces. President al-Atassi continued in office, and the progressive leaders, Gen. Salah al-Jadid and Yusuf Zeayen, a former prime minister, controlled the militia and al-Saiga, the Palestinian guerrilla movement.

About 70% of the population are Sunni but the Ba'thists relied for support mainly on the Alawi sect, which was estimated to be about 9% of the population. Gen. Asad and Gen. Jadid were Alawis and al-Atassi a Sunni. An open split between the generals would have led to division among their coreligionists, and, therefore, a compromise was necessary. President al-Atassi, in protest against the bickering among the Ba'thist leaders, resigned his posts in October 1970.

An emergency congress met in Damascus on 30 October and was attended by 80 Ba'thist leaders from Syria and other Arab states, but the meeting only led to further division among the two groups. The congress ended on 12 November after adopting resolutions supporting the position of the progressives.

Following his defeat at the congress, Gen. Asad staged a bloodless coup in Damascus on 13 November 1970. Gen. Jadid, Yusuf Zeayen, and a number of other progressive leaders were arrested. Nureddin al-Atassi was placed under guard. Radio and television stations were taken over by the army, and military police occupied the headquarters of al-Saiga and invited its members to enlist in "organizations whose objectives are limited

to the struggle for the recovery of the usurped fatherland."

No official statements were issued, and for three days the radio did not refer to the events. Nureddin al-Atassi was allowed to return to his home on 15 November. All those who had been arrested, with the exception of Gen. Jadid, were released. Gen. Asad failed to obtain al-Atassi's cooperation in forming a new government. On 16 November, it was announced that the Syrian command of the Ba'th Party had been removed and that it had been replaced by a provisional leadership, pending the convening of a party congress. The pan-Arab command then denounced the provisional leadership as illegal and expelled Gen. Asad from the Party.

A statement on 16 November declared that the previous leadership under Nureddin al-Atassi had fostered repeated crises in the party by using dictatorial powers. The former leadership, the statement said, had failed to act against "reaction" in Jordan and the "right wing" in Iraq. It had not mobilized Syria against "surrender" proposals made by the US. The statement went on to say that the new leadership would attempt to improve relations with progressive Arab states in all fields. The leadership welcomed moves toward Arab unity, such as the proposals for a federation of Egypt, Libya, and the Sudan. In Syria the provisional leadership would form a national front under Ba'thist leadership, and a People's Assembly would be convened within three months to decide on the country's future policies.

In March 1971, Gen. Asad was inaugurated as president (a new title) and was named Party secretary in May 1971, at the fifth congress of the Syrian Ba'th Party. On 7 March 1972, the Progressive Front of National Union was created to unite four other "progressive" groups under Ba'thist leadership; its directorate consisted of 17 members, 9 from the Ba'th Party, and 2 each from the Arab Socialist Union, the Socialist Unionist Movement, the Arab Socialist Party, and the Communist Party. Of these subsidiary groups, only the Communists were believed to have significant public support. Under the 1973 constitution, the president of Syria is also general secretary of the Ba'th Party and president of the Progressive Front of National Union.

In the March 1973 elections to the People's Council, the results were Ba'th Party, 111; Communist Party, 7; Arab Socialist Union, 6; Arab Socialist Party, 3; independents sponsored by the Progressive Front of National Union, 33; and others, 4.

14 LOCAL GOVERNMENT
Syria is divided into 14 provinces (muhafazat), each in the charge of a governor (muhafiz). Each province is in turn divided into counties (mantiqat), of which there are 48 in all, each headed by a qa'immaqam. Each county is further subdivided into municipal councils, each in the charge of a mudir. Local government is under the jurisdiction of the minister of local administration. Governors are appointed by and are directly responsible to the minister.

15 JUDICIAL SYSTEM
The Syrian legal system is based partly on French law and partly on Syrian statutes. The highest court of appeal is the Court of Cassation. Below it are 11 courts of appeal that try all criminal cases and some other cases; three judges, including the president, give decisions. Eighty-five summary courts try civil and minor penal cases, and 12 first-instance courts deal with matters not within the competence of special tribunals. In addition, there are Shari'ah courts, which apply Islamic law in cases involving personal status. The Druzes and non-Muslim communities have their own religious courts.

16 ARMED FORCES
In 1975, the army had an estimated 150,000 regular troops and 100,000 reserves; there were 2 armored divisions, 3 mechanized infantry divisions, 2 armored brigades, 3 mechanized brigades, 3 infantry brigades, 2 artillery brigades, 8 commando battalions, and 3 parachute battalions. The army had more than 2,000 heavy

and medium tanks, 36 missile batteries, and sophisticated antitank and antiaircraft weapons. The navy had 2,500 men and 2,500 reserves; naval vessels included 6 missile-equipped fast patrol boats, 11 torpedo boats, 1 minesweeper, and 1 coastal patrol vessel. The air force had 25,000 men; its 400 combat aircraft were under army command. Paramilitary forces totaled 9,500 men, including a 1,500-man desert frontier force. Armaments valued at $1,462 million were imported between 1971 and 1974; the USSR has been Syria's principal supplier. The military budget was estimated at $668 million in 1975.

[17] MIGRATION

In the past there was sizable emigration by Syrians to Europe, Africa, and the Western Hemisphere, but emigration virtually ceased by the late 1940s. Since World War I, there has been substantial internal migration from the crowded coastal mountains to the central plains and, in general, from the rural areas to the towns. There is considerable migration across the borders with Lebanon and Iraq.

[18] INTERNATIONAL COOPERATION

Syria is a member of the UN and all of its specialized agencies except GATT. Syria is also a charter member of the League of Arab States, set up in 1945 to foster cooperation in foreign and domestic affairs. In March 1972, Syria became a member of OAPEC.

Between February 1958 and September 1961, Syria and Egypt were joined in the United Arab Republic. During that period, the UAR was technically joined with Yemen in the United Arab States, with little practical effect. Another federation, established formally in April 1963 between Syria, Egypt, and Iraq, was never implemented; it was officially terminated in July 1963 after Nasirite loyalists attempted unsuccessfully to overthrow Syria's Ba'thist regime. On 1 January 1972, Syria formally became part of the Federation of Arab Republics with Egypt and Libya; the Federation, whose headquarters are in Cairo, also had little practical effect because of a deterioration in Egypt's relations with Syria and especially with Libya. In June 1974, Syria and Jordan established a joint commission to coordinate foreign and military policy. Diplomatic relations between Syria and the US were resumed on 16 June 1974, after US Secretary of State Henry Kissinger had successfully mediated a Golan Heights disengagement agreement; US-Syrian relations had been suspended since the June 1967 war.

[19] ECONOMY

Syria is traditionally an agricultural country; the livelihood of one-half of its work force and about one-fifth of its GDP are still provided by agriculture. In the past, agriculture was mainly on the subsistence level for domestic consumption, but in recent years, the government has begun to modernize production and marketing methods, has set a limitation on landholdings, and has undertaken projects to extend land cultivation; the most important of these is the Euphrates Dam. The third five-year economic plan (1971–75) envisaged investment of s£2.6 billion (33% of the total) on irrigation and land reclamation projects and other agricultural schemes.

Industry has been growing rapidly since World War II and especially in recent years. Under the third five-year plan, industry accounted for 23% of all government investment. The general index of industrial production (1970 = 100) rose from 127 in 1973 to 149 in 1974. The nascent state-owned oil industry based on the development of the Suwadiyah and Rumailah fields and the exploitation of other mineral resources, notably phosphates, are diversifying Syrian industry, which was formerly concentrated in light manufacturing and textiles. One of the major projects of the fourth plan (1976–80) is the construction of an iron-working complex at Hama.

Another element of the Syrian economy is oil transit. Two systems of international pipelines run across Syrian territory, carrying Iraqi and Sa'udi Arabian oil to the Mediterranean; these yield substantial transit royalties to Syria.

Foreign aid is important to Syrian economic development. Syria's attempts to expand its economy and living standards have depended heavily on financial assistance and technical aid from Socialist countries, especially the USSR, which agreed in 1966 to finance the foreign exchange cost of the Euphrates Dam by a loan of up to $157 million.

[20] INCOME

In 1974, the GDP was s£14,478 million in current prices, a 53.9% increase over 1973; in constant 1970 prices the increase was 18.7%. Per capita income rose from $201 in 1963 to about $400 in 1974.

Contributions to the 1974 GDP included agriculture, forestry, and fishing, 21%; wholesale and retail trade, 20.9%; manufacturing, 13.2%; mining, 9.7%; transport, storage, and communications, 6.9%; construction, 4.8%; and other sectors, 23.5%.

[21] LABOR

At the end of 1973, the labor force totaled 1,688,564 persons, or about 23% of the total population. It was estimated that 1,612,075 persons, or 95% of the work force, were employed, with 850,233 persons in agriculture and related fields and 271,121 in manufacturing, mining, and quarrying. Of the total female labor force of 343,956, the majority (279,177) were engaged in agriculture; however, small numbers of women were finding employment in industries or in technical professions.

There is a high level of unemployment and underemployment. Many unskilled persons in agriculture and industry work only seasonally. The government is attempting to meet the demand for trained workers by establishing vocational schools and encouraging apprenticeship training. Industrial employers must turn over to their employees 25% of all profits up to a maximum of s£750 per employee per annum. In 1973, the minimum wage stood at s£135 per month.

The basic law governing labor is Labor Law 91 of 1959. The code establishes the right of labor to form unions and empowers the government to regulate hours of work, vacations, sick leave, health and safety measures, and workmen's compensation. The government also is authorized to arbitrate labor disputes.

The average minimum monthly wage in 1974 ranged from s£250 to s£300. The average workweek for wage earners over 18 years of age was 46 hours in 1974. Although the number of unions decreased from 193 in 1966 to 160 in 1974, their combined membership increased from 99,201 to 184,916. In 1974, 36.7% of nonagricultural wage and salary earners were union members.

[22] AGRICULTURE

Of 18.5 million hectares of land, about 7.9 million hectares are arable, but the area actually cultivated is about 5.9 million hectares. Agriculture depends on rainfall, which is uncertain, and in lean years, Syria becomes a net importer of wheat and barley; this strains the whole economy and hampers development.

A primary aim of the government, therefore, is to replace dryland farming by irrigated cultivation. The total irrigated area of 619,000 hectares was expected to be nearly doubled through the Euphrates Dam project, which was virtually completed in 1975. Its aims are to control flooding, to irrigate about 500,000 hectares through a network of canals, and to generate about 1.5 billion kwh of electricity per year at the final stage. The government has allocated an increasing share of its investments (28% under the third plan) to irrigation; full development of irrigation schemes is expected to take 50 years.

Traditionally, Syria's agricultural land was held by landowners in tracts of more that 100 hectares; sharecropping was customary. This picture has been greatly altered since the government undertook agrarian reform in 1958. The law, as modified in 1963, fixed the maximum holding of irrigated land at between 15 and 50 hectares per person and that of nonirrigated land at 80 hectares per person. All expropriated land available for cultivation has now been allotted to farmers. In 1973 there were 1,725 agricultural cooperatives, with 134,562 members, covering 929,000 hectares.

The principal crops are cotton, cereals, vegetables, fruit, and tobacco. In 1973, Syria produced 593,000 tons of wheat, 269,000 tons of tomatoes, 152,400 tons of sugar beets, 110,500 tons of potatoes, 102,000 tons of barley, 98,600 tons of onions, 27,800 tons of peas, and 23,700 tons of pulses and lentils. Horticultural fruit production, in tons, included grapes, 147,000; olives, 73,000; apples, 41,000; and dried figs, 31,000. Cash crops included 404,300 tons of cotton, 288,000 tons of cottonseed, and 10,900 tons of tobacco.

The index of total agricultural production in 1972 (1970 = 100) was 197; in 1973, a poor year, the figure was 101. The index figure for cereal production was 128 in 1971, 281 in 1972, and 79 in 1973. Total agricultural production in 1973 was valued at s£1,267.7 million, of which cash crops were worth s£436.6 million.

The 1971–75 economic plan allocated 33% of total funds (s£2.6 billion) to agriculture, land reclamation, and irrigation. This included investment in the Euphrates project, the completion of smaller irrigation projects, the utilization of underground water resources in the southwestern part of the country—the arid zone—and general pest control, selective cotton raising, and use of fertilizers, which increased by 30% from 1969 to 1972. Mechanization is also encouraged; in 1973, 11,574 tractors and 1,709 harvester-threshers were in use.

23 ANIMAL HUSBANDRY
Steppe and pasture land occupies 6,497,000 hectares, or about 35% of Syria's total area. Stock raising contributes significantly to the Syrian economy; in 1973 there were 6,259,700 head of cattle, 4,840,000 sheep, 609,000 goats, 248,200 asses, 62,900 horses, 50,000 mules, and 5,800 camels. In 1973, Syria produced 394,000 tons of milk, 4,000 tons of beef and veal, 27,000 tons of mutton and lamb, and 370 million eggs. Animal products, in tons, also included cheese, 24,084; clarified butter (samneh), 6,166; butter, 1,092; and washed wool, 5,497. In 1972, 719,000 sheep, lambs, and goats and 54,000 head of cattle were exported; however, the numbers dropped to 198,000 and 29,000 respectively in 1973, when Syria became a net importer of live animals.

24 FISHING
There is some fishing off the Mediterranean coast, but the commercial catch is negligible.

25 FORESTRY
Syria is almost entirely denuded of forests. Although 481,000 hectares are officially listed as forests, some 340,000 hectares consist either of wholly barren land or range land with arboreous shrubs. The substantial forests are mainly on the northern slopes of the Ansariyah range, on the windward side of the Anti-Lebanon Mountains, and in the Latakia region.

26 MINING
Syria's mineral resources are not extensive, but there have been recent discoveries of valuable phosphate, iron, and oil deposits. Phosphate was found in two locations near al-Shargiyah, and production was begun in 1971; 270,000 tons were produced in 1973 and 650,000 tons in 1974. Iron deposits have been discovered near Palmyra, Aleppo, and Homs. Syria's iron reserves were estimated sufficient to operate for 90 years a factory with an annual capacity of 500,000 tons; exploitation will help reduce Syria's dependence on iron and steel imports, which in 1973 amounted to 253,479 tons and cost $54.7 million. In 1973, Syria produced 26,500 tons of asphalt and 35,100 tons of salt.

Oil in commercial quantities was first discovered in the late 1950s. Production rose from 1 million tons in 1968 to 5.7 million tons in 1974. Proved reserves in 1973 totaled 181 million tons. A 650-km pipeline linking the oil fields, the coast at Tartus, and the refinery at Homs was completed in 1968; its annual capacity was later expanded to 8 million tons. All oil concessions were granted exclusively in 1964 to the General Petroleum Authority, a government agency that owns the Homs refinery. In 1972, the pipelines and facilities in Syria of the Iraq Petroleum Co. were nationalized; the same year, Syria joined OAPEC. The value of Syria's oil exports in 1973 was $73.6 million.

27 ENERGY AND POWER
Much of the production of electricity is thermal, with oil used as fuel. Cost is high and the supply is limited. Installed capacity in 1973 was 437,000 kw, but facilities have been expanded in recent years. Production of electricity rose from 773 million kwh in 1968 to 1.2 billion kwh in 1973; about half was for industrial use. The Euphrates Dam is eventually expected to add 1.6 billion kwh of production per year.

28 INDUSTRY
Industry as a major factor in the Syrian economy is barely out of its infancy, but expansion has been rapid in recent years under government initiative. A series of nationalization measures since 1963 resulted in public control of most industry except construction, tourism, and small industries, but recent efforts have been made to stimulate the expansion of the private sector. The public industrial sector has been organized (since 1968) under three industrial unions: the Union of Food Industry, the Union of Engineering and Chemical Industries, and the Union of Textile Industries, supplemented by the General Petroleum Authority, the Organization of Syrian Electricity, and the Office of Phosphates and Mines. Production by the three chief unions in 1973 totaled s£898 million, 15% above 1972 levels. About 25% of all investment in 1971–75 was from the private sector, which in 1973 surpassed the public sector in the production of chocolate, cotton and silk fabric, stockings, paints, soap, and gas stoves.

Syria has been renowned since ancient times for such handicrafts as Damascus brocade and Syrian soap. Some of these traditions endured even after 1933, when the first mechanized plant for spinning and weaving was set up in Aleppo. The textile industry has remained the most important; it employs about 43,000 persons and in 1973 contributed approximately 49% of all manufactures and about 17% of all exports. Syria's production of cotton yarn was 28,500 tons in 1973 (4,700 in 1950). Local cotton is now ginned in Syrian factories; production in 1973 totaled 156,000 tons. In addition, 2,200 tons of wool yarn, 31,100 tons of cotton and silk textiles, 151,000 sq meters of wool carpets, 1,027 tons of wool textiles, and 966,000 dozen pieces of underwear were produced in 1973.

Also important are the chemical and engineering industries and the food industries. The largest component of the former sector is the cement industry, which produced 848,000 tons in 1973. A fertilizer plant (costing about $16 million) was built at Homs in 1968. Production of azotic fertilizers was 33,000 tons in 1973. The food industries include salt manufacture, sugar refining, fruit and vegetable canning, vegetable oil extraction, brewing of beer, and tobacco manufacture. In 1973, Syria produced 1,930 tons of tobacco, an estimated 3,465 million cigarettes, and 48,000 hectoliters of beer. A sugar refinery has been installed at Homs; production in 1973 totaled 142,000 tons. Vegetable and olive oils are traditional Syrian products; 42,400 tons were produced in 1973.

The oil refining industry was established with the completion of a petroleum refinery at Homs at a cost of s£54 million. Production of refinery products, in tons, in 1974 included motor fuel, 283,000; kerosine, 207,000; distillate fuels, 517,000; and residual fuel, 609,000.

29 DOMESTIC TRADE
Damascus and Aleppo are the principal commercial centers. Virtually all importers, exporters, and wholesalers have offices in one or both cities. The chief retail centers have general and specialized stores as well as large bazaars. Smaller bazaars and

open markets are found in many Syrian towns and villages.

An international fair is held every summer in Damascus. Advertising agencies use newspapers, magazines, moving picture theaters, buses, and other media.

Usual business hours are from 9 A.M. to 1 P.M. and from 3:30 P.M. to 7 P.M. Friday is the weekly day of rest. While the official language is Arabic, commercial firms commonly use English or French for business correspondence.

30 FOREIGN TRADE

Raw cotton was Syria's principal export in 1973, accounting for about one-third of all exports. Crude oil accounted for 22% in 1973, food and live animals for about 14%. By 1974, however, oil had become Syria's most important export, and receipts from crude petroleum exports were estimated at $450 million in 1975. Imports consist mostly of industrial raw materials and manufactured articles, especially machinery, transport equipment, metals, textile yarns, chemicals, and fuels. Annual trade deficits have been recorded since the mid-1950s. In 1974, Syria's exports were about $778 million and its imports $1,223 million, for a deficit of $445 million.

Principal exports in 1973 (in millions of dollars) were:

Raw cotton	113.3
Crude petroleum	73.6
Food and live animals	46.0
Textile yarns and fabrics	28.0
Wool	15.5
Clothing	13.8
Tobacco	11.4
Other exports	37.5
TOTAL	339.1

Principal imports in 1973 (in millions of dollars) were:

Food and live animals	141.8
Machinery	112.5
Chemicals	54.8
Iron and steel	54.7
Textile yarns and fabrics	44.9
Transport equipment	24.8
Other imports	161.2
TOTAL	594.7

Principal trade partners in 1973 (in millions of dollars) were:

	EXPORTS	IMPORTS	BALANCE
USSR	52.0	42.4	9.6
Italy	43.9	47.3	− 3.4
FRG	17.2	62.5	− 45.3
Lebanon	28.6	35.8	− 7.2
France	13.8	42.5	− 28.7
China	27.7	23.4	4.3
Other countries	155.9	340.8	−184.9
TOTALS	339.1	594.7	−255.6

Syria's trade patterns changed noticeably after the 1973 war with Israel. Trade with the EEC increased from 32.7% of Syria's total trade in 1973 to 36% in 1974, and the Federal Republic of Germany (FRG) emerged as Syria's leading import supplier and trade partner (13.3% of total trade in 1974). Greece became in 1974 the leading purchaser of Syria's exports, followed by the FRG, USSR, and UK, whose share of Syrian exports increased from 1.3% in 1973 to 9.8% in 1974. Although the USSR's share of total trade declined from 10.1% in 1973 to 7.9%, trade with other

East European countries increased, and the region's share of Syrian trade remained about 18%.

31 BALANCE OF PAYMENTS

After a period of overall surpluses, the balance of payments was in deficit between 1968 and 1971, and exchange reserves declined to $55 million by the end of 1970. From 1972 on, however, transfers of funds from other Arab governments have helped Syria register surpluses on current accounts and in the overall balance of payments despite a rising trade deficit. Exchange reserves increased from $135 million at the end of 1972 to $1,205 million as of 31 March 1975. The following are summaries (in millions of dollars) of Syria's balance of payments for 1973 and 1974:

	1973	1974
CURRENT ACCOUNTS		
Trade, net	−213	−353
Services, net	150	32
Transfers, net	401	459
TOTALS	338	138
CAPITAL ACCOUNTS		
Long-term capital	25	61
Short-term capital	14	189
TOTALS	39	250
Errors and omissions	− 49	− 28
Net change	328	360

32 BANKING

There are six government banks, with a total of 114 branches. The Central Bank, founded in 1956, is the bank of issue for currency, the financial agent of the government, and the cashier for the treasury. The Agricultural Bank makes loans to farmers at low interest; the Industrial Bank (nationalized in 1961), the Popular Credit Bank and the Real Estate Bank (both founded in 1966), and the Commercial Bank of Syria (formed in 1967 by a merger of five nationalized commercial banks) make loans in their defined sectors.

On 30 September 1974, the Central Bank's gold holdings were worth $33 million and its foreign exchange reserves $752 million. Its liabilities totaled $234 million. On the same date, the foreign assets of the commercial banks were s£291 million and their foreign liabilities s£185 million. The total money supply rose from s£1,868 million at the end of 1968 to s£5,134 million on 30 November 1974. The investments of the banks amounted to s£2,322 million in 1973, of which 77% was devoted to commerce, 12% to agriculture, and 7% to industry.

A decree promulgated in August 1970 raised the capital of the Agricultural Bank from s£100 million to s£150 million, entirely subscribed by the government. The increased capitalization and financing made available to the Bank is intended to promote agricultural production. In addition to short-term loans for crop financing, the bank makes loans of up to 5 years for financing livestock and machinery and up to 10 years for financing construction and irrigation projects. Other steps were taken in 1970 to encourage private savings and limit monetary and credit expansion, such as the elimination of tax on interest paid on deposits held for more than six months and an increase in bank lending rates.

33 INSURANCE

All insurance in Syria is controlled by the government-owned Syrian Insurance Co., founded in 1961; it has 13 offices and branches throughout the country. Motor vehicle insurance is compulsory, and a 1974 law exempts life policies of all taxes and stamp duties. In 1974, the total net premium income was s£62,780,337, a 60% increase over 1973.

³⁴SECURITIES

In the past, opportunities for investment were few. The government, however, has recently passed laws requiring companies to offer shares to the public and enacted measures to stimulate private investment in Syria. Capitalization increased from s£800 million in 1970 to s£2,400 million in 1974, of which s£400 million was private capital.

³⁵PUBLIC FINANCE

Syria maintains an ordinary budget and a development budget. In 1975, total budgeted expenditures were s£10,445,578,000, of which s£4,594,835,000 was for ordinary expenditures and s£5,850,743,000 for development expenditures. The following is a summary of consolidated budget estimates for 1974 and 1975 (in millions of Syrian pounds):

	1974	1975
REVENUES		
Taxes on income and production	397.8	444.5
Taxes on expenditure and consumption	571.8	670.8
Revenues from petroleum pipelines	608.0	575.0
Tax on wealth and capital	31.5	36.0
Other tax revenues and fees	131.0	149.7
Surpluses of government enterprises	1,682.0	3,153.0
Other receipts	3,554.0	5,416.6
TOTALS	6,976.1	10,445.6
EXPENDITURES		
National security	2,060.9	2,639.8
Industry and mining	1,583.5	2,546.4
Transportation and public works	754.8	907.3
Agriculture and land reclamation	726.3	1,254.0
Culture and information	607.6	880.9
Other expenditures	1,243.0	2,217.2
TOTALS	6,976.1	10,445.6

Syria's government expenditures are heavily subsidized by its wealthier Arab states.

³⁶TAXATION

Tax revenues are low relative to the GDP and in 1975 accounted for only 18% of total government revenue. Relatively low salaries have kept the tax base narrow, and price controls have restricted the taxable profits from industry. Of total tax revenues in 1975, taxes on income and production accounted for 23.7%, taxes on expenditure and consumption for 35.8%, and other tax revenues (in which the Syrian budget includes revenues from oil pipelines) 40.5%.

³⁷CUSTOMS AND DUTIES

Syria has a single-column tariff modified by trade agreements with other Arab countries and multilateral trade and transit agreements among the Arab League states. There are bilateral agreements with Lebanon, Iraq, Jordan, Sa´udi Arabia, Egypt, Libya, Kuwayt, and the Sudan under which these countries are granted preferential duties on certain products. Multilateral agreements provide for duty-free entry for certain agricultural, animal, and natural resources traded among the signatories and for a 25% reduction on certain manufactured products.

The amount of import duty charged varies widely with the product. Most items are dutiable on an ad valorem basis.

In the past, government policy was based on the protection of domestic production, on the foreign exchange situation, and to a lesser extent on the need for revenue. More recently, import restrictions have been relaxed to stimulate trade.

³⁸FOREIGN INVESTMENTS

The government's attitude to foreign investments is influenced by the priority given to public ownership of the principal means of production. Large companies are required to offer a majority of their shares to the public and to their employees. A 1952 decree required all firms acting as agents for foreign firms to be wholly owned by Syrian nationals. However, in 1969-71, the government issued a series of decrees to relax some restrictions on foreign investment, especially by Arab capital.

³⁹ECONOMIC POLICY

The transformation of Syria's economy began with the Agrarian Reform Law in 1958, which called for the expropriation of large tracts of land. During the union with Egypt, laws were passed for the nationalization of banks, insurance companies, and large industrial firms. After the Ba´th Party came to power in 1963, the socialist trend reasserted itself with greater force. A series of laws created a new banking system and instituted public ownership of all large industries. These were followed by laws setting limits to an individual's share in any joint-stock company and bringing the export-import trade under control. In 1970, Syria had a mixed economy, with an expanding public sector accounting for about 60% of the gross domestic capital and 85% of foreign trade.

By the early 1970s, however, the government had relaxed many restrictions on trade, foreign investment, and private-sector activity, in an effort to attract private and foreign, especially Arab, contributions to Syria's economic growth. A decree enacted on 29 December 1969 prohibited expropriation of Arab property without special legislation and immediate and equitable indemnity. An order issued on 7 March 1974 allowed foreign money in bank notes to be brought in or out of the country without restriction. In February 1973, a program of action presented to the People's Council called for specific delimitation of the sphere of activity open to private capital and increased efforts to promote investor confidence for operation within that sphere.

During 1973, 993 industrial projects were authorized within the private sector, with a capitalization of s£128 million, and private-sector foreign commerce accounted for 32% of the total volume.

The government's third five-year plan (1971–75) envisioned an 8% annual growth rate and an expenditure of s£8,120 million, of which 22.7% was targeted for industry and mining, 17.6% for energy, 12% for internal trade, 7.4% for public services, 6.3% for communications and transportation, 6.3% for agriculture; another 19% was allocated for a single project, construction of the Euphrates Dam. The first stage of the dam, financed by a $150-million Soviet loan, was completed in 1973.

The five-year plan for 1976–80 calls for an overall 80% growth in GNP, with an 89% growth in industry. The plan emphasizes development of the oil, phosphates, and iron and steel industries and the modernization of agricultural methods.

⁴⁰HEALTH

From 50% to 90% of the Syrian villagers examined in the latter part of World War II were found to have malaria, but since then the disease has been virtually eliminated, with the aid of WHO. Intestinal and other diseases associated with poor living conditions are still common, however. In 1972, the infant mortality rate was estimated at 21.7 per 1,000 live births. The average life expectancy in 1975 was estimated at 58.3 years for females and 54.8 years for males. In 1947, Syria had only 37 hospitals, with a total of 1,834 beds. By 1973, the number of hospitals had increased to 94, with 6,678 beds, or 1 bed per 1,087 inhabitants. In 1974 there were 2,666 physicians (1 for every 2,723 persons), 682 dentists, 3,102 nurses, 1,116 midwives, and 1,096 pharmacists. In 1974, the government maintained mobile hospital units, modern laboratories, X-ray centers, 287 sanatoriums and dispensaries, and 5 child welfare stations.

⁴¹SOCIAL WELFARE

The Ministry for Social and Labor Affairs was formed in 1956 to protect the interests of the working population, provide hygienic housing conditions for workers, and support philanthropic endeavors. A system of social insurance, introduced in August

1959, provides old age pensions and disability and death benefits. A total of 358,199 employees were covered by social security programs in 1974.

⁴²HOUSING
In 1970 there were 1,061,839 households (461,179 urban) with an average of 5.9 persons per household. In 1973, 16,439 residential dwellings were constructed, along with 6,583 commercial or industrial structures.

⁴³EDUCATION
Elementary schooling is now free and compulsory, but less than 50% of the population is literate. The school program starts with a five-year primary course, after which the student may obtain an elementary school certificate.

In 1973 there were 6,446 primary schools, with an enrollment of 1,102,652, and 967 secondary schools, with an enrollment of 388,473. The Syrian University in Damascus, founded in 1924, has 12 faculties; it had 36,535 students in 1972/73. The University of Aleppo, founded in 1961, had an enrollment of 11,172 in 1972/73. In 1973 there were 53 vocational technical schools with an enrollment of 15,922 (compared to 5,764 in 1967). There are also conservatories of music in Damascus and Aleppo and institutes for commerce, agriculture, and engineering.

In 1974, workers' education centers gave 167 courses and had 6,275 trainees.

⁴⁴LIBRARIES AND MUSEUMS
Al-Zahiriyah, founded in 1880, is the national library in Damascus and is an adjunct of the Arab Academy. It has about 68,000 volumes and is well known for rare books and manuscripts. There are three other national libraries, located in Aleppo, Homs, and Latakia. The library of the Syrian University in Damascus has 103,000 volumes. In 1971 there were 37 public libraries in Syria.

The most important museum is the National Museum in Damascus, founded in 1919. It contains ancient Oriental, Greek, Roman, Byzantine, and Islamic collections, and houses the Directorate-General of Antiquities, established in 1947, which supervises excavations and conserves antiquities under the Antiquities Law. There is a small museum in Aleppo, a museum attached to the Arab Academy of Damascus, and an archaeological museum at Palmyra.

⁴⁵ORGANIZATIONS
Syria has chambers of commerce, industry, and agriculture. The most prominent organizations are the Arab Academy and the Arab Club, both in Damascus. The Arab Academy, an ancient foundation devoted to literary and scholarly pursuits, maintains a large library. The Arab Club, founded just before World War I, was a center of Arab nationalism in the period of the Ottoman Empire. The General Women's Foundation was established in 1967 as one of several "popular organizations" through which the Ba'th Party has tried to mobilize popular energies and consolidate its control. The other popular organizations are the General Union of Peasants, the General Federation of Trade Unions, the General Union of Students, and the Revolutionary Youth Organization.

The cooperative movement is well developed. In 1974 there were 172 consumer cooperatives, with 117,838 members; 239 building cooperatives, with 79,435 members; and 177 professional cooperatives, with 31,437 members.

⁴⁶PRESS
In 1972 there were 5 daily newspapers and 12 nondailies. Each of the larger cities has its own daily newspapers. Principal papers in Arabic (with 1974 circulations) include *Al-Ba'th* (20,000) and *Al-Thawrah* (15,000), in Damascus; *Al-Jamahir* (15,000), in Aleppo; and *Al-Quruba* (8,000), in Homs. Newspapers are subject to government supervision.

⁴⁷TOURISM
Passports and visas are required. Group visas are also available. However, transit passengers by ship or plane need no visas. Exit visas are required only if the stay extends beyond six months. In 1974, 921,854 tourists spent 1,076,215 nights in Syria. Tourists included 304,127 Lebanese, 172,910 Jordanians, and 66,573 Iraqis. The principal non-Arab tourists were 116,360 Turks, 11,137 French, and 10,855 Iranians. In 1973 there were 588 hotels, with 8,704 rooms and 20,085 beds.

Syria has many famous tourist sights, such as the Krak des Chevaliers, a Crusaders' castle; Ras Shamrah, site of the ancient city of Ugarit; al-Risafa, with its early Christian monuments and a Muslim palace; and the ancient town of Dura Europos. Palmyra, the capital of Queen Zenobia, is a fairly well-preserved ruin of an Arabo-Hellenic city. The Ummayad Mosque and the adjacent Cathedral of St. John the Baptist, in Damascus, are also popular. Syria draws sizable income from tourism, which is expected to grow substantially in the future. Receipts from tourism were s£250 million in 1974.

⁴⁸FAMOUS SYRIANS
Among famous Syrians of an earlier period are the philosopher al-Farabi (Muhammad bin Muhammad bin Tarkhan abu Nasr al-Farabi, 872–950), considered by the Arab world as second only to Aristotle; the poet al-Mutanabbi (Abu al-Tayyib Ahmad bin al-Husayn al-Mutanabbi, 915–65); the mystic-philosopher Shihab al-din al-Suhrawardi (d.1191); and the theologian-philosopher Taqi al-Din Ahmad bin Taymiyah (1263–1328), from whom the Wahhabi and other modern movements in Islam have drawn inspiration. The modern poet Asad Rustrum, who ranks high among more recent writers, emigrated to the US and later wrote poetry with equal facility in both English and Arabic.

Of the Umayyad caliphs, Umar bin Abd-ad-Aziz (r.717–720) is still revered as a restorer of true Islam. In a later era, Nur al-Din (Nureddin, 1118–74), ruler of Aleppo, annexed Damascus, and brought Egypt under his control. By unifying Muslim forces against the Crusaders, he made possible the victories of the renowned Salah al-Din (Saladin, 1138–93), sultan of both Syria and Egypt, whose tomb is in Damascus.

Hafiz al-Asad (b.1928) has been president of Syria since 1970.

⁴⁹DEPENDENCIES
Syria has no territories or colonies.

⁵⁰BIBLIOGRAPHY
Altounyan, Taqui. *In Aleppo Once*. London: J. Murray, 1969.

Antonius, George. *The Arab Awakening: The Story of the Arab National Movement*. London: Hamilton, 1946.

Asfour, Edmund Y. *Syria: Development and Monetary Policy*. Cambridge: Harvard University Press, 1959.

Bliss, Frederick J. *Religions of Modern Syria and Palestine*. New York: AMS Press, 1912.

Castle, Wilfred Thomas Frogatt. *Syrian Pageant: The History of Syria and Palestine, 1000 B.C. to A.D. 1945. A Background to Religion, Politics and Literature*. London: Hutchinson, 1948.

Charles, Henri. *La Sédentarisation entre Euphrate et Balik*. Beirut, 1942.

Copeland, Paul W. *Land and the People of Syria*. Philadelphia: Lippincott, 1964.

Edde, Jacques. *Géographie du Liban et de la Syrie*. Beirut: Imprimerie Catholique, 1941.

Farra, Adnan. *L'Industrialisation en Syrie*. Geneva: Grivet, 1950.

Fedden, Henry Romilly. *Syria: An Historical Appreciation*. London: Hale, 1955.

Fisher, Sydney Nettleton (ed.). *Social Forces in the Middle East*. Ithaca, N.Y.: Cornell University Press, 1966.

Fisher, William Bayne. *The Middle East: A Physical, Social and Regional Geography*. London: Methuen, 1950.

Grant, Christina Phelps. *The Syrian Desert: Caravans, Travel and Exploration*. London: Black, 1937.

Haddad, George Meri. *Fifty Years of Modern Syria and Lebanon*. New York: Hafner, 1951.

Haddad, Robert M. *Syrian Christians in a Muslim Society*. Princeton, N.J.: Princeton University Press, 1970.

Helbaouri, Youssef. *La Syrie (Syria)*. Paris: Librairie de droit et de jurisprudence, 1956.

Hitti, Philip Khuri. *History of Syria, including Lebanon and Palestine*. London: Macmillan, 1957.

IBRD. *The Economic Development of Syria*. Baltimore: Johns Hopkins Press, 1955.

Jirku, Anton. *World of the Bible*. New York: World, 1968.

Kenyon, Kathleen M. *Amorites and Canaanites*. New York: Oxford University Press, 1966.

Kirk, George Edward. *The Middle East in the War*. London: Oxford University Press, 1952.

Kirk, George Edward. *The Middle East, 1945-50*. London: Oxford University Press, 1954.

Kupper, J. R. *Northern Mesopotamia and Syria*. New York: Cambridge University Press.

Lamens, Henri. *La Syrie: précis historique*. Beirut: Imprimerie Catholique, 1921.

Latron, André. *La Vie rurale en Syrie et au Liban*. Paris: Leroux, 1937.

Longrigg, Stephen Hemsley. *Syria and Lebanon under French Mandate*. New York: Oxford University Press, 1958.

Ma'oz, Moshe. *Ottoman Reform in Syria and Palestine 1840-61*. New York: Oxford University Press, 1968.

Nelson, Nina. *Your Guide to Syria*. New York: International Publications Service, 1966.

Patai, Raphael (ed.). *The Republic of Syria*. New Haven, Conn.: HRAF Press, 1956.

Poliak, A. N. *Feudalism in Egypt, Syria, Palestine, and the Lebanon, 1250-1900*. London: Luzac, 1939.

Rabinovich, Itamar. *Syria under the Ba'th, 1963-66*. Jerusalem: Israel University Press, 1972.

Sanjian, Avedis K. *Armenian Communities in Syria under Ottoman Dominion*. Cambridge: Harvard University Press, 1965.

Seale, Patrick. *Struggle for Syria: A Study of Post-War Arab Politics, 1945-1958*. New York: Oxford University Press, 1965.

Seltzer, Carl. *Racial Characteristics of Syrians and Armenians*. New York: Kraus, 1936.

Shair, Khaled A. *Planning for a Middle Eastern Economy: Model for Syria*. New York: Barnes & Noble, 1965.

Syria: Geography and History. Damascus: Directorate-General of Information, 1955.

Thoumin, Richard Lodois. *Géographie humaine de la Syrie centrale*. Paris: Leroux, 1936.

Tibawi, A. L. *A Modern History of Syria: Including Lebanon and Palestine*. New York: St. Martin's Press, 1969.

Torrey, Gordon H. *Syrian Politics and the Military, 1945-1958*. Columbus: Ohio State University Press, 1964.

Warriner, Doreen. *Land Reform and Development in the Middle East: A Study of Egypt, Syria, and Iraq*. New York: Oxford University Press, 1962.

Weulersse, Jacques. *Le Pays des Alaouites*. Tours: Arrault, 1940.

Weulersse, Jacques. *Paysans de Syrie et du Proche-Orient*. Paris: Gallimard, 1946.

Ziadeh, Nicola Abdo. *Syria and Lebanon*. New York: Praeger, 1957.

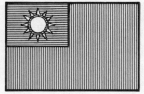

TAIWAN

Republic of China
Chung Hwa Min Kuo

CAPITAL: Taipei. **FLAG**: The flag is red with a twelve-pointed white sun on the blue upper left quadrant. The twelve points of the sun represent the 12 two-hour periods of the day in traditional Chinese horology and symbolize progress. The colors red, white, and blue represent the Three People's Principles (San Min Chu I) of Dr. Sun Yat-sen, father of the Republic of China, and symbolize the spirit of liberty, fraternity, and equality. **ANTHEM**: *Chung Hwa Min Kuo Kuo Ke (Chinese National Anthem)*. **MONETARY UNIT**: The new Taiwan dollar (NT$) of 100 cents is a nonconvertible paper currency. There are coins of 10, 20, and 50 cents, and notes of 1, 5, 10, and 50 new Taiwan dollars. NT$1 = US$0.0263(or US$1 = NT$38). **WEIGHTS AND MEASURES**: The metric system is employed in government and industrial statistics. Commonly used standards of weights and measures are the catty (1.10 lb or 0.4989 kg), the li (0.31 mile or 0.5 km), the shih chih (1.09 ft or 0.33 meter), and the chia (2.39 acres or 0.97 hectare). **HOLIDAYS**: New Year's Day and the Founding of the Republic of China (1912), 1 January; Youth Day (formerly known as Martyrs' Day), 29 March; Tomb-Sweeping Day, 5 April; Birthday of Confucius and Teachers' Day, 28 September; National Day (Double Tenth Day), 10 October; Taiwan Retrocession Day, 25 October; Dr. Sun Yat-sen's Birthday, 12 November; Constitution Day, 25 December. **TIME**: 8 P.M. = noon GMT.

¹LOCATION, SIZE, AND EXTENT

Taiwan lies in the western Pacific Ocean astride the Tropic of Cancer. To the NE, Okinawa lies 644 km (400 mi) away; to the E is the Pacific Ocean; the Philippine island of Luzon is 370 km (230 mi) to the S; to the W, the Taiwan (Formosa) Strait separates the island from the China coast by less than 161 km (100 mi) of water at the closest point. Taiwan has a coastline of *869 km (540 mi)*.

Besides the island proper, Taiwan comprises 13 islands in the Taiwan group and 63 islands in the Penghu group; the latter are also known as the Pescadores. The total area of Taiwan and all its outlying islands is 36,153 sq km (13,959 sq mi). Leaf-shaped Taiwan island extends *381 km (237 mi)* NNE–SSW and *139 km (86 mi)* ESE–WNW, with an area of 35,760 sq km (13,807 sq mi); the 13 other islands in the Taiwan group comprise an area of 74.8 sq km (28.9 sq mi). The Penghu group, lying 40 km (25 mi) west of Taiwan, has a total area of 127 sq km (49 sq mi).

Also under the control of the Republic of China are the Quemoy (Kinmen) and Matsu islands just off Fukien Province of the China mainland. Quemoy is the biggest of a group of six islands, two of which are occupied by the People's Republic of China. The main island is situated in Amoy Bay at 118° 23′E and 24°27′N and has a total area of 161.6 sq km (62.4 sq mi). The six islands of the Matsu group are located at 56′E and 26°9′N and have a total area of 29.2 sq km (11.3 sq mi).

²TOPOGRAPHY

Taiwan perches on the margin of the continental shelf. Along the west coast the sea is rather shallow, averaging 300 feet and not exceeding 700 feet at the deepest point; however, it deepens abruptly along the east coast, dropping to a depth of 13,000 feet only 31 miles offshore. The terrain is precipitous on the east coast, with practically no natural harbor except Suao Bay in the north. The west coast is marked by wide tidal flats where oceangoing vessels can approach the land only at a few river mouths, which are often choked with sandbars. Kaohsiung, the southern port, is situated in a long lagoon called Haochiung Bay. The north coast with its many inlets provides Taiwan with its best harbor, Keelung.

About two-thirds of the island is composed of rugged foothill ranges and massive mountain chains. Only about 35% of the land is less than 100 meters (328 feet) high. The mountains, towering along the eastern coast, run roughly from northeast to southwest. A low, flat coastal plain, extending from north to south, occupies the western third. Yu Shan, with an elevation of 13,114 feet, is the highest peak on the island. During the 20th century there have been more than 15,000 perceptible earthquakes, but most have been weak and sectional.

All the rivers originate in the mountains in the central part of the island. They have short courses and rapid streams. The longest river, Choshui, located in the western plain, is only 114 miles long. Tanshui, which flows past Taipei in the north, is the only navigable river in Taiwan.

³CLIMATE

Taiwan enjoys an oceanic, subtropical monsoon climate. The warm and humid summer lasts from May until September, the mild winter from December until February. The average lowland temperature in January is 15.6°C (60°F) in the north and 20°C (68°F) in the south; the average July temperature is 28°C (82.4°F) in the north and 27.6°C (81.7°F) in the south. The growing season lasts throughout the year, except on mountains above 4,000 feet in elevation where frost and snow occasionally occur.

The average rainfall is 101 inches, ranging from 50 inches at the middle of the western coast to 250 inches and more on exposed mountain slopes. Southwest monsoon winds blow from May through September and northeast monsoon winds from October to March. Only the extreme southwest has a distinct dry season. As a result of the tropical cyclonic storms that sweep out of the western Pacific, typhoons occur between June and October.

⁴FLORA AND FAUNA

The flora is closely related to that of South China and the Philippines. Taiwan has almost 190 plant families, about 1,180 genera, and more than 3,800 species, of which indigenous members constitute about one-third of the total flora. Mangrove forest is found in tidal flats and coastal bays. From sea level to a height of 2,000 meters is the zone of broad-leaved evergreen tropical and subtropical forest, where ficua, pandanus, palms, teak, bamboos, and camphors are commonly found. The mixed forest of broad-leaved deciduous trees and conifers occupies the next zone, extending from a height of 2,000 to 3,000 meters. Pines, cypresses, firs, and rhododendrons are grown in this region. Above 3,000 meters is the zone of coniferous forests, composed mainly of firs, spruce, juniper, and hemlock.

The mammals so far discovered number more than 60, 45 species of which appear to be indigenous to the island. The largest beast of prey is the Formosan black bear. Foxes, flying foxes, deer, wild boar, bats, squirrels, macaques, and pangolins are some of the mammals seen on the island. There are more than 330 species and subspecies of birds, of which 33 are common to the island, China, and the Philippines, and about 87 belong to peculiar forms. More than 65 species of reptiles and amphibians inhabit the island. There is an abundance of snakes, of which 13 species are poisonous. The insect life is extremely rich and varied. As of 1975, endangered species in Taiwan included the Formosan clouded leopard, dugong, and Formosan sika.

5 POPULATION

By the end of 1974, Taiwan had an estimated population of 15,852,200. The population density, among the world's highest, was 436 per sq km in 1974. The average annual rate of growth declined from 3.7% in 1952 to 2.7% in 1966 and 1.9% in 1974; 63.8% of the population is aged 15 or over. Taipei (T'ai-Pei), the capital and principal city, had an estimated population of 2,003,604 at the end of 1974. Other large cities are Kaohsiung (972,828), Taichung (527,399), Tainan (512,734), and Keelung (340,692).

6 ETHNIC GROUPS

The term "Taiwanese" is often used when referring to those Chinese who are natives of the island as distinct from those who migrated from the mainland after the end of World War II. Most Taiwanese are descendants of earlier immigrants from Fukien and Kwangtung provinces in South China. They form several distinct groups. More than 1 million Hakka are descendants of refugees and exiles from Kwangtung Province who came to Taiwan before the 19th century; they are farmers and woodsmen who occupy the frontiers of settlement. About 5 million Fukiens are descendants of peasants from Fukien Province who migrated to Taiwan in the 18th and 19th centuries; they form the bulk of the agricultural population. The native Taiwan population in 1944 was estimated to be 6.6 million. The influx of mainlanders to the island following the evacuation of the central government to Taiwan brought the mainland Chinese population on Taiwan to about 2 million. The mainlanders come from various provinces of China and are composed primarily of government employees, professionals, and technical personnel.

About 265,000 aborigines, primarily of Indonesian origin, live in the central and eastern mountains. They are divided into seven major tribes, with the Ami, Tyal, and Paiwan accounting for about 85%; the balance is distributed among the Bunnu, Saiset, Tsowu, and Yami. The aborigines generally have short stature, light brown skin, and straight black hair. Their language and customs suggest a close resemblance to the Malays. The assimilated aborigines are called Pepohuan.

7 LANGUAGE

Mainland Chinese in Taiwan generally speak Mandarin and a mixture of regional dialects. Taiwanese speak a variety of southern Chinese dialects, including Amoy, Swatow, and Hakka. Mandarin (Peking dialect) is the official language and is used in administration, jurisprudence, education, and, to a large extent, in commerce; it has come into increasingly common use during the last three decades. As a result of 50 years of Japanese rule, most Taiwanese and aborigines over 45 speak or understand Japanese. The tribesmen speak dialects of the Malay-Polynesian family. They do not have written scripts.

8 RELIGION

The Chinese are traditionally eclectic in their religious beliefs. The Taiwan folk religion is a fluid mixture of ancestor-worship, animism, Buddhism, and Taoism. Natural phenomena have been deified, and ancestors, sages, virtuous women, and historical personalities have been given the status of gods.

The first Westerners to bring Christianity to Taiwan were the Dutch (1624). However, a great persecution of Christians took place when the island was lost to Cheng Ch'eng-kung in 1662. Christianity made another beginning in 1860, when a missionary from Scotland came to the island. The English Presbyterian Mission started its work in the southern part of Taiwan about 100 years ago. Since the end of World War II, more than 80 Protestant denominations have been established on the island, and the activities of Christian missions, many coming over from the mainland, have become widespread. As of 1974, Christians totaled more than 605,000, nearly half of whom were Roman Catholics. Muslims number about 42,500.

9 TRANSPORTATION

The Taiwan Railway Administration operates two rail lines, totaling 1,000.4 km of track. Its trunk line of 408.5 km, linking Keelung, the main port in the north, with Kaohsiung in the south, connects major industrial centers and key cities. The other line connects Hualien and Taitung, on the Pacific coast. The 82-km North Link line, which will connect up with a previously isolated eastern line, is expected to be completed by 1978.

Taiwan has about 16,121 km of highways, of which 8,335 km are paved. By the end of 1973 there were 365,123 motor vehicles. As of mid-1975, Taiwan had invested more than $5 billion in public construction, most of which was in transportation projects. Top priority has been given to the 377-km limited-access toll road between the major port cities of Keelung and Kaohsiung on the west coast.

Shipping is the chief means of transportation between the coasts. Keelung in the north and Kaohsiung on the southwest coast are the island's two most important natural harbors. A new port on the east coast at Hualien has become Taiwan's third international harbor, and a fourth is being built in Taitung.

Taiwan's international main airport is situated at Sungshan, a suburb of Taipei. A second international airport has been added at Kaohsiung, and a third at Taoyuan (29 km south of Taipei) is expected eventually to replace the facility at Sungshan. The airfields at Tainan, Makung, and Pingtung are designated as supplementary airports for emergency landings. A domestic airline, the China Airlines, operates between Taipei and Hualien, Kaohsiung, Taichung, Tainan, and Makung and engages in international flights to Manila, Bangkok, Tokyo (resumed in October 1975), Hong Kong, Seoul, and the US. Foreign carriers operating in Taiwan include Japan Asia Airways (a subsidiary of JAL, whose Taiwan service was suspended during 1974–75), Northwest Orient Airlines, National Thai Airways, Korean National Airlines, Cathay Pacific Airways, and Philippine Airlines.

10 COMMUNICATIONS

Telecommunication services are owned by the government. By the end of 1974 there were more than 598,504 telephone subscribers in Taiwan, as compared with 88,209 in 1964. Some 93% of telephone service is automatic. Taipei earth-satellite stations were inaugurated for the Pacific region in 1969 and the Indian region in 1974. The postal service is managed by the Directorate General of Posts under the Ministry of Communications.

Radio broadcasting stations in Taiwan are under the supervision of the Ministry of Communications. By the end of 1974 there were 110 broadcasting stations. The largest network is the Broadcasting Corporation of China, which was founded in 1938 and was moved to Taipei in 1949. It operates three systems: overseas service, known as the Voice of Free China; the mainland service, known as the Central Broadcasting Station, aimed at the Chinese mainland; and the domestic service. These stations broadcast in some 17 languages and dialects. There are two other large networks: Armed Forces Radio Network and the Cheng Sheng

Broadcasting Co. At the end of 1974 there were 3.5 million radios. Television was introduced in 1962; the number of television sets in mid-1975 totaled 2.5 million.

11 HISTORY

Although Taiwan can be seen on a clear day from the China mainland, ancient Chinese chronicles contain few references to the island. Historians surmised from the brief information available in the early dynastic histories that Chinese emigration to Taiwan had begun as early as the T'ang dynasty (618–907). During the reign of Kublai Khan (1263–94), the first civil administration was established in the neighboring Pescadores. Taiwan itself, however, remained outside the jurisdiction of the Mongol Empire. During the Ming dynasty (1368–1644), Japanese pirates and Chinese outlaws and refugees wrested the coastal areas from the native tribes. The Chinese settled in the southwest region while the Japanese occupied the northern tip of the island.

In 1517, the Portuguese sighted the island and named it Ilha Formosa (Beautiful Island). The Dutch, who were disputing the monopoly of Far Eastern trade held by the Portuguese, captured the Pescadores in 1622 and used them as a base for harassing commerce between China, Japan, and the Philippines. Two years later, the Chinese offered the Dutch a treaty that gave them certain commercial privileges if they withdrew from the Pescadores, and occupied instead a trading post on Taiwan. The Dutch complied by building Fort Zeelandia and Fort Providentia in the southwestern part of the island. As a countermove, the Spaniards seized the northern part of Keelung in 1626, and later extended their domain to nearby Tanshui. The Japanese, constrained by the policy of national seclusion adopted by the Tokugawa Shogunate, withdrew voluntarily in 1628. The Dutch captured the Spanish settlement in 1642 and, after putting down a Chinese uprising in 1656 with the aid of the aborigines, gained complete control of the island.

While the Dutch were consolidating their hold on Taiwan, the Ming dynasty on the China mainland was being overthrown by the Manchus, who established the Ch'ing dynasty (1644–1912). Remnants of the Ming forces, led by Cheng Ch'eng-kung, son of a Chinese pirate and a Japanese mother, decided to establish an overseas base in Taiwan. They landed on the island in 1661 and ousted the Dutch in the following year. It was not until 1682 that the Manchus succeeded in wresting Taiwan from Cheng Ch'eng-kung's successors.

From 1683 to 1886, Taiwan was administered as a part of Fukien Province. During this period, Chinese colonization proceeded steadily as the aborigines were either assimilated into the Chinese population or pushed back into the mountains. The imperial government, however, paid scant attention to the island administration. As a result, official corruption and inefficiency often provoked armed rebellions. In the latter part of the 19th century, the strategic importance of Taiwan for the defense of the South China coast was recognized by the authorities, particularly after the French bombardment and blockade of the island in 1884 during the Sino-French War over Annam. The local administration was reorganized, and the island was made into a separate province in 1886.

Upon the conclusion of the Sino-Japanese War in 1895, Taiwan was ceded to Japan. Refusing to submit to Japanese rule, the islanders declared their independence and established a republic. Although organized resistance against the Japanese lasted only a few months, political uprisings against the occupation authorities continued for decades by Chinese and aborigines. Under the Japanese, the island's agricultural resources were developed rapidly to supply the needs of the home islands. Transportation was modernized. A policy of Japanization of the Taiwan population was adopted. During World War II, a beginning was made for the industrialization of the island in support of the Japanese southward expansion.

Allied bombings, however, had destroyed much of the industrial undertakings by the end of the war.

In accordance with the Cairo Declaration of 1943 and the Potsdam Proclamation of 1945, Taiwan was restored to China in September 1945. The malpractices of the Chinese officials, however, aroused the resentment of the local population. In February 1947, a police incident touched off a popular revolt, which was suppressed with bloodshed. The central government intervened by removing the governor and instituting a series of administrative reforms. On 8 December 1949, as the Chinese Communists were sweeping the Nationalist armies off the mainland, the government of the Republic of China was officially transferred to Taiwan.

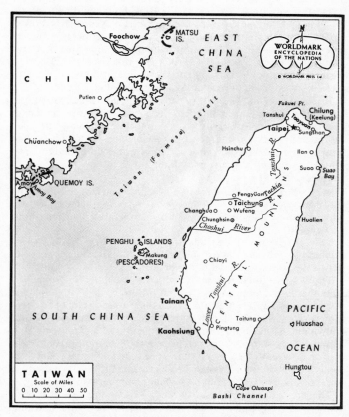

See continental political: front cover R7; physical: back cover Q7

LOCATION: 21°45'25" to 25°38'53"N; 119°18'3" to 122°6'25"E.
TERRITORIAL SEA LIMIT: 3 mi.

In 1951, Japan, in signing the San Francisco Peace Treaty, formally renounced its claim to the island of Taiwan. A Sino-Japanese Peace Treaty was concluded in Taipei the following year. Neither treaty specifically provided for the ceding of Taiwan to China. As a result, although the Republic of China is in effective occupation of the island, the island's legal status is still open to various and conflicting interpretations.

The question of which China—the People's Republic of China on the Chinese mainland or the Republic of China in Taiwan—should occupy China's seat at the United Nations was debated by the UN General Assembly for more than two decades, beginning in 1950. Support for Taiwan's representation gradually eroded over the years, and on 25 November 1971 the UN General Assembly voted 75–36 (with 17 abstentions) to expel the Republic of China (ROC-Taiwan) and seat the People's Republic of China (PRC). In a significant policy reversal, the US voted with the majority to seat the Peking government. Although maintaining full diplomatic ties with Taiwan, the US took the occasion of President Nixon's visit to China to acknowledge in what became known as the Shanghai communiqué of February 1972 that "all Chinese on either side of the Taiwan Strait maintain there is but one China and that Taiwan is part of China. The United States government does not challenge that position." The US thus formally abandoned its tacit "two Chinas" policy and, as a further concession to the PRC government, announced its intention ultimately to withdraw all US forces and military installations from Taiwan. Nonetheless, the 1954 US-ROC Mutual Defense Treaty, as well as massive economic ties between the two countries, remained in force. By 1975, most nations had shifted recognition from the ROC to the PRC and the number maintaining diplomatic ties with the ROC had dwindled to about 30. Among Asian nations only the Republic of Korea (ROK) continued to maintain an embassy in Taipei. Nonetheless, Taiwan successfully warded off isolation by maintaining a host of active contacts at other levels. By early 1975, relations with Japan, a critical economic contact, had improved measurably.

On 5 April 1975, President Chiang Kai-shek, leader of the ROC for nearly half a century, died at age 87. On 28 April, the leadership of the Nationalist Party (Kuomintang) and, hence, of the government, passed to Chiang's son, Chiang Ching-kuo, who had been in effective charge of the government since illness had incapacitated his father in 1972. Former vice-president Yen Chia-kan succeeded to the presidency.

12 GOVERNMENT

The constitution of the Republic of China was drafted by a constitutional convention at Nanking on 15 November 1946; it was adopted on 25 December 1946 and promulgated by the national government on 1 January 1947.

The government derives its powers from the National Assembly, which, according to the constitution, exercises political powers on behalf of the people.

The first National Assembly, which was elected in November 1947, had 2,961 delegates, selected on the basis of regional and occupational representations. It has the power to elect and recall the president and the vice-president, amend the constitution, and approve constitutional amendments proposed by the legislative council (Legislative Yuan). The number of delegates to the National Assembly has been sharply reduced over the years since some members did not reach Taiwan, while others have died. As of December 1974, National Assembly members totaled 1,349.

The president is the head of state. His tenure of office is six years, with eligibility for a second term. The constitutional prohibition against third terms was suspended in March 1960 to permit Chiang Kai-shek to continue in office. He was reelected in 1972 for a fifth six-year term. Chiang was granted special emergency powers in 1948, which were extended in 1954. He was empowered to govern by virtual decree, and some of the civil liberties provided in the constitution have been suspended in the interest of national security. Upon his death in April 1975, Chiang was succeeded as president by Yen Chia-kan, the former vice-president.

A special feature of the government organization is its system of five branches known as yuans (councils or departments). The Legislative Yuan, elected by popular vote, is the highest law-making organization. A 1972 amendment permitted the election of 51 new members to the Legislative Yuan-the last nationwide voting had taken place in 1948. As of March 1975, the body had 438 members (760 in 1948). Because of the impracticability of holding elections on the mainland, many members of the 1948 Legislative Yuan and the Control Yuan have continued to hold their seats.

The Executive Yuan, comparable to the cabinet in other countries, is the highest administrative organ in the government. There are eight ministries, two commissions, and a number of subordinate organs under the Executive Yuan. The premier is appointed by the president with the consent of the Legislative Yuan. The president is empowered to compel the premier to resign by refusing to sign decrees or orders presented by the latter for promulgation. Premier Chiang Ching-kuo, Chiang's son, has been premier and effective head of the government since 1972.

The Judicial Yuan is the highest judicial organ. Its members are nominated by the president and appointed with the consent of the Control Yuan.

The Control Yuan, the highest supervisory organ, exercises censorial power over and may impeach public functionaries. It also supervises the execution of the government budget and reviews the appointment of the president, vice-president, and grand justices of the Judicial Yuan, and the president, vice-president, and members of the Examination Yuan. The constitution provides that the members of the Control Yuan be elected for six-year terms by the provincial and municipal councils, the district councils of Mongolia and Tibet, and overseas Chinese groups. The total maximum membership is 223; the membership as of the end of 1974 was 74.

The Examination Yuan has its roots in the civil service examination system institutionalized in A.D. 132 by the Han emperor Shun. The Examination Yuan examines, appoints, registers, classifies, promotes, transfers, retires, and pensions government personnel. The president, vice-president, and a number of members of the Examination Yuan are appointed by the president of the Republic of China with the consent of the Control Yuan. Their term of office is six years.

13 POLITICAL PARTIES

The Chinese Nationalist Party (Chung-kuo Kuo-min-tang), better known as the Kuomintang (KMT), is the dominant political party in Taiwan. The teachings of Dr. Sun Yat-sen, which stress nationalism, people's rights, and people's livelihood, form the basic political doctrines of the party. After the fall of the mainland to the Communists in 1949, a reform committee was organized to chart a new program for the party. The paramount aim of the KMT has been the recovery of the mainland. It has also advocated encouragement of private enterprise and foreign investments for the economic reconstruction of the country, agrarian and urban land reforms, industrialization, an equitable system of taxation, protection of workers' rights and interests, and the development of local self-government. In February 1975, leadership of the KMT passed from the late Chiang Kai-shek to his son, Chiang Ching-kuo.

Besides the KMT, there are two small parties. The Young China Party (Ch'ing Nien Tang—CNT), founded in 1923, is highly nationalistic in outlook. The CNT has 75 members in the National Assembly, 13 members in the Legislative Yuan, and 4 members in the Control Yuan. The China Democratic Socialist Party (Ming Sheh Tang—MST), established in 1946, advocates political action to make China a democratic socialist country by democratic means. As of December 1974, the MST had 41 members in the National Assembly, 7 members in the Legislative Yuan, and 3 members in the Control Yuan.

14 LOCAL GOVERNMENT

The authority of the central government operating under emergency powers has limited the local autonomy that was granted to local bodies by the constitution. In recent years, however, the elective process has been restored at several levels.

The Taiwan provincial government holds jurisdiction over the main island of Taiwan, 13 smaller islands in adjacent waters, and the 63 islands of the Penghu (Pescadores) group. The provincial capital is located at Taichung. The province is divided into 16 county (hsien) administrative areas and 4 municipalities under the direct jurisdiction of the provincial government. Subdivisions of the county are the township (chen), the rural district or group of villages (hsiang), and the precinct.

The province is headed by a governor who is nominated by the president of the Executive Yuan and appointed by the president of the republic. Department heads and members of the provincial council are recommended by the governor for appointment by the Executive Yuan. The governor is the ex officio chairman of the appointed 21-member Provincial Council, the policy-making body, and holds veto power over its resolutions. The provincial government can issue ordinances and regulations for the administration of the province as long as they do not conflict with laws of the central government.

As of the 1972 elections, the Provincial Assembly was composed of 73 members elected for four-year terms by the people of the province; there is no restriction on reelection. The Assembly meets for two months every six months. Nominally it possesses broad legislative powers; however, its prerogatives are circumscribed by a provision in its organic law that in the event of a disagreement between the provincial government and the Assembly, the former may request a reconsideration. Should the Assembly uphold its original resolution, the provincial government may submit the dispute to the Executive Yuan for final judgment. The Executive Yuan may dissolve the Provincial Assembly and order a new election if it considers the Assembly is acting contrary to national policy.

At the lower level, the county government is headed by a magistrate (hsien-chang) and the municipal government by a mayor (shih-chang). Each county or municipality has a representative body called the hsien or municipal assembly. Further down are the councils and assemblies of townships and rural districts, each headed by a chief officer. All officials are elected by universal suffrage of citizens over age 20.

15 JUDICIAL SYSTEM
The Judicial Yuan interprets the constitution and other laws and decrees, adjudicates administrative suits, and disciplines public functionaries. The president and vice-president of the Judicial Yuan are nominated and appointed by the president with the consent of the Control Yuan. They, together with a number of grand justices, form the Council of Grand Justices, which is charged with the power and responsibility of interpreting the constitution, laws, and ordinances. The tenure of office of a grand justice is nine years. The judicial system is based upon the principle of three trials in three grades of courts: district court, high court, and supreme court. The Supreme Court, the highest tribunal of the land, consists of a number of civil and criminal divisions, each of which is formed by a presiding judge and four associate judges. The judges are appointed for life.

16 ARMED FORCES
Two years' military service is compulsory for all male citizens. The armed forces totaled 494,000 in 1974, a decrease of 56,000 from 1969. Of the 1974 total, the army had 340,000, the navy and marines 72,000, and the air force 82,000. In addition, militia and reserves totaled 305,000 men. The navy had 18 destroyers, 10 frigates, 18 coastal escort ships, and about 80 other craft. The air force had 216 combat aircraft. Taiwan began assembling its first fighter aircraft in late 1974. By the end of 1975, an estimated 2,800 US troops remained stationed on Taiwan, as compared with a peak of 9,000 in 1964-70.

17 MIGRATION
In 1963, the Nationalist government stated that since the completion of the Communist conquest of the mainland in 1949/50, a total of 146,772 Chinese refugees had come to Taiwan for resettlement. The number of refugees has varied from year to year. During 1974, 1,239 overseas Chinese came to settle, the overwhelming majority from elsewhere in Asia.

As of December 1974, the Taiwan government reported that there were 21,463,509 overseas Chinese, including those with dual nationality (20,385,459 in Asia, 794,599 in the Americas, 151,614 in Europe, 65,463 in Africa, and 66,374 in Oceania).

18 INTERNATIONAL COOPERATION
The Republic of China, a charter member of the UN, became the first government to be expelled from that body following a General Assembly vote on 25 November 1971 to seat the PRC as the sole legitimate representative of China. The ROC subsequently lost its membership in most (but not all) UN bodies as well as in several other international organizations—usually with its place taken by the PRC. As of 1976, however, it still belonged to the IBRD, IMF, IDB, and INTELSAT, among others. Taiwan has been extending technical assistance to African, Asian, and Latin American countries since 1961, although only a handful were still accepting aid in the mid-1970s.

US aid to Taiwan in the 1951–73 period was substantial, having totaled about US$1.5 billion. Cooperation between the US and the ROC came under two broad categories: military and economic. Under the Sino-US Mutual Defense Treaty of 1954, the US has committed itself to the defense of Taiwan against Communist aggression. The bulk of direct US military aid was terminated in July 1973, although assistance continues largely in the form of equipment underwriting by means of the US Foreign Military Sales Act. US economic grants were discontinued as of June 1965 by mutual agreement.

19 ECONOMY
Within the span of two decades, the economy of Taiwan has shifted its orientation from agriculture to industry. As of 1974, industry made up 30.9% of the net domestic product (compared with 19.6% in 1963), with agriculture accounting for 16.8% (26.6% in 1963). Taiwan remains, after Japan, the most intensely cultivated country in the world: although only a quarter of the entire land area is arable, nearly all the arable land is cultivated. Except for coal, mineral ores such as sulfur, pyrite, gold, and silver are found in limited quantities.

Under the Japanese, the island was developed as a major source of foodstuffs for Japan. As a result, although the production of rice and sugar increased rapidly, no textile or fertilizer industry was developed. After 1937, some effort was directed toward industrialization. Immediately after the war, the Japanese technicians were repatriated to Japan. Equipment and stocks were sold on the mainland market for quick profits. Agriculture was hampered by the lack of fertilizer. All these factors caused a rapid deterioration of the economy, which was aggravated by the influx of refugees from the mainland.

The situation improved with the removal of the Nationalist government to Taiwan. The arrival of technical and experienced personnel and capital equipment from the mainland facilitated the island's economic rehabilitation. Currency and tax reforms stabilized the monetary situation. The supply of fertilizer from the US and a land reform program aided the revival of agricultural production.

Through the early 1960s, energetic government measures supplemented by US aid resulted in substantial economic progress. In 1963, Taiwan registered its first favorable trade balance, which was further increased in 1964. The government's perennial reliance on US aid for meeting budgetary deficits decreased rapidly from 1957 to 1964, owing to the growth in domestic capital through the nation's rapid industrial expansion and to the increased confidence of overseas investors. By 1965, the economy appeared stable enough to warrant the cessation of US economic aid programs. During the 1963–73 period, the GNP grew by an average annual rate of 10.7% in real terms. Medium and light industry have led the expansion, with striking gains registered in electronics, household goods, and chemicals. During the mid-1970s, the economy showed impressive resiliency in the face of recession, inflation, and continued massive defense spending (about 40% of national government expenditures). The GNP grew by only 0.6% in 1974, but that rate was surpassed only in the Federal Republic of Germany (FRG). For the remainder of the 1970s, planners focused on further strengthening the infrastructure, with a target GNP growth rate of 6% annually.

[20] INCOME

During the last quarter-century, Taiwan's economy has experienced one of the highest growth rates in the world. National income at current prices rose from NT$13,047 million in 1952 to NT$418,300 million in 1974, an increase of 3,206% in 21 years. Net domestic product in 1974 was distributed as follows: industry, 30.9%; agriculture, 16.8%; commerce, 11.5%; construction, 5.5%; transport and communications, 5.1%; and other sectors, 30.2%. Per capita GNP was estimated at US$694 in 1975, as compared with US$697 in 1974 and US$396 in 1972.

[21] LABOR

In 1974, the employed labor force in Taiwan numbered 5,208,000. The share of persons employed in the primary activities of farming, forestry, and fishing has been declining steadily, with the proportion reaching 30% in 1974, as compared with 40% in 1968. Industry's share of the work force has meanwhile been on the rapid increase, although in the mid-1970s manufacturing still held a secondary position. The 1974 distribution of labor was as follows: agriculture, forestry, and fishing, 30%; industry, 26%; services, 15%; commerce, 14%; construction, 6%; transport, storage, and communications, 5%; and other sectors, 4%. As of October 1974, unemployed numbered 123,000 and workers classified as underemployed, 75,000.

Productivity has been improving. The law provides for an 8-hour day (which may be extended to 10 hours) and a six-day regular workweek; overtime is paid at $1\frac{1}{3}$ to $1\frac{2}{3}$ of the regular wage. A minimum of one week's vacation is provided after a year's employment. In 1975, the minimum monthly wage of NT$600 (US$15.78) set in 1968 was still in effect, although a proposal to raise the rate to NT$1,000 was under consideration by the government. In many cases, however, practice diverges from these provisions.

Trade unions are weak and cannot be called unions in the real sense of the term, for the law does not provide for effective collective bargaining and also prohibits strikes, shut-downs, and walkouts of any kind. The trade unions, organized under government supervision, tend to be used for carrying out government policies, but they carry on a considerable amount of welfare work. In 1974 there were 7 national labor organizations, 20 provincial labor organizations, 993 local labor unions, and 91 Taipei municipal labor organizations, with a total membership of 559,874 (compared with 367,885 in 1968).

[22] AGRICULTURE

Before Taiwan's land reform program was launched at the end of 1948, 35% of the land was held by owner-cultivators, 26% by part owners, and 39% by tenants.

The scarcity of land led to exorbitant land rental, which averaged 50% or more of the total yield per annum. The land reform program, which was formulated with the help of the Joint Commission on Rural Reconstruction, provided for the reduction of farm rent to 37.5% of the annual yield of the main crop. Security of tenure is guaranteed by providing that the farm lease shall not be shorter than six years. Public lands were offered for sale to farmers at a price fixed at 250% of the value of the annual main crop, which was to be paid off in annual installments. In 1953, the redistribution of private lands was inaugurated. All tenant-cultivated land exceeding 3 chia (7.19 acres) of medium-grade paddy field or 6 chia of medium-grade dry land was to be purchased by the government for resale to the tenant farmers. The resale price to the tenant farmer was the same as the purchase price plus 4% interest. The amount of land a tenant

farmer might purchase was restricted by the same rule that applied to owner-cultivators. By 1974, 90% of Taiwan's farmers were full landowners.

Although still important as both an export earner and a domestic food source, agriculture has fallen far from the preeminent position it long held in the Taiwan economy. Agriculture now accounts for less than 20% of national income; in 1974, agricultural products and processed agricultural products accounted for 15.5% of exports, as compared with 40% only a few decades earlier. A large segment of the agricultural work force has been drawn away by industry, which expanded by an average annual rate of 13.1% during 1953–74, as compared with a 3.4% growth rate for agriculture. The pressure of population on Taiwan's limited amount of arable land (about one-fourth of the total area) remains a serious impediment to major growth in the sector, which has already achieved high levels of efficiency in most areas.

Rice, the principal food crop, is grown on small farms along the western plain and in the south. In 1974, 2,452,417 tons were produced, a figure comparable to levels in the 1960s. Other food crops and their 1974 production were sweet potatoes, 2,851,385 tons; bananas, 317,380 tons; peanuts, 97,575 tons; soybeans, 67,181 tons; and corn, 109,344 tons.

Sugar (8.9 million tons in 1974), pineapples (293,690 tons), citrus fruits (350,000 tons), tea (24,269 tons), tobacco (17,713 tons), and asparagus (108,296 tons) are plantation-grown and are the principal cash and export crops.

The government's Taiwan Sugar Corporation dominates the sugar industry. Taiwan's world-famous oolong tea is grown in the north. Small amounts of cotton, tobacco, jute, and sisal are produced. Taiwan produces 60% of the world's supply of citronella oil, which is derived from citronella grass. A new but fast-rising industry, mushroom canning, led to the development of mushroom cultivation, a specialty crop well suited to Taiwan since it is labor-intensive and requires little space and small investment; 61,699 tons of mushrooms were produced in 1974.

Mechanization is confined largely to sugarcane, and standard farm tools are old and simple. Generally, Taiwanese agriculture is characterized by irrigation, terracing, multiple cropping, intertillage, and extensive use of fertilizers. Soil fertility is high when fertilizers are used. The government instituted irrigation, flood control, and conservation programs.

Since 1950, the farm population has increased by 50% but the amount of farmland has remained the same. As a result the average size of a farm is now about 2.5 acres; 67% of the farms are less than 2.5 acres and about 38% are less than 1.25 acres. The small-sized farms, together with the lack of cash and high interest rates, have discouraged farmers from buying modern agricultural machinery.

[23] ANIMAL HUSBANDRY

Hog raising is surpassed in importance only by rice and sugarcane in Taiwan's rural economy. In 1974 there were 2,809,000 hogs, 24,977 head of cattle (excluding 13,233 dairy cattle), and 188,176 goats. Chickens and ducks (about 28 million) are raised by most households. The production of beef cattle has been declining steadily in recent years, while poultry, dairy cattle, and goats have been on the increase. In 1974, 797 million chicken and 437 million duck eggs were produced, more than treble the quantities of 1953.

[24] FISHING

Coastal and inshore fishing furnishes more than 50% of the annual catch and serves as a source of income for more than 140,000 fishermen. Bonita, shark, sturgeon, tuna, red snapper, lobster, and shrimp are the main items of the catch. Deep-sea fishing, which in the prewar peak year surpassed all other types of catches, was practically wiped out by the war, and recovery for a time was slow owing to the need for heavy investments in vessels and harbors. Fish culture in ponds has about reached its limit because of limited land that can be used for ponds. In 1974, the total catch was 697,871 tons, about a 50% gain from a decade earlier.

25 FORESTRY
Approximately 64% of the land area is forest land. Of this area, 78% is productive forest while the rest is denuded or otherwise not producing timber. Artificial forests constitute 15.5% of the productive forest area. Of the forests, 34.2% are conifers and 65.8% are broad-leaved species. National forests and other government forest lands constitute 89.7% of the total forest area. The exploitation of the timber resources is limited by the inaccessibility of the forest lands. The total timber reserve is estimated at approximately 230 million cu meters. Production has been declining in recent years. The 1974 production was 982,963 cu meters. Forest products also included 205,321 tons of wood for industrial uses and 359,453 cu meters of wood for fuel. Principal timbers are oak, cedar, and hemlock. Although Taiwan is the world's largest producer of natural camphor and camphor oil, the low price of synthetic camphor has resulted in a 90% decrease in Taiwanese production.

26 MINING
The only significant mining operation in Taiwan is the production of bituminous coal, which totaled 2,934,427 tons in 1974, down sharply from 5,078,403 tons produced in 1967. Other minerals produced are small amounts of sulfur, pyrite, gold, silver, copper, manganese, mercury, petroleum, and natural gas. There are large reserves of volcanic sulfur; output in 1974 was 4,210 tons. The western third of the island has adequate amounts of sand, gravel, and limestone for building purposes, and the west coast produces more than 360,000 tons of salt annually by sea-water evaporation.

27 ENERGY AND POWER
Taiwan has several short, swift-flowing rivers estimated to possess a total hydroelectric potential of some 3.3 million kw. The island's installed power capacity reached 4,358,061 kw in 1974, 31.3% of which was hydroelectric. Total electric power output reached 20,534 million kwh in 1974 (compared with 1,966 million kwh in 1955); thermal power made up 77.2% of the total. There are at present 37 plants, of which 29 are hydro and 8 thermal. Of the net consumption of 18,881 million kwh in 1974, industry consumed a major portion, equaling nearly 78% of the total. Power is controlled by the Taiwan Power Co. (Taipower), a government-owned corporation, but some enterprises generate power for their own consumption. In the mid-1970s, Taipower embarked on a major development program for nuclear energy. The first plant was to be completed in the north in late 1976 with two generators of 636,000 kw each; the second plant, also in the north, will have two generators of 960,000 kw each. Plans for a third plant were also announced, to be built with a US$497-million loan from the US Eximbank.

River basin development is being vigorously pushed for irrigation, flood control, and power generation. Five dams are planned for the Techia River; the first, the 180-meter Tehchi Dam, was completed in late 1974 with a capacity of 334,000 kw.

Gasoline is manufactured in major refineries with a combined capacity of 5 million tons a year. Most crude petroleum for the refineries is imported from the US, but some gasoline is manufactured directly from four gasoline absorption plants at Taiwan's oil fields. Two natural gas strikes were made off Taiwan's southern coast by a US firm in 1974 and 1975.

28 INDUSTRY
Under the Japanese, about 90% of the industrial enterprises were owned by the government or by Japanese corporations with government assistance. After the restoration of Taiwan to China, the Nationalist government took over these enterprises. Some were sold to private owners, and the rest were grouped under the management of 18 public corporations, operated either by the national government or by the provincial government, or by both. Added to the confiscated enemy properties were public enterprises evacuated from the mainland. As a result, government-operated enterprises dominated Taiwanese industry. Although the proportion accounted for by these enterprises in the production value of manufacturing industries has been falling in recent years in contrast to the private sector, it still accounts for about one-fifth of total output. The average annual rate of industrial growth during the 1953–74 period averaged 19.7%, as compared with agriculture's 3.4%. In 1952, agriculture accounted for 35.7% of the net domestic product and industry for 17.9%. By 1974, the percentage had shifted significantly; industry's share was 30.9%, while agriculture's portion declined to 16.8%. The number of workers in manufacturing rose from 23,000 in 1945 to 733,000 in 1967, and to 1,421,000 by 1974.

Light and medium industries produce the bulk of industrial output. The food-processing sector, led by sugar refining, mushroom and pineapple canning, and tea packing, was traditionally the largest industrial earner of foreign exchange. Food processing has lately been surpassed in value by several other sectors, including electric and electronic products (notably transistor radios, television sets, fans, airconditioners, and refrigerators) and components, plastic goods, transport equipment (including bicycles), textiles, and chemicals. The chemical industries produce fertilizers, alkali products, cement, paper, alcohol, camphor, matches, and other consumer items. Textile products include cotton yarn and cloth, woolens, and gunny sacks. The production of basic metals includes aluminum, electrolytic copper, and a small quantity of pig iron and steel. Petroleum refining and shipbuilding have been expanded during the last few years. The drive for import substitution in the early 1970s produced major gains in tires, assembled automobiles, motorcycles, wheat flour, and cement. Lacking most raw materials, Taiwan relies on imports to supply the bulk of its new industry.

Production has risen spectacularly since the end of World War II, and especially since 1952. Cotton cloth production increased from 2.59 million sq meters in 1946 to 631 million sq meters in 1974; fertilizers from 4,843 to 1,465,000 tons; cement from 97,269 to 6,171,000 tons; and paper from 2,952 to 463,164 tons. Production of canned pineapple increased from 200,000 cases in 1945 to 2,670,000 cases in 1974 (down from 4,250,000 in 1973). Mushroom canning, which scarcely existed before 1960, produced 2,950,000 cases. Other major products in 1974 were plastic shoes, 197,037,000 pairs; refrigerators, 413,000; transistor radios, 16,100,000; assembled automobiles, 28,000; bicycles, 1,178,000; polyester staple, 73,576 tons; cement, 6,242,000 tons; and plywood, 3,762 million sq ft.

29 DOMESTIC TRADE
The marketing system is in part free and in part controlled. Salt, tobacco, alcoholic beverages, and certain commodities are produced and distributed by the government. Prices of some commodities are regulated and the movement of other commodities is controlled. Other commodities are controlled either in their production phase or in their distribution phase.

Retail sales in cities are handled by department stores, specialty shops, general stores, roadside stands, and peddlers. Since they have little overhead and are satisfied with a small margin of profit, their prices are generally lower than those of the large stores and shops.

Keelung and Taipei are the distribution centers for the northern end of the island, while Kaohsiung and Tainan are the principal distribution centers for the southern area. Most registered import and export trading firms are located in Taipei.

Accounts are usually settled during festival periods, according to Chinese custom.

Local markets open about 7 A.M. and close at 6 P.M. or later.

Business firms and stores usually open around 9 A.M and some stores close as late as 10 P.M Most stores are open seven days a week.

Advertising is becoming increasingly evident and is mainly carried by newspapers and on radio and television stations.

30 FOREIGN TRADE

Foreign trade is of great importance to the economy. To fulfill both production and consumer needs, Taiwan must import large quantities of industrial raw materials and manufactured goods. The export pattern is changing significantly. In 1952, industrial products represented only 10% of Taiwan's total exports and agricultural exports made up the rest; but by 1974, industrial exports (excluding processed agricultural products) had jumped to an overwhelming 84.5% share of the total.

Principal exports in 1967 and 1974 (in millions of US dollars) were:

	1967	1974
Textiles	121.0	1,594.3
Ores, metals, and machinery	80.6	1,518.3
Sugar	43.7	301.6
Canned mushrooms	32.7	45.2
Canned pineapple	19.3	20.8
Bananas	63.7	19.6
Other exports	314.1	2,139.2
TOTALS	675.1	5,639.0

Principal imports in 1967 and 1974 (in millions of US dollars) were:

	1967	1974
Machinery and tools	108.2	1,196.7
Ores, metals, and manufactures	124.0	776.0
Crude oil and fuels	39.1	715.4
Chemicals	38.0	657.6
Transport equipment	68.0	466.2
Cotton and other fibers	49.6	251.4
Wheat, flour, and cereals	31.2	211.9
Other imports	389.4	2,690.6
TOTALS	847.5	6,965.8

The US remains Taiwan's single most important trade partner, although Japan has made major gains, becoming Taiwan's major supplier in the 1970s.

Principal trade partners in 1974 (in millions of US dollars) were:

	EXPORTS	IMPORTS	BALANCE
US	2,036.6	1,679.9	356.7
Japan	844.0	2,214.9	−1,370.9
FRG	306.3	203.3	103.0
Hong Kong	338.3	117.0	221.3
Indonesia	127.5	181.7	− 54.2
UK	150.1	157.1	− 7.0
Thailand	68.9	176.8	− 107.9
Other countries	1,767.3	2,235.1	− 467.8
TOTALS	5,639.0	6,965.8	−1,326.8

31 BALANCE OF PAYMENTS

Taiwan's current stage of economic development requires the import of numerous raw materials and industrial equipment items, thus causing frequent deficits in goods and services. Private remittances from overseas Chinese and other foreign investors constitute an important source of payments inflow; such

funds reached a peak of $248 million in 1973, falling to $189 million in 1974 and to below $100 million (estimated) in 1975. During 1970–73, a surge in export earnings produced trade surpluses, although unfavorable world markets abruptly reversed this trend in 1974, producing a sizable deficit.

The following balance-of-payments summaries for 1971 and 1974 (in millions of US dollars) indicate the general trend in recent years:

	1971	1974
Merchandise exports (f.o.b.)	2,047	5,593
Merchandise imports (f.o.b.)	−1,755	−6,423
Trade balance	292	− 830
Services (net)	− 131	− 294
Surplus or deficit	161	−1,124
Transfer payments	11	11
Long-term capital	− 41	470
Short-term capital	− 69	630
Net errors and omissions	− 20	56
International reserves	− 40	− 42

Taiwan's international-reserve position remained fairly stable through the mid-1970s, despite unfavorable trends in foreign trade. As of 29 February 1976, foreign-exchange reserves stood at US$1,002 million, as compared with US$1,073 million in March 1975, and US$1,011 million in March 1974.

32 BANKING

Almost all banking institutions are either owned or controlled by the government. The Bank of Taiwan (with 47 branches) issued currency notes, handled foreign exchange, acted as the government's bank, and performed central banking functions in addition to its commercial banking activities before reactivation of the Central Bank.

The Central Bank of China was reactivated in Taipei in 1961. Its functions are regulation of the money market, management of foreign exchange, issuance of currency, and service as fiscal agent for the government. The Bank of China is a foreign exchange bank with branch offices in major world capitals. The Bank of Communications is an industrial bank specializing in industrial, mining, and transportation financing. The Central Trust of China acts as a government trading agency and handles most of the procurements of government organizations. The Postal Remittances and Savings Bank accepts savings deposits and makes domestic transfers at post offices.

There are 6 commercial banks: the First Commercial Bank of Taiwan, Chang Hwa Commercial Bank, Hua Nan Commercial Bank, Overseas Chinese Commercial Banking Corporation, the Shanghai Commercial and Savings Bank, and the International Commercial Bank of China. The City Bank of Taipei, established in 1969 as the fiscal agent for the Taipei municipal government, also functions as a commercial and savings bank. There are also 12 foreign banks, including 8 from the US and 1 each from Japan, Thailand, the Philippines, and Canada.

At the end of January 1976, total time and foreign-currency deposits of the commercial banks were NT$168.91 billion, while time and savings deposits of the Central Bank totaled NT$36.48 billion. At the end of 1975, savings institutions held NT$43.13 billion in time and savings deposits.

Under a new banking law that came into effect on 26 July 1975, fixed savings deposits were limited to nonjuridical depositors and could no longer be withdrawn before maturity; all deposits over NT$1 million were made subject to an income tax. As a result of the law, fixed savings declined during 1975/76 while time deposits rose sharply.

The money supply reached NT$121.11 billion as of 31 January 1976, as compared with NT$86.61 billion at the end of 1974, and NT$55.07 billion at the end of 1972.

33 INSURANCE

Insurance in Taiwan is supervised by the Ministry of Economic Affairs and may be written only by a limited liability company or a cooperative association.

Aside from group insurance operated by the government, life and annuity insurance are comparatively undeveloped in Taiwan. The Chinese tradition that the family should take care of its members in sickness and old age lessened somewhat the need for insurance protection. This sense of kinship obligation, however, is becoming less common in industrial areas.

In 1974 there were eight domestic life insurance companies, of which two were government-owned. Premium income in 1973 amounted to NT$1,920 million; total assets were NT$5,492 million, and liabilities were NT$4,810 million. Total life insurance in force was NT$68 billion in 1973, and policies numbered 612,835.

34 SECURITIES

The law stipulates that transactions in stocks and securities can by made only in the registered business places of stock dealers. Until recent years the capital market was not well developed and funds did not move readily from savers to investors. The bulk of capital needed by private industries was provided directly by the owners of the businesses and their relatives and friends. The first private corporate bond issue was floated in 1958.

The first stock exchange in Taiwan opened on 4 February 1962. Of its initial capital of NT$10 million ($250,000), 58% was underwritten by 27 private concerns and 42% by 15 public enterprises. The primary function of the exchange is to facilitate capital formation and to help the various industries of Taiwan raise needed capital. The volume of transactions remains relatively small and fluctuates widely. Average monthly turnover moved from NT$229 million in 1973 to NT95 million in 1974 and to NT$135 million for the first half of 1975. As of July 1975, the stock exchange index stood at 360.51 (1966 = 100).

35 PUBLIC FINANCE

Central government revenues come mostly from taxation, customs and duties, and income from government monopolies on tobacco and wines; other revenues are derived from profits realized by government enterprises; and finally, the recurring annual deficit in the government budget is made up by foreign loans (totaling NT$1,740 million at the end of 1975, mostly from the US Eximbank), the sale of public properties, and bond issues. The largest item of government expenditure is the cost of maintaining military establishments. Other central government expenditures include government investments in public enterprises, administrative outlays, allotments for propaganda, and overseas Chinese affairs.

Government accounts continued to show surpluses through the mid-1970s, despite adverse trends elsewhere in the economy. In 1974, total government expenditures were NT$62,795 million on current accounts and NT$23,452 million on capital accounts; total government revenues were NT$109,305 million, leaving a surplus of NT$23,058 million. Net revenues and expenditures of all levels of government in 1973 and 1974 (in millions of NT dollars) are summarized as follows:

REVENUES	1973	1974
Customs duties	14,364	24,904
Commodity tax	11,419	13,879
Income tax	7,732	13,777
Land tax	4,589	5,358
Business tax	3,763	5,737
Other taxes	11,226	17,260
Enterprises income	12,662	9,597
Monopolies revenue	7,634	7,926
Bond issues, loans	3,373	104
Other revenues	9,259	10,763
TOTALS	86,021	109,305

EXPENDITURES	1973	1974
Administration and defense	28,394	33,690
Economic development and communications	16,709	19,245
Education and culture	13,512	14,994
Public health and social welfare	8,662	9,719
Debt service	3,949	3,644
Security and police	2,677	3,208
Other expenditures	2,354	1,747
TOTALS	76,257	86,247

Principal revenues of the provincial government are the land tax and profits from government monopolies. The largest items of expenditures are for education and economic reconstruction. The local governments derive the bulk of revenues from local taxes on real estate, slaughtering, vehicles, boats, and entertainment. Most of their revenues are spent on education and police administration.

36 TAXATION

Taxes collected in Taiwan are classified as national, provincial, or local. In the mid-1970s, indirect taxes provided about three-fourths of government tax revenues. National taxes include customs duties, commodity taxes, income and inheritance taxes, stamp tax, and defense tax. Taxable commodities include salt, matches, cement, cotton yarn, woolen thread and yarn, non-alcoholic beverages, sugar, furs and hides, cosmetics, artificial silks, paper, lumber, and electric light bulbs. The income tax and inheritance and stamp taxes are administered by the provincial government, and their receipts are shared by all levels of the government. The tax-free floor for income-tax payment was raised from NT$12,000 to NT$15,000 in 1974.

The stamp tax is levied on all invoices, bills, vouchers, contracts, and other documents bearing a face value of NT$9 or more. Inheritance tax is collected on estates valued at NT$50,000 or more. The defense tax is a surtax on other taxes at varying rates.

Provincial taxes include land tax, business tax, and household tax. Land tax is collected in kind in the case of grain and in cash on other produce. The grain collected is delivered to the armed forces by the government and is rationed to civil servants. The increment of urban land value is taxed on a progressive scale. In 1974, the minimum value for payment of the house tax was raised from NT$15,000 to NT$24,000. Business tax is levied either on volume of business or net profit, according to the nature of the enterprise. Profits from the government tobacco and wine monopolies are shared by the central and provincial governments. The maximum rate on income of productive enterprises was lowered from 35% to 30% in 1974, with the ceiling on certain capital-intensive products (e.g., base metals and petrochemicals) fixed at 22%.

37 CUSTOMS AND DUTIES

Customs duties are important revenue earners and consist principally of import duties and tonnage dues; the former is levied on dutiable commodities, the latter on ships that call at Taiwan ports. The provincial government also levies a harbor reconstruction tax, a 2% ad valorem charge upon all nonexempt import cargo. Office equipment, movie projectors, phonographs, and bicycles are typical dutiable items. Duties on machinery range from 7.5% to 50% ad valorem. Articles imported for military use, for relief, or for educational or research purposes are exempted from import duty.

For all imports, a certificate of import showing that foreign exchange settlement has been made with the Bank of Taiwan must be presented to the customs. Imports are controlled and subject to licensing, which varies according to the need or desirability of the commodity. Capital equipment, raw materials, and essential consumer goods are on the permissible list, with tariffs generally ranging from zero to more than 40%. Items on a controlled list are taxed from 40% to 100%, while dangerous or luxury goods are often taxed more than 100%. Many tariff reductions were introduced in the 1970s as an economic stimulus.

Exports to mainland China are prohibited, and an export licensing system, designed to prevent diversion of Taiwan shipments to Communist-controlled areas, is in effect on many commodities.

38 FOREIGN INVESTMENTS

As of early 1976, total foreign investments in Taiwan from private sources surpassed US$1,300 million, with almost US$500 million coming from the US. The investment volume for 1975 was estimated at about US$100 million; for 1974, the total was US$189.3 million, of which overseas Chinese investments amounted to US$80.6 million and other foreign investments, US$108.7 million. Of the 1974 total, Japanese sources accounted for 35.8%; US sources for 35.6%; Western Europe, 13.6%; and 15% from other areas. Of the overseas Chinese total, 26.9% came from residents of Hong Kong. Some 36.8% of 1974 investments was absorbed by electronic and electrical-appliance industries, 19.1% went to nonmetal manufacturing, 6.7% to chemicals, and 37.4% to tourism and other sectors.

The government has accelerated economic development in Taiwan by obtaining capital resources from foreign investors. Since 1959, it has passed a series of acts prescribing legal, administrative, and economic reforms unusually beneficial to foreign capital. Tax concessions, liberalization of controls, easier acquisition of industrial land, financing at attractive terms, and assistance in finding sites, partners, skilled labor, and market outlets have made the investment climate extremely favorable. In late 1974, new liberalizations were enacted, including an income tax reduction from 30% to 20% for high-technology enterprises, and a withholding reduction from 35% to 20%. Agricultural land has been rezoned and requisitioned for industrial use. Foreign investors are permitted unlimited remittance of profits or interest derived from investment. Invested capital may be repatriated up to 15% annually, after a waiting period. New businesses are given a 20-year guarantee against expropriation, if aggregate foreign investment exceeds 5% of total capital stock. There are no restrictions against foreign ownership in the private sector, and completely foreign-owned businesses are permitted. In the public sector, the government has invited foreign capital by promoting joint public-private ventures, particularly in large-scale manufacturing and extractive industries.

39 ECONOMIC POLICY

Industrialization is the fundamental tenet of the government's economic policy. Further increases in agricultural production depend on better farming methods and improved agricultural techniques closely related to industrial development.

The government owns dominant enterprises in the lumbering, petroleum refining, pineapple, and sugar industries, and it has monopolies in camphor, tobacco, and wine. It owns almost 90% of the forests. It formerly owned the leading corporations in the cement, mining, paper and pulp, and other enterprises, but transferred the majority stock interests to private ownership in payment for land turned over for distribution to tenant and other farmers.

A four-year economic development plan (originally for 1953–56) set up production goals for the principal agricultural and industrial products. Primary consideration was given to rice production, fertilizer production, and the development of hydro-electricity. Under this and the succeeding plan (1957–60), national income rose 265.3% in current prices, or 72.5% in constant 1952 prices. Industry, agriculture, and foreign trade increased substantially.

A third four-year plan (1961–64) realized an increase in real gross national product of 55.5% and real national income of 59.5%, while real per capita income increased by 18.8%. The bulk of capital outlay was spent for industry (45.8%), agriculture (16.6%), and transport and communications (13.1%). Highest development priorities were on export industries, basic services and energy-generating industries, heavy industries, industries contributing to agricultural growth, new industries, and intensive exploration and utilization of natural resources. Resources were derived from net national savings (31%), depreciation provision (29%), external economic aid and private foreign investment (26%), and US counterpart funds (14%).

The fourth four-year plan (1965–68) constituted an integral part of a 10-year, long-range economic development plan running from 1965 through 1974. The implementation of the 10-year plan along with the fourth four-year plan resulted in an average annual increase in GNP exceeding 10% through 1973. Industry expanded at virtually all levels during the period, with exports of manufactured goods registering spectacular increases. The economic slowdown of the mid-1970s, however, forced a sudden disruption of the planning mechanism and in September 1975, Premier Chiang announced the remaining portion of the sixth four-year plan (1973–76) would be dropped at the end of the year. A six-year plan (1976–81) was being drafted in early 1976. The early stages of the new plan were expected to focus on completion of major infrastructural projects—dams, highways, port expansions, and steel and petrochemical industries—with new directions for the economy to await a reassessment in the plan's last years. Overall objectives were expected to include emphasis on precision, petrochemical, and heavy industry; rural modernization; continued search for oil and gas; development of resources in mountain areas; domestic supply of defense equipment; redistribution of wealth through taxation; and the maintenance of price stability. The annual growth rate was to be set at a relatively modest 6%.

40 HEALTH

The main diet of the people consists of rice and vegetables. It is generally considered adequate in proteins, minerals, and vitamins, except B2; but the protein is poor in quality, only about 10% of it being derived from animal sources. Fish furnishes about 50% of all animal protein consumed on the island. Dairy products have a low place in Taiwanese dietary habits. The Taiwan provincial government started a seven-year environmental sanitation improvement project in 1968. The project included the building of 420 tap water supply systems, 42,000 wells, 154,000 km of sewers, 1,792 public bathhouses, and 5,405 lavatories in rural areas.

Since the end of World War II, the most prevalent and menacing diseases have been tuberculosis, pneumonia, malaria, trachoma, leprosy, parasitic diseases, and diarrhea. Of lesser incidence are diphtheria, typhoid, typhus, plague, cholera, and venereal disease. Significant progress has been made in controlling malaria, tuberculosis, venereal disease, leprosy, and trachoma.

At the end of 1974, Taiwan's National Health Administration's facilities included 44 general hospitals, with 6,955 beds, and 346 health stations. The private health sector, including several missionary and charitable organizations, maintained 373 hospitals, with 18,984 beds. Medical personnel in 1974 included 14,668 physicians, 3,143 herb doctors, 2,315 dentists, 6,211 pharmacists, 14,129 registered nurses, and 10,262 midwives.

41SOCIAL WELFARE

Welfare activities are promoted and fostered by the government through legislation and supervision. All enterprises must set aside a certain portion of their capital stock and income for the establishment of "welfare units" such as cafeterias, low-rent housing, clinics, night classes, public baths, barber shops, nurseries, placement offices, laundries, and libraries. Labor unions participate in this program. Every general labor union and county federation has a labor welfare committee to improve living conditions and mitigate the hardships imposed by the low wage scale. Similarly, fishermen, farmers, and salt workers have their own welfare units. At the end of 1974, 1,446,242 persons (including dependents) were covered by a labor insurance program begun in 1950. Of the total, 1,042,621 (72.1%) were industrial workers. Labor insurance provides medical, disability, and other benefits. Employers bear 80% of the costs for their salaried workers.

42HOUSING

Housing remains inadequate throughout Taiwan, but the government has made substantial progress in alleviating the situation. The difficulty posed by the evacuation of more than 2 million persons from the mainland to an already densely populated island was intensified by one of the world's highest birthrates.

A National Housing Commission, assisted by US technical and financial aid, was created to ease the situation. The first project was the construction of housing units for the dock workers of Keelung, who formerly lived in empty crates or large sheds with no partitions separating families. The dockers agreed to provide part of the unskilled labor to reduce construction costs and to make amortization payments of 15% of their monthly incomes for about 10 years to pay for their houses. The success of this program encouraged other workers to institute similar programs.

The Commission also introduced new building materials for low-cost but strong construction and developed new sources of financing, such as cooperatives, savings and loan associations, and welfare funds. With US aid funds, it constructed dwellings for industrial workers, urban dwellers, and farmers.

Construction of public-financed low-cost housing projects has continued. In the 1970s, government housing programs focused on the cities, with slum clearance and the construction of high-rise apartment dwellings for low-income groups the major priorities.

43EDUCATION

About 85% of the population over 6 years of age can read and write.

A nine-year program of free education was inaugurated in September 1968. The new system adds three years to the compulsory six years of primary school. All primary-school graduates now may continue their education at tuition-free, publicly operated schools. Salaries of the teaching staff are paid by local governments. Textbooks and tuition are free, but children must buy their own notebooks and pencils. More than 98.4% of school-age children attended primary schools. In 1974/75, Taiwan had 660 preschools, with 110,403 pupils; and 2,354 primary schools, with 2,406,531 pupils. Some 88% of primary-school children go on to attend secondary schools. Some 1,433,255 students attended 586 three-year junior high schools, 209 senior high schools, and 173 senior vocational schools.

Academic middle schools are divided into junior and senior divisions, each of three years. Since 1950, some schools have experimentally adopted the so-called four-two system, four years in the junior division and two years in the senior division, so that pupils who cannot afford to go through the whole period of six years may stop at the end of the fourth year. Agriculture, engineering, commerce, maritime navigation, home economics, and nursing are some of the skills taught in vocational schools. The generally low salaries of teachers make the teaching profession not very attractive to promising students. As an encourage-ment, teacher-training schools offer free tuition, room and board, and uniform, with the understanding that the graduates must serve as teachers for at least three years.

In 1974/75, 9 national universities and 15 independent colleges had a combined enrollment of 134,187; 147,496 students were enrolled in 76 junior colleges. Sixteen overseas Chinese colleges are accredited by the Ministry of Education; 15 are in Hong Kong and 1 is in Manila.

There were 2,285 Taiwanese students approved for advanced education overseas in 1974, with 87% going to the US. There were 693 foreign students studying in Taiwan colleges and universities in 1974/75. Of these, the largest number was from Japan, followed by the US.

44LIBRARIES AND MUSEUMS

The National Central Library in Taipei has a collection of more than 500,000 volumes, including a collection of 143,974 volumes of rare Chinese books, the largest in the world. The Taiwan Provincial Taipei Library has more than 350,000 volumes. The National Taiwan University in Taipei has more than 1,000,000 volumes in collected holdings. There are also 2 provincial and 18 county and city libraries.

The major museums are the National Palace Museum, National Museum of History, and the Taiwan Provincial Museum. The National Palace Museum houses Chinese art treasures formerly divided between the National Palace Museum and the Central Museum. It has the world's largest collection of Chinese art. The National Museum of History, founded in 1955, has more than 30,000 items in its collections of oracle bones and ritual vessels of the Shang and Chou dynasties, earthenware of the Sui and T'ang dynasties, stone engravings of the Han dynasty, and jade articles of the Chou dynasty. The Taiwan Provincial Museum has the most complete collection of natural history specimens in the Republic of China. The National Science Hall in the Taipei Botanical Garden serves as a museum of science.

45ORGANIZATIONS

The most influential private organizations are the occupational or trade associations. These include associations of farmers, fishermen, trade unions, businessmen, and professional persons. Organizations devoted to social welfare and relief work are sponsored by the government, by religious groups, and by civic clubs. The Taiwan Federation of Chambers of Commerce has branches in all the principal cities.

Credit and consumers' cooperatives are an important adjunct to economic life, especially in the urban centers. In rural areas, agricultural cooperatives help the farmers transport and market special farm products such as fruits, tea, citronella oil, and handicrafts. Consumer cooperatives numbered 2,618 in 1974, with 1,137,682 members. Cooperative farms, organized with the help of the government, operate either on a community basis with the products distributed among the members or on an individual basis with the cooperative functioning as a purchasing, processing, and marketing agency. At the end of 1974, Taiwan had 176 cooperative farms with a total membership of 18,588.

Agricultural services and 4-H clubs in various parts of Taiwan provide training and social activities for more than 50,000 boys and 25,000 girls. Both the YMCA and YWCA are active in Taiwan.

The highest institution for scientific research on Taiwan is the Academia Sinica. Its nine associated institutes carry on research in mathematics, history and philology, economics, modern history, physics, botany, zoology, ethnology, and chemistry. An atomic energy committee promotes atomic research.

46PRESS

In 1975 there were 31 daily newspapers (including 2 in English), with a combined daily circulation of between 1.5 and 2 million. The leading newspapers, their orientation, and 1974 circulations are:

	ORIENTATION	CIRCULATION
China Times (Taipei)	Independent	450,000
Central Daily News (Taipei)	Government and KMT	300,000
United Daily News (Taipei)	Amalgamation of three independent papers	290,000
Taiwan Daily News (Tainan)	KMT	100,000
The China Post (Taipei)	English daily, independent	22,500

The Central News Agency was established in Canton by the KMT in 1924. The China News and Publication Service is privately owned and supplies to local newspapers the dispatches of foreign news agencies translated into the local vernaculars. In 1974 there were 44 news agencies, serving newspapers and radio and TV stations. As of June 1975 there were 1,375 magazines and a total of 1,260 publishing houses. The Chinese edition of *Reader's Digest* had the largest circulation, about 130,000.

The press law of 1954 stipulates that a publisher is liable to punishment should his paper be found to incite treason, disturb the public order, or commit acts of moral turpitude. There is no prior censorship, but all printed matter is checked by security officers after publication. Viewpoints diverging from Nationalist positions are rarely seen.

47 TOURISM

Tourism was comparatively undeveloped until 1961. In that year, about 43,000 tourists visited the island. In 1974, tourist arrivals totaled 819,821, bringing revenues of US$278 million. Of the total, 53.5% came from Japan and 13.3% from the US; overseas Chinese comprised 14.3%. Hotel construction has boomed as a result of government investment encouragement. At the end of 1974 there were 102 hotels, with 12,511 rooms of international standards (compared with 6,217 rooms in mid-1968). Aliens may apply to Chinese diplomatic or consular officers abroad for a temporary entry permit upon presentation of valid passports. The Tourism Bureau, under the Ministry of Communications, oversees tourist development.

In 1965, the government prescribed new, simplified entry regulations for visitors. A valid passport, visa, and a certificate of immunization against smallpox, typhoid and paratyphoid, typhus, and cholera are required.

48 FAMOUS TAIWANESE

Among the many Chinese scholars who have lived in Taiwan since 1949 are Hu Shih (1891–1962), philosopher and president of the Academia Sinica; Chiang Monlin (1886–1964), educator and chairman of the Joint Commission on Rural Reconstruction; Li Chi (b.1896) and Tung Tso-pin (1895–1963), archaeologists, whose discoveries at the Anyang site laid the foundation for modern Chinese archaeology; and Tsiang Ting-fu (Ting-fu Fuller Tsiang, 1895–1965), historian and long-time Chinese delegate to the UN. Chang Ta-chien (b.1900) is known for his painting of landscapes and figures and his copies of the famous Buddhist mural paintings of Tunhwang caves in Kansu Province. Two Chinese-born scientists now resident in the US who received the Nobel Prize for physics in 1957 are Dr. Tsung-dao Lee (b.1926) and Dr. Cheng-ning Yang (b.1922), who proved that parity is not always conserved; noted for her association with them in the experiments was Dr. Chien-Hsuing Wu (b.1912). Lin Yutang (1895–1976), poet, philosopher, lexicographer, and historian, was one of China's foremost interpreters for Western cultures.

The outstanding political and military figure of Nationalist China and postwar Taiwan was Chiang Kai-shek (Chiang Chung-cheng, 1887–1975), who was responsible for sustaining the spirit of anticommunism in Taiwan. His son, Chiang Ching-kuo (b.1910), assumed leadership of the Taiwan government following Chiang Kai-shek's demise.

49 DEPENDENCIES

Taiwan has no dependencies.

50 BIBLIOGRAPHY

Barclay, George W. *Colonial Development and Population in Taiwan.* Princeton, N. J.: Princeton University Press, 1954.

Barnett, A. Doak, and Edwin O. Reischauer. *The United States and China in World Affairs.* New York: Praeger, 1970.

Boorman, Howard, and Richard C. Howard (eds.). *Biographical Dictionary of Republican China.* 4 vols. New York: Columbia University Press, 1967–70.

Bueler, William M. *U.S. China Policy and the Problem of Taiwan.* Boulder, Colo.: Associated University Press, 1971.

Chang, Ching-hu. *Agricultural Geography of Taiwan.* Taipei: China Cultural Service, 1953.

China Yearbook. Taipei: China Publishing Company (annual).

Economic Progress in the Republic of China. Taipei: Central Bank of China and Council for International Economic Cooperation and Development, 1965.

Fairbank, John King. *The United States and China.* Cambridge: Harvard University Press, 1972.

Fitch, Geraldine Townsend. *Formosa Beachhead.* Chicago: Regnery, 1953.

Gallin, Bernard. *Hsin Hsing: A Chinese Village in Change.* Berkeley: University of California Press, 1966.

Goddard, William G. *Formosa: A Study in Chinese History.* East Lansing: Michigan State University Press, 1966.

Gordon, Leonard H. D. (ed.). *Taiwan: Studies in Chinese Local History.* New York: Columbia University Press, 1970.

Grieder, Jerome B. *Hu Shih and the Chinese Renaissance.* Cambridge: Harvard University Press, 1970.

Gurtov, Melvin. *Recent Developments on Taiwan.* Santa Monica, Calif.: Rand Corp., 1967.

Ho, Ch'un-sun. *Mineral Resources of Taiwan.* Taipei: Geological Survey of Taiwan, 1953.

Hsieh, Chiao-min. *Taiwan—Ilha Formosa.* Washington, D.C.: Butterworth, 1964.

Jackson, Denys Gabriel Maurice. *Formosa and the Chinese Nationalists.* Melbourne: Hawthorn, 1966.

Jacoby, Neil Herman. *U.S. Aid to Taiwan.* New York: Praeger, 1967.

Kerr, George H. *Formosa Betrayed.* Boston: Houghton Mifflin, 1965.

Levenson, Joseph R. *Liang Ch'i-ch'ao and the Mind of Modern China.* Berkeley: University of California Press, 1967.

Mancall, Mark (ed.). *Formosa Today.* New York: Praeger, 1963.

Mendel, Douglas H. *Politics of Formosan Nationalism.* Berkeley: University of California Press, 1970.

Pye, Lucian W. *Warlord Politics.* New York: Praeger, 1971.

Raper, Arthur Franklin. *Rural Taiwan: Problem and Promise.* Taipei: Joint Committee on Rural Reconstruction, 1953.

Taiwan (Formosa): A Geographical Appreciation. Ottawa: Department of Mines and Technical Surveys, Geographical Branch, 1952.

Thomson, James C. *While China Faces West.* Cambridge: Harvard University Press, 1969.

Tong, Hollington. *Chiang Kai-shek.* Taipei: China Publishing Co., 1953.

Williams, Lea E. *The Future of the Overseas Chinese in Southeast Asia.* New York: McGraw-Hill, 1966.

Wright, Mary. *China in Revolution: The First Phase, 1900–1913.* New Haven: Yale University Press, 1968.

Young, Arthur N. *China's Nation-Building Effort, 1927–1937.* Stanford, Calif.: Hoover Institution Press, 1971.

Yu, George T. *Party Politics in Republican China.* Berkeley: University of California Press, 1966.

THAILAND

Kingdom of Thailand
Pratet Thai

CAPITAL: Bangkok (Krung Thep). **FLAG:** The national flag, adopted in 1917, consists of five horizontal stripes. The outermost are red; those adjacent are white; the blue center stripe is twice as high as each of the other four. **ANTHEM:** There are three national anthems: *Pleng Sansen Phra Barami (Anthem Eulogizing His Majesty); Pleng Chard Thai (Thai National Anthem);* and *Pleng Maha Chati (Anthem of Great Victory),* an instrumental composition. **MONETARY UNIT:** The baht (B) is divided into 100 satangs. There are coins of 1, 5, 10, 25, and 50 satangs and 1 and 5 baht, and notes of 10, 20, and 100 baht. As of 29 February 1976, B1 = $0.04902 (or $1 = B20.40). **WEIGHTS AND MEASURES:** The metric system is the legal standard, but some traditional units also are used. **HOLIDAYS:** New Year's Day, 1 January; Coronation Day, 5 May; National Day, 24 June; Buddhist Lent Day, July; Queen's Birthday, 12 August; Chulalongkorn Day, 23 October; King's Birthday, 5 December; Constitution Day, 10 December; and several additional ceremonial holidays. **TIME:** 7 P.M. = noon GMT.

¹LOCATION, SIZE, AND EXTENT

Comprising an area of 514,000 sq km (198,456 sq mi) in Southeast Asia, Thailand extends almost two-thirds down the Malay Peninsula, with a length of *1,555* km *(966 mi)* N–S and a width of *790* km *(491 mi)* E–W. It is bordered on the NE and E by Laos, on the SE by Kampuchea (formerly Cambodia) and the Gulf of Siam, on the S by Malaysia, on the SW by the Andaman Sea, and on the W and NW by Burma, with a total boundary length of *7,547* km *(4,690 mi).*

²TOPOGRAPHY

Thailand may be divided into five major physical regions: the Central Valley, the Continental Highlands of the north and northwest, the Northeast, the Southeast Coast, and the Peninsula. The heart of both Thailand and the Thai people is the Central Valley, fronting the Gulf of Siam and enclosed on three sides by hills and mountains. This valley, the alluvial plain of the Chao Phraya River, its many tributaries and distributaries, is about 300 miles from north to south and has an average width of 100 to 150 miles. On this plain, and most especially on its flat deltaland bordering the Gulf, are found the main agricultural wealth and the main population concentration in Thailand.

The Continental Highlands lie north and west of the Central Valley. They include North Thailand, surrounded on three sides by Burma and Laos, which is a region of roughly parallel mountain ranges between which the Nan, Yom, Wang, Ping, and other rivers flow southward to join and create the Chao Phraya in the Central Valley. In the northernmost tip, drainage is northward to the Mekong, and on the western side, westward to the Salween in Burma. Most of the people of North Thailand live in small intermontane plains and basins which are generally widenings in the major river valleys. Doi Inthanon (8,468 feet) is the highest point in Thailand. Along the Burma border from North Thailand to the Peninsula is a sparsely inhabited strip of rugged mountains, deep canyons, and restricted valleys. One of the few natural gaps through this wild mountain country is Three Pagodas Pass along the Thailand-Burma boundary, used by the Japanese during World War II for their "death railway" (now dismantled) between Thailand and Burma.

The Northeast, much of it often called the Khorat, is a low, undulating platform, 400 to 700 feet above sea level in the north and west, gradually declining to 200 feet in the southeast. Hill and mountain ranges and scarps separate the Northeast from the Central Valley on the west and from Kampuchea on the south; its northern and much of its eastern boundaries are marked by the Mekong River. Most of the Northeast is drained by the Mun (La Moon) River and its major tributary, the Chi, which flow eastward into the Mekong. The Northeast, in the rain shadow of the Indo-China Cordillera, suffers from lack of water and from its often thin and poor soils.

The small Southeast Coast region faces the Gulf of Siam and is separated from the Central Valley and Kampuchea by hills and mountains that rise in places over 5,000 feet. This is a well-watered area and the vegetation is, for the most part, lush and tropical. Most of the people live along the narrow coastal plain and the restricted river valleys that drain southward to the Gulf.

Peninsular Thailand extends almost 600 miles from the Central Valley in the north to the boundary of Malaya in the south and is anywhere from 10 to 135 miles in width between the Gulf of Siam on the east and the Andaman Sea (Indian Ocean) and Burma on the west. At the Isthmus of Kra, the Peninsula itself is only 15 miles wide. A series of north-south ridges, roughly parallel, divide the Peninsula into distinct west and east coast sections. The west coastal plain is narrow—nonexistent in many places—and the coast itself is much indented and often very swampy. The east coastal plain is much wider, up to 20 miles in sections, and the coast is smooth, with long beach stretches and few bays. Well watered (especially the west coast), hot, and densely forested, the Peninsula, unlike the rest of Thailand except the Southeast Coast, is within the humid tropical forest lands.

³CLIMATE

Thailand has a tropical climate and for much of the country there are three distinct seasons: the hot season, from March through May; the rainy or wet monsoon, June to October; and the cool season, November through March. While continental Thailand receives most of its precipitation from June through October, rain occurs at all seasons in pensinular Thailand, the largest amount along the west coast from May to October, and along the east coast from October to January. For most of Thailand the temperature rarely falls below 13°C (55°F) or rises above 35°C (95°F), and the annual rainfall averages about 40 inches. Bangkok has an average annual temperature of 28.4°C (83°F), a low of 25°C (77°F) in December, a high of 30°C (86°F) in May, and rainfall of 59 inches.

353

⁴FLORA AND FAUNA

With at least 70% of Thailand covered by forests, many distinctive forms of plant and animal life are found. There are hardwoods, notably teak and pine, bamboos, and betel and coconut palms; in the coastal lowlands, mangroves and rattan abound. Among the larger mammals are the bear, otter, and civet cat. Climbing animals include the gibbon and many species of monkeys. There are also sheep, goats, oxen, single-horned rhinoceroses, deer, tapirs, wild cattle, wild hogs, and snakes. About 1,000 varieties of birds are indigenous, and crocodiles, lizards, and turtles are numerous. Fish abound in the rivers and coastal waters.

As of 1975, endangered species in Thailand included the pileated gibbon, Asiatic wild dog, clouded leopard, Indochinese tiger, leopard (*Panthera pardus*), Asian elephant, Malayan tapir, Javan rhinoceros, Sumatran rhinoceros, Fea's muntjac, Thailand brow-antlered deer, Asiatic buffalo, gaur, giant ibis, white-winged wood duck, river terrapin, Siamese crocodile, false gavial, and Burmese python.

⁵POPULATION

In 1975, Thailand's total population was estimated at 42,093,000; population for 1980 was projected at 49,473,000. The annual growth rate is high, averaging about 3.2% in the mid-1970s. The 1975 crude birthrate was estimated at 41.6 per 1,000, and the crude death rate was 9.3 per 1,000. Average density in 1975 was 82 per sq km, but there are great regional variations in density. Furthermore, in terms of cultivated land, the density of population exceeds 200 per sq km. Most Thais (about 83.5% in 1975) live in rural areas, and Bangkok (Krung Thep) is the single major urban area. Metropolitan Bangkok (including suburbs and satellite towns) was estimated to hold 4,000,000 persons in 1974. Outside of Bangkok, most other cities of any consequence are provincial capitals, each generally centered in a *changwat* (province or county) with the same name as the city. The largest of these (with 1972 official population estimates) included Nakhorn Ratchasima, 98,398; Chiengmai, 93,353; Phitsanulok, 70,649; and Udorn Thani, 70,110.

⁶ETHNIC GROUPS

Thailand contains more than 30 ethnic groups varying in history, language, religion, appearance, and patterns of livelihood. However, the Thai, akin to the Lao of Laos, the Shan of Burma, and the Thai groupings of southern China, comprise about 75% of the total population of Thailand.

The Thai in Thailand may be divided into three major groups and three minor groups. Major groups are the Thai (Siamese) of the Central Valley, the Peninsula, and the Southeast Coast; the Eastern Thai (Lao) of the Northeast (Khorat); and the Northern Thai (Lao) of North Thailand. Minor groups are the Puthai of northeastern Khorat, the Shan of the far northwestern corner of North Thailand, and the Lu in the northeastern section of North Thailand. The several branches of Thai are united by a common language.

Major ethnic minorities, and their approximate numbers, are the Chinese (3,000,000), engaged in business and commerce throughout the country; Malays (800,000) in the southern Peninsula near the border, and, to a lesser extent, along the Southeast Coast; Kampucheans (250,000), all along the Kampuchean border from the Mekong to the Gulf of Siam; and Vietnamese or Annamese (45,000), in the southern Khorat and on the southeast coast. Smaller numbers of residents from India, Europe, and the US live mainly in urban areas. Tribal groups, mainly hill peoples living in the north, total about 286,000. Principal among these are the Kui and Kaleung, in the Northeast; the Mons, living mainly on the Peninsula along the Burmese border; and the Karens, living along the northern Burmese border. There are, in addition, some 20 other minority groups including the Akha, Musso, Meo, Kamuk, Tin, Lawa, and So; most of these peoples, primitive and small in number, live by shifting cultivation in rugged, isolated mountain or dense forest terrain.

⁷LANGUAGE

The Thai language, with northern, eastern, central (Bangkok or official Thai), and southern dialects, all distantly related to Chinese, prevails in the country. Thai, written in a distinctive alphabet, is thought to be part of the Sino-Tibetan language family, although links to Indian languages are also evident. The Thai dialects for the most part are mutually intelligible. Although the ethnic minorities (including the 800,000 Malays) generally speak their own languages, Thai is widely understood. The Chinese population is largely bilingual. English, taught in many secondary schools and colleges, is used in official and commercial circles.

⁸RELIGION

Hinayana Buddhism is the state religion of Thailand; only Buddhists are employed by the government, and the Thai monarch is legally required to be a Buddhist. Although virtually all Thai are called Buddhists, the dominant form of religion in Thailand might be described as a spirit worship overlaid or mixed in varying degrees with Buddhist and Brahman beliefs imported from India. Among the ethnic minorities, the Chinese practice a traditional mixture of Mahayana Buddhism, Taoism, Confucianism, and ancestor worship. Most Malays are Muslims; the government provides financial assistance for the annual pilgrimage of 2,000–3,000 Muslims to Mecca. Most Vietnamese are Mahayana Buddhists, and most Indians, Hindus. Christians have been active in Thailand since the 17th century, and there are some 150,000 in the country.

⁹TRANSPORTATION

Thailand's transportation system is not fully developed, but it is growing rapidly. Owned and operated by the government, the railways, consisting in 1973 of 3,830 km of meter-gauge track, radiate from Bangkok to Malaysia in the south, to the Kampuchean border in the east, to Ubon and Nong Khai in the Northeast, and to Chiengmai in the north.

The highway system, significantly expanded during the 1960s and 1970s, serves many areas inaccessible to railways. In 1972 there were 17,686 km of highways, of which 11,507 km (65%) were national highways surfaced with asphalt or concrete compositions. In addition, there were 1,282 km of rural roads. The Friendship Highway, built with US assistance, now connects Bangkok with the northeastern plateau and the Laotian border. In 1973, registered motor vehicles totaled 393,600, of which 216,600 were passenger cars.

Waterways, both river and canal, are Thailand's most important means of inland transport; they carry more than three-fourths of the freight traffic over a network of some 1,600 km. The Chao Phraya River with its tributaries is the main traffic artery and Bangkok is its focal point. The modern port of Bangkok is the chief port for international shipping. Lying some 40 km inland from the sea, its harbor is navigable for vessels up to 10,000 tons, but constant dredging of the Chao Phraya is necessary. Phuket Harbor in southern Thailand has been improved to accommodate 15,000-ton cargo ships. Construction of new ports at Phuket and Songkhla was scheduled to begin in the late 1970s. An extensive shipping service also exists along the Gulf of Siam, and a small Thai merchant fleet plies between local and neighboring ports. In 1974, the merchant fleet included 26 vessels of more than 1,000 gross tons for a total of 143,000 gross tons.

Since the end of World War II, Bangkok has become an important center of international aviation; Don-Muang, a modern airfield outside Bangkok, handles all types of modern aircraft. Aeroflot, Air France, BA, Pan Am, KLM, and SAS are among over 30 foreign airlines servicing Thailand. Thai Airways International and Air-Siam Co. handle international flights. Domestic service and some regional flights are handled by the Thai Airways

Co. Thai Airways and Thai Airways International are government-owned.

¹⁰COMMUNICATIONS

The Ministry of Communications is responsible for Thailand's public postal, telegraph, and telephone services. Postal service, employing both railway and air mail, operates from the central post office in Bangkok and covers the entire country. Telephone service now reaches the principal towns, with some 34 provincial exchanges in service by 1976. In that year, the country had an estimated 416,000 telephone lines (compared with 98,000 in 1968), of which 310,000 were in greater Bangkok. Despite recent expansions, service remains highly erratic. Thailand is a member of INTELSAT and maintains trans-Pacific and Indian Ocean satellite communications stations.

Ownership of broadcasting is both public and private. The first mainland Asia television station was established in Bangkok in 1955; there were 48 transmitters in the country by 1973. In 1971 there were 241,000 television sets, and in 1973, 3,009,000 radios.

¹¹HISTORY

Archaeological excavations in the 1970s in Ban Chiang in northeastern Thailand have yielded traces of a Bronze Age people, dating as far back as 3600 B.C. and thus predating Bronze cultures in China and the Middle East. The technical achievements of the Ban Chiang society have challenged previous concepts of incipient civilization and technology, and Southeast Asia's role in it.

The Thai, descendants of ancient Pamir plateau stock, are racially related to the Chinese and were one of the major peoples that migrated from south China to mainland Southeast Asia. While in south China, the Thai had created the powerful Nan-Chao kingdom, but continued pressure from the Chinese and the Tibetans and final destruction by Kublai Khan in 1253 forced the Thai southward across the mountain passes into Southeast Asia. After entering the valley of the Chao Phraya River, they defeated and dispersed the Khmer settlers, ancestors of the Kampucheans, and established the kingdom of Thailand. By the mid-14th century, the Thai had expanded and centralized their kingdom at the expense of the Lao, Burmese, and Kampucheans. Although Thailand had had trading contacts with the Dutch and Portuguese in the 16th century and with the French and British in the 17th, it remained a feudal state with a powerful court of nobles. During the reigns of Mongkut (1851–68) and his son Chulalongkorn (1868–1910), however, Thailand emerged from feudalism and entered the modern world; a cabinet of foreign advisers was formed; commercial treaties of friendship were signed with the British (1855) and with the US and France (1856); the power of nobles was curtailed, slavery abolished, and many court practices, such as prostration in the royal presence, were ended.

Despite the progressive policies of Mongkut and Chulalongkorn, the Thai government continued as an absolute monarchy. In 1932, however, a bloodless revolution of Westernized intellectuals led to a constitutional monarchy. Since that time, Thailand has had several constitutions, changes of government, and palace and barracks revolutions. With the government in a state of flux, political parties have tended to cluster around strong personalities rather than political programs.

From 1932 through the 1940s, political life in Thailand centered around Pridi Banomyong and Marshal Phibul Songgram and thereafter around Marshal Sarit Thanarat, until his death in 1963. Sarit's handpicked heir, Marshal Thanom Kittikachorn, subsequently emerged as the country's political leader.

At the start of World War II, Thailand, after annexing Burmese and Malayan territories, signed an alliance with Japan and declared war on the US and the UK. After the war, however, Thailand became an ally of the US through their common

membership in SEATO, as well as through various bilateral treaties and agreements.

In January 1965, China announced the formation of the Thailand Patriotic Front whose purpose was to "strive for the

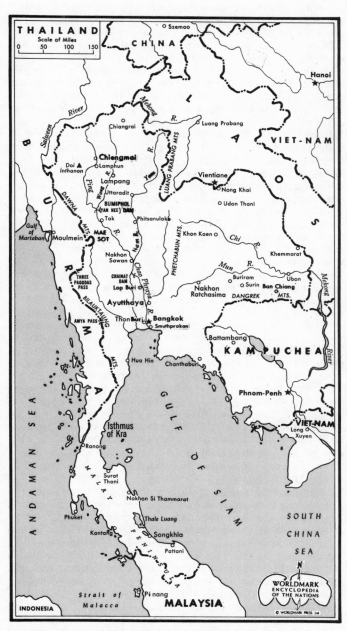

See continental political: front cover O8; physical: back cover O8

LOCATION: 97° to 106°E; 6° to 21°N. **BOUNDARY LENGTHS:** Laos, *1,754* km (*1,090* mi); Kampuchea, *803* km (*499* mi); Gulf of Siam coastline, *1,875* km (*1,165* mi); Malaysia, *576* km (*358* mi); Andaman Sea coastline, *740* km (*460* mi) Burma, *1,799* km (*1,118* mi). **TERRITORIAL SEA LIMIT:** 12 mi.

national independence" of Thailand. A limited insurgency subsequently developed in the north and northeast, growing in intensity in the late 1960s and early 1970s as the Southeast Asian conflict raged on Thailand's northern and northeastern borders. As a SEATO member, Thailand took a direct role in the Viet-Nam war by supplying a small number of troops in support of the Republic of Viet-Nam (RVN) government and, more important, by granting US forces the use of airbases in Thailand for massive bombing sorties against the Democratic Republic of Viet-Nam and Vietcong. US forces stationed in Thailand grew to a peak of 25,000 by the end of 1972. With the termination of the direct US combat role in Viet-Nam in early 1973, the US began a gradual withdrawal of military personnel from Thailand. In March 1976, the Thai government ordered the US to close its remaining military installations in the country and to remove all but a few military aid personnel by July. The insurgency within Thailand's borders had been contained but by no means stifled. Sporadic armed attacks on the government in remote northeastern border provinces continued through 1976, as the Thai government conceded control of some 640 villages and 200,000 people to forces of the banned Communist Party of Thailand.

Internally, Thailand weathered a series of political upheavals in the 1970s. In November 1971, Marshal Thanom, who had been reconfirmed as prime minister in the 1969 general elections, led a bloodless military coup that abrogated the constitution and imposed a state of martial law. An interim constitution that worked to preserve rule by the military was promulgated in December 1972. During 1973, student and labor groups began agitating for a more representative base in Thai government. By early October, demonstrations erupted into riots, and on 14 October Marshal Thanom resigned and quit the country. King Phumiphon stepped into the vacuum and named a National Legislative Assembly to draft a new constitution. On 7 October 1974, the new constitution—the tenth such document to be promulgated in Thailand since 1932—came into effect. On 26 January 1975, Thailand held its first truly open parliamentary elections since 1957. Some 42 parties competed in the balloting, which resulted in a fragile rightist coalition, formed during March 1975, and headed by Kukrit Pramoj, who was named prime minister. In January 1976, however, the ruling coalition collapsed and Kukrit resigned. New elections called for 4 April were preceded by numerous incidents of violence and assassination. Seni Pramoj, Kukrit's elder brother, emerged victorious with a solid front of 206 of the House's 279 members. On 6 October, however, the elected government was overthrown in a coup led by Adm. Sa-ngad Chaloryu. On 22 October, the king approved a new junta-dominated government headed by Thanin Kraivichien, and a new constitution.

12 GOVERNMENT

Thailand has been a constitutional monarchy since 1932. The present king is Phumiphon Adunyadet, invested as Rama IX on 5 May 1950. Until 1958, Thailand was governed under a constitution that was originally promulgated in December 1932. In October 1958, however, the constitution was suspended, and three months later the king proclaimed an interim basic law providing for a constituent assembly to draft a new constitution. Nine years in the making, the new constitution was promulgated in June 1968, and the first elections under it were held in 1969. The document was overturned in November 1971, however, by the man who was elected under it, Marshal Thanom Kittikachorn. A period of martial law under a National Executive Council ensued, with the military continued in power by virtue of an interim constitution of December 1972. Following Thanom's resignation in October 1974, the king appointed a 299-member National Legislative Assembly to draft a new constitution.

The new constitution, promulgated on 7 October 1974, called for a parliamentary government headed by a prime minister, with the king as chief of state. A bicameral legislature was established, consisting of a 100-member Senate, appointed by the king, and a House of Representatives of not more than 300 members, elected to four-year terms by direct universal suffrage. The constitution of 22 October 1976 excluded the extensive bill of rights

of the 1974 document. The new government announced its intention to appoint a new national legislative assembly.

13 POLITICAL PARTIES

Constitutional government in Thailand has been hindered by traditional public apathy, and political parties generally have been formed by military personalities rather than around political issues and programs.

Military leader Phibul Songgram became prime minister in 1938 and did not favor political parties. The pro-Japanese Phibul's immediate postwar successor, Pridi Banomyong, encouraged the growth of parties, but these were generally ineffective (primarily because of Thai inexperience with such institutions). The return of Phibul and the other military leaders to power in 1947 by means of yet another coup was followed by the banning of parties. In a move designed to undercut a growing threat from other soldiers, Phibul reinstated political parties in 1955, and such parties participated in the elections of 1957. A new coup, led by Marshal Sarit Thanarat, deposed Phibul in 1957, and political parties were again banned and did not exist in Thailand for a decade. Following the promulgation of a new constitution in June 1968, parties were again legalized and hotly contested the 1969 parliamentary elections. Prime Minister Thanom Kittikachorn's United Thai People's Party won a plurality (76) of the 219 seats in the House of Representatives, giving it a majority in partnership with 72 "independents" supported by Deputy Premier (and army chief) Praphas Charusathien. The Democratic Party, led by civilian politician Seni Pramoj, won 56 seats, thus becoming the chief opposition party. Following Marshal Thanom's coup of November 1971, political activity again subsided in favor of the military.

The collapse of military rule in October 1973 led to a resurgence of civilian political groups. In the parliamentary elections of 26 January 1975, 269 seats in the House of Representatives were contested by 2,193 candidates from 42 political parties. Voter apathy remained a problem, however, as only 47% of the electorate (33% in Bangkok) took part in the voting. The conservative Bangkok-based Democratic Party emerged with a meager plurality of 72 seats. The Democrats, however, failed to secure a majority coalition. On 13 March, Kukrit Pramoj, Seni's brother and leader of the Social Action Party (18 seats), was elected prime minister in a controversial vote in which 75 House members abstained. Kukrit thereupon formed a ruling right-wing coalition with the Social Justice Party (45 seats), the Chat Thai (28 seats), and four smaller groups. The Kukrit coalition collapsed in January 1975, and in new elections held on 4 April, Seni Pramoj, who first served as prime minister in 1945–46, gained the premiership. In the wake of the 1976 coup, massive arrests were made of liberal and leftist political elements.

14 LOCAL GOVERNMENT

Thailand is divided into 71 administrative provinces (changwats), each of which is under the control of an appointed commissioner directly responsible to the Ministry of the Interior. Provincial councils, comprised of 24 elected members, have limited authority in local affairs. Provinces in turn are subdivided into districts (amphoes) and villages (mubans). Districts are administered by state-appointed district officers (nai amphoes). Villages have locally elected headmen (puyaibans), who are directly responsible to their governor and district officer. Governments exist for cities (nakhorns), towns (muangs), and hamlets (tambols).

15 JUDICIAL SYSTEM

The 1974 constitution provides for an independent judiciary. Courts of the first instance, juvenile courts, and magistrate's courts exist in Bangkok, Thonburi, and in each of the provincial capitals. A court of appeal, sitting in Bangkok, hears cases for the entire kingdom. The Supreme Court, also in Bangkok, consists of at least three judges and decides only on points of law. Judges in Thailand are appointed (and removed) by the king. All appointments are subject to initial approval by a judicial commission. There is no trial by jury in Thailand.

The new constitution also provides for establishment of an administrative court, a court for labor, tax, and social affairs, and a nine-member constitutional tribunal to adjudicate disputes among the courts.

[16]ARMED FORCES

Males between the ages of 21 and 30 are liable for 2 years' active military duty and 23 years of various kinds of reserve status. The army, organized into five infantry divisions (including four tank battalions) and two independent regimental combat teams, numbered 135,000 personnel in 1975. The air force, reorganized with US assistance, consists of 110 combat aircraft, plus transport, training, and helicopter rescue units, and a complement of 42,000 personnel. The navy has 27,000 personnel (including 9,000 marines) and is equipped with 7 frigates, 14 patrol vessels, and some 90 smaller craft. In addition, a paramilitary volunteer defense corps of 49,000 is available for the maintenance of national security. Border police, numbering 14,000, are equipped with 54 helicopters.

[17]MIGRATION

Immigration to Thailand, except for the Chinese, has traditionally been comparatively small. The decade of the 1920s was a period of large-scale Chinese immigration: 70,000 to 140,000 a year. Strict immigration regulations have all but stopped the legal flow of Chinese into the country, but during the Franco-Indochinese war some 45,000 Vietnamese refugees settled in Thailand. An immigration quota was introduced in 1947, which limited migration from any one country to 200 persons annually.

In 1975, the establishment of a Pathet Lao government in Laos prompted the flight of 25,000 Meo hill people into Thailand, creating a tense climate on the border between the two countries. In addition, some 10,000 refugees from Kampuchea were living in camps inside Thailand following the victory in April 1975 of the Khmer Rouge. By mid-1976, an estimated 70,000 Laotian, Kampuchean, and Vietnamese refugees were living in Thailand.

[18]INTERNATIONAL COOPERATION

Thailand, a member of the UN since 1946 and of its specialized agencies, contributed military forces to the UN effort in Korea. Bangkok has served as regional headquarters for several UN agencies as well as the headquarters of SEATO. Prince Wan Waithayakon of Thailand was president of the 11th UN General Assembly in 1956–57. Identified more closely than most Asian countries with the Western nations, largely as a result of its alliances with the US, Thailand nevertheless is a member of the Afro-Asian Solidarity Conference. It also is a member of ASPAC, the IRC, IRSE, the International Tin Council, and ASEAN.

Thailand is a participant in the Colombo Plan, and it receives economic aid from the UN family for agricultural, industrial, and health projects. US assistance has been a vital factor in Thailand's economic development since World War II. During 1946–75, US economic grants totaled $600 million, while loan programs added another $174 million. Although never engaged in direct combat on Thai soil, the US has been Thailand's paramount military ally in recent years, supplying funds, equipment, advisers, and large-scale training programs for personnel. On order of the Seni government, the US military presence in Thailand was almost completely withdrawn in mid-1976, although a variety of US assistance measures, including a scheduled $54.1 million in military aid, continued in force.

Prior to the military and political upheavals of the 1970s, Kampuchea, Laos, Thailand, and the RVN, the four riparian countries, had been cooperating on the development of the Lower Mekong Basin in terms of hydroelectric power, irrigation, navigation improvement, and flood control. As of 1976, however, the prospect for future cooperation in the Lower Mekong remained in doubt, although initial talks toward rapprochement had begun among the parties. In July 1975, Thailand became the last country in the region to establish diplomatic ties with China.

[19]ECONOMY

Agriculture dominates the Thai economy, employing some 70% of the work force and producing about 30% of the GNP. Although rice remains the major crop, the area planted in rice increased by only 15% from 1950 to 1974, while areas planted in other cash crops increased by some 400%. In addition to new crops introduced—corn, cassava, and kenaf—strong gains were recorded in recent decades by rubber, cotton, sugarcane, and fruits and vegetables. The progressive diversification of Thai exports is underscored by the reduction in the share of exports of the major commodities—rice, rubber, tin, and teak—from some 90% prior to 1950 to less than 40% in 1974. Fish, abundant in the rivers and coastal waters, and teak forests are important natural resources. Tin is the most important commercial mineral extracted in Thailand. Heavy industry does not exist in Thailand, but many light industries flourish, such as textiles, rice milling, sugar refining, and native handicrafts. Industrial development has been inhibited by the scarcity of fuels, raw materials, technical skills, transportation and power facilities, and limited investment capital. The Thai economy registered steady if unspectacular growth during the 1960s, but declined during 1970–72. The GNP recovered to show an 8.7% real growth rate in 1973, slowing to 3.4% in 1974.

[20]INCOME

The GDP at current prices rose from B105,633 million in 1968 to B270,017 million in 1974. Of the GDP in 1974, agriculture, forestry, and fishing accounted for B86,225 million (31.9% of the total); wholesale and retail trade, B60,460 million (22.4%); industry, B47,137 million (17.5%); transport and communications, B15,534 million (5.8%); construction, B10,882 million (4%); mining, B4,788 million (1.8%); and other sectors, B44,991 (16.6%). Per capita income in 1974 stood at $280, as compared with $124 in 1967.

[21]LABOR

The labor force in 1974 totaled some 17.4 million (as compared with 15.1 million in 1967). Of the total, about 70% were engaged in agriculture, forestry, and fishing; 8.1% in services; 7.7% in industry; and 14.2% in other sectors. Unemployment in 1974 was estimated at 8.7%.

Because of the persisting government opposition to unions, organized labor was not a major factor in Thai economic life prior to the 1970s. The Settlement of Labor Disputes Act (1965) prescribed collective bargaining procedures that must be followed by representatives of employers and employees. In 1969, parliament passed legislation for formation of associations to negotiate. A 1969 labor bill also delineated workers' rights. Unions are now organized under the Thai Federation of Labor Unions. In 1973, labor groups joined with students in protests that forced the resignation of Marshal Thanom's government, leading to a return to civilian rule. After October, groups of students journeyed to the countryside to organize agricultural workers, who eventually formed the Farmers' Federation of Thailand. Strikes, heretofore an uncommon occurrence in Thailand, became commonplace during the year, involving the loss of 297,000 workdays. In 1974, several new unions having been formed, there were 357 strikes, involving 106,000 workers and 507,000 workdays. By 1975, a minimum wage of B25 (about $1.25) per day had been set in some provinces. Legislation regulating hours and conditions of work, wages, workmen's compensation, and welfare also exists.

[22]AGRICULTURE

With some 20 million hectares of arable land (12 million under cultivation), agriculture is the mainstay of the Thai economy. Rice farming, traditionally the most important agricultural activity, accounted for 60% (7.2 million hectares) of the cultivated acreage in 1974, and is carried on mostly in small, family-operated holdings. In recent years, however, tenancy has increased markedly as the population has expanded and the area of available arable land has declined. Farming is done by hand and with primitive implements. Nevertheless, Thailand has become one of the world's leading exporters of rice. In 1974, 14.2 million tons of paddy were produced. The government, highly dependent on rice revenues, has embarked on large-scale irrigation projects and introduced improved varieties of rice to provide a defense against floods and droughts.

Exports of rubber, theretofore the second-largest agricultural export, actually exceeded those of rice in 1973. Rubber is grown on the Peninsula and, to a lesser extent, on the southeast coast. Total production in 1974 was 380,000 tons, much of it exported to the US. Sugarcane production reached 12.7 million tons, while tapioca, traditionally important in Thailand, totaled 6.5 million tons. Corn production, which has increased significantly in recent decades, reached a record 2.5 million tons in 1974. Kenaf, tobacco, cotton, and kapok are cultivated mainly for domestic consumption, but quantities of jute, cocoa, peanuts, soybeans, and medical plants are exported.

The disparity between farm and nonfarm incomes in Thailand has become more apparent in recent years, and in the mid-1970s farmers began to organize to express their discontent over government neglect. In May 1976, the new Seni government announced land-reform proposals for the annual redistribution of 160,000 hectares to 40,000 families and for the curtailment of tenant farming.

23 ANIMAL HUSBANDRY

Cattle, used for plowing and harrowing, are important to rice farming, and most rural households have some cattle as well as hogs, chickens, and ducks. In 1973 there were 5.6 million water buffalo, 4.6 million head of cattle and oxen, 4.6 million hogs, and 168,000 horses. In the northwestern provinces, cattle and hogs are raised for export. Elephants, important as draft animals in rural areas, are used to haul teak.

24 FISHING

Fish is the major protein element in the Thai diet. Freshwater fish, abundantly found in rivers and canals, and marine fish (from the waters along the lengthy coastline) produced a catch of 1,692,300 tons in 1973 (as compared with 846,600 tons in 1967). Fishing now accounts for about 12% of the GDP, as compared with 4% in 1960. Plat-thu (rastrelliger species) is the most common fish in Thailand's diet. Thailand exports cured fish to neighboring countries, and frozen shrimp and prawns to Japan.

25 FORESTRY

With 56% of Thailand under forest, forest products continue to play a significant role in the economy, although the share of forestry has been dwindling steadily due to slash-and-burn practices still used by farmers. Teak, an important export, is found singly or in scattered small stands irregularly distributed through the mixed deciduous monsoon forest of northern Thailand up to an elevation of about 2,000 feet and accounts for about one-fourth of total lumber production. Teak felled for export is floated down the Ping, Yom, Nan, Wang, and other tributaries to the Chao Phraya and on to Bangkok for milling; some is sent down the Salween to Burmese ports. The teak industry suffers largely from past depletion of the forests through excessive cutting and inadequate replanting. In 1973, Thailand produced a total of 19.5 million cu meters of round wood.

Lac, a resinous insect substance found on trees, has always had value for the Thai, but its derivatives—seedlac, sticklac, and shellac—have also found a ready international market. Other important forestry products include charcoal, gums and resins, and kapok fiber and seed.

26 MINING

Thailand is relatively poor in mineral reserves. Those few deposits that are known and exploited, such as tin, provide an insubstantial basis for modern local industry.

In 1974, Thailand was the fourth-largest tin-producing country in the world. Tin ore, located mainly on the southern peninsula, is produced by UK, Australian, and local Chinese companies. The Thai Exploration and Mining Co. (TEMCO), a US-Dutch concession operating on the southwest coast, was shut down by the government in January 1975 following a public outcry alleging that former military officials had been direct beneficiaries of the concession; TEMCO had previously accounted for 15% of the total tin output. Tin production in 1974 totaled 27,767 tons, most of it exported.

Deposits of lignite have been developed with US aid and have begun to show a good yield; 437,000 tons were produced in 1974. A zinc ore deposit is now being exploited in the Mae Sod district near the Burmese border. By 1975, high-grade antimony ores were nearly exhausted. Thailand's first iron mine is located at Lop Buri; its production feeds a small smelting plant. Other minerals exploited on a small scale are coal, gold , silver, and many kinds of building stones. Rubies, sapphires, topaz, and zircons also are mined. The first commercial gypsum mine began operations in 1957. Production of both gypsum and fluorite were gaining significantly through the 1970s. Cement production in 1973 was 3,706,000 tons.

An oil field in Chiengmai Province is being developed, and drilling for oil goes on in Ayutthaya Province. A total of 6,000 tons of crude oil was produced in 1973.

Leading minerals (other than tin and lignite) in terms of tonnage produced in 1974 were iron ore, 36,300; fluorite, 420,000; gypsum, 309,000; lead, 3,600; manganese, 29,000; and antimony ore, 377. Tungsten, once Thailand's second leading mineral export, is now of lesser importance; 4,200 tons were produced in 1974.

27 ENERGY AND POWER

Until the mid-1960s, Thailand's power was supplied by firewood, rice stalks, and imported coal and oil. With the discovery and development of large lignite deposits, coal is no longer imported for power generation. During 1971–76, total installed generating capacity more than doubled, from 1,169,000 kw to 2,469,000 kw, of which 54.3% derived from thermal plants, 37.3% from hydroelectric facilities, and 8.4% from gas turbine and diesel plants. Distribution, however, is far from adequate, with only about two-thirds of the greater Bangkok population receiving electricity and only 4,000,000 persons, or about 13% of the rural population, having access to the system. The Metropolitan Electricity Authority serves Bangkok-Thonburi; the Provincial Electricity Authority provides service to 67 provinces. Total national output in 1972 was 6,209 million kwh (1,092 million kwh in 1964).

Power stations in Bangkok are mainly hydroelectric and steam turbine plants; provincial plants are of the diesel type. The government, which owns and operates the power system, has built several power projects. The Bhumiphol Dam (previously the Yan Hee Dam) Project on the Ping River is the largest of these and has a projected capacity of 350,000 kw. Other dams were due for completion in the late 1970s. Thus, Thailand's limited hydroelectric capacity is being rapidly harnessed, indicating a future stress on thermal and alternate sources.

28 INDUSTRY

Although there has been some expansion and diversification of industry in recent years, industrial development remains limited. Aside from textiles, which led virtually all other sectors in growth prior to 1974, manufacturing continues to exist on a modest scale—largely the processing of agricultural products and the production of building materials—and has not satisfied local demands. Thailand must continue to import manufactured goods.

Textile production averaging 500 million sq yards annually in the mid-1970s (compared with 277 million in 1966) was expected to reach 700 million by the end of 1976. After textiles, the most important industries are those processing agricultural products: rice milling, followed by rubber, sawmills, tobacco, cotton, jute, sugar, and cement. The older manufacturing industries, such as rice and sawmilling, are owned by private capital, mainly local Chinese and some Thai, but many more recent industrial enterprises are government-owned.

²⁹DOMESTIC TRADE
Bangkok, the port of entry and distribution point for the whole country, is the commercial center of Thailand; all foreign firms have their main offices there. Other commercially important cities are Chiengmai (teak, rice, and textiles), Ubon (lac, rice, jute, and leather), Phuket (tin), and Songkhla (rubber). A large segment of retailing is Chinese controlled.

Commercial credit is difficult to obtain. Importers, however, may obtain loans at high rates of interest from commercial bankers in the opening of letters of credit, but substantial margin deposits in baht are required. Small local sales are conducted on a cash basis, and installment purchasing is unusual.

Usual business hours are from 9 A.M. to 4 P.M., Monday through Friday, and from 9 A.M. to noon on Saturday.

Newspaper, billboard, radio, television, sound truck, and motion picture advertising is available. The annual Bangkok fair in December, originally conceived for entertainment, has developed into a trade fair.

³⁰FOREIGN TRADE
Thailand is primarily an importer of manufactured goods and exporter of agricultural products and raw materials. During 1970–74, the value of Thailand's exports expanded more than threefold, although trade deficits continued. Rice, traditionally the dominant export item, accounted for 45% or more of total export value in 1948. During the 1960s, however, it dropped to between 33% and 36%, and accounted for 20% by 1974; rubber, fluctuating between 10% and 30% in the 1960s, accounted for 10% of total exports in 1974; in that year, corn had risen to second place, accounting for 12% of the total.

Principal exports in 1970 and 1973 (in thousands of dollars) were:

	1970	1973
Rubber	107,357	224,294
Rice	120,998	176,314
Fruits and vegetables	78,432	156,330
Corn	89,280	140,347
Tin	77,814	99,807
Textile yarn and fabrics	8,704	87,847
Jute	34,567	50,791
Wood, lumber, and cork	10,907	37,222
Other exports	182,200	554,845
TOTALS	710,259	1,527,797

Principal imports in 1970 and 1973 (in thousands of dollars) were:

	1970	1973
Chemicals	167,288	325,229
Nonelectrical machinery	220,148	310,576
Transport equipment	135,078	239,546
Fuels and lubricants	113,172	233,341
Crude materials	67,282	174,570
Iron and steel	89,840	156,556
Electrical machinery and appliances	104,677	136,108
Other imports	395,931	497,364
TOTALS	1,293,416	2,073,290

Japan, Indonesia, Malaysia, and Hong Kong are the principal purchasers of Thailand's rice. Rubber, tin, and livestock shipped to Singapore are mainly for reexport. About half of Thailand's imports are supplied by two countries, Japan and the US.

Principal trade partners in 1973 (in thousands of dollars) were:

	EXPORTS	IMPORTS	BALANCE
Japan	410,242	741,097	−330,855
US	145,519	290,723	−145,204
FRG	37,073	157,778	−120,705
Netherlands	143,459	25,049	118,410
UK	30,019	133,437	−103,418
Singapore	117,615	29,397	88,218
Hong Kong	114,288	28,893	85,395
Malaysia	94,126	18,927	75,199
Australia	11,338	68,411	− 57,073
Sa'udi Arabia	19,936	48,231	− 28,295
Other countries	404,182	531,347	−127,165
TOTALS	1,527,797	2,073,290	−545,493

³¹BALANCE OF PAYMENTS
Thailand's balance-of-payments position was strengthened during the early Korean War and continued strong until late 1952. Since then, export returns have frequently fallen short of import expenditures.

Several factors account for Thailand's growing balance-of-payments problem. Probably the most important have been the fluctuations in the international market for its traditional primary exports. The value of rice and rubber exports dropped significantly between 1964 and 1968, and that of rice and tin during 1973–75. The needs of a modernizing economy are difficult to support by agricultural exports alone. In addition, Thailand imports large quantities of automobiles and machinery, as well as much fuel to run them, and many luxury and convenience manufactures. In recent years, the imbalance has been offset by foreign assistance, loans, and income from tourism.

Thailand's balance-of-payments position as of 1970 and 1974 (in millions of dollars) is summarized as follows:

	1970	1974
Goods and services	−299	−283
Private transfers	3	191
Government transfers	46	28
CURRENT BALANCE	−250	− 64
Long-term capital	109	379
Short-term capital	54	82
Errors and omissions	5	79
TOTALS	− 82	476

As of 29 February 1976, international reserves stood at $1,874 million, as compared with $1,858 million at the end of 1974.

³²BANKING
The Bank of Thailand (established 1942), the central bank, operates as an independent body under government supervision; its entire capital is owned by the government. The Bank issues notes, a function previously handled by the Ministry of Finance,

but the note issue is separate from banking activities. As of 29 February 1976, the Bank had gold holdings of $96 million and foreign exchange holdings of $1,704 million.

Of the 28 banks in Thailand, 14 are incorporated under Thai law and 14 are branches of foreign banks. About one-third of the country's 600 bank branches are located in Bangkok. As of 31 October 1975, demand deposits of the commercial banks totaled B10.98 billion and time and savings deposits, B66.72 billion.

Currency in circulation rose from B11.86 billion at the end of 1970 to B20.95 billion as of October 1975.

33 INSURANCE
Of the 11 life insurance companies in Thailand in 1973, 9 were domestically owned. Policies in force, including ordinary, group, and industrial, numbered 365,220, at a value of B8,212 million. Total assets of all life insurance companies were valued at B1,526 million; total income was B586 million.

Non-life companies in 1973 numbered 56, of which 47 were domestically incorporated; total assets as of 31 December 1973 were valued at B1,032 million. Gross premiums totaled B1,014 million; net premiums totaled B497 million. Of the total net premiums written, the largest class of non-life insurance was automobile (45%), followed by fire (34%), and marine and transport (14%).

34 SECURITIES
On 30 April 1975, the first public stock exchange was opened in Bangkok. All of its 30 members were Thai-owned securities firms. Initially, 11 companies were listed. Through September, the average monthly turnover was a relatively meager B70 million. Investors in Thailand showed a reluctance to leave their traditional modes of investment—land speculation, time deposits, and over-the-counter stock and monetary transactions.

35 PUBLIC FINANCE
Central government expenditures, which totaled B23,745 million in 1969/70 (1 October–30 September), rose to a record B45,672 million (estimated) by 1974/75. In recent years, about one-fifth of the total budget has been spent on national defense; another significant portion is devoted to economic development. It is the usual pattern for the Thai government to plan for a substantial budgetary deficit at the start of the year, based on an anticipated loss of receipts on rice exports. US aid and IBRD loans have contributed significantly to public revenues. Import duties and other indirect taxes make up more than 80% of the government's internally derived revenues.

Central government revenues and expenditures for 1969/70 and estimated for 1974/75 (in millions of baht) were broken down as follows:

REVENUES	1969/70	1974/75
Taxes on income and wealth	2,408	4,900
Import duties	5,394	9,580
Export duties	393	1,420
Rice export premium	654	1,020
Fiscal monopolies	672	1,236
Other indirect taxes	7,049	16,197
Other revenues	2,139	3,528
TOTALS	18,709	37,881

EXPENDITURES		
Education	3,899	10,288
Health	593	1,507
Other special services	1,770	2,312
Agriculture	2,604	4,153
Other economic services	4,346	5,991
Defense	4,160	8,289
Interest on public debt	1,362	4,018
Other expenditures	5,011	9,114
TOTALS	23,745	45,672

As of 31 December 1975, the domestic debt totaled B43,212 million (B23,644 million at the end of 1970), and the foreign-currency debt, B4,819 million (B3,671 million in 1970).

36 TAXATION
Less than 13% of the total estimated 1974/75 revenues of the Thai government was derived from direct taxes on income and wealth. Chief forms of taxation are transaction and consumption taxes, and import and excise duties. Foreign aid, particularly US military and economic assistance, has been used to make up most of the balance. Income tax rates in Thailand are graduated, rising from 10% on income of B10,000 to 50% on income of B2 million and over. Businesses and individual citizens are also subject to a host of indirect taxes, including customs duties, sales tax, and excise taxes. Corporate income taxes in 1975 were levied at the following rates: first B500,000, 20%; second B500,000, 25%; over B1 million, 35%. Stock dividends and capital gains are taxed as regular income. Thailand has no social security tax.

All companies and individuals engaged in industry, commerce, or services are subject to the sales tax (ranging from 1.5% to 25%); reductions are available under the Investment Promotion Act.

There are excise taxes on tobacco, alcoholic and soft beverages, and other products. Automobiles are subject to a special tax.

37 CUSTOMS AND DUTIES
Thailand's customs tariff is primarily for revenue, although in a limited fashion it protects local industry. Import duty rates have increased, and by 1974/75, they constituted 25.3% of government revenues. No preferential treatment is afforded any country, and all goods are subject to the general rate. Export duties exist for 23 classes of goods. Mineral exports, which provide revenue in the form of royalties, are not included. Rice exports provide revenue through an export duty and an "export premium" assessed on the individual trader's sales.

Most duties are ad valorem, with the impost ranging up to a high of 80%. More than 85% of the tariff items have duties of 30% or less, with the highest duties reserved for luxury and competitive items. Some tariffs are specific, and some are both specific and ad valorem. In order to encourage local industry, a standing government committee on customs tariffs can reduce duties on raw materials.

38 FOREIGN INVESTMENTS
Growth of the Thai economy has been directly related to the flow of investments from abroad. In order to stimulate such investment, the government passed the Investment Promotion Act (1962), which grants the following benefits to promoted industries: guarantees against nationalization and competition from government industries; exemption from import duties and business tax on plant, machinery, spare parts, and raw materials; exemption from duty on exports; exemption from tax on corporate income for a specified period; and repatriation of capital and remittance of profits abroad. The Board of Investment of Thailand considers applications for promotional benefits to both Thai and foreign investors. In 1973, foreign investments under the Promotion of Industrial Investment Act amounted to B4,323 million; the 1974 total reached B16,662 million. The rate of investment fell off sharply in mid-1975 following the change of regimes in Saigon and Phnom-Penh, but activity recovered somewhat thereafter. A major new project during the year was a lubricants plant to be built by Shell Oil at a cost of $115 million.

39 ECONOMIC POLICY
The Thai government, vulnerable in its financial dependence on a few primary commodities (rice, rubber, tin, and teak), has, in the 1960s and 1970s, pursued a policy of economic diversification through industrial development and increased agricultural production. With the beginning of the first development plan in 1961, the government committed itself to the primacy of private

enterprise and to a policy of fostering and assisting it. Government funds have been directed to private enterprise projects. The growth of industrialization has been handicapped by lack of venture capital and inadequacies in transportation, power generation, and communications. The government encourages private foreign enterprise and, with loans and assistance from abroad, is attempting to develop conditions for industrialization, including adequate fuel and power resources.

Since 1955, Thailand has also followed a policy of foreign trade and exchange liberalization. Foreign exchange control is nominal. Export controls are applied to rice and a few other commodities in order to prevent a shortage of supply and excessive domestic price rises.

Thailand's first economic plan covered the period 1961–66. The main aim of the plan was to raise the standard of living by means of greater agricultural, industrial, and power production. In the second development plan (1967–71), emphasis was placed on agricultural development, highways, irrigation, education, and industrial development in the private sector. The third development plan (1972–76) was introduced on 1 October 1972 and projected an average annual growth of 7% in GDP. A poor performance in domestic agriculture, coupled with the negative effects of inflation and the world recession, produced an actual GDP growth rate of 5.2% annually during 1972–75. Public development expenditures for the plan totaled B100,275 million, of which 17% derived from foreign loans and grants. The plan placed special emphasis on improvements in the rural infrastructure, growth in the financial and commercial sectors, and further assistance to crop diversification and to import-substitution industries. The government also committed itself to a reduction in the role of state-owned enterprises.

There are also regional development plans, including an accelerated rural development plan for 11 provinces of the northern and northeastern regions.

40 HEALTH
Owing largely to success in eradicating malaria and other tropical diseases, as well as to better sanitation and medical care, health conditions have steadily improved in Thailand. The government, with UN and US assistance, extended free medical treatment, expanded health education activities in schools and rural areas, and built many hospitals in the 1960s. Average life expectancy in 1975 was estimated at 60.3 years (45.2 years in 1950).

In 1970 there were 542 hospitals, with a total of 40,781 beds; the government expected to expand this total to some 51,300 by the end of 1976. In 1970 there were 4,313 physicians (1 for every 7,971 inhabitants), 389 dentists, 1,155 pharmacists, 5,171 nurses, and 9,974 midwives. The third national development plan called for the addition of 1,850 physicians and 7,595 nurses by the end of 1976.

41 SOCIAL WELFARE
Since 1940, social welfare has been the responsibility of the government (under its Department of Social Welfare) and it is only in recent years that private organizations have actively engaged in social welfare programs. Thailand has established a variety of social welfare benefits for its inhabitants. Services for the aged and the handicapped are available in the form of residential care and rehabilitation programs.

A nationwide social security system was under study in the mid-1970s. Insurance provisions covering birth, sickness, and work-related accidents and deaths were contemplated. The 1972–76 development plan called for expansion of family-planning services, with the goal of reducing the population growth rate to 2.5% by 1976.

42 HOUSING
Most families in Thailand live in dwellings that compare favorably with living facilities anywhere in Southeast Asia. In recent years, however, the Thai government embarked on two extensive housing and community development programs: (1) the housing plan, which provides government mortgages for building, renovation, or purchase of government land and houses; and (2) the self-help settlement scheme, under which the government sets up whole new communities, surveys sites, constructs roads and irrigation systems, provides public utilities and medical care.

In the 1970s, the government's National Housing Authority undertook overall responsibility for coordination of public and private housing programs. During the 1972–76 development plan, the government hoped to provide potable water facilities for some 20,000 villages. Water supply, drainage, slum clearance, and low-income housing projects were planned for urban areas.

43 EDUCATION
Literacy, estimated at 44.3% in 1947, rose to about 70% by 1974. Compulsory education provisions, first introduced in 1921, currently call for universal attendance starting at age 7 through the fourth year of primary school or through age 15. In 1974, however, lack of facilities and inadequate administration held school attendance to only 68% of children in the 7–10 age group. In 1974, some 4.3 million pupils attended lower-level (four-year) primary schools, while 900,000 were enrolled at the upper (three-year) level. In the mid-1970s, the government was planning conversion to a unitary, six-year primary program. Secondary enrollment in 1974 stood at about 1 million, with about three-fourths attending at the lower-middle-school (three-year) level. Both teacher-training and technical and vocational training (especially in agriculture) have been stressed in recent development plans.

In 1973, about 99,000 students were enrolled in institutes of higher education; 48,000 were attending eight universities. Chulalongkorn University (founded 1917), in Bangkok, is Thailand's most eminent university. The University of Thammasart in Bangkok (founded 1933), specializing in social and political sciences, is the country's largest university. Kasetsart University in Bangkok (founded 1943) specializes in agriculture. The University of Medical Sciences in Thon Buri was founded in 1942. Recent additions in provincial areas include Chiengmai University (founded in 1964), Khon Kaen University (founded in the Northeast in 1965), and the Prince of Songkhla University (founded in 1968). Eight colleges of education were combined into Srinakharinwirot University in Bangkok in 1974. A correspondence school, the Open University of Ramkamhaeng, opened in Bangkok in 1974.

An adult education program was established in 1938, and an educational broadcasting service in 1954.

44 LIBRARIES AND MUSEUMS
The National Library (founded in 1905) contains about 720,000 books and over 144,000 manuscripts. Other book collections are maintained by the Asian Institute of Technology (60,000 volumes), Chulalongkorn University (93,000 volumes), the University of Thammasart (211,000), Kasetsart University (60,000), the Siam Society, and the Swami Satyenanda Puri Foundation. The Neilson Hays Library is a private collection. Outside Bangkok, sizable collections are maintained at the University of Chiengmai and Khon Kaen University.

The National Museum in Bangkok (founded in 1926) has an extensive collection of Thai artifacts, including sculptures, textiles, ceramics, jewels, coins, weapons, and masks. Many of Bangkok's temples and palaces contain excellent examples of Thai frescoes and sculptures. The Temple of the Emerald Buddha has a famous mural of the Ramayana, the Sanskrit epic, and the Marble Temple contains a fine collection of bronze and stone Buddhas.

45 ORGANIZATIONS
Thailand has an extensive cooperative movement. Credit societies are the dominant type of cooperative. Consumer cooperatives are the next largest, followed by agricultural

marketing and processing cooperatives. Membership in the two last-named associations is still limited (about 8% of all Thai households), and the Ministry of National Development, which directs all organizational activity, intends to increase their membership in the rural areas. Other kinds of cooperatives, mostly formed during and since the 1930s, include colonization and land improvement cooperatives.

Trade organizations under the Ministry of Economic Affairs are significant in the promotion of commerce. They include the Thai Chamber of Commerce, the Board of Trade, and several foreign trade associations.

Cultural organizations include the Royal Institute of Arts and Sciences (founded 1933); the Thai-Bharat Cultural Lodge (founded 1940), which sponsors studies in the fields of linguistics, philosophy, and religion; and the Siam Society (founded 1904), which issues studies on Thai art, literature, and science. The Medical Association of Thailand and the Teachers' Institute issue journals.

46PRESS

The first daily newspaper, the *Siam Daily Advertiser,* appeared a century ago. In 1974 there were 28 daily newspapers, all of them published in Bangkok. Sixteen dailies are published in Thai, 8 in Chinese, and 4 in English. The provinces have weekly and semiweekly publications, all in Thai, but no daily papers. Bangkok also has a variety of weekly and monthly periodicals, most appearing in Thai. Bangkok's leading daily newspapers (with language medium and 1974 circulations) were as follows:

	LANGUAGE	CIRCULATION
Thai Rath (m.)	Thai	240,000
Daily News (m.)	Thai	230,000
Ban Muang (m.)	Thai	100,000
Prachatipatai (m.)	Thai	85,000
Siam (m.)	Thai	50,000
Sing Sian Wan Pao (m.)	Chinese	40,500
Thai Daily (m.)	Thai	38,000
Sing Thai Wan Pao (e.)	Chinese	37,500
Siam Rath (e.)	Thai	26,500
Bangkok Post (m.)	English	22,000

47TOURISM

Tourism has become a vital industry in Thailand, constituting in the mid-1970s the third-largest source of foreign exchange. In the late 1960s and early 1970s, the large US troop presence in Southeast Asia produced a surge in Thailand's tourism largely from US military personnel. In 1974, 1.1 million tourists visited the country, spending a total of B4,292 million. Bangkok offers a wide range of hotel accommodations, greatly expanded during the past decade.

All visitors must have passports and smallpox and cholera inoculation certificates; visitors from most countries may stay up to 15 days without a visa. Typhoid, tetanus, and gamma globulin immunizations are recommended, especially for travel in rural areas.

48FAMOUS THAI

Many ancient Thai kings enjoy lengendary reputations among their people: Rama Khamheng (the Great), 13th-century monarch, is traditionally regarded as the inventor of the Thai alphabet; Rama Tibodi I promulgated in the 14th century the first-known Thai laws; Trailok instituted lasting governmental reforms in the 15th century; and Phya Tak in the 18th century rebuilt a war-defeated Thailand. Two great monarchs, Mongkut (r.1851–68) and his son Chulalongkorn (r.1868–1910), became famous for introducing Thailand to the modern world. They are, respectively, the king and his young successor in Margaret Landon's *Anna and the King of Siam.* Further progress toward moder-

nization was accomplished in more recent times by three outstanding premiers: Phibul Songgram (1897–1964), Pridi Banomyong (b.1900), and Sarit Thanarat (1900–63). Prince Wan Waithayakon (b.1891), foreign minister and Thailand's representative to the UN, has played a major role in the diplomacy of recent years.

Marshal Thanom Kittikachorn (b.1911) was leader of Thailand from 1963 until October 1973, when political protests compelled his resignation as prime minister. Thanom, who left the country following his resignation, quietly reentered Thailand in December 1974, but was almost immediately expelled by the government.

The first modern novel in Thailand, *Yellow Race, White Race,* was written by Prince Akat Damkoeng in 1940. Modern styles in painting and sculpture are reflected in the work of Chitr Buabusaya and Paitun Muangsomboon, and the traditional manner in the art of Apai Saratani and Vichitr Chaosanket.

49DEPENDENCIES

Thailand has no territories or colonies.

50BIBLIOGRAPHY

American University. *Area Handbook for Thailand.* Washington, D.C.: Government Printing Office, 1971.

Basche, James R. *Thailand: Land of the Free.* New York: Taplinger, 1971.

Benedict, Ruth. *Thai Culture and Behavior.* Ithaca, N.Y.: Cornell University Press, 1952.

Bowie, Theodore (ed.). *The Arts of Thailand.* Bloomington: Indiana University Press, 1961.

Bowring, Sir John. *The Kingdom and People of Siam.* London: Parker, 1857.

Coedes, George. *The Making of Southeast Asia.* Berkeley: University of California Press, 1969.

Directory of Bangkok and Siam. Bangkok: Bangkok Times (annual).

Emery, R.F. *Financial Institutions of Southeast Asia: A Country by Country Study.* New York: Praeger, 1971.

Ingram, James C. *Economic Change in Thailand, 1850–1970.* Stanford, Calif.: Stanford University Press, 1971.

Kirk, Donald. *Wider War: The Struggle for Cambodia, Thailand and Laos.* New York: Praeger, 1971.

Le May, Reginald Stuart. *A Concise History of Buddhist Art in Siam.* Rutland, Vt.: Tuttle, 1963.

Le May, Reginald Stuart. *An Asian Arcady: The Land and Peoples of Northern Siam.* Cambridge: Heffer, 1926.

Leonowens, Anna Harriette. *The English Governess at the Siamese Court.* New York: Roy, 1954.

Moore, Frank J. *Thailand: Its People, Its Society, Its Culture.* New Haven, Conn.: HRAF Press, 1974.

Moorman, Michael. *Agricultural Choice and Peasant Choice in a Thai Village.* Berkeley: University of California Press, 1968.

Pendleton, Robert L., et al. *Thailand: Aspects of Landscape and Life.* New York: Duell, Sloan and Pearce, 1962.

Riggs, Fred W. *Thailand: The Modernization of a Bureaucratic Polity.* Honolulu: East-West Center, 1966.

Siffin, William J. *The Thai Bureaucracy: Institutional Change and Development.* Honolulu: East-West Center, 1966.

Silcock, Thomas Henry. *Thailand: Social and Economic Studies in Development.* Durham, N.C.: Duke University Press, 1968.

Skinner, George William. *Chinese Society in Thailand: Analytical History.* Ithaca, N.Y.: Cornell University Press, 1957.

Suvatti, Chote. *Fauna of Thailand.* Bangkok: Department of Fisheries, 1950.

Wells, Kenneth Elmer. *Thai Buddhism: Its Rites and Activities.* Bangkok: Bangkok Times Press, 1939.

Wilson, David A. *The United States and the Future of Thailand.* New York: Praeger, 1970.

TONGA

Kingdom of Tonga
Pule'anga Tonga

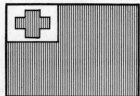

CAPITAL: Nuku'alofa. **FLAG**: The flag, adopted in 1862, is crimson with a cross of the same color mounted in a white canton. **ANTHEM**: *Koe Fasi Oe Tu'i Oe Otu Tonga (Tongan National Anthem)* begins "'E 'Otua Mafimafi Ko homau 'Eiki Koe" ("Oh Almighty God above, Thou art our Lord and sure defense"). **MONETARY UNIT**: The Tongan pa'anga (T$) of 100 seniti is a nonconvertible paper currency. Since 1967, the Tongan pa'anga has been at par with the Australian dollar. There are coins of 1, 2, 5, 10, 20, and 50 seniti and notes of $\frac{1}{2}$, 1, 2, 5, and 10 Tongan pa'angas. In April 1963, gold coins were issued in denominations of $\frac{1}{4}$, $\frac{1}{2}$, and 1 koula (1 koula equaled old T£20—T£1 equaled US$2.24). In July 1967, coronation palladium coins of $\frac{1}{4}$, $\frac{1}{2}$, and 1 hau were issued (1 hau equals T$100). T$1 = US$1.25 (or US$1 = T$0.80). **WEIGHTS AND MEASURES**: Imperial weights and measures are the legal standard. **HOLIDAYS**: Christian religious holidays are observed. **TIME**: 1:00 A.M. (the following day) = noon GMT.

¹LOCATION, SIZE, AND EXTENT

The Tonga archipelago, also known as the Friendly Islands, lies scattered east of Fiji in the South Pacific Ocean. Nuku'alofa, the capital, is about 692 km (430 mi) from Suva, Fiji, and about 1,770 km (1,100 mi) from Auckland, New Zealand. Comprised of 169 islands of various sizes, only 36 of which are inhabited, Tonga has an area, including inland waters and Minerva Reefs, of 749 sq km (289 sq mi). It extends *631 km (392 mi)* NNE–SSW and *209 km (130 mi)* ESE–WNW. The areas are: Tongatapu and 'Eua, 350 sq km (135 sq mi); Ha'apai, 119 sq km (46 sq mi); Vava'u, 143 sq km (55 sq mi); Niuatoputapu and Tafahi, 18 sq km (7 sq mi); Niuafo'ou, 52 sq km (20 sq mi); and other islands, 67 sq km (26 sq mi). Tonga's total coastline is about *560 km (348 mi)*.

²TOPOGRAPHY

The islands run roughly north and south in two parallel chains, of which the western eleven are volcanic and the eastern are coralline encircled by reefs. Tonga Deep is one of the lowest parts of the ocean floor, nearly 7 miles deep. The soil on the low-lying coral islands is porous, being a shallow layer of red volcanic ash, devoid of quartz, but containing broken-down limestone particles. The volcanic islands range in height between 150 and 3,389 feet, the latter being Kao. Falcon Island (Fonuafo'ou), about 40 miles northwest of Nuku'alofa, is famous for its periodic disappearances. There are few lakes or streams. Tofua, Vava'u, Nomuka, and Niuafo'ou each have a lake, and there are creeks on 'Eua and one stream on Niuatoputapu. Other islands rely on wells and the storage of rainwater.

³CLIMATE

The climate of Tonga is basically subtropical. Because it is in the southeast tradewind area, the climate is cooler from May to November; humidity is relatively low, and the temperature seldom rises above 26.7°C (80°F). Temperature varies from about 10°C (50°F) in winter to 32°C (90°F) in summer. Average rainfall, most of which occurs from December to March during the hot season, is 66 inches (67 inches on Tongatapu, 91.3 inches on Vava'u, and 74.3 inches on Niuatoputapu). The greatest variations are in relative humidity. The mean humidity is 80%.

⁴FLORA AND FAUNA

Coconut palms, hibiscus, and other tropical trees, bushes, and flowers are abundant. Tonga is particularly known for its flying foxes.

⁵POPULATION

In 1973, the estimated population was 92,587, as compared with 83,000 in mid-1969 and 52,838 at the 1956 census. Population density was 124 inhabitants per sq km in 1973 (320 per sq mi). The annual natural rate of population increase in 1973 was about 2.3%, based on a birthrate of 25.8 per 1,000 population, a death rate of 2.5 per 1,000, and a net natural increase of 23.3

More than half the inhabitants live on Tongatapu, where Nuku'alofa, the capital and chief port, had a population of about 25,000 in 1972. The next largest port city is Neiafu on Vava'u.

⁶ETHNIC GROUPS

The Tongans are a racially homogeneous Polynesian people. Less than 2% of the population is of European, part-European, or other origin.

⁷LANGUAGE

Tongan, a Polynesian language not written down until the 19th century, is the language of the kingdom, but government publications are issued in both Tongan and English, and English is taught as a secondary language in the schools. The word *Tonga* means "south."

⁸RELIGION

About 60% of Tongans are members of the Free Wesleyan Church of Tonga. Another 20% belong to the Church of Jesus Christ of Latter-day Saints, and the other 20% belong to various other Christian churches.

⁹TRANSPORTATION

There are 120 miles of all-weather roads. Graded earth roads total some 250 miles. There are no bridges in Tonga, but three islands in the Vava'u group are connected by two causeways. In 1973 there were an estimated 400 commercial vehicles, 900 private vehicles, and 343 motorcycles. Tonga has no railways.

Nuku'alofa on Tongatapu and Neiafu on Vava'u are ports of entry for overseas vessels. A New Zealand shipping company maintains bimonthly service on runs from New Zealand to Fiji to Tonga. There are regular services to Australia, and cargo ships visit the group from time to time for shipments of copra. Shipments entered and cleared in 1973 amounted to 610,889 tons. Sea connections within the kingdom are maintained by several motor ships and by sailing vessels. The Tonga Copra Board operates a 500-ton cargo and passenger boat and a transporter operates in the Ha'apai group. A 52-foot launch with cargo holds operates in the Vava'u group.

Fau'amotu, 14 miles from Nuku'alofa by road, is the site of an airfield. A new runway opened in 1973, allowing the first jet flights into Tonga by Air Pacific. Other air services are operated between Fiji and Tonga by Fiji Air and between Western Samoa and Tonga by Polynesian Airlines. In 1973, 405 planes arrived. Twice-daily flights between Tongatapu and ʻEua were begun in 1973 when construction of an airport at ʻEua was completed.

¹⁰COMMUNICATIONS

The government's radiotelegraph station at Nukuʻi alofa has substations at Neiafu (Vavaʻu), Pangai, Haʻafeva, and Nomuka (Haʻapai), ʻEua, and Niuatoputapu. There is also a direct overseas telegraph service between Nukuʻalofa and Wellington, Suva, and Apia. An internal radiotelephone service links Nukuʻalofa, ʻEua, Nomuka, Haʻafeva, Haʻapai, and Vavaʻu, and a direct overseas radiotelephone service links Nukuʻalofa to Suva, Apia, Niue, and Pago Pago. There were 1,090 telephones in Tonga in 1973.

The Tonga Broadcasting Commission's station, now named the Call of the Friendly Islands, was established in 1961. It has two medium-wave transmitters of 10 kw each, and broadcasts 60 hours a week in Tongan, English, Fijian, and Samoan. In 1972 there were 9,000 radios on the islands. There is no television in Tonga.

¹¹HISTORY

Since the Tongan language was not written down until the 19th century, the early history of the islands is based on oral tradition. Hereditary, absolute kings (Tuʻi Tonga) date back to Ahoeitu in the 10th century. About the 15th century the twenty-third king, Kauʻulufonua, while retaining his sacred powers, divested himself of much of his executive authority, transferring it to his brother Maʻungamotuʻa, whom he thereafter called the Tuʻi Haʻatakalaua. About the middle of the 17th century, the seventh temporal king, Fotofili, transferred the executive power to his brother Ngala, called the Tuʻi Kanokupolu, and thereafter the powers gradually passed into the hands of the latter and his descendants. In the mid-19th century, upon the death of the then Tuʻi Tonga, those powers were conferred upon the nineteenth Tuʻi Kanokupolu, Taufaʻahu Tupou, founder of the present dynasty, who took the name George in 1831 and was proclaimed king in 1845.

The island of Niuatoputapu was discovered by the Dutch navigators Jan Schouten and Jacob Le Maire in 1616. In 1643, Abel Tasman discovered Tongatapu, and from then until 1767, when Samuel Wallis anchored at Niuatoputapu, there was no contact with the outside world. James Cook visited Tongatapu and the Haʻapai groups in 1773 and again in 1777, and called Lifuka in the Haʻapai group the friendly island, whence the islands received their nickname, the Friendly Islands. It was in the waters of the Haʻapai group of islands that the mutiny on the *Bounty* occurred.

During the first half of the 19th century, there were civil wars, as the three lines of kings all sought dominance. They were finally checked during the reign of George Tupou I (1797–1893), who by conquest had gathered all power in his own hands.

In 1826, the first Wesleyan missionaries landed in Tonga. By the middle of the century, most chiefs and people had become Christians, the great majority being Wesleyans. George I came strongly under missionary influence and granted a constitution in 1875. In the latter part of the century, there were religious and civil conflicts between the Wesleyan Mission Church and the newly established Free Wesleyan Church of Tonga. After the dismissal of the prime minister, the Rev. Shirley Waldemar Baker, in 1890, the new government allowed full freedom of worship. In the 1920s, the dissenting factions were united in the Free Wesleyan Church of Tonga, of which King Taufaʻahau Tupou IV is now the head.

In 1900, during the reign of George II, a treaty of friendship was concluded between the UK and Tonga, and a protectorate was proclaimed. Queen Salote Tupou succeeded to the throne in

1918. Following her death, on 23 December 1965, she was succeeded by her eldest son, King Taufaʻahau Tupou IV, who was crowned in July 1967.

Two more treaties of friendship between the UK and Tonga were signed in 1958 and in May 1968, under which Tonga continued to be a state under UK protection, but with full freedom in internal affairs. External affairs generally remained the responsibility of the UK but certain aspects were conducted by the government of Tonga. On 4 June 1970, Tonga became an independent nation within the Commonwealth. The change in status from a UK protectorate foreshadowed few changes apart from the fact that it added Tongan control of foreign affairs to self-rule in domestic affairs.

In 1973, Tonga celebrated the bicentennial of Capt. Cook's first visit by inaugurating the new runway at Fuaʻamotu's airport with the islands' initial jet service by Air Pacific.

¹²GOVERNMENT

Tonga is an independent kingdom. According to the constitution of 1875, as amended, the government is divided into three main bodies: the sovereign, Privy Council, and cabinet; the Legislative Assembly; and the judiciary. The King-in-Council is the chief executive body, and the cabinet, presided over by the appointed prime minister, makes executive decisions of lesser importance. Lawmaking power is vested in the Legislative Assembly, which consists of a speaker appointed by the sovereign, the members of the Privy Council, 7 nobles elected by the 33 hereditary nobles of Tonga, and 7 representatives popularly elected every three years. The people's representatives are elected as independents, 3 from the Tongatapu island group, and 2 each from the Haʻapaoi and Vavaʻu groups. Sessions must be held at least once in every calendar year. Legislation passed by the Privy Council is subject to approval at the next meeting of the Legislative Assembly. Women voted for the first time in 1960. In July 1969, 40,000 Tongans voted in the election for the 7 people's representatives to the Legislative Assembly.

¹³POLITICAL PARTIES

There are no political parties.

¹⁴LOCAL GOVERNMENT

The islands are divided administratively into three districts, Vavaʻu in the north, Haʻapai in the center, and Tongatapu in the south. Haʻapai, Vavaʻu, and the outlying islands are administered by governors who are members of the Privy Council and are responsible to the prime minister. Minor officials perform statutory duties in the villages. Town and district officials have been popularly elected since 1965.

Titles of nobility were first bestowed in 1875, and later in 1882, 1887, 1903, and 1923. With the hereditary titles were granted villages and lands.

¹⁵JUDICIAL SYSTEM

The Supreme Court exercises jurisdiction in major civil and criminal cases. Other cases are heard in magistrates' courts or the Land Court, and appealed to the Supreme Court. Appeals from the Supreme Court and lower courts are made to the King-in-Council. With the ratification of the 1968 treaty, UK extraterritorial jurisdiction lapsed, and UK and other foreign nationals became fully subject to the jurisdiction of the Tongan courts.

¹⁶ARMED FORCES

The Tonga Defense Force was organized in World War II, became defunct in 1946, and was reactivated in 1952. It consists of a regular cadre and volunteers serving an initial training period, followed by attendance at annual training camps. The commander of the army is a New Zealand army officer. The minister of police heads a department consisting of more than 200 commissioned officers, noncommissioned officers, and policemen. A defense services patrol boat was commissioned in 1973 to patrol territorial waters.

[17]MIGRATION

There is considerable movement toward the larger towns, as the rapidly increasing population creates shortages of land. Some locally born non-Tongans migrate mainly to Fiji and New Zealand. Increasing emigration by Tongan workers, both skilled and unskilled, is of concern to the government.

Persons wishing to reside in Tonga must obtain a government permit. Permission is granted only to persons taking up approved employment. Immigrant settlement is not encouraged because of the land shortage.

[18]INTERNATIONAL COOPERATION

Tonga is a member of the Commonwealth of Nations, the South Pacific Forum, the Asian Development Bank, WHO, and the South Pacific Health Service. It avails itself of the advice and assistance of UNICEF. Tongan representatives have attended and taken a leading part at the South Pacific conferences. Since 1965, Tonga has received aid under the Australian South Pacific Technical Assistance Program. Tonga is a signatory of the Lomé Convention.

[19]ECONOMY

The economy is entirely agricultural, depending principally on the export of copra, bananas, and melons. There has been no development of mines, commercially exploitable forests, or large factories, although some ventures, especially in tourism, have been started. Potential development of an oil industry has been investigated since the discovery of small seepages of oil on Tongatapu and 'Eua in 1968. By 1975, however, test wells had yielded no positive indication of the extent of oil resources.

[20]INCOME

No recent figures on national income are available. In 1970/71, the GDP was T$13,300,000, nearly half of it derived from agriculture and fishing. Per capita income for that year was about T$149. Contributions to the GDP in 1970/71 included agriculture, forestry, and fishing, 47.4%; wholesale and retail trade, 9%; transport, storage, and communications, 5.3%; construction, 4.5%; and other sectors, 33.8%.

[21]LABOR

Most Tongans cultivate their own statutory holdings. Local firms, contractors, and leaseholders obtain their labor from those who offer their services. A Ministry of Labour, Commerce, and Industries was organized in 1973 with the goal of developing a labor code that would include a realistic wage structure, a system of job classification, and provisions for workmen's compensation. Holidays are prescribed by law. According to the constitution, it is not lawful to work, play games, or trade on Sunday. There are no trade unions.

The Public Works Department, the Nuku'alofa Electric Power Board, and the Tonga Visitors Bureau, the Tonga Copra Board, and its subsidiary, the Tonga Construction Company, all offer vocational training.

[22]AGRICULTURE

About 70% of Tonga is agricultural land, including small amounts of pasture and forest lands. With increasing population pressure on the land, more land is being intensively cultivated and less is available for fallow. The use of fertilizers, high-protein strains of corn, and similar methods to improve the efficiency of land use have become increasingly necessary.

According to the constitution of 1875, all the land in the kingdom belongs to the crown and cannot be alienated. Much of it, however, consists of hereditary estates that were bestowed upon various chiefs, who lease the lands to farmers at a nominal annual rent. Since 1890 the crown has been responsible for the collection of rents and the granting of allotments.

On reaching the age of 16, every Tongan male taxpayer is entitled under the constitution to a tax allotment of 1 'api (8.25 acres). These allotments are hereditary, pass from generation to generation in accordance with the law of succession, and may not be sold. A tenant may be ejected for nonpayment of rent or for failing to comply with the planting regulations under which every Tongan holder of a tax allotment is legally required to plant 200 coconut trees, which he must keep clean and free from weeds. Rapid population increases have made it impossible to guarantee the 'api to all those constitutionally entitled to one.

Principal subsistence crops are yams, taro, sweet potatoes, and manioc. Agricultural exports in 1973 included: 12,362 tons of copra, 17,466 bags of coconuts, 1,332 tons of desiccated coconut, 113,506 cases of bananas, 118,096 watermelons, 16,618 boxes of capsicum, and 46 cases of vanilla beans.

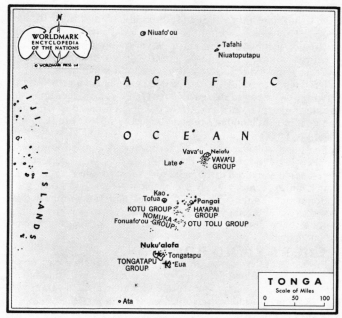

See Pacific Ocean map: front cover J8

LOCATION: 15° to 23°30'S; 173° to 177°W. **TERRITORIAL SEA LIMIT:** 12 mi.

The Department of Agriculture operates extension and farmer training programs, undertakes research in agronomy and pest control, and provides varied services, including machinery loan pools and the coconut replanting scheme. The experimental farms concentrate mainly on the production of corn and sweet potatoes for livestock feed, the development of vanilla plantations, and the cultivation of new vegetable crops, including tomatoes, Chinese and European cabbages, and bulb onions. The Tonga Copra Board and the Tonga Produce Board, two nonprofit organizations charged with exporting the two chief crops, enforce marketing control and ensure a maximum return to the producers. Cooperatives provide loans for agricultural development.

[23]ANIMAL HUSBANDRY

Beef cattle are generally raised and owned by Europeans, who use them for grazing in coconut plantations to keep the undergrowth in check and to provide additional income. Every householder has several hogs, which generally are not sold but are used for feasts. Sheep were brought into Tonga in 1954 but did not thrive, and in 1956 the entire flock was slaughtered. Livestock in 1973 included 34,491 hogs, 44,838 horses, and 2,689 head of cattle. The insufficient supply of fresh meat is supplemented by the importation of fresh, salted, and canned meats.

24 FISHING

Fish are abundant in the coastal waters, but the fishing industry has not been developed, and the supply of fish is insufficient to meet local demand. Thus, some fish must be imported. No organized commercial fishing by private or foreign enterprises is permitted within Tongan waters, although a Japanese firm has proposed establishment of a tuna base in the northern Vava'u group. The government-owned fishing vessel produces from 60 to 90 tons annually, principally tuna and shark. Turtles and shellfish are plentiful in local waters; however, there has been some concern about overharvesting of turtles during the December-January nesting period. An experimental project in oyster cultivation was begun in 1973.

25 FORESTRY

Forest lands cover about 14% of Tonga, mainly on 'Eua and Vava'u, but they have not been fully exploited, and wood for construction must be imported. Nine small local mills produce mostly shooks for banana cases. A government sawmill on 'Eua produces lumber for building and furniture. Ample timber reserves remain on 'Eua to satisfy local lumber needs.

The Department of Agriculture is carrying on a reforestation program; 430 acres were replanted and 12,000 seedlings distributed to farmers in 1973. Charcoal is manufactured from logs and coconut shell under a project begun with FAO funds.

26 MINING

Tonga has few known mineral resources. A limited amount of crushed stone is produced at local quarries. Oil is reported to have been discovered through its seepage into water wells. Tonga signed an agreement in 1970 with an international consortium under which Tonga will receive about half the profits if oil is found in commercially profitable quantities. However, exploration has been delayed, and reports from test drillings have been inconclusive.

27 ENERGY AND POWER

All power is derived from thermal sources. Installed capacity in 1972 was 1,400 kw. Electrical service has been expanded on Vava'u Island; in 1973, lines totaled about 1.2 miles serving 106 homes there. Output in 1973 totaled 5.3 million kwh.

28 INDUSTRY

Encouragement of new industries was a goal of the 1970–75 development plan, to be achieved in part by the Ministry of Labour, Commerce, and Industry, established in 1973. Industries at that time included coconut-processing, sawmills, local handicrafts, and tourism. There were 35 companies officially registered in Tonga in 1973, an increase from 31 in 1972.

29 DOMESTIC TRADE

Village stores carry a stock of flour, sugar, canned meats, textiles, hardware, soap, kerosene, tobacco, and matches. They are operated by Tongans or managed by Tongans for European trading firms in the larger towns. Storekeepers act as agents for the Copra Board and often extend credit to their customers until the end of the harvest. The Tonga Produce Board concerns itself with bananas, melons, and pineapples.

Development of cooperatives, of which there were 16 in 1973, was being actively pursued with a grant from the UK. They serve as savings and loan, produce marketing, and handicraft manufacturing organizations.

30 FOREIGN TRADE

Tonga's total exports in 1973 were valued at T$3,244,600, and imports at T$7,996,600. Major exports in 1973 (in thousands of pa'angas) were:

Coconut products	2,547
Bananas	306
Watermelons	157
Curios and handicrafts	34
Taro and sweet potatoes	27
Capsicum	22
Other exports	152
TOTAL	3,245

Major imports in 1973 (in thousands of pa'angas) were:

Meat	682
Flour	638
Textiles and clothing	503
Motor vehicles	472
Cigarettes	326
Timber	260
Hardware	244
Iron and steel	231
Other imports	4,641
TOTAL	7,997

Tonga's principal trading partners in 1973 (in thousands of pa'angas) were:

	EXPORTS	IMPORTS	BALANCE
New Zealand	673	2,773	− 2,100
Australia	732	2,399	− 1,666
UK	189	626	− 436
Japan	36	507	− 471
Fiji	54	428	− 373
Iran	0	368	− 367
Others	1,561	896	661
TOTALS	3,245	7,997	−4,752

31 BALANCE OF PAYMENTS

Since 1960, Tonga has had a growing trade deficit. In 1972/73, the deficit in goods and services reached T$5,159,684, up from T$2,888,028 in 1969/70. However, foreign funds received by Tonga have offset these deficits; these funds totaled T$7,695,170 in 1972/73. Invisibles (each category supplying over T$1 million in 1972/73) include remittances from Tongans working overseas, earnings from tourism, donations, and foreign bank transfers. Tonga's balance of payments for 1969/70 and 1972/73 (in pa'angas) were summarized as follows:

	1969/70	1972/73
GOODS AND SERVICES		
Exports	2,737,697	2,016,185
Imports	−5,625,725	−7,175,869
BALANCE	−2,888,028	−5,159,684
Invisibles	2,749,126	5,403,886
Loans and grants	597,050	77,807
TOTALS	458,148	322,009

32 BANKING

The Bank of Tonga was formed in 1971 with the government holding 40% of the shares and 20% each held by the Bank of Hawaii, Bank of New Zealand, and Bank of New South Wales. The overseas banks provided staff and supervision for the Bank of Tonga, which offers all commercial services and has assumed responsibility for government savings, traders' current accounts, and foreign exchange dealings.

33 INSURANCE

A single insurance firm, the Australian-based Queensland Insurance Co., operates in Tonga.

34 SECURITIES
There are no securities exchanges or stock issues in Tonga.

35 PUBLIC FINANCE
Total revenues in 1974/75 were T$4,196,936, and total expenditures were T$4,602,422. Principal revenues and expenditures for the fiscal years ending 30 June 1972 and 30 June 1973 (in thousands of pa'angas) were:

REVENUES	1971/72	1972/73
Import duties	1,051	1,182
Export duties	153	182
Port and wharf taxes	420	380
Income tax	205	206
Philatelic revenue	104	112
Interest	150	92
Other receipts	1,060	1,203
TOTALS	3,143	3,357

EXPENDITURES		
Education	500	549
Health	447	486
Prime minister's office	354	421
Works	274	289
Agriculture	223	227
Police	207	211
Wharf	90	98
Other expenditures	1,061	975
TOTALS	3,156	3,256

Tonga's total debt as of 30 June 1973 amounted to T$962,796, of which T$297,016 was external debt.

36 TAXATION
Income tax rates vary from 1.25 seniti on the first T$200 of taxable income to 38 seniti on each pa'anga of all taxable income over T$2,500. Businesses pay 25 seniti on the pa'anga.

All male Tongans 16 years of age and older, except the aged and infirm, pay an annual poll tax, the receipts of which are used to finance free education and medical benefits.

37 CUSTOMS AND DUTIES
Customs duties are the main source of revenue, accounting for about 40% of the total in 1972/73. They include specific ad valorem duties on imports and an export tax on copra. The general tariff ranges up to 33% ad valorem and the preferential tariff on Commonwealth items is up to 15% ad valorem. A port tax and customs service tax of 5% are payable on all imports. Various items are admitted free. The export tax on copra is about 10% of the f.o.b. value. Stamp duties are payable on bills of lading and other documents.

38 FOREIGN INVESTMENTS
Although some non-Tongans have leased large plantations and residential and business sites, there is relatively little foreign investment in Tonga.

In 1972, the UK granted an interest-free loan of about T$475,000 for protection of fisheries, airport development, electrification, road building, and other local needs. Other foreign aid in funds and services comes from New Zealand and Australia.

To offset the drain on reserves, the government is seeking new foreign investment. An announcement was made in April 1969 that foreign investment was welcome and that the government would arrange conditions for leasing of land, tax liberalization, and the arrangement of import and export licenses.

39 ECONOMIC POLICY
The 1970–75 development plan aimed at encouraging industries, diversification of agricultural production, and development of fisheries, transportation, and tourism. Expenditures under the plan, for the year ending 30 June 1973, were T$849,018, of which T$270,007 was on civil aviation and T$134,404 on marine shipping. Through the nonprofit Tonga Copra Board and the Tonga Produce Board, the government has a trading monopoly in copra, bananas, and melons.

40 HEALTH
Major diseases are tuberculosis, filariasis, typhoid fever, dysentery, eye conditions, and skin diseases. In comparison with other Pacific islands, however, Tonga is a healthy country. The crude death rate decreased from 8.9 per 1,000 in 1957 to 2.5 in 1973, and infant mortality declined from 68.9 per 1,000 live births to 5 during the same period. A joint WHO-UNICEF yaws eradication project was started in 1962, and by 1969, the incidence of yaws was low. Other projects in operation include the School Sanitation and Community Water Supply, the Maternal and Child Health, and Nursing Education programs.

Tongans receive free medical and dental treatment, but must pay for dentures. Non-Tongans are charged on a fixed scale. Tonga had 27 physicians, 8 dentists, and 181 nurses in 1973, along with 3 hospitals (266 beds) and 7 rural clinics.

Tonga is a member of the South Pacific Health Service, and receives aid from WHO, UNICEF, the UN Fund for Population Activities, and other agencies.

41 SOCIAL WELFARE
Every family is provided by law with sufficient land to support itself. There is no social welfare department. The medical and education departments and the missions provide what welfare services are available. There is no poor relief or old age pension scheme other than the provision made for pension payments to civil servants. Tonga has a family planning program which is integrated with maternal and child health services. Popular acceptance of family planning services increased notably between 1966 to 1974; the program had a total of 8,892 participants by the end of 1973.

42 HOUSING
Village houses usually are built of reed sides and a sloping roof thatched with sugarcane or coconut leaves; the posts are of ironwood, and braided cord takes the place of nails. More modern houses, especially in the towns, are built of wood, with roofs of corrugated iron. Unlike the village houses, they often contain more than one room and have verandas.

Rainwater is stored in concrete cisterns. With the help of WHO, a plan to tap underground fresh water was begun in 1958. The success of the plan has led to the extension of fresh water supplies to villages on all major islands.

Each Tongan taxpayer is entitled to a rent-free land allotment for urban residential purposes.

43 EDUCATION
The first schools in Tonga were started by the Wesleyan Mission in 1828, even before the conversion to Christianity of the Tongans, and practically all the primary education was controlled by the Mission until 1882, when the government took control of the educational system. In 1906, various mission bodies again were allowed to establish schools.

Education is compulsory for all Tongans between the ages of 6 and 14. Mission schools follow a government syllabus; mission primary schools, which enroll about 25% of all primary pupils, are annually inspected. Mission schools enroll more than 80% of students at postprimary level. Education is free in government schools except the high school, but small fees are charged at mission schools. Primary schools are coeducational, and most pupils enter at age 6. In 1973/74 there were 16,688 pupils in Tonga's primary schools and 10,217 in secondary schools. Elementary instruction is given in the Tongan language; English is also taught. Selected Tongan students prepare for the New Zealand school certificate examination.

A teacher-training college, established in 1944, provides a two-year course; in 1973/74, the college had an enrollment of 93. That same year there were 265 students in five technical and vocational schools. A government scholarship program provides higher education opportunities in foreign countries to 70 Tongans a year.

⁴⁴LIBRARIES AND MUSEUMS

There are small libraries in the larger towns. The teacher-training college also has a small library of approximately 5,000 volumes. There are no museums. Notable monuments include the great trilithon known as the Ha'amanga and some 45 langis, great rectangular platforms of recessed tiers of coral limestone blocks erected as the tombs of the medieval kings.

⁴⁵ORGANIZATIONS

Every Tongan village has a community house, with a thatched roof and open sides, where ceremonial cloth (tapa) is made by groups of women. The Tongan Women's Progressive Association, formed in 1956, conducts programs in the betterment of village conditions and holds classes in useful subjects. There are Boy Scout and Girl Guide groups. Christian Endeavor societies and Bible classes are well attended. Extension of cooperatives, which numbered 16 in 1973, is being actively encouraged by the government with aid from a UK grant.

⁴⁶PRESS

The government publishes a weekly, averaging 3,000 copies in Tongan and 800 in English. There are also church newspapers issued by missions at regular intervals. There is no news agency.

⁴⁷TOURISM

The minister of police grants prior-arrival visitors' permits up to a maximum of six months. Permits are not required from persons in direct transit, holders of Tongan passports, and any government officials traveling on official business.

Development of the tourist industry is seen as a potential source of overseas funds for Tonga. The entire industry earned T$1.5 million in 1973. The government-owned International Dateline Hotel in 1973 had a 23.5% rise in revenues over the previous year, to T$264,382. In 1973, 6,356 visitors arrived by air, a 38% increase over 1972. There were nearly 40,000 passengers on the 71 cruise ships that called at Tongan ports in 1973, an increase of 10,000 over 1972.

⁴⁸FAMOUS TONGANS

King George I (1797–1893) ruled for 48 years; during his reign, Tonga became a Christian nation and acquired a constitution. His prime minister, Shirley Waldemar Baker (1831–1903), was a Wesleyan clergyman, who, after being deposed in 1890, became an Episcopal minister and returned to Tonga. The most famous Tongan of this century was Queen Salote Tupou (1900–1964), whose rule began in 1918. Her dynasty, the Tupou, is the third branch of the royal family and traces its descent back 42 generations to Ahoeitu, first Tu'i Tonga of whom there is record. King Taufa'ahau Tupou IV (b. 1918) was crowned in 1967 and is Tonga's present sovereign.

⁴⁹DEPENDENCIES

Tonga has no dependencies.

⁵⁰BIBLIOGRAPHY

Adams, Emma Hildreth. *The Tonga Islands and Other Groups.* Oakland, Calif.: Pacific Press Pub. Co., 1890.

Bain, K. R. *The Friendly Islanders.* London: Hodder and Stoughton, 1959.

Bain, K. R. *The Official Record of the Royal Visit to Tonga, 19th-20th December, 1953.* London: Pitkin, 1954.

Beaglehold, Ernest. *Pangai, Village in Tonga.* Wellington: The Polynesian Society, 1941.

Blamires, Gwen G. *Little Island Kingdom of the South.* London: Stockwell, 1939.

Churchwood, C.M. *Tongan Dictionary.* London: Oxford University Press, 1959.

Collocott, Ernest Edgar Vyvyan. *Tales and Poems of Tonga.* Honolulu: Bishop Museum, 1928.

Cook, James. *A Voyage to the Pacific Ocean.* London: 1785. Vol. I, pp. 205–416.

Gifford, Edward Winslow. *Tongan Myths and Tales.* Honolulu: Bishop Museum, 1924.

Gifford, Edward Winslow. *Tongan Place Names.* Honolulu: Bishop Museum, 1923.

Gifford, Edward Winslow. *Tongan Society.* Honolulu: Bishop Museum, 1929.

Kennedy, T. F. *Geography of Tonga.* Nuku'alofa: Government Printer, 1957.

Latukefu, Sione. *Church and State in Tonga.* Honolulu: University of Hawaii Press, 1974.

Ledyard, Patricia. *Tonga: A Tale of the Friendly Islands.* New York: Appleton-Century-Crofts, 1956.

Luke, Sir Harry Charles Joseph. *From a South Seas Diary, 1938–1942.* London: Nicholson and Ward, 1945.

Luke, Sir Harry Charles Joseph. *Queen Salote and Her Kingdom.* London: Putnam, 1954.

McKern, Will Carleton. *Archaeology of Tonga.* Honolulu: Bishop Museum, 1929.

Macquarrie, Hector. *Friendly Queen.* London: Heinemann, 1955.

Martin, John. *An Account of the Natives of the Tonga Islands, with an Original Grammar and Vocabulary of Their Language, Compiled and Arranged from the Extensive Communications of Mr. William Mariner.* London: Murray, 1817.

Neill, James Scott. *Ten Years in Tonga.* London: Hutchinson, 1955.

Orange, James. *Life of the Late George Vason, of Nottingham, One of the Troop of Missionaries First Sent to the South Sea Islands.* London: 1840.

Parsonage, W. *The Story of Tonga (for Tonga Schools).* Auckland: 1941.

Rutherford, Noel. *Shirley Baker and the King of Tonga.* New York: Oxford University Press, 1972.

Thomson, Sir Basil Home. *The Diversions of a Prime Minister.* Edinburgh: Blackwood, 1894.

Vason, George. *An Authentic Narrative of Four Years' Residence at Tongataboo, One of the Friendly Islands, in the South Sea.* London: Longman, Hurst, Rees, and Orme, 1810.

Ward, John Manning. *British Policy in the South Pacific (1786–1893).* Sydney: Australasian Publishing Co., 1948.

West, Thomas. *Ten Years in South-Central Polynesia: Being Reminiscences of a Personal Mission to the Fiji Islands and Their Dependencies.* London: Nisbet, 1865.

TURKEY

Republic of Turkey
Türkiye Cumhuriyeti

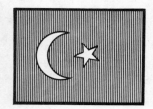

CAPITAL: Ankara. **FLAG**: The national flag consists of a white crescent (open toward the fly) and a white star on a red field. **ANTHEM**: *Istiklâl Marşi (March of Independence)*. **MONETARY UNIT**: The Turkish lira (TL) of 100 kuruş is a nonconvertible paper currency. There are coins of 5, 10, 25, 100, and 250 kuruş, and 1, 2½, and 25 liras, and notes of 5, 10, 50, 100, 500, and 1,000 liras. TL1 = $0.066 (or $1 = TL15.15). **WEIGHTS AND MEASURES**: The metric system is the legal standard. **HOLIDAYS**: New Year's Day, 1 January; National Sovereignty and Children's Day, 23 April; Spring Holiday, 1 May; Youth and Sports Holiday, 19 May; Constitution Day, 27 May; Victory Day, 30 August; Independence Day (Anniversary of the Republic), 29 October. Movable religious holidays include the Breaking of the Fast (three days) and the Sacrificial Festival (four days). **TIME**: 2 P.M. = noon GMT.

¹LOCATION, SIZE, AND EXTENT

The Republic of Turkey consists of Asia Minor, a small area in Thrace, and a few small offshore islands in the Aegean Sea, with a total area of 779,452 sq km (300,947 sq mi), extending 1,600 km (994 mi) SE–NW and 650 km (404 mi) NE–SW. Of the overall area, 97% is in Asia, and 3% in Europe. Turkey lies athwart the important Black Sea straits system—the Dardanelles, the Sea of Marmara, and the Bosporus. It is bordered on the N by the Black Sea, on the NE by the USSR, on the E by Iran, on the SE by Iraq, on the S by Syria and the Mediterranean Sea, on the W by the Aegean Sea, and on the NW by Greece and Bulgaria, with a total boundary length of 11,068 km (6,878 mi).

²TOPOGRAPHY

Other than the low, rolling hills of Turkish Thrace, the fertile river valleys that open to the Aegean sea, the warm plains of Antalya and Adana on the Mediterranean, and the narrow littoral along the Black Sea, the country is wrinkled by rugged mountain ranges that surround and intersect the high, semiarid Anatolian plateau. Average elevations range from 2,000 feet above sea level in the west to 6,000 feet amid the wild eastern highlands. The highest point is Mount Ararat (16,946 feet), which rises just within Turkey at the intersection of the Turkish, Soviet, and Iranian frontiers. There are 113 peaks with elevations of 10,000 feet or more. Other than the Tigris and Euphrates, which have their sources in eastern Turkey, rivers are relatively small. Because the watersheds of these streams are semibarren slopes, the seasonal variations in flow are very great. The largest lake is Lake Van (1,451 sq mi); the other major lake is Salt Lake (Tuz), whose water has a salinity so high that it serves as a commercial source of salt. Turkey's 5,167 miles of coastline (in addition to land frontiers of 1,711 miles) provide few good natural harbors. Most of Turkey lies within an earthquake zone, and recurrent tremors are recorded. On 29–30 March 1970 more than 1,000 earthquakes were felt in the Gediz region of western Turkey, killing 1,086 persons. Another quake, on 6 September 1975, 75 miles west of Lake Van, resulted in at least 2,300 deaths. The record destructive earthquake, however, was that of 29 December 1939—near Erzincan—which killed 30,000 persons.

³CLIMATE

Turkey's southern coast enjoys a Mediterranean climate. The Aegean coastal climate as far north as Izmir is much the same. The mean temperature range in these regions is 17°–20°C (63°–68°F), and the annual rainfall ranges from 27.6 to 43.3 inches. The northern Aegean-Marmara area is somewhat cooler, but also quite moist, the mean temperature range being 14°–17°C (57°–63°F) and annual rainfall between 21.6 and 27.6 inches. The Black Sea coast is also relatively mild (14°–15°C, or 57°–59°F) and very moist (27.6 to 98.4 inches of rainfall). The central Anatolian plateau is noted for its hot, dry summers and cold winters: the average annual temperature is 8°–12°C (46°–54°F) and annual precipitation is 11.8 to 29.5 inches. With the exception of some warmer pockets in the valleys, the eastern third of Turkey is colder (4°–9°C, or 39°–48°F), and rainfall averages 15.7 to 19.7 inches. On the central plateau, what little precipitation there is tends to be concentrated during the late fall and winter months.

⁴FLORA AND FAUNA

A wide variation of flora is found, semitropical to temperate, desert to alpine. In the mountains of southern, southwestern, and northern Turkey are extensive coniferous stands of commercial importance and some deciduous forest. Licorice, valonia oaks, and wild olive trees grow in the southwest. Principal varieties of wild animals are the fallow deer, red deer, roe deer, eastern mouflon, wild boar, hare, Turkish leopard, brown bear, red fox, gazelle, beech marten, pine marten, wildcat, lynx, otter, and badger. A large variety of birds is reported, including the snow partridge, quail, great bustard, little bustard, widgeon, woodcock, snipe, and a variety of geese, ducks, pigeons, and rails. About 30 species of snakes are listed. Bees and silkworms are grown commercially. As of 1975, endangered species in Turkey included the wolf, Anatolian leopard, cheetah, Mediterranean monk seal, Syrian wild ass, and waldrapp.

⁵POPULATION

According to the 1975 census (provisional results), Turkey's population was 40,197,669, an increase of 13% over the 1970 census figure of 35,605,176. A population of 45,363,000 was projected for 1980. About 57% of the population lives in rural communities; the urban population is about 43%. The average annual population increase during 1962–72 was 2.49%. Istanbul (formerly Constantinople), the largest city, had a 1974 population of 2,250,000. The six largest cities after Istanbul are Ankara, the capital, 1,236,152; Izmir (formerly Smyrna), 520,832; Adana, 347,454; Bursa, 275,953; Gaziantep, 227,652; and Ekişehir, 216,373.

⁶ETHNIC GROUPS

Major ethnic minorities (by mother tongue) in 1965 were Kurds 2,219,502, Arabs 365,340, Greeks 48,096, Circassians 58,339, Armenians 33,094, Georgians 34,330, Bosnians 17,627, and Lazes 26,007. Hundreds of thousands of Armenians were either killed or forced to flee during and immediately following World War I.

The Greek component in Turkey was reduced as a result of the 1919–22 hostilities with Greece, the 1923 Treaty of Lausanne (which provided for an exchange of population with Greece), and the post-World War II Cyprus controversy. The Kurds, though some were forcibly dispersed after an uprising in 1935, tend to be concentrated in the eastern provinces; the Arabs, in the south along the Syrian and Iraqi frontiers; and the Greeks, Armenians, and Jews in Istanbul and, to a lesser extent, in Izmir.

7 LANGUAGE

Turkish, a Ural-Altaic language, is the universal tongue. In addition to the Roman alphabet, modern Turkish uses the letters ç, ğ, ı (undotted), ö, ş, and ü, but no q, w, or x. With but minor exceptions, words are spelled phonetically. The language is agglutinative. A 1928 language reform substituted the Roman alphabet for the Arabic script, which had been used by the Turks since their conversion to Islam. During the 1930s, there was a state-sponsored effort to rid the language of Arabic and Persian words and grammatical constructions. Turkish grammatical rules are now applied for all words, regardless of origin, though many Persian and Arabic expressions persist. Traditionally, there was a great difference between vernacular Turkish and written Ottoman Turkish, the latter being heavily Arabicized and Persianized and almost unintelligible to the mass of Turks. This difference has been almost obliterated, though some regional difference in dialect, particularly in the villages, still makes effective communication difficult.

8 RELIGION

Religious freedom is provided for by the constitution. Although about 99% of the population is Muslim, there is no official state religion. Nonetheless, the state maintains urban mosques and other Muslim religious properties, licenses Muslim religious leaders, and provides Muslim religious education in the public schools. Non-Muslims may worship as they please. Proselytizing by either Muslim or non-Muslim is proscribed by law. Laws against the use of religion for political purposes are rigorously enforced. The vast majority of Turkish Muslims are Sunni, but there is a substantial Shi'i minority. Although at times suppressed by law, secret religious sects—various dervish orders—have remained active in some areas. According to the 1965 census there were 31,129,845 Muslims, 73,725 Greek Orthodox, 69,526 Gregorians, 25,833 Roman Catholics, 22,983 Protestants, and 14,785 unspecified Christians. There were an estimated 30,000 Jews in 1974.

9 TRANSPORTATION

The difficult terrain and its size, together with limited economic resources, have proved great obstacles to the construction of transportation facilities. When the republic was founded in 1923 there were 4,023 km of railways and 7,403 km of motor roads in Anatolia and Thrace, all in disrepair. In 1973, 8,141 km of railways connected most of the important points in the country with Ankara, Istanbul, and the Black Sea and Mediterranean ports. The railways are owned and operated by the Turkish State Railways, a public corporation. Most track is standard gauge (56.5 inches), replacing the old narrow- and broad-gauge lines. Turkish railways carried 117,500,000 passengers and 15,902,000 tons of freight in 1973. Credits of $47 million from the IBRD and $28 million from the Export-Import Bank were secured in 1973 to help finance a $223-million railway rehabilitation project.

Although animal transport still predominates in most of the country, it is gradually giving way to trucks and buses that use roads provided by extensive construction programs of the past 30 years. In 1972 there were 163,001 km of national, provincial, and village roads (including 35,221 km of state highways); 18,989 km were paved. In October 1973, the Bosporus Bridge in Istanbul was opened, facilitating the crossing of the Straits of the Bosporus by motorists. During the 1970s, the government has cooperated with other CENTO nations in creating road and rail links with Iran and Pakistan and improving the ports at Iskenderun and Trabzan. As of December 1972 there were 358,543 nonmilitary vehicles. These included 131,771 passenger cars and 36,896 buses.

The Turkish merchant fleet in 1974 consisted of 102 vessels totaling 830,000 GRT. In 1973, 14,712,000 tons of goods were loaded at Turkish ports, and 27,549,000 tons unloaded. The leading ports were Mersin, Istanbul, and Izmir.

With minor exceptions, domestic air transport is the monopoly of the semipublic Turkish Airways Corporation, which connects most major centers within the country on regular schedule and operates some international flights. Two international airports—Yesilkoy (Istanbul) and Esenboga (Ankara)—are served by numerous air carriers.

10 COMMUNICATIONS

Postal, telephone, and telegraph service is owned and operated by a semi-independent government enterprise under the jurisdiction of the Ministry of Communications. Telephones in 1973 numbered about 807,000. There are automatic telephone exchanges in the major cities, but manual exchanges are still found in many towns and villages. Direct radiotelephone communication links Turkey with the principal countries of Europe, and service is abailable to the US. A telegraph and short-wave wireless also provide continuous domestic and international communication. Ground mail service is universal, and air mail is carried between principal cities.

The state operates the 17 radio stations and the television networks. Daily broadcasts under the direction of the Ministry of Press, Broadcasting, and Tourism, and originating from 1 of the 3 Ankara stations, are beamed abroad in 11 foreign languages. The number of licensed radio sets in 1972 was 3,933,718. There were 157,226 registered television sets in 1972. The television networks transmit programs from 20 cities.

11 HISTORY

The Turks are a Ural-Altaic people who emerged from the plains between the Ural Mountains in Europe and the Altai Mountains in Asia. Climatic and demographic factors forced them to migrate in all directions. The immigrants to the north constituted what is known today as Finland; those who moved westward laid the foundations of present-day Hungary. The forerunners of the inhabitants of present-day Turkey reached Asia Minor about ten centuries ago. In the battle of Malazgirt (1071), they defeated the Byzantines and established themselves in Asia minor. Known as the Seljuk Turks from 1071 to 1243, they attained a pinnacle of Muslim culture in their great capital at Konya, in central Turkey. Their power was shattered in 1243 when a Mongol invasion under Genghis Khan swept across Asia Minor.

As the Mongols withdrew, Turkish power revived and expanded under the Ottoman Turks, a group of frontier warriors whose first Süleyman chief was Osman (whose name became Ottoman in the West). In 1453, the Ottomans under Mehmet II (the Conqueror) occupied Constantinople (now Istanbul) and made it their capital. In 1516, they conquered Syria; in 1517, Egypt. In 1529, they were at the gates of Vienna, at which point the expansion of the Turkish power westward was stopped. At its peak, generally identified with the reign of Sultan Süleyman I (the Magnificent), the Ottoman Empire encompassed Asia Minor, much of the Arabian Peninsula, North Africa, the islands of the eastern Mediterranean, the Balkans, the Caucasus, and Crimea. During the 18th and 19th centuries, as a result of the rise of nationalism, it gradually shrank in size, the independence of the remainder being maintained only by shrewd balance-of-power diplomacy.

The process of modernization began with the Imperial Rescript of 1839 (Sultan Abdul Mejid) and a body of reforms known as the Tanzimat, which to some extent curbed the absolute powers of the sultan-caliph. (The Turkish sultans had added the title "caliph" following the conquest of Egypt in 1517.) The Illustrious Rescript of 1856, largely dictated by Britain, France, and Austria as part of the negotiations leading to the settlement of the Crimean War, ensured equal rights for non-Muslims, provided for prison reform and the codification of Turkish law, and opened Turkey to European skills and capital. A constitution was introduced in 1876 (Sultan Abdul Hamid II) but was suspended the following year. Thereafter, an absolute monarchy prevailed until the Young Turk revolution of 1908, at which time the constitution of 1876 was reinstated. In 1913, leaders of the Committee for Union and Progress (the organizational vehicle of the Young Turks) took effective control of the government under Sultan Mehmet V. The principal leaders were Talat and Enver Paşa, who at the outbreak of World

Turkish nationalist resistance movement under the leadership of Mustafa Kemal (later called Atatürk) finally defeated them in 1922. The sultan, being virtually captive in Istanbul, was disgraced in Turkish eyes by his identification with Allied policy. After much maneuvering, a rival nationalist government under Mustafa Kemal was established in Ankara and gained national and international recognition. On 1 November 1922 the sultanate was abolished by Mustafa Kemal's provisional government. In 1923, the Ankara government negotiated the Treaty of Lausanne with the Allies, which recognized Turkish sovereignty over Asia Minor and a small area in Thrace. On 29 October 1923, a republic was proclaimed, with Ankara as its capital, and on 3 March 1924 the caliphate was abolished and all members of the dynasty banished.

See continental political: front cover G6; physical: back cover G6.

LOCATION: 25°33' to 44°50'E; 35°51' to 42°6'N. **BOUNDARY LENGTHS:** USSR, 610 km (379 mi); Iran, 454 km (282 mi); Iraq, 331 km (206 mi); Syria, 877 km (545 mi); Greece, 212 km (132 mi); Bulgaria, 269 km (167 mi); total coastline, 8,315 km (5,167 mi). **TERRITORIAL SEA LIMIT:** 6 mi.

War I were forced to commit the Empire to the side of the Central Powers. During the war, Turkey, after a heroic defense at the Dardanelles, was defeated. An armistice was concluded at Mudros on 30 October 1918, and Enver Paşa and his colleagues fled the country. On the basis of a series of earlier Allied agreements, the Ottoman Empire was to be stripped of all non-Turkish areas and much of what remained—Asia Minor—was to be divided among the UK, France, Greece, and Italy. A substantial portion was actually occupied. In 1919, with Allied assistance, the Greeks invaded Anatolia through Izmir, but a

During the next few years, a series of social, legal, and political reforms were accomplished, which, taken collectively, became known as the Atatürk Reforms. They included the substitution of secular law for religious law, the writing of a republican constitution based on popular sovereignty, suppression of religious education in Turkish schools, introduction of a Roman alphabet to replace the Arabic script, and the legal upgrading of the position of women. With but minor exceptions, political power resided in a single party, the Republican People's Party, and to a very substantial extent with Mustafa Kemal personally until his death in 1938. In 1946, a two-party system of government was officially established with the formation of the opposition Democratic Party (DP).

Although pro-Allied, Turkey remained neutral during most of World War II, but early in 1945 it declared war on the Axis and became a charter member of the UN. In 1947, the Truman Doctrine pledged US support to Turkey in the face of mounting Soviet pressure. This move was followed by large-scale military and economic assistance from the US. As a result of these circumstances, Turkey became firmly committed to the Western alliances—NATO; the Central Treaty Organization, or CENTO (Baghdad Pact); and the Balkan Pact.

The DP came to power in 1950. Under Prime Minister Adnan Menderes, the government stressed rapid industrialization and economic expansion at the cost of individual liberties. Restrictive press laws were passed in 1954 and 1956, and by 1960 the Menderes government had curtailed judicial independence, university autonomy, and the rights of opposition parties. On 27 May 1960, after student demonstrations (joined by War College cadets and some army officers) were harshly suppressed, Prime Minister Menderes, President Celal Bayar, and other government leaders were arrested by a newly formed committee of national unity. Gen. Cemal Gürsel became acting president and prime minister. A new constitution was popularly ratified in 1961, and elections were held in October. Gen. Gürsel was elected president by the new Grand National Assembly, and Ismet Inönü became prime minister of a coalition government. Former President Bayar was released from prison on 7 November 1963. On 17 November 1963, the opposition Justice Party (JP) won sweeping majorities in local elections. In the elections of October 1965, the JP won 52.3% of the vote, and a new government was formed by Süleyman Demirel. Four years later, the JP was returned to power, winning 260 of the 450 seats in the House of Representatives of the bicameral National Assembly, and Prime Minister Demirel began a new four-year term. On 12 March 1971, Turkey's four top military commanders forced the resignation of Demirel's government. They called for a "strong and credible government" that would restore economic and political stability and suppress student disorders, which had steadily grown more frequent and more violent since 1968. Martial law had been imposed from June to September 1970, and a new coalition government under Nihat Erim reimposed martial law in 11 provinces (including Ankara and Istanbul) in April 1971; the special government powers were extended at two-month intervals until January 1973 and were not completely lifted until May.

Political stability proved no easier to achieve: a succession of weak coalition governments held office between 1971 and 1974. The government of Bülent Ecevit was in power during the Greco-Turkish war on Cyprus in July–August 1974. Relations with Greece, strained by a dispute over mineral rights on the Aegean continental shelf, reached the breaking point on 15 July, when Cypriot President Makarios was overthrown in a Greek-led military coup. Turkish forces invaded on 20 July. A UN ceasefire came into effect on 22 July, but after peace talks at Geneva broke down, Turkish troops consolidated their hold over the northern third of the island by 16 August. As of February 1976, about 28,000 Turkish troops remained on Cyprus. In February 1975, Greece and Turkey agreed in principle to submit their dispute over the Aegean to the ICJ.

The Ecevit government resigned on 18 September 1974, leading to the longest of Turkey's cabinet crises. Not until 31 March 1975 was a new permanent government formed, with Süleyman Demirel returning to power.

12 GOVERNMENT

According to the 1961 constitution, Turkey is a "national, democratic, secular, social" republic "based on human rights and rule of law." The exercise of national sovereignty may not be handed over to any individual, group, or class. The Grand National Assembly consists of the House of Representatives with a fixed membership of 450 (elected for four-year terms) and the Senate of 165 members, of whom 15 are appointed by the president to review proposed legislation and to check political preferences. Senate membership is for six years and one-third of the members are elected every two years. Members of the Grand National Assembly are elected by universal, direct, and secret adult suffrage and through a system of proportional representation. Voting is by plurality and by party lists in each province. The minimum voting age is 18.

The president of the republic—the head of state—is elected for a single seven-year term by a joint session of the Grand National Assembly, and he must resign from his party immediately after his election. Upon expiration of his presidential term, he becomes a life member of the Senate. The president designates the prime minister from among Assembly members; the prime minister in turn chooses other cabinet ministers, who are collectively responsible for general government policy. The president may call for general elections if the government fails to receive a vote of confidence three times in 18 months. The parliamentary year starts on 1 November. The constitution provides for autonomy for the National Central Bank, the universities, and the state radio and television, which had previously been under government control.

13 POLITICAL PARTIES

The first significant nationwide party was organized by Mustafa Kemal in 1923, the Republican People's Party (Cumhuriyet Halk Partisi—RPP), successor to the earlier popular resistance organization, the Society for the Defense of the Rights of Anatolia and Thrace.

The RPP was identified with a program of forced-draft social and economic development via legislation and state enterprise. Strong, centralized authority and state economic planning marked its 27 years of power (1923–50). It deemphasized everything religious to the point of subordinating religious activity and organization to state control.

Minority parties appeared, such as the short-lived Liberal Party of 1930, but it was not until 1946 that a second popular party, the Democrat Party (Demokrat Parti—DP) came into being. Initially formed by a small group of dissident RPP members of parliament, the DP demanded greater political and economic liberalism and specifically a relaxation of central controls. When they came into power in 1950, winning 55.2% of the popular vote and 408 of 487 seats in the Assembly, the Democrats put into effect their policies of economic expansion through free enterprise; they also emphasized rural development through liberal credit terms to farmers and rapid mechanization. These policies, aimed at broadening the base of the economy, helped to return the Democrats to power three times in succession. After 1954, however, the Democratic regime reinstituted many of the former controls and instituted others, notably over the press. The RPP, however, condemned these moves as well as what they regarded as the lack of economic planning and adequate fiscal and commercial controls. Both the Democrats and RPP supported a firmly pro-Western, anti-Communist foreign policy.

The Republican National Party (Cumhuriyetşi Millet Partisi—RNP), a more conservative group, was established in 1948, and the Turkish Villagers' Party (TVP) in 1952. The Freedom Party (Hürriyet Partisi) was formed in 1955 by a group of second-echelon leaders of the DP, as a protest against the government's increasingly authoritarian posture, but it never gained wide popular support. In 1958, the RNP and the TVP merged, forming the Republican Peasants Nationalist Party (Cumhuriyetçi Köylü Millet Partisi), and in that same year the Freedom Party merged with the RPP.

In the first elections of the Second Republic (October 1961), none of the four parties won a controlling majority in either chamber. This forced a coalition government to be formed in 1962—a new experience for Turkey. The coalition, however, was short-lived, for the newly formed Justice Party (Adalet Partisi—JP) bolted the governing group of parties, becoming the chief political opposition.

The JP, which was to become the main political force in the country after the 1965 elections, is private enterprise oriented (in this respect it can be considered the successor of the DP, which was banned in 1960). Derived originally from local Democrat leaders, by the mid-1960s it reflected the views of modernization-minded professionals as well as workers and villagers.

In the 1965 elections, the JP won 53.8% of the seats in the House of Representatives and 61% of the Senate seats. The elections of October 1969 confirmed the JP's legislative predominance.

In December 1970, dissident members of the JP created the Democratic Party (Demokratik Parti—DCP). Another new organization, the Republican Reliance Party (Cumhuriyetçi Güven Partisi—RRP) put up its first candidates in the 1969 elections. The National Salvation Party (Milli Selâmet Partisi—NSP) was created in March 1973 for the purpose of preserving Islamic traditions and bringing about economic and social reforms. The general elections of 14 October 1973 resulted in the RPP's replacing the JP as the most popular party in Turkey, although it did not achieve a parliamentary majority. The distribution of seats in the House was RPP, 185; JP, 149; NSP, 48; DCP, 45; RRP, 13; National Action Party (Milliyetçi Hareket Partisi—NAP), 3; Turkish Unity Party (Türkiye Birlik Partisi), 1; and independents, 6. It was three months before the RPP and NSP formed a coalition under Bülent Ecevit.

After the Ecevit government fell on 18 September 1974, more than six months passed before a new permanent government was formed by Süleyman Demirel. His minority Government of the Nationalist Front included representatives of the JP, RRP, NSP, and NAP and commanded 214 out of 450 National Assembly seats. Voting on 12 October 1975 resulted in the following distribution of elective Senate seats: JP, 77; RPP, 63; RRP, 4; NSP, 4; others, 2. In Assembly by-elections, the RPP increased its share to 190 out of 450 seats.

14 LOCAL GOVERNMENT
The chief admisistrative official in each of Turkey's 67 provinces (vilayets or ils) is the provincial governor (vali), who is an appointee of the central government and responsible to the Ministry of Internal Affairs. Virtually all communications between officials of the provincial level and their respective ministries must pass through the governor's office. In addition, there is a locally elected provincial assembly, the size of which varies with the population of the province. Under national law, this assembly has the right to receive certain earmarked funds from the central government and to negotiate loans. Education, health, agriculture, and animal husbandry generally consume the bulk of an assembly's resources. For administration, provinces are subdivided into 571 districts (kazas or ilces), which in turn are divided into communes (nahiyes or bucaks), comprised of kasabas and villages. Chief administrator at each level is a central government appointee. In municipalities and villages, locally elected councils perform certain government functions. Both have specified sources of income and prepare budgets for the allocation of such income. Budgets are subject to approval by the central government. Most public revenue, however, is collected by the Ministry of Finance in Ankara.

15 JUDICIAL SYSTEM
Judicial powers are exercised by independent tribunals. Administrative functions, such as the selection, promotion, and transfer of judges and public prosecutors and the maintenance of

facilities, are responsibilities of the Ministry of Justice. There are nine types of courts: civil, commercial, criminal, labor, enforcement, appellate, military, a council of state, and a High Tribunal. Although the same justice may sit at different times at several kinds of court, courts of original jurisdiction of the first five types are found in many provincial seats. Enforcement courts deal with questions arising from the enforcement of court orders. Decisions of all courts of original jurisdiction are sent to a court of appeals in Ankara. The High Tribunal is a special court to try members of the cabinet and other high functionaries. A constitutional court, composed of members of the independent court system, is empowered to pass on the constitutionality of all legislative acts. In 1973, the State Security Court, which prosecutes all offenses against the state, was established by constitutional amendment.

16 ARMED FORCES
The Turkish military establishment is based on 20 months' compulsory service. The officer corps consist of both reservists and professionals. The total armed strength in mid-1975 was 453,000 (including 261,000 conscripts), plus 775,000 reserves. The army had 365,000 men, including 14 infantry divisions (2 mechanized) and 1 armored division; 3 missile battalions were equipped with Honest John missiles. At the beginning of 1976, an estimated 28,000 Turkish soldiers were stationed on Cyprus. In mid-1975, the navy had 40,000 men; naval strength included 16 submarines, 13 destroyers, 20 minesweepers, 9 minelayers, 70 patrol boats, 5 escort vessels, and about 50 landing craft. The air force had 48,000 men, 292 combat aircraft, and 6 antiaircraft squadrons equipped with Nike Ajax/Hercules missiles. Paramilitary forces totaled 750,000. The defense budget for 1975/76 was TL 32,830 million.

17 MIGRATION
Much Turkish emigration consists of workers under contract for employment in EEC countries, especially the Federal Republic of Germany (FRG). As of 7 July 1973, there were 647,537 Turkish workers employed abroad. The FRG's decision in late 1973 to halt the inflow of foreign workers sharply cut Turkish emigration in 1974. Immigration, being largely a result of external political pressures, varies greatly from year to year. An estimated 1.2 million foreign nationals entered Turkey in 1974, but only 50,000 were not tourists or through travelers.

18 INTERNATIONAL COOPERATION
Turkey is a member of the UN and most of its specialized agencies, NATO, OECD, the EMA, the Council of Europe, CENTO, and many other intergovernmental organizations. In December 1964, Turkey became an associate member of EEC. In April 1976, Turkey, Iran, and Pakistan agreed to establish a free trade zone and joint development bank.

Relations with the US, Turkey's principal aid benefactor, were strained during the 1970s over two issues. On 1 July 1974, over US objections, the Turkish government lifted the ban it had imposed in June 1971 on the cultivation of opium poppies; the US had already pledged up to $35 million in IDA grants to compensate farmers forced to stop growing opium poppies, from which much of the heroin and morphine smuggled into the US was derived. As of February 1975, the US Congress mandated an embargo on arms shipments to Turkey because of insufficient progress in negotiations toward a Cyprus settlement. After the Turkish government took over all but 2 of the more than 20 US military bases in Turkey on 27 July, the US Congress authorized limited resumption of arms shipments in October 1975, when negotiations on the future of the bases also began. One consequence of US-Turkish difficulties was a move toward détente with the USSR; the Russians had for centuries been the traditional enemy of the Turks.

19 ECONOMY
About 30% of Turkey's GDP is derived directly from agriculture.

Since the end of World War II, the agricultural share has been shrinking, and that of the industrial and construction sectors expanding. This shift in economic activity is in part the result of deliberate government policy. With the partial mechanization of agriculture, a significant shift in population has occurred. This has necessitated substantial urban and industrial development and hence a high rate of investment. This heavy investment, plus an explosion of consumer demand and the rural-urban movement, led to a serious inflationary situation and balance-of-payments problem by the mid-1950s. The cost of living index in Istanbul rose from 100 in 1938 to 981.2 in 1964; in Ankara, in the same period, it rose from 100 to 1,023.3. Anti-inflationary policies, particularly vigorously pursued after the 1960 coup, led to far less rapid—or damaging—inflation in the 1960s.

When the military regime came to power in May 1960, the economic situation was critical. There was a large national debt; development projects were overextended; money supply was drastically expanded; gold and foreign exchange were at a low ebb; and exports and imports resulted in a deficit. The austerity measures of 1958 and military reforms of 1960 were continued. Designed to stabilize the economy and relieve inflationary pressures, these measures included a reduction in expenditures, removal of price controls, devaluation of the currency, and revision in taxes, including for the first time a levy on agricultural income. Living standards and purchasing power remained relatively low, but by 1970 there had been considerable improvement. However, a resurgence of inflation in the 1970s (12.6% for the first half of 1975) forced the government to impose price controls.

The country is rich in natural resources, but their sale on the world market at competitive prices has required heavy investment in machinery or government subsidies. This situation holds for agriculture as well. To purchase the machinery with which to build a competitive economy, Turkey has gone heavily into debt to Western creditors, particularly the US. A major effort to advance the economic development of the country began in 1963 with the first five-year plan (1963–68), which realized an average annual economic growth of 6.7%. During the second five-year plan (1968–73) there was an average annual GNP growth of 7.1%. The third five-year plan (1973–78) projected an average increase in GNP of 7.9% annually. Real GNP growth was 5.5% in 1973 and 7% in 1974.

²⁰INCOME
The rise in GDP at factor cost from TL100,902 million in 1968 to TL368,040 million in 1974 represented an increase of 265% in current prices but only 45% in constant 1968 prices. Major contributors to the 1974 GDP were farming and livestock, 29.4%; manufacturing, 19.3%; wholesale and retail trade, 13%; government services, 10.3%; transport, storage, and communication, 8.6%; construction, 5.4%.

Estimated income per capita rose from $178 in 1960 to $435 in 1972.

²¹LABOR
Of a total estimated population of 35,605,176 in 1973, 15,223,000 persons were employed. Of these, 58% were in agriculture, indicating the basically farming character of the economy. The industrial labor force amounted to but 10.6% of the working population.

A 1946 law authorized the formation of labor unions and enabled them to engage in collective bargaining. Among the 746 employees' organizations in 1973 were 18 federations, 262 industrial unions, 116 regional unions, and 275 local unions. The major labor confederation was the Turkish Trade Union Federation, with 29 member unions covering about 1.2 million employees. Union membership is largest in the textile industry, tobacco manufacturing, public utilities, transport and communications and coal mining. Events since the 1960 overthrow of

the Menderes government, and especially since the 1961 elections, have favored trade union activity, indicated, for example, by the growing consolidation of the trade union movement. Through a series of demonstrations and mass meetings, the trade unions pressed the government to act upon their demands for the right to strike, for collective labor contracts, and for various social benefits, which were provided for in law but were not fully implemented.

A detailed labor code administered by the Ministry of Labor controls many aspects of labor-management relations. The law in effect bestows on the worker certain rights in his job and is designed to protect him against exploitation and poor working conditions. Turkey has a basic 48-hour workweek, with a maximum of 9 hours per day. Overtime is limited, and must be paid for at a 25% to 50% premium. No overtime is permitted in night work, underground work, or in industries considered dangerous to health. Work on Sundays and holidays is paid for at double-time rates. At each workplace covered by the law, workers' representatives are elected to negotiate with management. If a dispute cannot be resolved at the local level, it goes to a provincial arbitration body. Appeals may be taken to a supreme arbitration board in Ankara, decisions of which are final and legally binding. Compulsory accident and occupational disease insurance has been in effect since 1946, and workers enjoy a variety of other social security coverages.

In response to worker agitation, a new labor law was enacted on 12 August 1967, broadening existing protection and coverage of the nonagricultural workers. The law covers all establishments—other than agricultural enterprises—employing three or more persons. The hours of employed children are limited, and their employment may not interfere with their education. Annual vacations were made mandatory; these range from 12 to 24 working days. Strikes, though legal, may take place only after a prescribed period of negotiations and following notification to the government.

Since 1946, employment exchanges have operated under the direction of the Ministry of Labor. Of the 809,778 workers sent abroad between 1961 and 1974, 79.8% went to the FRG. In 1974, however, only 19,062 workers left Turkey to work in other countries, a sharp decrease of more than 100,000 from the previous year. Nevertheless, total remittances to Turkey exceeded $1.4 billion in 1974.

²²AGRICULTURE
In 1973, 25,013,000 hectares were considered arable; about 64% of arable land was under crops, and 36% was fallow. Little uncultivated arable land remains. The average holding is not more than 4 or 6 hectares. Dry grain farming—in which half the land must lie fallow each year—can sustain little more than a subsistence standard of living. The land distribution law of 1945 resulted in the distribution to 312,698 landless or near-landless farm families in 3,517 villages of some 2.5 million hectares of public lands at nominal cost, financed over 25 years by the state. In 1961 the State Planning Board stated that average farm income was only $106 per year, as against more than $300 for other occupations. The main reason for this low figure was stated to be that nearly 12 million persons in rural areas had small landholdings or, in some cases, no land at all. By 1973, the average wage of agricultural workers had risen substantially to about $3.60 a day. This figure is only about 8% below the average wage of a nonagricultural worker. Large farms are concentrated mainly in the Konya, Adana, and Izmir regions.

Agricultural methods still tend to be primitive, but modern machinery is being introduced. Much new land has been brought under cultivation since World War II, and the increased use of chemical fertilizers and expansion of irrigated lands have increased yields per acre overall. Nevertheless, crop yields are still extremely sensitive to variations in rainfall.

About 90% of the cultivated area is devoted to cereals. Wheat is the principal crop, accounting for 63% of the total grain production: 9,970,000 tons of wheat were grown in 1974, followed by barley with 3,000,000 tons. In 1974, Turkey also produced about 5,090,000 tons of sugar beets and 2,900,000 tons of grapes. Other agricultural products are grown in lesser but still important quantities: potatoes, 2,200,000 tons; corn, 1,110,000 tons; rye, 560,000 tons; and apples, 950,000 tons.

Since it is greatly influenced by weather conditions, cereal production varies from year to year. In good crop years, Turkey exports cereals (a record 1.4 million tons of wheat in 1954), but in drought years it must import (435,000 tons of wheat in 1957); 312,590 tons of grains were exported in 1973.

Turkish tobacco is world famous for its lightness and mildness. Most of the crop is grown in the Aegean region, but the finest tobacco is grown around Samsum on the Black Sea coast. Tobacco was replaced by cotton as the chief export in 1951 but still represents about one-tenth of total exports. Most of the cotton crop is grown around Adana and Izmir. Other crops of commercial importance are fruits, nuts, olives, vegetable oil, and seeds. Turkey leads the world in the production and export of hazelnuts and pistachio nuts and usually ranks second to the US in the production of raisins.

The government stimulates production through crop subsidies, low taxation, price supports, easy farm credit, research and education programs, and the establishment of model farms. The government also controls the conditions under which farm products can move into world markets. For some products, such as grain, the government is the sole exporter.

Turkey is one of seven countries authorized under the 1961 UN Convention on Narcotic Drugs to grow opium poppies for legitimate pharmaceutical purposes. In June 1971, after persistent US complaints that up to 80% of all opiates smuggled into the US were derived from Turkish poppies, the Turkish government banned poppy growing. Prime Minister Ferit Melen announced in September 1972 that 64,128 opium growers in seven provinces would receive compensation totaling $5.6 million beginning March 1973. However, after efforts to find substitute crops failed, the government decided to rescind the ban on 1 July 1974. Government steps to curtail illegal cultivation, refining, and export of opiates were reportedly successful.

23 ANIMAL HUSBANDRY

Turkey is heavily overgrazed. Many animals are used for transport and draft purposes as well as to supply meat and dairy products. The principal animals of commercial importance are mohair goats and sheep. The sheep wool is used mainly for blankets and carpets. Turkey ranks second in the world as a producer of mohair. Nevertheless, animal husbandry is generally poorly developed despite the great number of animals. In 1973 there were 38,806,000 sheep, 13,045,000 head of cattle, 1,701,000 asses, 962,000 horses, 312,000 mules, and 40,677,000 poultry. Production of wool was a record 61,000 tons in 1973. Other livestock products included milk, 4,224,000 tons; meat, 404,000 tons; and hen eggs, 127,900 tons.

24 FISHING

The total catch of fish by Turkey's deep-sea fishermen was 145,744 tons in 1971, most of it tuna and sardines caught as they migrate seasonally through the Bosporus. In addition, 5,869 tons of crustaceans and 14,442 tons of freshwater fish were caught. Great variations in quantity of catch occur annually. Improvements in fishing equipment and methods have been effected during recent years. For most of the population, the sea is not an important source of food.

25 FORESTRY

Forests, occupying 19,136,000 hectares, are classified into three types according to ownership. State forests include almost all the forest land. Community or municipal forests and private forests are small. Care of state forests and all cutting therein are the responsibility of the Directorate-General of Forestry within the Ministry of Agriculture. Round wood production in 1973 was an estimated 18.3 million cu meters; sawn wood output was 3.29 million cu meters in 1972.

26 MINING

Mineral resources are only partially developed, but Turkey has a wide variety of known minerals and is generally regarded as potentially very wealthy in terms of its mineral resources. About 75% of total mineral output is carried out by government-controlled organizations, principally the Coal Board and the Etibank, founded in 1935. Among the minerals actively exploited and marketed by the Etibank are copper, chromium, sulfur, copper pyrite, colemanite, mercury, lead, zinc, sulfuric acid, borax, and boric acid. In 1973, Turkey was the world's sixth-greatest producer of chrome ore; however, production had declined from 352,100 tons (ore content) in 1971 to 215,300 tons in 1973.

The bituminous coal field at Zonguldak on the Black Sea coast produces good coking coal. Turkey's total coal production in 1973 was 4,643,000 tons.

Several international oil companies as well as Turkish groups are exploring and drilling. Crude petroleum output in 1973 was 3,511,800 tons. Involved were three private companies, two of which were foreign. In 1967, a 494-km oil pipeline from Batman to Iskenderun was opened.

Other minerals produced in 1973 (in thousands of tons) were lignite, 4,574.5; antimony, 3,353; iron ore, 2,537; bauxite, 333; and copper, 22.5. Eskişehir in northwestern Anatolia is the world center of meerschaum.

According to law, mineral resources are state property, and private persons and corporations must apply to the state for the right of exploitation. The Council of Ministers may award concessions valid from 40 to 99 years. Private interests are involved in the mining of lignite or subbituminous coal, manganese, iron ore, chromite, and meerschaum.

27 ENERGY AND POWER

Hydroelectric and thermal power plants in 1973 produced 12,361 million kwh of electricity and had an installed capacity of 2.7 million kw in 1972. In the 1960s, lignite and water increased in importance as sources of energy, while coal and diesel oil dropped. But in the 1970s the importance of oil increased relative to other sources. The larger generating plants in the country are owned or operated either by Etibank or by municipal authorities.

28 INDUSTRY

Overall industrial production has tripled since 1962. Industrial revenues in constant prices increased 12.8% in 1973 and 9.1% in 1974. State enterprises, which account for more than one-half of total industrial production, have sparked the effort, but private industry is developing significantly. Major state industrial enterprises are textiles, sugar, alcoholic beverages, tobacco products, paper, petroleum, iron and steel, cement, and chemicals. The textile industry is the largest industrial unit in Turkey. Textile manufacture is centered in Izmir, Istanbul, Adana, and Kayşeri. Important extensions have been completed at the government-owned iron and steel mill at Karabük; the Ereğli iron and steel works began production in 1965. Other important Turkish enterprises are brick and tile, glass, leather, pharmaceuticals, metalworking, cordage, flour milling, vegetable-oil extraction, fats and oils, and rubber processing. The sugar-beet industry ranks first among food-processing industries, and produces more than domestic consumption requirements. The automobile industry expanded rapidly in the 1970s. Much of the production of machines, consumer goods, and tools takes place in hundreds of small machine shops and foundries, where little special-purpose machinery is used. Turkey exports few manufactured goods.

State textile enterprises in 1973 produced 218,780,000 meters of cotton fabric and 4,468,000 meters of woolen fabric. Other industrial commodities in 1973 (in thousands of tons) included coke, 1,457; crude steel, 1,492; fertilizers, 1,212; pig iron, 896; cement, 8,946; sugar, 677; and paper, 304. Selected consumer items produced in 1972 were beer, 537,000 hectoliters; wine, 520,000 hectoliters; cigarettes, 43,128 million; radios, 248,000; television receivers, 41,000; and passenger cars, 30,000. Output of petroleum products in 1974 (in thousands of tons) included motor fuel, 1,906; kerosene, 882; distillate fuels, 3,101; residual fuel, 5,545.

29 DOMESTIC TRADE

Individual retail firms tend to be small and specialized. There is virtually no commercial activity in villages; the villager comes into the market town to buy and to sell. Government-operated exchanges for cereals are located in municipalities. If the price of grain in the free market falls below the government price, the government-operated exchanges purchase the grain and market it. In this manner, the government controls the range of prices of cereals.

Because of the scarcity of some commodities, the government controls the distribution of various essential goods, notably cement, coal, lignite, and steel. Under a 1954 law, municipal authorities enforce specified profit margins on designated commodities. These margins are established at four levels: importer or manufacturer, distributor, wholesaler, and retailer. Packing and packaging, as well as standardization, constitute serious problems.

Customarily, a Turkish wholesaler supplies credit to retailers, who in turn often extend credit beyond their own means to consumers. Wholesalers' margins tend to be small because of low overhead and keen competition.

Most commercial firms belong to chambers of commerce, which exist in all cities. Chambers of industry are increasingly important in larger manufacturing centers. The government sponsors an international trade fair every year at Izmir.

Usual business hours are from 8 or 8:30 A.M. to 7 P.M., Monday through Saturday.

Advertising media are the newspapers, radio, motion pictures, and public displays. Because large numbers of consumers are illiterate, radio and motion pictures have been used to an increasing extent.

30 FOREIGN TRADE

Turkey's trade balance has long been negative, but the deficit reached crisis proportions in 1974 and 1975. The deficit, TL11,225.9 million in 1973, increased to TL32,089 million in 1974, on exports of TL21,273 million and imports of TL53,362 million. In 1975, the Turkish trade deficit was TL25,420 million for the first six months alone, with imports valued at nearly four times exports.

Agricultural products comprise about two-thirds of Turkey's exports. The leading exports are manufactured goods, cotton, and tobacco. The chief imports are machinery and transport goods, chemicals, mineral fuels (especially petroleum), and iron and steel.

Principal exports in 1973 (in millions of Turkish liras) were:

Manufactured goods	6,074.0
Cotton	4,189.0
Fruits and nuts	3,460.0
Tobacco	1,821.0
Cereals and legumes	889.2
Fish and shellfish	152.5
Wool	144.0
Other exports	1,307.7
TOTAL	18,037.4

Principal imports in 1973 (in millions of Turkish liras) were:

Machinery and transport equipment	12,332.0
Chemicals	5,648.0
Mineral fuels, lubricants	3,175.0
Iron and steel	2,568.0
Nonferrous metals	890.0
Textile fibers and waste	327.6
Textile yarn, fabrics	143.3
Other imports	4,179.4
TOTAL	29,263.3

In 1974, the EEC accounted for 45.7% of Turkey's total trade, the Middle East 17.1%, the US 9.3%, and EFTA 9.1%. Principal trade partners in 1973 (in millions of Turkish liras) were:

	EXPORTS	IMPORTS	BALANCE
FRG	3,031.2	5,826.3	− 2,795.1
US	1,792.0	2,545.1	− 753.1
Italy	1,581.6	2,301.9	− 720.3
Switzerland	1,586.8	1,781.3	− 194.5
France	996.2	1,878.4	− 882.2
USSR	690.3	1,798.0	− 1,107.7
Lebanon	1,422.0	1,004.9	417.1
Belgium-Luxembourg	589.0	1,156.6	− 567.6
Other countries	6,348.3	10,970.8	− 4,622.5
TOTALS	18,037.4	29,263.3	−11,225.9

31 BALANCE OF PAYMENTS

Despite chronic trade deficits, Turkey's payments balance was favorable between 1969 and 1973. Factors contributing to Turkey's favorable position were a continued high level of foreign assistance and investment; increasing net revenues from tourism (from $3,826,000 in 1970 to $78,464,000 in 1973); the rising value of remittances from Turkish workers employed abroad (over $1 billion in 1973); and continued income from US military bases on Turkish soil. In 1974, however, tourism dropped as a result of the Turkish role in the Cyprus war; at the same time, imports increased 78% while exports rose only 17.9%. Indications were that Turkey's payments position would show similar deterioration in 1975.

The following is a summary of Turkey's balance of payments for 1973 and 1974 (in millions of dollars):

	1973	1974
CURRENT ACCOUNTS		
Trade, net	−560	−1,830
Services, net	1,110	1,124
Transfers, net	75	72
TOTALS	625	− 634
CAPITAL ACCOUNTS		
Long-term capital	327	208
Short-term capital	−452	42
TOTALS	−125	250
Errors and omissions	34	− 50
Net change	534	− 434

32 BANKING

The Central Bank of Turkey was founded in 1930 as a privileged joint-stock company. It possesses the sole right of note issue and has the obligation of providing the monetary requirements of the state agricultural and commercial enterprises by discounting treasury-guaranteed bonds issued by these organizations. All foreign exchange transfers are handled exclusively by the Central Bank, which operates the clearing accounts under separate agreements with foreign countries.

At the end of 1973, 43 banking institutions were operating in Turkey, with over 3,900 branches. There were 30 commercial banks, 4 of which were foreign. Two of the most important banks, the Sümerbank and Etibank, are also state investment-holding companies. Another important state financial institution is the Agricultural Bank, which supplies credit to the farm population. The largest private commercial bank is the Business Bank. Another private bank, the Industrial Development Bank of Turkey, stimulates the growth of private industrial development and channels the flow of long-term debt capital into the private industrial sector for both short- and long-range development programs.

Bank deposits increased from TL87,536 million in 1972 to TL109,063 million by June 1974, while time and demand savings deposits increased from a negligible sum to TL55,589 million in June 1974. The money supply totaled TL73,430 million in June 1974, of which TL50,260 million was in demand deposits. In 1974, lending rates ranged from 3% to 14%, interest rates on time deposits ranged from 6% to 9%. Credits issued by all banks (excluding the Central Bank) reached TL104,400 million as of 31 May 1975.

³³INSURANCE

Government regulations in effect since 1929, amended in 1954, require all insurance companies to reinsure 30% of each policy with the National Reinsurance Corporation, a state organization. Since the 1954 amendment, life policies need not be so reinsured. It is possible to secure insurance policies for flood damage, third-party liability, earthquake, commercial shipments, theft, fire, accident, and life. There are 38 insurance companies, including 17 foreign companies (mainly Swiss, British, and French). Private insurance is the subject of a large amount of legislation. Varied social security insurances are administered directly by the state.

In 1973, domestic company premiums totaled TL1,250,014,000 and foreign company premiums, TL48,802,000. The premium volume increased by 32.7% over 1972. Payments by domestic insurance companies were TL502,339,000; by foreign companies, TL28,999,000.

³⁴SECURITIES

Turkey's only securities exchange is located in Istanbul. Because of the shortage of foreign exchange, there are no transactions in foreign bonds and stocks. With but few exceptions, trading is in government bonds. Virtually all of the securities that are issued by private enterprises are sold privately through personal arrangements between buyers and sellers.

³⁵PUBLIC FINANCE

The draft budget law is submitted by the government to the National Assembly prior to 1 December of each year. It must be enacted prior to 1 March of the following year, at which time the fiscal year begins. It is broken down into the general budget of the government (by ministry) and a number of annexed budgets, which relate to semiautonomous state activities such as the various universities. Additionally, each section is divided into operating and investment expenditures. The budget is invariably in deficit.

Estimated tax revenues for 1973/74 totaled TL65,883 million, including income taxes, TL28,900 million; customs duties and stamp taxes, TL14,130 million; taxes on production, TL11,603 million; and taxes and fees on services, TL7,050 million. Estimated consolidated expenditures for 1973/74 and 1974/75 (including current expenditures, investment expenditures, and transfers, in millions of Turkish liras) were as follows:

	1973/74	1974/75
Ministry of Finance	32,505	43,663
Ministry of Defense	13,427	20,839
Ministry of Education	12,775	14,366
Ministry of Health and Social Welfare	3,406	3,780
Ministry of Public Works	1,731	2,338
Ministry of Agriculture	1,579	1,795
Gendarmerie	1,653	2,008
Other departments	15,335	18,099
TOTALS	82,411	106,888

The total public debt was TL44,807.8 million as of 31 December 1973; 14% of the debt was foreign and 86% domestic.

³⁶TAXATION

All persons domiciled in Turkey, whether of Turkish citizenship or otherwise, are subject to taxation on income. Certain categories of foreigners are taxed only on income earned in Turkey, specifically foreign businessmen, scientists, experts, government officials, press correspondents, and others who have come to Turkey with no intention of becoming permanent residents, regardless of their length of residence. Income tax rates are progressive, from 2% to 68%. The tax for corporations and special partnerships with shares, limited-liability companies, cooperative societies, and all foreign companies of the same nature is 25% of net profit. The rate is 35% for state economic enterprises. A tax law of 1961 provided that farmers, not previously subject to income tax, must file a return.

Land and buildings are taxed on the basis of assessed value. The annual rate of the land tax ranges from 0.7% to 1% of assessed valuation. Rural land assessed at under TL60,000 is tax exempt. The building tax, levied by provinces, is 12% of net income from the building after deducting a 20% maintenance allowance from gross income, as estimated from the assessed value. The rate is less for homes.

Other taxes are stamp taxes on documents, vouchers, shares, and securities; fees on legal, bank, and insurance transactions; output taxes; petroleum production tax; a sales tax; service taxes; automobile taxes; inheritance and gift taxes; taxes on foreign travel, football pools, and sugar; and municipal taxes on advertising, entertainment, licenses, dogs, electricity and gas, and purchase of livestock.

All business establishments coming within the jurisdiction of the social security legislation are subject to an 8% old age insurance tax and a 4% illness and disability tax. Half is paid by the employer, half by the employee.

³⁷CUSTOMS AND DUTIES

Turkish customs duties are assessed on an ad valorem basis only. Present customs classification conforms with standardized international nomenclature. Duty-free entry is provided for some 30 types of imports; however, imports of nearly all consumer goods are banned. Tariffs varying from 5% to 10% are levied on raw materials, heavy production materials, steel, certain machinery, etc. Duties varying from 15% to 25% are assessed on semi-manufactured items and items considered essential or useful to the economy. Higher tariffs are levied on products deemed to be nonessential. Many imported items are also subject to import taxes.

Turkey became a member of GATT in 1951 and has granted tariff concessions to other GATT members. On 22 April 1975, Turkish, Iranian, and Pakistani leaders agreed to establish a free trade zone.

³⁸FOREIGN INVESTMENTS

Although Turkey was the recipient of considerable foreign aid in the 1950s and 1960s, including about $3 billion from the US, its leaders both before and since the 1960 coup have recognized the need for foreign private investment and have sought to attract such investment. By 1970, foreign capital could operate in any field of economic activity open to Turkish private capital. There was also no limit on the percentage of foreign participation in equity capital. This attitude toward foreign capital investment attracted considerable foreign investment in Turkish industries, especially from the US and FRG. As relations with the US have grown less cordial, Turkey has sought aid from other NATO nations, as well as from Eastern Europe. In July 1974, a $700-million development credit agreement was signed with the USSR. Government approval is necessary for new investment, but policies are generally liberal.

Measures designed to encourage foreign investment include possible exemption from corporate taxes until profits rise to a certain percentage of the basic investment (up to 80%), and partial or total exemption from customs and related taxes.

39 ECONOMIC POLICY

With the demonstrated failure of private enterprise to satisfy the needs of Turkey's economic targets in the 1920s, the state began to build industrial enterprises. During the 1930s, two state economic plans were laid out, and a policy of state capitalism became official. Following World War II, state enterprise, though necessarily expanded, was placed on a basis closer to that of private enterprise, and the state undertook by a variety of devices to encourage the development of private enterprise. Some state monopolies were relaxed. Nonetheless, government ownership and operation remained important in the fields of alcoholic beverages, tobacco, salt, tea, and a number of others.

Economic policy is formulated by the State Planning Organization. In June 1961, an integrated 15-year plan was announced. Its three five-year plans were designed to achieve a 7% yearly increase in national income. In March 1963, the first five-year plan, designed to facilitate economic growth, was inaugurated. The 1963–68 plan to some extent fell short of its goals, but its average annual increase of 6.7% in GNP was still impressive.

Three objectives were proclaimed by the Turkish government in 1968 at the start of the second five-year plan: a renewed effort to achieve a 7% annual growth-rate, economic viability, and social justice. The role of the public sector under the second five-year plan (1968–72) was twofold: creation and expansion of the economic and social infrastructure and the development of modern manufacturing industries. Economic policy, however, still sought the largest possible active role for private enterprise in the development of industries and encouraged private activity through fiscal concessions, financial assistance, and state participation in mixed enterprises.

The third five-year plan was inaugurated in 1973 with the objective of helping Turkey prepare for its future membership in the EEC. The long-term goals were to increase the per capita GNP from $400 in 1972 to $1,500 by 1995, to reduce agriculture's share of the GDP to 12%, and to increase industry's share to 37%. One of the main aims of the third five-year plan was to increase the efficiency of the tax-collection service by introducing a separate tax administration and a sales tax. In agriculture the objectives were to continue to increase food supplies for export and to feed a growing population through improved irrigation, technical advice to farmers, and the establishment of more cooperative farms.

40 HEALTH

Free medical treatment, given at the state hospitals or health centers, is provided by the state to any Turkish citizen who obtains a certificate of financial need from his local administrator. There are public and private hospitals and clinics in most provincial capitals. The number of beds in public and private health institutions rose from 15,691 in 1950 to more than 81,175 in 1973. Medical personnel by the end of 1973 included about 18,511 physicians (or 1 for each 2,093 persons), 4,279 dentists, 4,781

pharmacists, 13,410 registered nurses, and 13,556 midwives. The number of hospitals and health centers (public and private) in the country in 1973 was 791. Malaria, cholera, and trachoma have been effectively controlled by large-scale public preventive measures. Great efforts are exerted to improve health conditions in rural areas and in the slums of the larger cities. The infant mortality rate was estimated at 153 per 1,000 live births in 1967. Average life expectancy was an estimated 59.2 years in 1975.

41 SOCIAL WELFARE

Since 1936, various forms of social security have been introduced, all of which are administered by a public social insurance institution. Participation is compulsory for those employees and employers in establishments in which 10 persons or more are employed or, for 20 specified industries, for those employing 4 or more if located in cities with a population of more than 50,000 persons.

Forms of social security are industrial accident and disease, old age, sickness, and maternity insurance. The first is financed entirely by the employer's contribution, generally running about 2% of the payroll. Maximum benefit period is 52 weeks. The daily allowance of an insured person with dependents is 75% of his wages, and for others 50%. For permanent total disability, the insured person is entitled to a pension equal to 60% of the annual wage. Old age insurance premiums are 8%, half paid by the employer, half by the employee. The annual pension equals 20% of the total premiums paid, but less than TL400. To qualify, a worker must have completed his 60th year, worked at least 25 years in a qualified work place, and made contributions on at least 5,000 days' wages. Premiums for sickness and maternity are 4% of wages, contributed equally by employer and employee. Sickness benefits include medical assistance up to 180 days. Maternity benefits include two-thirds of one's pay for a period of three weeks preceding and six weeks following confinement. In some localities, the social insurance organization operates its own hospitals and other facilities.

The Social Insurance Institution covers all workers not employed in agriculture, who in 1973 numbered 1,649,179; in 1973, 236,836 people received benefits, and contributions totaling TL6,437,312,000 were received. In 1971, Bağ-kur, a social organization for artisans, craftsmen, and other self-employed workers, was established. Government workers are covered by the Government Employees Retirement Fund; in 1973, 336,370 former government employees received monthly pension benefits. Since February 1974, the government has taken steps to introduce an unemployment benefit system.

42 HOUSING

A traditional village house consists of sun-dried brick (adobe) or rough-hewn stone walls across which are laid timbers piled with brush and then topped with packed earth. The flat roof is often used for storage of feed grain. Floors are often bare earth covered with matting or light-weight carpets. Little furniture is used. Urban housing varies from houses similar to those in villages to modern, centrally heated apartment buildings. Owing to the massive rural-urban movement now under way, the government is attempting to stimulate cheap urban housing. The development of adequate housing has been given the greatest emphasis in the government's planning. The first five-year plan (1963–68) allocated 20.3% of its resources for this purpose. The second five-year plan increased this allocation by 49.1% (TL32.1 billion), and the third five-year plan aims for another increase of 37.1% (TL44 billion). In 1974, 161,047 housing units were constructed, of which 109,905 were in apartment buildings and 51,142 were in separate houses.

43 EDUCATION

In 1972, the literacy rate was 65% for persons living in towns and was considerably lower in villages. Primary, secondary, and a good deal of higher education is free. Education is compulsory for children aged 6 to 14 or until graduation from primary school (grade 5). However, owing to the inadequate number and distribution of schools and teachers, only about two-thirds of the children of primary-school age attend school.

The regular school system consists of five-year primary schools, three-year junior high schools, and four-year high schools. Parallel to this system is a variety of technical, trade, and commercial schools. The nine universities are the universities of Istanbul (founded 1453) and Ankara (founded 1946), the Technical University of Istanbul (founded 1773), the University of the Aegean at Izmir (founded 1955), the Middle East Technical University at Ankara (founded 1957), Atatürk University at Erzerum (opened 1958), Black Sea Technical University at Trabzon, Bosporus University (Istanbul), and Hacettepe University in Ankara.

Several private schools are in operation, including a number of foreign schools, and those maintained by ethnic or religious minorities.

In 1973/74 there were 40,342 primary schools, with 156,717 teachers and 5,327,000 students; 2,302 junior high schools, with 26,913 teachers and 927,000 students; 718 high schools, with 13,438 teachers and 304,000 students; 977 vocational and technical schools, with 16,848 teachers and 285,000 students; and 165 other institutions, with 11,773 teachers and 185,000 students. The nine universities and two other public higher institutions had 78,377 students and 8,101 faculty members in 1973/74.

44 LIBRARIES AND MUSEUMS

In 1972 there were 335 public libraries with total collections of 3,188,284 volumes, and 259 children's libraries with holdings of 677,440 volumes. The principal collections, however, are found at the National Library (550,000 volumes), the University of Ankara (395,000 volumes), the University of Istanbul (230,000 volumes), and the Middle East Technical University (110,000 volumes).

The most famous museums and ancient buildings are located in Istanbul. The old seraglio (Topkapi) is perhaps the most famous. The seat of the Ottoman government for many years, it now houses a large collection of paintings, manuscripts, and historically important items. Nearby is Saint Sophia Museum, the world-renowned Byzantine church, and next to it the Blue Mosque, famous for the beauty of its interior and the grace of its dome. Also in Istanbul are the museums of Archaeology and of the Ancient Orient, housing one of the finest collections of Greek art, including the sarcophagus of Alexander the Great. The Museum of Archaeology in Ankara contains the world's outstanding collection of Hittite works. In Konya are located museums of Islamic art, one of which is housed in the mausoleum of Mevlana. Along Turkey's Aegean coast are situated the ruins of Ephesus, Pergamum, Ilium, Halicarnassus, and other famous classical Greek cities. The only zoological garden is located in Ankara.

45 ORGANIZATIONS

The number and variety of private organizations in Turkey have increased substantially since World War II.

Professional organizations, labor unions, charitable associations, student organizations, athletic clubs, and chambers of commerce and industry are active in the major cities. There are several Masonic lodges and branches of the Rotary and Lions clubs. Women are active in a number of their own charitable organizations.

Since World War II, international cultural associations have appeared, chief among them being Turkish-American, Turkish-French, Turkish-German, and Turkish-English.

Chambers of commerce and chambers of industry have been serving as semiofficial agencies for the control of import license and foreign exchange allocations. Merchants and companies are required to register with their respective chambers.

46 PRESS

The constitution guarantees freedom of the press, but with the broadening influence of the press, the Menderes government in the pre-1960 period introduced severe personal libel and slander laws. It was a criminal offense to publish material that might undermine public confidence in the government or the economy or that might belittle or ridicule high government personages. Libel and slander were punishable by imprisonment or suspension. Repressive press laws were repealed on 6 October 1960 and greater freedom of the press ensued.

Since the development of a multiparty system, the press has expanded rapidly. In 1972 there some 433 dailies and 645 other periodicals.

Leading daily newspapers, their affiliations, and 1974 circulations were:

	AFFILIATION	CIRCULATION
ISTANBUL		
Hürriyet	Independent	505,000
Gunaydin	Independent	420,000
Halka Ve Olaylara Tercuman	Democratic	367,000
Milliyet	Independent	350,000
Saklambac	Independent	350,000
Cumhuriyet	Independent	100,000
Akşam	Independent	45,000
Dünya	RPP	18,000
ANKARA		
Bariş	Independent	17,000
Zafer	Democratic	13,000
Yeni Gun	Independent	4,412
IZMIR		
Yeni Asir	Pro-Democratic	68,500
Demokrat Ismir	Pro-RPP	7,135

47 TOURISM

Citizens of Australia, Austria, Finland, Ireland, Japan, Monaco, Pakistan, Sweden, Switzerland, and all NATO countries except Portugal may enter Turkey without visa if they possess valid passports, do not seek gainful employment, and remain not longer than three months. Visas are required for citizens of all other nations. For Soviet-bloc nationals a Turkish consulate issues a visa only after specific clearance from the Ministry of Foreign Affairs in Ankara. Foreigners entering without visa and remaining longer than three months must secure a residence permit from the police. No vaccinations or inoculations are required of visitors arriving directly from Europe or the US.

In 1973, 1,313,260 tourists visited Turkey; the total dropped to 1,110,300 in 1974, largely because of the Cyprus dispute. Net receipts from tourism were $44,412,000 in 1972 and $78,464,000 in 1973. During the first five-year plan (1963–68), Turkey's government invested the equivalent of $90 million in tourism for holiday villages, national parks, hotels, casinos, and the "road of pilgrimage" passing through the Balkan countries to Israel. Currency regulations were relaxed, enabling tourists to exchange their native currency for Turkish liras in shops, hotels, and restaurants. The government expenditure for tourism during the second five-year plan was about $70 million; about $119 million was allocated for the third five-year plan.

48 FAMOUS TURKS

Outstanding political figures include Sultan Mehmet II (1429–81), conqueror of Constantinople in 1453; Sultan Süleyman I (the Magnificent, 1495–1566); Sultan Abdul Hamid II (1842–1918), a despotic ruler whose tyranny led to the formation of the Young Turk movement; Mehmet Köprülü Paşa (1583–1661), Mehmet IV's grand vizier and founder of a family line of outstanding grand viziers; Barbaros Hayreddin Paşa (1473–1546), naval commander who established Turkish supremacy in the Mediterranean; Enver Paşa (1881–1922), Young Turk leader who was the ruler of Turkey during World War I; Mustafa Kemal Atatürk (1881–1938), World War I military commander, nationalist leader, and first president of the republic; Ismet Inönü (b.1884), Atatürk's chief of staff and prime minister, his successor as president (1938–50), and first prime minister of the Second Republic.

Outstanding religious figures are Haci Bektaş Veli (1242–1337), founder of the Bektashi dervishes, and Mevlana (Celâleddin-i Rumi or Jalal al-Din Rumi, 1207–73), author of the epic *Mesnevi* (or *Mathnavi*) and founder of the Mevlevi dervishes.

Revered literary figures include the mystical poets Yunus Emre (1238?–1320?) and Süleyman Çelebi (d.1422), author of *Mevlidi Sherif* (*Birth Song of the Prophet*). Other significant poets are Ahmedi (1334–1413), Şeyhi (d.1429?), Fuzuli (1494–1555), renowned for his lyrical verses about platonic love; the classical poets Ali Şir Nevâi (1441–1501), Nef'i (1582?–1636), Nabî (1642?–1712), Ahmet Nedim (1681–1730), perhaps Ottoman Turkey's greatest love poet; and Şeyh Galib (1757–98), the last great poet of the mystical and classical tradition. Renowned for his geographical and historical writings is Kâtip Çelebi (known in Europe as Haji Khalifa, 1609–57), and the great traveler Evliya Çelebi (1611–82), noted for his books on travel and history. The greatest folk poet was the 17th-century minstrel Karacaoğlan.

Sinasi (1826–71), dramatist, journalist, and essayist, was the first Turkish writer in the Western tradition. Other significant playwrights are Musaipzade Celal (1870–1959), Haldun Taner (b.1916), and Necati Cumali (b.1921). The poet Ziya Paşa (1825–80) was the outstanding literary figure of the reform period. Namik Kemal (Ahmed Kemal, 1840–88) and Mehmet Emin Yurdakul (1869–1944) dedicated their poetry to the achievement of political ideals. Four widely read novelists are Huseyin Rahmi Gurpinar (1864–1944), Ahmet Rasim (1864–1932), Halit Ziya Usakligil (1865–1945), and Mehmet Rauf (1871–1931). Omer Seyfettin (1884–1920) was a major short story writer. Ziya Gökalp (1875–1924) was a noted poet and sociologist. Significant contemporary novelists include Halide Edib Adivar (1884–1966), Yakup Kadri Karaosmanoglu (1888–1974), Reşat Nuri Güntekin (1892–1957), Refik Halit Karay (1888–1974), Kemal Tahir Demir (b.1910), Orhan Kemal (1914–70), and Yasar Kemal Gokceli (b.1922). Two fine modern poets were Yahya Kemal Beyatli (1884–1958) and Nazim Hikmet Ran (1901–1960). Two prominent journalists and political writers were Hüseyin Çahit Yalçin (1875–1957) and Ahmet Emin Yalman (1889–1973). Outstanding historians were Naima (1752–1815), Mehmet Fuat Köprülü (1890–1966), and Ahmet Zekî Velidî Toğan (1890–1970).

Other famous Turks include the architect Sinan (1490–1588), the miniaturist Abducelil Celebi Levni (d.1732), and the modern painter Bedri Rahmi Eyuboglu (1913–75). Famous contemporary composers include Ulvi Cemal Erkin (1906–1972) and Ahmed Adnan Saygun (b.1906). The operatic soprano Suna Korad (b.1934) and bass-baritone Ayhan Baran (b.1929) are well known in European musical circles.

⁴⁹DEPENDENCIES

Turkey has no territories or colonies.

⁵⁰BIBLIOGRAPHY

Bean, George E. *Aegean Turkey: An Archæological Guide.* New York: Praeger, 1966.

Bean, George E. *Turkey's Southern Shore: An Archæological Guide.* New York: Praeger, 1968.

Benoist-Mechin, Jacques. *Le Loup et la Léopard: Mustapha Kemal.* Paris: Michel, 1954.

Birge, John Kingsley. *A Guide to Turkish Area Study.* Washington, D.C.: American Council of Learned Societies, 1949.

Bisbee, Eleanor. *The New Turks: Pioneers of the Republic, 1920–1950.* Philadelphia: University of Pennsylvania Press, 1951.

Cohen, Edwin J. *Turkish Economic, Social, and Political Change.* New York: Praeger, 1970.

Creasy, Edward D. *History of the Ottoman Turks.* New York: Holt, 1878.

Dewdney, John C. *Turkey: An Introductory Geography.* New York: Praeger, 1971.

Ekrem, Selma. *Turkey, Old and New.* New York: Scribner, 1947.

Eliot, Sir Charles. *Turkey in Europe.* London: Arnold, 1908.

Eren, Nuri. *Turkey Today and Tomorrow.* New York: Praeger, 1963.

Eversley, Baron George John Shaw-Lefevre, and Sir Valentine Chirol. *The Turkish Empire from 1288 to 1922.* New York: Dodd, Mead, 1923.

Gibb, Elias John Williamson, and Edward G. Browne (eds.). *A History of Ottoman Poetry.* 6 vols. London: Luzac, 1900–1909.

Gökalp, Ziya. *Turkish Nationalism and Western Civilization.* New York: Columbia University Press, 1959.

Hasluck, Frederick William. *Christianity and Islam under the Sultans.* 2 vols. Oxford: Clarendon Press, 1929.

Heller, Deane Fons. *Hero of Modern Turkey: Atatürk.* New York: Messner, 1972.

Heyd, Uriel. *Foundations of Turkish Nationalism.* London: Luzac, 1950.

Inalcik, Halil. *The Ottoman Empire.* New York: Praeger, 1973.

IBRD. *The Economy of Turkey.* Baltimore: Johns Hopkins Press, 1951.

Karpat, Kemal H. *Turkey's Politics: The Transition to a Multi-party System.* Princeton: Princeton University Press, 1961.

Kiliç, Altemur. *Turkey and the World.* Washington, D.C.: Public Affairs Press, 1959.

Lewis, Bernard. *The Emergence of Modern Turkey.* London: Oxford University Press, 1961.

Lewis, Geoffrey. *Turkey.* New York: Praeger, 1965.

Mango, Andrew. *Turkey.* New York: Walker, 1968.

Orga, Irfan. *Portrait of a Turkish Family.* New York: Macmillan, 1957.

Peters, Richard F. *Story of the Turks from Empire to Democracy.* New York: Lundwall, 1959.

Ramsaur, Ernest Edmondson, Jr. *The Young Turks: Prelude to the Revolution of 1908.* Princeton: Princeton University Press, 1957.

Robinson, Richard D. *The First Turkish Republic.* Cambridge: Harvard University Press, 1963.

Stark, Freya. *Alexander's Path.* New York: Harcourt, Brace, 1959.

Stark, Freya. *Lycian Shore.* New York: Harcourt, Brace, 1956.

Szylowicz, Joseph S. *Political Change in Rural Turkey.* New York: Humanities, 1966.

Thomas, Lewis V., and Richard N. Frye. *The United States and Turkey and Iran.* Cambridge: Harvard University Press, 1951.

Toynbee, Arnold J. *The Western Question in Greece and Turkey: A Study in the Contact of Civilizations.* London: Constable, 1922.

Turkey and the United Nations. New York: Manhattan, 1961.

Ward, Barbara. *Turkey.* London: Oxford University Press, 1942.

Webster, Donald Everett. *The Turkey of Atatürk: Social Process in the Turkish Reformation.* Philadelphia: American Academy of Political and Social Science, 1939.

Weiker, Walter. *The Turkish Revolution 1960–61: Some Aspects of Military Politics.* Washington, D.C.: Brookings Institution, 1962.

Yalman, Ahmed Emin. *Turkey in My Time.* Norman: University of Oklahoma Press, 1956.

UNITED ARAB EMIRATES

The State of the United Arab Emirates
Dawlat al-Imarat al-ʿArabiyat al-Muttahidah

CAPITAL: Abu Dhabi (provisional). **FLAG**: The flag consists of a red vertical stripe at the hoist and three equal horizontal stripes of green, white, and black. **ANTHEM**: The National Anthem is an instrumental piece without words. **MONETARY UNIT**: The United Arab Emirates dirham (UD), introduced as the currency in May 1973, is divided into 100 fils. There are coins of 1, 5, 10, 25, 50, and 100 fils, and notes of 1, 5, 10, 100, and 1,000 dirhams. UD1 = $0.2533 (or $1 = UD3.947). **WEIGHTS AND MEASURES**: Both the British and the metric system are in general use; however, the government intends to convert fully to the metric system in the future. **HOLIDAYS**: New Year's Day, 1 January; National Day, 2 December; Christmas, 25 December; and Boxing Day, 26 December. Muslim religious holidays include ʿId al-Fitr, ʿId al-ʿAdha', and Milad al-Nabi. **TIME**: 4 P.M. = noon GMT.

¹LOCATION, SIZE, AND EXTENT
Comprising a total area of 77,700 sq km (30,000 sq mi), the United Arab Emirates (UAE), in the eastern Arabian Peninsula, consists of seven states: Abu Dhabi, with an area of 67,340 sq km (26,000 sq mi); Dubayy, 3,885 sq km (1,500 sq mi); Sharjah, 2,590 sq km (1,000 sq mi); Ra's al-Khaymah, 1,683 sq km (650 sq mi); Fujayrah, 1,166 sq km (450 sq mi); Umm al-Qaywayn, 777 sq km (300 sq mi); and ʿAjman, 259 sq km (100 sq mi). Extending *544* km *(338* mi) NE–SW and *361* km *(224* mi) SE–NW, the UAE is bordered on the N by the Persian Gulf, on the E by Oman, on the S by Saʿudi Arabia, and on the W by Qatar, with a total boundary length of *1,940* km *(1,206* mi). The boundary with Saʿudi Arabia is still in dispute.

²TOPOGRAPHY
The UAE consists mainly of sandy desert. It is bounded on the west by an immense sabkha or salt flat extending southward for nearly 70 miles. The eastern boundary runs northward over gravel plains and high dunes until it almost reaches the Hajar range of mountains in the Musandam Peninsula near al-ʿAyn. The flat coastal strip that makes up most of the UAE has an extensive area of sabkha subject to flooding. Some sand spits and mud flats tend to enlarge, and others enclose lagoons. A sandy desert with limestone outcroppings lies behind the coastal plain in a triangle between the gravel plain and the mountains of the east and the sands of Saʿudi Arabia to the south. Far to the south, the Liwa Oases are aligned in an arc along the edge of dunes that rise as high as 300 feet.

The main gravel plain extends inland and southward from the coast of Ra's al-Khaymah to al-ʿAyn and beyond. Behind Ra's al-Khaymah and separating Fujayrah from the Gulf is an area of mountains that rise over 3,000 feet in height with isolated cultivation. Finally, alluvial flats on the Gulf of Oman fill the bays between rocky spurs. South of Khor Fakkan (Sharjah), a continuous, well-watered fertile littoral strip, known as the Batinah Coast, runs between the mountains and the sea and continues into Oman. There are, in addition, many islands, most of which are owned by Abu Dhabi. These include Das Island, the site of oil operations, and Abu Musa, exploited for oil and red oxide.

³CLIMATE
The months between May and October are extremely hot, with shade temperatures of between 38°C and 49°C (100°F and 120°F) and high humidity near the coast. Winter temperatures can fall as low as 1.6°C (35°F), but the average winter minimum is 14°C (57°F). Average annual rainfall is between 2 and 4 inches, with considerably more in the mountains.

⁴FLORA AND FAUNA
Apart from cultivated plants, there are two categories of plant life in the UAE: the restricted salt-loving vegetation of the marshes and swamps, including the dwarf mangrove, and the desert plant community, which includes a wide range of flora that is most abundant after the fall of rain.

Animal and reptile life is similar to that of Bahrayn, with the addition of the fox, wolf, jackal, wildcat, and lynx. Hedgehogs have been seen. More than 250 species of small birds have been reported in the UAE similar to those found elsewhere along the Gulf, together with many of the larger birds—kites, buzzards, eagles, falcons, owls, and harriers. Sea birds include a variety of gulls, terns, ospreys, waders, and flamingos. Popular game birds include the Houbara (MacQueen's Bustard), as well as species of ducks and geese.

⁵POPULATION
Preliminary figures from UAE's first census, taken in 1975, show a total population for the seven emirates of 655,937, almost double the 1974 estimated figure of 350,000. Abu Dhabi had the largest population in 1975, with 235,662. Dubayy had 206,861, Sharjah 88,188, Ra's al-Khaymah 57,282, Fujayrah 26,498, ʿAjman 21,566, and Umm al-Qaywayn 16,879. At the time of the census 2,372 citizens were living abroad and 629 persons were living in areas whose sovereignty among the emirates remained unresolved. The towns of Dubayy and Abu Dhabi are the most important urban centers, both with more than 60,000 inhabitants. Abu Dhabi was expanding rapidly in the 1970s, attracting large numbers of internal and external migrants to its booming oil industry. There are about 20,000 nomads.

⁶ETHNIC GROUPS
The basic stock of the UAE is Arab, with a considerable admixture of Iranians, estimated at more than half of the population of Dubayy town. Preliminary figures of the 1975 census indicated that at least three-fourths of the resident population were foreign-born. There are also large numbers of Indians, Pakistanis, and Arabs from other parts of the Middle East. Jordanians, Palestinians, Egyptians, Iraqis, and Bahraynis are employed throughout the bureaucracy, including the educational system. An estimated 1,800 to 2,000 US citizens reside in Dubayy.

⁷LANGUAGE

Arabic is the universal language. Persian is spoken in Dubayy; and English is widely used in business.

⁸RELIGION

Virtually all UAE nationals are Muslims. Most are Sunnis, with the exception of a comparatively large Shi'i community in Dubayy. The non-Muslims are principally Christians and Hindus.

⁹TRANSPORTATION

With most of the population concentrated in coastal towns and the al-'Ayn oasis, road links between these centers have been given priority. There is now a paved coastal road linking Abu Dhabi, Dubayy, Sharjah, 'Ajman, Umm al-Qaywayn, and Ra's al-Khaymah. Roads to link the interior to the main towns are being constructed; of particular importance is a transpeninsular road from Fujayrah through the al-Hajar mountains. A two-lane highway has been built between Abu Dhabi and al-'Ayn, a distance of 209 km, and a bridge now connects Abu Dhabi island with the mainland. A highway now under construction will link the UAE coastal network with the trans-Arabian highway at al-Silah on the Qatar border.

The UAE is well provided with port facilities. Port Rashid, with its 15 deepwater berths, 1 tanker berth, and 12 warehouses, is the largest artificial harbor in the Middle East. A $170-million contract awarded in February 1976 called for Port Rashid's expansion to 47 berths. Abu Dhabi's Port Zayed has 6 berths, with construction of a further 6 under way. In Sharjah, Port Khalid is to have 7 berths in its initial stage. A UD360-million contract was awarded in mid-1975 for the construction of an 8-berth deepwater port at Ra's al-Khaymah, due for completion in mid-1977.

In March 1976, Ra's al-Khaymah airport was opened to traffic, bringing the total of international airports in the UAE to four; the other three are at Abu Dhabi, Dubayy, and Sharjah. Fujayrah is drawing plans for its own airport. Dubayy's is presently the largest in the country; in 1975, it handled nearly 1 million passengers (30% more than in 1974) and just over 12 million kg of freight (51% more than in 1974 and 195% over the 1971 total). In 1975, Abu Dhabi National Airlines purchased three Boeing-720s and one 707, for $35 million. International service to points in the Middle East, Asia, and Europe is also provided by BA, Gulfair, Air India, MEA, and PIA.

¹⁰COMMUNICATIONS

The communications system has been dramatically improved and expanded in recent years. In 1976, the government was setting up the UAE Communications Corporation to take over all telecommunications operations in the emirates with the exception of Ra's al-Khaymah, which declined to participate. Prior to its completion, each emirate was to continue its own telecommunications activities through joint ventures with either Cable & Wireless or International Airadio, both UK-owned. The government was to take a 60% holding in the new company, with the two UK firms controlling the remaining share. The Jebel Ali earth satellite station in Dubayy handles telephone and telegraph traffic, Telex data-transmission, and color television. Computer-controlled automatic Telex systems have also been installed in both Dubayy and Abu Dhabi.

In 1974, the UAE had some 26,000 telephones, 36% of which were located in Abu Dhabi. Sharjah has the most modern telephone exchange in the emirates; a 2,000-line system was installed in mid-1973, and 1,000 lines were added in 1974–75.

A color television network connects Abu Dhabi with Dubayy, Sharjah, Umm al-Qaywayn, Ra's al-Khaymah, and Fujayrah. Radio services exist in four emirates.

¹¹HISTORY

Although the Trucial Coast has for centuries been situated on one of the main trade routes between Asia and Europe, very little is known about the early history of the countries that now make up the UAE. The northern states of the UAE, and in particular Ra's al-Khaymah, first came into historic prominence during the period of Portuguese occupation in the 16th and early 17th centuries, when Portugal used the territories as a base to fight a rear-guard action against Persia. At that time and down to the mid-18th century, neighboring Oman played an integral role in the history of the maritime states.

Abu Dhabi island was settled by its present ruling family, al-Nayhan, toward the end of the 18th century, and Dubayy was founded by an offshoot of the same family in 1833. The late 18th and 19th centuries saw the division of the area between the Nayhan and the Qawasim, who ruled Ra's al-Khaymah and neighboring territories and whose clashes with British and Indian shipping led to British naval expeditions against what came to be known as the Pirate Coast. Subsequently, treaties concluded in 1820 and 1835 established a formal relationship between the states of the southern Gulf and Britain that was to last until 1971. Under a treaty signed in 1892, the UK promised to protect the Trucial Coast from all aggression by sea and to lend its good offices in case of land attack. In 1955, the UK effectively intervened on the side of Abu Dhabi in the latter's dispute with Sa'udi Arabia over the Buraymi Oasis, control of which is now shared by Abu Dhabi and the Sultanate of Oman.

When, in 1968, the UK announced its intention to withdraw its forces from the area, a decision to establish a federation of Arab emirates—embracing the seven Trucial States, Bahrayn, and Qatar—was agreed on in principle. However, it proved impossible to reconcile the differences among all the members and, in 1971, the six Trucial States (excluding Ra's al-Khaymah) agreed on the establishment of the United Arab Emirates. The UAE was officially proclaimed a sovereign, independent nation on 2 December 1971 and, as did Bahrayn and Qatar, signed a new treaty of friendship with Britain. Ra's al-Khaymah joined the UAE in early 1972.

Externally, the move to independence in 1971 placed the UAE in difficult straits with its two powerful neighbors, Sa'udi Arabia and Iran. Sa'udi Arabia asserted a territorial claim on a group of oases in the south of the UAE, and Iran laid claim to its offshore islands. In 1974 a border agreement on the Liwa Oases was signed with Sa'udi Arabia, after which full diplomatic relations were established.

¹²GOVERNMENT

According to the provisional constitution of the UAE, promulgated on 2 December 1971, the executive branch in the UAE government consists of three parts: the Supreme Federal Council (SFC), the Presidency, and the Council of Ministers. The SFC, composed of the rulers of the seven emirates, has responsibility for the formulation and supervision of all UAE policies, the ratification of federal laws, and oversight of the union's budget. The president and vice-president of the UAE, Shaykh Zayed of Abu Dhabi and Shaykh Rashid of Dubayy, respectively, inherited their posts and are to serve for life. The president is assisted by the Council of Ministers, or cabinet, presided over by the prime minister. The member states are represented in the cabinet in numbers relative to their size and importance. All member government institutions at the Shaykhdom level are considered to be UAE departments.

Legislative authority in the UAE is vested in the Federal National Council, or Consultative Assembly, comprised of 40 delegates from the member emirates. The delegates are appointed by their respective rulers for two-year terms. The constitution stipulates the distribution of 40 seats as follows: Abu Dhabi and Dubayy, 8 each; Sharjah and Ra's al-Khaymah, 6 each; and 'Ajman, Umm al-Qaywayn, and Fujayrah, 4 each.

In 1975, Abu Dhabi made a significant move in the direction of financial federalism by committing in advance half of its 1976 oil revenues to the federal budget. The outstanding federal issue is the merger of the principal defense forces.

13 POLITICAL PARTIES

No political parties exist in the UAE. Arab nationalist feeling is developing, however, and there is growing sentiment, particularly among urban youth, in favor of political liberalization and accelerated economic development. In Abu Dhabi, dissident local elements and others from nearby states had infiltrated the army and civil service in 1972–73, resulting in a number of arrests of alleged subversives. Those arrested were said to be members or supporters of the Palestinian Front for the Liberation of the Arab Gulf. Individuals with ties to the Palestinian fadayin, the Ba'th Party, and other leftist Arab organizations are known to be present in Abu Dhabi.

14 LOCAL GOVERNMENT

The major institutions of local government are the municipalities of Abu Dhabi town, al-'Ayn, Dubayy, Sharjah, Ra's al-Khaymah, Fujayrah, 'Ajman, and Umm al-Qaywayn, and a handful of traditional councils known as majalis and amiri diwans.

15 JUDICIAL SYSTEM

Abu Dhabi, Dubayy, and Sharjah have developed relatively sophisticated judicial systems based, as in other Gulf states, on a combination of Shari'a law for civil matters and contemporary legal codes. The constitution of the UAE established a Higher Court and an indeterminate number of courts of first instance. The Higher Court consists of a president and a maximum of five judges, all of whom are appointed by presidential decree upon approval of the SFC. The Higher Court president and member judges are deemed independent of the executive and legislative branches. Once appointed, the judges cannot be removed.

16 ARMED FORCES

The armed forces of the emirates have yet to be unified. The present defense system is based largely on the former Trucial Oman Scouts, which at independence became the nucleus of the UAE's armed forces and was renamed the Union Defense Force (UDF). Led by approximately 25 British officers and 100 non-commissioned officers, the UDF is responsible to the federal minister of defense and a higher Defense Council, the chairman of which is the UAE president. The force, equipped with armored cars and light artillery, numbers about 3,000.

Abu Dhabi continues to maintain its own army of 15,000 men, the most powerful force in the UAE. The air force was recently equipped with two squadrons of French Mirage fighter-bombers, bringing its combat force to 12 Hunters and 32 Mirages. Abu Dhabi's navy has 7 patrol craft, with 3 more to come in 1976. Ra's al-Khaymah has a 300-man Mobile Force. Dubayy's Defense Force numbers 2,000, including a small air unit.

17 MIGRATION

At least 75% of the UAE's population originates from outside its borders, mostly from Iran, other Arab countries, and the Indian subcontinent. The UAE cannot develop itself without foreign labor and skills, and immigration is a paramount issue.

18 INTERNATIONAL COOPERATION

In 1972, shortly after achieving independence, the UAE became a member of the UN, the Arab League, and numerous other international and Arab organizations, including the General Secretariat of the Islamic Conference, OPEC, UNICEF, WHO, IMF, IBRD, IAEA, and FAO. Loans and contributions by the UAE to developing countries in 1974 totaled $554 million; the allocation for 1975 was $1,243 million. The most important instrument in implementation of the aid policy is the Abu Dhabi Fund for Arab Economic Development (ADFAED). In 1975, its capital was raised to $500 million and its beneficiaries included Egypt, Bahrayn, Syria, Sudan, Tunisia, Jordan, the Arab Republic of Yemen, Morocco, Mauritania, and Bangladesh. The UAE has diplomatic relations with 34 countries, none of which is Communist-aligned.

19 ECONOMY

The economy of the UAE centers primarily on oil and oil-based industries, which have accounted for more than 85% of federal revenues in recent years. In Abu Dhabi, by far the wealthiest of the seven emirates, oil revenues accounted for more than 95.4% of all state income in 1974. Dubayy joined the ranks of oil-producing countries only in 1971, and entrepôt trade continues to play a major role in its economy. Most of the other members of the UAE depend on federal financial aid and aid in kind and in cash from Kuwayt, Sa'udi Arabia, and other oil-rich countries. Oil production in Sharjah began in July 1974, and the tourism potential there is being expanded. Ra's al-Khaymah and Fujayrah derive their principal income from traditional agriculture and fishing. The pace of development in various parts of the federation is thus necessarily uneven and, despite the sizable influx of foreign workers, the shortage of labor—both skilled and unskilled—remains a crucial constraint on sustained development.

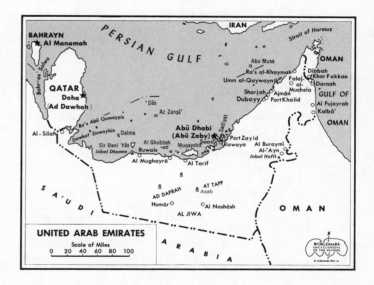

See continental political: front cover J7; physical: back cover J7

LOCATION: 51°3' to 56°23'E; 22°30' to 26°17'N. **BOUNDARY LENGTHS:** Persian Gulf coastline, 777 km (483 mi); Oman, 513 km (319 mi); Sa'udi Arabia, 586 km (364 mi); Qatar, 64 km (40 mi). **TERRITORIAL SEA LIMIT:** 3 mi.

20 INCOME

Overall calculations of the GNP are made difficult by the relative fiscal autonomy of the individual emirates. Per capita income in 1976 was the world's highest. Distribution, however, is uneven, both among the emirates and within the individual shaykhdoms.

21 LABOR

Indigenous labor is scarce, and even the large influx of immigrants has been insufficient to cope with the demand. The emirates lean heavily on skilled labor, technology, and management abilities provided by foreigners. Non-UAE Arabs are employed at all economic levels, including the government bureaucracy and civil service. Manual labor is largely performed by Pakistanis and Iranians; many Indians are to be found in clerical positions; there is a high proportion of Europeans at management levels.

The construction industry accounts for about 25% of the national labor force, followed by government administration (16%) and agriculture (12%). The highly mechanized petroleum sector accounts for only 5%. While in Abu Dhabi more than 40% of the labor force is employed in construction, more than 50% in Dubayy works in transport, trade, and service industries; nearly 80% of the labor force in Fujayrah is engaged in agriculture and fishing.

A recently drafted labor law guarantees a minimum wage, certain basic conditions of work, and some degree of social insurance. The right to organize is reserved to citizens.

²²AGRICULTURE

An overwhelming proportion of the emirates' 77,700 sq km is infertile. The most productive region is Ra's al-Khaymah, which receives underground water supplies from the nearby Oman mountains and enjoys the most plentiful rainfall. Agriculture still supports 50% of the population of Ra's al-Khaymah and supplies 50% of fresh food consumption, mainly fruits and vegetables, in the UAE. There are three other agricultural areas in the emirates: the Buraymi Oasis, the Liwa Oases, and portions of the discontinuous Batinah coastal plains on the Gulf of Oman.

The Digdagga Agricultural Trials Station in Ra's al-Khaymah is central to all agricultural research and education efforts in the emirates. The emirate of Abu Dhabi has its own experimental farm at al-'Ayn, and a new experimental farm at Rawaya is designed to encourage local Bedouins to take up settled farming. The Abu Dhabi Arid Lands Research Center on Sadiyat Island produces more than 400 tons of vegetables a year in an artificially controlled environment.

²³ANIMAL HUSBANDRY

Camels, goats, and sheep are raised in limited numbers, particularly in Abu Dhabi and Fujayrah. A 100-hectare dairy farm with a projected annual output of 1.4 million liters of milk was expected to start production near al-'Ayn in Abu Dhabi emirate in May 1976; some 600 head of Australian cattle were to be imported for the project.

²⁴FISHING

Fishing is an important source of domestic food and fodder. A recent FAO survey indicated that UAE coastal waters abound in fish and shellfish. The UAE borders two high-potential fishing regions: the Persian Gulf and the Gulf of Oman. Many varieties of fish, including rock cod, tuna, mackerel, sardines, anchovies, jack, marlin, red mullet, bream, and snapper, are now being caught. But full exploitation has been hampered by lack of a modern fishing fleet, good harbors, and modern land-based facilities. During 1971–75, the UAE Development Board financed the purchase of about 1,150 marine engines. Free maintainance workshops have been set up in some areas and marketing facilities are being improved. Refrigeration plants and a fish-meal factory are planned, and fisherman are being trained in modern techniques. Support thus far given to the fishing industry has already resulted in a major increase in catches: from 10,000 tons in 1963 to more than 60,000 tons in 1974.

²⁵FORESTRY

Wooded land is scarce, apart from palm groves along the northern and eastern coasts. The government of Abu Dhabi plans an extensive tree-planting program; 3,953 acres have already been planted.

²⁶MINING

The UAE, with crude oil production of 1.7 million barrels per day in 1974, ranked as the fifth-largest producer in the Middle East. Production is confined to Abu Dhabi, Dubayy, and Sharjah, which together have an estimated daily capacity of more than 2 million barrels. Abu Dhabi accounted for 84% of the total output of 612 million barrels in 1974. Total reserves are estimated at 21.5 billion barrels. Abu Dhabi's oil output, which rose steadily from 69 million barrels in 1964 to 515 million in 1974, comes almost exclusively from the onshore operations of the Abu Dhabi Petroleum Co. (ADPC) and the offshore operations of the Abu Dhabi Marine Areas Co. (ADMAC). Abu

Dhabi has a 60% participation share in the operations of ADPC and ADMAC, managed by the government-owned Abu Dhabi National Oil Co. (ADNOC). The remaining 40% of ADPC's ownership is divided mainly among UK, US, and Dutch interests; the balance of ADMAC is owned by UK, French, and Japanese firms.

All the oil of Dubayy, the UAE's second-leading oil producer, comes from the offshore Fateh field, which recently expanded its capacity to 330,000 barrels per day. In March 1975, the Dubayy government took over its oil industry after foreign interests (US, French, and Spanish) claimed they could not afford further expansion.

Production from a field off Sharjah's Abu Musa Island (with a capacity of 100,000 barrels a day) began in July 1974 under a consortium, 75%-owned by US interests. Profits are shared jointly by Sharjah and Iran. Onshore production was scheduled to commence in mid-1976. Drilling is also due to begin off Fujayrah in the Gulf of Oman, and onshore drilling has started in Ra's al-Khaymah under a joint venture with Dutch interests. Oil was reported to have been discovered in Umm al-Qaywayn in February 1976.

Abu Dhabi has also large reserves of natural gas. In March 1976, the Abu Dhabi government declared all natural gas reserves in the emirates to be the sole property of the state. ADNOC, which has been given the right to exploit all the emirate's gas reserves, has invited tenders for the design and building of a main liquefaction plant at Jebel Dhanna, and a $300-million plant with a 3 million-ton-a-year output is being built on Das Island.

²⁷ENERGY AND POWER

Power facilities have been expanding rapidly, but output still falls far short of demand. All electricity is thermally generated from oil or natural gas. In 1975, Abu Dhabi's total installed capacity was about 200 Mw. A 70-Mw generation and water-desalination plant was scheduled for commissioning in 1976. Dubayy's existing capacity of 100 Mw was to be more than doubled to 238 Mw in 1976 with the completion of two gas-turbine stations. In addition, the British National Enterprise Board is to provide the Dubayy Electric Co. with a 180-Mw power station and an associated desalination plant with a daily capacity of around 18 million gallons; full production is expected by 1980.

A federal electrification program designed to develop the northern emirates is going ahead with an investment of some UD800 million in immediate projects. Ra's al-Khaymah has a 12-Mw station; two units of 33 Mw each were to be commissioned in mid-1979. Sharjah's present output of 35 Mw is being expanded to more than 50 Mw.

²⁸INDUSTRY

Industrial development has been closely allied to the production of oil, with little movement thus far toward diversification. The major ongoing project in Abu Dhabi is a $600-million natural gas liquefaction plant on Das Island. The project is administered by the government-owned ADNOC, which owns 51%, and a consortium of four foreign companies, which together own the remaining 49%. Work on this project started in December 1973 and, upon completion in 1976, 3 million tons of liquid gas were expected to be exported annually, mainly to Japan. A $400-million liquefied natural gas plant on Das Island is also under way, with a proposed annual capacity of 5 million tons of natural gas liquids and condensate and 2 million tons of liquid petroleum gas.

Dubayy has begun construction of a $333-million dry dock, 70% owned by the government. The 100-acre complex for the repair of tankers is due to be completed in January 1979. A $300-million aluminum smelter with an annual capacity of 135,000 tons is also to be built. The project includes construction of a

400-Mw electricity station. Work is also well advanced on two other major state-sector ventures, a gas liquefaction plant and a cement factory.

Discussions are under way for a large cement plant at Fujayrah. In ʿAjman, a small dry dock, when completed, will repair and build ships up to 8,000 tons. Diversification of light industry has been painfully slow and, except for an occasional food-processing plant, has tended to center on the needs of the construction sector; four cement works with a combined annual capacity of about 1 million tons are either under construction or have been completed, one each at Raʾs al-Khaymah, Sharjah, Dubayy, and al-ʿAyn. Raʾs al-Khaymah has a rolled pipe plant, a fish-meal plant, and a factory producing steel reinforcing rods.

²⁹DOMESTIC TRADE

Dubayy remains the most important center of trade and commerce. The commercial facilities of Abu Dhabi have been growing rapidly during the past decade. Barter methods still prevail outside of the coastal towns, where specialized shops are becoming more common. Business hours tend to vary, although general hours of 8 A.M. to 1 P.M. and 3:30 to 6:30 P.M. are observed. Most offices are closed Thursday afternoon, and Friday is the weekly holiday.

³⁰FOREIGN TRADE

Virtually all export earnings derive from oil. In 1974, net government oil revenues amounted to UD16,917 million, representing a 456% increase over the 1973 total of UD3,711 million, despite the fact that production had been increased by less than 5%. As of the mid-1970s, the UAE remained a one-commodity state and was thus dependent on imports to fulfill the vast bulk of basic needs. The volume of imports doubled between 1973 and 1974, and continued to expand, although less markedly, through 1975. Total imports for the first eight months of 1975 were UD4,400 million, as compared with UD5,540 million in the whole of 1974. In 1974, the main imported items were transport equipment, foodstuffs, oil field equipment, pharmaceutical imports, tobacco and beverages, manufactured goods, machinery, building materials, textiles, and iron and steel. Imports through Dubayy accounted for 86% of imports into the UAE in 1974. The main suppliers were Japan (UD1,151 million), UK (UD705 million), US (UD632 million), Federal Republic of Germany (UD259 million), Italy (UD214 million), Iran (UD195 million), France (UD186 million), Lebanon (UD154 million), India (UD151 million), Switzerland (UD147 million), and the Netherlands (UD146 million).

³¹BALANCE OF PAYMENTS

In recent years, the UAE has registered a persistent overall balance-of-payments surplus induced by sharply higher foreign exchange receipts from transactions of the oil sector. During 1971–73, the surplus averaged $154 million. The quintupling of oil receipts in 1974 dramatically increased the magnitude of the surplus to $1.9 billion. In 1974, the net receipts from the oil sector of $4.3 billion (Abu Dhabi, $3.5 billion; Dubayy, $692 million; Sharjah, $28 million) were offset by a deficit in other trade services of $1.2 billion, resulting in a balance-of-payments surplus of about $3 billion on current account. Official transfers of capital, mostly foreign aid disbursed by Abu Dhabi, amounted to nearly $1.1 billion. After deducting the flow of private funds abroad, estimated at about $150 million, the overall surplus for 1974 probably exceeded $1.8 billion.

³²BANKING

The UAE's Currency Board came into existence with its issuance of the UAE dirham in May 1973. In 1975–76, statutes came into force providing for the Board's gradual transition to a central bank, including powers to impose minimum liquidity ratios and other credit regulations. In 1973–76, the number of banks operating in the UAE increased from 20 to 48 (with 202 operating branches), thus yielding the world's highest ratio of banks per capita. The largest bank is the British Bank of the Middle East, followed by the Bank of Credit and Commerce, the Bank of Oman (owned by Dubayy merchants), the Habib Bank (Pakistan), the National Bank of Abu Dhabi, the United Bank (Pakistan), and the Bank Saderat (Iran). Assets of the banking sector grew from UD9,800 million in January 1975 to UD10,500 million on 31 September 1975. Deposits have shown an overall upward trend. Credit extended by the banks grew considerably, from UD3,000 million in September 1974 to UD5,700 million a year later, comprising 43% of the total assets of deposit banks. Currency in circulation at the end of 1974 amounted to UD506 million, as compared with UD307 million at the end of 1973.

In February 1975, the UAE Currency Board declared a two-year moratorium on the proliferation of branches by foreign banks and laid down more stringent capital requirements, including the establishment of at least 80% local ownership, to provide a stimulus to local banks. During the first six months of 1975, six new locally incorporated banks were licensed.

³³INSURANCE

Some 33 companies are in operation, including Lebanese, Indian, and local insurance companies. Most of the business is in contractors' risk policies and in workers' compensation, which is required by law.

³⁴SECURITIES

Securities are bought and sold through the banks.

³⁵PUBLIC FINANCE

Oil receipts in Abu Dhabi, Dubayy, and Sharjah consist mainly of royalties and income tax payments by the foreign oil-producing concessionaires and, since 1973 in Abu Dhabi, of similar payments by ADNOC. Oil-derived receipts have contributed an average of more than 85% of annual revenues in the mid-1970s. The UAE federal budget for 1975/76 called for expenditures of UD2,778 million, an increase of more than 64% over the previous year's allocations of UD1,690 million, which was itself a massive 300% increase over 1973/74. Of the 1975/76 total, UD971 million was earmarked for development projects alone, almost double the 1974/75 sum. Education received the largest single share of current outlays, UD457 million.

Most of the UAE's revenue is provided by Abu Dhabi. The National Advisory Council of Abu Dhabi approved budget expenditures amounting to UD13,308 million for the emirate in 1975/76, almost five times as much as the UAE's federal budget outlays. Of Abu Dhabi's total current expenditures of UD12,877 million, UD3,500 million was earmarked for foreign aid and about $370 million for development projects.

³⁶TAXATION

Tax laws have as yet been enacted only by individual emirates. In Abu Dhabi and Dubayy, income tax is levied only on oil producers and banks. No distinction is made between local and foreign concerns. Rates apply after the first UD1 million, with a maximum of 50% on income of UD5 million and over. Individuals and firms are not subject to tax. There are no tax laws whatsoever in Raʾs al-Khaymah, Fujayrah, Umm al-Qaywayn, ʿAjman, or Sharjah. No other taxes of any kind exist in the UAE apart from customs duties.

³⁷CUSTOMS AND DUTIES

Dubayy, the major area for foreign trade, is a free-trade zone and free port with no restrictions on imports or exports. The individual governments exert no control over imports, except for licensing. Customs duties are levied ad valorem at rates from 2% to 10% for imported goods, and at a fixed rate of 0.25% for goods in transit. In 1975, customs duties were lifted on a variety of commodities, including foodstuffs and construction materials.

³⁸FOREIGN INVESTMENTS

All of the emirates are eager to attract foreign investment, with Dubayy and Sharjah affording the most liberal incentives in terms of customs and other concessions.

Abu Dhabi Investment Authority was established in February 1976 to take over Abu Dhabi's substantial overseas investment portfolio of about $2 billion, as well as the management of new funds expected to average around $1 billion annually.

³⁹ECONOMIC POLICY

Economic development policy in the UAE has three primary objectives; strengthening of physical as well as social infrastructure, diversification of the economy, and expansion of entrepôt trade. Abu Dhabi's authorities have stepped up efforts to encourage large-scale capital-intensive and export-oriented industries based on oil and gas as a means of diversifying the economy. Dubayy is using its rising oil income to finance projects designed to expand the emirate's trade and services capacities. The major thrust of the development effort in Sharjah has been to improve infrastructure and social services; the government is also encouraging the inflow of private foreign capital investment in small-scale industries. Priority is given by the federal government to the establishment of infrastructure projects in the poorer non-oil-producing emirates. In 1974, federal development outlays totaled about $40 million, while Abu Dhabi spent $235 million in that year, with $880 million earmarked for 1975.

⁴⁰HEALTH

Health facilities are being expanded rapidly, but trained personnel remains in short supply. In 1973, there were 211 doctors, 12 dentists, 16 pharmacists, and 800 nurses and midwives. Services vary greatly from region to region. Hospitalization for citizens is provided free of charge. In 1975, Abu Dhabi town had three hospitals, with a total of 540 beds. There are also a 132-bed hospital at al-ʿAyn and tuberculosis sanatoria at Saad and al-ʿAyn, each of which has 50 beds. In Dubayy there are 942 beds in three hospitals, as well as a sanatorium and hospital provided by Kuwayt and a 200-bed Iranian Red Lion and Sun hospital. In the other states, the largest facilities are the 100-bed al-Qasimi hospital in Sharjah town and three hospitals in Ra's al-Khaymah. Mobile clinics tour the more remote districts.

⁴¹SOCIAL WELFARE

There is no social security law in the UAE, but many welfare benefits are available to citizens, among them free hospital treatment and subsidies for education. Aid for any domestic catastrophe is provided from a disaster fund. If the father of a family is unable to work because of illness, disability, or old age, he receives help under the National Assistance Law; should he die or divorce his wife, the woman's future is secured. Food at subsidized prices can be bought at the UAE's Trading Company by both citizens and noncitizens.

⁴²HOUSING

The federal government is attempting to make modern low-cost homes available to poorer families, supplying them with amenities such as piped water, sewerage systems, and electricity. In early 1973, the Ministry of Housing constructed 1,720 houses for free distribution to poorer families. In March 1976, contractors were invited to bid for a scheme to build an additional 1,700 houses. In July 1975, the ruler of Dubayy set up a UD200-million loan fund to aid native citizens in developing property for both commercial and residential use, with free land provided and an interest rate of only 1%. Also in Dubayy, a contract worth UD300 million was signed in May 1975, providing for the construction of 1,710 units, including 1,000 houses for low-income workers; the project was to be completed by 1979.

⁴³EDUCATION

The educational system of the UAE has burgeoned since 1971. Education in the six northern emirates had previously been financed and administered by Kuwayt. Since 1972, it has been managed by the UAE Ministry of Education. Education is compulsory from age 6 and is free to all UAE citizens. School uniforms, books, equipment, and transport are also provided. During 1971–74, the number of schools of all types more than doubled to 147, although the system remains concentrated at the primary level. The traditional pattern has been for pupils to follow secondary-level courses abroad (in Qatar, Kuwayt, or elsewhere). In 1975 there were 32,000 pupils at the primary level, 14,000 at intermediate levels, 3,000 in secondary schools, and 700 in technical and vocational schools. In addition, 7,000 adults were receiving special education at 26 centers.

⁴⁴LIBRARIES AND MUSEUMS

There are government public libraries in Abu Dhabi, Dubayy, and Sharjah and British Council libraries in Abu Dhabi and Dubayy. Dubayy alone has three English-language libraries. There are excellent museums in Abu Dhabi town and al-ʿAyn, and a small museum in Dubayy.

⁴⁵ORGANIZATIONS

There are chambers of commerce in the larger states. Various social and sporting clubs provide outlets for philanthropic work and recreational facilities for members.

⁴⁶PRESS

Two Arabic-language daily newspapers are now published in the UAE: the official *Al-Ittihad* (*Federation*) and *Al-Wahdah* (*Unity*). Three newspapers are published weekly, with plans for daily circulation. There is also one official English-language daily, a daily Reuters service, and the Bahrayn-based *Gulf Weekly Mirror*.

⁴⁷TOURISM

Tourism is now encouraged by all the emirates, and museums, zoos, aquariums, and other amenities are being developed as tourist attractions. In 1976, 7 large hotels were operating in Abu Dhabi, with several more under construction. Dubayy has 5 hotels, with a 315-room facility to be completed by mid-1977, and a 300-room hotel to be included in the 33-story Dubayy trade center. In Sharjah, 12 hotels with more than 1,300 rooms are planned or in the process of construction. A 500-room hotel is planned for Khor Fakkan, with smaller buildings planned for Umm al-Qaywayn and the inland Falaj al-Muʿallah. Fujayrah's first hotel, of about 150 rooms, is now under construction by a French company. The east coast has begun to attract tourists from the cities. Ra's al-Khaymah has one international-class hotel and a second under construction. A British team of archaeologists is expected to examine local sites.

⁴⁸FAMOUS PERSONS

The UAE has no internationally famous citizens.

⁴⁹DEPENDENCIES

Several of the small islands have the status of dependencies.

⁵⁰BIBLIOGRAPHY

Anthony, John Duke. *Arab States of the Lower Gulf: People, Politics, Petroleum*. Washington, D.C.: Middle East Institute, 1975.

Belgrave, Sir Charles. *The Pirate Coast*. Beirut: Librairie du Liban, 1972.

Fenelon, Kevin G. *The United Arab Emirates: An Economic and Social Survey*. London: Longman, 1973.

Kumar, R. *India and the Persian Gulf, 1858–1907*. London: Asia Publishing House, 1965.

Lorimer, J. G. *Gazetteer of the Persian Gulf*. London: Gregg International Publishers, 1970.

Mann, Clarence. *Abu Dhabi: Birth of an Oil Shaikhdom*. Beirut: Khayats, 1964.

Sadik, Muhammed T., and William P. Snavely. *Bahrain, Qatar and the United Arab Emirates: Colonial Past, Present Problems and Future Prospects*. Concord, Mass.: Lexington Books, 1972.

Stanford Research Institute. *Area Handbook for the Peripheral States of the Arabian Peninsula*. Washington, D.C.: Government Printing Office, 1971.

Wilson, Sir Arnold. *The Persian Gulf*. London: Allen & Unwin, 1954.

UNITED KINGDOM ASIAN AND PACIFIC DEPENDENCIES

BRUNEI

The State of Brunei is a UK-protected sultanate, situated on the northwest coast of the island of Borneo and bordering on the South China Sea. It is made up of two parts, each enclosed on the land side by the Malaysian state of Sarawak. It has a land area of 5,765 sq km (2,226 sq mi) and 160 km (100 mi) of coastline. The terrain varies from steep rocky hills in the east to swamps in the west. The climate is tropical and humid, with heavy rainfall. Brunei's rain forests and swamps house a plethora of mammals, tropical birds, reptiles, amphibians, and insects. As of 1975, endangered species in Brunei included the estuarine crocodile, Siamese crocodile, and false gavial.

The population was estimated at 149,000 in 1974. More than 65% of the population is Malaysian; Chinese are the second-largest group. Other indigenous ethnic groups include Dayaks, Ibans, and Belaits. Bandar Seri Begawan (formerly the town of Brunei) had an estimated 37,000 inhabitants in 1974. Other important towns are Seria and Kuala Belait. The official religion is Islam, and the sultan is its head. The Chinese population is divided into Buddhist, Confucianist, and Christian groups.

From the 16th to the 19th century, Brunei was a powerful state, ruling all Borneo, the Sulu Archipelago, and other islands. It became a British-protected state in 1888. On 29 September 1959, the sultan of Brunei promulgated the country's first written constitution, which provided for assumed executive powers and an appointed chief minister (or mentri besar) to replace the UK resident. In 1965, the constitution was amended. The Council of Ministers is responsible to the sultan for the exercise of all executive powers. Presided over by the sultan, it consists of the high commissioner, six ex officio members (including the chief minister), and four assistant ministers appointed from the unofficial members of the Legislative Council. The Legislative Council has 10 elected members, 5 appointed, and 6 ex officio.

The UK is responsible for defense and external affairs, and an appointed high commissioner acts as adviser to the sultan on matters relating to external affairs, defense, and internal security.

There are two political parties: the People's Independence Front, and the People's National United Party. Brunei elected not to join the Federation of Malaysia upon its formation in September 1963.

In 1974 there were 733 miles of motorable roads. In that year, Brunei had about 15,000 motor vehicles. The Brunei Shell Petroleum Co. owns a short railway. Rivers are an important means of transportation, but the Brunei River is the only river navigable by oceangoing vessels (drawing up to 16 feet). There are three airports. Telephones in Brunei numbered about 4,500 in 1974. There is a central wireless station at Bandar Seri Begawan for international communications.

The economy depends largely on the production of oil, the principal industry, which accounts for 98% of the value of all exports. The Seria oil field, discovered in 1929, is exploited by the Brunei Shell Petroleum Co. The oil field, which extends offshore, passed its peak in the 1960s and a further search for new oil sources, conducted in the offshore areas, resulted in a dramatic increase in oil output during the 1970s. Production expanded

from 6,107,000 tons in 1969 to 11,053,000 tons in 1973. Reserves in 1973 were put at 294 million tons. Coal is no longer commercially mined. The main agricultural products are rubber, rice, jelutong, and sage. Local industries include boatbuilding, cloth weaving, and the manufacture of brassware and silverware.

Oil is by far the dominant export. Since 1971, rubber has been surpassed by rice as the second-leading export. Other exports include coconut, sago, pepper, vegetables and fruits, natural gas, and timber. Total exports in 1974 were valued at US$894.5 million (compared with US$101.2 million in 1970); imports totaled US$164.6 million (US$78.5 million in 1970). Most of Brunei's oil and, thus, most of its exports are shipped to Japan. Singapore and Japan supply most imports.

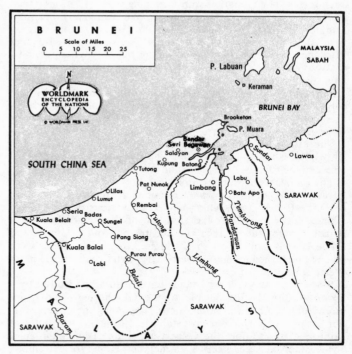

See continental political: front cover P9; physical: back cover P9

The local currency is the Brunei dollar (B$), which is interchangeable with the Malaysian ringgit and Singapore dollar. Individuals pay no income tax and Brunei has no public debt.

A five-year development plan for the 1974–78 period aimed at diversification of the economy and the creation of some 10,000 new jobs. Provisions were also made for the expansion of tourism. The plan called for expenditures of B$500 million.

A state welfare scheme provides pensions and allowances for the old, blind, disabled, lepers, and the mentally ill. Health services are good. In 1974 there were three major government hospitals. Brunei operates a flying doctor service and a chain of clinics that include a mobile dispensary. Land and river mobile units are also in use.

Education is free and compulsory up to the end of the six-year primary course. In 1973, 115 government schools and 41 private schools had an enrollment of 30,722 pupils at primary level and 12,500 at secondary level. There are five technical colleges and a teacher-training college.

GILBERT ISLANDS

The Gilbert Islands, a UK colony, situated in the Pacific Ocean between 3°20′N and 11°27′S and 150°13′W and 169°32′E, is made up of 28 coral atolls and islands. The land area is only some 813 sq km (314 sq mi), but the islands and the groups are scattered over a vast rectangle of sea covering about 5.2 million sq km (2 million sq mi). The islands form three groups: 16 Gilbert Islands, 8 Phoenix Islands, and 8 Line Islands; and Ocean Island, about 400 km (250 mi) west of the Gilbert Islands. Christmas Island is the largest of the Line group, with more than half the total land area. Two islands of the Phoenix group, Canton and Enderbury, have been under joint Anglo-US administration since 6 April 1939. The US also lays claim to 6 of the Line Islands and 6 of the Phoenix Islands.

Ocean Island is of volcanic origin; its 600 hectares (1,500 acres) contain rich deposits of phosphate of lime. All the other islands were formed by coral growth around the flanks of submerged mountains. Some lagoon islands have natural sheltered anchorages. The climate is warm, ranging from 21° to 32°C (70° to 90°F), with rainfall averaging 40 inches annually near the Equator. In 1975, the population of the Gilbert Islands was estimated at more than 52,000. A 1973 census reported 47,932 Micronesians on the islands, with a minority of Polynesians and a scattering of Europeans and Chinese. Tarawa and Ocean Island have the largest populations. The Phoenix and northern Line groups had no indigenous populations prior to colonization. The capital is Bairiki on Tarawa (Gilbert group). Population pressures are acute on several of the Gilbert Islands, and many persons work as laborers elsewhere.

There are ports of entry on Ocean, Tarawa, Fanning, and Christmas islands. Regular shipping services are maintained between the islands. Air Pacific and Air Nauru serve Tarawa.

The islands were probably first sighted by the Spanish explorer Alvaro de Mendaña in 1567–68, but officially recorded discovery is by the British navy, which landed on various of the Gilbert Islands between 1764 and 1824. Most of the islands became a British protectorate in 1892 and became part of the Gilbert and Ellice Islands Colony on 10 November 1915. The islands were placed under the jurisdiction of the UK High Commission for the Western Pacific.

Since 1972, the Gilbert Islands have been administered by a governor directly responsible to the UK Foreign and Commonwealth Office in London. Since November 1974, the governor has presided over a newly established 10-member Council of Ministers. In addition, the Gilbert and Ellice Islands Order of 1974 established an elective 28-member House of Assembly, headed by a chief minister. House membership was reduced to 20 following the separation of the Ellice Islands in 1975. The move, representing an initial step toward eventual independence for the islands, was greeted with widespread anxiety among the primarily Polynesian inhabitants of the Ellice Islands, who comprised a small minority within the predominantly Micronesian population of the other islands. In a referendum held in the presence of UN observers during August–September 1974, over 90% of the Ellice Islands electorate voted for separate status. On 2 January 1976, the Ellice Islands formally separated from the Gilbert and Ellice Islands, to become the UK Territory of Tuvalu. The Gilbert group, together with the remaining islands of the former territory, were reconstituted as the Gilbert Islands. A move toward independence on the part of residents of Ocean Island was meanwhile rejected by the UK and territorial governments.

The soil on most of the islands, only a few inches deep, consists largely of coral sand and lacks humus. Coconut trees grow everywhere, and copra plantations (estates) are worked on four islands. The only vegetable grown in quantity is a tuber cultivated in deep pits. Hogs and poultry abound on the islands, and there is subsistence fishing. The Australian dollar (A$) serves as the local currency.

The Gilbert Islands' economy is based on the mining of phosphates on Ocean Island by the British Phosphate Commission and on the production of copra on the other islands. Phosphates and copra account for 99% of the value of all exports (A$9,732,032 in 1973). Imports (A$6,669,563) consist mainly of foodstuffs and manufactured goods. The chief sources of local revenue are an export tax on phosphates and customs duties.

There is a comprehensive local system of welfare, supported by government activity in medicine and education and by missions in schools and churches. On each island with a resident population, there is a hospital with a dispensary and accommodation for 20 to 40 patients. A 142-bed general hospital on Tarawa has a mental ward and a leprosarium. School attendance is compulsory for all children between the ages of 7 and 16. In 1973 there were 133 government primary schools, with an enrollment of 14,308 pupils; 5 secondary schools, with 833 pupils; 1 teacher-training college, with 100 trainees; and 2 theological training centers. The islands had a total of about 500 teachers at all levels.

HONG KONG

Hong Kong is a UK colony consisting of 236 small islands off the southeast coast of China and a small peninsula of the mainland between 22°9′ and 22°37′N and 113°52′ and 114°36′E. With a total land area of 1,046 sq km (404 sq mi), it comprises the island of Hong Kong 75 sq km (29 sq mi), the Kowloon Peninsula 10 sq km (4 sq mi), and the New Territories (a leased section of the Chinese mainland) and the remaining islands 961 sq km (371 sq mi). Most of Hong Kong territory is rocky, hilly, and deeply eroded. Some 46 sq mi have been developed for industrial, commercial, and residential uses, 50 sq mi are cultivated, and the remaining 308 sq mi are mainly hillside and swamp. The climate is subtropical, with hot and humid summers. Rainfall is heavy, and there are occasional typhoons, some causing heavy damage and precipitating mud slides.

Total population, which was less than 600,000 in 1945, was estimated at 4,366,000 in mid-1975, making Hong Kong the world's most populous non-self-governing territory. The annual rate of growth (1970–75) was 1.5%. The population density in 1975 was 10,806 per sq mi. This phenomenal growth resulted from a large influx of mainland Chinese and the rapid natural increase. About 98% of the inhabitants are Chinese, and about 95% of the people live in the 46 sq mi of the urban area. The urban density is about 90,000 per sq mi. Chinese (Cantonese dialect) is the principal spoken language; both Chinese and English are official languages. The capital is Victoria, commonly known as Hong Kong.

Hong Kong has regular shipping, air, cable, and wireless services to every part of the world. Total length of all-concrete roads was 618 miles in 1974, and there were 203,000 registered vehicles (46.5 vehicles per 1,000 population), yielding the third-highest vehicle density per mile of roadway in the world (after Monaco and Gibralter). A tunnel connecting Hong Kong Island to Kowloon was opened in 1972. In 1976, five major new highways were under construction, along with a tunnel traversing Hong Kong Island. In November 1975, the government began construction of a 9.7-mile subway system; the largest infrastructure project in the colony's history, the line was expected to cost US$1.2 billion by the time of completion in 1980. The government owns and operates a 35-mile railway, known as the Kowloon-Canton Railway, part of which was being double-tracked in 1976. The railroad links up with the rail system of Kwangtung Province in China, and constitutes a major land-entry route to China. There are deepwater berths in Kowloon Peninsula and in Hong Kong; a new container terminal at Kwaichung in Kowloon handled some 60% of Hong Kong's exports in 1976. An extensive ferry service connects Hong Kong's islands; 11 hydrofoils provide service to Macao. The Hong Kong airport, Kai Tak, is suitable for both land and sea aircraft. The runway extends into the harbor on a spit of reclaimed land.

Telephones numbered about 760,000 in 1974 (174 per 1,000 inhabitants). Radio transmission is provided by a government station, Radio Hong Kong, and by a commercial station. By 1976, three commercial television stations were in operation. Broadcasting services are in both Chinese and English. In 1974 there were 730,000 licensed television sets.

A bleak fishermen's island for most of its early history, Hong Kong was occupied in 1841 by the British. Formal cession by China was made in 1842 by the Treaty of Nanking. The Kowloon Peninsula and adjacent islands were added in 1860, and in 1898, the New Territories were leased from China for 99 years. Hong Kong fell under Japanese occupation from 25 December 1941 to 30 August 1945.

The colony is ruled by a UK-appointed governor, with an advisory Executive Council headed by the local commander of UK forces, and an appointed Legislative Council presided over by the governor. The UK maintains a garrison of 10,000 troops (including three Gurkha battalions) in Hong Kong. About one-fourth of the cost of their maintenance is borne by the Hong Kong government. The currency unit is the Hong Kong dollar (HK$1 = US$0.203; US$1 = HK$4.925).

Within the past three decades, Hong Kong's economy has grown dramatically, to the point where it now exerts a major role both within Asia and on a world scale. Located at a major crossroad of world trade, Hong Kong has become a center of commerce, shipping, industry, and banking. Rapid industrialization, accelerated by the influx of new labor, skills, and capital, has changed the pattern of the economy since the end of World War II. The value of industrial exports wholly or principally of Hong Kong origin rose from 42% of the total value of exports in 1958, by which year industry was the most important sector of the economy, to 86% in 1974. While the heavy industries such as shipbuilding and repairing, iron, and steel remain important, light industry has developed more rapidly in recent years. The number of registered and recorded industrial enterprises rose from 8,215 (employing 350,174) in 1964 to 22,533 (employing 625,230) in 1974. Clothing and footwear manufactures, comprising the largest industrial sector, employed 171,692 workers, and textile firms, 101,119. In 1974, the GDP stood at HK$33,842 million. Electronics experienced the greatest rate of growth in the 1960s, while watch and clock manufactures led expansion in the 1970s. Toys and metal manufactures have also become important.

Agriculture, too, has been expanding and has changed from subsistence farming to intensive cultivation. Vegetables are the main crop. Agricultural produce still has to be imported (mainly from China). Hog raising has been intensified. Fishponds have been built to supplement the catch by fishermen, who operate up to 100 miles from shore. Total fishpond area now amounts to 5% of the total land area of Hong Kong. Production of minerals—iron ore (160,000 tons), tungsten, graphite, and kaolin—employed 4,518 people in 1974 and makes a small contribution to the economy.

Electricity is supplied by two companies. Water resources, for long a serious deficiency, have been increased by converting Plover Cove into a lake. Some 18,500 million gallons of water are purchased annually from China. In October 1975, the government opened a major new desalination plant. The largest such facility in the world, the plant will produce at full capacity 40 million gallons of water daily—about one-fifth of the colony's total consumption.

Imports in 1974 were valued at HK$34,120 million and exports at HK$30,036 million. Major import sources were Japan, China, the US, and UK; primary export destinations were the US, UK, Federal Republic of Germany, Japan, and Canada. Trade with China, which had been reduced drastically in the early 1960s, picked up again in 1966 and made up 18% of Hong Kong's imports by 1974. There are neither general tariffs nor export duties, and only a few import duties.

As a banking center, Hong Kong has received a continued flow of outside capital in the postwar years; 74 banks are authorized to deal in foreign exchange. In addition to the licensed banks, many Chinese firms handle Chinese remittances from overseas. At the end of 1974, bank deposits totaled HK$30,998 million (HK$24,613 million at the end of 1972).

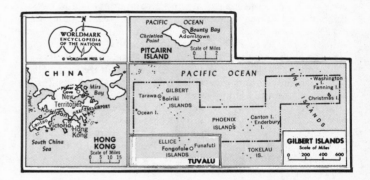

Pitcairn I. See Pacific Ocean map: front cover o8
Hong Kong See cont'l pol.: front cover P7; phys.: back cover P7
Gilbert Is. & Tuvalu See Pacific Ocean map: front cover H6

Some 80 insurance companies, mainly UK-based, operate in Hong Kong. The government regulates insurance companies. In 1975 there were four stock exchanges operating in Hong Kong.

Hong Kong is self-supportive except for external defense. Revenues in 1974/75 totaled HK$5,845 million, derived mainly from internal taxation and import duties. Expenditures amounted to HK$5,747 million. Currency in circulation as of 31 March 1975 was HK$3,996 million.

Tourism has become an important industry. In 1974, more than 1,291,950 tourists visited Hong Kong, spending HK$2.4 billion.

About 300 newspapers and magazines are published in the colony. Almost all of the newspapers are in Chinese; there are four English-language dailies.

In 1974 there were 17 general and special hospitals maintained by the government; 18 others were government-aided and 11 were private. Together they provided almost 17,000 beds. There are about 2,000 physicians and dentists. Despite law-enforcement efforts, opiate addiction remains widespread in Hong Kong, posing serious public-health and social problems.

Although attendance rates are high, education in Hong Kong is not compulsory. In 1971, provision was made for free attendance in government-operated (and, for the most part, government-assisted) primary schools. Education is under the general control of the director of education, who may order primary-school attendance in certain instances. Schools are of three types: Chinese, English, and Anglo-Chinese. There were 1,280,500 students in more than 2,700 schools in 1974. Higher education is provided by the University of Hong Kong and the Chinese University of Hong Kong; together they had a teaching staff of 830 and 6,399 students in 1974.

PITCAIRN ISLAND

Pitcairn is a mountainous island of volcanic origin about 5.2 sq km (2 sq mi) in area, in the South Pacific, at 25°4's and 130°5'w. Three smaller islands associated with Pitcairn are uninhabited. Pitcairn Island was discovered in 1767 by the British and settled in 1790 by *Bounty* mutineers and the Polynesian women who accompanied them from Tahiti. The population, mainly descendants of the *Bounty* mutineers, decreased from 120 in 1962 to 63 at the end of 1974. Some of the younger members of the community have migrated to New Zealand. The climate is warm, with very little change throughout the year.

There is one village, Adamstown. Pitcairn is administered, together with the three other small islands, as a UK colony by the UK high commissioner in New Zealand. The local government consists of an island magistrate and a 10-member Island Council. Four of the Council's members are elected. New Zealand dollars (NZ$) are used locally. There is no port or harbor; goods from ships are conveyed ashore in longboats. Ships plying between the UK and New Zealand on the Pacific route call periodically.

The main occupation is subsistence agriculture. A small surplus of fresh fruit and vegetables is sold to passing ships. Fish are abundant and the annual catch averages 2,000 pounds. Imports, consisting mainly of food, come from New Zealand. Fruit, woven baskets, carved curios, and stamps are sold to ships' passengers.

The islanders enjoy good health. There is one school on the island. Promising pupils are sent to New Zealand and Australia for secondary and higher education.

TUVALU

The Territory ot Tuvalu, situated in the Pacific Ocean between 5°38' and 10°46's and from 176°4' to 179°53'E, consists of the nine islands of the Ellice Islands group, with a total land area of about 26 sq km (10 sq mi), extending *677* km (*421* mi) SSE–NNW and *146* km (*91* mi) ENE–WSW. The principal island and seat of Tuvalu's territorial administration is Funafuti Island. Funafuti, Nukufetau, Nukulailai, and Nurakita islands are claimed by the US.

All of the Ellice Islands are coral atolls and are volcanic in origin. The climate is tropical, with rainfall averaging about 120 inches annually. Each of the islands in inhabited, with larger populations found on Funafuti, Nukufetau, Nukulailai, and Nanumea. In 1975, the total estimated population was about 7,000, of which the vast majority were Polynesian. Small groups of Micronesians, Chinese, and Europeans also live in the Territory.

The Ellice group, along with the Gilbert Islands to the north, were originally inhabited by Micronesians. In the 16th century, however, the Ellice Islands were attacked and occupied by Polynesians from Samoa. The population thus became predominantly Polynesian. Nanumea Island is thought to have first been sighted by the British navy in 1781, and Funafuti in 1819. During the 19th century, the population was drastically reduced by raiding parties of blackbirders, kidnappers who sold their captives into forced labor. On 10 November 1915, the Ellice and Gilbert groups were annexed by the UK at the request of local rulers and became the Gilbert and Ellice Islands Colony (GEIC). Until 1 January 1972, the territory was administered by the UK commissioner for the Western Pacific. In 1972, as a prelude to eventual independence, the GEIC was placed under direct rule of a UK-appointed governor. The Ellice islanders, apprehensive over the prospect of becoming a Polynesian minority in a Micronesian-dominated country, opted to seek separate territorial status. A referendum was conducted during August–September 1974 under observation by a UN decolonization committee. Over 90% of the Ellice Islands electorate voted for separation from the other islands and for establishment of the new Territory of Tuvalu. In November 1974, the newly created House of Assembly of the GEIC voted to support separation, a move acceded to by the UK. On 1 October 1975, the GEIC constitution was amended to accommodate the division, and on 2 January 1976, the Territory of Tuvalu was formally established.

The constitution of Tuvalu provides for a UK crown-appointed commissioner, with responsibilities for external affairs, defense, internal security, and public finance. Legislative authority is vested in a House of Assembly, consisting of two appointed and eight elected members. The House elects a chief minister, who in turn selects a cabinet. Initially, House seats were given to Ellice representatives in the GEIC House (elected in 1974). New elections were to be called by October 1977.

Most of Tuvalu's inhabitants live at a subsistence level. There is little natural topsoil. Fish, coconuts, and taro comprise the major commodities. Funafuti is served by scheduled shipping services and Air Pacific flights.

The Australian dollar (A$) is used as local currency in Tuvalu. Most expenditures through the 1970s are expected to be financed through UK grants. In 1976, government outlays were budgeted at A$1,687,150, of which A$440,000 was allocated for construction of a new capital on Funafuti. The UK grant-in-aid for 1976 totaled A$839,000, covering about 50% of expenditures. The bulk of locally derived revenues was expected to come from sale of Tuvalu stamps and coins to collectors overseas.

A small hospital is located on Funafuti. School attendance is compulsory from age 7 to 16. Schools are operated both by the government and by a variety of missionary groups.

UNITED STATES
PACIFIC DEPENDENCIES

AMERICAN SAMOA

American Samoa, an unincorporated insular US territory in the South Pacific Ocean, comprises that portion of the Samoan archipelago lying E of longitude 171°W. (The rest of the Samoan islands comprise the independent state of Western Samoa.) While the Samoan group as a whole has an area of 3,121 sq km (1,205 sq mi), American Samoa consists of only seven small islands (between 11° and 16°S and 167° and 171°W) with a total area (land and water) of 197 sq km (76 sq mi). Five of the islands are volcanic, with rugged peaks rising sharply, and two are coral atolls. The climate is hot and rainy; normal temperatures range from 24°C (75°F) in August to 32°C (90°F) during December–February; mean annual rainfall is 190 inches, the rainy season lasting from December through March. Hurricanes are common. The native flora includes flourishing tree ferns, coconut, hardwood, and rubber trees. There are few wild animals.

As of the 1970 census, the population was 27,159, an increase of more than 7,100 over the 1960 census figure. The 1975 population was estimated at 29,000. The inhabitants are almost pure Polynesian. Most Samoans are now Christians.

The capital of the territory, Pago Pago, on the island of Tutuila, has one of the finest natural harbors in the South Pacific. Two passenger liners call there every three weeks on a South Pacific tour, and a New Zealand vessel calls every month. Pan Am and Transocean Air Lines provide service between Honolulu and Samoa. There are regular air and sea services between American Samoa and Western Samoa. Radiotelegraph circuits connect the territory with Hawaii, Fiji, and Western Samoa.

The Samoan islands were visited in 1768 by the French explorer Louis Antoine de Bougainville, who named them the Iles des Navigateurs as a tribute to the skill of their native boatmen. Although the independence of the islands was recognized in 1889 by the US, the UK, and Germany, under the 1899 Treaty of Berlin the US was internationally acknowledged to have rights extending over all the islands of the Samoan group lying east of the 171st west meridian, while Germany was acknowledged to have similar rights to the islands west of 171°W. The islands of American Samoa were officially ceded to the US by the various ruling chiefs in 1900 and in 1904, and on 20 February 1929 the US Congress formally accepted sovereignty over the entire group. From 1900 to 1951, the territory was administered by the US Department of the Navy, thereafter by the Department of the Interior.

The executive branch of the government is headed by a governor, appointed by the secretary of the interior with the approval of the US president. A territorial secretary is similarly appointed. Village, county, and district councils have full authority to regulate local affairs.

The legislature is composed of the House of Representatives and the Senate. The 14 counties elect matais, who may be talking chiefs or high chiefs, to four-year terms in the Senate, while the House members are elected for two-year terms by popular vote within the counties. The Senate has 18 members and the House 20. The secretary for Samoan affairs, head of the Department of

Local Government, is appointed by the governor. Under his administration are three district governors, the county chiefs, village mayors, and police officials. The judiciary, an independent branch of the government, functions through the High Court and five district courts. Samoans living in the islands as of 17 April 1900 or born there since that date are nationals of the US; they may migrate freely to the US proper and may become US citizens after fulfilling the requirements of the Immigration and Nationality Act.

The economy is primarily agricultural. The median family income in 1972 was $2,840, among the lowest for all US territories. Small plantations—there are about 1,500, averaging 10 acres each—occupy about one-third of the land area; the principal crops are bananas, breadfruit, taro, papayas, pineapples, sweet potatoes, tapioca, coffee, cocoa, and yams. Hogs and poultry are the principal livestock raised; dairy cattle are few. The principal cash crop is copra. A California concern operates a modern tuna cannery (supplied with fish caught by Japanese fishing fleets); a second tuna cannery began operation in 1964. The two canneries now provide employment for about 1,000 Samoan men and women. The Pago Pago Intercontinental Hotel, opened in 1965 by the American Samoan Development Corporation, and a new jet air terminal have contributed to the further development of the tourist trade in the territory.

Owing largely to the cannery operations, American Samoa's balance of international trade has been highly favorable. In 1974, exports were valued at $19 million (compared with $1 million in 1970), while imports remained stable at about $1 million. American Samoa's trade is highly sensitive to fluctuations in the value of canned tuna shipments, which comprise more than 90% of the territory's total exports. Local revenue is supplemented by grants-in-aid and direct US appropriations. In 1972, local revenue amounted to $7.8 million, and grants by the US Congress and direct appropriations totaled $16.5 million. US currency is legal tender in the territory. Banking and credit are handled by the government-owned and -operated Bank of American Samoa.

Samoans are entitled to free medical treatment, including hospital care. Besides district dispensaries, the government maintains a central hospital, a tuberculosis unit, and a leprosarium. US-trained staff physicians work with Samoan medical practitioners and nurses. In general, the adult population is well nourished, but malnutrition is common—among infants, and skin diseases are common among preschool children. During 1969, the Department of Medical Services opened the 200-bed Lyndon B. Johnson Tropical Medical Center.

Education is a joint undertaking between the territorial government and the villages. School attendance is compulsory for all children from 7 through 15, and about 99% of the population 10 years of age and over is literate. The villages furnish the elementary-school buildings and living quarters for the teachers; the territorial government pays salaries and provides buildings and supplies for all but primary schools. Since 1964, educational television has served as the basic teaching tool in the school system. In 1972 there were 7,081 pupils enrolled at the preschool and primary levels (of which 16% were in primary schools) and

2,484 at the secondary level. There is one teacher-training school.

CANTON AND ENDERBURY ISLANDS

Canton Island (2°50's and 171°40'w) is an atoll in the Central Pacific Ocean 3,220 km (2,000 mi) w of Honolulu; it is about 6 km (4 mi) wide by 13 km (8 mi) long. To the SE is Enderbury Island (3°8's and 171°5'w), an uninhabited atoll. The total area (land and water) of the islands is 70 sq km (27 sq mi). The islands were claimed by the US under the Guano Act of 1856 and were worked for guano until late in the 19th century. The UK, regarding them as in the Phoenix Islands group, which forms part of the Gilbert Islands colony, claimed them in 1937 and built a radar station on Canton. The US formally claimed them in 1938 and placed them under department of the Interior jurisdiction. Both countries sent a few colonists to Canton in 1938, and it now serves as an emergency air field. The two islands were made a US-UK condominium in 1939 for a 50-year period.

GUAM

The largest and most populous of the Mariana Islands in the Western Pacific, Guam (13°30'N and 144°40'E) has an area (land and water) of 549 sq km (212 sq mi) and is about 48 km (30 mi) long and from 6 to 16 km (4 to 10 mi) wide. The island is of volcanic origin; in the south, the terrain is mountainous, while the northern part is a plateau with shallow fertile soil. The central part of the island, where the capital, Agaña, is located, is undulating country. Guam lies in the typhoon belt of the Western Pacific, and is occasionally subject to widespread storm damage. In May 1976, a typhoon with 190-mile-an-hour winds struck Guam, causing an estimated $300 million in damage and leaving 80% of the island's buildings in ruins. Guam has a tropical climate with little seasonal variation. Average temperature is 25.6°C (78°F); rainfall is substantial, reaching an annual average of more than 80 inches.

The 1970 census showed a population, excluding transient US military and civilian personnel and their families, of 84,996, a growth of 26.8% over the 1960 total. The 1974 total was estimated at about 97,000. The Chamorros, comprising about three-fourths of the permanent population, are descended from 18th-century settlers, who included Spaniards, Filipinos, and Mexicans, and later settlers from the US, UK, China, and Japan. Chamorro is the primary language of a large part of the people, but the official language is English. The predominant religion is Roman Catholicism. There are about 190 miles of paved and 47 miles of improved roads. Apra is the home port of the Pacific Micronesian Lines, which serves the Trust Territory of the Pacific Islands. Guam is a regular stop for Pan Am. Telephones numbered about 20,000 in 1975.

Guam was discovered in 1521 by Magellan, and a Spanish fort was established there in 1565. From 1696 until 1898, Guam was under Spanish rule. Under the Treaty of Paris that ended the Spanish-American War in 1898, the island was ceded to the US and placed under the jurisdiction of the Department of the Navy. During World War II, Guam was occupied by Japanese forces; US naval administration was restored in 1944. In 1950, the island's administration was transferred to the US Department of the Interior. Under the 1950 Organic Act of Guam, passed by the US Congress, the island was established as an unincorporated territory of the US; Guamanians were granted US citizenship; and internal self-government was introduced.

The governor is appointed by the US president for a term of four years. The Guam Elective Governor Act in late 1968 provided for the direct election of the governor and the lieutenant governor of Guam.

A 21-member unicameral legislature elected for two years by adult suffrage is empowered to legislate on all local matters, including taxation and appropriations. The US Congress reserves the right to annul any law passed by the Guam legislature, but

must do so within a year of the date it receives the text of any such law.

Judicial authority is vested in the District Court of Guam, and appeals may be taken to the regular US courts of appeal and ultimately to the US Supreme Court. An island court, a police court, and a juvenile court have jurisdiction over certain cases arising under the laws of Guam. The judge of the District Court is appointed by the US president; the judges of the other courts are appointed by the governor. Guam's laws were codified in 1953.

Guam is one of the most important US military bases in the Pacific, and the island's economy has been profoundly affected by the large sums of money spent by the US defense establishment. During the late 1960s and early 1970s, when the US took the role of a major combatant in the Viet-Nam conflict, Guam served as a base for long-range US bombers on sorties over Indochina. In 1975, Guam was a way station for more than 100,000 refugees from the Viet-Nam war.

Prior to World War II, agriculture and animal husbandry were the primary activities. By 1947, most adults were wage earners employed by the US armed forces, although many continued to cultivate small plots to supplement their earnings. Median family income in 1970 was $7,886.

Rice, coconuts, coffee, cocoa, tobacco, pineapples, and indigo grow in the fertile valleys, but agriculture generally has not returned to prewar levels, partly because a considerable amount of arable land is taken up by military installations. Only poultry raising has expanded notably, and by the late 1950s, egg production had become the most important single source of farm income. Copra is processed on a modest scale. Current fish catches are insufficient to meet local demand.

Guam has a vigorous and growing business community as well as a rapidly growing tourist industry, but its economy continues to be mainly military oriented. Business revenues peaked at $620 million in 1975. Retail trade is the largest nonagricultural sector, with 416 establishments employing 3,867 persons in 1972. In that year, 29 manufacturing enterprises had 1,201 employees. Guam's economy suffered a serious downturn in the mid-1970s, following the end of fighting in Southeast Asia. By 1976, unemployment had grown to 10%, in an economy that had frequently experienced shortages of workers.

Until the mid-1970s, tourism had been expanding rapidly. In 1973, some 215,000 visitors, mostly Japanese, spent about $100 million on the island. Seven major hotels were added in the early 1970s, although the worldwide recession at mid-decade left many of their rooms vacant.

The Guam Rehabilitation Act, a boon to the territory's capital improvement program, was given a further boost when the US Congress in 1969 raised the funding authorization of $45 million to $75 million. The increase made possible the continuation of Guam's vitally essential rehabilitation projects, although by 1975 the funds had largely run out. Electric power is derived from fuel-burning plants; the government of Guam controls the power distribution facilities.

Guam's trade usually shows substantial surpluses. Agricultural products are the major exports. In 1974, exports totaled $58 million (compared with $45 million in 1970), while imports cost $5 million ($1 million in 1970). The bulk of Guam's trade is with the US and Japan.

US income tax laws are applicable in Guam; all internal revenue taxes derived by the US from Guam are paid into the territory's treasury. US customs duties, however, are not applicable on Guam, which operates primarily as a free port. In its trade with the US mainland, Guam is required to use US shipping.

By local custom, the aged, the indigent, and orphans are cared for by their families. Some welfare work is carried out by a private organization on contract with the government, the organization contributing $1 for every $3 that the government allocates.

Typical tropical diseases are practically unknown today in Guam. Tuberculosis, long the principal killer, was brought under control by the mid-1950s. The Guam Memorial Hospital has a capacity of 285 beds and includes a special tuberculosis wing. Village dispensaries serve both as public health units and first-aid stations. In addition, there are a number of physicians in private practice. Specialists from the US Naval Hospital in Guam, assisting on a part-time basis, have made possible a complete program of curative medicine.

School attendance is compulsory from the age of 6 through 16. In 1972, enrollment in primary schools totaled 24,810 (17% in private schools) and in secondary schools, 7,512. The University of Guam in Agaña, made into a four-year college in 1961, has an enrollment of 6,000 students.

MIDWAY

The Midway Islands (28°12'–17'N and 177°19'–26'W) consist of an atoll and two small islets. Eastern Island (177°20'W) and Sand Island (177°22'–24'W), 2,102 km (1,306 mi) WNW of Honolulu. Total land and water area is 5 sq km (2 sq mi). Their population was 2,220 as of the 1970 census, a decline from 2,356 in 1960.

Discovered and claimed by the US in 1859 and formally annexed in 1867, Midway became a submarine cable station early in the 20th century and an airlines station in 1935. Made a US naval base in 1941, Midway was attacked by the Japanese in December 1941 and January 1942. In one of the great battles of World War II, a Japanese naval attack on 3–6 June 1942 was repelled by US airplanes. There is a naval station at Midway and the island is a US unincorporated territory under the administrative control of the US Department of the Navy. It is still a major refueling stop for transpacific airline flights.

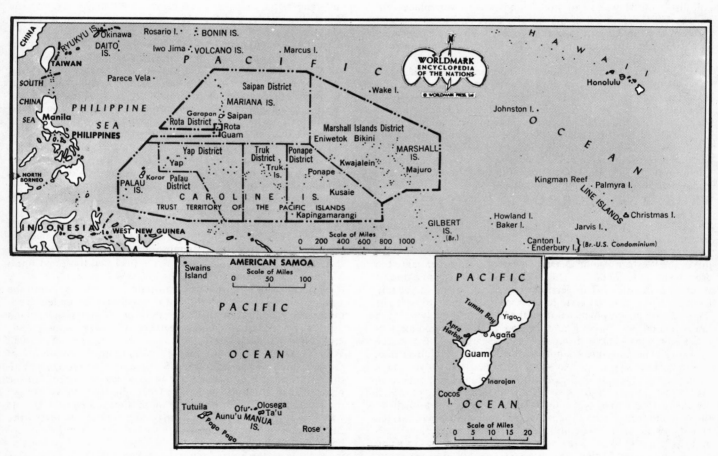

U.S. Pacific Dependencies See Pacific Ocean map front cover

JOHNSTON ATOLL

Johnston Atoll, located in the North Pacific 1,151 km (715 mi) SW of Honolulu, consists of two islands, Johnston (16°44'N and 169°31'W) and Sand (16°45'N and 169°30'W), with a total land and water area of less than 1.3 sq km (0.5 sq mi). It was discovered by English sailors in 1807 and claimed by the US in 1858. For many years, it was a bird reservation. Commissioned a naval station in 1941, it remains an unincorporated US territory under the control of the US Department of the Navy. In recent years, it has been used primarily for the testing of nuclear weapons. The 1970 census reported a population of 1,007.

PALMYRA ATOLL

Palmyra, an atoll in the Central Pacific Ocean, containing some 50 islets (with a total area of 197 hectares or 488 acres), is situated about 1,770 km (1,100 mi) SSW of Honolulu at 5°52'N and 162°6'W. It was discovered in 1802 by the USS *Palmyra*, formally annexed by the US in 1912, and was under the jurisdiction of the city of Honolulu until 1959, when Hawaii became the 50th state of the US. It is now the responsibility of the US Department of the Interior. The atoll is privately owned by the Fullard-Leo family of Hawaii.

Kingman Reef, NW of Palmyra Atoll at 6°25'N and 162°23'N,

was discovered by the US in 1874, annexed by the US in 1922, and became a naval reservation in 1934. Now abandoned, it is under the control of the US Department of the Navy.

HOWLAND, BAKER, AND JARVIS ISLANDS

Howland Island (0°48′N and 176°38′W), Baker Island (0°13′N and 176°28′W), and Jarvis Island (0°23′S and 160°1′W) are three small coral islands, each about 2.6 sq km (1 sq mi) in area, of the Line Islands group located in the Central Pacific Ocean. All are administered directly from Washington as US unincorporated territories. Howland was discovered in 1842 by US sailors, claimed by the US in 1857, and formally proclaimed a US territory in 1935-36. It was worked for its guano by US and British companies until about 1890.

Baker, 64 km (40 mi) S of Howland, and Jarvis, 1,770 km (1,100 mi) E of Howland, also were claimed by the US in 1857, and their guano deposits were similarly worked by US and British enterprises. Britain annexed Jarvis in 1889. In 1835, the US sent colonists from Hawaii to all three islands, which were placed under the US Department of the Interior in 1936. Baker was captured by the Japanese in 1942 and recaptured by the US in 1944. The three islands are uninhabited. They are visited annually by the US Coast Guard.

Malden Island (formerly known as Independence Island, 4°3′S and 154°59′W), about 8 km (5 mi) in length, and Starbuck Island (formerly known as Volunteer Island, 5°37′S and 155°53′W), although regarded by the UK as in the Phoenix Islands group of the Gilbert and Ellice Islands colony, also are claimed by the US. Once worked for their guano, they are now uninhabited. Starbuck was discovered in 1823 and claimed by the UK in 1866; Malden was discovered by the US in 1825 and claimed under the Guano Act of 1856. The UK claimed it in 1889. Malden contains Polynesian shrines of an undetermined period.

TRUST TERRITORY OF THE PACIFIC ISLANDS

The US-administered Trust Territory of the Pacific Islands consists of 2,141 islands and atolls with a total land area of 1,857 sq km (717 sq mi) scattered over some 7,700,000 sq km (3,000,000 sq mi) of the Western Pacific Ocean, an expanse almost equal to the area of the continental US. Only about 100 of the islands support resident populations. The Territory extends 4,345 km (2,700 mi), from 130° to 172°E and 2,414 km (1,500 mi), from 1° to 20°N; its approximate geographical center is the island of Truk, lying 8,047 km (5,000 mi) SW of San Francisco and 3,219 km (2,000 mi) E of the Philippines. Three groups of islands are included in the Territory: The Caroline Islands, to the S and W, include Palau, 487 sq km (188 sq mi), at 7°30′N and 138°8′E; Truk, 101 sq km (39 sq mi), at 7°25′N and 151°47′E; and Ponape, 334 sq km (129 sq mi), at 6°55′N and 158°15′E. The Marshall Islands, of which Kwajalein (8°43′ to 9°15′N and 167°30′E) is the largest atoll, lie to the E. Aside from Guam (a separate political entity) the Mariana Islands, to the N, include Rota, 85 sq km (33 sq mi), at 14°7′-12′N and 145°8′-18′E; Saipan, 122 sq km (47 sq mi), at 15°5′-17′N and 145°41′-50′E; and Tinian, 101 sq km (39 sq mi), at 14°58′N and 145°38′E.

The Marianas are a volcanic archipelago. Other volcanic islands are found in the western Carolines, and there are volcanic outcroppings on Truk, Ponape, and Kusaie (5°19′N and 162°59′E) in the eastern Carolines. Other islands, mostly atolls, are of coral formation. The climate is tropical, with relatively little seasonal change; the temperature averages 21°C to 29.4°C (70°F to 85°F), and relative humidity is generally high, ranging from an average of 77% in the Palaus to 86% at Ponape. Average rainfall varies from 82.2 inches per year in the northern Marianas to 185.5 inches in the eastern Carolines. In most of the territory, typhoons are ever-threatening from July through November, but the easternmost islands are relatively free of these disturbances.

The islands generally are covered with moderately heavy tropical vegetation. Forest trees, including excellent hardwoods, grow on the slopes of the higher volcanic islands. Coconut palms flourish on the coral atolls. Insects are numerous (about 7,000 species) and birds are common. The only native land mammal is the tropical bat; water buffalos, deer, goats, and rats have been introduced by man. Ocean fauna is abundant, and includes tuna, barracuda, sharks, sea bass, eels, flying fish, octopus, many kinds of crustaceans, and porpoises.

As of 1975, endangered species on Palau Island in the Carolines included the dugong and Palau varieties of megapode, ground dove, owl, and fantail; on Ponape Island, Ponape varieties of mountain starling and great white-eye; on Truk Island, Truk varieties of monarch and great white-eye. In the Marianas, endangered species included the Marianas megapode and Tinian monarch.

Total population in 1975 was estimated at 115,000; the 1970 census reported a total of 90,940. The principal islands, with their mid-1969 populations, are Truk, 32,000; Ponape, 23,300; the Marshalls, 25,000; and the Marianas, 14,000. Saipan is the administrative capital of the territory.

The local island people are classified broadly as Micronesians (literally, "peoples of the tiny islands"), and physically resemble the Malaysians. No native Micronesian culture encompasses the entire territory. Nine Micronesian languages, each with dialect variations, are spoken. Common cultural features are close kinship ties, a cult of ancestors, complex class distinctions, and local chieftainship. The Christian religion has been widely accepted, but earlier beliefs persist in certain forms. Japanese is widely spoken, but English is the official language.

Air Micronesia provides air service in the Territory. A modern airport, built at a cost of $10 million, was recently completed in Saipan. The logistic services in the Territory are operated by the Micronesian Interocean Line. Services between the islands of each district are supplied by government-owned vessels operated by Micronesian companies. The US Post Office provides postal facilities. Some of the larger centers have local telephone service; communication between most points is by radio.

The Marianas were discovered in 1521 by Ferdinand Magellan, who called them the Ladrone Islands, but as a whole the Micronesian islands were almost entirely unknown until the 19th century. By the late 19th century, Spain had extended its administrative control to include all three of the major island groups. The Marshall Islands were seized by Germany in 1885 and, following Spain's defeat by the US in the Spanish-American War (1898), the Carolines and Marianas (with the exception of Guam, which was ceded to the US) were sold to Germany. With the outbreak of World War I, Japan took over the islands of the present Trust Territory, and on 17 December 1920 they were entrusted to Japan under a League of Nations mandate. Upon its withdrawal from the League in 1935, Japan began to fortify the islands, and in World War II they served as important military bases. Several of the islands were the scene of heavy fighting during the war. In the battle for control of Saipan in June 1944, some 23,000 Japanese and 3,500 US troops lost their lives in one day's fighting. As each island was occupied by US troops, it became subject to US authority in accordance with the international law of belligerent occupation. On 18 July 1947, the islands formally became a UN trust territory under US administration, in accordance with a special strategic areas trusteeship agreement. The Territory was administered by the US Department of the Navy until 1 July 1951, when administration was transferred to the Department of the Interior. In 1953, the northern Marianas, with the exception of Rota, were transferred to the Department of the Navy's administrative control; the Department of the Interior resumed jurisdiction over these islands in 1962.

The atolls of Bikini and Eniwetok have become world famous

since 1946 as the sites of US nuclear and thermonuclear tests. The 167 inhabitants of Bikini and the 137 inhabitants of Eniwetok were resettled on other islands, and the people of two other islands, Utirik and Rongelap, had to leave their homes temporarily in 1954 because of unforeseen radioactive fallout.

On 28 September 1964, the US secretary of the interior issued an order for the establishment of the Congress of Micronesia, a bicameral legislature consisting of a General Assembly (21 members) and a House of Delegates (12 members). The Congress elected by universal suffrage, held its first session in July and August 1965. The Third Micronesian Congress held its first regular session in 1969 and its second in 1970. It is empowered to levy taxes, to participate in the preparation of the annual budget of the Trust Territory, and to refer legislation twice vetoed by the high commissioner to the secretary of the interior for further action.

On 24 March 1976, US President Gerald Ford signed the Northern Marianas Covenant, providing for the separation of the 14 Mariana Islands from the Caroline and Marshall groups and for the Marianas' transition, by 1981, to US commonwealth status. The Covenant followed a plebiscite, held in June 1975, in which 78.8% of Marianas voters opted for US citizenship and constitutional integration with the US. Formation of the new entity, to be known as the Northern Mariana Islands, must await approval by the UN Security Council.

The June 1975 plebiscite followed a rejection in 1970 of US commonwealth status by the Congress of Micronesia, representing all island groups in the Territory. In August 1975, the Congress called for a constitutional convention which, on 8 November, promulgated a document calling for establishment of the Federated States of Micronesia, once US trusteeship over the islands ends. The proposed federation would exclude the Marianas but would include the remaining Trust Territories of Truk, the Marshalls, Ponape, Palau, and Yap; Kusaie Island would be designated a separate district. The federation would be wholly self-governing, with defense and foreign-affairs responsibilities accorded to the US.

The Trust Territory is presently divided into six administrative districts: The Palau, Yap, Truk, and Ponape districts in the Caroline Islands; the Mariana Islands District; and the Marshall Islands District. Authority for all of the Trust Territory is vested in a high commissioner, appointed by the US president and under the immediate authority of the secretary of the interior. The high commissioner appoints a district administrator to each of the districts. Although the administering authorities must approve local legislation before it can come into force, the development of local representative government has been encouraged by the US. There are more than 100 local municipalities headed by magistrates or mayors, elected through universal adult suffrage. A municipality may consist of a group of villages on a larger island; in the case of smaller islands, the municipality may consist of an entire island or group of islands. Each administrative district has a district legislature.

The territorial judiciary is independent of the office of the high commissioner. It is headed by a chief justice and an associate justice appointed by and responsible to the US secretary of the interior. A high court (consisting of an appellate division and a trial division), district courts, and community courts are under the administrative supervision of the chief justice. All judges of the district and community courts are Micronesians, and two Micronesian judges sit on the trial division of the high court in murder cases. In all other cases involving local inhabitants, an assessor, often a district court judge, advises the court concerning local laws and customs.

All persons born in the Trust Territory are citizens of the Territory; they are not US citizens and, if they desire US citizenship, must acquire it in the same way as other immigrants.

Except for aliens whose permanent residence was in the Territory prior to the present administration, only indigenous inhabitants may own land. Until recently, persons not citizens or residents were required to obtain the specific authorization of the high commissioner to enter the Territory. In 1962, however, in response to some of the recommendations of the UN Trusteeship Council for accelerating preparations for eventual self-government and independence, US President Kennedy issued an executive order opening the Territory to US citizens, shipping, and investment without prior security clearance. With the planned establishment of US commonwealth status for the Marianas in 1981, all citizens of the Marianas will automatically receive US citizenship.

Law and order are maintained in the Trust Territory by an insular constabulary divided into district detachments.

The Trust Territory remains undeveloped economically. Median family income in 1970 was $773, by far the lowest of all US-affiliated regions. In the 1970s, only about 30% of the population over age 16 was part of the employed work force. The traditional economic activities are subsistence agriculture, livestock raising, and fishing. A considerable variety of tropical and semitropical food plants, including taro, arrowroot, yams, tapioca, pandanus, bananas, and coconuts, are cultivated. Hogs and chickens are widely raised; water buffalo (carabao), cattle, goats, and ducks are raised on the higher-elevated islands. Seafood is an important part of the diet, but, despite rich maritime resources, fishing has not been developed into an important industry by the Micronesians. A pilot fisheries project and a refrigeration plant are at Palau; a fisheries training school and a boatbuilding cooperative are at Koror. There is a training program in tuna-fishing methods for Micronesians in Hawaii.

Small processing and service industries are being developed and are increasing. Among them are soap factories, a starch-making factory, hollow-tile factories, an oil press, sawmills, and boatbuilding establishments.

The principal commercial products are copra and trochus shell (used to make pearl buttons). Trochus shell has been the second-largest cash export, but the shell beds have been dangerously depleted in recent years. In 1972, the value of copra exports amounted to $1.3 million. The commerce and trade in each district of the territory are conducted by one to three relatively large enterprises operating as general importers, wholesalers, and retailers, and by many small retailers who buy their stock from the large importing enterprises. A Micronesian products center on Guam serves as an outlet for handicrafts and other cottage-industry products of the Territory. Imports (about $30 million in 1972) traditionally far exceed exports ($3 million in 1972). Trade is mainly with the US and Japan.

US currency is the official medium of exchange. Each district is served by a branch bank, and banking services are provided by institutions in Guam, Hawaii, and the continental US. The Trust Territory Economic Development Loan Fund makes loans to trading companies from a revolving fund appropriated by the US Congress.

Tuberculosis continues to be the most serious health problem in the Trust Territory. Leprosy is on the wane, although occasional new cases are reported. Most major diseases are not found in the Territory. The medical services are supervised by a US director of public health. Eight well-equipped hospitals, 3 smaller field hospitals, and about 150 dispensaries serve the six districts.

The educational goal of the government has been a universal, free public-school system from primary though secondary levels, with advanced training in the trades and professions for those who can profit by further study. Adult and remedial education also is being stressed. Education is free and compulsory for children from 8 through 14 years of age, and more than 90% of the children in this age group attend school. In 1973 there were about 240 primary schools, both public and private (enrollment, 31,000 pupils), and 22 public and private secondary schools, with 7,328 students, including 226 enrolled in vocational programs. Mission schools play an important role in education, especially on the intermediate and secondary levels. There are no institutions of higher learning in the Territory, but each year several hundred students attend institutions of higher education in Guam, Fiji, Hawaii, and elsewhere.

The islands boast wide expanses of untrammeled beaches, and, by the 1970s, tourism emerged as the most important income-earner. The majority of those who visit the Trust Territory of the Pacific Islands—as well as the owners of most of the resort hotels—are Japanese.

WAKE ISLAND

Wake Island, actually a coral atoll and three islets (Wake, Peale, and Wilkes) 8 km (5 mi) long by 3.6 km (2.25 mi) wide, lies in the North Pacific 3,380 km (2,100 mi) W of Honolulu at 19°17′N and 166°35′E. The total land and water area is about 8 sq km (3 sq mi). Discovered by the British in 1796, it was long uninhabited. In 1898, a US expeditionary force en route to Manila landed on the island. The US formally claimed Wake in 1900. It was made a US naval reservation in 1934, and became a civil aviation station in 1935. Captured by the Japanese on 23 December 1941, it was subsequently the target of several US air raids. It was surrendered by the Japanese in September 1945 and has thereafter remained a US unincorporated territory under the jurisdiction of the Department of the Navy.

As of the 1970 census, 1,647 persons lived on the island, virtually all of them employees and dependents connected with its installations. Wake is a stopover and fueling station for civilian and military aircraft flying between Honolulu, Guam, and Japan.

VIET-NAM

Socialist Republic of Viet-Nam
Công Hỏa Xã Hôi Chủ Nghĩa ViêtNam

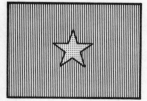

CAPITAL: Hanoi. **FLAG:** The flag is red with a five-pointed gold star in the center. **ANTHEM:** *Tien Quan Ça (Forward, Soldiers!).* **MONETARY UNIT:** The dong (D), subdivided into 10 hao and 100 xu (sou), is a nonconvertible paper currency. The Republic of Viet-Nam's piaster (P) was withdrawn from circulation on 22 September 1975 and replaced by the dong, issued by the Provisional Revolutionary Government. Coins exist for xu, hao, and 1 dong, and notes for 1, 5, and 10 dong. At the end of 1975, D1 = $0.2873 (or $1 =D3.48). **WEIGHTS AND MEASURES:** The metric system is the legal standard, but traditional units of measure such as the mau (0.89 acre in northern Viet-Nam; 1.24 acres in southern Viet-Nam), the gia (1.1 bushels), and the thung (0.55 bushel) still are used by the peasantry. **HOLIDAYS:** New Year's Day, 1 January; Liberation Day, 30 April; May Day, 1 May; Ho Chi Minh's Birthday, 19 May; National Day, 2 September; Resistance Day, 19 December; People's Army Day, 22 December. **TIME:** 7 P.M. = noon GMT.

¹LOCATION, SIZE AND EXTENT

Situated in Southeast Asia, the Socialist Republic of Viet-Nam (SRV) has an area of 332,559 sq km (128,401 sq mi), extending *1,650* km (*1,025* mi) N–S and *600* km (*373* mi) E–W. It is bordered on the N by China, on the E by the Gulf of Tonkin, on the E and S by the South China Sea, on the SW by the Gulf of Siam, and on the W by Kampuchea and Laos, with a total boundary length of *6,127* km (*3,807* mi). Prior to unification, proclaimed on 3 July 1976, Viet-Nam was divided in two by the 17th parallel—the former Republic of Viet-Nam (RVN, also known as South Viet-Nam) lying to the south and the Democratic Republic of Viet-Nam (DRV, also known as North Viet-Nam) to the north.

²TOPOGRAPHY

Before partition, Viet-Nam was frequently described as "a carrying pole with two rice baskets hanging from its ends." The description is a fitting one, for a single mountain chain, the Annamite or Hoanh Son Cordillera, extends along Viet-Nam's western border from north to south, connecting two "rice baskets," which are formed by the densely populated Red River Delta of the Tonkin region in the north and the rich Mekong Delta in the south.

A large portion of the intensively cultivated Red River Delta area is less than 10 feet above sea level. The region is dominated by a network of distributaries carrying off the water of the Red and other rivers. There are similar deltas to the south. Igneous mountains and plateaus of sandstone or limestone comprise the highlands terrain of the central region.

The Mekong Delta actually begins near Phnom-Penh in neighboring Kampuchea, where it divides into two major sections, which in turn subdivide before reaching the sea. This delta and the neighboring Vaico-Saigon Delta to the north are composed of sticky mud with occasional belts of fluvial sands. Cochinchina, the southwestern sector of Viet-Nam, comprising mainly the Mekong Delta, is one of the rich rice-growing areas of the world.

³CLIMATE

Viet-Nam's climate varies north and south of the central plateau region. The climate of northern Viet-Nam is intermediate between that of the continental area to the north and that of the insular region to the south. The rainy season of the year extends from mid-April to mid-October, with maximum rainfalls occurring in July and August. Hanoi has a mean annual rainfall of 68 inches; in areas of the Annamite Cordillera, annual rainfall exceeds 160 inches. Daily temperatures fluctuate widely in the Red River Delta region, particularly in the dry season, when the Delta is cooler than any other lowland region of Viet-Nam. The average temperature for Hanoi is 28°C (82°F) in June and 17°C (63°F) in January; the temperature drops as low as 6°C (43°F).

The climate of southern Viet-Nam is tropical, with temperatures in Ho Chi Minh City (formerly Saigon) between 18° and 33.4°C (64° and 92°F). Humidity is high. Temperatures in the highland areas are somewhat cooler, ranging from a mean of about 15.6°C (60°F) in winter to 20°C (68°F) in summer. The rainy season is from May or June to October or November, with annual rainfall amounting to 116 inches at Hue in the north and 79 inches in Ho Chi Minh City; annual average is 78 inches. The typhoon season in Viet-Nam lasts from July through November, the most severe storms occurring in the July–September period. Typhoons along the north and north-central portions of the eastern coastal area often lead to serious floods.

⁴FLORA AND FAUNA

The mountainous regions of Tonkin, as well as the Annamite Cordillera, are characterized by tropical rain forest broken by large areas of monsoon forest. In the higher altitudes of the western Tonkin mountains, there are pine forests. Shifting cultivation has resulted in many sections of secondary forest. Tranh, a tropical grass, is widespread, and there are mangrove forests fringing parts of the Red River Delta and along the coast in the southwest. Tropical evergreen forests predominate in the south, with pines providing a seemingly endless cover in the hills. During the war in the late 1960s and early 1970s, massive bombing raids and defoliation campaigns caused unparalleled destruction of natural foliage, especially in the central plateau regions. Savanna is extensive in the Cochinchina area.

Deer and wild oxen are among the animals found in the more mountainous areas. Many species of birds and insects exist, and fish of many varieties are plentiful along the coast and in inland waters.

As of 1975, endangered species in Viet-Nam included the douc langur, Asiatic wild dog, clouded leopard, Indochinese tiger, leopard (*Panthera pardus*), Asian elephant, Sumatran rhinoceros, Thailand brow-antlered deer, Asiatic buffalo, gaur, kouprey, giant ibis, Edward's pheasant, imperial pheasant, river terrapin, Siamese crocodile, and Burmese python.

5 POPULATION

The total population of Viet-Nam was officially estimated at 45,000,000 in 1975 (24 million in the north and 21 million in the south). The projection for 1980 was 48.6 million. The annual growth rate in 1975 was officially put at 3.5%; in 1975, the birthrate in the south was 42 per 1,000 and the death rate was 32 per 1,000; in the north, the birthrate was 37.5 and the death rate 16.1. Average overall population density was estimated at 135 per sq km (about 150 per sq km in the north and 113 per sq km in the south). Density in the Red River Delta is more than 800 per sq km. More than 80% of Viet-Nam's population is rural, with about 14% of the northern and 20% of the southern populations living in cities and urban areas. Saigon, the former capital of the RVN, was officially renamed Ho Chi Minh City in July 1976; it remained the largest city in Viet-Nam, with an estimated population of 3.5 million in 1975. Hanoi, the capital of the SRV and largest city in the north, had a population of about 1.4 million. Other large cities, with their 1975 populations, are Da Nang, about 500,000; Haiphong, 380,000; Hue 200,000; Nam-Dinh, 100,000; Vinh, 50,000; and Hong-Gai, 40,000.

6 ETHNIC GROUPS

Ethnically, Vietnamese comprise the vast majority (85–90%) of the inhabitants. Formerly called Annamites or Annamese, they are a mixture of Chinese and Thai ethnic stock and moved into Tonkin (present-day northern Viet-Nam) from central China from the 4th to the 2d century B.C. Vietnamese of direct Chinese ancestry, variously estimated to number between 800,000 and 1 million, constitute the largest single minority group, with the biggest concentration in Cholon, near Ho Chi Minh City. There are also more than 700,000 persons of Kampuchean ancestry and 35,000 Chams, descendants of the once powerful kingdom of Champa, destroyed by the Vietnamese in the 16th century. About 100 tribes of aborigines numbering 2 million live mainly in the high plateau region of central Viet-Nam. Formerly referred to as Montagnards, the tribal peoples are mainly of Thai, Chinese, Mon-Khmer, and Malayo-Polynesian origin, such as the Tay (formerly known as the Thô), the Muong, the Thai, and the Nung. Other Asians (mainly in the south) include several thousand Indians and Pakistanis and smaller numbers of Malays and Arabs. The French numbered about 10,000 in the early 1960s, some two-thirds of them Eurasians. By the mid-1970s, almost all Europeans (including the sizable US community that had built up in RVN during the late 1960s) had left the country. Many of the Chinese residents of the DRV had moved to the RVN during the 1954 exodus, but there were, as of the 1960 census, 174,000 ethnic Chinese in the north.

7 LANGUAGE

The national language is Vietnamese (Quôc-ngu). A tonal language, it bears similarities to Khmer, Thai, and Chinese, and at least one-third of the vocabulary is derived from Chinese. Formerly, Vietnamese was written in Chinese characters, but it has used a romanized alphabet since the 18th century. The Chinese living in Viet-Nam speak their own dialects, and most of the mountain tribes have their own languages or dialects, some of which are related to Lao and Thai. Several of the mountain languages have their own writing systems. French, a legacy of the colonial period, is known by many older, educated persons. Russian is important as a technical language in the north, where both Russian and Chinese are taught in the secondary schools. English is spoken in the south by many former RVN officials and army officers, as well as other segments of the population that were in frequent contact with US forces in the country.

8 RELIGION

The majority of Vietnamese derive their religious practices from the Chinese, borrowing elements of Mahayana Buddhism, Taoism, and Confucianism. Ancestor worship is a powerful force in Viet-Nam, with religious reverence also conferred on traditional, historical, and contemporary national figures. Consequently, apart from priests, monks, and other professional religionists, few Vietnamese have adhered exclusively to one religious system. Animist beliefs have also been present in Vietnamese worship, especially among the various mountain people. There are in addition about 2 million Roman Catholics. Some 700,000 Catholics fled to the RVN from the north following the Viet-Minh's victory over the French and partition of the country in 1954. The Hoa-Hao, a Buddhist-influenced sect, has about 1 million adherents, living mainly in the southwest region of the Mekong Delta. The Cao Dai, founded in 1926 as an eclectic combination of Buddhist, Christian, Confucianist, Taoist, and other beliefs, has about 2 million followers, mostly concentrated in Tay-Ninh Province in the south.

Traditional ways are being subjected to powerful modifying forces as a result of the atheist underpinning of the SRV's Marxist government. Nevertheless, the Roman Catholic community and segments of Buddhist and other faiths have retained a separate identity, even under the DRV government in the north. In 1975, the DRV's Archbishop Trinh Nhu Khue led a delegation of his country's Catholics to the Fourth World Synod of Bishops in Rome.

9 TRANSPORTATION

The war wreaked massive damage on Viet-Nam's transportation network, especially railways, roads, and bridges. Large-scale reconstruction is still under way, with much of the work undertaken by mass-organized labor brigades. In the mid-1960s, prior to the advent of US bombing raids, the DRV had some 13,500 km of roads, while in the RVN about 21,000 km of roads were in use. In 1973, the RVN had an estimated 66,100 passenger cars and 97,700 commercial vehicles.

Hanoi is the center of the rail network in the north and is linked to the Chinese railroad system. About 1,000 km of railway lines were in service in the north in 1975, comprising the region's major transport arteries. After the end of the war in April 1975, the principal north-south routing for freight transportation was an arduous one, by rail from Hanoi (or Haiphong) to Vinh, by road from Vinh to Da Nang, and by sea from Da Nang to Ho Chi Minh City. Work on restoring the complete rail link from Hanoi to Ho Chi Minh City—disrupted since 1946—was nearing completion in late 1976. By July 1975, rail service had been restored from Hanoi through to Da Nang. By mid-1975, Hanoi claimed to have rebuilt a total of 350 km of railways and repaired 54 bridges in the south. A major project under way in 1976 was construction, with Chinese aid, of a new bridge over the Red River, providing a vital link between Hanoi and Haiphong.

Water transportation, which suffered damage during World War II, the Franco-Viet Minh war of 1946–54, and the internecine fighting during 1960–75, has historically played an important role in Viet-Nam's economy. More than 95% of the total value and tonnage of goods imported and exported by the RVN and almost 50% of freight traffic in the DRV were shipped by sea. Haiphong, significantly expanded in 1975, is the major port in the north. A new harbor is currently being built with Cuban aid at Vinh, which is to be developed as a major sea outlet for Laos. Hong-Gai is an important port for the shipment of coal and other minerals. Ho Chi Minh City is the south's largest port, handling the bulk of cargo; the ports of Nha Trang, Qui Nhon, and Da Nang are also important. As during the war, the country relies heavily on foreign vessels for overseas shipping. In 1975, only 11 merchant ships totaling 27,000 gross tons were under Viet-Nam registry. The principal navigable river is the MeKong. Navigable inland waterways in the south—including rivers and canals—total 4,783 km. The Red River and its tributaries form the core of the inland waterway system in the north, which totals about 800 km.

Both Hanoi's Gia Lam Airport, Haiphong's Cat Bi Airport,

and Ho Chi Minh City's Tan Son Nhut Airfield are major civil air-ports, with Hanoi's handling most international traffic in the im-mediate postwar period. Hanoi is served by scheduled flights of the Civil Aviation Administration of China, Aeroflot, and Interflug. The national airline, Civil Aviation of Viet-Nam, flies domestic routes connecting Hanoi with Na San, Vinh, Don-Hoi, and Ho Chi Minh City.

¹⁰COMMUNICATIONS

Viet-Nam's postal, telegraph, and telephone services are under the Ministry of Communications. In 1974, the RVN had some 140,000 telephones, of which more than three-fourths were in Saigon. Hanoi has a strong central broadcasting station, the Voice of Viet-Nam, boosted by local relay transmitters. Since 1975, almost the entire country has been blanketed by a wired loudspeaker system. Radio programs beamed abroad include broadcasts in Chinese, English, French, Khmer, and Lao as well as special broadcasts to mountain tribes. An extensive television service, reaching some 80% of the population, was in operation in the RVN in the early 1970s. A pilot television station was in-augurated in the DRV in 1971. In 1975, the south had some 5 million radios and 1.2 million television sets, while the north had an estimated 510,000 radios.

¹¹HISTORY

In the 4th century B.C., the Viets, under pressure from their war-like neighbors, the Tsin, were forced to move southward from southern China, settling by the next century in northern Indo-china, in the region of present-day Tonkin and north Annam. There they encountered savage tribes of Proto-Malay origin, whom they subdued, and with whom they intermarried, thus forming the ethnic group known as the Vietnamese.

In 111 B.C., China expanded southward and overran the kingdom of Nam Viet. The grip exerted by China was powerful, but the Vietnamese succeeded in regaining short but significant periods of independence under the leadership of the Trung sisters (A.D. 40–43) and of Ly Nam De (544–602). The long period of political domination by the Chinese had a strong cultural im-pact on Viet-Nam and, as a result, the country today has more social characteristics in common with China than does any other country in Southeast Asia. The Chinese occupation of Viet-Nam came to an end in 938 when Ngo-Quyên defeated Chinese forces and formed a state whose independence was maintained, with few exceptions, until the late 19th century. During those thou-sand years, the area was ruled by various dynasties: the Dinh (967–68), the Le (980–1009), the Ly (1010–1224), the Tran (1225–1400), the Ho (1400–7), the Posterior Le (1428–1788), the Tay Son (1788–1802), and the Nguyên (1802–1945).

Further attempts by China to subjugate Viet-Nam occurred in 1075, 1257, 1284, and 1288, and China succeeded in regaining control from 1407 to 1427.

After achieving national independence, Viet-Nam gradually expanded southward, eventually gaining ascendancy over the Chams and Cambodians and completely occupying Annam, an area that later came to make up the Republic of Viet-Nam. Territorial expansion, however, contributed in part toward split-ting Viet-Nam into northern and southern sections from 1532 to 1592 and from 1674 to 1802, although one nominal sovereign was always recognized for the entire territory. Reunification was achieved in 1802 by Nguyên Anh, who, under the name of Gia Long, founded the Nguyên dynasty.

The division of Viet-Nam into two states, Tonkin in the north and Cochinchina in the south, and the long series of dynastic quarrels that followed permitted political intervention by the French, beginning in 1786, when a Roman Catholic bishop led a group of soldiers into Cochinchina to help Nguyên Anh in his fight for power against the Tay Son, his rivals. Long after his death, however, hostilities broke out between Viet-Nam, on the one hand, and France and Spain, on the other, over religious and

commercial issues. Unable to resist, Viet-Nam was forced to yield the three southern provinces of Cochinchina in 1862–67. In 1884, France established a protectorate in Annam and Tonkin

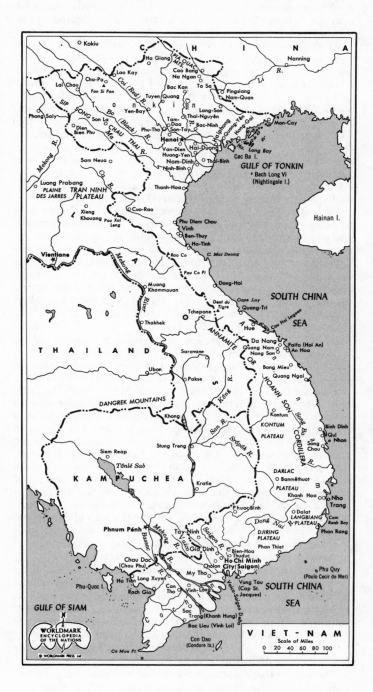

See continental political: front cover O8; physical: back cover O8

LOCATION: 102°10′ to 109°28′E; 8°22′ to 23°23′N. **BOUNDARY LENGTHS:** China, *1,281* km (*796* mi); total coastline, *2,309* km (*1,435* mi); Kampuchea, *982* km (*610* mi); Laos, *1,555* km (*966* mi). **TER-RITORIAL SEA LIMIT** (before unification): DRV, 12 mi; RVN, 3 mi.

(central and northern Viet-Nam). Gradually extending its in-fluence, by the end of the century France controlled all of In-dochina, including Laos and Cambodia (now Kampuchea) as well as Viet-Nam. Following World War I, resistance to the French began to assume the form of Western-style nationalism. Agitation for independence, strengthened by the return of Indochinese troops who had served in Europe, greatly increased over the next two decades, to culminate, shortly after the end of World War II, in open revolt.

After the collapse of France in the war against Germany in June 1940, the Japanese began to exert pressure on the French for transit and base rights in Viet-Nam. Following an initial French refusal, the Japanese attacked French border positions and bombed Haiphong on 22 September 1940. On orders from Vichy, the French in Indochina gave way to Japanese demands. In March 1945, the Japanese, nearing defeat, disarmed the French and removed them from the Indochinese administration to forestall their possible hostile action. Viet-Nam was thus deprived of all public administration. At the same time, the Japanese set up a puppet government, with Bao Dai, emperor of Annam, as nominal ruler. On 16 April 1945, Bao Dai formed a national government under Premier Tran Trong Kim, but when the war ended in August 1945 the vacuum created by more than 60 years of French rule and four years of Japanese occupation had not been filled. Tran Trong Kim resigned, and Bao Dai abdicated into the hands of Vietnamese revolutionaries who had entered northern Viet-Nam from China and had occupied Hanoi on 14 August 1945. On 2 September 1945, the League for the Independence of Viet-Nam, known as Viet-Minh, a nationalist coalition led by a Communist, Nguyên Ai Quoc (who had taken the name of Ho Chi Minh in 1943), proclaimed the Democratic Republic of Viet-Nam (DRV) in Hanoi.

Under the Potsdam agreements, Chinese Nationalist troops with US advisers occupied all of Indochina (Laos and Viet-Nam) north of the 17th parallel, while British troops occupied the rest of the land. France returned to the south in September and to the north after the French had recognized (6 March 1946) the DRV as a "free state within the French Union." Ho Chi Minh went to France and negotiated at Fontainebleau until a modus vivendi was signed between the DRV government and France on 16 September 1946. In the DRV itself, however, increasingly violent clashes occurred between French and Viet-Minh military units. On 19 December 1946, Viet-Minh forces in Hanoi attacked the French garrison, beginning a war that was to last eight years. The war was finally won by the Viet-Minh after its successful siege of Dien Bien Phu (13 March–8 May 1954). A cease-fire agreement was signed at Geneva on 21 July 1954 by the high commands of France and the Viet-Minh. This agreement provisionally partitioned Viet-Nam along the 17th parallel pending general elections to bring about the unification of the country.

After the withdrawal of the last French troops from Haiphong in May 1955, the DRV's Communist-dominated government was in full control of the north. In a referendum held in the south on 23 October 1955 to choose a form of government and a chief of state, Ngo Dinh Diem was elected president and the absentee chief of state, Bao Dai, was shorn of all claims to the Vietnamese throne. On 26 October, Diem proclaimed the Republic of Viet-Nam (RVN), with its capital at Saigon.

The Geneva signatories, meanwhile, had installed an International Control Commission, composed of Indian, Canadian, and Polish military and civilian personnel and chaired by India, whose task it was to see that both sides adhered to the provisions of the cease-fire agreement. Since the more populous north would be subject to Viet-Minh influence for two years before the elections, which were scheduled for July 1956, the south Vietnamese delegation, protesting the partition agreement, refused to sign it; the US likewise would not sign. The elections were never held, because the south Vietnamese premier, Ngo Dinh Diem, refused to prepare and hold elections under what he regarded as unfair conditions.

Beginning in 1959, Vietnamese guerrillas supported by Hanoi began widespread military activities against the Saigon government. The National Liberation Front (NLF), under the leadership of Nguyên Huu Tho, a Saigon lawyer, was formed in December 1960 to coordinate dissident guerrilla activities. The NLF, which drew its main strength from the Communists but whose Central Committee included members of other groups, conducted open insurrection against the government through its military arm, the National Liberation Army (referred to by the RVN as the Viet-Cong).

In April 1961, the US and the RVN signed a treaty of amity and economic relations, and in May the US announced that it would increase its military and economic assistance to the Saigon government. US military advisory personnel were increased from 685 at the end of 1960 to 7,500 at the end of 1962. Throughout 1963 and 1964, NLF and DRV forces, using the so-called Ho Chi Minh trail, steadily infiltrated the south from Laos and the DRV.

During 1963–64, the RVN's attempt to fight a counterguerrilla war against the NLF was hampered by constant internal political struggles, in part fomented by discontented Buddhists. Tensions between the government and the Buddhists led to the overthrow of the repressive Diem government on 1 November 1963 by a military junta led by Gen. Duong Van Minh (in the coup's aftermath, Ngo Dinh Diem was found shot to death). In December 1964, the military junta (which had undergone five internal upheavals since its takeover) dissolved the civilian High National Council (provisional legislature) and assumed control of the government. In June 1965 a military government headed by an air force commander, Nguyên Cao Ky, took control.

Ky, however, did not emerge as the military's choice to become president under the new republican regime, and instead he became the vice-presidential running mate of the army chief of staff, Gen. Nguyên Van Thieu, in the presidential election of September 1967. Thieu and Ky received about 35% of the total vote, sufficient for election.

The stepping-up of insurgent activity in the south in 1963 prompted increases in US military support to the Saigon government. On 2 August 1964, the US destroyer *Maddox*, patrolling the Tonkin Gulf, was claimed by the US to have been attacked by three of Hanoi's torpedo boats. The US then ordered retaliatory assaults on DRV naval installations and oil storage tanks at Vinh; torpedo-boat bases along the coast were also bombed. The DRV admitted involvement in the incident, but claimed that the *Maddox* had fired first. In February 1965, US President Lyndon B. Johnson ordered continuous bombing raids on the DRV below the 20th parallel. By mid-1966, US air strikes over DRV territory were averaging about 100 sorties a day, and in the ensuing three years inflicted awesome human and material destruction on the north.

On 30 January 1968, NLF and DRV forces launched a "Tet offensive" (referring to the last month of the Vietnamese lunar New Year), attacking Saigon and 30 provincial capitals in the RVN and occupying the city of Hue for 25 days. Record losses were incurred by both sides during the February fighting. Ground fighting between the allied NLF and DRV on the one hand, and the RVN on the other—the former assisted by supplies from the USSR, China, and other Communist countries, and the latter by a peak of 543,400 US fighting men (as of January 1969) as well as military equipment and economic aid—reached a peak in 1968. The pace of the fighting began to slow in 1969, however, and by the year's end reached its lowest level in two years. In an effort to encourage a negotiated settlement, President Johnson halted 90% of the US bombing of the DRV on 31 March 1968 as a prelude to the start of preliminary peace talks between the US and DRV in Paris on 10 May. In November, in one of his last major foreign policy acts as president, Johnson ordered a full halt to bombing.

On 18 January 1969, expanded peace negotiations began in Paris, with representatives of the RVN and NLF joining the talks. On 8 July 1969, the US began a graduated withdrawal of its troops from the RVN, after which the new US president, Richard M. Nixon, announced a "Vietnamization" policy, whereby the bulk of the fighting in the south would be taken over by RVN forces. The war lingered on inconclusively, however. On 30 April 1970, US and RVN forces mounted a massive invasion into Cambodia (which had declared itself neutral) in an effort to destroy their opponents' supply bases in border regions, but with little effect.

On 25 January 1972, President Nixon announced that secret talks had been ongoing since June 1971 between the US—represented by Secretary of State Henry A. Kissinger—and the DRV government. Hopes for a quick settlement were dashed, however, when on 30 March, the DRV launched a direct offensive across the 17th parallel and gained control of Quang Tri, the strategically important capital of the RVN's northernmost province. On 15 April, the US responded by resuming intensive bombing of the north (the first since 1968).

The last US combat troops were withdrawn from the RVN on 11 August 1972, and on 26 October the DRV announced that the secret talks between Kissinger and its representative, Le Duc Tho, had produced a tentative agreement. But during the ensuing weeks, the negotiations ran aground. On 18 December, President Nixon ordered the most intensive bombing assault yet to be inflicted on the DRV. For the first time, US high-altitude B-52 bombers struck Hanoi, causing widespread destruction of civilian as well as strategic sites. Peace negotiations resumed on 8 January 1973, and on 15 January, Nixon ordered a halt to all offensive operations. On 27 January, the Paris Peace Agreement was signed by the DRV, NLF, RVN, and US, and a cease-fire was instituted on the following day. The last of the US military left the RVN on 29 March; the US combat death toll in Viet-Nam as of 25 August 1973 was 46,079.

The Paris agreement and the withdrawal of US forces by no means signaled the end of the conflict. The internal parties to the dispute charged each other with constant violations of the truce, and a continuing—if less intense—war of attrition was waged in the south, with RVN forces gradually losing ground to incursions by the NLF and the DRV. At the start of 1975, events foreshadowing the demise of the RVN government began to follow one another with stunning rapidity. On 7 January, DRV and other insurgent forces captured Phuoc Binh, the capital of Phuoc Long Province, bordering Kampuchea (Cambodia). On 15 March, the central highlands north of Saigon had to be abandoned by RVN troops in the wake of their defeat at Banmêthuot. By the end of March, Hue and Da Nang (the second largest city in the RVN) also fell, with more than 100,000 RVN soldiers captured. Following a 12-day siege, the coastal town of Xuan Loc fell on 21 April, threatening Saigon's last viable defense perimeter. On that day, President Thieu announced his resignation. The US ordered a massive evacuation, first of some 2,000 orphans and then of remaining US personnel and some 135,000 Vietnamese. On 30 April, some two hours after the last US helicopters had left Saigon, Gen. Duong Van Minh, who had been appointed president to replace Thieu, announced the RVN's unconditional surrender. Shortly after noon that day, tanks of the NLF battered their way into the presidential palace, and the banner of the Provisional Revolutionary Government (PRG) was raised. The war, which had consumed the fortunes and the well-being of the Vietnamese people for much of three decades, had ended. In its wake, some 2,000,000 Vietnamese had been killed and another 4,000,000 maimed and injured, the total casualties accounting for 16.5% of the population. During 1965–74 alone, an estimated 57% of Viet-Nam's people were rendered homeless. In the north, US bombing was estimated to have destroyed 70% of the industrial infrastructure.

The PRG, which had functioned as the civilian authority in regions of the south that had fallen under NLF control, immediately placed Saigon under the direct command of a Military Management Committee (MMC), which undertook matters of day-to-day administration and security. On 21 January 1976, the MMC was replaced by a civilian administration. On 15 May, Pham Hung, secretary of the southern wing of the Lao-Dong Party, was named as the ranking leader in the south, with PRG Premier Huynh Thanh Phat as his deputy; Nguyên Huu Tho, nominal head of the NLF, was named chief of state.

Acting in concert, Hanoi and the PRG actively set about political programs and administrative procedures to bring about political reunification of the country. Nationwide elections for a new National Assembly were held on 25 April 1976; officials claimed that 99% of the country's electorate took part in the voting. The voters chose 492 deputies to the National Assembly, including 249 from the north and 243 from the south. During 24 June–3 July, the first Assembly of a unified Viet-Nam met in Hanoi and proclaimed the establishment of the Socialist Republic of Viet-Nam (SRV). Hanoi was declared the capital of the country (and Saigon renamed Ho Chi Minh City). Le Duan, as first secretary of the Lao-Dong Party's Central Committee, remained the effective leader of the government (as he had in the DRV), while Pham Van Dong was elected premier and Ton Duc Thang, president. A drafting commission was selected by the Assembly to draw up a new constitution for the SRV; the 1960 constitution was to remain in effect for the entire country until passage of a new code.

12 GOVERNMENT

The 1946 constitution for Viet-Nam, adopted before the war with the French, was never fully implemented because of wartime conditions. On 1 January 1960, a new constitution for the DRV was promulgated, instituting a largely presidential regime in the north. The unicameral National Assembly was declared the highest organ of state authority. It was to be elected for a four-year term by all citizens who had reached the age of 18. The Assembly was to meet twice yearly in regular sessions and in special sessions as needed. Between regular sessions, the Assembly's functions were performed by its Standing Committee, consisting of a chairman, vice-chairman, a secretary, and assistant secretaries and members. Since the legislature in effect met only for about one week twice a year, the burden of the legislative work rested on the Standing Committee.

The president and chief of state of the DRV, whose functions included appointing the premier and his cabinet, promulgating laws, conferring orders and medals, granting pardons, and dealing with foreign states, was elected for a four-year term by the National Assembly. The Council of Ministers, or cabinet, consisting of the premier, vice-premiers, and ministers, was the highest executive and administrative authority of the DRV. Actual governmental authority in the DRV, however, was exercised by the Central Committee of the Lao-Dong (Workers') Party, and by its first secretary.

On 25 April 1976, an electorate in both the south and north voted together for the first time to select a 492-member National Assembly. In the south, 281 candidates contested the 243 available seats; 249 persons were elected in the north, where no figure was released on the number of candidates. The Assembly—the sixth to be selected under terms of the 1960 constitution—proceeded to appoint members of a new Standing Committee, Council of Ministers, and National Defense Council.

Following the fall of the RVN government in 1975, full authority was taken over by the insurgency's Provisional Revolutionary Government. With the convening of the nationwide National Assembly in Hanoi in 1976, the PRG was absorbed under the unified SRV government.

13 POLITICAL PARTIES

The government of the SRV—as was that of the DRV—is ruled by a coalition consisting of the Lao-Dong (Workers) Party, which is in effect a Communist party, and the nominal Democratic and Socialist parties, which cooperate with the Lao-Dong. The Lao-Dong Party is the political successor to the Indochinese Communist Party, formed in 1930 and formally dissolved in 1951, after having been forced underground by the French in 1939. From 1941 to 1951, Communist activities and policies were pursued through the League for the Independence of Viet-Nam (Viet-Nam Doc Lap Dong Minh Hoi), known as the Viet-Minh, a front group consisting of Communists and several small splinter parties. In February 1951, Communist leaders met to reestablish a separate Communist party, which they named the Lao-Dong Party. The Lao-Dong is ostensibly administered through an assembly of national delegates. National party conventions elect a Central Committee to guide party affairs between sessions of the national convention. The Central Committee in turn elects the Politburo, the highest policy-making body, and a secretariat to direct the day-to-day party operations. The most important participant in party decision-making councils until his death in 1969 was long-time President Ho Chi Minh.

The Democratic Party, founded in 1944, is made up chiefly of intellectuals, petty bourgeoisie, small entrepreneurs, and merchants. The Socialist Party, formed in 1946, includes part of the intelligentsia. Neither group has asserted policies distinguishable from those of the Lao-Dong. In 1955, the Fatherland Front was established in the DRV as a device to group various elements in both north and south, including the Lao-Dong, the Democrats, and the Socialists, supporting the reunification of Viet-Nam under terms set forth by the Lao-Dong Party. The south's National Liberation Front, founded by Nguyên Huu Tho in 1960, in large measure consisted of members of the Lao-Dong's southern wing.

In the late 1950s, a group of Lao-Dong cadres, mainly southerners who were living in the north, went south and, together with other indigenous elements who opposed the Saigon government, began a political paramilitary effort that culminated in the creation of the National Liberation Front (NLF) in December 1960. The NLF was governed by a Central Committee responsible for policy formation and planning, a Presidium, and a Secretariat. Initially, about 30 provincial committees functioned as the chief operational units of the NLF and assigned military duties to local guerrilla units. The Communists joined the NLF while retaining their own organization, the People's Revolutionary Party (PRP); PRP membership was estimated at 100,000 in 1970.

Development of a political party system in the Western sense never passed the rudimentary state under the RVN government. The first elections under the 1956 RVN constitution were held on 30 August 1959. President Ngo Dinh Diem's party, the National Revolutionary Movement, won 76 of the 123 seats. Of the nearly 7.5 million registered voters, 85% participated.

Beginning in 1963 there was a significant increase in the political influence of the Buddhists. Under the leadership of the militant United Buddhist Church, the Buddhists protested their exclusion from the government. Protest marches and self-immolations ultimately led to the overthrow of the Ngo Dinh Diem government on 1 November 1963 and the revocation of discriminatory practices against the Buddhists. President Thieu, elected by a 35% plurality in 1967 while heading the People's Alliance for Social Revolution (PASR), tried in 1969 to consolidate anti-Communist political organizations in the RVN through the instrumentality of a multiparty National Social Democratic Front. In the 1970s, however, formal political organizations proved less potent than religious, regional, and ethnic loyalties. In the September 1970 voting for half the seats in the 60-member Senate, "militant Buddhists" drew the most votes. Following the NLF victory in 1975, all political groups not affiliated with the NLF in the south were disbanded, although some members of groups that had avoided association with either side during the war were elected to the NLF's Central Committee. Prior to the nationwide elections for a new National Assembly, held in April 1976, voting rights had been restored to 90% of former civil servants and military personnel of the RVN, all of whom had gone through "reeducation" programs undertaken by the government.

14 LOCAL GOVERNMENT

At the SRV's first National Assembly, convened in June 1976, Le Duan, first secretary of the Central Committee of the Lao-Dong, announced that three levels of local administration would be established throughout Viet-Nam: provincial and municipal, to be placed directly under the authority of the central government; district; and communal. At each of the three levels, people's councils would be set up, the councils in turn selecting executive organs—people's committees—to provide day-to-day administration.

Viet-Nam in the past was traditionally divided into provinces, of which there were 30 north of the 17th parallel. The DRV government consolidated these provinces to obtain a more centralized administration; as of 1975, the north had 23 provinces. In addition, the government had set up two autonomous ethnic regions in the mountainous hinterland; two municipalities, Hanoi and Haiphong; and a special zone, the Hong-Quang Zone, covering the Hong-Gai and Quang-Yên industrial area. The provinces were divided into districts, cities, and provincial capitals. The districts, in turn, were divided into villages and towns. Under the DRV government, people's councils at all levels were elected by direct suffrage for three-year terms at the province, autonomous region, and large-city levels, and for two-year terms at lower levels.

From the inception of PRG rule in 1975, people's committees were being set up as basic organs of local government throughout the south.

15 JUDICIAL SYSTEM

The judicial system of the SRV, as defined by the 1976 National Assembly, parallels that of the DRV. The highest court in Viet-Nam is the People's Supreme Court, whose members are appointed for five-year terms by the National Assembly. In addition, there are local courts, appointed to three-year terms by their corresponding local administrative committees, and military courts. The chief prosecutor, the director of the People's Office of Public Prosecution, is appointed by the National Assembly for five years and is charged with supervision of law enforcement in Viet-Nam; the director supervises a corps of procurators attached to each court but directly responsible to him.

Addressing the National Assembly on 24 June 1976, Le Duan called for the "gradual elaboration of a comprehensive legal system for the whole country. With regard to the laws now in force in the north, we propose that the National Assembly entrust the Council of Ministers with directing their implementation in a manner suited to the new situation, or studying amendments for their enforcement throughout the country."

The judicial organization in the RVN was based on a dual system of judicial and administrative courts, the former under the Court of Cassation, the latter under the Council of State. Relatively unimportant litigation was heard by 13 conciliation courts. More important civil, correctional, and criminal matters were heard by 6 provincial courts of first instance or by 23 justices of the peace, who also passed judgment on appeals from the conciliation courts. The courts of appeal, at Saigon and Hue, were superior to the provincial courts. Final appeals were heard by the Court of Cassation in Saigon.

¹⁶ARMED FORCES

The DRV's People's Army of Viet-Nam (PAVN) was established as a combat infantry force organized into 24 combat and 3 training divisions. At the war's end in April 1975, the PAVN had a strength of 685,000 personnel; an estimated 300,000 PAVN troops were operating in the RVN and in portions of Laos and Kampuchea (Cambodia) bordering Viet-Nam.

DRV naval forces were small and limited to coastal patrol duties. In 1975 there were 3,000 officers and enlisted men in the naval establishment. Ships and boats of the navy, almost all of Soviet or East European manufacture, included 2 coastal escorts, 4 missile-equipped patrol boats, 30 motor gunboats, 4 motor torpedo boats, and about 50 smaller patrol and landing craft. In 1975, the DRV air force had 2,000 personnel and 268 combat aircraft, including one light bomber squadron, 6 interceptor squadrons, and 6 fighter-bomber squadrons. Paramilitary forces in the DRV in 1975 included 1,500,000 persons in an armed militia and 50,000 personnel in frontier, coastal, and armed security forces.

The RVN's armed forces, disbanded after the NLF victory in April 1975, probably totaled about 400,000 at their peak in the 1970s, although large-scale defections and captures by NLF/DRV forces are thought to have reduced that number by about half at the war's end. The navy, including 13,000 marines, numbered about 44,000 men and officers. The RVN air force, organized as a separate service in 1955, had about 35,000 men and officers; its planes were largely acquired from the US in the middle and late 1960s. The RVN received massive military assistance from the US, and a US Military Assistance Group advised in the training of the armed forces. US personnel fighting in Viet-Nam reached a peak of 543,400 in April 1969, but thereafter declined until their final withdrawal in 1973. Regular Republic of Korea, Thai, and Australian forces also took part in the fighting on the side of the RVN. During 1950–74, direct US military assistance to the RVN totaled $16,121 million.

¹⁷MIGRATION

The 1954 partition of Viet-Nam resulted in a major exodus of refugees, a large number of them Roman Catholics, from the northern part of the country. Large-scale organized efforts aimed at assisting the departure of these refugees were permitted for the first year after the Geneva compromise, and more than 820,000 Vietnamese fled to the south during this period. At the same time, more than 100,000 Vietnamese from the south, many of whom were Viet-Minh troops and their dependents, moved north.

In the weeks prior to the collapse of the RVN government in April 1975, the US government participated in an air and sea evacuation of some 135,000 Vietnamese, many of them civil servants and officials of the RVN government, military personnel, and employees of the US official and military establishment in the south. Some 2,000 infants and children, most of them orphans, were also brought out. By 1976 almost all were in the process of being resettled among communities throughout the US.

The war caused severe disruption of living patterns within Viet-Nam and especially in the south, where in the early months of 1975 some 200,000 refugees, mainly from rural villages and tribal areas, fled toward Saigon to escape the fighting. During the 1965–74 decade alone, some 6.5 million persons in the south had become refugees, while about 57% of the population was left homeless. One of the initial undertakings of the PRG government was the dismantling of the refugee camps and the provision of transport and food rations to enable the displaced population to return to their villages. By March 1976, some 300,000 from the Saigon area had thus been resettled.

During 1975–76, government authorities in both the north and south pursued an overall policy of dispersing the population into the countryside to relieve congestion and (in the case of Ho Chi Minh City) severe unemployment. In the north, some 350,000 persons living in the overcrowded Red River plain were to be moved during 1975 to plateau and highland areas. The population of Ho Chi Minh City, meanwhile, was to be reduced over a somewhat longer period from its postwar peak of about 3.5 million to about 1 million.

¹⁸INTERNATIONAL COOPERATION

The SRV is not a member of the UN; in 1975, both the DRV and PRG formally applied for membership but were denied. In 1976, the observer missions of the two entities merged into a single group. The SRV is a member of the Afro-Asian Solidarity Conference, JINR, and OSZhd.

During the 1950–74 period, total US economic and military aid to Viet-Nam—almost entirely given in support of the RVN government in the south—was $23,899 million (including $16,121 million in direct military aid), representing the largest bilateral assistance program in modern history. Of that total, $4,296.5 million in economic assistance was provided through AID auspices during the 1962–74 period. In addition, $170 million was received from non-US sources, including the IBRD and IDA.

In 1959, China had agreed to extend to the DRV a loan of $126,575,000 and a grant of $42,200,000, repayable at 1% interest over a period of 10 years beginning in 1967. Between 1955 and 1965, the DRV was estimated to have received aid totaling D4,229,786,000, of which China provided D1,871,037,000 and the USSR D1,708,721,000. In 1971, Soviet aid to the DRV totaled $415 million (including $100 million in military assistance), while China provided $175 million; aid from East European sources amounted to an additional $185 million in 1971. Total Soviet and Chinese assistance reached an estimated $700 million in 1972. After 1973, the DRV also sought assistance from non-Communist countries. Substantial amounts were subsequently pledged by the Scandinavian countries, among others, with Sweden offering $160 million in equipment and technical assistance in 1974.

By the mid-1970s, the DRV had established formal ties with more than 60 nations. Following the conclusion of the 1973 Paris Peace Agreement with the US, many pro-Western countries—including Japan, Canada, the UK, and the Federal Republic of Germany (FRG)—established relations with Hanoi.

¹⁹ECONOMY

Wet-rice agriculture is the most important factor in Viet-Nam's economy. Some three-fourths of the country's total population is engaged in agriculture, with the Mekong Delta of the south comprising one of the most productive rice-growing regions in the world. Only about 15% of the northern region is arable; highly intensive rice cultivation is carried out in the Red River Delta and the coastal lowlands.

The most diversified area in Southeast Asia in terms of mineral resources, northern Viet-Nam is well endowed with coal, tin, tungsten, gold, iron, manganese, chromium, and antimony. Although still relatively underdeveloped, the potential for rapid industrialization exists. Cement, textiles, silk, matches, and paper are the main industrial products. Fishing and stock raising are important, and forestry may be expected to become so. Hydroelectric power potential is also considerable.

The range of natural resources, especially minerals, is more limited in the south, although great potential exists for further expansion in agriculture, forestry, and fishing. Before the war, the south was traditionally an important producer of rubber, and during 1975–76, production of this important export earner was resumed in earnest. Hydroelectric resources are also considerable, with more than half of current needs capable of being met by facilities completed—but heavily damaged—prior to the end of the war.

The war took its heaviest economic toll on Viet-Nam's infrastructure, which, even in the best of times, was far from adequate in affording access to and mobilization of the country's agricultural and industrial resources. While massive reconstruction efforts were under way in 1975-76, it was expected that several decades would be required to achieve full-scale modernization of the economy, even with a continued high volume of capital and technical assistance from external sources. Nevertheless, the industrial base of the north managed to last out the war with remarkable resilience, in part a function of the small scale and relatively mobile nature of many enterprises. Official pronouncements in late 1975 indicated that the south would be looked to in the immediate future as the country's source of food and export earnings, while the north would be primed for the rapid expansion of heavy and light industry and agricultural processing. Government policies in 1975-76 indicated that a state-controlled Socialist economy of the type in practice in the DRV would be gradually introduced in the south. In the meanwhile, a mixed economy continued in the south through the reunification period, with the state taking ownership of the major sources of production, and private businesses allowed to function in fields of both production and local commerce.

20 INCOME
Postreunification figures for the SRV are not available. GNP in the RVN was estimated at $3.1 billion in 1973, with per capita income in that year put at $154. In the DRV, Western estimates for 1970 put the GNP at $1.4 billion, with per capita income at less than $100.

21 LABOR
About three-fourths of the population in Viet-Nam are engaged in agricultural pursuits. Toward the end of the war in 1974, industrial activity occupied about 17% of the RVN's work force (estimated at 7.4 million) and about 10% of the employed population of the RVN. Given the sizable number of personnel drawn off into both sides of the war, however, the full work force potential of Viet-Nam could not be manifested in wartime figures. While full employment was claimed for the centrally controlled economy of the north, unemployment was reaching alarming proportions in the south, growing by an estimated 400,000 annually in 1973-74. The dismantling of the RVN's army, together with the PRG's reorganization of the south's economic base, increased the number of jobless workers in the south to more than 2.5 million by the end of 1975. Rural development was looked to as a short-term means of alleviating the problem, the government asserting that more than 1 million persons could immediately be absorbed into work in the rice paddies.

Trade unions in the north, which had a total membership of 1.3 million in 1974 (compared with 760,000 in the mid-1960s), are combined in the General Confederation of Labor of Viet-Nam. The principal functions of the labor unions are to ensure fulfillment of production plans and to administer the social welfare system, including hospitalization, disability, and survivor benefits. Prior to the advent of the PRG government in 1975, the largest organization in the south had been the Vietnamese Confederation of Labor, which had more than 300,000 members; its largest component, the 100,000-member Tenant Farmers Union, was agriculturally based.

22 AGRICULTURE
More than 75% of the total population of Viet-Nam derives its livelihood from agriculture. The total area planted as of the mid-1970s was about 5.5 million hectares, including 2.4 million hectares in the north and 3.1 million in the south. Only about 15% of the land in the north is arable, almost entirely (14.5%) under intensive cultivation. Agriculture is concentrated in the lowland areas—the densely populated Red River Delta and the smaller deltas along the coast of Annam. The Mekong Delta, among the great rice-producing regions of the world, is the dominant agricultural region of the south; 25% of the land area is arable, but only 17.8% was under cultivation in 1975.

Rice, the main staple of the Vietnamese diet, accounts for more than 60% of national agricultural production. In the north,

two and in some cases (as in Thai-Binh and Nam-Dinh provinces) three crops a year are made possible through an extensive system of irrigation, utilizing upward of 4,000 km of dikes. Single-cropping remains the rule in the south, where heavy rains fall for six months of the year, and virtually no rain at all during the other six months. The region's extensive network of canals is mainly used for transport and drainage, although some irrigational use was attempted under the RVN government. Rice production in the north, which has traditionally had to rely on large food imports, reached an estimated 6 million tons in 1974 (compared with 4.2 million tons in 1970, 3.5 million in 1971, and 4 million in 1973). Rice output and distribution in the south was seriously disrupted by the war, with the result that the region, once an important rice exporter, became a net importer during the 1964-74 period; in 1968, 4.4 million tons of rice were produced in the south, as compared with an average annual yield of 5 million tons during 1961-65; in 1973, a good crop year, output reached 7 million tons.

Prior to 1975, the separate governments in both the north and the south had been pressing for diversification of crops. Corn has become the north's second most important food crop, with an estimated 250,000 tons produced in 1973. Plans call for a doubling of available acreage, with eventual output projected at 1 million tons. In 1974, sweet-potato production reached a record 1.2 million tons, while the vegetable crop was said to have been twice that of 1965. Other important food crops in the north are manioc, beans, peanuts, and soybeans. The south grows significant quantities of sweet potatoes, pepper, manioc, sugar, peanuts, corn, and oilseeds.

Rubber, formerly a major crop and a leading source of Viet-Nam's foreign exchange, was grown mostly on large plantations organized during the French colonial period. Production in regions controlled by the RVN declined from 74,400 tons in 1964 (then the fifth-largest output in the world) to about 20,600 tons by 1973. Due to war activity, practically all large plantations in the RVN were shut down, and damage to trees was so severe that a full recovery of rubber will be limited for some time to come. Similarly, rubber plantations were expected to become an important element in the economy of the southernmost provinces of the DRV, but the war after 1965 eliminated the chance for such activity. In 1975, however, the government announced that rubber workers—soon to be joined by thousands of families from the cities—had resumed the extraction of latex from hundreds of thousands of rubber trees on plantations northwest and north of Ho Chi Minh City, most of which had lain fallow for years. Other industrial and export crops produced in Viet-Nam include coffee, cinnamon, tea, tobacco, kapok, kenaf, and copra.

Agriculture in the north has reached an advanced stage of collectivization, although the creation of agricultural communes is not contemplated for the immediate future. A land-reform program completed in 1956 distributed 810,000 hectares to 2,104,000 peasant families. The share of the Socialist sector in agricultural land had increased from 1% in 1955 to 95% in 1975. In that year, there were 26,790 cooperatives (comprising more than 90% of all peasant families); in 1975, the average cooperative in the north occupied 62 hectares and involved 120 families or 276 laborers. There existed, furthermore, some 63 state farms covering a total of more than 200,000 hectares, many of them operated by the PAVN. Of the total state loans for agricultural development in the DRV in 1953-74, 55.4% went to water conservation, 29.4% to state farms, and 15.2% to agricultural research.

In 80 years of colonial rule, the French built 12 water conservation projects; in the first 18 years of DRV rule, more than 1,000 water conservation projects were completed, supplying water to 80% of the cultivated acreage. Some 26% more electric power was used in agriculture in 1974 than in 1960. In the same period, the number of tractors increased 18 times. Most farmwork is still done by hand, however.

Rapid changes in agricultural policy accompanied the installation of the PRG government in the south. By 1976, two themes were apparent: In areas already under cultivation, small- and medium-scale landowners were permitted to continue operating their farms with the provision that they increase their hired laborers' share of the crops; the holdings of wealthy landlords or of those with connections to the former RVN government were, however, confiscated by the PRG and redistributed to landless peasants and families of NLF soldiers killed during the war. At the same time, the PRG government embarked on a major campaign to open new land to farming. Plans called for eventual resettlement of more than 1 million persons—mainly urban dwellers—in the countryside; in the Mekong Delta alone, more than 500,000 hectares were said to be lying fallow. Demobilized soldiers were also developing "new economic areas" in the central plateau regions and in areas directly north and east of Ho Chi Minh City. In contrast to existing farm areas, the reclaimed regions were being organized into collective farms.

23 ANIMAL HUSBANDRY
The most important aspect of animal husbandry in Viet-Nam remains the raising of draft animals, mainly water buffalo. Livestock rearing has traditionally been characterized as the weakest link in the agricultural activity of the north, with plans for expansion of stocks throughout the country severely hampered by the war. Lack of feed, shelter, and technical guidance, and an inability to control disease, continue to hamper animal husbandry.

Hogs are considered important both for the production of manure and for meat; pork comprised about 80% of the meat available for consumption in the north. The raising of both cattle and poultry is traditionally more important in the south, but there are no dairy farms. In 1973, the south had an estimated 853,000 head of cattle (compared with an annual average of 1,128,000 head during 1961–65) and 4,275,000 hogs (3,382,000 during 1961–65); in 1973, the north had some 890,000 head of cattle (812,000 average during 1961–65) and 5,500,000 hogs (4,310,000 during 1961–65). Water buffalo throughout the country are thought to number about 3,000,000.

24 FISHING
Fresh and dried fish and fish sauce (known as nuoc mam) are major ingredients of the Vietnamese diet (in many areas second in importance only to rice), and fishing is an important occupation. Shrimp, lobster, and more than 50 commercial species of fish are found in Vietnamese waters. Ha-Long Bay, the major fishing area of the north, is particularly rich in prawns and crayfish. Fish also abound in Viet-Nam's rivers and canals. In the north, the government has since 1975 been rapidly restoring and expanding fishing installations damaged during the war. The total catch of marine fish in 1957 was 114,000 tons, but by the late 1960s, the annual figure had risen to 150,000 tons. The government's announced annual target for fish and fish products is 200,000 tons.

The south is estimated to have more than 270,000 fishermen, and many farmers are part-time fishermen as well. The RVN government had been seeking to increase production through modernization of the country's fishing industry. In the late 1960s, some 76,000 vessels, including 23,000 motorized boats, were engaged in fishing in the south. The south's catch increased from 130,000 tons in 1957 to 397,000 tons in 1964 and to 713,500 tons by 1973.

25 FORESTRY
Forestry resources are important and relatively underexploited. In 1975, forests covered 40.3% of the total land area of Viet-Nam (48.7% in the north and 32.6% in the south). Forestry had long been stressed in the DRV where, even during the war years, productivity was sustained at levels twice that of 1939. More than

80% of total annual timber output in the north is produced by small enterprises on the local level. The DRV's timber output increased from 382,000 cu meters in 1957 to more than 1 million cu meters in 1964; by 1973, output was estimated to have reached 9.9 million cu meters. Important forestry products in the north include bamboo, resins, and lacquer.

A major part of woodlands in the south is comprised of secondary growth, and most forests are noncommercial. Virgin forests have been extensively exploited for local needs, including large amounts for firewood. About 7.7 million cu meters of timber were felled in 1968, but the war's expansion hampered output. Production in 1973 was put at 8.4 million cu meters. With the change of governments in 1975, added emphasis was placed on the development of the south's forest resources. The PRG's Department of Forestry announced plans to increase pine forests in the Dalat area by 20,000 hectares a year, thus enhancing supplies to the country's paper and textile industries. Afforestation was also planned for areas surrounding Ho Chi Minh City, with expectations of extracting tannin and oil, as well as supplying firewood to the city.

Quinine, resins, pine oil, turpentine, and pitch are produced locally in the south, and small quantities of lac and turpentine have been exported.

26 MINING
Viet-Nam has some important mineral resources. The principal reserves, located mainly in the northern regions, are anthracite coal, tin, chrome, apatite, and phosphate. The coal mines at Hong-Quang are the most important in Southeast Asia. The known mineral resources of the south include some coal near Nong Son, a gold mine at Bong Mieu, salt, peat beds, glass sand, and scattered deposits of molybdenum, lead, bismuth, and copper. Important phosphate deposits are found on the Paracel Islands (also claimed by China).

The production of coal dominates the mining sector. Anthracite reserves in Viet-Nam have been estimated at 12–14 billion tons. Coal output in the north rose from 1.2 million tons in 1956 to 2.8 million in 1961, and 3.2 million in 1964, a large part of which was exported. Production in 1974 stood at 3.4 million tons, with a goal of 5.3 million tons set for 1975. Production from the south's Nong Son mines rose from 12,373 tons in 1957 to 60,000 tons in 1962 and to 104,000 tons in 1963. However, production fell to 77,000 tons in 1964 and thereafter declined to insignificant amounts as a result of the war.

Tin production in the north, which amounted to 584 tons in 1939, dropped to insignificant levels during the Franco-Viet Minh War but reached its prewar level in 1961. Apatite production (mainly in Lao Kay Province) rose from 60,000 tons in 1957 to 750,000 tons in 1961 and 996,000 tons in 1964. About 300,000 tons of salt were being produced nationwide in the early 1970s; 500,000 tons of phosphate rock were produced in the north in 1973. Unknown quantities of uranium and tungsten are produced at Ta Sa and Na Ngan in the Pia Ouac Mountains.

In February 1975, the Mobil Oil Co., a US firm, struck oil off the southern coast, producing an initial outflow of 2,400 barrels per day. By mid-April, US oil firms—which had invested some $100 million in oil exploration in the RVN—had left the country. The PRG government, however, announced that it would permit foreign companies to resume the search for oil, and in 1976, several private concerns from the US, Japan, France, Canada, and the UK were quietly involved in negotiations to resume exploration. Offshore oil was thought also to have been discovered by Soviet geologists working in the Gulf of Tonkin. In August 1975, Hanoi announced formation of an Oil and Natural Gas Commission, functioning under the Council of Ministers; in that year the DRV granted offshore drilling rights to the Italian State Oil Corporation (ENI), with the understanding that Vietnamese would be taught how to operate the rigs.

²⁷ENERGY AND POWER

Most electric power is generated by steam and diesel stations, which accounted for about two-thirds of Viet-Nam's total capacity in the mid-1970s. The hydroelectric potential is significant, however, with several prospective sites for large plants available in both the northern and central regions. In 1972, the RVN had a total installed capacity of 838,000 kw, as compared with 271,000 kw in 1964. Of the 1972 total, 164,000 kw (32.3%) were hydroelectric. Production in the south in 1973 totaled 1,625 million kwh. Power facilities in northern Viet-Nam were estimated to have produced upward of 950 million kwh in 1975 (compared with 584 million kwh in 1964).

Power plants in the north utilize hydroelectric power in the mountainous hinterland and coal in the Red River Delta region. Although most of the north's generators are now fueled by coal, planned expansion of hydroelectric plants is expected to result in electrical capacity's being two-thirds hydroelectric by 1980. In 1975, large thermal plants were completed at Vong Bi and Ninh-Binh. Official projections called for a total output of 3-4 million Mwh by 1980. The USSR, China, Hungary, and Poland provided considerable assistance to the DRV in expanding its power-producing facilities. Inauguration of several major hydroelectric installations in the Red River Basin in 1966 virtually doubled the DRV's power-generating capacity, but the beginning of continuous US bombing of targets north of the 17th parallel in 1965 destroyed much of the power-producing infrastructure. Reconstruction of power plants and lines was accelerated after the US bombing was stopped in 1968 and in the mid-1970s.

The first stage of the south's Dan Him dam was completed in 1964, with an installed capacity of 80,000 kw. It was built with Japanese funds allocated as part of World War II reparations. The major escalation of the war in the mid-1960s forced abandonment of efforts to construct the second stage. In 1975, however, work on the dam was resumed, again with the help of Japanese technicians. When completed, the dam should provide fully half of the region's required capacity. Substantial quantities of power in the RVN were produced by private firms for their own use.

²⁸INDUSTRY

Viet-Nam's heavy and medium industries are concentrated in the north. Small-scale manufacturing is characteristic of industry in the south, which produces chiefly light manufactures and processed agricultural and forest products. The state-owned sector of industry in the north comprises that region's most important industries, including the coal, tin, chrome, and other mines, an engineering works at Hanoi, power stations, and modern tobacco, tea, and canning factories. Since 1975, major industrial enterprises in the south—including large utilities, cement works, and large food-processing plants—were brought under state control. As recently as June 1976, however, the Hanoi government reaffirmed its continued tolerance of a private industrial sector in Viet-Nam, which remained prevalent among small-scale enterprises throughout the country.

Most of the north's industries are concentrated in the Red River Delta area. Industrial development in the north before the onslaught of bombing by US aircraft in the mid-1960s was fairly considerable and rapid. A 170,000-ton-capacity steel mill at Thai Nguyên began production in December 1963. In 1964, an additional blast furnace was completed, as well as a coking plant with an annual capacity of 150,000 tons. The war disrupted such growth in several ways: Heavy US bombing destroyed large areas of capital plant, while forcing the Hanoi government to devote major amounts of manpower and materials to air defense as well as to repair of various vital activities interrupted by the air attacks (such as roads and communications facilities). In addition, much manpower and goods had to be diverted directly to the war effort. By the end of 1972, an estimated 70% of the DRV's in-

dustry had been destroyed, including the Thai Nguyên steel complex (the target of more than 120 bombing raids); chemical, sugar-refining, and pulping mills at the Viet-Tri light-industry complex (40 miles northwest of Hanoi); and the cement works in Haiphong. By early 1976, full recovery was still far from realized in these sectors. Official targets for the end of the year included 200,000 tons of pig iron and 170,000 tons of steel. Cement production, which totaled 300,000 tons in 1974, was to be doubled by early 1976 with the completion of new plants.

Some 80% of Viet-Nam's output is still produced by hand, and lack of experience has resulted in imported machines being operated at only 50% of their capacity. Since the diminution of the war in the mid-1970s, Hanoi has put great emphasis on machine-building industry. In 1975, 18% of the total state investment was to be allocated to machinery production, auto and truck parts, coastal vessels, diesel motors, batteries, and rubber products. The most sophisticated plant is the Hanoi Engineering Plant, producing lathes, planing and drilling machines, and other machine tools, already being exported to India and Kampuchea. Another engineering plant in Hanoi produces 12-horsepower tractors (as the first step in a process of mechanizing Viet-Nam's agriculture).

The north has a sizable complement of light industrial establishments. Major textile mills (at Nam-Dinh) and the "March 8" factory (in Hanoi) have a combined annual capacity of 80 million meters of fabric. Chemical production, especially of fertilizers, is also developing into an important industry. Apatite deposits at Lao Kay (near the Chinese border) are used for production of superphosphates. A plant for the production of antibiotics is also being constructed. Other enterprises produce soda and chlorine, bicycles, and tires and tubes. The north also produces glassware, porcelain, enamelware, plastics, hosiery, office equipment, canned fish and fruit, and soap.

Principal manufactured commodities in the south have included leather, sandals, soap, paper, bricks, tiles, matches, sugar, oxygen, acetylene, carbon dioxide, alcohol, rice, tobacco, beer, salt, and textiles. Major factors obstructing greater industrial development in the prewar period were lack of capital, technical skills, trained personnel, and raw materials. RVN government measures to promote industrial development included the establishment of an Industrial Development Center (IDC). The National Society for the Development of Industrial Zones (SONADEZI) was formed in 1963 as a subsidiary corporation of IDC. The first zone, or industrial park, under SONADEZI sponsorship began near Bien-Hoa in December 1963. The site was completed by the end of 1967 and by 1969, 19 plants were in operation and 26 more were nearing completion. The progress in implementing the Bien-Hoa industrial park was more the exception than the rule, however. No real industrial progress was registered in the late 1960s and early 1970s; almost all activity was directed at recovering from the considerable industrial construction setbacks suffered as a result of the Tet (lunar New Year) 1968 offensive and gradual attrition of the war during the subsequent years. Damage to the textile industry, particularly badly hit, was nearly 90%.

The nature of industrialization under the RVN was such that, in 1975, some 80% of Saigon's industries relied on imported raw materials. Following installation of the PRG government several firms—including those producing soft drinks, radios and television sets, pharmaceuticals, textiles, and agricultural machine tools—could continue production only through depletion of preexisting stocks. In some cases, alternatives to US and Japanese suppliers were sought in the USSR (which became the south's chief supplier of cotton), Eastern Europe, and other sources (donations of oil were received from Algeria and Iraq and aid for the purchase of pulp and yarn from Norway). Sewing machine and bicycle plants were trying to produce many of their needed parts on site, while other plants (including the 250,000-ton-capacity Ha Tien cement works) were substituting local firewood and coal for imported fuel oil.

29 DOMESTIC TRADE

Viet-Nam's distribution system is four-tiered, with state-owned trading companies topmost. Marketing cooperatives comprise the second channel of distribution and, together with the state organizations control almost all trading activities and retail sales in the northern part of the country (in the post-1975 period this system was also being gradually introduced in the south). There is a legal free market in both the north and the south, in which peasant collectives can sell or exchange sideline products and where private merchants can sell goods not requisitioned, purchased, or distributed by the state.

Although the level of domestic trade in the DRV was not announced in recent years, the circulation of retail goods sold on state-organized markets increased in 1974 by 2% over 1973, and doubled that of 1965. (In 1957, state companies and cooperatives controlled 61% of the wholesale trade, but only 31% of the retail trade, the rest being in private hands.) Although the share of private trade was being steadily decreased through the mid-1970s, both deep-set traditional patterns and an insufficient organizational and infrastructural base required continuing dependence on it.

Saigon was the commercial center of the RVN. The Saigon central market covered two city blocks, and there were 28 other large markets spread out around the city. There also were central marketplaces in villages, towns, and cities of the south. Resident Chinese traders traditionally predominated in the distribution of goods. During the war years, price controls were in effect on all imports and essential goods and services, with set wholesale and retail profit margins (more honored in the breach than in performance).

Business hours in the north are from 7:30 to 11:30 A.M. and from 2 to 6 P.M.; in the south, business hours are traditionally from 9 A.M. to noon and from 3 to 6 P.M.

Competitive advertising in the Western sense does not exist in the SRV. The RVN had several advertising agencies; motion-picture shorts and public displays, both influenced by US practices, were the chief advertising media.

30 FOREIGN TRADE

As separate entities in the post-World War II period, neither the DRV nor the RVN succeeded in establishing a viable foreign-trade balance. Profound disruptions in production and transportation brought about by the subsequent war accompanied an intrinsic liability imposed by each side's inaccessibility to the other's resources and capacities. The north had never produced enough rice to support its population and, until 1954, had relied heavily on supplies from the Mekong Delta. And the south, while traditionally a net exporter of rice and rubber, lacked both the raw materials and infrastructure to sustain industrial development.

The DRV had not realized a positive commodity trade balance since its inception, and relied heavily on credits from China and the USSR. Although official trade statistics have not been available since 1963, Western estimates placed the DRV's 1971 export volume at $60 million and imports at $650 million. Anthracite traditionally accounted for 40% of the DRV's exports to all other countries; other mineral products (including apatite and cement) accounted for 6%; agricultural, forestry, and handicraft products constituted the balance. Imports in the early 1970s consisted largely of machinery, petroleum products, foodstuffs, textiles, and technical apparatus. In 1975, the government predicted a 30% increase in export volume over 1974, and a 24% increase over the peak year of 1964.

From 85% to 90% of the DRV's trade in the early 1970s was estimated to be with other Socialist countries. China is thought to

have been the most important traditional trade partner, followed by the USSR and Czechoslovakia. The USSR had traditionally accounted for about 10% of the DRV's foreign trade, but its share steadily increased through the 1960s and 1970s. Trade between the USSR and the DRV (in rubles) rose from 51.7 million in 1957 to 76 million in 1962 and to 94.9 million in 1965. Imports of Soviet petroleum products reached 121,000 tons in 1965. The USSR has since supplied the DRV with all its gasoline, kerosine, and other petroleum products. The DRV also had important commercial relations with Albania, Bulgaria, Cuba, the GDR, Mongolia, Poland, Hungary, and Romania. Since 1975, important new trade relations have been established with the new governments of Kampuchea and Laos. Viet-Nam is expected to provide Laos with vital outlets to the sea, through Haiphong and, eventually, the reconstructed port of Vinh.

Trade with non-Communist countries declined in the late 1960s, largely because of the cessation of anthracite shipments to France and of pig iron to Japan. Following the signing of the 1973 Paris peace accord, however, the trend reversed itself, especially in the case of Japan. By the end of 1973, more than 15 Japanese trading firms were dealing directly with the DRV. In 1974, two-way trade between Japan and the DRV totaled $50 million, representing a 300% increase over 1973 levels; the annual volume was expected to exceed $200 million by the late 1970s. Japan expressed special interest in Viet-Nam's coal deposits, and by mid-decade was importing 600,000 tons of Vietnamese anthracite coal a year. In exchange, Viet-Nam has been considering the purchase of Japanese steel, chemicals, fertilizer, and industrial plants. Significant trade dealings were also being pursued with the Scandinavian countries.

The RVN had a large chronic trade deficit that widened increasingly under the impact of the war. Exports never exceeded about 20% of the annual value of imports; in 1968, they represented only about 2.5% of the total value of imports, recovering to only 8.2% by 1973. Formerly a rice exporter, the RVN had to import rice after the mid-1960s. The postcolonial low in exports—due to war—was reached in 1968; exports in that year were limited to 25,600 tons of rubber and small quantities of fish, tea, duck feathers, and cinnamon. By 1972, rubber exports had fallen to 22,900 tons. In 1972, RVN exports totaled $13,313,000, while imports reached $706,904,000—leaving a deficit of $693,591,000. The situation was met by large-scale US economic assistance, principally in the form of grants.

By 1973, the US share of RVN imports had grown to 43% of the total, with Japan, Singapore, and France the other major suppliers. Traditional markets for RVN goods were France, Japan, and the UK.

In mid-1975, the US declared a trade embargo against the PRG government, denying export licenses for all but humanitarian supplies to the south.

31 BALANCE OF PAYMENTS

The northern region of Viet-Nam has traditionally had an adverse trade balance. As long ago as 1939, the north accounted for 42% of imports of French-ruled Viet-Nam but for only 18% of the exports. Trade deficits have continued since the division of the country in 1954, but have been largely offset by credits and assistance from the USSR, China, and other Socialist countries. In the mid-1970s, the DRV requested and received assistance from both Socialist and non-Socialist states. Sweden contributed some $160 million in 1974; the USSR remained the DRV's largest single source of trade assistance. In September 1975, Japan agreed to pay the DRV $43.8 million in World War II reparations.

The southern segment of Viet-Nam has also suffered perennial trade deficits, at least since World War II. During the 1960s and early 1970s, the US provided the RVN substantial aid and import subventions. Foreign assets of the RVN's National Bank of Viet-Nam fell from P21.9 billion in 1968 to a negative balance of P2.7

billion by the end of 1971. By November 1974, claims on the government reached P297.2 billion, as against foreign assets of P134.6 billion.

³²BANKING

The State Bank of the Democratic Republic of Viet-Nam, created in 1951, has been the central bank of issue for the DRV, with numerous branches throughout the territory and an extensive agricultural and industrial loan service that lends to individuals as well as to cooperatives and to state-owned enterprises. Foreign exchange is regulated by the Foreign Trade Bank. The Bank of China, the USSR Popular Bank, the Czechoslovakian State Bank, and the Bank of Northern Europe and Paris have offices in Hanoi to receive payments for imports. In 1973, two Japanese banks—Sanwa and Mitsui—established financial ties with the Foreign Trade Bank.

Financial chaos became a constant threat during the final years of the RVN. During 1974 alone, rampant inflation forced 10 separate devaluations of the piaster, the last by 24.5% in December 1974. The National Bank of Viet-Nam (NBV) was established in 1954 as the RVN's sole authority for issuing notes, controlling credit, and supervising the formation of new banks and changes in banking establishments. Currency in circulation rose from P12.8 billion in 1962 to P85 billion in 1967, and to P245.7 billion by the end of 1974. US, French, UK, and Chinese (Taiwan-linked) banks, which were equipped to do general banking business, handled foreign exchange dealings and granted loans.

During April 1975, the last month of RVN control in the south, more than P150 billion were withdrawn from the banks. In early May, the newly installed PRG government ordered the temporary closure of all banks in the south, although the RVN piaster continued to circulate as the only legal tender. After two months of stock taking, the NBV was reopened under new management. Stringent regulations were announced, in part as an effort to curb inflation: Depositors with less than P100,000 in savings were permitted to make withdrawals of P10,000 at a time, once having received authorization from local committees. All private Vietnamese and foreign banks were to be permanently closed by 1 December and their assets liquidated. Then, on 22 September, the government ordered a complete withdrawal from circulation of the old RVN currency and its replacement by a dong issued by the PRG. The PRG dong was placed on a par with that of the DRV, a major initial step in the economic reunification of the country. A conversion ceiling of P200,000 (convertible to D400) was set for individuals (much higher ceilings were permitted for industries and businesses), with excess funds to be registered in NBV savings accounts. Thus, by the year's end, the currency of the south had been brought firmly under the control of the PRG authorities.

³³INSURANCE

Prior to May 1975, life and property insurance were available in the RVN from three small Vietnamese insurance companies and through local representatives of about 70 French, UK, and US insurance firms. Regulatory legislation was modeled on French law. By late 1975, all private insurance facilities had ceased to operate, in accord with the practice of the DRV. Old age insurance and pensions were introduced in the DRV in 1962.

³⁴SECURITIES

There are no securities exchanges in Viet-Nam, and trading in securities, a routine activity in the RVN until 1975, is not permitted.

³⁵PUBLIC FINANCE

Viet-Nam's first unified budget was expected to be issued by the SRV government in late 1976. From 1964 on, the DRV did not make any figures available on its state budget. More than half the state budget in the years 1966–74 was probably devoted directly to different dimensions of the war with the RVN and the US, although the proportion of military spending probably declined

through the early 1970s. By contrast, in 1960, the government was reportedly spending only 13.8% of its public budget on military matters. In 1970, military expenditures were estimated at D2,150 million ($584 million). Even as early as the late 1950s, however, one-third of the DRV budget was made up of contributions from the other Communist countries, particularly the USSR and China. Taxation provided 28% of domestic revenues in 1959, and 22.1% of all government receipts in 1963. In the 1968/69 fiscal year, the government made only the following statement on public finance: "On the basis of...increased production, the people's contributions and the assistance of the brotherly countries, there is always a rapid increase in the revenue of the state budget."

In 1962, the RVN reorganized its public finance procedures, listing its accounts in three separate budgets: (1) the civilian ordinary budget, subject to legislative approval; (2) the extraordinary security budget, implemented by presidential decrees; and (3) the economic development budget, subject to "advice" by the Economic Council. Budgeted military expenditures rose from P30.4 billion in 1965 to P92 billion in 1969, and to P274 billion by 1974. Since 1954, the US had assumed a major share of the RVN's budget commitments, and during 1961–74 the US supported virtually all military expenditures. The projected 1974 budget showed revenues of P454 billion and expenditures of P561 billion, leaving a deficit of P107 billion. Foreign debt as of 31 December 1973 stood at $172.8 million.

³⁶TAXATION

Taxes on the incomes of individuals and enterprises are thought to have comprised about one-fourth of the central government's internal revenue in the DRV. A 1956 income tax law tightened controls over the remaining private businessmen. Yearly taxes were due by the end of January, the business year ending a month earlier. The Tax Service—not the individual businessman—calculates the tax. Real estate taxes, codified on 12 January 1956, have been levied at a rate of 1.8% of the value of the house minus exemptions granted for building new houses or repairing old ones. An agricultural tax law passed the same year chiefly affected private landowners.

Tax revenues of the RVN government were derived from income, land, production, and commercial licenses (taxes paid to establish and operate various businesses). Wages and salaries were taxed at rates ranging from 1% to 5%. Profits earned by individuals and the self-employed were taxed at 16%, corporate profits at 24%. However, the collection of taxes in the RVN was frequently erratic.

³⁷CUSTOMS AND DUTIES

Pursuant to prior policies in the DRV, all foreign currency now entering Viet-Nam must be declared upon entry and exchanged at the state's banks. Import duties on objects considered of interest to the DRV economy (e.g., machinery and pharmaceuticals) have been very low. Luxury items are taxed at above 100% of declared value.

In the RVN, comparatively low duty rates were applied to raw materials, essential consumer items, and machine tools and agricultural equipment. Higher rates were levied on luxury items. In addition, there were protective tariffs on items that competed with certain local products. Exports of rubber, rice, and their derivatives, pepper, and ores were taxed at 5%.

³⁸FOREIGN INVESTMENTS

France was the dominant foreign investor in Indochina before World War II. Resident Chinese, however, played a major role in rice milling, retailing, and other activities (and continued to do so in the south through the early 1970s). Following the 1954 partition agreement, the French economic position in the DRV was completely liquidated, and the participation of private foreign investments in the DRV economy were prohibited.

The RVN government traditionally encouraged the introduction of private capital. In March 1957, a presidential declaration provided guarantees against nationalization and expropriation without due compensation; temporary exemption from various taxes; and remittance of profits within existing regulations. Despite these efforts, relatively little new private foreign investment was attracted to the country, apart from a few ventures by US interests (which committed some $100 million to offshore oil exploration in the 1970s) and by the Japanese (in electronics and other consumer-goods manufactures). Some French interests were retained in rubber and other export sectors.

³⁹ ECONOMIC POLICY

The primary goal of the SRV, as officially reaffirmed upon reunification in June 1976, is "to transform the economy along Socialist lines." Added to that, for the late 1970s, loomed the formidable task of integrating the often divergent economic lifestyles of the formerly free-enterprise south with the Socialist patterns of the north. However, while the SRV government was speaking in terms of "15 or 20 years" for "laying the material and technical basis of socialism" for Viet-Nam, it was expected that substantial integration of resources in the formerly divided north and south could be accomplished much sooner. By early 1976, postal and telegraph services, railways, and banks in the south as well as north were wholly state-owned and -operated, and an integrated national currency system had been established. Le Duan, in addressing the Vietnamese National Assembly on 25 June 1976, set the theme for the SRV's economic policies in the wake of reunification: "It is necessary to carry out Socialist transformation of the private capitalist economy in production, transport and communications, and building, this transformation being effected through the use of different measures to suit concrete situations: Private enterprises may be turned into joint state-private ones, or they may be allowed to continue in existence and encouraged to serve socialism under the guidance of the Socialist state and within the framework of state plans."

By the beginning of the DRV's first five-year plan (1961), the bulk of industry in the north had been transferred to state ownership. Much of the handicraft economy (in 1960 it still represented D1.01 billion out of a GNP of D4.3 billion) is now under joint state-private ownership or completely cooperativized. Meanwhile, the share of state industry in the total industrial output rose from 12% in 1955 to 57.6% in 1961, and was said to have surpassed 90% by 1970.

The number of state farms has been decreasing, while the number of cooperatives has been growing. In 1961, however, the "supplementary family economy" (e.g. what cooperative farmers grew on their own private plots) still provided 55.5% of the average real income of cooperative farmers. In 1975, it was asserted that 95% of agricultural income derived from the Socialist sector.

In 1965, goals of the DRV's five-year plan launched in 1960 were announced to be near fulfillment. Targets provided at the plan's inception included raising food production by 44% (4.9 million tons in 1960), raising coal production by 92% (2.6 million tons in 1960), and cement production by 74% (408,000 tons in 1960). Plans for a second five-year plan were abandoned in 1965, and a two-year plan was adopted; the major focus of the plan was on building air-raid defenses.

The years of vigorous warfare between 1965 and 1973 could not help but profoundly influence the DRV's economic policy. The impact took two forms: various setbacks in fields of apparent previous progress and adoption of different measures to minimize the conflict's consequences for the economy. In a public report in late August 1970, the government admitted that the war had inflicted heavy damage on an "already very poor and backward" economy. Production "on the whole," it was said, maintained its previous level—implying no progress and some setbacks.

With the final defeat of RVN forces in early 1975, Hanoi moved quickly to place production and development back on a firm footing, with primary attention given to continued restoration of infrastructure and agriculture to prewar levels, while pressing for material advances in energy production. In late 1975, Premier Pham Van Dong indicated that the south "will soon become a prosperous center for agricultural production and fishing," while the north was to expand rapidly "the existing heavy industries which are very necessary to itself and to the whole country." Production of consumer goods would also be stressed in the north, "especially those which it has the capacity to produce in great quantities, with high output and low production costs." Long-range planning for the country was to resume with a 1976–80 development plan placing major emphasis on heavy industries. In 1975, the government spoke of the country producing, by 1980, 3–4 billion kwh of electricity, 10 million tons of coal, 3 million tons of cement, 1 million tons of fertilizers, and new items of machinery, including 100-horsepower engines. While heavy industry would be concentrated in large urban areas, light industry was to be dispersed among new regional centers, with planners pointing to a policy of guided urbanization whereby the development of towns of 50,000–200,000 population would be encouraged. The south, which faced more pressing problems of unemployment and disorganization, was to be led through a period of "advanced democracy," whereby massive restructuring of the rural economy would apparently await restoration of the region to a productive footing.

⁴⁰ HEALTH

Viet-Nam is afflicted with tropical diseases. Despite significant contributions by France during the colonial period, health facilities before World War II were insufficient and badly organized. France established three centers of the Pasteur Institute in Viet-Nam for conducting research in tropical diseases, distributing vaccines, and solving the problems of hygiene and sanitation that accompanied Indochinese urbanization. Important contributions were made to the knowledge of tropical diseases, but health facilities under the colonial regime were insufficient, particularly in the heavily populated rural areas. Both the RVN and DRV governments tried to improve rural health standards. The wars since 1946 have done much damage to existing health facilities, particularly to urban hospitals in the north struck in the course of US bombing raids. A 1976 WHO report indicated the dimensions of that destruction: 24 research institutes and specialized hospitals, 28 provincial hospitals, 94 district hospitals, and 533 community health centers were destroyed, mainly as the result of bombings.

Health problems in the north appeared to have been stabilized in recent decades despite destruction to medical facilities. In 1976, Hanoi claimed that infant mortality had been reduced to a rate of 1.2%, as compared with 20–40% before 1945. In addition, smallpox, malaria, polio, and tuberculosis were said to have been effectively eliminated in the north. Each district (compared with about one-fourth of the districts before 1965) was supplied with a 100-150-bed hospital, yielding a national ratio of 22 beds per 1,000 population (or about 530,000 beds in 1975). In 1975, some 4,000 beds were added in rural areas, and a new Hanoi children's hospital was being constructed, the former facility having been destroyed by bombs. In addition, more than 90% of the villages in the north were said to have been supplied with infirmaries, each usually equipped with at least one physician, two nurses, a pharmaceutical technician, and two midwives. In 1975, the north had 3,400 civilian doctors and 18,000 practitioners of traditional medicine.

Three decades of intermittent war appeared to have had a devastating effect on health conditions in the south. At the war's end in 1975, many endemic diseases were observed to be on the increase, in alarming contrast to trends among other affected countries in Southeast Asia. WHO reported in 1976 that malaria was both widespread and increasing in the south in 1975. During 1965-74, 5,000 cases of bubonic plague were occurring annually, with a mortality rate of 5%. Saigon was said to have had a tuberculosis rate two to three times that of neighboring countries, while leprosy—involving an estimated 80,000–160,000 cases—was increasing. Venereal and paravenereal diseases were said to have affected 1 million persons in the south (about 5% of the total population) and, the WHO claimed, 80%of RVN soldiers. Opiate addiction, it was said, affected about 500,000 persons. In 1972, the RVN had 1,579 hospitals and other health establishments with a total of 34,750 beds (or less than 2 for every 1,000 population). Health personnel included 1,883 physicians, 370 dentists, 2,399 pharmacists, 7,631 nurses, and 2,767 midwives. During the war the US became an important source of medical supplies and services in the south, and the US departure created a considerable vacuum in the health care sector.

In 1975, average life expectancy was estimated at 51 years in the north and 47.6 years in the south.

41 SOCIAL WELFARE
The war hindered the systematic provision of social services in both the DRV and RVN. In June 1976, Le Duan spoke of his government's obligation to "take good care of wounded and sick soldiers and of the families of those who have laid down their lives for their country, bring up war orphans, provide help to the aged and invalids who have lost all means of support." There are no orphanages in the north, the tradition having been to place all orphans with relatives or other families.

Social security legislation under the RVN was embodied in the workmen's compensation provisions of the labor code of 1952, which required that some degree of medical care be given employees under contract, and to an employer-financed family-allowances system established by law in 1953, a system that covered about 15% of the population.

Under the PRG in the south, a variety of welfare provisions and special concessions were made available to the dependents of wounded or deceased soldiers who had fought on the side of Hanoi or the NLF.

42 HOUSING
Housing in the countryside of the north is generally more adequate than that in the urban areas of Hanoi and Haiphong, where serious problems of overcrowding occurred even before the war. The congestion was due in part to the population increase, but also to planning priorities that put maximizing of agricultural and industrial production ahead of personal comforts. The war took a heavy toll, primarily in terms of displacement of large numbers of urban inhabitants to the country as part of the process of industrial dispersion occasioned by US bombing. In the mid-1970s, four- and five-story apartment buildings were being erected near Hanoi to accommodate 50,000 workers and civil servants. Plans in 1975 called for the construction of up to 10 medium-sized industrial cities to be populated by urban workers and rural cooperative members. One such city under construction was Viet-Tri, 40 miles upriver from Hanoi, with a population of 50,000.

A major housing problem was created in the 1950s in the south by the influx of refugees from the DRV. With the help of economic assistance from France and the US, the RVN government established a number of resettlement projects, which provided refugee families with land and homes. A second massive wave of dislocations occurred during the late 1960s and early 1970s, when the fighting (and consequent political changes in various regions) left more than half of the population homeless. The PRG policy since 1975 has been to disperse urban dwellers to the villages and countryside.

43 EDUCATION
In the mid-1970s, literacy in the south was estimated at about 65%, while in the north a rate of 85% was claimed in 1975. Both rates represented substantial improvements over World War II levels, when less than one-fourth of Viet-Nam's population could read and write.

Following the end of the war, the DRV government announced in July 1975 that fees for education would be reduced to an annual charge to parents of about D2 per child. Primary education in the north lasts for 10 years (ages 7-17), segmented into three levels of 4, 3, and 3 years. As of 1974, enrollment was virtually universal for the first level (grades 1-4), but was 60% for the second stage (grades 5-7) and only 40% at the final primary stage (grades 8-10). In 1973/74, 6.5 million students were enrolled at all levels (including preschool), in some 11,560 general education (primary) schools and 240 higher-level schools. The plan for 1975/76 called for 400,000 infants (3 months to 2 years of age) in day-care centers, 480,000 children (aged 3-6 years) in nursery schools and kindergartens, 5.6 million students in general education, 87,500 in specialized schools, and 65,000 in universities. Some 20,000–25,000 new schoolrooms, accommodating 500,000 children, were to be built during 1975 alone. The north has 39 universities and schools of higher learning. The University of Hanoi (founded in 1918) is the largest. Several thousand Vietnamese students from the north attend universities in the USSR, China, and other Communist lands; the total abroad was expected to reach 10,000 in 1976. In 1974, about 3,000 students, the largest single group, were attending school in the USSR.

In the south, more than 500,000 adults in the 1960s attended RVN government-sponsored night courses, intended to wipe out illiteracy. In 1972/73, the RVN had more than 8,000 primary schools, with 2,891,424 pupils, as compared with 1,660,968 in 1964/65 (and only 441,000 pupils in all of Viet-Nam in 1954). In 1968 there were 935,185 secondary-level students, as contrasted with 381,562 in 1964/65.

The University of Ho Chi Minh City includes faculties of letters and sciences, a teachers' college, and schools of medicine, pharmacy, and dental surgery. A second university was opened in Hue in 1959, and a third at Da'lat in 1960. Institutions of higher learning in the RVN had a total enrollment of 88,104 in 1972/73 (28,410 in 1964/65).

Under the PRG, educational patterns in the south were being restructured to reflect those of the DRV. The 12-year school cycle was reduced to 10 years, and the more than 20,000 teachers in the south were subjected to "reeducation" programs. By 1976, some 1,400 tons of DRV textbooks were shipped to the south, all textbooks in use under the RVN having been burned. In addition, more than 1,000 formerly private schools in the south were brought under state control, as were larger independent universities in Dalat, Tay Ninh, and Long Xuyen.

44 LIBRARIES AND MUSEUMS
The Ecole Française d'Extrême-Orient maintained an extensive research library in Hanoi which was transferred intact to the DRV, as was the Hanoi City Library. Now the National Library, it has about 1,000,000 volumes; the bulk of the present collection was added since 1954, and includes a substantial number of Russian titles. There are also 76 municipal and provincial libraries, each with between 5,000 and 20,000 volumes. The RVN's National Library in Saigon had 160,000 volumes in the 1970s. There were also several libraries belonging to private associations or institutes. Most university libraries had limited collections of about 20,000 volumes. The PRG burned a number of books in the south's library system, especially in the larger libraries at Ho Chi Minh City, Hue, and Da Nang.

Collections of the Musée Louis-Finot, an excellent archaeological and cultural museum established by the French in Hanoi, were also transferred intact to the DRV. The collections are now part of the Historical Museum and contain valuable additions resulting from recent archaeological discoveries in

Thanh-Hoa and Yen-Bay, including a 2,500-year-old burial boat and an excellent array of bronze implements. Hanoi's Museum of Fine Arts includes a folk-art collection and Vietnamese Bronze Age artifacts. There exists, too, the Museum of the Revolution, grouping memorabilia of Viet-Nam's struggle for independence from the French since the early 1900s. The Army Museum, housed in the Hanoi Citadel, contains a collection of weapons and documents concerning the Indochina War. Museum facilities are not extensive in the South. Religious edifices and former Vietnamese imperial structures, however, provide an opportunity to view the products of the country's cultural heritage in the settings for which they were designed. There are archaeological and cultural museums in Ho Chi Minh City, Hue, and Da Nang.

45 ORGANIZATIONS
The principal mass organization in the DRV has been the Fatherland Front of Viet-Nam, which is led by the Lao-Dong Party and includes other political and social organizations. The Fatherland Front draws up single slates of candidates in all elections and seeks to implement the political, economic, and social policies of the Lao-Dong Party. Other organizations that form part of the Fatherland Front are the Peasant Union, with some 5 million members; the Federation of Vietnamese Youth; and the Federation of Vietnamese Women, with 4 million members. The youth federation, in turn, consists of the Union of Working Youth, an equivalent of the Young Communist League; the Vietnamese Student Union; the Vietnamese Pupils' Union; and sports societies with a combined membership of more than 1 million. Industrial and commercial enterprises are represented by the Chamber of Commerce of the DRV.

Most of the various types of economic, professional, and social organizations found in Western countries had been developing in the RVN since the 1950s. It was assumed, however, that most of these would be disbanded or phased out during the immediate post-1975 period. Among them were the Boy Scouts and Girl Scouts, cooperatives, sports organizations, and various cultural, professional, and youth associations.

46 PRESS
The DRV press is controlled by the government, either directly or through various party organs and agencies. Seven daily newspapers and some 25 weekly and monthly periodicals are published in Hanoi; about 100 newspapers and bulletins are published outside of Hanoi, including one daily in each province. Plans in 1975 called for the printing of 210 million copies of newspapers and periodicals in that year, a 7% increase over 1974. The dailies include Nhan Dan (The People's Daily), organ of the Lao-Dong Party, with an estimated 1975 circulation of 100,000; Nhan Dan Nong Thong (The Peasantry), an agricultural supplement, with a circulation of 21,000; Thoi Moi (New Times), circulation 25,000; and Thu Do Hanoi (Free Hanoi), published by the Hanoi Lao-Dong Party, with a circulation of 30,000. Quan Doi Nhan Dan (People's Army) is an army daily, and Chinh Nghia (Justice) is an organ of the Catholic community. Principal periodicals and their publishers are Cu'u Quoc (National Salvation), organ of the Fatherland Front, circulation 20,000; Lao-Dong (Labor), organ of the Federation of Trade Unions, circulation 10,000; and Tien Phong (Avant-Garde), youth federation organ, circulation 16,000. Hoc Tap (Study) is an important theoretical journal published by the Lao-Dong Party.

The number of dailies in the RVN increased from 32 in 1965 to 56 in 1970, but declined to 26 by 1974; 16 were published in Vietnamese, 10 in Chinese, and 1 each in English and French. Officially, censorship existed only for the foreign-language newspapers, but in fact all papers practiced a policy of self-censorship in order to avoid difficulty. Newspapers were closed down periodically because of the government's objection to their news policies or editorial line. Total circulation of Vietnamese-language dailies was 1,221,000 in 1970; Chinese-language dailies circulated to about 80,000 readers. The English-language newspapers—which often appeared with large blank spaces in the middle of the front page as a result of disagreement with the censor—catered primarily to the US community. Most newspapers in the south were shut down by the PRG in 1975, but some papers that had been sympathetic to the NLF/DRV cause were allowed to continue publication. Giai Phong is now the government newspaper of the south.

The Viet-Nam News Agency is Viet-Nam's national news service.

47 TOURISM
Prior to World War II, northern Viet-Nam contained some of Indochina's most attractive resort areas. The beauty of Ha-Long Bay, with its countless grottoes and rock spits jutting vertically out to sea, is well known. Hanoi itself, with its historical monuments, its lakes and pagodas, is extremely picturesque, but hotel facilities are sparse and expensive. Before 1965 there were guided tours from Eastern Europe, but these were discontinued with the war's intensification. Tourism on an experimental basis was resumed in the mid-1970s. In 1975, a Danish travel agency was awarded a franchise for Western Europe. Officials in the south announced in February 1976 that the region would be reopened to tourism that spring. Preparations were under way for receiving 10,000 tourists (including visitors from the US), with facilities being developed at coastal beaches, highland resorts, Hue, and Ho Chi Minh City. The former US airbase at Nha Trang was being transformed into a tourist resort.

48 FAMOUS VIETNAMESE
Personages in Vietnamese history who are esteemed in modern Viet-Nam include the sisters Trung Trac and Trung Nhi, national heroines who led a revolt (A.D. 40–43) against China when that nation was imperial master of Tonkin and North Annam; Ngo Quyên, who regained Vietnamese independence from China in 938; Tran Hung Dao, who defeated the forces of Kublai Khan in 1288; Emperor Le Loi, national hero and brilliant administrator, in whose reign the Vietnamese legal code was promulgated in 1407; Emperor Gia Long (d. 1820), who reunified Viet-Nam in the early 19th century; and Le Van Duyet (1763–1832), military leader who helped the emperor to unify the country.

The 13th-century writer Nguyên Si Co is regarded as one of the first truly Vietnamese authors; he is best known for his collection entitled Chieu Quan Cong Ho. Other leading literary figures are two 15th-century poets, Ho Huyen Qui and Nguyên Binh Khien; the latter's collection, Bach van thi tap, is a classic of Vietnamese literature. Nguyên Du (1765–1820) wrote a famous novel in verse, Kim Van Kieu. Hoang Ngoc Phach, who wrote the romantic novel To Tam (1925), is credited with the introduction of Western literary standards into Vietnamese literature.

Phan Boi Chau (1875–1940) was Viet-Nam's first modern nationalist and, like China's Sun Yat-sen, is claimed by Vietnamese Communists and nationalists alike as their spiritual leader. Ho Chi Minh ("He Who Shines," 1890–1969), a man of many other pseudonyms, was a founding member of the French Communist Party in 1920 and founded the Vietnamese Communist Party in 1930. He was president of the DRV from 1945 until his death. Referred to by his countrymen before and after his death as "Uncle Ho," Ho Chi Minh has acquired the symbolic status of father of the country. Gen. Vo Nguyên Giap (b. 1912), a professor of history turned strategist, organized the first anti-French guerrilla groups in 1944, led the PAVN in its eight-year-long struggle against France, and defeated the French at Dien Bien Phu. He has been minister of defense, commander in chief of the PAVN, and vice-premier of the DRV. Truong Chinh ("Long March," b. 1909), the DRV's foremost Communist thinker, was secretary-general of the Vietnamese Communist Party from 1940 until 1956, when he was purged from his post for having mismanaged the land reform. The author of several important books on the Vietnamese revolution, he has been since 1960 chairman of the Standing Committee of the National Assembly. Pham Van Dong (b.1906), a member of the nobility, joined the Vietnamese revolutionary movement at its inception, and became minister of foreign affairs in 1954, premier of the DRV in 1955, and of the SRV in 1976. Le Duan (b.1907), first secretary of the Lao-Dong Party, presided over Viet-Nam's reunification and the formation of the SRV. Le Duc Tho (b.1911), a member of the Lao-Dong Politburo but with no post in the government, was the DRV's chief negotiator in talks that led to the 1973 Paris Peace Agreement; for his role, Le was awarded the 1973 Nobel Prize for Peace.

Prominent political figures in the formation of the RVN included Bao Dai (b.Nguyên Vinh Thuy, 1913 in France), who had served as nominal emperor of Annam under the Japanese and had attempted to form a unified national government after the war; and Ngo Dinh Diem (1901–63), who served as president of the RVN from its founding on 26 October 1955 until his overthrow and death in November 1963. Nguyên Cao Ky (b.1930), an RVN air force commander, took control of the government in the coup of June 1965. Gen. Nguyên Van Thieu (b.1923) was elected president of the RVN in the elections of September 1967 (with Ky as his vice-presidential running mate), an office he retained until the RVN's defeat in 1975. Both Thieu and Ky left the country in 1975, Thieu taking up residence in Taiwan and Ky in the US.

The new leadership in the south following the 1975 NLF victory was headed by Pham Hung (b.1913), since 1967 chairman of the southern wing of the Lao-Dong Party; Huynh Thanh Phat (b.1913), the PRG premier; and Nguyên Thi Binh (b.1927), the PRG's foreign affairs minister, who had headed the NLF delegation at the Paris talks.

⁴⁹DEPENDENCIES

Both the DRV and the RVN laid claim to the Paracel Islands and the Spratly Islands, located in the South China Sea. Although uninhabited, they are rich in minerals and have good fishing grounds. In January 1974, China occupied the Paracels after fighting a brief battle with RVN forces. On 5 May 1975, the NLF navy was reported to have occupied six of the Spratly Islands. The Vietnamese claims to both groups have been disputed by China, the Philippines, Malaysia, and France. In June 1976, China strongly reiterated its claim to the 96-island Spratly group.

⁵⁰BIBLIOGRAPHY

Bloodworth, Dennis. *An Eye for the Dragon*. New York: Farrar, Straus, and Giroux, 1970.

Buttinger, Joseph. *A Dragon Defiant: A Short History of Vietnam*. New York: Praeger, 1972.

Chomsky, Noam, and Howard Zinn (eds.). *The Pentagon Papers*. 4 vols. Boston: Beacon Press, 1971.

Cooper, Chester L. *The Lost Crusade: America in Viet-Nam*. New York: Dodd, Mead, 1972.

Devillers, Philippe. *Histoire du Viet-Nam de 1940 à 1952*. Paris: Editions du Seuil, 1952.

Devillers, Philippe, and Jean Lacouture. *End of a War: Indochina, 1954*. New York: Praeger, 1969.

Fall, Bernard B. *Last Reflections on a War*. New York: Doubleday, 1967.

Fall, Bernard B. *The Two Viet-Nams: A Political and Military Analysis*. New York: Praeger, 1967.

Fall, Bernard B. *The Viet-Minh Regime*. New York: Institute of Pacific Relations, 1956.

Fall, Bernard B. *Viet-Nam Witness, 1953–66*. New York: Praeger, 1966.

FitzGerald, Frances. *Fire in the Lake*. Boston: Little, Brown, 1972.

Hammer, Ellen J. *The Struggle for Indochina, 1940–1955*. Stanford, Calif.: Stanford University Press, 1966.

Hoang Van Chi. *From Colonialism to Communism: A Case History of North Vietnam*. New York: Praeger, 1964.

Ho Chi Minh on Revolution: Selected Writings, 1920–66. Edited by Bernard B. Fall. New York: Praeger, 1967.

Honey, Patrick J. *Communism in North Vietnam*. Cambridge: MIT Press, 1963.

Lancaster, Donald. *The Emancipation of French Indochina*. New York: Oxford University Press, 1961.

Le Duan. *On the Socialist Revolution in Vietnam*. 3 vols. Hanoi: Foreign Languages Publishing House, 1965.

McAlister, John T., Jr., and Paul Mus. *The Vietnamese and Their Revolution*. New York: Harper & Row, 1970.

Oberdorfer, Don. *Tet*. New York: Doubleday, 1971.

Pike, Douglas. *Vietcong: The Organization and Techniques of the National Liberation Front of South Vietnam*. Cambridge: MIT Press, 1966.

Robequain, Charles, et al. *The Economic Development of French Indo-China*. London: Oxford University Press, 1944.

Salisbury, Harrison E. *Behind the Lines—Hanoi, December 23, 1966–January 7, 1967*. New York: Harper & Row, 1967.

Shaplen, Robert. *The Road from War: Viet-Nam 1965–70*. New York: Harper & Row, 1970.

Shaplen, Robert. *Time Out of Hand: Revolution and Reaction in Southeast Asia*. New York: Harper & Row, 1969.

U.S. Senate, Committee on Foreign Relations. *Background Information Relating to Southeast Asia and Viet-Nam*. 6th rev. ed. Washington, D.C.: Government Printing Office, 1970.

Vo Nguyen Giap. *Banner of People's War: The Party's Military Line*. New York: Praeger, 1970.

Vo Nguyen Giap. *People's War, People's Army: The Viet Cong Insurrection Manual for Underdeveloped Countries*. New York: Praeger, 1962.

WESTERN SAMOA

The Independent State of Western Samoa
Samoa i Sisifo

CAPITAL: Apia. **FLAG:** The first quarter of the flag is blue and bears five white, five-rayed stars representing the Southern Cross. The remainder of the flag is red. **ANTHEM:** *The Flag of Freedom.* **MONETARY UNIT:** The Western Samoa tala (WS$) of 100 sene is a convertible currency. There are coins of 1, 2, 5, 10, 20, and 50 sene, and notes of 1, 2, and 10 talas. WS$1=US$1.28 (or US$1=WS$0.781). **WEIGHTS AND MEASURES:** British weights and measures are used. **HOLIDAYS:** New Year's Day, 1 January; Anzac Day, 25 April; Independence Holidays, 3, 4, 5 June; Christmas Day, 25 December; Boxing Day, 26 December. Movable holidays are Good Friday, Easter Monday, and Whitmonday. **TIME:** 1 A.M. = noon GMT.

¹LOCATION, SIZE, AND EXTENT

Western Samoa consists of the islands of Savai'i and Upolu and several small islands, of which only Manono and Apolima are inhabited. The group, situated almost centrally both in the Pacific Ocean and among the South Sea islands, has a total land area of approximately 2,841 sq km (1,097 sq mi), extending *150* km (*93* mi) ESE–WNW and *39* km (*24* mi) NNE–SSW. Savai'i and Upolu, separated by a strait nearly 18 km (11 mi) long, have a combined coastline of *371* km (*231* mi).

²TOPOGRAPHY

The islands are volcanic, with coral reefs surrounding most of them. Rugged ranges rise to 3,608 feet in Upolu and 6,094 feet in Savai'i. Apolima is a volcanic crater whose wall is pierced by a passage that connects its harbor with the sea. Manono, about 230 feet high, consists chiefly of coral sand. The islands are in an area of active volcanism. Severe eruptions occurred in Savai'i in 1905–11.

³CLIMATE

The climate is tropical, but because of the oceanic surroundings temperature ranges are not considerable. The hottest month is December, and July is the coldest. The mean daily temperature is about 27°C (80°F). The year is divided into a dry season (May to October) and a wet season (November to April). Rainfall averages 113 inches annually, and the average yearly relative humidity is 83%. Although the islands lie outside the normal track of hurricanes, occasionally there are severe storms. Trade winds from the southeast are fairly constant throughout the dry season.

⁴FLORA AND FAUNA

Lush vegetation covers much of the land. Along the coast there are mangrove forests, pandanus, Barringtonia, hibiscus, and strand vegetation commonly found throughout the Pacific. Adjacent lowland forest, which originally stretched inland over the lower slopes of the mountains, has been cut down extensively on Upolu and in more limited areas on Savai'i. Inland and at higher elevations, the rain forests contain trees and lianas of many genera and species. The higher elevations of Savai'i contain moss forest and mountain scrub.

Fifty species of birds are found; 16 of these are seabirds, many of which visit Samoa only during the breeding season. Sixteen of the 34 species of land birds are indigenous. Among the latter are small doves, parrots, pigeons, and a wild duck. The most interesting bird, scientifically, is the tooth-billed pigeon (Didunculus strigirostris Peale), which some ornithologists regard as the connecting link between bird life of the present and the tooth-billed birds of zoological antiquity.

The only indigenous mammals in Western Samoa are the rat (Mus exulans Peale) and the flying Fox (Pteropus samoensis Peale). Numerous species of birds and mammals, chiefly domesticated, have been introduced by the Samoans and Europeans. Two species of snakes, several different lizards, and a gecko are found. Insect life includes many species of moths, beetles, spiders, and ants. The mosquito (Stegomyia pseudoscutellaris) is a carrier of human filaria.

⁵POPULATION

The population of Western Samoa in mid-1974 was estimated at 160,000, compared with the 1966 census figure of 131,377. The annual rate of increase in 1966–74 was 1.5%, and the population density in 1974 was about 146 per sq mi. Upolu, including the islands of Manono and Apolima, had a population of 106,063 in 1971; the population of Savai'i was 40,572. Apia is the only town in the country; it is the administrative and commercial center, with a population of 28,880.

⁶ETHNIC GROUPS

Samoans comprise nearly 90% of the total population. The Samoans are the second-largest branch of the Polynesians, a people occupying the scattered islands of the Pacific from Hawaii to New Zealand and from eastern Fiji to Easter Island. Most of the remaining population are of mixed Samoan and European or Asian descent. Europeans, other Pacific islanders, and Asians number about 1,500.

For many years, all inhabitants of Western Samoa had been accorded a domestic status as Samoan or European. Residents are now officially classed as either citizens or foreigners. Among Western Samoan citizens, however, the distinction between persons of Samoan or European status is still recognized. Most Samoans live in foreshore villages; non-Samoans predominate in Apia and its environs.

⁷LANGUAGE

Samoan is the universal language but both Samoan and English are official languages. Most of the part-Samoans and many others speak English, and it is taught in the schools.

⁸RELIGION

All Samoans profess some form of Christianity, and religious observance is strong among all groups. The Congregational Christian Church of Western Samoa, a successor to the London Missionary Society, is self-supporting and has more adherents than any other religious body in the country. The Roman Catholic and Methodist churches also have large followings. The Mormon and Seventh Day Adventist churches and a number of other denominations have smaller congregations located in various parts of the country.

⁹TRANSPORTATION

Western Samoa has no railroads. The road system in 1973 totaled 582 miles, most of which were on the northern coast of Upolu. There were 251 miles of main roads, of which 74 miles were bitumen-sealed or concrete. Buses and taxis provide public transport. In 1973 there were 2,712 private motor vehicles and 223 government vehicles.

Diesel-powered launches carry passengers and freight around the islands, and small motor vessels maintain services between Apia and Pago Pago in American Samoa. Fortnightly cargo and passenger services are maintained with New Zealand, and scheduled trans-Pacific services connect Western Samoa with Australian and North American ports. British and Norwegian ships also call at regular intervals. There are daily air connections with Pago Pago and five flights weekly to Naudi and Fiji. Through Pago Pago and Naudi there are connecting flights to New Zealand, Australia, the US, and Europe. Faleolo Airport, near Apia, is the principal facility. Internal air services link Upolu and Savai'i.

¹⁰COMMUNICATIONS

Postal facilities conform to standards of the New Zealand Post Office. In addition to the Apia Post Office, there are 21 sub-post offices. The telephone system serves about 1,800 subscribers. Internal and overseas wireless telegraph services are maintained.

The Apia radio station is government-owned and has two transmitters. The station transmits 85 hours of scheduled programming weekly, in addition to direct broadcasts from the Legislative Assembly.

¹¹HISTORY

Little is known about Samoan history before the middle of the 13th century, but archaeology indicates that the Samoans had settled in the islands long before that time. The genealogies, important titles, traditions, and legends give considerable information on the main political events from about 1250 on. The first Europeans to sight the islands were the Dutch explorer Jacob Roggeveen in 1722 and the French navigator Louis de Bougainville in 1768. But the world knew little about Samoa until after the arrival of the missionary John Williams in 1830 and the establishment of the London Missionary Society two years later.

Williams' arrival coincided with the victory of one group of chiefs over another, ending a series of violent internecine wars. Runaway sailors and other Europeans had already settled among the Samoans and had assisted the chiefs in their campaigns. Whalers also visited the islands, and from time to time the warships of great powers visited Apia to oversee the activities of whaling crews and settlers. Naval officers and missionaries both began to consult with the dominant group of chiefs as if it represented a national government and to treat its leader as a king. In 1893, this group agreed to and promulgated a set of commercial regulations, drawn up by British and US naval commanders, controlling the port of Apia and the relations of Samoans and Europeans. In a short time, semiofficial representatives of Great Britain and the US were stationed in Apia. Between 1847 and 1861, the US appointed a commercial agent and Britain and the city of Hamburg appointed consuls.

Factional rivalries took a new turn as British, US, and German consular agents, aided sometimes by their countries' warships, aligned themselves with various paramount chiefs. Intrigues among the chiefs and jealousies among the representatives of the great powers culminated in civil war in 1889. In the Berlin Treaty that followed, Britain, the US, and Germany set up a neutral and independent government under King Malietoa Laupepea, and their consuls were authorized to constitute Apia as a separate municipality. The death of King Malietoa in 1898 led to a dispute over the succession, and the three powers intervened once again. In 1899, they abolished the kingship; in 1900, they signed a series of conventions that made Western Samoa a German protectorate. The German administration continued to experience difficulties, leading to the exile of several Samoan leaders and the suspension of others from office. With the outbreak of World War I in 1914, New Zealand military forces occupied Western Samoa, and from 1919 to 1946, New Zealand administered the islands as a mandate of the League of Nations.

In 1927, local opposition to the New Zealand administration among both the Samoan and the European communities resulted in the formation of a nationalistic organization known as the Mau, which embarked on a program of civil disobedience. Its members withdrew from political life, from schools, and from all contact with the government. The protests lasted in one form or another until 1936, when leaders of the Mau reached an agreement with the administration and reentered the political life of the territory.

In 1946, a trusteeship agreement was approved by the UN General Assembly, and New Zealand formally committed itself to promote the development of Western Samoa toward ultimate self-government. The passage of the Samoa Amendment Act of 1947 and a series of further amendments governed Western Samoa's subsequent evolution toward independence. An Executive Council was reconstituted in 1957, and the New Zealand high commissioner withdrew from the Legislative Assembly, which thenceforth was presided over by an elected speaker. In 1959, an executive cabinet was introduced, and in 1960 the constitution of the Independent State of Western Samoa was adopted. This was followed by a plebiscite under UN supervision in 1961 in which an overwhelming majority of voters approved the adoption of the constitution and supported the course toward independence.

On 1 January 1962, Western Samoa became an independent nation. Tupua Tamasese Meaoli and Malietoa Tanumafili II became joint heads of state. When the former died on 5 April 1963, the latter became the sole head of state. Fiame Faumuina Mataafa became Western Samoa's first prime minister. In 1970, Western Samoa became a member of the British Commonwealth. In 1975, on the death of Prime Minister Mataafa, Tupua Tamasese Lealofi IV was appointed his successor.

¹²GOVERNMENT

Executive power is vested in the head of state. Although Malietoa Tanumafili has lifetime tenure, the constitution provides for his successors to be elected for a term of five years by the Legislative Assembly. The powers and functions of the head of state are far-reaching. All legislation must have his assent before it becomes law. He also has power to grant pardons and reprieves and to suspend or commute any sentence by any court, tribunal, or authority. Executive authority is administered by a cabinet consisting of a prime minister (a member of the Legislative Assembly chosen by a majority of its members) and eight other ministers appointed by him. The head of state and the cabinet members comprise the Executive Council.

The parliament consists of the head of state and the Legislative Assembly. The Assembly is composed of 1 elected member from each of the 45 Samoan constituencies, and 2 members elected by persons whose names appear on the individual voters' roll. The election of the 45 Samoan members is by adult suffrage on a franchise confined to matais—persons of Samoan status who qualify for registration. Citizens of non-Samoan origin who qualify for registration on the individual voters' roll elect the two other members by universal suffrage. The Assembly serves for three years unless dissolved sooner by the head of state.

¹³POLITICAL PARTIES

Organized political parties have not emerged in Western Samoa. Candidates for office campaign as individuals, usually seeking the support of electors by stressing their civic virtues and past experience in business and administrative affairs, rather than by articulating broad policies or ideologies.

[14] LOCAL GOVERNMENT

With the exception of the Apia area, local government is carried out by the village fono, or council of chiefs and orators, and, where and when necessary, through meetings of chiefs and orators of a district. The main administrative link between the central government and the outside districts is provided by the part-time officials in each village who act as government agents in such matters as the registration of vital statistics; local inspectors represent the various government departments.

[15] JUDICIAL SYSTEM

Court procedure is patterned after practices in British courts. Samoan custom is taken into consideration in certain cases. English is the official language of the court, but Samoan is also used. The Supreme Court has full civil and criminal jurisdiction for the administration of justice in Western Samoa. It is under the jurisdiction of the chief judge, who is appointed by the head of state, acting on the advice of the prime minister. The court of appeals consists of three judges who may be judges of the Supreme Court or other persons with appropriate qualifications.

Magistrates' courts are subordinate courts with varying degrees of authority. The highest, presided over by the senior magistrate, may hear criminal cases involving imprisonment up to three years or cases involving only fines. The Land and Titles Court has jurisdiction in disputes over Samoan land and succession to Samoan titles. Samoan assessors and associate judges possessing a good knowledge of Samoan custom must be present at all sittings of the court. Lawyers are not permitted to appear in the Land and Titles Court; each party appoints its own leader, usually a chief or an orator. Court decisions are based largely on Samoan custom.

[16] ARMED FORCES

Western Samoa has no armed forces.

[17] MIGRATION

Permanent resident status may be granted only to persons who have resided in Western Samoa for more than five years. There is generally an annual loss of population through migration. Migration consists mainly of students going to New Zealand to continue their education, of European families going there to settle, and of Samoans seeking work there.

[18] INTERNATIONAL COOPERATION

Western Samoa does not belong to the UN, but it is a member of WHO and it cooperates with other specialized agencies. The UNDP's regional representative for the Western Pacific was located in Apia until July 1974, when he was transferred to Manila. Although it has not been a member of the South Pacific Commission, Western Samoa has had representatives at conferences and has actively participated in many of the Commission's projects. An Inter-Samoa Consultative Committee, made up of representatives from Western Samoa and American Samoa, holds meetings alternately in both countries to discuss matters of mutual interest. By treaty, New Zealand is the exclusive representative of Western Samoa in the conduct of its foreign affairs outside the Pacific region. New Zealand is also the main source of technical and financial aid. The New Zealand high commissioner in Apia is the only officially accredited diplomatic representative in the country. In 1975, diplomatic relations were established with China.

[19] ECONOMY

The economy has been based almost entirely on agriculture, in which the subsistence farming of food crops predominates. The main exports are copra, cocoa, and bananas. The government is actively promoting tourism as well as a large-scale timber-milling industry. Samoan farmers grow almost all the bananas, most of the copra, and an increasing amount of the cocoa. Plantation agriculture, private or controlled by the Western Samoa Trust Estates Corporation, accounts for the remainder of agricultural production.

[20] INCOME

There are no detailed national income statistics. Although the urban population in and around Apia is becoming increasingly dependent on a money economy, Samoans living in the villages obtain the greater part of their food, housing, and fuel through the traditional domestic economy, and the government has no reliable indication of their income.

[21] LABOR

The majority of workers are engaged in agricultural pursuits in which cash crops are raised as supplements to subsistence crops. No Samoan is entirely dependent on wages for sustenance; all share in the products of their family lands and can always return to them. Some 12,000 persons are wage earners, with about half employed by the government or the Trust Estates Corporation. About 17,500 persons are primarily engaged in village agriculture.

Although trade unions are not prohibited, none has been established. Labor is generally restricted to a 40-hour week. Payment is in cash, and in many cases rations are also supplied to workers either as part of their wages or in addition to them. In most cases, quarters are supplied to plantation workers.

Over the years, thousands of skilled and semiskilled Samoans have left the islands, mainly drawn away by better economic opportunities in New Zealand.

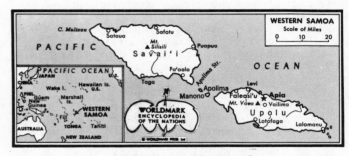

See Pacific Ocean map: front cover J7.

LOCATION: 13° to 15°s; 171° to 173°w. **BOUNDARY LENGTHS:** Savai'i coastline, 188 km (117 mi); Upolu coastline, 183 km (114 mi). **TERRITORIAL SEA LIMIT:** 12 mi.

[22] AGRICULTURE

Agriculture is the mainstay of the economy, and most Samoans grow food crops for home consumption and cash crops for export. The chief method of production, known as "village agriculture," is confined to Samoan villages, where the productive unit is the family. It involves the largest areas of land, occupies the greatest labor force, and produces the major portion of food and cash crops. Copra, cocoa, and bananas are produced for export, and bananas, taro, and ta'amu are grown for local sale. Village plantings are invariably mixed, containing some or all of the following crops: coconuts, cocoa, bananas, taro, ta'amu, breadfruit, sugarcane, yams, manioc, and various fruits. In 1973, 13,946 tons of copra and 1,228 tons of cocoa were exported.

Plantation agriculture is controlled mainly by Europeans. The main products are cocoa, copra, and bananas for export and small quantities of taro and ta'amu for local sale. Apart from the efforts of the planter and his family, labor is supplied, either on a contract or wage basis, by Samoans.

[23] ANIMAL HUSBANDRY

Cattle form the bulk of the livestock. About 500 are kept primarily for milk; the remainder are raised for beef and to control plantation weed growth. About one-half of the cattle population is owned by the Western Samoa Trust Estates Corporation, the most progressive cattle breeder. In 1970, cattle were estimated at 20,000. Hogs (about 40,000) are common in the villages, as are poultry. Horses and donkeys are used extensively for plantation work. Lack of refrigeration hampers the further development of animal husbandry.

24 FISHING
No organized commercial fisheries exist, but there is a great deal of "subsistence" fishing along the reefs and coasts. Deep-sea fishing, save for bonito and shark, is not general. Fish are caught by line, net, fixed traps, and underwater spearing. The catch amounts to about 2,000 tons annually.

25 FORESTRY
There are some 760 sq mi of forests under cultivation (about 70% of the total land area); less than 30 sq mi remain virgin forests and bush. A few experimental forest areas are under the supervision of the Department of Agriculture, Forests, and Fisheries. Until recently there had been no planned utilization of the forest areas; but in 1968, a joint Samoan/Japanese timber-milling company was established in Upolu. A large-scale timber-milling enterprise was established on Savai'i in 1970 and began to produce kiln-dried sawn timber and veneer sheets for export. In 1974, the value of timber and plywood exports totaled US$400,000.

26 MINING
No minerals of commercial value are known to exist.

27 ENERGY AND POWER
In 1973, the total capacity of the government-owned power sector (excluding village schemes and other private plants) was 6,910 kw, of which 5,600 kw was in diesel plants and 1,310 kw in hydroelectric plants. Production for the year was 4.73 million kwh. Hydroelectric and diesel installations in and around Apia serve the population with a peak demand of nearly 1,100 kw. In addition, approximately 80 small lighting plants, each of 2-kw to 4-kw capacity, are operated privately throughout the islands, and five villages are supplied by 20-kw to 30-kw diesel plants.

28 INDUSTRY
Industries are few and small. They consist of timber milling and dressing, and small individual enterprises for processing coffee and for manufacturing curios, soap, carbonated drinks, and other consumer products. Although the government has begun to encourage industrial growth, agriculture continues to attract the major share of available funds for economic development.

29 DOMESTIC TRADE
Apia, the only port of entry and the only town, is the center of commercial life. Many firms act as agents for shipping and air lines and for overseas commercial organizations generally. Outside Apia, trading stations, linked with it by launch and road transport, collect produce and distribute consumer goods. Five major firms operate about 200 stations in the outer districts and secure a large share of the total commercial business. There are also several smaller firms and a number of independent traders. In Apia, various firms and small shops sell imported commodities and domestic products.

Stores are open generally from A.M. until noon and from 1:30 P.M. to 4:30 P.M. Shops close at 12:30 P.M. on Saturdays and are closed on Sundays.

Products are advertised through window displays, the local newspapers, and motion picture slides.

30 FOREIGN TRADE
The fact that Western Samoa has only three exports of any significance renders its economy extremely vulnerable to reduced shipments or drops in market prices. The government's marketing division handles the collection and shipment of bananas, and the marketing of copra is controlled by the Copra Board, which also operates a stabilization fund.

During the early 1970s, the cost of imports was often far more than double the value of exports. In 1973, total exports were

valued at WS$4,000,635, of which copra represented 42% and cocoa 28%. Imports were valued at WS$14,433,069, consisting chiefly of food, machinery, transportation equipment, and other manufactured articles. The trade deficit for 1973 amounted to approximately WS$10,433,000.

New Zealand is Western Samoa's most important single trading partner, accounting for 34% of total volume in 1973. Principal trade partners in 1973 (in thousands of talas) were:

	EXPORTS	IMPORTS	BALANCE
New Zealand	1,439	4,769	− 3,330
Australia	32	3,022	− 2,990
Japan	72	1,826	− 1,754
US	268	1,215	− 947
FRG	713	440	273
Fiji	218	788	− 570
UK	33	838	− 808
Netherlands	547	69	478
Other countries	678	1,466	− 788
TOTALS	4,000	14,433	−10,433

31 BALANCE OF PAYMENTS
In the 1970s, Western Samoa's large trade deficits have been largely offset by tourist revenues and by long-term investment capital, the latter totaling US$14.7 million during 1972–74. The balance of payments in 1970 and 1974 (in millions of US dollars) was as follows:

	1970	1974
Merchandise balance	−7.3	−14.5
Services balance	−0.4	− 0.5
Government transfers, net	0.4	2.8
Private transfers, net	2.2	7.2
Long-term capital, n.i.e.	2.9	6.7
Short-term capital, n.i.e.	2.7	− 2.3
Errors and omissions	0.1	0.1
TOTALS	−0.6	− 0.6

32 BANKING
Western Samoa is served by one commercial bank, the Bank of Western Samoa, which also acts as the bank of issue. The Bank is a limited-liability company with a paid-up capital of WS$500,000; 50% of the Bank's capital is owned by the government and 50% by the Bank of New Zealand. The Bank offers all normal commercial banking services, and operates a savings division. As of 30 April 1975, foreign-exchange holdings of the Bank amounted to US$4.61 million. The post office also operates a savings bank; deposits totaled WS$800,000 at the end of 1974.

33 INSURANCE
In 1974 there were five foreign insurance companies in operation, covering all categories of insurance.

34 SECURITIES
There are no securities exchanges in Western Samoa.

35 PUBLIC FINANCE
Western Samoa's financial year ends on 31 December. Government budgets have commonly shown deficits in recent years. Government revenues and expenditures for 1973 (in thousands of Western Samoa talas) were reported as follows:

REVENUES	
Customs	5,042.0
Inland revenue	1,454.6
Public works	765.0
Treasury stores	702.0
Post office	333.5
Other sources	1,292.1
TOTAL	9,589.2

EXPENDITURES

Education	1,348.7
Health	1,092.7
Customs	789.1
Treasury stores	731.4
Public works	643.1
Other expenditures	3,464.4
CURRENT ACCOUNTS TOTAL	8,069.4
Development expenditures	2,744.9
TOTAL	10,814.3

36 TAXATION

Individuals and companies are liable for the payment of income tax. Nonresident corporate rates are based on a graduated scale, ranging from 10 to 55 sene on the tala. Personal and resident corporate rates range from 5 to 40 sene on the tala. There is no property tax in Western Samoa.

37 CUSTOMS AND DUTIES

Approximately one-half of government revenues come from import and export duties. The duties on the three primary exports are as follows: a 10% ad valorem tariff on copra; 5% ad valorem on cocoa when the price is less than ws$400 per ton, and 10% plus .01% for each ws$2 per ton in excess of ws$400; and a flat rate of 10 sene per case on bananas. On imported goods there are two types of duties: Commonwealth preferential and general. In addition, a duty of 7.5% ad valorem is attached to all goods, whether dutiable or duty-free, unless specifically exempted.

38 FOREIGN INVESTMENTS

The government formerly did not encourage outside investment in Western Samoa; it is now active in promoting the establishment of industries financed by overseas companies. These include milling and logging operations by a US company on Savai'i and by a joint Japanese-Samoan enterprise on Upolu, and a US hotel resort center near Apia. In 1973, 17 new companies incorporated in Western Samoa and one incorporated outside were registered. They brought the total number of companies registered to 120. Their nominal share capital amounted to ws$15,216,380.

All foreign investments in Western Samoa, whether direct or in the form of licensing or royalty agreements, require the prior approval of the government. All development proposals also require government approval. Government policy favors investments that utilize indigenous raw materials, or imported raw materials in their most basic form. Similarly, preference is given to activities that contribute to export income, strengthen capital goods production, or improve the country's base of technical knowledge and skills. To encourage foreign investment, the government allows the remittance of profits, interests, and dividends earned by overseas investors.

39 ECONOMIC POLICY

Throughout the 1960s and 1970s, the government has consistently stressed the diversification of agriculture. It has also adopted a policy under the Enterprises Incentives Act of stimulating secondary industries by giving an income tax holiday, duty-free imports, and other incentives to new or expanding industries. A capital development program has included a hydroelectric scheme on Upolu, improving the road between Apia and the Faleolo Airport, and upgrading the airport to accommodate larger aircraft.

40 HEALTH

The main health facility is the Apia Hospital, with 298 beds. Outstation hospitals have an additional 357 beds. In 1973, the medical staff of the Department of Health included 45 doctors trained in Fiji, 5 trained in New Zealand, and 2 trained elsewhere; and 14 dentists and 235 registered nurses. District nurses are stationed at strategic points throughout the islands. Child health clinics, and particularly clinics for young children and infants, are a regular feature of their work. A mobile dental clinic operates in the villages, while all schools in Apia are visited at regular intervals by a team of dental practitioners.

Western Samoa is remote from the areas of the major pestilential diseases, and most of the scourges of the tropics are unknown in the islands. However, filariasis, a parasitic disease, is endemic.

41 SOCIAL WELFARE

There are no community welfare services, although the various district hospitals, with the aid of the women's committees in the villages, perform some public health services. All treatment at hospitals and dispensaries, including maternity treatment, is free.

42 HOUSING

Most Samoans live in villages in traditional Samoan houses called fales. A fale is usually round or oval with pebble floors and a thatch roof. It has no walls, being supported on the sides by posts. Coconut-leaf blinds can be lowered to exclude wind and rain. In areas more affected by contact with Europeans, the fale may have a concrete floor, corrugated-iron roof, and lattice-work walls. Another fused Samoan-European type, much used by chiefs and pastors, is an oblong concrete house with some walls, and often, rooms in each corner; but like the fale it is open at the sides. Fales are grouped around an open area in the center of the village and have separate cookhouses behind them.

In 1969, there were 15,438 thatched fale dwellings, 1,149 iron-roof fale dwellings, 1,738 open houses of imported materials, and 2,699 closed houses of imported materials. There was an average of 6.2 persons per dwelling.

43 EDUCATION

Formal education is provided by the Department of Education and five religious missions. Government and mission schools have a uniform syllabus and common examinations. The government school system is the more comprehensive, with almost all its teachers holding Samoan teachers' certificates. Village schools provide four years of primary schooling. District schools draw the brighter pupils from village schools and educate them through the upper primary level. In the Apia area, urban schools provide a lower- through upper-primary curriculum. A major educational goal has been to make Samoans bilingual, with English as their second tongue. In the senior classes of the primary schools, all instruction is in English.

The government maintains three secondary schools in which the medium of instruction is English. Samoa College is patterned after a New Zealand secondary school; each year, 100 pupils from government and mission schools are selected by competitive examination for entry to it. Vaipouli High School, in Savai'i, provides a general secondary curriculum and Avele Agricultural College offers training in modern agricultural methods. The medium of instruction in mission secondary schools is English, with curriculum and textbooks similar to those used in New Zealand. General, commercial, and academic courses are offered.

In 1973 there were 30,388 primary pupils, of whom 26,363 were in government schools; 7,072 intermediate pupils, of whom 6,212 were in government schools; and 4,435 secondary students, of whom 2,249 were in government schools. There were 1,137 primary-level teachers, and 152 teachers in secondary and vocational schools and in the teacher-training college.

44 LIBRARIES AND MUSEUMS

The Nelson Memorial Library in Apia has over 28,000 volumes. A bookmobile service operates on Upolu and Savai'i. There are no museums in Western Samoa, but the government has plans to establish a small museum of Samoan artifacts and historical relics.

45 ORGANIZATIONS

Among the numerous clubs, societies, and organizations in

Western Samoa are the Chamber of Commerce, Red Cross, Catholic Club, Returned Servicemen's Association, Mothers' Club, Calliope Lodge of Freemasons, Federation of Women's Committees, and the South-East Asia and Pan-Pacific Women's Association.

⁴⁶PRESS

Two weekly bilingual newspapers (English and Samoan) have a combined circulation of 7,600. A Samoan-language newspaper for outlying areas is published monthly by the government.

⁴⁷TOURISM

Until 1965, official policy in Western Samoa was opposed to tourism, but in the two years that followed there was a complete reversal of policy. The government hired international tourist consultants to advise it on long-term means of developing a tourist industry. Various immediate steps were also taken. Western Samoa joined the Pacific Area Travel Association, extended tax holidays and import-duty concessions to hotel building, and appropriated money for the building of new hotels. In 1974, excluding cruise ship passengers, 10,931 tourists visited the country. Tourism remains hampered by limited hotel accommodations and the inability of Fieolo Airport to take jet aircraft.

Visitors for a period of no longer than seven days do not require an entry permit; a passport and onward tickets, however, are necessary. Visitors' visas may be extended up to a maximum of three months. In addition, a smallpox vaccination is required for entry.

⁴⁸FAMOUS WESTERN SAMOANS

There are no internationally famous Western Samoans.

⁴⁹DEPENDENCIES

Western Samoa has no dependencies.

⁵⁰BIBLIOGRAPHY

Davidson, J.W. *Samoa mo Samoa.* London: Oxford University Press, 1967.

Gilson, R. P. *Samoa 1830 to 1900: The Politics of a Multi-Cultural Community.* New York: Oxford University Press, 1970.

Keesing, Felix Maxwell. *Modern Samoa: Its Government and Changing Life.* London: Allen & Unwin, 1934.

Keesing, Felix Maxwell and Marie Margaret. *Elite Communication in Samoa: A Study of Leadership.* Stanford: Stanford University Press, 1956.

Lockwood, Brian. *Samoan Village Economy.* New York: Oxford University Press, 1971.

Mead, Margaret. *Coming of Age in Samoa.* London: Penguin, 1961.

O'Grady, John P. *No Kava for Johnny.* Sidney: Smith, 1960.

Pitt, David. *Tradition and Economic Progress in Samoa.* Oxford: Clarendon Press, 1970.

Report by the New Zealand Government to the General Assembly of the United Nations on the Administration of Western Samoa, 1960. Wellington: Government Printer, 1961.

Rowe, Newton Allan. *Samoa under the Sailing Gods.* London: Putnam, 1930.

Stair, John Bettridge. *Old Samoa; or, Flotsam and Jetsam from the Pacific Ocean.* London: Religious Tract Society, 1897.

Stevenson, Robert Louis. *A Footnote to History: Eight Years of Trouble in Samoa.* New York: Scribner, 1892.

Stevenson, Robert Louis. *Vailima Letters: Being Correspondence Addressed by Robert Louis Stevenson to Sydney Colvin, November, 1890–October, 1894.* 2 vols. Chicago: Stone & Kimball, 1895.

Trade, Commerce, and Shipping of the Territory of Western Samoa, 1969. Wellington: Government Printer, 1970.

Turner, George. *Samoa a Hundred Years Ago and Long Before...* London: Macmillan, 1884.

Watson, R. W. *A Short History of Samoa.* Wellington: Whitcombe and Tombs, 1918.

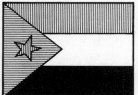

PEOPLE'S DEMOCRATIC REPUBLIC OF YEMEN

Jumhuriyat al-Yamaniyyah al-Dimuqratiyah al-Shaʿabiyah

CAPITAL: Aden (Adan). Madinat al-Shaʿab (al-Ittihad) is the administrative capital. **FLAG**: The national flag is a tricolor of red, white, and black horizontal stripes, with a red star on a blue triangle at the hoist. **ANTHEM**: *Al-Salaam al-Gumhuri (The Presidential Salute)*. **MONETARY UNIT**: The South Yemen dinar (SYD) of 1,000 fils is a nonconvertible paper currency. There are coins of 1, 25, and 50 fils, and notes of 250 and 500 fils and of 1, 5, and 10 dinars. SYD1 = $2.8952 (or $1 = SYD0.3454). **WEIGHTS AND MEASURES**: Local weights and measures are used. **HOLIDAYS**: Revolution Day, 14 October; Independence Day, 30 November. Muslim holidays include ʿId al-Fitr, ʿId al-ʿAdhaʾ, and Milad al-Nabi. **TIME**: 3 P.M. = noon GMT.

¹LOCATION, SIZE, AND EXTENT
The People's Democratic Republic of Yemen (PDRY), formerly Southern Yemen, occupies most of the southern fringe of the Arabian Peninsula, from at-Turbah on the Red Sea coast, where it borders on the Yemen Arab Republic (YAR), to Raʾs Dharbat ʿAli, where it borders on Oman. The PDRY has an area of 287,683 sq km (111,075 sq mi), extending *1,127* km *(700* mi) NE–SW to *412* km *(256* mi) SE–NW. It is bordered on the N by Saʿudi Arabia, on the E by Oman, on the S by the Indian Ocean and the Gulf of Aden, and on the W by the YAR, with a total boundary length of *2,909* km (*1,808* mi).

²TOPOGRAPHY
There are four geographical regions: (1) the mountainous west, rising to a plateau, with peaks over 8,000 feet (Jabal Thamir, 8,245 feet); (2) the arid coastal plain, from the Red Sea coast along the Gulf of Aden; (3) the northern desert, a part of the Rub ʿal-Khali (the Empty Quarter), Arabia's great desert (an average of 2,500 feet above sea level); and (4) a plateau ranging in height from 3,000 to 5,000 feet, whose main feature is the great Wadi Hadramawt, the longest and most fertile of the southern valleys.

³CLIMATE
Except for the mountainous regions of the west and the plateau, where temperatures in the winter dip near or below 0°C (32°F), the climate is hot. During the southwest monsoon (late spring through fall), the temperature, frequently in excess of 54.4°C (130°F), is combined with high humidity and strong, dust-laden winds. Rainfall is generally restricted to the winter months and is rare except in the western highlands. Average annual rainfall is less than 3 inches.

⁴FLORA AND FAUNA
Vegetation is generally restricted to desert plants and shrubs, except in the highlands and wadis where date palms, fruit trees, flowers, and herbs are found. Without forest cover, larger animals find it difficult to survive. However, there are many varieties of birds and insects.

As of 1975, endangered species in the PDRY included the Arabian gazelle, African lammergeyer, and South Arabian leopard.

⁵POPULATION
The first official census in the PDRY was taken in May 1973; however, its results had not yet been published in 1976. The UN population estimate for 1975 was 1,660,000. The annual rate of increase was 3%, based on a crude birthrate of 48.3 per 1,000 and a death rate of 18.5, for a net natural increase of 29.8. Population was projected to reach 1,930,000 by 1980. About 67% of the population is rural and 33% urban, with a nationwide density of 6 per-

sons per sq km (15 persons per sq mi). Some 15% of the nation's people reside in greater Aden, while the majority live along the coast. In 1972, the population of Aden, the capital, was said to have fallen from 225,000 to fewer than 80,000, at least in part because of the economic crisis caused by the closing of the Suez Canal. Other towns of some size are al-Mukalla (65,000), Lahij, Sayʿun, and Lawdar.

⁶ETHNIC GROUPS
Until independence in 1967, the population was about 90% Arab; the remainder, concentrated in Aden and a few port towns, consisted of sizable communities of Indians, Pakistanis, Somalis, and a sprinkling of Danakils, Ethiopians, Indonesians, Malaysians, Baluchis, and Europeans. By 1968, most non-Arabs and Yemenis from the YAR had returned to their homelands.

⁷LANGUAGE
Arabic, the national language, is spoken in a variety of dialects. It is a West Semitic language related to the ancient South Arabian languages spoken prior to the coming of Muhammad. Traces of these languages are noted in the dialects of the remoter districts. Mahri, a rare and relatively unstudied language of unknown origins, is still spoken in the extreme east. English is widely understood.

⁸RELIGION
Islam is the religion of 96% of the population; the majority of the inhabitants adhere to the Shafiʿi school of law. Until relatively recently there was also a sizable community of Jews, primarily in Aden, but most of them had emigrated by 1975. No Jews were permitted in the east, where a holy site alleged to be the tomb of the biblical prophet Ebir (in Arabic, Hud) is located. In remote areas there are evidences of shamanism, animism, and forms of paganism.

⁹TRANSPORTATION
There are no railroads (although there once was one from Aden to Lahij), and overland transportation is almost solely via truck or animal transport. In 1973 there were 12,973 cars and 3,948 trucks and buses registered. Some 5,633 km of tracks and rough roads connect the towns and villages. In 1971–74, 175 km were asphalted and 880 km were constructed or improved.

Shipping traffic through the port of Aden after the reopening of the Suez Canal in May 1975 averaged 150 ships a month, as compared with an average of 500 before the 1967 closure.

The airport at Khormaksar is serviced regularly by more than 12 international airlines. The state airline, Alyemda Airways, provides both domestic and international services.

10 COMMUNICATIONS

Aden is a major telecommunications center, with public telegraph, radiotelephone, and Telex services. Outside Aden, postal, telegraph, and telephone services are limited, but under the three-year development plan for 1971–74, a telephone exchange of 1,000 lines was built in al-Mukalla, existing lines were improved, and telegraph and postal services were improved. There were 9,558 telephones in 1972.

Besides the government's Central Broadcasting Service of Radio Aden, there are three regional radio stations. Television broadcasts are made by the government stations from Aden and three other cities for about $4\frac{1}{2}$ hours daily. In 1973 there were about 100,000 radios and 20,000 television sets.

11 HISTORY

The area now known as the PDRY was part of Arabia Felix—the "happy" southwestern corner of the Arabian Peninsula in which a series of wealthy and highly civilized empires (including the Sabaean, Minaean, and Himyarite) rose and fell over a period of about 1,500 years prior to the birth of Muhammad in the 6th century A.D. Islam came to the area early in the 7th century, but never succeeded in completely eliminating traces of the pre-Islamic past or in converting all the fiercely independent tribes. Throughout much of the period, the area was at least lightly under the political suzerainty of the imams of Yemen, but it did not regain its former economic or political importance. With the British conquest of Aden in 1834 and the opening of the Suez Canal in 1869, southernmost Arabia began its ascent to world importance; by the mid-1960s, Aden had become the fourth busiest port in the world.

Until the end of World War I, the UK signed a few treaties of "protection and advice" with rulers of the tribes and states in the hinterland, leading to the adoption of the names the Western Aden Protectorate (WAP) and the Eastern Aden Protectorate (EAP). While Yemen (now the YAR) remained at least nominally a part of the Ottoman Empire, relations on the frontier between the UK (in southernmost Arabia) and the Turks (in Yemen) were relatively peaceful. But the defeat of the Ottomans in World War I brought independence to Yemen, and an opportunity to reassert its claims to British-held territories on its southern frontier. The Kingdom of Yemen invaded and occupied some of the principalities, and although a treaty was signed in 1934 to regularize the Anglo-Yemeni relationship, border frictions and disputes continued.

In 1959, the UK formed the Federation of Arab Emirates of the South by joining the six WAP states, with others joining later. The inhabitants of Aden, who were more politically, socially, and economically advanced than those of the protectorates, vigorously opposed adherence to the Federation. Nevertheless, Aden was merged into the Federation in 1963, resulting in the new Federation of South Arabia.

The dispute over the future form and direction of the new political entity, as well as what other states would join, produced violence for five years, while the political parties, labor organizations, and other groups fought for political ascendancy. Finally, in 1967, the National Liberation Front (NLF) emerged as the strongest political group, and the UK agreed to negotiate with it concerning future independence. On 30 November 1967, all the states of the WAP and EAP were amalgamated, the last British soldiers withdrew, and the NLF declared the independence of the People's Republic of South Yemen. On 22 June 1969, the head of the NLF, Qahtan al-Sha'bi, was deposed by a group of young leftists of the NLF. The new regime, headed by a five-man council led by Salein Rubai, renamed the country the People's Democratic Republic of Yemen, and developed close ties with the USSR and secured economic aid from it and from China.

From its inception, the Republic has been embroiled with all three of its neighbors. A separatist movement was supported in Oman; there were border skirmishes with Sa'udi forces; and although the two Yemens at times have declared their wish to unite, border incidents have marred their relations.

12 GOVERNMENT

On 30 November 1970, the constitution of the PDRY was ratified by the general command of the National Front Political Organization (NFPO), which leads political activity. The People's Supreme Council, which has 101 elected members, is the legislative body. It enacts laws; makes decisions; elects the president, the Presidential Council, the prime minister, and the Council of Ministers; and exercises control over the executive branch of the government. Executive power is held jointly by the Presidential Council and the Council of Ministers. The Presidential Council, which consists of the president, prime minister, and NFPO secretary-general, represents the PDRY internally and externally, proposes draft laws, issues the laws approved by the People's Supreme Council, and nominates the prime minister and the Council of Ministers.

13 POLITICAL PARTIES

The National Liberation Front (NLF), which emerged in 1967 as the strongest faction in the disputes before independence, is the only legal party, and under the 1970 constitution, became known as the National Front Political Organization. Elements of the defeated contestants for power, notably the South Arabian League and the Front for the Liberation of Occupied South Yemen, have continued to operate illegally from the neighboring YAR.

14 LOCAL GOVERNMENT

In an effort to deemphasize older loyalties and associations, the PDRY created a highly centralized state and divided the country into six governorates, all closely controlled by the central government. Each has an appointed governor, and each is divided into districts, which are also administered by appointed officials.

15 JUDICIAL SYSTEM

Aden has secular codes for criminal and civil affairs (except those involving matters of personal status). The rest of the PDRY has a mixed system of Muslim law (Shari'ah) courts, tribal courts, and civil courts. Appeals are possible within all systems. In 1968, a Supreme State Security Court, composed of representatives of the NLF, the army, and the minister of justice, was established to try former rulers and political prisoners.

16 ARMED FORCES

The armed forces in 1975 had 18,000 men, including 300 in the navy and 2,500 in the air force. The army of 15,200 comprised 9 infantry brigades, 2 armored battalions, and artillery, signals, and training battalions. The PDRY has an unknown number of national security units and NFPO militia.

17 MIGRATION

Prior to 1967 independence, Aden attracted many immigrants, including more than 80,000 Yemenis from the YAR, who provided much of the unskilled labor, and Indians and Pakistanis, who were active in trade and commerce. The closing of the Suez Canal caused a drastic decline in Aden's commercial significance and contributed to the exodus of most of the Yemenis from the YAR, as well as many others.

Persons from the EAP traditionally had gone to Indonesia and Malaysia to work, returning later in life to retire. In the interim, their remittances had contributed substantially to the relative prosperity of the EAP.

18 INTERNATIONAL COOPERATION

The PDRY is a member of the AL and of the UN and many of its agencies. It has economic and technical cooperation agreements with Bulgaria, China, Romania, Hungary, the German Democratic Republic, and the USSR.

[19] ECONOMY

Prior to independence in November 1967, the economy of the PDRY was dominated by trade and services. Petroleum refining was the major industrial activity, while subsistence agriculture provided the livelihood of most of the people outside the Aden area. The closing of the Suez Canal and the achievement of independence in 1967, with the subsequent withdrawal of British troops, created a deep recession, and the authorities were compelled to impose an austere fiscal regime and tight restrictions on foreign exchange transactions.

[20] INCOME

In 1974, the PDRY had a per capita GNP of $120, one of the lowest in the world according to the IBRD. While there are no recent data on national income, it is believed that the growth rate overtook the 3% rate of population increase in 1973/74 and remained ahead in 1974/75.

[21] LABOR

Since independence, the once powerful Aden Trades Union Congress has been replaced by the Confederation of the Yemeni Workers, and its influence has been limited. Unions conclude working and wage agreements, supervise social insurance, and aid in settlement of industrial disputes. The labor force was estimated at 250,000 in 1970.

[22] AGRICULTURE

Agriculture employs about three-fourths of the country's labor force. Of the 1.5 million acres with potential agricultural value, 246,500 were irrigated and an added 227,800 cultivated by the end of the 1973/74 fiscal year. Production increased in 1973/74; harvests (in tons) included fodder, 264,200 (140,000 in 1969/70); corn, 70,300 (57,000); fruit, 62,000 (57,500); wheat, 17,700 (12,500); and cotton, 15,000 (13,900).

[23] ANIMAL HUSBANDRY

Poor or inadequate grazing land has limited livestock raising. However, the FAO estimated that, by 1973, the number of cattle had risen to 96,000 head; sheep to 225,000; and goats to 900,000. In 1973/74 meat production totaled SYD9.5 million, and fodder production reached 264,200 tons. All meat and milk are consumed locally; hides and skins exported.

[24] FISHING

The PDRY's coast is adjacent to some of the richest fishing grounds in the world, which UN studies indicate have 300 species of fish. Production rose to 126,800 tons in 1973. A modern fishing port is being established and fish-processing plants are being built at al-Mukalla.

[25] FORESTRY

There are no forests in the PDRY.

[26] MINING

The PDRY has announced a program of oil and mineral exploitation. Oil explorations are planned for a 4.4-million acre area on Socotra Island and the surrounding continental shelf.

[27] ENERGY AND POWER

Aden has a complete range of power facilities. All power is generated through diesel machinery using imported petroleum products. Total electric production in 1972 was 186 million kwh.

[28] INDUSTRY

Development priority is being given to projects that depend mainly upon locally available raw materials or produce commodities that are normally imported.

In 1974, about 80% of industrial output came from the British Petroleum refinery at Little Aden, the only major industrial concern that has not been nationalized. During the development plan for 1971–74, 14 new industrial projects were completed, including factories for making cloth, plastic housewares, leather goods, paint, and agricultural spare parts. Industrial production totaled SYD10.2 million in 1973/74, an increase of 9.7% over 1972/73.

[29] DOMESTIC TRADE

Consumer needs are increasingly being met by new public sector industries. Retail prices are controlled, and major food items are subsidized. Profits from domestic trade are limited to 5% on wholesale and 2–6% on retail sales.

[30] FOREIGN TRADE

Imports in 1974 were valued at about $243 million, and exports at $256 million. Major imports in 1972 were manufactured goods, oil, machinery, vehicles, foodstuffs, tobacco, and textiles. Petroleum products made up 77% of the exports, which also included coffee, textiles, cotton, hides and skins, and grains. The major trading partners in 1974 were: Canada (23%), Iraq (7%), Kuwayt (7%), Australia (7%), Japan (6%), Iran (5%), the UK (4%), and the US (4%).

[31] BALANCE OF PAYMENTS

The 1974 balance of payments showed an overall deficit of $34.4 million, as compared with a deficit of only $3.5 million in 1973. This was partly the result of an estimated 46% rise in the total value of imports over the year.

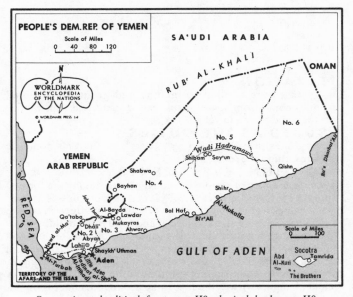

See continental political: front cover H8; physical: back cover H8

LOCATION: 12°7' to 19°N; 42°32' to 53°5'E.   BOUNDARY LENGTHS: Sa'udi Arabia, *830 km (516 mi)*; Oman, *288 km (179 mi)*; total coastline, *1,210 km (752 mi)*; YAR, *581 km (361 mi)*.   TERRITORIAL SEA LIMIT: 12 mi.

[32] BANKING

Prior to November 1969, eight commercial banks operated in the PDRY. These have since been nationalized and consolidated into the National Bank, which had reserves of SYD6.6 million on 30 September 1975, and at the same time had SYD13.61 million in demand deposits and SYD13.11 million in time and savings deposits. The Central Bank began operations in July 1972 by taking over the assets and liabilities of the Yemen Currency Authority. Its foreign assets on 30 September 1975 were SYD24.03 million, and reserves were SYD43.54 million.

Money in circulation increased from SYD29.8 million in 1967 to SYD52.3 million in 1975, while reserve money increased from SYD21.1 million in 1967 to SYD43.5 million in September 1975.

[33] INSURANCE

All insurance and reinsurance companies were nationalized in November 1969, and were amalgamated into the National Insurance and Reinsurance Co., based at Aden.

³⁴SECURITIES

There are no securities exchanges in the PDRY.

³⁵PUBLIC FINANCE

Budget summaries for fiscal years 1972/73, 1973/74, and 1974/75 (in millions of South Yemen dinars) were:

	1972/73	1973/74	1974/75 (Estimated)
REVENUES			
Taxes on income and profits	2.5	3.2	2.9
Import duties	4.4	5.1	3.6
Excise taxes	1.3	2.2	2.4
Other tax revenues	0.8	1.0	1.0
Nontax revenue	3.0	3.8	3.9
TOTALS	12.0	15.3	13.8
EXPENDITURES	21.7	22.7	29.4
Deficit	−9.7	−7.4	−15.6
FINANCING			
External (foreign aid)	0.3		
Domestic	9.6	7.5	15.6

³⁶TAXATION

Direct taxes are applied to income and profits. Additional revenues come from stamp taxes, excise taxes, customs duties, port fees, and road and vehicle taxes.

³⁷CUSTOMS AND DUTIES

Import duties provided from 23% to 37% of PDRY's domestic revenues from 1969 to 1974.

³⁸FOREIGN INVESTMENTS

In 1971, in a series of nationalization measures taking the form of "spontaneous workers' revolts," almost all businesses still in private hands were taken over by workers' committees. A decree of 1972 nationalized all commercial and residential buildings.

In 1975, the government announced programs of oil and mineral exploration in cooperation with foreign nations. Western companies were offered exploration concessions with the opportunity for production-sharing ventures in the event of oil finds. A Canadian company was the first to be awarded a concession under these terms.

³⁹ECONOMIC POLICY

Capital investment in the five-year plan for 1974–79 was to total SYD75 million, or double the investment in the three-year development plan for 1971–74. The overall objective of the plan is a gradual changeover from a service economy to one based on agricultural and industrial production, with greater employment opportunities. Top priority was given to oil and mineral exploitation.

⁴⁰HEALTH

In 1970 there were 17 hospitals, with 1,248 beds; and in 1969, there were 103 doctors and 17 dentists. The departure of many British technicians, nurses, and other skilled personnel after 1967 independence created significant shortages.

During the three-year development plan for 1971–74, newly completed facilities included 11 health centers, with a capacity of 425 beds; 142 health units; and 5 hospitals, with a total capacity of 220 beds. Medical facilities outside Aden are extremely limited. In 1975, average life expectancy was estimated at 47.4 years.

⁴¹SOCIAL WELFARE

Traditional means of providing assistance to the sick, handicapped, widows, and orphans predominate. Only in Aden have sophisticated welfare programs been developed. A state retirement scheme under which public employees will become eligible for pensions at age 60 for men and 55 for women, after a minimum of 25 years' continuous service, was established in April 1975.

⁴²HOUSING

While Aden has an excess of modern housing, the economic decline after 1967 produced difficulties in the building and construction industry. Outside of Aden, housing is still traditional, with multistory stone houses for the wealthy and small houses of stone or baked brick for the poor.

⁴³EDUCATION

In Aden, nearly all children obtain the required 4 years of primary, 3 years of intermediate, and 4–6 years of secondary education. As a result of the school building program in 1971–74, there was a total of 216,368 students in the PDRY in 1973/74, up from 152,154 students in 1970/71. A college for training teachers for secondary and intermediate schools was opened in 1970, with 110 students and 13 teachers. In September 1975, the PDRY's first university, the University of Aden, was established.

⁴⁴LIBRARIES AND MUSEUMS

The largest library is the Miswat Library, the former Lake Library, administered by the municipality of Aden, with some 35,000 volumes in Arabic, English, and Urdu. It also maintains a traveling library of some 10,000 volumes. The Yemen Center for Cultural Research collects documents for a planned Central National Library. Two museums in Aden specialize in archaeological materials, and the Department of Antiquities operates a museum in al-Mukalla.

⁴⁵ORGANIZATIONS

The Confederation of Workers in the PDRY and the General Union of Yemeni Women are the two leading organizations in the country. Trade unions, marketing cooperatives, and similar organizations are permitted and encouraged. In addition, there are three employers' associations. The Aden Society of Arts is the only learned society in the PDRY.

⁴⁶PRESS

The Aden News Bulletin is published twice daily in Arabic and English. Other Arabic dailies include 14th October and Al-Shararah.

⁴⁷TOURISM

With the reopening of the Suez Canal in May 1975, improved facilities were planned for the tourist trade, which was expected to be revitalized with renewed ship traffic.

⁴⁸FAMOUS YEMENIS

There are no internationally famous persons from the PDRY.

⁴⁹DEPENDENCIES

The PDRY controls island territories that were part of the former British colony: Perim, in the Red Sea; and Socotra and the Kuria Muria Islands, off the coast of Oman. Kamaran Island was occupied in October 1972 by YAR troops.

⁵⁰BIBLIOGRAPHY

American University. *Area Handbook for the Peripheral States of the Arabian Peninsula.* Washington, D.C.: Government Printing Office, 1971.

Brinton, J. Y. *Aden and the Federation of South Arabia.* Washington: American Society of International Law, 1964.

Ingrams, Harold. *Arabia and the Isles.* London: Murray; New York: Praeger, 1966.

King, Gillian. *Imperial Outpost—Aden.* London: Oxford University Press, 1964.

Little, Tom. *South Arabia.* New York: Praeger, 1968.

O'Ballance, Edgar. *The War in the Yemen.* Hamden, Conn.: Archon Books, 1971.

Reilly, Sir Bernard. *Aden and the Yemen.* London: HMSO, 1960.

YEMEN ARAB REPUBLIC

Al-Jumhuriyah al-ʿArabiyah al-Yamaniyah

CAPITAL: Sanʿaʾ. **FLAG**: The national flag is a tricolor of red, white, and black horizontal stripes, with a green star on the white stripe. **ANTHEM**: Al-Watani (*Peace to the Land*). **MONETARY UNIT**: The Yemeni riyal (YR) of 100 fils (formerly 40 buqsha) replaced the Maria Theresa thaler in 1964. There are coins of $\frac{1}{2}$, 1, 5, 10, and 25 fils and notes of 1, 5, 10, 20, and 50 riyals. As of 31 January 1976, YR1 = $0.21918 (or $1 = YR4.5625). **WEIGHTS AND MEASURES**: The unit of weight is the waqiyah, about 1.2 ounces. The multiple of waqiyah is the rotl. The small rotl (about 17 waqiyah) is used for weighing coffee, sugar, dates, and other products; the medium rotl (20 waqiyah), for meats; and the large rotl (24 waqiyah), for petroleum. The unit of length is the dhraʾ, about 26 inches. The unit of capacity is the qadah, about 35 dry quarts. The qadah is divided into 64 nafar. The metric system is being introduced. **HOLIDAYS**: Movable Muslim holidays include ʿId al-Fitr, ʿId al-ʿAdhaʾ, Milad al-Nabi, First of Muharram; Republic Day is celebrated on 26 September. **TIME**: Solar time.

¹LOCATION, SIZE, AND EXTENT
Situated in the southwestern corner of the Arabian Peninsula, the Yemen Arab Republic (YAR) has an estimated total area of 195,000 sq km (75,290 sq mi), extending *540* km (*336* mi) N–S and *418* km (*260* mi) E–W. It is bounded by Saʿudi Arabia on the N and NE, by the People's Democratic Republic of Yemen (PDRY) on the E and S, and by the Red Sea on the W, with a total boundary length of *1,661* km (*1,032* mi).

²TOPOGRAPHY
Essentially mountainous, the YAR encloses the southern limits of the great tablelands that stretch from the northern heights of ʿAsir to the southwestern tip of the Arabian Peninsula. Except for the coastal plain, the Tihamah, which runs the entire length of the territory and averages 30 miles in width, the country is composed of fertile highland plateaus rising from 4,000 to 10,000 feet. The highest known point, the summit of Jabal Hadhur, rises 12,336 feet above the Red Sea coast. Beyond the Tihamah are foothills of the maritime ranges. These ranges sometimes culminate in vast isolated mountains reaching between 4,000 and 7,000 feet in height. The enormous escarpment formed by the main mountain range provides the western wall of the great central plateau. The height of the plateau averages 8,000 feet, and several of its peaks rise to more than 10,000 feet.

Rainfall on the western slopes is carried away (in exceptional circumstances to the sea) by a series of parallel wadis flowing in a westerly direction. To the northeast rise tributaries of Wadi Najran and of the great Dawasir system, while, farther south, two other trunk wadis drain into the sands of the Rubʿ al-Khali. Wadi Bana and Wadi Tiban drain the southern slopes into the Gulf of Aden, and on the southeastern ranges rise many of the minor tributaries of the great trunk Wadi Hadramawt.

³CLIMATE
Along the Tihamah, extreme humidity combines with high temperatures—as high as 54.4°C (130°F) in the shade—to produce a stiflingly hot climate. Winds blowing northwest in summer and southwest in winter bring little rain but cause severe sandstorms. During January and February, however, temperature averages about 20°C (68°F). The climate of the highlands is generally considered the best in Arabia. Summers are temperate and winters are cool, with some frost. Temperature varies from 21.6°C (71°F) in June, the hottest month, to 14°C (57°F) in January. Rainfall in the highlands ranges from 16 inches at Sanʿaʾ to 32 inches in the monsoon area of the extreme southwest. The average year-round temperature at Sanʿaʾ is 17.5°C (63.5°F).

⁴FLORA AND FAUNA
Vegetation is sparse along the coast, but in the highlands and wadis it is plentiful. Acacia, date palm, and many fruit trees are common. Custard apple, euphorbia, and spurge grow in abundance. Alpine roses, balsam, basil, wild elder, and Judas tree are among the flowers and herbs. Wild animals include baboon, gazelle, leopard, and mountain hare. Scorpions and millipedes are everywhere, but snakes are less common. Many varieties of birds are found, including the bustard, hawk, vulture, raven, parrot, hornbill, honeysucker, and weaver finch. Scott's expedition collected 27,000 varieties of insects and over 600 specimens of flowering plants.

As of 1975, endangered species in the YAR included the South Arabian leopard, dugong, Arabian gazelle, and African lammergeyer.

⁵POPULATION
The YAR's first official census, conducted in 1975, indicated a total population of 6,471,000, with a density of 33 persons per sq km (86 per sq mi). The YAR is the second most densely populated country on the Arabian Peninsula, after Kuwayt. Projected 1980 population was 7,690,000. Most of the population is concentrated in the Tihamah foothills and in the central highlands. In 1975, about 91% of the population was rural, mostly engaged in settled agriculture. The principal towns, with their 1975 population, are Sanʿaʾ, 134,571, situated at an altitude of 7,260 feet; Taʿizz, about 80,000, situated at an altitude of 4,600 feet; and al-Hudaydah, about 80,000, the chief port. Other towns with populations of more than 10,000 are Dhamar and Yarim.

⁶ETHNIC GROUPS
Many ethnologists contend that the purest "Arab" stock is to be found in the YAR. Classified as Joktanic Semites, the Yeminis claim descent from Himyar, great-grandson of Joktan, who in turn was descended from Shem, the son of Noah. The purest Joktanic types are to be found in any numbers only in the remoter confines of the mountainous parts of the YAR. The Tihamah has been subjected to occupation and infiltration by many conquerors, and its people have strong admixtures of other racial types, including Negroid peoples.

The history of the Yemenite Jews, who lived in their own secluded communities and left for Israel in 1949, predates by centuries the Islamic Hijra (622 A.D.). How they came to settle in the region has not been determined.

⁷LANGUAGE

Arabic in a Yemeni dialect is spoken throughout the YAR. In vocabulary and other features there is a considerable difference between the classical language used for writing and formal speaking and the spoken dialect used for ordinary discourse.

⁸RELIGION

The YAR is a Muslim country. About half of the inhabitants are Sunnis, who belong to the Shafi'i school, one of the four major schools of Islamic law. They reside in the coastal plains and the southwestern part of the country. Most of the dwellers in the highlands are Shi'is of the Zaydi sect. This sect, originating in the 9th century A.D., takes its name from Zayd bin 'Ali (d.740), a descendant of the Prophet. In addition, there are about 50,000 Isma'ilis, members of another Shi'i sect.

⁹TRANSPORTATION

The YAR's transportation system before the early 1960s consisted of a few primitive mud tracks connecting the larger towns. In 1961, technicians from China completed a 139-mile road between San'a' and al-Hudaydah—the YAR's first asphalt highway. The US then completed the 240-mile Ta'izz San'a'-Mocha highway, a seven-year project, in 1968. In 1969, the USSR completed a road from Ta'izz to al-Hudaydah. By 1975 there were 648 miles of paved roads in the YAR. Another 448 miles were expected to be completed by 1980, including a 162-mile road between al-Hudaydah and Jizan. In 1974, the YAR had 2,727 private cars (736 in 1972), 3,517 taxis (1,028), and 3,575 trucks (1,649). The country has no railways.

Improvements to al-Hudaydah port were completed by Soviet engineers in 1961, and additional berthing, storage, and handling facilities were added by Egypt. The port can now accommodate oceangoing vessels. In 1974, 22,941 tons of cargo were loaded and 578,068 tons unloaded. Some 453 ships called at al-Hudaydah in 1974. Other ports are Mocha and al-Salif, which have sheltered harbors and deepwater ports capable of taking 10,000-ton ships.

Progress in air transportation has been rapid in recent years. Yemen Airways, the national airline, operates services between San'a', Ta'izz, al-Hudaydah, and al-Beidha and also schedules flights to Egypt, Kuwayt, PDRY, Sa'udi Arabia, the United Arab Emirates (UAE), and to Asmara in Ethiopia and Djibouti in the Territory of the Afars and the Issas; during 1970–74, its passenger volume nearly doubled, reaching 71,098. Aeroflot, Sa'udi Arabian airlines, Ethiopian Air Lines, and Air Djibouti also have flights to the YAR. The only airport capable of handling modern jet aircraft is al-Rahba International Airport, located north of San'a'. In 1974, 71,451 passengers arrived there.

¹⁰COMMUNICATIONS

Postal, telegraph, and telephone services are expanding, but remain limited. Two-way radio links the YAR directly with Cairo, Rome, and the PDRY. Telephone and telegraph facilities are available in major cities. A modern dial telephone system has been installed in San'a', Ta'izz, and al-Hudaydah. By 1974, the country had 4,930 telephone subscribers, as compared with 3,400 in 1972. Radio San'a' operates four transmitters regularly on both short- and medium-wave frequencies. There were about 86,000 radios in 1973; there is no television.

¹¹HISTORY

Classical geographers divided Arabia into three regions: Arabia Petræa, Arabia Deserta, and Arabia Felix. The last, the southwestern corner, included the territory now occupied by the Yemen Arab Republic, as well as 'Asir and Hadramawt. The region was the site of a series of rich kingdoms that dominated world trade. The wealthy kingdom of Sheba (Saba), with its capital at Ma'rib, is the best known of the South Arabian kingdoms. The prosperity of this kingdom (10th century to 2d

century B.C.) was based on the incense trade. Competition from new trade routes undermined Sabæan prosperity and caused the kingdom to decline. From the 2d century B.C. to the 6th century A.D., the Himyarite dynasty, of ethnic stock similar to the Sabaeans, ruled in Arabia Felix, and paganism gave way to Christianity and Judaism.

Himyarite hegemony was ended in 525 by invading Christian Ethiopians, whose rule lasted until 575, when they were driven out by Persian invaders. Islam was accepted in the next century. As a Muslim country, Yemen became the site of religious schisms. The coastline (Tihamah) was held by the Sunnis of the Shafi'i rite while the highlands were held by the Zaydis, a Shi'i sect.

The 9th century is especially important in the history of Yemen. The Zaydi imam Yahya al-Hadi ila'l Haqq founded a line of imams (rulers) that survived until the second half of the 20th century. Nevertheless, Yemen's medieval history is a tangled chronicle of contesting local imams. The Fatimids of Egypt helped the Isma'ili maintain dominance in the 11th century. Saladin (Salah al-Din) annexed Yemen in 1173. The Rasulid dynasty (Kurdish and Turkish in origin) ruled Yemen, with Zabid as its capital, from about 1230 to the 15th century. In 1516, the Mamluks of Egypt annexed Yemen.

The entry of the West was manifested by the Portuguese attack on Aden in 1513. In 1517, the Mamluk governor surrendered to the Ottoman Turks, and from 1536 Turkish armies overran the country. But they were challenged by the Zaydi imam, Qasim the Great (imam from 1597 to 1620), and expelled from the interior around 1630. From then until the 19th century, the Ottomans retained control only of the coastal area, while the highlands generally were ruled by the Zaydi imams.

Early in the 19th century, Yemen was overrun by Wahhabis, but in 1818, Ibrahim Pasha, the son of Muhammad 'Ali of Egypt, drove them out of Yemen and reestablished Zaydi control. Egyptian troops occupied the main ports of Yemen until 1840, when they were withdrawn. The Zaydi imams recognized Ottoman suzerainty and paid a large annual subsidy to the Ottoman sultan. After 1840, the situation was anarchic, and law and order in any form were not reestablished until 1872, when the Ottomans again occupied San'a' and consolidated their control. During World War I they kept a large force in Yemen, but under the armistice terms evacuated it in 1918.

During the war, the British had supported the Idrisi tribe's attempt to establish itself in Yemen. In 1919, the UK occupied al-Hudaydah, which came into Idrisi hands when the British withdrew in 1921. The Zaydis, now led by Imam Yahya ibn Muhammad al-Hamid al-Din, who had founded a hereditary dynasty in 1891, waged an armed struggle against the Idrisis that ended when Imam Yahya seized al-Hudaydah in 1925. The imam also moved into the states of the Western Aden Protectorate in an attempt to reestablish his suzerainty in these former Yemeni-held territories. The Idrisis came under the protection of King Ibn Sa'ud, and in 1934, a war broke out between the Sa'udis and Yemenis. By the Treaty of Ta'if (May 1934), Yemen lost 'Asir to Sa'udi Arabia, but won UK and Sa'udi recognition of its independence. However, Imam Yahya's actions against the areas of the UK protectorate in Aden (later known as Southern Yemen and, since 1970, as the People's Democratic Republic of Yemen—PDRY), continued until 1937.

Yemen joined the Arab League in 1945 and in 1958 formed a federation, the United Arab States, with the newly established United Arab Republic (UAR). In December 1961, however, the federal connection with Egypt was severed, and in September 1962, the days-old government of Imam Muhammad al-Badr was overthrown by revolutionary forces led by the then Brigadier 'Abdallah al-Sallal, who proclaimed himself president and commander in chief of the army, and declared the establishment of the Yemen Arab Republic. Muhammad al-Badr escaped to the northern regions of the YAR, and there was able to organize a counterrevolutionary force.

A civil war between the royalists (defenders of the imamate) and the republican government broke out, and appeals by both sides for support brought about the active intervention of other Arab states: Sa'udi Arabia supported the royalist cause and the UAR came to the assistance of the Republic, dispatching up to 70,000 troops to the YAR. Beginning in 1963, the YAR government represented the country at the UN. The civil war, however, continued until 1969, with fighting particularly bitter during the winter of 1963–64. As Sa'udi Arabia began to withdraw support from the royalist forces, fighting dwindled in 1969. Talks between republican leaders and Sa'udi Arabia in March 1970 at Jiddah concluded with an agreement that ended the civil war and left the republicans in control.

In June 1974, 'Abd al-Rahman al-Iryani (who had been president since 1967) resigned, thrusting the country into a state of political confusion. In November, a Command Council took over the government. The Council, headed by an appointed president, former deputy chief of the armed forces Lt. Col. Ibrahim Muhammad al-Hamadi, restored the constitution (suspended in June), with modifications to accommodate the new government's strong central control.

¹²GOVERNMENT
Amended in 1965, 1967, 1971, and 1974, the YAR's constitution affirms Islamic law as the basis of all legislation and a unicameral Consultative Assembly as the supreme legislative body. The Assembly is to nominate the president and is authorized to appoint a ruling executive council.

In 1971, the YAR held its first national elections. Voters selected 119 members of the Consultative Assembly; the 40 remaining members were appointed by the president. In November 1974, an amended version of the constitution was put into effect, with executive rule passing to a seven-member Presidential Council. An appointed prime minister also serves on the Council. In 22 October 1975, Lt. Col. al-Hamadi dissolved the Council with a view toward holding elections for a new, fully elective body. As of mid-1976, no date had been set for the voting.

¹³POLITICAL PARTIES
Political parties were prohibited under the imamate. Political parties in the Western sense have not developed under the YAR. Tribal allegiances remain an important political factor in the country.

¹⁴LOCAL GOVERNMENT
The YAR is divided into 10 governorates (muhafaza), each headed by a governor (emir). Each governorate contains a varying number of districts (qada), which are divided into sectors (nahyah). Traditional divisions still extant include the ozlah, a group of villages (qarya) whose inhabitants belong to the same tribe, headed by a shaykh; and the mahallah, a group of houses administratively subordinate to a village. The central government retains ultimate authority over local officials, although certain administrative sanctions have been granted to traditional local rulers. In 1974, the YAR had 41 qada, 165 nahyah, 1,680 ozlah, 15,418 qarya, and 14,384 mahallah.

¹⁵JUDICIAL SYSTEM
The Muslim community is governed primarily according to Islamic religious law, the Shari'ah, which is administered in each district by a hakim. Litigants may appeal against the decision of a hakim to another hakim, and from him there is a final appeal to the Istinaf, the highest court of appeal, in San'a'. Two other legal systems operate—civil law and tribal law.

Civil law is administered by the president through the Ministry of Justice. The president appoints civil judges. The central administration tries to discourage the use of tribal law (urf), but it is deeply rooted, especially in outlying districts. New penal and civil codes have been drafted under the paramountcy of Islamic law. The Supreme Shari'ah Court was empowered in 1964 to deal with political cases and to try senior government officials.

¹⁶ARMED FORCES
Under the Republic, the armed forces have been completely reorganized, largely along Egyptian lines. In 1975, the army had 30,000 personnel. The air force had 1,700 personnel and 24 combat aircraft, mostly of Soviet manufacture. A small navy of 300 personnel operated five patrol boats. Tribal paramilitary forces numbered about 20,000.

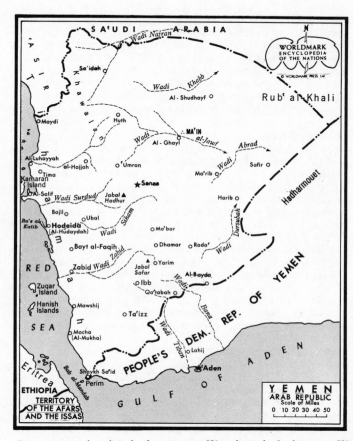

See continental political: front cover H8; physical: back cover H8

LOCATION: 12°41' to 17°32'N; 42°8' to 46°19'E. **BOUNDARY LENGTHS:** Sa'udi Arabia, 628 km (390 mi); PDRY, 581 km (361 mi); Red Sea coastline, 452 km (281 mi). **TERRITORIAL SEA LIMIT:** 12 mi.

¹⁷MIGRATION
Although the imamate discouraged both immigration and emigration, many Yemenis (mainly Shafi'is) emigrated to the principal trading centers of the Arab world as well as to the Indian subcontinent, Indonesia, and Singapore. Some 80,000 to 90,000 Yemenis emigrated to Aden alone.

The creation of the Republic in 1962 encouraged some émigrés to return to the YAR, especially those with special skills who had been unable to find employment in the primitive economy of the imamate. As of the mid-1970s, however, an estimated 1 million Yemenis lived abroad, including some 400,000 migratory workers, mostly in Sa'udi Arabia.

Internal migration from rural areas to the towns has been growing in recent years.

¹⁸INTERNATIONAL COOPERATION

Yemen joined the Arab League in 1945, and was admitted to UN membership in 1947. The YAR participates in FAO, ITU, UPU, WHO, and UNESCO. In 1970, it took up membership in the IMF, IBRD, IFC, and IDA.

Both the YAR and PDRY governments have espoused a goal of eventual unification into a "Greater Yemen." In 1972, both states acted to set up unification committees, although ideological differences and regional rivalry have made the prospect of action remote.

¹⁹ECONOMY

The YAR, traditionally an agricultural country, maintains the largest farming sector on the Arabian Peninsula. Until the 18th century, Yemen was the source of nearly all the world's coffee. Since 1971, cotton has surpassed coffee as the principal export crop, followed by tobacco and qat, a narcotic. The YAR is largely self-sufficient in foodstuffs and produces a sizable export surplus, upon which the country relies for its foreign exchange. In ancient times, Yemen was noted for its leatherwork, sword-making, and other handicrafts, and it still produces fine craftwork, particularly shawls. In terms of infrastructure, however, the YAR is among the dozen or so least developed countries in the world.

²⁰INCOME

In 1974, GDP totaled YR4,305 million, as compared with YR2,895 million in 1971. The 1974 total was distributed as follows: agriculture, 54.1%; commerce, 14.2%; government, 8.8%; construction, 7.4%; industry, 6%; and other sectors, 9.5%. Per capita income is among the lowest in the world; in 1972, it was put at about $85, and was thought to have slightly exceeded $100 by 1975.

²¹LABOR

In the mid-1970s, some 90% of the YAR's population was engaged in subsistence agriculture. In 1973, industrial establishments employed a total of 7,900 persons. Under the imamate, primitive guild associations existed in some crafts and economic enterprises. In 1963, the YAR's first trade union, the Yemen General Trade Union, was formed, in Ta'izz. Its members include only laborers on construction projects undertaken by foreign contractors.

²²AGRICULTURE

Yemenis, unlike most inhabitants of the Arabian peninsula, have long led lives as sedentary farmers. The highlands of the YAR contain areas of great fertility. Though primitive tools are used, the YAR's agriculture employs more advanced techniques than most Asian and African countries. In most areas, nearly all the serviceable land is under cultivation. More than 80% of farm families work as tenants under a sharecropping system. Agriculture yields more than half of the national income and generates virtually all exports. Until the 1970s, coffee had always been the principal export crop, and mocha, the famous Yemeni coffee, derives its name from the once-prosperous coffee port of Mocha. In the 1970s, the YAR produced about 5,000 tons of coffee annually. Since 1971, cotton, grown mainly in the Tihamah, has emerged as the leading cash crop. Tobacco (5,000 tons produced in 1973) and the qat shrub, the leaves of which are narcotic when chewed, are also major export crops. Food crop production in 1974/75, in tons, included dhurra, 1,570,000; barley, 220,000; corn, 107,000; wheat, 78,000; pulses, 84,000; potatoes, 78,000; vegetables, 168,000; and fruits, 60,000.

²³ANIMAL HUSBANDRY

Animal husbandry is the second most important sector of the economy, and the export of hides and skins has long been an important source of foreign exchange. In 1973, the livestock population was estimated to include 1,220,000 head of cattle, 3,470,000 sheep, 10,000,000 goats, and large numbers of camels and horses.

²⁴FISHING

An estimated 2,000 persons are engaged in fishing. An FAO mission estimated the annual catch at 2,000 tons. A fish-processing plant has been built at al-Hudaydah. Pearl and coral diving have been practiced for centuries.

²⁵FORESTRY

Large forests once covered Yemen. The systematic cutting of timber for fuel and construction and the ravages of goats have almost completely eliminated the forest areas. Forestry production in 1973 was estimated at 8.4 million cu meters.

²⁶MINING

The only significant commercial mining enterprise extracts rock salt from a deposit at al-Salif. Operated by the government, the mine produces about 100,000 tons annually, much of which is exported. There is a thin stratum of coal near San'a'. Small quantities of gypsum, soapstone, and agate are produced and used locally; some agate is exported. No oil in commercial quantities has been found.

²⁷ENERGY AND POWER

Although progress in electrification has been made in the 1960s and 1970s, only about 5% of the population has electric service. Total electricity production increased from 2.3 million kwh in 1966 to 22 million kwh in 1973.

²⁸INDUSTRY

Traditional industries in Yemen flourish as they have for millennia. Almost all clothing, jewelry, shoes, implements, and even weapons are made by hand from domestic materials. Modern industry is in its infancy. The textile industry, utilizing locally grown cotton, is the leading producer. In 1974, 7,956 tons of lint cotton and 11.5 million yards of fabric were produced. Other import-substituting industries process foods and produce construction materials. Since 1970, the modern industrial sector has expanded by more than 10% annually, although the total contribution to the GNP came to only 6% in 1974. Projects constructed during the 1970s include a cement factory and a cigarette factory at Bajil, a pharmaceutical plant at Ta'izz, and a canning and soft drinks factory at al-Hudaydah. The largest sectors, by value of production, in 1973 were bakeries, textiles, cement, cigarettes, and soft drinks.

²⁹DOMESTIC TRADE

At the center of most towns is a marketplace (suq), the lanes of which are lined with open-front booths where food and implements are displayed and sold. Merchants specialize in particular items. Some shops sell miscellaneous items. Some things are bartered; others are sold for cash, usually after bargaining.

³⁰FOREIGN TRADE

Foreign trade is controlled by the government. In 1974, the YAR's exports were estimated at $13 million and imports at $190 million. Exports were thus less than 7% of imports in 1974.

Principal exports in 1971 and 1973 (in thousands of dollars) were:

	1971	1973
Raw cotton	1,597	3,945
Coffee	916	1,334
Hides and skins	408	1,213
Cotton seed	155	472
Fruits and vegetables	64	171
Other food and live animals	10	597
Salt	477	7
Other exports	687	243
TOTALS	4,314	7,982

Principal imports in 1971 and 1973 (in thousands of dollars) were:

	1971	1973
Sugar and sugar preparations	3,564	16,413
Wheat flour	1,632	10,978
Other food and live animals	8,785	32,754
Chemicals	1,881	7,960
Transport equipment	2,777	7,642
Textiles	1,268	7,569
Petroleum and products	1,691	6,174
Other imports	15,370	35,359
TOTALS	36,968	124,849

Principal trade partners in 1973 (in thousands of dollars) were:

	EXPORTS	IMPORTS	BALANCE
Japan	1,773	16,892	− 15,119
Afars and Issas	263	15,056	− 14,793
PDRY	1,019	8,975	− 7,956
Sa'udi Arabia	926	8,118	− 7,192
France	13	7,977	− 7,964
China	1,317	4,819	− 3,502
FRG	23	5,797	− 5,774
Singapore	1,320	3,239	− 1,919
Other countries	1,328	53,976	− 52,648
TOTALS	7,982	124,849	−116,867

31 BALANCE OF PAYMENTS
The YAR has consistently had a deficit in its balance of payments; the deficit has been financed largely by foreign aid (development assistance projects and commodity agreements) and remittances by overseas Yemenis. Summaries of the YAR's balance of payments in 1970 and 1973 (in millions of SDRs) are as follows:

	1970	1973
Export balance	5.8	7.4
Import balance	−88.4	−130.0
Invisible receipts and remittances from Yemenis overseas	45.0	90.9
Official and private grants	17.7	19.5
CURRENT BALANCE	−19.9	− 12.2
Official loans	26.7	14.4
Errors and omissions	3.2	12.0
TOTALS	10.0	14.2

32 BANKING
The republican government set up the Yemen Currency Board in 1964 with a capital of YR2 million. Paper currency was then first introduced. In July 1971, the Currency Board was replaced by the Central Bank of Yemen.

The banking sector was expanding rapidly in the 1970s. The Yemeni Bank for Reconstruction and Development (YBRD), which incorporated the only bank existing before the revolution, the Sa'udi National Commercial Bank, is state-owned and, with a capital of YR10 million, finances development activities and also operates as a commercial bank. In the mid-1970s, the YBRD continued to dominate the banking business, controlling some 70% of the loans outstanding in the country. During 1970–74, five foreign commercial banks opened offices in the YAR: the Arab Bank, British Bank of the Middle East, Citibank, Indo-Chinese Bank, and the Sa'udi National Commercial Bank.

33 INSURANCE
The only domestic insurance firm in the YAR is the Yemen Insurance Co. Much insurance is handled through firms in Aden.

34 SECURITIES
There is no stock exchange. Since 1961, the republican govern-ment has offered public shares in a number of enterprises, including the Yemeni Bank for Reconstruction and Development, the National Cigarette and Tobacco Co., Yemen Airways, and the San'a' and Ta'izz power companies.

35 PUBLIC FINANCE
The YAR's budgetary procedures underwent broad reforms in the 1970s, including the creation of a Central Budget Bureau in 1972. In 1974, the new Ministry of Finance introduced the government's first comprehensive system of budgeting and accounting. The 1973/74 budget was the first ever to be approved by the Consultative Assembly prior to implementation.

Principal revenues and expenditures for 1973/74 (in thousands of Yemeni riyals) were as follows:

REVENUES	
Taxes	232,776
Nontax revenues	42,904
Cash grants	109,220
TOTAL	384,900

EXPENDITURES	
Defense	184,177
Health and education	30,338
Other current expenditures	109,158
Capital expenditures	139,261
TOTAL	462,934

As of 30 June 1974, the public debt totaled YR78,035,000, as compared with YR77,362,000 in mid-1972. Of the mid-1974 total, foreign indebtedness totaled YR140,710,000, while domestic accounts yielded an offsetting surplus of YR62,675,000.

36 TAXATION
Taxes for exit, tobacco imports, defense, and on miscellaneous account are added on customs duties—the government's largest source of revenue. Zakat (the religious charity tax) is state-enforced. Taxes were increased substantially in the 1970s, with taxes on imports providing about 70% of total tax revenues. There are excise duties, road and vehicle taxes, port fees, a tax on rents, and telegraph fees, and income from state domain that consists of confiscated property of the imamate. Total government tax revenues increased from YR122,891,000 in 1971/72 to YR262,060,000 in 1974/75.

37 CUSTOMS AND DUTIES
Import duties are levied at the rate of 10% on essential goods and 20% on luxury items. A surcharge of 10% is added to these basic rates to finance schools and orphanages and to assist the poor. Export duties are levied on a variety of products.

38 FOREIGN INVESTMENTS
The republican government has passed legislation that actively encourages foreign investment. The law grants foreign firms a five-year exemption on income taxes, exemption from customs duties for necessary machinery and materials, and repatriation of profits in the currency of the country of origin.

During 1946–67, the YAR received $42.8 million in grants from the US, but in 1967, it announced that it would no longer accept US aid. Assistance subsequently came from the USSR and China. From 1954 to 1964, capital worth $119 million was provided by the Communist countries. Other recent donors have been Kuwayt, Iraq, the UAE, The Federal Republic of Germany (FRG), and the German Democratic Republic. Since 1971, Sa'udi Arabia has been the single largest contributor, followed by IDA and FRG, providing a large share of funding for the $205.8-million 1973/74–1974/75 development plan. Direct Sa'udi assistance in 1974 was estimated to exceed $100 million. US aid, resumed in 1972, totaled $25.6 million in 1972/73.

39 ECONOMIC POLICY
Until 1970, the civil war and lack of statistical information hampered economic planning. For the first decade of its ex-

istence, the YAR was concerned with establishing the bare rudiments of a modern economic life in the form of a national budget, paper currency, and administrative machinery for compilation of statistics and planning. In 1973, the newly established Central Planning Office, aided by the IBRD, issued the country's first three-year development plan (1973/74–75/76). The plan called for expenditures of YR935.6 million ($205.8 million), some 75.1% of which was to be financed from foreign grants and loans. The plan's major focus was development of the YAR's infrastructure. Funds for the three-year period were to be distributed as follows: transport and communications, 31.2%; education, 20.9%; agriculture, 14.8%; public utilities, 10.4%; industry and energy, 9.8%; health, 5.2%; and other sectors, 7.7%.

⁴⁰HEALTH
Undernourishment and the diseases associated with it are the YAR's major health problems. Malaria, typhus, tuberculosis, dysentery, whooping cough, measles, hepatitis, schistosomiasis, and typhoid fever are widespread. Sewage disposal of the most rudimentary type constitutes a great menace to health. Addiction to qat (a narcotic) is endemic, and is both psychologically and economically ruinous in the YAR. Life expectancy in 1975 was estimated at about 45 years.

Within the last decade, more than 20 hospitals and 12 health dispensaries have been established. In 1974 there were 33 hospitals, with 4,119 beds, and 25 dispensaries. In that year there were 265 physicians, 14 dentists, 21 pharmacists, and 1,036 medical assistants. Many physicians are non-Yemenis and are subsidized through foreign aid.

⁴¹SOCIAL WELFARE
Families and tribes care for their sick, handicapped, unemployed, and widows and orphans. Those without family or tribal ties beg or have recourse to Islamic pious foundations (waqfs). The state operates orphanages and finances other rudimentary welfare measures. While the YAR government has expanded its role in providing assistance, traditional means still predominate.

⁴²HOUSING
In the hot coastal region most dwellings, except those of the ruling classes, are straw huts. In the highlands, poorer people live in huts of stone or baked brick. Wealthier Yemenis live in large houses whose style is unique to southwestern Arabia. The lower parts are generally built of sandstone, basalt, or granite. The upper part, which may rise from two to eight stories, is usually of baked brick with windows outlined in decorative designs. Often a loggia topped with brass and open on all sides rises from the roof. New construction is undertaken in concrete and cement.

⁴³EDUCATION
Although knowledge of the Qur'an (Koran) is widespread, only 15–20% of the total population is literate. Traditional education is provided mainly by the kuttab and the madrasah, old types of religious schools, and in religious colleges in the mosques. These schools offer Arabic, Muslim law, history, Qur'anic commentaries, and philosophy.

The educational system calls for 6 years' primary schooling, 3 years' intermediate, and 3 years' secondary training. In 1974 there were 1,540 schools at the primary level, with a total of 178,755 pupils (compared with 74,900 in 1966). There were 81 intermediate schools, with 9,362 pupils, and 15 secondary schools, with 3,098 students. In addition, the YAR had 5 teacher-training schools, with 1,349 students; 1 technical school, with 292 students; and 3 commercial schools, with 174 students. A

program of educational expansion was under way in the mid-1970s.

Development of higher education in the YAR began in 1970/71 with the opening of two facilities at the University of San'a'; by 1974, the university had 1,730 students and 42 faculty.

⁴⁴LIBRARIES AND MUSEUMS
The 10,000-volume main library, in the great mosque in San'a', consists mostly of religious texts and old Arabic manuscripts; it is presently not open to the public. A Kuwayti library was established in 1971. Under the imamate, the government maintained two museums, at Ma'rib and San'a'. The museums served as storage facilities for the bronzes, statues, pottery, and other archæological artifacts of the ancient pre-Islamic Yemeni civilizations.

⁴⁵ORGANIZATIONS
The republican government has encouraged the formation of economic cooperatives, but private associations with political overtones are still suspect.

⁴⁶PRESS
There are two dailies, *Al-Thawrah*, published in San'a', and *Al-Jumhuriyyah*, in Ta'izz. A weekly, *Al-Sabah*, is published in al-Hudaydah, and there are six fortnightlies.

⁴⁷TOURISM
Under the imamate, foreigners were forbidden to visit Yemen as tourists. The republican government has taken steps to encourage tourism, but the lack of facilities as well as the civil war has discouraged travel to the country. There are small hotels in San'a', Ta'izz, and al-Hudaydah. Visas may be obtained from YAR embassies. Smallpox, yellow fever, cholera, and typhoid immunization and gamma globulin inoculations are recommended for visitors.

⁴⁸FAMOUS YEMENIS
Imam Yahya ibn Muhammad al-Hamid al-Din (c.1868–1948) declared himself king in 1926; he was murdered during an uprising in 1948. No other Yemeni in modern times has won fame outside the country.

⁴⁹DEPENDENCIES
Yemen has no territories or colonies.

⁵⁰BIBLIOGRAPHY
American University. *Area Handbook for the Peripheral States of the Arabian Peninsula.* Washington, D.C.: Government Printing Office, 1971.
Deffarge, Claude, and Troeller Gordian. *Yémen, '62–69: De la Révolution sauvage à la trêve des guerriers.* Paris: Laffont, 1969.
Ingrams, Harold. *The Yemen.* London: John Murray, 1963.
Macro, Eric. *Bibliography on Yemen.* Coral Gables, Fla.: University of Miami Press, 1960.
O'Ballance, Edgar. *The War in the Yemen.* Hamden, Conn.: Archon Books, 1971.
Reilly, Sir Bernard. *Aden and the Yemen.* London: HMSO, 1960.
Sanger, Richard. *The Arabian Peninsula.* Ithaca, N.Y.: Cornell University Press, 1954.
Schmidt, Dana Adams. *Yemen: The Unknown War.* New York: Holt, 1968.
Scott, Hugh. *In the High Yemen.* London: Murray, 1942.
Van der Meulen, D. *Faces in Shem.* London: Murray, 1961.
Vocke, Harold. *Das Schwert und die Sterne.* Stuttgart: Deutsche Verlags-Anstalt, 1965.
Wenner, Manfred W. *Modern Yemen, 1919–1966.* Baltimore: Johns Hopkins Press, 1967.

G   Worldmark encyclopedia of
103   the nations.
W67
1976
v.4

G   Worldmark encyclopedia of the
103   nations.
W67
1976
v.4

ASIA
PHYSICAL

Copyright by C.S. HAMMOND & CO., N.Y.

SCALE OF MILES
0   150   300   600   900   1200

SCALE OF KILOMETRES
0   300   600   900   1200

Mountain Altitudes in Feet

Metres		Feet
5000		16400
4000		13120
3000		9840
2000		6560
1000		3280
500		1640
200		656
Sea		Level
Depression		Depression
200		109
3000		1640
Metres		Fathoms